BENSON and HEDGES
Cricket Year
FIRST EDITION

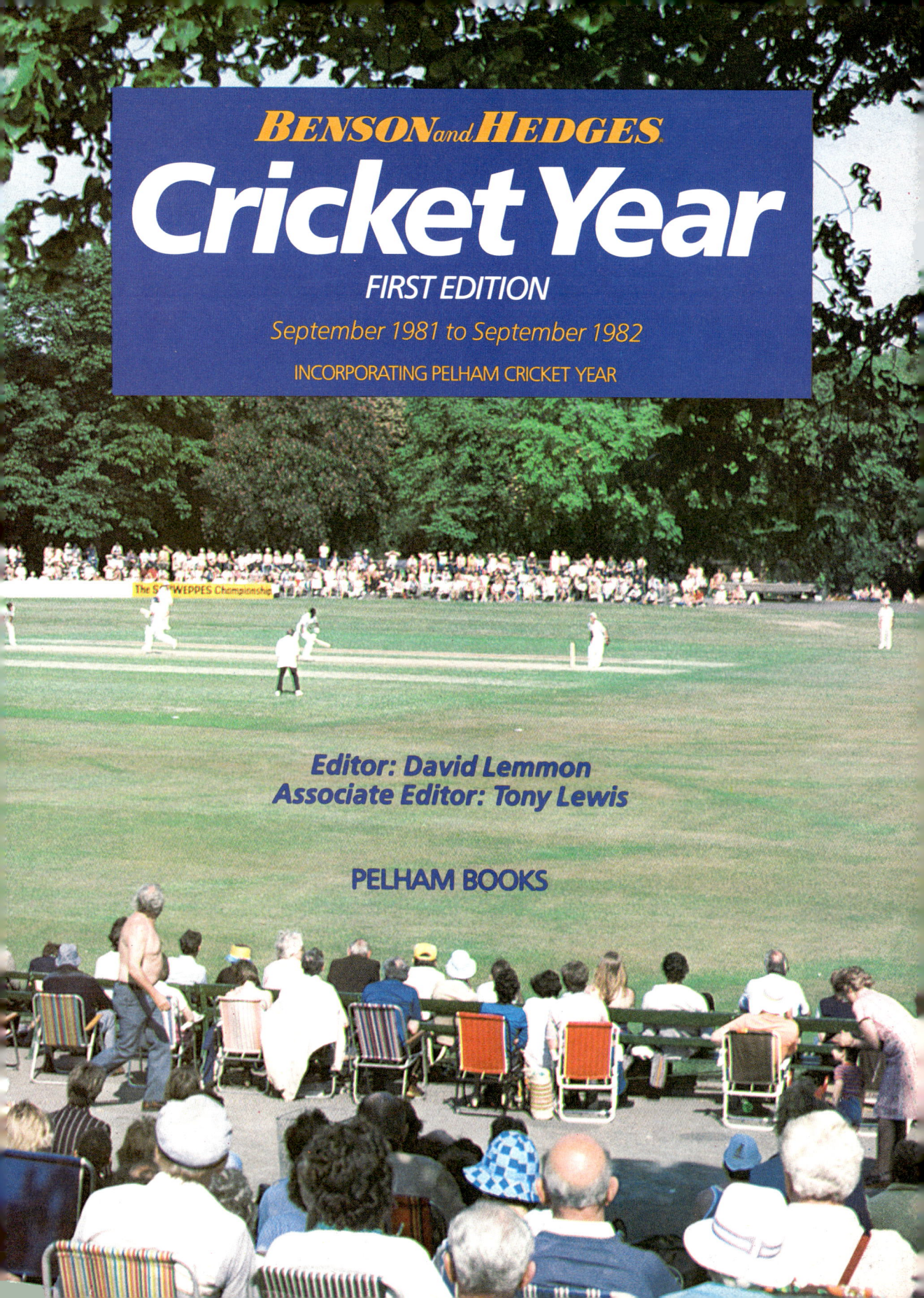

Photo credits

The publishers are grateful to the following for permission to reproduce their photographs in this book:

Danie Coetzer page 414; Robin Craze pages 109, 110, 111, 112, 113, 114, 115, 116, 117, 118, 121; *Daily News*, Durban pages 148, 149, 151, 152; Patrick Eagar pages 12, 13, 21, 54, 59, 78, 101, 103, 106, 107, 216, 217, 223, 227, 229, 230, 235, 237, 252, 253, 259, 260, 261, 274, 275, 292, 293, 308, 315, 316, 317, 318, 319, 320, 321, 322, 353, 356 (top and bottom left), 357 (top and bottom left), 393; John Grainger Picture Agency pages 429, 430; Jan Hamman page 413; Ken Kelly pages 213, 215, 233, 246, 248, 263 (top), 264, 299, 300, 301, 302, 327, 330 (bottom right), 332, 342 (bottom), 343, 348 (bottom), 355, 356 (bottom right), 357 (bottom right), 364 (bottom), 365, 366 (bottom), 367, 368, 369, 373 (top), 379, 383, 407, 463; Stewart Kendall pages 335, 419; Adrian Murrell title page and pages 13, 15, 17, 19, 33, 38, 39, 41, 43, 45, 81, 83, 84, 85, 88, 90, 93, 96, 97, 191, 192, 196, 199, 219, 221, 225, 226, 236, 239, 245, 255, 262, 263 (bottom), 265, 266, 269, 273, 283, 285, 289, 290, 291, 292, 293, 297, 305 (bottom), 310, 311, 312, 323, 325, 326, 329, 330 (top and bottom left), 331 (bottom left and right), 333, 336, 339, 340, 342 (top), 344, 345, 346, 347, 348 (top and middle), 349, 350, 358, 362, 363, 364 (top), 366 (top and centre), 371, 372, 373 (bottom), 376, 381, 385, 453, 455, 461, 465, 469, 473, 477, 479; Norbert Phillip page 431; Sporting Pictures pages 241, 243, 298, 305 (top), 307, 331 (top), 351, 399, 401, 403, 435; *The Age*, Melbourne pages 47, 48, 49, 50, 51, 53; *The Argus*, Cape Town pages 145, 150, 154, 157; *The Pretoria News* pages 135, 136, 138, 139, 146; *The Star*, South Africa page 140; John Traylen pages 250, 251; Universal Pictorial Press and Agency page 433. The publishers are also grateful to the various county clubs for their help in supplying photographs to accompany the form charts.

First published in Great Britain by
Pelham Books Ltd
44 Bedford Square
London WC1B 3DU
1982

© 1982 by Pelham Books Ltd

All Rights Reserved. No part of this publication may be reproduced, stored in a retrieval system, or transmitted, in any form or by any means, electronic, mechanical, photocopying, recording or otherwise, without the prior permission of the Copyright owner

British Library Cataloguing in Publication Data
Benson and Hedges cricket year
1. Cricket
I. Lemmon, David   II. Lewis, Tony
796.35'8   GV917

ISBN 0 7207 1429 X

Typeset by Northumberland Press Ltd, Gateshead
Printed in Great Britain by Blantyre Printing and Binding Company Limited, Glasgow and bound by Hunter & Foulis Limited, Edinburgh

Foreword

We are very proud to be closely associated with the publication of the *Benson and Hedges Cricket Year*, which comes exactly ten years after we announced our sponsorship of the Benson and Hedges Cup.

The Benson and Hedges Cup, a 55-over one day competition, is now established as one of the most sought-after titles in the British cricketing season and every year the Final at Lord's attracts capacity crowds of enthusiastic supporters.

It therefore seems fitting that we, and Pelham Books who have also made a major contribution to the British cricketing scene, should now come together to produce the *Benson and Hedges Cricket Year*, a chronological record of first-class cricket played during the past season in this country and abroad.

As well as information and comment from such leading experts on the game as Tony Lewis, Bob Willis, Robin Marlar, Christopher Martin-Jenkins and David Lemmon, the *Benson and Hedges Cricket Year* has over 50 colour pages including a centre colour section of dramatic photographs taken at this year's Benson and Hedges Cup Final by top cricket photographer Patrick Eagar.

Cricket provides a most satisfying medium for photographers and on pages 6 and 480 are details of the *Benson and Hedges Cricket Year* Amateur Photography Photographic Competition, and Professional Photographers' Awards.

We are confident the *Benson and Hedges Cricket Year* published so soon after the end of the season, will become an invaluable companion for every follower of the game.

DEREK WILSON,
Managing Director
Gallaher Ltd.

BENSON and HEDGES

Amateur Photographers' Competition

£3,000 worth of prizes to be won

Your cricket photograph could win you a VIP all expenses paid day at the 1984 Final of the Benson & Hedges Cup – probably one of the most sought after championships in the British cricketing calendar, plus £500 worth of camera equipment or, one of the 50 runner-up prizes of Benson & Hedges photographic equipment bags.

What You Have To Do
Using any format and type of photographic equipment that you desire, submit one or more colour prints, taken at any cricket match, in Britain during the 1983 season. It can be exciting, dramatic, humorous, or spectacular, just as long as it depicts the spirit of the sport. The judges will also be looking for originality and overall picture quality.

Rules of Entry
Entrants must be aged 18 or over and be resident in the United Kingdom. Employees of Gallaher Limited, Benson & Hedges Limited, Pelham Books Limited and their advertising agents or representatives are not eligible.

Each photograph must be in the form of a colour print with the name and address of the entrant clearly written in Block Capitals on the reverse.

Closing date for the Competition is 30th September, 1983. Entries arriving after this date will be disqualified. No responsibility can be accepted for entries that are damaged, lost or delayed in the post. Entries will be returned only if accompanied by a stamped addressed envelope. The judging panel will include David Lemmon and Tony Lewis, the Editor and Associate Editor of the Benson & Hedges Cricket Year, Patrick Eager, one of the country's leading cricket photographers and representatives of Benson & Hedges

Limited and Pelham Books Limited. Their decision will be final and no correspondence will be entered into. The results will be announced in November 1983 and the prizes presented at a luncheon, to be held in London. Entrants will automatically permit Benson & Hedges Limited to use and reproduce the photographs submitted to the competition and will assign the copyright therein on request by Benson & Hedges Limited, All entrants will be deemed to have accepted and agreed to be bound by the Competition rules and instructions.

How to Enter
Select your photographs, clearly mark the back of each colour print with your name and address, state when and where taken, enclose a stamped, addressed envelope if you require the prints returned, and send to:

The Benson & Hedges Cricket Year Amateur Photographers' Competition, Room 217a, Baker Street, London W1M 1DL.

Ensure that your entry is well packed. No responsibility can be accepted for entries that are damaged or lost.

Contents

SECTION A
Internationals Galore   11

Pakistan and West Indies in Australia. Australia v Pakistan First Test 13. Second Test 16. Third Test 21. Averages 23. Australia v West Indies First Test 26. Second Test 28. Third Test 37. Averages 39. Benson and Hedges World Series Averages 41-44. Charts 40-43.

SECTION B
Southern Revival   45

The Australian domestic season. Sheffield Shield final table 57. McDonald's Cup final 57. First Class averages 58. Frank Tyson's review of the season 60. Charts 62-73.

SECTION C
The Lost Cause   77

England tour of India and Sri Lanka. India v England First Test 80. Second Test 83. Third Test 86. Fourth Test 87. Fifth Test 89. Sixth Test 91. Sri Lanka v England Inaugural Test 95. Charts 99. Robin Marlar's review of the tour 99.

SECTION D
The New Zealand Season   101

Shell Trophy final table 109. Shell Cup final 109. Australian tour of New Zealand. New Zealand v Australia First Test 116. Second and Third Tests 119. Test averages 120. Don Cameron's review of the season 121. Charts 122-132.

SECTION E
The Great Rebellion   135

Cricket in South Africa compiled by Robert Brooke. Datsun Shield final 155. Castle Bowl final 156. Currie Cup final log 159. Castle Bowl final logs 159. Charts 158-189. SAB England XI tour 159. First Class averages 181.

SECTION F
The Small Rebellion   191

Pakistan v Sri Lanka First Test 192. Second Test 192. Third Test 194. Test averages 197.

SECTION G
Calypso Cricket   199

West Indian domestic season. Charts 200-211. Shell Shield final table 211.

SECTION H
The English Season   213

The South African Problem by David Frith 214. Christopher Martin-Jenkins on the State of Cricket 217. Combined Universities chart 238. Minor Counties chart 240. Scotland chart 242. Benson and Hedges Cup Zonal Round final table 244. Prudential Trophy 250. England v India First Test 262. Second Test 274. Cambridge University charts 278. Oxford University charts 280. ICC Trophy final group tables 288. Third Test 290. Indian touring team charts 296. Test averages 298. ICC Trophy final 299. Prudential Trophy England v India First Test 262. Second Test 274. England v Pakistan first match 306. Second match 310. Benson and Hedges final 315. England v Pakistan First Test 326. Second Test 342. Third Test 362. Averages 369. National Westminster Bank Trophy final 376. County form charts 378. John Player League final table 397. Schweppes County Championship final table 405. The Problem of Wickets by Bob Willis 409. A Season to Remember by Tony Lewis 413. First class averages 421. Review of the Season by David Lemmon 429. Book reviews 437.

Editor's Note

The aim of *Benson and Hedges Cricket Year* is that the cricket enthusiast shall be able to read through the happenings in world cricket, from each October until the following September (the end of the English season). Form charts are printed and a player's every appearance will be given on these charts, and date and place allow those appearances to be readily found in the text.

The symbol * indicates 'not out' or 'wicket-keeper' according to the context and the symbol † indicates captain.

The editor wishes to express his deepest thanks to VICTOR ISAACS, the Hampshire C.C.C. scorer, for his corrections and advice in the preparation of the English Counties form charts which appear at the end of this book.

Mr Isaacs is one of the country's leading statisticians, with particular reference to limited-over cricket. His research and pursuit of accuracy are renowned and we are deeply indebted to him.

SECTION A
Internationals Galore

West Indies and Pakistan in Australia.
The Test Matches, tour matches and
Benson & Hedges World Series.

Before one Cricket Year has ended, another has begun. The dust had barely settled at Lord's after Derbyshire's victory in a wonderful NatWest Final before there was a purge in the victors' camp. Mike Hendrick left for Nottinghamshire. David Steele returned to Northamptonshire and Geoff Miller, captain at the beginning of 1981 and vice-captain of England only a few months earlier, severed his connection with the county.

Quickly and quietly John Hampshire left behind the wrangles of Yorkshire and joined Derbyshire. The agonies of the White Rose continued with public and private debate as to the respective qualities of Messrs Illingworth and Boycott. There were many inside and outside the county who felt that Mercutio's dying curse, 'A plague o' both your houses!', was the most apt comment on the situation that existed.

While the thunder of Botham's doings against Australia still reverberated in our ears Pakistan were preparing themselves to do battle with Kim Hughes' men who were to have little respite before they began another Test series.

Once more the Australian season was to be dominated by two touring teams who would play six Tests and at least seventeen one-day internationals between them. Once more it seemed a daunting prospect and a not altogether healthy one.

With Greg Chappell available once more, it seemed unlikely that Hughes would continue as Australia's captain. His record as captain of his country is not a good one and it is apparent that, like Botham, he is a better player under someone else's leadership, certainly at international level.

There was not a general display of rejoicing in Pakistan at the appointment of Javed Miandad as captain of the party to tour Australia. He was blamed in some quarters for the poor showing against the West Indies. It was difficult to see who else could have been chosen to lead the side, however, and the perseverance with Javed, still short of his twenty-fifth birthday, seemed right and just.

For several years Pakistan have looked to be a strong side with several players of outstanding talent, but their record has not been a good one and the selectors must have been well aware that their record was unlikely to improve for Imran Khan is now thirty, Majid thirty-six, Wasim Bari thirty-four, Wasim Raja thirty, Sarfraz thirty-four and Zaheer Abbas thirty-five.

The awareness that their star players were growing older must have prompted the Pakistan selectors to include two exciting young players in their party, Saleem Malik, eighteen years old, and Rizwan Uz-Zaman, a nineteen-year-old opening batsman, although it must be admitted that Pakistan have ever been willing to encourage youth at international level.

The West Indies who were to begin their tour of Australia a month after Pakistan showed few surprises in their team. Nanan and Parry were unlucky to be omitted, the spinner's place going to Harold Joseph, and Lawrence Rowe, Everton Mattis and Alvin Kallicharran could also find no place in the side. Kallicharran had struggled for his place in the Warwickshire side for most of 1981 and his omission, though sad, was not surprising.

It would seem that the Test career of this elegant and exciting batsman is at an end, but as one had thought over the past few years that we had seen the last of Willis, Brearley, Lloyd, Walters and Knott in Test cricket, only to see them reappear, it would be unwise to make too hasty a mourning at Kallicharran's passing from the scene.

One of the most interesting of the newcomers to the West Indian side was Jeff Dujon. In these pages last year we commented upon his thrilling batting in Shell Shield matches and as he is an able wicket-keeper, his inclusion as reserve keeper to David Murray was axiomatic.

The preparation for Test cricket in the double tour Australian seasons is inadequate. West Indies were to have only one first-class game before becoming involved in the Benson and Hedges World Series Cup while Pakistan played Western Australia, Queensland and Victoria before flying back to Perth for the first Test. One felt that many would be limp from travel, if not cricket, by the end of the tour.

23, 24, 25 and 26 October 1981

at Perth

Pakistanis 380 for 9 dec (Majid Khan 110, Ejaz Faqih 61 not out, Mudassar Nazar 57, B. Yardley 4 for 100, M. F. Malone 4 for 111) and 92 for 2
Western Australia 545 (G. M. Wood 151, G. Shipperd 131, K. J. Hughes 55, Iqbal Qasim 5 for 136)
Match drawn

The opening match of the Pakistan tour ended in a draw when rain restricted play on the last day. Before then batsmen on both sides had flourished. Mudassar and Rizwan Uz-Zaman had begun the tour with a century opening stand. There was a mild collapse before Majid Khan, enjoying a little luck, hit 110 from 129 deliveries. Bruce Yardley bowled his off-breaks impressively and it was the left-arm spin of Iqbal Qasim and the off-breaks of all-rounder Ejaz Faqih that proved most effective in the Western Australian innings. For the best part of two days the Pakistan bowlers toiled. Wood and Shipperd added 180 for the second wicket. Wood's 151 was the highest score of his career and he hit twelve fours in his innings which lasted for over six and a half hours, an uncharacteristic grind for him, but one which consolidated his Test place.

30, 31 October, 1 and 2 November 1981

at Brisbane

Pakistanis 328 (Javed Miandad 138, Zaheer Abbas 84, D. J. Lillie 4 for 77)
Queensland 375 for 5 (G. S. Chappell 162, M. F. Kent 91)
Match drawn

Rain followed Pakistan to Brisbane where the last two days of the match with Queensland were washed out. Pakistan lost Rizwan Uz-Zaman at 0 and Mudassar at 45, but Javed and Zaheer effected a fine recovery. Javed was at his punishing best and Zaheer was in the elegant vein that had delighted Gloucestershire all the previous season. The second day belonged to Greg Chappell. He shared a stand of 192 with Martin Kent for the second wicket and gave every indication that he would return to lead Australia at his majestic best. The most impressive bowler on view was the leg-spinner Lillie who took three wickets in nineteen deliveries and showed admirable control of length and flight.

6, 7, 8 and 9 November 1981
at Melbourne

Victoria 311 for 8 dec (J. M. Wiener 83, R. D. Robinson 71, Imran Khan 5 for 83) and 242 for 7 dec (G. N. Yallop 68, G. M. Watts 59)
Pakistan 317 (Imran Khan 93 not out, Saleem Malik 62, Rizwan Uz-Zaman 50) and 99 for 5 (M. H. N. Walker 4 for 45)

Match drawn

Once more rain brought play to an early close, but on this occasion Pakistan were thankful for they seemed to be facing defeat, having lost five wickets for 99 and Zaheer unable to bat. On the opening day Wiener, who two years ago had looked to be assured of the Australian number one position for several seasons, did much to repair his loss of confidence with a patient innings which lasted just over three and a half hours. Imran Khan bowled with fire and was obviously working up to full pace for the Test match. Robinson showed more aggression than the earlier batsmen and Scholes declared, but thanks to some fierce hitting by Imran, Pakistan took a narrow lead on the first innings. He hit eight fours and two sixes in an innings which lasted two and three quarter hours. Zaheer, who was captaining the side, found himself unable to bat. He had been struck in the ribs by a ball from Thomson in the match against Queensland and the injury forced him to withdraw not only from this match, but from the first Test. Yallop hit 68 in the second innings and was called into the Australian side as a replacement for the injured Kent. Pakistan were set to make 237 in three hours, but after a brisk start they lost four wickets in twenty minutes for 8 runs and with Max Walker swinging the ball as of old in the humid conditions, they were glad to escape further torment when the rain returned.

FIRST TEST MATCH

Javed took the brave decision of asking Australia to bat when he won the toss and although there was no immediate reward for his bowlers, by the end of the first day, with Australia 159 for 7, his action had been proved fully justified. The Pakistan attack was determined and relentlessly accurate with Imran, who dismissed Chappell with a marvellous break-back, particularly impressive. The blot on the day was an over-rate of twelve an hour. The Australian batting was mediocre. Yallop batted over two and a half hours for twenty and he was not alone in his ineptitude. Whatever the failings of the Australian batsmen on the first day, they were as nothing compared to those of the Pakistanis on the second. In under twenty-two overs Pakistan were dismissed for 62 and but for some bold hitting by Sarfraz at number eight, they would have struggled to reach 30. It was a bleak performance. The tourists were totally demoralised by Lillee and Alderman. Lillee began with a no-ball in his first over, but Alderman had the debutant Rizwan Uz-Zaman lbw with his first delivery. It was Alderman's first Test in his own country. Wasim Bari was playing his fifty-ninth Test, a Pakistan record. With an unexpected lead of 118, Australia now totally dominated the game. Wood and Laird gave them a good start in the second innings and Chappell alone failed. Kim Hughes re- captured the grace and elegance of his pre-English season and Australia moved into a massive lead.

The Pakistan innings had lasted only 108 minutes and in that time the game had been completely transformed. Chappell declared with a lead of 542 and as Mudassar and Rizwan Uz-Zaman left quickly, it was soon apparent that we were not going to see history made and a dramatic Pakistan victory snatched against all the odds. What we did see, in fact, was one of the most disgraceful scenes that have been witnessed on a cricket field. As Javed was taking a comfortable single Dennis Lillee obstructed him and Javed knocked into the bowler. Before Lillee bowled the next ball words were exchanged between the two players after which Javed turned his back and prepared to take up the normal position of the non-striker. It was then that Lillee kicked at Javed, touching him behind the left knee. Javed turned and brandished his bat. The umpire, Crafter, stepped between the two players. The punishment was a suspension of two one-day matches for Lillee, a punishment which, ultimately, with an apology, Pakistan accepted. Once more it was felt that the Australian Board was an organisation that lacked authority or courage, probably both. One longs for the day when the flabby leadership that has prevailed in world cricket over the past few years is replaced by integrity and a positivity which does not flinch in the face of the television magnet or the player who acts as if he is more important than the game itself. The rest of the match was predictable, but victory finally came to Australia through some splendid off-spin bowling by Bruce Yardley who had his best ever figures in a Test match.

Wasim Bari

FIRST TEST MATCH – AUSTRALIA v. PAKISTAN
13, 14, 15, 16 and 17 November 1981 at Perth

AUSTRALIA

	FIRST INNINGS		SECOND INNINGS	
B. M. Laird	c Bari, b Imran	27	(2) c Bari, b Imran	85
G. M. Wood	lbw, b Sikhander	33	(1) b Qasim	49
G. S. Chappell†	lbw, b Imran	22	b Imran	6
K. J. Hughes	b Sarfraz	14	c Majid, b Imran	106
G. N. Yallop	c and b Qasim	20	c Imran, b Sikhander	38
A. R. Border	c Bari, b Sarfraz	3	c Mudassar, b Sikhander	37
R. W. Marsh*	c Qasim, b Sikhander	16	c Mansoor, b Raja	47
B. Yardley	c Bari, b Imran	9	st Bari, b Qasim	22
D. K. Lillee	c Bari, b Raja	16	not out	4
J. R. Thomson	b Imran	2	not out	5
T. M. Alderman	not out	0		
Extras	b 5, w 1, nb 12	18	b 1, lb 9, w 1, nb 14	25
		180	(for 8 wkts dec)	424

	O	M	R	W	O	M	R	W
Imran Khan	31.4	8	66	4	39	12	90	3
Sarfraz Nawaz	27	10	43	2	27	5	88	—
Sikhander Bakht	21	4	47	2	23	3	79	2
Iqbal Qasim	3	1	6	1	26	4	81	2
Wasim Raja	1	1	0	1	20	3	58	1
Javed Miandad					1	—	2	—
Mudassar Nazar					2	1	1	—

FALL OF WICKETS
1–45, 2–81, 3–89, 4–113, 5–119, 6–136, 7–154, 8–165, 9–180
1–92, 2–105, 3–192, 4–262, 5–327, 6–360, 7–412, 8–416

PAKISTAN

	FIRST INNINGS		SECOND INNINGS	
Mudassar Nazar	c Marsh, b Lillee	0	lbw, b Alderman	5
Rizwan Uz-Zaman	lbw, b Alderman	0	c Marsh, b Alderman	8
Mansoor Akhtar	c Marsh, b Alderman	6	c Hughes, b Thomson	36
Javed Miandad†	c Hughes, b Alderman	6	b Yardley	79
Majid Khan	c Marsh, b Lillee	3	c Marsh, b Yardley	0
Wasim Raja	c Thomson, b Lillee	4	c Hughes, b Yardley	48
Imran Khan	c Yardley, b Lillee	4	c Alderman, b Yardley	31
Sarfraz Nawaz	c Marsh, b Alderman	26	c and b Yardley	9
Wasim Bari*	c Marsh, b Lillee	1	c Border, b Yardley	20
Iqbal Qasim	c Alderman, b Thomson	5	c Alderman, b Lillee	4
Sikhander Bakht	not out	3	not out	0
Extras	nb 4	4	lb 1, nb 15	16
		62		256

	O	M	R	W	O	M	R	W
Lillee	9	3	18	5	20	3	78	1
Alderman	10.2	2	36	4	16	4	43	2
Thomson	2	1	4	1	12	4	35	1
Yardley					25.5	5	84	6

FALL OF WICKETS
1–1, 2–1, 3–14, 4–17, 5–21, 6–25, 7–25, 8–26, 9–57
1–8, 2–27, 3–96, 4–99, 5–174, 6–198, 7–229, 8–236, 9–254

Australia won by 286 runs

13, 14, 15 and 16 November 1981
at Adelaide

West Indians 294 (H. A. Gomes 95, D. A. Murray 72, G. J. Winter 7 for 65) and 236 for 5 dec (M. D. Marshall 66, S. F. A. Bacchus 58 not out, D. L. Haynes 53)
South Australia 79 and 225 (W. M. Darling 88, J. Garner 5 for 45)

West Indians won by 226 runs

While the Pakistanis were engaged in the First Test the West Indians began their tour under Richards' captaincy, Lloyd not yet having arrived from England where he had had a back operation. Richards batted for 26 minutes but made only one and South Australia had the tourists at 106 for 5. Larry Gomes and David Murray added 165 and from that point, in spite of Graham Winter's career best 7 for 65, West Indies were always on top. Graham Winter had never come closer to the state side than twelfth man before this season.

In an inept batting performance the home side made only 79 in 33 overs against the four pace bowlers, opening bat Harris carrying his bat for 19. Some sparkling second innings batting by Bacchus and Marshall, who made 103 in 94 minutes, meant that South Australia needed 452 to win in 425 minutes.

Darling and Harris began with a stand of 141, but the later order collapsed before Garner and Marshall, the last five wickets falling for 24 runs.

18 November 1981
at Midura

West Indians 250 for 5 dec (A. L. Logie 57 not out, C. H. Lloyd 55, C. G. Greenidge 51)
Victorian Country XI 92 for 8 (H. Joseph 4 for 13)

Match drawn

Clive Lloyd quickly established his fitness with a competent fifty in his first game of the tour. The home side began well, but Harold Joseph took 4 for 13 in 12 overs of off-spin as they tumbled from 38 for 0 to 65 for 8 before Cleary and Arthur saved the day. Dujon was impressive behind the stumps.

Benson and Hedges World Series

FIRST ONE-DAY INTERNATIONAL – PAKISTAN v. WEST INDIES

Dropped at slip by Iqbal Qasim off the bowling of Imran Khan before he had scored, Desmond Haynes shared in an opening stand of 182 with Gordon Greenidge that was the basis of the West Indian victory in the first of the one-day internationals.

Greenidge was at his best and hit a six and five fours in his 103. He was aided by some slack fielding from Pakistan which made the task of their batsmen greater than it should have been.

FIRST ONE-DAY INTERNATIONAL: PAKISTAN v. WEST INDIES
21 November 1981 at Melbourne

WEST INDIES							PAKISTAN						
C. G. Greenidge	c Rizwan, b Sarfraz				103		Mudassar Nazar	b Marshall					51
D. L. Haynes	b Mudassar				84		Rizwan Uz-Zaman	c Roberts, b Garner					14
I. V. A. Richards	b Imran				17		Javed Miandad†	c Murray, b Roberts					74
S. F. A. Bacchus	c Rizwan, b Sarfraz				8		Mansoor Akhtar	b Marshall					2
C. H. Lloyd†	b Sarfraz				10		Majid Khan	c Bacchus, b Roberts					56
A. M. E. Roberts	c Mansoor, b Imran				0		Imran Khan	c Murray, b Roberts					0
J. Garner	c Ashraf, b Imran				0		Wasim Raja	not out					10
M. D. Marshall	not out				9		Ashraf Ali*	not out					1
H. A. Gomes	c and b Sarfraz				0		Sarfraz Nawaz						
D. A. Murray*	not out				1		Sikhander Bakht						
C. E. H. Croft							Iqbal Qasim						
Extras	lb 13				13		Extras	b 2, lb 7, w 4, nb 6					19
	(for 8 wkts)				245			(for 6 wkts)					227
		O	M	R	W				O	M	R	W	
Sarfraz Nawaz		9	2	37	4		Roberts		10	1	42	3	
Imran Khan		10	2	23	3		Marshall		10	1	27	2	
Sikhander Bakht		9	—	46	—		Garner		10	—	30	1	
Iqbal Qasim		10	—	49	—		Croft		10	1	57	—	
Majid Khan		5	—	34	—		Richards		10	—	52	—	
Mudassar Nazar		7	—	43	1								

FALL OF WICKETS
1–182, 2–203, 3–222, 4–223, 5–223, 6–224, 7–244, 8–244

FALL OF WICKETS
1–53, 2–120, 3–124, 4–212, 5–212, 6–221

West Indies won by 18 runs

Imran Khan

Pakistan batted with determination, but the West Indian pace attack was well supported in the field and it was the Caribbean out cricket which won the day and maintained West Indies' hundred per cent record against Pakistan in one-day internationals.

Benson and Hedges World Series

SECOND ONE-DAY INTERNATIONAL – AUSTRALIA v. PAKISTAN

Without a victory in the first five matches of their tour the Pakistanis, reinforced by the return of Zaheer, beat Australia in a thrilling game in Melbourne, their victory coming with only four balls remaining. Australia were without the suspended Lillee.

Wood and Darling gave Australia a good start, but Sikhander Bakht then took the wickets of Darling, Chappell and Border and they were reduced from 48 for 0 to 102 for 5. It was Hughes who revived Australia with an elegant and brisk 67. He and Yardley added 86 for the sixth wicket.

Pakistan began poorly, losing Mansoor and Zaheer for 21, both dismissed by Alderman, but Javed Miandad, who had been top scorer against West Indies the previous day, again played a captain's innings. With Mudassar Nazar, he added 105 for the third wicket.

Greg Chappell dismissed both batsmen and brought about a minor collapse so that Pakistan needed 58 from the last ten overs with five wickets in hand. Imran Khan batted with great sense and experience of limited over cricket and Ejaz Faqih, who had bowled well, gave fine support.

Ejaz was bowled by Thomson and, crucially, Imran was dropped at cover by Darling. There were no more alarms and Pakistan won with four balls to spare.

SECOND ONE-DAY INTERNATIONAL: AUSTRALIA v. PAKISTAN
22 November 1981 at Melbourne

AUSTRALIA				PAKISTAN			
G. M. Wood	run out		23	Mudassar Nazar	c Marsh, b Chappell		44
W. M. Darling	c Sarfraz, b Sikhander		41	Mansoor Akhtar	c Yardley, b Alderman		12
G. S. Chappell†	c Raja, b Sikhander		3	Zaheer Abbas	c Marsh, b Alderman		2
A. R. Border	b Sikhander		6	Javed Miandad†	c Lawson, b Chappell		72
K. J. Hughes	c Mudassar, b Sikhander		67	Wasim Raja	c Darling, b Chappell		8
R. W. Marsh*	b Sarfraz		15	Imran Khan	not out		28
B. Yardley	b Imran		28	Ejaz Faqih	b Thomson		17
S. F. Graf	run out		8	Ashraf Ali*	not out		15
G. F. Lawson	not out		4	Sarfraz Nawaz			
J. R. Thomson	run out		3	Sikhander Bakht			
T. M. Alderman				Tahir Naqqash			
Extras	b 2, lb 3, w 3, nb 3		11	Extras	lb 7, w 3, nb 2		12
	(for 9 wkts)		209		(for 6 wkts)		210

	O	M	R	W		O	M	R	W
Imran Khan	10	1	42	1	Thomson	9.2	—	47	1
Sarfraz Nawaz	10	—	44	1	Alderman	10	—	20	2
Tahir Naqqash	10	—	46	—	Graf	10	—	34	—
Sikhander Bakht	10	1	34	4	Lawson	8	1	43	—
Ejaz Faqih	10	1	32	—	Yardley	3	—	21	—
					Chappell	9	1	33	3

FALL OF WICKETS
1–48, 2–51, 3–71, 4–80, 5–102, 6–188, 7–197, 8–204, 9–209

FALL OF WICKETS
1–19, 2–21, 3–126, 4–139, 5–151, 6–184

Pakistan won by 4 wickets

23 and 24 November 1981

at Canberra

Pakistanis 200 for 6 dec (Saleem Malik 51 not out) and 153 for 3 (Zaheer Abbas 91 not out)
Capital Territory 200 for 7 dec

Match drawn

The importance of this match to Pakistan was in the form of Zaheer Abbas who, in struggling to get fully fit after his fractured rib, scored 41 and 91 not out.

Benson and Hedges World Series

THIRD ONE-DAY INTERNATIONAL – AUSTRALIA v. WEST INDIES

For Australia the third of the limited over internationals was vitally important as defeat would have left them adrift at the bottom of the table. In the first two matches Miandad had put the opposition in when he won the toss, but at Sydney, in the day and night match, Lloyd elected to bat first.

The West Indian batting was in its usual mould of effective exuberance. A four over burst from Thomson in which he dismissed Greenidge, Haynes and Bacchus changed the pattern of the game as West Indies tumbled from 64 for 0 to 98 for 3, but Richards and Lloyd restored West Indian supremacy with a stand of 72. Lloyd was the dominant partner and scored 63 off 59 deliveries including seven fours. The Australians were fined £375 for bowling only 49 overs in the first session instead of the required 50. The number bowled would have been most welcome in Test cricket.

The Australians began dreadfully when they lost Darling and Chappell with only eight runs scored. Laird and Border then put on 82 in 73 minutes and although Border was run out, the scoring rate was maintained. Hughes and Laird scored 147 in 25 overs to win the match for Australia with two overs to spare. It was magnificent batting and Laird's century and Hughes' exciting stroke play made a mockery of the fear that had been engendered by the West Indian pace quartet.

SECOND TEST MATCH – AUSTRALIA v. PAKISTAN

Pakistan introduced Mohsin Khan who had been asked to join the side when Zaheer was injured. Zaheer, in fact, played as did Ejaz Faqih; the three players losing their places in the side being Rizwan, Mansoor and Iqbal Qasim. Wellham replaced the injured Yallop for Australia for whom Lillee returned after missing the two one-day internationals through suspension.

Although the wicket appeared to be perfect, Chappell asked Pakistan to bat when he won the toss and it was only a fine innings from Zaheer with able support from Wasim Raja and Ejaz Faqih that halted a Pakistan slump. They were bowled out on the first day and Dennis Lillee's 5 for 81 took him past the three hundred wicket mark in Test cricket, only the third player to reach this target.

Laird and Wood gave Australia a splendid start, but the innings was dominated by Greg Chappell who scored his

B. M. Laird

THIRD ONE-DAY INTERNATIONAL: AUSTRALIA v. WEST INDIES
24 November 1981 at Sydney

WEST INDIES					AUSTRALIA			
C. G. Greenidge	b Thomson		39		B. M. Laird	not out		117
D. L. Haynes	c and b Thomson		30		W. M. Darling	c Murray, b Holding		5
I. V. A. Richards	run out		47		G. S. Chappell†	lbw, b Roberts		1
S. F. A. Bacchus	c Hughes, b Thomson		4		A. R. Border	run out		29
C. H. Lloyd†	c Thomson, b Lawson		63		K. J. Hughes	not out		62
D. A. Murray*	c Graf, b Lawson		5		G. M. Wood			
M. D. Marshall	not out		16		R. W. Marsh*			
A. M. E. Roberts	run out		15		S. F. Graf			
J. Garner	lbw, b Alderman		1		G. F. Lawson			
M. A. Holding	not out		2		J. R. Thomson			
C. E. H. Croft					T. M. Alderman			
Extras	lb 7, w 5, nb 2		14		Extras	b 1, lb 13, w 4, nb 5		23
	(for 8 wkts)		236			(for 3 wkts)		237

	O	M	R	W		O	M	R	W
Lawson	10	2	28	2	Holding	10	—	34	1
Alderman	10	—	35	1	Roberts	9	—	44	1
Thomson	10	—	55	3	Marshall	10	—	45	—
Graf	9	—	56	—	Garner	9	—	43	—
Chappell	10	—	48	—	Croft	9	—	48	—

FALL OF WICKETS
1–64, 2–89, 3–98, 4–170, 5–197, 6–197, 7–229, 8–232

FALL OF WICKETS
1–7, 2–8, 3–90

Australia won by 7 wickets

SECOND TEST MATCH – AUSTRALIA v. PAKISTAN
27, 28, 29, 30 November and 1 December 1981 at Brisbane

PAKISTAN

	FIRST INNINGS		SECOND INNINGS	
Mudassar Nazar	c Marsh, b Lillee	36	c Laird, b Lillee	33
Mohsin Khan	c Border, b Chappell	11	c Marsh, b Lillee	43
Majid Khan	c Chappell, b Lillee	29	c Chappell, b Yardley	15
Javed Miandad†	b Lillee	20	lbw, b Lillee	38
Zaheer Abbas	b Lillee	80	lbw, b Yardley	0
Wasim Raja	c Laird, b Lillee	43	b Lillee	36
Imran Khan	c Marsh, b Alderman	0	c Wellham, b Yardley	3
Ejaz Faqih	b Yardley	34	c Chappell, b Thomson	21
Sarfraz Nawaz	c Border, b Alderman	4	c Alderman, b Yardley	13
Wasim Bari*	c Marsh, b Thomson	7	not out	4
Sikhander Bakht	not out	1	b Thomson	2
Extras	b 12, lb 1, w 1, nb 12	26	b 2, lb 3, w 1, nb 9	15
		291		**223**

AUSTRALIA

	FIRST INNINGS		SECOND INNINGS	
B. M. Laird	c Zaheer, b Ejaz	44	(2) not out	3
G. M. Wood	c Mudassar, b Raja	72	(1) not out	0
G. S. Chappell†	c Zaheer, b Sikhander	201		
A. R. Border	b Imran	36		
K. J. Hughes	b Imran	28		
D. M. Wellham	b Imran	36		
R. W. Marsh*	c Zaheer, b Imran	27		
B. Yardley	b Sarfraz	2		
D. K. Lillee	b Sarfraz	14		
J. R. Thomson	not out	22		
T. M. Alderman	not out	5		
Extras	b 1, lb 5, w 2, nb 17	25		
	(for 9 wkts dec)	**512**	(for no wkt)	**3**

	O	M	R	W	O	M	R	W
Lillee	20	3	81	5	19	4	51	4
Alderman	25	6	74	2	15	3	37	—
Thomson	15	2	52	1	15	3	43	2
Chappell	3	1	6	1				
Yardley	15	1	51	1	24	4	77	4
Border	1	—	1	—				

	O	M	R	W	O	M	R	W
Imran Khan	40	6	92	4	1.2	1	2	—
Sarfraz Nawaz	35	4	121	2				
Sikhander Bakht	24	2	81	1	1	—	1	—
Ejaz Faqih	22	1	76	1				
Wasim Raja	17	—	68	1				
Mudassar Nazar	2	—	10	—				
Javed Miandad	3	—	18	—				
Majid Khan	9	1	21	—				

FALL OF WICKETS
1–40, 2–60, 3–105, 4–111, 5–236, 6–237, 7–245, 8–263, 9–285
1–72, 2–90, 3–115, 4–115, 5–177, 6–178, 7–189, 8–216, 9–219

FALL OF WICKETS
1–109, 2–149, 3–219, 4–298, 5–429, 6–448, 7–469, 8–470, 9–492

Australia won by 10 wickets

---

fourth double century in Test cricket and made the highest score by an Australian against Pakistan in Australia. He batted for 411 minutes, faced 296 deliveries and hit 22 fours. He gave one chance, a caught and bowled to Sarfraz when he had made 187, and survived a confident lbw appeal by Imran twelve runs later. After his run of low scores it was a majestic and welcome knock.

There were smaller contributions from everybody and Australia took a first innings lead of 221. It proved too big a lead for Pakistan to counter and it was only a brief, late flourish that forced Australia to bat again.

Lillee had four more wickets which brought him closer to Gibbs' Test record. Among his wickets was Mohsin who gave a polished display. Yardley bowled well and took the most important wicket, that of Zaheer, for nought.

27, 28, 29 and 30 November 1981
at Sydney

New South Wales 278 for 9 dec (J. Dyson 98, R. B. McCosker 64) and 319 (J. Dyson 123, I. C. Davis 52, A. M. E. Roberts 4 for 48)
West Indians 482 for 7 dec (D. L. Haynes 139, J. Dujon 104 not out, S. F. A. Bacchus 83) and 117 for 1 (S. F. A. Bacchus 53 not out, I. V. A. Richards 53 not out)

West Indians won by 9 wickets

Two splendid innings by John Dyson, rejected by the Australian selectors, failed to save New South Wales from defeat by the West Indians. Dyson batted with his usual patience and, in the first innings, had an opening stand of 102 with another former Test opener, Rick McCosker, but the middle order failed. Haynes and Bacchus began the West Indian reply with a stand of 168 and Haynes hit a six and nineteen fours in his innings which lasted 316 minutes. The most exciting batting, however, came from Dujon who hit 104 in under three hours and looked a fine player. New South Wales seemed to be in no danger of defeat, but they lost their last seven wickets to Roberts and Croft for 26 runs and Richards and Bacchus scored at five an over to give West Indies victory with nearly five overs to spare.

2 December 1981
at Orange

West Indians 235 for 6 (M. D. Marshall 65 not out, A. L. Logie 63 not out)
New South Wales Country XI 181 for 8 (R. Oakley 78)

West Indians won by 54 runs

In a forty-five over match, West Indians were struggling at 112 for 6, but Logie and Marshall rallied them with a stand of 123 in 19 overs. Only a spirited 78 by skipper Bob

Oakley, two sixes and ten fours, offered the country eleven any hope of avoiding defeat.

3 December 1981
at Port Lincoln
South Australian Country XI 161 for 8 (P. Schmerl 50)
Pakistanis 214 for 4 (Ejaz Faqih 83, Iqbal Qasim 51)
Pakistanis won by 8 wickets

Benson and Hedges World Series

FOURTH ONE-DAY INTERNATIONAL – PAKISTAN v. WEST INDIES

For the first time in a one-day international Pakistan triumphed over West Indies. This victory was as unexpected and dramatic as it was historic. There was no hint of Pakistan victory as they dragged to 68 for 7, Zaheer alone showing any confidence. When Zaheer was dismissed by Roberts, Ejaz Faqih and Sarfraz Nawaz gave Pakistan some hope with an eighth wicket stand of 57, but the final total of 140 all out in the forty-ninth over, seemed highly unlikely to present the West Indies with any problems. West Indies made the worst of starts, however, when Sarfraz dismissed Greenidge and Richards and Tahir had Haynes caught behind so that they were 38 for 3. Bacchus and Lloyd appeared to have rallied the side and set the course for a comfortable win, but the sensations came when Wasim Raja, with his leg-spin, almost unheard of in one-day cricket, took 3 for 8 in 23 balls. Imran Khan destroyed late resistance and Pakistan bowled out the West Indies in 38.5 overs to gain a memorable victory by 8 runs. Wasim Raja was Man of the Match and one wondered how long we would have to wait before a leg-spinner again took four wickets in a one-day international.

Tahir Naqqash

FOURTH ONE-DAY INTERNATIONAL: PAKISTAN v. WEST INDIES
5 December 1981 at Adelaide

PAKISTAN					WEST INDIES			
Mudassar Nazar	c Greenidge, b Holding			11	C. G. Greenidge	b Sarfraz		4
Mohsin Khan	run out			11	D. L. Haynes	c Ashraf, b Tahir		7
Zaheer Abbas	c Murray, b Roberts			46	I. V. A. Richards	c Ashraf, b Sarfraz		9
Javed Miandad†	lbw, b Marshall			1	S. F. A. Bacchus	b Raja		37
Wasim Raja	b Garner			1	C. H. Lloyd†	c Tahir, b Ejaz		28
Imran Khan	c Murray, b Marshall			1	P. J. Dujon	b Raja		0
Ejaz Faqih	c Lloyd, b Holding			20	M. D. Marshall	b Raja		20
Ashraf Ali*	c Bacchus, b Richards			3	D. A. Murray*	lbw, b Raja		0
Sarfraz Nawaz	not out			34	A. M. E. Roberts	b Imran		4
Tahir Naqqash	run out			1	M. A. Holding	c Raja, b Imran		8
Sikhander Bakht	run out			3	J. Garner	not out		1
Extras	b 1, lb 4, w 2, nb 1			8	Extras	lb 7, w 2, nb 5		14
				140				132

	O	M	R	W		O	M	R	W
Roberts	10	3	19	1	Imran Khan	9.5	—	13	2
Holding	10	1	28	2	Sarfraz Nawaz	6	—	24	2
Garner	10	3	32	1	Sikhander Bakht	4	—	11	—
Marshall	9	—	18	2	Tahir Naqqash	6	—	25	1
Richards	10	1	35	1	Ejaz Faqih	6	—	20	1
					Wasim Raja	7	—	25	4

FALL OF WICKETS
1–16, 2–27, 3–31, 4–34, 5–35, 6–63, 7–68, 8–125, 9–127

FALL OF WICKETS
1–7, 2–19, 3–38, 4–85, 5–88, 6–107, 7–107, 8–120, 9–120

Pakistan won by 8 runs

Benson and Hedges World Series

FIFTH ONE-DAY INTERNATIONAL – AUSTRALIA v. PAKISTAN

Over twenty thousand people saw Australia take the lead in the Benson and Hedges World Series by defeating Pakistan with some ease. Australia batted evenly, but were dismissed in 48.3 overs for 208. Javed declined to use Wasim Raja, the hero of the previous day, relying instead upon six overs of trundle from Zaheer Abbas, a rare sight. Pakistan began well enough, but their scoring was never brisk and they fell well short of their target although they were aided by some sloppy Australian fielding. Chappell added three wickets, key ones, to his competent 38 and was named Man of the Match. Sadly, there still seemed to be a verbal battle between Javed and the Australians and one cannot help but recollect that there have been too many incidents of an unpleasant nature between these two sides over the past few years.

The sixth one-day international, a day and night game due to be played in Sydney, was postponed because of a strike by power workers. Australia and Pakistan agreed to an earlier start, but they would not agree to putting the match back for a day as both insisted that this placed it too close to the final Test. The other item of news was that Ian Chappell was suspended for three weeks for making a blasphemous remark, involuntarily, while broadcasting. Since retiring from cricket Chappell had become a television commentator.

7, 8 and 9 December 1981
at Hobart

Tasmania 204 (P. Mancell 50) and 100 for 2
West Indians 203 (I. V. A. Richards 57, C. H. Lloyd 51, F. Stephenson 5 for 46)

Match drawn

Gales and rain restricted play to eleven overs on the first day and brought play to an early close on the last day. Clive Lloyd batted for nearly two hours in his first first-class innings of the tour, but the honours went to another West Indian, Franklyn Stephenson. Stephenson had made an incredible debut in first-class cricket in October with ten wickets against Victoria whom Tasmania beat convincingly. Now he numbered Richards and Bacchus among his victims and generally gave the West Indian batsmen a torrid time with his speed.

11, 12, 13 and 14 December 1981
at Brisbane

West Indians 539 for 7 dec (H. A. Gomes 200 not out, I. V. A. Richards 121, S. F. A. Bacchus 85, C. H. Lloyd 68)
Queensland 165 (G. M. Ritchie 55, M. D. Marshall 5 for 31) and 282 (G. M. Ritchie 71, K. C. Wessels 57, R. B. Phillips 51, I. V. A. Richards 5 for 88)

West Indians won by an innings and 92 runs

Taking advantage of missed chances, Viv Richards recorded

FIFTH ONE-DAY INTERNATIONAL: AUSTRALIA v. PAKISTAN
6 December 1981 at Adelaide

AUSTRALIA

Batsman	Dismissal	Runs
B. M. Laird	lbw, b Sikhander	20
W. M. Darling	run out	35
G. S. Chappell†	c Raja, b Ejaz	38
A. R. Border	c Raja, b Mudassar	25
K. J. Hughes	c Mudassar, b Sarfraz	14
G. M. Wood	not out	43
R. W. Marsh*	c Ashraf, b Mudassar	10
G. F. Lawson	b Sarfraz	2
D. K. Lillee	c Sarfraz, b Imran	7
J. R. Thomson	b Imran	6
T. M. Alderman	c Ashraf, b Imran	1
Extras	lb 2, w 3, nb 2	7
		208

Bowler	O	M	R	W
Imran Khan	9.3	3	19	3
Sarfraz Nawaz	10	—	44	2
Sikhander Bakht	9	—	29	1
Ejaz Faqih	7	—	43	1
Zaheer Abbas	6	—	41	—
Mudassar Nazar	7	—	25	2

FALL OF WICKETS
1-43, 2-84, 3-103, 4-136, 5-136, 6-169, 7-176, 8-187, 9-199

PAKISTAN

Batsman	Dismissal	Runs
Mudassar Nazar	run out	14
Mohsin Khan	c Marsh, b Chappell	27
Zaheer Abbas	c Alderman, b Lawson	38
Javed Miandad†	c Alderman, b Chappell	4
Wasim Raja	c Darling, b Lawson	2
Imran Khan	c Darling, b Alderman	18
Ejaz Faqih	c Marsh, b Thomson	18
Sarfraz Nawaz	c Darling, b Chappell	5
Tahir Naqqash	not out	21
Ashraf Ali*	not out	11
Sikhander Bakht		
Extras	lb 8, w 1, nb 3	12
	(for 8 wkts)	170

Bowler	O	M	R	W
Alderman	10	1	26	1
Lawson	10	1	33	2
Chappell	10	1	31	3
Lillee	10	—	23	—
Thomson	10	—	45	1

FALL OF WICKETS
1-41, 2-57, 3-79, 4-84, 5-91, 6-121, 7-134, 8-138

Australia won by 38 runs

Allan Border run out twice in the Third Test at Melbourne v. Pakistan.

his first century of the tour and led the onslaught on the weakened Queensland attack with a six and eighteen fours. He and Gomes added 127 for the third wicket after Haynes and Greenidge had gone for 40. Bacchus also played well, but Gomes, who batted for eight hours and hit twenty-one fours, dominated the innings with the first double century of his career. Lloyd hit fiercely and shared a sixth wicket stand of 136 with Gomes. Facing a huge total, Queensland disintegrated before the West Indian pace attack, Malcolm Marshall taking five wickets. There was more determined batting at the second attempt with Greg Ritchie again the most positive of the state players. Wessels and Phillips also batted well, but Viv Richards took 5 for 88, the best bowling figures of his career.

THIRD TEST MATCH – AUSTRALIA v. PAKISTAN

With the series already decided and Pakistan without a first-class win on the tour, the Australian public showed little interest in the final Test, but the Pakistan batsmen at last revealed their true ability. Once more the Melbourne wicket was severely criticised, but Javed had no hesitation in batting when he won the toss. Mohsin Khan was out with the score at 40, but from that point onwards the Pakistan batsmen dominated the Australian attack. Majid at last reminded us of former glories and Mudassar completed a thousand runs in Test cricket. Javed and Zaheer, now completely fit, continued the onslaught on the second day and Wasim Raja and Imran Khan savaged some late runs. Throughout the two days Bruce Yardley was the Australian hero. He sent down 396 balls and, in his nineteenth Test, returned his best figures, 7 for 187, on a wicket which gave him no assistance.

As Australia batted solidly on the third day there seemed no possibility of them facing defeat. Wood took six and a quarter hours to reach his hundred, but Australia, on the fourth day, collapsed from 232 for 4 to 293 all out and so failed to save the follow-on by 8 runs. Imran took the last three wickets to become Pakistan's leading wicket-taker in Test cricket, surpassing Fazal Mahmood's record which had stood for nineteen years.

When Australia batted again their beginning was a nightmare. Wood was caught off Sarfraz and Chappell, now in a neurotic state about the pitch, fell to the same bowler. Border was run out for the second time in the match and Australia were 13 for 3. Worse was to follow and they finished the day at 78 for 5.

Only 82 minutes play was necessary on the last morning for Pakistan to achieve their first ever innings victory over Australia, Qasim and Imran doing the final damage.

Yardley was named Man of the Match and Imran Khan Man of the Series. It was all some consolation for Pakistan.

Majid Khan hooks Lillee in the Third Test at Melbourne. For Majid it was not a happy tour.

THIRD TEST MATCH – AUSTRALIA v. PAKISTAN
11, 12, 13, 14 and 15 December 1981 at Melbourne

PAKISTAN

	FIRST INNINGS	
Mudassar Nazar	c Lillee, b Yardley	95
Mohsin Khan	c Thomson, b Yardley	17
Majid Khan	c Wood, b Yardley	74
Javed Miandad†	lbw, b Yardley	62
Zaheer Abbas	c and b Yardley	90
Wasim Raja	c Laird, b Yardley	50
Imran Khan	not out	70
Sarfraz Nawaz	c Yardley, b Chappell	0
Wasim Bari*	b Yardley	8
Iqbal Qasim	not out	16
Sikhander Bakht		
Extras	b 1, lb 5, nb 12	18
	(for 8 wkts dec)	500

	O	M	R	W
Lillee	36.3	9	104	—
Alderman	27	8	62	—
Chappell	9	2	17	1
Thomson	25	2	85	—
Yardley	66	16	187	7
Border	4	1	16	—
Hughes	3	1	2	—
Laird	1	—	9	—

FALL OF WICKETS
1–40, 2–181, 3–201, 4–329, 5–363, 6–443, 7–444, 8–456

AUSTRALIA

	FIRST INNINGS		SECOND INNINGS	
G. M. Wood	c Mohsin, b Sarfraz	100	c Bari, b Sarfraz	1
B. M. Laird	lbw, b Qasim	35	c Sarfraz, b Qasim	52
G. S. Chappell†	c Bari, b Raja	22	c Miandad, b Sarfraz	0
A. R. Border	run out	7	run out	1
K. J. Hughes	c and b Qasim	34	c Majid, b Qasim	11
D. M. Wellham	c Mudassar, b Sarfraz	26	b Sarfraz	13
R. W. Marsh*	c Mudassar, b Imran	31	c Mohsin, b Qasim	21
B. Yardley	b Qasim	20	b Imran	0
D. K. Lillee	lbw, b Imran	1	c Bari, b Qasim	4
J. R. Thomson	not out	3	b Imran	17
T. M. Alderman	lbw, b Imran	1	not out	4
Extras	b 4, lb 6, nb 3	13	b 1	1
		293		125

	O	M	R	W	O	M	R	W
Imran Khan	24.1	7	41	3	14.1	5	21	2
Sarfraz Nawaz	14	3	43	2	15	10	11	3
Wasim Raja	37	7	73	1	13	2	34	—
Iqbal Qasim	55	17	104	3	24	11	44	4
Sikhander Bakht	2	—	9	—				
Majid Khan	2	—	10	—	4	1	5	—
Javed Miandad					2	—	9	—

FALL OF WICKETS
1–75, 2–118, 3–127, 4–173, 5–232, 6–235, 7–286, 8–288, 9–289
1–1, 2–9, 3–13, 4–29, 5–77, 6–78, 7–79, 8–92, 9–121

Pakistan won by an innings and 82 runs

Australia v. Pakistan – Test Match Averages

AUSTRALIA BATTING

	M	Inns	NOs	Runs	HS	Av	100s	50s
G. M. Wood	3	6	1	255	100	51.00	1	1
G. S. Chappell	3	5		251	201	50.20	1	
B. M. Laird	3	6	1	246	85	49.20		2
K. J. Hughes	3	5		193	106	38.60	1	
R. W. Marsh	3	5		192	47	28.40		
D. M. Wellham	2	3		75	36	25.00		
J. R. Thomson	3	5	3	49	22*	24.50		
A. R. Border	3	5		84	37	16.80		
B. Yardley	3	5		53	22	10.60		
T. M. Alderman	3	4	3	10	5*	10.00		
D. K. Lillee	3	5	1	39	16	9.75		

Played in one Test – G. N. Yallop 20 and 38

PAKISTAN BATTING

	M	Inns	NOs	Runs	HS	Av	100s	50s
Zaheer Abbas	2	3		170	90	56.66		2
Javed Miandad	3	5		205	79	41.00		2
Wasim Raja	3	5		181	50	36.20		1
Mudassar Nazar	3	5		169	95	33.80		1
Imran Khan	3	5	1	108	70*	27.00		1
Majid Khan	3	5		121	74	24.20		1
Mohsin Khan	2	3		71	43	23.66		
Iqbal Qasim	2	3	1	25	16*	12.50		
Sarfraz Nawaz	3	5		52	26	10.40		
Wasim Bari	3	5	1	40	20	10.00		
Sikhander Bakht	3	4	3	6	3*	6.00		

Played in one Test – Rizwan Uz-Zaman 0 and 8; Mansoor Akhtar 6 and 36; Ejaz Faqih 34 and 21

AUSTRALIA BOWLING

	Overs	Mds	Runs	Wkts	Av	Best	5/inn
G. S. Chappell	12	3	23	2	11.50	1/6	
D. K. Lillee	104.3	22	332	15	22.13	5/18	2
B. Yardley	130.5	26	399	18	22.16	7/187	2
T. M. Alderman	93.2	23	252	8	31.50	4/36	
J. R. Thomson	69	12	219	5	43.80	2/43	

Also bowled – A. R. Border 5-1-17-0 (two innings); K. J. Hughes 3-1-2-0; B. M. Laird 1-0-7-0.

PAKISTAN BOWLING

	Overs	Mds	Runs	Wkts	Av	Best	5/inn
Imran Khan	150.2	39	312	16	19.50	4/66	
Iqbal Qasim	108	33	235	10	23.50	4/44	
Sarfraz Nawaz	118	32	306	9	34.00	3/11	
Sikhander Bakht	71	9	257	5	51.40	2/79	
Wasim Raja	88	13	233	4	58.25	1/0	

Also bowled – Majid Khan 15-2-36-0 (three innings); Mudassar Nazar 4-1-11-0 (two innings); Ejaz Faqih 22-1-76-1 (one innings); Javed Miandad 6-0-29-0 (three innings).

AUSTRALIA CATCHES

11—R. W. Marsh; 4—B. Yardley and T. M. Alderman; 3—K. J. Hughes, A. R. Border, G. S. Chappell and B. M. Laird; 2—J. R. Thomson; 1—D. M. Wellham, D. K. Lillee and G. M. Wood.

PAKISTAN CATCHES

9—Wasim Bari (ct 8/st 1); 4—Mudassar Nazar; 3—Iqbal Qasim and Zaheer Abbas; 2—Majid Khan and Mohsin Khan; 1—Imran Khan, Mansoor Akhtar, Sarfraz Nawaz and Javed Miandad.

The record breaker at rest – Dennis Lillee.

16 December 1981

at Caloundra

West Indians 214 for 7 (S. F. A. Bacchus 103 not out)
Queensland Country XI 146 for 8
West Indians won by 68 runs

After Bacchus had hit a fine century for the West Indians the Country XI found batting difficult even though Richards withdrew his pace bowlers from the attack very quickly. Eight bowlers shared the forty-five overs and proved too much for the locals.

Benson and Hedges World Series

SIXTH ONE-DAY INTERNATIONAL – AUSTRALIA v. PAKISTAN

This match was originally due to be played on 8 December but, as recorded already, it had been postponed because of a strike by power workers. Now, with the inspiration of their innings victory in the Third Test, Pakistan produced one of their very best performances to win by six wickets with just under seven overs to spare. There seemed no indication that they would gain such a comfortable victory earlier in the day when Darling and Laird began well enough for Australia. Wood and Darling continued with confident aggression, but there was a mid-innings collapse brought about by some accurate bowling from Mudassar. He bowled Wood, who played too soon, had Border caught behind when he hung his bat out and Chappell, not fully fit, caught on the leg-side. After 33 overs Australia had been reduced to 132 for 5 from 106 for 1.

Marsh and Wellham batted with great sense and added 90 in the last seventeen overs so that the target for Pakistan was by no means an easy one. Mohsin went quickly to Lawson and Australia were on top.

Mudassar and Zaheer took complete charge of the match, however, Mudassar with a practical approach and Zaheer with his elegance and fire. Mudassar was caught off a top edge and Zaheer was twice dropped before completing a century of charm. He was bowled by Chappell and Javed was lbw to the same bowler, but the game had long since passed to Pakistan who went to the top of the table.

Mudassar Nazar's all-round performance won him the Man of the Match award.

SIXTH ONE-DAY INTERNATIONAL: AUSTRALIA v. PAKISTAN
17 December 1981 at Sydney

AUSTRALIA				PAKISTAN			
W. M. Darling	run out		74	Mudassar Nazar	c Alderman, b Thomson		50
B. M. Laird	b Sikhander		12	Mohsin Khan	b Lawson		2
G. M. Wood	b Mudassar		25	Zaheer Abbas	b Chappell		108
A. R. Border	c Ashraf, b Mudassar		2	Javed Miandad†	lbw, b Chappell		22
D. M. Wellham	run out		42	Majid Khan	not out		20
G. S. Chappell†	c Miandad, b Mudassar		0	Wasim Raja	not out		9
R. W. Marsh*	not out		54	Imran Khan			
D. K. Lillee				Ashraf Ali*			
G. F. Lawson				Sarfraz Nawaz			
J. R. Thomson				Tahir Naqqash			
T. M. Alderman				Sikhander Bakht			
Extras	b 2, lb 7, w 1, nb 3		13	Extras	b 2, lb 5, w 4, nb 1		12
	(for 6 wkts)		222		(for 4 wkts)		223

	O	M	R	W		O	M	R	W
Imran Khan	10	—	47	—	Lawson	9	—	43	1
Sikhander Bakht	8	—	48	1	Alderman	10	1	41	—
Sarfraz Nawaz	9	—	38	—	Lillee	8	1	38	—
Tahir Naqqash	3	—	21	—	Thomson	7	—	27	1
Majid Khan	10	—	35	—	Border	3	—	24	—
Mudassar Nazar	10	4	20	3	Chappell	6.2	—	38	2

FALL OF WICKETS
1–40, 2–106, 3–110, 4–132, 5–132, 6–222

FALL OF WICKETS
1–15, 2–120, 3–174, 4–205

Pakistan won by 6 wickets

Benson and Hedges World Series

SEVENTH ONE-DAY INTERNATIONAL – PAKISTAN v. WEST INDIES

With West Indies languishing at the bottom of the table with only one win from three games and Pakistan in a state of elation at recent successes, it was felt that West Indian dominance in limited over cricket was under threat for the first time. Clive Lloyd was quoted as saying that his team faced a crisis and he looked for a drastic improvement in application. A close and tense struggle was expected, but as it transpired West Indies overwhelmed their inconsistent opponents who were most unfortunate to lose Majid who was injured when he slipped in the dressing room and took no part in the match.

After twenty-nine overs Pakistan were 109 for 2, but the spin of Richards changed the course of the game and the later Pakistani batsmen wilted before pace and fine fielding.

West Indies began badly, losing Bacchus and Richards for 21, but Desmond Haynes played a fine innings which blossomed from early caution into a cascade of brilliant shots. Lloyd gave him good support until he was magnificently caught and bowled by Wasim Raja, but this was Pakistan's last success. Haynes, who was named Man of the Match, and Gomes scored the last 66 runs in 53 minutes and West Indies won with 7.4 overs to spare and such talents as Dujon and Logie were not required to bat.

Benson and Hedges World Series

EIGHTH ONE-DAY INTERNATIONAL – AUSTRALIA v. WEST INDIES

If people still had doubts as to the efficiency of the West Indians in the one-day game, those doubts were quickly dispelled when the West Indians routed Australia in Perth with twenty overs to spare.

The game belonged to the West Indians from the very start when Holding, bowling at a brisk pace and making the ball lift disconcertingly, dismissed both Darling and Chappell. Laird was out to Marshall and Australia never totally recovered from 30 for 3.

Border batted with the restraint of one for whom things have not gone well of late and Hughes flourished very briefly. Wood and Lillee batted with bravery and aggression, but 188 was a score that was unlikely to strike terror into the visitors.

Haynes and Bacchus went early and Lloyd joined Richards with the total 37 for 2. What followed was a display of devastating hitting which both delighted and stunned the record crowd of twenty-six thousand.

In 92 minutes these two great players added 153 runs. Richards hit three sixes and eight fours in his innings of 72 which came off only 62 balls, but for once he was almost overshadowed by his captain who hit eleven of the 82 deliveries that he received to the boundary. The Australian attack was left limp and the crowd in a state of ecstatic, if stunned, admiration.

SEVENTH ONE-DAY INTERNATIONAL: PAKISTAN v. WEST INDIES
19 December 1981 at Perth

PAKISTAN					WEST INDIES			
Mudassar Nazar	c Richards, b Marshall		30		D. L. Haynes	not out		82
Mohsin Khan	c Lloyd, b Garner		6		S. F. A. Bacchus	c Bari, b Imran		4
Zaheer Abbas	c Dujon, b Richards		35		I. V. A. Richards	c Bari, b Sarfraz		8
Javed Miandad†	c Bacchus, b Richards		21		C. H. Lloyd†	c and b Raja		32
Wasim Raja	c Haynes, b Richards		17		H. A. Gomes	not out		26
Imran Khan	not out		29		P. J. Dujon*			
Ejaz Faqih	c Haynes, b Garner		2		A. L. Logie			
Sarfraz Nawaz	c Roberts, b Garner		0		M. D. Marshall			
Wasim Bari*	run out		4		M. A. Holding			
Sikhander Bakht	c Dujon, b Marshall		0		J. Garner			
Majid Khan	absent injured		0		A. M. E. Roberts			
Extras	b 4, lb 3, w 2, nb 7		16		Extras	b 1, lb 3, w 2, nb 3		9
			160			(for 3 wkts)		161

	O	M	R	W		O	M	R	W
Holding	8	1	15	—	Imran Khan	8.2	—	38	1
Roberts	8	1	21	—	Sarfraz Nawaz	10	1	29	1
Garner	9	1	23	3	Sikhander Bakht	6	—	27	—
Marshall	9.4	1	33	2	Mudassar Nazar	1	—	1	—
Richards	10	—	52	3	Ejaz Faqih	6	—	30	—
					Wasim Raja	10	1	26	1
					Javed Miandad	1	—	1	—

FALL OF WICKETS
1–29, 2–61, 3–106, 4–107, 5–148, 6–151, 7–152, 8–156, 9–160

FALL OF WICKETS
1–5, 2–21, 3–95

West Indies won by 7 wickets

EIGHTH ONE-DAY INTERNATIONAL: AUSTRALIA v. WEST INDIES
20 December 1981 at Perth

AUSTRALIA					WEST INDIES			
W. M. Darling	b Holding		7		D. L. Haynes	c Chappell, b Lillee		9
B. M. Laird	lbw, b Marshall		7		S. F. A. Bacchus	c Thomson, b Alderman		21
G. S. Chappell†	c Haynes, b Holding		0		I. V. A. Richards	not out		72
A. R. Border	c Bacchus, b Marshall		27		C. H. Lloyd†	not out		80
K. J. Hughes	c Holding, b Marshall		18		H. A. Gomes			
G. M. Wood	run out		54		P. J. Dujon*			
R. W. Marsh*	c Logie, b Richards		0		A. L. Logie			
D. K. Lillee	not out		42		M. D. Marshall			
G. F. Lawson	b Garner		0		A. M. E. Roberts			
J. R. Thomson	run out		5		M. A. Holding			
T. M. Alderman	not out		9		J. Garner			
Extras	lb 12, w 5, nb 2		19		Extras	w 4, nb 4		8
	(for 9 wkts)		188			(for 2 wkts)		190

	O	M	R	W		O	M	R	W
Holding	10	—	37	2	Lillee	6	1	36	1
Roberts	10	1	26	—	Alderman	8	1	41	1
Garner	10	1	32	1	Thomson	5	—	24	—
Marshall	10	—	31	3	Lawson	6	—	46	—
Richards	10	—	43	1	Chappell	5	—	35	—

FALL OF WICKETS
1–10, 2–20, 3–30, 4–62, 5–78, 6–80, 7–150, 8–150, 9–166

FALL OF WICKETS
1–23, 2–37

West Indies won by 8 wickets

22 December 1981

at Albany

West Indians 290 for 2 (D. L. Haynes 94 retired, S. F. A. Bacchus 91 retired, H. A. Gomes 55)
Western Australia Country XI 184 (L. Scott 62, A. Logie 4 for 61)

West Indians won by 106 runs

Haynes and Bacchus put on 188 for the first wicket in the 110 minutes play before lunch at which point they retired. The local side could never hope to recover from this blistering attack and they had further problems against the spin of Joseph later in the day.

FIRST TEST MATCH – AUSTRALIA v. WEST INDIES

When Australia were 8 for 3 in the twelfth over of the first day, Greg Chappell having recorded his fourth consecutive duck in thirteen days, there were few who would have given much hope for their chances of either survival or recovery. Border left at 26 and Wellham at 59 so that there seemed to be unending misery for the Australian supporters.

Holding, at his fearsome best, had taken three of the first four wickets and Garner and Croft were no less demanding than the two opening bowlers. Marsh and Yardley batted with courage and determination, but the Australian hero was Kim Hughes. Mixing his natural aggression with discipline and unrelenting concentration, he scored the seventh, and greatest, Test century of his career. That he was able to reach his memorable century was due in no small measure to Terry Alderman.

When Geoff Lawson was bowled by Holding, Australia were 155 for 9. Alderman, with a first-class average of just over six, gave little confidence that he would be able to stay for long. He lasted for 56 minutes, however, during which time 43 invaluable runs were scored. Sustaining two nasty blows, Alderman scored ten before giving Murray his fifth catch of the day behind the stumps. Before this Hughes had square cut Garner mightily for four to reach his hundred and as the crowd of over thirty-nine thousand rose to him he punched the air in elation and acclaim.

Lillee began the bowling for Australia needing five wickets to beat Lance Gibbs' record as the most prolific wicket-taker in Test history. By close of play on the first day he needed only two more wickets. Facing Australia's 198, West Indies were shattered to 10 for 4. Lillee dismissed Haynes, Croft and Richards in the space of eleven balls and Alderman sent back Bacchus. He had to wait until after lunch on the second day to reach the target. Dujon hooked him high and Hughes took a spectacular running catch at backward square-leg and then Gomes edged to Chappell at slip to give Lillee his 310th wicket in Test cricket.

By the end of the day West Indies were hanging on grimly at 187 for 9 and on the next morning Garner and Murray took this to 201, a first innings lead of three. Lillee finished with a marvellous 7 for 83.

Wood and Laird batted with great tenacity in the second innings and although Chappell again failed, Border ended a miserable spell with a determined and invaluable knock.

FIRST TEST MATCH – AUSTRALIA v. WEST INDIES
26, 27, 28, 29 and 30 December 1981 at Melbourne

AUSTRALIA

	FIRST INNINGS		SECOND INNINGS	
B. M. Laird	c Murray, b Holding	4	(2) lbw, b Croft	64
G. M. Wood	c Murray, b Roberts	3	(1) c Murray, b Garner	46
G. S. Chappell†	c Murray, b Holding	0	c Murray, b Garner	6
A. R. Border	c Murray, b Holding	4	b Holding	66
K. J. Hughes	not out	100	b Holding	8
D. M. Wellham	c sub (Logie), b Croft	17	lbw, b Holding	2
R. W. Marsh*	c Richards, b Garner	21	c Murray, b Holding	2
B. Yardley	b Garner	21	b Garner	13
D. K. Lillee	c Gomes, b Holding	1	c Murray, b Holding	0
G. F. Lawson	b Holding	2	not out	0
T. M. Alderman	c Murray, b Croft	10	b Holding	1
Extras	b 1, lb 6, nb 8	15	b 5, lb 4, w 1, nb 4	14
		198		**222**

	O	M	R	W	O	M	R	W
Holding	17	3	45	5	21.3	5	62	6
Roberts	15	6	40	1	18	4	31	—
Garner	20	6	59	2	18	5	37	3
Croft	16.1	3	39	2	20	2	61	1
Richards					5	—	17	—

FALL OF WICKETS
1-4, 2-4, 3-8, 4-26, 5-59, 6-115, 7-149, 8-153, 9-155
1-82, 2-106, 3-139, 4-184, 5-190, 6-199, 7-215, 8-218, 9-220

WEST INDIES

	FIRST INNINGS		SECOND INNINGS	
D. L. Haynes	c Border, b Lillee	1	c Lillee, b Yardley	28
S. F. A. Bacchus	c Wood, b Alderman	1	lbw, b Alderman	0
C. E. H. Croft	lbw, b Lillee	0	(11) not out	0
I. V. A. Richards	b Lillee	2	(3) b Alderman	0
C. H. Lloyd†	c Alderman, b Yardley	29	(4) c Border, b Lawson	19
H. A. Gomes	c Chappell, b Lillee	55	(5) b Yardley	24
P. J. Dujon	c Hughes, b Lillee	41	(6) c Marsh, b Yardley	43
D. A. Murray*	not out	32	(7) c Marsh, b Yardley	10
A. M. E. Roberts	c Marsh, b Lillee	18	(8) lbw, b Lillee	10
M. A. Holding	c and b Alderman	2	(9) lbw, b Lillee	7
J. Garner	c Laird, b Lillee	7	(10) lbw, b Lillee	0
Extras	b 1, lb 3, nb 9	13	b 1, lb 10, nb 9	20
		201		**161**

	O	M	R	W	O	M	R	W
Lillee	26.3	3	83	7	27.1	8	44	3
Alderman	18	3	54	2	9	3	23	2
Lawson	9	2	28	—	17	3	36	1
Chappell	2	2	0	—				
Yardley	7	2	23	1	21	7	38	4

FALL OF WICKETS
1-3, 2-5, 3-6, 4-10, 5-62, 6-134, 7-147, 8-174, 9-183
1-4, 2-4, 3-38, 4-80, 5-88, 6-116, 7-150, 8-154, 9-154

Australia won by 58 runs

Michael Holding could not be denied by the remaining batsmen, however, and Australia went from 184 for 3 to 222 all out.

It was not expected that West Indies would fail a second time, but Alderman produced a match winning burst in which he had Bacchus lbw and bowled Richards for nought. There was recovery, but Lillee took another three wickets and Yardley proved the value of spin by dismissing Haynes, Gomes, Dujon and Murray who had earlier set a West Indian record with nine catches behind the wicket.

The interest in the game was immense and Australia's victory grandly acclaimed. On the last day when only seven minutes was needed for the Australians to capture the one remaining West Indian wicket, three thousand people turned up to celebrate the Australian triumph. It was a Test match of splendour and heroic deeds of which Kim Hughes' first innings hundred was deemed the greatest.

26, 27, 28 and 29 December 1981
at Adelaide

Pakistanis 358 for 4 dec (Rizwan Uz-Zaman 126, Javed Miandad 90, Mansoor Akhtar 81) and 415 (Zaheer Abbas 117, Mansoor Akhtar 86, Javed Miandad 74, G. J. Winter 4 for 89)

South Australia 404 for 6 dec (W. M. Darling 132, W. B. Phillips 106, D. W. Hookes 91) and 125 for 1 (W. M. Darling 58 not out, W. B. Phillips 54)

Match drawn

A run-saturated match began with Rizwan playing his best innings of the tour in an opening stand of 139, but South Australia responded positively when openers Phillips and Darling both scored centuries and put on 228 for the first wicket. Hookes recalled past glories and his side dominated as Pakistan slumped to 180 for 5, but on the last day, Zaheer, batting at number eight, hit a sparkling hundred and there was a good innings from Javed. As the game ended in a tame draw Pakistan's main concern was that Majid Khan was likely to return to Pakistan because of his injured back.

SECOND TEST MATCH – AUSTRALIA v. WEST INDIES

In spite of concern over an injured knee, Gordon Greenidge started briskly for West Indies in their attempt to draw level in the series. The West Indian innings was given a reassuring foundation by Larry Gomes who reached his third Test hundred, all of them against Australia. He batted five and three quarter hours and hit nine fours in his 126. The West Indian total was an insurance against defeat and they took a grip on the match when Holding took two wickets at the close of the second day. The Australian discomfort continued the next day when only the determination of Yardley and Border, in contrasting styles, brought them to within 117 of the West Indian total.

A splendid display of off-spin bowling by Yardley gave Australia hope of an improbable victory. He controlled length and flight in conditions which gave him just a little assistance and his total of 7 for 98 brought his Test Wickets for the season to 33. He was aided by splendid catching, the catch by

SECOND TEST MATCH – AUSTRALIA v. WEST INDIES
2, 3, 4, 5 and 6 January 1982 at Sydney

WEST INDIES

	FIRST INNINGS		SECOND INNINGS	
C. G. Greenidge	c Laird, b Lillee	66	c Yardley, b Lillee	8
D. L. Haynes	lbw, b Thomson	15	lbw, b Lillee	51
I. V. A. Richards	c Marsh, b Lillee	44	c Border, b Alderman	22
H. A. Gomes	c Chappell, b Yardley	126	c Border, b Yardley	43
C. H. Lloyd†	c Marsh, b Thomson	40	c Hughes, b Yardley	57
P. J. Dujon	c and b Thomson	44	c and b Yardley	48
D. A. Murray*	b Yardley	13	c Laird, b Yardley	1
M. A. Holding	lbw, b Lillee	9	c Dyson, b Yardley	5
S. T. Clarke	b Yardley	14	c Dyson, b Yardley	5
J. Garner	c Marsh, b Lillee	1	(11) b Yardley	0
C. E. H. Croft	not out	0	(10) not out	4
Extras	lb 3, nb 9	12	lb 1, w 5, nb 5	11
		384		**255**

AUSTRALIA

	FIRST INNINGS		SECOND INNINGS	
B. M. Laird	c Dujon, b Garner	14	c Murray, b Croft	38
G. M. Wood	c Murray, b Holding	63	(6) not out	7
J. Dyson	lbw, b Holding	28	(2) not out	127
T. M. Alderman	b Clarke	0		
G. S. Chappell†	c Dujon, b Holding	12	(3) c Murray, b Croft	0
K. J. Hughes	b Garner	16	(4) lbw, b Gomes	13
A. R. Border	not out	53	(5) b Gomes	9
R. W. Marsh*	c Holding, b Gomes	17		
B. Yardley	b Holding	45		
D. K. Lillee	c Garner, b Holding	4		
J. R. Thomson	run out	8		
Extras	b 1, lb 2, w 2, nb 2	7	b 2, lb 1, nb 3	6
		267	(for 4 wkts)	**200**

	O	M	R	W	O	M	R	W
Lillee	39	6	119	4	20	6	50	2
Alderman	30	9	73	—	12	2	46	1
Thomson	20	1	93	3	15	3	50	—
Yardley	26.2	3	87	3	31.4	6	98	7
Border	1	1	0	—				

	O	M	R	W	O	M	R	W
Holding	29	9	64	5	19	6	31	—
Clarke	16	4	51	1	16	9	25	—
Garner	20	4	52	2	12	3	27	—
Croft	20	7	53	—	27	5	58	2
Richards	13	7	21	—	13	3	33	—
Gomes	9	1	19	1	15	7	20	2

FALL OF WICKETS
1–37, 2–128, 3–133, 4–229, 5–325, 6–346, 7–363, 8–379, 9–380
1–29, 2–52, 3–112, 4–179, 5–208, 6–225, 7–231, 8–246, 9–255

FALL OF WICKETS
1–38, 2–108, 3–111, 4–112, 5–128, 6–141, 7–172, 8–242, 9–246
1–104, 2–104, 3–149, 4–169

Match drawn

Alderman bowled Holding 1, Australia's second innings, Melbourne Test.

which Dyson dismissed Clarke being of the highest quality. At deep mid-wicket Dyson held a tremendous blow from Clarke high over his head as he leapt in the air.

Dyson's form continued as he and Laird began with a stand of 104. Chappell failed again and now looked to have lost all confidence in his batting, but as Dyson reached his second Test century Australia drew the match with ease and West Indies were forced to contemplate that spin might have given them victory.

Yardley's fine bowling rightly earned him the Man of the Match award.

1, 2, 3 and 4 January 1982

at Launceston

Tasmania 158 (R. Jeffrey 64, Iqbal Qasim 5 for 31) and 316 (B. F. Davison 72, Tahir Naqqash 4 for 60)
Pakistanis 472 for 5 dec (Javed Miandad 158 not out, Rizwan Uz-Zaman 118, Mansoor Akhtar 73, Saleem Malik 51 not out) and 4 for 0

Pakistanis won by 10 wickets

The left-arm spin of Iqbal Qasim destroyed Tasmania on the opening day and once the tourists, in their last first-class match, had asserted themselves with some brilliant batting, the outcome of the match was never in doubt. Rizwan played another fine innings, but he was overshadowed by his captain Javed who was in devastating form. Davison, who had been forced to retire hurt in the first innings, batted well in the second, but Pakistan were not to be denied.

6 January 1982

at Stawell

Victorian Country XI 178 for 8 (R. Scott 52, W. Walsh 50 not out, Tahir Naqash 6 for 32)
Pakistanis 179 for 5 (Zaheer Abbas 81 not out, R. Davis 4 for 50)

Pakistanis won by 5 wickets

The country side lost three wickets for 1 run but recovered well. Then Pakistan struggled and lost 5 for 58 before Zaheer and Ejaz saw them to victory.

Benson and Hedges World Series

NINTH ONE-DAY INTERNATIONAL – AUSTRALIA v. PAKISTAN

An exhilarating innings of 84 in 110 minutes, during which time he dominated two vital partnerships, by Zaheer Abbas gave Pakistan control of the fourth one-day match between the two sides. Nevertheless, Australia should have considered the target of 219 in 50 overs well within their reach. The target would have been smaller had Laird not dropped Zaheer when he had scored 29. Worse was to follow for Laird when he was needlessly run out with only five runs scored. Dyson also left quickly, but Wood and Chappell revived hope with a careful stand which ended when Wood was caught at square-leg. After this only Border showed the necessary application as Darling, Lillee and Lawson emulated Laird's suicidal tendencies.

TENTH ONE-DAY INTERNATIONAL – AUSTRALIA v. WEST INDIES

78,142 people, the largest crowd ever to attend a limited over match, saw Australia give another inept display and, by losing to the West Indies, make their chances of reaching the World Series Final seem remote.

The Australians recalled two senior players in McCosker and Malone, both of whom performed creditably, but, in spite of Chappell's determined knock, they could muster only 146 and were out in under 43 overs. Certainly the wicket was not good and the bowling, Holding's in particular, was hostile and accurate, but much of the batting was feeble.

The West Indians began badly, losing both openers for 18, but when Dujon came to the wicket with the score at 52 for 4 he made it look a different game, batting with a flair and confidence that mocked the efforts of the earlier batsmen.

ELEVENTH ONE-DAY INTERNATIONAL – PAKISTAN v. WEST INDIES

Playing under floodlights for the first time, Pakistan were well beaten by West Indies who thereby assured themselves of a place in the final. Pakistan batted limply and when they were 75 for 5 it seemed that there would be little contest. Imran Khan then played a splendid innings and Wasim Raja and Tahir Naqqash made contributions that ensured that West Indies would have a target of more than moderate size to chase.

Haynes again failed, but Greenidge was at his most belligerent and, with Richards and Lloyd also finding form, West Indies won with just under eight overs to spare.

TWELFTH ONE-DAY INTERNATIONAL – AUSTRALIA v. PAKISTAN

An exciting innings from Kim Hughes who shared a stand of 87 with Greg Chappell after Australia had threatened to falter. They had started well through Wood and Laird with McCosker maintaining the momentum, but it was the final ten overs, from which 76 runs were scored, that gave them the decisive advantage. Hughes was quite magnificent in his approach, his belligerence never marring his elegance as he scored his runs in 18 overs.

NINTH ONE-DAY INTERNATIONAL: AUSTRALIA v. PAKISTAN
9 January 1982 at Melbourne

PAKISTAN				AUSTRALIA			
Mansoor Akhtar	c Marsh, b Alderman		5	G. M. Wood	c Raja, b Mudassar		38
Mudassar Nazar	lbw, b Thomson		40	B. M. Laird	run out		4
Zaheer Abbas	c Laird, b Thomson		84	J. Dyson	lbw, b Sikhander		11
Javed Miandad†	c Laird, b Lillee		37	G. S. Chappell†	b Ejaz		35
Imran Khan	run out		3	A. R. Border	not out		75
Wasim Raja	not out		19	W. M. Darling	run out		5
Ejaz Faqih	run out		1	R. W. Marsh*	c Javed, b Ejaz		2
Sarfraz Nawaz	not out		14	D. K. Lillee	run out		8
Wasim Bari*				G. F. Lawson	run out		1
Tahir Naqqash				J. R. Thomson	b Imran		2
Sikhander Bakht				T. M. Alderman	b Sikhander		0
Extras	lb 10, w 1, nb 4		15	Extras	b 4, lb 8		12
	(for 6 wkts)		218				193

	O	M	R	W		O	M	R	W
Lawson	10	—	36	—	Imran Khan	9	2	21	1
Alderman	10	—	37	1	Sarfraz Nawaz	8	—	34	—
Lillee	10	1	37	1	Tahir Naqqash	8	—	35	—
Thomson	10	—	55	2	Sikhander Bakht	8	—	33	2
Chappell	10	3	38	—	Mudassar Nazar	6	—	24	1
					Ejaz Faqih	10	—	34	2

FALL OF WICKETS
1–10; 2–79, 3–169, 4–172, 5–193, 6–199

FALL OF WICKETS
1–5, 2–41, 3–74, 4–135, 5–147, 6–153, 7–175, 8–181, 9–190

Pakistan won by 25 runs

In reply Pakistan mounted no real challenge and although Australia were still without the injured Alderman, their attack was strong enough to stem any threatened flow of runs. Mansoor Akhtar alone played with certainty and his driving was particularly impressive.

Mudassar, recovered from food poisoning, was bowled in the third over and Zaheer promised only briefly before hitting Lawson to cover. Javed was lbw playing across the line and when Mansoor was caught at mid-on Pakistan had surrendered the match.

TENTH ONE-DAY INTERNATIONAL: AUSTRALIA v. WEST INDIES
10 January 1982 at Melbourne

AUSTRALIA

Batsman	How Out	Runs
B. M. Laird	hit wkt, b Holding	4
G. M. Wood	c Greenidge, b Holding	3
R. B. McCosker	run out	20
G. S. Chappell†	c Logie, b Roberts	59
A. R. Border	b Marshall	6
W. M. Darling	c Holding, b Gomes	20
R. W. Marsh*	c Logie, b Gomes	0
B. Yardley	c Logie, b Holding	23
D. K. Lillee	c Holding, b Roberts	1
G. F. Lawson	not out	0
M. F. Malone	b Holding	1
Extras	lb 4, w 1, nb 4	9
		146

WEST INDIES

Batsman	How Out	Runs
C. G. Greenidge	c Border, b Malone	9
D. L. Haynes	lbw, b Lawson	1
I. V. A. Richards	c Lawson, b Yardley	32
H. A. Gomes	c Laird, b Malone	7
C. H. Lloyd†	lbw, b Lawson	37
P. J. Dujon*	not out	51
M. D. Marshall	not out	5
A. M. E. Roberts		
A. L. Logie		
M. A. Holding		
J. Garner		
Extras	lb 3, w 1, nb 1	5
	(for 5 wkts)	147

Bowler	O	M	R	W
Holding	7.5	1	32	4
Roberts	7	—	23	2
Garner	6	—	13	—
Marshall	5	—	12	1
Richards	10	1	31	—
Gomes	7	1	26	2

Bowler	O	M	R	W
Lillee	10	—	34	—
Lawson	9.1	—	31	2
Malone	10	5	9	2
Chappell	9	1	33	—
Yardley	6	—	25	1
Border	3	—	10	—

FALL OF WICKETS
1–7, 2–16, 3–33, 4–41, 5–99, 6–101, 7–140, 8–144, 9–145

FALL OF WICKETS
1–7, 2–18, 3–48, 4–52, 5–137

West Indies won by 5 wickets

ELEVENTH ONE-DAY INTERNATIONAL: PAKISTAN v. WEST INDIES
12 January 1982 at Sydney

PAKISTAN

Batsman	How Out	Runs
Mohsin Khan	b Marshall	17
Mansoor Akhtar	run out	13
Zaheer Abbas	run out	1
Javed Miandad†	c Dujon, b Garner	26
Wasim Raja	c Logie, b Roberts	33
Saleem Malik	b Garner	0
Imran Khan	not out	62
Ejaz Faqih	b Garner	5
Tahir Naqqash	not out	23
Wasim Bari*		
Sikhander Bakht		
Extras	b 1, lb 5, w 7, nb 3	16
	(for 7 wkts)	191

WEST INDIES

Batsman	How Out	Runs
C. G. Greenidge	lbw, b Imran	84
D. L. Haynes	b Imran	2
I. V. A. Richards	b Tahir	41
C. H. Lloyd†	not out	35
H. A. Gomes	not out	15
P. J. Dujon*		
A. L. Logie		
M. D. Marshall		
A. M. E. Roberts		
M. A. Holding		
J. Garner		
Extras	lb 5, w 5, nb 5	15
	(for 3 wkts)	192

Bowler	O	M	R	W
Holding	10	1	37	—
Roberts	10	—	47	1
Marshall	10	1	33	1
Garner	10	1	17	3
Richards	10	—	41	—

Bowler	O	M	R	W
Imran Khan	10	—	42	2
Sikhander Bakht	7	1	40	—
Wasim Raja	9.1	—	37	—
Tahir Naqqash	10	—	31	1
Ejaz Faqih	6	—	27	—

FALL OF WICKETS
1–26, 2–32, 3–32, 4–75, 5–75, 6–122, 7–144

FALL OF WICKETS
1–37, 2–107, 3–155

West Indies won by 7 wickets

Allan Border is bowled by West Indian fast bowler Malcolm Marshall for 6 in the Tenth One-Day International.

TWELFTH ONE-DAY INTERNATIONAL: AUSTRALIA v. PAKISTAN
14 January 1982 at Sydney

AUSTRALIA							PAKISTAN					
G. M. Wood	b Mudassar			42			Mudassar Nazar	b Lillee				5
B. M. Laird	c Bari, b Mudassar			45			Mansoor Akhtar	c Lawson, b Chappell				40
R. B. McCosker	lbw, b Mudassar			13			Zaheer Abbas	c Border, b Lawson				12
G. S. Chappell†	c Raja, b Sikhander			36			Javed Miandad†	lbw, b Chappell				8
K. J. Hughes	not out			63			Wasim Raja	b Malone				16
R. W. Marsh*	c Zaheer, b Imran			3			Imran Khan	b Thomson				39
A. R. Border	not out			11			Ejaz Faqih	c Marsh, b Malone				0
D. K. Lillee							Sarfraz Nawaz	c Hughes, b Lillee				5
G. F. Lawson							Tahir Naqqash	c Lillee, b Lawson				13
J. R. Thomson							Wasim Bari*	retired hurt				9
M. F. Malone							Sikhander Bakht	not out				0
Extras	b 3, lb 8, w 3, nb 3			17			Extras	lb 6, w 1				7
	(for 5 wkts)			230								154

	O	M	R	W				O	M	R	W
Imran Khan	10	—	37	1			Lillee	7.3	1	23	2
Sarfraz Nawaz	9	—	45	—			Thomson	7	1	19	1
Tahir Naqqash	5	2	20	—			Lawson	8	—	45	2
Sikhander Bakht	9	—	43	1			Malone	10	2	36	2
Mudassar Nazar	10	1	36	3			Chappell	8	—	24	2
Ejaz Faqih	7	—	32	—							

FALL OF WICKETS
1–80, 2–108, 3–111, 4–198, 5–206

FALL OF WICKETS
1–8, 2–30, 3–66, 4–71, 5–89, 6–89, 7–99, 8–129, 9–150

Australia won by 76 runs

Benson and Hedges World Series

THIRTEENTH ONE-DAY INTERNATIONAL – PAKISTAN v. WEST INDIES

With the knowledge that victory in this, their last game would clinch them a place in the final of the Benson and Hedges World Series, Pakistan welcomed back Majid Khan. West Indies, on the other hand, were troubled by injuries. Murray was still absent with a broken finger and Logie was out with a broken nose, but still Pakistan were thwarted.

Pakistan made a promising start with Mudassar in brave and determined form. In thirty overs they had reached 100 for 2 and seemed set for a good score, but then there was a minor collapse and to add to their problems Wasim Raja pulled a hamstring. Garner bowled with frustrating economy and Pakistan finished on a disappointing 177.

An hour's delay through rain reduced the West Indian target to 107 in 30 overs. With a zest in the field and a fire and accuracy in their bowling that they had not always produced in previous matches, Pakistan made the West Indian task extremely difficult; Greenidge went at 12, Richards for nought, Haynes at 36 and Lloyd was out at 38. Bacchus alone played with the necessary mixture of sense and aggression, but the eighth wicket fell at 90. Pakistan dreamed of success and then Holding played a vital miniature and Garner stayed while the two last runs were scored.

Pakistan's defeat gave Australia hope of qualifying for the final.

FOURTEENTH ONE-DAY INTERNATIONAL - AUSTRALIA v. WEST INDIES

Another large crowd saw Australia narrowly beaten in a match which rain interruption reduced to forty overs. Laird and Wood gave Australia a sound start, but then wickets fell steadily and only the determination of Greg Chappell, playing by far his best innings for several weeks, lifted the home side to a reasonable score.

West Indies once more began badly and Richards, captaining the side as Lloyd had a mild bout of flu, played wildly before hitting Thomson high to extra cover. It was the dependable Gomes who gave the innings the substance that was needed to achieve victory. Bacchus had a brief flourish and Lloyd played well in spite of his illness. He was calm when calmness was most needed and West Indies moved to a tense, but unflustered victory.

18 January 1982

at Junction Oval, Melbourne
Victorian XI 151 for 9
Pakistanis 156 for 1 (Majid Khan 78 not out)
Pakistanis won by 9 wickets

This match was hastily added to the programme in order to give Pakistan some practice as they were likely to reach the final of the Benson and Hedges series. The tourists won easily with Majid Khan displaying his talents excitingly and showing that he had completely recovered from his back injury.

THIRTEENTH ONE-DAY INTERNATIONAL: PAKISTAN v. WEST INDIES
16 January 1982 at Brisbane

PAKISTAN				WEST INDIES			
Mudassar Nazar	run out		40	C. G. Greenidge	b Sarfraz		7
Mansoor Akhtar	c Greenidge, b Holding		4	D. L. Haynes	c sub (Mohsin), b Sarfraz		13
Zaheer Abbas	c Lloyd, b Richards		17	I. V. A. Richards	c Imran, b Sarfraz		0
Javed Miandad†	c Lloyd, b Roberts		25	H. A. Gomes	b Sikhander		13
Imran Khan	c Dujon, b Garner		31	C. H. Lloyd†	c Mudassar, b Sikhander		1
Wasim Raja	retired hurt		12	S. F. A. Bacchus	not out		36
Majid Khan	c Dujon, b Holding		10	A. M. E. Roberts	c Sarfraz, b Mudassar		1
Ashraf Ali*	run out		3	P. J. Dujon*	c and b Sikhander		13
Sarfraz Nawaz	c Clarke, b Garner		10	S. T. Clarke	c Ashraf, b Imran		1
Iqbal Qasim	c Greenidge, b Garner		2	M. A. Holding	c Ashraf, b Mudassar		8
Sikhander Bakht	not out		1	J. Garner	not out		1
Extras	b 2, lb 12, w 6, nb 2		22	Extras	b 4, lb 4, w 5		13
	(for 9 wkts)		177		(for 9 wkts)		107

	O	M	R	W		O	M	R	W
Holding	10	3	23	2	Imran Khan	10	1	23	1
Clarke	10	2	28	—	Sarfraz Nawaz	10	1	31	3
Roberts	10	1	33	1	Sikhander Bakht	6.5	—	29	3
Garner	10	1	19	3	Mudassar Nazar	2	—	11	2
Richards	10	—	52	1					

FALL OF WICKETS
1–16, 2–57, 3–101, 4–111, 5–115, 6–161, 7–165, 8–175, 9–177

FALL OF WICKETS
1–12, 2–12, 3–36, 4–38, 5–61, 6–69, 7–83, 8–90, 9–105

West Indies won by 1 wicket (Target reduced to 107 in 30 overs by rain)

FOURTEENTH ONE-DAY INTERNATIONAL: AUSTRALIA v. WEST INDIES
17 January 1982 at Brisbane

AUSTRALIA					WEST INDIES				
B. M. Laird	b Garner			26	C. G. Greenidge	c Wood, b Chappell			16
G. M. Wood	c Lloyd, b Richards			15	D. L. Haynes	c Marsh, b Lillee			11
R. B. McCosker	c Bacchus, b Clarke			18	I. V. A. Richards	c Lillee, b Thomson			34
G. S. Chappell†	c Greenidge, b Garner			61	H. A. Gomes	not out			56
K. J. Hughes	st Dujon, b Richards			2	S. F. A. Bacchus	run out			20
A. R. Border	c Garner, b Holding			20	C. H. Lloyd†	c Border, b Thomson			30
R. W. Marsh*	c Greenidge, b Garner			7	P. J. Dujon*	not out			6
J. R. Thomson	b Holding			0	A. M. E. Roberts				
D. K. Lillee	c Holding, b Garner			11	S. T. Clarke				
G. F. Lawson	not out			4	M. A. Holding				
M. F. Malone	not out			0	J. Garner				
Extras	b 2, lb 9, w 9, nb 1			21	Extras	lb 7, w 4, nb 2			13
	(for 9 wkts)			185		(for 5 wkts)			186

	O	M	R	W		O	M	R	W
Holding	8	1	38	2	Lillee	9	2	32	1
Clarke	9	1	22	1	Thomson	10	2	40	2
Garner	9	—	45	4	Malone	10	1	34	—
Roberts	5	1	11	—	Chappell	4	—	22	1
Richards	7	—	36	2	Lawson	5.4	—	45	—
Gomes	2	—	12	—					

FALL OF WICKETS
1–51, 2–58, 3–97, 4–113, 5–159, 6–161, 7–165, 8–181, 9–181

FALL OF WICKETS
1–27, 2–32, 3–94, 4–116, 5–174

West Indies won by 5 wickets

Imran Khan

Benson and Hedges World Series

FIFTEENTH ONE-DAY INTERNATIONAL – AUSTRALIA v. WEST INDIES

In front of 52,053 people Australia, with a lateness and closeness that were the essence of melodrama, beat West Indies and so passed into the final ahead of Pakistan on account of their faster run rate.

Asked to bat, and with the gates closed an hour after the start, West Indies started disastrously when Greenidge played on in the first over. Once more Haynes could not find his touch and Gomes too was out of form. With a long injured list and some of the walking wounded pressed into action, West Indies were struggling, but Richards played some characteristic shots and some one-day swipes. Bacchus, Dujon and Marshall all gave sound and pugnacious displays and the West Indies climbed to 189.

When Wood went for 1 and Chappell for another nought this seemed an immense score. Darling and Dyson both played with good sense, but at 97 for 4 Australia's hopes of a place in the final were dwindling fast.

Hughes batted with authority from the start and although his stay was not long, it was vital in increasing the tempo. Lillee and Marsh flung their bats with abandon, but Border punctuated his aggressive shots with sound defence and, ultimately, it was to him that Australia were indebted. He had just hit a boundary that made the Australian scoring rate 3.89 to West Indies 3.78 when the rains came and the players were forced to leave the field. No more play was possible and Australia went into the final ahead of Pakistan on the faster scoring rate. Whether they would have made the last 22 runs needed for victory had the game run its course is open to question. To support Border there remained only Pascoe, Thomson and Malone.

FIFTEENTH ONE-DAY INTERNATIONAL: AUSTRALIA v. WEST INDIES
19 January 1982 at Sydney

WEST INDIES

Batsman	Dismissal	Runs
C. G. Greenidge	b Lillee	1
D. L. Haynes	b Malone	5
I. V. A. Richards†	b Thomson	64
H. A. Gomes	c Marsh, b Pascoe	3
S. F. A. Bacchus	c Marsh, b Malone	20
P. J. Dujon*	b Thomson	30
M. D. Marshall	not out	32
A. M. E. Roberts	c Wood, b Pascoe	9
M. A. Holding	c Marsh, b Pascoe	0
S. T. Clarke	b Lillee	16
J. Garner	run out	2
Extras	lb 5, w 1, nb 1	7
		189

AUSTRALIA

Batsman	Dismissal	Runs
G. M. Wood	c Roberts, b Holding	1
W. M. Darling	c Clarke, b Roberts	34
J. Dyson	b Garner	37
G. S. Chappell†	lbw, b Roberts	0
K. J. Hughes	b Roberts	25
A. R. Border	not out	30
R. W. Marsh*	c Greenidge, b Marshall	12
D. K. Lillee	b Holding	6
L. S. Pascoe	not out	0
J. R. Thomson		
M. F. Malone		
Extras	lb 16, w 5, nb 2	23
	(for 7 wkts)	**168**

Bowler	O	M	R	W
Lillee	10	—	47	2
Thomson	10	1	36	2
Pascoe	10	—	44	3
Malone	10	1	27	2
Chappell	10	—	28	—

Bowler	O	M	R	W
Holding	6.1	—	34	2
Clarke	10	1	20	—
Marshall	10	—	43	1
Roberts	10	3	15	3
Garner	7	—	33	1

FALL OF WICKETS
1–2, 2–23, 3–40, 4–79, 5–103, 6–137, 7–155, 8–156, 9–182

FALL OF WICKETS
1–6, 2–57, 3–61, 4–97, 5–125, 6–144, 7–157

Australia won on faster run rate

Benson and Hedges World Series Cup – Qualifying League

Final Table	P	W	L	Pts
West Indies	10	7	3	14
Australia	10	4	6	8
Pakistan	10	4	6	8

20 January 1982

at Geelong

Geelong 191 for 6 (C. Lynch 82)
Pakistanis 192 for 7

Pakistanis won by 7 wickets

In the last match of their tour Pakistan won by seven wickets with two overs to spare. It had been an arduous tour and the preparation for Test cricket allowed by the fixture list was once more unsatisfactory. There was much travelling and a plethora of one-day matches that left the players tired and ill-equipped mentally for the sterner tests.

Benson and Hedges World Series

FIRST FINAL

A second wicket stand between Greenidge and Richards which realised 112 put West Indies in a position of strength which was never threatened for the rest of the match. Richards was at his exciting best and his 78 took only 96 minutes. Wickets fell as batsmen attempted to press for runs, but the final West Indian total proved more than adequate. Australia slumped to 64 for 6 and though there was a brief recovery, the outcome of the match was really decided before it was half over.

SECOND FINAL

With the Melbourne wicket again providing substance for much criticism, Australia were overwhelmed by West Indies for the second day running and this time they barely escaped humiliation.

Greenidge and Haynes put on 65 for the first West Indian wicket and Greenidge and Richards 85 for the second. After that it was a pillage of quick runs with Larry Gomes finding himself relegated to number eleven as the hitters were promoted. Pascoe gained some glory at the end with four wickets, but Australia looked a beaten side.

With the ball keeping low, Australia struggled from the start of their innings and it looked doubtful whether they would make a hundred. That they did was due to some hard hitting at the end, but even this could not lessen the ignominy of the defeat.

THIRD FINAL

Back in their happier hunting ground of Sydney, Australia gained a well-deserved victory over West Indies and so kept alive their hopes of winning the World Series.

There was little indication at the start that Australia would fare any better in this encounter than they had done in the first two finals for Laird and Chappell, again for nought, were out with only twenty scored. Wood played well and Hughes helped to rectify the bad start, but it was Border who, first with Marsh and then with Pascoe, gave the Australian innings respectability and with it some hope of victory.

That hope became more positive when the pace attack of Lillee, Thomson and Pascoe dismissed the first four West

INTERNATIONALS GALORE

BENSON AND HEDGES WORLD SERIES – FIRST FINAL: AUSTRALIA v. WEST INDIES
23 January 1982 at Melbourne

WEST INDIES

Batsman	Dismissal	Runs
C. G. Greenidge	b Lillee	59
D. L. Haynes	c Marsh, b Pascoe	13
I. V. A. Richards	c Wood, b Chappell	78
C. H. Lloyd†	c Pascoe, b Thomson	20
S. F. A. Bacchus	c Marsh, b Thomson	2
P. J. Dujon*	c Hughes, b Pascoe	6
H. A. Gomes	run out	6
A. M. E. Roberts	run out	5
M. A. Holding	not out	7
S. T. Clarke	not out	0
J. Garner		
Extras	lb 5, w 12, nb 3	20
	(for 8 wkts)	216

Bowler	O	M	R	W
Lillee	10	3	35	1
Thomson	10	1	44	2
Malone	10	2	25	—
Pascoe	9	1	33	2
Chappell	10	—	59	1

FALL OF WICKETS
1–26, 2–138, 3–179, 4–184, 5–197, 6–198, 7–204, 8–210

AUSTRALIA

Batsman	Dismissal	Runs
W. M. Darling	c Bacchus, b Garner	14
G. M. Wood	run out	19
J. Dyson	b Clarke	0
G. S. Chappell†	lbw, b Garner	4
K. J. Hughes	b Richards	4
A. R. Border	c and b Gomes	16
R. W. Marsh*	c Bacchus, b Clarke	32
D. K. Lillee	b Clarke	11
J. R. Thomson	b Holding	5
L. S. Pascoe	not out	3
M. F. Malone	st Dujon, b Gomes	10
Extras	b 4, lb 5, w 2, nb 1	12
		130

Bowler	O	M	R	W
Holding	8	1	19	1
Roberts	5	1	16	—
Clarke	9	1	22	3
Garner	6	3	7	2
Richards	5	1	29	1
Gomes	4.4	—	25	2

FALL OF WICKETS
1–30, 2–30, 3–43, 4–43, 5–56, 6–64, 7–107, 8–110, 9–117

West Indies won by 86 runs

BENSON AND HEDGES WORLD SERIES – SECOND FINAL: AUSTRALIA v. WEST INDIES
24 January 1982 at Melbourne

WEST INDIES

Batsman	Dismissal	Runs
C. G. Greenidge	c Marsh, b Malone	47
D. L. Haynes	c Dyson, b Pascoe	52
I. V. A. Richards	c Dyson, b Chappell	60
S. F. A. Bacchus	c Malone, b Thomson	31
C. H. Lloyd†	not out	22
P. J. Dujon*	b Lillee	5
A. M. E. Roberts	b Pascoe	0
S. T. Clarke	b Pascoe	5
M. A. Holding	b Pascoe	0
J. Garner	run out	0
H. A. Gomes		
Extras	b 2, lb 9, w 2	13
	(for 9 wkts)	235

Bowler	O	M	R	W
Lillee	10	—	53	1
Pascoe	10	1	39	4
Thomson	10	1	31	1
Malone	10	—	37	1
Chappell	10	—	62	1

FALL OF WICKETS
1–65, 2–150, 3–200, 4–204, 5–220, 6–225, 7–235, 8–235, 9–235

AUSTRALIA

Batsman	Dismissal	Runs
G. M. Wood	c Haynes, b Clarke	7
B. M. Laird	c Haynes, b Roberts	13
A. R. Border	c Dujon, b Roberts	13
G. S. Chappell†	b Garner	1
K. J. Hughes	lbw, b Garner	0
J. Dyson	b Clarke	18
R. W. Marsh*	b Gomes	15
D. K. Lillee	c Dujon, b Gomes	0
J. R. Thomson	b Gomes	15
L. S. Pascoe	lbw, b Gomes	0
M. F. Malone	not out	15
Extras	b 2, lb 3, w 4, nb 1	10
		107

Bowler	O	M	R	W
Holding	10	3	25	—
Clarke	6.2	1	15	2
Garner	5	2	10	2
Roberts	5	1	16	2
Gomes	6	1	31	4

FALL OF WICKETS
1–14, 2–42, 3–43, 4–43, 5–43, 6–65, 7–65, 8–81, 9–81

West Indies won by 128 runs

Indian batsmen before fifty had been scored. West Indies never recovered from that position. Their recovery, when it came, was too late to threaten the Australian supremacy. Seven men were out before the hundred was passed. Lloyd batted well, but the honours were all Australian. They fielded magnificently. Wood ran out Bacchus by hitting the one stump he could see and Marsh and substitute Dyson pulled off splendid catches. It was a good day and evening for Australia who, in winning this match, beat West Indies for the sixth time in six day/night matches.

BENSON AND HEDGES WORLD SERIES – THIRD FINAL: AUSTRALIA v. WEST INDIES
26 January 1982 at Sydney

AUSTRALIA					
B. M. Laird	c Richards, b Clarke	14			
G. M. Wood	c and b Gomes	45			
G. S. Chappell†	b Garner	0			
K. J. Hughes	b Holding	28			
A. R. Border	not out	69			
D. W. Hookes	c Dujon, b Holding	1			
R. W. Marsh*	b Clarke	20			
D. K. Lillee	b Clarke	1			
J. R. Thomson	c Dujon, b Roberts	7			
L. S. Pascoe	not out	15			
M. F. Malone					
Extras	lb 13, nb 1	14			
	(for 8 wkts)	214			
		O	M	R	W
Holding		10	2	32	2
Clarke		10	2	30	3
Garner		10	—	42	1
Roberts		10	1	50	1
Gomes		10	—	46	1

FALL OF WICKETS
1–19, 2–20, 3–94, 4–100, 5–103, 6–145, 7–147, 8–167

WEST INDIES					
C. G. Greenidge	lbw, b Lillee	5			
D. L. Haynes	c Chappell, b Pascoe	26			
I. V. A. Richards	lbw, b Lillee	4			
H. A. Gomes	c Marsh, b Thomson	0			
C. H. Lloyd†	not out	63			
S. F. A. Bacchus	run out	19			
P. J. Dujon*	c sub (Dyson), b Malone	10			
A. M. E. Roberts	lbw, b Chappell	1			
M. A. Holding	c Thomson, b Chappell	6			
S. T. Clarke	run out	16			
J. Garner	c sub (Dyson), b Pascoe	3			
Extras	b 1, lb 3, w 9, nb 2	15			
					168
		O	M	R	W
Lillee		10	4	18	2
Thomson		6	—	38	1
Pascoe		6.5	1	21	2
Malone		10	1	33	1
Chappell		10	1	43	2

FALL OF WICKETS
1–20, 2–34, 3–41, 4–41, 5–68, 6–88, 7–95, 8–113, 9–164

Australia won by 46 runs

Benson and Hedges World Series

FOURTH FINAL

West Indies overcame the hoodoo of Sydney and the Australians to win the World Series Cup by 3–1. The last match in the series was a good one in which the West Indies always held the upper hand although Australia battled bravely to the end.

Lillee produced a fine opening spell in which he conceded only 4 runs in 7 overs for the wicket of Haynes. Following the dismissal of Haynes at 13 came the crucial stand of the match between the two most exciting of batsmen, Greenidge and Richards. In two hours they advanced the score by 138 and Richards' 70 was scored off only 89 balls. Australia had a cruel piece of misfortune when Richards was given not out when Border threw down his wicket from mid-on and appealed for run out. Richards had not opened his score at this time and video recordings of the incident suggested that he was lucky to have survived the appeal.

What followed after this, however, was Richards at his most exhilarating and with Lloyd plundering some swift runs, West Indies reached a comfortable 234 in their fifty overs.

For a time Australia had hopes of matching this total for Wood batted with aggression and confidence. He was caught at mid-on straight after the drinks' break when driving at Holding. This made the score 135 for 4, but Border was batting well and Australia were by no means beaten. At 163 Border was bowled pulling at Richards and Australia's real hopes went with him.

Imran Khan. Man of the Series. Pakistan v. Australia

INTERNATIONALS GALORE/37

BENSON AND HEDGES WORLD SERIES – FOURTH FINAL: AUSTRALIA v. WEST INDIES
27 January 1982 at Sydney

WEST INDIES				AUSTRALIA			
C. G. Greenidge	b Malone		64	G. M. Wood	c Lloyd, b Holding		69
D. L. Haynes	lbw, b Lillee		8	B. M. Laird	lbw, b Garner		13
I. V. A. Richards	run out		70	G. S. Chappell†	c Richards, b Clarke		10
S. F. A. Bacchus	b Thomson		17	K. J. Hughes	c Lloyd, b Richards		27
C. H. Lloyd†	not out		41	A. R. Border	b Richards		23
P. J. Dujon*	b Pascoe		13	D. W. Hookes	c Greenidge, b Garner		17
A. M. E. Roberts	b Thomson		5	R. W. Marsh*	c Gomes, b Roberts		5
S. T. Clarke	not out		2	L. S. Pascoe	b Roberts		7
H. A. Gomes				J. R. Thomson	not out		19
M. A. Holding				D. K. Lillee	b Roberts		4
J. Garner				M. F. Malone	not out		5
Extras	lb 14		14	Extras	b 4, lb 10, w 2, nb 1		17
	(for 6 wkts)		234		(for 9 wkts)		216

	O	M	R	W		O	M	R	W
Lillee	10	4	30	1	Holding	10	1	36	1
Thomson	10	—	60	2	Clarke	10	3	40	1
Pascoe	10	1	46	1	Garner	10	1	27	2
Malone	10	1	50	1	Roberts	10	—	48	3
Chappell	10	—	34	2	Richards	10	—	48	2

FALL OF WICKETS
1–13, 2–151, 3–155, 4–198, 5–224, 6–229

FALL OF WICKETS
1–37, 2–57, 3–102, 4–135, 5–163, 6–173, 7–194, 8–198

West Indies won by 18 runs

THIRD TEST MATCH – AUSTRALIA v. WEST INDIES

Clive Lloyd won the toss and asked Australia to bat on a wicket which had a little surface moisture. Within fifty minutes of the start his decision was seen as a stroke of genius for Laird, Wood, Dyson and Hughes were out and only 17 runs had been scored. Roberts and Holding bowled with great hostility and, as ever, this hostility was mirrored in the attitude of the fielders who grasped everything that came within reach.

Greg Chappell who had had a most miserable time of late was joined by Allan Border in a stand of courage and responsibility. Chappell, who needed some good fortune, was dropped on 22 and 23, but played by far his best innings for several months. He became the third Australian batsman in history to score 6,000 runs in Test cricket.

Border's innings was a monument to disciplined strokeplay and he finished the first day 78 not out with Australia having recovered to 204 for 6 although Marsh had been forced to retire hurt when struck by a ball from Croft.

Marsh added only two to his score when he returned the next morning and Border was out without addition and Australia were out for 238.

It was the Australian bowlers that gave their side renewed hope when they reduced West Indies to 204 for 6 by the end of the second day. Jeff Thomson gave his best bowling display in international cricket for some time and Australia nursed dreams of winning the series against West Indies.

Australia had received a severe blow when Lillee had been forced to retire injured before completing his fifth over and now his loss was felt most assuredly as Gomes and Dujon revived West Indies. Gomes reached his second hundred of the series and Dujon's was a sparkling innings. He is a batsman of exciting potential. Roberts also made a valuable contribution and West Indies led by a formidable 151. Hughes was unable to field because of an injured toe and at one time Australia fielded three substitutes.

It was now an uphill struggle for Australia and matters worsened when Wood and Dyson were both dismissed while 35 were scored. Border and Laird rescued Australia with a four hour stand of 166. It was a stand of determination, pugnacity and resolution. When Laird went Hughes, limping and batting with a runner, Dyson, joined Border in a stand of 66. It was heroic stuff. Border batted with great dignity and tenacity and completed his ninth Test hundred. His innings lasted 5½ hours and Australia entered the last day with a lead of 191. It was a wonderful performance and West Indies must have longed for a spinner of Yardley's class in their side. The occasional spinners, Richards and Gomes, bowled 32 unproductive overs; Joseph, of course, was in the dressing room.

On the last morning the Australians could manage only another 45 runs as their last six wickets went down. It was a bitter disappointment, but it was brought about by some magnificent bowling by the mighty Joel Garner who took 4 for 5 in 9 overs, 7 of which were maidens. So West Indies needed 236 to win in 4¾ hours.

Haynes was caught behind driving at Thomson, but Greenidge and Richards added 100 in brisk time. Then Greenidge drove at Thomson and was magnificently caught by Marsh diving to his right. Richards was bowled by a leg-cutter from Pascoe and Australia hoped again.

Gomes, the most consistent and quietly efficient of the West Indian batsmen, steadied the innings in company with Lloyd. When the last 20 overs were reached West Indies needed 74, but at 176 Gomes was bowled by Pascoe. Bacchus was dropped by Pascoe off Yardley when he had made 4 and Lloyd was dropped off the same bowler on 55.

THIRD TEST MATCH – AUSTRALIA v. WEST INDIES
30, 31 January, 1, 2 and 3 February 1982 at Adelaide

AUSTRALIA

	FIRST INNINGS		SECOND INNINGS	
B. M. Laird	c Dujon, b Roberts	2	(2) c Dujon, b Croft	78
G. M. Wood	c Garner, b Roberts	5	(1) c and b Holding	6
J. Dyson	c Dujon, b Holding	1	c Lloyd, b Garner	10
K. J. Hughes	c Greenidge, b Holding	5	(6) c Bacchus, b Garner	84
G. S. Chappell†	c Garner, b Holding	61	(7) lbw, b Holding	7
A. R. Border	c Dujon, b Roberts	78	(4) c Dujon, b Roberts	126
R. W. Marsh*	c Dujon, b Holding	39	(5) c Haynes, b Holding	38
B. Yardley	b Croft	8	b Garner	6
D. K. Lillee	b Roberts	2	c Dujon, b Garner	1
J. R. Thomson	not out	18	c Bacchus, b Garner	0
L. S. Pascoe	b Holding	10	not out	0
Extras	b 1, lb 2, w 1, nb 5	9	b 7, lb 10, nb 13	30
		238		**386**

	O	M	R	W	O	M	R	W
Holding	25	5	72	5	29	9	70	3
Roberts	19	7	43	4	24	7	64	1
Croft	23	4	60	1	32	4	90	1
Garner	17	4	44	—	35	15	56	5
Gomes	7	3	10	—	14	1	38	—
Richards					18	3	38	—

FALL OF WICKETS
1–3, 2–8, 3–8, 4–17, 5–122, 6–193, 7–206, 8–209, 9–210
1–10, 2–35, 3–201, 4–267, 5–362, 6–373, 7–383, 8–383, 9–383

WEST INDIES

	FIRST INNINGS		SECOND INNINGS	
C. G. Greenidge	c Border, b Thomson	8	c Marsh, b Thomson	52
D. L. Haynes	c Marsh, b Thomson	26	c Marsh, b Thomson	4
I. V. A. Richards	c Laird, b Yardley	42	b Pascoe	50
H. A. Gomes	not out	124	b Pascoe	21
S. F. A. Bacchus	c Laird, b Pascoe	0	(6) c Lillee, b Pascoe	27
C. H. Lloyd†	c Marsh, b Thomson	53	(5) not out	77
C. E. H. Croft	b Thomson	0		
P. J. Dujon*	c Thomson, b Yardley	51	(7) not out	0
A. M. E. Roberts	c sub (Hookes), b Yardley	42		
M. A. Holding	b Yardley	3		
J. Garner	c Wood, b Yardley	12		
Extras	b 4, lb 7, w 3, nb 14	28	lb 2, w 1, nb 5	8
		389	(for 5 wkts)	**239**

	O	M	R	W	O	M	R	W
Lillee	4.5	3	4	—	4	—	17	—
Thomson	29	1	112	4	19.1	4	62	2
Yardley	40.5	10	132	5	16	—	68	—
Pascoe	30	3	94	1	22	3	84	3
Border	5	—	19	—				

FALL OF WICKETS
1–12, 2–72, 3–85, 4–92, 5–194, 6–194, 7–283, 8–365, 9–369
1–7, 2–107, 3–114, 4–176, 5–235

West Indies won by 5 wickets

Bacchus was out when two were needed, but with seventeen balls remaining, Lloyd pulled Thomson over mid-wicket for four and victory. Garner, Holding and Croft ran on to the field to chair their captain from the field at the end of this glorious game.

It was a triumph for Test cricket and put the nineteen one-day internationals into true perspective. It was also gratifying that Yardley, a spinner, was chosen as Benson and Hedges International Cricketer of the Year.

Border was named Man of the Match and Holding Man of the Series, but this last Test had seen several heroic performances, not the least of which was Hughes' determined batting with broken toe and bruised instep.

H. A. Gomes

The West Indies fast bowling menace.

Australia v. West Indies – Test Match Averages

AUSTRALIA BATTING

	M	Inns	NOs	Runs	HS	Av	100s	50s
A. R. Border	3	6	1	336	126	67.20	1	3
J. Dyson	2	4	1	166	127*	55.33	1	
K. J. Hughes	3	6		226	100*	45.20	1	1
B. M. Laird	3	6		200	78	33.33		2
G. M. Wood	3	6	1	130	63	26.00		1
R. W. Marsh	3	5		117	39	23.40		
B. Yardley	3	5		93	45	18.60		
G. S. Chappell	3	6		86	61	14.33		1
J. R. Thomson	2	3	1	26	18*	13.00		
T. M. Alderman	2	3		11	10	3.66		
D. K. Lillee	3	5		8	4	1.60		

Played in one Test: G. F. Lawson 2 and 0*; L. S. Pascoe 10 and 0*; D. M. Wellham 17 and 2

AUSTRALIA BOWLING

	Overs	Mds	Runs	Wkts	Av	Best	5/inn
D. K. Lillee	121.3	26	317	16	19.81	7/83	1
B. Yardley	142.5	28	446	20	22.30	7/98	2
J. R. Thomson	83.1	9	317	9	35.22	4/112	
T. M. Alderman	69	17	196	5	39.20	2/23	

Also bowled: A. R. Border 6–1–19–0; G. S. Chappell 2–2–0–0; G. F. Lawson 26–5–64–1; L. S. Pascoe 52–6–178–4.

AUSTRALIA CATCHES

10—R. W. Marsh; 5—A. R. Border and B. M. Laird; 2—T. M. Alderman, J. Dyson, K. J. Hughes, G. S. Chappell, J. R. Thomson, G. M. Wood, D. K. Lillee, B. Yardley; 1—substitute (D. W. Hookes)

WEST INDIES BATTING

	M	Inns	NOs	Runs	HS	Av	100s	50s
H. A. Gomes	3	6	1	393	126	78.60	2	1
C. H. Lloyd	3	6	1	275	77*	55.00		3
P. J. Dujon	3	6	1	227	51	45.40		1
C. G. Greenidge	2	4		134	66	33.50		2
I. V. A. Richards	3	6		160	50	26.66		1
A. M. E. Roberts	2	3		70	42	23.33		
D. L. Haynes	3	6		125	51	20.83		1
D. A. Murray	2	4	1	56	32*	18.66		
S. F. A. Bacchus	2	4		28	27	7.00		
M. A. Holding	3	5		26	9	5.20		
J. Garner	3	5		20	12	4.00		
C. E. H. Croft	3	5	3	4	4*	2.00		

Played in one Test: S. T. Clarke 14 and 5

WEST INDIES BOWLING

	Overs	Mds	Runs	Wkts	Av	Best	5/inn
M. A. Holding	140.3	37	344	24	14.33	6/62	4
J. Garner	122	37	275	12	22.91	5/56	1
H. A. Gomes	45	12	87	3	29.00	2/20	
A. M. E. Roberts	76	24	178	6	29.33	4/43	
C. E. H. Croft	138.1	25	361	7	51.57	2/39	
I. V. A. Richards	49	13	109	0	—	0/17	

Also bowled: S. T. Clarke 32–13–76–1.

WEST INDIES CATCHES

12—D. A. Murray; 9—P. J. Dujon; 3—J. Garner; 2—S. F. A. Bacchus and M. A. Holding; 1—H. A. Gomes, C. G. Greenidge, C. H. Lloyd, D. L. Haynes, I. V. A. Richards and substitute (A. L. Logie)

Pakistan in Australia 1981–82
First Class Matches

BATTING

	v. Western Australia (Perth) 23–26 October 1981	v. Queensland (Brisbane) 30 Oct–2 Nov. 1981	v. Victoria (Melbourne) 6–9 November 1981	First Test Match (Perth) 13–17 November 1981	Second Test Match (Brisbane) 27 Nov–1 Dec. 1981	Third Test Match (Melbourne) 11–15 December 1981	v. South Australia (Adelaide) 26–29 December 1981	v. Tasmania (Launceston) 1–4 January 1982
Mudassar Nazar	57 48*	20 —		0 5	36 33	95 —	— 1	
Rizwan Uz-Zaman	44 11	0 —	50 27	0 8		80 0	90 126 47	118 —
Zaheer Abbas	24 15	84		6 79	20 38	62	36* 117	15 —
Javed Miandad	6 11*	138			29 15	74	90 74	158* —
Majid Khan	110 —	26	5 2	3 0				
Wasim Raja	0 —	9 —	38 10	4 48	43 36	50	— 1	
Imran Khan	43 —		93* —	4 31	0 3	70*		— —
Ejaz Faqih	61* —		1 18*		34 21		— 29	
Wasim Bari	26 —	0 —		1 20	7 4*	8	— 2	
Tahir Naqqash	4 —	25* —					— 10	— —
Iqbal Qasim	— —	0 —		5 4			— 16*	
Sarfraz Nawaz		4 —	7 —	26 9	4 13	0		— —
Sikhander Bakht		11 —	0 —	3* 0*	1* 2		— 4*	
Saleem Malik			62 0				16 30	51* —
Ashraf Ali			17 10*					4 4*
Mansoor Akhtar			33 30	6 36			81 86	73 —
Mohsin Khan					11 43	17 —		28 0*
Byes	1 3	3	1	12	2	1	6 4	
Leg-byes	2 2	1	7 2	1	1 3	5	1 5	7
Wides	1 1				1	1	4 2	6
No-balls	1 1	7	3	4 15	12 9	12	4 1	8
Total	380 92	328	317 99	62 256	291 223	500	358 415	472 4
Wickets	9 2	10	9† 5	10 10	10 10	8	4 10	5 0
Result	D	D	D	L	L	W	D	W

Catches
15 – Wasim Bari (ct 12/st 3)
6 – Javed Miandad
5 – Ashraf Ali, Iqbal Qasim, Majid Khan, Mudassar Nazar and Zaheer Abbas
3 – Ejaz Faqih
2 – Mohsin Khan, Wasim Raja and subs.
1 – Imran Khan, Rizwan Uz-Zaman, Mansoor Akhtar, Saleem Malik and Sarfraz Nawaz

† Zaheer Abbas absent hurt

BOWLING

	Imran Khan	Tahir Naqqash	Ejaz Faqih	Iqbal Qasim	Mudassar Nazar	Wasim Raja	Javed Miandad	Rizwan Uz-Zaman
v. Western Australia (Perth) 23–26 October 1981	36-6-92-0	26-1-97-1	31.4-1-93-3	44-5-136-5	9-3-22-0	7-2-12-0	8-3-21-0	3-0-7-0
v. Queensland (Brisbane) 30 October–2 November 1981				19-3-76-1	2-0-7-0	15-2-55-0	2-0-21-0	2-0-8-0
v. Victoria (Melbourne) 6–9 November 1981	28-5-89-5 19-4-50-1		8-2-22-0 24-10-32-3			21-8-49-3 14-3-45-0		
First Test Match (Perth) 13–17 November 1981	31.4-8-66-4 39-12-90-3			3-1-6-1 26-4-81-2	2-1-1-0	1-1-0-1 20-3-58-1	1-0-2-0	
Second Test Match (Brisbane) 27 November–1 December 1981	40-6-92-4 1.2-1-2-0		22-1-76-1		2-0-10-0	17-0-68-1	3-0-18-0	
Third Test Match (Melbourne) 11–15 December 1981	24.1-7-41-3 14.1-5-21-2			55-17-104-3 24-11-44-4		37-7-73-1 13-2-34-0	2-0-9-0	
v. South Australia (Adelaide) 26–29 December 1981		24-5-84-1 6-3-19-0	27-4-74-1 12-2-27-1		2-0-21-0 5-2-17-0	12-2-59-0 6-0-27-0	14-0-46-0	1-1-0-0
v. Tasmania (Launceston) 1–4 January 1982	18-4-59-3 30-8-84-3	2-0-12-0 23-6-60-4		21.4-8-31-5 22-7-54-2			8-1-20-1	
	281.2-66- 686-28 av. 24.50	81-15- 272-6 av. 45.33	124.4-20- 324-9 av. 36.00	214.4-56- 532-23 av. 23.13	22-6- 78-0 —	163-30- 480-7 av. 68.57	38-4- 137-1 av. 137.00	6-1- 15-0 —

A. Saleem Malik 4-0-19-0
B. Wasim Bari 2-1-1-0
Mansoor Akhtar 2-1-3-0, Saleem Malik 3-0-14-0

† B. F. Davison retired hurt

INTERNATIONALS GALORE/41

Benson and Hedges World Series Averages

AUSTRALIA BATTING

	M	Inns	NOs	Runs	HS	Av	100s	50s
A. R. Border	14	14	4	352	75*	35.20		2
K. J. Hughes	11	11	2	310	67	34.44		3
G. M. Wood	14	13	1	384	69	32.00		2
B. M. Laird	11	11	1	275	117*	27.50	1	
W. M. Darling	9	9		235	74	26.11		1
G. S. Chappell	14	14		248	61	17.71		2
R. B. McCosker	3	3		51	23	17.00		
J. Dyson	4	4		66	37	16.50		
M. F. Malone	8	5	3	31	15*	15.50		
R. W. Marsh	14	13	1	175	54*	14.58		1
L. S. Pascoe	5	5	3	25	15*	12.50		
D. K. Lillee	12	10	1	91	42*	10.11		
J. R. Thomson	13	9	1	62	19*	7.75		
T. M. Alderman	6	3	1	10	9*	5.00		
G. F. Lawson	9	6	3	11	4*	3.66		

Also batted: B. Yardley 28 and 23 (two matches); S. F. Graf 8 (two matches); D. M. Wellham 42 (one match); D. W. Hookes 1 and 17 (two matches)

AUSTRALIA BOWLING

	Overs	Mds	Runs	Wkts	Av	Best	5/inn
L. S. Pascoe	45.5	4	183	12	15.25	4/39	
J. R. Thomson	114	6	521	19	27.42	3/55	
M. F. Malone	80	13	251	9	27.88	2/9	
G. S. Chappell	121.2	7	528	17	31.05	3/31	
T. M. Alderman	58	3	200	6	33.33	2/20	
D. K. Lillee	110.3	18	406	12	33.83	2/23	
G. F. Lawson	75.5	4	350	7	50.00	2/28	

Also bowled: B. Yardley 9–0–46–1; A. R. Border 6–0–34–0; S. F. Graf 19–0–90–0

AUSTRALIA CATCHES

14—R. W. Marsh; 4—W. M. Darling, J. R. Thomson and J. Dyson (inc. 2 as sub.); 3—G. F. Lawson, K. J. Hughes, T. M. Alderman, B. M. Laird, A. R. Border and G. M. Wood; 2—G. S. Chappell and D. K. Lillee; 1—B. Yardley, L. S. Pascoe, M. F. Malone and S. F. Graf

Allan Border

West Indies in Australia 1981–82
First Class Matches

BATTING	v. South Australia (Adelaide) 13–16 November 1981	v. New South Wales (Sydney) 27–30 November 1981	v. Tasmania (Hobart) 7–9 December 1981	v. Queensland (Brisbane) 11–14 December 1981	First Test Match (Melbourne) 26–30 December 1981	Second Test Match (Sydney) 2–6 January 1982	Third Test Match (Adelaide) 30 Jan.–3 Feb. 1982
C. G. Greenidge	28 4	—	12 —	1 —	—	66 8	8 52
D. L. Haynes	44 53	139 10	—	12 —	1 28	15 51	26 4
I. V. A. Richards	1 —	44 53*	57 —	121 —	2 0	44 22	42 50
S. F. A. Bacchus	12 58*	83 53*	0 —	85 —	1 0	—	0 27
H. A. Gomes	95 —	13 —	11 —	200* —	55 24	126 43	124* 21
A. L. Logie	5 4	43 —	29 —	—	—	—	—
D. A. Murray	72 —	—	11* —	6 —	32* 10	13 1	—
C. E. H. Croft	4* 34	—	—	6 —	0 0*	0* 4*	0 —
M. D. Marshall	0 66	—	—	—	—	—	—
S. T. Clarke	0 —	—	—	—	—	14 5	—
J. Garner	18 —	—	—	12 —	7 0	1 0	12 —
C. H. Lloyd	—	—	51 —	68 —	29 19	40 57	53 77*
P. J. Dujon	—	104* —	—	1 —	41 43	44 48	51 0*
A. M. E. Roberts	—	33 —	—	0* —	18 10	—	42 —
H. Joseph	—	7 —	4 —	—	—	—	—
M. A. Holding	—	—	6 —	24 —	2 7	9 5	3 —
Byes	2 2	2	—	4	1 1	—	4
Leg-byes	3 8	6 1	2	4	3 10	3 1	7 2
Wides	5	—	—	—	—	5	3 1
No-balls	10 2	8	2	19	9 9	9 5	14 5
Total	294 236	482 117	203	539	201 161	384 255	389 239
Wickets	10 5	7 1	10	7	10 10	10 10	10 5
Result	W	W	D	W	L	D	W

Catches
19 – D. A. Murray
16 – P. J. Dujon
4 – J. Garner, I. V. A. Richards and S. F. A. Bacchus
3 – C. G. Greenidge, C. E. H. Croft, D. L. Haynes, M. A. Holding, C. H. Lloyd and subs.
1 – A. M. E. Roberts, H. Joseph and H. A. Gomes

BOWLING	S. T. Clarke	M. D. Marshall	C. E. H. Croft	J. Garner	M. A. Holding	A. M. E. Roberts	H. Joseph	I. V. A. Richards
v. South Australia (Adelaide) 13–16 November 1981	11–2–28–3 10–0–43–0	10–2–23–3 12–3–29–3	6–3–11–1 21–1–86–2	6–3–6–3 18–6–45–5				
v. New South Wales (Sydney) 27–30 November 1981	11–1–40–1		17–3–43–2 41.4–10–78–3		16–2–44–2	14–4–30–2 33–11–48–4	31–8–89–1 33–8–73–1	1–0–4–0 33–8–71–1
v. Tasmania (Hobart) 7–9 December 1981			17–0–52–2 11–1–42–1	16.3–5–41–3 3–0–5–0	20–3–48–2 9–2–34–1		21–7–45–3 6–2–10–0	
v. Queensland (Brisbane) 11–14 December 1981	7–1–23–1 18–1–51–3	18–8–31–5 6–1–22–0			12–3–29–2 17–2–36–1	12–4–26–1 12–1–36–0		15–3–32–0 22.5–4–88–5
First Test Match (Melbourne) 26–30 December 1981			16.1–3–39–2 20–2–61–1	20–6–59–2 18–5–37–3	17–3–45–5 21.3–5–62–6	15–6–40–1 18–4–31–0		5–0–17–0
Second Test Match (Sydney) 2–6 January 1982	16–4–51–1 16–9–25–0		20–7–53–0 27–5–58–2	20–4–52–2 12–3–27–0	29–9–64–5 19–6–31–0			13–7–21–0 13–3–33–0
Third Test Match (Adelaide) 30 January–3 February 1982			23–4–60–1 32–4–90–1	17–4–44–0 35–15–56–5	25–5–72–5 29–9–70–3	19–7–43–4 24–7–64–1		18–3–38–0
	89–18– 261–9 av. 29.00	46–14– 105–11 av. 9.54	251.5–43– 673–18– av. 37.38	165.3–51– 372–23 av. 16.17	214.3–49– 535–32 av. 16.71	147–44– 318–13 av. 24.46	91–25– 217–5 av. 43.40	120.5–28– 304–6 av. 50.66

INTERNATIONALS GALORE/43

Benson and Hedges World Series Averages

WEST INDIES BATTING

	M	Inns	NOs	Runs	HS	Av	100s	50s
M. D. Marshall	8	5	4	82	32*	82.00		
C. H. Lloyd	13	13	5	462	80*	57.75		3
I. V. A. Richards	14	14	1	536	78	41.23		5
C. G. Greenidge	12	12		438	103	36.50	1	3
D. L. Haynes	14	14	1	343	84	26.38		3
H. A. Gomes	12	9	3	126	56*	21.00		1
S. F. A. Bacchus	12	12	1	219	37	19.90		
P. J. Dujon	12	9	2	134	51*	19.14		1
S. T. Clarke	7	6	2	40	16	10.00		
M. A. Holding	13	7	2	31	8	6.20		
A. M. E. Roberts	14	9		40	15	4.44		
D. A. Murray	3	3	1	6	5	3.00		
J. Garner	14	7	2	8	3	1.60		

C. E. H. Croft played in two matches and A. L. Logie in four matches but did not bat

WEST INDIES BOWLING

	Overs	Mds	Runs	Wkts	Av	Best 5/inn
J. Garner	121	13	373	24	15.54	4/45
H. A. Gomes	29.4	2	140	9	15.55	4/31
S. T. Clarke	64.2	11	177	10	17.70	3/22
M. D. Marshall	73.4	3	242	12	20.16	3/31
M. A. Holding	118	15	390	19	20.52	4/32
A. M. E. Roberts	119	14	411	18	22.83	3/15
I. V. A. Richards	92	3	419	11	38.09	3/52

Also bowled: C. E. H. Croft 19-1-105-0

WEST INDIES CATCHES

11—P. J. Dujon (ct 9/st 2); 8—C. G. Greenidge; 7—C. H. Lloyd; 5—D. A. Murray, S. F. A. Bacchus, D. L. Haynes and A. L. Logie; 4—M. A. Holding; 3—A. M. E. Roberts and I. V. A. Richards; 2—C. G. Greenidge, S. T. Clarke and H. A. Gomes; 1—J. Garner

Clive Lloyd

Benson and Hedges World Series Averages

PAKISTAN BATTING

	M	Inns	NOs	Runs	HS	Av	100s	50s
Majid Khan	4	3	1	86	56	43.00		1
Zaheer Abbas	9	9		343	108	38.11	1	1
Imran Khan	10	9	3	211	62*	35.16		1
Mudassar Nazar	8	8		280	51	35.00		1
Javed Miandad	10	10		290	74	29.00		2
Tahir Naqqash	7	4	2	58	23*	29.00		
Wasim Raja	10	10	4	127	33	21.16		
Sarfraz Nawaz	9	6	2	68	34*	17.00		
Ashraf Ali	6	5	3	33	15*	16.50		
Wasim Bari	4	2	1	13	9*	13.00		
Mansoor Akhtar	6	6		76	40	12.66		
Mohsin Khan	5	5		63	27	12.60		
Ejaz Faqih	7	7		63	20	9.00		
Sikhander Bakht	10	4	2	4	3	2.00		

Also batted: Iqbal Qasim 2 (two matches); Rizwan Uz-Zaman 14 (one match); Saleem Malik 0 (one match).

PAKISTAN BOWLING

	Overs	Mds	Runs	Wkts	Av	Best	5/inn
Mudassar Nazar	43	5	160	12	13.33	3/20	
Wasim Raja	26.1	1	88	5	17.60	4/25	
Imran Khan	96.4	9	305	15	20.33	3/19	
Sarfraz Nawaz	81	4	326	13	25.07	4/37	
Sikhander Bakht	76.5	2	340	12	28.33	4/34	
Ejaz Faqih	52	1	218	4	54.50	2/34	
Tahir Naqqash	42	2	178	2	89.00	1/25	

Also bowled: Javed Miandad 1–0–1–0; Zaheer Abbas 6–0–41–0; Majid Khan 15–0–69–0; Iqbal Qasim 10–0–49–0

PAKISTAN CATCHES

8—Ashraf Ali; 7—Wasim Raja; 4—Sarfraz Nawaz; 3—Wasim Bari and Mudassar Nazar; 2—Javed Miandad and Rizwan Uz-Zaman; 1—Mansoor Akhtar, Tahir Naqqash, Zaheer Abbas, Sikhander Bakht and substitute (Mohsin Khan).

Opposite: *David Hookes, captain of Sheffield Shield winners South Australia.*

SECTION B
Southern Revival
The Australian domestic season

Once more the Australian season was cluttered with a surfeit of delights. Unfortunately, the delights were centred upon the plethora of international matches and Tests and the Sheffield Shield once more shrunk into the background as the State sides were deprived of their best players for most of the season. A glance at the form charts at the end of this section will reveal just how much cricket Marsh, Lillee, Hughes, Alderman, Chappell and Border played for their respective states. Western Australia were severely hit and this accounts for the fact that in nine first-class matches, no fewer than twenty-five players represented the state. Wood, Marsh, Laird, Hughes, Yardley and Alderman played only in the first three matches and did not represent Western Australia after the game against New South Wales which finished on 2 November.

It is a sorry story and one which must not be repeated if domestic cricket in Australia is to flourish as it must. The picture was not all gloom, however, and the Sheffield Shield was keenly contested, reaching its climax on the last day of the season which brought about a revival in the fortunes of South Australia.

16, 17, 18 and 19 October 1981

at Brisbane

Queensland 247 and 399 for 6 dec (K. C. Wessels 168, T. V. Hohns 58 not out, A. R. Border 52)
Victoria 315 (G. N. Yallop 82, G. M. Watts 60) and 268 (P. A. Hibbert 89, T. V. Hohns 4 for 85)

Queensland won by 63 runs
Queensland 12 pts, Victoria 4 pts

at Perth

Western Australia 186 (D. K. Lillee 54 not out, G. J. Winter 5 for 67) and 253 for 6 dec (B. M. Laird 110 not out, K. J. Hughes 80, G. J. Winter 4 for 76)
South Australia 107 (T. M. Alderman 7 for 49) and 180 (I. R. McLean 70, B. Yardley 4 for 54)

Western Australia won by 152 runs
Western Australia 16 pts, South Australia 0 pts

The season began most positively with victories for Queensland and Western Australia.

At Brisbane, where Victoria have not won for sixteen years, the home side were 42 for 4 and 72 for 5 against the bowling of McCurdy and Walker. Ritchie and Hohns effected a recovery and there were some useful contributions from Dymock and Thomson who scored 45 at number 10, adding 35 with both Dymock and Lillee. A fine attacking innings by Yallop was not built upon and Victoria slipped from 187 for 2 to 315 all out. Nevertheless, they took first innings points and a lead of 68. Martin Kent retired hurt when hit by a Graf bouncer, but Wessels was in dominant form when Queensland batted again. He hit twenty-seven fours in an innings which lasted 296 minutes and swung the game Queensland's way. Dymock dismissed Watts and Yallop and then the left-arm spin of Hohns and the leg-spin of Lillie brought Queensland victory.

Western Australia started disastrously at Perth where South Australian debutants, Sayers, McLellan and Winter, reduced them to 116 for 8. Dennis Lillee hit 54 off 79 deliveries, although twice being dropped, and helped boost the score to 186. Bad weather restricted play on the second day, but the third day belonged entirely to Terry Alderman. He took six wickets in the morning session and finished with a career best 7 for 49. When Western Australia batted again Hughes and Laird shared a third wicket stand of 113. Laird's hundred took four hours and Hughes made 80 off 90 deliveries. Phillips went quickly when South Australia began the task of chasing 333 to win, but Darling and McLean added 56 before Darling was caught behind, one of Marsh's eight catches in the match. Thereafter, McLean apart, South Australia disintegrated before the bowling of Yardley and Alderman who had match figures of 10 for 92. The game was over before tea on the final afternoon and South Australia's only solace was the exciting debut of Graham Winter.

22, 23, 24 and 25 October 1981

at Newcastle

New South Wales 322 for 6 dec (J. Dyson 65, G. R. Beard 62 not out, T. M. Chappell 58, I. C. Davis 52)
Queensland 269 (K. C. Wessels 103, A. R. Border 58, G. R. Beard 5 for 67)

Match drawn
New South Wales 2 pts, Queensland 2 pts

The first Sheffield Shield game to be scheduled for Newcastle had a most unhappy beginning, the first two days being lost to rain. When play began New South Wales batted slowly and McCosker did not declare until the final morning. Wessels again batted brilliantly for Queensland, hitting fifteen fours in an innings which lasted 3¼ hours, but the end was stalemate. Graeme Beard had a good all-round match although his batting was somewhat tedious.

30, 31 October and 1 November 1981

at Melbourne

Tasmania 215 (D. C. Boon 79) and 155
Victoria 191 (F. D. Stephenson 4 for 27, S. L. Saunders 4 for 82) and 83 (F. D. Stephenson 6 for 19)

Tasmania won by 96 runs
Tasmania 16 pts, Victoria 0 pts

at Perth

New South Wales 215 (G. R. Beard 75, T. M. Alderman 7 for 59) and 117 (T. M. Alderman 7 for 28)
Western Australia 367 (K. J. Hughes 113, R. S. Langer 77, G. F. Lawson 6 for 70)

Western Australia won by an innings and 35 runs
Western Australia 16 pts, New South Wales 0 pts

Both matches ended in three days and both contained some sensational cricket.

On the much criticised Melbourne wicket, Tasmania won their first match on the mainland since being admitted to the Sheffield Shield. It was the first time in Shield matches

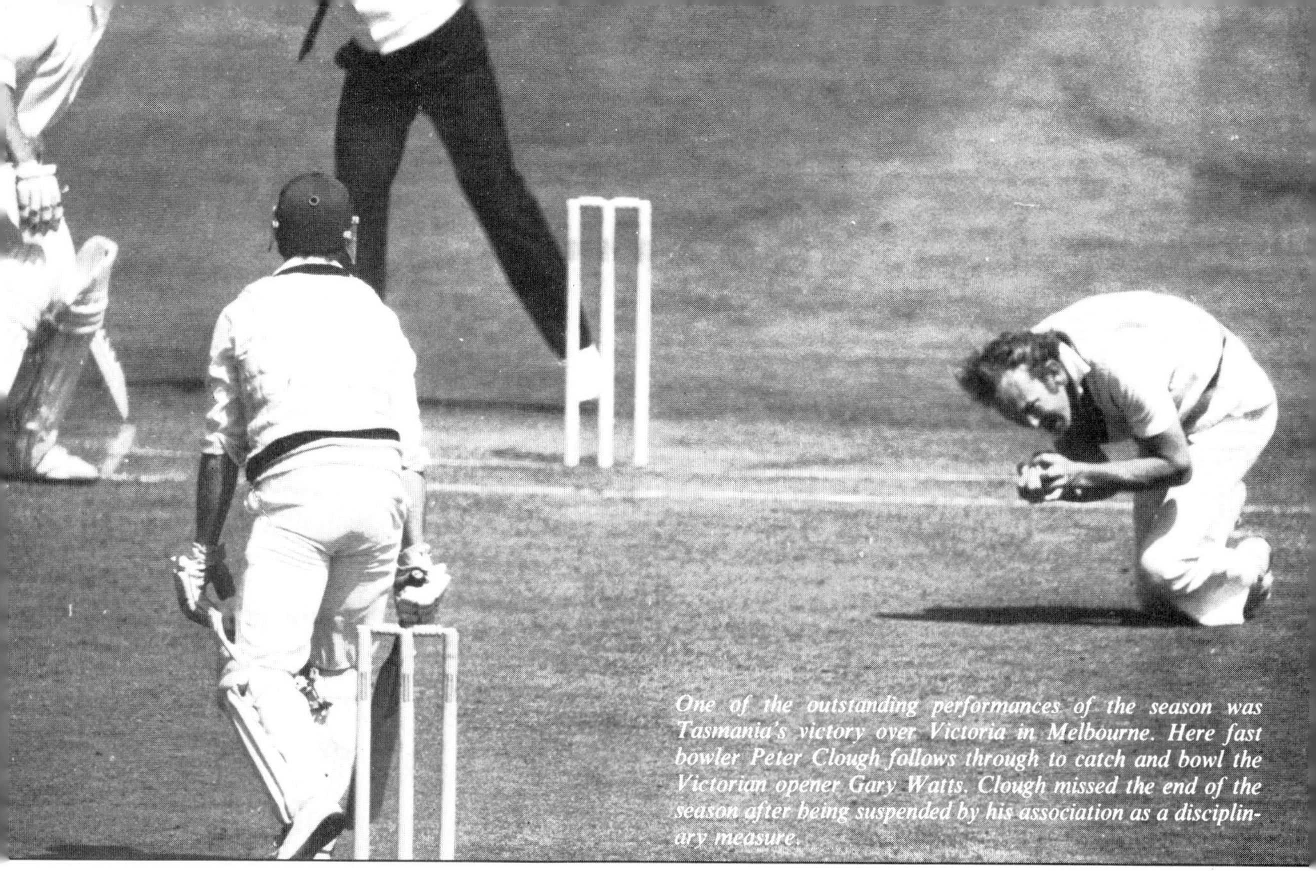

One of the outstanding performances of the season was Tasmania's victory over Victoria in Melbourne. Here fast bowler Peter Clough follows through to catch and bowl the Victorian opener Gary Watts. Clough missed the end of the season after being suspended by his association as a disciplinary measure.

Roger Woolley had a splendid season for Tasmania, both as wicket-keeper and batsman. Here is one of his less happy moments when he receives treatment after being hit on the ankle by a 'shooter' while keeping wicket.

Jim Higgs and wicket-keeper Ian Maddocks in balletic mood as they both converge on the same return from the outfield.

that they had twice bowled out the opposition. On the opening day Tasmania struggled against the bowling of Graf and Higgs, but were saved from disaster by David Boon who batted for 209 minutes. Victoria seemed to be heading for a comfortable first innings lead when they passed 100 with only two men out, but leg-spinner Stuart Saunders and West Indian pace bowler Franklyn Stephenson brought about a collapse and with Clough taking two wickets, Victoria were out for 191, the last eight wickets falling for 60 runs. Spinners Higgs and Bright troubled Tasmania in the second innings, but the Islanders batted doggedly for five hours. Set to make 180, Victoria lost both openers for 11, then a sustained spell of hostile fast bowling from Stephenson removed all further opposition as Victoria were bowled out for their lowest score against Tasmania for forty-eight years. Stephenson finished with career best match figures of 10 for 46 and Tasmania celebrated a great victory.

Terry Alderman was in an equally destructive mood in Perth. He took 7 for 59 on the opening day as New South Wales were bowled out for 215, a career best equal by Beard raising them from the depths of 113 for 7. Western Australia struggled also and were 92 for 4, but Hughes and Langer added 178 for the fifth wicket to put their side in a commanding position in spite of some fine bowling by Geoff Lawson. Batting again, New South Wales found no answer to Alderman who demoralised them with his control of late movement and variety of pace. His match figures were 14 for 88, the best ever match performance by a Western Australian bowler, and his second innings 7 for 28 bettered his career best of a fortnight earlier. In the first two Shield matches of the season he had taken 24 wickets at 7.46 runs apiece. Following upon his great success in England, this marked him as one of Australia's outstanding bowlers of all time.

7, 8, 9 and 10 November 1981

at Adelaide

South Australia 551 for 9 dec (J. J. Crowe 157, D. W. Hookes 106, W. M. Darling 71, R. J. Inverarity 54)
New South Wales 220 for 2 (J. Dyson 108, R. B. McCosker 90)

Match drawn
South Australia 2 pts, New South Wales 2 pts

South Australia batted until tea time on the second day as their batsmen prospered against an attack in which only Lawson showed necessary application. When New South Wales batted they showed no haste and with play lost to rain, a draw became inevitable. Dyson and McCosker put on 191 for the first wicket.

McDonald's Cup – First Round Matches
7 November 1981

at Brisbane

Tasmania 225 for 7 (R. J. Jeffery 58, D. C. Boon 53)
Queensland 229 for 3 (G. S. Chappell 92, A. R. Border 55 not out)

Queensland won by 7 wickets

8 November 1981

at Brisbane

Western Australia 148 for 8
Queensland 149 for 4 (R. B. Kerr 50)

Queensland won by 6 wickets

Queensland made a splendid start in the McDonald's Cup 50 over competition with two resounding wins in the opening matches.

In the first match a stand of 125 in 83 minutes between Chappell and Border was the foundation of the easy win over Tasmania which was accomplished with 3.5 overs to spare. The second match, watched by over eight thousand people, saw Western Australia struggle after they had been put in to bat and Queensland won with 14.1 overs in hand.

19 November 1981

at Sydney

New South Wales 260 for 2 (R. B. McCosker 111 not out, J. Dyson 78)
Victoria 213 for 8 (J. M. Wiener 108 not out)

New South Wales won by 47 runs

An opening stand of 169 by McCosker and Dyson put New South Wales in an impregnable position. Only 65 runs came from the first twenty overs, but 195 came from the last thirty, Graf, Bright and Ross were the main sufferers. Victoria fielded poorly and batted little better, only a courageously aggressive innings by Wiener saving their dignity.

20, 21, 22 and 23 November 1981
at Brisbane

Western Australia 351 (R. S. Langer 140, T. V. Hohns 4 for 97)
Queensland 308 for 9 (K. C. Wessels 72, A. L. Mann 4 for 78)
Match drawn
Queensland 2 pts, Western Australia 2 pts

No play on the first day and restricted play on other days made it certain that the game would end indecisively. Rob Langer, recalled to the side as many players were absent on Test duty, batted well, and another who was recalled to the Western Australian side, Tony Mann was the state's best bowler, but Brabon and Maguire defied the visiting attack in the closing stages to give their side a share of the points.

27, 28, 29 and 30 November 1981
at St Kilda, Melbourne

Victoria 487 for 2 dec (J. M. Wiener 221 not out, J. K. Moss 200 not out)
Western Australia 208 (G. D. Porter 64, J. D. Higgs 4 for 24) and 209 for 6 (G. D. Porter 51)
Match drawn
Victoria 4 pts, Western Australia 0 pts

This match was transferred from the M.C.G. to Junction Oval and the wicket prepared made it possible for Julien Wiener and Jeff Moss to write their names indelibly in the record books of Australian cricket. They added an unbeaten 390 for the third wicket as both reached double centuries. For Wiener it was a career best. Their stand was the best for any Victorian wicket in a Sheffield Shield match and a record for Australia's third wicket, beating the 389 of Ponsford and McCabe v. M.C.C. at Lord's in 1934. Wiener batted for 561 minutes and hit eighteen fours. Moss batted for 410 minutes and hit a six and ten fours. Play was restricted on the third day and Western Australia had no difficulty in saving the game when forced to follow-on. Makeshift opener Graeme Porter batted well in both innings.

Because the Melbourne Cricket Ground, the venue for so many famous Test matches, was deemed sub-standard, Victoria played at St Kilda's Junction Oval. Unfortunately in the game against Western Australia the covers were blown off the wicket and Western Australia were forced to bat on a damp pitch. Victorian fielders cluster round eagerly.

50/BENSON & HEDGES CRICKET YEAR

For twenty-three year old Mark O'Neill the season was a bitter disappointment after he had promised so much in his first two seasons and had spent a year at Lord's. Below: *He enjoys a brief moment of glory as he despatches a ball for four after it had slipped out of the bowler's hand. Wiener looks on philosophically.* Right: *He edges Jim Higgs to slip. Ian Maddocks is keeping wicket.*

Opposite below: *An Australian record for the third wicket.*
Jeff Moss 200 not out
Julien Wiener 221 not out
The stand is worth 390 and Scholes declares at 487 for 2.

SOUTHERN REVIVAL/51

McDonald's Cup – First Round Match
3 December 1981

at Sydney

New South Wales 310 for 4 (R. B. McCosker 164, J. Dyson 100)
South Australia 199 (P. R. Sleep 90)
New South Wales won by 111 runs

A woefully weak South Australian attack was savaged by Dyson and McCosker who set up a record for the competition with an opening stand of 253. McCosker achieved the best individual score recorded. Sleep batted bravely for South Australia in a one-sided match.

10, 11, 12 and 13 December 1981

at Sydney

New South Wales 271 (P. M. Toohey 84, R. J. Inverarity 5 for 40) and 252 for 5 dec (R. B. McCosker 146 not out)
South Australia 268 (W. B. Phillips 79, P. R. Sleep 65, R. G. Holland 6 for 64) and 245 for 2 (J. J. Crowe 137 not out, W. M. Darling 52)
Match drawn
New South Wales 4 pts, South Australia 0 pts

South Australia recovered dramatically from their mauling in the McDonald's Cup match and, with a stronger side, came close to beating New South Wales. Peter Toohey, who had been left out of the side earlier in the season, scored a fine 84 for New South Wales who recovered from a poor start only to collapse again to the slow left-arm of veteran John Inverarity. South Australia started well. Phillips and wicket-keeper Wright, who opened in place of Darling who was unwell, put on 86, but then Holland's leg-spin confused the later batsmen and only Peter Sleep's good sense brought them in touch with New South Wales' score. McCosker continued his brilliant form with an innings of 146, including fourteen fours, and with Inverarity taking three more wickets, he declared at the end of the third day as he believed the wicket was breaking up. South Australia had a day in which to score 256. Phillips and Crowe began with 125 and then Crowe and Darling added 106. Rain began to fall and with South Australia only 11 short of victory, the umpires led the players from the field. Hookes and Crowe stayed at the wicket in protest and Hookes was later fined for describing the umpires' action as 'unsportsmanlike and shameful'.

17, 18, 19 and 20 December 1981

at Brisbane

Queensland 389 for 8 dec (G. M. Ritchie 126, G. Dymock 101 not out) and 249 for 8 dec (R. B. Kerr 103 not out, P. R. Sleep 5 for 117)
South Australia 404 for 5 dec (R. J. Inverarity 100 not out, P. R. Sleep 78, K. J. Wright 64 not out, K. P. Harris 52, D. W. Hookes 51) and 198 for 9 (K. P. Harris 97, A. B. Henschell 4 for 34)
Match drawn
South Australia 4 pts, Queensland 0 pts

19, 20, 21 and 22 December 1981

at Sydney

Victoria 254 (J. M. Wiener 72, R. G. Holland 4 for 73) and 232 (G. M. Watts 71, J. K. Moss 67, G. R. Beard 4 for 54)
New South Wales 255 for 4 dec (R. B. McCosker 123 not out, P. M. Toohey 76) and 233 for 2 (R. B. McCosker 118 not out, J. Dyson 83)

New South Wales won by 8 wickets
New South Wales 16 pts, Victoria 0 pts

In a game of fluctuating fortunes, South Australia, who led on the first innings, were saved from defeat by their last pair, Inverarity and Lewis after Henschell and Lillie had brought Queensland close to victory. The home state had been well served by Greg Ritchie who played an exciting innings and further enhanced his claims for a Test place. At 244 for 7, however, Queensland could not be satisfied, but De Jong and Dymock added 145 and skipper Geoff Dymock reached his maiden first-class century at the age of thirty-six. South Australia replied with a consistently even batting display and John Inverarity, a year older than Dymock, reached the twenty-fourth hundred of his career. Kerr starred in the Queensland second innings and Dymock declared, setting South Australia 235 to win. In his first Shield match, Kim Harris batted splendidly, but his side faltered under the attack of Henschell and Lillie after a good start.

The dominance of Rick McCosker continued. At Sydney, he hit two unbeaten hundreds, bringing his number of centuries to 22, and on this, his hundredth appearance in first-class cricket, he was on the field for the whole of the match. Bob Holland's leg-spin allied to the pace of Pascoe and Skilbeck brought about the destruction of Victoria in the first innings and McCosker was content to obtain first innings points and then declare. Toohey played another delightful knock. In their second innings, Victoria stood at 199 for 3, but Beard and Holland brought about a collapse which saw seven wickets fall for 33 runs. Needing 232 for victory, New South Wales were given the best possible start, McCosker and Dyson adding 174 in 228 minutes before Dyson was stumped off Bright. Chappell was bowled by Higgs, but Toohey and McCosker strode to victory. The win helped to keep New South Wales in touch with Western Australia and Tasmania, one win from one match, at the top of the table. South Australia sadly languished at the bottom.

McDonald's Cup – First Round Matches

1 January 1982

at Adelaide

South Australia 249 for 5 (P. R. Sleep 81, D. W. Hookes 56, R. J. Inverarity 54 not out)
Victoria 253 for 4 (J. M. Wiener 89, J. W. Scholes 62 not out, G. M. Watts 52)

Victoria won by 6 wickets

7 January 1982

at Perth

Western Australia 215 for 3 (R. S. Langer 99 not out, G. Shipperd 86)
Tasmania 202 for 9 (D. J. Boyd 4 for 35)

Western Australia won by 13 runs

South Australia and Tasmania both departed from the competition, but both gave much improved performances.

Victoria beat South Australia with one ball to spare thanks to a captain's innings by John Scholes who assured that the opening stand of 144 between Wiener and Watts should not go unwasted. Earlier Hookes and Sleep had a fourth wicket stand of 63 which included 50 off 65 deliveries.

In Perth, Langer, Man of the Match, and Shipperd shared a third wicket stand of 172, the runs coming in 33 overs. The Tasmanian fielding and catching was dreadful and, in spite of some hard hitting by Davison and Boon, they were never really scoring at the required rate. Left-arm bowler David Boyd took 4 for 35 in his first game for the state. Wayne Daniel again had an unhappy time.

Qualifying Round Final Tables

Group A	P	W	L	Pts
Queensland	2	2	—	4
Western Australia	2	1	1	2
Tasmania	2	—	2	—

Group B	P	W	L	Pts
New South Wales	2	2	—	4
Victoria	2	1	1	2
South Australia	2	—	2	—

8, 9 and 10 January 1982

at Adelaide

South Australia 552 for 4 dec (W. B. Phillips 260, D. W. Hookes 88, P. R. Sleep 62 not out)
Queensland 297 (G. M. Ritchie 103, A. B. Henschell 50, M. C. Dolman 4 for 114) and 162 (R. B. Kerr 66, P. R. Sleep 4 for 19)

South Australia won by an innings and 93 runs
South Australia 16 pts, Queensland 0 pts

9, 10, 11 and 12 January 1982

at Perth

Tasmania 234 (B. F. Davison 68) and 279 (S. L. Saunders 106, R. F. Jeffery 67, T. G. Hogan 4 for 64)
Western Australia 328 (K. H. Macleay 83 not out, R. S. Langer 75) and 186 for 5 (G. Shipperd 67)

Western Australia won by 5 wickets
Western Australia 16 pts, Tasmania 0 pts

South Australia crushed Queensland to win their first game of the season in either competition. A magnificent innings of 260 by Wayne Phillips, which more than doubled his previous best score, dominated the match and gave more ammunition to those who consider the twenty-four-year old opener to be worthy of a place in the Australian Test team. He hit two sixes and twenty-five fours and batted for 7½ hours. He shared an opening stand of 168 with Kim Harris, who made 45, and a third wicket stand of 178 in 132 minutes with David Hookes who hit leg-spinner Lillie for four consecutive sixes. Greg Ritchie, another Test claimant, gave an impressive display for Queensland, but the spin of Dolman and Inverarity proved too much for the rest of the Queensland batsmen. Following-on, Queensland again succumbed to spin with Peter Sleep taking the last four wickets.

Tasmania collapsed from 160 for 3 to 234 all out against the bowling of Boyd and Macleay who also batted well to give Western Australia a 96-run lead. Hogan and Mann spun the ball well to reduce Tasmania to 159 for 9 in their second innings, but a thrilling last wicket stand of 120 in 3 hours between Saunders and Clough gave hope to Tasmania. It was a last wicket Sheffield Shield record for Tasmania and Saunders hit his maiden first-class hundred in 251 minutes, an impressive performance by a twenty-one year old with only a handful of first-class matches. Shipperd and Langer overcame early alarms and Western Australia moved to a five wicket victory.

15, 16, 17 and 18 January 1982

at Geelong

South Australia 244 (K. J. Wright 59, I. W. Callen 4 for 76) and 279 for 6 dec (W. M. Darling 134, J. J. Crowe 62)
Victoria 160 and 252 for 6 (G. M. Watts 64, B. C. Green 63 not out)

Match drawn
South Australia 4 pts, Victoria 0 pts

Merv Hughes. In his debut season he was hailed as an Australian Test fast bowler of the future.

at Hobart

New South Wales 281 (I. C. Davis 133, T. M. Chappell 81, F. D. Stephenson 4 for 51, P. M. Clough 4 for 57) and 262 (G. R. Beard 67)
Tasmania 345 (S. L. Saunders 84, R. D. Woolley 83, A. J. Skilbeck 4 for 94) and 135 (D. C. Boon 63 not out, L. S. Pascoe 8 for 41)

New South Wales won by 63 runs
New South Wales 12 pts, Tasmania 4 pts

The retirement of Richie Robinson and Max Walker and the inclusion of new players in an attempt to rebuild the side gave the Victorian team a strange look and there was early success for one of the newcomers, Merv Hughes, as well as for Callen. South Australia were 143 for 6, but the tail wagged and Parkinson and the spinners continued the good work by bowling out Victoria for 160 so giving the visitors a substantial first innings lead. Darling and Crowe built upon this lead with a second wicket stand of 143. Darling batted 5¼ hours for his 134. Victoria were set to make 364 in 379 minutes and passed the hundred for the loss of Wiener, but then wickets tumbled and the match was drawn.

Having looked to be likely winners for most of the game, Tasmania collapsed before Len Pascoe on the last day and lost to New South Wales by 63 runs. Pascoe's 8 for 41 was his best bowling in first-class cricket. Davis and Trevor Chappell had begun the match with a stand of 219 only to see their colleagues disintegrate before Clough and Stephenson. Tasmania, on the other hand, began badly, but some splendid batting by Davison, Woolley and Saunders took them to a first innings lead. Once more Saunders made an invaluable late contribution as he and Mancell added 96 for the ninth wicket. Mancell had success with the ball as well, but New South Wales recovered from 133 for 6 to add 129 for the last four wickets. Still Tasmania seemed winners until Pascoe produced his magnificent spell of bowling.

29, 30, 31 January and 1 February 1982

at Brisbane

Queensland 183 (G. M. Ritchie 52, G. F. Lawson 4 for 37) and 334 (K. C. Wessels 106, T. V. Hohns 89)
New South Wales 448 for 6 dec (P. M. Toohey 137, I. C. Davis 113, S. B. Smith 50, J. N. Maguire 4 for 86) and 72 for 2

New South Wales won by 8 wickets
New South Wales 16 pts, Queensland 0 pts

at Perth

Western Australia 307 (C. S. Serjeant 80, T. G. Hogan 70, I. W. Callen 4 for 88) and 263 (G. Shipperd 69, G. R. Marsh 67, J. D. Higgs 5 for 68)
Victoria 316 (B. C. Green 82, G. N. Yallop 55) and 120 for 6

Match drawn
Victoria 4 pts, Western Australia 0 pts

New South Wales beat Queensland with ease, their first victory in Brisbane for twelve years, and moved to the top of the Sheffield Shield table. Lawson destroyed late resistance after Skilbeck and Gordon had taken early wickets and then Davis and Toohey led the assault on the Queensland bowling well supported by the impressive newcomer, Steve Smith. Wessels batted superbly in Queensland's second innings with the reliable Hohns also batting well, but New South Wales were not to be denied.

The match in Perth developed into a struggle for first innings points, a struggle won narrowly by Victoria who omitted Moss as part of their rebuilding policy. Callen showed further evidence of return to his best pre-injury form and Jim Higgs bowled better than he had done all season as well as sharing a last wicket stand of 31 with Callen which gave Victoria the points. Callen's 34 was his best score for Victoria.

McDonald's Cup – Semi-Finals

6 February 1982

at Perth

New South Wales 245 for 5 (J. Dyson 101, R. B. McCosker 67, I. C. Davis 51)
Western Australia 186 (B. M. Laird 56, T. M. Chappell 4 for 35)

New South Wales won by 59 runs

7 February 1982

at Brisbane

Queensland 238 for 8 (W. R. Broad 59, A. R. Border 59, I. W. Callen 4 for 47)
Victoria 217 for 7 (J. M. Wiener 79, J. W. Scholes 60)

Queensland won by 21 runs

The fragmented nature of the first round matches had almost destroyed interest in the limited over competition so that when time arrived for the semi-finals people had nearly forgotten who had qualified. In the event, Queensland gained a solid victory over Victoria for whom Wiener, Watts and Scholes had batted well at the start of their innings. No one had been able to capitalise on the good start, however, and Thomson, Maguire and Dymock bowled Queensland to victory.

Opposite: *Terry Alderman. In two Sheffield Shield games he took 24 wickets at 7.46 runs each and then played no more for his state because of Test and international matches.*

McCosker and Dyson had an opening stand of 118 for New South Wales and Dyson and Davis added 106 for the second wicket so that the visitors were in a commanding position all through the match at Perth.

11, 12, 13 and 14 February 1982

at Sydney

Western Australia 439 (G. R. Marsh 176, C. S. Serjeant 106, R. G. Holland 4 for 124) and 56 for 2
New South Wales 523 for 9 dec (R. B. McCosker 130, T. M. Chappell 89, I. C. Davis 72, S. B. Smith 60, T. G. Hogan 4 for 154)

Match drawn
New South Wales 4 pts, Western Australia 0 pts

12, 13, 14 and 15 February 1982

at Geelong

Queensland 282 (R. B. Phillips 111 not out, M. G. Hughes 4 for 69) and 340 (K. C. Wessels 173)
Victoria 536 for 7 dec (J. M. Wiener 165, G. N. Yallop 111 not out, J. W. Scholes 94, B. C. Green 64, G. W. Brabon 4 for 106) and 57 for 3

Match drawn
Victoria 4 pts, Queensland 0 pts

at Launceston

Tasmania 298 (B. F. Davison 86, S. Reid 65 not out, R. D. Woolley 53, P. R. Sleep 4 for 60) and 265 (R. D. Woolley 83, S. L. Saunders 70, S. D. H. Parkinson 4 for 50, B. A. Vincent 4 for 64)
South Australia 462 (W. M. Darling 88, J. J. Crowe 79, W. B. Phillips 67, P. R. Sleep 66, G. J. Winter 50 not out, F. D. Stephenson 5 for 97) and 102 for 5 (W. M. Darling 52 not out, S. L. Saunders 4 for 29)

South Australia won by 5 wickets
South Australia 16 pts, Tasmania 0 pts

Western Australia batted for most of the first two days which were dominated by a record fourth wicket partnership of 260 between Geoff Marsh and Craig Serjeant. Marsh hit his maiden century in first-class cricket. McCosker and Davis began New South Wales' reply with a stand of 145 which launched the home side on its way to a huge score as first innings points became the only interest.

Victoria had dreams of recording their first win of the season, but they were blighted by a defiant innings from Kepler Wessels who will be qualified to play for Australia by October, 1982. In their first innings Queensland had been saved from complete disaster by a brave hundred from wicket-keeper Phillips. Merv Hughes had again impressed as an opening bowler. Victoria attacked the bowling from the start and a second wicket stand of 209 in just over three hours between Wiener and Scholes saw the Queensland attack torn to shreds. With a first innings lead of 254, Victoria had every hope of an outright win, but Wessels denied them with an innings of great maturity which lasted for 5 hours, 20 minutes. Victoria made a brave, almost suicidal, attempt to get the 87 runs that they needed for victory, but ten an over was more than they could manage.

Displaying great all round batting strength, South Australia built up a substantial first innings lead and beat Tasmania with some ease after a few stumbles to the leg-spin of Saunders. Davison, Woolley and debutant Stan Reid saved Tasmania after a bad start and Franklyn Stephenson again bowled splendidly, but he could not prevent South Australia from taking a lead of 164 on the first innings. Tasmania lost 6 wickets in clearing off the arrears, but Woolley, Reid and Saunders again batted well. Saunders' batting grew more impressive with every match, and it was he who gave the visitors some trouble with his spin before they clinched victory and moved into a challenging position for the Shield title.

19, 20, 21 and 22 February 1982

at Adelaide

South Australia 507 for 7 dec (W. M. Darling 121, K. J. Wright 104 not out, D. W. Hookes 97, R. J. Inverarity 75, G. J. Winter 64, M. F. Malone 4 for 134) and 19 for 1
Western Australia 245 and 280 (G. R. Marsh 59, A. T. Sincock 5 for 56)

South Australia won by 9 wickets
South Australia 16 pts, Western Australia 0 pts

at Devonport

Tasmania 405 (R. D. Woolley 116, F. D. Stephenson 90, D. C. Boon 88)
Queensland 411 for 4 (K. C. Wessels 220, G. M. Ritchie 136 not out, F. D. Stephenson 4 for 58)

Match drawn
Queensland 4 pts, Tasmania 0 pts

at St Kilda, Melbourne

Victoria 161 (S. N. Graf 55, G. F. Lawson 4 for 63) and 235 (G. N. Yallop 54, T. M. Chappell 4 for 12)
New South Wales 305 for 8 dec (S. J. Rixon 124, M. G. Hughes 4 for 71) and 93 for 2

New South Wales won by 8 wickets
New South Wales 16 pts, Victoria 0 pts

New South Wales won their last match of the season and headed the Sheffield Shield table with 72 points; only South Australia, with one match to play, could overtake them. New South Wales were confronted by some very limp Victorian batting at St Kilda and Geoff Lawson quickly brushed it aside. When New South Wales batted their hero was wicket-keeper Steve Rixon who, coming in as night-watchman, stayed to make 124 and put his side in a strong position. New South Wales never lost their grip on the game. Whitney took quick wickets and only Yallop showed sufficient concentration although he was batting with a severe arm injury – it was later discovered to be broken. Trevor Chappell brought the innings to a close with 4 for 12 in 8 overs.

Only 47 minutes were possible on the second day at

Devonport so that the game became a battle for first innings points. Tasmania were 71 for 4, but Woolley and Boon added 137. Then came a marvellous flourish from Franklyn Stephenson who, batting at number ten, hit 90 of the last 122 runs. Queensland were 91 for 2, but Wessels, again in marvellous form, and the equally impressive Ritchie had a record stand of 304 in 375 minutes and Queensland swept to first innings points in spite of another splendid bowling performance by Stephenson.

The South Australian late surge on the title was maintained when they thrashed Western Australia in Adelaide. Darling was in fine form, adding 113 with Inverarity for the third wicket. Hookes joined Inverarity in a stand of 132 and Kevin Wright hit the second century of his career to raise the score to 500. The spin of Sleep and Inverarity soon had Western Australia in trouble and when they followed-on they succumbed to the veteran medium pacer Sincock who had been called into the side for the first time since the opening match of the season because of an injury to Brian Vincent.

26, 27, 28 February and 1 March 1982

at Perth

Western Australia 353 (S. C. Clements 73, G. R. Marsh 51) and 301 for 3 dec (G. R. Marsh 120, S. C. Clements 86, G. Shipperd 70 not out)
Queensland 331 (R. B. Kerr 158, K. C. Wessels 62, T. G. Hogan 4 for 103) and 276 for 7 (R. B. Kerr 101, A. B. Henschell 76)

Match drawn
Western Australia 4 pts, Queensland 0 pts

at Adelaide

Victoria 297 (J. M. Wiener 116, J. W. Scholes 64, A. T. Sincock 4 for 85) and 286 (J. W. Scholes 71, P. J. Davies 57)
South Australia 423 for 8 dec (J. J. Crowe 126, D. W. Hookes 63, P. R. Sleep 53, I. W. Callen 4 for 98) and 161 for 1 (W. B. Phillips 84 not out)

South Australia won by 9 wickets
South Australia 16 pts, Victoria 0 pts

A tedious innings by Shipperd had much to do with condemning the game at Perth to a draw, particularly as it followed a fine opening stand of 127 between Marsh and newcomer Shane Clements. They had an opening stand of 171 in the second innings and this took them only 132 minutes and under 35 overs. For Queensland Robbie Kerr, opening with Wessels, hit a century in each innings, only the fourth Queenslander to do this.

The main interest was in the game at Adelaide, however, where South Australia had to beat Victoria outright to win the Sheffield Shield. There seemed little hope that South Australia would achieve their ambition when Wiener hit a hundred on the opening day and the score stood at 230 for 1, but Victoria collapsed, losing their last nine wickets for 67, mainly due to a fine spell by Andrew Sincock. Jef, Crowe played splendidly when the home side batted, but once more it was the consistent application of their batsmen right down the order that made it possible for them to take a first innings lead of 126. Once more Victoria started well and once more they collapsed, losing their last eight wickets for 118 runs which included a lively eighth wicket stand of 64 between Callen and Sacristani whose wicket-keeping had impressed in his first few matches for the state. Needing 161 to win, South Australia took the match and the title with a joyful flourish. Darling and Phillips began with 101 in 85 minutes and Crowe joined Phillips, who finished a fine season unbeaten on 84, to score the last 60 runs in 37 minutes. South Australia had won the Sheffield Shield for the first time since Hookes' golden days of 1976 and this time it was his enthusiastic leadership that had much to do with their success.

Sheffield Shield Final Table

	P	W	1st inn points	NR	L	Pts
South Australia	9	4	6	1	1	74
New South Wales	9	4	6	2	1	72
Western Australia	9	3	4	1	1	54
Tasmania	5	1	2	—	3	36
Queensland	9	1	2	2	2	20
Victoria	9	—	4	—	5	16

Points – 12 for a win; 4 for first innings lead; 2 for a match without decision on the first innings. Tasmania's points are multiplied by 9 and divided by 5.

McDonald's Cup
6 March 1982

at St Kilda, Melbourne
Third Place Match
Victoria 171 for 8
Western Australia 172 for 8
Western Australia won by 2 wickets

Final
at Sydney
Queensland 224 for 8 (W. R. Broad 85)
New South Wales 197 (P. M. Toohey 66, G. Dymock 5 for 27)

Queensland won by 27 runs

Playing the final match of his illustrious career, Geoff Dymock ended on a note of personal and team triumph that pleased all. Queensland had reached a good total after a disastrous start and for this they had to thank Wayne Broad who won the Man of the Match award for his determined 85. It was Dymock, however, who immediately put the game out of New South Wales' reach as he took 3 wickets and Maguire 1 to leave the home side floundering at 14 for 4.

First Class Averages

BATTING

	M	Inns	NOs	Runs	HS	Av	100s	50s
W. M. Darling	9	17	3	1011	134*	72.71	3	6
R. B. McCosker	9	15	3	796	146*	66.33	4	2
K. C. Wessels	11	18		1094	220	60.77	5	3
G. M. Ritchie	10	16	2	833	136*	59.50	3	3
M. F. Kent	3	4	1	167	91	55.66		1
J. Dyson	8	14	1	709	127*	54.53	3	8
G. R. Marsh	5	10		545	176	54.50	2	3
J. M. Wiener	9	17	1	847	221*	52.93	3	2
P. A. Hibbert	2	3		153	89	51.00		1
K. J. Hughes	9	15	1	706	113	50.42	3	3
J. J. Crowe	10	18	4	704	157	50.28	3	2
W. B. Phillips	10	19	1	857	260	47.61	2	4
R. B. Kerr	8	14	1	613	158	47.15	3	1
B. M. Laird	9	16	2	659	110*	47.07	1	4
P. M. Toohey	8	13	2	511	137	46.45	1	2
J. K. Moss	5	9	1	358	200*	44.75	1	1
D. W. Hookes	11	17	1	703	106	43.93	1	5
D. C. Boon	7	13	2	473	88	43.00		3
I. R. McLean	2	3		126	70	42.00		1
G. Shipperd	10	17	2	613	131	40.86	1	3
S. B. Smith	5	7	1	245	60	40.83		2
A. R. Border	9	15	2	530	126	40.76	1	5
G. M. Wood	9	16	2	569	151	40.64	2	2
B. C. Green	5	10	2	318	82	39.75		3
K. P. Harris	4	7		275	97	39.28		2
K. J. Wright	9	14	4	392	104*	39.20	1	2
R. S. Langer	8	14	1	506	140	38.92	1	2
R. J. Inverarity	9	12	3	348	100*	38.66	1	
T. M. Chappell	10	17	3	533	89	38.07		3
I. C. Davis	9	14		523	133	37.35	2	3
R. D. Woolley	7	13		482	116	37.07	1	3
B. F. Davison	7	12	1	397	86	36.09		3
G. N. Yallop	9	18	1	647	111*	36.05	1	4
B. A. Vincent	5	5	2	107	47	35.66		
G. S. Chappell	9	15		532	201	35.46	2	1
S. J. Rixon	10	12	3	310	124	34.44	1	
G. R. Beard	10	13	2	378	75	34.36		3
R. B. Phillips	11	16	3	414	111*	31.84	1	1
D. L. Boyd	4	7	2	149	43*	29.80		
J. W. Scholes	10	18	1	505	94	29.70		3
A. L. Mann	6	10	2	236	47	29.50		
T. V. Hohns	11	18	3	442	89	29.46		2
P. R. Sleep	11	16	1	438	78	29.20		5
C. S. Serjeant	10	16	3	376	106	28.92	1	1
S. L. Saunders	7	12	1	308	106	28.00	1	2
R. F. Jeffery	7	12	1	305	67	27.72		2
G. D. Porter	5	8	1	194	64	27.71		2
G. M. Watts	10	19	1	495	71	27.50		4
K. H. MacLeay	7	10	1	242	83*	26.88		1
R. W. Marsh	9	14		342	47	24.42		
R. D. Robinson	4	8	1	170	71*	24.28		1
A. B. Henschell	6	11		263	76	23.90		2
G. Dymock	11	15	4	260	101*	23.63	1	
T. G. Hogan	6	8	1	159	70	22.71		1
R. J. Bright	7	12	1	247	39	22.45		
J. R. Thomson	8	11	5	129	45	21.50		
T. J. Zoehrer	7	10	1	188	46	20.88		
P. J. Davies	4	7		143	57	20.42		1
I. W. Callen	6	7	2	102	34	20.40		
S. F. Graf	8	13	2	230	55	19.16		1
R. N. Travers	5	10		177	29	17.70		
F. D. Stephenson	7	12	1	192	90	17.45		1
G. J. Winter	10	11	2	156	64	17.33		2
W. R. Broad	5	7		116	33	16.57		
B. Yardley	9	14		226	45	16.14		
I. R. Beven	5	10	1	139	40	15.44		
D. M. Wellham	7	11		153	36	15.30		
P. J. Mancell	7	12		179	50	14.91		1
H. K. De Jong	4	7		100	41	14.28		
D. K. Lillee	8	12	3	125	54*	13.88		1

(Qualification 100 runs, average 10.00)
(S. C. Clements, 86 and 73, also scored 100 runs, but played in only one match)

BOWLING

	Overs	Mds	Runs	Wkts	Av	Best	5/inn
T. M. Alderman	240.5	60	627	37	16.94	7/28	3
T. M. Chappell	59.4	17	174	10	17.40	4/12	
F. D. Stephenson	229.5	57	630	36	17.50	6/19	3
R. J. Inverarity	343.2	117	639	30	21.30	5/40	1
P. M. Clough	148.3	42	390	18	21.66	4/57	
D. K. Lillee	301	66	819	37	22.13	7/83	3
G. F. Lawson	200.4	48	533	24	22.20	6/70	1
B. Yardley	360.4	73	1105	49	22.55	7/98	4
R. G. Holland	332.4	128	661	27	24.48	6/64	1
I. W. Callen	265.1	45	789	31	25.45	4/76	
G. J. Winter	318.4	97	773	29	26.65	7/65	2
S. D. H. Parkinson	310.5	79	851	28	30.39	4/50	
M. G. Hughes	192.4	37	567	18	31.50	4/59	
B. A. Vincent	99	18	320	10	32.00	4/64	
K. H. MacLeay	144.2	34	330	10	33.00	3/34	
L. S. Pascoe	234.3	45	760	23	33.04	8/41	1
A. J. Skilbeck	162.4	44	465	14	33.21	4/94	
P. R. Sleep	343.3	102	878	26	33.76	5/117	1
D. L. Boyd	113	18	406	12	33.83	3/40	
G. R. Beard	355	116	747	22	33.95	5/67	1
M. H. N. Walker	167.1	42	482	14	34.42	4/45	
G. W. Brabon	119.3	18	417	12	34.75	4/106	
A. L. Mann	220.4	60	533	15	35.33	4/78	
A. T. Sincock	103.4	21	354	10	35.40	5/56	1
T. G. Hogan	303.3	83	735	20	36.75	4/64	
R. J. Bright	348.2	108	741	20	37.05	3/23	
J. R. Thomson	246.1	46	788	21	37.52	4/112	
S. L. Saunders	136	22	467	12	38.91	4/29	
J. D. Higgs	393.3	83	1142	29	39.37	5/68	1
S. F. Graf	238.3	49	671	17	39.47	3/37	
M. F. Malone	264	45	763	19	40.15	4/111	
M. C. Dolman	167.1	44	492	12	41.00	4/114	
G. Dymock	381.2	106	919	22	41.77	3/82	
J. N. Maguire	276	62	773	18	42.94	4/86	
T. V. Hohns	367.3	62	1182	23	51.39	4/85	
D. J. Lillie	129.2	20	577	11	52.45	4/77	

Leading Fielders

37 R. W. Marsh
33 K. J. Wright (ct 31/st 2)
24 S. J. Rixon (ct 21/st 3)
23 C. S. Serjeant
17 R. B. Phillips (ct 16/st 1)
16 T. J. Zoehrer (ct 13/st 3)
14 R. D. Woolley (ct 12/st 2)
13 D. W. Hookes and B. M. Laird
12 A. R. Border and J. W. Scholes
11 R. B. McCosker and R. D. Robinson (ct 8/st 3)
10 J. J. Crowe and P. G. Sacristani (ct 8/st 2)

Opposite: Greg Chappell. No longer the dominant force of Sheffield Shield and Australian cricket. Now thirty-four, he has been playing first-class cricket for sixteen years, yet it would be unwise to suggest that this majestic player will never again dominate Australian cricket.

FRANK TYSON, *the former England fast bowler, now a leading cricket writer and coach, reviews the Australian season.*

In early December 1981 Rick McCosker and John Dyson established a new first wicket record of 253 for New South Wales in its one-day McDonald's Cup annihilation of South Australia by 111 runs and six wickets. As I watched that 50-over massacre I little dreamed that its losers would eventuate as the winners of the Sheffield Shield in the following March. One-day cricket is vastly different from the four-day variety; but it must surely reflect, in some small degree, the comparative abilities of the contestants. There was nothing in the performances of Rick Darling, Wayne Phillips, Jeff Crowe, Peter Sleep, Kevin Wright, Brian Vincent and Graham Winter on that day in Sydney to suggest that they were champions in the making, capable of winning the Sheffield Shield for South Australia for the first time since 1975–76.

Yet, in spite of all the early season jeremiads, David Hookes' youthful South Australians swept to a narrow and spectacular success in the 1981–82 domestic competition by winning four of their last five games by an innings. Yet as late as the first day of the final match of the season against Victoria, the Shield appeared to have eluded the grasp of the South Australians; at one stage of the game Victoria were a promising 1/230 and the chances of the home side gaining the sixteen points necessary for its ultimate triumph seemed remote. David Hookes had other ideas, however, and his men counter-attacked to such telling effect that the sixteenth point and $56,000 in prize money fell into their laps at 5.32 p.m. on the last afternoon.

The champions' forte lay in their batting; Darling, Crowe, Phillips and Hookes each exceeded 500 runs and a mean figure of 40 for the first-class season. The team provided five names in the first sixteen places in the national batting averages and only failed to score less than a collective 400 runs in an innings once in the last seven games in Adelaide. The astonishing aspect of the Adelaide side's march to its Shield triumph was the manner in which it repeatedly dismissed good batting combinations with an attack which would not have been out of place in the middle of the Schweppes' County Championship table. Its fastest bowler was the left-handed Sam Parkinson: a poor man's Fred Rumsey but a striker effective enough to capture twenty-two wickets. Peter Sleep's leg-spinners brought him twenty-four victims – a fact which might surprise many Lancashire League readers; but the undoubted star with the ball was the former Western Australian skipper and veteran orthodox left-handed spinner, John Inverarity, whose thirty wickets cost him only just over 19 each.

Inverarity's influence extended beyond the bowling crease and there is no doubt that, under his mentorship, the impetuous Hookes matured and the youth and enthusiasm of the South Australians were blended into the stuff of which champions are made.

After a disappointing start to the season with three draws and a loss to Western Australia, Rick McCosker's New South Welshmen recovered, reeled off four outright wins and, until early March, never looked likely to lose the Shield. The Sydney side concluded its programme on 22 February with a lead of 12 points and had to wait for the agonising remainder of the season with the sword of Damocles and the possibility of a last minute South Australian triumph in its final match hanging over its head. Ultimately the two-edged sword fell, not only on New South Wales' Sheffield Shield aspirations, but also on its hopes of winning the McDonald's Cup which it lost to Queensland. The reversal of New South Wales' early indifferent form came when, with South Australia just 11 runs from victory with eight wickets in reserve, the local umpires abandoned a Sydney match because of persistent rain and saved the home side from defeat; an act which the visiting skipper, Hookes, denounced as 'unsportsmanlike and shameful'. That caustic comment cost the insubordinate Hookes a fine of $130; but, more importantly, it aroused New South Wales from its earlier lethargy. McCosker's men then proceeded to account for Victoria by eight wickets, Tasmania by 63 runs, Queensland by eight wickets and, after denying Western Australia any points, Victoria once more by eight wickets. In final sprint to the line, it proved to be the sluggish beginning of the season which cost the Sydney-siders the Shield.

No blame for his side's failure could attach to captain Rick McCosker, who enjoyed a wonderful summer with the bat, scoring 709 first-class runs and topping the national averages. Toohey and Beard exceeded 40 runs per innings whilst the former Test man, Ian Davis, notched hundreds against Tasmania and Queensland. Dirk Wellham, the hero of the 1981 Oval Test against England, fell victim to the uncertainty of cricket and spent most of the summer carrying the drinks of his state side; he ended the season reputedly speculating on the possibility of the greater Test opportunities available in Victoria.

After missing the tour of England because of injury, fast bowler, Len Pascoe's early season form fell below expectations. His speedy colleague Geoff Lawson, however, more than made amends for the dark-haired quickie's shortcomings by capturing twenty-three wickets at 20.39. The surprise packet of the New South Wales' attack, however, was 'Dutch' Holland, the experienced leg-spinner from provincial Newcastle, whose twenty-seven wickets prompted many New South Welsh partisans to advocate his inclusion in the national team.

The Western Australian Governor, Sir Richard Trow-bridge, remarked to me, with some justification, at an official reception, that his state could hardly be blamed for finishing so far down the premiership ladder in 1981–82 because it fielded its second eleven for most of the summer. Seven of the West Australian regulars played in only two of their State's nine Shield fixtures because of the demands of Tests, One-Day Internationals and the New Zealand tour; both of these state games were won by the decisive margins of 152 runs and an innings and 35. The last time that a full strength Perth combination took the field in 1981–82 was on 1 November, a bare fortnight after the opening of the season! This ludicrous programming of domestic first-class matches resulted in Bruce Laird, Graeme Wood, Kim Hughes and Rod Marsh failing to qualify for a place in the averages. Only one Western Australian batsman, Geoff Marsh, gained a mention in the Shield honours list, finishing fifth with the figures of 545 runs at an average of 54.5. Terry Alderman was the best of the Shield bowlers with the astonishingly low average of 7.46. Even more astonishing was the fact that the twenty-four wickets which earned the young medium-pacer the premier place amongst his peers were all captured in the first two matches played by the full-strength Perth team. With the departure of its Test brigade, success deserted Western Australia. Under its surrogate skipper, Craig Serjeant, it struggled to supplement its previously earned 32 points with a further 22 from seven games.

Tasmania played an abridged programme of five matches for the last time in 1981–82; in 1982–83, the island side will compete on an equal nine game footing with its mainland rivals. Three of the Apple Isle's clashes produced outright losses, but Australia's southernmost cricketers were far from disgraced. In the course of the season Leicestershire's Brian Davison led them to a notable 96 run victory over Victoria, inspired them to a 63 run first innings lead over New South Wales and showed his men the way to a massive 405 total against Queensland. The imported Barbadian beanpole, Franklyn Stephenson, captured thirty wickets with his medium-fast inswing and only conceded pride of place in the averages to Terry Alderman. David Boon's consistency with the bat yielded him 329 runs at an average of 41.12 and again made one wonder what this stocky Taswegian must do to gain the recognition of the Australian selectors. Whilst Davison's aggregate of 301 proved disappointing after his prolific 1980–81 season, Roger Woolley exceeded all expectations by complementing his sporadically brilliant wicket-keeping with a bonus of 417 runs. By far the most improved player in Tasmanian ranks, however, was leg-spinner Stuart Saunders, who returned to Hobart, after a summer in county second eleven cricket on an Esso scholarship, a transformed and improved batsman. He scored his maiden hundred from the disadvantaged lower order against Western Australia, followed that achievement with 84 against New South Wales and 70 against South Australia and underlined his season's worth to the side by contributing ten wickets with his wrist-spinners.

Like Western Australia, Queensland was blessed with the presence of its stars, Greg Chappell, Allan Border and Jeff Thomson, for only two of its nine Shield matches. Like its Perth counterpart, the Northern State began with a convincing win and might easily have earned more points from its clash against New South Wales in Newcastle, had not rain curtailed the match by two days. Once again the incongruity occurred of three of Australia's leading cricketers failing to gain a mention in the averages because of their lack of opportunity; as was the case with Western Australia, the performances of Queensland tailed off miserably after the departure of its stars for international pastures. The only consolations which Queenslanders gained from the season, after their initial win, was a first innings victory against Tasmania and an exhilarating triumph over New South Wales in the McDonald's Cup.

On the individual plane, however, the summer was far from unproductive for the Sunshine State. Its adopted Springbok opener, Kepler Wessels, aggregated 1015 runs: 253 more than his closest home-grown rival, the Victorian, Julien Wiener. The development of young middle-order batsman, Greg Ritchie progressed to the extent of his being deemed unfortunate not to accompany his state captain's Australian contingent across the Tasman Sea to New Zealand and produced 653 classical runs at an average of 55.25. The elegant opener Rob Kerr was not far behind his more acclaimed team-mate and collected 577 runs, including a brace of centuries in one match against Western Australia. Much of the credit for the nurturing of Queensland's burgeoning talent must go to the veteran paceman, Geoff Dymock, who assumed the reins of command after the departure of Greg Chappell and so inspired his young charges that they wrested the one-day championship of Australia from the much-fancied New South Wales.

The glory which was Victoria in its premiership years of 1978–80 was nowhere in evidence two seasons later. The newly-appointed captain, John Scholes, with a wealth of experience at his disposal, was unable to imbue his men with any collective drive and the southern state finished the season as wooden spoonists of the first-class competition, without a win to its name and with only four first innings advantages and 16 points to its credit. Wiener stood out from the Victorian ruck of batting mediocrity with 762 runs and an average of 54.42: a feat which gained him a prize of $10,000 from the Victorian eleven's sponsors, Federation Insurance Ltd. Jeff Moss notched 358 runs but was jettisoned from the team on the grounds of ostensibly approaching senility, whilst Ian Callen was the outstanding bowler in the Melbourne side with thirty-one victims at an individual cost of 25.45 in his seasonal account. Misfortune courted Victoria's international batsman, Graham Yallop, who fell completely from selectorial favour when he was compelled to withdraw from the Test scene with a back strain after the Brisbane clash against Pakistan: to add further injury to insult and injury, the left-hander sustained a fractured wrist during a subsequent game against New South Wales and was eliminated from the closing stages of the Sheffield Shield season. The darling of the Melbourne Cricket Ground, Max Walker, was also far from fit and was finally forced into retirement half-way through the season, together with the former state captain and wicket-keeper, Richie Robinson. With Gary Watts, John Scholes and Jeff Moss producing only ephemeral form, Victoria were constantly prone to sudden middle-order collapses.

On the bowling scene, leg-spinner Jimmy Higgs, took twenty-seven expensive wickets in nine matches; towards the end of the season, his control and penetration evaporated completely, leaving a residue of only ten victims from his last six appearances at the bowling crease. The orthodox left-handed spinner, Ray Bright, twice in the course of the summer received his call-up papers for Australia; he was also chosen to tour New Zealand, where he was bowled sparingly, and has been included in Kim Hughes' contingent to visit Pakistan in late 1982. In Bright's case, selection has been the sincerest form of flattery, since his Shield figures of twenty wickets at a cost of 34.35 in 1981–82 scarcely warranted such consistent favours. Shaun Graf, once considered a blossoming Test all-rounder, failed to live up to his early promise and had a disappointing season with both bat and ball.

The truth about the Victorian side in 1981–82 was that it was an aging collection of talents which the complacent selectors neglected to prune and re-invigorate; when they did make changes and introduce Jones, Davies, Hughes and Sacristani to first-class ranks, it was too late to salvage any prestige from the wreckage of the disaster which was the 1981–82 season. It is impossible to envisage any harvest from Victoria's newly planted crop of ability for two years.

New South Wales 1981-82
First Class Matches

BATTING	v. Queensland (Newcastle) 22-25 October 1981	v. Western Australia (Perth) 30 Oct-2 Nov. 1981	v. South Australia (Adelaide) 6-9 November 1981	v. West Indians (Sydney) 27-30 Nov. 1981	v. South Australia (Sydney) 10-13 Dec. 1981	v. Victoria (Sydney) 19-22 Dec. 1981	v. Tasmania (Hobart) 15-18 January 1982	v. Queensland (Brisbane) 29 Jan.-1 Feb. 1982	v. Western Australia (Sydney) 11-14 February 1982	v. Victoria (St Kilda) 19-22 February 1982
R. B. McCosker	18 — 0 4	90 —	64 23	49 146* 123*	118*	20 6	130 —	5 0		
J. Dyson	65 — 10 19	108 —	98 123	5 26	6 83					
T. M. Chappell	58 — 31 12	4* —	6 44	34 18	1 10	81 12	26 22*	89 —	38 47*	
I. C. Davis	52 — 0 36	— —	15 52	0 1		133 6	113 11	72 —	16 16	
P. M. Toohey	16 — — —	— —	11 44	84 39	76 19*	11 20	137 26*	1 —	27 —	
G. R. Beard	62* — 75 30	— —	4 2	48 2	12* —	0 67	40 —	17 —	19 —	
S. J. Rixon	4* — 18 7	— —	25 2	17 14*	— —	5 39	18* —	37 —	124 —	
M. Ray			21* 11*	17 —	— —					
L. S. Pascoe	— — 39 5*	— —	23 0	4 —	— —	1 10*				
M. R. Whitney	— — 3* 0	— —	0 0	1* —						
A. J. Skilbeck		— 0				6* 2	— —	34 —	33* —	
D. M. Wellham	24 — 2 0	7* —				1 25				
D. W. Hourn	— — 24 0	— —								
G. F. Lawson	— — 4 0	— —					14* —	25 —	2 —	
R. P. Done			— —							
R. G. Holland				2 —		1 5	— —	12* —	— —	
S. B. Smith					35 —	7 46	50 —	60 —	17 30*	
D. A. H. Johnston						13 14				
E. Gordon						— —	30* —			
Byes		1	2 5	2		7 10	1	3	1	
Leg-byes	9	3 2 4	7 7	4	1 2	11 2	3 7	4	10	
Wides	1	1 1	1 3	1	1		1		2	
No-balls	13	5 2 5	1 3	5	3 1	1 4	4 25	9	11	
Total	322	215 117 220	278 319	271 252	255 233	281 262	448 72	523	305 93	
Wickets	6	10 10 2	9 10	10 5	4 2	10 10	6 2	9	8 2	
Result	D	L D	L D	W	W	W	D		W	
Points	2	0 2	— 4	16	12	16	4		16	

Catches
24 – S. J. Rixon (ct 21/st 3)
11 – R. B. McCosker
9 – I. C. Davis and P. M. Toohey
6 – J. Dyson
5 – T. M. Chappell and R. G. Holland
4 – G. R. Beard
2 – S. B. Smith and D. M. Wellham
1 – A. J. Skilbeck, M. Ray, L. S. Pascoe, E. Gordon, G. F. Lawson, M. R. Whitney and D. A. H. Johnston

BOWLING	L. S. Pascoe	M. R. Whitney	A. J. Skilbeck	M. Ray	G. R. Beard	T. M. Chappell	R. B. McCosker	E. Gordon
v. Queensland (Newcastle) 22-25 October 1981	13-5-28-2	17-3-65-2			24-5-67-5	5.4-1-13-0		
v. Western Australia (Perth) 30 October-2 November 1981	17-5-46-0	28-4-89-2			22-2-65-0			
v. South Australia (Adelaide) 6-9 November 1981		31-6-85-0			32-8-75-2	4-2-7-1		
v. West Indians (Sydney) 27-30 November 1981	26-4-112-3	16-2-79-0	14-4-41-0	33.5-8-112-2 4-0-20-0	31-8-71-1 4-0-26-0	14-3-34-1 5-0-40-1	3-1-17-0 3.1-0-29-0	
v. South Australia (Sydney) 10-13 December 1981	14-2-51-0 8.4-0-53-1	15-4-49-1 3-0-10-0		13-7-17-2 20-6-46-0	37-13-64-1 19-5-59-1	1-0-2-0		
v. Victoria (Sydney) 19-22 December 1981	27.4-3-93-3 16-3-47-0		17-9-34-3 13-3-39-2	3-0-13-0 4-1-18-0	17-9-17-0 34.5-17-54-4	2-0-11-0		
v. Tasmania (Hobart) 15-18 January 1982	38-7-111-2 22.1-10-41-8		26.4-3-94-4 17-3-54-1		16-8-25-1 15-4-19-0	10-1-35-1		
v. Queensland (Brisbane) 29 January-1 February 1982			12-2-33-1 15-3-46-1		10-4-22-1 25.1-7-56-3	2-1-4-1		16-3-49-2 15-5-34-1
v. Western Australia (Sydney) 11-14 February 1982			22-8-56-0 8-4-13-0		54-19-109-3	5-3-6-0		14-1-47-0 10-3-28-0
v. Victoria (St Kilda) 19-22 February 1982		20.1-6-33-2 18-3-55-2	12-3-36-1 6-2-19-1		2-1-1-0 12-6-17-0	3-1-10-1 8-5-12-4		
	182.3-39-763-19 av. 40.15	148.1-28-465-9 av. 51.66	162.4-44-465-14 av. 33.21	77.5-22-226-4 av. 56.50	355-116-747-22 av. 33.95	59.4-17-174-10 av. 17.40	6.1-1-46-0 —	55-12-158-3 av. 52.66

A. R. P. Done 26-2-117-0 B. P. M. Toohey 1-0-1-0 C. P. M. Toohey 1-1-0-0 D. S. B. Smith 1-0-1-0

The South Australian hunt for Shield honours began inauspiciously in Perth against Western Australia, who, after being unceremoniously bundled out for 186 by Graham Winter's medium-pace swing, recovered to knock its opponents to the canvas for 107 and 180 and triumph by 152 runs. Laird's 110, Hughes' 80 and Alderman's match analysis of 10/92 were the catalysts which stimulated their side's eventual supremacy: an ascendancy which would have been all the greater, had it not been for a defiant 70 in 207 minutes from Ian McLean and a nine wicket match performance from Winter.

The Adelaide clash against New South Wales produced the frustration of a high scoring draw with the home side reaching 9/551 and nearly all of the fourth day's play being lost to rain. Former New Zealand schoolboy star, Jeff Crowe, who had carried the drinks in the previous game in Perth, accumulated 157, pillaging the Sydneysider's attack to the tune of 103 runs in the final session of the first day. He was well supported by 106 from David Hookes and 71 from the bat of Rick Darling. New South Wales' skipper, McCosker, was in no hurry to overhaul the South Australian total and he and Dyson dawdled along to reach 191 in six hours before the first wicket fell. New South Wales had reached 2/220 when the merciful umpires called time.

The return game in Sydney ended in pouring rain and with a display of fireworks which was far from an exhibition of damp squibs. New South Wales led South Australia by three runs on the first innings after being hauled back from the brink of a huge supremacy by Inverarity, whose left-handed spinners returned him a seasonal best of 5/40 and occasioned a five wicket collapse for 24 runs. McCosker lambasted a rapid-fire 146 in his side's second innings of 5/252, before declaring to leave Hookes and his men the task of scoring 256 on the final day of the match. Crowe obliged with an unbeaten 137 and Darling contributed 52 to the South Australian total of 2/245. It was at this juncture that the local umpires suspended play with the visitors just 11 runs short of their goal. The South Australian skipper, Hookes, exploded with indignation at being baulked of his victory – and was fined his match fee for showing his resentment at the umpires' decision.

It was South Australia's turn to escape defeat by the skin of its teeth when the Adelaide men met Queensland in their next sally on to the field in Brisbane. At the conclusion of play, South Australia's last pair, Inverarity and Lewis were at the crease, with their side 37 runs from victory after being set the task of scoring 235 to win in four sessions and thirty minutes by Queensland's substitute skipper, Geoff Dymock. Both sides closed their first innings with only 15 runs separating their collective efforts. For South Australia, the thirty-seven year old Inverarity notched his twenty-first first-class hundred in 330 minutes; a knock which was matched by Greg Ritchie's 126 and a maiden century from Geoff Dymock in his retirement season. In Queensland's second innings Rob Kerr contributed 103 to his side's declared score of 8/249. Kim Harris thereupon all but scored a century on his first appearance for his state, before becoming one of Henschell's four quick wickets, in a spell which wrote *finis* to any hopes of a South Australian victory.

Hookes more than turned the tables on Dymock when the northerners journeyed to Adelaide. The South Aus-

Queensland 1981-82
First Class Matches

BATTING

	v. Victoria (Brisbane) 16-19 October 1981	v. New South Wales (Newcastle) 22-25 October 1981	v. Pakistanis (Brisbane) 30 Oct.-2 Nov. 1981	v. Western Australia (Brisbane) 20-23 Nov. 1981	v. West Indians (Brisbane) 11-14 Dec. 1981	v. South Australia (Brisbane) 17-20 Dec. 1981	v. South Australia (Adelaide) 8-10 January 1982	v. New South Wales (Brisbane) 29 Jan.-1 Feb. 1982	v. Victoria (Geelong) 12-15 February 1982	v. Tasmania (Devonport) 19-22 February 1982	v. Western Australia (Perth) 26 Feb.-1 Mar. 1982
K. C. Wessels	11 168 103	— 9	— 72	— 13	57 23	29 22	4 8	106 2	173 220	— 62	12
M. F. Kent	25 25* 26	— 91	—								
G. S. Chappell	10 21 2	— 162	—								
W. R. Broad	18 13 0	— 11	— 33	—						22	19
G. M. Ritchie	49 14 22	— 44*	— 44	55 71	126 47	103 1	52 8	40 21	136*			
T. V. Hohns	36 58* 4	— 32	— 25	18 18	33 10	26 4	23 89	2 48*	2*	— 4	10
A. R. Border	0 52 58	— 0*	—								
R. B. Phillips	19 27 5	—	— 46	— 16*	51 6	14 6	27 0	22 111*	12	— 40	12*
G. Dymock	22 — 22*	—	— 33	— 10	8 101*	0* 37	6 10	0 1	0	— 10	0*
D. J. Lillie	4* — —	— —	—	0 15*	— 0	2* 1					
J. R. Thomson	45 9* 0	— —	—								
R. B. Kerr				4 20	16 6	103* 14	66 37	26 24	9	29 —	158 101
M. A. Gaskell				19 —	0 6						
A. D. Parker				6 —	8 0						
H. K. De Jong					1 20	41 5	— 0	19 4	4 1	5 —	0 —
J. N. Maguire				0*	— 0	0 —	0 19	4 4	1 6	0	2 1* —
G. W. Brabon		1* —	—	0*							
R. N. Travers					25 25	24 7	28 4	2 27			6 29
A. B. Henschell					19 0	50 15	0 38	33 16	1	— 15	76
C. G. Rackemann						0 6*	0* 0*				
I. D. C. Kelly								31 15		— 1	3
Byes	1 1	4	7	10 12	11 5	3	5 4	4	2	2
Leg-byes	3 3 7	8	3	4 4	6 2	3 2	3 7	17 5	6	7 10
Wides	5 4				1 2	1	2	4	2	1 1
No-balls	5 3 14	14	16	10 4	2 1	4 1	1 6	4 5	13	2 1
Total	247 399 269	375	308	165 282	389 249	297 162	183 334	282 340	411	331 276
Wickets	10 6 9	5	9	10 10	8 10	10 10	10 10	10 10	4	10 7
Result	W	D	D	D	L	D	L	L	D	D	D
Points	12	2	—	2	—	0	0	4	0	4	0

Catches
17 — R. B. Phillips (ct 16/st 1) 6 — G. Dymock and K. C. Wessels 5 — R. B. Kerr 4 — A. R. Border, G. M. Ritchie and W. R. Broad (inc. one as sub) 3 — G. S. Chappell, T. V. Hohns a R. N. Travers

BOWLING

	J. R. Thomson	G. Dymock	D. J. Lillie	G. S. Chappell	W. R. Broad	T. V. Hohns	J. N. Maguire	H. K. De Jong
v. Victoria (Brisbane) 16-19 October 1981	29-6-76-3 19-5-47-1	31-6-82-3 8-1-33-2	8-4-21-0 19.2-3-68-3	14-4-43-0 8-0-17-0		24.3-4-74-3 29-7-85-4		
v. New South Wales (Newcastle) 22-25 Oct. 1981	24-9-53-0	33-14-75-1		11-4-42-1	3-0-13-0	10-0-38-0		
v. Pakistanis (Brisbane) 30 Oct.-2 Nov. 1981	22-5-76-3	28-7-74-2	20-3-77-4	3-1-8-0	10-3-35-0	11-0-44-1		
v. Western Australia (Brisbane) 20-23 November 1981		39-19-66-1			18-8-28-1	27.3-3-97-4	35-11-90-2	
v. West Indians (Brisbane) 11-14 December 1981		30-10-73-1	32-3-166-1			37.4-9-105-2	27-6-97-1	16-2-71-2
v. South Australia (Brisbane) 17-20 December 1981		21-7-38-0 2-0-11-0	31-5-122-1 12-1-69-2			42-8-122-2 21-6-58-1	26-7-52-2 3-2-3-0	9-3-21-0 2-1-2-1
v. South Australia (Adelaide) 8-10 January 1982		36-3-95-1	7-1-54-0			31-2-125-1	21-0-82-2	
v. New South Wales (Brisbane) 29 Jan.-1 Feb. 1982		26-7-59-0 8-2-26-1				30-1-110-1 8-0-25-0	29-6-86-4	13-1-62-1 0.3-0-14-0
v. Victoria (Geelong) 12-15 February 1982		32-9-57-1 4-0-29-1				32-2-130-0	34-5-102-2 4-0-21-2	
v. Tasmania (Devonport) 19-22 February, 1982		42-12-88-3				27.5-3-77-2	42-9-105-2	9-1-31-1
v. Western Australia (Perth) 26 February-1 March 1982		33-9-86-3 8.2-0-27-2			4-2-14-0 4-0-32-0	40-16-81-2 4-1-36-0	33-11-55-1 14-5-55-0	
	94-25- 252-7 av. 36.00	381.2-106- 919-22 av. 41.77	129.2-20- 577-11 av. 52.45	36-9- 110-1 av. 110.00	39-13- 122-1 av. 122.00	367.3-62- 1182-23 av. 51.39	276-62- 773-18 av. 42.94	49.3-8- 201-5 av. 40.20

A. A. R. Border 6-1-20-0   C. R. B. Kerr 1-0-3-0, R. N. Travers 1-0-5-0,   27-6-114-0
B. A. R. Border 1-0-3-0   G. M. Ritchie 1-0-2-0, C. G. Rackemann   D. C. G. Rackemann 13-3-55-0

tralian skipper did not even allow the Queenslanders the opportunity of escaping from the match with dignity and a draw; his side completely annihilated its opponents by an innings and 93 runs. The left-handed opener, Wayne Phillips, demonstrated that he had benefited immensely as a result of playing in county second eleven cricket as an Esso scholarship holder in 1981 and scored 260. This contribution plus 88 from Hookes and 62 from the bat of Sleep, boosted the South Australian total to the immensity of 4/552. Thereafter Queensland were never in the race, and, in spite of a valiant 103 from Greg Ritchie, were compelled to follow on after lagging by 255 on the first innings. The second innings proved an even graver disappointment than the first, with Dymock's batsmen surrendering for a mere 162, of which Rob Kerr notched 66.

South Australia's away fixture against Victoria was played at Geelong because of the unsatisfactory condition of the Melbourne Cricket Ground surface. The switch of venues proved to be a case of going from one extreme to the other, for the Kardinia Park wicket defied all the efforts of the bowlers on both sides and the game died to a fall. Poor first innings batting by Victoria permitted Hookes' men to enjoy an initial advantage of 88 runs: a lead which was expanded to 367 when Darling exploited the ideal batting conditions to the tune of 134 runs. South Australia thereupon declared, leaving the home state 379 minutes in which to score the required runs. Scholes' batsmen progressed impressively to 1/104, but slumped, according to form, against the seven bowlers employed by Hookes. Brad Green's unbeaten 63 and Gary Watts' 64 proved the final stumbling blocks obstructing the South Australian march towards victory.

At Launceston, the Adelaide batsmen outscored their Taswegian counterparts by 164 on the first innings in spite of an enterprising 86 in 87 deliveries from Brian Davison. No fewer than five South Australians scored half-centuries and, with Parkinson and Vincent each snaring four victims in the home team's second innings, the visitors were set to score 102 runs for victory in their second batting attempt. They made heavy weather of their task against the accurate leg-spin of Stuart Saunders and lost five wickets before reaching their goal.

Adelaide and its flawless batting pitch was the setting for a super 500 batting performance from the home side for the third successive occasion on 19 February. This time the suffering bowlers hailed from Western Australia; they toiled fruitlessly as Darling composed a faultless 121 in 142 deliveries, adding 113 for the third wicket with Inverarity who went on to collaborate with Hookes in a joint 132 for the fourth wicket. Hookes failed to add to his overnight score of 97 on the second day, but keeper Kevin Wright capitalised on the excellent foundations laid by the earlier South Australian batsmen to reach three figures and bolster his sides' total to 7/507 declared. It was the height of irony that two of the major contributors to the South Australian innings, Inverarity and Wright, were former Western Australian players: one of them a reject. Disheartened by the enormity of the scoring task facing them, the Perth men succumbed twice in succession for 245 and 280, with Andrew Sincock, introduced into the Adelaide team at the last moment as a replacement for the injured Vincent, taking five wickets in the Western Australian second innings.

South Australia 1981–82
First Class Matches

BATTING	v. Western Australia (Perth) 16-19 October 1981	v. New South Wales (Adelaide) 6-9 November 1981	v. West Indians (Adelaide) 13-16 Nov. 1981	v. New South Wales (Sydney) 10-13 Dec. 1981	v. Queensland (Brisbane) 17-20 Dec. 1981	v. Pakistanis (Adelaide) 26-29 Dec. 1981	v. Queensland (Adelaide) 8-10 January 1982	v. Victoria (Geelong) 15-18 January 1982	v. Tasmania (Launceston) 12-15 February 1982	v. Western Australia (Adelaide) 19-22 February 1982	v. Victoria (Adelaide) 26 Feb.–1 Mar. 1982
W. M. Darling	23 32	71 —	7 88	16 52	— —	132 58*	— —	46 134	88 52*	121 8*	36 47
W. B. Phillips	13 4	— 19	10 79	41 15	0 106	54 260	— 14	8 67	16 20	7 40	84*
I. R. McLean	13 70	43 —									
R. J. Inverarity	18 9	54 —	— 2	— 100*	4* 4	— 38*	0 11	— —	75 —	33 —	
D. W. Hookes	7 10	106 —	8 42	11 7*	51 32	91 —	88 —	21 34	26 9	97 —	63 —
P. R. Sleep	0 1	29 —	4 0	65 —	— 78	22 7	— 62*	42 4	66 0	5 —	53 —
K. J. Wright	7 21	33 —	0 1	38 —	64* 3	— —	— —	59 16*	22 6*	104* —	18 —
G. J. Winter	1 2	4 —	5 4	19 —	— —	0 2*	— —	5 —	50* —	64 —	
A. T. Sincock	0 6								6* —	11*	
D. K. Sayers	5* 1	— 1*	0								
R. M. McLellan	5 14*										
J. J. Crowe		157 —	1 9	1 137*	24 16	28 9*	22 —	1 62	79 3	0 4*	126 25*
S. D. H. Parkinson		26 —	1 0	12 —	— 7	— —	— —	1 —	4 —	— 9*	
R. W. Dugan		1* —	3 0*								
K. P. Harris			19 49	— —	52 97	— —	45 —	— 0	13 —		
W. Prior				0 —	— —	4 —					
K. J. Lewis				2* —	— 0*	— —					
B. A. Vincent						7* —	— —	47 7*	23 —	23 —	
M. C. Dolman							— —	0* —	6 —		
J. R. Davey							— —				
Byes	4	4 5	1 1	6 7	4 1	3 5	2 6	4			
Leg-byes	12 6	11 2	5 5	2 6	4 6	10 5	3 19	5 4	3		
Wides				1		4		2			
No-balls	3 16	5 12	17 5	8 1	17 4	22	7 1	2 3	2		
Total	107 180	551 79	225 268	245 404	198 404	125 552	244 279	462 102	507 19	423 161	
Wickets	10 10	9 10	10 10	2 5	9 6	1 4	10 6	10 5	7 1	8 1	
Result	L	D	L	D	D	D	W	D	W	W	W
Points	0	2	—	0	4	—	16	4	16	16	16

Catches
33 – K. J. Wright (ct 31/st 2)   13 – D. W. Hookes   10 – J. J. Crowe   8 – W. B. Phillips   7 – R. J. Inverarity   6 – K. P. Harris and J. R. Davey (ct 4/st 2)   5 – S. D. H. Parkinson and G. J. Winter   4 – P. R. Sleep   3 – W. M. Darling

BOWLING	M. C. Dolman	A. T. Sincock	G. J. Winter	D. K. Sayers	P. R. Sleep	S. D. H. Parkinson	R. W. Dugan	R. J. Inverarity
v. Western Australia (Perth) 16-19 October 1981		12-1-40-0 20-4-70-1	36.4-10-67-5 25-5-76-4	21-8-43-2 4-0-19-0	4-2-5-0 6-0-36-0			
v. New South Wales (Adelaide) 6-9 November 1981			8-2-15-0	17-8-26-0	20-2-54-0	34.2-8-69-2	23-14-21-0	19-7-24-0
v. West Indians (Adelaide) 13-16 November 1981			36-15-65-7 19-7-42-0	14-4-50-1 16-7-34-0	14-6-37-0 12-2-35-1	28-5-87-1 18-5-52-2	19-3-40-0 16.3-4-56-1	
v. New South Wales (Sydney) 10-13 December 1981			13-2-41-1 6-1-23-0		3-1-14-0 11-4-27-0	17-4-43-1 13-4-38-1		12.3-2-40-5 26-8-51-3
v. Queensland (Brisbane) 17-20 December 1981			23-7-57-2 3-1-11-0		25-7-80-0 39-11-117-5	20-5-46-1 2-1-1-0		21-7-50-1 20.1-8-46-3
v. Pakistanis (Adelaide) 26-29 December 1981			16-4-41-1 24-3-89-4		10-6-26-0 12-3-41-1	21-2-79-1 26-5-88-2	20-5-41-0	31-11-70-0 14-6-21-2
v. Queensland (Adelaide) 8-11 January 1982	26-2-114-4 11.1-1-47-2		27-7-68-2 12-5-32-1		20-9-39-0 8-3-19-4	14-4-42-1 5-1-13-0		20-5-40-2
v. Victoria (Geelong) 15-18 January 1982	14-3-38-0 24-8-53-2		12-2-28-0 14-5-26-0		9-3-14-2 16-4-44-1	12-4-20-3 21-4-66-2		16-9-15-3 33-12-45-1
v. Tasmania (Launceston) 12-15 February 1982	22-6-56-2 12-2-60-0		13-3-44-0 7-5-9-1		17.4-4-60-4 33-14-60-1	15-1-59-2 17.3-7-50-4		
v. Western Australia (Adelaide) 19-22 February 1982	20-7-46-1 18-8-36-1	7-1-21-0 25.4-8-56-5	9-5-13-0 15-8-26-1		22-9-33-3 28-4-59-1	13-6-24-2 5-4-4-0		35.4-15-67-3 33-9-63-2
v. Victoria (Adelaide) 26 Feb.-1 Mar. 1982	14-5-30-0 6-2-12-0	22-3-85-4 17-4-82-0			12-0-35-0 21.5-8-43-3	17-7-44-2 12-2-26-1		25-5-38-2 37-13-69-3
	167.1-44- 492-12 av. 41.00	103.4-21- 354-10 av. 35.40	318.4-97- 773-29 av. 26.65	72-27- 172-3 av. 57.33	343.3-102- 878-26 av. 33.76	310.5-79- 851-28 av. 30.39	78.3-26- 158-1 av. 158.00	343.2-117- 639-30 av. 21.30

A. R. M. McLellan 10-3-30-1 and 11-3-47-1   B. W. Prior 18-2-53-2 and 8-0-47-0   C. W. Prior 26-4-84-3

Hookes' batsmen knocked off the 19 runs required for victory for the loss of Phillips' wicket.

A measure of the spirit within the South Australian ranks was provided by the manner in which the Adelaide men fought back in the final and crucial encounter of the season against Victoria. Needing all the points which the game offered, the home side was at one stage on the first day in a hopeless position with Victoria on the threshold of non-losing total at 1/230. When the linch-pin of the Victorian batting, Julien Wiener, was run out for 116, however, the Melbourne team's last nine wickets surrendered tamely for a paltry 67. This collapse enabled South Australia to take command of the game by compiling 8/423, mainly through the agency of a splendid 126 from Jeff Crowe. In spite of a first innings lead of 126, however, it seemed unlikely that Hookes' men would gain the necessary maximum points from the game to win the Shield when Victoria again began well to be 2/168 in its second innings. Predictably Scholes' last eight batsmen succumbed for 118 runs and South Australia raced to the required 161 runs in 122 minutes to win by nine wickets and pip New South Wales on the Sheffield Shield winning post.

The Sydneysiders probably lost the trophy in the first few weeks of the summer. Their indifferent beginning to the Shield programme saw them draw their first fixture against Queensland in Newcastle; it was sheer bad luck that rain and a flooded outfield restricted play to two days and only permitted each side a single innings. In retrospect, however, McCosker must have rued more than bad luck the lack of bowling urgency which allowed Queensland's last two batsmen Dymock and Brabon to survive eighteen deliveries and deny New South Wales the extra two points which would have placed them on an equal footing with South Australia when the final accounting for the summer was done. In the New South Wales' score of 6/322, Dyson, Trevor Chappell and Beard all surpassed the half-century mark, whilst Wessel's contributed 103 and Ritchie 58 to Queensland's total of 9/269.

McCosker's cohorts more than met their match in Perth, where a full strength Western Australian combination took just three days to send them back to Sydney with a flea in their ear and a defeat by an innings and 35 runs registered in their scorebook. Skipper Hughes and Rob Langer rescued the home side from the precarious situation of 4/94 with a 178 run stand for the fifth wicket; but whilst Hughes scored 113 and Langer 77 in the Western Australian total of 367, the game really belonged to Terry Alderman, the medium-pace bowler who was the Australian star of the 1981 rubber against England. His 14/87 in the game sent the New South Welshmen back to the pavilion for scores of 215 and 117; his analysis was the best by a Western Australian bowler in first-class cricket and would have been improved had not the Perth men dropped four catches in New South Wales' second innings.

When two more draws eventuated from successive meetings with South Australia it appeared that McCosker's men were out of the race for Shield honours; but like their South Australian opponents in the contentious game in Sydney, they were spurred on to adopt a more positive approach to their remaining matches by the abrasiveness of David Hookes. So it was that New South Wales turned the corner and headed home towards victory with an eight

Tasmania 1981–82
First Class Matches

BATTING	v. Victoria (Melbourne) 30 Oct.–1 Nov. 1981	v. West Indians (Hobart) 7–9 December 1981	v. Pakistanis (Launceston) 1–4 January 1982	v. Western Australia (Perth) 9–12 January 1982	v. New South Wales (Hobart) 15–18 January 1982	v. South Australia (Launceston) 12–15 February 1982	v. Queensland (Devonport) 19–22 February 1982
D. B. Robinson	7 12			48 4	1 0		
R. F. Jeffery	4 32	10* —	64 37	31 67	31 9	9 11	0 —
R. L. Knight	7 0						
D. C. Boon	79 1	21 40*	34 49	37 24	12 63*	25 0	88 —
B. F. Davison	27 15	9 —	15* 72	68 25	48 9	86 9	14 —
R. D. Woolley	6 37	24 4	0 37	12 1	83 26	53 83	116 —
P. J. Mancell	2 6	50 —	12 2	6 4	16 14	2 38	27 —
S. L. Saunders	21 15	2 —	4 2*	0 106	84 0	0 70	4 —
F. D. Stephenson	26 5	13 —	12 9	1 2	1* 0	33 0	90 —
M. B. Scholes	24* 1*						
P. M. Clough	1 15	0 —	0 34	0* 31*	11 2		
I. R. Beven		40 37*	0 21	12 4	15 5	0 5	
N. J. Allanby		9 10	0 8		26 0		
D. Mullett		13 —					
P. A. Blizzard			1* 4	4 0			
S. Reid						65* 21	9 —
G. J. Wilson						7 5	19* —
M. F. Leedham						3 4*	
D. A. Smith							12 —
E. Benjamin							6 —
Byes	2 9	4 4	4 19	6	1 1	7 6	1
Leg-byes	6 7	7 3	4 9	5 4	10 4	3 8	8
Wides		1	1 2	1		1 2	5
No-balls	3	1 2	7 11	3 7	6 1	3	11
Total	215 155	204 100	158 316	234 279	345 135	298 265	405
Wickets	10 10	10 2	9† 10	10 10	10 10	10 10	10
Result	W	D	L	L	L	L	D
Points	16	—	—	0	4	0	

Catches
14 – R. D. Woolley (ct 12/st 2)   7 – F. D. Stephenson   3 – I. R. Beven
8 – D. B. Robinson (inc. 4 as sub)   5 – B. F. Davison   2 – S. L. Saunders, R. F. Jeffery and P. M. Clough
                                       4 – D. C. Boon

BOWLING	F. D. Stephenson	P. M. Clough	P. J. Mancell	S. L. Saunders	G. J. Wilson	D. Mullett	P. A. Blizzard	N. J. Allanby
v. Victoria (Melbourne) 30 Oct.–1 Nov. 1981	18–9–27–4 15–7–19–6	13.1–8–19–2 10–2–20–1	16–6–13–0 18–8–22–2	22–1–82–4 3–0–10–1	3–0–21–0			
v. West Indians (Hobart) 7–9 December 1981	17.5–3–46–5	19–4–48–3	13–1–54–0	9–1–30–2		7–2–21–0		
v. Pakistanis (Launceston) 1–4 January 1982	25–4–85–1	23–4–96–1	13–4–38–0 1.1–1–4–0	17–4–46–0			27–6–94–2	18–2–53–1
v. Western Australia (Perth) 9–12 January 1982	26–8–67–2 17.4–1–72–2	26.2–7–64–3 13–3–44–2	24–7–59–2	12–3–49–0			9–2–34–1 3–0–10–0	
v. New South Wales (Hobart) 15–18 January 1982	17.2–6–51–4 25–2–78–3	23–9–57–4 21–5–42–2	13–3–31–1 23–4–66–3	14–5–42–0 6–0–18–0				12–0–50–0 11–5–18–1
v. South Australia (Launceston) 12–15 February 1982	32–9–97–5 5–0–30–0		21–5–59–0 11.2–4–23–1	15–2–68–1 9–0–29–4	21–3–68–1 2–0–17–0			
v. Queensland (Devonport) 19–22 February 1982	31–8–58–4		27–7–63–0	29–6–93–2	21–6–51–0			
	229.5–57– 630–36 av. 17.50	148.3–42– 390–18 av. 21.66	180.3–50– 432–9 av. 48.00	136–22– 467–12 av. 38.91	47–9– 157–1 av. 157.00	7–2– 21–0 —	39–8– 138–3 av. 46.00	41–7– 121–2 av. 60.50

A. M. B. Scholes 3–0–21–0   D. M. F. Leedham 12–1–50–0, S. Reid   E. E. Benjamin 23–0–81–0, D. A. Smith
B. R. D. Woolley 2–2–0–0   5–0–20–0   1–0–6–0
C. D. B. Robinson 2–0–7–0

wicket win over Victoria in Sydney just before Christmas. The triumph was engineered almost solely by skipper Rick McCosker, who recorded two unbeaten hundreds and was on the field for the whole of the match. It was the second occasion on which McCosker had performed the dual century feat in the same game and his repetition of the achievement earned him a unique niche in the annals of New South Welsh cricket. The home side lost only six wickets in the game, scoring 4/255 and 2/233 to outplay the Victorians who could only manage 254 and 232. Holland captured seven wickets in the clash and he was well supported by Skilbeck's five and Beard's four wickets. For Victoria, Wiener top-scored with 72 in its first knock, whilst Watts reached 71 and Moss 67 when their side batted again. This latter batting attempt was again characterised by the traditional collapse which saw the last seven Victorian wickets fall for 33 runs.

The match against Tasmania eventually went the way of New South Wales by 63 runs; but it was not without its moments of anxiety for McCosker's men who were outscored by the Apple Islanders by 44 on the first innings. The visitors to Hobart began in impressive fashion with Ian Davis compiling a century and combining with Trevor Chappell to add 219 for their side's first wicket; the remainder of the New South Welsh batsmen thereupon squandered this advantage by capitulating for an additional 62 runs. Davison's gamble of sending his opponents in to bat appeared to have miscarried when Tasmania floundered to 6/134 in reply, but the local skipper's 48 and a ninth wicket partnership of 96 between Saunders and Mancell gave his side a slight but invaluable advantage at the half-way mark in the game. This supremacy became even more significant when New South Wales could only manage 262 in its second attempt with the bat, thus setting the home team the moderate task of scoring 199 in its final innings to win the match. It was at this timely juncture that Len Pascoe shrugged off the lethargic fast bowling form which had dogged him all summer to return his best first-class figures of 8/41, win the game for his side and regain his place in the Australian team.

An eight wicket victory in Brisbane against Queensland yielded a further 16 points to the Sydneysiders who owed a debt of gratitude for the result to Jupiter Pluvius and the Queenslanders' lack of batting resolution. After being 3/147 on the first day, the home side proceeded to sacrifice its last seven wickets for a mere 36 on a rain-affected pitch. New South Wales blasted a rapid 6/448 reply with Davis and Toohey each reaching three figures and an aggressive Stan Smith 50. In spite of its 265 run deficit on the first innings, Queensland fought back gallantly through an opening stand of 138 between Kepler Wessels and Rob Kerr. The left-handed Wessels batted like a man inspired to claim 106 of the first 149 runs recorded by the scorers. Only Hohns, however, lent his wholehearted support to the opening pair and, with Queensland being dismissed a second time for 334, Trevor Chappell and Peter Toohey experienced little difficulty in knocking off the 72 runs needed for victory, after losing Davis and McCosker en route.

The excellent Sydney wicket burked any hope of a result in the home side's return game against Western Australia: the sole conquerors of New South Wales in 1981–82. The visitors amassed 439 with the ersatz opener Geoff Marsh

Victoria 1981–82
First Class Matches

BATTING	v. Queensland (Brisbane) 17–19 October 1981	v. Tasmania (Melbourne) 30 Oct.–1 Nov. 1981	v. Pakistanis (Melbourne) 6–9 November 1981	v. Western Australia (Melbourne) 27–30 Nov. 1981	v. New South Wales (Sydney) 19–22 Dec. 1981	v. South Australia (Geelong) 15–18 January 1982	v. Western Australia (Perth) 29 Jan.–1 Feb. 1982	v. Queensland (Geelong) 12–15 February 1982	v. New South Wales (St Kilda) 19–22 February 1982	v. South Australia (Adelaide) 26 Feb.–1 Mar. 1982
J. M. Wiener		2	4	83	2	221*	—	72	2	3	25	42	33	165	8	26	1	116	42
G. M. Watts	60	2	46	4	29	59	4	—	2	71	6	64	6	20	42	11*	10	20	35	4
G. N. Yallop	82	31	46	3	36	68		—	24	10	19	9	55	7	111*	20	14	54		
P. J. Davies				12	0									9	—	0	33	32	57
J. W. Scholes	13	1	22	13	25	6	—	—	15	48	32	37	0	25	94	11*	6	22	64	71
R. D. Robinson	30	0	2	8	71*	29			22	8										
S. F. Graf	4	25	7	24	3	32*	—	—	13	0					12	—	55	39	8	8
R. J. Bright	39	23	0	5	28	15	—	—	35*	6	34	26	30	6						
M. H. N. Walker	0	31	11	0	9	—	—	—	28	8										
R. J. McCurdy	30	32	3	0					0	4*										
J. D. Higgs	0*	0*	0*	5*	—	—	—	—	0	0	0	—	10*	—	—	—	0*	1*	0	6
P. A. Hibbert	26	89				38	—													
J. K. Moss	12	16	23	5		200*	—	30	67											
I. L. Maddocks					—	—					6	16*								
I. W. Callen					—	—					0		34	—	2*		26	0	6*	34
B. C. Green											39	63*	82	15*	64	0	0	37	12	6
M. G. Hughes											1*		4	—	—		17	1	0	1*
D. M. Jones													39	6					0	8
P. G. Sacristani											3	3*	12	—		2	0	0	36	

Byes		6	11	8		11			2	2	2	1		1			6	5	4	
Leg-byes	2	3	8	2	5	12	6		4	12	4	1	1	13	6		2	6	8	3
Wides	3	1		1		1				1	1						2	6	2	1
No-balls	14	8	10	2	9	8	17		9	4		5	8	3	12		3	9	9	5

Total	315	268	191	83	311	242	487		254	232	160	252	316	120	536	57	161	235	297	286
Wickets	10	10	10	10	8	7	2		10	10	10	6	10	7	3	10	10	10	10	10
Result	L		L		D		D		L		D		D		D		L		L	
Points	4		0		—		4		0		0		4		4		0		0	

Catches
12 – J. W. Scholes
11 – R. D. Robinson (ct 8/st 3)
10 – P. G. Sacristani (ct 9/st 1)
9 – G. N. Yallop
8 – G. M. Watts
7 – I. L. Maddocks (ct 4/st 3)
5 – B. C. Green
4 – J. K. Moss, I. W. Callen and R. J. Bright

BOWLING	R. J. McCurdy	S. F. Graf	M. H. N. Walker	R. J. Bright	J. W. Scholes	J. D. Higgs	G. N. Yallop	I. W. Callen
v. Queensland (Brisbane) 16–19 October 1981	16–2–60–3	9–3–22–0	24–2–89–3	20–8–42–1		4.4–0–26–2		
	8–1–45–0	15–1–66–2	20.2–2–106–1	31–5–96–1		24–6–74–2		
v. Tasmania (Melbourne) 30 Oct.–1 Nov. 1981	9–3–26–1	18.3–7–37–3	15–3–31–1	23–7–39–1		29–6–71–3		
	9–2–28–1	15–5–31–2	5–1–17–0	29.3–18–23–3		23–7–40–3	1–1–0–0	
v. Pakistanis (Melbourne) 6–9 November 1981	17–1–86–0	25–6–52–2	14.5–5–37–2	23–6–54–0	3.1–0–8–0	23.3–8–69–2		
	4–0–22–0	12–3–29–1	18–5–45–4			2–1–1–0		
v. Western Australia (Melbourne) 27–30 Nov. 1981		15–3–41–1	19–7–36–1	26–11–42–1		14–7–24–4		23–8–54–3
		11–2–19–0	21–7–42–1	21–9–22–0	1–0–3–0	29–5–55–3		18–4–46–2
v. New South Wales (Sydney) 19–22 December 1981	12–1–27–1	7–0–23–0	13–4–39–1	35–8–76–1		30–5–88–0		
	3–1–4–0	9–3–26–0	17–6–40–0	29.3–7–69–1		29–6–91–1		
v. South Australia (Geelong) 15–18 January 1982				30–9–65–3		21–6–40–0		26.1–2–76–4
				27–9–62–2		14–0–62–1	4–1–12–0	25–3–81–3
v. Western Australia (Perth) 29 Jan.–1 Feb. 1982				28.2–8–59–3		23–4–68–0		30–5–88–4
				25–3–92–3		18.2–4–68–5		18–3–52–2
v. Queensland (Geelong) 12–15 February 1982		22–4–54–1				20–3–71–0		21.5–5–43–3
		25–5–68–3				41–8–107–2		28.1–4–74–3
v. New South Wales (St Kilda) 19–22 February 1982		27–5–66–1				7–1–24–0		31–4–120–2
						6–0–22–0		4–0–25–1
v. South Australia (Adelaide) 26 Feb.–1 Mar. 1982		25–2–108–1				26–6–82–0		32–7–98–4
		3–0–29–0			1–0–4–0	9–0–59–1		8–0–32–0

	R. J. McCurdy	S. F. Graf	M. H. N. Walker	R. J. Bright	J. W. Scholes	J. D. Higgs	G. N. Yallop	I. W. Callen
	78–11–	238.3–49–	167.1–42–	348.2–108–	5.1–0–	393.3–83–	5–2–	265.1–45–
	298–6	671–17	482–14	741–20	15–0	1142–29	12–0	789–31
	av. 49.66	av. 39.47	av. 34.42	av. 37.05	—	av. 39.37	—	av. 25.45

A. Zaheer Abbas absent hurt   B. D. M. Jones 3–1–10–0

	Inns	NOs	Runs	HS	Av
	17	1	847	221*	52.93
	19	1	495	71	27.50
	16	1	589	111*	39.26
	7	—	143	57	20.42
	18	1	505	94	29.70
	8	1	170	71*	24.28
	13	1	230	55	19.16
	12	1	247	39	22.45
	7	—	87	31	12.42
	6	1	69	32	13.80
	12	7	22	6	4.40
	3	—	153	89	51.00
	9	1	358	200*	44.75
	2	1	22	16*	22.00
	7	2	102	34	20.40
	10	2	318	82	39.75
	6	2	24	17	6.00
	4	—	53	39	13.25
	7	1	56	36	9.33

3 – J. D. Higgs, J. M. Wiener and S. F. Graf
2 – D. M. Jones and P. J. Davies (one as sub)
1 – M. H. N. Walker, R. J. McCurdy and M. G. Hughes

J. M. Wiener	M. G. Hughes	B. C. Green	B	Lb	W	Nb	Total	Wkts
				3		5	247	10
			1	3	5	3	399	6
			2	6		3	215	10
			9	7			155	10
			1	7		3	317	9A
				2			99	5
			1	2	1	7	208	10
1-0-3-0			6	9		4	209	6
				1		1	255	4
				2		1	233	2
	21-5-53-3	2-0-2-0	3	5			244	10
	19-3-52-0	2-0-7-0		3			279	6
	25-5-60-2		5	9	1	7	307	10B
	11-2-41-0	2-1-1-0	1	3	5		263	10
	24-7-69-4	9-3-16-2	4	17	4	4	282	10
	20-2-73-2	2-1-4-0	4	5		5	340	10
	30.4-6-71-4	2-2-0-0	1	10	2	11	305	8
	3-0-19-1	6-0-27-0					93	?
	31-6-97-2	6-1-27-0	4	4		3	423	8
	8-1-32-0			3		2	161	1
1-0-	192.4-37-	31-8-						
3-0	567-18	84-2						
—	av. 31.50	av. 42.00						

and Craig Serjeant each contributing centuries and establishing a new Western Australian fourth wicket record of 260. Complacency at the enormity of their score misled the Perth batsmen into the mistake of throwing away their last seven wickets for a mere 55 runs. The error cost Serjeant's side first innings points, as McCosker, with a knock of 130, led by example and steered his side to an 84 lead on the first innings. For New South Wales the reliable Davis reached 72, and assisted his captain in setting his side on the road to a first innings victory with an opening stand of 145; Chappell took over where Davis left off, notching 89, whilst Stan Smith enhanced his burgeoning reputation with 60. Holland was by far the most impressive of the bowlers on display, sending down a marathon 68 overs in the Western Australian first innings to capture 4/124, and snatching 2/6 when Serjeant's men batted a second time.

The mediocrity of the Victorian batting provided New South Wales with its grand winning finale to the season by eight wickets, in a game played on the St Kilda club ground in Melbourne. In its first innings the totally dispirited home side capitulated for 161, after being 7/75 before a 57 run Graf–Callen revival. Fast bowler Geoff Lawson proved the principal destroyer of Victorian hopes with figures of 4/63. New South Wales replied with 3/305 declared, thanks to 124 from night-watchman Steve Rixon: a specialist in that position whose highest score for New South Wales had also been at the expense of Victoria four years previously at the Melbourne Cricket Ground. Batting a second time, the Victorians again proved totally inadequate to the crisis facing them. They were dismissed for 235, with only Yallop adding to his reputation with a determined 54, scored in spite of the handicap of what later proved to be a broken wrist. Whilst Davis and McCosker failed for the second time against the impressive opening attack of Hughes and Callen, Trevor Chappell and Stan Smith experienced little trouble in knocking off the required 93 runs to hasten their team to victory in a mere 70 minutes. The sixteen points earned by New South Wales in this final climacteric took its season's tally to 72; its fixtures were concluded but its anguish was just beginning. It now had to live in suspense for another week until the outcome of the South Australia–Victoria match was decided.

After beginning the summer with two comfortable conquests of South Australia and New South Wales, Western Australia's hopes of retaining the Sheffield Shield, wrested from Victoria in the previous season, received its first setback in its third encounter against Queensland. International calls upon the services of Hughes, Wood, Laird, Marsh, Alderman, Yardley and Lillee compelled the Perth selectors to fall back upon the talents of Porter, O'Neill, Zoehrer, Baker, MacLeay, Mann and the West Indian import, fast bowler Wayne Daniel. Queensland, too, were not at full strength and took the field without Greg Chappell, Allan Border and Jeff Thomson. The equilibrium between the abilities within the two depleted teams and the loss of eight hours play to the Brisbane weather produced the inevitable corollary of a draw. Rob Langer followed his innings of 77 against New South Wales with a sound 140 in 310 minutes: a knock which enabled Western Australia to reach the security of 351. Queensland's last two batsmen were at the crease with their side still 44 runs from a first innings lead and four points when time expired.

Western Australia 1981–82
First Class Matches

BATTING	v. South Australia (Perth) 16–19 October 1981	v. Pakistanis (Perth) 23–26 October 1981	v. New South Wales (Perth) 30 Oct.–2 Nov. 1981	v. Queensland (Brisbane) 20–23 Nov. 1981	v. Victoria (Melbourne) 27–30 Nov. 1981	v. Tasmania (Perth) 9–12 January 1982	v. Victoria (Perth) 29 Jan.–1 Feb. 1982	v. New South Wales (Sydney) 11–14 February 1982	v. South Australia (Adelaide) 19–22 February 1982	v. Queensland (Perth) 26 Feb.–1 Mar. 1982
G. M. Wood	4	12	151	—	17	—				
B. M. Laird	26	110*	47	—	30	—				
G. Shipperd	24	3	131	—	3	—	47	—	33	4	3	67	43	69	21	16*	1	30	48	70*
K. J. Hughes	39	80	55	—	113	—				
M. D. O'Neill	7	1	1	—			15	—	26	39
C. S. Serjeant	9	9*	24	—	8	—	10	—	1	3	19	29*	80	23	106	—	23	18	3	11*
R. W. Marsh	3	7	34	—	39	—				
B. Yardley	3	26	32	—	19	—				
D. K. Lillee	54*	—		—	24*	—				
M. F. Malone	8	—	15	—	2	—	27*	—	2*	—			17*	—	6	0	11	—
T. M. Alderman	8	—		—	1	—				
G. D. Porter			23*	—			12	—	64	51	14	6	13	11				
D. J. Baker			3	—			5	—										
R. S. Langer					77	—	140	—	10	48	75	46	3	21	31	2*	27	3	20	3
K. H. MacLeay							16	—	34	1	83*	—	3	27	11	—	24	24	19	—
A. L. Mann							31	—	2	40*	47	14*	17	24	4	—	40	17		
T. J. Zoehrer							13	—	23	4*	3	—	13	2	19	—	34	46	31	—
W. W. Daniel							21	—	2	—										
T. G. Hogan							0	—	4	—	70	3	2		19*	49	12	
G. R. Marsh									24	7	1	67	176	20	20	59	51	120
W. M. Clark									3	—	0*	1*	0	—				
D. L. Boyd									37	4	42	6			17	0*	43*	—
R. R. McFarlane															22	10	6	13		
S. C. Clements																			73	86
G. A. Millar																			20	—
Byes		4	4	4	1	6	12	6	5	1	10		8	3	3	1
Leg-byes	3	11	9	5	2	9	2	6	9	3	9	1	12	9	13	2
Wides		1	2	8		1		1		1		1		5	1		1
No-balls	1	1	12	13	5		7	4	1	1	7	5	10	7	3	8	6	7
Total	186	253	545	367	351	208	209	328	186	307	263	439	56	245	280	353	301
Wickets	10	6	10	10	10	10	6	10	5	10	10	10	2	10	10	10	3
Result	W	D	W	D	D	W	D	D	L	D
Points	16	—	16	2	0	16	0	0	0	4

Catches 16 – R. W. Marsh and T. J. Zoehrer (ct 13/st 3)   6 – B. M. Laird and T. G. Hogan   3 – M. F. Malone and G. D. Porter
23 – C. S. Serjeant   7 – G. Shipperd   4 – R. R. McFarlane   2 – K. J. Hughes and A. L. Mann

BOWLING	D. K. Lillee	T. M. Alderman	M. F. Malone	B. Yardley	G. D. Porter	W. M. Clark	D. L. Boyd	A. L. Mann
v. South Australia (Perth) 16–19 October 1981	25-6-43-3 16-4-38-1	24.2-5-49-7 19-6-43-3	11.2-1-35-1	20-4-54-4				
v. Pakistanis (Perth) 23–26 October 1981			36-10-111-4 10-3-35-2	33-10-100-4 3-0-9-0	17-3-56-0			
v. New South Wales (Perth) 30 Oct.–2 Nov. 1981	21-5-49-1 13-3-40-1	18.1-4-59-7 17-5-28-7	13-2-46-1	15-3-52-1 14-2-45-2				
v. Queensland (Brisbane) 20–23 November 1981			29-5-72-3		6-1-15-0			30-5-78-4
v. Victoria (Melbourne) 27–30 November 1981			41.4-6-102-1		20-3-66-0			11-1-39-0
v. Tasmania (Perth) 9–12 January 1982					12-2-23-0 3-1-5-0	11-1-27-1 30-5-63-1	17-3-40-3 16-2-68-2	27-6-72-3 34-17-54-3
v. Victoria (Perth) 29 Jan.–1 Feb. 1982					13-6-23-0	19-6-50-1 11-1-26-2	18-6-37-1 7-1-30-0	29.4-12-63-2 11-5-15-1
v. New South Wales (Sydney) 11–14 February 1982			39-8-76-0			24-3-64-1		52-10-139-2
v. South Australia (Adelaide) 19–22 February 1982			42-5-134-4 1-0-10-0			23-1-125-2 2-0-9-1		26-4-73-0
v. Queensland (Perth) 26 Feb.–1 Mar. 1982			21-2-72-2 20-3-70-1			21-4-56-2 9-1-41-1		
	75-18- 170-6 av. 28.33	78.3-20- 179-24 av. 7.45	264-45- 763-19 av. 40.15	85-19- 260-11 av. 23.63	71-16- 188-0 —	95-16- 230-6 av. 38.33	113-18- 406-12 av. 33.83	220.4-60- 533-15 av. 35.53

A. M. D. O'Neill 2-1-7-0, D. J. Baker 27-5-101-1   B. D. J. Baker 9-0-41-0   C. W. W. Daniel 30-9-66-1, D. J. Baker 23-5-51-1   D. W. W. Daniel 33-4-114-0

Serjeant's bowlers encountered a beautiful wicket and the confident and in-form Julien Wiener and Jeff Moss when they journeyed east to Melbourne. Wiener and Moss both notched undefeated double centuries to establish a new Australian record of 390 for the fourth wicket, surpassing the previous best of 389 set by McCabe and Ponsford against the M.C.C. at Lord's in 1934. When it was Western Australia's turn to bat, it was discovered that the covers at the new venue of the Junction Oval, St Kilda, were not as efficient as those at the recently abandoned Melbourne Cricket Ground and that overnight rain had penetrated the tarpaulins half-way down the wicket. In spite of this misfortune which drew understandably sharp protest from Western Australian skipper, Craig Serjeant, the visitors defied the Victorian bowlers' attempts to dislodge them twice and drew the encounter with scores of 208 and 6/209. Opening bat Graeme Porter was the hero of the Western Australian resistance with scores of 64 and 51.

The taste for victory returned to the west with a five wicket triumph over Brian Davison's Taswegians. Davison's personal 68 failed to avert a first innings decline from 3/160 to 234 all out: a score which the host team outstripped by 94 thanks to 75 from the ebullient Langer and 83 not out from the future Esso scholarship winner, the promising all-rounder Ken MacLeay. Tasmania did better in its second batting effort, making a more substantial if luckier 279. That total would have been infinitely smaller had it not been for a Tasmanian best partnership of 120 for the last wicket between Stuart Saunders and Peter Clough. Saunders continued his purple patch with the bat by registering an incredible 106 batting at number eight in the Tasmanian order. It was Saunders' maiden Shield century, but it was not enough to set Serjeant's batsmen more than 186 to score in their last knock: a task which they completed with ease, thanks to a competent 67 from Shipperd.

Western Australia's home game against Victoria produced a close tussle on the first innings. Tail-enders Hogan and Boyd helped their captain, Serjeant, to boost the Perth side's total to 307 after it had languished earlier against the hostility of pace bowlers Hughes and Callen at 5/94 and subsequently 6/138. Western Australia should have gained first innings points after half-centuries from Brad Green and Graham Yallop could not take the eastern state's total beyond 9/285; but wicket-keeper Zoehrer dropped Higgs off leg-spinner Mann and Scholes' side gained an unexpected if slender lead of nine, together with its accompanying four points. Leg-spinner Higgs produced his best figures of the season – 5/68 – to send the home team back to the pavilion for the second time in the match for 263, leaving Victoria to score 255 for victory in 210 minutes. Illusions of their first win of the season were quickly dispelled from Victorian minds by left-handed, orthodox spinner Tom Hogan, who captured 3/33 to send the visitors' batsmen reeling in typically fragile fashion to 6/120 when stumps were drawn.

Its high scoring draw against New South Wales in Sydney and a nine wicket defeat at the hands of South Australia in Adelaide put an end to any fond hopes which the Western Australians might have entertained about retaining the Sheffield Shield. When Dymock's Queenslanders headed for Perth and their final match of the season only prestige was at stake and for the second time in three months the two sides shared the honours of an inconclusive contest. The home side moved into stride at a spanking pace with Geoff Marsh and debutant Shane Clements assembling an opening stand of 127 in 165 minutes. Shipperd, however, put a damper on proceedings by occupying the crease on the first day for 193 minutes and scoring only 44 runs. Queensland replied to the Western Australian total of 353 with an innings of 158 from Rob Kerr and a tally of 331. On a batsman's paradise, however, Marsh and Clements once more gave their side an excellent start of 171 runs in 132 minutes: a beginning which was quickly expanded by the following batsmen into a declared advantage of 324. Queensland were only afforded 274 minutes in which to accomplish this scoring task. Kerr made the job look possible by scoring his second hundred of the game, but in the final analysis his side fell 68 runs short of its target and Western Australia still required three wickets to win when time ran out.

The beginning of Queensland's summer fortunes was vastly different to its conclusion. The season started with a bang and the traditional innings defeat of the luckless Victorians whose record in Brisbane in recent years has been nothing short of abysmal. In the early stages of the game, however, Victoria seemed certain to reverse the trend of its modern misfortune in the far north when it reduced the strong Queensland batting line-up to an ineffectual 5/72, dismissed the home state for a moderate 247 and then reached 2/187 in reply. The expectations of Victorian skipper Scholes that his batsmen might scale great heights were disappointingly dashed when his star left-hander, Graham Yallop, received a dubious lbw decision just as he was poised to score a big hundred; thereafter it was all downhill for the visitors to the Sunshine State. The possibility of a large first-innings lead was whittled down to an eventual 68. Kepler Wessels thereupon exploited the good luck of his being dropped at 43 by Ray Bright off the bowling of Graf to plunder 168 runs off the flagging Victorian bowlers and enable his captain Greg Chappell to declare at 6/399, thereby setting Scholes the target of 332 to win. The left-handed opener Hibbert was the only batsman to offer any sort of resistance when the Melbourne side batted a second time; his 89 in a total of 268, however, could not avert defeat. It was a doubly disappointing knock for Hibbert, for not only did his side lose, but his defiant and meritorious innings was destined the last he would play in first-class cricket in 1981–82; an injury subsequently sidelined him and the ensuing successes of the opening pair of Wiener and Watts strangely prevented his regaining any position in a deplorably weak Victorian batting combination.

Wessels scored his second hundred in as many games against New South Wales but his efforts could secure no more than a draw for his fellow Queenslanders. Another Wessels' innings of 72 highlighted the match against Western Australia, but again the match proved inconclusive. The following clashes against South Australia and New South Wales produced results, but they were far from the liking of substitute skipper, Dymock, and his now depleted side. South Australia overcame the 103 run resistance of Greg Ritchie in Adelaide to win by an innings and 93, whilst an incomparable 106 from Wessels proved insufficient to prevent an eight wicket drubbing at the hands of New South Wales before the eyes of Queensland's mortified home supporters.

Against Victoria in Geelong the leading batsmen failed and Queensland would not have reached even its moderate score of 282 had it not been for a redeeming 111 runs from the unexpected source of wicket-keeper Ray Phillips. Victoria's gargantuan answer on an ideal batting strip was 7/536: a tally to which Wiener contributed 165, Yallop 111 not out and Scholes 94. Thereafter the match became a question of the visitors saving their sinking ship: a salvage act which they accomplished by kind permission of the Victorian fieldsmen who dropped Wessels at 33 and 145, thus enabling him to score 173, add 142 for his team's second wicket with Roger Traves, and shepherd Queensland to the security of a second innings total of 340.

Wessels continued his phenomenally prolific spell with the bat in the north-western Tasmanian town of Devonport. After the home state's batsmen Woolley, Boon and Stephenson had demoralised the touring northern bowlers with a total of 405, it seemed certain that the Taswegians must at least gain first innings points from the game. Wessels had other thoughts on the subject; he and Rob Kerr added 91 for the first wicket before Tasmania's West Indian speedster, Franklyn Stephenson, removed Kerr and De Jong with successive deliveries. It was then that Ritchie took root and compiled an undefeated 136 which assisted Wessels to add 304 for their side's fourth wicket, easily surpassing the twenty-year-old record of 296 established by Peter Burge and Ken Mackay against South Australia. The Tasmanian score was only eight runs distant when fatigue and Stephenson, the only successful bowler in the host team, claimed the wicket of Wessels for 220. Hohns and Ritchie subsequently guided the Queenslanders to a four point reward for their marathon batting chase.

In Perth it was Western Australia's turn to take four points off Queensland. It only managed the task by 24 runs; nonetheless the home side were very much on top and only three wickets from an outright victory at the end of the fourth day. With Kerr dismissed after completing his brilliant pair of hundreds with 101 in the second innings, it was unlikely that the Queensland later batsmen would have spanned the 48 run chasm which separated them from an innings win.

The pinnacle of Tasmania's achievements in 1981–82 was scaled in its first game against Victoria. On a grassless Melbourne pitch which deteriorated from the first ball of the match until it was virtually impossible to bowl anything but shooters, Brian Davison was fortunate enough to win the toss and bat. Not surprisingly his Tasmanians won the game by ungratefully bowling out their hosts for 83 in their second innings. It was the lowest score by Victoria against Tasmania for forty-seven years and gave the visitors victory by 96 runs. David Boon scored 79 for the Apple Islanders before he was caught sweeping at Ray Bright. His was the main contribution to the Tasmanian first innings score of 215, which, when the Victorian reply stood at 2/131, hardly seemed a winning total. It was at this point that the Victorian batsmen established a pattern of batting supineness which they were to observe all season. The last eight wickets fell for 60 runs and at the end of its second knock, Davison's side had translated its first innings 15 run ascendancy into an overall advantage of 170. On the then bounceless Melbourne pitch, the Victorians had as much chance of scoring those runs to win as they had of reaching the moon without a Saturn rocket. The gangling West Indian fast bowler, Franklyn Stephenson, took off his transistor radio ear-muffs just long enough to take 6/19 for his adopted state and bring his match analysis to 10/46 and the discomfiture of Victoria was completed.

Except for the four points which Davison's team gained for its first innings lead over New South Wales, the sixteen which it won against its closest mainland neighbour were its only material return for the season. The rest of the Tasmanian story was told in two five wicket losses to Western Australia and South Australia, a hard fought 63 run reverse at the hands of New South Wales and a meritorious batting performance in the high-scoring draw against Queensland. When converted according to the proportional mathematical formula outlined by the Australian Cricket Board, Tasmania's 20 points underwent a metamorphosis into 36 points: a tally large enough in this bonus-pointless season to win it fourth place in the Shield table.

The tale of Victoria's 1981–82 season amounted to stark tragedy, unalleviated by a single happy moment of victory. Each time that Scholes' men created opportunities to win it seemed that they frittered away their chances with inexplicable batting failures at the most inopportune times. Against Western Australia in Melbourne and Queensland in Geelong, the Melbourne side established substantial first innings leads without capitalising on its advantage when its opponents went in again. An initial supremacy of 68 in Brisbane was surprisingly translated into an eventual 63 run defeat. In Perth, a slight ascendancy of nine runs was almost transformed into a crushing reverse because of the almost habitual batting collapse of the Victorian middle-order. New South Wales twice completely outplayed its most inveterate rival by eight wickets, whilst South Australia enjoyed the better of its draw against the Victorians in Geelong and dispatched them with embarrassing ease by nine wickets in the deciding contest of the Sheffield Shield season. But by far the most humiliating moment for the formerly proud Victorians in their crow-eating summer of 1981–82 was the hour of their defeat against the Australian Cinderella state, Tasmania. Four rations of four points for first innings leads in its quartet of matches against Queensland and Western Australia were all that Victoria had to show for its efforts at the end of its dismal summer. After two years of plenty, the years of famine had descended on the southern state with a vengeance.

The one-day side show of the Australian season, the McDonald's Cup, produced an upset 27 run win in the final by Queensland over the popular favourite, New South Wales. The Sydney team had been untroubled by any opposition from the very first ball of the competition, principally because of the superlative form of its opening batsmen Rick McCosker and John Dyson, who never failed to hoist the hundred before they were separated. Indeed, the New South Wales middle-order was never put to the test until the last one-day encounter of the summer, as their side lost only eleven wickets in its three-match preface to the final.

New South Wales' royal progress to the limited-over apogee of the season began with an opening stand of 169 between McCosker and Dyson and an untroubled 47 run defeat of Victoria: an accomplishment completed in spite of a brilliantly defiant Wiener century. The next game against the seemingly untalented South Australia saw the New South Wales' numbers one and two go 84 runs better by scoring 253 runs before they were separated. Their opening partnership was the highest ever recorded since the inception of one-day cricket in Australia. McCosker's 164 outstripped his previous fifty-over innings by 53, whilst Dyson added 22 to his earlier 78 to notch a precise hundred. The eventual 4/310 New South Welsh tally proved to be 111 runs too rich for Hookes' Adelaide side, for whom Sleep notched a wide-awake 90. It was at this stage of the season that I mistakenly dispelled, as the fantasy of a disordered mind, any thought of South Australia winning the Sheffield Shield.

In the semi-final of the trophy in Perth McCosker and Dyson did it again! They steered their side to 118 before the first wicket fell. After McCosker was caught behind the wicket by Marsh off Alderman for 67, Dyson continued serenely to 101 before he was run out in the forty-ninth over. Davis' 51 helped raise the visitors' score to 5/245: a figure which proved 59 runs too many for Hughes' West Australians, who were in such a hurry to reach their goal that they failed to utilise 5.2 overs of allowable quota. For New South Wales Trevor Chappell captured four wickets, Beard three, whilst Laird salvaged 56 runs from the West Australian wreck.

In the early stages of the McDonald's Cup, Queensland was almost as impressive as its neighbouring state to the south. In Brisbane, Tasmania accumulated a creditable 7/225 with Boon and Jeffery each registering a half-century; Greg Chappell and Allan Border were in fine fettle with the bat, however, and this total fell well short of victorious standards. The two Queensland Test players added 125 in 83 minutes for the third wicket, to lay the foundations of a Queensland win with 2.5 overs to spare. The following day's defeat of Western Australia saw an even better performance from Greg Chappell's side. Firstly, the fast attack of Thomson, Dymock, Brabon and Maguire complemented one another so effectively that the first five Western Australian wickets tumbled for 81; only Marsh's 48 in 92 minutes enabled the Perth side to reach its eventual, if unsatisfactory, 8/148. Malone bowled well when it was Queensland's turn to bat, conceding only 21 runs and taking two wickets in his statutory 10 overs; but the medium-pacer strove in vain, for, whilst Queensland's big guns failed to fire, Rob Kerr stepped into the breach with a solid 50, which was instrumental in bringing an easy victory to the 'Banana-Benders' with 12.1 overs of their innings remaining.

The Brisbane semi-final against Victoria was never really in doubt from the first loose over sent down by the southern bowlers. The Melbournites were far too prodigal in their approach and conceded 238 runs whilst taking eight wickets in the space of 49 overs. At one stage Queensland was a dominant 3/198 and, had not five local batsmen not surrendered for 21 runs, the Victorians would have been chasing a far larger score. Scholes' side began solidly but without pace or panache; it was never in the scoring race and whilst the ever reliable Wiener contributed 79 runs and Scholes 60, when the final whistle blew, it was still 21 runs short of the Queensland total. Perhaps it should be added that the Victorians were fortunate to reach the final stages of the competition, since they only qualified for the semi-finals by virtue of a last ball win over South Australia in a *repechage* round.

The Queensland 27 run victory in the McDonald's Cup final was a triumph of team effort over individualistic brilliance. Dymock's batsmen opened proceedings in the worst possible style, losing both Wessels and Kerr with only eight runs on the board. On a lively pitch, Wayne Broad and the young Mark Gaskell fought back against the pace of Lawson, Whitney, Skilbeck, Beard and Trevor Chappell; there is no doubt that the 81 run third wicket partnership between the two Queenslanders turned the tide of the game. Henschell's 45 augmented Broad's 85 and the Brisbane men finally clawed their way to 8/224 in 47 overs. The total was not beyond the capabilities of the one-day brilliance of the New South Welsh batsmen. It was true that Dyson was on tour with the Australian side in New Zealand; but there was always the in-form Ian Davis on whom to fall back.

When Dymock's inswinger trapped Davis lbw with only three on the board and then hit the off stump of McCosker and the leg stump of Chappell in quick succession, the Queensland bowling cat was really amongst the New South Welsh batting pigeons. And what a killing he made! In his last game for his state, Geoff Dymock – the bowler who was for years sorely underestimated by the Australian selectors – snared five New South Welsh wickets for 27 to lead his team by example to a clear-cut win with 2.2 overs of the home side's batting ration still unused. Toohey fought the good fight for the Sydneysiders, reaching 66 before he was bowled by Maguire attempting a desperate big hit. Rixon lent him valuable support with a handy knock of 41.

In the final analysis, however, the last day of the 1981–82 Australian season – 7 March – belonged to Queensland. Rick McCosker and his New South Welshmen were left to ponder on the cruel pathos of the summer: a period of just over five months which, at one stage or another, had promised both the Sheffield Shield and the McDonald's Cup to the Sydney team, but which, in the end, flattered only to deceive – twice!

Opposite: *Cricket still plays to capacity and above capacity crowds in India.*

SECTION C
The Lost Cause
England tour of India and Sri Lanka

At the end of the 1981 season English cricket was in a state of euphoria. The heroics of Botham, the endeavour of Willis and the leadership of Brearley had raised England from the depths of Lord's and brought about victory in the 'Incredible Tests'. The excitement of the matches at Headingley and Edgbaston and Old Trafford throbbed long after the last celebratory pint had been sunk.

Only in the shortening days of October did the real world begin to intrude again. The names of Boycott and Cook were linked with cricket in South Africa and for weeks the tour to India and Sri Lanka was in doubt. There was much diplomacy behind the scenes and ultimately the tour went ahead because, it was said, Boycott had denounced apartheid in a recently published book.

Then, when we reflected upon the team chosen to tour India and Sri Lanka, it became apparent that what Botham's heroics had done was to paper over cracks which, in more sober times, became all too obvious again.

Brearley had passed from the scene once more although one could never be sure that he would not return in the future when his country called; England's answer to General de Gaulle. His place as captain had been taken by Keith Fletcher who had led Essex during the most successful period in their history. Fletcher was an expected and generally popular choice. He had a reputation for being a fine tactician with a thorough knowledge of the game; the doubts that surrounded his selection were whether, as his success as a captain had been essentially of a domestic nature, he could get the best from men at international level, whether he could expand from his rather conservative approach to leadership to the more imaginative demands needed to succeed at Test standard, and whether he could eradicate what some considered to be a tendency to unwise team selections that had certainly hampered Essex in 1981. On the credit side the man was a Test player of proven ability who had served a long apprenticeship before being appointed captain. There certainly seemed to be no other reasonable choice.

There were considerable doubts as to the composition of the side which he took with him. Cook was chosen mainly on the strength of a century in the NatWest Final while Larkins and Parker were omitted simply because they had failed in the final Test at The Oval. The non-selection of Parker was very hard to understand. Here is a batsman and a fielder of very high class. He is a player of beauty and quality and such men should be encouraged, for they are all too rare.

Contrary to expectations the side was packed with medium and quick bowlers which left only Emburey and Underwood as the spinners. The thinking behind these selections was that the Indian batsmen were reputed to be vulnerable to anything above medium pace. On Indian wickets this remained something of a doubtful premise, particularly as the Indian selectors were likely to put much trust in their spinners, Doshi and Shastri.

England's batting remained a worry, but confidence was in the air. We had beaten Australia 3–1, and there was Botham fighting fit. Defeat was unthinkable.

Indian victory draws near. Dilley bowled Madan Lal for 9, First Test.

11 November 1981

at Bombay

England XI 154 for 9 (G. Cook 56)
Cricket Club of India President's XI 107

England XI won by 47 runs

After an uncertain beginning England won their opening fixture, a limited over game, with some ease. Put in to bat, England struggled to 154 in 48 overs and owed much to a determined 56 from Geoff Cook. He and Gower added 59 for the third wicket, but no one else established himself. The President's XI struggled even more painfully as Underwood's figures of 2 for 10 in his ten overs would indicate. The biggest stand was one of 29 for the last wicket. However mediocre much of the cricket, it was watched with enjoyment by a crowd of forty thousand.

13, 14 and 15 November 1981

at Poona

Indian Under 22 XI 339 for 7 dec (Gursharan Singh 101 not out, K. Srikkanth 87) and 180 for 2 dec (K. Srikkanth 74)
England XI 219 for 1 dec (G. Boycott 101 not out, K. W. R. Fletcher 56 not out, C. J. Tavare 56) and 303 for 4 (I. T. Botham 98, D. I. Gower 94)

England won by 6 wickets

On the opening day England toiled in the sun. Srikkanth who was captaining the Indian side batted excitingly and emphasised the opinions that had been passed on him that here was a batsman who would serve India with distinction. Gursharan was more sedate, but this was his debut in first-class cricket and, at the age of eighteen, he reached his hundred off the penultimate ball of the day. It was a splendid performance. On the second day, at his usual pace, Boycott reached the 125th century of his career, but his first in India and then Fletcher declared although England were still 120 behind. Srikkanth responded to this challenging declaration with another exciting knock and then set England 301 to win in 3½ hours. Gower and Gatting began with a stand of 77 and when Gatting was lbw to Srikkanth Botham joined Gower. They added 144 in 73 minutes of stunning cricket. At tea England were 143 for 1 in 25 overs. In the next 6 overs 66 runs came. Gower was run out and Botham was caught hooking in his blind manner, but by then he had scored 98 from 67 deliveries. England won with 4 overs to spare and they had scored at 6½ an over. It was a thrilling way to start a tour.

17, 18 and 19 November 1981

at Nagpur

Board of Control President's XI 202 (K. Srikkanth 66, D. L. Underwood 6 for 64) and 176 (Yashpal Sharma 61 not out, D. L. Underwood 5 for 72)
England XI 243 (C. J. Tavare 51, Kirti Azad 7 for 63) and 136 for 5

England XI won by 5 wickets

Although Srikkanth once more showed his ability to play exciting shots, the first day honours went to Derek Underwood as he took six of the last nine Indian wickets which fell for 79 runs. England fared little better and that they gained a lead was due to some resourceful batting at the last by Emburey, Lever and Underwood. Tavare and Botham had shown differing ways of approaching a difficult situation and the contributions of both were valuable, but the honours went to Kirti Azad whose medium pace off-breaks gave him the best figures by an Indian against England outside Test matches for over fifty years. The President's XI were soon in trouble at 10 for 3, but Chopra and Yashpal Sharma made sure that England would face a difficult task on an uneasy wicket which Underwood and Emburey exploited well. It was the common sense application of Fletcher and Cook and some lusty blows from Botham that gave England their third win of the tour.

21, 22 and 23 November 1981

at Baroda

England XI 278 for 4 dec (C. J. Tavare 96, G. Boycott 66) and 171 for 2 dec (G. Boycott 73 not out)
West Zone 178 and 197 for 4

Match drawn

In their last game before the one-day international and the first Test England gained useful practice and fielded the side that was likely to do battle in the first of the internationals and Tests. The only worry from England's point of view was that Gooch was having a lean time, suffering from uncertain umpiring decisions at a time when he was struggling to find form. His importance to the side was seen in that although Tavare and Boycott batted safely, neither of them could advance the score at a rate necessary to force a win. Gooch's attacking style is an essential complement to their solidity.

FIRST ONE-DAY INTERNATIONAL – INDIA v. ENGLAND

Fletcher won the toss and asked India to bat on a wicket which looked a little uneven. Srikkanth had a testing start before playing on in Botham's second over and Gavaskar was taken at slip off a ball which pitched on off-stump and left him.

Vengsarkar and Kirti Azad were the batsmen who ensured that England would have a reasonable total to chase, but, for the most part, the England bowling was tight throughout and few liberties could be taken as was shown when Vengsarkar eventually drove unwisely at Underwood.

Kirti Azad hit Lever over cover for six and there was some scampering from Kirmani and Shastri which lifted the score to 156 in 46 overs.

Boycott went quickly, but Gooch and Cook looked confident until falling in successive overs, Gooch well caught down the leg-side and Cook taken at first slip. Gower and Fletcher promised quick victory, but Gower spooned a catch to the bowler.

With Doshi and Shastri operating together, England began to fall behind the required run rate and although Gatting and Fletcher batted securely, their fifty partnership

FIRST ONE-DAY INTERNATIONAL: INDIA v. ENGLAND
25 November 1981 at Ahmedabad

INDIA

Batsman	Dismissal	Runs
S. M. Gavaskar†	c Gooch, b Willis	0
K. Srikkanth	b Botham	0
D. B. Vengsarkar	c and b Underwood	46
G. R. Viswanath	c Cook, b Gooch	8
Kirti Azad	b Botham	30
S. Madan Lal	c Lever, b Underwood	6
S. M. H. Kirmani*	not out	18
R. J. Shastri	run out	19
R. Binny	not out	2
D. R. Doshi		
Randhir Singh		
Extras	b 4, lb 13, w 7, nb 3	27
	(for 7 wkts)	156

Bowler	O	M	R	W
Willis	9	3	17	1
Botham	10	4	20	2
Lever	10	—	46	—
Gooch	7	—	28	1
Underwood	10	3	18	2

FALL OF WICKETS
1–2, 2–8, 3–39, 4–91, 5–113, 6–119, 7–154

ENGLAND

Batsman	Dismissal	Runs
G. A. Gooch	c Kirmani, b Binny	23
G. Boycott	lbw, b Madan Lal	5
G. Cook	c Viswanath, b Binny	13
D. I. Gower	c and b Binny	8
K. W. R. Fletcher†	b Doshi	26
M. W. Gatting	not out	47
I. T. Botham	not out	25
C. J. Richards*		
J. K. Lever		
D. L. Underwood		
R. G. D. Willis		
Extras	lb 7, w 2, nb 4	13
	(for 5 wkts)	160

Bowler	O	M	R	W
Madan Lal	10	2	30	1
Randhir Singh	6	—	18	—
Binny	7.5	3	35	3
Shastri	10	1	24	—
Doshi	10	1	40	1

FALL OF WICKETS
1–5, 2–43, 3–46, 4–61, 5–126

England won by 5 wickets

occupied 18 overs. With 9 overs remaining, England needed 41 runs.

Fletcher was out in the fortieth over and Botham arrived with 31 wanted from 6 overs. In spite of Gavaskar circling the boundary with seven fielders, Botham launched his attack and finished the game with two sixes off Binny so that England won with 13 balls to spare.

FIRST TEST MATCH – INDIA v. ENGLAND

For the First Test Match England brought in Taylor for Richards, Tavare for Cook and played both spinners so that Gatting was relegated to twelfth man. India welcomed back Kapil Dev whilst Patil was preferred to Binny.

The omission of Gatting from the England side revealed a frightening imbalance, Emburey finding himself batting at number seven, a position he rarely attains for Middlesex. The misgivings about England were quickly dispelled as India struggled from the start on a pitch where the bounce was uneven. Having survived a confident appeal for a catch behind, Srikkanth lobbed an easy catch to Fletcher at gully. Gavaskar was missed by Fletcher and he was never able to take command. Vengsarkar was caught at slip when the ball rebounded off Botham and Viswanath was taken at third slip off Botham's outswinger. Patil was out of touch and after two hours and fifty minutes at the wicket, Gavaskar touched another Botham outswinger to Taylor.

Kapil Dev swung his bat to effect and he and Kirti Azad added 52 before Azad was caught at short-leg by Gatting who was fielding while Willis had repairs to a cut eye. Dilley took the last wickets to finish with rather flattering figures for the day really belonged to Botham and although Gooch was lbw to Madan Lal before the close, the ball keeping low, England ended the day in high spirits.

The optimism remained until lunch when England were 95 for 1 after much good sense batting and application by Boycott and Tavare, although 49 runs in 31 overs was hardly seizing the initiative. After 27 overs the England innings had stood at 35 for 1.

Boycott was caught at forward short-leg and this heralded a period of disaster and distaste for England. Gower was sent back and run out. He chose to question the decision. The sweep shot accounted for Fletcher and the England batting now took on the air of sweeping suicide that it had had against Bright at Edgbaston a few months earlier. This time the batsmen set most of the blame on the umpires, which is never a wise thing to do and on this occasion brought about a paralysing neuroticism in the side. It was a point of decline from which England never truly recovered. While the umpiring was not of the best, it was also apparent that Doshi and Shastri are far better bowlers than Bright and he had not needed umpires' help to unsettle England.

The innings trembled to insignificance, but still there was hope for England as Botham once more tore the heart out of the Indian batting and reduced them to 90 for 5. Shastri, promoted in the order, and Kirti Azad stayed together for an hour before Azad, who was all excitement, succumbed leadenly to Emburey's spin. Dilley was upset when an appeal against Azad for lbw was turned down and England bore the air of one who is being martyred.

Shastri played an important innings of mature calm, remarkable in one still short of his twentieth birthday, but it was Kapil Dev who snatched the game away from England

Opposite: Madan Lal, an unexpected hero, has Fletcher lbw in the First Test.

FIRST TEST MATCH – INDIA v. ENGLAND
27, 28, 29 November and 1 December 1981 at Bombay

INDIA

	FIRST INNINGS			SECOND INNINGS		
S. M. Gavaskar†	c Taylor, b Botham	55		c Taylor, b Botham	14	
K. Srikkanth	c Fletcher, b Willis	0		run out	13	
D. B. Vengsarkar	c Tavare, b Dilley	17		c Tavare, b Botham	5	
G. R. Viswanath	c Boycott, b Botham	8		c Taylor, b Botham	37	
S. M. Patil	lbw, b Botham	17		lbw, b Botham	13	
Kirti Azad	c sub (Gatting), b Underwood	14		(7) lbw, b Emburey	17	
Kapil Dev	c Taylor, b Botham	38		(8) lbw, b Willis	46	
S. Madan Lal	c Taylor, b Dilley	0		(10) not out	17	
S. M. H. Kirmani*	lbw, b Dilley	12		(9) c Taylor, b Emburey	0	
R. J. Shastri	not out	3		(6) lbw, b Dilley	33	
D. R. Doshi	c Taylor, b Dilley	0		b Botham	7	
Extras	lb 5, nb 10	15		b 8, lb 8, nb 9	25	
		179			**227**	

	O	M	R	W	O	M	R	W
Willis	12	5	33	1	13	4	31	1
Botham	28	6	72	4	22.3	3	61	5
Dilley	13	1	47	4	18	5	61	1
Underwood	4	2	12	1	11	4	14	0
Emburey					13	2	35	2

ENGLAND

	FIRST INNINGS			SECOND INNINGS		
G. A. Gooch	b Lal	2		c Kirmani, b Dev	1	
G. Boycott	c Srikkanth, b Azad	60		lbw, b Lal	3	
C. J. Tavare	c Shastri, b Doshi	56		c Gavaskar, b Dev	0	
D. I. Gower	run out	5		lbw, b Dev	20	
K. W. R. Fletcher†	lbw, b Doshi	15		lbw, b Lal	3	
I. T. Botham	c Gavaskar, b Doshi	7		c Azad, b Dev	29	
J. E. Emburey	lbw, b Doshi	0		c Gavaskar, b Lal	1	
G. R. Dilley	b Shastri	0		b Lal	9	
R. W. Taylor*	not out	9		b Lal	1	
D. L. Underwood	c Kirmani, b Dev	8		not out	13	
R. G. D. Willis	c Gavaskar, b Doshi	1		c Kirmani, b Dev	13	
Extras	b 1, lb 2	3		b 4, lb 3, nb 2	9	
		166			**102**	

	O	M	R	W	O	M	R	W
Kapil Dev	22	10	29	1	13.2	—	70	5
Madan Lal	12	2	24	1	12	6	23	5
Doshi	29.1	12	39	5	1	1	0	—
Shastri	19	6	27	1				
Patil	3	—	9	—				
Kirti Azad	15	4	35	1				

FALL OF WICKETS
1–1, 2–40, 3–70, 4–104, 5–112, 6–164, 7–164, 8–168, 9–179
1–19, 2–24, 3–43, 4–72, 5–90, 6–138, 7–154, 8–157, 9–203

FALL OF WICKETS
1–3, 2–95, 3–105, 4–131, 5–143, 6–146, 7–147, 8–147, 9–163
1–2, 2–4, 3–28, 4–29, 5–42, 6–50, 7–73, 8–74, 9–75

India won by 138 runs

---

as he played with a bravado and a flourish which had not been seen earlier in the match. He and Madan Lal added 46 invaluable runs for the ninth wicket and Kapil Dev scored all but 5 of them. He was lbw to one that kept very low and this in itself was an ominous sight for England.

After a rest day which, for England, must have been fretful, play resumed with Madan Lal and Doshi adding another 24 runs and so England were left the best part of two days in which to make 241. After an hour they were 42 for 5 and at lunch they were 57 for 6. The pitch was not good and there was a frightening tendency for the ball to keep low, but the England batting was poor, weak in technical application and low in spirit and determination.

Boycott concentrated on strokeless defence as all about him fell and Gower flirted with danger, essaying the occasional shot of elegance. Botham played a few good shots and some edges and joined Sobers and Benaud as the only players in Test history to have scored 2000 runs and taken 200 wickets. He on-drove Kapil Dev for a superb six and next ball was caught at mid-off. With him went England's last hope.

Recalled to Test cricket at the age of thirty, Madan Lal bowled with accuracy and persistence and deserved his success. He had last played for India in 1977 and he now seemed a far better bowler than he had done then. He and Kapil Dev bowled unchanged as England slumped close to ignominy as well as defeat. They were 75 for 9 and then Willis and Underwood gave some hint of respectability.

Madan Lal was taken off, but Doshi bowled only one over before Kapil Dev, named Man of the Match, had Willis caught behind by the excellent Kirmani to give India a remarkable and memorable victory by 138 runs.

4, 5 and 6 December 1981
at Hyderabad

South Zone 247 for 9 dec (M. V. Narasimha Rao 51 not out, R. G. D. Willis 4 for 35) and 241 for 7 dec (B. P. Patel 68, V. Mohanraj 59)
England XI 186 for 0 dec (G. A. Gooch 119 not out, G. Boycott 55 not out) and 223 for 4 (K. W. R. Fletcher 108, M. W. Gatting 71)

Match drawn

A strong South Zone side found the speed of Bob Willis a little disconcerting on the opening day and Willis' bowling and a splendid return to form by Gooch on the second day were heartening performances for a somewhat deflated England side. Once more England's over-rate caused much concern – 13 overs an hour was hardly entertaining stuff. South Zone, with three spinners, including Test off-spinner Yadav, managed 16 an hour. Declining South Zone's invitation to score 303 in just under four hours, England settled for batting practice and Keith Fletcher hit his first hundred of the tour while Mike Gatting also batted encouragingly.

India's spin pair: (left) Ravi Shastri and (right) Dilip Doshi.

SECOND TEST MATCH – INDIA v. ENGLAND

England brought in Lever for Willis who was declared unfit and Gatting replaced Emburey who had not bowled well in the previous game. India, not surprisingly, were unchanged.

On the first day 81 overs and 3 balls were bowled and England scored 181 for 4 wickets, one of which was the nightwatchman, John Lever. At lunch England were 84 for 0, a splendid start, and Gooch in spanking form. At 88 Boycott was caught at slip and eight runs later Gooch unwisely pulled at the immaculate Shastri and was caught at mid-wicket. What followed was tedium as the afternoon session produced 46 runs from 30 overs.

The England policy was to consolidate a position from which they could reach a big score and so force a win. In theory this may have been admirable, but the point at which shots should have been played disappeared into the past and with it went any hopes England may have nurtured. Tavare batted for 177 minutes, faced 135 balls for his 22 runs before he missed with a defensive prod and was lbw.

The second day saw England grind on remorselessly and their innings closed on the last ball of the day when Dilley, who had had an entertaining ninth wicket partnership of 69 with Bob Taylor, was caught at long-off to give Shastri his fourth wicket. There were some fine shots from Botham and Gower showed a return to former glories was in embryo, but sadly the most talked about incident was Fletcher's knocking down the stumps when given out caught behind off Shastri. It was explained that he was angry at himself, but, whatever the reason, it was a stupid and unnecessary action.

What had become a certain draw dragged into tedium on the third day's play when England bowled only 71.2 overs and India scored 189 for 1. Sadly, the one wicket was that of Srikkanth who had begun to show an exciting range of strokes before he edged to second slip.

England's conservative approach to the game did not deserve success. In response India had batted as if bent on attrition. Gavaskar had batted through the third day's play and scored 71; by the end of the fourth he was 163. There had been some hope of incident when Lever found himself able to swing the ball in the earlier part of the day, but Gavaskar was immovable and when he reached his century with a push to mid-on he had been batting nearly seven hours. His innings lasted for 11 hours, 42 minutes and he was ninth out so failing by only 4 minutes to be on the field for the whole of the match. The rest should be silence.

16, 17 and 18 December 1981

at Jammu

North Zone 167 (A. Malhotra 80, P. J. W. Allott 5 for 54, J. K. Lever 4 for 57) and 200 for 5 dec (A. Malhotra 67 not out, J. E. Emburey 4 for 72)
England XI 154 and 127 for 0 (G. A. Gooch 60 not out, G. Boycott 59 not out)
Match drawn

Fletcher is unhappy and knocks down the wicket on being out in the Second Test.

SECOND TEST MATCH – INDIA v. ENGLAND
9, 10, 12, 13 and 14 December 1981 at Bangalore

ENGLAND

	FIRST INNINGS		SECOND INNINGS	
G. A. Gooch	c Gavaskar, b Shastri	58	lbw, b Dev	40
G. Boycott	c Gavaskar, b Dev	36	b Doshi	50
C. J. Tavare	lbw, b Lal	22	c Patil, b Shastri	31
D. I. Gower	lbw, b Shastri	82	not out	34
J. K. Lever	lbw, b Dev	1		
K. W. R. Fletcher†	c Kirmani, b Shastri	25	(5) not out	12
I. T. Botham	c Lal, b Doshi	55		
M. W. Gatting	lbw, b Dev	29		
G. R. Dilley	c Gavaskar, b Shastri	52		
R. W. Taylor*	c Dev, b Doshi	33		
D. L. Underwood	not out	2		
Extras	lb 2, nb 3	5	lb 6, nb 1	7
		400	(for 3 wkts)	174

INDIA

	FIRST INNINGS	
S. M. Gavaskar†	c and b Underwood	172
K. Srikkanth	c Gooch, b Botham	65
D. B. Vengsarkar	c Taylor, b Lever	43
G. R. Viswanath	lbw, b Lever	3
R. J. Shastri	lbw, b Lever	1
S. M. Patil	lbw, b Lever	17
Kirti Azad	c Fletcher, b Underwood	24
Kapil Dev	c Taylor, b Lever	59
S. M. H. Kirmani*	lbw, b Botham	9
S. Madan Lal	not out	7
D. R. Doshi	c Boycott, b Underwood	0
Extras	b 2, lb 14, w 3, nb 9	28
		428

	O	M	R	W	O	M	R	W
Kapil Dev	40	3	136	3	12	2	49	1
Madan Lal	24	7	46	1	4	2	14	—
Doshi	39	15	83	2	21	8	37	1
Kirti Azad	12	1	47	—	12	3	36	—
Shastri	43	14	83	4	20	7	31	1

	O	M	R	W
Botham	47	9	137	2
Dilley	24	4	75	—
Lever	36	9	100	5
Underwood	43	21	88	3

FALL OF WICKETS
1–88, 2–96, 3–180, 4–181, 5–223, 6–230, 7–278, 8–324, 9–393
1–59, 2–105, 3–152

FALL OF WICKETS
1–102, 2–155, 3–208, 4–214, 5–242, 6–284, 7–376, 8–412, 9–428

Match drawn

After a splendid first day when only Ashok Malhotra could withstand some fine bowling by Paul Allott and John Lever England batted wretchedly. Gooch and Boycott had given the foundation necessary to force a win with an opening stand of 76, but this stand was followed by what appeared to be a total lack of concentration and application so that, in spite of the efforts of Allott and Lever, England were 13 behind on the first innings. Malhotra again batted well, but England declined Amarnath's suggestion that they should try to make 214 in two hours, ten minutes and Boycott and Gooch practised against eight different bowlers.

SECOND ONE-DAY INTERNATIONAL – INDIA v. ENGLAND

Early morning mist reduced the game to 36 overs and the mist had not cleared completely when England began their innings. They started badly and then became sedentary against some accurate and confident Indian bowling. Gavaskar left the field unwell and Kirmani took over the captaincy. He led the side shrewdly and maintained the pressure on England.

At 48 for 4 England looked very unhappy, but Gatting and Gower added 109 in 17 overs of exciting batting. The last six overs of the innings produced 59 runs and included a marvellous effort by Gatting who hit Shastri for four sixes in one over.

(Left) Bob Taylor's hundredth Test victim. Vengsarkar caught off Lever. Second Test.

SECOND ONE-DAY INTERNATIONAL: INDIA v. ENGLAND
20 December 1981 at Jullundur

ENGLAND

Batsman	Dismissal	Runs
G. A. Gooch	b Madan Lal	12
G. Boycott	run out	6
I. T. Botham	lbw, b Madan Lal	5
K. W. R. Fletcher†	c Azad, b Patil	5
D. I. Gower	run out	53
M. W. Gatting	not out	71
G. Cook	b Kapil Dev	1
C. J. Richards*	lbw, b Kapil Dev	0
J. K. Lever		
D. L. Underwood		
R. G. D. Willis		
Extras	b 2, lb 4, w 1, nb 1	8
	(for 7 wkts)	161

Bowler	O	M	R	W
Kapil Dev	8	1	26	2
Madan Lal	7	—	33	2
Nayak	7	2	25	—
Patil	7	—	16	1
Shastri	7	—	53	—

FALL OF WICKETS
1–18, 2–22, 3–25, 4–48, 5–158, 6–161, 7–161

INDIA

Batsman	Dismissal	Runs
K. Srikkanth	lbw, b Botham	17
D. B. Vengsarkar	not out	88
Kirti Azad	c Gower, b Gooch	14
S. M. Patil	b Gooch	3
Kapil Dev	c Willis, b Underwood	6
Yashpal Sharma	not out	28
S. M. Gavaskar†		
S. Nayak		
S. Madan Lal		
S. M. H. Kirmani*		
R. J. Shastri		
Extras	b 3, lb 3, nb 2	8
	(for 4 wkts)	164

Bowler	O	M	R	W
Willis	7.3	2	41	—
Lever	7	—	31	—
Gooch	7	—	25	2
Botham	7	—	33	1
Underwood	7	1	26	1

FALL OF WICKETS
1–41, 2–69, 3–78, 4–89

India won by 6 wickets

India had asked England to bat and must have been well pleased with their decision when Srikkanth and Vengsarkar began with a stand of 41 in 10 overs before Srikkanth fell to Botham's first ball. There followed a period of Indian uncertainty as Kirti Azad fell to a splendid catch by Gower at extra cover, Patil swung wildly at Gooch and Kapil Dev drove Underwood high to mid-off.

Vengsarkar remained calm and positive as wickets fell at the other end and now he gained the partner he needed in the determined Yashpal Sharma. The light was fading rapidly, but with five overs remaining India needed 29 to win. With two overs left this had been reduced to 10.

From the first ball of the thirty-fifth over Yashpal Sharma hit Botham back over his head for two, but he could make nothing of the next four deliveries. Then, off the last ball of the over, he hit a wonderful six over long-off, a shot that drew admiration from Botham himself.

The first ball of the last over was driven through the covers by Vengsarkar, Man of the Match, and India had beaten England in a one-day international for the first time, and most deservedly so. It was only India's sixth win in 25 limited over matches.

THIRD TEST MATCH – INDIA v. ENGLAND

After protest by Subba Row, the England manager, Mohammad Ghouse was replaced as umpire by Sharoup Kishan before the Third Test began in Delhi. The only meaningful change was on the field where Willis replaced Dilley.

There had been talk of runs needed more quickly and Gooch certainly answered the call with some powerful shots, but once more the first day saw England score only 190 runs in 78 overs, 43 of them bowled by spinners.

Ten minutes before the close of play Boycott reached a personal milestone when he passed Gary Sobers' Test aggregate of 8,032 runs and so became the highest scorer in Test cricket, a task which he no doubt set himself some twenty years ago. He achieved his goal through dedication and single-mindedness, but only his most blinkered fan would suggest that he has given constant pleasure, and one regrets that he could not find it in him to play more often as he did at Lord's in the Gillette Cup Final of 1965.

Boycott duly reached his century on the second day and he was joined by Chris Tavare who, in his seventh Test, scored his first Test hundred and finally reached 149 including 18 fours. His innings lasted for 455 minutes. In the press for runs, England lost five wickets for 17 and then declared.

The game went very much with England for a time. Srikkanth, still too excited, was bowled by Willis, Vengsarkar was caught bat and pad and Gavaskar was taken low down by Taylor, a splendid catch.

Viswanath, with no kind of form behind him, blunted the England attack with some fine shots and careful defence. His 107 took 4½ hours and was the most assured and pleasing century recorded in the series to date. It heralded a thoroughly miserable fourth day for England in which Kirmani and Shastri not only saved the follow-on, but engaged in a stand of 128 for the eighth wicket. Shastri and Madan Lal then had a record stand of 104 for the ninth wicket. Young Shastri played a dedicated innings and saw India from a position of some peril to a lead of 13, but it was all pretty meaningless and, with an average of around 13½ overs an hour from each side, very tedious. Luckily the record books remember only the statistics and, in the span of Test history, Boycott's was a monumental achievement.

THIRD TEST MATCH – INDIA v. ENGLAND
23, 24, 26, 27 and 28 December 1981 at Delhi

ENGLAND

	FIRST INNINGS		SECOND INNINGS	
G. A. Gooch	c Dev, b Doshi	71	not out	20
G. Boycott	c Lal, b Doshi	105	not out	34
C. J. Tavare	b Lal	149		
D. I. Gower	lbw, b Lal	0		
K. W. R. Fletcher†	b Patil	51		
I. T. Botham	c Azad, b Lal	66		
M. W. Gatting	b Lal	5		
R. W. Taylor*	lbw, b Lal	0		
J. K. Lever	b Dev	2		
D. L. Underwood	not out	2		
R. G. D. Willis				
Extras	lb 15, nb 10	25	b 9, nb 5	14
	(for 9 wkts dec)	476	(for no wicket)	68

INDIA

	FIRST INNINGS	
S. M. Gavaskar†	c Taylor, b Lever	46
K. Srikkanth	b Willis	6
D. B. Vengsarkar	c Fletcher, b Underwood	8
G. R. Viswanath	b Botham	107
S. M. Patil	b Willis	31
Kirti Azad	st Taylor, b Underwood	16
Kapil Dev	c Gooch, b Botham	16
R. J. Shastri	lbw, b Gooch	93
S. M. H. Kirmani*	lbw, b Lever	67
S. Madan Lal	b Gooch	44
D. R. Doshi	not out	0
Extras	b 20, lb 8, w 4, nb 21	53
		487

	O	M	R	W	O	M	R	W
Kapil Dev	40.4	5	126	1	4	1	18	—
Madan Lal	32	4	85	5	3	1	4	—
Doshi	40	15	68	2				
Shastri	27	3	109	—				
Kirti Azad	9	2	35	—				
Patil	8	1	28	1	3	1	10	—
Srikkanth					6	1	10	—
Gavaskar					3	—	12	—

	O	M	R	W
Willis	26	3	99	2
Lever	37	7	104	2
Underwood	44	18	97	2
Botham	41	7	122	2
Gooch	8.1	1	12	2

FALL OF WICKETS
1–132, 2–248, 3–248, 4–368, 5–459, 6–465, 7–465, 8–474, 9–476

FALL OF WICKETS
1–11, 2–41, 3–89, 4–174, 5–213, 6–237, 7–254, 8–382, 9–486

Match drawn

FOURTH TEST MATCH – INDIA v. ENGLAND

Emburey for Lever and Yadav for Kirti Azad were the only changes for the Fourth Test which England felt confident that they could win for the Calcutta wicket more than any other of the Test wickets promised a surface on which a result could be achieved.

Fletcher won the toss and England batted. Boycott began with a flourish of aggression and confidence, but he touched a late outswinger from Kapil Dev to Kirmani and a quarter of an hour later Tavare went the same way. On the last ball before lunch Gower swatted at Shastri and Kirmani held his third catch. It would have been a dreadful stroke at any time; in the context in which it was played it was appalling.

Gooch and Fletcher seemed to be righting matters, but Gooch flashed at Doshi and edged to first slip. Fletcher and Botham did restore England's challenge and added 93 good runs before Botham was held at second slip, second attempt off a very hard chance. England ended the day at 198 for 5 and more interest was abroad than at Bangalore.

The last five England wickets went down for 32 and India dug in. It was a hard day's grind and Underwood removed first Srikkanth and then Gavaskar, but India finished at 105 for 2.

Forty-five minutes into the third day Emburey seized the initiative for England when he dismissed Viswanath and Patil in the same over. Vengsarkar batted well, but he showed dissent when given out caught behind. The disease appeared to be spreading. England snatched a lead of 40, but England failed to press home their advantage, scoring only 49 for the loss of Boycott in the 25 overs that India bowled at them.

The fourth day's play was good for England. Gooch, Gower, Tavare, Botham and Fletcher paced the innings well. It was positive cricket and Fletcher declared so that India faced an uncomfortable twenty minutes at the end of the day. They needed 305 in 5½ hours, but the odds were very much on England.

What England desperately wanted on the final morning was to be able to exploit the early haze with their quicker bowlers and so open the way for the spinners later. The heavy atmosphere seemed perfect for England's purposes, but after one ball the umpires decided that the light was bad and India agreed and Gavaskar and Srikkanth left the field. England sat dazed and hopeful in the middle of the field, but seventy minutes play was lost and with it went England's hope of victory. Gavaskar once more proved immovable and England finished on a note of frustration.

Shortly after the Test it was announced that Boycott would be returning home as he felt unwell. Medical tests had failed to diagnose anything wrong, but it was agreed that he had a listlessness and that if the mental attitude was not right, then it would be pointless to insist that he remain on the tour.

As he left India, his Test record aggregate achieved, there was speculation that we had seen him with an England side for the last time.

Cricket in India. The Fourth Test at Calcutta.

FOURTH TEST MATCH – INDIA v. ENGLAND
1, 2, 3, 5 and 6 January 1982 at Calcutta

ENGLAND

	FIRST INNINGS		SECOND INNINGS	
G. A. Gooch	c Viswanath, b Doshi	47	b Doshi	63
G. Boycott	c Kirmani, b Dev	18	lbw, b Lal	6
C. J. Tavare	c Kirmani, b Dev	7	run out	25
D. I. Gower	c Kirmani, b Shastri	11	run out	74
K. W. R. Fletcher†	lbw, b Lal	69	(6) not out	60
I. T. Botham	c Gavaskar, b Dev	58	(5) c Yadav, b Doshi	31
D. L. Underwood	c Patil, b Dev	13		
M. W. Gatting	c Kirmani, b Dev	0	(7) not out	2
J. E. Emburey	lbw, b Dev	1		
R. W. Taylor*	c Vengsarkar, b Doshi	6		
R. G. D. Willis	not out	11		
Extras	lb 3, nb 4	7	lb 4	4
		248	(for 5 wkts dec)	265

INDIA

	FIRST INNINGS		SECOND INNINGS	
S. M. Gavaskar†	b Underwood	42	not out	83
K. Srikkanth	b Underwood	10	c Botham, b Emburey	25
D. B. Vengsarkar	c Taylor, b Botham	70	c Tavare, b Fletcher	32
G. R. Viswanath	c and b Emburey	15	c Gooch, b Emburey	0
S. M. Patil	c Fletcher, b Emburey	0	not out	17
Kapil Dev	c Tavare, b Underwood	22		
R. J. Shastri	run out	8		
S. M. H. Kirmani*	b Botham	10		
S. Madan Lal	c Gooch, b Willis	1		
Shivlal Yadav	c Taylor, b Willis	5		
D. R. Doshi	not out	7		
Extras	b 2, lb 4, w 1, nb 11	18	lb 2, nb 11	13
		208	(for 3 wkts)	170

	O	M	R	W	O	M	R	W
Kapil Dev	31	6	91	6	21	3	81	—
Madan Lal	20	4	58	1	19	3	58	1
Doshi	19.2	8	28	2	27	5	63	2
Yadav	17	7	42	—	3	—	11	—
Shastri	21	10	22	1	17	4	35	—
Patil					3	—	13	—

	O	M	R	W	O	M	R	W
Willis	14	3	28	2	6	—	21	—
Botham	27	8	63	2	11	3	26	—
Underwood	29	13	45	3	31	18	38	—
Emburey	24	11	44	2	30	11	62	2
Gooch	6	1	10	—	2	—	4	—
Fletcher					3	1	6	1

FALL OF WICKETS
1–23, 2–39, 3–68, 4–95, 5–188, 6–216, 7–218, 8–224, 9–230
1–24, 2–88, 3–107, 4–154, 5–259

FALL OF WICKETS
1–33, 2–83, 3–117, 4–117, 5–143, 6–180, 7–184, 8–187, 9–196
1–48, 2–116, 3–120

Match drawn

8, 9 and 10 January 1982
at Jamshedpur
East Zone 242 (P. Nadi 97, P. J. W. Allott 5 for 77) and 74 for 0
England XI 356 for 8 dec (M. W. Gatting 127, G. A. Gooch 79, D. I. Gower 57, Paranjit Singh 5 for 108)
Match drawn

In the absence of both Fletcher and Willis, Gooch led England for the first time. Allott and Dilley bowled well and quite quickly for England after Gooch had put the opposition in, but Palash Nadi played an excellent innings, far outshining his international team-mates. Gooch hit fiercely and Gower batted encouragingly, but the England batting honours went to Mike Gatting who completed his first hundred overseas before the game subsided into a draw and farce.

FIFTH TEST MATCH – INDIA v. ENGLAND

There were doubts about the fitness of Botham and Taylor before the start of the game, but both played. Dilley and Allott came in for Boycott and Emburey, Tavare moving up to open with Gooch so that Cook remained in reserve. For India, Roy replaced Srikkanth as Gavaskar's partner, and Yashpal Sharma and Malhotra replaced Yadav and Patil.

Intent on victory, Fletcher gave India first use of the pitch when he won the toss, but his bold gesture was nullified by dropped catches. There was success for England early on when Roy was caught behind off Dilley, but both Gavaskar and Vengsarkar were dropped at slip off straightforward chances brought about by Allott's bowling and England were never again in the contest.

Vengsarkar batted with dash and elegance to reach 71 before he was hit by a ball from Willis which did not lift as expected and retired hurt. He was not needed again. In only 66 overs which England bowled on the first day India scored 178 for 2 with Viswanath on 64 not out.

England failed to take a wicket on the second day as Viswanath and Yashpal Sharma added another 217 runs and both reached centuries. In the course of the day Viswanath was put down at slip by the luckless Tavare off the suffering Allott. By the end England had dissolved into petulance.

Viswanath and Sharma actually put on 316 together, a figure only once surpassed for India. The third wicket realised 415 in all. Sharma batted 8 hours 10 minutes and hit two sixes and eighteen fours; Viswanath's 222 was a record against England. It lasted 10 hours 38 minutes and included 31 fours. He was generously applauded by the England team at the end who recognised a great adversary and a great batsman. It was incredible to ponder that only

FIFTH TEST MATCH – INDIA v. ENGLAND
13, 14, 15, 17 and 18 January 1982 at Madras

INDIA

	FIRST INNINGS		SECOND INNINGS	
S. M. Gavaskar†	c Taylor, b Willis	25	c Botham, b Willis	11
P. Roy	c Taylor, b Dilley	6	not out	60
D. B. Vengsarkar	retired hurt	71		
G. R. Viswanath	b Willis	222		
Yashpal Sharma	c Tavare, b Botham	140	(4) c Botham, b Underwood	25
Kapil Dev	not out	6	(5) not out	15
A. Malhotra			(3) run out	31
R. J. Shastri				
S. M. H. Kirmani*				
S. Madan Lal				
D. R. Doshi				
Extras	lb 1, w 1, nb 9	11	b 12, lb 1, nb 5	18
	(for 4 wkts dec)	481	(for 3 wkts dec)	160

ENGLAND

	FIRST INNINGS	
G. A. Gooch	c and b Shastri	127
C. J. Tavare	c Gavaskar, b Doshi	35
K. W. R. Fletcher†	b Doshi	3
D. I. Gower	lbw, b Shastri	64
I. T. Botham	c Kirmani, b Shastri	52
M. W. Gatting	c Viswanath, b Doshi	0
G. R. Dilley	c and b Dev	8
R. W. Taylor*	b Doshi	8
D. L. Underwood	c Kirmani, b Dev	0
P. J. W. Allott	c Roy, b Dev	6
R. G. D. Willis	not out	1
Extras	b 1, lb 9, nb 14	24
		328

	O	M	R	W		O	M	R	W
Willis	28.1	7	79	2		7	2	15	1
Botham	31	10	83	1		8	1	29	—
Dilley	31	4	87	1		5	1	13	—
Allott	33	4	135	—					
Underwood	22	7	59	—		15	8	30	1
Gooch	9	2	27	—		8	2	24	—
Fletcher						1	—	9	—
Taylor						2	—	6	—
Tavare						2	—	11	—
Gower						1	—	1	—
Gatting						1	—	4	—

	O	M	R	W
Kapil Dev	25.5	7	88	3
Madan Lal	9	1	41	—
Shastri	63	23	104	3
Doshi	57	31	69	4
Gavaskar	1	—	2	—

FALL OF WICKETS
1-19, 2-51, 3-466, 4-481
1-16, 2-69, 3-122

FALL OF WICKETS
1-155, 2-164, 3-195, 4-279, 5-283, 6-307, 7-307, 8-311, 9-320

Match drawn

a few weeks previously his Test place had been in jeopardy.

The England reply was brilliant in character. Before the close of the third day Gooch had scored 117 out of 144. It was an innings of power, clean and devastating hitting. He added only ten on the fourth morning and England faltered a little, but Botham and Gower saved the follow-on. It became very painful cricket as England amassed only 163 runs from the 80 overs bowled in the day. In the end Doshi's 57 overs cost him only 69 runs, incredible figures on such a wicket.

Once more the game drifted to farce and a draw.

Two Indian batting heroes
Right: *Viswanath, 223 in the Fifth Test. Fletcher in pensive mood.*
Below: *Gavaskar, 182 in the Second Test. Gatting ducks, Fletcher looks on.*

22, 23 and 24 January 1982
at Indore

England XI 436 for 7 dec (I. T. Botham 122, M. W. Gatting 111, G. R. Dilley 52) and 210 for 1 (G. Cook 104 not out, C. J. Tavare 81)
Central Zone 311 (Ved Raj 59)

Match drawn

A century in 50 minutes off 48 balls by Ian Botham dwarfed all else in this match which fizzled to a draw as England's seven previous matches had done. In all Botham hit seven sixes and sixteen fours in a stay of 55 minutes during which time he faced 55 deliveries. It was a mighty performance even by his standards. Gatting and Botham put on 137 for the fourth wicket, Botham getting 122 of them. In the context of the innings Gatting's hundred became overshadowed, but he batted well, sharing a fifth wicket stand of 127 in 93 minutes with Bob Taylor. Gatting reached his hundred in 168 minutes with thirteen fours and three sixes. England batted into the second day and found Central Zone unwilling to surrender. Batting practice followed, which Cook at least enjoyed, and another match died.

THIRD ONE-DAY INTERNATIONAL – INDIA v. ENGLAND

With England's unhappiness manifesting itself with more discussions about umpires off the field, they had a bitter disappointment on the field when they lost the third one-day international to India so giving the home country their first ever victory in a limited over series by 2–1.

It seemed that England had done enough with the bat to win the match. They recovered from the early loss of Gooch and provided some exciting stroke play. Gower and Botham were good, but Fletcher played his best innings as England's captain. Dropped off a skier, he responded by hitting Madan Lal for sixes over mid-on and extra-cover. He moved from 11 to 50 in 3 overs, hitting Madab Lal for three successive fours and Nayak for a six over mid-wicket on the way.

Having set India a target of more than five an over, England seemed in a good position, but Gavaskar began with a flurry of strokes. The loss of Arun Lal and Vengsarkar did not deter him. He and Patil added 76 in 14 overs before Gavaskar stepped out to Underwood and missed. Patil continued the assault and although Kapil Dev went quickly, Yashpal Sharma and Malhotra saw India home to emotional applause, and there were still 4 overs to spare.

SIXTH TEST MATCH – INDIA v. ENGLAND

Gooch again began brightly for England and Botham and Gower added 92 in the last 25 overs of the first day, but when rain restricted play on the second day to an hour before lunch, England's slender hopes of squaring the series evaporated.

Two more hours were lost on the third day which saw Botham reach the ninth hundred of his Test career and emphasise his growing stature as a very great batsman. England did capture the wicket of Roy before the close, but they captured only two wickets the next day and the game was dead.

There was some excitement on the last day when India recovered from 207 for 6 to 376 for 7. The architect of the recovery was Kapil Dev, already India's national hero, who hit a hundred off 83 balls. He hit two sixes and sixteen fours in his 116 and India had won their fourth Test series against England, their first since 1973.

Not surprisingly, it was announced that Sunil Gavaskar would lead the Indian side to tour England later in the year.

THIRD ONE-DAY INTERNATIONAL: INDIA v. ENGLAND
27 January 1982 at Cuttack

ENGLAND					INDIA			
G. A. Gooch	c Arun Lal, b Madan Lal		3		S. M. Gavaskar†	st Taylor, b Underwood		71
G. Cook	c Nayak, b Patil		30		Arun Lal	c Gooch, b Botham		9
C. J. Tavare	c Madan Lal, b Shastri		11		D. B. Vengsarkar	c Willis, b Gooch		13
D. I. Gower	c and b Patil		42		S. M. Patil	b Underwood		64
I. T. Botham	b Nayak		52		Yashpal Sharma	not out		34
K. W. R. Fletcher†	b Madan Lal		69		Kapil Dev	c Gooch, b Underwood		0
M. W. Gatting	not out		8		A. Malhotra	not out		28
R. W. Taylor*	not out		2		S. M. H. Kirmani*			
J. K. Lever					S. Nayak			
D. L. Underwood					S. Madan Lal			
R. G. D. Willis					R. J. Shastri			
Extras	lb 9, w 1, nb 3		13		Extras	lb 7, w 2, nb 3		12
	(for 6 wkts)		230			(for 5 wkts)		231

	O	M	R	W		O	M	R	W
Kapil Dev	8	3	23	—	Willis	6	1	29	—
Madan Lal	8	—	56	2	Botham	8	—	48	1
Nayak	10	1	51	1	Lever	10	—	55	—
Shastri	10	1	34	1	Gooch	8	—	39	1
Patil	10	—	53	2	Underwood	10	—	48	3

FALL OF WICKETS
1–13, 2–33, 3–86, 4–101, 5–181, 6–228

FALL OF WICKETS
1–16, 2–59, 3–135, 4–184, 5–184

India won by 5 wickets

SIXTH TEST MATCH – INDIA v. ENGLAND
30, 31 January, 1, 3 and 4 February 1982 at Kanpur

ENGLAND

FIRST INNINGS

G. A. Gooch	b Doshi	58
C. J. Tavare	b Doshi	24
K. W. R. Fletcher†	b Dev	14
D. I. Gower	lbw, b Dev	85
I. T. Botham	st Kirmani, b Doshi	142
M. W. Gatting	c Lal, b Doshi	32
G. R. Dilley	lbw, b Shastri	1
R. W. Taylor*	b Shastri	0
J. E. Emburey	run out	2
D. L. Underwood	not out	0
R. G. D. Willis		
Extras	b 2, lb 5, w 6, nb 7	20
	(for 9 wkts dec)	378

	O	M	R	W
Kapil Dev	34	3	147	2
Madan Lal	24	4	79	—
Doshi	34.2	8	81	4
Shastri	23	6	51	2

FALL OF WICKETS
1–82, 2–89, 3–121, 4–248, 5–349, 6–354, 7–354, 8–360, 9–378

INDIA

FIRST INNINGS

S. M. Gavaskar†	run out	52
P. Roy	b Botham	5
D. B. Vengsarkar	c Fletcher, b Dilley	46
G. R. Viswanath	c Gower, b Willis	74
Yashpal Sharma	not out	55
A. Malhotra	lbw b Willis	0
R. J. Shastri	c Taylor, b Willis	2
Kapil Dev	c Dilley, b Gower	116
S. M. H. Kirmani*	not out	1
S. Madan Lal		
D. R. Doshi		
Extras	b 1, lb 7, w 2, nb 16	26
	(for 7 wkts)	377

	O	M	R	W
Willis	23	5	75	3
Botham	25	6	67	1
Dilley	14	2	67	1
Underwood	25	8	55	—
Emburey	32	7	81	—
Fletcher	2	1	5	—
Gower	1	—	1	1

FALL OF WICKETS
1–12, 2–79, 3–166, 4–197, 5–197, 6–207, 7–376

Match drawn

India v. England – Test Match Averages

INDIA BATTING

	M	Inns	NOs	Runs	HS	Av	100s	50s
Yashpal Sharma	2	3	1	220	140	110.00	1	1
S. M. Gavaskar	6	9	1	500	172	62.50	1	3
G. R. Viswanath	6	8		466	222	58.25	2	1
Kapil Dev	6	8	2	318	116	53.00	1	1
D. B. Vengsarkar	6	8	1	292	71*	41.71		2
P. Roy	2	3	1	71	60*	35.50		1
R. J. Shastri	6	6	1	140	93	28.00		1
Madan Lal	6	5	2	69	44	23.00		
K. Srikkanth	4	6		119	65	19.83		1
S. M. H. Kirmani	6	6	1	99	67	19.80		1
S. M. Patil	4	6	1	95	31	19.00		
Kirti Azad	3	4		71	24	17.75		
A. Malhotra	2	2		31	31	15.50		
D. R. Doshi	6	5	2	14	7*	4.66		

Played in one Test: S. Yadav 5

INDIA BOWLING

	Overs	Mds	Runs	Wkts	Av	Best	5/inn
D. R. Doshi	267.5	103	468	22	21.27	5/39	1
Madan Lal	159	34	432	14	30.85	5/23	2
Kapil Dev	243.5	40	835	22	37.95	6/91	2
R. J. Shastri	233	73	462	12	38.50	4/83	
Kirti Azad	48	10	153	1	153.00	1/35	

Also bowled: S. M. Gavaskar 4–0–14–0; S. M. Patil 17–2–60–1; K. Srikkanth 6–1–10–0; S. Yadav 20–7–53–0.

INDIA CATCHES
11—S. M. H. Kirmani (ct 10/st 1); 9—S. M. Gavaskar; 3—Kapil Dev and Madan Lal; 2—R. J. Shastri, Kirti Azad, S. M. Patil and G. R. Viswanath; 1—D. B. Vengsarkar, P. Roy, K. Srikkanth and S. Yadav.

ENGLAND BATTING

	M	Inns	NOs	Runs	HS	Av	100s	50s
I. T. Botham	6	8		440	142	55.00	1	4
G. A. Gooch	6	10	1	487	127	54.11	1	4
D. I. Gower	6	9	1	375	85	46.88		4
G. Boycott	4	8	1	312	105	44.57	1	2
C. J. Tavare	6	9		349	149	38.77	1	1
K. W. R. Fletcher	6	9	2	252	69	36.00		3
G. R. Dilley	4	5		70	52	14.00		1
M. W. Gatting	5	6	1	68	32	13.00		
R. G. D. Willis	5	4	2	26	13	13.00		
D. L. Underwood	6	7	4	38	13*	12.66		
R. W. Taylor	6	7	1	57	33	9.50		
J. K. Lever	2	2		3	2	1.50		
J. E. Emburey	3	4		4	2	1.00		

Played in one Test: P. J. W. Allott 6

ENGLAND BOWLING

	Overs	Mds	Runs	Wkts	Av	Best	5/inn
K. W. R. Fletcher	6	2	20	1	20.00	1/6	
J. K. Lever	73	16	204	7	29.14	5/100	1
R. G. D. Willis	129.1	29	381	12	31.75	3/75	
J. E. Emburey	99	32	222	6	37.00	2/35	
G. A. Gooch	33.1	6	77	2	38.50	2/12	
I. T. Botham	240.3	52	660	17	38.82	5/61	1
D. L. Underwood	228	99	438	10	43.80	3/45	
G. R. Dilley	105	17	350	7	50.00	4/47	

Also bowled: P. J. W. Allott 31–4–135–0; M. W. Gatting 1–0–4–0; R. W. Taylor 2–0–6–0; D. I. Gower 2–0–2–1; C. J. Tavare 2–0–11–0.

ENGLAND CATCHES
16—R. W. Taylor (ct 15/st 1); 5—K. W. R. Fletcher and C. J. Tavare; 4—G. A. Gooch; 3—I. T. Botham; 2—G. Boycott; 1—G. R. Dilley, J. E. Emburey, D. I. Gower, D. L. Underwood and M. W. Gatting (substitute).

Cricket in Sri Lanka. England XI v. Board XI at Kandy.

After the disappointments of India England moved on to Sri Lanka. They appeared tired and jaded, but they could not fail to be moved by the state of excited anticipation that prevailed in the island which was about to witness something for which it had striven for several years, its first Test match.

9, 10 and 11 February 1982

at Kandy

President's XI 273 for 5 dec (R. S. Madugalle 142 not out, B. Perera 56 not out) and 125 for 6 (R. S. A. Jayasekera 52)

England XI 360 (G. Cook 104, M. W. Gatting 54, J. R. Ratnayake 5 for 120)

Match drawn

John Lever produced a sharp opening spell which had the President's XI struggling, but a splendidly positive hundred by Madugalle took all the honours and delighted the enthusiastic crowd. He and Perera had an unbeaten stand of 164 for the sixth wicket. Geoff Cook asserted his right to a Test place with another century and Gatting gave good support, but a draw again became inevitable.

FIRST ONE-DAY INTERNATIONAL – SRI LANKA v. ENGLAND

Uncertain at the start, Gooch recovered his poise to give England the chance of a substantial score. Cook had been eminently dependable and Botham arrived to provide the injection of power that was needed. All seemed to be going according to plan as 191 was reached with only three men out, but the last seven English wickets went down in 24 balls while only another 20 runs were added and England looked vulnerable.

At tea, Sri Lanka were 62 for 1 from 15 overs and so they were well set for the final push towards an epic victory.

England concentrated their efforts on the basic virtues of line and length to a well set field and Sri Lanka began to falter. They were revived by Ranasinghe who hit 51 from 40 balls. He was out at 187 in the forty-second over so that Sri Lanka needed 25 from three overs for victory.

In his efforts at containment Fletcher had used Willis and Botham to the full and now found himself obliged to use Gooch for the last over with only 12 runs needed, but Gooch bowled well and conceded only three singles so that England won by 5 runs.

It was gratifying to see the excellent and economical use that Sri Lanka made of her spinners. Refreshingly, they had not yet fallen into the inhibited medium pace pattern of one-day internationals.

FIRST ONE-DAY INTERNATIONAL: SRI LANKA v. ENGLAND
13 February 1982 at Colombo

ENGLAND				SRI LANKA			
G. A. Gooch	b G. R. A. de Silva		64	B. Warnapura†	c Gower, b Allott		10
G. Cook	c G. R. A. de Silva, b Kaluperuma		28	S. Wettimuny	c Richards, b Allott		46
D. I. Gower	run out		15	R. S. A. Jayasekera*	c Gooch, b Willis		17
I. T. Botham	b de Mel		60	R. L. Dias	c and b Underwood		4
K. W. R. Fletcher†	b D. S. de Silva		12	L. R. D. Mendis	c Gower, b Underwood		2
M. W. Gatting	c Mendis, b de Mel		3	R. S. Madugalle	b Willis		22
C. J. Richards*	b G. R. A. de Silva		3	A. N. Ranasinghe	c Cook, b Botham		51
J. E. Emburey	lbw, b de Mel		0	D. S. de Silva	b Botham		8
P. J. W. Allott	run out		0	A. L. F. de Mel	not out		13
D. L. Underwood	b de Mel		4	L. W. Kaluperuma	not out		14
R. G. D. Willis	not out		2	G. R. A. de Silva			
Extras	b 6, lb 2, w 2, nb 10		20	Extras	b 5, lb 10, w 2, nb 1		19
			211		(for 8 wkts)		206

	O	M	R	W		O	M	R	W
de Mel	8.4	1	34	4	Willis	9	1	32	2
Ranasinghe	8	2	20	—	Botham	9	—	45	2
Kaluperuma	7	—	35	1	Emburey	5	—	18	—
D. S. de Silva	9	—	31	1	Allott	8	—	40	2
G. R. A. de Silva	9	—	56	2	Gooch	6	1	18	—
Wettimuny	3	—	15	—	Underwood	7	—	34	2

FALL OF WICKETS
1–55, 2–83, 3–152, 4–191, 5–197, 6–202, 7–205, 8–205, 9–205

FALL OF WICKETS
1–37, 2–75, 3–84, 4–92, 5–92, 6–160, 7–175, 8–187

England won by 5 runs

SECOND ONE-DAY INTERNATIONAL – SRI LANKA v. ENGLAND

In a memorable match which produced a dramatic climax, Sri Lanka beat England by three runs and instigated an evening of national rejoicing and celebration.

Each side made strengthening changes from the previous day and the inclusion of the specialist wicket-keeper, Goonatillake, was to prove valuable to Sri Lanka. They started badly losing Warnapura and Mendis for 5 runs in Botham's fourth over. After 17 overs they were 43 for 3, having lost Dias whose helmet had fallen into his stumps.

The eighteen-year-old left-hander, Ranatunga, played with confident aggression and he and Wettimuny added 87 in 16 overs. Ranasinghe failed, but Wettimuny and his last three partners increased the score by 70 in the last 10 overs when Botham, who had bowled so tightly in his opening spell, was quite expensive. Wettimuny carried his bat. He faced 109 balls and hit eight fours.

Gooch and Cook began with smooth efficiency and England looked set for an easy victory. Gooch hit a six and nine fours, but, in successive overs from the slow left-arm bowling of Ajit de Silva, he and Cook were both beaten through the air and stumped. The leg-breaks of D. S. de Silva were also causing consternation and when the last 10 overs were reached England were 74 short of victory and the light was fading.

There was ecstasy among the crowd when the great Botham gave Warnapura a simple return catch, but Fletcher replied for England by taking 16 runs off the thirty-eighth over which was bowled by D. S. de Silva. The leg-spinner retaliated by bowling Tavare with the first ball of his next over so that England needed 46 for 35 balls.

Seventeen runs came in the forty-first over. This time it was Ajit de Silva who was punished and the over included an on-driven six from Gatting. 27 were needed from 4 overs, 19 from 3, and 14 from the last 2. It was at this point that corporate insanity gripped England.

Gatting was run out from the first ball of the penultimate over. Fletcher was run out on the third ball of the same over. De Mel bowled the last over and the first ball went through to the wicket-keeper. Taylor was run out going for the second run for a leg-glance on the second ball. Underwood was run out next ball, the first he received. Lever took a single off the next ball.

This left Willis facing the bowling with two balls left and four runs needed for victory. De Mel had bowled his fast medium splendidly throughout and now Willis swung at him fiercely for what would have been the winning hit, but Madugalle held a splendid catch at mid-wicket and Sri Lanka had won a memorable victory.

As the crowd of 20,000 swept on to the field in adulation we reflected that England had lost their last six wickets in 11 balls.

SECOND ONE-DAY INTERNATIONAL: SRI LANKA v. ENGLAND
14 February 1982 at Colombo

SRI LANKA				ENGLAND		
B. Warnapura†	c Taylor, b Botham	4		G. A. Gooch	st Goonatillake, b G. R. A. de Silva	74
S. Wettimuny	not out	86		G. Cook	st Goonatillake, b G. R. A. de Silva	32
L. R. D. Mendis	c and b Botham	0		D. I. Gower	lbw, b de Mel	6
R. L. Dias	hit wkt, b Lever	26		I. T. Botham	c and b Warnapura	13
A. Ranatunga	run out	42		K. R. W. Fletcher†	run out	38
A. N. Ranasinghe	c Gooch, b Underwood	0		C. J. Tavare	b D. S. de Silva	5
R. S. Madugalle	c Taylor, b Lever	12		M. W. Gatting	run out	18
A. L. F. de Mel	run out	14		R. W. Taylor*	run out	3
D. S. de Silva	not out	9		J. K. Lever	not out	2
H. M. Goonatillake*				D. L. Underwood	run out	0
G. R. A. de Silva				R. G. D. Willis	c Madugalle, b de Mel	0
Extras	b 2, lb 18, w 1, nb 1	22		Extras	lb 19, w 1, nb 1	21
	(for 7 wkts)	215				212

	O	M	R	W		O	M	R	W
Willis	9	1	26	—	de Mel	8.5	—	14	2
Botham	9	4	29	2	Ranasinghe	9	—	37	—
Lever	9	—	51	2	Warnapura	9	—	42	1
Gooch	9	—	50	—	D. S. de Silva	9	—	54	1
Underwood	9	—	37	1	G. R. A. de Silva	9	1	44	2

FALL OF WICKETS
1–5, 2–5, 3–43, 4–130, 5–130, 6–158, 7–186

FALL OF WICKETS
1–109, 2–122, 3–122, 4–147, 5–170, 6–203, 7–206, 8–211, 9–211

Sri Lanka won by 3 runs

THE INAUGURAL TEST

Sri Lanka's great day arrived and Warnapura celebrated by winning the toss although his decision to bat first surprised many people. It was fitting that the captain should score the first run for Sri Lanka in Test cricket, but after that things went badly for the home side. There was a hesitancy and nervousness in the batting and with Willis and Botham extracting life from a slightly damp pitch, Sri Lanka were shattered at 34 for 4.

They were revitalised by the batting of two young men, Madugalle and the eighteen-year old Ranatunga. Both batted with maturity and crispness in a stand of 99 that had the crowd, smaller than anticipated, in raptures. Much of their good work was underdone by Underwood who took four wickets in a fourteen over spell for only 18 runs.

Underwood dismissed Madugalle the next morning and the innings closed for 218. England's start was little better than Sri Lanka's. De Mel bowled quite superbly after an indifferent couple of overs. Cook, on his debut, slashed wildly and was taken in the gully, Tavare was yorked second ball and then Gooch, who had looked menacing, was lbw. Fletcher should have been caught, but he survived and lunch was taken at 44 for 3.

Fletcher and Gower then rallied England with a stand of 80, but as well as dismissing Fletcher, Sri Lanka captured the prize wicket of Botham before the end of the day which England ended only 32 runs behind with five wickets in hand.

On the third day Sri Lanka celebrated their first Test match in a way which delighted their supporters and made the defeat of England a real possibility. The last five English wickets fell to the left-arm spin and leg-break combination of the de Silva's, who are unrelated, while only 37 were added to the overnight score. Then Sri Lanka's batsmen showed a delightful array of strokes and although Roy Dias, their top scorer, was dismissed by Underwood shortly before the close, Sri Lanka ended the day at 152 for 3, a position of authority on a wearing pitch.

The next day will remain in Sri Lanka's memory for a long time as the day when a dream of glory turned into a nightmare. John Emburey recorded his best figures in Test cricket, at one time taking 5 for 5 in 33 deliveries as Sri Lanka lost their last seven wickets for 8 runs in 45 minutes. They were destroyed not only by some excellent spin bowling, but also by their own inexperience and the shades of fear that attended the beckoning finger of success.

Cook failed again and Gooch played a somewhat bizarre innings technically, however Tavare batted with fluency and sense and England won with surprising ease, but by now Sri Lanka's bitter disappointment was very apparent. It was good for England to finish an uneasy tour with a win, but it was something of a sad ending to a celebratory occasion.

THE INAUGURAL TEST – SRI LANKA v. ENGLAND
17, 18, 20 and 21 February 1982 at Colombo

SRI LANKA

	FIRST INNINGS		SECOND INNINGS	
B. Warnapura†	c Gower, b Willis	2	c Gooch, b Emburey	38
S. Wettimuny	c Taylor, b Botham	6	b Willis	9
R. L. Dias	c Cook, b Willis	0	c Taylor, b Underwood	77
L. R. D. Mendis	lbw, b Botham	17	c Willis, b Emburey	27
R. S. Madugalle	c Gower, b Underwood	65	c Cook, b Emburey	3
A. Ranatunga	b Underwood	54	c Fletcher, b Emburey	2
D. S. de Silva	c Gower, b Underwood	3	c Fletcher, b Underwood	1
A. L. F. de Mel	c Fletcher, b Underwood	19	c Gower, b Emburey	2
L. W. Kaluperuma	c Cook, b Underwood	1	c Taylor, b Emburey	0
H. M. Goonatillake*	not out	22	not out	2
G. R. A. de Silva	c Emburey, b Botham	12	c Willis, b Underwood	0
Extras	b 2, lb 4, w 2, nb 9	17	lb 6, nb 8	14
		218		**175**

ENGLAND

	FIRST INNINGS		SECOND INNINGS	
G. A. Gooch	lbw, b de Mel	22	b G. R. A. de Silva	31
G. Cook	c Kaluperuma, b de Mel	11	lbw, b de Mel	0
C. J. Tavare	b de Mel	0	st Goonatillake, b G. R. A. de Silva	85
D. I. Gower	c Goonatillake, b D. S. de Silva	89	not out	42
K. W. R. Fletcher†	c Warnapura, b G. R. A. de Silva	45	not out	0
I. T. Botham	b de Mel	13		
R. W. Taylor*	not out	31		
J. E. Emburey	lbw, b G. R. de Silva	0		
P. J. W. Allott	c Kaluperuma, b D. S. de Silva	3		
D. L. Underwood	c Mendis, b D. de Silva	0		
R. G. D. Willis	run out	0		
Extras	lb 3, nb 6	9	b 7, lb 5, nb 1	13
		223	(for 3 wkts)	**171**

	O	M	R	W	O	M	R	W
Willis	19	7	46	2	9	3	24	1
Botham	12.5	1	28	3	12	1	37	—
Allott	13	4	44	—				
Emburey	19	3	55	—	25	9	33	6
Underwood	18	6	28	5	37.3	15	67	3

	O	M	R	W	O	M	R	W
de Mel	17	2	70	4	13.1	4	33	1
Warnapura	3	1	9	—	1	—	1	—
D. S. de Silva	27.5	11	54	3	15	5	38	—
Kaluperuma	9	1	29	—	12	3	40	—
G. R. A. de Silva	30	12	52	2	17	6	46	2

FALL OF WICKETS
1–9, 2–11, 3–29, 4–34, 5–133, 6–149, 7–181, 8–183, 9–190
1–30, 2–113, 3–140, 4–167, 5–169, 6–170, 7–172, 8–173, 9–174

FALL OF WICKETS
1–34, 2–34, 3–40, 4–120, 5–151, 6–200, 7–207, 8–216, 9–216
1–3, 2–84, 3–167

England won by 7 wickets

Below: *R. S. Madugalle.* Right: *A. N. Ranasinghe.*

Opposite: *The cares of captaincy. Warnapura, Sri Lanka's captain in their first Test match.*

England in India and Sri Lanka 1981–82
First Class Matches

BATTING

	v. Indian u/22 XI (Poona) 13–15 November 1981	v. President's XI (Nagpur) 17–19 November 1981	v. West Zone (Baroda) 21–23 November 1981	First Test Match (Bombay) 27 Nov.–1 Dec. 1981	v. South Zone (Hyderabad) 4–6 December 1981	Second Test Match (Bangalore) 9–14 December 1981	v. North Zone (Jammu) 16–18 December 1981	Third Test Match (Delhi) 23–28 December 1981	Fourth Test Match (Calcutta) 1–6 January 1982	v. East Zone (Jamshedpur) 8–10 January 1982	Fifth Test Match (Madras) 13–18 January 1982	v. Central Zone (Indore) 22–24 January 1982
G. Boycott	101* —		66 73*	60 3	55* —	36 50	35 59*	105 34*	18 6			
C. J. Tavare	56 —	51 7	96 —	56 0		22 31	7 —	149	7 25	15 —	35 —	14 81
K. W. R. Fletcher	56* —	2 35*	39* —	15 3	108 —	25 12*	0 —	51 —	69 60*		3 —	32 —
D. I. Gower	— 94		39 33*	5 20	8 82	34* —	0 —	0 —	11 74	57 —	64 —	
M. W. Gatting	— 42	2 8				71 29	26 —	5 —	0 2*	127 —	0 —	111 —
I. T. Botham	— 98	32 25	6* 24	7 29		55 —		66 —	58 31		52 —	122 —
G. R. Dilley	— 36*	3 5*	— —	0 9		52 —				23 —	8 —	52 —
C. J. Richards	— 18*				— 11*		5 —			1* —		16* —
J. E. Emburey	— 10	33 —		0 1	— 11*		2 —		1 —	7 —		9* —
P. J. W. Allott	— —				— —		4 —		0 —	6 —		
R. G. D. Willis	— —			1 13	— —		0* —		11* —		1* —	
G. A. Gooch		17 16	17 32	2 1	119* —	58 40	42 60*	71 20*	47 63	79 —	127 —	
R. W. Taylor		4 —		9* 1		33 —		0 —	6 —		8 —	40 —
D. L. Underwood	— 22*			8 13*	2* —		1 —	2* —	13 —		0 —	
J. K. Lever	— 16						15 —	2 —				
G. Cook		39 30			0 —		8 —			37 —		39 104*
Byes	1 14	5 4		1 4	5 4		8	9		1	8	
Leg-byes	4 4	6 3	2 3	3 8	2 6	1 8	15	3 4	3	9	2 7	
Wides		1						5				
No-balls	6 4	4 1	4 6	2 4	2 3	1 1	10	4	7	14	7 2	
Total	219 303	243 136	278 171	166 102	186 223	400 174	154 127	476 68	248 265	356	328	436 210
Wickets	1 4	10 5	4 2	10 10	0 4	10 3	10 0	9 0	10 5	8	10	7 1
Result	W	W	D	L	D	D	D	D	D	D	D	D

Catches 28 – R. W. Taylor (ct 27/st 1)   11 – G. A. Gooch (one as sub.) and   9 – K. W. R. Fletcher   6 – M. W. Gatting (one as su
12 – C. J. Richards (ct 11/st 1)   C. J. Tavare (one as sub.)   7 – I. T. Botham and D. I. Gower   5 – J. E. Emburey and G. Co

BOWLING

	R. G. D. Willis	I. T. Botham	P. J. W. Allott	G. R. Dilley	M. W. Gatting	J. E. Emburey	K. W. R. Fletcher	J. K. Lever
v. Indian u/22 XI (Poona) 13–15 November 1981	11–1–65–1 4–0–18–0	11–2–55–1 3–0–26–0	18–1–67–1 8–2–25–0	12–1–58–1 7–0–43–1	6–1–16–1	23–7–67–2 17–3–51–1	2–0–9–0	
v. President's XI (Nagpur) 17–19 November 1981		6–0–27–0		6–0–31–1		14–1–43–3 24–5–76–3		8–0–27–0 6–2–19–2
v. West Zone (Baroda) 21–23 November 1981	12–4–28–2 5–0–16–0	16–4–30–2 7–2–26–1		11–0–47–1 8–0–38–0		17–6–33–2 17–1–59–2		
First Test Match (Bombay) 28 November–1 December 1981	12–5–33–1 13–4–31–1	28–6–72–4 22.3–3–61–5		13–1–47–4 18–5–61–1		13–2–35–2		
v. South Zone (Hyderabad) 4–6 December 1981	17–6–35–4 5–0–31–1		16–3–48–1 3–1–9–0			15–3–38–2 24–8–71–3	20–0–82–1	19–2–83–2 5–0–24–0
Second Test Match (Bangalore) 9–14 December 1981		47–9–137–2		24–4–75–0				36–9–100–5
v. North Zone (Jammu) 16–18 December 1981	11–4–21–0 20–8–22–1		16–4–54–5 17.5–8–41–0			3.1–0–7–1 25–6–72–4		19–7–57–4 12–1–59–0
Third Test Match (Delhi) 23–28 December 1981	26–3–99–2	41–7–122–2						37–7–104–2
Fourth Test Match (Calcutta) 1–6 January 1982	14–3–28–2 6–0–21–0	27–8–63–2 11–3–26–0				24–11–44–2 30–11–62–2	3–1–6–1	
v. East Zone (Jamshedpur) 8–10 January 1982			26.5–6–77–5 6–3–7–0	29–3–93–3 5–2–6–0	4–0–20–0	8–3–13–0		20–3–46–1 3–2–10–0
Fifth Test Match (Madras) 13–18 January 1982	28.1–7–79–2 7–2–15–1	31–10–83–1 8–1–29–0	33–4–135–0	31–4–87–1 5–1–13–0	1–0–4–0		1–0–9–0	
v. Central Zone (Indore) 22–24 January 1982		9–2–39–1		13.2–4–57–1		21–5–94–3	1–0–10–0	24–5–74–1
Sixth Test Match (Kanpur) 30 January– 4 February 1982	23–5–75–3	25–6–67–1		14–2–67–1		32–7–81–0	2–1–5–0	
v. President's XI (Kandy) 9–11 February 1982			21–4–70–2 5–0–24–1	7–1–26–0 7–1–18–0		18–3–81–1 11–2–48–3		18–4–45–2 7–2–17–1
Test Match (Colombo) 17–21 February 1982	19–7–46–2 9–3–24–1	12.5–1–28–3 12–1–37–0	13–4–44–0			19–3–55–0 25–9–33–6		
	242.1–62– 687–24 av. 28.62	317.2–65– 928–25 av. 37.12	183.4–40– 601–15 av. 40.06	210.2–29– 767–15 av. 51.13	11–1– 40–1 av. 40.00	380.1–96– 1063–42 av. 25.30	29–2– 121–2 av. 60.50	214–44– 665–20 av. 33.25

A. C. J. Richards 2–1–5–0   C. J. Tavare 2–0–7–0   D. I. Gower 1–0–1–0   C. D. I. Gower 1–0–1–1
D. I. Gower 3–2–4–0   B. R. W. Taylor 2–0–6–0   C. J. Tavare 2–0–11–0

Robin Marlar, *Secretary of the Cricket Writers' Society, former captain of Sussex and forthright cricket correspondent of* The Sunday Times, *reviews England's sad tour of India and Sri Lanka.*

There is no adversary more dangerous than the one whose quality you underestimate. That was England's mistake in India. After being knocked down in the first round they could never get on terms again. From time to time Keith Fletcher's team held the initiative but their own shortcomings apart, ways were discovered to prevent their advantage being pressed home. A single result in a six match series tells its own tale. The cricket was often boring to the point of being unwatchable. The visitors marvelled at the patience of the huge crowds of Indians who seemed to take delight from the tiniest of cricketing morsels. Those who had been before noted that their numbers were in decline and were therefore worried for the future of the game in a land where two hundred million people have regularly been listening to the radio commentary.

Against that backcloth, it was clear which captain held the issue in his sights. Sunil Gavaskar, often a controversial figure in Indian cricket but never a negligible one, came into the captaincy late but mature. He is the dominant cricketer in India, has been for years, and once he had achieved a Test victory over England no one could gainsay him nor indeed did the Chairman of Selectors, Polly Umrigar, nor the President of the Board, S. K. Wankhede wish to do other than give their man his head. A scene flashes across, in the ballroom at the West End Hotel in Bangalore where Gavaskar, master of the stage and of the sponsors' invited audience alike, amusingly introduced the team he held in the hollow of his hand whilst the England honours were undertaken not by Keith Fletcher but by his manager, Raman Subba Row.

Not that a skipper should be judged by the smoothness of his speeches. In Gavaskar's case he also proved the vital run maker, stroking five hundred runs at an average of over 60, making more than forty in seven of his nine innings, whilst his twenty-five on the opening morning of the Madras Test where England hoped to deploy their seamers on a helpful pitch was worth many a hundred in easier conditions. That innings opened the way for Viswanath's double century which effectively condemned that match to a draw, the fifth, just as Gavaskar's own century at Bangalore and Vishy's gallant knock on the steps of the selectors' scaffold at Delhi, had secured the draws in the second and third. Endless delays, bad light and a slow pitch allowed India to get off the hook in Calcutta, the fourth, and the last Test, at Kanpur the textile city in central India, was as wet and miserable as any that have been played on Manchester's Old Trafford.

The England players claimed, vociferously at times, that they were having a hard time of it. To some extent they were. They felt that the itinerary that had been agreed for them had them travelling up and down India like a fever patient. Finishing the tour at Kanpur instead of Bombay was certainly odd, and a break with tradition, but it helped the Indian coffers. More revealing was the siting of the one-day matches at places like Cuttack. There was a reason for this, a debt paid to an old and by then deceased Board colleague but one could not help feeling that the reason the large centres were avoided for the limited-over games was because of the dire contrast in entertainment value: the last minute finish against the five day yawn.

The selection of the England party showed the Indians that Fletcher, who was the prime mover behind the concentration on pace bowling, was going to have scant regard for niceties like overrate. Thus India, taking a message from former captain Bishen Bedi, resolved to continue to slow the game down even with their spinners. So successful were they that at one stage a figure of 9 overs an hour was achieved by Doshi and Shastri. This was never checked by the umpires and became such a scandal that even some of the more intelligent of the England side were beginning to believe that the legislators must do something quickly to speed up the conduct of the game.

The genesis of a growing sense of outrage about the tour lay in a complete loss of confidence in Indian umpiring during the Bombay Test. England's preparations for this first important encounter had gone so well but they had never seen the front line Indian bowlers: and the wicket at the newish Wankhede Stadium had an uneven bounce and more pace than was to be the case as the Indians decided to slow them all down by late watering during the rest of the series – much to Kapil Dev's annoyance. However it was this fine all-rounder, the player most underestimated by an England side apparently unable to reconcile his subsequent record-breaking feats with the player they had seen in England in 1979, who began to swing that game. Certainly the Indians were in credit when it came to totting up all the bad umpiring decisions in that match. India, too, were at fault in continuing their policy of selecting umpires on the basis of Buggins' turn when it was clear that Buggins was incompetent. All this, however, paled into insignificance besides the incompetence of the England batsmen, including Fletcher, who claim to be seasoned professionals and yet one after another were dismissed playing the sweep shot on a dodgy wicket against umpires with trigger happy fingers. In the history of English cricket I doubt if there was a more inept, more wrongheaded approach to an important match than this.

By seeking to plant the blame for their comeuppance anywhere but in their own shortcomings, at least initially, this England team forfeited respect. When they did get a grip of themselves they were clearly thwarted time and time again by an Indian team determined to hang on grimly to their Koh-in-Noor victory: the Indians defended a single goal by packing their goalmouth for months on end. Fletcher apparently did not see the need to communicate with Gavaskar on this, pleading the longer term interest of the game. Such pleas would fall on deaf ears, thought the England camp. It was worth a try.

Was anything gained? Gooch played the best innings for England – at Madras – but we now know that he was disliking it all so much that he resolved to go to South Africa. Boycott also hated the tour and bowed out of Test cricket for ever after a bizarre request for a game of golf following the record breaking century at Delhi which put him on top of England's Test batsmen in the aggregate list. There was comfort in the more disciplined approach of both Botham and Gower to their batting: they dug England out of the only holes that threatened after Bombay. The bowlers tried their utmost but they were wrong for the wickets: Underwood and Emburey were outbowled by their opponents. Apart from winding up Gavaskar and Viswanath, the Indian batting looked to be more solid, and in greater depth especially against fast bowling. Helmets have helped their resolution. Like England, India are also finding it hard to develop young players into stars at Test level. But Shastri at least looks as if he will become a taller, more elegant version of Vinoo Mankad. There can be no higher praise or aspiration than that.

When all is said and done what mattered to the Indians was the victory. Nationally, they were exultant winners. It is some comfort to know that they still regard England as the team they most want to beat.

Opposite: *John Wright – 'now the bold, graceful attacker'.*

SECTION D
The New Zealand Season

The New Zealand Season

The recent success of the New Zealand Test team had raised interest in cricket in the country to a level rarely experienced before and the New Zealand public was able to look forward to a season when the Test stars would be playing in the Shell competitions and when the Australians would arrive for a Test series at the end of the season.

The stability of the Test side under Howarth's leadership and the mature skills of such as Hadlee, Wright and Edgar had captured public imagination. New Zealand had beaten West Indies and India in the last two home series and had reached the final of the Benson and Hedges World Series on their last tour to Australia. These successes had lifted the quality of the domestic game and young players like Cooper, Bruce Blair and Robertson were pushing their way to the top and jostling established Test players for places.

There were pre-season movements between associations. John Wiltshire, captain of Auckland in 1981, had moved to Central Districts while Lance Cairns had moved to Northern Districts, his third provincial side. Brendon Bracewell, once hailed as New Zealand's fast bowling hope and still only 22, was to play for Otago.

Wellington gained the services of the Central Districts' wicket-keeper Ervin McSweeney and they had also enlisted a Jamaican fast bowler, Junior Williams. Wellington looked a strong side on paper, but in recent years they had consistently failed to realise their potential. Auckland, double winners in 1981, were still considered to be favourites with their solid batting and all-round bowling strength, but none could dismiss the challenge of Northern Districts lightly.

Auckland began the defence of their title in most convincing fashion. Their all-round bowling strength proved too much for Central Districts for whom Anderson and Edwards alone showed the necessary determination and solid batting down the order gave the home side an advantage they never relinquished.

Wellington gave early indication that they would be challengers with a fine win over Canterbury who once more relied very heavily on Richard Hadlee. Chatfield sent back Dempsey and Brown with only 5 scored and wickets continued to fall so that when Hadlee came to the wicket Canterbury were 121 for 6. He hit lustily, first in partnership with skipper Cran Bull, then receiving support from Steve Bateman so that his side reached some respectability. In harness with Steve McNally, he had Wellington stumbling at 137 for 5, but Coney stood firm and there was some splendid batting by the late order with McSweeney hitting a career best on his Wellington debut. Wellington had a lead of 123, the last three wickets having added 167. Chatfield and the impressive Gray wore down Canterbury's opposition and when Wellington threatened to falter Morrison and Ormiston steered them to victory.

Otago never really recovered from John Wright's century and the first innings lead that they surrendered was the margin by which they failed to win the match. It was the Otago spinners, John Bracewell and Stephen Boock, who caused Northern most discomfort, but there was a career best for the visitors' David White.

Shell Trophy
27, 28 and 29 December 1981
at Molyneux Park, Alexandra

Northern Districts 286 (J. G. Wright 124, G. P. Howarth 58, J. G. Bracewell 6 for 91) and 227 (B. L. Cairns 58, S. L. Boock 6 for 95)
Otago 228 for 9 (B. R. Blair 82, D. J. White 6 for 45) and 226 for 6 (B. R. Blair 52, C. W. Dickeson 5 for 59)

Match drawn
Northern Districts 7 pts, Otago 6 pts

at Basin Reserve, Wellington

Canterbury 233 (R. J. Hadlee 61 not out, E. J. Chatfield 4 for 67) and 248 (D. A. Dempsey 63, E. J. Chatfield 4 for 76, E. J. Gray 4 for 92)
Wellington 356 (E. B. McSweeney 96 not out, R. W. Ormiston 80, J. V. Coney 72, R. J. Hadlee 5 for 81, S. R. McNally 4 for 57) and 129 for 4

Wellington won by 6 wickets
Wellington 20 pts, Canterbury 4 pts

at Eden Park, Auckland

Central Districts 191 (R. W. Anderson 73, L. W. Stott 4 for 57) and 181 (G. N. Edwards 57, M. C. Snedden 4 for 28, J. M. McIntyre 4 for 63)
Auckland 288 (G. K. Robertson 4 for 57, D. R. O'Sullivan 4 for 88) and 85 for 2

Auckland won by 8 wickets
Auckland 18 pts, Central Districts 3 pts

Shell Cup
30 December 1981
at Molyneux Park, Alexandra

Otago 132
Northern Districts 134 for 5

Northern Districts won by 5 wickets

at Basin Reserve, Wellington

Canterbury 189 for 8
Wellington 192 for 3 (B. A. Edgar 96)

Wellington won by 7 wickets

at Eden Park, Auckland

Auckland 185 (J. F. Reid 53, D. C. Aberhart 4 for 32)
Central Districts 188 for 7

Central Districts won by 7 wickets

Central Districts gained revenge on Auckland when they defeated the holders in a tense struggle at Eden Park. Dennis Aberhart was the most successful of the Central bowlers, sending down seven maidens in his ten overs and winning the man-of-the-match award, but it was John Wiltshire who kept cool and took Central to victory with three overs to spare when there were signs of panic. Steve Gill's quick 25 had a great influence on the result for it was 143 for 6 when he went in and 37 invaluable runs were added with Wiltshire.

Bruce Edgar savaged Canterbury to give Wellington a

Bruce Edgar ... 'was quite obviously the man of the season'.

Shell Trophy

1, 2 and 3 January 1982

at Carisbrook, Dunedin

Auckland 287 for 6 (J. F. Reid 95, M. D. Crowe 72, B. Abernethy 4 for 85)
Otago 85 (A. T. R. Hellaby 4 for 17, G. B. Troup 4 for 17) and 214 for 7 (W. K. Lees 63)
Match drawn
Auckland 7 pts, Otago 2 pts

at Lancaster Park, Christchurch

Northern Districts 132 (R. J. Hadlee 5 for 49) and 202 (G. P. Howarth 53)
Canterbury 109 (B. L. Cairns 5 for 32) and 164 (R. J. Hadlee 68, B. L. Cairns 4 for 39)
Northern Districts won by 61 runs
Northern Districts 16 pts, Canterbury 4 pts

at Basin Reserve, Wellington

Central Districts 215 (E. J. Chatfield 4 for 69) and 168 (E. J. Chatfield 5 for 29)
Wellington 398 (E. J. Gray 126, R. W. Ormiston 93, B. A. Edgar 64, D. C. Aberhart 4 for 94)
Wellington won by an innings and 15 runs
Wellington 19 pts, Central Districts 4 pts

With their second win in two games Wellington planted themselves firmly at the top of the table, aided by Auckland's failure to beat Otago.

There was some remarkable cricket in the game at Basin Reserve and the confidence with which Wellington had begun the season was confirmed. Only some solid middle order batting from Wiltshire and Hodgson enabled Central Districts to reach 215, but, in spite of a sparkling 64 from Bruce Edgar, Wellington lost 5 wickets for 120. It was then that Ross Ormiston, whose time with Central Districts had not been very productive in terms of runs scored, joined Evan Gray. Gray, an all-rounder intent on attracting the notice of the Test selectors, reached his maiden century and Ormiston a career best 93. They added 226 for the sixth wicket, a sixth wicket stand bettered in New Zealand only by that of Victor Trumper and Clem Hill in 1905. The record stand knocked the heart out of Central, Ormiston's first three innings of the season for Wellington had produced only 39 runs less than he scored in three seasons with Central Districts, and they succumbed by an innings.

Tom Hellaby's medium pace bowling gave him a career best and helped rout Otago. He conceded only 30 runs in 29 overs when they followed-on, but it was dogged batting which gained the home side a draw. Reid and Crowe put on 134 for Auckland's third wicket on the opening day.

Canterbury suffered their second defeat of the season. On a spiteful wicket John Parker batted with great resolution to score 41 not out. When Cairns and Carrington destroyed Canterbury the value of Parker's innings became apparent. Howarth played a captain's innings at the second attempt and although the magnificent Hadlee roused Canterbury from the depths of 103 for 9 in a last wicket stand of 61 with Mackle, the result was never in doubt.

Shell Cup

4 January 1982

at Rangiora

Northern Districts 247 (B. L. Cairns 95, A. D. G. Roberts 51)
Canterbury 199
Northern Districts won by 48 runs

at Oamaru

Otago 162 (L. W. Stott 5 for 44)
Auckland 163 for 4 (M. D. Crowe 79 not out, A. T. R. Hellaby 68 not out)
Auckland won by 6 wickets

at Basin Reserve, Wellington

Wellington 271 for 4 (B. A. Edgar 97, J. F. M. Morrison 81, J. V. Coney 57)
Central Districts 205 (J. R. Wiltshire 78)
Wellington won by 66 runs

The triumph of Wellington continued with a fine display of batting at Basin Reserve. Vance was caught behind off Robertson with the score at 6 after which there were stands of 96 between Edgar and Coney, and 142 between Edgar and Morrison. Central lost too many wickets in pursuit of quick runs and were all out with five overs and one ball of their fifty still remaining.

Tom Hellaby emphasised his all-round ability when he helped Martin Crowe to give Auckland victory when they threatened to stutter. Warren Stott's medium pace had given Auckland the chance of a comfortable win.

A typically violent assault on the bowling by Lance Cairns, obviously enjoying his move from Otago to Northern Districts, completed the Canterbury misery of having lost all of their four games, two in the Cup and two in the Trophy.

Shell Trophy

6, 7 and 8 January 1982

at Lancaster Park, Christchurch

Canterbury 285 and 180 for 6 dec
Auckland 245 for 7 dec (A. J. Hunt 58) and 77 for 8 (R. J. Hadlee 6 for 26)
Match drawn
Canterbury 6 pts, Auckland 6 pts

at Harry Barker Reserve, Gisborne
Northern Districts 354 for 5 dec (J. G. Wright 90, J. M. Parker 80 not out, M. J. E. Wright 62, A. D. G. Roberts 59) and 213 for 5 dec (A. D. G. Roberts 65 not out)
Wellington 263 for 9 (B. A. Edgar 141 not out, R. H. Vance 50, C. W. Dickeson 4 for 56) and 195 for 2 (J. V. Coney 76 not out)
Match drawn
Northern Districts 9 pts, Wellington 5 pts

at McLean Park, Napier
Otago 224 (I. A. Rutherford 92, D. C. Aberhart 5 for 61) and 205 for 6 dec (W. K. Lees 66 not out, B. Abernethy 57 not out)
Central Districts 157 (B. P. Bracewell 4 for 41) and 191 for 8 (I. D. S. Smith 63, S. Gill 60, J. G. Bracewell 4 for 51)
Match drawn
Otago 6 pts, Central Districts 5 pts

Auckland's draw with Canterbury was their 23rd first-class game without defeat so beating their own record of 22 matches set up between 1943 and 1944. In the end, however, they drew the game at Lancaster Park by the skin of their teeth. Canterbury took a first innings lead of 40 and declared setting Auckland to make 221 to win. From the moment that Franklin was caught by substitute Hart off Richard Hadlee for a duck Auckland were always struggling. Hadlee's performances seem to demand one superlative after another. In twenty-overs of hostile bowling he totally demoralised Auckland who, hanging on at 77 for 8, were thankful for a draw.

Wellington were thwarted for the first time in a high scoring game at Gisborne. Mike and John Wright began with a stand of 139 and this set the tone of the match. Wellington were 1 for 2, but Bruce Edgar, batting at number four, was again in superb form and he and Vance added 122. Runs were never difficult to score and a draw became an obvious conclusion early on the last day.

Central Districts achieved a draw at Napier through the efforts of Smith and Steve Gill. Chasing a target of 273, Central were 61 for 6 when Gill joined the Test wicketkeeper. They added 123 and saved the day. Gill had also bowled impressively and was voted man-of-the-match.

Shell Cup

9 January 1982

at Harry Barker Reserve, Gisborne
Wellington 283 for 3 (B. A. Edgar 147 not out, R. H. Vance 74)
Northern Districts 278 for 9 (A. D. G. Roberts 68, G. P. Howarth 54)
Wellington won by 5 runs

at Lancaster Park, Christchurch
Auckland 159
Canterbury 160 for 2 (D. A. Dempsey 57)
Canterbury won by 8 wickets

at McLean Park, Napier
Central Districts 163
Otago 142
Central Districts won by 21 runs

Wellington's hundred percent record was maintained in the Shell Cup in a marvellous game at Gisborne. Edgar, in magnificent form, and Vance put on 191 for Wellington's first wicket, and Northern Districts faced the immense task of making 284 in 50 overs. 54 for 3 was not an impressive start, but Geoff Howarth and Andrew Roberts added 76 and all the later order batsmen added useful scores. The ninth wicket went down at 262, but Scott and Carrington scampered 16 more runs, a brave effort, but it left them 6 short of victory.

Denied a win in the Trophy match, Canterbury overwhelmed Auckland in the one-day game, reaching their target with just over 17 overs to spare.

In a low scoring game at Napier, Otago never batted with enough stability to snatch a win when needing only 164 for victory.

Shell Cup

11 January

at Basin Reserve, Wellington
Otago 137
Wellington 141 for 2 (B. A. Edgar 106 not out)
Wellington won by 8 wickets

at Eden Park, Auckland
Auckland 233 for 6 (T. J. Franklin 102, J. F. Reid 62)
Northern Districts 230 for 8 (G. P. Howarth 81)
Auckland won by 3 runs

Wellington assured themselves of a place in the Shell Cup Final when they annihilated Otago at Basin Reserve. Led by West Indian Junior Williams the Wellington bowlers dismissed bottom of the table Otago in 49.2 overs. Edgar and Vance began Wellington's reply. The first wicket realised 41 of which Vance scored 3, the second wicket added 17 with Coney failing to score and the unfinished third wicket put on 83 of which Gray contributed 16. Bruce Edgar hit 106 not out in 40.2 overs of regal stroke play. Only one other batsman in the match, Osborne, reached twenty. This meant that Edgar's scores in the four cup games were 96, 97, 147 not out and 106 not out, and he won the man-of-the-match award in each of the four games. His form in the first-class matches was equally impressive.

For the second time in three days Northern Districts were beaten by a very narrow margin. A second wicket stand of 143 between John Reid and Trevor Franklin was the backbone of the Auckland innings. Northern started badly in reply, but Howarth batted splendidly in a bid to give his side victory, and when he was caught and bowled by Stott the rest of the batsmen could not quite manage to muster the runs required.

Richard Hadlee – he bore a tremendous load for New Zealand and for Canterbury.

Shell Trophy

11, 12 and 13 January 1982

at Fitzherbert Park, Palmerston North

Central Districts 241 (G. J. Langridge 76, G. C. Bateman 5 for 60) and 187 (R. W. Anderson 80, R. J. Hadlee 6 for 40)
Canterbury 225 (R. J. Hadlee 83 not out, D. W. Stead 56, M. F. Gill 6 for 56) and 205 for 3 (P. E. McEwan 103 not out, P. J. Rattray 82)

Canterbury won by 7 wickets
Canterbury 18 pts, Central Districts 6 pts

12, 13 and 14 January

at Eden Park, Auckland

Auckland 249 (M. D. Crowe 99, J. F. Reid 58, M. S. Carrington 4 for 57, S. R. Gillespie 4 for 64) and 367 for 6 dec (P. N. Webb 116, J. F. Reid 82, M. D. Crowe 60, A. E. W. Parsons 53 not out)
Northern Districts 335 (J. G. Wright 113, L. W. Stott 5 for 113) and 282 for 5 (J. G. Wright 105, B. G. Cooper 56)

Northern Districts won by 5 wickets
Northern Districts 20 pts, Auckland 6 pts

at Basin Reserve, Wellington

Otago 274 (W. L. Blair 132, B. W. Cederwall 4 for 65) and 246 for 9 dec (G. Dawson 52, I. A. Rutherford 51)
Wellington 253 (S. L. Boock 4 for 28) and 269 for 6 (E. B. McSweeney 60 not out, B. A. Edgar 58)

Wellington won by 4 wickets
Wellington 19 pts, Otago 7 pts

Auckland's unbeaten run came to an end when Northern Districts scored at nearly six an over to reach the target of 282 which Reid had set them. Reid and Crowe added 142 for the third wicket after both openers had gone for 1, but the hero of the match was John Wright with a century in each innings. His second century assured Northern of the victory which kept them in touch with the leaders, Wellington. Peter Webb scored the fourth hundred of his career when he and John Reid added 147 for the second wicket in Auckland's second innings. Mark Carrington showed his promise with some fierce fast bowling which brought him the best return of his brief career.

Canterbury at last gained reward for the Herculean efforts of Richard Hadlee. He scored 83 of the last 105 as Canterbury recovered from 120 for 6 to 225 all out, a deficit of 16. Then he tore Central Districts apart with another magnificent piece of fast bowling. His 6 for 40 left Canterbury needing 204 to win and this was achieved when Rattray and McEwan took the score from 8 for 2 to 182, their stand of 174 was a Canterbury record.

Without a win in either competition, Otago ran Wellington closer than might have been expected. They led by 21 on the first innings thanks to a fine innings by Wayne Blair and the slow left-arm of Stephen Boock, the forgotten man of New Zealand cricket. Wellington were set 268 to win at more than five an over, but resolute batting down the order and a great flourish by Ervin McSweeney brought victory for the third time in four Trophy matches and kept them eleven points ahead of Northern Districts at the top of the table.

Shell Cup

14 January 1982

at Wanganui

Central Districts 244 for 8 (J. G. Wiltshire 56)
Canterbury 247 for 4 (P. J. Rattray 66, D. A. Dempsey 64, R. J. Hadlee 63)

Canterbury won by 6 wickets

16 January 1982

at Dunedin

Otago 177 for 9 (I. A. Rutherford 53)
Canterbury 182 for 5

Canterbury won by 5 wickets

at Eden Park, Auckland

Wellington 204 for 8 (R. H. Vance 106)
Auckland 191 (M. D. Crowe 54, G. Wheeler 4 for 42)

Wellington won by 13 runs

at Seddon Park, Hamilton
Northern Districts 120 (R. A. Pierce 4 for 26)
Central Districts 121 for 1 (R. W. Anderson 66 not out)
Central Districts won by 9 wickets

By beating Central Districts, Canterbury needed only a win over Otago in their last match to qualify to meet Wellington in the final of the Shell Cup. Their task of scoring 245 in 50 overs to beat Central did not seem an easy one, but David Dempsey gave them a bubbling start with 64 out of 109 for the first wicket. Peter Rattray and Richard Hadlee, who batted at number four, carried on the attack and Canterbury won with three overs to spare.

Hadlee was again to the fore with 42 not out and ten economic overs in the win over Otago.

Wellington maintained their hundred percent record and Vance took the man-of-the-match award at Eden Park while a blistering innings by Bob Anderson gave Central Districts victory with ten overs to spare at Hamilton where Northern Districts batted well below form.

Qualifying table

	P	W	L	Pts
Wellington	5	5	—	10
Canterbury	5	3	2	6
Central Districts	5	3	2	6
Northern Districts	5	2	3	4
Auckland	5	2	3	4
Otago	5	—	5	0

Shell Trophy

17, 18 and 19 January 1982

at Carisbrook, Dunedin
Canterbury 243 (R. T. Latham 95, P. W. Hills 4 for 71) and 121 (P. E. McEwan 52, J. G. Bracewell 7 for 9)
Otago 164 (J. G. Bracewell 51, R. J. Hadlee 4 for 32) and 202 for 3 (B. R. Blair 98 not out, R. N. Hoskin 62 not out)
Otago won by 7 wickets
Otago 17 pts, Canterbury 6 pts

at The Domain, Tauranga
Northern Districts 241 (J. M. Parker 117, D. Stirling 6 for 75) and 278 for 6 dec (J. M. Parker 102 not out, A. D. G. Roberts 56)
Central Districts 228 (I. D. S. Smith 74, M. Jamieson 59, B. L. Cairns 5 for 48) and 192
Northern Districts won by 99 runs
Northern Districts 16 pts, Central Districts 6 pts

at Eden Park, Auckland
Wellington 277 (F. J. Gray 114, F. B. McSweeney 68, M. C. Snedden 4 for 58, I. T. Donnelly 4 for 70) and 204 for 7 dec (J. F. M. Morrison 83)
Auckland 157 (E. J. Chatfield 4 for 30) and 178 (A. E. W. Parsons 53, E. J. Gray 4 for 58)
Wellington won by 146 runs
Wellington 19 pts, Auckland 5 pts

John Morrison – his astute leadership was a vital factor in Wellington's double success.

In one of the most remarkable games in New Zealand cricket history, Otago won their first match of the season when they beat Canterbury by 7 wickets at Dunedin. A career best innings from Rodney Latham and the usual contribution with the ball from Richard Hadlee had given Canterbury a first innings advantage of 77. At 117 for 3, Canterbury stood poised to reach a big second innings score and clinch the game. John Bracewell and Stephen Boock had just joined the Otago attack and an hour later Canterbury were all out, 7 wickets had fallen for the addition of 4 runs. Bracewell's off-spin had returned the figures of 10.1 overs, 6 maidens, 9 runs, 7 wickets – the best analysis ever returned in New Zealand cricket for a bowler taking seven or more wickets. Boock had taken 1 for 6 in 8 overs, 6 of them maidens. Dizzy at this unexpected success, Otago set about the task of scoring 202 to win. They lost 3 for 75, but Bruce Blair and Richard Hoskin had the scent of victory and keeping Hadlee at bay, they attacked the other bowlers to give Otago their first success of the season in either competition, and John Bracewell's name was written indelibly in the record books.

A century in each innings by John Parker and some good bowling from Lance Cairns gave Northern Districts victory over Central Districts for whom Derek Stirling took a career best and caught the eye of the selectors who were choosing the Rest side to play New Zealand. Northern's win kept them in contact with Wellington at the top, but only just.

Wellington made it four wins in five games when they trounced Auckland. Another century by Evan Gray rescued Wellington from 73 for 6. He and McSweeney, a most valuable acquisition, added 142. Chatfield and Maguiness bowled Wellington to a 120 run lead and some quick runs from Gray and astute skipper Morrison put the game out of Auckland's reach. Gray completed a fine match with 4 for 58 in 27 overs and Wellington had one hand on the Shell Trophy.

Shell Trophy
23, 24 and 25 January 1982
at Recreation Ground, Lower Hutt

Wellington 251 for 8 dec (E. J. Gray 71 not out) and 262 (J. F. M. Morrison 56, R. H. Vance 52, M. S. Carrington 5 for 69)
Northern Districts 200 (J. M. Parker 57 not out, E. J. Chatfield 5 for 42, J. Williams 4 for 39) and 159 (J. G. Wright 88, J. Williams 4 for 26)

Wellington won by 154 runs
Wellington 19 pts, Northern Districts 5 pts

at Queens Park, Invercargill

Otago 161 for 7 (R. N. Hoskin 53, D. C. Aberhart 5 for 46)
v. **Central Districts**

Match abandoned as a draw
Otago 6 pts, Central Districts 6 pts

at Eden Park, Auckland

Canterbury 281 (D. J. Boyle 58, P. E. McEwan 55, G. B. Troup 4 for 63) and 163 for 4 dec (D. W. Stead 50)
Auckland 184 (A. J. Hunt 53, R. J. Hadlee 4 for 27) and 262 for 7 (J. F. Reid 72, G. C. Bateman 4 for 49)

Auckland won by 3 wickets
Auckland 17 pts, Canterbury 6 pts

Wellington won the Shell Trophy when they crushed nearest rivals Northern Districts on a wicket which gave their bowlers some assistance. It was a thoroughly deserved triumph for a side which had played with confidence and authority from the beginning of the season. Gray and Morrison were once more in good form with the bat and Junior Williams had a career best bowling performance in the first innings which he bettered in the second as only John Wright, in an accomplished performance on a wearing wicket, could cope with the seam attack.

Rain ruined the game at Invercargill, but at Eden Park, Auckland gained a splendid victory after looking well beaten for most of the match. Solid batting throughout the order saw Canterbury to 281 and Hadlee and Glenn Bateman bowled them to a 97 run first innings lead. Cran Bull felt confident enough to declare his second innings and set Auckland a target of 261. Parsons fell to Bateman at 2, but Franklin and Reid added 103 for the second wicket.

Reid and Crowe saw the total past 150, but Bateman produced a good spell which had Auckland nervous at 197 for 6. As he had done in the first innings when he scored 46 not out, Martin Snedden now batted with great good sense and snatched victory for Auckland with an innings of 49 not out.

Shell Trophy
29, 30 and 31 January 1982
at Lancaster Park, Christchurch

Canterbury 261 (D. W. Stead 88, E. J. Chatfield 4 for 74) and 158 (R. T. Latham 72 not out, S. J. Maguiness 4 for 42)
Wellington 123 (R. J. Hadlee 5 for 35) and 297 for 4 (J. F. M. Morrison 100 not out, B. A. Edgar 65, R. W. Ormiston 59 not out)

Wellington won by 6 wickets
Wellington 16 pts, Canterbury 7 pts

30 and 31 January 1982
at Seddon Park, Hamilton

Otago 114 (M. S. Carrington 4 for 43) and 82 (B. L. Cairns 6 for 19)
Northern Districts 194 (A. D. G. Roberts 59, S. L. Boock 4 for 44) and 7 for 0

Northern Districts won by 10 wickets
Northern Districts 17 pts, Otago 4 pts

30, 31 January and 1 February 1982
at Pukekura Park, New Plymouth

Central Districts 194 (J. R. Wiltshire 73, R. A. Pierce 52) and 200
Auckland 342 for 8 (M. D. Crowe 150, T. J. Franklin 57, D. R. O'Sullivan 4 for 118) and 53 for 3

Auckland won by 7 wickets
Auckland 20 pts, Central Districts 4 pts

Wellington ended the season in glorious style. Their sixth win in seven matches was achieved in the heroic manner of worthy champions. They trailed Canterbury by 138 runs on the first innings and in spite of Chatfield and Maguiness dismissing Canterbury for 158 at the second attempt, they looked a well beaten side. Edgar scored 65 and was third out at 104. Coney went at 163 and Morrison was then joined by Ormiston. They added 134 to take Wellington to a most improbable victory. Morrison's first hundred of the season was a fitting climax to the season for one whose leadership had done so much to bring about the Wellington triumph.

Otago's miserable season was underlined when they were beaten in two days at Seddon Park. Their second innings score of 82 was the lowest Trophy score of the season. It was brought about by the bowling of Lance Cairns, but the batting lacked all substance.

Auckland, on the other hand, finished with a marvellous

flourish. Martin Crowe hit his maiden century in first-class cricket and reached 102 before lunch on the second day. His hundred was the fastest of the season and was reached off 94 balls.

Shell Trophy Final Table
(1981 positions in brackets)

	P	W	L	D	Bonus bat	Bonus bowl	Pts
Wellington (4)	7	6	—	1	19	26	116
Northern Districts (6)	7	4	1	2	17	27	92
Auckland (1)	7	3	2	2	15	28	78
Canterbury (2)	7	1	5	1	15	24	51
Otago (5)	7	1	2	4	9	22	42
Central Districts (3)	7	—	5	2	9	22	30

(Wellington, Auckland, Otago and Central Districts each had one point deducted for slow over rate.)

Shell Cup Final

6 February 1982

at Lancaster Park, Christchurch

Canterbury 204 for 7 (R. Carter 66)
Wellington 205 for 2 (B. A. Edgar 79 not out, R. H. Vance 69)

Wellington won by 8 wickets

It was right and proper that Wellington should win the Shell Cup Final for they had swept all before them throughout the competition. They won with ease, eight wickets and 4.1 overs still remaining.

Canterbury had problems before the match. David Dempsey, who had done well in the early rounds of the Shell Cup, had been dropped from the Shell Trophy side because of lack of form. Recalled to the side for the Cup Final, he made some scathing remarks in public about inconsistency of selection and was omitted from the team. Sadly, his cricketing future remains uncertain. His place was taken by the Northamptonshire all-rounder Bob Carter who had a fine match, scoring 66 and taking the wickets of Vance and Coney.

Bob Vance was in punishing form as he and Edgar put on 120 for the first wicket and he took the man-of-the-match award.

8, 9 and 10 February 1982

at Basin Reserve, Wellington

New Zealand 422 (B. A. Edgar 143, P. N. Webb 70, J. F. Reid 67, M. S. Carrington 4 for 90)
The Rest 80 and 182 (E. J. Gray 61)

New Zealand won by an innings and 160 runs

This representative 'trial' match proved a very one-sided affair with Bruce Edgar again in dominant form. Mark Carrington, a raw and strong young fast bowler, took 4 for 90 in 29 overs and was selected as New Zealand's young cricketer to go to Lord's and gain the benefits from being on the ground staff for 1982 season.

When the Australian team to tour New Zealand was announced it was greeted with much criticism. It was hard to defend the inclusion of Bright ahead of Sleep or Holland, difficult to understand why Pascoe was chosen instead of Lawson and why no place could be found for Boon, the promising young Tasmanian.

Whatever the criticisms set against the Australian side, they had beaten Pakistan with some conviction and drawn a marvellous series with the great West Indian side. New Zealand cricket was at its highest peak of achievement and interest, but Australia would be no easy opposition. They never are.

First One-Day International

That interest in cricket in New Zealand was at its highest was emphasised when a record crowd saw the first match of the Australian tour and, in spite of a fine hundred from Greg Chappell, they were able to cheer a convincing New Zealand victory.

Once more New Zealand's success was built upon the solid foundation of excellent team work with every player contributing. Bruce Edgar was top scorer, but every wicket produced a sound partnership.

Jeremy Coney hitting for four in the one-day international at Eden Park, his best innings in a generally disappointing series for the tall right-hander.

Australia started badly when Wood was needlessly run out and Laird fell to Cairns. Hadlee bowled with great economy and after the left-arm medium pace of Gary Troup had accounted for Dyson, Chappell could find no one to stay with him long enough to make a serious challenge and the New Zealand bowling quickly exposed the length of the Australian tail.

Left: *For whom the bail falls: Bruce Edgar, the New Zealand opening batsman, looking anywhere but at the fallen leg bail – the first incident of the first one-day international, and Greg Chappell's cool acceptance of the umpires' not out decision had much to do with the smooth course of the tour.*

Below: *Umpire John Hastie surrounded by Australians after the Edgar-bail incident at Eden Park. Rod Marsh is communing with himself but Graeme Wood, Terry Alderman (the bowler) and Allan Border seem unconcerned.*

Opposite: *Greg Chappell made his own rules about batting style during his superb 100 in the one-day international at Eden Park ... this time a 'flamingo' four through extra cover. Ian Smith is the keeper and Dennis Lillee the other batsman.*

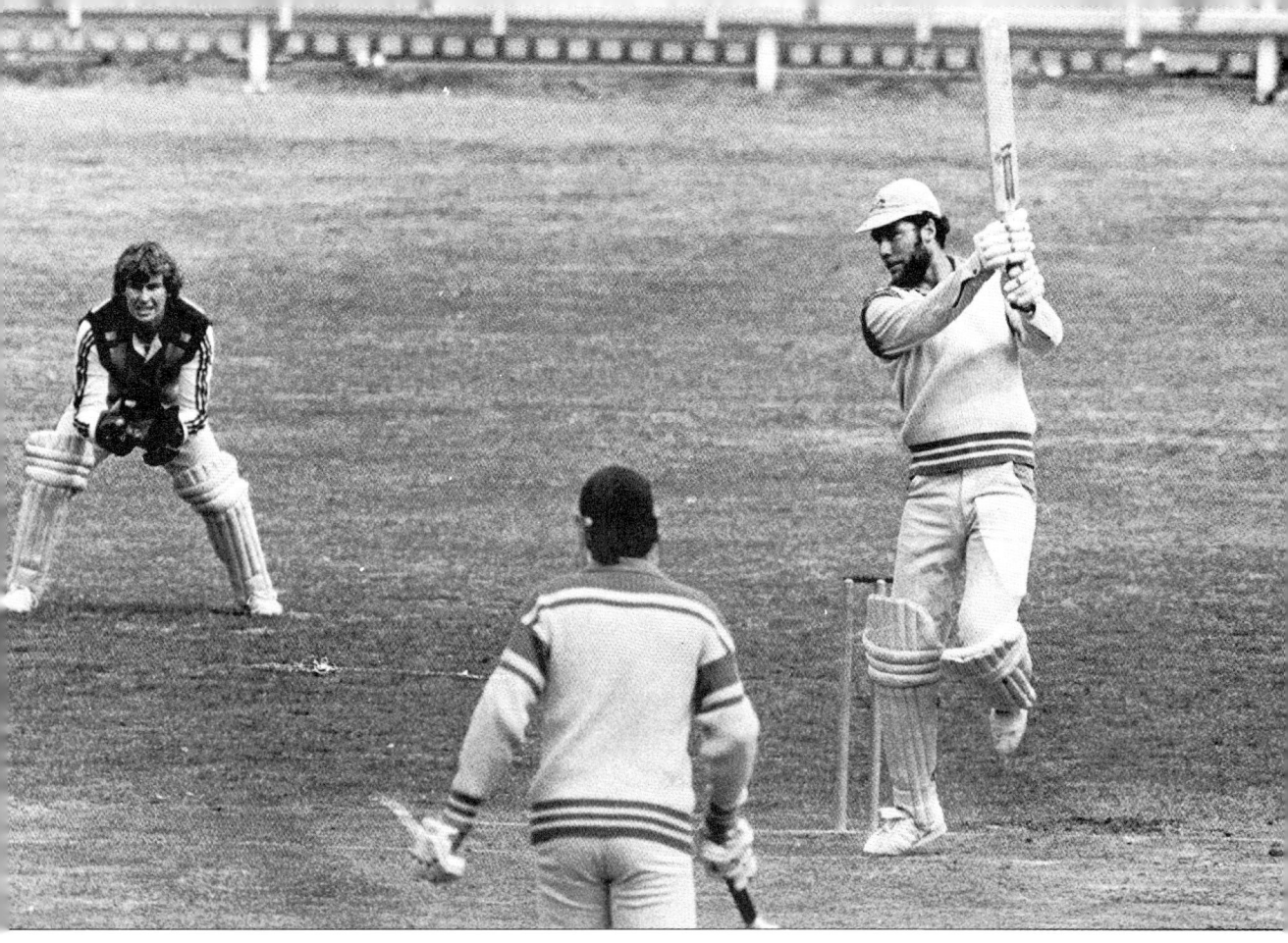

FIRST ONE-DAY INTERNATIONAL: NEW ZEALAND v. AUSTRALIA
13 February 1982 at Auckland

NEW ZEALAND

Batsman	Dismissal	Runs
J. G. Wright	run out	18
B. A. Edgar	b Pascoe	79
J. F. Reid	c Alderman, b Chappell	20
G. P. Howarth†	c Marsh, b Lillee	34
J. V. Coney	run out	45
R. J. Hadlee	b Alderman	11
B. L. Cairns	not out	18
M. D. Crowe		
M. C. Snedden		
I. D. S. Smith*		
G. B. Troup		
Extras	lb 13, w 1, nb 1	15
	(for 6 wkts)	240

Bowler	O	M	R	W
Thomson	10	2	36	—
Alderman	10	3	41	1
Pascoe	10	—	35	1
Chappell	10	—	57	1
Lillee	10	—	56	1

FALL OF WICKETS
1–28, 2–89, 3–148, 4–184, 5–210, 6–240

AUSTRALIA

Batsman	Dismissal	Runs
G. M. Wood	run out	1
B. M. Laird	c Crowe, b Cairns	11
J. Dyson	c Crowe, b Troup	32
G. S. Chappell†	c Howarth, b Troup	108
K. J. Hughes	c Crowe, b Coney	16
A. R. Border	b Crowe	6
R. W. Marsh*	b Troup	1
J. R. Thomson	c Snedden, b Troup	0
D. K. Lillee	c Wright, b Crowe	1
L. S. Pascoe	not out	2
T. M. Alderman	b Snedden	1
Extras	b 4, lb 9, nb 2	15
		194

Bowler	O	M	R	W
Cairns	10	1	31	1
Hadlee	8	3	15	—
Snedden	7.5	1	35	1
Coney	7	—	45	1
Troup	10	1	44	4
Crowe	2	—	9	2

FALL OF WICKETS
1–1, 2–21, 3–109, 4–144, 5–182, 6–187, 7–189, 8–190, 9–192

New Zealand won by 46 runs

Above: *Richard Hadlee losing his off bail in the first one-day international at Auckland.*

14 February 1982

at Hamilton

Northern Districts 260 (G. P. Howarth 72, B. Yardley 5 for 58)
Australians 236 (J. Dyson 79, B. M. Laird 63)
Northern Districts won by 24 runs

Australia suffered defeat for the second day running in a 50-over game in which neither side lasted for its full quota of overs, Northern Districts being dismissed in 46 overs and the Australians in 47.2 overs. Once more it was the consistency of the home side's batting which was their strength with skipper Geoff Howarth top scorer. He and John Wright put on 85 for the second wicket.

Wood was run out early in the Australian innings for the second day running, but Dyson and Laird then added 138 and the Australians seemed set for victory. Chappell batted at number eight, but even he could not prevent the collapse as the last seven wickets went down for 62 runs.

Second One-Day International

Another record crowd, this time of 15,000, 3,000 more than the previous best in Dunedin, saw the Australians give a truer indication of their ability when Lillee and Alderman exploited a dry pitch of uneven bounce to restrict New Zealand to 159 in 49 overs.

Below: *Rod Marsh takes time from his out-fielding to please three earnest youngsters during the one-day match against Northern Districts.*

The home side's position would have been worse but for a stand of 85 for the fifth wicket between Coney and Bruce Blair who was making his international debut.

Australia were in desperate trouble at 45 for 4, but Laird and Border won the match with an unbeaten stand of 115.

Greg Chappell giving himself acres of room in the one-day 'slog' against Northern Districts – a merry afternoon of 496 runs, and no-one really worried about a winner, in this case Northern Districts. Mike Wright is the keeper.

SECOND ONE-DAY INTERNATIONAL: NEW ZEALAND v. AUSTRALIA
17 February 1982 at Dunedin

NEW ZEALAND				AUSTRALIA			
B. A. Edgar	lbw, b Alderman	3		G. M. Wood	b Chatfield	4
J. G. Wright	b Lillee	5		B. M. Laird	not out	71
M. D. Crowe	c Hughes, b Alderman	3		J. Dyson	c Smith, b Cairns	18
G. P. Howarth†	c Chappell, b Thomson	12		G. S. Chappell†	c Howarth, b Hadlee	0
J. V. Coney	b Alderman	54		K. J. Hughes	b Hadlee	5
B. R. Blair	c Laird, b Lillee	29		A. R. Border	not out	53
R. J. Hadlee	b Lillee	7		R. W. Marsh*		
I. D. S. Smith*	not out	14		D. K. Lillee		
B. L. Cairns	c Dyson, b Pascoe	3		J. R. Thomson		
M. C. Snedden	run out	3		L. S. Pascoe		
E. J. Chatfield	not out	2		T. M. Alderman		
Extras	lb 11, w 1, nb 12	24		Extras	lb 8, nb 1	9
	(for 9 wkts)	159			(for 4 wkts)	160

	O	M	R	W		O	M	R	W
Thomson	10	1	30	1	Chatfield	10	1	30	1
Alderman	10	3	22	3	Hadlee	9	3	24	2
Lillee	10	3	24	3	Snedden	9	1	41	—
Chappell	10	1	30	1	Coney	9	1	32	—
Pascoe	9	—	29	1	Cairns	8	1	24	1

FALL OF WICKETS
1-14, 2-26, 3-27, 4-39, 5-124, 6-132, 7-136, 8-143, 9-150

FALL OF WICKETS
1-12, 2-37, 3-39, 4-45

Australia won by 6 wickets

Above: *Ian Smith (keeper) and Richard Hadlee watch John Dyson tee off a straight six from Jeremy Coney's bowling in the second one-dayer at Dunedin.*

Above right: *Lance Cairns, now a first-rate bowler at test and one-day level, all bustle and business during the one-day international at Dunedin.*

Opposite: *To the victors the spoils. Greg Chappell and Terry Alderman hold up the new Rothmans gold cup after winning the one-day international series. Alderman was Man of the Match in the deciding third match with his 5 for 17, and also won a prize for the bowler with the best strike rate.*

Third One-Day International

Put in to bat and losing John Wright to the first ball of the match, caught at slip by Terry Alderman, New Zealand never really recovered and suffered a shattering defeat which could have done their morale for the forthcoming Test series little good.

An eighth wicket stand of 34 by Hadlee and Cairns served only to prolong the innings a little, but by the time that they came together Alderman had already ensured an Australian victory with bowling of the calibre which had disturbed England the previous year. It was devastating fast medium bowling of sustained accuracy allied to late swing.

Although they lost Laird and Marsh, Australia were never seriously troubled and Chappell and Dyson won the game with ease. New Zealand's disappointment at losing the limited over series by 2–1 after their triumph in the first match was apparent, but it was the rain-soaked pitch which had been the prime cause of their undoing in this match. It was not a surface on which to have to face Lillee, Alderman, Thomson and Pascoe.

Right: *Richard Hadlee, the man of the series, bound to hit the seam in the one-day international at Wellington.*

THIRD ONE-DAY INTERNATIONAL: NEW ZEALAND v. AUSTRALIA
20 February 1982 at Wellington

NEW ZEALAND						AUSTRALIA			
J. G. Wright	c Alderman, b Thomson			0		B. M. Laird	lbw, b Hadlee		10
B. A. Edgar	b Alderman			11		R. W. Marsh*	b Cairns		3
M. D. Crowe	c Laird, b Alderman			7		J. Dyson	not out		26
G. P. Howarth†	b Alderman			7		G. S. Chappell†	not out		24
J. V. Coney	c Hughes, b Lillee			3		K. J. Hughes			
B. R. Blair	lbw, b Alderman			2		G. M. Wood			
I. D. S. Smith*	c Border, b Alderman			0		A. R. Border			
R. J. Hadlee	c Hughes, b Lillee			18		J. R. Thomson			
B. L. Cairns	c Alderman, b Pascoe			14		D. K. Lillee			
M. C. Snedden	b Lillee			1		L. S. Pascoe			
G. B. Troup	not out			2		T. M. Alderman			
Extras	lb 6, w 1, nb 2			9		Extras	lb 5, w 2, nb 5		12
				74			(for 2 wkts)		75

	O	M	R	W			O	M	R	W
Thomson	5	1	11	1		Hadlee	8.3	2	25	1
Alderman	10	2	17	5		Cairns	4	1	12	1
Lillee	10	3	14	3		Troup	6	1	23	—
Pascoe	4	1	23	1		Snedden	2	1	3	—

FALL OF WICKETS
1–0, 2–20, 3–23, 4–30, 5–32, 6–35, 7–37, 8–71, 9–71

FALL OF WICKETS
1–4, 2–28

Australia won by 8 wickets

Even Rod Marsh sometimes misses, and Allan Border and Jeff Thomson show their alarm when Marsh made a mess of a snick from John Morrison in the First Test.

22, 23 and 24 February 1982
at Napier
Australians 134 for 4 (G. M. Wood 66)
v. North Island
Match abandoned as a draw

Play was brought to a close two hours before the end of the first day and rain made no further play possible. Wood returned to form with a patient 66. Coney took the wickets of Wood and Border in seven overs for 13 runs.

First Test Match

Greg Chappell won the toss and put New Zealand in to bat on a damp pitch. Only five hours play was possible over the first four days during which New Zealand scored 127 for 2.

There was a full day's play on the last day, but by then it had ceased to matter.

The main points of interest were in the composition of the New Zealand side where Martin Crowe, who had played in the one-day internationals, won his first Test cap at the age of 19 and John Morrison, 35, was recalled to the side after an absence of six years.

THE NEW ZEALAND SEASON/117

FIRST TEST MATCH – NEW ZEALAND v. AUSTRALIA
26, 27, 28 February, 1 and 2 March 1982 at Wellington

NEW ZEALAND
FIRST INNINGS

B. A. Edgar	lbw, b Alderman	55
J. G. Wright	c Chappell, b Yardley	38
J. F. M. Morrison	b Thomson	15
G. P. Howarth†	not out	58
J. V. Coney	lbw, b Yardley	1
M. D. Crowe	run out	9
R. J. Hadlee	b Thomson	21
I. D. S. Smith*	c Chappell, b Yardley	11
B. L. Cairns	not out	19
M. C. Snedden		
E. J. Chatfield		
Extras	b 5, lb 19, w 4, nb 11	39
	(for 7 wkts dec)	266

	O	M	R	W
Thomson	26	13	35	2
Alderman	44	20	93	1
Lillee	15	5	32	—
Chappell	8	2	18	—
Yardley	23	10	49	3

FALL OF WICKETS
1–86, 2–120, 3–149, 4–162, 5–186, 6–212, 7–246

AUSTRALIA
FIRST INNINGS

G. M. Wood	b Cairns	41
B. M. Laird	not out	27
J. Dyson	not out	12
G. S. Chappell†		
K. J. Hughes		
A. R. Border		
R. W. Marsh*		
D. K. Lillee		
B. Yardley		
J. R. Thomson		
T. M. Alderman		
Extras	lb 2, nb 3	5
	(for 1 wicket)	85

	O	M	R	W
Hadlee	7	2	15	—
Snedden	8	1	24	—
Cairns	11	4	20	1
Chatfield	8	5	7	—
Crowe	4	1	14	—

FALL OF WICKET
1–65

Match drawn

Geoff Howarth trying one-stump cricket in the rain-hit First Test at Wellington. Jeff Thomson, the bowler, had chipped two stumps when he bowled John Morrison with the previous ball. Howarth survived Thomson's bowl from about 55 yards and afterwards he, Rod Marsh and Bruce Edgar got back to serious business.

4 March 1982

at Nelson

Australians 195 (J. Dyson 97, D. C. Aberhart 4 for 37)
Nelson–Marlborough 132

Australia won by 63 runs

A fine innings by John Dyson which lasted nine minutes short of three hours including a six and thirteen fours was the backbone of the Australian innings. Denis Aberhart's medium pace troubled the tourists and he was also top scorer for the combined side with 21 not out.

6, 7 and 8 March 1982

at Christchurch

President's XI 250 (J. G. Bracewell 62, V. R. Brown 52) and 338 for 8 (V. R. Brown 121 not out)
Australians 357 (G. M. Wood 93, G. S. Chappell 78, K. J. Hughes 66)

Match drawn

The Australians were able to indulge in some necessary batting practice on the second day, but the last day belonged to left-hander Vaughan Brown. The twenty-three year old enhanced his Test claims with a violent attack on the Australian spinners and reached a career best, particularly gratifying after what had been a lean season for him.

Wood was again in good form for the Australians and appeared to have recovered completely from his traumatic start to the tour.

9 March 1982

at New Plymouth

Australians 171 (A. R. Border 70)
Central Districts 172 for 9 (T. M. Alderman 4 for 21)

Central Districts won by 1 wicket

Border and Dyson alone showed any confidence with the bat and Central Districts snatched a thrilling victory.

The Second and Third Test matches are reported by DON CAMERON in his review of the season.

THE NEW ZEALAND SEASON

SECOND TEST MATCH – NEW ZEALAND v. AUSTRALIA
12, 13, 14, 15 and 16 March 1982 at Auckland

AUSTRALIA

	FIRST INNINGS		SECOND INNINGS	
B. M. Laird	c Smith, b Troup	38	(2) lbw, b Hadlee	39
G. M. Wood	c Smith, b Cairns	9	(1) c Snedden, b Cairns	100
J. Dyson	b Snedden	33	b Cairns	33
K. J. Hughes	c Smith, b Troup	0	b Cairns	17
G. S. Chappell†	run out	32	c Edgar, b Hadlee	24
A. R. Border	run out	0	c Howarth, b Morrison	38
R. W. Marsh*	b Troup	33	c Crowe, b Hadlee	3
B. Yardley	b Hadlee	25	c Coney, b Hadlee	0
J. R. Thomson	lbw, b Hadlee	13	lbw, b Hadlee	4
D. K. Lillee	c Crowe, b Troup	9	c Smith, b Morrison	5
T. M. Alderman	not out	0	not out	0
Extras	lb 2, nb 16	18	b 4, lb 5, nb 8	17
		210		**280**

	O	M	R	W	O	M	R	W
Hadlee	20	7	38	2	28	9	63	5
Troup	18.3	3	82	4	15	4	31	—
Cairns	17	7	38	1	44	10	85	3
Snedden	12	5	26	1	8	2	22	—
Howarth	1	—	8	—	4	2	4	—
Coney					4	1	6	—
Morrison					35	16	52	2

FALL OF WICKETS
1–19, 2–75, 3–76, 4–120, 5–120, 6–131, 7–173, 8–187, 9–203
1–106, 2–167, 3–196, 4–202, 5–241, 6–254, 7–254, 8–260, 9–277

NEW ZEALAND

	FIRST INNINGS		SECOND INNINGS	
B. A. Edgar	c and b Yardley	161	c Lillee, b Yardley	29
J. G. Wright	c Yardley, b Lillee	4	c Laird, b Alderman	1
J. F. M. Morrison	b Lillee	11	c Marsh, b Lillee	8
G. P. Howarth†	run out	56	c Chappell, b Yardley	19
J. V. Coney	b Yardley	73	(6) not out	5
M. D. Crowe	c Wood, b Lillee	2		
R. J. Hadlee	c Chappell, b Yardley	25	not out	6
I. D. S. Smith*	lbw, b Yardley	5		
B. L. Cairns	c Lillee, b Alderman	14	(5) b Border	34
M. C. Snedden	not out	18		
G. B. Troup	c Border, b Alderman	4		
Extras	b 4, lb 7, w 1, nb 2	14	lb 4	4
		387	(for 5 wkts)	**109**

	O	M	R	W	O	M	R	W
Thomson	23	8	52	—				
Alderman	24.3	5	59	2	7	—	30	1
Lillee	39	7	106	3	13	5	32	1
Yardley	56	22	142	4	7.4	2	40	2
Border	3	—	11	—	2	1	3	1
Chappell	5	2	3	—				

FALL OF WICKETS
1–15, 2–35, 3–122, 4–276, 5–291, 6–326, 7–345, 8–352, 9–366
1–4, 2–17, 3–44, 4–97, 5–103

New Zealand won by 5 wickets

THIRD TEST MATCH – NEW ZEALAND v. AUSTRALIA
19, 20, 21, 22 and 23 March 1982 at Christchurch

AUSTRALIA

	FIRST INNINGS		SECOND INNINGS	
B. M. Laird	c Smith, b Troup	12	(2) c Edgar, b Snedden	31
G. M. Wood	c Hadlee, b Snedden	64	(1) c Coney, b Hadlee	15
J. Dyson	c Crowe, b Hadlee	1	not out	14
G. S. Chappell†	c Smith, b Coney	176	not out	3
K. J. Hughes	b Hadlee	12		
A. R. Border	b Snedden	6		
R. W. Marsh*	c Cairns, b Hadlee	23		
B. Yardley	c Cairns, b Hadlee	8		
J. R. Thomson	b Hadlee	25		
D. K. Lillee	c and b Hadlee	7		
T. M. Alderman	not out	1		
Extras	b 2, lb 8, nb 8	18		0
		353	(for 2 wkts)	**63**

	O	M	R	W	O	M	R	W
Hadlee	28.5	5	100	6	8	2	10	1
Troup	11	1	53	1				
Snedden	18	2	89	2	4	—	15	1
Cairns	21	3	74	—	9	1	28	—
Coney	8	2	15	1	1	—	2	—
Morrison	3	—	4	—	2	1	6	—
Wright					1	—	2	—
Crowe					0.3	—	0	—

FALL OF WICKETS
1–50, 2–57, 3–82, 4–128, 5–145, 6–237, 7–256, 8–340, 9–352
1–24, 2–60

NEW ZEALAND

	FIRST INNINGS		SECOND INNINGS	
B. A. Edgar	c Dyson, b Alderman	22	c Marsh, b Alderman	11
J. G. Wright	c Marsh, b Lillee	13	b Alderman	141
J. F. M. Morrison	lbw, b Thomson	8	lbw, b Chappell	4
G. P. Howarth†	c Alderman, b Thomson	9	c and b Border	41
J. V. Coney	b Lillee	0	b Border	0
M. D. Crowe	c Marsh, b Lillee	0	b Yardley	9
R. J. Hadlee	c Marsh, b Thomson	40	c Alderman, b Yardley	0
I. D. S. Smith*	b Thomson	0	c Wood, b Yardley	0
B. L. Cairns	run out	3	lbw, b Yardley	16
M. C. Snedden	b Alderman	32	b Border	20
G. B. Troup	not out	0	not out	8
Extras	b 8, lb 2, w 1, nb 11	22	b 4, lb 7, w 2, nb 9	22
		149		**272**

	O	M	R	W	O	M	R	W
Thomson	21	5	51	4	19	5	54	—
Alderman	19.2	2	63	2	23	5	66	2
Lillee	12	6	13	3				
Chappell					18	5	30	1
Yardley					27	7	80	4
Border					10.3	4	20	3

FALL OF WICKETS
1–33, 2–57, 3–57, 4–57, 5–67, 6–82, 7–82, 8–87, 9–149
1–21, 2–36, 3–129, 4–133, 5–162, 6–166, 7–166, 8–215, 9–249

Australia won by 8 wickets

New Zealand v. Australia – Test Match Averages

NEW ZEALAND BATTING

	M	Inns	NOs	Runs	HS	Av	100s	50s
B. A. Edgar	3	5		278	161	55.60	1	1
G. P. Howarth	3	5	1	183	58*	45.75		2
J. G. Wright	3	5		200	141	40.00	1	
M. C. Snedden	3	3	1	70	32	35.00		
R. J. Hadlee	3	5	1	92	40	23.00		
B. L. Cairns	3	5	1	86	34	21.50		
J. V. Coney	3	5	1	79	73	19.75		1
G. B. Troup	2	3	2	12	8*	12.00		
J. F. M. Morrison	3	5		46	15	9.20		
M. D. Crowe	3	4		20	9	5.00		
I. D. S. Smith	3	4		16	11	4.00		

E. J. Chatfield played in one Test but did not bat

AUSTRALIA BATTING

	M	Inns	NOs	Runs	HS	Av	100s	50s
G. S. Chappell	3	4	1	235	176	78.33	1	
G. M. Wood	3	5		229	100	45.80	1	1
B. M. Laird	3	5	1	147	39	36.75		
J. Dyson	3	5	2	93	33	31.00		
R. W. Marsh	3	3		59	33	19.66		
A. R. Border	3	3		44	38	14.66		
J. R. Thomson	3	3		42	25	14.00		
B. Yardley	3	3		33	25	11.00		
K. J. Hughes	3	3		29	17	9.66		
D. K. Lillee	3	3		21	9	7.00		
T. M. Alderman	3	3	3	1	1*	—		

NEW ZEALAND BOWLING

	Overs	Mds	Runs	Wkts	Av	Best	5/inn
R. J. Hadlee	91.5	25	226	14	16.14	6/100	2
J. V. Coney	13	3	23	1	23.00	1/15	
J. F. M. Morrison	40	17	62	2	31.00	2/52	
G. B. Troup	44.3	9	166	5	33.20	2/89	
M. C. Snedden	50	10	176	4	44.00	2/89	
B. L. Cairns	102	25	245	5	49.00	3/85	

Also bowled – E. J. Chatfield 8-5-7-0; J. G. Wright 1-0-2-0; M. D. Crowe 4.3-1-14-0; G. P. Howarth 5-2-12-0

AUSTRALIA BOWLING

	Overs	Mds	Runs	Wkts	Av	Best	5/inn
A. R. Border	15.3	5	34	4	8.50	3/20	
B. Yardley	113.4	41	311	13	23.92	4/80	
D. K. Lillee	79	23	183	7	26.14	3/13	
J. R. Thomson	89	31	192	6	32.00	3/13	
T. M. Alderman	117.5	32	311	8	38.87	2/59	
G. S. Chappell	31	9	51	1	51.00	1/30	

NEW ZEALAND CATCHES

6—I. D. S. Smith; 3—M. D. Crowe; 2—B. A. Edgar, J. V. Coney, R. J. Hadlee and B. L. Cairns; 1—G. P. Howarth and M. C. Snedden

AUSTRALIA CATCHES

5—R. W. Marsh; 4—G. S. Chappell; 2—B. Yardley, G. M. Wood, D. K. Lillee, A. R. Border and T. M. Alderman; 1—J. Dyson and B. M. Laird

First Class Averages

Batting	M	Inns	NOs	Runs	HS	Av	100s	50s
J. M. Parker	7	13	7	618	117	103.00	2	2
B. A. Edgar	11	19	1	934	161	51.88	3	4
J. G. Wright	11	18		872	141	48.44	4	3
J. F. Reid	8	14	1	585	95	45.00		5
E. B. McSweeney	8	10	3	295	96*	42.14		3
V. R. Brown	4	8	2	250	121*	41.66	1	1
E. J. Gray	10	15		623	126	41.53	2	2
M. C. Snedden	12	15	6	342	49*	38.00		
R. W. Ormiston	8	14	3	411	93	37.36		3
J. F. M. Morrison	13	20	3	616	100*	36.23	1	2
D. W. Stead	7	13	1	417	88	34.75		3
M. D. Crowe	12	18	1	582	150	34.23	1	3
A. D. G. Roberts	7	14	3	371	65*	33.72		4
R. J. Hadlee	10	18	3	500	83*	33.33		3
P. E. McEwan	6	12	2	327	100*	32.70	1	1
A. E. W. Parsons	6	11	2	266	53*	29.55		2
G. P. Howarth	11	18	2	463	58*	28.93		4
R. W. Anderson	7	12		340	80	28.33		2
P. N. Webb	7	12		336	116	28.00	1	1
B. Abernethy	6	11	5	165	57*	27.50		
R. T. Latham	6	11	2	273	95	27.30		2
G. J. Dawson	7	12	1	298	52	27.09		1
C. Webb	5	8	1	188	45	26.85		
W. G. Hodgson	3	6		161	49	26.83		
A. J. Hunt	5	9	2	182	58	26.00		
M. J. E. Wright	7	13		325	62	25.00		1
B. R. Blair	9	17	1	398	98*	24.87		3
I. A. Rutherford	5	10		244	92	24.40		2
J. R. Wiltshire	9	14		325	73	23.21		1
J. V. Coney	12	19	2	384	76*	22.58		3
J. G. Bracewell	9	17	1	355	62	22.18		2
P. J. Rattray	7	14		308	82	22.00		1
G. J. Langridge	4	6		132	76	22.00		1
W. L. Blair	7	13		274	132	21.07	1	
W. K. Lees	9	16	3	274	66*	21.07		2
B. L. Cairns	11	19	2	357	58	21.00		1
R. H. Vance	7	12		247	52	20.58		1
R. N. Hoskin	7	13	1	247	62*	20.58		2
R. A. Pierce	4	6		115	52	19.16		1

Batting	M	Inns	NOs	Runs	HS	Av	100s	50s
A. T. R. Hellaby	5	7	1	115	46	19.16		
I. D. S. Smith	11	17		322	74	19.00		2
D. A. Dempsey	5	10		190	63	19.00		1
T. J. Franklin	10	17		302	57	17.76		1
B. G. Cooper	7	14	1	226	56	17.38		1
C. L. Bull	7	13	1	183	46	15.25		
G. N. Edwards	8	14		201	57	14.35		1
B. P. Bracewell	9	13	2	124	23	11.27		
S. R. McNally	7	11	1	105	40	10.50		

(Qualification 100 runs, average 10.00)

Bowling	Overs	Mds	Runs	Wkts	Av	Best	5/inn
R. J. Hadlee	425.1	130	870	59	14.74	6/26	7
E. J. Chatfield	396.2	135	868	51	17.01	5/29	2
G. C. Bateman	159.4	57	321	17	18.88	5/60	1
D. C. Aberhart	206	79	455	23	19.78	5/46	2
B. L. Cairns	373.3	110	816	41	19.90	6/19	3
J. M. McIntyre	195.4	88	379	19	19.94	4/63	
S. L. Boock	236	84	592	27	21.92	6/95	1
J. V. Coney	116	38	253	11	23.00	3/54	
B. P. Bracewell	152.3	39	393	17	23.11	4/41	
S. J. Maguiness	142.4	31	398	17	23.41	4/42	
M. S. Carrington	202	40	611	26	23.50	5/69	1
J. G. Bracewell	239.4	74	661	28	23.61	7/9	2
G. B. Troup	272.1	61	827	34	24.32	4/29	
L. W. Stott	265.3	76	657	27	24.33	5/115	1
C. W. Dickeson	239	84	498	20	24.90	5/59	1
J. A. Williams	188.3	43	549	22	24.95	4/26	
S. R. Gillespie	172	53	402	16	25.13	4/64	
D. J. White	101.2	25	319	12	25.75	6/45	1
M. C. Snedden	341.5	73	1051	40	26.27	4/76	
P. W. Hills	82	29	290	11	26.36	4/76	
E. J. Gray	265.1	86	661	24	27.54	4/58	
S. R. McNally	230	59	558	17	32.82	4/57	
M. F. Gill	148.3	34	495	15	33.00	6/56	1
D. W. Stead	204.4	69	532	13	40.92	3/39	
D. R. O'Sullivan	302.3	85	747	17	43.94	4/88	

(Qualification 10 wickets)

THE NEW ZEALAND SEASON

LEADING FIELDERS

24—I. D. S. Smith (ct 23/st 1)
18—M. J. E. Wright (ct 17/st 1)
17—J. M. Parker
16—E. B. McSweeney
15—M. D. Crowe
13—R. W. Ormiston and W. K. Lees (ct 11/st 2)
10—G. N. Edwards (ct 9/st 1), G. P. Howarth and A. W. Hart (ct 8/st 2) (Hart's catches include 2 while acting as substitute)

DON CAMERON, New Zealand's leading cricket writer, reviews the New Zealand season in general and the Test matches in particular.

When 41,000 flooded into Eden Park for the first one-day international between Australia and New Zealand – the crowd lapping down to and then over the boundary ropes – the message was vividly clear. New Zealand had moved into the bold, brassy atmosphere of jet-age cricket.

The old record for the park, and for any cricket ground in New Zealand, was the 30,000 who came and watched in 1960 the MCC side led by Dennis Silk against an invitation side arranged by Lord Cobham, the then Governor-General who not only played in the match but found an imperishable place in New Zealand cricket by hitting a ball from Don Wilson over long-on for six.

Those were 22 long years ago and between times New Zealand cricket has ebbed and flowed, and so had the size of the faithful crowds who had been sustained not so much by victory after victory, but by an old-fashioned affection for the game and its traditions. The traditionalists looked askance at Packerdom, but they could not hold back the modern version of cricket progress; especially as the arrival of Packer rather coincided with a marked up-turn in the fortunes of New Zealand in home test series. A tied one-all series with England led temporarily by Geoff Boycott, the stormy one-nil victory over Clive Lloyd's West Indians followed by the placid grace of a similar margin over Sunil Gavaskar's Indians.

En passant, so to speak, New Zealand had competed, along with Australia and India in a Packer-style one-day series in Australia, a kaleidoscope of colour and controversy borne across the Tasman Sea by live television.

So the arrangement in the last southern summer of a tour by Greg Chappell and his Australians came at the perfect time for New Zealand – the three forces of a successful test side, a public thirsting for this technicoloured toy of one-day cricket and the controversies of New Zealand's expedition to Australia 12 months before all combining to produce a promoter's dream.

The Hadlee haka ready to start – youngsters at Lancaster Park have their cans ready to beat out their noisy tribute to their hero Richard Hadlee.

Auckland 1981-82
First Class Matches

BATTING	v. Central Districts (Eden Park) 27-29 December 1981		v. Otago (Dunedin) 1-3 January 1982		v. Canterbury (Christchurch) 6-8 January 1982		v. Northern Districts (Auckland) 12-14 January 1982		v. Wellington (Auckland) 17-19 January 1982		v. Canterbury (Auckland) 23-25 January 1982		v. Central Districts (New Plymouth) 30 Jan.-1 Feb. 1982	
A. E. W. Parsons	40	34*	41	—	31	5	1	53*	5	53	1	2		
T. J. Franklin	36	21	30	—	11	0	0	22	20	4	7	47	57	6
J. F. Reid	43	26	95	—	17	12	58	82	37	27	11	72	29	9*
M. D. Crowe	36	1*	72	—	24	9	99	60	4	3	25	34	150	8
P. N. Webb	11	—					9	116	16	1	21	12	32	16
A. T. R. Hellaby	46	—	5*	—	15	3			1	16			29	—
M. C. Snedden	33	—	5	—	41*	1	16	14*	12	39	46*	49*	6	—
J. M. McIntyre	7	—	3	—	7	1*					0*	11*	14*	—
L. W. Stott	13	—			27*	0	0		32	13	0	—	7*	
N. A. Scott	6*	—					0*	17						
G. B. Troup	0	—			—	—	11*	—	4	1	—	—		
A. J. Hunt			10*	—	58	32	0	0			53	9	6	14*
I. Donnelly			—	—					0*	1*				
W. Fowler							29	6						
P. Kelly									14	11	10	6	4	—
Byes	4		2		7	4		2	2	1	2	10		
Leg-byes	6	2	5		6	8	5	4	2	3	8	8	4	
Wides	2		1							1		1		
No-balls	5	1	18		1	2	4	8	8	4		1	4	
Total	288	85	287		245	77	249	367	157	178	184	262	342	53
Wickets	10	2	6		7	8	10	6	10	10	8	7	8	3
Result	W		D		D		L		L		W		W	
Points	18		7		6		6		5		17		20	

Catches
- 12 – M. D. Crowe
- 8 – N. A. Scott
- 7 – P. Kelly (ct 5/st 2)
- 5 – M. C. Snedden and A. T. R. Hellaby (one as sub)
- 4 – P. N. Webb, G. B. Troup and J. F. Reid
- 3 – T. J. Franklin and A. E. W. Parsons
- 2 – L. W. Stott and J. M. McIntyre
- 1 – A. J. Hunt

BOWLING	G. B. Troup	M. C. Snedden	L. W. Stott	A. T. R. Hellaby	J. M. McIntyre	J. F. Reid	I. Donnelly	M. D. Crowe
v. Central Districts (Eden Park) 27-29 December 1981	16-2-51-2 / 13-2-45-2	14-6-40-2 / 16.1-5-28-4	19-6-57-4 / 8-2-17-0	2-0-5-0	12.2-5-24-2 / 31-12-63-4	2-0-14-0		
v. Otago (Dunedin) 1-3 January 1982	14-5-29-4 / 26.1-6-53-3	9-1-32-2 / 30-10-58-1		6-1-17-4 / 29-15-30-1	24-17-30-2		8-2-19-0	
v. Canterbury (Christchurch) 6-8 January 1982	17-4-68-2 / 4-0-13-0	21-3-77-2 / 12-2-47-1	20-9-44-3 / 29-10-63-2	6-2-17-0	31.4-14-55-2 / 22-7-45-2			
v. Northern Districts (Auckland) 12-14 January 1982	23-8-58-1 / 9-0-60-1	28-3-95-3 / 13-0-76-1	38.5-13-115-5 / 12-0-66-1			0.2-0-2-0		3-0-19-0
v. Wellington (Auckland) 17-19 January 1982	13-3-37-0 / 9-2-24-2	20-5-58-4 / 19-4-62-0	29-6-57-2 / 24.5-6-56-3	10-3-26-0 / 7-1-22-0		3-1-5-0	22.2-2-70-4 / 7-2-17-0	2-0-7-0
v. Canterbury (Auckland) 23-25 January 1982	24.3-5-63-4 / 6-1-19-0	30-9-93-2 / 11-3-17-0	26-3-49-2 / 24.5-7-71-2		18-7-40-1 / 17-6-53-1			
v. Central Districts (New Plymouth) 30 January-1 February 1982	14-4-26-1 / 16-5-51-1	16-4-39-3 / 16-2-58-3	21-8-38-1 / 13-6-24-2	15-6-33-2 / 8-2-22-1	23.4-11-38-3 / 16-9-31-2			
	204.4-47-597-23 av. 25.95	255.1-57-780-28 av. 27.85	265.3-76-657-27 av. 24.33	83-30-172-8 av. 21.50	195.4-88-379-19 av. 19.94	5.2-1-21-0 —	37.2-6-106-4 av. 26.50	5-0-26-0 —

And so it proved that madcap afternoon at Eden Park when Geoff Howarth's New Zealanders won the first of the three one-day internationals. And so, through sunshine and rain, triumph and trauma, through a one-day series taken by Australia 2–1 and a test series shared one-all, cricket dominated the New Zealand sporting scene as never before. The threats of boycotts at the Brisbane Commonwealth Games were forgotten, and the ill-advised visit to South Africa of five New Zealand Rugby Union councillors went virtually unnoticed until Chappell's men had left.

It was, in so many ways a marvellous summer, for once past the frantic atmosphere of the one-day internationals the tests – apart from the first at Wellington which was ruined by rain – produced cricket of drama and quality and, best of all, of thorough sportsmanship.

This was the greatest triumph of them all, a tour and a test series throbbing with life and vigour, and blessedly free of acrimony or any sour aftertaste.

Perhaps it is a commentary of modern cricket that a tour which enhanced the character of the game and the men who played it should be regarded as, if not the exception, something unusual. Yet it needs to be mentioned for it is the counterpoint to much that had gone before, and the very reason why 41,000 Aucklanders streamed into Eden Park that February afternoon.

For the seeds of this tour had been sewn 14 months before, especially on one Sunday afternoon at the Melbourne Cricket Ground when the umpires chose not to watch the New Zealander Martin Snedden taking an utterly brilliant catch in the outfield, and when Greg Chappell chose to end that one-day international by having his young brother Trevor bowl the last ball underarm.

Over the next 12 months these incidents, especially the underarm, became embedded in the New Zealand psyche, rivalled only by the fact that the 1905 All Blacks had been diddled out of the try which would have drawn, perhaps won, the rugby test against Wales at Cardiff Arms Park.

Wittingly or not the New Zealand Cricket Council produced a nicely orchestrated itinerary, with the tour starting with three televised one-day internationals and then into three five-day tests. Rothmans, who had sponsored cricket generously for years, stepped up their promotion work. Various other people tossed, unintentionally, a few logs on the fire. One was Sir Donald Bradman who, in an article he donated to the tour booklet, referred to 'a blot on the spirit of the game which no apology from the Australian captain could erase.' This remark re-echoed round New Zealand, and in Australia where Chappell was trying to win two battles – the one a search for his own batting form, the other a tough contest against the West Indians.

There was, then much speculation that Chappell might withdraw from the tour, for his form was not good and there was the prospect that four or five weeks in New Zealand would become a personal ordeal.

It says much for the character and personal pride of the man that Chappell did not take the easy way out. And five weeks later there was the indelible memory that Chappell, by his own efforts, had done more than any man to restore good sense and good humour to the game, and the tour.

Soon after the first one-day international at Eden Park a cartoon appeared in an Australian cricket magazine which

Canterbury 1981-82
First Class Matches

BATTING

	v. Wellington (Wellington) 27-29 December 1981	v. Northern Districts (Christchurch) 1-3 January 1982	v. Auckland (Christchurch) 6-8 January 1982	v. Central Districts (Palmerston North) 11-13 January 1982	v. Otago (Dunedin) 17-19 January 1982	v. Auckland (Auckland) 23-25 January 1982	v. Wellington (Christchurch) 29-31 January 1982
D. A. Dempsey	3 63	13 16	0 41	2 2	16 34		
P. J. Rattray	36 1	0 5	44 36	7 82	20 20	4 35	4 14
V. R. Brown	0 6	42 1	16 12*				
P. E. McEwan	20 49	3 7	19 7	3 103*	11 52	55 42*	19 0
R. T. Latham	5 23		24 4	2 6*	95 0	40 2	0 72*
C. L. Bull	42 0	5 7	15 2	31 —	0 4	29 0*	46 2
D. W. Stead	12 37	21 16	32 42*	56 —	35 5	12 50	88 11
R. J. Hadlee	61* 35	4 68	32 24	83* —	22 0	0 31	41 7
S. N. Bateman	25 2						
J. M. Mackle	6 13	1* 21*		11 1			
S. R. McNally	1 0*	1 6	39 —	1 —	0 2	0 —	40 15
B. D. Ritchie		17 2	40 —			2 0	
G. C. Bateman		1 0	0* —	16 —		4* —	3* 10
R. I. Leggat				0 —	23 1		
A. W. Hart					13* 0	24 —	6 13
A. J. Farrant					2 1*		
D. G. Farrant					33 —		0 0
D. J. Boyle					58 —		

Byes	2 9	6 6	6	5			2	
Leg-byes	7 3	1 3	12 6	7 4	6 2	10 2	4 7	
Wides	1	1		1 1				
No-balls	13 6	5 6		5 1		12 1	8 5	

Total	233 248	109 164	285 180	225 205	243 121	281 163	261 158	
Wickets	10 10	10 10	10 6	10 3	10 10	10 4	10 10	
Result	L	L	D	W	L	L	L	
Points	4	4	6	18	6	6	7	

Catches
10 – A. W. Hart (ct 8/st 2) (inc. 2 catches as sub)
7 – J. M. Mackle (ct 5/st 2) and P. E. McEwan
6 – D. W. Stead
4 – D. A. Dempsey
3 – B. D. Ritchie, R. I. Leggatt and R. J. Hadlee
2 – A. J. Farrant (one as sub), R. T. Latham and P. J. Rattray
1 – S. N. Bateman, V. R. Brown, C. L. Bull and S. R. McNally

BOWLING

	R. J. Hadlee	S. R. McNally	P. E. McEwan	D. W. Stead	V. R. Brown	D. A. Dempsey	R. T. Latham	G. C. Bateman
v. Wellington (Wellington) 27-29 December 1981	35-10-81-5 16-6-24-2	30.1-10-57-4 9-4-32-0	12-0-44-0	7-1-41-0 13-2-47-2	13-6-29-0 4-1-4-0	1-0-9-0	0.2-0-4-0	
v. Northern Districts (Christchurch) 1-3 January 1982	26-8-49-5 22-6-46-2	13-4-24-1 18-8-35-3	7-2-25-3 5-1-14-0	20.3-6-39-3	16-1-31-2			21.3-13-23-1 9-3-22-0
v. Auckland (Christchurch) 6-8 January 1982	31-9-72-0 22-8-26-6	16-3-44-2 8-1-19-1	1-1-0-0	24-11-58-3 10.1-7-10-0				28-9-57-2 11-6-8-1
v. Central Districts (Palmerston North) 11-13 January	26-7-63-2 19.5-6-40-6	14-4-49-1 20-4-48-0	7-1-15-1 7-2-22-2	9-0-39-0 5-1-11-0		1-0-1-1		18.1-2-60-5 7-3-11-0
v. Otago (Dunedin) 17-19 January 1982	19-5-32-4 22-12-34-1	14-5-46-1 15.5-4-46-2	3.5-1-6-2 9-2-26-0	16-9-28-2 16-4-50-0			1-0-4-0	
v. Auckland (Auckland) 23-25 January 1982	22-9-27-4 26.3-10-62-1	17-7-27-1 20-3-54-1	4-3-1-0 4-0-20-0	27-6-76-0 9-2-26-0				20-9-29-3 15-3-49-4
v. Wellington (Christchurch) 29-31 January 1982	20-5-35-5 26-4-53-2	7-1-18-0 18-1-59-0		12-3-35-2 36-17-72-1			2-0-5-0	10-2-20-1 20-7-42-0
	333.2-105-644-45 av. 14.31	220-59-558-17 av. 32.82	59.5-13-173-8 av. 21.62	204.4-69-532-13 av. 40.92	33-8-64-2 av. 32.00	2-0-10-1 av. 10.00	3.2-0-13-0 —	159.4-57-321-17 av. 18.88

A. S. N. Bateman 18-7-54-1   B. P. J. Rattray 1-0-4-0

THE NEW ZEALAND SEASON/125

rather said it all. It showed several Colonel Blimpish characters sitting in the New Zealand Cricket Council holy of holies, a jam-packed ground visible through the windows, and the old buffers sitting in chairs almost submerged by piles of dollar notes. And one is saying: 'Terrible thing, that underarm. I wonder whether he would do it again.'

But back to the realities. Chappell may have felt like a martyr in the Coliseum as he led his team out for the first act at Eden Park. The noise was vast, boos mixing with cheers, and if Chappell had reacted badly the day, perhaps the whole tour might have been a disaster. That searing afternoon Chappell was at the centre of several incidents any of which could have produced uproar.

The first came when Bruce Edgar, who was to become the backbone of the New Zealand innings, walked round a ball from Terry Alderman, and a second or two later Rod Marsh pointed eagerly at the leg bail lying on the ground. Everyone, including the umpires, seemed mystified by the event, so much so that the umpires gave Edgar the benefit of the doubt.

On the field, and afterwards, Chappell played down the incident, and got on with the game.

Ironically, Chappell's next act which helped to break down any further crowd resentment was his bowling. Jeff Thomson, Alderman and Len Pascoe had the New Zealand batsmen pinned down, and Chappell, usually very successful in such matches against New Zealand, tried to maintain the pressure. Instead he conceded runs at a furious rate, and he was cheered every time he started an over. So New Zealand, with Edgar going on from the bail incident (which came at 14 for one wicket) to 79, scored 240, and very quickly removed Graeme Wood and Bruce Laird.

Chappell arrived, to the usual turmoil, but there was fun rather than fury when from the crowd a lawn-bowl waddled out on to the field. The fury came from Chappell's batting, a marvellous century as his team-mates fell at the other end. Even the most churlish among the crowd could not fail to recognise the majesty of Chappell's batting, and he gained due tribute. As Chappell was out at 192 for nine some of the crowd rushed on to the field, and Chappell was knocked over by a spectator.

Again, no protest, rather Chappell's calm statement afterwards that he had sensed out of the corner of his eye a young girl heading across his bows, they collided, Chappell off-balance fell over, and then regained his feet.

So the mad merry afternoon put the tour precisely on the right path. New Zealand had won, Chappell had reacted with dignity, and played like a champion. The incidents were forgotten, simply because Chappell afterwards dismissed them quickly and with humour. The crowd had come to bay and bray at Chappell, and then found he was not a villain, rather a fine and fair cricketer.

From that point onward the tour went smoothly along. Chappell did get a ritual jeer when he appeared on other grounds, but the crowds, while still large and vibrant, did not become offensive. And, in the final match, the third test at Lancaster Park, Chappell played an innings of such majesty that he signed off the tour with a superb flourish. He scored 176, the last 100 between the start of play and lunch on the second day, in the Australian first innings of 353, which eventually led to an Australian victory by eight wickets. The man who had come as an apparent villain left

Central Districts 1981–82
First Class Matches

BATTING	v. Auckland (Eden Park) 27–29 December 1981		v. Wellington (Wellington) 1–3 January 1982		v. Otago (Napier) 6–8 January 1982		v. Canterbury (Palmerston North) 11–13 January 1982		v. Northern Districts (Tauranga) 17–19 January 1982		v. Otago (Invercargill) 23–25 January 1982		v. Auckland (New Plymouth) 30 Jan.–1 Feb. 1982	
R. W. Anderson	73	20	47	9	19	11	17	80	1	25	—	—	0	38
A. H. Jones	0	0	2	38	3	6			*					
M. H. Toynbee	0	20	0	3										
G. N. Edwards	33	57	15	10	0	10	37	10	0	14	—	—	10	0
J. R. Wiltshire	12	12	45	29	23	0	16	14	29	23	—	—	73	33
W. G. Hodgson	21	27	49	6	48	10								
I. D. S. Smith	5	22	24	36	13	63	4	28	74	1	—	—	0	32
G. K. Robertson	8	8	2	0	4	—								
D. C. Aberhart	1	0	8*	11	11	4*	5	1			—	—	18	27
D. R. O'Sullivan	20	1	0	12	0	1*	22	0	0	20	—	—	3	4
M. F. Gill	4*	0*	7	0*			4*	1*	0*	16			0	0
C. Webb					14	21	44	25	7	45	—	—	12	20*
S. J. Gill					17*	60	2	15						
R. A. Pierce							0	4	29	13	—	—	52	17
G. J. Langridge							76	0	21	18	—	—	5	12
M. D. Jamieson									59	7	—	—	1*	3
D. Stirling									0	0*	—	—		
Byes		2	3	1			6	3	1	4				3
Leg-byes	7	10	3	7	3	2	7	5	4	5			11	5
Wides				1										
No-balls	7	2	10	5	2	3	1	1	3	1			9	6
Total	191	181	215	168	157	191	241	187	228	192			194	200
Wickets	10	10	10	10	10	8	10	10	10	10			10	10
Result	L		L		D		L		L		D		L	
Points	3		4		5		6		6		6		4	

Catches
13 – I. D. S. Smith (ct 12/st 1)
10 – G. N. Edwards (ct 9/st 1)
6 – R. W. Anderson
4 – G. J. Langridge and S. J. Gill (1 as sub)
3 – D. R. O'Sullivan, J. R. Wiltshire, C. Webb and D. C. Aberhart
2 – M. D. Jamieson, M. F. Gill (as sub), D. Stirling (as sub) and R. A. Pierce
1 – G. K. Robertson and W. G. Hodgson

BOWLING	G. K. Robertson	M. F. Gill	D. R. O'Sullivan	D. C. Aberhart	M. H. Toynbee	W. G. Hodgson	S. J. Gill	R. A. Pierce
v. Auckland (Eden Park) 27–29 December 1981	29.4–8–57–4	17–3–66–0	42–15–88–4	25–12–32–2	13–4–28–0			
	7–2–12–0	4–0–26–1	14.4–0–38–0		3–1–6–1			
v. Wellington (Wellington) 1–3 January 1982	28–9–86–1	24–5–72–0	25–7–73–1	38–10–94–4	9.1–2–34–3	3–0–13–0		
v. Otago (Napier) 6–8 January 1982	10–5–9–0		33.5–12–83–2	29–13–61–5			27–9–60–3	
			46–15–66–0	29–12–44–3		8–0–34–1	26–10–49–2	
v. Canterbury (Palmerston North) 11–13 January 1982		25.3–11–56–6	15–6–31–1	24–6–70–2			11–1–55–1	
		15–2–64–1	19.4–2–71–2	15–8–49–0				6–2–10–0
v. Northern Districts (Tauranga) 17–19 January 1982		14–4–37–1	26–7–65–1					5–2–12–0
		19–2–69–2	23.2–5–66–1					10–3–28–0
v. Otago (Invercargill) 23–25 January 1982			17–7–48–1	26–11–46–5				
v. Auckland (New Plymouth) 30 January–1 February 1982		24–5–79–2	40–9–118–4	20–7–59–2				7–2–26–0
		6–2–26–2						
	74.4–24– 164–5 av. 32.80	148.3–34– 495–15 av. 33.00	302.3–85– 747–17 av. 43.94	206–79– 455–23 av. 19.78	25.1–7– 68–4 av. 17.00	11–0– 47–1 av. 47.00	64–20– 164–6 av. 27.33	28–9– 76–0 av. —

A. I. D. S. Smith 0.1–0–3–0;
R. W. Anderson 2–1–1–0;
J. R. Wiltshire 1–0–4–0

as a very real hero – and now Chappell had a special place of honour in New Zealand cricket memories.

The record crowd at Eden Park produced gate-takings of $190,000 and when the subsequent one-dayers at Carisbrook and the Basin Reserve produced more records (Carisbrook had 16,000 for a mid-week match) the prospect was that the NZCC, like those characters in the cartoon, would be rolling in money.

The NZCC had to find $400,000 before the tour went into profit, and the prospect was that the NZCC would clear perhaps $300,000 on the tour, an unheard-of profit for a sports body not used to bandying around six-figure gains.

Unfortunately after the drama and excitement of the one-day internationals, with Australia winning a tight match at Dunedin and then romping away with the third, the rains cut the heart out of the tour. A three-day match against North Island at Napier became a dreary two-hour exercise. The first test at the Basin Reserve in Wellington, which promised capacity crowds for at least three of the five days, became a soggy affair with barely a full day of play.

The second test, before more modest crowds at Eden Park, went amiably along on a docile pitch until Chappell and Allan Border were run out from consecutive balls and Australia struggled to 210 in their first innings. Edgar, who had an enormously successful season at all levels, put together a long innings of 161, leading New Zealand to 387 and a lead of 177. Wood replied with a crisp 100 and time was running out for New Zealand as Australia started the fifth and last day at 241 for four, 64 runs on, Chappell and Border together. The pitch had become so low and slow, with some turn for Bruce Yardley, but New Zealand had chosen not to play a spinner.

Richard Hadlee's first ball of the fifth morning was fairly routine, but Chappell rather choked on a drive and the catch looped out to Edgar at cover. That was the start of one of New Zealand's more incredible charges to victory. Hadlee, snorting fire, snatched three more wickets and John Morrison, bowling left-arm slows of impeccable straightness, winkled out two to finish the Australian innings at 280, leaving New Zealand 104 for victory with time to spare.

Still, New Zealand hearts were in their mouths, for this was precisely the same winnings score needed against West Indies two years before, and after a vast amount of agony New Zealand only took that victory with the last batsmen at the crease.

There were tremors this time, too, as John Wright and Morrison departed quickly, but the diligent Edgar stuck fast, and Geoff Howarth went out and did precisely the right thing – he played strokes. And when he was out Howarth brought off another coup by promoting Lance Cairns to No 5.

In 29 nerve-jangling minutes Cairns scored 32 (three fours, two sixes) of a stand of 50 with Edgar. They were both out before the end, which came with a six by Hadlee.

It was a famous victory, the more so because for four-fifths of the match it seemed unlikely that anyone could drag a result from the humourless pitch. But it also showed that, after losing ground in the one-dayers, New Zealand were a highly competitive team even if Edgar as the run-maker and Hadlee as the wicket-taker, had to bear the heaviest loads. It also showed that the Australian batting relied much too much on Chappell and that on pitches

Northern Districts 1981-82
First Class Matches

BATTING	v. Otago (Alexandra) 27-29 December 1981	v. Canterbury (Christchurch) 1-3 January 1982	v. Wellington (Gisborne) 6-8 January 1982	v. Auckland (Auckland) 12-14 January 1982	v. Central Districts (Tauranga) 17-19 January 1982	v. Wellington (Lower Hutt) 23-25 January 1982	v. Otago (Hamilton) 30-31 January 1982
M. J. E. Wright	7 30	13 9	62 27	36 9	1 46	41 13	31 —
J. Wright	124 20	4 23	90 31	113 105	26 22	26 88	0 —
G. P. Howarth	58 16	2 53	20* —	41 41	11 0	3 6	9 —
B. G. Cooper	21 12	20 14	0 26	25 56	8 9	5 5	19 6*
J. M. Parker	47 44*	41* 17	80* 38	45* 14*	117 102*	57* 12	4 —
A. D. G. Roberts	3 12	14 42	59 65*	7 15*	28 56	10 0	59 1*
D. J. White	4 20	4 8	— —	6 —	0 16		
B. L. Cairns	2 58	10 16	25 17	38 29	0 14*	3 13	32 —
C. W. Dickeson	6 1	4 5	— —	0 —	1 —	1 0	1 —
S. R. Gillespie	2 6	2 0	— —	1 —	18* —	9 8	4 —
S. J. Scott	0* 4						
M. Carrington		7 0*	— —	4* —	23 —	0 5	0* —
N. D. Pollock						24 0*	
C. M. Kuggeleijn							17 —
Byes	2	2 5	3		5	4 4	
Leg-byes	7 3	6 8	(18) (9)	14 10	4 (13)	5	5
Wides							
No-balls	3 1	3 2	5	4	11	5	9
Total	286 227	132 202	354 213	335 282	241 278	200 159	194 7
Wickets	10 10	10 10	5 5	10 5	10 6	10 10	10 0
Result	D	W	D	W	W	L	W
Points	7	16	9	20	16	5	17

Catches
18 – M. J. E. Wright (ct 17/st 1)
17 – J. M. Parker
8 – G. P. Howarth and C. W. Dickeson
6 – J. G. Wright and D. J. White (2 as sub)
4 – B. G. Cooper and A. D. G. Roberts
2 – S. R. Gillespie, M. S. Carrington, B. L. Cairns and C. M. Kuggeleijn
1 – S. J. Scott and sub (Parala)

BOWLING	S. R. Gillespie	B. L. Cairns	S. J. Scott	A. D. G. Roberts	C. W. Dickeson	D. J. White	G. P. Howarth	B. G. Cooper
v. Otago (Alexandra) 27-29 December 1981	14-5-25-0 11-3-21-0	18-6-29-0 14-1-42-0	12-4-42-0	9-5-12-2 4-2-14-0	24-8-42-0 38-16-59-5	22-10-45-6 19-2-55-0	6-3-9-0 13-4-22-1	1-0-1-0
v. Canterbury (Christchurch) 1-3 January 1982	8-3-18-1 18-6-41-3	18.4-5-32-5 26-9-39-4		9-5-7-1 7-1-21-1	1-0-1-0		1-0-2-0 5.1-3-5-1	
v. Wellington (Gisborne) 6-8 January 1982		22-6-55-3	13-3-38-0 4-0-30-0		33-12-56-4 23-8-60-1	11-3-34-2 11-5-32-0	12-2-31-0 15-5-26-1	
v. Auckland (Auckland) 12-14 January 1982	25-9-64-4 6-1-15-0	21-4-64-0 17-6-39-0		2-0-9-0 8-6-16-0	20-5-40-1 37-8-106-3	1.5-0-6-1 21-2-96-2	7-1-23-0	
v. Central Districts (Tauranga) 17-19 January 1982	19-6-53-1 18-5-33-2	28-10-48-5 17-3-35-3		6-4-7-1 7-1-26-0	7-1-27-0 25-14-35-3	10-3-30-0 5.3-0-21-1	3-1-10-0	
v. Wellington (Lower Hutt) 23-25 January 1982	18-7-31-1 13-2-34-0	23.3-7-61-2 25-8-43-3		8-2-15-0 4-2-6-0	16-5-40-2 15-7-32-1			
v. Otago (Hamilton) 30-31 January 1982	11-3-36-3 11-3-31-1	15-8-24-2 14.1-8-19-6		3-2-8-1			5-3-5-2	
	172-53- 402-16 av. 25.12	259.2-81- 530-33 av. 16.06	29-7- 110-0 —	67-30- 141-6 av. 23.50	239-84- 498-20 av. 24.90	101.2-25- 319-12 av. 26.58	67.1-22- 133-5 av. 26.60	1-0- 1-0 —

A. J. Wright 5-1-12-0

without speed or bounce Dennis Lillee, Thomson, Alderman and Pascoe were good, but scarcely great, bowlers.

So New Zealand went two days later to the last match, the third test, at Lancaster Park with heads and hopes high, even if the pitch there seemed likely to have the sharpness which Lillee and company could use. Howarth won a very useful toss and put Australia in on a pitch sure to help the seamers, and with the bonus that the Australians had to bat on a grey wintry day. The Australians prefer the warmth of the sun on their backs, and after four hours five were gone for 202. Wood had scored a crisp 64 and Chappell was still there on 76, with Rod Marsh a solid lieutenant, when bad light prevented any play after tea. The Australians had scored quickly, but lost half their batting, and on the surface it seemed a useful start by New Zealand.

But really it was not. Hadlee had bowled superbly, but the rest – Gary Troup, Martin Snedden and Lance Cairns – had been rather flattered by the waywardness of the Australian batting.

The next morning Chappell hit two twos and four fours from Troup's first over to race past his 100, and he just kept racing onward. Again only Hadlee had the control to keep the master in check – the others conceded runs at bewildering speed. Chappell's 100 had come from 141 balls, his 150 from 193, at 170 he had a century in boundaries, at 176 a century before lunch with 14 minutes to spare. As the utter anticlimax Chappell then chased a wide ball from Jeremy Coney and was caught at the wicket. Hadlee finished off the innings to have six for 100, the 13th time he had taken five or more in a test.

As if triggered by Chappell's magnificent batting Australia found for a golden hour or two that over-powering presence which made them quite unbeatable in the 1970s. Four of the old characters were there – Lillee and Thomson bowling at furious pace, Marsh leading the aggressive fielding, Chappell coldly directing the assault. As many other teams had done seven or eight years before the New Zealanders withered under this onslaught. The Australians regarded Edgar and Wright as New Zealand's only solid batting armour, and once that was cracked open the rest of the batting was vulnerable.

It was, to a dispassionate viewer, a superb hour or two of cricket ... Thomson all bounce and belligerence, Lillee rather slower than at his best, but with marvellous control. In 12 overs Lillee took three wickets for 13 runs before an old knee injury flared up. He went away to have his bionics adjusted, came back, limped after a ball, and was gone. Perhaps it was the last of Lillee in test cricket. If so, he finished in rampant mood, as he should be remembered.

Only a brave little rally by Hadlee and Martin Snedden brought New Zealand to within four runs of avoiding the follow-on, and Chappell rather gambled by making New Zealand bat again with Lillee off the field and with Alderman worried by injuries, and far from the effective bowler he had been in England. But Chappell shrewdly reasoned that even if the pitch was now steady the New Zealand batsmen would be deflated by their first innings failure, and in no mood to counter-attack. The sun was shining and perhaps Chappell took the sensible view that in an erratic climate like New Zealand's he must make best use of the fine weather.

Again Chappell read the position perfectly, and again

Otago 1981-82
First Class Matches

BATTING	v. Northern Districts (Alexandra) 27-29 December 1981	v. Auckland (Dunedin) 1-3 January 1982	v. Central Districts (Napier) 6-8 January 1982	v. Wellington (Wellington) 12-14 January 1982	v. Canterbury (Dunedin) 17-19 January 1982	v. Central Districts (Invercargill) 23-25 January 1982	v. Northern Districts (Hamilton) 30-31 January 1982
I. A. Rutherford	20 29	0 27	92 11	13 51	1 0		
J. G. Bracewell	15 33	10 26	12 15	0 23	51 8	15 —	36 0
R. N. Hoskin	27 33	0 15	7 17	25 0	62* 53	—	5 3
B. R. Blair	82 52	42 4	10 22	12 4	20 98*	4 —	0 0
W. L. Blair	22 9	17 5	13 10	132 1	6 27	10 —	5 17
G. J. Dawson	4 27*	1 49	15 5	48 52	15 —	42 —	2 38
W. K. Lees	8 0	3 63	14 66*	7 41	25* —	0 —	0 0
B. Abernethy	6 31*	1 16*	19 57*	2 9		6* —	10 8*
B. P. Bracewell	8 —	4 —	1 —	12 19	23 —	16* —	3 0
P. W. Hills	4* —		20 —	6* 3*	0 —	—	7 0
S. L. Boock	8* —	0 —	2* —	12 —	0 —	—	1* 6
D. J. Walker		0* 0*					
G. Osborne				8 —			
S. J. McCallum						12 —	
J. K. Lindsay							42 5
Byes	7 3	1 6	7	4 4	3 4	—	1
Leg-byes	6 4	1 6	4 11	6 10	10 1	3	2
Wides		1 2	6 1				1
No-balls	11 4	3 6		3 4	2 2	3	1
Total	228 226	85 214	224 205	274 246	164 202	161 —	114 82
Wickets	9 6	10 7	10 6	10 9	10 3	7 —	10 10
Result	D	D	D	L	W	D	L
Points	6	2	6	7	17	6	4

Catches
9 – W. K. Lees (ct 7/st 2) and G. J. Dawson
7 – W. L. Blair
5 – P. W. Hills
4 – S. L. Boock, B. R. Blair and R. N. Hoskin
3 – I. A. Rutherford
2 – G. Osborne and J. G. Bracewell
1 – B. P. Bracewell and sub (Mawhinney)

BOWLING	B. P. Bracewell	P. W. Hills	B. Abernethy	J. G. Bracewell	S. L. Boock	D. J. Walker	B. R. Blair	G. Osborne
v. Northern Districts (Alexandra) 27-29 December 1981	11-4-25-0 11-2-30-1	8-2-30-0 3-1-13-0	9-4-17-0 4-2-8-0	34-7-91-6 31-10-77-3	34-5-111-3 39-18-95-6			
v. Auckland (Dunedin) 1-3 January 1982	8-3-13-0		31-9-85-4	13-2-36-1	14-6-32-0	23-5-78-0	11-3-17-1	
v. Central Districts (Napier) 6-8 January 1982	15-4-41-4 4-1-5-0	10-4-27-2 14-4-52-1	2-0-12-0 8-3-16-1	11-5-36-1 32-16-51-4	14-3-36-3 30-13-62-1			
v. Wellington (Wellington) 12-14 January 1982	25-5-45-3 3-0-10-0	14-3-43-2 3-1-5-0	4-0-17-1 20-1-96-2	22-4-87-0 5-0-43-1	13.5-4-28-4 19.4-2-87-3		10-2-27-0	
v. Canterbury (Dunedin) 17-19 January 1982	12.3-3-33-2 6-1-20-0	16-2-71-4 8-1-27-0		10-4-24-1 10.1-6-9-7	9-3-22-2 8-6-6-1		20-8-52-1 12-2-47-1	16-6-35-0 7-2-10-1
v. Central Districts (Invercargill) 23-25 January 1982								
v. Northern Districts (Hamilton) 30-31 January 1982	15-2-55-3	6-1-22-2		24-9-55-1	32.3-18-44-4			
	110.3-25-277-13 av. 21.30	82-19-290-11 av. 26.36	78-19-251-8 av. 31.37	192.1-63-509-25 av. 20.36	213.3-78-523-27 av. 19.37	23-5-78-0 —	53-15-143-3 av. 47.66	23-8-45-1 av. 45.00

much of the New Zealand batting faded away, apart from Wright and, for a time, Howarth. This time Yardley carried most of the bowling burden, and recaptured some of his amazing form of the Australian home series by taking four for 80, three of them in a middle-innings collapse.

Only Wright escaped, and played a long, lonely innings as the others departed. But this was a new Wright, not the strokeless, worried defender of so many unsatisfactory test innings, but the bold, graceful attacker. He had 17 boundaries in his century, and on the last morning sprinted from 91 to 141 with ten fours. But no-one could stay with him, and eventually Australia needed only 69 to win, which they reached for the loss of two wickets.

So the vibrant series was over, and afterwards Chappell won a special award as the sportsman of the series, which he thoroughly deserved. Hadlee won a car as the player of the one-day and test series, and this despite the strong challenge from Edgar and Chappell.

And, in many ways, Hadlee was very much the centre-point of the series for he seemed to be involved in whatever controversy was about. Much of it concerned Hadlee's wish that he bowl from a short run-up rather than present the flamboyant figure which his can-banging army of spectators (especially at Eden Park) had come to expect.

Hadlee had moved to his shorter run for Nottinghamshire in the 1981 county championship, and with resounding success he was the only man to take 100 wickets, and headed the averages. Playing again for Canterbury Hadlee remained on his short run, again with startling success – 45 wickets in seven matches. During this triumphant progress Hadlee maintained he would bowl from his short run in the tests, and just as strenuously Frank Cameron, manager and chairman of selectors, announced that New Zealand would want Hadlee from his long run. Howarth was of the same view, and told Hadlee this on two occasions.

Yet even after Howarth had gambled by putting Australia in to bat in the second test at Auckland, Hadlee started from his short run, and without noticeable success. There was a large amount of comment, and my own reference in the *New Zealand Herald* about Hadlee bowling 'from his pop-gun run-up' when New Zealand rather needed heavier artillery specially seemed to touch a raw nerve. Soon afterwards I was taken to task by Walter Hadlee, the bowler's father, but not by the bowler himself – we parted conversational company for a time. Hadlee's New Zealand team-mates were not especially impressed, either.

For whatever reason, Hadlee during that innings returned to his long run, his faithful army resumed their clamour for 'Had-leeee' and, from his long run, Hadlee bowled superbly at Auckland and, if anything, better at Christchurch.

But at the end of the series Hadlee was still out of sorts. He had, he said, been upset by the criticism, and he was eager to return to Notts, 'where they appreciate what you do.' There was, too, some dispute with the NZCC over a contract, and the suggestion that Hadlee might retire, but in the end all was solved, apparently amicably. But the short-run, long-run problem will probably remain next season.

On the domestic front Wellington were the dominant side, winning both the Shell Trophy for the three-day competition, and the concurrent one-day Shell Cup competition. They won both because they were a nicely balanced team,

Wellington 1981-82
First Class Matches

BATTING

	v. Canterbury (Wellington) 27-29 December 1981		v. Central Districts (Wellington) 1-3 January 1982		v. Northern Districts (Gisborne) 6-8 January 1982		v. Otago (Wellington) 12-14 January 1982		v. Auckland (Auckland) 17-19 January 1982		v. Northern Districts (Lower Hutt) 23-25 January 1982		v. Canterbury (Christchurch) 29-31 January 1982	
B. A. Edgar	30	9	64	—	141*	41	14	58	20	31	26	12	2	65
R. H. Vance	3	17	24	—	50	23	12	18	2	—	15	52	4	27
J. V. Coney	72	5	13	—	0	76*	48	28	1	0	1	0	11	14
B. W. Cederwall	1	—	0	—			38	0			17*	19	0	—
J. F. M. Morrison	2	45*	7	—	24	47*	11	43	18	83	41	56	21	100*
E. J. Gray	18	11	126	—	0	—	35	13	114	43	71	43	21	—
R. W. Ormiston	80	33*	93	—	5	—	6	21*	1	4	48	18	18	59*
E. B. McSweeney	96*	—	7	—	0	—	29	60*	68	16*	4	6	9	—
S. Maguiness	1	—	6	—	2	—			24	0	0	12*	15	—
J. Williams	0	—	13	—	3	—	18	—	5*	—	18*	8	7	2
E. J. Chatfield	3	—	19	—	24*	—	4	—	3	—	—	3	7*	—
P. J. Holland					1	—			4	4				
G. Wheeler							32*	—						
Byes	13	4	2				2	8	4	5	1	8	1	13
Leg-byes	24	1	1		(13)	(8)	1	15	6	12	8	24	7	16
Wides	2		6						1	1				
No-balls	11	4	17				3	5	6	5	1	1		1
Total	356	129	398		263	195	253	269	277	204	251	262	123	297
Wickets	10	4	10		9	2	10	6	10	7	8	10	10	4
Result	W				D		W		W		W		W	
Points	20		19		5		19		19		19		16	

Catches
16 – E. B. McSweeney
12 – R. W. Ormiston
8 – J. F. M. Morrison
7 – J. V. Coney, E. J. Chatfield and S. Maguiness
6 – B. W. Cederwall (one as sub)
5 – E. J. Gray and R. H. Vance
2 – B. A. Edgar
1 – J. Williams and P. J. Holland

BOWLING

	J. A. Williams	E. J. Chatfield	B. W. Cederwall	S. Maguiness	E. J. Gray	J. V. Coney	J. F. M. Morrison	P. J. Holland
v. Canterbury (Basin Reserve) 27-29 December 1981	18-4-52-2	28-9-67-4	6-2-17-1	5-0-15-1	9-2-28-0	16-1-32-1		
	8-1-31-1	35-13-76-4		6.4-4-11-1	37-11-92-4	14-7-19-0		
v. Central Districts (Wellington) 1-3 January 1982	16.4-2-48-3	29-9-69-4	3-0-33-0	11-2-37-2		12-7-12-1		
	17-3-47-1	19.4-7-29-5		21-5-40-2	4-3-1-0	2-0-8-0		
v. Northern Districts (Gisborne) 6-8 January 1982	13-0-46-0	26-4-79-0		15-2-65-1	12-2-52-0	20-3-54-3		12-2-40-1
	6-1-18-0	21-2-71-3		1-0-4-0	27-8-82-2	2-0-13-0		2-0-16-0
v. Otago (Wellington) 12-14 January 1982	15-5-36-0	24-6-58-3	26.4-5-65-4		23-7-58-3	8-4-27-0		
	21-8-49-2	28-12-68-3	7.5-1-26-2		38-18-56-2	2-0-16-0		
v. Auckland (Auckland) 17-19 January 1982	10-4-42-1	25.3-12-30-4		13-3-24-3	13-6-28-1			5-1-21-1
	10-0-35-1	23-7-45-3		5-1-17-0	27-8-58-4	1-0-6-0		5-2-8-1
v. Northern Districts (Lower Hutt) 23-25 January 1982	20-6-39-4	27-11-42-5	15-2-38-0	18-7-52-1	1-0-8-0			
	12-6-26-4	16-5-54-2	1-0-8-0	10-1-29-2	11.1-4-33-2			
v. Canterbury (Christchurch) 29-31 January 1982	9.4-1-41-2	23-3-74-4	4-1-11-0	24-4-62-0	9-2-37-2	7-2-24-2		
	12-2-39-1	19-10-31-3		13-2-42-4	13-5-26-1	5-2-6-1		
	188.2-43-549-22 av. 24.95	344.1-110-793-47 av. 16.87	63.3-11-198-7 av. 28.28	142.4-31-398-17 av. 23.41	229.1-77-587-22 av. 26.68	91-29-210-8 av. 26.25	2-0-8-0 av. —	24-5-85-3 av. 28.33

	Inns	NOs	Runs	HS	Av
	13	1	513	141*	42.75
	12	—	247	52	20.58
	13	1	269	76*	22.41
	7	1	75	38	12.50
	13	3	498	100*	49.80
	11	—	495	126	45.00
	12	3	386	93	42.88
	10	3	295	96*	42.14
	8	1	60	24	8.57
	9	2	74	18*	10.57
	8	1	60	24	8.57
	3	—	9	4	3.00
	1	1	32	32*	—

	B	Lb	W	Nb	Total	Wkts
G. Wheeler						
	2	7		13	233	10
	9	3	1	6	248	10
	3	3		10	215	10
	1	7	1	5	168	10
		(18)			354	5
		(9)			213	5
3-0-17-0	4	6		3	274	10
7-2-13-0	4	10		4	246	9
	2	2		8	157	10
	1	3	1	4	178	10
	5	5		11	200	10
	4			5	159	10
		4		8	261	10
	2	7		5	158	10
10-2-30-0						

with a steady flow of runs coming from Edgar (513), Morrison (498), Evan Gray (495) and Ross Ormiston (396), but with the comparatively minor offering of 269 from Coney. Their bowling was similarly businesslike, with Ewen Chatfield taking 47 wickets, and the rest supporting him steadily. Northern Districts never really mounted a challenge, for they leaned too heavily on Wright (692) and John Parker (618) for their runs, and never really had a sharp enough bowling attack to force the wins.

Despite Hadlee's bowling, Canterbury never scored enough runs, Auckland lacked a hostile bowling attack, and Otago and Central Districts laboured along at the rear of the field.

Edgar was quite obviously the man of the season, and the doughty little left-hander has now acquired both a hearty appetite for runs, and no little skill in scoring them. He followed his 513 runs for Wellington with 143 for New Zealand versus the Rest in a trial. In the one-day Shell Cup matches he had the quite staggering scores of 96, 97, 147 not out, 106 not out, 3 and 79 not out. In the one-dayers against Australia Edgar scored 79, 3 and 11, and in the tests 55, 161, 29, 22 and 11. As these figures might indicate Edgar is now reaching the peak of his form, and is becoming much more confident with his stroke-play, as his one-day batting would suggest.

But even now with Wright, Howarth and Edgar established as test-ranking batsmen New Zealand must look closely at the middle-order problems. Coney had a modest season, and Martin Crowe, the 19-year-old, had a gruelling and none too successful start in international cricket. Morrison was recalled to the test side, but rather confirmed that his ability against quick bowling is declining – even if he performed some startling feats with his bowling.

Happily, at least in the short term, the New Zealand batting may soon be improved by the return of Glenn Turner, after his century of centuries. At the time of writing Turner was talking seriously of making this his last season with Worcestershire, and of returning to Dunedin where a prospective, and challenging job, would require him to play cricket. Before he returned to Worcester Turner mentioned that he might well be available again, especially as there was a tour of Australia next summer, and the prospect of trying his hand at day–night cricket represented a new challenge.

It is encouraging, too, that the NZCC and the New Zealand Sports Foundation have combined to provide financial backing for Howarth, Wright and Hadlee in between county seasons. Howarth and Hadlee will receive $20,000 each, and Wright $10,000, for coaching and promotion duties during the home season – and for that they can thank both the foundation, and the thousands of spectators who, especially on that mad, merry afternoon in Auckland, jolted New Zealand into the mega-world of modern cricket.

Opposite: *Jim Cook (Transvaal) is bowled by Frank Joubert of Northern Transvaal when pressing for runs on the last day of the Currie Cup game in Pretoria.*

SECTION E
The Great Rebellion
Cricket in South Africa

One of the most controversial seasons, details of which will appear in subsequent pages. Unfortunately controversy often overshadowed the cricket which was sometimes disappointing and often sub-standard. The same could be said of the wickets, and the players' attitudes.

Ominously for the future of cricket in the Republic the outstanding players were mainly those who had learned their cricket in the previous decade. Of the comparatively few younger players to make an impression mention should be made of Transvaal's Mandy Yachad, who fell away somewhat after a brilliant start but is a slightly built right-hander with plenty of strokes, a good defence and, most important, a touch of class, and Pienaar Anker who made his mark as an off-spinner with Castle Bowl winners Boland. He was the third highest wicket taker behind Sprinboks van der Bijl and Jefferies. These two young players seem to have the style and ability to reach the top but their development, as with others, may well depend on South Africa's position in world cricket. The next few seasons will be vital, and *could* be fatal.

South African domestic first-class cricket saw substantially the same set-up as in the previous season. The Currie Cup saw each competitor play the others home and out, with champions Natal again having to contend with Transvaal, Northern Transvaal, and the Eastern and Western Province sides. The Castle Bowl was again divided into two sections, but the advent of Northern Transvaal's 'B' string saw some re-organisation. Griqualand West, Orange Free State and Natal 'B' were joined in the erstwhile 'Northern' section by Western Province 'B', while the other section received reigning holders Transvaal 'B', Northern Transvaal 'B' also joining Border, Boland and Eastern Province 'B'. The two section winners were to meet in the final at the season's end.

The first-class season started at Bloemfontein – Griqualand West visiting Free State, on last season's form hardly a battle of the giants. The feature of a rain-interrupted opening day was a hat-trick by Free State pace-man, eighteen-year-old Johannes van Heerden. This put the skids under a promising Griquas start and some good Free State batting – beefy Geoff Humpage well to the fore with two aggressive fifties eventually saw them to a comfortable win.

Castle Bowl
16, 17 and 18 October
at Ramblers, Bloemfontein

Griqualand West 247 (T. Smit 52 not out, C. J. van Heerden 4 for 45) and 243 (A. D. Methven 67, M. J. D. Doherty 53)
Orange Free State 309 (J. J. Strydom 85, G. W. Humpage 64) and 182 for 3 (G. W. Humpage 61 not out, R. J. East 53 not out)

Orange Free State won by 7 wickets
Orange Free State 19 pts, Griqualand West 7 pts

Alan Barrow (Northern Transvaal) hooks Hanley to celebrate the start of the season.

DATSUN SHIELD ROUND ONE: WESTERN PROVINCE 'B' v. ORANGE FREE STATE

24 October 1981 at Newlands, Cape Town

ORANGE FREE STATE

L. W. Griessel	b Mahoney		7
C. J. van Heerden	lbw, b Mahoney		19
S. N. Hartley	b Taljaard		39
G. W. Humpage	b Nieuwoudt		99
R. J. East	b Pagden		21
E. Schmidt	c Nieuwoudt, b Pagden		0
W. M. van der Merwe	not out		44
J. J. Strydom	not out		7
G. Grobler			
C. J. P. G. van Zyl			
L. J. Wenzler			
Extras			17
	(for 6 wkts)		253

	O	M	R	W
Nieuwoudt	11	3	26	1
Mahoney	11	3	19	2
Taljaard	11	—	41	1
Pagden	11	1	67	2
van Niekerk	4	—	30	—
Clarke	7	—	53	—

FALL OF WICKETS
1–12, 2–44, 3–141, 4–192, 5–192, 6–218

WESTERN PROVINCE 'B'

P. M. Thompson	c East, b Schmidt	9
E. Muntingh	b Schmidt	2
J. Seeff	c East, b van der Merwe	7
P. Rayner	c Wenzler, b van der Merwe	143
T. A. Clarke	b van Zyl	22
H. M. Ackerman	c East, b Grobler	4
A. van Niekerk	c sub, b van Heerden	1
N. Pagden	run out	14
M. Taljaard	lbw, b van der Merwe	6
J. Mahoney	not out	16
A. B. Nieuwoudt	b van der Merwe	0
Extras		9
		233

	O	M	R	W
Schmidt	11	3	20	2
van der Merwe	10.5	1	49	4
van Zyl	10	1	41	1
Grobler	8	1	37	1
van Heerden	10	1	57	1
Hartley	4	—	20	—

FALL OF WICKETS
1–5, 2–16, 3–18, 4–68, 5–81, 6–84, 7–152, 8–183, 9–232

Orange Free State won by 20 runs

DATSUN SHIELD ROUND ONE: NORTHERN TRANSVAAL v. BORDER

24 October 1981 at Berea Park, Pretoria

NORTHERN TRANSVAAL

A. Barrow	c Hagemann, b Hayes	27
V. F. du Preez	c Kent, b Hayes	45
N. G. Featherstone	b Gower	70
C. S. Stirk	c Hagemann, b Hayes	27
A. M. Ferreira	not out	44
R. C. Ontong	not out	13
A. H. Wilkins		
F. E. Joubert		
W. F. Morris		
B. McBride		
K. G. Motley		
Extras		6
	(for 4 wkts)	232

	O	M	R	W
Hartley	11	4	54	
Lyons	11	2	27	
Davies	6	1	22	
Ranger	6	1	16	
Hayes	11		51	3
Gower	10	1	56	1

FALL OF WICKETS
1–65, 2–94, 3–148, 4–196

BORDER

I. D. Harty	c McBride, b Joubert	1
R. A. Stretch	lbw, b Wilkins	4
R. Kent	c McBride, b Joubert	2
E. T. Laughlin	c McBride, b Joubert	7
G. L. Hayes	b Ferreira	11
D. Hagemann	c Morris, b Wilkins	0
R. B. C. Ranger	c Stirk, b Ontong	11
A. Lyons	c Motley, b Ferreira	0
G. M. Gower	c Ontong, b Morris	12
J. Hartley	b Morris	5
C. Davies	not out	0
Extras		8
		61

	O	M	R	W
Joubert	8	4	11	3
Wilkins	7	3	12	2
Ontong	5.3	2	9	1
Ferreira	6	1	15	2
Morris	4	2	6	2

FALL OF WICKETS
1–2, 2–8, 3–16, 4–16, 5–23, 6–29, 7–29, 8–47, 9–59

Northern Transvaal won by 171 runs

Currie Cup

30, 31 October and 2 November 1981

at Berea Park, Pretoria

Northern Transvaal 356 (C. S. Stirk 124, V. F. du Preez 115, N. V. Radford 4 for 93) and 181 (R. W. Hanley 4 for 34)
Transvaal 347 for 9 dec (K. A. McKenzie 67, C. E. B. Rice 66, R. G. Pollock 65, A. M. Ferreira 5 for 63) and 66 for 4

Match drawn
Transvaal 8 pts, Northern Transvaal 5 pts

Castle Bowl

at Wanderers, Johannesburg

Northern Transvaal 'B' 173 and 207 (J. P. Ackermann 52, I. F. Weideman 4 for 39)
Transvaal 'B' 260 (M. Yachad 154, H. W. Raath 5 for 53) and 121 for 4 (M. Yachad 59)

Transvaal 'B' won by 6 wickets
Transvaal 'B' 19 pts, Northern Transvaal 'B' 5 pts

The Currie Cup season opened at Pretoria, with Transvaal the visitors to their Northern neighbours. The home team

Lee Barnard of Transvaal is bowled by Ferreira in the Currie Cup match with Northern Transvaal. Clive Rice, his skipper, looks on unamused.

started well, a third wicket stand of 224 by Craig Stirk and Vernon Du Preez (a Northern Transvaal first-class record) putting them in a strong position on the opening day. The visitors replied with an equally impressive display of aggressive and consistent batting, with only Anton Ferreira commanding respect among the Northern bowlers. Northern gave a disappointing display against the pace of Hanley and Radford on the third morning but Transvaal in their turn struggled in their second innings and the match finished with them grateful to hang on for a draw.

The feature of the Castle Bowl match at Wanderers between the respective 'B' teams was a glorious 154 in 5 hours by twenty-year-old Transvaal opener Mandy Yachad. After a slow start the diminutive Maccabeean dominated the Northern bowling, his driving being especially impressive and only left armer Heinrich Raath really kept him in check. Northern's second innings batting was little better than the mediocre efforts of the first, Francois Weideman breaking their back with a 4 for 6 spell when a draw seemed just possible. Needing 121 to win Transvaal coasted home, with Yachad again dominating proceedings with a delightful 59.

Currie Cup
6, 7 and 8 November 1981
at Newlands, Cape Town

Eastern Province 172 (D. J. Brickett 55, G. S. le Roux 5 for 30) and 158 (S. T. Jefferies 4 for 51, D. L. Hobson 4 for 65)
Western Province 284 (P. N. Kirsten 114, W. K. Watson 4 for 52) and 50 for 0

Western Province won by 10 wickets
Western Province 17 pts, Eastern Province 2 pts

Castle Bowl
at Ramblers, Bloemfontein

Western Province 'B' 129 (C. van Zyl 6 for 50, A. Sidebottom 4 for 32) and 278 (H. M. Ackerman 86 not out, T. A. Clarke 82, A. Sidebottom for 50)
Orange Free State 218 (R. J. East 54, J. D. du Toit 5 for 46) and 190 for 8

Orange Free State won by 2 wickets
Orange Free State 17 pts, Western Province 'B' 5 pts

Rupert Hanley of Transvaal bowling to left-handed opener Brian Whitfield of Northern Transvaal. Whitfield had a splendid season.

7, 8 and 9 November 1981

at Kemsley Park, Port Elizabeth

Border 113 (I. Howell 4 for 22) and 133
Eastern Province 'B' 339 (I. Howell 112, M. K. van Vuuren 75, R. G. Fensham 68, J. Hartley 4 for 57)

Eastern Province 'B' won by an innings and 93 runs
Eastern Province 'B' 22 pts, Border 5 pts

at Kingsmead, Durban

Griqualand West 242 (A. P. Beukes 55) and 91 for 2
Natal 'B' 313 (P. H. Williams 67, D. K. Pearse 55 not out, A.P. Beukes 5 for 101)

Match drawn
Natal 'B' 10 pts, Griqualand West 7 pts

Western Province started their Currie Cup campaign well with a convincing home victory over their Eastern neighbours. Eastern made a bad start on the first morning, losing openers Dennis Broad and Keith Gradwell for 15 runs and needed a ninth wicket stand of 66 from skipper Dave Brickett and Kenny Watson to reach respectability. Kirsten's first Currie Cup hundred for two years ensured a lead of 112 and with the Eastern batsmen again unconvincing against the seam of Stephen Jefferies and Denys Hobson's spin the 10 wicket win was a formality.

Reigning Castle Bowl holders Western Province 'B' commenced their campaign disappointingly. Winning the toss on a lively Ramblers wicket their batsmen put up a painful exhibition of spineless batting against the pace of Corrie van Zyl. Seven wickets fell for 30 before the last 3 wickets added 99. Orange Free State in their turn struggled, only an aggressive half century from skipper Robbie East ensuring a lead. A solid fifth wicket stand of 138 between Hylton Ackerman and Bossie Clarke gave Westerns cause for hope, but a fine spell by Yorkshireman Arnie Sidebottom caused a late collapse and although Free State never found their task easy they finally achieved a 2 wicket win with 15 overs remaining.

Meanwhile at Port Elizabeth Border confirmed fears of a struggling season with an innings defeat by Eastern Province 'B'. Batting first, wickets fell steadily after opener Richard Kent had gone at 7 and when Easterns batted a century on the first-class debut by Ian Howell, plus fifties from Russ Fensham and van Vuuren put Border's backs against the wall. Needing 226 to make Eastern bat again, Border again fell apart to lose with a day to spare. With 112 and 5 wickets for 47 Ian Howell made an outstanding, and match-winning first-class debut for Easterns.

The winner at Durban was the weather. Griqualand West batted solidly on the first day but Natal 'B''s great aggression paid off to bring a first innings lead and bonus points. Griquas had levelled the scores with 2 wickets down on the second afternoon when bad light curtailed play and rain restricted the third day to only 13 overs.

Castle Bowl

12, 13 and 14 November 1981

at Country Club, Kimberley

Western Province 'B' 282 for 8 dec (P. M. Thompson 90, E. Muntingh 69) and 166 for 5 (P. M. Thompson 52)
Griqualand West 288 (A. G. D. Methven 68, M. J. D. Doherty 55, T. A. Clarke 5 for 30)

Match drawn
Griqualand West 7 pts, Western Province 'B' 7 pts

at Oude Libertas, Stellenbosch

Boland 346 for 3 dec (A. du Toit 117, E. J. Barlow 107, H. N. Basson 64)
Border 116 and 169 (R. Kent 52, G. L. Hayes 52, P. Anker 6 for 83, E. L. Barlow 4 for 25)

Boland won by an innings and 61 runs
Boland 21 pts, Border 1 pt

Currie Cup

13, 14 and 15 November 1981

at St Georges Park, Port Elizabeth

Northern Transvaal 177 (R. C. Ontong 75, J. A. Carse 6 for 50) and 183 (V. F. du Preez 70)
Eastern Province 216 (C. M. Old 4 for 54) and 114 (C. M. Old 4 for 29)

Northern Transvaal won by 30 runs
Northern Transvaal 15 pts, Eastern Province 7 pts

Champions Western Province 'B' batted carefully on the first day of their Castle Bowl match with Griqualand West; opener Peter Thompson's 90 in over 3½ hours, and his second wicket stand of 86 in 2 hours with Eugene Muntingh probably put them safe from defeat, but, barring a Griqua collapse, safe too from victory. An opening stand of 88 between Yorkshireman Kevin Sharp and veteran Mike Doherty, and some tail-wagging by Winkie Dobson and Tienie Smit, saw there was no crucial collapse despite Bossie Clarke's 5 wickets and when rain washed-out proceedings at lunch on the third day a draw seemed certain.

Border continued their catastrophic season when their visit to Stellenbosch ended in another, two-day, slaughter. Led for the first time by Eddie Barlow, Boland began with a stand of 180, by a long way their best for the first wicket, both Barlow and Andre du Toit posting hundreds. As the Border bowlers wilted in the afternoon the openers increased the scoring rate and when they departed Bosie Basson and Andre Odendaal completed the destruction with a stand of 83 in under an hour. The demoralised Border lost 3 wickets to fast bowler Charl Coetzee before the close and on the second day they crumbled depressingly to a humiliating defeat before the off-spin of Pienaar Anker, who achieved match figures of 9 for 123 on his first-class debut and, latterly, the seamers of the irrepressible Barlow.

In the Currie Cup, Port Elizabeth hosted a meeting of last season's stragglers, Eastern Province and Northern Transvaal. The seamers found the overcast conditions to their liking and only a fighting 75 from Rod Ontong avoided disaster for Northerns, against seamers James Carse and Ken Watson revelling in the conditions. Chris Old put

Dave Richardson

DATSUN SHIELD SECOND ROUND: EASTERN PROVINCE 'B' v. BOLAND
21 November 1981 at St Georges Park, Port Elizabeth

BOLAND

E. J. Barlow	b Carse		19
A. du Toit	c Ogilvie, b van Vuuren		38
H. N. Basson	b Carse		0
A. Odendaal	c Richardson, b Carse		42
P. D. Swart	b Watson		24
S. A. Jones	not out		31
M. van Blommenstein	run out		5
H. Bergins	c Ogilvie, b Brickett		0
R. C. Schultz*	c Richardson, b Watson		2
P. Anker	not out		4
C. J. Coetzee			
Extras			19
	(for 8 wkts)		184

	O	M	R	W
Watson	11	2	44	2
Ogilvie	11	1	27	—
Carse	11	2	21	3
Brickett	11	3	32	1
van Vuuren	11	1	41	1

FALL OF WICKETS
1–36, 2–36, 3–95, 4–122, 5–147, 6–170, 7–170, 8–180

EASTERN PROVINCE 'B'

R. J. B. Whyte	c Swart, b Coetzee	2
K. W. Gradwell	c Bergins, b Coetzee	3
R. L. S. Armitage	c Odendaal, b Barlow	18
D. J. Richardson	c van Blommenstein, b Anker	3
M. van Vuuren	c Schultz, b Barlow	12
R. G. Fensham	c van Blommenstein, b Bergins	28
D. J. Brickett	c Barlow, b Bergins	17
D. H. Howell	run out	0
W. K. Watson	b Bergins	10
J. D. Ogilvie	c Schultz, b Bergins	15
J. A. Carse	not out	0
Extras		10
		118

	O	M	R	W
Barlow	11	3	23	2
Coetzee	6	2	8	2
Anker	9	1	22	1
Swart	6	—	14	—
Bergins	8.2	3	18	4
Jones	7	—	23	—

FALL OF WICKETS
1–6, 2–7, 3–20, 4–30, 5–42, 6–71, 7–75, 8–95, 9–118

Boland won by 66 runs

Easterns into trouble on their first evening but as conditions eased on the second day the seamers lost their venom. Dave Richardson and Russell Fensham played well to add 98 for the fifth wicket and some vigorous tail wagging brought a first innings advantage. Northerns made another disastrous start in the second innings but this time Vernon du Preez, supported by some lusty blows from Anton Ferreira provided the rescue act. Needing 145 for victory Eastern's specialist batsmen again failed and although Dave Richardson and the tail again fought hard Northerns fully deserved their 30 run win.

DATSUN SHIELD SECOND ROUND: WESTERN PROVINCE v. NORTHERN TRANSVAAL

21 November 1981 at Newlands, Cape Town

NORTHERN TRANSVAAL
B. J. Whitfield	c McEwan, b Jefferies		0
A. Barrow	lbw, b During		27
V. F. du Preez	c Nel, b le Roux		5
C. S. Stirk	c Seeff, b Hobson		1
N. G. Featherstone	c Ryall, b During		1
R. C. Ontong	c During, b Pienaar		12
P. D. de Vaal	run out		0
A. M. Ferreira	c Nel, b Jefferies		26
C. M. Old	not out		10
B. McBride	c Ryall, b Jefferies		0
F. E. Joubert	c Ryall, b le Roux		9
Extras			7
			98

	O	M	R	W
le Roux	8	1	16	2
Jefferies	8	3	17	3
Hobson	11	4	20	1
During	11	4	22	2
Pienaar	6	2	16	1

FALL OF WICKETS
1–1, 2–17, 3–37, 4–38, 5–39, 6–39, 7–75, 8–85, 9–85

WESTERN PROVINCE
L. Seeff	not out	42
M. J. Nel	b Old	0
P. N. Kirsten	c Joubert, b Ontong	32
A. J. Lamb	not out	23
K. S. McEwan		
S. T. Jefferies		
R. J. Ryall*		
J. During		
R. F. Pienaar		
D. L. Hobson		
G. S. le Roux		
Extras		4
	(for 2 wkts)	101

	O	M	R	W
Old	7	4	4	1
Joubert	3	1	12	—
Ontong	7	1	42	1
Ferreira	8	1	25	—
de Vaal	1.2	—	14	—

FALL OF WICKETS
1–1, 2–55

Western Province won by 8 wickets

DATSUN SHIELD SECOND ROUND: ORANGE FREE STATE v. NATAL

21 November 1981 at Ramblers, Bloemfontein

ORANGE FREE STATE
L. J. Wenzler	c Procter, b Taylor	4
C. J. van Heerden	c Clift, b Taylor	0
L. W. Griessel	not out	59
G. W. Humpage	b Cooper	16
R. J. East	c Daniels, b Cooper	16
J. J. Strydom	lbw, b Bentley	4
G. N. Lister-James	c Smith, b Cooper	0
W. M. van der Merwe	c Wilkins, b Taylor	31
A. Sidebottom	run out	3
C. J. P. G. van Zyl	lbw, b Taylor	3
G. Grobler	not out	2
Extras		15
	(for 9 wkts)	153

	O	M	R	W
van der Bijl	11	3	22	—
Taylor	11	6	15	4
Clift	11	1	34	—
Cooper	11	4	21	3
Bentley	11	1	46	1

FALL OF WICKETS
1–2, 2–10, 3–32, 4–62, 5–75, 6–76, 7–128, 8–134, 9–147

NATAL
B. A. Richards	c van der Merwe, b van Heerden	66
C. P. Wilkins	lbw, b van der Merwe	0
R. M. Bentley	b Grobler	15
M. J. Procter	b van Zyl	39
D. Bestall	not out	7
N. P. Daniels	not out	17
V. A. P. van der Bijl		
P. B. Clift		
L. B. Taylor		
A. J. S. Smith		
K. R. Cooper		
Extras		13
	(for 4 wkts)	157

	O	M	R	W
van der Merwe	6	—	26	1
van Zyl	9	1	28	1
Sidebottom	11	—	22	—
Grobler	3	—	19	1
van Heerden	6	—	34	1
Humpage	4	1	15	—

FALL OF WICKETS
1–5, 2–31, 3–115, 4–136

Natal won by 6 wickets

Currie Cup

27, 28 and 30 November 1981

at Berea Park, Pretoria

Northern Transvaal 129 (S. T. Jefferies 5 for 46) and 208 (B. J. Whitfield 70, D. L. Hobson 5 for 82)
Western Province 368 for 9 dec (P. N. Kirsten 86, S. T. Jefferies 63, K. S. McEwan 53)

Western Province won by an innings and 31 runs
Western Province 19 pts, Northern Transvaal 4 pts

Castle Bowl

27, 28 and 30 November 1981

at Constantia, Cape Town

Griqualand West 108 (J. D. du Toit 6 for 26) and 203 (M. J. D. Doherty 82, J. D. du Toit 4 for 41)
Western Province 'B' 210 (T. A. Clarke 54, T. Smit 5 for 68) and 104 for 5

Western Province 'B' won by 5 wickets
Western Province 'B' 17 pts, Griqualand West 5 pts

DATSUN SHIELD SECOND ROUND: GRIQUALAND WEST v. TRANSVAAL
21 November 1981 at Kimberley

TRANSVAAL

S. J. Cook		c Dobson, b Smit	5
A. I. Kallicharran		c Dobson, b Canny	32
H. R. Fotheringham		c Smit, b Liebenberg	42
R. G. Pollock		b Beukes	66
C. E. B. Rice		c Dobson, b Parker	33
K. A. McKenzie		not out	37
L. J. Barnard		not out	0
N. V. Radford			
R. W. Hanley			
J. Fairclough			
R. V. Jennings			
Extras			22
		(for 5 wkts)	237

	O	M	R	W
Smit	11	4	16	1
Canny	6	—	23	1
McLaren	11	3	29	1
Liebenberg	10	1	49	1
Beukes	9	—	43	1
Parker	8	—	55	1

FALL OF WICKETS
1–16, 2–65, 3–121, 4–175, 5–237

GRIQUALAND WEST

K. Sharp	b Barnard	27
M. J. D. Doherty	c & b Barnard	29
P. L. Symcox	c Radford, b Kallicharran	10
A. D. Methven	lbw, b Kallicharran	20
A. P. Beukes	not out	47
E. F. Parker	c & b Radford	19
H. Liebenberg	run out	1
K. McLaren	not out	0
T. Smit		
R. Canny		
W. Dobson		
Extras		15
	(for 6 wkts)	168

	O	M	R	W
Rice	5	2	7	—
Hanley	6	2	22	—
Radford	9	3	15	—
Fairclough	11	5	16	—
Barnard	11	2	33	2
Kallicharran	5	—	22	2
Fotheringham	3	—	19	—
McLaren	5	—	19	—

FALL OF WICKETS
1–65, 2–66, 3–92, 4–98, 5–158, 6–167

Transvaal won by 69 runs

5, 6 and 7 December 1981
at Wanderers, Johannesburg

Western Province 269 (A. P. Kuiper 63, A. J. Lamb 62, J. Fairclough 5 for 44) and 118 for 2 (L. Seeff 57 not out)
Transvaal 397 for 6 dec (A. I. Kallicharran 129, R. G. Pollock 70, C. E. B. Rice 70, J. During 4 for 114)

Match drawn
Transvaal 8 pts, Western Province 4 pts

at Pietermaritzburg

Natal 358 for 8 dec (R. M. Bentley 88, B. A. Richards 62, V. A. P. van der Bijl 53 not out) and 184 for 7 dec (B. A. Richards 87 not out)
Northern Transvaal 277 (B. J. Whitfield 100, P. D. de Vaal 64, P. B. Clift 4 for 45) and 120 for 1 (B. J. Whitfield 58 not out)

Match drawn
Natal 6 pts, Northern Transvaal 4 pts

4, 5 and 7 December 1981
at Constantia, Cape Town

Western Province 'B' 252 (A. Sidebottom 4 for 36, W. M. van der Merwe 4 for 38) and 215 for 8 dec (W. M. van der Merwe 4 for 37)
Orange Free State 92 (O. Henry 5 for 34) and 132 (J. D. du Toit 4 for 24, O. Henry 4 for 48)

at Oude Libertas, Stellenbosch

Northern Transvaal 'B' 241 (J. P. Ackermann 61, P. J. Marneweck 54, P. Anker 4 for 42) and 172 (P. J. A. Visagie 95, P. Anker 4 for 55)
Boland 164 (P. D. Swart 54, H. W. Raath 4 for 25, W. F. Morris 4 for 67) and 168 (H. W. Raath 4 for 41)

Northern Transvaal 'B' won by 81 runs
Northern Transvaal 'B' 18 pts, Boland 5 pts

Western Province maintained their good early Currie Cup form as they quite over-played Northern Transvaal at Pretoria. Northerns could never get to grips with the keen Western attack though more enterprise may have brought more positive results against the fire and swing of le Roux and Jefferies. Westerns in reply made light of the home team's highly-rated seamers, Chris Old especially suffering at the hands of Kirsten and Co., and declared leaving Northerns requiring 239 to avoid the innings defeat. Whitfield and Barrow achieved an opening stand of 105 but once this was broken Hobson steadily chipped away at the middle-order before During and le Roux returned to complete the job.

Western Province, atop the table at the end of November next travelled to Johannesburg. Winning the toss, Westerns had early struggles against the lively Transvaal pace attack but sensible batting by Alan Lamb and Adrian Kuiper, helped by some uncharacteristic fielding lapses helped pull them round, before the veteran Fairclough dealt with the tail in expert fashion. Main feature of the Transvaal reply was a century by Alvin Kallicharran; his third wicket stand with Graeme Pollock added 155 in less than 3 hours, while Clive Rice's 70 in 1¾ hours drove home Transvaal's advantage. Unfortunately the declaration came too late for a result to be anything but a remote possibility and rain finally curtailed proceedings with two hours remaining.

Last season's champions, Natal finally made their bow at Pietermaritzburg against Northern Transvaal. This match marked the return of Barry Richards after a long absence, and he stroked his way to a sedate 62 before falling to Joubert. A fine 88 from Rob Bentley and tail end aggression saw the home side to a formidable total but they were frustrated on the second day by a stubborn 6 hour century from former team-mate Brian Whitfield. Tight seam bowling foiled Natal's quest for quick runs on the third morning and despite a declaration Northerns, with Whitfield again defying his old colleagues played out the game easily.

The Castle Bowl continued with Griqualand West travelling to Constantia to confront the reigning champions. The visitors struggled against Western Province seamers Mahoney and du Toit and Westerns in their turn also had early setbacks before Eugene Muntingh and Bossie Clarke tilted the balance in their favour with a 72 run fourth wicket stand. Griqualand made a promising start to their second innings but after du Toit had dismissed the consistent Michael Doherty a collapse ensued and Westerns knocked off the 104 required for victory before lunch on the third day.

Next visitors to Constantia's Jack Burt Oval were Free State. Westerns won the toss and consistent batting saw them to a reasonable total against the keen pace of Willem van der Merwe and Arnold Sidebottom. Free State were soon in dire straits, finishing the first day at 55 for 6. Henry and du Toit soon completed the rout on the second morning and more remarkable consistent batting (Henry's unbeaten 43 was the highest score for his side in a match which saw them obtain 467 runs for 18 wickets) enabled them to set Free State 376 for victory. Despite an opening stand of 54 they never looked remotely like achieving their presumed goal and Omar Henry and Danie du Toit again sparked a disappointing collapse.

Meanwhile at Stellenbosch Boland came down to earth with a bump. Steady batting by visitors Northern Transvaal 'B' established a sound base, though off-spinner Anker produced a good spell in mid-innings to keep things under control. Boland struggled disappointingly against left armers Heinrich Raath (seam) and Bill Morris (spin) and found themselves with a first innings deficit of 77. Northerns in their turn found things difficult in their second knock and owed everything to a best ever 95 by Peter Visagie, who remained at the crease for 2¼ hours while wickets fell around him. Chasing 250 with a whole day remaining, Boland's batting was again disappointingly inept. Again the left armers did the damage, Mel Davies joining in with his seamers, and Northerns achieved victory 65 minutes after lunch.

First-class friendly match

15, 17 and 18 December 1981

at Newlands, Cape Town

Western Province 130 and 309 (A. J. Lamb 69, L. Seeff 54, J. D. du Toit 5 for 59)
S.A. Universities 249 (R. J. East 63, R. F. Pienaar 4 for 64) and 106 (O. Henry 7 for 22)

Western Province won by 84 runs

Sent in to bat Westerns suffered acute embarrassment on a wet wicket on the opening day and found themselves considerably in arrears on first innings. Acting skipper Alan Lamb and Larkie Seeff led a second innings recovery however and Universities collapsed against the spin of Omar Henry, who achieved a career best 7 for 22 in 16.1 overs supported by Roy Pienaar. With a first innings lead of 119, and with the whole of the third day in which to achieve the 191 needed to win, Universities should *never* have lost.

DATSUN SHIELD SEMI-FINAL, FIRST LEG: TRANSVAAL v. NATAL

19 December 1981 at Wanderers, Johannesburg

NATAL

B. A. Richards	run out	7
C. P. Wilkins	c Fairclough, b Rice	66
R. M. Bentley	b Radford	11
D. Bestall	c Cook, b Hanley	10
M. J. Procter	c Fairclough, b Radford	37
N. P. Daniels	c Pollock, b Fairclough	0
A. J. S. Smith	c Kourie, b Radford	10
P. B. Clift	not out	18
V. A. P. van der Bijl	c Pollock, b Radford	14
K. R. Cooper	not out	30
L. B. Taylor		
Extras		27
	(for 8 wkts)	230

	O	M	R	W
Rice	11	—	43	1
Fairclough	11	—	51	1
Kourie	11	2	17	—
Radford	11	3	25	4
Hanley	11	—	67	1

FALL OF WICKETS
1–16, 2–50, 3–67, 4–146, 5–147, 6–151, 7–167, 8–184

TRANSVAAL

S. J. Cook	c Smith, b Daniels	60
H. R. Fotheringham	c Procter, b Daniels	44
R. G. Pollock	c Taylor, b Cooper	36
K. A. McKenzie	lbw, b Procter	1
A. I. Kallicharran	not out	70
C. E. B. Rice	not out	15
J. Fairclough		
A. J. Kourie		
N. V. Radford		
R. W. Hanley		
R. V. Jennings		
Extras		8
	(for 4 wkts)	234

	O	M	R	W
Taylor	9	—	38	—
van der Bijl	9	—	30	—
Procter	9	1	41	1
Cooper	11	—	50	1
Clift	7	—	41	—
Daniels	6	1	2	2
Richards	0.3	—	5	—

FALL OF WICKETS
1–105, 2–109, 3–190, 4–197

Transvaal won by 6 wickets

Currie Cup

26, 27 and 28 December 1981

at Kingsmead, Durban

Western Province 157 (A. P. Kuiper 89, V. A. P. van der Bijl 7 for 31) and 144 (V. A. P. van der Bijl 4 for 33, L. B. Taylor 4 for 47)
Natal 143 (R. F. Pienaar 5 for 24) and 160 for 5 (D. Bestall 57, S. T. Jefferies 4 for 50)

Natal won by 5 wickets
Natal 15 pts, Western Province 5 pts

DATSUN SHIELD SEMI-FINAL, FIRST LEG: WESTERN PROVINCE v. BOLAND

19 December 1981 at Newlands, Cape Town

WESTERN PROVINCE
L. Seeff	c Schultz, b Swart		15
R. F. Pienaar	c Coetzee, b Bergins		67
K. S. McEwan	b Anker		12
A. J. Lamb	c de Villiers, b Coetzee		90
P. N. Kirsten	not out		57
A. P. Kuiper	not out		8
S. T. Jefferies			
J. D. du Toit			
J. During			
D. L. Hobson			
R. J. Ryall			
Extras			9
	(for 4 wkts)		258

	O	M	R	W
Barlow	11	4	34	—
Coetzee	7	—	37	1
Swart	11	2	54	1
Anker	11	1	40	1
Jones	9	—	52	—
Bergins	6	1	32	1

FALL OF WICKETS
1-45, 2-72, 3-134, 4-239

BOLAND
E. J. Barlow	b J. D. du Toit		43
A. du Toit	c During, b Kuiper		9
C. van der Merwe	b Pienaar		42
A. Odendaal	c Kuiper, b During		2
P. D. Swart	c McEwan, b Jefferies		51
J. de Villiers	c Seeff, b Pienaar		5
S. A. Jones	c During b Pienaar		0
R. C. Schultz	not out		19
P. Anker	b Kuiper		3
C. J. Coetzee	b Kuiper		0
H. Bergins	not out		0
Extras			10
	(for 9 wkts)		184

	O	M	R	W
Jefferies	11	1	45	1
Kuiper	7	2	16	3
J. D. du Toit	11	3	22	1
During	11	2	34	1
Hobson	5	—	25	—
Pienaar	10	3	32	3

FALL OF WICKETS
1-30, 2-70, 3-83, 4-120, 5-128, 6-129, 7-176, 8-184

Western Province won by 74 runs

at Wanderers, Johannesburg

Eastern Province 178 (J. Fairclough 5 for 52) and 80 (N. V. Radford 4 for 20)
Transvaal 359 for 5 dec (R. G. Pollock 124, C. E. B. Rice 108)

Transvaal won by an innings and 101 runs
Transvaal 22 pts, Eastern Province 3 pts

Castle Bowl

at Uitenhage

Transvaal 'B' 149 and 297 (L. J. Barnard 69, N. T. Day 63)
Eastern Province 'B' 232 (H. Losper 7 for 86) and 177 for 9 (J. W. Furstenburg 57)

Match drawn
Eastern Province 'B' 8 pts, Transvaal 'B' 5 pts

at East London

Border 110 (P. J. Marneweck 6 for 12) and 158 (P. J. Marneweck 4 for 37)
Northern Transvaal 'B' 343 for 9 dec (C. P. L. de Lange 112, W. F. Morris 99, G. M. Gower 5 for 66)

Northern Transvaal 'B' won by an innings and 75 runs
Northern Transvaal 'B' 17 pts, Border 3 pts

at Constantia, Cape Town

Western Province 'B' 349 for 5 dec (J. Seeff 113 not out, S. D. Bruce 100 not out, P. M. Thompson 55) and 14 for 0
Natal 'B' 99 (R. R. Lawrenson 5 for 50) and 260 (M. D. Tramantino 69, M. Hedley 53, L. L. Louw 4 for 52)

Western Province won by 10 wickets
Western Province 17 pts, Natal 'B' 2 pts

What promised to be the match of the season had a disappointing start at Durban when rain permitted only one ball to be bowled after lunch on the first day. Currie Cup leaders had then scored 83 for 6 against defending champions and due entirely to the battling of Adrian Kuiper (49 not out) had recovered from 12 for 3 and 24 for 5. Van der Bijl's figures at this point were 4 for 12 from 11.5 overs. The following morning Kuiper, playing the innings of his life advanced to 89 and Western finally totalled 157. Natal's batsmen found conditions equally difficult as they struggled to 143 all out. On the third morning yet another collapse saw Natal requiring only 159 for victory. Steve Jefferies quickly removed the openers but a stand of 99 between Rob Bentley and Daryl Bestall took Natal to the brink of victory with Neville Daniels eventually making the winning hit.

The other Currie Cup match, at Wanderers, saw lowly Eastern Province visiting the ambitious Transvaal. Eastern Province won the toss but let themselves down with yet another inept batting display. Transvaal made an indifferent initial reply, losing both openers for 29 but a century third wicket stand between Kallicharran and Pollock righted the ship, while the 197 added for the fourth wicket by Pollock and Rice completely demoralised the visitors. Pollock reached his thirtieth Currie Cup century in 4½ hours, and when twenty became the first player to score 10,000 runs in the Currie Cup. Rice's third Currie Cup hundred took him just under 3 hours. Any slight hopes Eastern Province held of drawing were shattered when Radford and Hanley shared 4 wickets for only 13 runs on the second evening and the match was soon over on the third day. Ray Jennings' six wicket-keeping catches in the second innings brought his match total to nine, to equal the South African record.

In the Castle Bowl Northern section, Northern Transvaal 'B', owing much to match figures of 10 for 49 by pace bowler

Peter Marneweck and debutant Laurens de Lange's 112, went to the top of the Northern section with an innings victory over the poor Border team while in a match of changing fortunes at Uitenhage Transvaal 'B' and Eastern Province played out a draw – Easterns being lucky to survive, finishing 37 behind with only one wicket to fall. In the Southern section holders Western Province 'B' kept up their bid to retain the Shield with a crushing victory over Natal 'B'. Centuries from Stephen Bruce and Jonathan Seeff ensured a big total and although after a dismal first innings performance had meant a follow-on Natal showed much improved form to force Western Province to bat again – albeit needing only 14 runs for victory.

Currie Cup

1, 2 and 3 January 1982

at St Georges Park, Port Elizabeth

Eastern Province 295 (R. L. S. Armitage 118)
Natal 145 (C. Wulfsohn 6 for 18) and 254 for 5 (M. J. Procter 76)

Match drawn
Eastern Province 7 pts, Natal 5 pts

at Newlands, Cape Town

Western Province 353 for 9 dec (S. D. Bruce 89, A. P. Kuiper 72, O. Henry 53, A. J. Kourie 6 for 88) and 186 for 7 dec (A. J. Kourie 5 for 102)
Transvaal 251 (K. A. McKenzie 78, S. J. Cook 72, G. S. le Roux 5 for 63) and 118 for 3

Match drawn
Western Province 9 pts, Transvaal 6 pts

Castle Bowl

1, 2 and 3 January 1982

at Kingsmead, Durban

Natal 'B' 295 for 7 dec (P. J. Allan 75 not out, D. K. Pearse 70, R. A. Smith 58) and 160 for 7 dec
Orange Free State 250 (C. J. van Heerden 57, I. Ebrahim 5 for 75) and 81 for 1

Match drawn
Natal 'B' 6 pts, Orange Free State 5 pts

at Berea Park, Pretoria

Northern Transvaal 'B' 284 (D. N. Edwards 62, C. P. L. de Lange 61, L. Reid-Ross 6 for 78) and 221 for 6 dec (D. N. Edwards 50, M. K. van Vuuren 5 for 71)
Eastern Province 'B' 195 and 251 for 6 (G. S. Cowley 98 not out)

Match drawn
Northern Transvaal 6 pts, Eastern Province 4 pts

at East London

Transvaal 'B' 230 (N. Day 78, G. E. McMillan 64) and 203 (N. E. Wright 65)
Border 335 (E. T. Laughlin 101, R. B. C. Ranger 75) and 102 for 6

Border won by 4 wickets
Border 17 pts, Transvaal 'B' 6 pts

Ken McEwan (Western Province – and Essex) under siege from Transvaal. Clive Rice watches Barnard and wicket-keeper Jennings dive for a half chance. Bowler Graham Johnson looks on hopefully.

A splendid hundred from Robert Armitage gave Eastern Province their best start of the season so far and when Natal, handicapped by an injury to Barry Richards collapsed in the face of a fine spell of pace bowling from Clive Wulfsohn the follow-on was enforced. Unfortunately for Eastern Wulfsohn was unable to work the oracle again and Natal, showing no aggression or aggressive intent were able to plod to a dreary draw, thus averting humiliation. An interesting feature of the Natal second innings was an 'over' of 9 legitimate balls by James Carse; Carse also bowled four successive away swinging wides at one stage.

While the potential wooden spoonists were trying to force their first win, log leaders Western Province were fighting a somewhat grim draw with second placed Transvaal. Westerns made a bad start, losing 5 for 90 as left arm spinner Alan Kourie bowled his best spell of the season thus far. However two big stands – 157 for the sixth wicket by Kuiper and Bruce, and 92 for the eighth between le Roux and Henry changed the position, enabling them to declare at 353 for 9. Transvaal's reply was cautious and, at times, almost comatose, McKenzie and Cook taking over 3½ hours to add 151 for the third wicket, Cook's 72 actually occupying over 4 hours. Having saved the follow-on Transvaal suffered a late collapse but as losing four early wickets persuaded Westerns to take no risks in the second innings, they lost any slight chance of a win. Finally set a target of 289 in 110 minutes plus 20 overs Transvaal showed no interest in trying to win and the match drifted to a boring, and farcical draw.

Clive Rice

DATSUN SHIELD SEMI-FINAL, SECOND LEG: BOLAND v. WESTERN PROVINCE

9 January 1982 at Oude Libertas, Stellenbosch

WESTERN PROVINCE			
L. Seeff	c Schultz, b Jones		17
R. F. Pienaar	c Schultz, b Swart		42
P. N. Kirsten	c Schultz, b Jones		4
K. S. McEwan	b Barlow		32
A. P. Kuiper	run out		0
S. D. Bruce	b Jones		47
O. Henry	c Jones, b Swart		2
G. S. le Roux	not out		42
J. D. du Toit	c Anker, b Jones		42
S. T. Jefferies	run out		0
J. During	not out		0
Extras			8
	(for 9 wkts)		236

	O	M	R	W
Coetzee	11	1	49	—
Jones	11	1	52	4
Barlow	11	1	20	1
Swart	9	—	50	2
Bergins	1	—	9	—
Anker	7	—	31	—
de Villiers	5	—	17	—

FALL OF WICKETS
1–25, 2–32, 3–93, 4–93, 5–127, 6–133, 7–162, 8–222, 9–223

BOLAND		
C. van der Merwe	c Bruce, b le Roux	8
A. du Toit	c Bruce, b Jefferies	3
A. Odendaal	b Jefferies	8
P. D. Swart	lbw, b le Roux	0
E. J. Barlow	c Henry, b Jefferies	0
J. de Villiers	c During, b Jefferies	2
H. Bergins	c Bruce, b During	13
S. A. Jones	c Pienaar, b J. D. du Toit	40
R. C. Schultz	c McEwan, b During	14
P. Anker	b During	15
C. J. Coetzee	not out	2
Extras		13
		118

	O	M	R	W
le Roux	11	3	13	2
Jefferies	11	2	34	4
Henry	5	—	12	—
During	9.1	2	20	3
Pienaar	2	—	16	—
J. D. du Toit	3	—	10	1

FALL OF WICKETS
1–10, 2–20, 3–20, 4–28, 5–29, 6–30, 7–65, 8–101, 9–101

Western Province won by 118 runs to go through to the final

The position at the end of these two matches was a ten point lead for Westerns over Transvaal, who had a match in hand. Defending champions Natal were struggling in fourth place, five points ahead of Eastern Province, still winless.

In the Castle Bowl Southern section Natal 'B' recovered from a bad start against Free State at Durban, Allan and Pearse adding 136 for the seventh wicket, and the steady spin from Ebrahim kept Free State down to 250. Natal's second innings declaration left Free State to get 206 for victory in

DATSUN SHIELD SEMI-FINAL, SECOND LEG: NATAL v. TRANSVAAL

9 January 1982 at Kingsmead, Durban

NATAL

R. M. Bentley	b Rice	11
C. P. Wilkins	b Rice	84
M. J. Procter	c Jennings, b Rice	1
D. Bestall	c Jennings, b Fairclough	3
R. A. Smith	c McKenzie, b Fairclough	10
A. J. S. Smith	c Jennings, b Hanley	0
N. P. Daniels	run out	17
P. B. Clift	c Kourie, b Hanley	14
V. A. P. van der Bijl	c Cook, b Radford	4
K. R. Cooper	c McKenzie, b Radford	29
L. B. Taylor	not out	1
Extras		17
		191

	O	M	R	W
Hanley	11	1	34	2
Radford	9.1	—	39	2
Kourie	11	—	47	—
Rice	9	2	29	3
Fairclough	11	3	25	2

FALL OF WICKETS
1–49, 2–59, 3–75, 4–114, 5–115, 6–119, 7–153, 8–159, 9–185

TRANSVAAL

S. J. Cook	c A. Smith, b Clift	43
H. R. Fotheringham	c Procter, b van der Bijl	0
K. A. McKenzie	lbw, b Procter	0
A. I. Kallicharran	c A. Smith, b Cooper	20
C. E. B. Rice	c Procter, b Cooper	14
L. J. Barnard	c A. Smith, b Clift	2
A. J. Kourie	lbw, b Procter	22
R. V. Jennings	b van der Bijl	42
N. V. Radford	not out	13
R. W. Hanley	b Taylor	2
J. Fairclough	not out	3
Extras		22
	(for 9 wkts)	183

	O	M	R	W
van der Bijl	11	5	14	2
Procter	11	1	48	2
Taylor	11	2	39	1
Cooper	11	4	17	2
Clift	11	—	43	2

FALL OF WICKETS
1–9, 2–14, 3–60, 4–85, 5–91, 6–97, 7–142, 8–169, 9–181

Natal won by 8 runs, deciding match to be played

DATSUN SHIELD SEMI-FINAL, PLAY-OFF: NATAL v. TRANSVAAL

13 January 1982 at Durban

TRANSVAAL

S. J. Cook	c Wilkins, b Procter	16
A. J. Kourie	b Clift	10
A. I. Kallicharran	b Procter	2
C. E. B. Rice	b Taylor	76
K. A. McKenzie	c van der Bijl, b Cooper	0
H. R. Fotheringham	c A. Smith, b Taylor	17
N. Day	c A. Smith, b Cooper	10
R. V. Jennings	c A. Smith, b Cooper	5
N. V. Radford	lbw, b Cooper	1
R. W. Hanley	not out	2
J. Fairclough	not out	0
Extras		26
	(for 9 wkts)	165

	O	M	R	W
van der Bijl	11	2	23	—
Procter	11	5	18	2
Clift	11	3	35	1
Cooper	11	2	24	2
Taylor	11	1	39	2

FALL OF WICKETS
1–32, 2–36, 3–38, 4–42, 5–78, 6–124, 7–134, 8–136, 9–157

NATAL

A. J. S. Smith	c Kallicharran, b Radford	9
C. P. Wilkins	c Radford, b Fairclough	3
R. M. Bentley	c Day, b Radford	39
D. Bestall	c Jennings, b Hanley	13
M. J. Procter	c Jennings, b Rice	19
R. A. Smith	c Jennings, b Hanley	18
N. P. Daniels	c Jennings, b Radford	23
P. B. Clift	not out	22
V. A. P. van der Bijl	not out	0
K. R. Cooper		
L. B. Taylor		
Extras		20
	(for 7 wkts)	166

	O	M	R	W
Radford	11	2	37	3
Fairclough	11	4	14	1
Rice	10.2	2	31	1
Kourie	11	2	28	—
Hanley	11	2	36	2

FALL OF WICKETS
1–12, 2–14, 3–51, 4–86, 5–116, 6–116, 7–161

Natal won by 3 wickets and so proceeded to the final v. Western Province

160 minutes but the prospect of an interesting finish was ruined by rain with Free State well on target.

Northern section leaders Northern Transvaal 'B' lost some ground when gaining only 6 points from a draw with second placed Eastern Province 'B'. Gaining a good first innings lead Northerns ended the second day 188 ahead with only 2 second innings wickets down. However on the third day Easterns, set 311 fought all the way and an unbeaten 98 by skipper Gavin Cowley, who shared in a seventh wicket stand of 81 with Ian Howell put defeat out of the question.

In the other Northern match a fine hundred by Errol Laughlin gave Border a lead of 105 and the smell of their first victory. A superb spell by Gary Gower kept the Transvaal 'B' score down in the second innings – his 21 overs for 26 runs and 3 wickets are a testimony to his accuracy and although they suffered some hiccups Border, set 99 to win finally reached the target, with the winning boundary fittingly coming from Laughlin.

Mike Procter, the Natal skipper, and wicket-keeper Tich Smith show their delight at the province's victory over Transvaal in mid-January.

Currie Cup
16, 17 and 18 January 1982
at Kingsmead, Durban

Transvaal 209 and 151 (V. A. P. van der Bijl 7 for 64)
Natal 174 (M. J. Procter 55, R. W. Hanley 6 for 33) and 187 for 8

Natal won by 2 wickets
Natal 15 pts, Transvaal 7 pts

Castle Bowl
15, 16 and 17 January
at Wanderers, Johannesburg

Transvaal 'B' 106 and 135
Boland 169 (E. J. Barlow 65, I. F. Weideman 4 for 55) and 73 for 4

Boland won by 6 wickets
Boland 15 pts, Transvaal 5 pts

Smarting from the two Datsun Shield defeats Transvaal batted without conviction on the first day against steady but not impossible bowling but 'Spook' Hanley's best performance for several seasons skittled Natal for 174 to give his side a 33 run lead. Another disappointing Transvaal batting performance against a marathon 3¾ hour van der Bijl spell which brought him 7 for 64 in 32.3 overs left Natal to score 187 at about one a minute and despite stalling tactics from Clive Rice – at one time Transvaal bowled only 6 overs in half an hour – Natal achieved their target with 2 overs and wickets remaining. An unhappy match for Rice who stood his ground when given out caught at shortleg, the umpire having to repeat his finger-raising, as well as indulging in time wasting and negative tactics – not for the first time this season. Natal were now in third place with 39 points from 4 matches, 12 behind Transvaal, 14 behind Western Province, but both these had played 5 matches.

In the Northern Castle Bowl section there was another triumph for Eddie Barlow. 'Bunter's' Boland restricted Transvaal 'B' to a first innings 106 at less than 2 per over and although Boland themselves collapsed after good innings from Barlow and Peter Swart a lead of 63 was obtained. The second innings saw Transvaal 'B' struggling apprehensively in indifferent light – a run rate again less than 2 per over suggested more enterprise may have paid off – and Boland were left to make only 73 for victory. Despite worry over the

Jim Cook survives a confident appeal for lbw. Transvaal v Natal. Mike Procter, the Natal skipper, looks pained.

weather this was easily obtained as the Vine growers logged another convincing victory to get nearer the coveted Castle Bowl final place.

Currie Cup
23, 24 and 25 January 1982
at Wanderers, Johannesburg

Northern Transvaal 86 and 153 (C. E. B. Rice 5 for 45)
Transvaal 226 (K. A. McKenzie 56, R. C. Ontong 5 for 69)
Transvaal won by 10 wickets
Transvaal 18 pts, Northern Transvaal 5 pts

Castle Bowl
22, 23 and 25 January 1982
at Berea Park, Pretoria

Transvaal 'B' 268 (A. Videgauz 57, H. W. Raath 6 for 95) and 249 for 3 dec (N. E. Wright 85, L. J. Barnard 65)
Northern Transvaal 'B' 219 (I. F. Weideman 4 for 52) and 121 for 3
Match drawn
Transvaal 'B' 9 pts, Northern Transvaal 'B' 7 pts

at Ramblers, Bloemfontein

Natal 'B' 238 (T. R. Madsen 55, A Sidebottom 4 for 43) and 346 for 7 dec (M. B. Logan 107 not out)
Orange Free State 249 (A. Sidebottom 66, E. J. Hodkinson 4 for 76) and 204 for 5 (S. N. Hartley 72 not out, R. J. East 53)
Match drawn
Natal 'B' 8 pts, Orange Free State 8 pts

The recently criticised Transvaal pulled themselves together and in beating their struggling Northern neighbours went top of the Currie Cup log for the first time. Put in to bat on a dubious pitch Northerns showed little heart or enterprise as they collapsed abjectly to the Transvaal pace battery, whereas the Northern pacemen, Ontong excepted seemed nowhere near as formidable. Owing much to a sound 2½ hour 56 from Kevin McKenzie and late aggression from Gordon McMillan, Transvaal attained a lead of 140 and with the Northern batsmen again failing dismally were left to get only 14 for a 10 wicket victory.

Meanwhile the respective 'B' teams met at Pretoria. Again the seamers dominated the first innings, and no batsmen played major knocks, but when Transvaal commenced their second innings 49 ahead, much more enterprise was shown. Mandy Yachad and Neville Wright shared a bright opening stand before the stylish Yachad departed and Lee Barnard kept up the pressure so that a pre-lunch declaration was possible. Set to get 299 at less than one a minute, Northerns seemed to be playing themselves out of contention by a too cautious approach but it all became academic when a thunderstorm interrupted play and then water blown off the covers as they were removed ruined the pitch and caused the abandonment of the match.

At Ramblers Trevor Madsen's 55 was the backbone of Natal 'B''s first innings, while a tenth wicket stand of 91, to which Arnold Sidebottom contributed 66 enabled Free State to attain a narrow lead. However a maiden hundred by Mark Logan put Natal 'B' virtually safe from defeat; set to get 336 in 160 minutes plus 20 overs, Free State lost an early wicket and then played out time, Neil Hartley contributing a valuable unbeaten 72.

Currie Cup
29, 30 January and 1 February 1982
at Newlands, Cape Town

Northern Transvaal 251 (N. G. Featherstone 99, B. J. Whitfield 53, G. S. le Roux 6 for 44) and 75 (S. T. Jefferies 4 for 25)
Western Province 422 for 9 dec (P. N. Kirsten 130, K. S. McEwan 61, L. Seeff 50)

Western Province won by an innings and 96 runs
Western Province 21 pts, Northern Transvaal 7 pts

30, 31 January and 1 Febuary 1982
at Kingsmead, Durban

Natal 279 (R. A. Smith 91, J. A. Carse 4 for 59) and 8 for 0
Eastern Province 120 (V. A. P. van der Bijl 5 for 48) and 164 (V. A. P. van der Bijl 5 for 56)

Natal won by 10 wickets
Natal 20 pts, Eastern Province 5 pts

Below: *Stephen Jefferies appeals as Lawrence Seeff dives to catch the ball, but Vernon du Preez, the batsman, was judged not out. Jefferies appeared for Derbyshire against Pakistan during the English season.*

Opposite: *Robin Smith, a young batsman of immense promise, during his innings of 91 for Natal against Eastern Province. Smith, like his elder brother, 'Kippy', will be qualified to play for Hampshire in 1983.*

Above: *James Carse of Eastern Province beats Roy Bentley of Natal outside the off-stump.*

Left: *Rob Armitage is caught at leg-slip for nought off the bowling of Vincent van der Bijl. Van der Bijl raises his arms in acclaim – Armitage of Eastern Province was van der Bijl's 500th victim in Currie Cup matches.*

Castle Bowl
28, 29 and 30 January 1982
at Country Club, Kimberley

Griqualand West 296 (F. W. Swarbrook 71, A. D. Methven 57, M. Clare 4 for 61) and 236 for 7 dec (F. W. Swarbrook 70, M. J. D. Doherty 62, I. Ebrahim 5 for 57)
Natal 'B' 251 for 8 dec (T. R. Madsen 92, H. Liebenberg 5 for 55) and 245 for 8 dec (C. L. Smith 78)

Match drawn
Griqualand West 8 pts, Natal 'B' 7 pts

30 January, 1 and 2 February 1982

at Uitenhage

Eastern Province 'B' 263 (J. W. Stephenson 83, P. Anker 5 for 55) and 136 (P. Anker 5 for 50)
Boland 378 for 6 dec (E. J. Barlow 202 not out) and 22 for 1

Boland won by 9 wickets
Boland 17 pts, Eastern Province 'B' 7 pts

Going hard for the championship Western Province slaughtered the lowly Northern Transvaal outfit at Newlands. A fine spell by Garth le Roux gave Northerns early troubles despite a sound fifty from Brian Whitfield and there was then a middle order collapse before skipper Norman Featherstone, with support from the tail guided his side to a reasonable total, Featherstone unluckily missing his hundred by a single run.

Westerns lost Roy Pienaar for 5 but a century stand between Larkie Seef and Peter Kirsten for the second wicket, and another for the fourth between Kirsten, who completed his twenty-seventh first-class hundred and finally batted four hours for 130, and Ken McEwan, plus fifty stands for the eighth and ninth wickets put Westerns into an impregnable position. Needing 171 to make Westerns bat again, Northerns virtually surrendered themselves. Le Roux took the top off the innings on the second evening and Steve Jefferies completed the rout the following morning. Thus Westerns went top, and Northerns went flop, and must do some contemplating.

Defending Champions Natal needed a win to retain hopes of another title. Natal were soon in trouble on the notorious Kingsmead wicket and against keen East Province bowling and fielding were soon 76 for 5. An inexplicable change of tactics – Easterns employing a run-saving field and negative bowling then enabled eighteen-year-old Roger Smith to lead a fightback. Neville Daniels supported him in an 85 runs stand while van der Bijl's late aggression also improved matters. Van der Bijl then got among the Eastern batsmen, quickly taking the two wickets needed to be the first to take 500 in the Currie Cup, and with Les Taylor supporting him well, and Mike Procter mopping up the tail, Easterns were forced to follow on. Van der Bijl, in his last home match for Natal again did most damage and although Easterns, through a wagging tail avoided the innings defeat Natal needed only 6 for a victory which at least put them on the edge of the Championship race. Easterns tightened their grip at the foot of the log – their position seemingly hopeless.

In the Castle Bowl an inconclusive and remarkably even match at Kimberley saw Natal 'B' finish 36 short of victory with Griqualand West requiring only two wickets. Trevor Madsen and Chris Smith batted well for Natal 'B', but Henning Liebenberg's first innings figures of 5 for 55 in 23.4 overs were his best ever for Griqualand. While skipper Mike Doherty as ever batted well and ex-Derbyshire favourite Fred Swarbrook returned to the fray with two seventies. Griquas just had their noses in front at the finish.

The Eddie Barlow/Boland saga continued at Uitenhage. Pienaar Anker seemed to be running through the Eastern 'B' batting before 'keeper John Stephenson slammed 83 in 93 minutes to help his side to 263. Day two belonged to Barlow, as with his first competitive double century in the Republic for 15 years, he was enabled to declare and give Eastern 30 minutes at the day's end. His forty-first first class century put him behind only Richards and Pollock among South Africans. On the third morning Easterns collapsed to Anker, and left arm paceman Stephen Jones, setting Boland a nominal target of 22, and virtually ensuring them of a quite sensational place in the Bowl final.

Castle Bowl
4, 5 and 6 February 1982

at Jan Smuts, East London

Boland 191 (S. A. Jones 59) and 240 for 7 dec (P. D. Swart 92, J. Hartley 4 for 56)
Border 136 (C. J. Coetzee 4 for 49) and 249 (D. S. Scott 62, E. T. Laughlin 56)

Boland won by 46 runs
Boland 16 pts, Border 5 pts

5, 6 and 7 February 1982

at Wanderers, Johannesburg

Transvaal 'B' 305 for 7 dec (H. R. Fotheringham 115)
Eastern Province 'B' 146 (H. Page 4 for 47) and 104 (H. Page 4 for 49)

Transvaal 'B' won by an innings and 55 runs
Transvaal 'B' 19 pts, Eastern Province 'B' 4 pts

Currie Cup
6, 7 and 8 February 1982

at St Georges Park, Port Elizabeth

Eastern Province 182 (R. J. D. Whyte 58, R. W. Hanley 5 for 31, G. E. McMillan 4 for 43) and 249 (N. V. Radford 4 for 53, C. E. B. Rice 4 for 49)
Transvaal 354 for 8 dec (K. A. McKenzie 101 not out, R. G. Pollock 72, A. I. Kallicharran 61) and 78 for 1

Transvaal won by 9 wickets
Transvaal 21 pts, Eastern Province 5 pts

Boland, Castle Bowl Southern champions elect travelled to take on the wooden-spoonists and had a big shock losing their first 4 wickets for 29 and 7 for 96. A record eighth wicket stand of 85 between Robbie Schultz and Stephen Jones saved them from disaster but a total of 191 was most disappointing on a hard and apparently true wicket. Border, absolutely luckless had then to contend with bad light and rain and undid all their good work losing 3 for 3 by the close of day one. On the second morning Brad Osborne batted well for 46 but generally Border lacked concentration and at the close of the second day Boland had established a lead of 222 with 6 wickets standing. Set 296 on the third morning Border made a real fight of it, fifties from Scott and Laughlin helping make Barlow sweat before, in the last 20 overs a sudden collapse saw the last 4 wickets fall for 15, and another Boland triumph.

Meanwhile in what was virtually a fight for second place at Johannesburg, a century by Henry Fotheringham – dropped from the Transvaal Currie Cup side helped the 'B' team to a good score against the Eastern 'B' side and then incisive medium pace bowling from nineteen-years-old Hugh Page induced two collapses to give Transvaal 'B' an innings victory, no Eastern player doing himself justice in a miserable performance.

In the Currie Cup Transvaal went to the top of the log against Eastern Province. Easterns gave a characteristically pathetic first innings performance until Bob Whyte and Dickie Ogilvie put some back bone and character into the batting but with a 2½ hour century from Kevin McKenzie, and stylish support from Kallicharran and Pollock Transvaal achieved a powerful position at the end of the second day. Easterns made a much better fist of their second innings without a major performance to make Transvaal worry and eventually they achieved a 9 wicket triumph with 80 minutes remaining.

Currie Cup

12, 13 and 15 February 1982

at Newlands, Cape Town

Natal 169 (O. Henry 4 for 22) and 243 (M. J. Procter 63, S. T. Jefferies 4 for 65)
Western Province 363 (K. S. McEwan 117, A. J. Lamb 89, A. P. Kuiper 50) and 51 for 3

Western Province won by 7 wkts
Western Province 18 pts, Natal 3 pts

Peter Kirsten in all his glory drives Natal spinner Daniels back over his head.

Ken McEwan, 117 for Western Province against Natal.

at Berea Park, Pretoria

Northern Transvaal 220 (A. M. Ferreira 60) and 246 (V. F. du Preez 84, C. S. Stirk 59, I. Foulkes 4 for 92, R. L. S. Armitage 4 for 65)
Eastern Province 350 for 6 dec (R. L. S. Armitage 171 not out, I. Foulkes 53) and 14 for 3

Match drawn
Eastern Province 6 pts, Northern Transvaal 6 pts

Castle Bowl

13, 14 and 15 February 1982

at Pietermaritzburg

Western Province 'B' 212 (T. A. Clarke 63, E. J. Hodkinson 4 for 31) and 281 for 9 dec (R. R. Lawrenson 87, E. J. Hodkinson 6 for 68)
Natal 'B' 238 (C. L. Smith 65, K. D. Verdoorn 61) and 176 for 8 (H. M. Ackerman 4 for 61)

Match drawn
Natal 'B' 8 pts, Western Province 'B' 7 pts

A fourth wicket stand of 152 between Kirsten and Lamb led the way for Western Province to build a good lead in the vital Currie Cup game with Natal, after Omar Henry had cut into the Natal middle order. Despite improved batting in the second innings, with Procter hitting 63 in 69 minutes they could only reach 243 leaving Western Province ample time to score the 50 runs required. Westerns thus went back to the top of the log, becoming favourites to stay there. Natal on the other hand saw their hopes of retaining the title disappear.

Meanwhile a career-best unbeaten 171 in 6 hours helped Eastern Province to a good position in the 'battle of the stragglers' against Northern Transvaal, but dogged second innings batting, with Vernon du Preez scoring 84 in over 3½ hours enabled Northerns to force a draw, despite fine bowling by batting hero Armitage and Ivor Foulkes. Thus Easterns stayed rooted to the bottom, with only one game remaining.

In the Castle Bowl a good first innings by Bossie Clarke helped Western Province 'B' recover from a bad start but pace man Evan Hodkinson was mainly instrumental in limiting the Western score to 212. Natal 'B' also started poorly, losing 2 for 12 but a stand of 111 for the third wicket between Kippy Smith and Kevin Verdoorn put them on the track to a first innings lead. Western's second innings started poorly and at 97 for 7 Evan Hodkinson already having 5 wickets, defeat seemed certain. However a stand of 115, dominated by Bob Lawrenson (87) enabled Westerns to reach 281 for 9 before declaring and Natal never seriously attempted the 256 in 210 minutes required for victory.

Western Province won the Datsun Shield for the fourth time, and performed the first part of its first outright 'double'. Natal won the toss and invited Westerns to take first innings. Westerns never really recovered from the loss of Seeff at 1 and despite a good looking wicket neither Pienaar or Kirsten was able to score at the required rate, and only when Kuiper and Lamb came together in a fifth wicket stand of 40 was there any real aggression. The final score of 178 did not look enough but Natal's disastrous start, with Tich Smith and Wilkins both falling in the first over redressed the balance. Bestall and Bentley steadied the ship with a third wicket stand of 73 and with useful knocks from Richards and Procter the forty-first over was reached with 62 runs needed, and four wickets only down. There was then a minor slump and although Daniels then played well he could get no-one to stay with him. The last ball was reached with 3 runs still required. They were not scored and Westerns had won by almost the narrowest possible margin. The match and result were marred by two must unfortunate incidents. During the Western Province innings van der Bijl bowled to Kuiper who played the ball back. Kuiper immediately began signalling for a new bat while van der Bijl picked up the ball and made as if to walk back to his mark. Lamb strayed inches out of his crease and van der Bijl suddenly threw the wickets down. Umpire Perry Hurwitz reluctantly gave Lamb out.

The second incident occured with Natal needing seven for victory. Van der Bijl, facing Jefferies, appeared to snick a catch to wicket-keeper Bruce but the batsman refused to walk and Hurwitz turned down confident appeals. The 'keeper then threw the ball to Kirsten at mid off. While the fieldsmen discussed the 'catch' at the batsman's end, and non-striker Clift strolled up the wicket to talk to van der Bijl Kirsten calmly strolled towards the bowler's wicket and broke it. Hurwitz declared Clift run out. Both sets of players blamed the others for the unpleasant incidents and unsporting behaviour; from a distance, and taking an indepen-

DATSUN SHIELD FINAL: NATAL v. WESTERN PROVINCE
20 February 1982 at Wanderers, Johannesburg

WESTERN PROVINCE

L. Seeff	c Smith, b Procter		1
R. F. Pienaar	lbw, b Taylor		12
P. N. Kirsten	c Bestall, b Clift		35
A. J. Lamb	run out		16
K. S. McEwan	run out		3
A. P. Kuiper	c Richards, b Taylor		38
S. D. Bruce	b Taylor		17
G. S. le Roux	b Taylor		8
O. Henry	not out		17
S. T. Jefferies	not out		1
J. During			
Extras			30
	(for 8 wkts)		178

	O	M	R	W
van der Bijl	11	1	39	—
Procter	11	5	15	1
Taylor	11	3	26	4
Cooper	11	1	51	—
Clift	11	1	17	1

FALL OF WICKETS
1–1, 2–35, 3–63, 4–69, 5–109, 6–136, 7–143, 8–177

NATAL

A. J. S. Smith	b Jefferies		0
C. P. Wilkins	run out		0
R. M. Bentley	c Bruce, b Pienaar		28
D. Bestall	c Kirsten, b le Roux		47
B. A. Richards	c Jefferies, b le Roux		29
M. J. Procter	c Seeff, b Jefferies		24
N. P. Daniels	b Jefferies		23
P. B. Clift	run out		3
V. A. P. van der Bijl	not out		1
K. R. Cooper	not out		3
L. B. Taylor			
Extras			18
	(for 8 wkts)		176

	O	M	R	W
Jefferies	11	3	17	4
le Roux	11	5	21	2
Kuiper	6	1	14	—
During	11	—	45	—
Pienaar	10	—	40	1
Kirsten	4	—	16	—
Henry	2	—	5	—

FALL OF WICKETS
1–0, 2–1, 3–47, 4–117, 5–118, 6–167, 7–172, 8–172

Western Province won by 2 runs

dent view neither came out of the match with any credit whatsoever and van der Bijl and Kirsten, who actually performed the 'run outs' should be ashamed of themselves. On the wider issue, many may feel 'If this is the way South Africans play their cricket ...!'

Castle Bowl
25, 26 and 27 February 1982
at Ramblers, Bloemfontein

Orange Free State 202 (R. A. le Roux 67, K. van Rensburg 4 for 45) and 216 for 4 (R. A. le Roux 102 not out)
Griqualand West 246 for 8 dec (M. J. D. Doherty 112 not out, H. Liebenberg 63)

Match drawn
Griqualand West 6 pts, Orange Free State 5 pts

26, 27 February and 1 March 1982
at Oude Libertas, Stellenbosch

Eastern Province 'B' 212 (P. Anker 4 for 83) and 202 (G. Long 98, D. H. Howell 54, P. Anker 5 for 70)
Boland 201 (J. de Villiers 61, P. D. Swart 57, M. K. van Vuuren 5 for 38) and 163

Eastern Province 'B' won by 50 runs
Eastern Province 'B' 17 pts, Boland 7 pts

at Berea Park, Pretoria

Northern Transvaal 'B' 215 (C. P. L. de Lange 72) and 190 (A. H. Jordaan 57, B. Osborne 7 for 25)
Border 144 (T. Wheelwright 4 for 35) and 153

Northern Transvaal 'B' won by 108 runs

Free State required 19 points to overtake Western Province 'B' at the top of the Southern section Bowl competition, but if this was the signal for aggression and a 'death or glory' bid for victory over Griquas they gave few signs. Much of the first day was taken up with Free State's first innings, and a pedestrian 67 from Raymond le Roux which just about destroyed any chance Free State may have had to attain sufficient batting points for their purpose. Mike Doherty's 7 hour marathon 112 not out was the backbone of Griqua's draw seeking first innings and the point of the third day was elusive – unless purely to give Raymond le Roux his maiden hundred – not surprisingly a grim, unsmiling affair of nearly six hours – an anti-spectator effort which can have pleased no-one bar himself.

In the Northern section Boland were already mathematically champions so the final two games had little real point. At Stellenbosch Mike van Vuuren caused the champions some early embarrassment against Eastern Province 'B' and although Grant Long's career best 98, and a sixth wicket stand of 135 between Long and David Howell caused more frustration in the second innings more fine spin bowling by Pienaar Anker left Boland starting the third day needing only 206 for victory. It was not to be, they batted without conviction and slithered to a disappointing defeat; but they were still champions!

Finally wooden spoonists Border sent in Northern Transvaal 'B' but were foiled by a valuable, if laboured 72 by Laurens de Lange. Border's reply was disappointing but a superb spell of off spinning by Brad Osborne, who achieved a career best 7 for 25 in the Northern second innings put them back in the game. Unfortunately they never looked likely to achieve the 262 needed for victory on the final day. In fact they threw in the towel, losing their last five wickets for a mere 34 runs.

Currie Cup
8, 9 and 10 March 1982
at Berea Park, Pretoria

Northern Transvaal 221 (V. A. P. van der Bijl 6 for 64) and 110 (V. A. P. van der Bijl 8 for 47)
Natal 148 (T. Wheelwright 5 for 47) and 186 for 4 (D. Bestall 80 not out)

Natal won by 6 wickets
Natal 14 pts, Northern Transvaal 7 pts

Natal, still with a very outside chance of retaining the Currie Cup championship had mixed fortunes on the opening day of their game with Northern Transvaal – themselves seeking a few points to make sure of avoiding last place for the third successive season. Vince van der Bijl, on his 100th Currie Cup appearance quickly got among the Northern batsmen but stubbornness in the middle order enabled them to reach 221, albeit in over 6¼ hours. Natal then lost 2 wickets cheaply before the close, and the second day saw them bundled out rather ignominiously for 148 in 3½ hours, paceman Trevor Wheelwright having career best figures of 5 for 47. When Northerns batted again however van der Bijl was in irresistable form. He took 8 for 47 in 21 overs as Northerns crumbled to a most disappointing 110 all out in 3 hours and although Wheelwright again caused some early troubles an unbeaten 80 by Darryl Bestall steered them to an eventually comfortable win. Van der Bijl's match figures, 14 for 111 in 50 overs were a career best, surpassing figures of 13 for 53 in 1970–71.

The tour of the English Players caused postponement of the final three domestic matches until late March.

Castle Bowl – final
24, 25, 26 and 27 March 1982
at Oude Libertas, Stellenbosch

Boland 237 (T. A. Clarke 4 for 35) and 291 (P. D. Swart 89 J. L. Louw 7 for 57)
Western Province 'B' 115 and 264 (E. Muntingh 67, M. D. Mellor 60, P. Anker 5 for 73)

Boland won by 149 runs

It was Glory Glory! all the way as Boland, in only their second season as a first-class side annexed the Castle Bowl with an easy win over Western Province 'B'. Eddie Barlow had no hesitation in batting on a bare pitch, feeling it would become more favourable to bowlers as the game developed. Three wickets fell for 48 but the middle order, led by Jac de Villiers and Sol Barnard staged a recovery, albeit with somewhat stolid and stodgy methods, which were shown to be justified when on the second day Westerns collapsed disappointingly and with Boland batting far more enterprisingly on the third day Westerns entered the last day needing 259 for victory with the valuable wickets of Thompson and Seeff already gone. They did in fact put up a most disappointing show on the last day, losing their last 8 wickets for 76 runs, finding diminutive off-spinner Pienaar Anker particularly hard to master as he finished with 5 for 73 in 44.1 overs – thus confirming himself as one of the 'finds' of the season.

Currie Cup
31 March, 1 and 2 April 1982
at St Georges Park, Port Elizabeth

Eastern Province 120 (G. S. le Roux 5 for 28, S. T. Jefferies 4 for 48) and 307 (S. J. Bezuidenhout 110, G. S. le Roux 5 for 51)
Western Province 384 for 3 dec (P. N. Kirsten 151 not out, A. J. Lamb 106 not out, L. Seeff 79) and 46 for 0

Western Province won by 10 wickets
Western Province 23 pts, Eastern Province 2 pts.

at Wanderers, Johannesburg

Natal 371 (C. L. Smith 112, D. Bestall 68, N. P. Daniels 66) and 175 for 5 dec (N. P. Daniels 51)
Transvaal 277 for 7 dec (A. I. Kallicharran 103, R. G. Pollock 72 not out, C. J. Cook 50, V. A. P. van der Bijl 4 for 62) and 270 for 7 (C. E. B. Rice 102 not out, V. A. P. van der Bijl 5 for 129)

Transvaal won by 3 wickets
Transvaal 17 pts, Natal 7 pts

The Currie Cup went to Western Province despite a victory by their only challengers, Transvaal. At Port Elizabeth it was 'top v. bottom' and on the first day Eastern Province's faltering batting was swept aside by the pace of Steve Jefferies and Garth le Roux. In reply Seeff and Kirsten hammered the bowling with a second wicket stand of 189 in 3¾ hours and on Seeff's dismissal Lamb came in to continue the assault. Kirsten eventually reached 151 in 295 minutes, while Lamb's unbeaten 106 occupied 141 minutes. Going in against arrears of 264 Easterns did much better second time round. They owed much to a magnificent century by Simon Bezuidenhout in only 121 balls but although the Western bowling, especially le Roux, became somewhat ragged, with frustration showing through in, from le Roux, shows of petulance a late collapse left Westerns needing only 44 for victory – and the title.

At Johannesburg Transvaal, who had prepared the wicket specially for spinner Alan Kourie found the scheme backfire when he sustained a groin injury and had to stop bowling early on the first afternoon. Despite batting on a wicket which they considered to be a disgrace Natal finished the first day on 345 for 7, with a superb century from Kippy Smith the highlight. Although they were now fighting a lost cause Transvaal fought back on the second day. Kallicharran stroked a fine century in 220 minutes and he was well

The mighty fallen. Barry Richards is bowled by Garth le Roux.

Boland 1981-82

BATTING	v. Border (Stellenbosch) 12, 13 November 1981	v. Northern Transvaal 'B' (Stellenbosch) 4, 5, 7 December 1981	v. Transvaal 'B' (Johannesburg) 15, 16, 18 January 1982	v. Eastern Province 'B' (Uitenhage) 30 Jan.–1, 2 Feb. 1982	v. Border (East London) 4, 5, 6 February 1982	v. Eastern Province 'B' (Stellenbosch) 26, 27 Feb.–1 Mar. 1982	v. Western Province 'B' (Stellenbosch) 24, 25, 26, 27 March 1982 (Bowl Final)
E. J. Barlow	107 33	30 65	3 202*	— 17	0 15	47 17	48
A. du Toit	117 4	19 3	4 36	10* 7	5 0	1 18	30
H. N. Basson	64 0	17					
A. Odendaal	37* 7	4 5	15* 0	— 36	29 3	5 5	31
J. de Villiers	—	17 —	21 —	11 27*	61 14	46 33	
P. D. Swart	—	54 11	40 29*	5 —	0 92	57 26	30 89
R. C. Schultz	—	16 5	10 —	— 38	7* 0	17 10	5
S. A. Jones	—	2 29	14 —	42* 59	2 0	0 20	9
P. Anker	—	0 20	2* —	— 1	— 27*	17* 10*	9*
M. van Blommenstein	—	20 0					
C. J. Coetzee	—	14* 6*	3 —	— 0*	— 0	4 5	11
H. F. H. Bergins		0 10					18 10
C. van der Merwe			1 1	26 0	1 34	14 7	
D. Malan			0 19	5 5*	12 35		
C. Viljoen						0 5	
S. Barnard							40 5
Extras	21	14 17	9 2	41 7	9 9	24 20	18 11
Total	346	164 168	169 73	378 22	191 240	201 163	237 291
Wickets	3	10 10	10 4	6 1	10 7	10 10	10 10
Result	W	L	W	W	W	L	W
Points	21	5	15	17	16	7	—

BOWLING	S. A. Jones	C. J. Coetzee	P. D. Swart	P. Anker	E. J. Barlow	H. F. H. Bergins
v. Border (Stellenbosch) 12, 13 November 1981	12–4–21–2 9–2–19–0	13–4–32–3 7–3–16–0	8.4–2–19–2 8–3–14–0	12–3–40–3 33.2–9–83–6	12–4–25–4	
v. Northern Transvaal 'B' (Stellenbosch) 4, 5, 7 December 1981	14–2–41–1 18–5–31–3	14–5–40–2 12.4–3–29–2	16–5–51–1 11–0–31–1	13.1–4–42–4 20–6–55–4		14–4–50–2 2–0–17–0
v. Transvaal 'B' (Johannesburg) 15, 16, 18 January 1982	16–8–22–2 19–7–43–2	12–2–23–2 18–7–22–3	15.3–4–22–3 9–0–15–0	12–4–24–2 20–6–55–5	12–4–21–2 10.3–3–17–2	
v. Eastern Province 'B' (Uitenhage) 30 January–1, 2 February 1982	17–2–44–2 18–5–36–3	17–6–35–2 19–4–35–2	14–4–67–0 4–1–9–0	20–6–55–5 30.4–12–50–5	14–5–37–0	
v. Border (East London) 4, 5, 6 February 1982	11.1–3–17–2 11–5–15–3	15–2–49–4 21–3–49–3	7–3–13–1 16–3–37–0	8–2–23–1 26–6–93–3	9–4–20–1 20–5–31–1	
v. Eastern Province (Stellenbosch) 26, 27 February–1 March 1982	15–4–36–1 16–4–35–3	14.5–3–36–2 12–1–47–2	15–2–47–2 9–1–43–0	29–6–83–4 21.2–2–70–5		
v. Western Province (Stellenbosch) 24, 25, 26, 27 March 1982 (Bowl Final)	23–6–29–1	21–6–35–3 28–4–79–1	13–0–27–1 21–7–37–1	25.5–8–40–3 44.1–18–73–5	11–9–4–3 17–4–36–2	3–1–2–0
	199.1–57– 389–25 av. 15.56	224.3–53– 527–31 av. 17.00	167.1–35– 432–12 av. 36.00	295.3–86– 731–50 av. 14.62	105.3–38– 191–15 av. 12.73	19–5– 69–2 av. 34.50

Inns	NOs	Runs	HS	Av
12	1	584	202*	53.09
13	1	254	117	21.17
3	—	81	64	27.00
12	2	177	37*	17.70
8	1	230	61	32.86
11	1	433	92	43.30
9	1	108	38	13.50
10	1	177	59	19.67
8	5	86	27*	28.67
2	—	20	20	10.00
8	3	43	14*	8.60
4	—	38	18	9.50
8	—	84	34	10.50
6	1	76	35	15.20
2	—	5	5	2.50
2	—	45	40	22.50

ROs	Extras	Runs	Wkts
	4	116	10
	12	169	10
	17	241	10
	9	172	10
1	18	106	10
1	14	135	10
1	25	263	10
	6	136	10
1	14	136	10
	24	249	10
1	10	212	10
	7	202	10
	9	115	10
	8	264	10

supported by Jimmy Cook with a sound fifty and Graeme Pollock, who went in late because of eye trouble but reached an unbeaten 72 in 140 minutes. The third day saw a Natal declaration setting Transvaal a target of 270 in 130 minutes plus 20 overs. Although this meant a rate of virtually six an over, and they already knew that Western Province were beating Easterns and almost assured of the title Transvaal went for the runs in cavalier fashion and with Clive Rice hitting an unbeaten 102 in 150 minutes they achieved their target in thrilling fashion in semi-darkness with only 5 balls remaining.

THE CURRIE CUP FINAL LOG

	G	W	D	L	Bonus pts	Total pts
Western Province	8	5	2	1	66	116
Transvaal	8	4	3	1	67	107
Natal	8	4	2	2	43	83
Northern Transvaal	8	1	3	4	42	52
Eastern Province	8	0	2	6	37	37

THE SAB CASTLE BOWL FINAL LOGS

Southern section	G	W	D	L	Bonus pts	Total pts
Western Province 'B'	6	3	2	1	42	72
Orange Free State	6	2	2	2	39	59
Natal 'B'	6	0	5	1	42	42
Griqualand West	6	0	4	2	40	40
Northern section						
Boland	6	4	0	2	41	81
Northern Transvaal 'B'	6	3	2	1	40	70
Transvaal 'B'	6	2	2	2	43	63
Eastern Province 'B'	6	2	2	2	42	62
Border	6	1	0	5	25	25

Boland defeated Western Province 'B' in the final

SOUTH AFRICAN BREWERIES ENGLAND ELEVEN TOUR OF SOUTH AFRICA 1982

In 1970 the South African tour of England was cancelled and subsequently the Cricket Council made it absolutely clear that South Africa would not return to the International cricket fold until their teams were selected on a multi-racial basis.

The result was that throughout the 1970s unprecedented changes were made within the fabric of South African cricket. Under the leadership of Rashid Varachia, coloured president of the newly-formed South African Cricket Union, enormous strides were made towards making cricket in the Republic non-racial. Progress was slower than some would have wished but in 1979 members of an ICC delegation were 'greatly impressed by the progress made towards non-racial cricket and the amount of non-racial cricket being played ... There is no hindrance to any non-white cricketer playing at the very highest level of the game in South Africa for any reason other than cricket ability.' Thus South Africa had fulfilled the conditions laid down by the ICC nine years before. Disappointingly the delegation added that fully representative cricket should not yet be started, but that a strong 'unofficial' team could usefully be sent to the Republic.

This very minor concession to South African cricket had no hope of being carried out. The optimists among us reckoned without other influences, such as the political expediency which is so often regarded with more importance

Border 1981-82

BATTING

	v. Eastern Province 'B' (Port Elizabeth) 7, 8, 9 November 1981	v. Boland (Stellenbosch) 12, 13 November 1981	v. Northern Transvaal 'B' (East London) 26, 28, 29 December 1981	v. Transvaal 'B' (East London) 1, 2, 3 January 1982	v. Boland (East London) 4, 5, 6 February 1982	v. Northern Transvaal 'B' (Pretoria) 26, 27 Feb.–1 Mar. 1982
R. Kent	0 36	2 52	47* 1	14 3	3 48	0 22
J. Lawrence	12 8	30 15	0 26	2 44	0 5	19 32
R. B. C. Ranger	16 4	0 10		75 0		1 2
E. T. Laughlin	16 10	8 6	3 0	101 4*	17 56	
G. L. Hayes	10 19	22 52			20 16	40 36
G. C. G. Fraser	36 2	0 1	0 0	43 1*	13 0	
D. Hagemann	0 16	2 5				
A. R. Lyons	0 10	31 13				
T. R. Ball	0 5	16 1				
J. Hartley	2 2	0* 0	0 1*		0 0	11 7
A. Jones	0* 3*	1 2*				
I. D. Harty			1 10			
R. A. Stretch			5 9	16 0		
B. M. Osborne			0 40	10 18	46 5	21 11
D. G. W. Alers			2 0	0* —	6 0	
G. M. Gower			8 27	0 —	8 31*	1 9*
D. S. Scott			38 21	29 —	9* 62	0 1
G. Nelson				7 15		
G. Pfuhl					0 2	19* 6
P. Cowan						0 7
A. Wells					13 2	
Extras	21 18	4 12	6 23	38 17	14 24	19 18
Total	113 133	116 169	110 158	335 102	136 249	144 153
Wickets	10 10	10 10	10 10	10 6	10 10	10 10
Result	L	L	L	W	L	L
Points	5	1	3	17	5	4

BOWLING

	A. Jones	A. Lyons	G. L. Hayes	J. Hartley	G. C. G. Fraser	E. T. Laughlin	R. B. C. Ranger	D. G. W. Alers
v. Eastern Province 'B' (Port Elizabeth) 7, 8, 9 November 1981	16.3-3-94-2	14-1-57-1	4-2-11-0	23-6-57-4	17-6-70-1	4-1-23-1	4-1-13-0	
v. Boland (Stellenbosch) 12, 13 November 1981	5-0-14-0	15.4-1-43-1	21-4-52-1	16-4-56-0	12-2-36-1	12-2-60-0	12-1-64-0	
v. Northern Transvaal 'B' (East London) 26, 28, 29 December 1981				22-5-54-1	3-1-12-0	8-1-27-0		33-5-104-1
v. Transvaal 'B' (East London) 1, 2, 3 January 1982					11-3-28-1		14-4-28-1	21-7-52-3
							4-1-8-0	14-4-44-2
v. Boland (East London) 4, 5, 6 February 1982			2-2-0-0	10-2-26-3	11-3-30-0			12-2-46-2
			5-1-12-1	17-5-56-4		9-2-21-1		7-0-32-1
v. Transvaal 'B' (Pretoria) 26, 27 February–1 March 1982			17-5-37-3	17-6-38-2			18-5-35-2	
			2-1-2-0	11-3-28-0			26-4-75-1	
	21.3-3-108-2 av. 54.00	29.4-2-100-2 av. 50.00	51-15-114-5 av. 22.80	116-31-315-14 av. 22.50	54-15-176-3 av. 58.67	33-6-131-2 av. 65.50	78-16-223-4 av. 55.75	87-18-278-9 av. 30.89

A. G. Nelson 10-5-11-0 and 21-12-26-3

	Inns	NOs	Runs	HS	Av
	12	1	228	52	20.73
	12	—	193	44	16.08
	8	—	108	75	13.50
	10	1	221	101	24.55
	8	—	215	52	26.88
	10	1	96	43	10.67
	4	—	23	16	5.75
	4	—	54	31	13.50
	4	—	22	16	5.50
	10	2	23	11	2.88
	4	3	6	3*	—
	2	—	11	10	5.50
	4	—	30	16	7.50
	8	—	151	46	18.88
	5	1	8	6	2.00
	7	2	84	31*	16.80
	7	1	160	62	26.67
	2	—	22	15	11.00
	4	1	27	19*	9.00
	2	—	7	7	3.50
	2	—	15	13	7.50

G. M. Gower	D. S. Scott	B. M. Osborne	ROs	Extras	Runs	Wkts
			1	14	339	10
				21	346	3
35–12–66–5	10–4–32–0	7–1–25–2		23	343	9
22–5–55–3	14.1–5–31–2	3–1–12–0		13	230	10A
35–16–51–3	16–4–48–2			26	203	10
22–8–36–2	13.2–4–28–2	8–1–16–0	1	9	191	10
25–7–57–0	11–0–53–0			9	240	7
22–10–44–0	16.3–5–39–2		1	22	215	10
14–4–25–0	8–3–24–2	8.5–1–25–7		11	190	10
175–62–334–13	89–25–255–10	26.5–4–78–9				
av. 25.69	av. 25.50	av. 8.67				

than principles. Britain's administrators caved in to 'warnings' from several other cricketing countries, and political organisations, many of which were themselves hardly paragons of racial and political principle; to be fair another more understandable reason for again rejecting South Africa was the threat of 'Rentamob'; it was likely that a South Africa tour to Britain would cause mob-violence never before experienced on the British sporting scene. The isolationists had won, not only for the present but for the foreseeable future. Meanwhile South African cricket, already showing signs of decline was in danger of withering on the bough and eventually, to all intents and purposes, dying.

Early season rumours of a 'pirate' tour of South Africa were rife but nothing materialised. In February the whispers again started and suddenly at the end of the month cricket's best-kept secret was out, and the 'Dirty Dozen' began arriving in South Africa. Tour mastermind was an English-born owner of a South African record company, Peter Cooke. For some time he had been concerned at the apparent decline of cricket standards at grass-roots level in South Africa and for more than a year had been travelling to Britain and, on one occasion, the West Indies, making personal contacts with players. Finally he was able to sign up several English players (and had also had several refusals) and with sponsorship from South African Breweries, and the blessing of the SACU, the tour finally got under way at the beginning of March. The original twelve tourists were D. L. Amiss (Warwicks), G. Boycott (Yorks), J. E. Emburey (Middlesex), G. A. Gooch (Essex elected captain), M. Hendrick (Notts), A. P. E. Knott (Kent), W. Larkins (Northants), J. K. Lever (Essex), C. M. Old (Yorks), L. B. Taylor (Leics), D. L. Underwood (Kent) and P. Willey (Northants). Later additions were G. W. Humpage (Warwicks), A. Sidebottom (Yorks) and R. A. Woolmer (Kent).

Although a strongish looking combination it could not, by any stretch of the imagination be regarded a representative England side. In fact only Gooch and Emburey could definitely be said to have had any Test career in front of them. The other Test players were over the hill or approaching the end of their first-class careers anyway, while Humpage and Taylor, were of really uncertain quality due to their never having had an opportunity with the England Test team. Thus, though the South African authorities awarded 'colours' and some newspapers treated the matches as bona fide Tests, they were no such thing and indeed they attracted to themselves the sort of publicity and apparent importance out of all proportion to their actual standing in world cricket.

Similarly the reaction of the TCCB. All the members of the English side were summarily barred from Test cricket for three years, while in addition their counties undertook not to pick them for matches against the touring Indian and Pakistani teams during the 1982 season. Thus in order to preserve Test cricket as currently constituted the TCCB in effect announced that in future all England Test teams must be submitted to the controlling bodies of the opposition – a far cry indeed from the trenchant views expressed in the West Indies only a year earlier when the Georgetown Test match was cancelled 'as it is no longer possible for the Test team to be chosen without restrictions being imposed'.

As to the tour itself, the action commenced with a two day game against a South African Under-25 team at Pretoria,

Eastern Province 1981-82

BATTING

	v. Western Province (Cape Town) 6, 7, 9 November 1981	v. Northern Transvaal (Port Elizabeth) 13, 14, 15 November 1981	v. Transvaal (Johannesburg) 26, 27, 28 December 1981	v. Natal (Port Elizabeth) 1, 2, 3 January 1982	v. Natal (Durban) 30, 31 Jan.–1 Feb. 1982	v. Transvaal (Port Elizabeth) 6, 7, 8 February 1982	v. Northern Transvaal (Pretoria) 12, 13, 15 February 1982	v. Western Province (Port Elizabeth) 31 Mar–1, 2 Apr. 1982
D. Broad	10 12							
K. W. Gradwell	4 23	2 2						
R. L. S. Armitage	20 37	1 4	26 0	118	0 2	3 24	171* —	25 34
R. J. B. Whyte	8 1	8 2	7 3	48	1 17	58 23	12 7*	0 46
I. Foulkes	20 4		6 5	40		0	38 53 —	5 3
D. H. Howell	6 18							
D. J. Brickett	55 12	5 6	4 11* 20		17 5	13 15	11* —	4 1
G. Long	0 0							
J. W. Stephenson	1 21							
W. K. Watson	36 10	27 24	23 0 2		0* 13	0 8	— —	0 13
J. A. Carse	6* 0*	0* 16*	2 9 4		0 19	0 3*	— —	
T. G. Shaw		7 2						
D. J. Richardson		47 18	20 38 5		21 32	5 39	0 —	16 34
R. G. Fensham		37 0	15 0 4		10 6	6 6	28 0	38* 39
J. D. Ogilvie		21 17			23 21*	42* 6	— —	6 0
M. K. van Vuuren		25 10						0 0*
S. J. Bezuidenhout			38 3 25		0 22	31 43	34 2	10 110
J. A. Hopkins			7 3 19		25 5	5 33	20 2	
C. Wulfsohn			17* 1 3*					
J. W. Furstenburg					2 0			9 15
Extras	6 20	36 13	13 7 7	21	22 19	11 21	3 7	12
Total	172 158	216 114	178 80 295	120	164 182	249 350	14 120	307
Wickets	10 10	10 10	10 10 10	10	10 10	10 6	3 10	10
Result	L	L	L D		L	L D		L
Points	2	7	3 7		5	5 6		2

BOWLING

	W. K. Watson	J. A. Carse	D. J. Brickett	G. Long	I. Foulkes	R. L. S. Armitage	M. K. van Vuuren	J. D. Ogilvie
v. Western Province (Cape Town) 6,7,9 November 1981	26–5–52–4 6–1–14–0	20–3–52–2 7.4–3–23–0	11–2–21–2	28–4–58–0	16–3–45–1	7–1–25–1 3–2–2–0		
v. Northern Transvaal (Port Elizabeth) 13, 14, 15 November 1981	16–10–11–2 22–11–27–3	17.5–5–50–6 18–4–67–3				4–2–7–0	11–3–30–0 11.4–1–29–3	14–2–50–1 13–3–42–1
v. Transvaal (Johannesburg) 26, 27, 28 December 1981	28–7–79–2	20–3–78–1	15–1–39–1			7–0–38–0		
v. Natal (Port Elizabeth) 1, 2, 3 January 1982	16–5–34–1 17–1–54–1	13–3–44–1 9–2–27–0	6–3–12–0 9–0–23–0			16–6–32–2 38–15–71–2	1–0–1–0 15–5–26–1	
v. Natal (Durban) 30, 31 January–1 February 1982	21–5–62–2	17–3–59–4 0.4–0–8–0	18–2–40–1				11.2–3–32–2	13–2–63–1
v. Transvaal (Port Elizabeth) 6, 7, 8 February 1982	28–6–73–2 7–0–33–1	21–3–74–3	18–2–41–1 6–0–14–0		3–0–18–0 2–1–14–0	13–0–58–1		14–2–63–0 2.3–0–15–0
v. Northern Transvaal (Pretoria) 12, 13, 15 February 1982	12–2–25–0 12–5–31–0	19–5–48–1 13–3–14–1	12–3–17–1 6–2–13–1		19.4–4–60–3 38–11–92–4	11–3–25–2 37.1–11–65–4		13–3–35–2 8–4–20–0
v. Western Province (Port Elizabeth) 31 March–1, 2 April 1982	25–4–81–2		22–2–65–1		11–0–66–0	6–0–22–0	18–1–81–0 5–1–16–0	9–1–56–0 5–1–19–0
	236–62– 576–20 av. 28.80	176.1–37– 544–22 av. 24.73	123–17– 285–8 av. 35.63	28–4– 58–0 —	143.4–40– 398–12 av. 33.17	115.3–27– 301–11 av. 27.36	45.4–6– 156–3 av. 52.00	91.3–18– 363–5 av. 72.60

FIRST LIMITED OVERS MATCH
6 March 1982
at Port Elizabeth

SAB ENGLAND XI

G. A. Gooch†	c and b le Roux	114
G. Boycott	c Rice, b Procter	5
W. Larkins	c Jennings, b Procter	14
D. L. Amiss	not out	71
P. Willey	c Cook, b Jefferies	13
A. P. E. Knott*	c Cook, b van der Bijl	5
G. W. Humpage	not out	2
L. B. Taylor		
J. K. Lever		
D. L. Underwood		
C. M. Old		
Extras		16
	(for 5 wkts)	240

	O	M	R	W
Procter	10	5	20	2
Jefferies	10	2	44	1
le Roux	10	—	70	1
van der Bijl	10	1	56	1
Kourie	10	3	34	—

FALL OF WICKETS
1–7, 2–44, 3–182, 4–229, 5–237

SOUTH AFRICA

S. J. Cook	b Old	82
B. A. Richards	b Gooch	62
P. N. Kirsten	c Larkins, b Underwood	4
R. G. Pollock	not out	57
C. E. B. Rice	not out	24
M. J. Procter		
G. S. le Roux		
R. V. Jennings		
V. A. P. van der Bijl		
A. J. Kourie		
S. T. Jefferies		
Extras		15
	(for 3 wkts)	244

	O	M	R	W
Taylor	10	2	36	—
Lever	7	—	56	—
Gooch	8	—	27	1
Old	9	1	48	1
Willey	3	—	17	—
Underwood	10	—	40	1
Boycott	0.2	—	5	—

FALL OF WICKETS
1–125, 2–147, 3–176

South Africa won by 7 wickets

and the Under-25s had slightly better of a somewhat tame draw, and they then travelled to Port Elizabeth for the first of the three limited overs matches with a representative South African XI. The English team batted first and after a slowish start followed a brilliant innings by Gooch – he was 97 not out at lunch and finally scored 114 in 172 minutes from 132 balls, with 14 fours and 4 sixes. Gooch added 138 for the third wicket with Dennis Amiss, whose invaluable unbeaten 71 occupied 150 minutes and 102 balls, and England gave the home side a target of 241 in their 55 overs. They were given the right start with an opening stand of 125 in 28 overs

Eastern Province 'B' 1981-82

BATTING

	v. Border (Port Elizabeth) 7, 8, 9 November 1981	v. Transvaal 'B' (Uitenhage) 26, 27, 28 December 1981		v. Northern Transvaal 'B' (Pretoria) 1, 2, 4 January 1982		v. Boland (Uitenhage) 30 Jan.–1, 2 Feb. 1982		v. Transvaal 'B' (Johannesburg) 5, 6, 7 February 1982		v. Boland (Stellenbosch) 26, 27 Feb.–1 Mar. 1982	
J. W. Furstenburg	12	36	57	29	43			13	24	8	0
C. Boshoff	12										
B. Hopley	12										
R. G. Fensham	68										
G. S. Cowley	13	7	33*	18	98*	6	0	10	18	36	2
W. Fensham	6										
D. G. Emslie	0										
I. Howell	112	22	1	17	18*	24	12	18*	9*	17	10*
L. Reid-Ross	8	14	0*	4*	—						
M. K. van Vuuren	75	33*	0	10	—	8*	6*	4	0	7	12
C. Wulfsohn	7*										
D. Broad		11	3	0	0						
T. G. Shaw		1	5	31	5	22	38	17	0	46	9
B. de K. Robey		0	0	12	—						
D. H. Howell		41	0	41	30	34	0	29	17	1	54
J. W. Stephenson		0	24	20	4	83	27	18	0	32	5
G. Long		38	44	3	37	6	4	6	10	23	98
P. A. Amm						32	27	2	1	23	0
T. C. Seaman						7	15	19	10	9	5
I. Foulkes						12	1				
S. Brookes						4	0	0	0	0*	0
Extras	14	29	10	10	16	25	6	10	15	10	7
Total	339	232	177	195	251	263	136	146	104	212	202
Wickets	10	10	9	10	6	10	10	10	10	10	10
Result	W	D		D		L		L		W	
Points	22	8		4		7		4		17	

BOWLING

	M. K. van Vuuren	C. Wulfsohn	G. S. Cowley	L. Reid-Ross	I. Howell	W. Fensham	B. de K. Robey	G. Long
v. Border (Port Elizabeth) 7, 8, 9 November 1981	17–7–35–2 9–3–18–1	9–3–14–2 12.5–5–24–1	7–3–15–0 6–3–7–1	5–3–6–1 6–3–16–1	13–5–22–4 12–5–25–1	13–5–25–3		
v. Transvaal 'B' (Uitenhage) 26, 27, 28 December 1981	19–7–45–2 21–7–39–3		12–3–17–1 13.2–3–29–3	8.5–4–12–2 11–3–45–0	10–6–8–1 23–7–51–2		14–7–21–1 36–11–75–2	15–7–31–2 8–3–16–0
v. Northern Transvaal 'B' (Pretoria) 1, 2, 4 January 1982	16–4–36–1 18.5–3–71–5		6–3–14–0 17–4–44–0	38–10–78–6 5–1–14–0	18–2–53–1 5–2–10–1		19–8–31–0 10–1–38–0	10–2–24–2 3–1–29–0
v. Boland (Uitenhage) 30 January–1, 2 February 1982	23–4–53–0 4–1–6–0		10–2–28–0		29–8–69–2			30–8–89–2
v. Transvaal 'B' (Johannesburg) 5, 6, 7 February 1982	25–7–66–2		14–3–44–2		13–5–39–1			13–1–42–0
v. Boland (Stellenbosch) 26, 27 February–1 March 1982	16.1–3–38–5 20–6–32–3		15–4–38–2 12–3–28–2		11–6–26–1 11–5–33–1			9–2–35–0
	189–52– 439–24 av. 18.29	21.5–8– 38–3 av. 12.67	112.2–31– 264–11 av. 24.00	73.5–24– 171–10 av. 17.10	145–51– 336–15 av. 22.40	13–5– 25–3 av. 8.33	79–27– 165–3 av. 55.00	88–24– 266–6 av. 44.33

between Jimmy Cook and Barry Richards and after a brief series of set-backs, with 3 wickets falling quickly a brilliant unbeaten 57 off 44 balls by Graeme Pollock marked South Africa's return to International cricket with a win.

The tourists then moved on to Cape Town, for a match on 8, 9 and 10 March against the strongest current domestic side in South Africa, Peter Kirsten's Western Province. Westerns made a sticky start and after 19 overs were 14 for 3, three wickets to off-spinner John Emburey. A middle-order recovery was led by Adrian Kuiper, the Stellenbosch University student staking a claim for full Sprinbok status with an aggressive 90 in 166 minutes. Bossie Clarke and Stephen Bruce gave hard hitting support while Omar Henry's batting suggested he may achieve Springbok recognition during the coming series. The English response was disappointing, only Gooch and to some extent, Amiss attempting dominance over the steady spin of Denys Hobson. Westerns finished the second day 141 ahead with 8 second innings wickets in hand and declared the following afternoon setting the tourists to get 249 runs, with about 4 hours to get them out. Unfortunately a draw seemed the limit of the Englishmen's ambitions. Boycott ground out a dreary 95, effectively destroying any hopes of a result either way, while Larkins and Woolmer also made no attempt to force the pace. Amiss flourished briefly, while Humpage and Old showed the right intentions, but it was all too little too late, and England held on for the draw.

The SAB England XI next moved to Johannesburg for the first of the three games with a representative South African eleven. This game took place on 12, 13, 14 and 15 March. In some circles they were styled 'Tests', but they were of course nothing of the sort, though they *were* the first opportunities for South Africa to get a realistic idea as to the current strength of their cricket. Only Richards, Pollock and Procter of the home team had had genuine Test match experience, whereas the tourists had a massive collective total of caps between them.

The first day belonged to the Springboks. Against a miserable over-rate (13¼ per hour) they compiled 277 for the loss of Barry Richards. Richards had added 117 for the first wicket with Jimmy Cook and the latter, who finished the day unbeaten at 114 was then involved in an unbroken second wicket stand of 160 with Peter Kirsten. A fine spell by Les Taylor on the second morning heralded a Springbok collapse, and when the English batted a typical innings of 5 in an hour by Boycott enabled the Springbok bowlers to dominate proceedings and finish the day well and truly on top, the Englishmen struggling to avoid following-on with 5 men out. This they failed to do on the third morning but then a magnificent century by Gooch, plus a typically dour effort from Boycott enabled the tourists to put up a fight before going down by 8 wickets on the fourth afternoon.

The next port of call was Durban, for the second limited overs match, and for the second time the tourists were thoroughly thrashed. Although no major innings was played there was good batting all down the order as South Africa reached 231 for 6 in their 50 overs and any hopes that the English may make a game of it evaporated when Gooch fell to van der Bijl in the third over and then Boycott helped put his side far behind the required rate. Larkins, with 47 off 66 balls, attempted to up the run rate while Willey also batted soundly but with Amiss failing for the first time, and

Griqualand West 1981-82

BATTING	v. Orange Free State (Bloemfontein) 16, 17, 19 October 1981	v. Natal 'B' (Durban) 7, 8, 9 November 1981	v. Western Province 'B' (Kimberley) 12, 13, 14 November 1981	v. Western Province 'B' (Constantia) 27, 28, 30 November 1981	v. Natal 'B' (Kimberley) 28, 29, 30 January 1982	v. Orange Free State (Bloemfontein) 25, 26, 27 February 1982
J. Pearson	34	6				
M. J. D. Doherty	22	53	47	48* 55	34 82	40 62 112*
K. Sharp	47	5	0	31 44	17 40	34 27
P. L. Symcox	24	13	0	0	5 46	34 2 8
A. D. Methven	48	67	41	0 68	7 6	57 13 0
A. P. Beukes	0	25	55	— 49	6 10	0 29 26
H. Liebenberg	0	35	8	— 0	5 0	7 3* 63
W. Dobson	0	23	12	— 18	2 5	12* 2* 0
T. Smit	52*	1	13	— 26*	3 3*	
R. Engelbrecht	12	2*	8*	—		
R. Canny	5	2			1* 2	—
K. McLaren			26	11* 2	24 0	
E. F. Parker			20	— 2	0 4	
R. N. Martin				4		
J. R. Gray				5	31 8	0
F. W. Swarbrook					71 70	18
K. van Rensburg					0 —	1
P. McLaren					1 —	0*
Extras	3	11	12	1 15	4 5	9 20 18
Total	247	243	242	91 288	108 203	296 236 246
Wickets	10	10	10	2† 10	10 10	10 7 8
Result	L	D	D	L	D	D
Points	7	7	7	5	8	6

† P. L. Symcox retired hurt

BOWLING	R. Canny	H. Liebenberg	R. Engelbrecht	T. Smit	A. P. Beukes	K. McLaren	M. J. D. Doherty	E. F. Parker
v. Orange Free State (Bloemfontein) 16, 17, 19 October 1981	18-2-58-3 4-1-13-0	24-7-79-2 17.4-3-87-2	14.5-2-54-2 12-4-32-1	16-5-63-1 4-0-22-0	21-6-44-1 2-0-15-0			
v. Natal 'B' (Durban) 7, 8, 9 November 1981		13-1-56-0	6-0-31-0	8-0-32-1	36.1-8-101-5	21-5-62-2	2-0-15-0	
v. Western Province 'B' (Kimberley) 12, 13, 14 November 1981		24-9-57-2 22-5-71-3		20-5-54-2 5-1-10-0	32-14-62-1 6-2-23-0	10-4-31-0 20-7-30-1	5-0-15-0	16-4-46-3 8-2-17-1
v. Western Province 'B' (Constantia) 27, 28, 30 November 1981	10-1-34-3	17-6-48-0 19-5-40-3		18.3-1-68-5 17-1-50-1	21-10-28-1 3-1-6-1	1-0-3-0		6-1-19-1
v. Natal 'B' (Kimberley) 28, 29, 30 January 1982		23.4-8-55-5 12-2-61-1			20-5-63-1 17.3-3-65-0	23-7-49-3	2-0-5-0	
v. Orange Free State (Bloemfontein) 25, 26, 27 February 1982	9-1-19-0 14-1-39-1	11-1-35-1 16-1-38-2			21-13-20-0		1-0-2-0	
	55-6- 163-7 av. 23.29	199.2-48- 627-21 av. 29.86	32.5-6- 117-3 av. 39.00	88.3-13- 299-10 av. 29.90	202.4-69- 476-13 av. 36.62	52-16- 126-3 av. 42.00	10-0- 37-0 —	30-7- 82-5 av. 16.40

A P. L. Symcox 7-2-19-0

Woolmer failing again, nothing of use came from the middle order and the tourists finally collapsed to a most disappointing 79 run defeat.

The English, allegedly masters of the limited overs game, had twice been outplayed, and with their poor form in the other matches the tour was now threatening to be a monumental flop.

WESTERN PROVINCE v. SAB ENGLAND XI
8, 9 and 10 March 1982 at Newlands, Cape Town

WESTERN PROVINCE

	FIRST INNINGS		SECOND INNINGS	
L. Seeff	c Knott, b Emburey	12	c Humpage, b Emburey	48
R. F. Pienaar	run out	0	not out	2
P. N. Kirsten†	c Knott, b Emburey	10	not out	67
K. S. McEwan	b Emburey	0	c Knott, b Old	2
A. P. Kuiper	b Gooch	90	c Emburey, b Hendrick	1
S. D. Bruce*	c Boycott, b Gooch	42	c and b Gooch	10
T. A. Clarke	c Knott, b Old	41	b Gooch	11
O. Henry	not out	33	c Knott, b Old	6
S. T. Jefferies	b Emburey	17	c Woolmer, b Emburey	45
J. During	not out	10		
D. L. Hobson				
Extras		8		12
	(for 8 wkts dec)	263	(for 7 wkts dec)	204

	O	M	R	W	O	M	R	W
Old	18	7	61	1	11	5	26	2
Lever	0.2	—	—	—				
Hendrick	16.4	2	52	—	12	2	27	1
Gooch	17	4	54	2	14	2	45	2
Emburey	26	7	88	4	21.5	3	65	2
Larkins					6.1	—	23	—
Humpage					2	—	6	—

FALL OF WICKETS
1–7, 2–22, 3–22, 4–25, 5–100, 6–195, 7–203, 8–242
1–21, 2–26, 3–103, 4–108, 5–110, 6–133, 7–197

SAB ENGLAND XI

	FIRST INNINGS		SECOND INNINGS	
G. Boycott	c Clarke, b Jefferies	20	run out	95
W. Larkins	b Jefferies	24	c Kuiper, b Hobson	22
D. L. Amiss	b Hobson	52	b Henry	30
R. A. Woolmer	lbw, b Hobson	3	c Seeff, b Pienaar	27
A. P. E. Knott*	lbw, b Jefferies	27	c Kirsten, b Jefferies	0
G. A. Gooch†	c McEwan, b Clarke	58	c Jefferies, b Pienaar	0
G. W. Humpage	b Hobson	1	c During, b Henry	10
J. E. Emburey	c Kirsten, b Clarke	13		
C. M. Old	not out	5	c Kuiper, b Hobson	20
M. Hendrick	b Hobson	1	not out	0
J. K. Lever	did not bat injured		not out	10
Extras		15		11
		219	(8 wkts)	225

	O	M	R	W	O	M	R	W
Jefferies	19	3	47	3	13	1	37	1
Kuiper	3	—	15	—	9	2	20	—
Pienaar	11	4	24	—	16	2	41	2
During	5	2	7	—				
Hobson	21.1	8	57	4	21	6	48	2
Henry	8	3	34	—	11	1	61	2
Clarke	4	1	20	2	2	—	2	—
Kirsten					1	—	5	—

FALL OF WICKETS
1–45, 2–52, 3–72, 4–133, 5–133, 6–134, 7–202, 8–215, 9–219
1–62, 2–135, 3–138, 4–165, 5–166, 6–190, 7–211, 8–220

Match drawn

	Inns	NOs	Runs	HS	Av
	2	—	40	34	20.00
	10	2	555	112*	69.38
	9	—	245	47	27.22
	9	1	132	46	16.50
	10	—	307	68	30.70
	9	—	200	55	22.22
	9	1	121	63	15.13
	9	2	74	23	10.57
	6	3	98	52*	32.67
	3	2	22	12	—
	4	1	10	5	3.33
	5	1	63	26	15.75
	4	—	26	20	6.50
	1	—	4	4	—
	4	—	44	31	11.00
	3	—	159	71	53.00
	2	—	1	1	0.50
	2	1	1	1	—

P. McLaren	K. van Rensburg	A. D. Methven		ROs	Extras	Runs	Wkts
				1	11	309	10
					13	182	3
				2	16	313	10
					17	282	8
					15	166	5
					10	210	10
					8	104	5
21–2–63–2	17–2–64–0				6	251	8
9–1–27–3	13–0–60–2	2–0–18–0		2	9	245	8
11–1–40–1	27–11–45–4			1	14	202	10
18–7–37–1	8–1–24–0	10–3–14–0			23	216	4A
59–11–	65–14–	12–3–					
167–7	193–6	32–0					
av. 23.86	av. 32.17	—					

Natal 1981–82

BATTING

	v. Northern Transvaal (Pietermaritzburg) 5, 6, 7 December 1981		v. Western Province (Durban) 26, 27, 28 December 1981		v. Eastern Province (Port Elizabeth) 1, 2, 3 January 1982		v. Transvaal (Durban) 16, 17, 18 January 1982		v. Eastern Province (Durban) 30, 31 Jan.–1 Feb. 1982		v. Western Province (Cape Town) 12, 13, 15 February 1982		v. Northern Transvaal (Pretoria) 8, 9, 10 March 1982		v. Transvaal (Johannesburg) 31 Mar.–1, 2 Apr. 1982	
B. A. Richards	62	87*	6	3	39*	—				38	34	5	32	2	31*
C. P. Wilkins	10	5	10	1	29	37	2	32	2	0*	22	15	6	33	46	44
R. M. Bentley	88	21	39	48	13	39	18	4*	16	—	6	24	4	5	0	12
D. Bestall	31	8	25	57	32	19	41	34	1		43	37	35	80*	68	17
M. J. Procter	1	10	11	24	6	76	55	0	22	—	20	63	9	17*		
N. P. Daniels	3	14	8	8*	7	20*	5	31	40	—	1	32	20*	—	66	51
A. J. S. Smith	47	—	1	0*	2	39	11	18	25	8*	0	0	10	—	4	—
P. B. Clift	14	—	29	—	9	11*	0	28			17	4	35	9		
V. A. P. van der Bijl	53*	12	4	—	4	—	18*	17*	42		6	0	3	—	13*	—
K. R. Cooper	38*	16	3*	—	0	—	3	1	6	—			17	—	36	—
L. B. Taylor	—	—	2	—	0	—	12	—	0*	—	2*	6*				
R. A. Smith							6	10	91	—	2	0				
D. K. Pearse									11	—					3	—
E. J. Hodkinson													0	—	1	—
C. L. Smith															112	6
Extras	11	11	5	19	4	13	3	12	23	—	12	28	4	10	20	14
Total	358	184	143	160	145	254	174	187	279	8	169	243	148	186	371	175
Wickets	8	7	10	5	10	5	10	8	10	0	10	10	10	4	10	5
Result	D		W		D		W		W		L		W		L	
Points	6		15		5		15		20		3		14		7	

BOWLING

	V. A. P. van der Bijl	L. B. Taylor	M. J. Procter	K. R. Cooper	P. B. Clift	N. P. Daniels	R. M. Bentley	C. P. Wilkins
v. Northern Transvaal (Pietermaritzburg) 5, 6, 7 December 1981	31–9–56–1 11–2–22–0	22–9–50–1 11–4–23–0	16.5–7–30–3 14–5–30–0	13–1–47–0 4–0–12–0	22–10–45–4 11–2–21–1	11–3–32–0	4–2–4–0	1–0–2–0
v. Western Province (Durban) 26, 27, 28 December 1981	23.5–10–31–7 23–9–33–4	14–3–43–1 19.5–6–47–4	17–11–15–2	10–3–25–1 5–2–9–0	8–2–31–1 7–2–13–0			
v. Eastern Province (Port Elizabeth) 1, 2, 3 January 1982	34–6–74–3	21.5–7–59–2	12–3–40–1	23–7–56–3	27–11–52–1		4–2–7–0	
v. Transvaal (Durban) 16, 17, 18 January 1982	23–6–42–2 32.3–11–64–7	14.5–3–55–3 13–2–29–0	9–4–14–0	19–5–53–3 11–3–20–1	15–6–28–2 7–0–25–0	1–0–1–2		
v. Eastern Province (Durban) 30, 31 January–1 February 1982	27–3–48–5 21–8–56–5	27–9–26–3 13–3–38–1	4.4–1–9–2 8–5–10–2	6–1–16–0 11–3–28–1		2.2–1–9–1		
v. Western Province (Cape Town) 12, 13, 15 February 1982	30–9–61–0 6–2–15–0	14–3–34–2	20–3–61–3		23–3–78–2 4–2–10–1	27–3–78–3 5–1–13–1	6–3–11–0	
v. Northern Transvaal (Pretoria) 8, 9, 10 March 1982	29–8–64–6 21–6–47–8		12–4–36–0	12–1–44–0	18–6–35–2 11–2–22–1	4–1–3–1 13–6–19–1		
v. Transvaal (Johannesburg) 31 March–1, 2 April 1982	28–8–62–4 23.1–2–129–5			14–0–57–1 9–1–39–0		28–4–75–2 11–3–42–2	4–0–14–0 2–0–17–0	1–0–8–0 10–0
	359.3–103– 804–53 av. 14.11	163.3–49– 404–17 av. 23.76	113.3–43– 245–13 av. 18.85	137–27– 406–10 av. 40.60	153–46– 360–15 av. 24.00	102.2–22– 272–13 av. 20.92	20–7– 53–0 —	2–0– 10–0 —

A A. J. S. Smith 0.5–0–6–0
B C. L. Smith 1–0–14–0

THE GREAT REBELLION/169

SOUTH AFRICA v. SAB ENGLAND XI
12, 13, 14 and 15 March 1982 at the Wanderers, Johannesburg

SOUTH AFRICA

	FIRST INNINGS			SECOND INNINGS	
S. J. Cook	c Gooch, b Taylor	114		c and b Old	2
B. A. Richards	c Amiss, b Underwood	66		lbw, b Lever	4
P. N. Kirsten	c Gooch, b Taylor	88		not out	20
R. G. Pollock	not out	64		not out	9
C. E. B. Rice	c Knott, b Taylor	1			
M. J. Procter†	c Knott, b Lever	1			
A. J. Kourie	lbw, b Old	14			
R. V. Jennings*	c Knott, b Lever	24			
G. S. le Roux	not out	6			
V. A. P. van der Bijl					
S. T. Jefferies					
Extras		22			2
	(for 7 wkts dec)	400		(for 2 wkts)	37

	O	M	R	W	O	M	R	W
Taylor	31	7	73	3				
Old	28	10	76	1	6	1	8	1
Lever	32	3	122	2	5.4	1	27	1
Underwood	23	1	92	1				
Gooch	2	—	15	—				

FALL OF WICKETS
1–117, 2–278, 3–286, 4–290, 5–295, 6–331, 7–388
1–8, 2–14

SAB ENGLAND XI

	FIRST INNINGS			SECOND INNINGS	
G. A. Gooch†	b le Roux	30		c Jennings, b van der Bijl	109
G. Boycott	c Cook, b van der Bijl	5		lbw, b van der Bijl	36
W. Larkins	lbw, b van der Bijl	2		c Kourie, b van der Bijl	20
D. L. Amiss	not out	66		c Procter, b Jefferies	24
R. A. Woolmer	c Jennings, b Kourie	14		lbw, b le Roux	21
P. Willey	lbw, b Jefferies	1		lbw, b le Roux	24
D. L. Underwood	c Cook, b van der Bijl	8		lbw, b van der Bijl	6
A. P. E. Knott*	c Richards, b van der Bijl	5		lbw, b van der Bijl	9
C. M. Old	c Kourie, b van der Bijl	1		b le Roux	11
J. K. Lever	b Kourie	9		not out	10
L. B. Taylor	b Jefferies	0		c Pollock, b le Roux	0
Extras		9			13
		150			283

	O	M	R	W	O	M	R	W
van der Bijl	22	8	25	5	32	10	79	5
Jefferies	20	5	59	2	27	4	88	1
Kourie	11	2	19	2	16	7	53	—
le Roux	10	2	38	1	22.2	5	44	4
Procter					6	3	6	—

FALL OF WICKETS
1–38, 2–38, 3–42, 4–73, 5–80, 6–90, 7–124, 8–130, 9–142
1–119, 2–174, 3–179, 4–207, 5–229, 6–252, 7–258, 8–267, 9–278

South Africa won by 8 wickets

Natal 'B' 1981–82

BATTING	v. Griqualand West (Durban) 7, 8, 9 November 1981	v. Western Province 'B' (Constantia) 26, 28, 29 December 1981	v. Orange Free State (Durban) 1, 2, 3 January 1982	v. Western Province (Pietermaritzburg) 13, 14, 15 January 1982	v. Orange Free State (Bloemfontein) 22, 23, 25 January 1982	v. Griqualand West (Kimberley) 28, 29, 30 January 1982
A. Warman	1					
R. A. Smith	49	8	8	58	14	
C. L. Smith	49	14	40	1	32	65	1*	30	48	38	78
P. H. Williams	67	8	10	46	11	22	2	20	35	3	34
M. Hedley	15	1	53	32	10						
T. R. Madsen	35	9	22	1	43	5	4	55	26	92	8
P. J. Allan	13	5	5	75*	30*	19	41	12	27	29	18
D. K. Pearse	55*	23*	13	70	12	11	8	11	44		
I. Ebrahim	8	0	12*	—	1*		9	—		0	0*
P. Geyer	0										
E. J. Hodkinson	5	10	11	—	—	24	5*	23	—	6*	15
M. D. Tramontino		19	69	0	1	0	33	12	4	0	49
M. Clare		0	5	—	—			5*	—	—	—
M. B. Logan						4	8	8	107*	12	7*
K. D. Verdoorn						61	47	22	27	47	23
G. Smith						7	20			18*	4
M. K. Thompson						0*	—				
Extras	16	2	12	12	6	20	7	31	28	6	9
Total	313	99	260	295	160	238	176	238	346	251	245
Wickets	10	10	10	7	7	10	8	10	7	8	8
Result	D	L		D		D		D		D	
Points	10	2		6		8		8		7	

BOWLING	E. J. Hodkinson	P. Geyer	D. K. Pearse	P. J. Allan	I. Ebrahim	C. L. Smith	P. H. Williams	M. Clare
v. Griqualand West (Durban) 7, 8, 9 November 1981	24–7–52–3 7.1–0–23–0	15–2–34–0 4–0–14–0	20–9–42–1 12–6–12–1	13–3–31–0	23–9–64–3 12–3–22–1	4–2–7–2 1–0–4–0	0.5–0–0–1 4–0–15–0	
v. Western Province 'B' (Constantia) 26, 28, 29 December 1981	24–6–56–1		30–7–55–2		32–3–133–1	7–0–21–0	4–0–25–0	17–4–47–1
v. Orange Free State (Durban) 1, 2, 3 January 1982	26.3–8–55–2 10–1–42–1		8–3–12–0	17–4–38–2	24–10–75–5 9–0–29–0			15–5–47–1
v. Western Province 'B' (Pietermaritzburg) 13, 14, 15 February 1982	18–7–31–4 31–12–68–6		16–2–34–3 4–0–16–0	7–2–15–0 7–3–12–0		1–0–1–0 1–0–5–0	15.4–4–32–2 18–3–57–2	
v. Orange Free State (Bloemfontein) 22, 23, 25 January 1982	25–5–76–4 8–1–24–0		12–4–45–2	3.2–1–3–1 7–2–14–1	17–0–78–3 19–0–86–3	10–1–26–0 13–3–49–0		4–2–2–0 10–2–27–0
v. Griqualand West (Kimberley) 28, 29, 30 January 1982	20–5–54–2 18–5–39–1			15–4–46–1 10–1–44–0	28–10–92–1 20–3–57–5		3–1–2–0	19–2–61–4 22–5–76–1
	211.4–57–520–24 av. 21.67	19–2–48–0 —	102–31–216–9 av. 24.00	79.2–20–203–5 av. 40.60	184–38–636–22 av. 28.91	37–7–113–2 av. 56.50	45.3–8–131–5 av. 26.20	87–20–260–7 av. 37.14

A M. D. Tramontino 2–2–0–0

THE GREAT REBELLION/171

SECOND LIMITED OVERS MATCH
17 March 1982 at Kingsmead, Durban

SOUTH AFRICA

S. J. Cook	c Knott, b Sidebottom	35
B. A. Richards	c Lever, b Underwood	34
P. N. Kirsten	lbw, b Willey	14
R. G. Pollock	run out	41
C. E. B. Rice	c Woolmer, b Lever	23
M. J. Procter	c Gooch, b Lever	30
R. V. Jennings*	not out	21
G. S. le Roux	not out	19
V. A. P. van der Bijl		
S. T. Jefferies		
A. J. Kourie		
Extras		14
	(for 6 wkts)	231

	O	M	R	W
Lever	10	—	49	2
Hendrick	10	2	53	—
Sidebottom	10	1	31	1
Gooch	5	1	24	—
Underwood	10	1	46	1
Willey	5	—	14	1

FALL OF WICKETS
1–65, 2–77, 3–123, 4–134, 5–182, 6–193

SAB ENGLAND XI

G. A. Gooch†	c Jennings, b van der Bijl	10
G. Boycott	c Jennings, b le Roux	10
W. Larkins	c Jennings, b Jefferies	47
D. L. Amiss	c Richards, b Kourie	8
A. P. E. Knott*	run out	14
R. A. Woolmer	b le Roux	0
P. Willey	b van der Bijl	31
A. Sidebottom	st Jennings, b Kourie	10
J. K. Lever	b van der Bijl	5
D. L. Underwood	c Kourie, b Kirsten	10
M. Hendrick	not out	1
Extras		6
		152

	O	M	R	W
van der Bijl	7	2	19	3
Procter	10	1	24	—
le Roux	8	2	30	2
Jefferies	7	2	25	1
Kourie	10	1	45	2
Kirsten	1.2	—	3	1

FALL OF WICKETS
1–16, 2–38, 3–49, 4–88, 5–88, 6–99, 7–133, 8–139, 9–148

South Africa won by 79 runs

Before the start of the second 'International' match, at Newlands, came the news from England that the members of the touring side had been banned for three years from Test cricket, but if this 'punishment' was to spur the 'rebels' to greater efforts there was little sign on the first day. With rain reducing play by half they crawled to 101 for 1, from 45 overs. Boycott's was the wicket to go down, and an appalling decision it was. The Yorkshireman edged the ball hard into the ground, it then bounced onto his ankle and was taken at silly point. After a long pause umpire Barry Smith incredibly gave the batsman out caught. As usual the English middle order failed to do its job and they collapsed disappointingly, but with the Springboks losing Richards, Cook and Pollock

Northern Transvaal 1981-82

BATTING

	v. Transvaal (Pretoria) 30, 31 Oct.–2 Nov. 1981	v. Eastern Province (Port Elizabeth) 13, 14, 15 November 1981	v. Western Province (Pretoria) 27, 28, 30 November 1981	v. Natal (Pietermaritzburg) 5, 6, 7 December 1981	v. Transvaal (Johannesburg) 23, 24, 25 January 1982	v. Western Province (Cape Town) 29, 30 Jan.–1 Feb. 1982	v. Eastern Province (Pretoria) 12, 13, 15 February 1982	v. Natal (Pretoria) 8, 9, 10 March 1982
B. J. Whitfield	31 3	0 3	24 70	100 58*	5 6	53 5	8 0	30 8
A. Barrow	13 37	6 7	1 45	6 19				
V. F. du Preez	115 33	0 70	48 1	12 33*	5 0	24 4	8 84	18 16
C. S. Stirk	124 11	1 5	0 24	0 —	25 5	4 2	45 59	27 31
N. G. Featherstone	9 4	14 7	19 11	10 —	2 26	99 18	5 0	
R. C. Ontong	18 4	75 4	8 36*	38 —	3 33	0 4	5 12	45 20
A. M. Ferreira	0 12	4 40	8 1	30 —	11 20	2 0	60 12	29 0
C. M. Old	1 30	20 7	0 2	4 —	4 6	4 14*	1 2	
B. McBride	2 5	0* 1	4* 0	0* —	2* 15	10* 12		
W. F. Morris	6* 27					16 0		
F. E. Joubert	12 3*	6 9*	0 3	0 —	1 22*		0 13	
P. D. de Vaal		15	19 13	6 64				
J. P. Ackermann					14 2	5 2		
C. P. L. de Lange					1 0	19 6		
K. Jennings							18 25	26 1
P. J. A. Visagie							47 12	5 0
N. Rynners							13* 16*	
G. Tullis							21	22
H. W. Raath							6*	1
A. H. Wilkins							2	2
T. Wheelwright							2	1*
Extras	25 12	36 11	4 9	13 10	13 18	15 8	10 11	10 8
Total	356 181	177 183	129 208	277 120	86 153	251 75	220 246	221 110
Wickets	10 10	10 10	10 10	10 1	10 10	10 10	10 10	10 10
Result	D	W	L	D	L	L	D	L
Points	5	15	4	4	5	7	5	7

BOWLING

	C. M. Old	F. E. Joubert	A. M. Ferreira	R. C. Ontong	W. F. Morris	P. D. de Vaal	J. P. Ackermann	N. G. Featherstone
v. Transvaal (Pretoria) 30, 31 Oct.–2 Nov. 1981	23-3-108-2 6-1-26-2	14-3-51-1 6-0-28-2	25-8-63-5 3-0-8-0	21-4-65-1	8-0-44-0			
v. Eastern Province (Port Elizabeth) 13, 14, 15 November 1981	19.5-9-54-4 17-5-29-4	21-8-37-1 10-6-15-1	26-9-43-2 10-5-21-2	19-4-46-3 8.5-1-26-2		6-3-10-0		
v. Western Province (Pretoria) 27, 28, 30 November 1981	23-4-80-1	15-1-59-1	29-5-81-3	23-2-83-2		15-2-54-1		
v. Natal (Pietermaritzburg) 5, 6, 7 December 1981	18-2-79-1 7-0-21-1	16-1-69-2 12-2-36-1	32-9-92-3 7-0-40-1	10-2-36-0 11-1-51-1		25-8-71-2 2.3-0-25-2		
v. Transvaal (Johannesburg) 23, 24, 25 January 1982	24-8-35-2	10-1-29-1	20-4-51-1	27-10-69-5			2-1-4-0	2.4-0-4-0
v. Western Province (Cape Town) 29, 30 Jan.–1 Feb. 1982	30-9-75-3		31-8-114-2	20-5-96-1	24-2-76-2		1-0-9-1	1-0-11-0
v. Eastern Province (Pretoria) 12, 13, 15 February 1982	18-5-35-1 2-0-8-0	25-3-82-1 1.3-0-3-3	32-7-89-2	19-7-62-2				4-1-12-0
v. Natal (Pretoria) 8, 9, 10 March 1982			17-5-31-2 26-12-34-0	11-1-39-2 6-3-17-0				
	187.5-46- 550-21 av. 26.19	130.3-25- 409-14 av. 29.21	258-72- 667-23 av. 29.00	175.5-40- 590-19 av. 31.05	32-2- 120-2 av. 60.00	48.3-13- 160-5 av. 32.00	3-1- 13-1 av. 13.00	7.5-1- 27-0 —

A C. S. Stirk 1-0-3-0
B H. W. Raath 12.1-3-31-1

for 43 on the second evening honours were about even at the close. A splendid six hour 114 by Peter Kirsten prevented a humiliating collapse on the third day. The only support came from Jennings but this was sufficient to ensure a narrow first innings lead. On the fourth day sound batting from Gooch, Larkins and Amiss put the tourists safe from another defeat though the point of declaration was somewhat elusive as the game petered out into the inevitable draw.

SOUTH AFRICA v. SAB ENGLAND XI
19, 20, 21 and 22 March 1982 at Newlands, Cape Town

ENGLAND XI

	FIRST INNINGS		SECOND INNINGS	
G. A. Gooch†	hit wicket, b Kourie	83	c Kourie, b Hobson	68
G. Boycott	c Kuiper, b Kourie	16	c Jennings, b Jefferies	1
W. Larkins	c Richards, b Kourie	29	lbw, b Kirsten	95
D. L. Amiss	c Jennings, b Jefferies	13	not out	73
R. A. Woolmer	c and b Kourie	2	not out	1
P. Willey	c Kourie, b van der Bijl	39		
A. P. E. Knott*	b van der Bijl	16		
C. M. Old	c Jennings, b Jefferies	1		
J. K. Lever	b Jefferies	8		
D. L. Underwood	c Richards, b van der Bijl	0		
L. B. Taylor	not out	10		
Extras		6		11
		223	(for 3 wkts dec)	249

	O	M	R	W	O	M	R	W
van der Bijl	33	12	61	3	21	6	53	—
Jefferies	24.4	8	56	3	14	5	39	1
Hobson	13	3	48	—	30	7	86	1
Kourie	32	14	52	4	16	4	38	—
Kirsten					4	2	7	1
Kuiper					8	2	15	—

FALL OF WICKETS
1–27, 2–104, 3–140, 4–144, 5–148, 6–189, 7–199, 8–205, 9–207
1–8, 2–112, 3–231

SOUTH AFRICA

	FIRST INNINGS		SECOND INNINGS	
S. J. Cook	c Knott, b Lever	18		
B. A. Richards†	lbw, b Taylor	8		
P. N. Kirsten	lbw, b Lever	114		
R. G. Pollock	c Knott, b Lever	0		
C. E. B. Rice	lbw, b Taylor	12		
A. P. Kuiper	c Willey, b Underwood	1	not out	9
A. J. Kourie	c Knott, b Lever	18		
R. V. Jennings*	c sub, b Lever	32	not out	28
S. T. Jefferies	c Knott, b Lever	3		
V. A. P. van der Bijl	not out	4		
D. L. Hobson	b Taylor	2		
Extras		23		1
		235	(for no wkts)	38

	O	M	R	W	O	M	R	W
Taylor	27	8	49	3				
Lever	37	11	86	6	3	—	22	—
Old	18	6	33	—	4	—	15	—
Underwood	22	9	36	1				
Willey	4	1	8	—				

FALL OF WICKETS
1–11, 2–43, 3–43, 4–85, 5–87, 6–144, 7–212, 8–218, 9–232

Match drawn

Northern Transvaal 'B' 1981-82

BATTING	v. Transvaal 'B' (Johannesburg) 30, 31 Oct.–1 Nov. 1981		v. Boland (Stellenbosch) 4, 5, 7 December 1981		v. Border (East London) 26, 28, 29 December 1981		v. Eastern Province 'B' (Pretoria) 1, 2, 4 January 1982		v. Transvaal 'B' (Pretoria) 22, 23, 25 January 1982		v. Border (Pretoria) 26, 27 Feb.–1 Mar. 1982	
J. P. Ackermann	16	52	61	10	38		18	2			4	4
D. E. Robinson	23	10	9	7								
A. H. Jordaan	10	32	1	11	2		38	38	42	3	41	57
L. J. E. Coetzee	11	22										
D. N. Edwards	4	13	31	0	7		62	50	40	6	13	1
K. G. Motley	19	17	2	1	30		20	36	7	16*	20	0
A. G. Elgar	30	25										
H. W. Raath	1	4	0	6	7		13	—	0	—	10	5
N. Rynners	15	9	2	16*	0		10	—	29*	—		
P. J. Marneweck	17*	8	54	0	18*		2	23*			24	25
M. G. Davies	10	1*	9*	0	—		10*	—	2			
P. J. A. Visagie			31	95	7		10	7	34	35		
W. F. Morris			24	17	99		17	23*	4		0	43
C. P. L. de Lange					112		61	27			72	26
K. Jennings									41	48*		
G. W. Jones									0	—		
D. Malan									5			
A. Geringer											4	17
B. McBride											5	0
T. Wheelwright											0*	1*
Extras	17	14	17	9	23		23	15	15	13	22	11
Total	173	207	241	172	343		284	221	219	121	215	190
Wickets	10	10	10	10	9		10	6	10	3	10	10
Result	L		W		W		D		D		W	
Points	5		18		17		6		7		17	

BOWLING	P. J. Marneweck	M. G. Davies	J. P. Ackermann	H. W. Raath	A. G. Elgar	K. G. Motley	A. H. Jordaan	W. F. Morris
v. Transvaal 'B' (Johannesburg) 30, 31 October–1 November 1981	21.5–5–78–3 5–0–17–0	21–3–60–1 5–0–16–0	10–3–24–1 4.1–0–8–1	22–5–53–5 10–0–32–0	3–0–18–0 7–2–14–2	6–2–19–1	1–0–3–0	
v. Boland (Stellenbosch) 4, 5, 7 December 1981	3–1–19–0 11–3–33–1	8–2–12–0 12–3–27–2	13–2–27–1	22–14–25–4 24–8–41–4				26–6–67–4 23–9–50–3
v. Border (East London) 26, 28, 29 December 1981	10.2–4–12–6 19–4–37–4	13–4–21–3 16–9–30–1	6–3–4–0 15–5–31–2	13–3–20–0 6.2–2–8–2				12–1–47–1 19–7–29–1
v. Eastern Province 'B' (Pretoria) 1, 2, 4 January 1982	13–5–26–2 12–1–43–1	11–3–31–0 14–3–41–0	9–0–26–1 7–1–20–0	11–3–20–1 20–0–50–3		1–0–1–0	7.5–2–12–3 11–5–13–0	26–5–70–3 23–8–54–1
v. Transvaal 'B' (Pretoria) 22, 23, 25 January 1982		9–0–36–0 16–2–82–2		32–4–95–6 7–2–25–0			16.4–5–38–2	10–3–27–0 16–2–73–1
v. Border (Pretoria) 26, 27 February–1 March 1982	10.2–2–4–0–3 11–1–35–1		9–3–12–2 8–3–15–3	11–3–23–0 5–3–12–0				8–3–15–1 15–5–27–2
	116.3–26– 340–21 av. 16.19	125–29– 356–9 av. 39.56	81.1–20– 167–11 av. 15.18	183.2–47– 404–25 av. 16.16	10–2– 32–2 av. 16.00	7–2– 20–1 av. 20.00	36.3–12– 66–5 av. 13.20	178–49– 459–17 av. 27.00

A D. Malan 7–0–26–0 and 7–2–19–0

THE GREAT REBELLION/175

The now-dead three match limited overs series was completed at Johannesburg, and the home side gained a 3 to 0 whitewash when they were controversially awarded the match on faster run-rate after rain had limited the tourists to only 23 overs. A whirlwind 54 from Adrian Kuiper, and more staid efforts from Cook and Rice helped the Springboks to an impressive 243 for 5 in 50 overs and after a long break for rain the Englishmen scored 111 for 7 in 23 overs. This gave them a run-rate of 4.826 runs per over as against the Springboks' 4.86 and they and the scorers believed that under South African rules they had won. After a long discussion however International rules were applied, with South Africa awarded the match on a least wickets lost basis.

THIRD LIMITED OVERS MATCH
24 March 1982 at Johannesburg

SOUTH AFRICA

S. J. Cook	run out		62
B. A. Richards	c Boycott, b Sidebottom		13
P. N. Kirsten	c Taylor, b Sidebottom		32
R. G. Pollock	c Knott, b Sidebottom		3
C. E. B. Rice	not out		58
A. P. Kuiper	c Gooch, b Taylor		54
R. V. Jennings*	not out		7
V. A. P. van der Bijl			
W. K. Watson			
G. S. le Roux			
A. J. Kourie			
Extras			14
(for 5 wkts)			243

	O	M	R	W
Taylor	10	4	35	1
Hendrick	10	—	54	—
Underwood	10	—	53	—
Sidebottom	10	1	35	3
Gooch	2	—	17	—
Willey	8	1	35	—

FALL OF WICKETS
1–43, 2–118, 3–119, 4–126, 5–209

SAB ENGLAND XI

G. A. Gooch	run out		38
G. Boycott	c Rice, b le Roux		26
W. Larkins	b le Roux		10
P. Willey	b van der Bijl		1
D. L. Amiss	c Jennings, b van der Bijl		19
G. W. Humpage	b van der Bijl		1
A. P. E. Knott*	not out		0
A. Sidebottom	run out		1
L. B. Taylor			
M. Hendrick			
D. L. Underwood			
Extras			15
(for 7 wkts)			111

	O	M	R	W
van der Bijl	9	—	30	3
Watson	7	—	26	—
le Roux	5	—	32	2
Kuiper	2	—	8	—

FALL OF WICKETS
1–60, 2–85, 3–86, 4–88, 5–108, 6–110, 7–111

South Africa won on faster scoring rate

Orange Free State 1981-82

BATTING

	v. Griqualand West (Bloemfontein) 16, 17, 19 October 1981	v. Western Province 'B' (Bloemfontein) 6, 7, 9 November 1981	v. Western Province 'B' (Constantia) 4, 5, 7 December 1981	v. Natal 'B' (Durban) 1, 2, 3 January 1982	v. Natal 'B' (Bloemfontein) 22, 23, 25 January 1982	v. Griqualand West (Bloemfontein) 25, 26, 27 February 1982
E. Grobler	16 17	5 23				
C. J. van Heerden	4 36		7 21	57 45*	2 32	21 22
L. W. Griessel	11 2	43 47	0 8	9 —		
G. W. Humpage	64 61*	15 19	0 15	15 12*		
R. J. East	25 53*	54 25	0 0	47 —	22 53	6 31
J. J. Strydom	85 —		3 1	12 —	12 9	8 2*
L. J. Wenzler	9 —					
R. A. le Roux	21 —				10 3	67 102*
W. M. van der Merwe	48* —	28* 19	4 2	5 —	17 —	6 —
C. J. P. G. van Zyl	15 —	0 —	7* 14	0 —	24* —	9* —
G. Grobler	0 —		8 12*	46 —		
D. P. le Roux		37 4				
G. N. Lister-James		13 25*			20 8	
S. Regenstein		15 6	31 19	28 —	1 23*	
L. J. Coetzee		0 11				
A. Sidebottom		0 6*	16 2		66 —	3 —
L. J. Wenzler			10 22	3 14		
S. N. Hartley				28 —	10 72*	28 34
E. Schmidt				23* —		
M. Michav					38 2	
P. Grobler					1 —	
G. Martin					1 —	
Extras	11 13	8 5	6 16	23 10	19 4	14 23
Total	309 182	218 190	92 132	250 81	249 204	202 216
Wickets	10 3	10 8	10 10	10 1	10 5	10 4
Result	W	W	L	D	D	D
Points	19	17	5	5	8	5

BOWLING

	W. M. van der Merwe	C. J. P. G. van Zyl	G. Grobler	C. J. van Heerden	L. J. Wenzler	R. A. le Roux	G. W. Humpage	A. Sidebottom
v. Griqualand West (Bloemfontein) 16, 17, 19 October 1981	14-3-58-0 18-7-38-1	16.4-4-58-3 22-7-51-3	13-4-41-1 13-5-41-3	13-5-45-4 18-1-54-3	7-2-32-1 5-2-18-0	3-1-10-1 9-3-19-0	5-1-11-0	
v. Western Province 'B' (Bloemfontein) 6, 7, 9 November 1981	9-3-25-0 16.1-3-48-2	15-7-50-6 29-9-60-1					19-2-53-1	14.3-4-32-4 26-10-50-5
v. Western Province 'B' (Constantia) 4, 5, 7 December 1981	14-3-38-4 13-2-37-4	17-6-54-1 15-4-37-3	8-0-40-0 8-2-23-0	2-0-11-0			8.1-1-28-1	22-9-36-4 10-3-19-0
v. Natal 'B' (Durban) 1, 2, 3 January 1982	13-4-23-1 19-2-42-2	19-6-70-1 11-1-30-1		12.5-2-59-2 7-3-13-2			8-1-29-0	
v. Natal 'B' (Bloemfontein) 22, 23, 25 January 1982	12.1-1-45-0 16.5-0-79-2	7-0-18-0 16-3-56-0	15-5-41-2 9-0-40-0	9-2-34-1 9-5-12-1		10-1-37-1		19-5-43-4 14-3-49-1
v. Griqualand West (Bloemfontein) 25, 26, 27 February 1982	22-8-50-1	20-4-53-3		11-5-18-1				22-8-31-1
	167.1-36- 483-20 av. 24.15	187.4-51- 537-22 av. 24.41	66-16- 226-6 av. 37.67	81.5-23- 246-14 av. 17.57	12-4- 50-1 av. 50.00	22-5- 66-2 av. 33.00	40.1-5- 121-2 av. 60.50	127.3-42- 260-19 av. 13.68

A L. J. Coetzee 6-3-12-0
B L. J. Wenzler 4-0-21-0
C P. Grobler 8-4-11-1

THE GREAT REBELLION

Not for the first time a limited overs match had a farcical result, with the spectators leaving the ground without a clue as to the winners. Something is badly wrong with a game where that can happen.

The 'Rebel' tour finished with the third representative match, played at Durban on 26, 27, 28 and 29 March at the Kingsmead ground. Despite previous failings Gooch's team stuck to the same basic players. With the repeated failures of the middle-order ir was a mystery why Humpage, a fierce striker of the ball who of late has outscored Woolmer and Willey in the county game, was not given a fair chance. South Africa lost the toss and with the wicket green and grassy were invited to bat first. Les Taylor, as previously on this tour, looked far faster and more dangerous than his more celebrated colleagues and after getting the prize wicket of Graeme Pollock, ran through the late order to send the Springboks crashing to 181 for 9; they then declared to give England half an hour's batting. This they negotiated without mishap. Desperately needing a win to square the series England unaccountably seemed intent on defence. This especially applied to Boycott. His 31 in over three hours lost his side the chance to make a big score on the second day. A very good hundred by Woolmer – the only time on the tour that he showed any form partly made up for the early sloth but then rain butted in and the final day was a pointless exercise. Gooch declared far too late for anything but a draw to be feasible and the match was finally abandoned with seven overs unbowled.

Thus the SAB England team completed its tour, arguably the most controversial in modern times. Joe Pamensky, new president of the SACU voted it a resounding success; Ahmed Mangera, his counterpart in the rival SA Cricket Board felt it was a gimmick of no lasting consequence. One suspects that the latter assessment was nearer to the truth. Certainly the poor crowds and, from the tourists, indifferent play and, at times, attitudes, did not help matters. If the aim was to strike a blow against international double standards it was felt that a point had been proved, yet it also served to accentuate and increase the hypocritical attitudes which ensure South Africa remains in the cricket wilderness. The tour did nothing to prove, or disprove the belief prevalent in South Africa and, to some extent, abroad, that its cricketing standards are as high as any in the world. Certainly the struggles of so many county players in domestic competitions in recent years added fuel to the flames, and now came this series of, at times, overwhelming victories against a team of English internationals. Frankly most of Gooch's side are manifestly over the hill, some having been in cricket so long, all fire and enterprise has been ground out of them. Sometimes they seemed to be merely going through the motions. After all, whatever they did, their money was safe.

The tourists returned home barred from Test cricket but happy (one assumes) in the knowledge that their income is assured for the next three years at least. But what of South Africa's Test future? One doubts really whether many of the 'rebels' really care.

No report of the tour would be complete without a mention of Rashid Varachia, who died suddenly in Johannesburg on 11 December. No-one had worked harder to make South African cricket non-racial, and likewise no-one

	Inns	NOs	Runs	HS	Av
	4	—	61	25	15.25
	10	1	247	57	27.44
	7	—	120	47	17.14
	8	2	201	64	33.50
	11	1	316	54	31.60
	8	1	132	85	18.86
	1	—	9	9	—
	5	1	203	102*	50.75
	8	2	129	48*	21.50
	7	3	69	24*	17.25
	4	1	66	46	22.00
	2	—	41	37	20.50
	4	1	66	25*	22.00
	7	1	123	31	20.50
	2	—	11	11	5.50
	6	1	93	66	18.60
	4	—	49	22	12.25
	5	1	172	72*	43.00
	1	1	23	23*	—
	2	—	40	38	20.00
	1	—	1	1	—
	1	—	1	1	—

S. Regenstein	E. Schmidt	G. Martin	ROs	Extras	Runs	Wkts
			3	247	10	
			11	243	10	
1-0-4-0			18	129	10	
15-7-39-1			16	278	10	
4-0-23-0			22	252	10	
13-4-64-1			14	215	8	
19-6-44-0	26-11-58-3		12	295	3	
11-2-38-1	12-3-31-1		6	160	7	
8-1-26-0			31	238	10	
12-5-45-0			2	28	346	7
		26-9-65-0	1	18	246	8
83-25-	38-14-	26-9-				
283-3	89-4	65-0				
av. 94.33	av. 22.25	—				

Transvaal 1981-92

BATTING

	v. Northern Transvaal (Pretoria) 30, 31 Oct.-1 Nov. 1981	v. Western Province (Johannesburg) 5, 6, 7 December 1981	v. Eastern Province (Johannesburg) 26, 27, 28 December 1981	v. Western Province (Cape Town) 1, 2, 4 January 1982	v. Natal (Durban)	v. Northern Transvaal (Johannesburg) 16, 17, 18 January 1982	v. Eastern Province (Port Elizabeth) 23, 24, 25 January 1982	v. Natal (Johannesburg) 6, 7, 8 February 1982	v. Natal (Johannesburg) 31 Mar.-1, 2 Apr. 1982	
S. J. Cook	9	19	48	15	72	28	30	2	34	9*	9	28*	50	28
A. I. Kallicharran	34	0	129	42			24	29			61	45*	103	17
H. R. Fotheringham	12	12		8	12	5	4	9	16	—				
R. G. Pollock	65	14*	70	124	2	41*					72	—	72*	26
K. A. McKenzie	67	1	13	5*	78	23	7	4	56		101*		5	30
C. E. B. Rice	66	16*	70	108	35	17*	34	20	9		22	—	1	102*
L. J. Barnard	36	—			5	—								
R. V. Jennings	1	—	23*	—	3	—	0	23	5		14	—	3	1
N. V. Radford	16*	—	—	—	12	—	21	0	0		3*	—		
G. E. McMillan	13						33	13	43*		2	—	0	6
R. W. Hanley	12*	—					2*	0*	6		—	—		
M. Yachad			8											
A. J. Kourie			10*	13*	3	—	11	29	10		25		27*	12*
J. Fairclough			—	—	9*						—	—		
G. W. Johnson					9				—					
N. T. Day							26	10	4					
M. S. Venter									9	4*	18	3		
H. Page													3	26
Extras	16	4	26	44	11	4	17	12	34	1	27	2	13	22
Total	347	66	397	359	251	118	209	151	226	14	354	78	277	270
Wickets	9	4	6	5	10	3	10	10	10	0	8	1	7	7
Result	D		D	W	D		L		W		W		W	
Points	8		8	22	6		7		18		21		17	

BOWLING

	C. E. B. Rice	R. W. Hanley	G. E. McMillan	N. V. Radford	L. J. Barnard	J. Fairclough	A. J. Kourie	G. W. Johnson
v. Northern Transvaal (Pretoria) 30, 31 Oct.-2 Nov. 1981	28-10-60-2 / 19-4-64-2	41-15-79-2 / 20-8-34-4	26.4-11-44-2 / 2-1-8-0	28-4-93-4 / 13-2-53-3	22-7-55-0 / 6.4-4-10-1			
v. Western Province (Johannesburg) 5, 6, 7 December 1981	21-9-43-2 / 10-4-16-1	28-8-70-1 / 7.4-1-17-0		25-10-45-0 / 5-1-14-0		29-12-44-5 / 8-0-19-0	16-4-50-1 / 22-6-46-1	
v. Eastern Province (Johannesburg) 26, 27, 28 December 1981	13-7-16-0 / 10.3-2-18-3	12.2-5-20-1 / 15-6-23-3		9-1-30-1 / 13-5-20-4		27-10-52-5 / 8-4-4-0	23-7-47-2 / 7-3-8-0	
v. Western Province (Cape Town) 1, 2, 4 January 1982	22-6-43-1 / 14-4-20-0			13-2-58-0 / 10-2-21-2		26-4-87-2 / 12-3-27-0	25.3-9-88-6 / 33.5-11-102-5	17-3-61-0 / 2-0-9-0
v. Natal (Durban) 16, 17, 18 January 1982	15-5-51-0 / 10-1-37-3	19-4-33-6 / 13-2-63-0	9-0-33-1	14-4-40-2 / 8-1-24-2			5-1-14-1 / 15-1-51-1	
v. Northern Transvaal (Johannesburg) 23, 24, 25 January 1982	15.2-4-19-3 / 21.3-5-45-5	13-6-10-3 / 21-4-51-3	8-4-14-2 / 7-3-16-0	10-2-30-1 / 13-3-23-2				
v. Eastern Province (Port Elizabeth) 6, 7, 8 February 1982	12-1-23-1 / 19.4-4-49-4	15.3-7-31-5 / 19-5-51-1	20-9-43-4 / 20-5-55-1	12-0-39-0 / 17-4-53-4			10-3-27-0 / 20-9-30-0	
v. Natal (Johannesburg) 31 March-1, 2 April 1982		23.5-5-95-3 / 13-2-28-1	20-3-74-3 / 10-2-25-0			22-4-53-0 / 8-2-21-1	24.4-9-44-2	
	231-66- 504-27 av. 18.67	261.2-78- 605-33 av. 18.33	122.4-38- 312-13 av. 24.00	190-41- 543-25 av. 21.72	28.4-11- 65-1 av. 65.00	140-39- 307-13 av. 23.62	202-63- 507-19 av. 26.67	19-3- 70-0 —

had done more to try and persuade the ICC that South Africa deserved another chance. As President of the SACU he was in London to attend the ill-fated ICC conference in August 1981 and was desperately disappointed at the renewed rejection of his country. It is fair to say that he probably worked himself into an early grave on behalf of South African cricket; one is told it is not possible to die of a broken heart.

SOUTH AFRICA v. SAB ENGLAND XI
26, 27, 28 and 29 March 1982 at Kingsmead, Durban

SOUTH AFRICA

	FIRST INNINGS			SECOND INNINGS	
S. J. Cook	c Gooch, b Lever	11		not out	50
B. A. Richards†	c Knott, b Hendrick	41		retired hurt	17
P. N. Kirsten	c Gooch, b Hendrick	11		c Knott, b Lever	14
R. G. Pollock	b Taylor	15		c Hendrick, b Larkins	12
C. E. B. Rice	c Gooch, b Hendrick	9		not out	39
A. P. Kuiper	b Taylor	0			
A. J. Kourie	not out	50			
R. V. Jennings*	c Knott, b Taylor	22			
G. S. le Roux	c Knott, b Taylor	0			
V. A. P. van der Bijl	c Knott, b Taylor	0			
W. K. Watson	not out	4			
Extras		18			11
	(for 9 wkts dec)	181		(for 2 wkts)	143

	O	M	R	W	O	M	R	W
Taylor	25.3	5	61	5	8	2	23	—
Lever	13	1	53	1	16	9	25	1
Old	11	3	21	—	6	2	18	—
Hendrick	21	9	28	3	12	3	37	—
Larkins					5	—	24	1
Knott					1	—	5	—

FALL OF WICKETS
1–48, 2–61, 3–77, 4–92, 5–92, 6–111, 7–168, 8–170, 9–170
1–61, 2–91

SAB ENGLAND XI

	FIRST INNINGS	
G. A. Gooch†	c Kourie, b le Roux	48
G. Boycott	c Jennings, b van der Bijl	31
W. Larkins	lbw, b van der Bijl	39
D. L. Amiss	c Cook, b van der Bijl	50
R. A. Woolmer	c Kourie, b Watson	100
P. Willey	b Watson	15
A. P. E. Knott*	c Kirsten, b van der Bijl	6
C. M. Old	c Rice, b van der Bijl	10
J. K. Lever	not out	4
M. Hendrick		
L. B. Taylor		
Extras		8
	(for 8 wkts dec)	311

	O	M	R	W
van der Bijl	40	14	97	5
Watson	25.2	4	79	2
le Roux	25	5	71	1
Kourie	17	3	43	—
Kuiper	3	1	8	—
Kirsten	2	1	5	—

FALL OF WICKETS
1–67, 2–95, 3–137, 4–217, 5–259, 6–270, 7–301, 8–311

Match drawn

Transvaal 'B' 1981-82

BATTING

	v. Northern Transvaal 'B' (Johannesburg) 30, 31 Oct.–1 Nov. 1981	v. Eastern Province 'B' (Uitenhage) 26, 27, 28 December 1981	v. Border (East London) 1, 2, 3 January 1982	v. Boland (Johannesburg) 15, 16, 18 January 1982	v. Northern Transvaal 'B' (Pretoria) 22, 23, 25 January 1982	v. Eastern Province 'B' (Johannesburg) 5, 6, 7 February 1982
D. D. Dyer	10 16			17 20	14 28*	20
M. Yachad	154 59	1 21	8 13	0 3	5 49	48
W. J. van der Linden	4 30*					
N. T. Day	30 0	25 63	78 39			9
N. Jurgensen	9 4					
R. W. Adair	8 0*	5 27*	17 7			
K. P. Skjoldhammer	0 —					
I. F. Weideman	0 —			18 8	21 —	31*
A. Viljoen	1 —		0 0	0 0		—
B. L. Mare	8 —	1 0				
J. Fairclough	9*					
M. S. Venter		40 14	6 17	3 33		
N. E. Wright		34 46	11 65	6 8	43 85	5
L. J. Barnard		1 69		9 3	45 65	
A. H. Drake		2 1	24 14	2 3	6 —	
G. E. McMillan		15 0	64 9*			
A. J. Plint		7 29	3 0			
H. Losper		3* 1	0* 0	9 8		
R. Reid			6 13			
H. Page				1 13	5 —	21*
T. Knodell				23* 22*	39 —	
A. Videgauz					57 3*	2
K. J. Kerr					18 —	24
M. Park					1*	
H. R. Fotheringham						115
Extras	27 12	15 26	13 26	18 14	14 19	30
Total	260 121	149 297	230 203	106 135	268 249	305
Wickets	10 4	10 10	10 10	10 10	10 3	7
Result	W	D	L	L	D	W
Points	19	5	6	5	9	19

BOWLING

	J. Fairclough	B. L. Mare	I. F. Weideman	K. P. Skjoldhammer	A. Viljoen	H. Losper	G. E. McMillan	A. J. Plint
v. Northern Transvaal 'B' (Johannesburg) 30, 31 Oct.–1 Nov. 1981	24–12–29–1 22–11–22–1	16–5–49–3 26–12–42–1	14.1–4–20–1 13.4–5–39–4	16–9–22–2 22–10–46–2	15–4–36–2 6–2–11–0			
v. Eastern Province 'B' (Uitenhage) 26, 27, 28 December 1981		15–3–37–0 10–0–40–0				25.5–7–86–7 17–6–39–3	20–8–43–3 18–6–40–3	3–0–17–0 1–0–2–0
v. Border (East London) 1, 2, 3 January 1982					22–7–54–3 5–3–8–0	25–8–57–2 9–4–13–1	24–8–76–2 6–1–12–1	17–5–58–0 4–0–15–1
v. Boland (Johannesburg) 15, 16, 18 January 1982			24–10–55–4 9–1–22–2		18–3–42–1 4–0–24–2	5–1–17–0 3–0–10–0		
v. Northern Transvaal 'B' (Pretoria) 22, 23, 25 January 1982			28–1–52–4 14–3–32–1					
v. Eastern Province 'B' (Johannesburg) 5, 6, 7 February 1982			18–10–35–3 8–3–7–2		8–2–12–2 7–3–13–2			
	46–23– 51–2 av. 25.50	67–20– 168–4 av. 42.00	128.5–37– 262–21 av. 12.48	38–19– 68–4 av. 17.00	85–24– 200–12 av. 16.67	84–26– 222–13 av. 17.08	68–23– 171–9 av. 19.00	25–5– 92–1 av. 92.00

A W. J. van der Linden 10–4–24–1
   R. W. Adair 6–0–9–1
B R. W. Adair 13–2–36–0;
   N. E. Wright 9.2–4–15–1;

A. H. Drake 1–0–1–1;
C N. E. Wright 7–4–12–0;
   M. Yachad 3–0–13–0;
   N. T. Day 2–1–5–0;

R. Reid 1–0–5–2;
A. H. Drake 1–0–2–1
D A. H. Drake 0.2–0–3–0
   K. J. Kerr 19–6–49–0 and 15–5–34–1

THE GREAT REBELLION

First-Class Averages

BATTING

	M	Inns	NOs	Runs	HS	Av	100s	50s
M. J. D. Doherty (Griqualand West)	6	10	2	555	112	69.38	1	4
R. G. Pollock (Transvaal)	9	14	5	586	124	65.11	1	5
D. L. Amiss (SA Breweries)	4	7	2	308	73*	61.60		4
P. N. Kirsten (Western Province)	12	19	3	948	151	59.25	3	3
G. A. Gooch (SA Breweries)	4	7		396	109	56.57	1	3
A. I. Kallicharran (Transvaal)	6	10	1	484	129	53.78	2	1
S. D. Bruce (Western Province)	6	7	2	268	100*	53.60	1	1
E. J. Barlow (Boland)	7	12	1	584	202*	53.09	2	1
C. E. B. Rice (Transvaal)	11	16	4	561	108	46.75	2	2
J. Seeff (Western Province 'B')	5	9	2	322	113*	46.00	1	
P. D. Swart (Boland)	7	11	1	433	92	43.30		4
A. J. Lamb (Western Province)	9	14	3	472	106*	42.91	1	3
C. L. Smith (Natal)	7	13	1	514	112	42.83	1	2
K. A. McKenzie (Transvaal)	8	12	2	390	101*	39.00	1	3
D. Bestall (Natal)	8	15	1	528	80*	37.72		3
I. Howell (Eastern Province 'B')	7	13	5	299	112	37.38	1	
B. A. Richards (Natal)	9	16	3	475	87*	36.54		3
L. Seeff (Western Province)	10	18	3	547	79	36.47		4
S. J. Cook (Transvaal)	11	19	3	576	114	36.00	1	3
C. P. L. de Lange (Northern Transvaal)	5	9		324	112	36.00	1	2
R. L. S. Armitage (Eastern Province)	8	14	1	465	171*	35.78	2	
O. Henry (Western Province)	10	13	5	281	53	35.13		1
S. T. Jefferies (Western Province)	9	10	4	209	63	34.83		1
K. S. McEwan (Western Province)	10	14	1	430	117	33.08	1	2
W. Larkins (SA Breweries)	4	7		231	95	33.00		1
J. de Villiers (Boland)	6	8	1	230	61	32.86		1
A. P. Kuiper (Western Province)	10	15	1	457	90	32.64		5
A. J. Kourie (Transvaal)	10	12	5	222	50*	31.72		1
R. J. East (Orange Free State)	7	13	1	380	63	31.67		4
V. F. du Preez (Northern Transvaal)	8	16	1	471	115	31.40	1	2
N. E. Wright (Transvaal 'B')	6	11		344	85	31.27		1
M. Yachad (Transvaal)	7	12		369	154	30.75	1	1
A. D. Methven (Griqualand West)	6	10		307	68	30.70		3
P. J. Allan (Natal 'B')	6	11	2	274	75*	30.44		1
G. Boycott (SA Breweries)	4	7		204	95	29.14		1
L. J. Barnard (Transvaal)	5	8		233	69	29.13		2
D. K. Pearse (Natal)	7	11	2	261	70	29.00		2
S. J. Bezuidenhout (Eastern Province)	6	11		318	110	28.91	1	
P. Anker (Boland)	7	8	5	86	27*	28.67		
P. J. Marneweck (Northern Transvaal 'B')	5	9	3	171	54	28.50		1
N. T. Day (Transvaal)	6	10		284	78	28.40		2
R. A. Woolmer (SA Breweries)	4	7	1	168	100	28.00	1	

(Partial batting table, left)

Inns	NOs	Runs	HS	Av
7	1	125	28*	20.83
11	—	361	154	32.82
2	1	34	30*	—
7	—	244	78	34.86
2	—	13	9	6.50
6	2	64	27*	16.00
1	—	0	0	—
5	1	78	31*	19.50
5	—	1	1	0.20
3	—	9	8	3.00
1	1	9	9*	—
6	—	113	40	18.83
9	—	303	85	33.67
6	—	192	69	32.00
7	—	52	24	7.43
4	1	88	64	29.33
4	—	39	29	9.75
6	2	21	9	5.25
2	—	19	13	9.50
4	1	40	21*	13.33
3	2	84	39	—
3	1	62	57	31.00
2	—	42	24	21.00
1	1	1	1*	—
1	—	115	115	—

Bowling (partial)

L. J. Barnard	H. Page	M. Park	ROs	Extras	Runs	Wkts
			1	17	173	10
				14	207	10A
				29	232	10
				10	177	9
			1	38	335	10B
				17	102	6C
7–2–20–0				9	169	10
21–8–46–3				2	73	4
			1	15	219	10D
				13	121	3
13–7–20–2	11.5–2–26–3					
	8.3–3–15–0					
16–5–28–2	13–4–28–0	15–2–47–3				
10–3–9–0	6–1–17–0	6–0–13–1				
				10	146	10E
	16–4–47–4	11–4–31–1				
	12–2–49–4	8–3–20–2		15	104	10
67–25–123–7	67.2–16–182–11	40–9–111–7				
av. 17.57	av. 16.55	av. 5.86				

E K. J. Kerr 4–1–11–0

Western Province 1981-82

BATTING

	v. Eastern Province (Cape Town) 6, 7, 9 November 1981	v. Northern Transvaal (Pretoria) 27, 28, 30 November 1981	v. Transvaal (Johannesburg) 5, 6, 7 December 1981	v. SA Universities (Cape Town) 14, 15, 17 December 1981	v. Natal (Durban) 26, 27, 28 December 1981	v. Transvaal (Cape Town) 1, 2, 4 January 1982	v. Northern Transvaal (Cape Town) 29, 30 Jan.–1 Feb. 1982	v. Natal (Cape Town) 12, 13, 15 February 1982	v. SAB England XI (Cape Town) 8, 9, 10 March 1982	v. Eastern Province (Port Elizabeth) 31 Mar.–1, 2 Apr. 1982
L. Seeff	47 20*	37	20 57*	5 56	0 4	44 31	50	10 6	12 48	79 21*
M. J. Nel	5 19*			12 24						
P. N. Kirsten	114 —	86	14 38		3	19 22	14 130	5 28*	10 67*	151
R. J. Ryall	7 —	4*	13* —	6 21	0 6					106*
A. J. Lamb	32 —	38	62 9*	10 69	8 28	4 1	12	89 4*	0 2	28*
K. S. McEwan	21 —	53	4 —	27 37	1 34	3 42	61	117 —	0 2*	7 25*
R. F. Pienaar	4 —	3	20 8	12 0	1 0	7 8	5		0	
O. Henry	6 —			36 3		53 30*	31	22*	33* 6	
G. S. le Roux	12 —	6	34 —		1 8	43 10	42	3		
S. T. Jefferies	3* —	63	14 —		17* 0*		35*	12	17 45	—
D. L. Hobson	2 —	11*	4 —	4 0				5		
A. P. Kuiper		27	63 —		89 9	72 28		50 0	90 1	—
J. During		29	4 —		6 9	0* —		5 10	10*	
E. Muntingh				0 28						
T. A. Clarke				10 21					41 11	
R. R. Lawrenson				0 24						
J. E. Mahoney				10* 3*						
S. D. Bruce						89 15*	7	5 —	42 10	—
J. D. Du Toit							8			
Extras	31	11	17 6	2 23	27 27	16 7	41	40 3	8 12	13 —
Total	284 39	368	269 118	130 309	157 144	353 186	422	363 51	263 204	384 46
Wickets	10 0	9d	10 2	10 10	10 10	9d 7	9d	10 3	8d 7d	3d 0
Result	W	W	D	W	L	D	W	W	D	W
Points	17	19	4	—	5	9	21	18	—	23

BOWLING

	G. S. le Roux	S. T. Jefferies	R. F. Pienaar	D. L. Hobson	O. Henry	J. During	A. P. Kuiper	R. R. Lawrenson
v. Eastern Province (Cape Town) 6, 7, 9 November 1981	19–4–30–5 18–9–22–2	20.3–5–56–2 28–9–51–4	11–4–11–0	9–3–29–0 27.1–11–65–4	18–5–40–2			
v. Northern Transvaal (Pretoria) 27, 28, 30 November 1981	14.4–5–22–3 18.4–6–31–2	20–6–46–5 21–6–51–1	6–0–11–0	14–3–24–1 30–11–82–5		18–7–33–1 13–4–20–2	2–1–4–0	
v. Transvaal (Johannesburg) 5, 6, 7 December 1981	8–3–18–0	35–7–128–1	14–1–56–0	15–2–55–1		35–6–114–4		
v. SA Universities (Cape Town) 14, 15, 17 December 1981			20–4–64–4 18–4–34–3			23–4–75–2 16.1–7–22–7		24–6–54–3 9–0–39–0
v. Natal (Durban) 26, 27, 28 December 1981	10–0–37–1 5–0–14–0	15.4–4–49–2 15–5–50–4	12–4–24–5 9–3–28–0	3–0–13–0		18–5–28–1 6.5–1–28–0	5–2–8–1	
v. Transvaal (Cape Town) 1, 2, 4 January 1982	27.3–6–63–5 8–0–27–1	32–6–73–3 11–4–29–0	9–1–18–1 3–0–3–0			27–9–53–1 15–5–28–2	4–0–21–0	
v. Northern Transvaal (Cape Town) 29, 30 Jan.–1 Feb. 1982	21.4–7–44–6 14–7–23–3	18–5–41–1 14–6–25–4	6–4–6–0		30–10–84–2 15.2–6–19–2	11–1–45–1		
v. Natal (Cape Town) 12, 13, 15 February 1982	17–5–50–2 19–4–64–3	23–11–40–3 21.3–7–65–4		7–1–31–1 31–17–53–3	14–8–26–0	10.5–4–22–4	10–3–14–0	
v. SAB England XI (Cape Town) 8, 9, 10 March 1982		19–3–47–3 13–1–37–1	11–4–24–0 16–2–41–2	21.1–8–57–4 21–6–48–2	8–3–34–0 11–1–61–2	5–2–7–0	3–0–15–0 9–2–20–0	
v. Eastern Province (Port Elizabeth) 31 March–1, 2 April 1982	18.3–8–28–5 20.3–1–51–5	19–8–48–4 23–2–88–3	6–2–11–0 8–0–43–0	4–2–14–0 28–3–68–0	11–2–35–1		3–1–12–1 3–1–10–1	
	239.3–65–524–43 av. 12.19	348.4–95–924–45 av. 20.53	149–33–374–15 av. 24.93	255.4–83–642–25 av. 25.68	165–49–441–22 av. 20.06	109.5–28–265–8 av. 33.13	23–7–69–3 av. 23.00	33–6–93–3 av. 31.00

A L. Seeff 2–0–10–0   B J. D. du Toit 5–2–9–0

BATTING continued

	M	Inns	NOs	Runs	HS	Av	100s	50s
N. P. Daniels (Natal)	8	14	3	306	66	27.82		2
W. F. Morris (Northern Transvaal)	7	12	2	276	99	27.60		1
C. J. van Heerden (Orange Free State)	5	10	1	247	57	27.44		1
T. R. Madsen (Natal 'B')	6	11		300	92	27.27		2
K. Sharp (Griqualand West)	5	9		245	47	27.22		
B. J. Whitfield (Northern Transvaal)	8	16	1	404	100	26.93	1	3
G. L. Hayes (Border)	4	8		215	52	26.88		1
G. S. Cowley (Eastern Province 'B')	6	11	2	241	98*	26.78		1
D. S. Scott (Border)	4	7	1	160	62	26.67		1
G. W. Humpage (Orange Free State)	5	10	2	212	64	26.50		2
P. M. Thompson (Western Province 'B')	7	14	1	341	90	26.23		3
P. J. A. Visagie (Northern Transvaal)	6	11		283	95	25.73		1
T. A. Clarke (Western Province)	9	17		434	82	25.53		3
R. R. Lawrenson (Western Province)	8	12	2	253	87	25.30		1
A. H. Jordaan (Northern Transvaal 'B')	6	11		275	57	25.00		2
R. A. Smith (Natal)	6	10		246	91	24.60		2
E. T. Laughlin (Border)	5	10	1	221	101	24.55	1	1
M. J. Procter (Natal)	8	14	1	315	76	24.23		3
C. S. Stirk (Northern Transvaal)	8	15		363	124	24.20	1	1
R. M. Bentley (Natal)	8	15	1	337	88	24.07		1
M. J. Nel (Western Province)	5	10	2	192	38	24.00		
P. H. Williams (Natal 'B')	6	11		258	67	23.45		1
E. Muntingh (Western Province)	8	15		350	69	23.33		2
D. H. Howell (Eastern Province)	6	12		271	54	22.58		1
G. Long (Eastern Province)	6	12		269	98	22.42		1
A. P. Beukes (Griqualand West)	6	9		200	55	22.22		1
G. E. McMillan (Transvaal)	7	11	2	198	64	22.00		1
V. A. P. van der Bijl (Natal)	11	13	5	176	53*	22.00		1
N. Rynners (Northern Transvaal)	6	9	4	110	29*	22.00		
D. J. Richardson (Eastern Province)	8	14		307	47	21.93		
H. M. Ackerman (Western Province 'B')	7	13	2	241	86*	21.91		1
R. C. Ontong (Northern Transvaal)	8	15	1	305	75	21.79		1
W. M. van der Merwe (Orange Free State)	6	8	2	129	48*	21.50		
H. R. Fotheringham (Transvaal)	6	9		193	115	21.44	1	
A. du Toit (Boland)	7	13	1	254	117	21.17	1	
D. D. Dyer (Transvaal 'B')	4	7	1	125	28*	20.83		
R. Kent (Border)	6	12	1	228	52	20.73		1
D. N. Edwards (Northern Transvaal 'B')	6	11		227	62	20.64		2
S. Regenstein (Orange Free State)	4	7	1	123	28	20.50		
R. G. Fensham (Eastern Province)	9	16	1	307	68	20.47		1
S. A. Jones (Boland)	7	10	1	177	59	19.67		1
C. P. Wilkins (Natal)	8	16	1	294	46	19.60		

Western Province 'B' 1981-82

BATTING

	v. Orange Free State (Bloemfontein) 6, 7, 9 November 1981	v. Griqualand West (Kimberley) 12, 13, 14 November 1981	v. Griqualand West (Constantia) 27, 28, 30 November 1981	v. Orange Free State (Constantia) 4, 5, 7 December 1981	v. Natal 'B' (Constantia) 26, 28, 29 December 1981	v. Natal 'B' (Pietermaritzburg) 13, 14, 15 February 1982	v. Boland (Stellenbosch) 24, 25, 26, 27 March 1982 (Bowl Final)
P. M. Thompson	20 23	90 52	4 7	0 15	55 14*	20 2	3 36
P. W. Martin	1 9	17 44					
E. Muntingh	0 36	69 7	46 21	21 20	0 —	0 35	0 67
P. Rayner	0 0	4 11					
T. A. Clarke	0 82	26 12	54 11	24 19	31 —	63 3	1 25
H. M. Ackerman	5 86*	29 23*	23 0	31 2	0 —	0 9	21 12
J. D. Du Toit	0 4		0 4*	43 27		4 2	9 17
S. Vercucil	9 2	9* —	13	16 6*			
R. R. Lawrenson	39 10	9 —	21*	24* 1	— —	21 87	12 5
M. B. Minnaar	30* 0	— —					
N. Lotter	7 10						
O. Henry		2 2*		14 43*	—		
R. J. Bowley		10* —					
M. J. Nel			10 10	38 36	38 0*		
J. Seeff			15 43*	17 32	113* —	2 38	32 30
M. Taljaard			0			4* 0*	
J. E. Mahoney			14				
S. Bose				2 —			
S. D. Bruce					100* —		
L. L. Louw					— —	4* 7*	3 2
B. P. Martin					— —		
M. D. Mellor						14 0	19 60
R. F. Pienaar						23 34	
R. J. Ryall						21 39*	2 2
Extras	18 16	17 15	10 8	22 14	12 —	40 25	9 8
Total	129 278	282 166	210 104	252 215	349 14	212 281	115 264
Wickets	10 10	8 5	10 5	10 8	5 0	10 9	10 10
Result	L	D	W	W	W	D	L
Points	5	7	17	19	17	7	—

BOWLING

	R. R. Lawrenson	N. Lotter	J. D. du Toit	M. B. Minnaar	H. M. Ackerman	T. A. Clarke	O. Henry	J. E. Mahoney
v. Orange Free State (Bloemfontein) 6, 7, 9 November 1981	16-5-40-3 11-3-37-1	9-2-35-0 2-0-2-0	19-7-46-5 35.4-11-66-3	22.2-4-72-2 24-6-58-3	4-1-17-0	8-3-22-1		
v. Griqualand West (Kimberley) 12, 13, 14 November 1981	19-5-55-2			19-1-28-1		13-6-30-5	30-3-96-2	
v. Griqualand West (Constantia) 27, 28, 30 November 1981	7-1-30-0 15-1-59-3		16-6-26-6 18.1-3-41-4		4-0-19-0	6-0-15-1 7-0-24-1		17.2-8-33-3 14-4-29-1
v. Orange Free State (Constantia) 4, 5, 7 December 1981	8-2-24-2 12-4-20-0		8-2-22-1 15-4-24-4			2-0-8-0	16.3-5-34-5 23.2-11-48-4	
v. Natal 'B' (Constantia) 26, 28, 29 December 1981	16-5-50-5 20-5-56-2				6-3-12-0	15-5-25-0 3-2-4-0	12.5-3-17-1 23-4-59-3	
v. Natal 'B' (Pietermaritzburg) 13, 14, 15 February 1982	28-7-85-3 5-1-18-0		13-3-36-2 11-1-43-3		13-1-61-4			
v. Boland (Stellenbosch) 24, 25, 26, 27 March 1982	22-7-53-3 11-1-34-0		24-7-42-3 8-0-42-0		2-0-3-0	15.3-5-35-4 2-1-8-1		
	190-47- 561-24 av. 23.38	11-2- 37-0 —	167.5-44- 388-31 av. 12.52	65.2-11- 158-6 av. 26.33	29-5- 112-4 av. 28.00	71.3-22- 171-13 av. 13.15	105.4-26- 254-15 av. 16.93	31.2-12- 62-4 av. 15.50

A R. J. Bowley 21-5-64-0   B S. Base 7-5-6-2 and 9-3-16-1   C B. P. Martin 3-1-10-2 and 18-5-44-1

BATTING continued

	M	Inns	NOs	Runs	HS	Av	100s	50s
J. W. Stephenson (Eastern Province)	6	12		235	83	19.58		1
J. W. Furstenberg (Eastern Province)	7	13		248	57	19.08		1
M. K. van Vuuren (Eastern Province)	8	14	4	190	75	19.00		1
B. M. Osborne (Border)	4	8		151	46	18.88		
J. J. Strydom (Orange Free State)	5	8	1	132	85	18.86		1
M. D. Mellor (Western Province)	3	6		113	60	18.83		1
M. D. Tramantino (Natal 'B')	5	10		187	69	18.70		1
A. Odendaal (Boland)	7	12	2	177	37*	17.70		
J. P. Ackermann (Northern Transvaal)	7	13		228	61	17.54		2
J. D. Ogilvie (Eastern Province)	6	10	2	140	42*	17.50		
P. B. Clift (Natal)	6	10	1	156	35	17.33		
N. G. Featherstone (Northern Transvaal)	7	13		224	99	17.23		1
R. J. B. Whyte (Eastern Province)	8	15	1	241	58	17.21		1
K. R. Cooper (Natal)	7	9	2	120	38*	17.14		
L. W. Griessel (Orange Free State)	4	7		120	47	17.14		
K. G. Motley (Northern Transvaal 'B')	6	11	1	168	36*	16.80		
A. Barrow (Northern Transvaal)	4	8		134	45	16.75		
P. L. Symcox (Griqualand West)	5	9	1	132	46	16.50		
M. S. Venter (Transvaal)	5	10	1	147	40	16.33		
R. V. Jennings (Transvaal)	11	13	2	179	32	16.27		
J. Lawrence (Border)	6	12		193	44	16.08		
I. Foulkes (Eastern Province)	7	12		187	53	15.58		1
A. M. Ferreira (Northern Transvaal)	8	15		229	60	15.27		1
T. G. Shaw (Eastern Province)	6	12		183	46	15.25		
R. J. Ryall (Western Province)	7	11	3	121	39*	15.13		
H. Liebenberg (Griqualand West)	6	9	1	121	63	15.13		1
A. J. S. Smith (Natal)	8	13	2	165	47	15.00		
D. J. Brickett (Eastern Province)	8	14	2	179	55	14.92		1
J. During (Western Province)	7	10	3	104	29	14.86		
R. C. Schultz (Boland)	7	9	1	108	38	13.50		
R. B. C. Ranger (Border)	4	8		108	75	13.50		1
W. K. Watson (Eastern Province)	9	14	2	160	36	13.33		
J. A. Hopkins (Eastern Province)	5	9		119	33	13.22		
E. J. Hodkinson (Natal)	8	10	2	100	24	12.50		
R. F. Pienaar (Western Province)	10	17	2	159	34	10.60		
J. D. du Toit (Western Province)	7	13	1	124	43	10.33		

(Qualification – 100 runs, average 10, 7 innings)

	Inns	NOs	Runs	HS	Av
	14	1	341	90	26.23
	4	—	71	44	17.75
	13	—	322	69	24.78
	4	—	15	11	3.75
	13	—	351	82	27.00
	13	2	241	86*	21.91
	10	1	110	43	12.22
	6	2	55	16	13.75
	10	2	229	87	28.63
	2	1	30	30*	—
	2	—	17	10	8.50
	4	2	61	43*	30.50
	1	1	10	10*	—
	6	1	132	38	26.40
	9	2	322	113*	46.00
	3	2	4	4*	—
	1	—	14	14	—
	1	—	2	2	—
	1	1	100	100*	—
	4	2	16	7*	8.00
	—	—	—	—	—
	4	—	93	60	23.25
	2	—	57	34	28.50
	4	1	64	39*	21.33

M. Taljaard	L. L. Louw	M. D. Mellor		ROs	Extras	Runs	Wkts
					8	218	10
					5	190	8
					15	288	10A
					4	108	10
9-3-26-1					5	203	10
					6	92	10B
				1	16	132	10
	10-2-20-2				2	99	10C
	25-8-52-4				12	260	10
	17.3-5-30-3	4-0-7-1			20	238	10D
	6-1-15-1	6-2-16-0			7	176	8
13-5-25-0	22-5-45-0	7-0-16-0			18	237	10
27-6-106-1	26-7-57-7	7-0-33-0		1	11	291	10
49-14-	106.3-28-	24-2-					
157-2	219-17	72-1					
av. 78.50	av. 12.88	av. 72.00					

D R. F. Pienaar 15-2-50-1 and 3-1-12-0
E. Muntingh 3-1-6-0 and 2-1-4-0

South Africa 1981-82

BATTING

	v. SAB England XI (Johannesburg) 12, 13, 14, 15 March 1982		v. SAB England XI (Cape Town) 19, 20, 21, 22 March 1982		v. SAB England XI (Durban) 26, 27, 28, 29 March 1982	
S. J. Cook	114	2	18		11	50*
B. A. Richards	66	4	8		41	17
P. N. Kirsten	88	20*	114		11	14
R. G. Pollock	64*	9*	0		15	12
C. E. B. Rice	1		12		9	39*
M. J. Procter	1					
A. J. Kourie	14		18		50*	
R. V. Jennings	24		32	28*	22	
G. S. le Roux	6*				0	
V. A. P. van der Bijl	—		4*		0	
S. J. Jefferies	—		3			
A. P. Kuiper			1	9*	0	
D. L. Hobson			2			
W. K. Watson					4*	
Extras	22	2	23	1	18	11
Total	400	37	235	38	181	143
Wickets	7	2	10	0	9	3
Result	W		D		D	

BOWLING

	V. A. P. van der Bijl	S. T. Jefferies	A. J. Kourie	G. S. le Roux	M. J. Procter	D. L. Hobson	P. N. Kirsten	A. P. Kuiper
v. SAB England XI (Johannesburg) 12, 13, 14, 15 March 1982	22-8-25-5 32-10-79-5	20-5-59-2 27-4-88-1	11-2-19-2 16-7-53-0	10-2-38-1 22.2-5-44-4	6-3-6-0			
v. SAB England XI (Cape Town) 19, 20, 21, 22 March 1982	33-12-61-3 21-6-53-0	24.4-8-56-3 14-5-39-1	32-14-52-4 16-4-38-0			13-3-48-0 30-7-86-1	4-2-7-1 2-1-5-0	8-2-15-0 3-1-8-0
v. SAB England XI (Durban) 26, 27, 28, 29 March 1982	40-14-97-5		17-3-43-0	25-5-71-1				
	148-50- 315-18 av. 17.50	85.4-22- 242-7 av. 34.57	92-30- 205-6 av. 34.17	57.2-12- 153-6 av. 25.50	6-3- 6-0 —	43-10- 134-1 av. 134.00	6-3- 12-1 av. 12.00	11-3- 23-0 —

BOWLING

	Overs	Mds	Runs	Wkts	Av	5/inn	10 mtch
T. Wheelwright (Northern Transvaal)	61.4	16	147	12	12.25	1	
I. F. Heideman (Transvaal 'B')	128.5	37	262	21	12.48		
J. D. du Toit (Western Province)	210.4	57	496	39	12.72	3	1
E. J. Barlow (Boland)	105.3	38	191	15	12.73		
J. L. Louw (Western Province 'B')	106.3	28	219	17	12.88	1	
T. A. Clarke (Western Province)	88.3	27	212	16	13.25	1	
A. Sidebottom (Orange Free State)	127.3	42	260	19	13.68	1	
G. S. le Roux (Western Province)	297.2	77	677	49	13.82	5	1
P. Anker (Boland)	295.3	86	731	50	14.62	5	1
V. A. P. van der Bijl (Natal)	507.3	153	1119	75	14.92	10	4
J. P. Ackermann (Northern Transvaal)	84.1	21	180	12	15.00		
S. A. Jones (Boland)	199.1	57	389	25	15.56		
C. Wulfsohn (Eastern Province)	73.5	18	177	11	16.09	1	
P. J. Marneweck (Northern Transvaal 'B')	116.3	26	340	21	16.19	1	1
A. Viljoen (Transvaal 'B')	85	24	200	12	16.67		
H. W. Raath (Northern Transvaal)	195.3	50	435	26	16.73	2	
C. J. Coetzee (Boland)	224.3	53	527	31	17.00		
H. Losper (Transvaal 'B')	84	26	222	13	17.08	1	
L. Reid-Ross (Eastern Province 'B')	73.5	24	171	10	17.10	1	
C. J. van Heerden (Orange Free State)	81.5	23	246	14	17.57		
R. W. Hanley (Transvaal)	261.2	78	605	33	18.33	2	
C. E. B. Rice (Transvaal)	231	66	504	27	18.67	1	
O. Henry (Western Province)	271.4	75	695	37	18.78	2	
M. J. Procter (Natal)	119.3	46	251	13	19.31		
H. Page (Transvaal)	89.3	18	250	12	20.83		
N. P. Daniels (Natal)	102.2	22	272	13	20.92		
N. V. Radford (Transvaal)	190	41	543	25	21.72		
L. B. Taylor (Natal)	255	71	610	28	21.79	1	
G. E. McMillan (Transvaal)	190.4	61	483	22	21.95		
M. M. van Vuuren (Eastern Province)	234.4	58	595	27	22.04	2	
S. T. Jefferies (Western Province)	434.2	117	1166	52	22.42	1	
J. Hartley (Border)	116	31	315	14	22.50		
E. J. Hodkinson (Natal)	239.4	61	604	26	23.23	1	1
J. Fairclough (Transvaal)	186	62	358	15	23.87	2	
P. B. Clift (Natal)	153	46	360	15	24.00		
G. S. Cowley (Eastern Province 'B')	112.2	31	264	11	24.00		
W. M. van der Merwe (Orange Free State)	167.1	36	483	20	24.15		
R. R. Lawrenson (Western Province)	223	53	654	27	24.22	1	
I. Howell (Eastern Province)	165	58	389	16	24.31		
C. J. P. G. van Zyl (Orange Free State)	187.4	51	537	22	24.41	1	
J. A. Carse (Eastern Province)	176.1	37	544	22	24.73	1	
D. S. Scott (Border)	89	25	255	10	25.50		
G. M. Gower (Border)	175	62	334	13	25.69	1	

SAB England XI 1981-82

BATTING

	v. Western Province (Cape Town) 8, 9, 10 March 1982		v. South Africa (Johannesburg) 12, 13, 14, 15 March 1982	v. South Africa (Cape Town) 19, 20, 21, 22 March 1982		v. South Africa (Durban) 26, 27, 28, 29 March 1982	
G. Boycott	20	95	5	36	16	1	31
W. Larkins	24	22	2	20	29	95	39
D. L. Amiss	52	30	66*	24	13	73*	50
R. A. Woolmer	3	27	14	21	2	1*	100
A. P. E. Knott	27	0	5	9	16	—	6
G. A. Gooch	58	0	30	109	83	68	48
G. W. Humpage	1	10					
J. E. Emburey	13						
C. M. Old	5*	20	1	11	1		10
M. Hendrick	1	0*					
J. K. Lever	—	10*	9	10*	8		4*
P. Willey			1	24	39		15
D. L. Underwood			8	6	0		
L. B. Taylor			0	0	10*		—
Extras	15	11	9	13	6	11	8
Total	219	225	150	283	223	249	311
Wickets	9	8	10	10	10	3	8
Result		D	L		D		D

BOWLING

	C. M. Old	J. K. Lever	M. Hendrick	G. A. Gooch	J. E. Emburey	W. Larkins	G. W. Humpage	L. B. Taylor
v. Western Province (Cape Town) 8, 9, 10 March 1982	18-7-61-1 11-5-26-2	0.2-0-0-0	16.4-2-52-0 12-2-27-1	17-4-54-2 14-2-45-2	26-7-88-4 21.5-3-65-2	6.1-0-23-0	2-0-6-0	
v. South Africa (Johannesburg) 12, 13, 14, 15 March 1982	28-10-76-1 6-1-8-1	32-3-122-2 5.4-1-27-1		2-0-15-0				31-7-73-3
v. South Africa (Cape Town) 19, 20, 21, 22 March 1982	18-6-33-0 4-0-15-0	37-11-86-6 3-0-22-0						27-8-49-3
v. South Africa (Durban) 26, 27, 28, 29 March 1981	11-3-21-0 6-2-18-0	13-1-53-1 16-9-25-1	21-9-28-3 12-3-37-0			5-0-24-1		25.3-5-61-5 8-2-23-0
	102-34- 259-5 av. 51.60	107-25- 335-11 av. 30.45	61.4-16- 144-4 av. 36.00	33-6- 114-4 av. 28.50	47.5-10- 153-6 av. 25.50	11.1-0- 47-1 av. 47.00	2-0- 6-0 —	91.3-22- 206-11 av. 18.73

THE GREAT REBELLION/189

BOWLING *continued*

	Overs	Mds	Runs	Wkts	Av	5/inn	10 mtch
R. F. Pienaar (Western Province)	167	36	436	16	27.25	1	
R. I. S. Armitage (Eastern Province)	115.3	27	301	11	27.36		
J. During (Western Province)	140.5	35	341	12	28.42		
A. J. Kourie (Transvaal)	294	93	712	25	28.48	2	1
I. Ebrahim (Natal 'B')	184	38	636	22	28.91	2	
A. M. Ferreira (Northern Transvaal)	258	72	667	23	29.00	1	
W. K. Watson (Eastern Province)	261.2	66	655	22	29.78		
D. L. Hobson (Western Province)	298.4	93	776	26	29.85	1	
H. Liebenberg (Griqualand West)	199.2	48	627	21	29.86	1	
T. Smit (Griqualand West)	88.3	13	299	10	29.90	1	
J. K. Lever (SA Breweries)	107	25	335	11	30.45	1	
W. F. Morris (Northern Transvaal)	210	51	579	19	30.47		
R. C. Ontong (Northern Transvaal)	175.5	40	590	19	31.05	1	
I. Foulkes (Eastern Province)	157.4	43	428	12	35.67		
P. D. Swart (Boland)	167.1	35	432	12	36.00		
A. P. Beukes (Griqualand West)	202.4	69	476	13	36.62	1	
K. R. Cooper (Natal)	137	27	406	10	40.60		

(*Qualification – 10 wickets*)

Leading Wicket-keepers
35 (32ct/3st) R. V. Jennings
26 (24ct/2st) R. J. Ryall
25 (24ct/1st) A. J. S. Smith
24 (22ct/2st) R. C. Schultz
20 (14ct/6st) T. R. Madsen

Leading catchers in field
14 A. P. Kuiper
12 K. S. McEwan, L. Seeff
11 P. N. Kirsten, P. D. Swart
10 J. During, E. J. Barlow, A. J. Kourie, A. J. Lamb, E. Muntingh

---

	Inns	NOs	Runs	HS	Av
	7	—	204	95	29.14
	7	—	231	95	33.00
	7	2	308	73*	61.60
	7	1	168	100	28.00
	6	—	63	27	10.50
	7	—	396	109	56.57
	2	—	11	10	5.50
	1	—	13	13	—
	6	1	48	20	9.60
	2	1	1	1	—
	5	3	41	10*	20.50
	4	—	79	39	19.75
	3	—	14	8	4.67
	3	1	10	10*	5.00

D. L. Underwood	P. Willey	A. P. E. Knott	ROs	Extras	Runs	Wkts
			1	8	263	8
				12	204	3
23–1–92–1				22	400	7
				2	37	2
22–9–36–1	4–1–8–0			23	235	10
				1	38	0
				18	181	9
		1–0–5–0		11	143	2
45–10– 128–2 av. 64.00	4–1– 8–0	1–0– 5–0				

Opposite: *Javed Miandad*

SECTION F
The Small Rebellion

Pakistan v Sri Lanka

Sri Lanka's first tour as a Test nation could not have begun in unhappier circumstances. They arrived in Pakistan to find that their hosts were in a state of cricket revolution. The dissension came from the unwillingness of eight Test men to play under the captaincy of Javed Miandad. There had been some unrest when Javed was chosen to take the side to Australia and events in Australia had convinced some of the senior players that they did not wish to play again under his leadership. There were emergency meetings of the Pakistan Board of Control, but when the team for the first Test was announced the eight players – Majid Khan, Zaheer Abbas, Imran Khan, Sarfraz Nawaz, Mohsin Khan, Wasim Bari, Sikhander Bakht and Mudassar Nazar – were not in the side.

While Pakistan were having their domestic struggle Sri Lanka also had problems in that the first match of the tour, the three-day game against the BCCP Patron's XI, the only first-class game of the tour outside the three Tests, was abandoned without a ball being bowled.

FIRST TEST MATCH

The internal conflict continued as Ejaz Butt, Pakistan's chief selector, resigned and accused Nur Khan, the President of the Pakistan Cricket Control Board, of adopting a rigid attitude towards the rebellious eight.

In the Test itself, Pakistan were in some trouble at 126 for 6, but Haroon Rashid played a fine innings, his third, and highest, Test century and with Tahir Naqqash and Rashid Khan adding valuable fifties, they recovered to 396.

Pakistan bowled tightly, but Sri Lanka batted with great application and consistency and finished only 52 behind on the first innings. Rizwan was caught behind off de Mel so that at the end of the third day, Pakistan were 16 for 1 and Sri Lanka still very much in the match.

The last two days belonged entirely to Pakistan. Nightwatchman Iqbal Qasim reached a praiseworthy fifty and when he was third out at 107 Saleem and Javed proceeded to devastate the Sri Lankan attack. Somachandra de Silva was again the most successful of the Pakistan bowlers, but with Warnapura unwell and Ratnayake injured, the bowlers struggled as Saleem reached a hundred in his first Test and shared a stand of 161 with his captain.

Sri Lanka seemed unable to last the five days and were visibly tired as they began their second innings. They began badly, losing Warnapura to the third ball. Sri Lanka lunched at 67 for 3 and after lunch they succumbed to the spin combination of Tausif and Iqbal Qasim. It was a quiet and disappointing end for them in a game which had promised them a chance to record a first Test win, but it was also a triumph for the Pakistan 'reserves' and a reminder to the rebels that in cricket one can quickly become one of yesterday's men.

FIRST ONE-DAY INTERNATIONAL

This match, scheduled for forty overs an innings, was reduced to thirty-three overs each by a riot that occurred in the crowd shortly before lunch. There was a crowd of twenty thousand and the trouble happened when people outside the ground began pouring in through a broken gate. Spectators swarmed on to the pitch and about thirty-five minutes play was lost.

Sri Lanka had won the toss and had reached 147 for 2 when trouble broke out. They were obviously at a disadvantage when the number of overs was reduced and Pakistan won comfortably with more than three overs to spare.

SECOND TEST MATCH

The Pakistan Cricket Board had said that they would review the question of the captaincy at the end of the series with Sri Lanka and this seemed to have resolved the argument with the rebels, but, although selected, Majid Khan, Zaheer Abbas, Imran Khan and Mudassar Nazar declined to play in the Second Test.

Whatever Pakistan's problems, nothing could detract from the achievement of Sidath Wettimuny who became the first Sri Lankan to hit a Test hundred. Sri Lanka were 270 for 1 at the end of the first day. On the second day both Dias and Madugalle came close to emulating Wettimuny in scoring a hundred, but Dias was caught two short of his

Wettimuny who scored the first Test century in Sri Lanka's history.

FIRST TEST MATCH – PAKISTAN v. SRI LANKA
5, 6, 7, 9 and 10 March 1982 at Karachi

PAKISTAN

	FIRST INNINGS		SECOND INNINGS	
Mansoor Akhtar	c Goonatillake, b de Mel	6	c Mendis, b S. de Silva	23
Rizwan Uz-Zaman	c Goonatillake, b Ratnayake	42	c Goonatillake, b de Mel	10
Saleem Malik	b S. de Silva	12	(4) not out	100
Javed Miandad†	c Goonatillake, b de Mel	4	(5) st Goonatillake, b S. de Silva	92
Wasim Raja	c Dias, b de Mel	31	(6) not out	12
Haroon Rashid	run out	153		
Salim Yousuf*	c Goonatillake, b S. de Silva	4		
Tahir Naqqash	c Mendis, b S. de Silva	57		
Iqbal Qasim	lbw, b S. de Silva	1	(3) c sub (Wijesuriya), b S. de Silva	56
Rashid Khan	c Madugalle, b A. de Silva	59		
Tausif Ahmed	not out	5		
Extras	lb 9, w 4, nb 9	22	b 5, lb 1, w 1, nb 1	8
		396	(for 4 wkts dec)	301

	O	M	R	W	O	M	R	W
de Mel	28	2	124	3	23.2	3	100	1
Ratnayake	16	6	49	1	5.4	2	20	—
D. S. de Silva	38	8	102	4	26	3	99	3
G. R. A. de Silva	17.2	2	69	1	35	5	74	—
Warnapura	2	—	9	—				
Wettimuny	2	—	21	—				

FALL OF WICKETS
1–6, 2–46, 3–53, 4–72, 5–113, 6–126, 7–231, 8–232, 9–359
1–16, 2–53, 3–107, 4–268

SRI LANKA

	FIRST INNINGS		SECOND INNINGS	
B. Warnapura†	lbw, b Tahir	13	b Tahir	0
S. Wettimuny	c Mansoor, b Rashid	71	c Yousuf, b Rashid	14
R. L. Dias	lbw, b Qasim	53	lbw, b Tahir	19
R. S. Madugalle	c Yousuf, b Rashid	29	c Tausif, b Qasim	18
J. R. Ratnayake	c Rizwan, b Qasim	24	(10) c Malik, b Raja	0
L. R. D. Mendis	c Rashid, b Tahir	54	(5) c Yousuf, b Qasim	15
A. Ranatunga	st Yousuf, b Tausif	13	(6) c Yousuf, b Tausif	33
D. S. de Silva	b Tausif	26	(7) st Yousuf, b Qasim	12
H. M. Goonatillake*	c Yousuf, b Tahir	14	(8) c Haroon, b Raja	13
A. L. F. de Mel	run out	9	(9) c Miandad, b Qasim	2
G. R. A. de Silva	run out	10	not out	0
Extras	b 1, lb 12, w 3, nb 12	28	b 9, lb 11, w 1, nb 2	23
		344		149

	O	M	R	W	O	M	R	W
Tahir Naqqash	32	11	83	3	9	1	34	2
Rashid Khan	36	7	53	2	8	3	25	1
Iqbal Qasim	28	7	88	2	15.1	8	27	4
Tausif Ahmed	21.4	6	64	2	12	1	39	1
Wasim Raja	5	1	28	—	3	2	1	2

FALL OF WICKETS
1–24, 2–120, 3–152, 4–199, 5–221, 6–242, 7–285, 8–301, 9–322
1–1, 2–27, 3–41, 4–68, 5–91, 6–121, 7–125, 8–139, 9–149

Pakistan won by 204 runs

FIRST ONE-DAY INTERNATIONAL: PAKISTAN v. SRI LANKA
12 March 1982 at Karachi

SRI LANKA

B. Warnapura†	b Qasim	77
S. Wettimuny	b Jalaluddin	2
R. L. Dias	c and b Tahir	57
L. R. D. Mendis	not out	5
A. Ranatunga	not out	15
R. S. Madugalle		
D. S. de Silva		
A. L. F. de Mel		
R. S. A. Jayasekera*		
J. R. Ratnayake		
R. A. Wijesuriya		
Extras	b 3, lb 1, w 1, nb 10	15
	(for 3 wkts)	171

	O	M	R	W
Tahir Naqqash	6	—	19	1
Rashid Khan	8	—	40	—
Iqbal Qasim	5	—	32	1
Jalaluddin	5	1	14	1
Wasim Raja	5	—	29	—
Javed Miandad	4	—	22	—

FALL OF WICKETS
1–5, 2–144, 3–151

PAKISTAN

Mansoor Akhtar	b Wijesuriya	20
Mohsin Khan	c Mendis, b Ratnayake	85
Javed Miandad†	not out	56
Wasim Raja	not out	0
Saleem Malik		
Haroon Rashid		
Tahir Naqqash		
Rashid Khan		
Iqbal Qasim		
Salim Yousuf*		
Jalaluddin		
Extras	b 3, lb 5, w 2, nb 3	13
	(for 2 wkts)	174

	O	M	R	W
de Mel	6	2	28	—
Ratnayake	6.2	—	40	1
Wijesuriya	8	—	48	1
D. S. de Silva	6	—	30	—
Ranatunga	3	—	15	—

FALL OF WICKETS
1–52, 2–157

Pakistan won by 8 wickets

SECOND TEST MATCH – PAKISTAN v. SRI LANKA
14, 15, 16, 18 and 19 March 1982 at Faisalabad

SRI LANKA

	FIRST INNINGS		SECOND INNINGS	
S. Wettimuny	b Raja	157	c Ashraf, b Tahir	13
H. M. Goonatillake*	c Saleem, b Qasim	27	b Qasim	56
R. L. Dias	c Saleem, b Qasim	98	c Mohsin, b Tahir	7
L. R. D. Mendis†	b Qasim	16	(5) run out	0
R. S. Madugalle	not out	91	(4) lbw, b Qasim	12
A. Ranatunga	b Qasim	0	c Ashraf, b Tausif	2
A. N. Ranasinghe	c Miandad, b Qasim	6	c Miandad, b Tausif	5
A. L. F. de Mel	c Miandad, b Qasim	4	(9) not out	25
D. S. de Silva	lbw, b Rizwan	25	(8) st Ashraf, b Tausif	8
L. W. Kaluperuma	b Rizwan	0	not out	11
G. R. A. de Silva	lbw, b Rizwan	5		
Extras	lb 11, w 2, nb 12	25	lb 8, w 1, nb 6	15
		454	(for 8 wkts dec)	154

PAKISTAN

	FIRST INNINGS		SECOND INNINGS	
Rizwan Uz-Zaman	b A. de Silva	36	b de Mel	16
Mohsin Khan	c Wettimuny, b de Mel	12	c de Mel, b S. de Silva	74
Saleem Malik	b de Mel	23	lbw, b de Mel	4
Javed Miandad†	c Ranatunga, b S. de Silva	18	c Madugalle, b S. de Silva	36
Wasim Raja	c Madugalle, b S. de Silva	22	c Wettimuny, b S. de Silva	0
Haroon Rashid	c de Mel, b S. de Silva	25	b S. de Silva	0
Ashraf Ali*	b Ranasinghe	58	not out	29
Tahir Naqqash	c de Mel, b A. de Silva	1	c Dias, b S. de Silva	13
Iqbal Qasim	run out	5		
Rashid Khan	not out	43	(9) not out	3
Tausif Ahmed	c Madugalle, b S. de Silva	18		
Extras	lb 1, nb 8	9	b 3, lb 7, nb 1	11
		270	(for 7 wkts)	186

	O	M	R	W	O	M	R	W
Tahir Naqqash	26	4	108	—	12	3	52	2
Rashid Khan	13	3	52	—	1	—	4	—
Iqbal Qasim	65	18	141	6	30	9	52	2
Tausif Ahmed	12	3	35	—	14	4	18	3
Wasim Raja	26	6	66	1				
Rizwan Uz-Zaman	12	3	26	3	5	2	13	—
Javed Miandad	1	—	1	—				

	O	M	R	W	O	M	R	W
de Mel	23	4	73	2	17	2	71	2
Ranasinghe	7	1	23	1	5	—	17	—
D. S. de Silva	31.5	2	103	4	18	2	59	5
G. R. A. de Silva	24	10	38	2	19	4	28	—
Kaluperuma	6	—	24	—				

FALL OF WICKETS
1-77, 2-294, 3-304, 4-341, 5-341, 6-355, 7-385, 8-446, 9-448
1-19, 2-43, 3-82, 4-82, 5-86, 6-104, 7-114, 8-114

FALL OF WICKETS
1-19, 2-54, 3-83, 4-116, 5-124, 6-154, 7-156, 8-185, 9-222
1-24, 2-40, 3-132, 4-132, 5-132, 6-137, 7-174

Match drawn

century and Madugalle ran out of partners when in his nineties. The stand between Wettimuny and Dias added 217 for the second wicket and the Sri Lankan total was their highest in Test cricket, but there were honours too for Pakistan as Iqbal Qasim took 6 for 141 and reached 100 wickets in Test cricket. Rizwan Uz-Zaman had his best bowling with 3 for 26.

Somachandra de Silva bowled Sri Lanka to a position of strength on the third day when Pakistan closed with 8 wickets down and still 45 short of avoiding the follow-on. But the follow-on was avoided on the fourth morning when Ashraf Ali and Rashid Khan continued their splendidly defiant innings.

Sri Lanka went for brisk runs to try to force victory and declared on the last morning, setting Pakistan 339 in 5½ hours.

There seemed no concern for Pakistan at the outset, but they sank from 132 for 2 to 137 for 6 and Sri Lanka scented victory. It was Ashraf, who had a fine match, and Tahir who thwarted Sri Lanka and the game was drawn. Nevertheless, Sri Lanka had once more shown their tremendous potential as a Test side and Somachandra de Silva had taken 5 for 59 with some wonderful leg-break bowling so becoming the first of his countrymen to take five wickets in a Test.

THIRD TEST MATCH

To bring peace to cricket in Pakistan, Javed Miandad asked that he should not be selected as captain of the side to tour England. Majid Khan, Mudassar Nazar, Zaheer Abbas and Imran Khan returned to the Pakistan side after their self-inflicted exile and the balance which had existed between the two sides in the first two Tests tilted heavily in favour of Pakistan.

Sri Lanka were saved from rout on the first day by a courageous knock from Roy Dias. He came in at 17 for 2 and hit 33 in the first three overs from Tahir Naqqash. His first fifty came in sixty-nine minutes and his was a glorious display.

Dias' innings came to an end early on the second morning and Imran's pace was far too much for the rest of the Sri Lankan batsmen. He finished with 8 for 58 and reached his 150 wickets in Test cricket. Pakistan began briskly and by the close had reached 168 for 1 in under three hours.

There was only a slight hindrance to Pakistan's dominance when de Mel had Javed and Wasim Raja caught behind in successive overs, but Mohsin Khan hit his first Test century and Zaheer Abbas his seventh as Pakistan moved into a lead of 260. Zaheer reached 3,000 runs in Test cricket.

Warnapura and Wettimuny began with a cautious stand

THIRD TEST MATCH – PAKISTAN v. SRI LANKA
22, 23, 24, 26 and 27 March 1982 at Lahore

SRI LANKA

	FIRST INNINGS		SECOND INNINGS	
B. Warnapura†	c Mohsin, b Imran	7	c Miandad, b Tausif	26
S. Wettimuny	c Qasim, b Imran	20	c Majid, b Imran	41
R. S. A. Jayasekera	b Imran	0	(6) b Imran	2
R. L. Dias	c Tausif, b Imran	109	(3) c Raja, b Tausif	9
R. S. Madugalle	c Ashraf, b Imran	0	(4) b Tausif	5
L. R. D. Mendis	c and b Tausif	26	(5) c Mudassar, b Tausif	5
D. S. de Silva	b Imran	7	not out	35
A. L. F. de Mel	st Ashraf, b Qasim	34	lbw, b Imran	0
H. M. Goonatillake*	b Imran	15	c and b Imran	22
R. A. Wijesuriya	lbw, b Imran	0	(11) b Imran	3
J. R. Ratnayake	not out	1	(10) b Imran	0
Extras	lb 11, w 6, nb 4	21	b 4, lb 2, w 1, nb 3	10
		240		**158**

PAKISTAN

	FIRST INNINGS	
Mudassar Nazar	c Madugalle, b S. de Silva	37
Mohsin Khan	b Ratnayake	129
Majid Khan	c sub (Ranasinghe), b Ratnayake	63
Javed Miandad†	c Goonatillake, b de Mel	26
Zaheer Abbas	b Ratnayake	134
Wasim Raja	c Goonatillake, b de Mel	1
Imran Khan	c Mendis, b de Mel	39
Ashraf Ali*	not out	45
Tahir Naqqash	not out	1
Iqbal Qasim		
Tausif Ahmed		
Extras	b 5, lb 4, w 6, nb 10	25
	(for 7 wkts dec)	**500**

	O	M	R	W	O	M	R	W
Imran Khan	29.3	8	58	8	22.5	3	58	6
Tahir Naqqash	10	–	54	–	6	–	22	–
Iqbal Qasim	12	5	21	1	1	–	1	–
Mudassar Nazar	8	1	23	–				
Tausif Ahmed	12	1	50	1	25	7	58	4
Wasim Raja	5	1	13	–	7	3	9	–
Majid Khan					1	1	0	–

	O	M	R	W
de Mel	28	3	120	3
Ratnayake	28	3	121	3
D. S. de Silva	29	4	129	1
Wijesuriya	24	3	105	–

FALL OF WICKETS
1-17, 2-17, 3-79, 4-83, 5-141, 6-171, 7-209, 8-231, 9-239
1-56, 2-78, 3-84, 4-90, 5-93, 6-95, 7-96, 8-142, 9-142

FALL OF WICKETS
1-79, 2-230, 3-247, 4-297, 5-306, 6-406, 7-494

Pakistan won by an innings and 102 runs

---

of 56, but after Javed had taken a diving catch off Tausif to dismiss Warnapura, the innings disintegrated. At the close Sri Lanka were 95 for 5 and next day they were beaten by an innings, Imran returning 14 for 116, his best figures in Test cricket.

The only real resistance came from de Silva and Goonatillake in an eighth wicket stand of 46. The match ended just before lunch.

Sri Lanka had revealed more than at any other time during the series their inexperience. In each of the three Tests they played well for half the match, but appeared to lose concentration as the game wore on. Nevertheless, as against England, they displayed undoubted talent and should become a force within a few years.

SECOND ONE-DAY INTERNATIONAL

Warnapura won the toss and asked Pakistan to bat and his decision seemed a good one when, with the help of two run outs, Pakistan were reduced to 94 for 3, but Zaheer and Haroon Rashid added 121 for the fourth wicket. Zaheer hit a sparkling 123 and the last twenty overs of the innings brought 144 runs.

Warnapura fell to Sikhander at 10, but thereafter Sri Lanka were always in command and were coasting to victory when bad light brought the match to a premature close after they had batted for only 33 of their 40 overs. The match was decided on the scores after 20 overs and as Sri Lanka had made 126 for 2 compared to Pakistan's 95 for 3, they were declared winners and justice was done.

It was their first victory of the tour.

THIRD ONE-DAY INTERNATIONAL

With Javed Miandad unwell, Zaheer Abbas took over the captaincy of Pakistan and asked Sri Lanka to bat when he won the toss.

Sri Lanka began comfortably enough, but Imran was at his most niggardly and run scoring was difficult. In the last mad rush for runs wickets tumbled and Sri Lanka were dismissed for 218 with nine balls of their quota unused.

Mudassar and Mohsin gave Pakistan a fine start and Mudassar, in particular, batted with real authority. Mansoor and Wasim Raja stopped any thought of a Sri Lanka victory with defiant innings after Zaheer and Haroon had gone quickly and Pakistan won with eleven balls to spare.

So Pakistan won the one-day series 2–1 and Sri Lanka ended their first tour as a Test nation. In results the tour had been disappointing for them, but they had acquitted themselves well and they can view the future with confidence.

Above: *A. Ranatunga* (right) *Roy Dias*.

SECOND ONE-DAY INTERNATIONAL: PAKISTAN v. SRI LANKA
29 March 1982 at Lahore

PAKISTAN

Mudassar Nazar	b D. S. de Silva		27
Mohsin Khan	run out		6
Zaheer Abbas	c Madugalle, b Ratnayake		123
Javed Miandad†	run out		1
Haroon Rashid	not out		63
Imran Khan	not out		9
Mansoor Akhtar			
Ashraf Ali*			
Tahir Naqqash			
Rashid Khan			
Sikhander Bakht			
Extras	lb 2, w 8		10
	(for 4 wkts)		239

	O	M	R	W
Ratnayake	8	1	44	1
Ranasinghe	6	—	33	—
Warnapura	2	—	21	—
D. S. de Silva	8	—	49	1
Ratnatunga	8	—	52	—
de Mel	8	1	30	—

FALL OF WICKETS
1–14, 2–86, 3–94, 4–215

SRI LANKA

B. Warnapura†	c Miandad, b Sikhander		5
S. Wettimuny	c Ashraf, b Mudassar		32
R. L. Dias	c Imran, b Mudassar		81
L. R. D. Mendis	b Tahir		52
R. S. Madugalle	not out		36
A. Ranatunga	not out		5
D. S. de Silva			
H. M. Goonatillake*			
A. L. F. de Mel			
J. R. Ratnayake			
A. N. Ranasinghe			
Extras	lb 7, w 7, nb 2		16
	(for 4 wkts)		227

	O	M	R	W
Imran Khan	5	1	19	—
Sikhander Bakht	5	1	15	1
Tahir Naqqash	8	—	65	1
Mudassar Nazar	8	—	56	2
Rashid Khan	7	—	56	—

FALL OF WICKETS
1–10, 2–87, 3–160, 4–185

Sri Lanka won on faster scoring rate

THIRD ONE-DAY INTERNATIONAL: PAKISTAN v. SRI LANKA
31 March 1982 at Karachi

SRI LANKA

S. Wettimuny	c Mansoor, b Mudassar	27
H. M. Goonatillake*	c Imran, b Sikhander	5
R. L. Dias	b Mudassar	49
L. R. D. Mendis†	b Tausif	44
R. S. Madugalle	st Yousuf, b Raja	46
A. Ranatunga	b Imran	6
A. N. Ranasinghe	c and b Imran	24
A. L. F. de Mel	run out	5
D. S. de Silva	run out	2
J. R. Ratnayake	not out	0
G. R. A. de Silva	b Sikhander	1
Extras	lb 4, w 5	9
		218

PAKISTAN

Mudassar Nazar	c sub, b Ranatunga	79
Mohsin Khan	c Madugalle, b Ranasinghe	36
Zaheer Abbas†	b G. R. A. de Silva	1
Mansoor Akhtar	st Goonatillake, b G. R. A. de Silva	31
Haroon Rashid	c and b G. R. A. de Silva	4
Wasim Raja	not out	41
Imran Khan	not out	15
Salim Yousuf*		
Rashid Khan		
Tausif Ahmed		
Sikhander Bakht		
Extras	lb 10, w 2, nb 3	15
	(for 5 wkts)	**222**

	O	M	R	W
Imran Khan	7	1	10	2
Sikhander Bakht	5.3	—	34	2
Rashid Khan	4	—	37	—
Mudassar Nazar	8	—	42	2
Tausif Ahmed	8	—	41	1
Wasim Raja	6	—	45	1

	O	M	R	W
de Mel	7	—	35	—
Ratnayake	4.1	—	34	—
Ranasinghe	8	1	27	1
D. S. de Silva	4	—	34	—
Ranatunga	7	—	36	1
G. R. A. de Silva	8	—	41	3

FALL OF WICKETS
1–7, 2–54, 3–113, 4–147, 5–170, 6–196, 7–211, 8–213, 9–214

FALL OF WICKETS
1–90, 2–91, 3–154, 4–162, 5–170

Pakistan won by 5 wickets

Pakistan v. Sri Lanka – Test Match Averages

PAKISTAN BATTING

	M	Inns	NOs	Runs	HS	Av	100s	50s
Ashraf Ali	2	3	2	132	58	132.00		1
Rashid Khan	2	3	2	105	59	105.00		1
Mohsin Khan	2	3		215	129	71.66	1	1
Haroon Rashid	2	3		178	153	59.33	1	
Saleem Malik	2	4	1	139	100*	46.33	1	
Javed Miandad	3	5		176	92	35.20		1
Rizwan Uz-Zaman	2	4		104	42	26.00		
Tahir Naqqash	3	4	1	72	57	24.00		1
Tausif Ahmed	3	2	1	23	18	23.00		
Iqbal Qasim	3	3		62	52	20.66		1
Wasim Raja	3	5	1	66	31	16.50		

Played in one Test: Mansoor Akhtar 6 and 23; Salim Yousuf 4; Mudassar Nazar 37; Majid Khan 63; Zaheer Abbas 134; Imran Khan 39

SRI LANKA BATTING

	M	Inns	NOs	Runs	HS	Av	100s	50s
S. Wettimuny	3	6		316	157	52.66	1	1
R. L. Dias	3	6		295	109	49.16	1	2
R. S. Madugalle	3	6	1	155	91*	31.00		1
H. M. Goonatillake	3	6		147	56	24.50		1
D. S. de Silva	3	6	1	113	35*	22.60		
L. R. D. Mendis	3	6		116	54	19.33		1
G. R. A. de Silva	2	3	2	15	10*	15.00		
A. L. F. de Mel	3	6	1	74	34	14.80		
A. Ranatunga	2	4		48	33	12.00		
B. Warnapura	2	4		46	26	11.50		
J. R. Ratnayake	2	4		25	24	6.25		

Played in one Test: A. N. Ranasinghe 6 and 5; L. W. Kaluperuma 0 and 11*; R. S. A. Jayasekera 0 and 2; R. A. Wijesuriya 0 and 3

PAKISTAN BOWLING

	Overs	Mds	Runs	Wkts	Av	Best	5/inn
Imran Khan	52.2	11	116	14	8.28	8/58	2
Rizwan Uz-Zaman	17	5	39	3	13.00	3/26	
Iqbal Qasim	151.1	47	330	15	22.00	6/141	1
Tausif Ahmed	96.4	22	264	11	24.00	4/58	
Wasim Raja	46	13	117	3	39.00	2/1	
Rashid Khan	58	13	134	3	44.66	2/53	
Tahir Naqqash	95	19	353	7	50.42	3/83	

Bowled in one innings: Javed Miandad 1-0-1-0; Majid Khan 1-1-0-0; Mudassar Nazar 8-1-23-0

SRI LANKA BOWLING

	Overs	Mds	Runs	Wkts	Av	Best	5/inn
D. S. de Silva	142.5	19	492	17	28.94	5/59	1
A. N. Ranasinghe	12	1	40	1	40.00	1/23	
A. L. F. de Mel	119.2	14	488	11	44.36	3/120	
J. R. Ratnayake	49.4	11	190	4	63.33	3/121	
G. R. A. de Silva	95.2	21	209	3	69.66	2/38	

Bowled in one innings: R. A. Wijesuriya 24-3-105-0; B. Warnapura 2-0-9-0; S. Wettimuny 2-0-21-0; L. W. Kaluperuma 6-0-24-0

PAKISTAN CATCHES
7—Salim Yousuf (ct 5/st 2); 5—Javed Miandad and Ashraf Ali (ct 3/st 2); 3—Saleem Malik and Tausif Ahmed; 2—Mohsin Khan; 1—Mansoor Akhtar, Rizwan Uz-Zaman, Rashid Khan, Haroon Rashid, Imran Khan, Mudassar Nazar, Wasim Raja, Majid Khan, Iqbal Qasim

SRI LANKA CATCHES
8—H. M. Goonatillake (ct 7/st 1); 5—R. S. Madugalle; 3—L. R. D. Mendis and A. L. F. de Mel; 2—R. L. Dias and S. Wettimuny; 1—A. Ranatunga and substitute (A. N. Ranasinghe)

Joel Garner - his bowling had much to do with Barbados winning the Shell Shield for the tenth time

SECTION G
Calypso Cricket

West Indian domestic season

Barbados 1982
Shell Shield

BATTING	v. Trinidad and Tobago (Bridgetown) 5–8 March 1982	v. Windward Islands (Bridgetown) 12–15 March 1982	v. Leeward Islands (Basseterre) 20–23 March 1982	v. Jamaica (Bridgetown) 27–29 March 1982	v. Guyana (Georgetown) 2–5 April 1982		
C. G. Greenidge	101	25	64	26	—	—	—
D. L. Haynes	34	16	34	11	32	26	11
A. T. Greenidge	31	48*	39	12	5	8	172
E. N. Trotman	3	5	7	11		55	—
C. L. King	42	56	87	24	6	88*	16
L. N. Reifer	0	41	22	19	0	1	
D. A. Murray	38	—	2	55	55*	29*	
S. T. Clarke	7	0*					31
A. L. Padmore	25	—	3	2	5	—	8*
E. A. Moseley	16*	—	5	9	29	—	21
W. W. Daniel	5	—	0*	1*			
G. Linton			0	—			
G. N. Reifer					0	0	
F. D. Stephenson					165	12	10
T. R. O. Payne					2	3	
J. Garner					0	—	0
C. A. Best							75
R. L. Skeete							32
Byes	5	1			1		3
Leg-byes	6	4	1	2	2	2	5
Wides	1		1				5
No-balls	12	1	4	12	6	4	21
Total	326	197	269	184	308	173	465
Wickets	10	5	10	9†	10	6	10
Result	W		L		W	W	D

Catches
12 – D. A. Murray
6 – R. L. Skeete and L. N. Reifer
5 – E. N. Trotman (one as sub)
4 – E. A. Moseley
2 – S. T. Clarke, C. G. Greenidge, A. T. Greenidge, C. L. King, C. A. Best, T. R. O. Payne and G. N. Reifer (one as sub)
1 – J. Garner, F. D. Stephenson and A. L. Padmore

† G. Linton absent injured

BOWLING	S. T. Clarke	W. W. Daniel	E. A. Moseley	A. L. Padmore	C. L. King	G. Linton	J. Garner	F. D. Stephenson
v. Trinidad and Tobago (Bridgetown) 5–8 March 1982	19–5–45–2 31–7–99–2	14–3–40–2 23–4–81–2	15.2–1–67–3 21–7–58–3	11–5–25–3 29–9–56–0	6.4–1–19–3			
v. Windward Islands (Bridgetown) 12–15 March 1982			15–0–73–2 21–4–76–1	23.5–4–66–4 36–6–66–2	21–6–37–3 42–12–71–2	6–2–13–1 10–5–13–0	6–4–7–0	
v. Leeward Islands (Basseterre) 20–23 March 1982			15–4–44–1 14–1–57–2	14–5–22–2 29–6–83–3	3–1–14–0		23.2–8–56–5 22.2–5–65–2	13–4–39–1 24–5–58–2
v. Jamaica (Bridgetown) 27–29 March 1982	18–4–50–1 8–0–33–1		20–3–48–1 6–0–35–2	8–1–29–0			26.4–5–74–6 6.2–1–24–3	14–4–23–2 8–1–27–3
v. Guyana (Georgetown) 2–5 April 1982	8–1–40–0		9–2–35–0	14–1–37–1			13–5–33–0	5–1–26–1
	84–17– 267–6 av. 44.50	73–11– 270–7 av. 38.57	160.1–28– 476–18 av. 26.44	168–45– 360–14 av. 25.71	25.4–9– 59–4 av. 14.75	6–4– 7–0 —	91.4–24– 252–16 av. 15.75	64–15– 173–9 av. 19.22

Inns	NOs	Runs	HS	Av
4	—	216	101	54.00
7	—	164	34	23.42
7	1	315	172	52.50
5	—	81	55	16.20
7	1	319	88*	53.16
6	—	83	41	13.83
5	2	179	55*	59.66
3	1	38	31	19.00
5	1	43	25	10.75
5	1	80	29	20.00
3	2	6	5	6.00
1	—	0	0	—
2	—	0	0	—
3	—	187	165	62.33
2	—	5	3	2.50
2	—	0	0	—
1	—	75	75	75.00
1	—	32	32	32.00

B	Lb	W	Nb	Total	Wkts
4	1	1	10	193	10
1	4		11	329	10
	(17)			213	10
2	7	3	3	241	5
2	3		14	194	10
4	9		8	284	10
6	5	1	6	242	10
2	3		4	128	10
	4		1	176	3

With the Shell Shield winners of 1981, Combined Islands, separated into Windward Islands and Leeward Islands, the fifteen match competition had an intense and compact look. With no Test matches in the Caribbean, all public interest was focussed on domestic cricket and the West Indian side returned from Australia in time for the leading players to participate in the Shell Shield. Unfortunately, Michael Holding was unable to play because of a cartilage operation and Marshall, Clarke and Garner also suffered injuries. More disconcerting was the moderate form of batsmen Dujon and Logie of whom much had been expected.

In Dujon's case, his form behind the stumps was also below average and it would probably be better if he could relinquish this post and concentrate on his batting, for the absence of promising young batsmen in the West Indies is troubling and Dujon's talents will certainly be needed over the next decade.

4, 5, 6 and 7 March

at Roseau

Leeward Islands 384 (I. V. A. Richards 92, A. L. Kelly 71, R. M. Otto 62) and 115 (N. Phillip 7 for 33)
Windward Islands 302 (L. A. Lewis 115, N. C. Guishard 6 for 33) and 140 (A. M. E. Roberts 5 for 52)

Leeward Islands won by 57 runs

5, 6, 7 and 8 March

at Bridgetown

Trinidad and Tobago 193 and 329 (T. Cuffy 88, R. S. Gabriel 71)
Barbados 326 (C. G. Greenidge 101, H. Joseph 4 for 97) and 197 for 5 (C. L. King 56, R. Nanan 4 for 64)

Barbados won by 5 wickets

at Kingston

Jamaica 211 (E. H. Mattis 98, C. E. H. Croft 4 for 26) and 435 for 6 dec (H. S. Chang 155, R. A. Austin 118, P. J. Dujon 66 not out)
Guyana 285 (S. F. A. Bacchus 50, R. Haynes 5 for 87) and 309 (S. F. A. Bacchus 79, A. A. Lyght 69, R. Haynes 6 for 119)

Jamaica won by 52 runs

It was fitting that the tournament should open with a keenly contested match between the two new teams. Under the wise leadership of the veteran Irvine Shillingford and coached by Wes Hall, Windward Islands quickly put aside ideas that they would be the weakest side in the Shell Shield. After Kelly and Otto had put on 128 for the Leeward Islands second wicket only Viv Richards batted with real authority, but the tail wagged effectively, Baptiste and Roberts getting useful runs.

When Windward Islands batted Lewis became the first St Vincent Islander to score a century in Shell Shield cricket. Batting at number five for Windward was Wilf Slack, the Middlesex opener, who had returned to St Vincent for the first time since leaving for England as a boy. He was

Guyana 1982
Shell Shield

BATTING	v. Jamaica (Kingston) 5–8 March 1982	v. Trinidad and Tobago (Pointe-à-Pierre) 12–15 March 1982	v. Barbados (Georgetown) 2–5 April 1982			
A. R. Lyght	44	69	0	1	103	—
T. R. Etwaroo	11	8	38	10	20	—
Timur Mohammed	17	22	102	45	35	—
S. F. A. Bacchus	50	79	59	126	12*	—
C. H. Lloyd	0	38				
M. R. Pydanna	37	17	1	2	—	—
I. D. Kallicharran	21	13	19	6	—	—
R. A. Harper	7	9	37	34	—	—
C. Butts	35	14	5*	20	—	—
C. E. H. Croft	27*	1	1	15	—	—
R. F. Joseph	2	0*	2*	0*		
M. A. Harper			5	2	—	—
W. Whyte					1*	—
Byes	20	20	4	6		
Leg-byes	8	11	3	2	4	
Wides						
No-balls	6	8	3		1	
Total	285	309	279	269	176	
Wickets	10	10	9	10	3	
Result	L		D		D	

Catches
5 – R. A. Harper
4 – M. R. Pydanna
3 – C. H. Lloyd
2 – C. Butts and T. R. Etwaroo
1 – I. D. Kallicharran, S. F. A. Bacchus, Timur Mohammed and W. Whyte (as sub)

BOWLING	C. E. H. Croft	R. F. Joseph	R. A. Harper	I. D. Kallicharran	C. Butts	T. R. Etwaroo	S. F. A. Bacchus
v. Jamaica (Kingston) 5–8 March 1982	12.2–0–26–4 24–6–81–1	11–1–50–0 11–2–58–0	10–5–15–2 40–10–95–3	20–3–71–3 29–3–116–1	12–3–31–1 16–2–60–0	2–0–10–0	
v. Trinidad and Tobago (Pointe-à-Pierre) 12–15 March 1982	14–2–33–0 31–5–83–3	9–2–40–1 8–1–34–0	6.2–2–11–2 28–5–63–2	28–6–63–5 16–2–69–0	14–5–40–1 21–10–30–0		1–1–0–0
v. Barbados (Georgetown) 2–5 April 1982							
	81.2–13– 223–8 av. 27.87	39–6– 182–1 av. 182.00	84.2–22– 184–9 av. 20.44	93–14– 319–9 av. 35.44	63–20– 161–2 av. 80.50	2–0– 10–0 —	1–0– 0–0 —

making his debut in the competition and though having little success with the bat, took 2 for 15 in the first innings.

Windward Islands stuttered before the bowling of spinner Noel Guishard and trailed by 82 on the first innings. Norbert Phillip bowled them back into contention with a career best 7 for 33, but a target of 198 proved too much against Roberts and Guishard on a wearing wicket.

The might of Barbados was soon in evidence as Sylvester Clarke, Wayne Daniel, so unsuccessful for Western Australia, Ezra Moseley and off-spinner Albert Padmore reduced Trinidad to 185 for 8 before rain interrupted and then quickly finished the innings. Gordon Greenidge was at his best and he and Haynes began with a stand of 88. When the side threatened to collapse Collis King hit well and Barbados took a lead of 133.

Solid batting down the order gave Trinidad renewed hope when they batted again and Barbados were set to make 197 to win. Alvin Greenidge provided the substance and Collis King the fireworks as Barbados, scoring at more than four an over, won by 5 wickets.

At Sabina Park all the honours went to a seventeen-year-old Kingston College schoolboy Robert Haynes who, on his first-class debut, had match figures of 11 for 186 with his leg-breaks.

Jamaica trailed by 74 on the first innings, but some fine batting by Austin and Chang, who shared a fifth wicket stand of 159, turned the game in the home side's favour and although Guyana batted with resolution, the leg-breaks of the six feet four inch Haynes gave Jamaica victory. Clive Lloyd appeared in his only game of the series, scoring 0 and 38 run out.

12, 13, 14 and 15 March

at Pointe-à-Pierre

Guyana 279 for 9 dec (Timur Mohammed 102, S. F. A. Bacchus 59, R. Nanan 4 for 78) and 269 (S. F. A. Bacchus 126, S. Jumadeen 4 for 58)
Trinidad and Tobago 196 (I. D. Kallicharran 5 for 63) and 313 for 7 (H. A. Gomes 93, D. Furlonge 71)

Match drawn

at Bridgetown

Barbados 269 (C. L. King 87, C. G. Greenidge 64, T. Kentish 6 for 69) and 184 (D. A. Murray 55, N. Phillip 4 for 21)
Windward Islands 213 (S. Julien 52, E. A. Moseley 4 for 66) and 241 for 6 (W. N. Slack 68 not out, N. Phillip 62, L. C. Sebastien 60)

Windward Islands won by 4 wickets

at Kingston

Jamaica 372 (G. Powell 95, M. C. Neita 84, P. J. Dujon 81, A. M. E. Roberts 6 for 54) and 305 for 5 dec (E. H. Mattis 77, H. S. Chang 57, R. A. Austin 55)
Leeward Islands 240 (I. V. A. Richards 73, A. L. Kelly 64, R. Haynes 4 for 68) and 174 (I. V. A. Richards 50, R. Haynes 5 for 72)

Jamaica won by 263 runs

Inns	NOs	Runs	HS	Av
5	—	217	103	43.40
5	—	87	38	17.40
5	—	221	102	44.20
5	1	326	126	81.50
2	—	38	38	19.00
4	—	57	37	14.25
4	—	59	21	14.75
4	—	87	37	21.75
4	1	74	35	24.66
4	1	44	27*	14.66
4	3	4	2*	4.00
2	—	7	5	3.50
1	1	1	1*	—

B	Lb	W	Nb	Total	Wkts
	1	1	6	211	10
6	8		11	435	6
		2	7	196	10
13	9		12	313	7
			Abandoned		

Jamaica 1982
Shell Shield

BATTING	v. Guyana (Kingston) 5-8 March 1982		v. Leeward Islands (Kingston) 12-15 March 1982		v. Trinidad and Tobago (Port of Spain) 19-22 March 1982		v. Barbados (Bridgetown) 27-29 March 1982		v. Windward Islands (St Vincent) 2-4 April 1982	
R. A. Austin	2	118	0	55	5	2	20	19	2	2
G. Powell	48	2	95	12						
E. H. Mattis	98	41	21	77	51	50*	18	24	30	31
L. G. Rowe	3	13	29	1	73	—	21	0	16	22
P. J. Dujon	20	66*	81	35*	25	—	0	0	17	26
H. S. Chang	19	155	15	57	6	—	97	26	1	50
M. C. Neita	6	12*	84	48*	4	—	4	16	0	8
M. A. Tucker	2*	3								
C. U. Thompson	4	—								
R. Haynes	1	—	11	—	16	—	16	5	28	19
R. R. Wynter	0	—	2*	—	3*	—	0*	5*	5*	0*
D. O. Malcolm			3	—	5	—	5	19	12	21
C. A. Walsh			15	—	21	—	0	0	2	0
C. W. Fletcher					122	24*	43	5	7	31
Byes		6	8	10	8		6	2	6	
Leg-byes	1	8	4	7	5		5	3	4	2
Wides	1						1			
No-balls	6	11	4	3	2	1	6	4	12	1
Total	211	435	372	305	346	77	242	128	142	213
Wickets	10	6	10	5	10	1	10	10	10	10
Result	W		W		D		L		L	

Catches
10 – P. J. Dujon (ct 9/st 1)
9 – L. G. Rowe
5 – R. R. Wynter
4 – H. S. Chang and D. O. Malcolm
3 – G. Powell
2 – R. A. Austin, E. H. Mattis, C. W. Fletcher and sub (Peters)
1 – M. C. Neita, C. A. Walsh and R. Haynes

BOWLING	R. R. Wynter	C. U. Thompson	R. A. Austin	R. Haynes	M. A. Tucker	E. H. Mattis	C. A. Walsh	D. O. Malcolm
v. Guyana (Kingston) 5-8 March 1982	20-3-69-1	15-2-25-2	6.1-1-39-1	29-5-87-5	13-3-30-0	2-1-1-1		
	12-0-43-1	10-3-28-0	11-3-31-0	34-7-119-6	13.2-1-49-1			
v. Leeward Islands (Kingston) 12-15 March 1982	7-1-45-2		20-7-54-3	23-6-68-4			10-2-52-0	6.1-0-17-1
	15-4-46-2			20-5-72-5			8-2-16-1	13-7-25-2
v. Trinidad and Tobago (Port of Spain) 19-22 March 1982	31.1-6-98-2		28-2-79-2	18-3-69-0			35-8-119-4	15-0-77-1
v. Barbados (Bridgetown) 27-29 March 1982	20-1-98-3		10-0-50-0	29-2-107-0		1-0-1-0	31.1-7-95-6	25-3-80-1
v. Windward Islands (St Vincent) 2-4 April 1982	13.2-0-41-3		6-2-12-0	24-5-57-2			21-1-70-2	7-0-15-2
	3-0-20-0		4-0-15-0	7.5-1-45-1			9-1-26-2	7-2-29-0
	121.3-15-460-14	25-5-53-2	85.1-15-280-6	184.5-34-624-23	26.2-4-79-1	3-1-2-1	114.1-21-378-15	73.1-12-243-7
	av. 32.85	av. 26.50	av. 46.66	av. 27.13	av. 79.00	av. 2.00	av. 25.20	av. 34.71

After the second round of matches Jamaica remained the only unbeaten side. Once more it was the leg-break bowling of Robert Haynes which brought them victory. They lost Austin in Roberts' opening over on the first morning, but thereafter they dominated the match. Roberts bowled splendidly, but he lacked adequate support and consistent batting took Jamaica to a good score. In reply, Kelly and Richards were the only batsmen to offer real resistance, but the score was boosted by the tail-enders.

When Jamaica batted again Viv Richards took three catches in a spell behind the stumps, but the home side consolidated their strong position and the issue was never in doubt.

The weakness of the Trinidad attack was illustrated when Larry Gomes again had to use himself to open the bowling against Guyana. Surviving the early loss of Lyght and inspired by a fine innings from Timur Mohammed, Guyana were able to declare at a reasonable total after rain had scarred their innings. Against the spin of the younger Kallicharran Trinidad faltered and Guyana batted again with a lead of 83.

Bacchus played a captain's innings of authority, but he gained scant support and Guyana's total was only boosted by late flourishes from Harper, Butts and Croft.

Set to make 353, Trinidad batted valiantly with Furlonge and skipper Gomes leading the charge, but wickets fell in the rush after tea and the scoring rate was never quite high enough.

Windward Islands provided the great surprise with a memorable victory over Barbados at Kensington Oval. There was authority in the early batting of Barbados and they reached 216 for the loss of 4 wickets, but Kentish and Winston Davis brought about a collapse and six men fell for 53.

In reply Windward Islands struggled, but Shane Julien, a prolific scorer in club cricket in Barbados where he now lives, batted doggedly and a total collapse was avoided.

Without the injured Linton, Barbados had an unhappy time against the bowling of Norbert Phillip and Windward Islands found themselves needing 241 to win, a total within their capabilities.

They started badly, losing Lewis and John for 12. Julien followed at 50 and Sebastien, who had batted well, and Cadette were both out by 110. Norbert Phillip then played a remarkable innings, hitting powerfully to score 62 out of 113 in a stand with Slack. Windward now sighted victory and Slack and Shillingford finished the job.

19, 20, 21 and 22 March

at Port of Spain

Jamaica 346 (C. W. Fletcher 122, L. G. Rowe 73, E. H. Mattis 51, B. D. Julien 9 for 97) and 77 for 1 (E. H. Mattis 50 not out)

Trinidad and Tobago 480 for 9 dec (A. L. Logie 171, K. G. D'Heurieux 61, H. A. Gomes 59, A. Rajah 52, C. A. Walsh 4 for 119)

Match drawn

Leeward Islands 1982
Shell Shield

BATTING	v. Windward Islands (Roseau) 4–7 March 1982	v. Jamaica (Kingston) 12–15 March 1982		v. Barbados (Basseterre) 20–23 March 1982		v. Trinidad and Tobago (Antigua) 2–5 April 1982	
E. E. Lewis	15	4	2	11			
A. L. Kelly	71	49	64	20	47	8	25	4
R. M. Otto	62	5	3	32	18	38	13	24
I. V. A. Richards| 92	1	73	50	4	46	167	—
J. C. Allen	8	34	25	2	48	28		
S. I. Williams	18	2	10	12	0	13	2	—
D. R. Parry	11	5	20	15	27*	25	17	6*
E. A. Baptiste	46	0	28*	0	25	3	24	—
N. C. Guishard	14	0	2	0*	1	13	4*	43
A. M. E. Roberts	22	2*	3	2	4	0	2	—
J. B. Harris	0*	0			1*	13*		
V. A. Eddy			6	15				
R. Richardson					0	76	24	11
S. Liburd							7	48*
A. C. M. White							11	—
Byes	14	8	1	6	2	4	3	1
Leg-byes	3	3	2	2	3	9	3	9
Wides								
No-balls	8	2	1	7	14	8		
Total	384	115	240	174	194	284	302	146
Wickets	10	10	10	10	10	10	10	4
Result	W		L		L		D	

Catches
12 – I. V. A. Richards
7 – S. I. Williams (ct 6/st 1)
6 – A. L. Kelly
3 – E. A. Baptiste, D. R. Parry, E. E. Lewis and J. C. Allen (one as sub)
2 – A. M. E. Roberts and A. C. M. White
1 – R. M. Otto and N. C. Guishard

BOWLING	A. M. E. Roberts	J. B. Harris	D. R. Parry	E. A. Baptiste	I. V. A. Richards	N. C. Guishard	V. A. Eddy	A. C. M. White
v. Windward Islands (Roseau) 4–7 March 1982	22–6–59–2 18–7–52–5	14–1–73–1 5–2–9–0	27–9–78–1 13–2–29–1	8–1–30–0 3–0–4–0	6–2–15–0 5–2–11–1	25–9–33–6 18–7–27–3		
v. Jamaica (Kingston) 12–15 March 1982	21–7–54–6 13–1–26–1		16–1–72–0 31–4–82–1	20–3–105–2 16–2–57–2	10–1–29–0 4–0–9–0	35–8–96–2 38–5–105–1	2–0–6–0	
v. Barbados (Basseterre) 20–23 March 1982	20.2–4–53–4 16–1–53–2	12–1–36–1 4–0–14–1	36–7–92–2 27–7–49–3	9–0–43–0	7–2–12–0 1–0–2–0	20–6–63–2 12–2–49–0		
v. Trinidad and Tobago (Antigua) 2–5 April 1982	17.2–5–45–2 16–3–56–2		21–5–86–2 26–11–37–3	17–3–48–2 17–3–62–3	5–1–19–0 4–0–6–0	12–4–27–2 19–4–48–2		13–0–64–2 6–0–31–0
	143.4–34–398–24 av. 16.58	35–4–132–3 av. 44.00	197–46–525–13 av. 40.38	90–12–349–9 av. 38.77	42–8–103–1 av. 103.00	179–45–448–18 av. 24.88	2–0–6–0 —	19–0–95–2 av. 47.50

20, 21, 22 and 23 March

at Basseterre

Leeward Islands 194 (J. Garner 5 for 56) and 284 (R. Richardson 76)
Barbados 308 (F. D. Stephenson 165, D. A. Murray 55 not out, A. M. E. Roberts 4 for 53) and 173 for 6 (C. L. King 88 not out)

Barbados won by 4 wickets

The match between Guyana and Windward Islands was abandoned without a ball being bowled.

The match at Queen's Park Oval was dominated by batsmen and ended early by rain. There was a career best from Gus Logie and a fine century from Fletcher, but these splendid performances were totally eclipsed by the bowling of Bernard Julien. The former Kent all-rounder, now thirty-two, took a career best 9 for 97, a brilliant display on a good wicket. There was also some impressive fast bowling from eighteen-year-old Courtenay Walsh, six feet four inches tall and a disciple of Michael Holding.

Joel Garner returned to shoot out Leeward Islands on the opening day at Warner Park, but the Islanders responded by dismissing Reifer and Alvin Greenidge for 8. Franklyn Stephenson, playing his first match for Barbados following his success with Tasmania, was sent in as night-watchman. The following day Stephenson hit four sixes and nineteen fours in a devastating attack on the home side's bowling. He finally fell run out with the score at 238, his contribution having been 165 out of 230. He then dismissed Kelly and Allen as Leeward Islands were bowled out for 284.

Needing 171 to win, Barbados lost 6 wickets for 73, but Collis King, who had come in at 50 for 4, hit 88 out of 123 scored while he was at the wicket and Barbados took the match.

27, 28, 29 March

at Bridgetown

Barbados 465 (A. T. Greenidge 172, C. A. Best 75, E. N. Trotman 55, C. A. Walsh 6 for 95)
Jamaica 242 (H. S. Chang 97, J. Garner 6 for 74) and 128

Barbados won by an innings and 95 runs

27, 28, 29 and 30 March

at St George's

Windward Islands 332 (L. D. John 69, S. Julien 58, L. C. Sebastien 50, B. D. Julien 4 for 59, R. Nanan 4 for 98) and 192 (R. Nanan 5 for 51)
Trinidad and Tobago 281 (H. A. Gomes 72, K. G. D'Heurieux 70 not out) and 158 (W. W. Davis 5 for 42)

Windward Islands won by 85 runs

The match between Guyana and Leeward Islands was abandoned without a ball being bowled.

In spite of some more impressive pace bowling by young

Inns	NOs	Runs	HS	Av
4	—	32	15	8.00
8	—	288	71	36.00
8	—	195	62	24.37
7	—	433	167	61.85
6	—	145	48	24.16
7	—	57	18	8.14
8	2	126	27*	21.00
7	1	126	46	21.00
8	2	77	43	12.83
7	1	35	22	5.83
4	3	14	13*	14.00
2	—	21	15	10.50
4	—	111	76	27.75
2	1	55	48*	55.00
1	—	11	11	11.00

B	Lb	W	Nb	Total	Wkts
	(14)			302	10
6	2			140	10
8	4		4	372	10
10	7		3	305	5
1	2		6	308	10
	2		4	173	6
4	6		5	304	10
3	5		5	253	10

Trinidad and Tobago 1982
Shell Shield

BATTING	v. Barbados (Bridgetown) 5-8 March 1982		v. Guyana (Pointe-à-Pierre) 12-15 March 1982		v. Jamaica (Port of Spain) 19-22 March 1982		v. Windward Islands (St George's) 27-30 March 1982		v. Leeward Islands (Antigua) 2-5 April 1982	
R. S. Gabriel	34	71	44	39	13	—	13	34	75	85
K. Miller	1	44								
H. A. Gomes	26	19	16	93	59	—	72	31	51	1
A. L. Logie	42	24			171	—	7	17	29	27
P. Moosai	23	28	7	0						
T. Cuffy	0	88	0	42			22	19	42	0
B. D. Julien	19	7	37	2	0	—	1	1*		
R. Sampath	24	20			40	—			34	31
R. Nanan	4	6*	24	11*	40	—	19	13*	2	3
J. R. Lyon	0*	1	1	—	—	—	11	0	18	4
H. Joseph	4	5	0*	—						
D. Furlonge			23	71			4	8	9	49
A. Rajah			25	21	52	—	44	0*		
S. Jumadeen			10	0*	2*	—	2	8		
K. R. Bainey					12	—				
K. G. D'Heurieux					61	—	70*	12	23	27
P. Ramnath									6	13
K. Williams									0*	0*
Byes	4	1		13	6		3	3	4	3
Leg-byes	1	4	2	9	12		3	6	6	5
Wides	1				1		1			
No-balls	10	11	7	12	11		10	5	5	5
Total	193	329	196	313	480		281	158	304	253
Wickets	10	10	10	7	9		10	8†	10	10
Result	L		D		D		L		D	

Catches
11 – J. R. Lyon (ct 7/st 4)
7 – B. D. Julien
6 – R. S. Gabriel
4 – T. Cuffy, D. Furlonge and S. Jumadeen
3 – P. Moosai (one as sub)
2 – K. G. D'Heurieux
1 – R. Nanan, H. Joseph, A. Rajah, H. A. Gomes, R. Sampath and P. Ramnath (as sub)

† B. D. Julien and A. Rajah retired hurt

BOWLING	B. D. Julien	H. A. Gomes	R. Nanan	H. Joseph	S. Jumadeen	R. Sampath	A. Rajah	J. R. Lyon
v. Barbados (Bridgetown) 5-8 March 1982	26-3-100-3 8-0-38-0	20-8-46-0 9-0-44-1	38.2-18-59-3 18.3-6-64-4	33-7-97-4 9-1-45-0				
v. Guyana (Pointe-à-Pierre) 12-15 March 1982	9-1-34-1 8-1-30-2	9-3-25-0 7-1-22-0	34-14-78-4 48-17-75-3	16-0-82-2 19-2-76-0	19-5-50-2 21-4-58-4			
v. Jamaica (Port of Spain) 19-22 March 1982	32.2-4-97-9 8-3-12-1	15-1-47-0	31-6-76-0 7-2-13-0		24-6-44-1 4-2-4-0	18-3-67-0 4-0-29-0	1-0-1-0	5-0-13-0
v. Windward Islands (St George's) 27-30 March 1982	18.4-2-59-4 18-4-51-1	16-3-47-1 11.2-4-30-3	39-11-98-4 35-10-51-5		33-8-112-1 19-8-38-1			
v. Leeward Islands (Antigua) 2-5 April 1982		1-1-0-0 4-1-4-0	34.4-11-109-7 25-10-54-2		6-1-25-0 2-0-6-0			
	128-18- 421-21 av. 20.04	92.2-22- 265-5 av. 53.00	310.3-105- 677-32 av. 21.15	77-10- 300-6 av. 50.00	120-33- 306-9 av. 34.00	30-4- 127-0 —	1-0- 1-0 —	5-0- 13-0 —

Walsh, Barbados reached 465 by lunch on the second day with Alvin Greenidge hitting his highest score in the Shell Shield and sharing stands of 169 with Best for the second wicket and 116 with Trotman for the third.

Garner destroyed Jamaica, having among his six victims Chang who batted quite heroically. Following-on, Jamaica succumbed weakly to the all pace attack of Clarke, Moseley, Garner and Stephenson, and the match was over in three days. This victory assured Barbados of the Shell Shield for the tenth time in the sixteen seasons of its history.

An opening stand of 100 between John and Sebastien put Windward Islands on the way to a tempestuous victory over Trinidad. Gomes and D'Heurieux batted well, but Windward Islands led by 51 on the first innings.

Their confidence was shattered a little by Nanan's spin, however, and Trinidad were left needing 244 to win. Some furious fast bowling by Winston David demoralised them. He took 5 for 42 and both Rajah and Bernard Julien had to retire hurt after being hit. Hinds' spin acted as a perfect foil.

2, 3, 4 and 5 April

at Georgetown

Guyana 176 for 3 (A. A. Lyght 103)
v. **Barbados**

Match abandoned as a draw

at Antigua

Trinidad and Tobago 304 (R. S. Gabriel 75, H. A. Gomes 51) and 253 (R. S. Gabriel 85)
Leeward Islands 302 (I. V. A. Richards 167, R. Nanan 7 for 109) and 146 for 4

Match drawn

at St Vincent

Jamaica 142 (N. Phillip 6 for 41) and 213 (H. S. Chang 50)
Windward Islands 217 (L. D. John 57) and 139 for 3

Windward Islands won by 7 wickets

The only play possible in Guyana throughout the series was three-quarters of the opening day during which time Lyght reached a hundred.

Viv Richards scored his highest innings of the series on his home ground, the Recreation Ground, Antigua. He was the only one to counter Nanan's spin and the first innings ended in stalemate. Gabriel and Furlonge started the Trinidad second innings with a partnership of 118, but the game was always drifting to a draw.

The main excitement was at St Vincent where more devastating fast bowling from Phillip and Davis routed Jamaica on the opening day. Only John, Slack and Phillip, Man of the Match, reached double figures when Windward Islands batted, but they still took a first innings lead of 75.

Jamaica showed more resolution at the second attempt, but Windward Islands were left needing only 139 to win, a target they reached for the loss of three wickets so gaining victory in three days and a most commendable second place in the Shell Shield.

Windward Islands 1982
Shell Shield

BATTING	v. Leeward Islands (Roseau) 4–7 March 1982		v. Barbados (Bridgetown) 12–15 March 1982		v. Trinidad and Tobago (St George's) 27–30 March 1982		v. Jamaica (St Vincent) 2–4 April 1982	
L. C. Sebastien	0	34	6	60	50	33	4	0
L. A. Lewis	115	2	38	1	0	0		
S. Julien	5	19	52	20	58	5	4	51*
I. T. Shillingford	48	11	10	5*	34	2	2	—
W. N. Slack	13	23	12	68*	47	40	45	42
A. Tesheira	16	2					0	13*
N. Phillip	2	10	2	62	43*	23	44	—
I. Cadette	3	17	21	8	7	11	3	—
T. Kentish	31*	7	0	—	0	24	8	—
S. J. Hinds	47	6*	21*	—	4	1*	18	
W. W. Davis	8	1	0	—	4	0	10*	
L. D. John			34	2	69	32	57	29
Byes		6		2	6	13	7	
Leg-byes	(14)	2	(17)	7	7	4	4	
Wides					3		4	
No-balls			3	3	4	7	4	
Total	302	140	213	241	332	192	217	139
Wickets	10	10	10	6	10	10	10	3
Result	L		W		W		W	

Catches
- 11 – I. Cadette (ct 3/st 8)
- 6 – W. N. Slack
- 5 – A. Tesheira (two as sub)
- 4 – I. T. Shillingford
- 3 – S. J. Hinds
- 2 – S. Julien, L. C. Sebastien, N. Phillip and T. Kentish
- 1 – W. W. Davis, L. D. John, and L. A. Lewis

BOWLING	N. Phillip	W. W. Davis	T. Kentish	S. J. Hinds	W. N. Slack	L. C. Sebastien
v. Leeward Islands (Roseau) 4–7 March 1982	21–4–80–1	30–5–88–3	32–8–85–2	31–4–91–2	6.1–2–15–2	
	13–0–33–7	8–2–30–1	12–3–12–2	7–1–22–0	1–0–5–0	
v. Barbados (Bridgetown) 12–15 March 1982	11–3–44–0	19–3–86–3	16.1–2–69–6	18–6–64–1		
	14–5–21–4	19–6–43–0	18.3–2–44–2	24–6–62–3		
v. Trinidad and Tobago (St George's) 27–30 March 1982	24–3–68–2	31–4–97–3	18–3–40–0	21.4–2–60–3		
	1–0–4–0	26–5–42–5	6–1–11–0	24.2–4–72–3		3–0–14–0
v. Jamaica (St Vincent) 2–4 April 1982	19–6–41–6	18–3–45–4		8–1–34–0		
	18–3–51–1	22–6–70–3	18.4–3–44–2	17–4–45–3		
	121–24–342–21 av. 16.28	173–34–501–22 av. 22.77	121.2–22–305–14 av. 21.78	151–28–450–15 av. 30.00	7.1–2–20–2 av. 10.00	3–0–14–0 —

† G. Linton absent injured   ‡ A. Rajah and B. D. Julien retired hurt

SHELL SHIELD – FINAL TABLE

	P	W	L	D	Ab	Points
Barbados	5	3	1	1	—	57
Windward Islands	5	3	1	—	1	52
Jamaica	5	2	2	1	—	36
Guyana	5	—	1	2	2	25
Leeward Islands	5	1	2	1	1	24
Trinidad & Tobago	5	—	2	3	—	20

Inns	NOs	Runs	HS	Av
8	—	187	60	23.37
6	—	156	115	26.00
8	1	214	58	30.57
7	1	112	48	18.66
8	1	290	68*	41.42
4	1	31	16	10.33
7	1	186	62	31.00
7	—	70	21	10.00
6	1	70	31*	14.00
6	3	97	47	32.33
6	1	23	10*	4.60
6	—	223	69	37.16

B	Lb	W	Nb	Total	Wkts
14	13		8	384	10
8	3		2	115	10
	1	1	4	269	10
	2		12	184	9†
3	3		10	281	10
3	6	1	5	158	8‡
6	4		12	142	10
	2		1	213	10

Mike Brearley leaves first-class cricket on a misty September morning at Worcester. He is clapped from the field after he has made the winning hit.

SECTION H
The English Season

Schweppes County Championship, John Player League,
NatWest Trophy, Benson and Hedges Cup.
Cornhill and Prudential matches v India and Pakistan.
Full season's results and form charts.
Review of the season by Tony Lewis.
Book reviews.

The English season began with what have become customary movements and the inevitable trauma.

Glamorgan, as ever, were in the forefront of change. Malcolm Nash resigned as captain and Javed Miandad, rejected as captain of Pakistan, was contacted to take over from him. As Javed would be spending half the season with the Pakistan touring side, this would place a great responsibility on Barry Lloyd who had the distinction of being vice-captain and an uncapped player. Norman Featherstone decided not to return and Charles Rowe came from Kent.

Geoff Miller made his peace with Derbyshire and there was calm in Yorkshire. Tavare and Cowdrey became joint vice-captains of Kent and Mike Brearley announced that this would be his last season.

Tim Lamb entered hospital for an operation which meant that he would miss the first month of the season and Joel Garner's services were denied to Somerset for the same reason. Steve Perryman left Warwickshire for Worcestershire and Jim Cumbes left Worcestershire for Warwickshire.

All these events were dwarfed, however, by the news from South Africa that a party of English cricketers, including Gooch, Boycott, Emburey, Knott and Underwood, were to play a series of representative matches under the sponsorship of the South African Breweries. The South African Board elevated these matches to the standard of 'Test Matches' by awarding caps to the South African players taking part in them. These matches were not, nor can they ever be, Test matches for the simple reason that the South Africans were not opposed by an England side which had been chosen by the English selectors. They were opposed by a hastily gathered group of players who, by no stretch of imagination, could be considered as fully representative of their country.

It was all very sad and there must have been many, like the present writer, who woke every morning hoping that it had not really happened and that Gooch would be at Twickenham on Saturday or at Upton Park the following Tuesday. But it did happen and the consequence was that the players involved were banned from Test cricket for three years which, in some cases, certainly meant the end of their Test careers.

We were confronted by a paradox. The editor of this annual abhors apartheid and over the years has made some gestures, however slight and futile, against it. He is, of course, not alone in his abhorrence and the reason for the distaste of the segregational policies of the South African government is that they deny a group of individuals the right to go where they like and mix with whom they please.

Now we were asked to criticise a group of English cricketers for doing just that. They affirmed that they had no interest in politics and certainly did not support apartheid. They became the shuttlecocks in a game of badminton played between opposing political factions, naively allowing themselves to be exploited by one side while they were unwittingly, and even undeservedly, castigated by the other.

Where they stood condemned was in the deceitfulness that had gone into the planning of the expedition, for it was only their words of honour that had saved the tour to India and Sri Lanka.

There had been a precedent in the defection of players to World Series Cricket, but those who went to South Africa could look at that affair and know that after a temporary ban players had been reinstated through legal action and had soon appeared in the Honours' List so could they have too much to fear?

Although the severity of the Test ban may have surprised them, none of them could have expected that the incident would have gone unnoticed or unpunished. But then, if Test cricket was what some of them had just played in India, did it matter very much if one was banned from it. It is an inescapable fact that most of those who played in the Tests in India found it an experience that gave little joy and one which they would not seek again.

Whoever was responsible for the drudgery and boredom of the series between India and England cannot be determined. It was a corporate responsibility. But the sufferers, albeit some of their wounds were self-inflicted, were ripe for the temptation when business men offered them large sums of money to play cricket for a couple of weeks in a beautiful country with a serene climate. Did they stop to think of politics? Did they even remember that it was the South African government which brought politics firmly into cricket when they refused an England touring side which included Basil D'Oliveira?

We live in a material world and the money offered was a further step in the pursuit of happiness. Are they now in a position to answer the question that Estragon poses to Vladimir in *Waiting for Godot* – 'What do we do now, now that we're happy?'

The action of the English cricketers caused much debate, not all of it valuable, some of it hypocritical. DAVID FRITH, *editor of* Wisden Cricket Monthly, *a man of energy and intelligence, clarifies the debate in his characteristically precise and balanced manner.*

When the fifteen English cricketers who toured South Africa in March – against the TCCB edict of the previous autumn – had a three-year Test ban lowered upon them, several absurdities struck the man in the street. What was happening to cricket if England's most dynamic top-order batsman, Graham Gooch, was forbidden from representing his country against India and Pakistan, while Allan Lamb, Ian Greig and Brian Davison, all born in southern Africa, were eligible to play for England and free to do so? Gooch had broken no law; had broken no contract.

What he and his fourteen fellow-tourists *had* done was flout an urgent TCCB recommendation, the *raison d'etre* for which was the protection of the financial security of the British first-class game in the face of mounting pressure from India, Pakistan and West Indies.

The pressure, more insistent with every international tour, was upon those countries and individuals tempted to re-engage in cricket contact with South Africa. The aim of those who adhere to this pressure line, whether naturally or at the behest of their government, is to compel the South African government to abandon apartheid. The oppression and deprivation suffered by non-whites in that country will eventually be swept away, it is held, as sporting isolation cuts deep.

The 1982 England selectors; (left to right) Norman Gifford, Peter May, Alec Bedser and Alan Smith.

There are some observers, however, who feel that this isolation will never amount to more than an irritation to South Africa. The world action which would eventually squeeze Pretoria into reform, into according all South African citizens equality of opportunity and reward, would be economic sanctions. Sporting sanctions alongside would make more sense, providing a morale-bruising back-up to the economic measures.

Thus, even a cricketer who was torn between the two views – or perhaps who felt in all sincerity that sporting contact was desirable – will have had little hesitation in accepting the cash offer of a lifetime for a one-month tour. Why, he would have asked, are individuals allowed to play and coach in South Africa, but a group (team) not? The difference, as many a man in the street professed to see it, was subtle. But it was important.

County cricketers are not tied to their clubs in the off-season. The restraint-of-trade aspect had been aired thoroughly – and for the TCCB with disastrous effect – in 1977 when an attempt was made to ban those who joined Kerry Packer's World Series Cricket. How, then, could the TCCB expect to get away with a warning to players not to tour South Africa as a team? The answer to that came soon after the whispered-about venture became a reality. The TCCB carefully laid its reasons for instituting the ban. They all had to do with protecting the revenues – and with them the jobs of over three hundred county cricketers. No replacement tour could reasonably have been set up if India and Pakistan had cancelled their 1982 tours to England in a spirit of indignation heavily but not totally government-inspired.

Where the TCCB may have got the tone wrong was in its omission to make clear that the punishment was meted out to the fifteen Englishmen because the *TCCB itself* disapproved of this 'big-time' contact with South Africa. It was all made to seem as if the TCCB was capitulating to others' demands – something they had clearly refused to do when Robin Jackman was deported from Guyana in February 1981, for having strong playing links with South Africa. Here the right of the individual was defended by Lord's, a

principle reasserted at the time of the banning of the fifteen a year later.

Meanwhile, South African cricket, lodged in a slough of despond, took heart from the unofficial tour and hoped for more. There would naturally have been a preference for legitimate re-entry to international cricket home and away, but, having done all in their power to make the game multiracial in their own country, the administrators and players knew, after all, that the promise made a dozen years ago – that they could come back when South African cricket, from top to bottom, was non-descriminatory – was not to be honoured now that the world disapproval of their government's policies had intensified.

This situation jarred the sense of justice. Who could blame the Springboks, backed by commerce and perhaps even by their government, from importing whatever talent they could secure? They could not tempt Ian Botham, not even with £200,000, and that took the ginger from the March 1982 enterprise. Yet plans to import a mature and attractive

Two exciting young players: (left) *David East of Essex and* (below) *Mike Benson of Kent.*

Australian team, a World XI, and possibly even a Pakistan side were under way as the year progressed. Without such alternative arrangements, cricket in South Africa was certain to continue to falter in appeal, and then to border on extinction, as in the USA, where it had once shown signs of flourishing. Such a decline in the sport would hardly affect the government's racial policies.

And yet ... While argument over the March '82 tour raged, occasional news bulletins came from the Republic to indicate that genuine relaxations in apartheid were in the wind. The reasons for such a shift are necessarily complex and speculative, and are part of another story. Those who fostered the sports boycott throughout would claim some credit, while cynics might insist that Prime Minister Botha and the more enlightened members of his cabinet were merely buying time by talking about reform and instituting it in meaningless, cosmetic dollops.

However South Africa arrives at a just society of its own, it will take much time. Graeme Pollock may not see it. Graeme Pollock's grandson might. In the interim, the key question concerns the willingness or otherwise of various national cricket control bodies, in the shadows of their respective governments, to join afresh in official Test matches against the long-accursed Springboks. The option is this or unofficial tours which, against the threat of individual Test bans, will feature only players in the last years of their effectiveness ... that is, until the money becomes so large and irresistible that younger men will think little of throwing up their Test careers.

There is another possibility, even more unpalatable: Test cricket will be divided into racial sections, a spectacle which would have the instigators of apartheid holding their sides with laughter.

Partners. Botham and Willis for England at Headingley, Prudential Trophy.

The solemn cloud that hung over cricket could only be dispelled by the inevitable joys of an advancing season. CHRISTOPHER MARTIN-JENKINS, *editor of* The Cricketer *and talented broadcaster, reflects the opening days of the season and* The State of Cricket.

You cannot keep a good optimist down. There are any number of reasons for pessimism about the future of cricket as the 1982 season begins but who, with cricket in his veins, can feel depressed at the start of *any* season? The most important thing of all is that the game should continue to be played and enjoyed and as to a Christian the Easter Festival is a time for hope and a fresh start, so it is with happy coincidence of spring and another new season.

When you come to think about it, the whole of life tends to be a battle between realism and romanticism. There is danger round every corner, but there is also pleasure, beauty, excitement. The realist in cricket has no difficulty in stressing the perils ahead – less variety and, in some respects, falling standards, the domination of the game in some quarters by commercial interests, and political disruption. But against that one may weigh the buoyancy of the game in schools and clubs, at amateur levels, the improvements in the terms of those playing cricket for a living and the determination of most of them not to sacrifice the game's best traditions, exemplified by the voluntary resolution of the Cricketers' Association not to show any dissent towards umpires.

Commentators, cricket-writers and editors tend, I fear, to be censorious of first-class cricket (*sometimes*, no doubt, unfairly) so let me at least begin by counting a few blessings. The freshest in my mind are two happy reversals of recent trends evident in the first few matches of the season. An engaging character called Asif Din, who arrived at Birmingham from Kampala courtesy of Big Daddy Amin and returned there via the Lord's Ground Staff, took five wickets in Warwickshire's first Championship match bowling leg-spinners. Moreover a journey I made to watch Somerset in practice before the season started revealed what looked like an authentic member of this apparently extinct species bowling with a good, natural loop to Brian Rose. It turned out to be young Russell, son of Colin, McCool, who was so keen to come to England that he came over in 1981 at his own expense, only to twist his knee so badly after a week in the nets that he had to have an operation and return home. As Roy Kerslake explained, however, 'We had seen enough to take a gamble when we knew that Denis Breakwell was retiring and that we were not going to get a good left-armer'. Once upon a time, of course, a leg-spinner would not have been considered a gamble. I noticed that Somerset decided not to play McCool in their first Championship match, though when I was at Taunton at the end of April they had been intending to. By the time this book is published we shall know whether or not McCool has been able to strike a blow for the smallest union in cricket.

I must not let my optimism die so soon, but the realist gets the better of the romantic here: the leg-spinner will not come back in any numbers until groundsmen find how to quicken up pitches without leaving them too green and the lbw law is altered to enable the right-arm bowler delivering from over the wicket to win an affirmative decision if the ball has pitched outside leg-stump, struck the pad within crease and wicket, and would have hit the stumps. Even in present circumstances leg-spinners *would* get more wickets than they do if only captains would accept that they are bound to be less accurate than other types of spinner. Ask one hundred club batsmen (in England, at any rate) whether they would rather face a good leg-spinner or a good off, or orthodox left-arm, spinner and I guarantee that ninety per cent would prefer not to play against the leg-break and googly man – simply because they have so little practice against that type and no longer understand the mystery. (Since the Editor has recently published a very good book about Tich Freeman, I know I am on safe ground here!)

The other encouraging sign that not everything is changing was the positive flurry of hundreds by Oxford and Cambridge undergraduates amidst the chill of late April and early May. After Ian Hodgson had taken the first eight wickets of the first-class season against Glamorgan (for whom Alan Jones proved that another thing has not changed by getting a century himself) Derek Pringle, Robin Boyd-Moss, Ralph Cowan, and Simon Halliday all scored good hundreds off reputable county attacks and Steve Henderson of Cambridge made Worcestershire wonder about their decision to release him by scoring a double century against Middlesex. The Oxbridge contribution to English cricket remains extremely valuable and it is steadily being reinforced by strength in other universities, especially Durham.

There are other good signs as I write. Sixteen countries from almost all parts of the globe will be staying under one roof in Solihull in June and July whilst playing a great many matches against enterprising and hospitable clubs in the West Midlands as well as competing amongst themselves for the ICC Trophy and the chance to go through to the 1983 Prudential (World) Cup. What a wonderful feat of organisation this competition is; what a vindication for Ben Brocklehurst who first had the idea; for John Gardiner who sold the competition to Lord's and pushed it through to a successful conclusion in 1978; for Jack Bailey who offered encouragement and official blessing; and for Bob Evans and the Midlands Club Cricket Conference, who have made the 1982 competition into a unique festival of cricket. Would that Argentina, one of the most popular competitors in 1978, had been in a position to come this time. For the rest, let us hope that cricket conquers politics for a change. Zimbabwe for the cup!

There are those who would say that at the higher level of the game cricket has sold out to politics and will never recover. This is, however, where reality defeats romanticism by an innings. Why, ask the majority of British cricket followers, did the TCCB ban the fifteen players who went to South Africa in March to play representative games when so many had been there before (including those who went on four tours under the aegis of Derrick Robins to play games of similar standing) without being punished? Why did the TCCB allow the threat of the cancellation of the Indian and Pakistan tours this summer to force them into a policy of appeasement? Why did they abandon their oft-stated policy not to be dictated to when it came to selecting the England team? It goes against the grain to admit it, but although a great injustice has been done to South African cricket (as opposed to the stubborn South African Government) by the other cricket nations who refuse to play them, despite the achievement of genuinely multi-racial cricket at all levels, the TCCB took the only realistic decision possible when they banned the players to defend the summer's tours and therefore the stability of county cricket.

The simple truth is that Governments are more powerful than Cricket Boards and if the players had not been banned, the tours would not have taken place. If England had then invited South Africa, to salvage county finances, the winter tour to Australia would have been cancelled, because the main sporting preoccupation of the Australian Government at the time was the Commonwealth Games. There would, until a compromise was reached at least, have been no more Tests for England against any other countries except perhaps New Zealand (and presumably South Africa) and no Prudential World Cup in 1983. The whole fragile structure of international cricket would have collapsed. Quite apart from this the TCCB had issued a warning in 1981 of their own volition, although this in turn had been to protect the England tour to India. Theirs was a choice between two evils and they chose the lesser. Whether the bans should have been for so long a period is another matter. Once they had decided to take a stand, however, they were no doubt right to take a strong one. Young players, at least, with genuine hopes of Test cricket, are unlikely to follow the Krugerrand trail.

Money and politics! Oh that they could be ignored, but they make the realist's world go round.

Rightly or wrongly the first-class season goes ahead and it promises well. India, away from the seething, demanding crowds of home, look a well organised side who will give England a serious testing before the arrival of the even more talented Pakistanis. The latter have too seldom pulled together in the past but maybe Imran Khan will succeed as captain where Javed Miandad failed. Ninety-six overs at least will be bowled on fine days in the Test series. Hooray for action on that, at last. England have got to find some new faces, especially some new opening batsmen and bowlers of all types. They do not, now, look likely to hold on to the Ashes in Australia in the winter. But I am an optimist . . . .

21, 22 and 23 April

at Cambridge

Glamorgan 281 for 9 dec (A. Jones 103, G. C. Holmes 68, K. I. Hodgson 8 for 68) and 266 for 3 dec (R. C. Ontong 106 not out, M. J. Llewellyn 61 not out)
Cambridge University 222 (D. R. Pringle 127, B. J. Lloyd 5 for 58) and 256 for 5 (D. R. Pringle 73 not out, J. P. C. Mills 56)

Match drawn

The season opened with three days of uninterrupted cricket. It was right and just that the first century of the season should go to Alan Jones, at forty-three the oldest man playing first-class cricket in England, and still one of the very best and most underpraised of opening bats. Jones' performance was overshadowed by a remarkable piece of bowling by the South African born law student, Ian Hodgson, who took eight wickets, including that of Jones. Cambridge were 2 for 2, but Pringle batted with great authority to equal his highest score. There was then a stand of 140 between Ontong and Llewellyn before Lloyd declared, setting the University 326 in 4¾ hours. Doggart and Pringle added 103 at a brisk pace, but when Daniels bowled Doggart both sides settled for a draw.

24, 26 and 27 April

at Cambridge

Cambridge University 259 for 8 dec (D. R. Pringle 81, S. J. G. Doggart 64, R. J. Boyd-Moss 52, E. E. Hemmings 5 for 71) and 154 (R. J. Boyd-Moss 82)
Nottinghamshire 280 for 8 dec (P. A. Todd 52, R. W. M. Palmer 4 for 96) and 134 for 0 (P. A. Todd 104 not out)

Nottinghamshire won by 10 wickets

at Oxford

Northamptonshire 366 for 4 dec (A. J. Lamb 140, P. Willey 100 not out) and 211 for 6 dec (R. G. Williams 106 not out)
Oxford University 338 for 5 dec (R. S. Cowan 143 not out, G. D. R. Toogood 54) and 93 for 3

Match drawn

For Oxford University the season began well. They withstood the battering given them by Lamb and Willey who added 215 for the fourth wicket on the opening day. It was ironic that the South African destined to play for England should combine with the Englishman banned for his South African jaunt. Lamb was at his exciting belligerent best, but Ralph Cowan, born in Germany, and Giles Toogood were equally impressive for the University. Williams, surely an England player of the future, hit the fourth century of the match before the game subsided to a draw. Pringle again batted well for Cambridge and had good support from Doggart and Boyd-Moss, but Notts batted unevenly after a bright start by Todd and French. Then Illingworth took valuable second innings wickets and Cambridge floundered. A depleted Cambridge attack could not contain Todd. He reached his hundred in 75 minutes as he and Randall gave

The season's first centurion, Alan Jones, the pillar of Glamorgan.

Notts a ten wicket victory by scoring at six an over. They were helped by poor bowling and some missed chances, none of them difficult.

To add to the Cambridge woe, Oxford beat them in a limited over friendly match on the Sunday.

28, 29 and 30 April

at Cambridge

Cambridge University 380 for 6 dec (S. P. Henderson 209 not out, J. P. C. Mills 98) and 142 for 2 dec (D. R. Pringle 72 not out, D. W. Varey 51 not out)
Middlesex 231 for 2 dec (W. N. Slack 114, J. M. Brearley 60) and 292 for 2 (M. W. Gatting 164 not out, C. T. Radley 72)

Middlesex won by 8 wickets

at Oxford

Worcestershire 401 for 2 dec (G. M. Turner 239 not out, Younis Ahmed 70 not out, J. A. Ormrod 66)
Oxford University 211 (G. D. R. Toogood 83, R. S. Cowan 76) and 202 for 3 (R. G. P. Ellis 92, R. P. Moulding 67)

Match drawn

Rejected by Worcestershire at the end of the 1981 season, Steve Henderson affirmed the belief in his own ability with a thumping innings of 209 not out against Middlesex. Cambridge had been 50 for 3, but Henderson and Peter Mills put on 220 for the fourth wicket. Henderson hit 31 boundaries and his first hundred came in 84 minutes. His previous best score had been 64 and his first-class average 14.59. Slack hit a century amid the showers and Middlesex were finally set 292 in 195 minutes. Gatting and Radley began with a stand of 145 and Gatting hit four sixes and eighteen fours in his superb innings which won the game with eight overs to spare.

At Oxford, Glenn Turner hit the ninety-ninth hundred of his career and his highest score in county cricket. Cowan and Toogood saved the University from complete disaster, but Oxford still had to follow-on. Toogood's form was again encouraging and he showed why he had been singled out for a Cricket Society scholarship a few years ago. The main Oxford heroes, however, were Richard Ellis, the captain, and Roger Moulding who put on 162 for the first wicket when Oxford batted again and saved the match.

The Oxford side looked to be their most promising for several seasons.

1, 3 and 4 May

at Lord's

M.C.C. 269 for 8 dec (V. J. Marks 71 not out) and 125 for 4 dec (D. I. Gower 62)
Nottinghamshire 131 for 3 dec (D. W. Randall 52 not out) and 61 for 2

Match drawn

at Cambridge

Cambridge University 274 (R. J. Boyd-Moss 123) and 265 for 4 dec (R. J. Boyd-Moss 119, D. W. Varey 63)
Warwickshire 244 for 4 dec (T. A. Lloyd 95) and 7 for 0

Match drawn

at Oxford

Oxford University 306 for 8 dec (S. J. Halliday 113 not out, R. S. Cowan 108) and 55 for 5
Kent 616 for 6 dec (N. R. Taylor 127, R. A. Woolmer 126, C. J. Tavare 125, M. R. Benson 120, D. G. Aslett 51 not out)

Match drawn

The match at Lord's was ruined by rain, but there was sufficient play for Gower, Rice, Marks and Randall to demonstrate their batting skills and for Randall to take his first wickets in first-class cricket, those of Butcher, Gower and Richards for 15 runs. Paul Newman dismissed Paul Todd with the first ball of each innings and displayed lively pace.

In a rain scarred match at Cambridge Robin Boyd-Moss hit his maiden century and followed with another in the second innings. At Oxford six centuries were scored. On the Saturday Simon Halliday hit his maiden hundred and Ralph Cowan hit his second of the season in another impressive Oxford batting display. Their efforts were vanquished in the next couple of days when the first four batsmen in the Kent order hit centuries and Kent reached 616 for 6 before Cowdrey declared. It was the highest score in first-class cricket for 33 years and Oxford batted again dejectedly until rain put an end to their suffering.

5, 6 and 7 May

at Southampton

Leicestershire 281 (B. F. Davison 172, T. E. Jesty 6 for 71) and 214 (N. G. Cowley 6 for 48)
Hampshire 301 for 9 dec (N. G. Cowley 104) and 81 for 1

Match drawn
Hampshire 8 pts, Leicestershire 7 pts

at Old Trafford

Lancashire 120 (K. E. Cooper 6 for 46) and 129 (R. J. Hadlee 6 for 65)
Nottinghamshire 286 (J. D. Birch 71, D. W. Randall 61, R. J. Hadlee 59, L. L. McFarlane 4 for 64)

Nottinghamshire won by an innings and 37 runs
Nottinghamshire 23 pts, Lancashire 4 pts

at Lord's

Essex 355 for 8 dec (K. W. R. Fletcher 120, G. A. Gooch 58, B. R. Hardie 50) and 0 for 0 dec
Middlesex 8 for 0 dec and 348 for 8 (M. W. Gatting 90, J. E. Emburey 67 not out, J. M. Brearley 59)

Middlesex won by 2 wickets
Middlesex 18 pts, Essex 4 pts

at Northampton

Yorkshire 368 for 8 dec (G. Boycott 138, D. L. Bairstow 77) and 189 for 5 dec (J. D. Love 64 not out)
Northamptonshire 223 (W. Larkins 118 not out, A. Sidebottom 5 for 57) and 160 for 4 (W. Larkins 59)

Match drawn
Yorkshire 8 pts, Northamptonshire 5 pts

at Taunton

Somerset 212 (I. T. Botham 66, V. J. Marks 51, G. S. le Roux 5 for 47) and 150 for 9 dec
Sussex 192 (H. R. Moseley 5 for 40) and 125 for 3

Match drawn
Somerset 6 pts, Sussex 5 pts

at The Oval

Surrey 205 (C. J. Richards 52 not out, S. T. Clarke 52, G. R. Dilley 6 for 96) and 90 for 0 dec (A. R. Butcher 59 not out)
Kent 48 for 3 dec and 229 (N. R. Taylor 82, R. A. Woolmer 62, S. T. Clarke 5 for 52)

Surrey won by 18 runs
Surrey 19 pts, Kent 4 pts

at Edgbaston

Glamorgan 303 (R. C. Ontong 73, A. M. Ferreira 4 for 81) and 190 (Javed Miandad 96 not out, Asif Din 5 for 100)
Warwickshire 280 (G. W. Humpage 78, T. A. Loyd 74)

Match drawn
Glamorgan 7 pts, Warwickshire 6 pts

Alvin Kallicharran. A splendid contribution to Warwickshire cricket. He remains a batsman of grace and charm.

at Worcester

Derbyshire 198 (A. E. Warner 4 for 73) and 247 for 8 dec (J. G. Wright 60, S. P. Perryman 5 for 97)
Worcestershire 194 (D. J. Humphries 52, P. J. Hacker 5 for 61) and 192 for 5

Match drawn
Worcestershire 5 pts, Derbyshire 5 pts

at Oxford

Oxford University 230 (R. G. P. Ellis 65, C. R. Trembath 5 for 91) and 217 (R. S. Cowan 60 not out, K. A. Hayes 52, D. Surridge 4 for 42)
Gloucestershire 411 for 5 dec (Zaheer Abbas 144, B. C. Broad 95, J. N. Shepherd 57 not out, S. P. Ridge 4 for 128) and 37 for 0

Gloucestershire won by 10 wickets

5 May

at Arundel

Indians 201 for 5 (Yashpal Sharma 66 not out, A. Malhotra 54)
Lavinia, Duchess of Norfolk's XI 202 for 0 (Sadiq Mohammad 107 not out, A. W. Stovold 90 not out)

Lavinia, Duchess of Norfolk's XI won by 10 wickets

THE ENGLISH SEASON/221

In very chilly conditions at Arundel the Indians began their tour and were trounced. Malhotra was impressive in his stroke play and Yashpal Sharma batted very well, but Sadiq and Andy Stovold won the game for the home side with one ball of the forty-five overs to spare.

The more serious business of the Schweppes County Championship got under way and Notts, the reigning champions, took only two days to beat a feeble looking Lancashire. There was some solid batting from Notts, but it was the pace attack of Hadlee, Cooper and Hendrick which looked to be the strength of the side and it was apparent that they would not relinquish their title easily.

In spite of losing a day's play, Surrey beat Kent at The Oval. Dilley reduced Surrey to 80 for 7 on the opening day, but Jack Richards and Sylvester Clarke hit them to 205. Some brisk runs and declarations on the last morning left Kent with 248 to make in 210 minutes. Woolmer hit 62 out of 79 in 24 overs for the first wicket, but Kent always had a little too much to do. They appeared to be cruising to victory, however, at 189 for 3. Then Clarke brought about a collapse and, although Dilley played some lusty blows, 7 wickets went down for 40 runs. Nineteen were needed off the last three overs, but Wilson had Jarvis caught behind with only two balls of the match remaining.

There were contrived declarations at Lord's where Fletcher made a patient century and Essex forfeited their second innings. Needing 348, Middlesex won with nearly 4 overs to spare. At 246 for 7, Middlesex looked beaten for Gatting's aggression had been ended. Williams and Emburey took Middlesex to victory with an unbeaten ninth wicket stand of 59. A splendid win, but Essex contributed to their own defeat with indifferent bowling, fielding and tactics.

Boycott hit his hundredth century in England, but Larkins responded by carrying his bat and Northants forced a dour draw. An unbeaten 96 in 96 minutes by Javed Miandad and a career best 5 for 100 by leg-spinner Asif Din were the highlights of the tame draw at Edgbaston.

The match at Taunton was evenly balanced, but Sussex, a team of abundant talent, were left to make 170 in 110 minutes on a doubtful wicket in dubious weather. They made a gallant effort through Mendis and Parker, but a defensive field saved the day for Somerset. Oxford could not be saved from the graceful power of Zaheer who led the Gloucestershire onslaught on their bowling. Broad and John Shepherd, in his first game for the county, also made useful contributions, but the main cause for Gloucestershire excitement was the bowling of Chris Trembath on his debut and of David Surridge, a pace bowler of rich but as yet unfulfilled promise, in the second innings. Hayes, Ellis and Cowan all batted well for Oxford.

Warner, Perryman and Hacker were all making first appearances for new counties at Worcester and all three gave impressive bowling performances. Wright batted courageously on a difficult wicket and both sides were content to settle for a draw.

Brian Davison hit 99 before lunch on the opening day at Southampton, but he got little support from the rest of the Leicestershire side who succumbed to Trevor Jesty. Tolchard, with 24, was next highest scorer to Davison's 172. Hampshire took a first innings lead and maximum batting points thanks to a fine hundred from Cowley who followed this up with his best ever bowling performance, 6 for 48.

Benson and Hedges Cup

8 May

at Bristol
Gloucestershire 187 (A. W. Stovold 59)
Glamorgan 183 (A. Jones 67)
Gloucestershire (2 pts) won by 4 runs
(Gold Award – J. H. Childs)

at Canterbury
Kent 217 for 9 (N. R. Taylor 61)
Hampshire 198 (J. M. Rice 66, C. G. Greenidge 56, G. R. Dilley 4 for 44)
Kent (2 pts) won by 19 runs
(Gold Award – N. R. Taylor)

at Old Trafford
Scotland 154 (O. Henry 59, C. E. H. Croft 6 for 10)
Lancashire 156 for 0 (D. Lloyd 76 not out, A. Kennedy 72 not out)
Lancashire (2 pts) won by 10 wickets
(Gold Award – C. E. H. Croft)

at Leicester
Derbyshire 232 for 6 (P. N. Kirsten 77 not out, J. G. Wright 60)
Leicestershire 233 for 5 (J. C. Balderstone 89 not out, M. A. Garnham 55)
Leicestershire (2 pts) won by 5 wickets
(Gold Award – M. A. Garnham)

at Northampton
Nottinghamshire 234 for 7 (J. D. Birch 69)
Northamptonshire 195 (A. J. Lamb 95, M. Hendrick 6 for 33)
Nottinghamshire (2 pts) won by 39 runs
(Gold Award – A. J. Lamb)

at Taunton
Combined Universities 147 (D. R. Pringle 68)
Somerset 150 for 2 (B. C. Rose 58)
Somerset (2 pts) won by 8 wickets
(Gold Award – D. J. S. Taylor)

at The Oval
Surrey 276 for 6 (G. S. Clinton 79, G. P. Howarth 51 not out)
Essex 191 for 8 (G. A. Gooch 66)
Surrey (2 pts) won by 85 runs
(Gold Award – M. A. Lynch)

at Leeds
Yorkshire 209 for 9 (K. Sharp 71, C. W. J. Athey 57)
Worcestershire 210 for 8 (G. B. Stevenson 5 for 50)
Worcestershire (2 pts) won by 2 wickets
(Gold Award – G. B. Stevenson)

The Benson and Hedges Cup got off to an uninterrupted start and all the matches were completed on the first day. Somerset, the holders, easily accounted for Combined Universities for whom only Pringle showed the necessary application. All else in this game was dominated by the performance of Derek Taylor who, in taking eight catches behind the stumps, set up a record for limited over cricket. In *Pelham Cricket Year First Edition* we wrote of Taylor as one of the two most consistent 'keepers in the country and nothing in the past three years has happened to change that assessment.

After a laborious opening stand of 33 in 16 overs Gloucestershire recovered to beat Glamorgan by four runs with four balls to spare. The Welshmen faded into frenzy after Alan Jones and John Hopkins gave them a fine start. John Childs' left-arm spin bemused the rest of the batsmen. Steve Barwick's 3 for 30 was his best in the competition. It could not compare with Colin Croft's best for Lancashire. His pace demoralised Scotland.

There was a competition best for Clinton at The Oval. Without Fletcher who was injured, Essex again bowled badly and batted indifferently, but Lynch's 45 off 30 balls towards the end of the Surrey innings was a vital factor in putting the score beyond the reach of the visitors.

There was a thrilling finish at Headingley. Kevin Sharp hit his first Benson & Hedges fifty and then fine bowling by Stevenson reduced Worcestershire to 187 for 8, but Gifford and Pridgeon added 23 to win the game for the visitors with an over to spare.

Some solid middle order batting gave Notts a substantial score at Northampton. Allan Lamb batted brilliantly for the home side, but no other batsman reached 20, and Northants, without Willey who had a broken thumb, were destroyed by Hendrick whose six wickets represented his best in the competition.

Balderstone provided the backbone for Leicestershire as they beat Derbyshire with an over to spare. The match was in the balance until Garnham made a brisk fifty.

Hampshire appeared to be beating Kent with ease when Greenidge and Rice gave them an opening stand of 74, but the innings fell apart before Jarvis and Dilley and Kent were surprised winners. Dilley's early season sharpness was encouraging.

Phil Neale, the new Worcestershire captain, did not play in the match at Headingley as he was in the Lincoln City side trying to win promotion from the Third Division. They won at Chester.

An English hope – fast bowler Paul Newman of Derbyshire.

John Player League

9 May

at Bristol
Middlesex 184 for 7 (C. T. Radley 107 not out)
Gloucestershire 164

Middlesex (4 pts) won by 20 runs

at Old Trafford
Glamorgan 148 (C. J. C. Rowe 54)
Lancashire 152 for 3 (C. H. Lloyd 64 not out)

Lancashire (4 pts) won by 7 wickets

at Leicester
Leicestershire 239 for 4 (D. I. Gower 100, B. F. Davison 53)
Derbyshire 172 (J. F. Steele 4 for 24)

Leicestershire (4 pts) won by 67 runs

at Northampton
Northamptonshire 196 for 6
Somerset 184 for 9

Northamptonshire (4 pts) won by 12 runs

at Trent Bridge
Hampshire 201 for 6 (T. E. Jesty 79)
Nottinghamshire 186 for 7

Hampshire (4 pts) won by 15 runs

at The Oval
Kent 235 for 7 (M. R. Benson 97)
Surrey 128 for 7 (G. R. J. Roope 51 not out)

Kent (4 pts) won by 107 runs

at Hove
Essex 115
Sussex 116 for 5

Sussex (4 pts) won by 5 wickets

at Huddersfield
Yorkshire 185 for 7 (D. L. Bairstow 55)
Worcestershire 188 for 8

Worcestershire (4 pts) won by 2 wickets

The Sunday League programme opened in sunshine. At Hove the champions, Essex, were put in to bat and then destroyed by the Sussex pace attack backed by some brilliant fielding and catching. But for some brave swipes from Turner and Pont, the Essex humiliation would have been great indeed. Essex bowled better than they batted, but the wicket had grown easier and Sussex had few doubts about victory.

A splendidly forceful innings by Benson settled the issue at The Oval. Surrey lost early wickets to Dilley, Jarvis and the improving Cowdrey and the game drifted away from the reach of the home side.

Middlesex appeared to be in much trouble at Bristol where they lost their first four wickets for 18 runs and were 51 for 6. Throughout these calamities, brought about by Shepherd and Surridge, Clive Radley stood firm and, finding an eager partner in Edmonds, then dominated the bowling in an innings of calm, grace and power almost out of context on a Sunday. Gloucestershire were 78 for 2 after 20 overs, but Sadiq and Shepherd then went quickly and thereafter, in spite of Graveney's bravery, they were struggling.

For the second day running Worcestershire snatched victory from Yorkshire in the closing stages of the match. Yorkshire had omitted Boycott from their side in order to give chances to some of the younger members of their staff. It was, however, the senior players, Old and Bairstow, who gave the Yorkshire innings substance with a fifth wicket stand of 72. Worcestershire were 111 for 6 in reply to Yorkshire's 185, but Neale and Inchmore added 39 and the visitors won with three balls to spare.

McFarlane and Simmons curtailed Glamorgan for whom Rowe hit fifty and Clive Lloyd steered Lancashire to an easy win. Leicestershire's successful start was maintained with a convincing win over Derbyshire. Gower hit a hundred and shared an opening stand of 140 with Briers. Davison again batted well and John Steele's naggingly accurate slow left-arm stifled Derby's hopes.

Somerset faltered at Northampton and Notts were overwhelmed by Hampshire for whom Jesty had a fine all-round game.

8, 9 and 10 May

at Edgbaston
Indians 243 (D. B. Vengsarkar 72, G. R. Viswanath 67) and 351 for 5 (S. M. Gavaskar 172, A. Malhotra 79, D. B. Vengsarkar 57 not out)
Warwickshire 447 for 7 dec (A. M. Ferreira 112 not out, Asif Din 91, T. A. Lloyd 87, R. G. D. Willis 72)

Match drawn

On the friendliest of batting pitches the Indians were dogged rather than fluent on the opening day, but Warwickshire batted into the last morning as Ferreira, Asif Din and Willis all recorded career bests. For Willis it was a maiden fifty in first-class cricket. Prospering after being missed, Gavaskar gave note that he has lost none of his strength, timing and class as he and Malhotra added 168 in 32 overs when the Indians batted again against some rather undemanding bowling.

12, 13 and 14 May

at Derby
Somerset 219 (I. T. Botham 63, S. Oldham 6 for 63) and 177
Derbyshire 291 (B. Wood 62, G. Miller 61, H. R. Moseley 4 for 40) and 108 for 1 (J. G. Wright 59 not out)

Derbyshire won by 9 wickets
Derbyshire 23 pts, Somerset 5 pts

at Bristol
Worcestershire 222 (P. A. Neale 61, D. Surridge 5 for 78) and 184 (Younis Ahmed 84, D. A. Graveney 7 for 37)
Gloucestershire 158 (J. D. Inchmore 7 for 53) and 237 (Zaheer Abbas 91, D. N. Patel 4 for 19, A. P. Pridgeon 4 for 56)

Worcestershire won by 11 runs
Worcestershire 18 pts, Gloucestershire 5 pts

at Dartford
Kent 300 for 7 dec (N. R. Taylor 143 not out, Asif Iqbal 55) and 297 for 5 dec (Asif Iqbal 115 not out, C. J. Tavare 66, R. A. Woolmer 55)
Warwickshire 255 for 8 dec (T. A. Lloyd 87, D. L. Underwood 5 for 63) and 327 for 9 (A. I. Kallicharran 105, G. W. Humpage 64, D. L. Amiss 54, D. L. Underwood 4 for 104)

Match drawn
Kent 7 pts, Warwickshire 6 pts

at Hove
Sussex 378 (Imran Khan 85, I. J. Gould 74, G. S. le Roux 69, G. D. Mendis 54, J. K. Lever 5 for 91) and 40 for 0
Essex 170 (K. W. R. Fletcher 64, G. A. Gooch 56, Imran Khan 4 for 40) and 244 (N. Phillip 56, A. C. S. Pigott 4 for 53)

Sussex won by 10 wickets
Sussex 24 pts, Essex 5 pts

Neil Taylor (Kent) a first century in the Schweppes County Championship, v Warwickshire at Dartford, was followed by two centuries in the Benson and Hedges Cup. An opening batsman of rich promise.

Early season form revealed a vastly improved and more mature player – Chris Cowdrey of Kent.

at Leeds
Yorkshire 380 for 7 dec (G. Boycott 134, C. W. J. Athey 77, J. D. Love 65) and 248 for 5 dec (C. W. J. Athey 100, R. G. Lumb 67, R. C. Ontong 4 for 80)
Glamorgan 322 for 9 dec (J. A. Hopkins 80, R. C. Ontong 75, Javed Miandad 50, A. Sidebottom 4 for 83) and 112 for 2 (J. A. Hopkins 64 not out)

Match drawn
Yorkshire 7 pts, Glamorgan 6 pts

at Trent Bridge
Nottinghamshire 141 (Kapil Dev 5 for 39) and 251 for 4 dec (R. T. Robinson 52, D. W. Randall 51)
Indians 259 (P. Roy 51, K. Saxelby 4 for 47, M. K. Bore 4 for 52) and 97 for 6

Match drawn

at Leicester
Surrey 358 (G. S. Clinton 102, D. M. Smith 89, C. J. Richards 61) and 260 for 5 dec (A. R. Butcher 151 not out)
Leicestershire 351 (D. I. Gower 99, J. C. Balderstone 94, S. T. Clarke 4 for 101) and 292 for 5 (B. F. Davison 111, D. I. Gower 61, M. A. Garnham 55)

Leicestershire won by 5 wickets
Leicestershire 24 pts, Surrey 7 pts

at Lord's
Middlesex 379 for 5 dec (J. M. Brearley 165, J. E. Emburey 100 not out, B. J. Griffiths 5 for 105) and 67 for 1
Northamptonshire 220 (A. J. Lamb 55, D. S. Steele 52) and 225 (D. S. Steele 66)

Middlesex won by 9 wickets
Middlesex 24 pts, Northamptonshire 4 pts

at Cambridge
Lancashire 304 (D. P. Hughes 106, D. Lloyd 54) and 128 (D. R. Pringle 6 for 33)
Cambridge University 274 (J. P. C. Mills 73, K. I. Hodgson 50, D. P. Hughes 4 for 28, I. Folley 4 for 40) and 159 for 3 (D. R. Pringle 61 not out)

Cambridge University won by 7 wickets

Derek Pringle. His all-round performances for Cambridge University caught the eye of the England selectors.
Opposite: Mark Nicholas. He matured into a fine batsman. A vital component in the Hampshire revival.

at Oxford
Hampshire 370 for 4 dec (M. C. J. Nichols 206 not out, C. L. Smith 71)
Oxford University 169 (J. G. Varey 68, S. J. Malone 7 for 55) and 139 (S. J. Malone 5 for 55)

Hampshire won by an innings and 62 runs

The triumph of Sussex continued and with it the discomfiture of Essex. Splendidly aggressive batting throughout the innings compensated for the loss of Barclay who retired hurt when struck in the face by a ball from Foster. Imran and le Roux were particularly sparkling. Imran destroyed the Essex first innings. In a welter of extravagant strokes Essex went from 131 for 2 to 170 all out and lost the first four wickets of their second innings to Pigott. A career best of 36 not out from David East delayed the Sussex triumph only a little on the last morning.

Gloucestershire were as profligate as Essex. They dismissed Worcestershire for 222 with David Surridge returning a career best, but John Inchmore tilted the game Worcestershire's way with a sustained spell of seam bowling that brought him seven wickets. David Graveney snatched the initiative back with some spin bowling of the highest class and Gloucestershire, needing 249 to win, were 171 for 4 with Zaheer in command and the match seemingly theirs. Sadly they collapsed to Pridgeon and Patel and Worcestershire won a narrow and exciting victory.

There was no such closeness at Lord's where Middlesex, unwisely put in to bat by Cook, dominated from start to finish. Griffiths alone was at his best for Northants who fielded badly. Brearley batted for five hours and came within 8 runs of his best score in England. John Emburey hit his maiden century and obviously enjoyed it and then the all-round quality of the Middlesex attack twice proved too good for Northants.

Somerset faltered badly at Derby where Steve Oldham returned the best figures of his career. Geoff Miller and Barry Wood edged Derbyshire into a first innings lead and Somerset failed again so that the home side ran out convincing winners. The Maltese born slow left-arm bowler from Scotland, Gordon Moir had 3 for 60 in the Somerset second innings.

Geoff Boycott hit his second century in successive matches and Bill Athey played two fine innings, but after a courageous knock by John Hopkins who returned from hospital to keep Yorkshire at bay, the match always looked to be heading for a draw. Glamorgan were in no way bettered by the Yorkshiremen.

A fine game at Grace Road ended in a spectacular Leicestershire victory by five wickets with four overs and one ball to spare. On a beautiful wicket both sides prospered. Clinton and Butcher hit centuries and Balderstone and Gower, who was run out at 99, also batted with authority. Surrey led by 27 on the first innings and, ultimately, they set Leicestershire 288 to win in five minutes under 3 hours. Gower and Davison added 114 in 70 minutes for the third wicket and Garnham also helped Davison in the plunder. They took 67 off the first five overs bowled in the final hour and Davison's 111 was made off 94 balls. Roberts completed a memorable victory with two straight sixes into the pavilion off Pocock.

There was an exciting finish of a different nature at Dartford where Warwickshire, having been set 343 to win, finished on 327 for 9. Kallicharran and Humpage had made victory seem possible, but Underwood ended their dreams as he had done in the first innings. There were two fine knocks by the Kent skipper, Asif Iqbal, but Kentish honours went to Neil Taylor who hit his highest score and his first championship hundred. The exciting Benson had an experience of a different kind as he bagged his first *pair*. Kent looked a more efficient and organised side than they had done for two or three years.

Oxford's confidence appeared to have evaporated. Mark Nicholas hit the first double century of his career in a stunning display on the first day and then Steve Malone routed the University twice with his pace. His match figures, 12 for 110, and his first innings bowling, 7 for 55, were both career bests and he made his point for a regular place in the Hampshire side in most emphatic fashion.

Whilst Oxford were once more licking their wounds, Cambridge were celebrating their first win over a county side for eleven years. All else in the match was dwarfed by the all-round performance of Derek Pringle who had career best bowling figures as he destroyed some feeble Lancashire resistance in the second innings.

Bowlers were mostly on top at Trent Bridge where a weakened Notts side fought back to draw with the Indians in a not very satisfactory match. It ended in farce when, chasing 134 in 19 overs, the Indians showed an urgency which none had shown earlier in the match. Kapil Dev displayed his prowess with bat and ball, and once more there was much to admire in the bowling of Mike Bore.

Benson and Hedges Cup

15 May

at Derby
Minor Counties 201
Derbyshire 202 for 2 (G. Miller 88 not out, P. N. Kirsten 58)

Derbyshire (2 pts) won by 8 wickets
(Gold Award – G. Miller)

at Chelmsford
Essex 178 (K. S. McEwan 55 not out, D. L. Underwood 4 for 24)
Kent 180 for 5 (R. A. Woolmer 55)

Kent (2 pts) won by 5 wickets
(Gold Award – D. L. Underwood)

at Bournemouth
Sussex 248 for 9 (P. W. G. Parker 77)
Hampshire 129

Sussex (2 pts) won by 119 runs
(Gold Award – P. W. G. Parker)

at Lord's
Somerset 98
Middlesex 99 for 4

Middlesex (2 pts) won by 6 wickets
(Gold Award – N. F. Williams)

at Trent Bridge
Nottinghamshire 244 for 7 (B. S. Hassan 99 not out, R. J. Hadlee 70)
Warwickshire 205 (G. W. Humpage 62, Asif Din 61)

Nottinghamshire (2 pts) won by 39 runs
(Gold Award – S. B. Hassan)

at Worcester
Leicestershire 278 for 3 (J. C. Balderstone 100, B. F. Davison 69 not out)
Worcestershire 272 for 8 (D. N. Patel 90, J. A. Ormrod 87, L. B. Taylor 6 for 35)

Leicestershire (2 pts) won by 6 runs
(Gold Award – J. C. Balderstone)

at Glasgow
Northamptonshire 259 for 5 (W. Larkins 126, A. J. Lamb 81)
Scotland 82 (Sarfraz Nawaz 4 for 21)

Northamptonshire (2 pts) won by 177 runs
(Gold Award – W. Larkins)

at Oxford
Gloucestershire 300 for 4 (A. W. Stovold 123, B. C. Broad 53)
Combined Universities 216 for 8 (D. R. Pringle 64)

Gloucestershire (2 pts) won by 84 runs
(Gold Award – A. W. Stovold)

Stuart Turner. In the midst of Essex's disastrous start to the season his defiantly aggressive batting reached heights of heroic grandeur. (Here he is batting v Kent, Benson & Hedges Cup. Knott is behind the stumps.)

The second round of matches in the Benson and Hedges Cup are always vital for those left pointless after two matches have only the faintest hopes of survival in the competition.

At Chelmsford, Essex suffered their fifth defeat in five matches. Their batting was dreadful. Wasteful and profligate strokes encouraged Derek Underwood to his first individual award and he was supported by some fine fielding, especially from the greatly improved Cowdrey. The Essex bowling and fielding were far superior to their inept batting and they made Kent fight hard, but a steady fifty from Woolmer was supported by some fine strokes from the exciting Benson and a decisive piece of aggression from Knott.

Minor Counties scored quite well, but far too few to trouble Derbyshire who won with more than sixteen overs to spare, and Combined Universities died bravely after Andy Stovold and Chris Broad had put on 154 for the first Gloucestershire wicket. In Glasgow Wayne Larkins hit a hundred in 128 minutes with thirteen fours after which a boxing referee would have stopped the contest to save the Scots from further punishment.

Chris Balderstone's hundred was the foundation of the Leicestershire innings, but they seemed about to suffer their first defeat of the season when Ormrod and Patel added 160 for the second Worcestershire wicket, but, in the gathering gloom, the pace of Taylor proved decisive and Leicestershire, with a little good fortune, were narrow winners for the second week running.

Notts, through Hassan and Hadlee, who added 125, recovered from 30 for 4 to reach a total too big for Warwickshire in spite of a brave effort by Humpage and Asif Din.

Sussex also recovered after losing Barclay and Wells for 13. It was Paul Parker who was most instrumental in bringing about the recovery and the power and elegance of his shots left one wondering again why this man is not batting regularly for England. Hampshire surrendered tamely to the all-round power of the Sussex attack. Barclay had three wickets with his off-spin.

Somerset crumpled alarmingly at Lord's and new Middlesex pace bowler Neil Williams had Viv Richards as one of his three victims, a bowling feat which won him the Gold Award. Middlesex made heavy weather of getting the runs, but they still preserved their one hundred per cent record with plenty of overs and wickets to spare. Somerset were out in 39.3 overs and Middlesex made the runs in 37.4 overs. The decline of Somerset, as with the decline of Essex, was hard to understand.

Asif Iqbal, bowled Stuart Turner 1 Essex v Kent, Chelmsford, Benson and Hedges Cup, May. Asif walks away as Turner and David East celebrate. Alan Lilley joins them.

John Player League

16 May

at Derby
Essex 160 for 9 (B. Wood 4 for 8)
Derbyshire 161 for 6 (P. N. Kirsten 72)
Derbyshire (4 pts) won by 4 wickets

at Bournemouth
Hampshire 185 for 7
Middlesex 186 for 6 (C. T. Radley 60 not out)
Middlesex (4 pts) won by 4 wickets

at Canterbury
Glamorgan 205 for 6 (R. C. Ontong 84, Javed Miandad 70)
Kent 206 for 3 (C. J. Tavare 103 not out, Asif Iqbal 56 not out)
Kent (4 pts) won by 7 wickets

at Old Trafford
Lancashire 216 for 4 (C. H. Lloyd 72, A. Kennedy 54, I. Cockbain 53 not out)
Gloucestershire 110 for 8
Lancashire (4 pts) won by 116 runs

at Leicester
Leicestershire 169 for 9 (S. Stuchbury 5 for 16)
Yorkshire 168 for 8 (C. W. J. Athey 54, P. B. Clift 4 for 35)
Leicestershire (4 pts) won by 1 run

at Trent Bridge
Nottinghamshire 118
Worcestershire 122 for 4 (G. M. Turner 50)
Worcestershire (4 pts) won by 6 wickets

at Hove
Sussex 153
Somerset 134 for 9
Sussex (4 pts) won by 19 runs

at Edgbaston
Surrey 229 for 7 (G. S. Clinton 63)
Warwickshire 141
Surrey (4 pts) won by 88 runs

The Essex misery continued. The nagging accuracy of Barry Wood reduced them to 95 for 8, having been 94 for 4, but David East, with his highest John Player League score, and John Lever took them to a brave and creditable 160. Kirsten was at his best, however, and against some wayward Essex bowling, Lever being particularly inaccurate, he steered Derbyshire close to victory. There was a stumble as three wickets went down for one run, but the home side won easily enough with seven balls to spare.

A rather uninspiring game at Bournemouth saw Clive Radley nudge Middlesex to victory with ten balls to spare, but at Canterbury there was far more exhilarating stuff. Rodney Ontong and Javed Miandad had a third wicket stand of 154 in 26 overs after Asif had put Glamorgan in. Ontong's score was his best in the competition and both he and Javed fell to fine catches in the deep, by Cowdrey and Potter respectively. Glamorgan had a right to feel encouraged by their batting and by the bowling of Nash who dismissed Taylor at 1. Kent were 82 for 3 and then Tavare and Asif Iqbal added the 124 needed for victory in 16 overs so that the home side won with five overs to spare. Tavare's hundred came in 100 minutes and included a six and seven fours. Any who have only seen this courteous and charming man bat in a Test match have been denied one of the joys of cricket.

Lancashire's one-day power continued when they severely mauled Gloucestershire. Kennedy and Clive Lloyd began the afternoon with a stand of 102. There was another good opening stand at Trent Bridge where Turner and Ormrod started with 88. Notts declined into obscurity and one feels that they have no real appetite for the Sunday game.

Surrey, for whom Clinton again hit with force and correctness to reach his half century in 77 minutes, overwhelmed Warwickshire who never recovered from losing Amiss for 1.

At Hove, Sussex, bubbling with confidence and ability, were put in by Somerset and were in disarray at 70 for 6. Phillipson, le Roux and Barclay lifted them to 153, but this hardly seemed a winning total. Imran and le Roux gave them a fierce start in the field, however, when they sent back Denning and Richards, out of sorts with himself and all around him, for 8. Popplewell and Taylor played well, but Barclay caught and bowled Botham for nought and Sussex snatched a remarkable victory by 19 runs.

There was an even closer contest at Leicester where, led by Gower's 45, the home side made 169. Yorkshire reached the last over needing eight to win with three wickets standing. Three runs came off the first ball and then Bairstow was yorked by Clift, who took four wickets. The last three balls produced only three singles and Leicestershire had maintained their winning start with a one-run victory. The most remarkable performance of the day came from the Yorkshire left-arm seam bowler Steve Stuchbury who took five for 16 in his eight overs, a performance which should have given his side victory.

15, 17, and 18 May

at Bradford
Indians 376 for 5 dec (G. A. M. H. Parkar 146, S. M. Gavaskar 79) and 171 for 5 dec
Yorkshire 260 for 3 dec (K. Sharp 115, C. W. J. Athey 61 not out, R. G. Lumb 57) and 35 for 0
Match drawn

Bad light and rain brought this match to an early close, but a result hardly seemed likely. Parkar emphasised his claim for the position of Gavaskar's opening partner, but the main interest lay in the fine hundred by Kevin Sharp, a young player whom the gods of cricket have not treated kindly, but one for whom there is still time to realise his abundant talent. Athey, another forgotten man, also batted commendably, but once more the tourists' match had little to give as a contest.

Yorkshire rested their three players with South African connections.

19, 20 and 21 May

at Cardiff
Leicestershire 327 (R. W. Tolchard 93 not out, M. A. Garnham 53)
Glamorgan 134 (A. M. E. Roberts 5 for 27) and 184 (Javed Miandad 51, L. B. Taylor 4 for 31)
Leicestershire won by an innings and 9 runs
Leicestershire 23 pts, Glamorgan 3 pts

at Old Trafford
Derbyshire 216 (J. H. Hampshire 54, A. Hill 54, C. E. H. Croft 7 for 88) and 242 for 5 (P. N. Kirsten 81)
Lancashire 287 (D. Lloyd 114, C. H. Lloyd 73, P. J. Hacker 5 for 51)
Match drawn
Lancashire 7 pts, Derbyshire 6 pts

at Northampton
Surrey 272 (G. R. J. Roope 108, D. M. Smith 74) and 171 (R. D. V. Knight 65, Sarfraz Nawaz 4 for 33)
Northamptonshire 133 (R. D. Jackman 5 for 39, S. T. Clarke 5 for 58) and 215 (A. J. Lamb 63, S. T. Clarke 5 for 51)
Surrey won by 95 runs
Surrey 23 pts, Northamptonshire 4 pts

at Trent Bridge
Nottinghamshire 180 (S. J. Malone 4 for 53) and 218 for 5 dec (B. N. French 65 not out)
Hampshire 70 (R. J. Hadlee 7 for 25) and 56 (M. Hendrick 5 for 21, K. Saxelby 4 for 18)
Nottinghamshire won by 272 runs
Nottinghamshire 21 pts, Hampshire 4 pts

at Hastings
Gloucestershire 98 (Imran Khan 4 for 26) and 222 (A. W. Stovold 54)
Sussex 218 (C. M. Wells 88, J. N. Shepherd 6 for 75, D. Surridge 4 for 74) and 104 for 3

Sussex won by 7 wickets
Sussex 22 pts, Gloucestershire 4 pts

at Edgbaston
Warwickshire 158 and 166 (D. L. Amiss 75, C. M. Old 6 for 76)
Yorkshire 292 (G. B. Stevenson 115 not out, G. Boycott 79, G. C. Small 7 for 68) and 33 for 1

Yorkshire won by 9 wickets
Yorkshire 23 pts, Warwickshire 5 pts

at Worcester
Worcestershire 199 (D. J. Humphries 69 not out, J. W. Lloyds 6 for 62) and 198
Somerset 298 (P. W. Denning 71, D. J. S. Taylor 67, P. M. Roebuck 50, D. N. Patel 4 for 82) and 101 for 5 (A. P. Pridgeon 4 for 39)

Somerset won by 5 wickets
Somerset 21 pts, Worcestershire 4 pts

at Lord's
M.C.C. 319 for 4 dec (D. W. Randall 130 not out, C. J. Tavare 99, D. I. Gower 55) and 126 for 2 dec (C. J. Tavare 75 not out)
Indians 180 (D. B. Vengsarkar 96, G. R. Dilley 5 for 69) and 143 for 4 (G. A. M. H. Parkar 92)

Match drawn

at Cambridge
Cambridge University 99 (N. Phillip 5 for 41) and 258 (R. J. Boyd-Moss 81, W. E. J. Barrington 59, S. P. Henderson 52, N. Phillip 6 for 50)
Essex 399 (D. E. East 78, R. E. East 58, K. S. McEwan 51, A. J. Pollock 5 for 108)

Essex won by an innings and 42 runs

a

a

ABOVE
a *Warwickshire v Yorkshire, 20 May 1982. Geoff Boycott first in, last out, determination written on his face as he joins Stevenson in Yorkshire's record last wicket stand.*
b *The end of the stand. The last wicket has added 149.*
c *Graham Stevenson, a century at number eleven. Humpage is keeping wicket. Amiss is in the gully.*

BELOW
a *Boycott congratulates Stevenson on reaching his century.*
b *Stevenson waves his bat in acknowledgement of the crowd's applause as he reaches his hundred.*
c *Boycott is bowled by Asif Din and the heroes leave the field.*

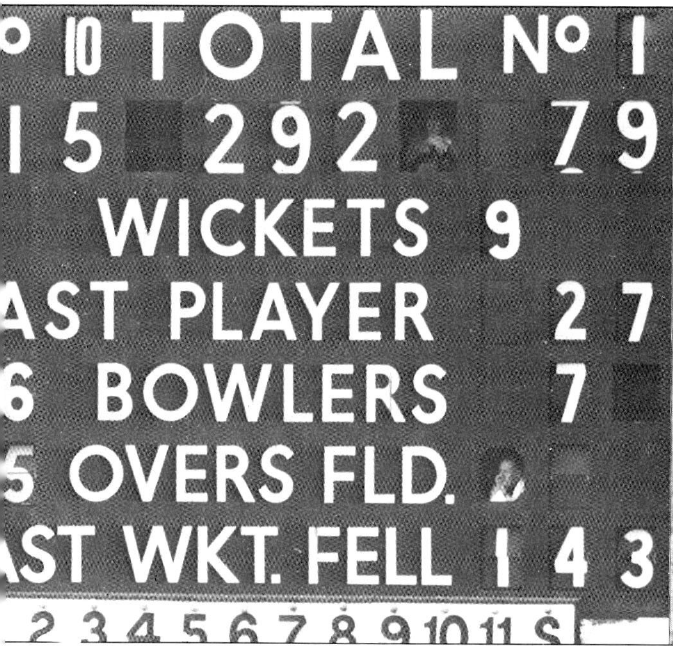
10 TOTAL Nº 1
15 292 79
WICKETS 9
AST PLAYER 27
6 BOWLERS 7
5 OVERS FLD.
AST WKT. FELL 143
2 3 4 5 6 7 8 9 10 11 S

c
c

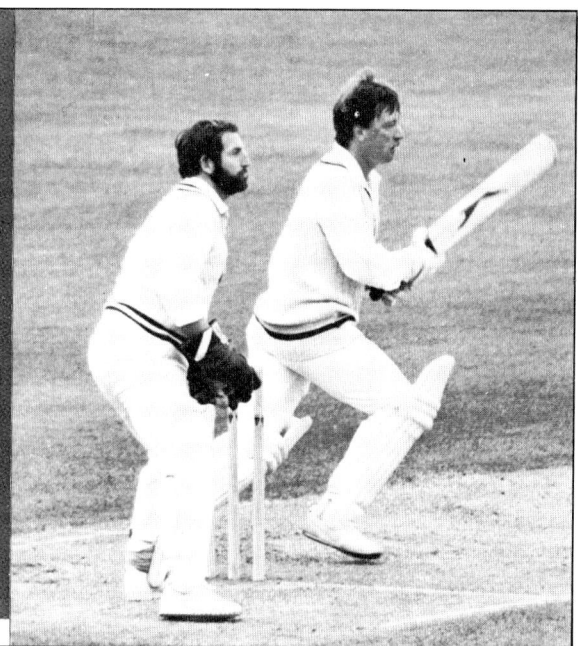

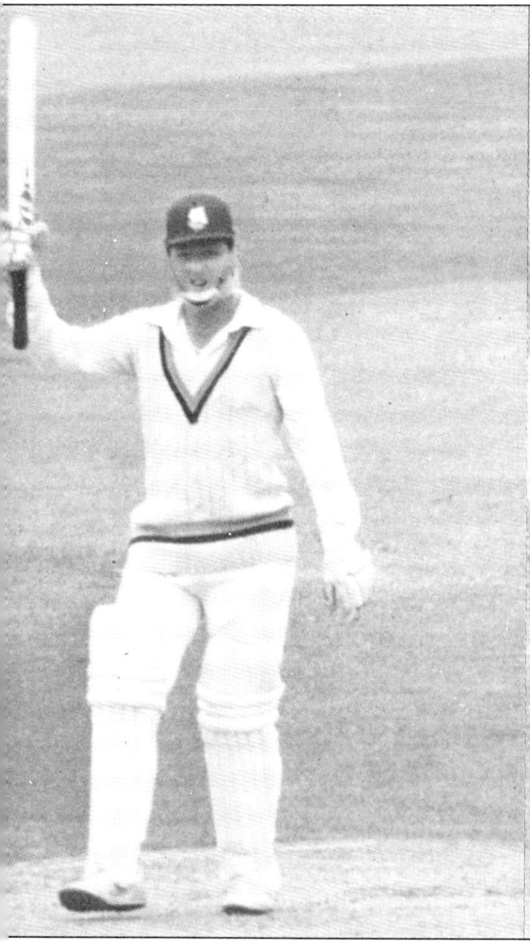

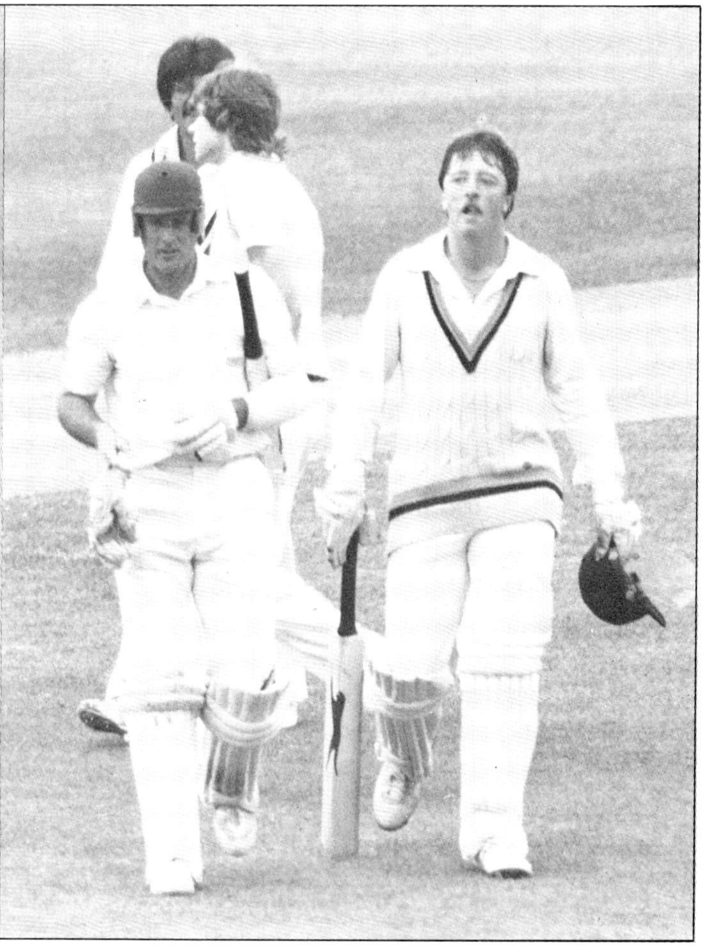

at Oxford
Oxford University 228 and 143 (R. J. Maru 4 for 30, N. F. Williams 4 for 38)
Middlesex 478 for 5 dec (W. N. Slack 203 not out, K. P. Tomlins 146)

Middlesex won by an innings and 107 runs

David Gower led the M.C.C. side against the Indians and showed a most positive attitude to captaincy. Madan Lal was the only Indian bowler to give the M.C.C. batsmen any problems, but Tavare, Randall and Gower himself all batted with aggression and authority. Randall's century assured him of a recall to the England side and he and Tavare added 166 in 155 minutes of exciting batting for the second wicket. Vengsarkar saved India from humiliation after both Dilley and Pringle had bowled well. Parkar emphasised his claim to be Gavaskar's opening partner with some good shots in the second innings as the game petered to a draw. The most interesting selection in the M.C.C. side was that of Derek Pringle who had begun the season well as captain of Cambridge University. He took 3 for 53 in the first innings and was obviously on the selectors' long list for Australia, but his performances with Essex had been far from satisfactory and one feels that a sterner sense of application at county level is needed before he can be a serious candidate at Test level. At the conclusion of the M.C.C. match with the Indians, Bob Willis was named as England skipper for the forthcoming series, a surprising and obviously short term selection although one can have nothing but admiration for the man. There was some sympathy for Fletcher who, it was felt, had been hastily and impolitely discarded.

Leicestershire's success continued with a trouncing of Glamorgan at Cardiff. At Old Trafford Colin Croft destroyed the later Derbyshire batting, the last six wickets falling for 51 runs. He was well supported by Ian Folley who had made an impressive debut at Cambridge. David Lloyd and Clive Lloyd combined to give Lancashire promise of a big lead, but Hacker cut short their aspirations and rain on the last afternoon condemned the match to a draw.

There were fiery happenings at Trent Bridge where Hampshire asked Notts to bat and Marshall and Malone shot them out for 180. Hampshire fared even worse. With the ball leaping menacingly, Greenidge was forced to retire with a cut eye and Richard Hadlee tore the heart out of the innings. Paul Todd bagged his second pair of the season and his third first ball dismissal in six innings in which he had registered 4 and five ducks. French, however, batted with surprising confidence and a demoralised Hampshire side were bowled out for 56, the lowest score of the season.

Surrey, struggling at 55 for 4, were rescued by Roope and Smith who added 152 in 99 minutes. Roope reached the twenty-sixth hundred of his career and Clarke and Jackman then bowled Surrey into a strong position so that they took a grip on the game which they never relinquished.

The all-round power of Sussex was demonstrated once more when they beat Gloucestershire with ease at Hastings. The visitors were routed by the Sussex pace attack on the opening morning and although Sussex batsmen did not find the pitch easy when confronted by Shepherd and Surridge, who continued to impress, Wells batted with an assurance that he had been unable to find the previous summer.

Somerset ended their run of poor form with a comfortable win at Worcester. Jeremy Lloyds, in the Somerset side because Marks had been called to Lord's to replace the injured Edmonds in the M.C.C. team, took 6 for 62 on the opening day, one run more than the career best he had achieved with his off-breaks two years earlier. The second day was marked by some fine left-arm slow bowling from eighteen-year old Richard Illingworth who dismissed Roebuck, Rose and Botham, an impressive first three victims in first-class cricket. Somerset gained a good lead, however, and when Worcestershire faltered a second time to Lloyd and Richards they needed only 100 to win. They had alarms when Pridgeon took four wickets in seven overs, but won with 22 balls to spare.

Essex gained their first win of the season when David East hit a career best at Cambridge. Phillip and Turner were too much for the undergraduates for whom Pollock bowled with distinction. At Oxford, Wilf Slack hit a violent double century and Keith Tomlins a maiden hundred. In five years it was only Tomlins' thirty-third first-class match.

The most sensational happenings were at Edgbaston. Old asked Warwickshire to bat and had a hand in dismissing them for 158, but Yorkshire finished the day in gloom at 91 for 7, Boycott unbeaten on 38. Old hit strongly, but when Stevenson came in at number eleven the score was 143. In 140 minutes Stevenson and Boycott added 149 for the last wicket before Boycott was bowled by Asif Din. Stevenson's 115 was only the third century recorded by a number eleven in the county championship, and only the eighth ever recorded by a number eleven in the first-class game. The stand of 149 beat the Yorkshire record for the tenth wicket which had stood for eighty-four years and was previously held by Lord Hawke and David Hunter. Amid the Yorkshire rejoicing it was almost forgotten that Gladstone Small had returned a career best 7 for 68. A stunned Warwickshire succumbed to Old and Yorkshire had an easy win.

Benson and Hedges Cup

22 May

at Chelmsford
Hampshire 130 (J. K. Lever 4 for 19)
Essex 131 for 9 (S. Turner 55 not out, K. St J. Emery 5 for 24)

Essex (2 pts) won by 1 wicket
(Gold Award – S. Turner)

at Cardiff
Glamorgan 232 for 5 (J. A. Hopkins 70)
Combined Universities 86 (B. J. Lloyd 4 for 26)

(Gold Award – J. A. Hopkins)

at Leicester
Yorkshire 207 for 9 (G. Boycott 82)
Leicestershire 210 for 4 (J. C. Balderstone 50)

Leicestershire (2 pts) won by 6 wickets
(Gold Award – G. Boycott)

at Northampton
Northamptonshire 102 (A. J. Lamb 63, B. W. Reidy 4 for 27)
Lancashire 105 for 2

Lancashire (2 pts) won by 8 wickets
(Gold Award – B. W. Reidy)

at Edgbaston
Scotland 166 (A. M. Ferreira 4 for 42)
Warwickshire 167 for 1 (D. L. Amiss 105 not out)

Warwickshire (2 pts) won by 9 wickets
(Gold Award – D. L. Amiss)

at Wellington
Worcestershire 226 (G. M. Turner 79, D. Nicholls 6 for 43)
Minor Counties 129 (S. P. Perryman 4 for 28)

Worcestershire (2 pts) won by 97 runs
(Gold Award – D. Nicholls)

22 and 24 May

at Bristol
Gloucestershire 226 for 3 (A. W. Stovold 65, Sadiq Mohammad 62, A. J. Hignell 56 not out)
Middlesex 229 for 6 (J. M. Brearley 70)

Middlesex (2 pts) won by 4 wickets
(Gold Award – J. M. Brearley)

at The Oval
Surrey 231 (A. R. Butcher 80, R. D. V. Knight 57)
Sussex 235 for 7 (C. P. Phillipson 66 not out, I. J. Gould 56)

Sussex (2 pts) won by 3 wickets
(Gold Award – I. J. Gould)

Roger Knight. His coverage and determination as Surrey's captain earned him a late call to the England party for the Prudential Trophy.

Having dismissed Hampshire for 130, at 3.30 on Saturday afternoon, Essex stood at 14 for 6. Young Bob Parks, a delightful man and a wicket-keeper of outstanding talent, had equalled the Hampshire Benson and Hedges record with four catches, and Emery, with impressive quick bowling, had taken four of the six wickets. Essex stood on the verge of another defeat. Turner joined Pont and they added 38 before Pont was bowled by Tremlett. David East who in one week had scored his highest score in the John Player League and in first-class cricket, now hit his highest Benson and Hedges score as he and Turner added 71 for the eighth wicket. Ray East was out with the score at 126, but John Lever scored four of the five needed for victory and Essex had won a remarkable victory. Stuart Turner's innings, one of the bravest ever seen in the tournament, won him his second Gold Award and gave to Essex supporters a sense of pride and of hope that something might yet be salvaged from the season.

There was no such close encounter at Cardiff where Tony Cordle made a surprise reappearance for Glamorgan. He celebrated by removing both the Universities' openers for 1. With Eifion Jones injured, Terry Davies kept wicket for Glamorgan in a competitive match for the first time. He celebrated with four catches. The Universities had nothing to celebrate and crept from the tournament.

The all-round batting strength of Leicestershire was too much for Yorkshire and so they qualified for the quarter-finals. In spite of a splendid bowling performance by Nicholls, Minor Counties succumbed to Worcestershire whose batting lacked conviction.

Warwickshire overwhelmed Scotland, Amiss reaching his century in 38 overs. Lancashire needed only 36.1 overs to beat Northamptonshire for whom nothing was going well. Only Allan Lamb was finding consistent form with the bat where Williams, Willey, Cook and Yardley were all out of touch. It should be said, however, that to the surprise of many, Lancashire were looking a useful one-day side.

Rain at Bristol and The Oval meant that the games there were carried over until the Monday. Middlesex paced things perfectly with Embury and Edmonds supporting Brearley well with the bat. Brearley's form was better than any other opener in the country.

Chasing Surrey's total of 231, Sussex finished Saturday evening at 106 for 6 from 34 overs and seemingly facing defeat. Gould and Phillipson who had added 39 on the Saturday added another 53 on Monday morning and Sussex smelt victory. Phillipson achieved it with 10 balls remaining. The deciding over was Pocock's last when le Roux hit him for two sixes and a four. Eighteen in all came from the over and Sussex had no further worries.

One of the fiercest opening attacks in the world. Garth le Roux of Sussex and (right) Imran Khan.

22, 23 and 24 May

at Canterbury

Kent 302 for 7 dec (L. Potter 96, N. R. Taylor 62) and 248 for 4 dec (L. Potter 118)
Indians 282 for 3 dec (A. Malhotra 154 not out, Yashpal Sharma 77) and 68 for 3

Match drawn

With Woolmer, Knott and Underwood out of the Kent side because of their South African connection, many Kent members refused to attend this match as a protest against other countries dictating the composition of English county sides and the England Test team. They missed a fine opening stand of 101 by Potter and Taylor on the first day and some sparkling batting from Malhotra and Yashpal Sharma in a fourth wicket stand of 198 in just over three hours. It was the most impressive Indian batting of the tour. The third day belonged entirely to Laurie Potter who followed up his 96 in the first innings with a maiden century. His hundred came off 130 balls and of the opening stand of 124 Taylor made only 18. It was stirring stuff from Potter, a naturally aggressive batsman, certain in his approach and still six months to go before his twentieth birthday.

John Player League

23 May

at Chelmsford

Hampshire 144 for 7 (C. G. Greenidge 64)
Essex 52 for 5

Hampshire (4 pts) won on faster scoring rate

at Cardiff

Leicestershire 88 for 3
v. **Glamorgan**. Match abandoned.

Leicestershire 2 pts, Glamorgan 2 pts

at Bristol

Worcestershire 202 for 6 (G. M. Turner 73)
Gloucestershire 128 for 5 (B. C. Broad 54)

Gloucestershire (4 pts) won on faster scoring rate

at Lord's

Nottinghamshire 112 for 1 (C. E. B. Rice 58 not out)
Middlesex 32 for 5. Match abandoned.

Middlesex 2 pts, Nottinghamshire 2 pts

at Bedford

Lancashire 56 for 2
v. **Northamptonshire**. Match abandoned.

Lancashire 2 pts, Northamptonshire 2 pts

at Taunton

Somerset 235 for 6 (I. T. Botham 105)
Derbyshire 236 for 3 (J. H. Hampshire 91 not out, G. Miller 81)

Derbyshire (4 pts) won by 7 wickets

at Bradford

Yorkshire 193 for 9
Warwickshire 194 for 4 (D. L. Amiss 60)

Warwickshire (4 pts) won by 6 wickets

For the first time in the season rain caused the abandonment of some matches and delays in most. Leicestershire, Lancashire and Middlesex all lost their hundred per cent records because of the weather although Middlesex were scoring at a frantic 6.4 runs an over at Lord's when the rains came.

Essex got their arithmetic and all else wrong at Chelmsford and gave a miserable performance in losing to Hampshire for whom Greenidge batted splendidly and Parks again impressed with his wicket keeping. At Bradford Warwickshire brushed aside Yorkshire to win their first Sunday League game of the season with twenty balls and six wickets to spare.

Glenn Turner became the first batsman to reach 6,000 runs in Sunday League cricket and he and Ormrod put on 102 for the first wicket, but Gloucestershire's target was reduced to 128 in 24 overs by the weather and they reached it with five balls to spare.

Botham hit a hundred off 77 balls with six sixes and twelve fours, but Derbyshire's confidence was such that Wright and Hampshire began with 53 in 13 overs and then Hampshire and the rejuvenated Miller hit 118 in 16 overs. Miller's 81 came in 52 minutes and included two sixes and nine fours. Hampshire hit nine fours and Derbyshire won with 9 balls remaining.

238/BENSON & HEDGES CRICKET YEAR

Benson and Hedges Cup

25 May

at Swansea
Somerset 174 for 6 (P. M. Roebuck 50)
Glamorgan 162 (C. J. C. Rowe 54)
Somerset (2 pts) won by 12 runs
(Gold Award – I. T. Botham)

at Canterbury
Surrey 217 (C. Penn 4 for 34)
Kent 220 for 9 (C. S. Cowdrey 66, M. R. Benson 65)
Kent (2 pts) won by 1 wicket
(Gold Award – C. S. Cowdrey)

at Old Trafford
Lancashire 239 for 8 (A. Kennedy 79, C. H. Lloyd 60)
Warwickshire 201 (K. D. Smith 83, I. Folley 4 for 34)
Lancashire (2 pts) won by 38 runs
(Gold Award – A. Kennedy)

at Hove
Essex 327 for 2 (G. A. Gooch 198 not out, K. W. R. Fletcher 101 not out)
Sussex 213
Essex (2 pts) won by 114 runs
(Gold Award – G. A. Gooch)

at Worcester
Derbyshire 284 for 6 (B. Wood 106, P. N. Kirsten 53)
Worcestershire 278 for 9 (G. M. Turner 78, P. G. Newman 4 for 48)
Derbyshire (2 pts) won by 6 runs
(Gold Award – B. Wood)

at Glasgow
Nottinghamshire 242 for 8 (C. E. B. Rice 130 not out, P. A. Todd 59)
Scotland 149 for 8 (R. G. Swan 69)
Nottinghamshire (2 pts) won by 93 runs
(Gold Award – C. E. B. Rice)

at Cambridge
Combined Universities 105
Middlesex 107 for 1 (W. N. Slack 60 not out)
Middlesex (2 pts) won by 9 wickets
(Gold Award – P. H. Edmonds)

25 and 26 May

at Bradford
Minor Counties 192 for 8 (N. A. Riddell 63)
Yorkshire 193 for 4 (R. G. Lumb 76, C. W. J. Athey 61 not out)
Yorkshire (2 pts) won by 6 wickets
(Gold Award – C. W. J. Athey)

Combined Universities of Oxford and Cambridge 1982
Benson and Hedges

BATTING	v. Somerset (Taunton) 8 May 1982	v. Gloucestershire (Oxford) 15 May 1982	v. Glamorgan (Cardiff) 22 May 1982	v. Middlesex (Cambridge) 25 May 1982
R. G. P. Ellis	4	5	0	0
G. D. R. Toogood	14	8	1	10
R. J. Boyd-Moss	1	4	1	30
D. R. Pringle	68	64	22	0
S. P. Henderson	0	15	18	1
K. A. Hayes	7	10	6	7
S. J. G. Doggart	16	18	4	3
J. G. Varey	20	33*	6	27
A. J. Pollock	8		18	11
C. F. E. Goldie	0	3*	3	0
I. J. Curtis	0*	—	1*	
K. I. Hodgson		41		
C. C. Ellison				0*
Byes	2		2	1
Leg-byes	6	11	2	9
Wides	1	2	2	3
No-balls		2		3
Total	147	216	86	105
Wickets	10	8	10	10
Result	L	L	L	L
Points	0	0	0	0

Catches
3 – S. P. Henderson
2 – C. F. E. Goldie
1 – J. G. Varey, K. I. Hodgson and A. J. Pollock

BOWLING	A. J. Pollock	D. R. Pringle	J. G. Varey
v. Somerset (Taunton) 8 May 1982	6.5–1–44–0	5–1–8–0	7–0–37–0
v. Gloucestershire (Oxford) 15 May 1982		11–1–52–1	11–2–44–2
v. Glamorgan (Cardiff) 22 May 1982	11–0–39–1	11–1–41–0	11–0–62–2
v. Middlesex (Cambridge) 25 May 1982	6–0–18–0	6–1–7–1	5–0–14–0

Middlesex moved into the quarter-finals of the Benson and Hedges Cup with predictable ease. Edmonds, Selvey and Williams posed too many problems for the Universities and Slack and Brearley got to within two runs of the home side's total in 32 overs.

Notts and Lancashire also qualified from Group B. Todd had a welcome fifty for Notts, but Clive Rice dominated a somewhat erratic innings with his highest score in the

The Parks. Home of Oxford University.

S. P. Henderson	I. J. Curtis	S. J. G. Doggart	K. I. Hodgson	R. J. Boyd-Moss	C. C. Ellison	B	Lb	W	Nb	Total	Wkts
–0–29–1	6–1–9–0	6–0–19–1				1	1	1	1	150	2
–0–3–0	9–0–41–0	11–0–67–0	11–0–53–0	1–0–4–0		3	18	11	4	300	4
	11–2–30–1	11–0–31–1				10	11	5	3	232	5
		5–1–19–0		6–0–25–0	5–0–20–0	1	1	2		107	1

competition. He and Todd put on 161 for the third wicket. Scotland died bravely, three batsmen being stumped and skipper Swan hitting 69. Lancashire always had a few too many for Warwickshire after Kennedy and Clive Lloyd had put on 102 for the third wicket. A fighting stand by David Smith and Ferreira came a little too late for the visitors.

Somerset kept alive hopes of qualifying by beating Glamorgan at Swansea. Somerset batted indifferently and owed much to Peter Roebuck's steadiness. They owed even more to Botham who sent back Alan Jones, Hopkins and Ontong with only 11 scored. Javed and Rowe gave some hope, but in the late flurry Somerset always had their noses in front.

Bad light stopped play on the first day at Bradford with Minor Counties having some hope of victory, Gemmell had dismissed Boycott for 2. Lumb and Athey continued their

Sacked as England's captain, Keith Fletcher enjoys the confidence of a good season with the bat.

Minor Counties 1982
Benson and Hedges

BATTING	v. Derbyshire (Derby) 15 May 1982	v. Worcestershire (Wellington) 22 May 1982	v. Yorkshire (Bradford) 25-26 May 1982	v. Leicestershire (Wellington) 27 May 1982
M. Norton	36			
J. G. Tolchard	24	26	23	1
S. G. Plumb	15	47	1	24
P. D. Johnson	28	2	13	12
G. I. Burgess	0	1		
D. Bailey	6	7	34	8
N. A. Riddell	34	9	63	31
N. T. O'Brien	27	0		
F. E. Collyer	4	10		
I. J. Gemmell	1	0	4*	
R. J. Halley	1*			
J. Smith		6*		17
D. Nicholls		2	15	
W. Osman			21	44
A. Griffiths			0	13*
S. A. Davies			1*	
R. W. Flower			—	
B. M. Brain				—
Byes	1	2		9
Leg-byes	12	6	11	10
Wides	7	5	6	10
No-balls	5	6		8
Total	201	129	192	187
Wickets	10	10	8	7
Result	L	L	L	W
Points	0	0	0	2

Catches
3 – F. E. Collyer, A. Griffiths and S. G. Plumb
2 – J. G. Tolchard and N. A. Riddell
1 – G. I. Burgess, D. Bailey, I. J. Gemmell and R. W. Flower

BOWLING	I. J. Gemmell	N. T. O'Brien	D. Bailey
v. Derbyshire (Derby) 15 May 1982	8-0-44-0	6-1-25-0	4-0-21-0
v. Worcestershire (Wellington) 22 May 1982	11-1-53-1	11-1-31-1	
v. Yorkshire (Bradford) 25-26 May 1982	11-1-35-1		1.3-0-12-0
v. Leicestershire (Wellington) 27 May 1982			

A. B. M. Brain 8-3-18-2

stand on the second morning, however, and it realised 109 to make a Yorkshire victory assured. It was their first of the season in limited over competition.

The match at Hove provided one of the greatest innings ever seen in limited over competition. In the sixteenth over of the Essex innings Hardie was run out and McEwan was caught at slip first ball. In the remaining 39 overs of the innings Gooch and Fletcher scored 268 runs. Fletcher's 101 was his first century in limited over competitions and Gooch's 198 not out was the highest score ever hit in a limited over competition in England. It included five sixes and twenty-two fours and it was made off the strongest attack in the country, none of whom was spared. The stand between the two was a record for the third wicket in the Benson and Hedges Cup and it was poignant in that Fletcher had just been deposed as England's captain and Gooch, of course, the most forceful batsman of his generation and the most exciting, was barred from international cricket for three years.

Sussex had a hopeless task. They struck some lusty blows and died, Turner took three wickets and so did Gooch. And still that handsome face under the sad moustache revealed nothing.

Unbelievably, Essex now had a hope of qualifying for the quarter-finals for Kent beat Surrey in a thrilling match at Canterbury. Thanks to a late 46 by Jackman, Surrey made 217 and Kent were struggling at 68 for 4. Those two most entertaining batsmen, Cowdrey and Benson, put on 93 in 23 overs before Benson was run out as he tried to take a leg-bye to the wicket-keeper. Knott fluttered briefly and with three overs left Kent needed 25 to win. Clarke bowled Johnson, but Cowdrey kept attacking until he was lbw to Clarke on the first ball of the final over. Jarvis came in with two

Derby County Cricket Ground.

G. I. Burgess	S. G. Plumb	N. A. Riddell	R. J. Halley	J. Smith	D. Nicholls	S. A. Davies	R. W. Flower	B	Lb	W	Nb	Total	Wkts
7-0-39-1	2-0-9-1	0.5-0-8-0	11-3-45-0					1	4	6		202	2
11-1-28-0				11-1-41-0	11-0-43-6			1	18	9	2	226	10
	7-0-38-0				11-2-31-3	11-2-24-0	11-1-42-0	6		3	2	193	4
				6.2-2-8-4		9-6-11-4	3-2-1-0		2	15	1	56	10A

needed and snicked Clarke for four to win the match. Cowdrey took the Gold Award, but Kent had another hero in Chris Penn from Dover who took four of the first five wickets to fall. He is eighteen years old and was playing as Underwood was injured.

The most vital game was at Worcester where a marvellous innings by Barry Wood, arguably the best he has ever played in a limited over game, set Derbyshire on the way to victory. Turner and Ormrod responded well, but Derbyshire had given the home side just a little too much to do.

26 May

at Belfast

Indians 179 for 2 (P. Roy 84 not out)
v. **Ireland**. Match abandoned.

27 May

at Belfast
Ireland 134 for 9 (E. A. McDermott 50, D. R. Doshi 4 for 11)
Indians 137 for 5
Indians won by 5 wickets

Benson and Hedges Cup

at Chesterfield
Yorkshire 178 (J. D. Love 60)
Derbyshire 181 for 3 (J. H. Hampshire 66 not out)
Derbyshire (2 pts) won by 7 wickets
(Gold Award – J. H. Hampshire)

at Southampton
Surrey 207 for 8 (G. R. J. Roope 53)
Hampshire 194 for 7 (J. M. Rice 56)
Surrey (2 pts) won by 13 runs
(Gold Award – G. R. J. Roope)

at Trent Bridge
Nottinghamshire 216 for 8 (R. J. Hadlee 56)
Lancashire 194 for 9 (G. Fowler 59)
Nottinghamshire (2 pts) won by 22 runs
(Gold Award – R. J. Hadlee)

at Bristol
Somerset 307 for 6 (P. W. Denning 129, I. V. A. Richards 72)
Gloucestershire 294 for 7 (P. Bainbridge 80)
Somerset (2 pts) won by 13 runs
(Gold Award – P. W. Denning)

at Wellington
Minor Counties 187 for 7
Leicestershire 56 (J. Smith 4 for 8, S. Davis 4 for 11)
Minor Counties (2 pts) won by 131 runs
(Gold Award – S. Davis)

27 and 28 May

at Hove
Sussex 305 for 8 (C. M. Wells 80, I. J. Gould 72, Imran Khan 65 not out)
Kent 252 (N. R. Taylor 121, G. S. le Roux 4 for 59)
Sussex (2 pts) won by 53 runs
(Gold Award – N. R. Taylor)

at Edgbaston
Northamptonshire 258 for 8 (W. Larkins 132)
Warwickshire 259 for 4 (A. I. Kallicharran 86)
Warwickshire (2 pts) won by 6 wickets

Scotland 1982
Benson and Hedges

BATTING	v. Lancashire (Old Trafford) 8 May 1982	v. Northamptonshire (Glasgow) 15 May 1982	v. Warwickshire (Edgbaston) 22 May 1982	v. Nottinghamshire (Glasgow) 25 May 1982
G. J. Warner	0	17		
R. R. Jones	2			
R. G. Swan	1	3	14	69
A. Brown	47	0	6	2
O. Henry	59	1	37	8
H. G. F. Johnston	10	0	6	13*
W. G. D. Loudon	17*	0	16	11
D. L. Snodgrass	9	6	10	0
J. E. Ker	0			
G. F. Goddard	1	14		—
J. Clark	0	0*	0*	—
B. K. Kunderan		3		
R. S. Weir		31	26	18
W. A. Donald			35	3
A. B. M. Ker			2	12
A. R. Taylor				0
Byes				4
Leg-byes	8	3	10	7
Wides		2	2	1
No-balls		2	2	1
Total	154	82	166	149
Wickets	10	10	10	8
Result	L	L	L	L
Points	0	0	0	0

Catches
2 – A. Brown (ct 1/st 1)
1 – B. K. Kunderan, G. J. Warner, D. L. Snodgrass and R. G. Swan

BOWLING	D. L. Snodgrass	W. G. D. Loudon	G. F. Goddard
v. Lancashire (Old Trafford) 8 May 1982	5.2–1–21–0	7–1–26–0	10–1–28–0
v. Northamptonshire (Glasgow) 15 May 1982	10–0–43–1	7–0–32–1	11–3–37–1
v. Warwickshire (Edgbaston) 22 May 1982	5–0–31–0	8–2–23–0	
v. Nottinghamshire (Glasgow) 25 May 1982	11–1–44–3	11–1–53–1	8–1–36–0

28 May

at Lord's
Glamorgan 195 for 8 (Javed Miandad 59, A. Jones 52)
Middlesex 199 for 3 (M. W. Gatting 88 not out, R. O. Butcher 50 not out)
Middlesex (2 pts) won by 7 wickets
(Gold Award – M. W. Gatting)

The Best appointed ground in England, Edgbaston.

J. Clark	O. Henry	J. E. Ker	H. G. F. Johnston	A. R. Taylor		B	Lb	W	Nb	Total	Wkts
3-4-0	11-1-35-0	6-1-20-0	4-0-14-0				5	2	1	156	0
)-40-0	9-1-41-1		10-0-42-0				20		4	259	5
-21-0	11-1-47-1		5-0-21-0	2-0-20-0			1		3	167	1
-32-2	11-2-26-0		8-0-34-0			3	8	3	3	242	6

The final round of matches in the Benson and Hedges Cup qualifying tournament produced some notable performances and settled outstanding issues. Surrey, Middlesex and Warwickshire gained victories which had no bearing on settling who was to go into the quarter-finals. The proceeds from the game at Edgbaston were given to the Falkland Islands' Fund. Hampshire lost their fifteenth Benson and Hedges Cup game in their last sixteen outings.

John Hampshire led the onslaught on his old county which put Derbyshire into the last stages of the competition from Group A where Leicestershire had already qualified. Derbyshire won with 13 overs to spare after there had been a stoppage for rain.

It was as well that Leicestershire had already qualified for Minor Counties provided the outstanding performance of the competition by beating them at Wellington in sensational manner. Chasing a target of 188, Leicestershire were bowled out for 56, a record low score for the competition. On a wearing wicket their early batting was destroyed by the Australian pace bowler Simon Davis who plays for Durham. He sent back Briers, Gower, Davison and Garnham, and Smith and the veteran Brian Brain made sure that there was no recovery. The eccentric state of the wicket meant that there were 15 wides bowled, the only double figure score in the Leicestershire innings.

Notts beat Lancashire in the match that decided who was to be top of Group B and Somerset edged out Gloucestershire for the second place in Group D. Denning and Roebuck put on 124 for the first wicket and Denning and Richards added the same amount for the second. Graveney had put Somerset in, but Peter Denning was in his very best form and scored a lovely hundred, full of urgency and power. Gloucestershire slumped to 95 for 5 before Bainbridge and Shepherd gave belated hope with a stand of 105, but the Gloucestershire effort had come too late to alter the result.

Sussex rightfully took the final place in Group C although Kent long kept alive the hopes of Essex. On the Thursday Sussex reached a mammoth score which left Kent needing to break the record for the second innings to win. Undaunted, Taylor and Potter opened with a stand of 162, but only Cowdrey and Aslett posed any further threat to Sussex and Kent lost their last five wickets for 20 runs. Taylor's innings was quite magnificent. He hit four sixes and thirteen fours before he was third out at 183, bowled by Barclay as he went down the wicket.

Benson and Hedges Cup Zonal Round – Final Tables

Group A	P	W	L	Pts
Derbyshire	4	3	1	6
Leicestershire	4	3	1	6
Worcestershire	4	2	2	4
Minor Counties	4	1	3	2
Yorkshire	4	1	3	2

Group B	P	W	L	Pts
Nottinghamshire	4	4	—	8
Lancashire	4	3	1	6
Warwickshire	4	2	2	4
Northamptonshire	4	1	3	2
Scotland	4	—	4	0

Group C	P	W	L	Pts
Kent	4	3	1	6
Sussex	4	3	1	6
Essex	4	2	2	4
Surrey	4	2	2	4
Hampshire	4	—	4	0

Group D	P	W	L	Pts
Middlesex	4	4	—	8
Somerset	4	3	1	6
Gloucestershire	4	2	2	4
Glamorgan	4	1	3	2
Combined Universities	4	—	4	0

John Player League
30 May

at Chesterfield
Warwickshire 183 for 7
Derbyshire 187 for 3 (J. H. Hampshire 79)
Derbyshire (4 pts) won by 7 wickets

at Swansea
Glamorgan 186 for 7 (J. A. Hopkins 56, C. H. Dredge 4 for 32)
Somerset 187 for 3 (P. W. Denning 84 not out)
Somerset (4 pts) won by 7 wickets

at Gloucester
Gloucestershire 209 for 4 (A. W. Stovold 85, B. C. Broad 59)
Sussex 210 for 7
Sussex (4 pts) won by 3 wickets

at Lord's
Middlesex 245 for 5 (J. M. Brearley 98, W. N. Slack 52)
Essex 194 (K. S. McEwan 69, M. W. W. Selvey 4 for 27)
Middlesex (4 pts) won by 57 runs

at Trent Bridge
Nottinghamshire 230 for 5 (C. E. B. Rice 117)
Northamptonshire 207 for 8 (G. Cook 71)
Nottinghamshire (4 pts) won by 23 runs

at The Oval
Surrey 214 for 7 (D. M. Smith 57)
Leicestershire 213 for 8 (D. I. Gower 115)
Surrey (4 pts) won by 1 run

at Worcester
Kent 219 for 6 (C. S. Cowdrey 61 not out)
Worcestershire 189 (K. B. S. Jarvis 4 for 41)
Kent (4 pts) won by 30 runs

Peter Denning maintained his good form at Swansea where Somerset gained their first John Player League win of the season. Dredge had restricted Glamorgan after Hopkins and Ontong had threatened to build a big score. Botham hit 39 not out off 21 deliveries. It was one of his non-textbook innings.

There was a first win, too, for Notts who, as ever, owed much to Clive Rice. His 117 was scored off 83 balls in 86 minutes.

The top teams all maintained their challenge. Kent won comfortably at Worcester, recovering from 114 for 5 in 30 overs through some fine hitting by Cowdrey, Knott and Dilley which produced 105 runs in the last ten overs. Jarvis, Dilley and Penn bowled well enough to make the Kent total too formidable for Worcestershire.

Opposite: *An English Sunday in Summer. Derbyshire v. Warwickshire at Chesterfield, John Player League, May 1982.*

Middlesex, put in to bat, routed Essex. Brearley and Slack put on 136 for the first wicket. Brearley was in dominant form in front of a crowd of twelve thousand and after Slack had been missed first ball Essex were always trailing.

The confidence of Derbyshire exuded as they despatched a dispirited Warwickshire with two balls to spare, and Sussex came back from the brink of defeat to beat Gloucestershire. They needed 59 off seven overs on a wicket which was slow. Le Roux gave them victory with a fiercely struck 43 not out. They also owed much to some tidy spin bowling by Waller and Barclay.

The finest match of the day was at The Oval. Surrey, helped by some indifferent bowling, reached 214 in 40 overs. Briers and Gower gave Leicestershire a good start with a stand of 74 before Briers fell to Knight, but the visitors were ahead of the asking rate. Gower continued to hit cleanly, but his colleagues faltered and when the last over was reached 12 were needed for victory. Gower was still there and he and Parsons nearly snatched victory, but Gower was run out off the last ball of the match and Surrey had won by 1 run. Gower hit a six and nine fours and in the words of those who played against him, 'He has never batted better. He has now cut out the bat waving on the off.' It was cheering news for England.

So May ended with Middlesex at the top of the league with fourteen points from four matches. Kent, Sussex and Derbyshire were two points behind them, the first two having won all of their three matches and Derbyshire having lost one in four. Essex and Yorkshire were embedded at the bottom of the table pointless from four and three matches respectively.

29, 30 and 31 May

at Southampton

Hampshire 336 for 6 dec (T. E. Jesty 156 not out, M. C. J. Nicholas 72) and 236 for 2 dec (C. G. Greenidge 156, M. C. J. Nicholas 54 not out)
Indians 277 for 6 dec (G. R. Viswanath 100, S. M. H. Kirmani 65) and 298 for 7 (D. B. Vengsarkar 86)

Indians won by 3 wickets

at Leeds

Lancashire 351 for 8 dec (D. P. Hughes 126 not out, J. Abrahams 57, C. M. Old 4 for 91) and 255 for 6 dec (D. Lloyd 81)
Yorkshire 317 for 6 dec (C. W. J. Athey 90, D. L. Bairstow 70 not out) and 197 for 5 (R. G. Lumb 72, G. Boycott 68)

Match drawn
Yorkshire 6 pts, Lancashire 5 pts

29, 31 May and 1 June

at Chesterfield

Nottinghamshire 320 for 9 dec (C. E. B. Rice 87, J. D. Birch 60, K. Saxelby 59 not out, D. G. Moir 4 for 62) and 209 for 7 dec (D. W. Randall 67, B. N. French 55)
Derbyshire 259 (J. G. Wright 141 not out, R. J. Hadlee 5 for 64) and 123 for 6 (G. Miller 53, E. E. Hemmings 4 for 48)

Match drawn
Nottinghamshire 7 pts, Derbyshire 6 pts

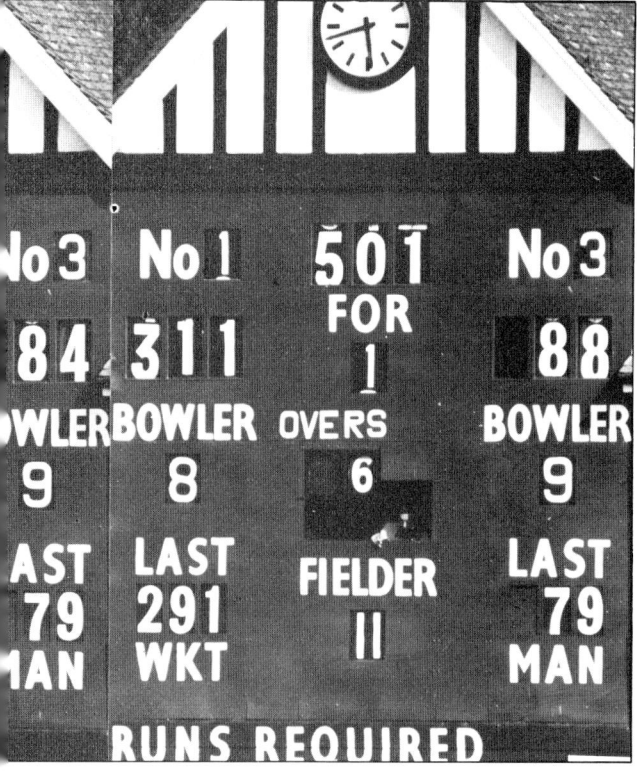

The scoreboard at Worcester records the stages of Turner's memorable innings, 29 May 1982.

a *12.55 Turner 102 not out after 115 minutes. No. 2. Ormrod is 41 not out.*
b *3.03 p.m. 201 not out in 65 overs.*
c *5.35 p.m. 303 not out. Patel is 84 not out.*
d *5.43 p.m. Neale declares with the Worcestershire score at 501 for 1.*

at Chelmsford
Essex 228 (S. Turner 74, P. I. Pocock 5 for 73) and 288 for 5 dec (K. W. R. Fletcher 122, G. A. Gooch 71, A. W. Lilley 67)
Surrey 132 (N. Phillip 6 for 60) and 175 (M. A. Lynch 69, J. K. Lever 5 for 61)
Essex won by 209 runs
Essex 22 pts, Surrey 4 pts

at Swansea
Glamorgan 308 (S. A. B. Daniels 73, T. Davies 66 not out, C. J. C. Rowe 55, P. Bainbridge 6 for 59) and 321 for 4 dec (R. C. Ontong 152 not out, A. Jones 94)
Gloucestershire 325 for 6 dec (P. Bainbridge 101 not out, D. A. Graveney 55 not out) and 172 for 5 (Zaheer Abbas 60, A. J. Hignell 50 not out)
Match drawn
Gloucestershire 8 pts, Glamorgan 5 pts

at Leicester
Northamptonshire 354 for 5 dec (G. Cook 125, A. J. Lamb 102) and 233 for 8 dec (P. Willey 88 not out, J. C. Balderstone 4 for 51)
Leicestershire 319 for 9 dec (J. C. Balderstone 98, N. E. Briers 71, D. I. Gower 54, D. S. Steele 4 for 96) and 174 for 7 (D. I Gower 52, B. F. Davison 52)
Match drawn
Northamptonshire 7 pts, Leicestershire 5 pts

at Lord's
Middlesex 230 (W. N. Slack 85, A. C. S. Pigott 5 for 47, I. A. Greig 4 for 62) and 199 for 8 dec
Sussex 168 (P. H. Edmonds 4 for 40) and 193 (P. H. Edmonds 8 for 80)
Middlesex won by 68 runs
Middlesex 22 pts, Sussex 5 pts

at Taunton
Somerset 362 for 7 dec (I. V. A. Richards 146, B. C. Rose 89, D. L. Underwood 4 for 65) and 200 for 7 dec (P. M. Roebuck 73)
Kent 302 for 7 dec (C. J. Tavare 122 not out) and 192 for 5 (N. R. Taylor 81 not out, R. A. Woolmer 50)
Match drawn
Somerset 7 pts, Kent 7 pts

at Worcester
Worcestershire 501 for 1 dec (G. M. Turner 311 not out, D. N. Patel 88 not out, J. A. Ormrod 79) and 167 for 6 dec
Warwickshire 380 for 9 dec (A. I. Kallicharran 235, D. L. Amiss 64, R. K. Illingworth 4 for 85) and 197 for 5 (K. D. Smith 62 not out)
Match drawn
Worcestershire 5 pts, Warwickshire 3 pts

The Bank Holiday week-end brought the Indians their first victory of the tour. Hampshire batted with considerable aplomb in both innings. Jesty came within three runs of a career best with a fine innings on the Saturday and Gordon Greenidge was at his most devastating on the Monday morning reaching his hundred in under three hours. In 70 minutes on the Sunday night after India had declared, following a fine hundred from Viswanath and a good performance from Kirmani as an opener, Greenidge scored only 19, but by lunch on the Monday he was 150. He hit five sixes, all of them out of the ground. Pocock, returning to Hampshire after pre-season injury, set the Indians 296 in 227 minutes and, with consistent batting supporting the elegant fury of Vengsarkar, they reached the target with 22 balls to spare.

There were not quite the same thrills in the Roses match where bad light ended play early, but Yorkshire had made a positive attempt to get 290 in three hours. On the first day David Hughes had rescued Lancashire from 87 for 4 with a stand of 134 in 140 minutes with John Abrahams. Hughes' batting appears to be improving with age and it is hard to remember that, initially, he was selected as a left-arm bowler. Athey batted with great confidence on the Sunday until missing a full toss from Abrahams which he was attempting to hit out of the ground.

Glenn Turner holds the chalice presented to him by the county to commemorate his hundred hundreds. He shares champagne with 'Billy' Ibadulla who had much to do with bringing Turner to England and guiding him through the early part of his career. Worcester Cathedral smiles approvingly.

Derbyshire clung on against Notts and it was Miller's stubborn batting that saved them in the end. Notts had been 43 for 3 in their first innings, but Birch, back in the side, Rice, Hemmings and Saxelby restored their pride. Hemmings and Saxelby added 102 for the eighth wicket, Saxelby hitting a maiden fifty in first-class cricket. John Wright alone withstood the Notts seam attack and reached a fine hundred.

Essex showed that they were emerging from their nightmare with a comfortable win over Surrey. Once more it was Stuart Turner who rescued them from the depths. Going in at 80 for 5, he got off the mark with a six and steered Essex to 228, including a last wicket stand of 32 with David Acfield who got 1 not out. Surrey disintegrated before Phillip and Lever and closed at 49 for 6 on the Saturday. Clarke struck a few lusty blows, but when Essex batted again Gooch, dropped badly on 13, Lilley and Fletcher who hit a chanceless century in 216 minutes plundered a Surrey attack that was operating without Pocock who had injured his back. Surrey succumbed a second time to Lever and Phillip after some big hitting from Clarke and Lynch.

There were some notable achievements at Swansea where Glamorgan were 165 for 9 on the Saturday when Simon Daniels joined Terry Davies who was keeping wicket because Eifion Jones was injured. They added 143, a county record and a wonderful performance by two uncapped players. Bainbridge added a century to his five wickets and then Ontong hit a career best in a second wicket stand of 142 with Alan Jones, the unquenchable. Gloucestershire declined Javed's invitation to try to score 305 in three hours, even though Malcolm Nash retired injured from the Glamorgan attack.

Centuries by Cook and Lamb, the first one of relief to a much out of form batsman, the second a celebration on being selected for the England side, dominated Saturday's play at Leicester. The home side countered with a good all round batting performance, but the game was always moving towards a draw.

The meeting of the giants at Lord's saw Middlesex slump from 175 for 3 to 230 all out against the bowling of Tony Pigott. Sussex found runs hard to get as the wicket began to turn and Phil Edmonds bowled with intelligence and control. In the second innings he was supreme and his 8 for 80, a career best, not only maintained Middlesex's hundred per cent record, but emphasised his right to a recall to the England side. Needless to say he was aided by fine fielding and astute leadership by Brearley.

Viv Richards scored his first hundred of the season for Somerset as he and Rose shared a third wicket stand of 155 to put their side into a commanding position. Chris Tavare batted Kent into contention with one of his more studious innings. Ultimately, Rose asked Kent to make 261 in 175 minutes. Woolmer and the impressive and ever-improving Taylor gave them a good start, but the game ebbed to a draw.

When all else has been forgotten one innings will remain in the memory from Whitsun Bank Holiday, 1982. On Saturday, 29 May, at Worcester, Glenn Turner scored 311 not out for Worcestershire against Warwickshire. It was the first triple century in the county championship since Jack Robertson of Middlesex scored 331 not out at Worcester in 1949. More significantly, it was the thirty-five-year old Turner's hundredth hundred in first-class cricket. It was his 779th innings since he first played in 1964, and he became only the nineteenth batsman in the history of the game to reach a hundred hundreds.

His self-imposed exile from Test cricket has tended to diminish Turner's achievements in most eyes. Yet his 39 Tests have seen him score nearly 3,000 runs at an average of 43.62, an impressive record. Perhaps secretly we are critical of his total application, his consistent search for purity of technique, his dedication to the art of batsmanship which has tended to take over the man. Whatever it may be, we have held back from giving the man his full due. He has indicated that this is his last year for Worcestershire and that he will make himself available for New Zealand at the end of 1982. It is much to be desired for New Zealand have commanded great respect in the past three or four years and with Turner in the side they could be strong contenders for the Prudential World Cup in 1983.

On the second day of this remarkable match, Alvin Kallicharran hit his first double century for Warwickshire. It was perhaps typical of this delightful cricketer and charming man that he should choose an occasion when another stole the limelight to play such an historic innings.

As May gave way to June, Middlesex led the Schweppes County Championship with 64 points, Leicestershire, Sussex and Surrey were on their heels. Glenn Turner led the batting averages and Richard Hadlee the bowling averages. Of course, they both came from New Zealand.

Opposite: Glenn Turner's innings of 311 not out. Gladstone Small looks on as Turner turns the ball to leg. It was Turner's hundredth hundred.

Prudential Trophy

FIRST ONE-DAY INTERNATIONAL

The first interest in this game lay in the selection of the England side, the first under Peter May's chairmanship of the selection committee. Not unexpectedly, Allan Lamb was chosen to represent England for the first time. The surprising choices were Geoff Miller, whose record did not seem to suggest he was worthy of a place in representative cricket, Barry Wood and Vic Marks. Even more surprising was the selection of Roger Knight as reserve when there were doubts about Wood's fitness. Apparent in the constitution of the side was that it was chosen with the specific job of winning a one-day game and could not be taken as an indication of the selectors' real thinking on the Test side.

Bob Willis captained England for the first time. His selection had been seen as a short term measure. The man deserves every honour that has come his way, for none tries harder, but his appointment did not help to solve the problem as to who was to lead the side to Australia.

Willis won an important toss and put India in on a wicket which had been affected by a violent storm the previous afternoon. Gavaskar was twice dropped and Dilley, unrecognisable as the quick bowler who had torn in at Dartford and Chelmsford, plodded at medium pace. Allott bowled splendidly and Botham proved his irresistible self. On a wicket giving the bowlers much assistance, India wilted. Only a marvellously defiant flourish by Kapil Dev gave them any respectability.

Their total of 193 gave England no problems. The wicket was now easier. Tavare and Wood were confident and efficient. Kapil Dev and Madan Lal apart, the Indian bowling was indifferent. Wood made his best score in a one-day international and Lamb had an encouraging start. Wood was Man of the Match.

FIRST PRUDENTIAL ONE-DAY INTERNATIONAL: ENGLAND v. INDIA
2 June 1982 at Headingley

INDIA				ENGLAND		
S. M. Gavaskar†	c Botham, b Allott	38		B. Wood	not out	78
G. A. M. H. Parkar	c Tavare, b Willis	10		C. J. Tavare	lbw, b Madan Lal	66
D. B. Vengsarkar	c Taylor, b Botham	5		A. J. Lamb	not out	35
G. R. Viswanath	b Botham	9		D. I. Gower		
S. M. Patil	c Taylor, b Botham	0		I. T. Botham		
Yashpal Sharma	c Taylor, b Allott	20		D. W. Randall		
R. J. Shastri	run out	18		G. Miller		
Kapil Dev	run out	60		G. R. Dilley		
S. M. H. Kirmani*	c Taylor, b Botham	11		R. W. Taylor*		
S. V. Nayak	c Tavare, b Willis	3		P. J. W. Allott		
Madan Lal	not out	1		R. G. D. Willis†		
Extras	b 4, lb 9, w 1, nb 4	18		Extras	b 1, lb 7, w 3, nb 4	15
		193			(for 1 wkt)	194

	O	M	R	W		O	M	R	W
Willis	11	—	32	2	Kapil Dev	9	2	21	—
Dilley	5	1	20	—	Madan Lal	9	3	21	1
Allott	11	4	21	2	Nayak	9	—	37	—
Botham	11	—	56	4	Shastri	11	—	37	—
Wood	7	2	17	—	Patil	7	—	29	—
Miller	10	—	29	—	Yashpal Sharma	5.1	—	34	—

FALL OF WICKETS
1–30, 2–54, 3–58, 4–59, 5–68, 6–113, 7–114, 8–154, 9–192

FALL OF WICKETS
1–133

England won by 9 wickets

PRUDENTIAL TROPHY AT HEADINGLEY

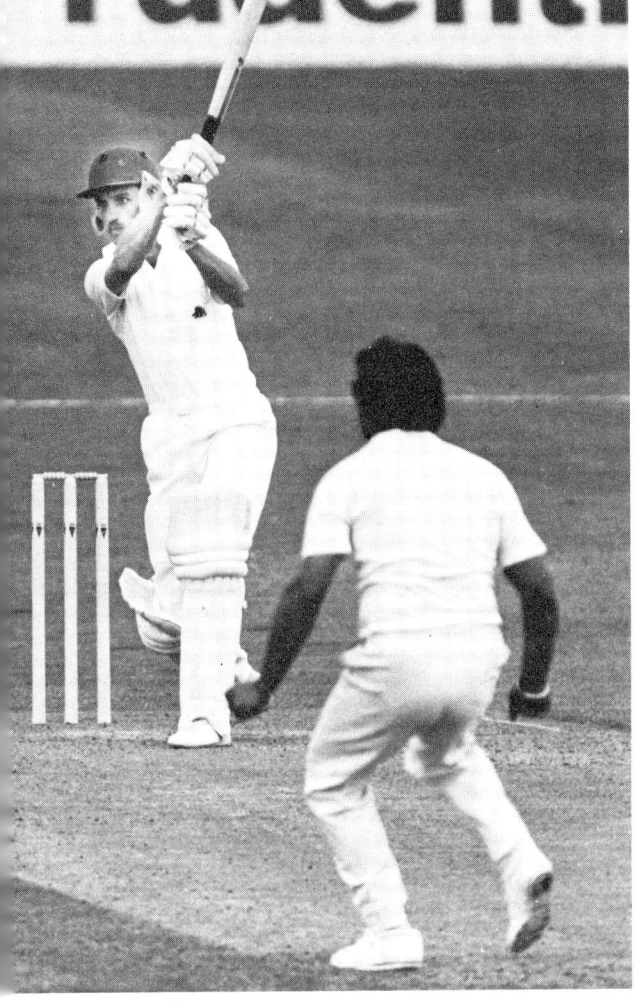

Above: *A recall to glory. Barry Wood, man of the match.* Left: *Chris Tavare drives Sharma during his innings at 66. Kirmani keeping wicket.* Below: *India's saving grace. Kapil Dev cuts Miller. Taylor keeping wicket.*

Prudential Trophy

SECOND ONE-DAY INTERNATIONAL

England fielded an unchanged side; India replaced Viswanath by Malhotra. Gavaskar won the toss and asked England to bat. Kapil Dev and Madan Lal again bowled well and Patil disconcerted both openers before bowling them. Wood had had an unhappier stay than at Leeds.

Lamb and Gower settled quickly with Gower the dominant partner looking a more assured, safer player than at any time since his quality was first recognised. Shastri once more proved an ineffectual bowler in the limited over context and it was surprising that he had been played in preference to the more experienced Doshi.

Gower and Lamb added 159 in 27 overs for the third wicket, a record. The Indians laboured in the field until Gower lifted Sharma to deep mid-off. The remaining overs were a scramble for bonus runs as the four run-outs testify.

Lamb batted splendidly until he became bogged down on 99 and swung fretfully at Madan Lal to whom he skied a caught and bowled. Lamb looked as if he would be an England batsman for many years to come and it was humanly refreshing that one to whom runs seem to come so easily should show emotion and concern on nearing the century that he deserved.

India batted dreadfully and it looked for a time as they would be dismissed for a record low score, but Kapil Dev and Madan Lal once more gave them respectability and, surprisingly, they lasted their full quota of overs.

Right: *Chaos at The Oval. Gower, Kirmani and Yashpal Sharma end in a heap with the wicket broken and Gower 'in'.*

SECOND PRUDENTIAL ONE-DAY INTERNATIONAL: ENGLAND v. INDIA
4 June 1982 at The Oval

ENGLAND

Batsman	Dismissal	Runs
B. Wood	b Patil	15
C. J. Tavare	b Patil	27
A. J. Lamb	c and b Madan Lal	99
D. I. Gower	c Vengsarkar, b Sharma	76
I. T. Botham	run out	4
D. W. Randall	run out	24
G. Miller	run out	0
G. R. Dilley	c Sharma, b Madan Lal	1
R. W. Taylor*	not out	3
P. J. W. Allott	run out	5
R. G. D. Willis†		
Extras	b 3, lb 10, w 6, nb 3	22
	(for 9 wkts)	276

Bowler	O	M	R	W
Kapil Dev	11	1	39	—
Madan Lal	11	—	50	2
Nayak	11	1	48	—
Shastri	8	—	53	—
Patil	11	—	37	2
Yashpal Sharma	3	—	27	1

FALL OF WICKETS
1-43, 2-53, 3-212, 4-218, 5-260, 6-260, 7-267, 8-268, 9-276

INDIA

Batsman	Dismissal	Runs
S. M. Gavaskar†	c Willis, b Miller	15
G. A. M. H. Parkar	c Botham, b Willis	2
D. B. Vengsarkar	c Taylor, b Dilley	15
Yashpal Sharma	lbw, b Allott	2
A. Malhotra	b Botham	4
S. M. Patil	b Miller	1
Kapil Dev	c Gower, b Wood	47
S. M. H. Kirmani	c Botham, b Miller	8
Madan Lal	not out	53
R. J. Shastri	not out	9
S. V. Nayak		
Extras	b 1, lb 3, w 2	6
	(for 8 wkts)	162

Bowler	O	M	R	W
Willis	7	2	10	1
Dilley	7	1	19	1
Botham	9	2	22	1
Allott	8	3	24	1
Miller	11	3	27	3
Wood	11	—	51	1
Tavare	2	—	3	—

FALL OF WICKETS
1-5, 2-28, 3-36, 4-42, 5-42, 6-43, 7-66, 8-131

England won by 114 runs

Above: *Again India's saviour – Kapil Dev hits out at The Oval.* Below: *Man of the Match at The Oval. Allan Lamb pulls Sandeep Patil in his innings at 99.*

2, 3 and 4 June

at Swansea
Somerset 330 for 6 dec (B. C. Rose 97 not out, P. M. Roebuck 90) and 196 for 8 dec (B. C. Rose 63 not out, P. M. Roebuck 53 not out, S. R. Barwick 5 for 44)
Glamorgan 226 (J. A. Hopkins 75, J. W. Lloyds 6 for 114) and 187 for 7 (C. J. C. Rowe 58 not out)

Match drawn
Somerset 8 pts, Glamorgan 4 pts

at Gloucester
Gloucestershire 267 (Zaheer Abbas 162 not out, C. E. H. Croft 4 for 39) and 350 for 5 (Zaheer Abbas 107, Sadiq Mohammad 91)
Lancashire 375 for 5 (D. Lloyd 108, G. Fowler 100, D. P. Hughes 66 not out)

Match drawn
Lancashire 7 pts, Gloucestershire 4 pts

at Bournemouth
Hampshire 158 (J. M. Rice 60) and 221 (T. E. Jesty 52, D. L. Underwood 7 for 79)
Kent 274 (D. G. Aslett 80, M. D. Marshall 5 for 84) and 106 for 4 (L. Potter 54)

Kent won by 6 wickets
Kent 23 pts, Hampshire 5 pts

at Hinckley
Leicestershire 329 for 7 dec (N. E. Briers 106, J. C. Balderstone 67, P. Carrick 4 for 106) and 141 for 8 dec.
Yorkshire 229 for 8 dec (R. G. Lumb 70, L. B. Taylor 5 for 52) and 192 for 6 (G. Boycott 56, C. W. J. Athey 50, N. G. B. Cook 4 for 74)

Match drawn
Leicestershire 7 pts, Yorkshire 4 pts

at Lord's
Derbyshire 228 for 9 dec (J. E. Embury 5 for 50) and 208 for 1 dec (J. G. Wright 103 not out, P. N. Kirsten 80 not out)
Middlesex 89 for 0 dec and 340 for 9 (M. W. Gatting 140, P. H. Edmonds 67)

Match drawn
Middlesex 4 pts, Derbyshire 2 pts

at Northampton
Northamptonshire 253 for 5 dec (G. Cook 81, R. G. Williams 52 not out, P. Willey 51) and 187 for 8 dec
Nottinghamshire 195 (J. D. Birch 64, B. J. Griffiths 4 for 53) and 134 for 8

Match drawn
Northamptonshire 7 pts, Nottinghamshire 3 pts

at Worcester
Worcestershire 222 for 9 dec (M. J. Weston 63, Younis Ahmed 63, A. J. Traicos 5 for 56) and 181 for 7 dec (Younis Ahmed 75 not out, P. W. E. Rawson 5 for 42)
Zimbabwe 156 for 3 dec (A. J. Pycroft 62 not out, D. A. G. Fletcher 56 not out) and 52 for 2

Match drawn

at Oxford
Oxford University 305 for 4 dec (K. A. Hayes 152, R. Marsden 60) and 162 for 8 dec (J. Cumbes 4 for 47)
Warwickshire 239 for 8 dec (K. D. Smith 64, G. C. Small 57 not out, I. J. Curtis 4 for 57) and 230 for 1 (G. W. Humpage 121 not out, T. A. Lloyd 63)

Warwickshire won by 9 wickets

We often ignore achievement and give the greatest praise only when there is a hint of failure, of vulnerability. Middlesex had won their three Schweppes County Championship games, all of their Benson and Hedges Cup qualifying matches and all but one of their John Player League games, the one with Notts which was abandoned. Then they entertained Derbyshire at Lord's and suffered hours of frustration with the rain. Brearley hastily closed his first innings and thereby challenged Kirsten, captaining Derbyshire in the absence of Wood. Wright completed his second hundred of the week as he and Kirsten shared in a second wicket stand of 263, and Middlesex were set to make 348 to win in just over four hours, a formidable task. They lost their first four batsmen for 88 before Gatting and Emburey added 82.

When Emburey was run out Edmonds joined Gatting and in 25 overs they added 152 runs before they were dismissed in successive overs. A brief flurry of rain cost Middlesex two of the last 20 overs and wickets fell to some fine catches as they tried to get the 49 that they needed off the last 38 balls. The last two batsmen still went for the runs, but Middlesex, having been asked to score at 85 runs an hour, were just eight runs short. It was a glorious failure and the cricket world was stunned in admiration. Gatting's hundred came in three hours and there was a general sense of bewilderment as to why he was not with the England party.

The reigning champions, Notts, held on for a draw in the rain-affected game at Northampton where Richard Williams showed a happy return to form. Notts were chasing 249 in 155 minutes when Willey, Steele and Williams took quick wickets and Bore and Hemmings batted out the final sixteen overs to save the day for the visitors.

There was no saviour for Hampshire at Bournemouth where Derek Underwood's lift and turn gave Kent their first championship win of the season. Captained by Chris Cowdrey, Kent fielded six uncapped players and were without Tavare, Dilley and the injured Benson. Aslett and Knott revived their fortunes after Marshall had threatened to put Hampshire on top and Potter batted well in the second innings. It was the forty-first time in his career that Underwood had taken ten wickets in a match.

Another notable record was at Gloucester where Zaheer Abbas hit a century in each innings for the seventh time and

Wayne Daniel. In June he swept aside all opposition as Middlesex went on their conquering way.

so equalled Wally Hammond's record. The match ended tamely, but in the first innings Zaheer had stood alone as wickets tumbled, the last seven going down for 19 runs. David Lloyd and Fowler added 182 for the second wicket, but until Hughes arrived Lancashire were never scoring quickly enough. When Gloucestershire batted again Zaheer and Sadiq, in rejuvenated form, added 162 for the third wicket.

Rain and some slow scoring by Leicestershire in their first innings when Briers hit the eighth hundred of his career always made a result at Hinckley seem unlikely and three declarations could not bring it about.

There were changing fortunes at Swansea where Roebuck and Rose dominated the first day and Hopkins alone held his own against the spin of Jeremy Lloyds on the second day. Lloyds was playing only because Marks was with the England party. Steve Barwick bowled Glamorgan back into contention with an opening burst on the second evening which removed Lloyds, Popplewell, Denning and Slocombe, and the next morning he added Taylor for a career best. Once more Rose and Roebuck were Somerset's heroes, but Roebuck retired ill.

Glamorgan went for victory, but Viv Richards took 3 for 6 and halted their chase and it was the good sense of Charles Rowe that saw them to a deserved draw.

Zimbabwe opened their short tour with an impressive display in the drawn, rain-ruined game at Worcester. Athanasios John Traicos, thirty-five years old and Egyptian born, showed that he had lost none of his cunning with his off-breaks which had won him a Test place for South Africa against Australia twelve years ago. Damien D'Oliveira made his first-class debut for Worcestershire and did well enough to suggest that he would live firmly on his own reputation and not the reputation of his accomplished father.

Kevin Hayes hit a maiden century for Oxford University against Warwickshire and his score was the highest by an Oxford batsman for eight years. Oxford appeared to be winning until Small and Sutcliffe added 68 for the ninth wicket. In the end Warwickshire were asked to score at more than five an over, a task they accomplished with some ease thanks to an opening stand of 129 between Lloyd and acting skipper Humpage who hit a fierce century.

5, 6 and 7 June

at Northampton

Indians 203 for 5 dec (G. R. Viswanath 106 not out) and 197 for 4 (S. V. Nayak 67 not out, Yashpal Sharma 56)
Northamptonshire 204 (R. M. Carter 79, S. V. Nayak 5 for 54)

Match drawn

5, 7 and 8 June

at Chelmsford

Essex 238 (B. R. Hardie 76, K. W. R. Fletcher 72, V. J. Marks 7 for 59) and 249 for 9 dec (K. W. R. Fletcher 61, J. W. Lloyds 7 for 88)
Somerset 111 (J. K. Lever 4 for 28) and 203 (B. C. Rose 83 not out, R. E. East 6 for 80)

Essex won by 173 runs
Essex 22 pts, Somerset 4 pts

at Gloucester

Gloucestershire 354 for 5 dec (Sadiq Mohammad 85, A. W. Stovold 60, J. N. Shepherd 57 not out, A. J. Hignell 52 not out) and 194 (D. G. Moir 4 for 46)
Derbyshire 301 for 4 dec (P. N. Kirsten 143, J. H. Hampshire 52) and 157 for 8 (D. A. Graveney 4 for 49)

Match drawn
Derbyshire 6 pts, Gloucestershire 5 pts

at Tunbridge Wells

Kent 276 (N. R. Taylor 100, D. G. Aslett 53, J. E. Emburey 5 for 68, P. H. Edmonds 4 for 91) and 90 (W. W. Daniel 5 for 37)
Middlesex 438 for 9 dec (C. T. Radley 141 not out, M. W. Gatting 114, W. N. Slack 51)

Middlesex won by an innings and 72 runs
Middlesex 24 pts, Kent 4 pts

at Old Trafford

Lancashire 240 (D. P. Hughes 99, R. C. Ontong 4 for 53) and 212 for 6 dec (C. H. Lloyd 53 not out, G. Fowler 52)
Glamorgan 115 and 131

Lancashire won by 206 runs
Lancashire 22 pts, Glamorgan 4 pts

Unobtrusively, he has completed the Middlesex jig-saw and provided them with the needed stability and aggression in the opening partnership with Brearley. Wilf Slack pulls viciously in his innings of 51 v Kent at Tunbridge Wells at the beginning of June.

at Trent Bridge

Worcestershire 166 (G. M. Turner 54) and 186 (Younis Ahmed 65)
Nottinghamshire 290 (D. W. Randall 76, R. T. Robinson 65, N. Gifford 6 for 48) and 63 for 1

Nottinghamshire won by 9 wickets
Nottinghamshire 23 pts, Worcestershire 5 pts

at The Oval

Hampshire 148 (T. E. Jesty 55, S. T. Clarke 4 for 44, R. D. Jackman 4 for 52) and 170 (C. G. Greenidge 84, D. J. Thomas 4 for 39)
Surrey 214 (M. A. Lynch 67) and 101 (M. D. Marshall 7 for 38)

Hampshire won by 3 runs
Hampshire 20 pts, Surrey 6 pts

at Edgbaston

Sussex 343 (I. A. Greig 109, J. R. T. Barclay 77, G. S. le Roux 53) and 174 for 3 dec (P. W. G. Parker 84 not out)
Warwickshire 205 (A. I. Kallicharran 89) and 43 (C. E. Waller 4 for 11)

Sussex won by 269 runs
Sussex 24 pts, Warwickshire 6 pts

at Leicester

Zimbabwe 249 for 9 dec (I. P. Butchart 54, R. Brown 51) and 286 for 9 dec (G. J. Heron 83, A. J. Pycroft 50)
Leicestershire 284 for 7 dec (R. A. Cobb 64, J. F. Steele 63) and 78 for 5

Match drawn

In their last game before the First Test the Indians were hampered by the weather, but Viswanath hit a confidence boosting hundred and Nayak gave a fine all-round performance which did not, however, win him a place in the Test side. Carter hit a career best for Northants.

At Chelmsford, Essex were 142 for 1 before Vic Marks destroyed them after lunch with his career best bowling performance and nine wickets fell for 96 runs. Lever and Phillip struck back for Essex and on the Monday the West Indian pace bowler, enjoying a fine season, again supported Lever to rout the west countrymen. Essex had gained a surprisingly big lead and increased on it despite some more fine off-spin bowling, this time from Lloyds who, like Marks, had a career best performance. Thereafter Somerset wilted to Ray East on a crumbling wicket.

The relentlessly efficient Middlesex continued their triumphant progress. Kent failed to prosper sufficiently on a beautiful Tunbridge Wells wicket on the Saturday. Neil Taylor gave another most impressive display of forceful batting and he was well supported by Aslett, but some highly intelligent bowling by Edmonds who dismissed Woolmer, Tavare, Cowdrey and Knott dampened Kent's hopes of a large score. Embury mopped up the tail and Radley and Gatting, in contrasting styles of accumulation and pugnacity, took Middlesex to a formidable total. In their second innings, Kent batted ineptly and surrendered lamely to the pace of Daniel. Their problems appeared to be ones of concentration rather than any caused by the wicket.

Fortunes fluctuated at Gloucester, but, in the end, Derbyshire were happy to manage a draw.

Lancashire always had the better of Glamorgan at Old Trafford. David Hughes, improving daily with the bat like a good wine, was run out on 99, but the variety of the Lancashire attack twice proved too much for Glamorgan.

Sussex won in splendid style at Edgbaston. Ian Greig hit his first hundred of the season and John Barclay showed a returning confidence with the bat. Garth le Roux once more hit to great effect and Sussex built a good total. Kallicharran apart, the Warwickshire batting was dismal, and when Sussex batted again they capitalised on their good position. Sussex started the last morning at 78 for 2, a lead of 216. They increased that lead to 312 at which point they declared, shortly before lunch. Parker was totally magnificent. He hooked and cut Willis and twice drove Sutcliffe for six and then he finished the Sussex innings in sensational fashion when he hit 32 in one over off Kallicharran, four sixes and two fours. Parker is a batsman of the highest quality and his attitude is right. Surely, he will find a place in the England side in the near future.

Warwickshire's troubles had not finished. Lloyd was out before lunch and in the afternoon, with Oliver absent hurt, they were dismissed for 43. It was a miserable performance and over the three days Sussex had outclassed them.

Once more the Trent Bridge wicket was cause for concern

and this time it was Glenn Turner who was injured and forced to retire. The Notts victory was founded on a second wicket stand of 128 between Randall and Robinson after poor Todd had bagged another 'duck'. Notts had the all-round attack to exploit the wicket, but one could not help but feel that a better batting track would be desirable at Trent Bridge.

Zimbabwe again showed that they are a fine side, but a little courage in the timing of their declaration might have brought them victory.

There was a mighty contest on a doubtful wicket at The Oval, a wicket which gave much assistance to the seam bowlers. Clarke and Jackman dismissed Hampshire cheaply on the opening day and Lynch's powerful hitting gave Surrey a lead of 66 which, in the context of the match, looked as if it would be decisive. A marvellous innings of 84 by Greenidge, which made the efforts of all other batsmen on this wicket seem puny in comparison, gave Hampshire some hope and that hope blossomed when Marshall reduced Surrey to 13 for 5 before the close.

Chasing 105 for victory, Surrey's discomfiture continued as Marshall exploited the conditions perfectly and Surrey faced certain defeat when Monkhouse joined Thomas, who had bowled well, with the score on 68 for 9. Thomas batted heroically and Monkhouse was a splendid foil as the last pair added 33 before Thomas edged the first ball of Marshall's fourteenth over of the morning to Pocock at third slip where it was smartly taken to give Hampshire victory by three runs.

John Player League

6 June

at Chelmsford

Essex 92 (I. V. A. Richards 4 for 9)
Somerset 91 for 6

Essex (4 pts) won by 1 run

at Old Trafford

Lancashire 93 for 4
Sussex 97 for 3

Sussex (4 pts) won by 7 wickets

at Leicester

Leicestershire 211 for 5 (D. I. Gower 96, N. E. Briers 58, K. St. J. Emery 4 for 21)
Hampshire 202 for 8

Leicestershire (4 pts) won by 9 runs

at Edgbaston

Warwickshire 164 for 9
Kent 169 for 3

Kent (4 pts) won by 7 wickets

at Worcester

Worcestershire 201 for 7
Derbyshire 203 for 2 (J. G. Wright 103, J. H. Hampshire 64 not out)

Derbyshire (4 pts) won by 8 wickets

at Bradford

Match abandoned
Yorkshire 2 pts, Glamorgan 2 pts

Yorkshire and Essex gained their first John Player League points of the season; Yorkshire by reason of rain causing the abandonment of their match with Glamorgan and Essex with a thrilling one run victory over Somerset in a match brought down to ten overs.

Batting first, Essex reached 88 for 4 when Richards, bowling at medium pace, did the hat-trick, Phillip, McEwan and Fletcher being the victims. Then, with the first two balls of the next over, the last, Botham dismissed Pont and David East so that five wickets had fallen in five balls. Pringle and Lever scrambled four runs from the rest of the over and these runs proved invaluable as Essex, bowling well and fielding bravely, thwarted Somerset's dash for victory.

Sussex had the advantage of the weather at Manchester where Lancashire had already used valuable overs when the match was curtailed. Mendis and Parker batted with grace and aggression to give Sussex a comfortable win which placed them second in the table to Kent who strolled to victory at Edgbaston with more than five overs to spare. Potter batted with supreme confidence and he and Tavare built the platform to victory with a second wicket stand of 67. Underwood had been at his most miserly conceding only 8 runs in his 8 overs and taking the wickets of Kallicharran and Oliver.

Derbyshire won most emphatically at Worcester with John Wright reaching a fine hundred before being dismissed when his side were only three short of victory.

Hampshire asked Leicestershire to bat and then proceeded to drop catches in abundance. Even Parks was guilty as he missed two skiers and Gower and Briers thrived. Parsons restricted the early Hampshire batting, but Jesty, Marshall and Parks made a brave, but unsuccessful bid for victory.

9 June

at Trent Bridge

Nottinghamshire 218 for 3 (C. E. B. Rice 60, J. D. Birch 58 not out)
Zimbabwe 142

Nottinghamshire won by 76 runs

10 June

at Sheffield

Yorkshire 203 for 7 (G. Boycott 98 not out)
Zimbabwe 202 (D. A. G. Fletcher 53)

Yorkshire won by 3 wickets

9, 10 and 11 June

at Chesterfield

Derbyshire 199 for 9 dec (J. H. Hampshire 64) and 241 for 4 (J. G. Wright 106, J. H. Hampshire 81 not out)
Essex 386 for 7 dec (K. S. McEwan 150 not out, S. Turner 56)

Match drawn
Essex 8 pts, Derbyshire 4 pts

at Swansea
Glamorgan 191 (Javed Miandad 66, M. W. Gatting 5 for 34) and 202 (Javed Miandad 52, W. W. Daniel 9 for 61)
Middlesex 352 (R. O. Butcher 122, M. W. Gatting 81, M. A. Nash 4 for 95) and 45 for 0
Middlesex won by 10 wickets
Middlesex 24 pts, Glamorgan 5 pts

at Southampton
Lancashire 210 (J. Simmons 50, M. D. Marshall 5 for 48) and 359 (D. Lloyd 112, D. P. Hughes 65, C. H. Lloyd 60)
Hampshire 458 for 8 dec (N. E. J. Pocock 164, M. D. Marshall 116 not out, N. G. Cowley 71) and 115 for 0 (C. G. Greenidge 62 not out, J. M. Rice 50 not out)
Hampshire won by 10 wickets
Hampshire 24 pts, Lancashire 5 pts

at Tunbridge Wells
Sussex 204 (G. S. le Roux 78) and 251 (I. J. Gould 65, G. D. Mendis 52)
Kent 424 for 6 dec (R. A. Woolmer 203, Asif Iqbal 73) and 35 for 0
Kent won by 10 wickets
Kent 24 pts, Sussex 3 pts

at Leicester
Warwickshire 381 for 6 dec (A. I. Kallicharran 210) and 177 (P. Smith 59, A. M. E. Roberts 6 for 61)
Leicestershire 302 for 7 dec (N. E. Briers 58 not out, J. F. Steele 58, J. C. Balderstone 51) and 196 for 7 (M. A. Garnham 57, R. W. Tolchard 50 not out)
Match drawn
Warwickshire 7 pts, Leicestershire 5 pts

at Worcester
Worcestershire 369 for 2 dec (J. A. Ormrod 200 not out, Younis Ahmed 114 not out) and 268 for 3 dec (J. A. Ormrod 93, P. A. Neale 79 not out, M. J. Weston 51)
Gloucestershire 320 for 4 dec (Zaheer Abbas 77, Sadiq Mohammad 72, P. Bainbridge 55 not out) and 197 for 6 (A. W. Stovold 68, P. Bainbridge 62, N. Gifford 4 for 73)
Match drawn
Worcestershire 5 pts, Gloucestershire 4 pts

at Cambridge
Northamptonshire 372 for 5 dec (R. G. Williams 141, D. S. Steele 65 not out, P. Willey 64) and 179 for 4 dec (W. Larkins 52)
Cambridge University 272 for 9 dec (D. W. Varey 158 not out, P. Willey 4 for 43) and 146 (R. G. Williams 4 for 25)
Northamptonshire won by 133 runs

at Oxford
Surrey 345 for 5 dec (G. S. Clinton 175 not out, C. J. Richards 61, R. D. Jackman 52) and 261 for 1 dec (A. R. Butcher 131, R. D. V. Knight 104 not out)
Oxford University 276 (K. A. Hayes 65, R. D. Jackman 4 for 66, K. S. Mackintosh 4 for 77) and 187 for 5 (R. G. P. Ellis 105 not out)
Match drawn

While Ray Illingworth was turning out for Yorkshire at the age of fifty and Zimbabwe were losing their two one-day games, Middlesex took a firm grip on the Schweppes County Championship. Captained by Mike Gatting, as Mike Brearley was involved in paternal duties, Middlesex brushed away the constraints of the weather and overwhelmed Glamorgan. Gatting returned career best bowling figures and batted with his usual chunky aggression, but the outstanding batting performance for Middlesex came from Roland Butcher who reached his hundred in eighty-three minutes. Butcher and Gatting put on 195 for the fourth wicket and Butcher hit three sixes and twenty fours in his blistering assault. With the rain threatening to deny Middlesex the victory that they deserved Wayne Daniel produced the best bowling performance of the season, 9 for 61. His pace was too much for Glamorgan and it was sobering to realise that he is not among the first half dozen quick bowlers to be considered by the West Indian selectors.

Sussex lost ground on Middlesex when they lost ineptly at Tunbridge Wells. The hitting of Garth le Roux was their only salvation in the first innings and then Bob Woolmer hit the first double century of his career, his previous career best had been against Sussex in 1980. He was at his mightiest. It was one of those occasions when he combined his solid defence with his power of shot that, sadly, he reveals too infrequently. In his pugnacious mood he is a very fine player indeed, even bringing glimpses of Wally Hammond. He and Potter put on 125 for the first wicket and he shared a third wicket stand of 164 with Asif Iqbal in 105 minutes.

Gould and Mendis gave hope of a Sussex revival with an opening stand of 120 in 40 overs, but Kent got on top after Woolmer had caught Mendis off Underwood and they ran to an easy victory against some unexpectedly limp batting.

Essex's dreams of a third championship win were ended by the weather although they had the better of the game with Derbyshire for the first two days. The home county batted very slowly after a late start and Essex took a good lead through a fine hundred from Ken McEwan and some swashbuckling from Turner and Foster, but Wright and Hampshire batted Derbyshire to safety, refusing the bait of some friendly bowling.

Warwickshire threw off the despair of their game with Sussex to have an exciting draw with Leicestershire. Alvin Kallicharran hit his second double century of the season, but, in the second innings, Warwickshire were struggling at 61 for 6 against some fine bowling by Roberts and Parsons, a rapidly maturing and impressive medium pace bowler. Paul Smith and Lethbridge added 89, a crucial stand, and Small and Sutcliffe brought them close to victory after Garnham's sixty minute fifty had given Leicestershire a chance to win. Tolchard blunted Warwickshire's ambitions.

At Worcester the wicket again took its toll of the bowlers, only fifteen wickets fell in the three days while 1,154 runs were scored. The batsman to take the biggest share of plunder was Ormrod who reached the second double century of his career in the first innings and followed it with 93 in the second. Gloucestershire were set to make 318 in 212 minutes, but Gifford restricted them and the draw which had looked inevitable for so long became an actuality.

Hampshire, considered by many to be the Cinderellas of the championship, refuted such allegations with their second

Mike Gatting. Ignored by the England selectors for the Tests and Prudential Internationals against India, he responded with a ferocity which made him the leading English run-maker in first-class cricket in the opening matches of the season.

win in a week and it was achieved in splendid style. Marshall and the other pace men bowled Lancashire out on the opening day, but Hampshire closed on 98 for 4. The next day Nick Pocock, a firm and courageous captain, reached a career best 164 to halt Lancashire's progress and then Malcolm Marshall also hit a career best with a maiden century. Nigel Cowley gave good support and Hampshire reached their highest score for seven years.

A David Lloyd century and some dogged batting by Clive Lloyd, David Hughes and Jack Simmons threatened to deny Hampshire, but Jesty, Marshall and Emery finally broke through, Reidy alone defying them.

Hampshire were left to make 112 in 18 overs, a task that Greenidge and Rice accomplished in the grandest manner with eight balls to spare.

Williams had a fine all-round match at Cambridge where the University succumbed to off-spin, but the highlight of the game was a splendid maiden century by David Varey.

Not to be outdone, Richard Ellis hit a maiden century for Oxford University to save the game against Surrey for whom Butcher, after going to hospital with hay-fever, Clinton and Knight all hit hundreds. Clinton's score was the highest of his career.

The Lancashire team against Hampshire included wicket-keeper Chris Maynard who had been transferred from Warwickshire and played under special registration.

THE ENGLAND TEAM FOR THE FIRST TEST v INDIA AT LORD'S.
(Back row) *Derek Randall; Chris Tavare; Paul Allott; Derek Pringle; Phil Edmonds; Geoff Cook; Allan Lamb*
(Front row) *Bob Taylor; David Gower; Bob Willis (capt.); Ian Botham; Geoff Miller*

First Cornhill Test Match

The England selectors made a couple of surprise choices. Against the form book Cook was chosen to open the innings and, more surprisingly, Derek Pringle, with a very poor record in county cricket as opposed to his performances for Cambridge University, was included. It was hard to support the choice of Pringle when one considered those professionals who had produced outstanding performances for their counties season after season and remained ignored by the selectors, but Pringle was obviously considered a young man of great potential although his fielding was weak and his appetite for the game unproven. Allan Lamb's selection surprised none, but few could understand why Gatting found no place in the side. In 1979, he was chosen for the Prudential World Cup squad when he was quite clearly well below the required standard, now he had matured into a good player and an aggressive one, he was ignored.

India left out Nayak and Patil, choosing Parkar as opener and playing only two seam bowlers.

Willis won the toss, a good start to his captaincy, but England made a dreadful start against some fine bowling by Kapil Dev. Cook and Lamb went lbw and Tavare hung his bat out to give first slip a catch and Kapil Dev his 150th wicket in Test cricket. Gower was superbly taken at slip by Viswanath and, after some belligerent shots which gave England respectability, when it was desperately needed, fell to the perservering and deserving Madan Lal. Pringle's debut was brief and Edmonds joined Randall with England at 166 for 6 in mid-afternoon and India were well on top although the great Kapil Dev could well have wished for the support of another seamer as well as the untiring Madan Lal.

It was the end of India's triumph. Randall celebrated his return to Test cricket with a century which, if a little more circumspect than of yore, still bubbled happily. Phil Edmonds confirmed his all-round ability with an intelligent innings which produced his highest score in Test cricket. When he was superbly caught behind on the leg-side on Friday morning he and Randall had added 125. The Indian agony was not over yet.

Randall hit Kapil Dev lazily to cover where Parkar's brilliant fielding was rewarded with a simple catch. Bob Taylor enjoyed himself and then Willis and Allott shared a last wicket record partnership of 70. The last four wickets had produced 267 runs.

Kapil Dev had bowled marvellously for his six wickets, but he badly needed more support. Of the spinners, Shastri was bitterly disappointing.

Further disappointments followed as Willis and Botham broke the heart of the Indian batting and Pringle gave good support to get a wicket in his first over in Test cricket, and then he followed by dismissing Malhotra. 45 for 5. Kapil Dev

THE INDIAN TEAM WHICH TOURED ENGLAND, 1982.
(Back row) *P. Roy; Yashpal Sharma; Ashok Malhotra; Ghulam Parkar*
(Middle row) *Shivlal Yadav; Randhir Singh; Ravi Shastri; Kapil Dev; Sandeep Patil; S. Nayak; Dilip Doshi; G. Saulez*
(Front row) *Raj Singh (Manager); Dilip Vengsarkar; G. Viswanath; Sunil Gavaskar; S. Madan Lal; S. Kirmani*

joined Gavaskar in some good sense batting, but on a Saturday decimated by showers, India were bowled out and followed on.

Parkar was agonisingly out of his class. He shuffled and fidgeted before offering no stroke to Willis and being bowled. It was a merciful release. When Gavaskar was caught at leg-slip off a ball that leapt nastily and took the shoulder of the bat, it seemed that India would not last beyond Monday lunch time.

That this was not the fact was due to an innings of courage, charm and sheer good sense by Vengsarkar, a man whose every movement is graceful. India had begun the fourth day at 61 for 2, but Shastri stayed with Vengsarkar until the score reached 107 when he was bowled by Allott who had spent most of his time fielding at fine-leg both ends, Willis seemingly considering all his other fielders as specialists.

In the over following Shastri's dismissal Viswanath was out to a poor delivery from Pringle which he touched as it wandered down the leg-side. Yashpal Sharma pronounced the necessary concentration and the Indian recovery, aided by some missed catches, asserted itself again.

Vengsarkar reached his century off 205 balls, but England players had clearly believed that he had been caught behind off Pringle when 65. This does not detract from the quality of his innings which ended when he hooked at the new ball and was caught at long leg.

Yashpal Sharma was beaten for pace and Malhotra was brilliantly caught by Taylor diving in front of first slip. It was Willis' two hundred and fiftieth victim in Test cricket and he had taken three wickets in nine balls to deny India's ambitions once more.

Gower caught Kirmani at slip and Pringle dropped Kapil Dev there off Botham. It was a costly miss. When the chance was dropped Kapil Dev had scored 5. He now assaulted the bowling in a most belligerent manner. He hit three sixes and thirteen fours in an innings of 89 which came off only 55 deliveries. It was breathtaking stuff and when he was caught at short mid-wicket off Botham he still had sixteen balls left to make the eleven runs he needed for the fastest century in Test cricket.

He was not yet done with England. They needed only 65 to win and had a half an hour's batting at the close of the day. Bowling like a man inspired, which is how he plays all his cricket, Kapil Dev sent back both openers and nightwatchman Taylor with only 18 scored. The next morning England duly completed their victory, but the spirit that India had shown on the Monday had breathed some life into a series which had threatened to be stillborn.

The saddest reflection of the Test was that India had refused to accept David Constant as umpire. It was generally believed that this was retaliation for England's attitude to the Indian umpires during the series in India earlier in the year.

Above: *Kirmani, c Gower, b Willis 3. Second Innings, First Test at Lord's.*

Opposite: *Captain of England. Bob Willis in three moods. Above: Joyful at meeting Her Majesty the Queen. Below left: Pensive on the field. Below right: Reflective on the balcony.*

FIRST CORNHILL TEST MATCH – ENGLAND v. INDIA
10, 11, 12, 14 and 15 June 1982 at Lord's

ENGLAND

	FIRST INNINGS		SECOND INNINGS	
G. Cook	b Dev	4	lbw, b Dev	10
C. J. Tavare	c Viswanath, b Dev	4	b Dev	3
A. J. Lamb	lbw, b Dev	9	(4) not out	37
D. I. Gower	c Viswanath, b Dev	37	(5) not out	14
I. T. Botham	c Malhotra, b Lal	67		
D. W. Randall	c Parkar, b Dev	126		
D. R. Pringle	c Gavaskar, b Doshi	7		
P. H. Edmonds	c Kirmani, b Lal	64		
R. W. Taylor*	c Viswanath, b Doshi	31	(3) c Sharma, b Dev	1
P. J. W. Allott	not out	41		
R. G. D. Willis†	b Lal	28		
Extras	b 1, lb 5, nb 9	15	lb 2	2
		433	(for 3 wkts)	67

	O	M	R	W	O	M	R	W
Kapil Dev	43	8	125	5	10	1	43	3
Madan Lal	28.1	6	99	3	2	1	2	—
Shastri	34	10	73	—	2	—	9	—
Doshi	40	7	120	2	5	3	11	—
Yashpal Sharma	3	2	1	—				

INDIA

	FIRST INNINGS		SECOND INNINGS	
S. M. Gavaskar†	b Botham	48	c Cook, b Willis	24
G. A. M. H. Parkar	lbw, b Botham	6	b Willis	1
D. B. Vengsarkar	lbw, b Willis	2	c Allott, b Willis	157
G. R. Viswanath	b Botham	1	(5) c Taylor, b Pringle	3
Yashpal Sharma	lbw, b Pringle	4	(6) b Willis	37
A. Malhotra	lbw, b Pringle	5	(7) c Taylor, b Willis	0
Kapil Dev	c Cook, b Willis	41	(8) c Cook, b Botham	89
R. J. Shastri	c Cook, b Willis	4	(4) b Allott	23
S. M. H. Kirmani*	not out	6	c Gower, b Willis	3
Madan Lal	c Tavare, b Botham	6	lbw, b Pringle	15
D. R. Doshi	c Taylor, b Botham	0	not out	4
Extras	lb 1, nb 4	5	lb 2, nb 11	13
		128		369

	O	M	R	W	O	M	R	W
Botham	19.4	3	46	5	31.5	7	103	1
Willis	16	2	14	3	28	3	101	6
Pringle	9	4	16	2	19	4	58	2
Allott	4	1	15	—	17	3	51	1
Edmonds	2	1	5	—	15	6	39	—
Cook					1	—	4	—

FALL OF WICKETS
1-5, 2-18, 3-37, 4-96, 5-149, 6-166, 7-291, 8-363, 9-363
1-11, 2-13, 3-18

FALL OF WICKETS
1-17, 2-21, 3-22, 4-31, 5-45, 6-112, 7-116, 8-116, 9-128
1-6, 2-47, 3-107, 4-110, 5-252, 6-252, 7-254, 8-275, 9-341

England won by 7 wickets

Derek Pringle takes a wicket in his first over in Test cricket. Yashpal Sharma, lbw, b Pringle 4. Above: Gower, Botham, Tavare, Taylor and Edmonds join in the appeal. Below: *Yashpal Sharma leaves disconsolately as the England players run to congratulate Pringle.*

Derek Randall hits out to celebrate his recall to the England side. Teeth gritted in endeavour, he hit one six (the shot shown) and eleven fours in his 126. Viswanath is at slip, Kirmani is keeping wicket. First Test Match at Lord's.

Vengsarkar, elegance and belligerence, India's saving grace at Lord's.

12, 14 and 15 June

at Cardiff
Warwickshire 391 for 7 dec (T. A. Lloyd 122, G. W. Humpage 90 not out) and 169 (Asif Din 55, S. R. Barwick 4 for 10, R. C. Ontong 4 for 61)
Glamorgan 250 (A. L. Jones 72, Javed Miandad 68, C. Lethbridge 5 for 68) and 166 for 6 (R. C. Ontong 56)
Match drawn
Warwickshire 8 pts, Glamorgan 5 pts

at Liverpool
Lancashire 237 (J. Abrahams 53) and 367 for 5 (G. Fowler 122, J. Abrahams 90, D. P. Hughes 85 not out)
Essex 300 for 5 dec (K. S. McEwan 92 not out, K. W. R. Fletcher 73 not out, G. A. Gooch 66)
Match drawn
Essex 8 pts, Lancashire 3 pts

at Northampton
Northamptonshire 302 for 5 dec (W. Larkins 137, P. Willey 65) and 257 for 3 dec (R. G. Williams 87 not out, P. Willey 70, D. J. Capel 60 not out)
Somerset 203 for 1 dec (J. W. Lloyds 132 not out, P. M. Roebuck 51) and 152 for 0 (J. W. Lloyds 102 not out)
Match drawn
Northamptonshire 4 pts, Somerset 4 pts

at Trent Bridge
Kent 157 (A. P. E. Knott 52) and 57 (M. Hendrick 4 for 4)
Nottinghamshire 183 (B. Hassan 66, G. W. Johnson 5 for 36, D. L. Underwood 5 for 70) and 35 for 0
Nottinghamshire won by 10 wickets
Nottinghamshire 21 pts, Kent 5 pts

at The Oval
Gloucestershire 239 for 8 dec (P. Bainbridge 57) and 163 for 4 dec (Zaheer Abbas 58)
Surrey 150 for 5 dec (G. R. J. Roope 53 not out) and 253 for 5 (A. R. Butcher 79, R. D. V. Knight 54, J. N. Shepherd 4 for 81)
Surrey won by 5 wickets
Surrey 20 pts, Gloucestershire 4 pts

at Hove
Worcestershire 85 and 153
Sussex 275 for 8 dec (P. W. G. Parker 74, I. J. Gould 66)
Sussex won by an innings and 37 runs
Sussex 23 pts, Worcestershire 3 pts

at Sheffield
Yorkshire 203 (W. W. Daniel 6 for 60) and 236 for 5 dec (P. Carrick 81, S. N. Hartley 60 not out)
Middlesex 158 (G. B. Stevenson 4 for 46, C. M. Old 4 for 48) and 39 for 2
Match drawn
Yorkshire 6 pts, Middlesex 5 pts

With Middlesex having the worst of a drawn game at Sheffield which was finally ended early by rain, Sussex closed the gap at the top of the Schweppes County Championship by beating Worcestershire in two days at Hove.

Everything went wrong for Worcestershire. Younis was declared unfit and Scott was called in as a late replacement, but, although play began an hour and a half late, Worcestershire were bowled out by Imran, Greig and le Roux before Scott could reach the ground. Barclay's decision to put the opposition in was fully justified when Parker and Gould shared a fourth wicket stand of 95 to put Sussex on top. Gould hit fiercely and Parker stabilised the innings so that Sussex gained a lead of 190. This was too much for Worcestershire who succumbed to the Sussex pace attack for a second time.

There was rain at Liverpool where Essex dominated the early stages of the match. They bowled Lancashire out on the Saturday and scored quickly to gather maximum bonus points, but there were interruptions for rain and the last day became a frenzy of scoring as against the bowling of Fletcher and McEwan, offering runs, Fowler hit six sixes in his 122 and Hughes scored 85 not out in 42 minutes before rain ended play.

At The Oval, Gloucestershire and Surrey defied the rain interruptions with a series of declarations, but, ultimately, Graveney's declaration which asked Surrey to score 253 in 203 minutes seemed a little over-generous and Surrey, pacing their innings well, won with eight balls to spare. Butcher and Clinton gave them a fine start and Knight and Lynch maintained the scoring rate required before falling to Shepherd and leaving the final flourish to Roope and Richards.

A massive first innings total founded on fine innings by Andy Lloyd and Humpage gave Warwickshire ascendancy over Glamorgan who only avoided the follow-on through a last wicket stand of 20 between Daniels and Barwick. Earlier Javed and A. L. Jones had saved them from a threat of extinction and then Ontong and Barwick, bowling well, even gave the Welshmen an outside chance of victory, but Lethbridge and Small were threatening as rain brought play to an early close.

There was a rain restricted day on the Saturday at Northampton, but Wayne Larkins completed a very good century on the Monday. On a placid pitch batsmen thrived. Jeremy Lloyds hit a career best 132 and followed this with a second innings century, the first time he had hit two hundreds in a match, but as a contest, it died.

The Trent Bridge wicket was again under debate as Kent struggled on the opening day against the Notts seamers. Only Knott's improvisations gave them any respectability and after rain Notts fared little better although Asif pressured them with spin. Notts, thanks mainly to an opening stand of 96 by Hassan and Robinson, scrambled a first innings lead of 26 which took on gigantic proportions when Kent closed the second day with Woolmer, Potter, Dilley and Underwood all out to Hendrick and only three runs on the board. They never recovered and it was more the total lack of application and determination in their batting and the accuracy and aggression of the Notts bowling than the wicket which caused their downfall. Hassan and Robinson scored the runs needed for victory at five an over.

Zaheer, Imran and Sarfraz were playing their last games for their counties before joining the Pakistan touring side.

John Player League

13 June

at Portsmouth

Derbyshire 193 for 5 (J. G. Wright 67)
Hampshire 194 for 9

Hampshire (4 pts) won by 1 wicket

at Old Trafford

Essex 269 for 3 (G. A. Gooch 122, K. S. McEwan 76, B. R. Hardie 53)
Lancashire 187 (F. C. Hayes 87, N. Phillip 6 for 13)

Essex (4 pts) won by 82 runs

at Leicester

Leicestershire 172 for 8 (N. E. Briers 61)
Middlesex 173 for 6 (C. T. Radley 58 not out)

Middlesex (4 pts) won by 4 wickets

at Northampton

Northamptonshire 203 for 6 (D. J. Capel 79, R. G. Williams 66, K. B. S. Jarvis 4 for 39)
Kent 142

Northamptonshire (4 pts) won by 61 runs

at The Oval

Surrey 210 for 5 (M. A. Lynch 55 not out, A. R. Butcher 55)
Gloucestershire 182 for 5 (Zaheer Abbas 63 not out)

Surrey (4 pts) won by 28 runs

at Horsham

Sussex 206 for 8 (P. W. G. Parker 73)
Worcestershire 208 for 7

Worcestershire (4 pts) won by 3 wickets

at Edgbaston

Somerset 261 for 3 (P. W. Denning 112 not out, I. V. A. Richards 79)
Warwickshire 177 (C. Lethbridge 57 not out)

Somerset (4 pts) won by 84 runs

at Hull

Yorkshire 232 for 6 (J. D. Love 70)
Nottinghamshire 232 for 8 (C. E. B. Rice 82)

Match tied
Yorkshire 2 pts, Nottinghamshire 2 pts

A violent assault on the Lancashire bowling by Graham Gooch which brough him five sixes and ten fours in his highest John Player League score was a reminder to England selectors what had been denied them. Gooch and Hardie opened with a stand of 107 and he and McEwan added 161 for the second. Facing the massive Essex total, Lancashire were reduced to 49 for 4 by Norbert Phillip. Frank Hayes resisted bravely until he was struck on the chin by a bouncer from Phillip and trod on his wicket.

Middlesex disposed of their near challengers Leicestershire after an uneasy time at Grace Road. The home side always threatened more than they achieved, but Middlesex were still 25 short of victory when they lost their sixth wicket. Downton then joined the durable Radley and there were no more alarms.

Kent's unbeaten run came to an end at Northampton where Williams and Capel put on 113 for the third wicket for Northants. Nineteen year-old Capel batted with great maturity and he emphasised the qualities which had won him an assured place in the Northants side.

Lynch's fierce hitting which inspired 70 runs in the last nine overs, his own contribution being 55 from 38 balls, proved decisive in Surrey's win at The Oval.

Somerset showed something of their true form when their batsmen savaged Warwickshire at Edgbaston. Denning hit his highest John Player League score, carrying his bat throughout the forty overs, and he and Richards, at his brilliant best, added 148 in nineteen overs for the second wicket. In reply Warwickshire never recovered from 35 for 4. It was the first time in the season that Somerset were able to field both Garner and Richards.

The Sussex challenge on Middlesex was surprisingly frustrated by Worcestershire. Some splendid wicket-keeping by Humphries who caught Mendis, Gould and Wells, and stumped Greig in exciting fashion off Younis helped the visitors to restrict Sussex to 116 for 5. Some forceful stroke play by Parker gave hope to Sussex and he raised hopes further with a brilliant catch to dismiss Hemsley, but big hitting from Humphries, Inchmore and skipper Neale won the day for Worcestershire with an over to spare.

Yorkshire came very close to winning their first limited-over game of the season, only to be thwarted at the last by Saxelby of Notts. Jim Love played a belligerent innings and Yorkshire felt safe with their 232 for 6. Clive Rice gave the Notts innings authority and substance, but when Stuchbury bowled the last over they were ten short of victory. Hendrick and Saxelby scored off every ball, but Stuchbury's dive to stop Saxelby's drive off the last ball denied the batsmen the two that they needed and the game was tied.

There were equally thrilling events at Portsmouth where Derbyshire were beaten narrowly and thrillingly and so lost the chance to be top of the league. Chasing a target of 194, Hampshire were given a good start, but they lost four middle order batsmen for 19 runs. Cowley batted with good sense, but the first batsman to suggest that Hants could really win was Bobbie Parks who hit with a majesty reminiscent of his father and indicating that he was two or three places too low in the batting order. When he lofted Oldham to Wood the responsibility fell on Tremlett who responded with calm and dignity. Eight runs were needed off the last over. There was a brilliant stop by Hill and then Tunnicliffe bowled Emery so that Malone came in with five needed from three balls. Malone thankfully hit the first for a single and then Tremlett drove and overpitched delivery through the covers for a regal four. As Tremlett had also dismissed top scorer Wright, who had shared a 101 partnership with John Hampshire, he could be said to have enjoyed his day.

I.C.C. Trophy

17 June

at Old Silhillians

Gibraltar 80
Kenya 81 for 1 (A. Rehman 53 not out)
Kenya won by 9 wickets

at Blossomfield

Netherlands 150 for 9
East Africa 127
Netherlands won by 23 runs

at Bournville

Hong Kong 100
Papua New Guinea 101 for 6
Papua New Guinea won by 4 wickets

at Moseley

Zimbabwe 332 for 4 (D. L. Houghton 135, K. M. Curran 126 not out)
U.S.A. 141 (P. W. Rawson 4 for 34)
Zimbabwe won by 191 runs

at Wednesbury

Bermuda 348 for 9 (W. Reid 128, G. Brown 100)
Malaysia 64 (E. G. James 5 for 2)
Bermuda won by 284 runs

at West Bromwich

Bangladesh 246 (G. Ashraf 77)
West Africa 170 for 9
Bangladesh won by 76 runs

Benson and Hedges Cup – Quarter Finals

17 June

at Canterbury

Kent 207 (N. R. Taylor 121, I. T. Botham 4 for 52)
Somerset 208 for 7 (B. C. Rose 52, P. M. Roebuck 50)
Somerset won by 3 wickets
(Gold Award – N. R. Taylor)

at Derby

Derbyshire 190 (P. N. Kirsten 60)
Sussex 194 for 6 (P. W. G. Parker 72)
Sussex won by 4 wickets
(Gold Award – P. W. G. Parker)

at Lord's

Lancashire 191 for 9 (C. H. Lloyd 66)
Middlesex 139 (C. T. Radley 66, I. Folley 4 for 18)
Lancashire won by 52 runs
(Gold Award – C. H. Lloyd)

17 and 18 June

at Trent Bridge

Nottinghamshire 156
Leicestershire 154 for 9
Nottinghamshire won by 2 runs
(Gold Award – G. J. Parsons)

Having swept all before them throughout the season and being unbeaten in all competitions, Middlesex fell at the most vital hurdle when their batting failed miserably to reach the meagre target which their bowling had earned for them. Some powerful hitting by Clive Lloyd and some stubborn aggression from the venerable Simmons lifted Lancashire with a fifth wicket stand of 74 after four wickets had gone for 72. It proved to be the biggest, and most crucial stand of the day. Middlesex began badly and in spite of the brave defiance of Radley, they never really recovered. The young left-arm seam bowler Ian Folley bowled Radley and with him went Middlesex's hopes. As well as Folley's fine bowling, Lancashire had much to thank Jack Simmons for. He took the wickets of Butcher and Barlow in his eleven over spell which cost only 17 runs and he was very unlucky not to be named for the Gold Award. Apart from Radley's knock and the

Their indestructability increases with age. Pillars of the Lancashire side. All-rounders – (left) David Hughes. He has ripened into a most dependable batsman. (Right) Jack Simmons. It is hard to understand why he did not receive the Gold Award in the Benson & Hedges Quarter Final at Lord's. A good and faithful servant.

steadiness of their bowling, Middlesex could be pleased with some brilliant wicket-keeping by Paul Downton. Lancashire could be pleased that they had become the first side in the season to lower the Middlesex colours and they had done it when it mattered most.

Neil Taylor, who had hit 121 against Sussex in the last of the Benson and Hedges qualifying games, hit exactly the same score against Somerset at Canterbury. A punching batsman, strong in the fore-arms like a championship boxer, Taylor mocked the efforts of his team-mates who crumpled before the varied Somerset attack. Kent were floundering at 54 for 4 when Chris Cowdrey joined Taylor in a stand of 119 in 27 overs, Cowdrey was finally adjudged lbw to Garner although he was well down the wicket. No other batsman reached double figures, but Somerset too started circumspectly. Denning followed an outswinger from Jarvis in the seventh over and was caught behind with only 12 on the board. Richards hit three fours and then pulled outrageously at Jarvis and was lbw. Wisdom now took control and Rose and Roebuck accumulated quietly. Their stand for the third wicket realised 83 and it gave the Somerset innings its much needed hardcore. Roebuck tried to pull Woolmer but was caught and bowled. The dependable Rose pulled Dilley into mid-on's hands and Lloyds, looking nothing like a batsman who had just scored two hundreds in a match, was caught at long on. Botham heaved all about him and looked like settling the match on his own when he square cut Jarvis into Woolmer's hands at cover. Somerset now needed 23 off 28 balls. Marks slashed Dilley into Cowdrey's hands but Somerset always had their noses in front and a heave by Garner, the coolness of Taylor and a wide by Dilley gave them victory with two balls to spare.

Asked to bat, Derbyshire made only 189 and owed much to Kirsten although once more it was the all round steadiness of the Sussex attack that caught the eye. Sussex lost Imran and Wells with only six scored but first Mendis and then Parker, in one of his less flamboyant innings, assured them of victory.

The match at Trent Bridge moved into a second day. The Notts batting was rather uninspired, but the home side had to contend with an accurate seam attack in which the economic Parsons was outstanding. Leicestershire's batting was no more confident than Notts' had been. Briers went in the fourth over and Gower scored only five in his first hour at the wicket. Just as he seemed to be getting into his stride he was caught sweeping at Hemmings. The Leicestershire middle order disintegrated in worsening light and a halt was called with the score at 118 for 7 with eight overs remaining and Notts poised for victory.

Steele and Parsons had other ideas and on the Thursday morning they nudged and scrambled runs so that in the fifty-third over they had taken the score to 143 when Steele flicked Saxelby off his legs for what looked to be a four until French took a fine diving catch behind the wicket. In the end Parsons needed to hit the last ball of the match for four which he just failed to do.

In the first round of matches in the I.C.C. Trophy Gladstone Brown and Winston Reid put on 211 for Bermuda's first wicket and their side's total of 348 for 9 was a record score for the competition.

17 and 18 June

at Cambridge

Combined Universities 288 for 7 dec (R. G. P. Ellis 90, R. J. Boyd-Moss 63, S. N. Yadav 5 for 107) and 234 for 7 dec (K. A. Hayes 62, D. R. Pringle 51)
Indians 354 for 6 dec (S. M. Gavaskar 120, R. J. Shastri 93, Yashpal Sharma 55) and 51 for 1
Match drawn

I.C.C. Trophy

18 June

at Alvechurch

Gibraltar 42 for 4
v. **U.S.A.**
Match abandoned

at Wolverhampton

Zimbabwe 192 for 4 (D. L. Houghton 73, J. G. Heron 50)
Kenya 71 for 4
Zimbabwe won by 121 runs

at Colwall

Fiji 31 for 2
v. **Malaysia**
Match abandoned

at Studley

Hong Kong 207 for 7 (A. A. Lorimer 53)
Israel 84
Hong Kong won by 123 runs

at Walsall

East Africa v. **Singapore**
No play

at Rugby

West Africa v. **Netherlands**
No play

The rain which had come close to wrecking the first I.C.C. Trophy competition in 1979 returned to savage the second competition. The Zimbabwe match was reduced to 25 overs and the Hong Kong game to 45 although most of those were played in a light drizzle. It was sad that these delightful and happy cricketers from all over the world could not have been welcomed with better weather, sad too that Argentina were forced to withdraw from the competition for political reasons and Denmark could not compete for financial ones.

19, 20 and 21 June

at Bristol

Indians 245 for 5 dec (Madan Lal 51 not out, R. J. Shastri 51, Yashpal Sharma 50 not out) and 200 for 4 dec (Madan Lal 58 not out)
Gloucestershire 200 for 6 dec (B. C. Broad 73, P. Bainbridge 61) and 39 for 4 (Madan Lal 4 for 28)
Match drawn

19, 21 and 22 June

at Ilford

Essex 252 for 7 dec (N. Phillip 61, B. R. Hardie 55, H. L. Alleyne 4 for 92)
Worcestershire 64 (G. A. Gooch 7 for 14) and 17 for 1
Match drawn
Essex 7 pts, Worcestershire 3 pts

at Canterbury

Kent 250 for 8 dec (Asif Iqbal 65, C. J. Tavare 54, C. J. Tunnicliffe 5 for 73) and 28 for 0
Derbyshire 151 for 3 dec
Match drawn
Kent 3 pts, Derbyshire 3 pts

at Lord's

Lancashire 280 (C. H. Lloyd 93)
Middlesex 267 for 6 (M. W. Gatting 133 not out, R. O. Butcher 82, C. E. H. Croft 4 for 100)
Match drawn
Middlesex 6 pts, Lancashire 4 pts

at Trent Bridge

Warwickshire 74 for 3
v. **Nottinghamshire**. Match abandoned.
Nottinghamshire 1 pt, Warwickshire 0 pts

at Bath

Hampshire 259 (N. G. Cowley 50, I. T. Botham 5 for 48) and 85 for 1
Somerset 248 (I. T. Botham 66, K. St. J. D. Emery 5 for 80)
Match drawn
Hampshire 7 pts, Somerset 6 pts

at Hove

Sussex 313 for 9 dec (J. R. T. Barclay 87, G. S. le Roux 83) and 85 for 3 (I. J. Gould 55 not out)
Surrey 243 (R. D. V. Knight 69, C. E. Waller 7 for 67)
Match drawn
Sussex 7 pts, Surrey 5 pts

at Middlesbrough

Northamptonshire 382 for 3 dec (W. Larkins 186, G. Cook 112 not out)
Yorkshire 142 for 4 (C. W. J. Athey 54)
Match drawn
Northamptonshire 5 pts, Yorkshire 1 pt

at Cambridge
Leicestershire 256 for 9 dec (N. E. Briers 94, D. I. Gower 77) and 40 for 1
Cambridge University 230 for 8 dec (D. W. Varey 72)
Match drawn

at Swansea
Oxford University 250 (R. Edbrooke 84 not out, R. S. Luddington 65) and 154 for 6 (R. S. Luddington 62 not out)
Glamorgan 317 (A. Jones 98, C. J. C. Rowe 60 not out, T. Davies 52, T. J. Taylor 5 for 118, I. S. Curtis 5 for 140)
Match drawn

Rain totally destroyed the matches that began on 19 June. Play was possible on the first day, but there were only a few balls bowled at Cambridge and Swansea on the last day, none elsewhere.

There were some performances of note before the deluge. Madan Lal had a splendid all-round match for India who looked to be on their way to a victory. Norbert Phillip's lusty blows revived Essex and then, in the absence of the injured Lever, Gooch was used as first change bowler. In sultry conditions he bowled eleven overs and took seven for 14, a career best, and a demoralised Worcestershire followed on but were saved by the rain.

Ferocious hitting by Roland Butcher supported yet another splendid innings by Mike Gatting at Lord's. In 140 minutes, 35 overs, they added 178 for the fourth wicket; this was after Middlesex had been 24 for 3. There was also some fierce hitting by Botham, 66 off 38 deliveries, but Emery kept Hampshire in contention with some good pace bowling.

Cook and Larkins had an opening stand of 278 for Northants at Middlesbrough with Larkins making 186 of them.

Barclay scored welcome runs for Sussex and le Roux helped him to revive his side with a seventh wicket stand of 130 and then Chris Waller came very clsoe to a career best with some beautifully controlled left arm spin. Parker took four fine catches and Gould hit belligerently in the late evening.

The most sensational news came from Yorkshire where it was announced that Chris Old was being relieved of the captaincy and that Ray Illingworth was returning to first-class cricket at the age of fifty to lead the side.

The unluckiest news came from Lord's where, on the opening day, Frank Hayes fell when taking a run, was carried from the field and it was discovered that he had broken his ankle. The gods of cricket have not treated the man kindly since he burst on the scene like a comet some dozen years ago.

John Player League
20 June
at Ilford
Essex 247 for 6 (K. S. McEwan 105 not out)
Worcestershire 138 (M. J. Weston 61)
Essex (4 pts) won by 109 runs

at Canterbury
Kent 193 for 7
Derbyshire 186
Kent (4 pts) won by 7 runs

at Lord's
Middlesex 198 for 7 (W. N. Slack 63)
Lancashire 178 (C. H. Lloyd 52, W. W. Daniel 5 for 27)
Middlesex (4 pts) won by 20 runs

at Trent Bridge
Nottinghamshire 161 for 9
Warwickshire 139 for 9
Nottinghamshire (4 pts) won by 22 runs

at Bath
Surrey 175 (I. T. Botham 4 for 47)
Somerset 179 for 6 (J. Garner 59 not out)
Somerset (4 pts) won by 4 wickets

at Hastings
Sussex 251 for 4 (G. S. le Roux 88, C. M. Wells 81 not out)
Glamorgan 132
Sussex (4 pts) won by 119 runs

at Middlesbrough
Northamptonshire 282 for 4 (W. Larkins 79, G. Cook 73, A. J. Lamb 67 not out)
Yorkshire 227 (A. Sidebottom 52 not out, D. J. Capel 4 for 30)
Northamptonshire (4 pts) won by 55 runs

In their third meeting with Lancashire in three different competitions within the space of five days Middlesex triumphed to maintain a seven point lead at the top of the table. The Middlesex innings was founded on a second wicket stand of 70 between Slack and Gatting. Clive Lloyd opened the Lancashire innings at his aggressively exciting best and completed a fine fifty before he was run out by Daniel in the eighteenth over. Daniel took 5 for 27 in a hostile and accurate spell confirming his magnificent run of success.

A glorious century by Ken McEwan and a thrilling display of hitting by Alan Lilley put all hopes of a Worcestershire victory aside. They added 69 in 4 overs at one time and Pringle had a fine opening spell in which he dismissed Turner, Ormrod and Patel so that the issue was quickly decided. Worcestershire's consolation was a maiden half-century in the competition by Weston.

For the second day running Yorkshire suffered at the hands of the Northants openers. This time Cook and Larkins began with a stand of 128. Allan Lamb added a brisk half-century and the target got beyond Yorkshire's capabilities.

A sodden wicket at Trent Bridge produced a low scoring game in which the Notts spinners were the decisive factor.

Garth le Roux hit 88 off 56 balls and he and Colin Wells shared a spectacular stand of 128 in 15 overs against a rather sad Glamorgan attack. The all round bowling strength of

Sussex easily accounted for the Glamorgan batting to give the home side a massive victory.

Kent also maintained the challenge on Middlesex with an exciting win over Derbyshire. Derbyshire needed 79 to win over the last 10 overs and soon lost Wood and Barnett which left them 56 from 5 overs. Bob Taylor and Bill Fowler brought them renewed hope. Bill Fowler, the English born player with Auckland, was playing his first game in the competition. He was bowled by Jarvis for 29 and Jarvis run out for 18. Dilley was barracked by the crowd when 17 runs were scored from one over that he bowled. Dilley was not fully fit and this was a disgraceful outburst which was later censured by Kent manager Brian Luckhurst. It was Dilley who caught Oldham off Jarvis off the first ball of the final over to give Kent victory by 7 runs.

The most devastating innings of the day was at Bath where, chasing 176, Somerset were 94 for 6. Garner then arrived and hit 25 in one over from Needham including four gigantic sixes. He then hit two more sixes off Knight and Somerset cruised to an astonishingly easy victory which left Surrey a little bewildered.

I.C.C. Trophy
21 June

at Lichfield
U.S.A. v. **Kenya**
No play

at Brewood
Zimbabwe v. **Gibraltar**
No play

at Cheltenham
Israel 167 for 9 (S. B. Periman 75 not out)
Papua New Guinea 171 for 1 (N. Agonia 86 not out, T. Val 75 not out)
Papua New Guinea won by 9 wickets

at Burton
Hong Kong v. **Canada**
No play

at Swindon
Bangladesh 143 (W. A. Bourne 4 for 33)
East Africa 117
Bangladesh won by 26 runs

at Bromsgrove
Bermuda 153 for 5
Fiji 102 for 6
Bermuda won by 51 runs

at Fordhouse
Netherlands v. **Singapore**
No play

Rain again curtailed the I.C.C. Trophy when the third round of matches was scheduled. The match at Bromsgrove was reduced to twenty overs and in four places there was no play at all. Nigel Agonia and Taunao Val added 157 for the second wicket to give Papua New Guinea a surprisingly easy victory at Cheltenham C.C. and Bangladesh recovered from the early devastations of former Warwickshire seamer Bill Bourne to beat East Africa.

I.C.C. Trophy
23 June

at Lutterworth
Bangladesh v. **Singapore**
No play

at Nuneaton
Canada v. **Gibraltar**
No play

at Bridgnorth
Malaysia v. **East Africa**
No play

at Barnt Green
Fiji v. **West Africa**
No play

at Pershore
Israel 74 for 6
v. **Kenya**
Match abandoned

at Warwick
Papua New Guinea v. **U.S.A.**
No play

Rain so ravaged the tournament that in the six matches the twenty-four overs bowled at Pershore were the only overs bowled. Poor Singapore had not got onto the field in any of their three scheduled matches.

23, 24 and 25 June

at Ilford
Yorkshire 152 for 8 dec (R. G. Lumb 52, G. A. Gooch 4 for 60)
Essex 90 for 1
Match drawn
Essex 3 pts, Yorkshire 1 pt

at Cardiff
Worcestershire 217
Glamorgan 86 for 1 (A. Jones 53)
Match drawn
Glamorgan 4 pts, Worcestershire 2 pts

at Basingstoke
Hampshire 200 for 2 dec (M. C. J. Nicholas 127 not out J. M. Rice 60) and 8 for 1
Sussex 106 for 6 dec (M. D. Marshall 4 for 42)
Match drawn
Hampshire 4 pts, Sussex 0 pts

at Leicester
Kent 53 for 1
v. **Leicestershire**
Match drawn
No points

at Northampton
Warwickshire 41 for 2 dec and 123 for 4 (A. I. Kallicharran 52 not out)
Northamptonshire 65 for 2 dec
Match drawn
No points

at Bath
Somerset 200 for 8 dec (P. W. Denning 51)
Gloucestershire 104 for 3
Match drawn
Somerset 3 pts, Gloucestershire 3 pts

at The Oval
Surrey 128 for 5 dec
Lancashire 78 for 5
Match drawn
Surrey 2 pts, Lancashire 2 pts

at Lord's
Middlesex 144 for 9 (W. N. Slack 64) and 30 for 4 (Imran Khan 4 for 10)
Pakistanis 31 for 1
Match drawn

The Pakistanis' tour had a sodden beginning, but their bowlers displayed enough talent at Lord's to make England pause and consider.

The Schweppes County Championship programme was totally ruined by the weather. Illingworth's come-back was restricted to 18.5 overs of fielding at Ilford where Gooch again demonstrated his ability to move the ball in heavy conditions.

At Basingstoke Mark Nicholas had time to complete an impressively efficient century and confirm his advance as a batsman, but the rain was the only winner everywhere.

I.C.C. Trophy
25 June
at Banbury
Fiji *v.* **Bangladesh**
No play

Chris Maynard, a mid-season transfer from Warwickshire to Lancashire.

at Moseley
Bermuda *v.* **Netherlands**
No play

at Leamington
Canada 9 for 0
v. **Zimbabwe**
Match abandoned

at Wishaw
Israel 42 for 2
v. **Gibraltar**
Match abandoned

at Aldridge
U.S.A. *v.* **Hong Kong**
No play

at Wightwick
Singapore *v.* **West Africa**
No play

Second Cornhill Test Match

England made one change from the side which won at Lord's, Miller replaced Allott about whose fitness there were doubts. Jarvis of Kent had been called to join the party when Allott was reported likely to be unfit. The inclusion of Pringle in the England side meant that the Cambridge captain would miss the Varsity match, a most unfortunate happening and one which, it was felt, the selectors should have been sensitive enough to avoid. Nayak replaced Parkar in the Indian side, Shastri moving up to open the innings.

Willis again won the toss and Cook and Tavare began with a century which, if statistically impressive and of great value, was hardly a partnership that suggested an England opening pair of class and distinction. Its worth was sharpened in perspective, however, when in 14 overs India captured five

Second Test Match, Old Trafford. Geoff Miller off-drives. Kirmani echoes the batsman's concentration. Again Miller fell short of the hundred.

Opposite: *Sandeep Patil. An innings to remember. In all his glory, he hits Bob Willis for 4 at Old Trafford. Second Test.*

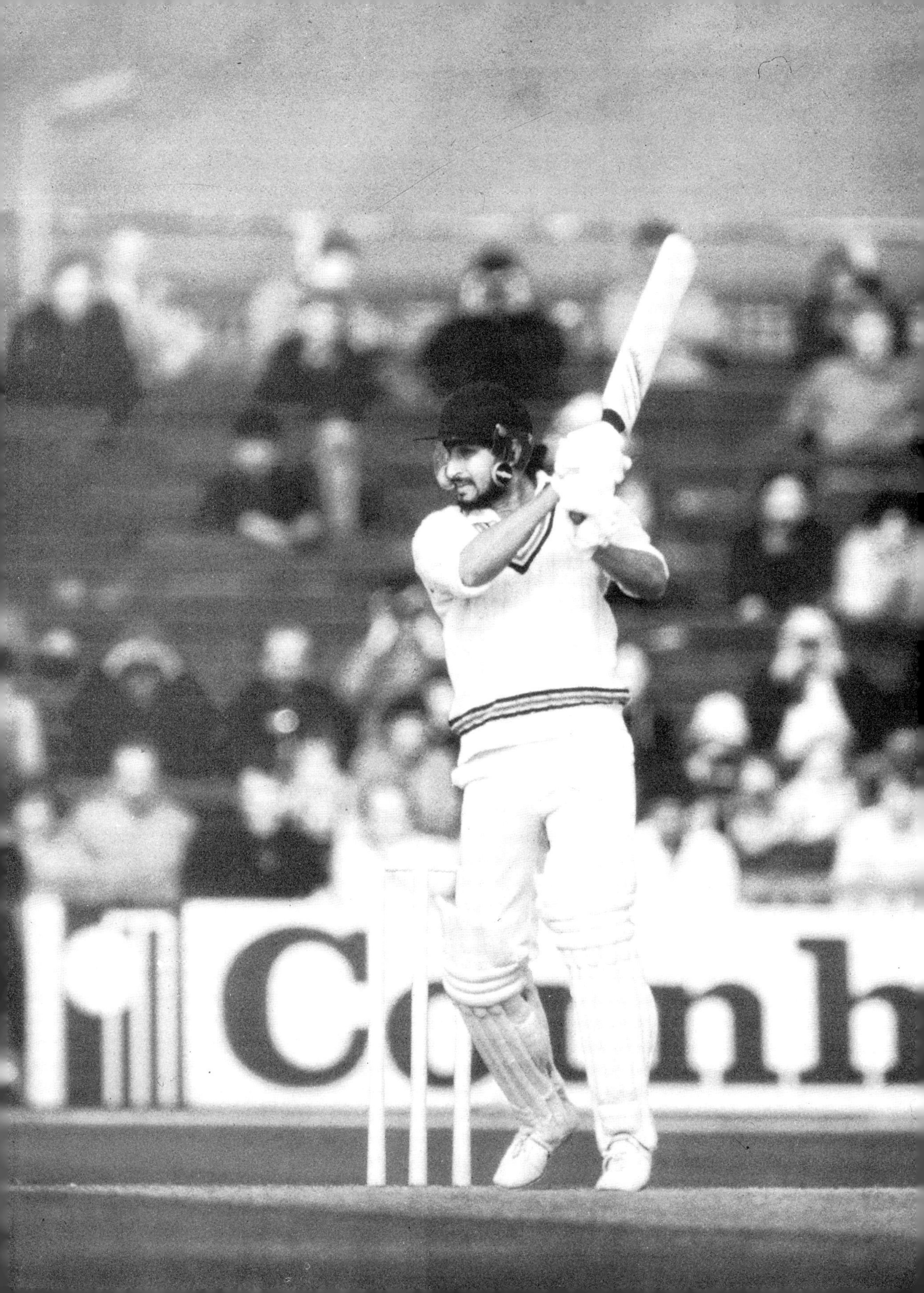

wickets for 55 runs. Doshi had 3 for 29 in 15 balls of intelligently attacking spin and England were thankful for Cook's maiden Test fifty.

They were even more thankful for what followed when Botham and Miller added 169, the last 91 from 23 overs. Botham was again like a Colossus as he smote two sixes and nineteen fours, his 128 coming from 169 deliveries. The last part of his innings was with the help of a runner after he had been hit hard on the toe by a ball from Nayak which he had edged.

Rain closed the second day with England on 340 for 6, a formidable score on a doubtful wicket.

On a Saturday that was punctuated by rain, thunder and lightning, England grasped a position of total dominance although their efforts to score quick runs earlier in the day were not successful. Pringle tried hard, but he was stumped giving Doshi the charge after lunch and all interest centred on Miller. In all he batted for six minutes short of 5½ hours and hit thirteen fours. After a stoppage of forty minutes Edmonds was caught behind off Madan Lal and then Miller square cut Doshi for four to reach 98, the first century of his career now, it seemed, a formality, but the next ball was well up to Miller and pushing forward he was caught bat and pad at silly point.

Many felt that Willis would have been advised to declare early in the day, but when play closed he had bowled England into an unbeatable position. He had Gavaskar and Shastri caught, the first low down at second slip, the second at backward short leg. Shastri was out with the score at 5, Gavaskar at 8. Vengsarkar fell to Pringle who had opened the bowling with Willis and India ended at 35 for 3.

As it transpired the next day, the Sunday, was the last, rain washing out play completely on the Monday. The Sunday, however, was a day of glorious batting. India lost five more wickets in the day, but they scored 344 runs and put to shame England's ditherings of the previous day.

Viswanath and Kirmani attacked from the start and reached 112 before Viswanath was caught cutting. Yashpal Sharma went back to Edmonds and was bowled and this brought in Patil. He batted with great fluency from the moment he arrived and was undeterred when Kirmani, who had done a fine job, was bowled by Edmonds.

Kapil Dev and Patil added 96 for the seventh wicket of which Kapil Dev scored 65, his fifty coming off 33 balls. It was mighty stuff once more and the Indian all-rounder had taken on an awesome power and grandeur in this series. He was caught behind when he hesitated in trying to force Miller through the off-side field.

The centre of the stage now belonged entirely to Sandeep Patil. He responded with the dynamism of one who knows that the occasion belongs to him. He moved from 72 to his century in nine balls.

England had taken the new ball and Patil hit the last two balls of a Botham over for four and three. This brought him facing Willis who bowled an over which will long live in the memory of those who witnessed it. It included a no-ball and from the seven deliveries Patil hit six fours, two cover drives, one flat batted back over the bowler's head, two square cuts of ferocious power and a mighty hook. These 24 runs from the over constituted a record for a Test in England and Patil's flashing blade stamped its image indelibly on the memory.

Opposite: Kapil Dev. All fire and joy. Man of the Series and hopefully a man for many more seasons.

SECOND CORNHILL TEST MATCH – ENGLAND v. INDIA
24, 25, 26, 27 and 28 June 1982 at Old Trafford

ENGLAND

	FIRST INNINGS	
G. Cook	b Doshi	66
C. J. Tavare	b Doshi	57
A. J. Lamb	c Viswanath, b Madan Lal	9
D. I. Gower	c Shastri, b Madan Lal	9
I. T. Botham	b Shastri	128
D. W. Randall	c Kirmani, b Doshi	0
G. Miller	c Vengsarkar, b Doshi	98
D. R. Pringle	st Kirmani, b Doshi	23
P. H. Edmonds	c Kirmani, b Madan Lal	12
R. W. Taylor*	not out	1
R. G. D. Willis†	c Gavaskar, b Doshi	6
Extras	b 2, lb 5, nb 9	16
		425

	O	M	R	W
Kapil Dev	36	5	109	—
Madan Lal	35	9	104	3
Nayak	12	1	50	—
Doshi	47.1	17	102	6
Shastri	23	8	44	1

FALL OF WICKETS
1–106, 2–117, 3–141, 4–161, 5–161, 6–330, 7–382, 8–413, 9–419

INDIA

	FIRST INNINGS	
S. M. Gavaskar†	c Tavare, b Willis	2
R. J. Shastri	c Cook, b Willis	0
D. B. Vengsarkar	c Randall, b Pringle	12
G. R. Viswanath	c Taylor, b Botham	54
S. M. H. Kirmani*	b Edmonds	58
Yashpal Sharma	b Edmonds	10
S. N. Patil	not out	129
Kapil Dev	c Taylor, b Miller	65
Madan Lal	b Edmonds	26
S. V. Nayak	not out	2
D. R. Doshi		
Extras	b 6, lb 2, w 3, nb 10	21
	(for 8 wkts)	379

	O	M	R	W
Willis	17	2	94	2
Pringle	15	4	33	1
Edmonds	37	12	94	3
Botham	19	4	86	1
Miller	16	4	51	1

FALL OF WICKETS
1–5, 2–8, 3–25, 4–112, 5–136, 6–173, 7–269, 8–366

Match drawn

Cambridge University 1982
First Class Matches

BATTING	v. Glamorgan (Cambridge) 21-23 April 1982		v. Nottinghamshire (Cambridge) 24-27 April		v. Middlesex (Cambridge) 28-30 April 1982		v. Warwickshire (Cambridge) 1-4 May 1982		v. Lancashire (Cambridge) 12-14 May 1982		v. Essex (Cambridge) 19-21 May 1982		v. Northamptonshire (Cambridge) 9-11 June 1982		v. Leicestershire (Cambridge) 19-22 June 1982		v. Oxford University (Lord's) 26-29 June	
J. P. C. Mills	0	56	0	1	98	10	4	9	73	15	24	19	9	31	20	—	9	11
D. W. Varey	0	41	10	22	0	51*	24	63	16	28	7	3	156*	17	72	—	22	16*
R. J. Boyd-Moss	15	18	52	82	14	0	123	119	39	3	2	81	0	16	12	—	41*	100
C. F. E. Goldie	13	—	28	1	—	19	—	31	—	4	8	10	1	—	—	—	—
D. R. Pringle	127	73*	81	8	0	72*	37	—	24	61*					38	—		
S. P. Henderson	0	23	0	13	209*	—	2	15	8	46*	8	52	2	30	34	—	39*	50
S. J. G. Doggart	8	34	64	16	16	—	7	47*	1	—	10	10	7	5	27	—	—	—
K. I. Hodgson	34	—	13	11	25	—	20	—	50	—			8	0	16	—		36*
C. C. Ellison	15	—	1*	3	—	—	16	—	0*	—	11*	10*					—	—
R. S. Dutton	0	—	0*	0														
R. W. M. Palmer	0*	—	—	0*	—	—	2*	—	3	—	12	0	3*	0*			—	—
A. J. Pollock			—	—	13		5*	19	—	—	0	5	4	17	0*	—	—	—
W. E. J. Barrington											2	59	45	20	0	—	—	48*
A. G. Davies											13	4						
P. D. Griffiths													1	0				
Byes	4	1	7		9	3		2					2	4	1	5		1
Leg-byes	2	5	2	7	7	4	4	3	5	4	4	3	8	3	5		1	9
Wides	1	5			1			1							1		1	
No-balls	3		1		1	2	3	1	5	2	2	2	15	5			1	1
Total	222	256	259	154	380	142	274	265	274	159	99	258	272	146	230		114	272
Wickets	10	5	8	10	6	2	10	4	10	3	10	10	9	10	8		2	3
Result	D		L		L		D		W		L		L		D		W	

Catches
23 – C. F. E. Goldie (ct 19/st 4)
12 – S. P. Henderson
6 – D. W. Varey
3 – R. J. Boyd-Moss, S. J. G. Doggart and J. P. C. Mills
2 – R. W. M. Palmer, A. G. Davies and C. C. Ellison
1 – D. R. Pringle and W. E. J. Barrington

BOWLING	R. W. M. Palmer	R. S. Dutton	K. I. Hodgson	S. J. G. Doggart	C. C. Ellison	S. P. Henderson	R. J. Boyd-Moss	D. R. Pringle
v. Glamorgan (Cambridge) 21-23 April 1982	22-3-73-0 13-2-66-0	6-0-29-0 4-1-22-0	32-12-68-8 22-5-71-2	20-3-55-1 20-1-86-1	8-1-28-0	4-3-6-0	3-8-11-0 7-3-17-0	
v. Nottinghamshire (Cambridge 24-27 April 1982)	18-2-96-4 7-0-26-0	4-0-44-0 5-0-35-0	22-4-55-3 6.4-1-38-0	19-3-55-0	8-2-20-1		4-0-34-0	
v. Middlesex (Cambridge) 28-30 April 1982	10.2-0-51-0 7-0-37-0		6-0-27-0 5-1-24-0	4-1-18-0 13-2-77-2	10-1-35-0 9-1-42-0			6-3-41-1 9.3-0-45-0
v. Warwickshire (Cambridge) 1-4 May 1982	18-8-57-2 3-1-7-0			16-4-39-0	11-1-44-0			18-5-47-0 2.4-2-0-0
v. Lancashire (Cambridge) 12-14 May 1982	14-3-39-1 8-2-32-0		18-5-72-1 14-5-22-0	10-3-30-2	14-5-37-1 17.5-7-30-3			18.1-7-54-3 27-13-33-6
v. Essex (Cambridge) 19-21 May 1982	23-1-102-1			16-3-57-1	11-1-48-0	2-0-2-0	24-8-68-3	
v. Northamptonshire (Cambridge) 9-11 June 1982	19-5-63-1 13-3-48-1		16-1-72-2 9-1-29-1	24-1-73-0 14-3-38-0			1-0-10-1	
v. Leicestershire (Cambridge) 19-22 June 1982	11.2-0-49-2 6-2-16-1		24-4-71-3 1.1 0 5 0	20-4-57-0			22-7-54-3 4-0-14-0	
v. Oxford University (Lord's) 26-29 June 1982	17-2-52-1 10-0-35-0		26-4-89-3 3-0-20-0		6-1-23-0 2-0-7-0		11-1-51-1 9-0-42-4	
	219.4-34- 849-14 av. 60.64	19-1- 130-0 —	198.1-42- 625-23 av. 27.17	182.4-29- 623-7 av. 89.00	96.5-20- 314-5 av. 62.80	6-3- 8-0 —	64-15- 233-9 av. 25.88	117.2-37- 288-13 av. 22.15

26, 27 and 28 June

at Hove

Pakistanis 450 for 2 dec (Mudassar Nazar 211 not out, Mohsin Khan 151, Javed Miandad 52 not out)
Sussex 209 (Abdul Qadir 7 for 44) and 229 (G. D. Mendis 114, C. M. Wells 59, Abdul Qadir 6 for 78)

Pakistanis won by an innings and 13 runs

26, 28 and 29 June

at Lord's

Oxford University 249 for 5 dec (R. G. P. Ellis 86) and 136 for 6 dec (R. J. Boyd-Moss 4 for 42)
Cambridge University 114 for 2 dec and 272 for 3 (R. J. Boyd-Moss 100, S. P. Henderson 50)

Cambridge University won by 7 wickets

at Derby

Leicestershire 126 (B. F. Davison 61, D. G. Moir 5 for 40, C. J. Tunnicliffe 4 for 53) and 175 for 5 dec (R. W. Tolchard 53)
Derbyshire 73 for 1 dec and 229 for 2 (P. N. Kirsten 121 not out, J. H. Hampshire 62 not out)

Derbyshire won by 8 wickets
Derbyshire 20 pts, Leicestershire 0 pts

at Bristol

Hampshire 0 for 0 and 99 (D. Surridge 4 for 26, F. D. Stephenson 4 for 48)
Gloucestershire 0 for 0 and 101 for 6

Gloucestershire won by 4 wickets
Gloucestershire 16 pts, Hampshire 0 pts

at The Oval

Middlesex 330 for 9 dec (M. W. Gatting 192, J. E. Emburey 54, R. D. Jackman 4 for 55) and 63 for 3 dec
Surrey 144 for 4 dec (N. F. Williams 4 for 40) and 137 for 8 (W. W. Daniel 6 for 37)

Match drawn
Middlesex 5 pts, Surrey 3 pts

at Edgbaston

Somerset 305 for 4 dec (I. V. A. Richards 135, B. C. Rose 102 not out) and 83 for 0 (C. H. Dredge 54 not out)
Warwickshire 323 (D. L. Amiss 156, V. J. Marks 7 for 121)

Match drawn
Somerset 7 pts, Warwickshire 5 pts

at Worcester

Worcestershire 0 for 0 and 264 for 7 dec (G. M. Turner 115, L. McFarlane 4 for 64)
Lancashire 0 for 0 and 175 (D. N. Patel 7 for 46)

Worcestershire won by 89 runs
Worcestershire 12 pts, Lancashire 0 pts

Oxford University 1982
First Class Matches

BATTING	v. Northamptonshire (Oxford) 24-27 April 1982		v. Worcestershire (Oxford) 28-30 April 1982		v. Kent (Oxford) 1-4 May 1982		v. Gloucestershire (Oxford) 5-7 May 1982		v. Hampshire (Oxford) 12-14 May 1982		v. Middlesex (Oxford) 19-21 May 1982		v. Warwickshire (Oxford) 2-4 June 1982		v. Surrey (Oxford) 9-11 June 1982		v. Glamorgan (Swansea) 19-22 June 1982		v. Cambridge University (Lord's) 26-28 June 1982	
R. G. P. Ellis	34	27	25	92	3	8	65	36	15	15	35	8	35	2	39	105*	15	7	86	14
R. P. Moulding	1	0	2	67	5	2	8	5	6	13	48	0	7*	28	12	0	0	10	20*	8
K. A. Hayes	27	37	0	23*	5	7	0	52	23	13	24	0	152	32	65	8	0	10	13*	—
R. S. Cowan	143*	12*	76	3	108	0	37	60*	19	10			10	0					33	4
G. D. R. Toogood	54	1*	83	5*	0	15*	7	9	3	16	15	28	31*	26	28	2			31	38
J. Chesser	47	—	1	—	1	18*														
J. G. Varey	4*						6	0	68	5	23	48	—	28*	0	13*			32*	12*
R. S. Luddington	—	—	15	—	12	—	38	13	1	32	10	2	—	0	27	—	65	62*	6	7
T. J. Taylor	—	—	0	—													20	17*	—	—
I. S. Curtis	—	—	0*	—									—	20*			0	—	—	—
S. J. Ridge	—	—	0	—	6*	—	13*	5	22	4*	0	4*	—	0	4*	—	4	0	—	2*
H. T. Rawlinson			1	—	21	0					4	0			4	—				
S. J. Halliday					113*	—	1	27	4	15					18	35				
A. J. Gilfillan							—	—	31	0	2	7								
P. J. Crowe							11	0												
M. E. Lawrence									0*	0*	2*	18	—	—	0	—				
R. Marsden											46	4	60	9	49	11	12	21*	13	39
A. Miller											0	20								
P. Armstrong																	34	0		
R. Edbrooke																	84*	16		
J. Cassidy																	0	—		
Byes	1		1		4	5	1				3	4			5	3	3	4		6
Leg-byes	3	8	2	7	7	2	4			3	4	5	2	4	8	12	8	7	5	10	4
Wides				1		3			3	1	1	2		2					4	1
No-balls	24	8	4	1	17	2	9	7	2	1	10	9	4	4	15	2	5	2	4	2
Total	338	93	211	202	306	55	230	217	169	139	228	143	305	162	276	187	250	154	249	136
Wickets	5	3	10	3	8	5	10	10	10	10	10	10	4	8	10	5	10	6	5	6
Result	D		D		D		L		L		L		L		D		D		L	

Catches
7 – R. G. P. Ellis
6 – R. S. Luddington (ct 5/st 1)
4 – K. A. Hayes and G. D. R. Toogood
3 – S. J. Ridge, R. S. Cowan and subs
2 – J. G. Varey
1 – I. S. Curtis, R. Marsden and H. T. Rawlinson

BOWLING	S. J. Ridge	R. S. Cowan	J. G. Varey	I. S. Curtis	T. J. Taylor	H. T. Rawlinson	K. A. Hayes	A. J. Gilfillan
v. Northamptonshire (Oxford) 24-27 April 1982	13-1-43-0 17-1-51-1	19-1-19-1 8-2-37-1	7-2-24-0	35-4-108-2 29-3-66-2	23-3-95-1			
v. Worcestershire (Oxford) 28-30 April 1982	10-0-51-0	12-2-33-1		24.1-2-85-0	35-1-127-0	10-0-57-1	4-0-23-0	
v. Kent (Oxford) 1-4 May 1982	43.1-3-161-3	23-8-80-0				22-3-95-0	12-0-51-0	39-2-177-2
v. Gloucestershire (Oxford) 5-7 May 1982	36-6-128-4 6-3-5-0	4-0-11-0	25-2-116-0			1-1-0-0		3-2-1-0
v. Hampshire (Oxford) 12-14 May 1982	17-6-37-2	15-2-58-1	25-1-109-1					9-1-40-0
v. Middlesex (Oxford) 19-21 May 1982	24-1-100-1			19-1-88-1		28.1-4-117-2		
v. Warwickshire (Oxford) 2-4 June 1982	8-1-17-0	24-3-75-2 13-0-83-0	16-2-52-0 9-0-42-0	42-15-57-4 19.3-1-96-1			1-0-1-0	
v. Surrey (Oxford) 9-11 June 1982	24-2-96-1 16-3-65-0		12-4-27-0 14-3-60-0			22-1-102-2 14-1-64-0	2-0-20-0	
v. Glamorgan (Swansea) 19-22 June 1982	12-4-28-0				53-18-140-5	47-11-118-5	1-0-1-0	
v. Cambridge University (Lord's) 26-29 June 1982	6-0-14-0 8-1-33-1	7-0-49-0 6-0-42-0	2-0-13-1 3-0-19-0		5-0-17-0 22-2-119-1	16-4-46-1		
	240.1-32- 829-13 av. 63.76	131-18- 559-6 av. 93.16	132-15- 550-3 av. 183.33	214.4-45- 659-15 av. 43.93	149-24- 469-9 av. 52.11	96.1-9- 435-5 av. 87.00	22-1- 96-0 —	51-5- 218-2 av. 109.00

A. G. D. R. Toogood 3-0-22-0   B. J. Cassidy 4-2-12-0

at Harrogate
Yorkshire v. Nottinghamshire
Match abandoned

As if warning England of what was in store for them later in the summer, the Pakistan touring side totally devastated Sussex at Hove. Once more Sussex were open to criticism that they failed to treat a match with a touring side with the seriousness that it deserved. They were hampered by injury, it is true, and that situation worsened during the match as both Parker and Jones were injured. The injury to Parker was a grave blow to Sussex as it prevented this fine player from playing in the semi-final of the Benson and Hedges Cup.

Mudassar Nazar and Mohsin Khan routed the Sussex attack on the Saturday with an opening stand of 319, a partnership of majestic shots and awesome power. Sussex crumpled before the leg-spin of Abdul Qadir and there was excitement in the air that we may well see a leg-spinner operating in a Test match in England again. When Sussex followed on Mendis hit his first hundred of the season and shared a second wicket stand of 171 with Colin Wells before Abdul Qadir again took the initiative and sad Sussex were beaten just after three o'clock, neither Parker nor Jones batted.

The silly arrangement of fixtures which allowed the Varsity match to clash with a Test match tended to devalue the contest at Lord's in the public's eyes. The devaluation was aided by the Test selectors' decision to deprive Cambridge University of their elected skipper. It must be added that the way in which the University match has been played in the last few years has not won the fixture much respect. How refreshing it is to report then that the 1982 Varsity match was played in a most positive spirit with both captains, Ellis and Mills, doing their utmost to beat the weather and bring about a definite result.

There was only half an hour's play possible on the Saturday which Ellis remedied with a superbly aggressive innings during the period that play was possible on the Monday. He then declared and was rewarded with the wickets of Mills and Varey, dismissed by his brother, before the close. Cambridge added only another 40 runs the following morning before declaring 135 runs behind. Oxford responded to this declaration with some brisk hitting although, sadly, Cambridge were handicapped by the absence from their attack of Doggart who had dislocated a finger while fielding.

Ellis set Cambridge to make 272 in 3½ hours and if they were to win, the light blues needed an innings of quality and bravado from somebody. They got it from Robin Boyd-Moss who hit a hundred in as many minutes. David Varey had been forced to retire hurt when hit on the toe and Mills went lbw to Ridge at 26, but Henderson and Boyd-Moss added 144 in 22 overs and Boyd-Moss' hundred came out of 164 after which Barrington and Hodgson steered Cambridge to a splendid victory.

Efforts to beat the weather elsewhere were not always so successful. The forfeiture of innings at Bristol led to a bizarre match in which Surridge and the Tasmanian West Indian star Stephenson routed Hampshire and Gloucestershire's batsmen limped to victory.

Brian Rose settled for a plodding maximum batting point draw at Edgbaston where Vic Marks again excelled with the ball.

Glenn Turner equalled Don Kenyon's record of 70 centuries for Worcestershire when he reached his hundred in 81 minutes before lunch at Worcester where the game was played under the one-day rule. Dipak Patel spun a career best 7 for 46 to give Worcestershire a remarkably easy victory.

Dallas Gordon Moir's left-arm spin delivered from 6 feet 8 inches and more combined with Colin Tunnicliffe's left-arm medium pace to destroy Leicestershire whose early season form had evaporated. Brian Davison again hit excitingly, but he could rally none of his team-mates. Rain forced Barry Wood to declare 53 behind and he then fed Leicestershire with some part-time bowling. Tolchard declared and left Derbyshire 154 minutes in which to make 229. Hampshire and Kirsten shared an unbeaten third wicket stand of 179 to give Derbyshire victory with eight wickets and twenty balls to spare.

Another wonderful innings by Mike Gatting and some astute leadership by Brearley nearly snatched victory for Middlesex in the rain-saturated game at The Oval. Surrey went from 70 for 2 to 93 for 8 against the hostile bowling of Wayne Daniel, now bowling better than at any other time for Middlesex. Daniel sustained pace and accuracy and with a ring of fielders swooping round the bat like vultures he was a menacing sight indeed. Surrey found their own heroes in the injured Clinton and Robin Jackman who defied Daniel and all else to save the game. One felt that with Daniel in such form and aided by an attack of variety and subtlety allied to Gatting's batting of the very highest quality and Brearley's captaincy Middlesex must surely win at least one of the three titles still remaining in their grasp.

John Player League

27 June

at Derby

Yorkshire 202 for 5 (C. W. J. Athey 76, G. Boycott 54)
Derbyshire 183 for 9

Yorkshire (4 pts) won by 19 runs

at Harlow

Essex 144 for 8 (G. J. Parsons 4 for 19)
Leicestershire 95 for 8 (N. Phillip 4 for 11)

Essex (4 pts) won by 49 runs

at Ebbw Vale

Glamorgan v. **Gloucestershire**
Match abandoned

Glamorgan 2 pts, Gloucestershire 2 pts

at Basingstoke

Hampshire 116 for 4
Kent 84 for 9 (M. D. Marshall 5 for 31)

Hampshire (4 pts) won on faster scoring rate

at Lord's

Surrey 161 (D. M. Smith 50, M. W. W. Selvey 4 for 32)
Middlesex 162 for 7

Middlesex (4 pts) won by 3 wickets

at Bath

Somerset 185 for 6 (P. W. Denning 71, E. E. Hemmings 5 for 44)
Nottinghamshire 72 (H. R. Moseley 5 for 40, J. Garner 4 for 6)

Somerset (4 pts) won by 113 runs

at Edgbaston

Warwickshire 227 for 5 (T. A. Lloyd 79)
Northamptonshire 185 (P. Willey 89, C. Lethbridge 5 for 47)

Warwickshire (4 pts) won on faster scoring rate

at Worcester

Lancashire 160 for 4 (G. Fowler 59)
Worcestershire 138 (C. E. H. Croft 4 for 29)

Lancashire (4 pts) won by 22 runs

Widespread rain meant reduced overs and reduced targets. Only at Derby and Lord's were the full quota of overs played. Middlesex hung on after a middle order collapse which saw four wickets fall for 14 runs. Downton and Selvey restored sanity.

Kent disintegrated before Marshall and Emery and Derbyshire provided Illingworth and Yorkshire with their first victory of the season. The Yorkshire success was founded on an opening stand of 123 by Boycott and Athey.

In a game reduced to 28 overs at Bath, Notts were bowled out in 19 overs, the last four wickets falling to Garner while one run was scored.

Northants left all to Willey after Warwickshire had batted with consistency. Lethbridge had his best league figures and tilted the game in Warwickshire's favour.

Croft was too much for Worcestershire and Norbert Phillip scored a vital 44 as he and Turner (35) rescued Essex from 28 for 5 with a stand of 77. Phillip then took 4 for 11 in his 6 overs and Essex won comfortably to move to fifth in the table behind Middlesex, Sussex, Kent and Derbyshire. Gloucestershire and Glamorgan to whom the weather had been most unkind shared bottom place.

I.C.C. Trophy

28 June

at Kidderminster

Bangladesh 122 for 7
Malaysia 121 for 6

Bangladesh won by 1 run

at Burton

Singapore 115 (W. H. Trott 4 for 27)
Bermuda 116 for 4

Bermuda won by 4 wickets

at Kenilworth
Papua New Guinea 231 for 7 (V. Pala 103 not out)
Canada 211 (T. Javed 50, K. V. Vagl 4 for 26)
Papua New Guinea won by 20 runs

at Dudley
East Africa 53 for 2
v. **West Africa**
Match abandoned

at Hinckley
Netherlands 251 for 6 (R. Elferink 154 not out)
Fiji 79 for 2
Netherlands won on faster scoring rate

at Walmley
Gibraltar 129 for 8
Hong Kong 130 for 2 (D. Reeve 56 not out, D. G. Greenwood 56 not out)
Hong Kong won by 8 wickets

at Bloxwich
Israel 65 (A. J. Traicos 4 for 21)
Zimbabwe 66 for 1
Zimbabwe won by 9 wickets

Vavine Pala reached his hundred off the last ball of Papua New Guinea's innings against Canada when the sixth round of the I.C.C. Trophy was treated more kindly by the weather than the previous five. Singapore at last played a match, losing to the strong Bermuda side. Zimbabwe took only seven overs to get the required runs against Israel who had batted for 31.2 overs for their 65. David Houghton made 43 of Zimbabwe's runs, but the batting honours of the day went to Holland's Elferink. He hit 154 not out before rain returned late in the day at Hinckley.

Benson and Hedges Cup – Semi-Finals
30 June

at Taunton
Sussex 110 (J. Garner 4 for 24)
Somerset 112 for 2 (P. W. Denning 68 not out)
Somerset won by 8 wickets
(Gold Award – J. Garner)

at Trent Bridge
Lancashire 182 (C. Maynard 60)
Nottinghamshire 184 for 6 (R. J. Hadlee 55 not out)
Nottinghamshire won by 4 wickets
(Gold Award – R. J. Hadlee)

The semi-finals of the Benson and Hedges Cup produced games of totally different nature.

At Taunton, a Sussex side weakened and dispirited by injury collapsed lamely before the all round might of the Somerset attack. In the fifth over Garner had Mendis lbw

Colin Dredge, one of the wreckers of Sussex in the Benson and Hedges Semi-Final at Taunton. Constant professional application by a fine seam bowler, he represents all that is good in county cricket.

and bowled Green. In the next over Barclay was caught in the gully by Garner off Botham. In the eighth over Gould was bowled by Botham and Sussex were 20 for 4. It was simply a case of the bowling being better than the batting. There were some brave blows by le Roux, but Marks had him stumped and also dismissed Colin Wells and Phillipson so that Sussex were all out in 41.1 overs. Roebuck and Denning began with 91 and Denning went on untroubled by the loss of Roebuck and Richards and there were nearly nineteen overs to spare when the winning runs were made.

There was no such one-sidedness at Trent Bridge where Lancashire made 182 on a very brown wicket. Their leading batsman was Chris Maynard, the newly acquired wicket-keeper from Warwickshire, who had been promoted to number three in order to break up Lancashire's abundant supply of left-handers. In reply, Notts began badly when they lost both openers to Croft. The light was not good and Randall was uneasy against Croft, but he held on and he and Rice had taken the score to 63 for 2 at tea. Notts seemed to be just ahead until, with his first ball, Reidy bowled Rice middle stump and in the next over Simmons beat Randall through the air and had him stumped floundering – 97 for 4 after 36 overs.

Birch was lbw to Reidy who was bowling admirably and at 116 French was bowled by Croft. Hadlee, suffering from a damaged hamstring, was completely unable to time his shots and made only 9 in 13 overs. When he had scored 8 and the total was 117 for 6, he hit Croft high to long on where Folley, running in, missed the catch. It proved to be the only miss of the match and, for Lancashire, a disastrous one.

In the forty-ninth over of the innings, bowled by Reidy, Notts still needed 56 to win and they were losing. Suddenly Hadlee swung into action with a succession of thrilling shots. He hit the ball high for six, drove mightily off the back foot for four and pulled ferociously. Hemmings supported him with sense and encouragement. The forty-ninth over produced 18 runs, the fiftieth 12 and the fifty-first 10. Notts cantered home with eleven balls to spare and Hadlee limped from the wicket to receive the gold award due to a hero.

I.C.C. Trophy
30 June

at Sutton Coldfield
Canada 233 (T. Javed 68)
U.S.A. 95 (R. J. Stevens 4 for 26)
Canada won by 138 runs

at Wombourne
Papua New Guinea 94
Zimbabwe 96 for 1
Zimbabwe won by 9 wickets

at Streetly
Hong Kong 105 for 9
Kenya 108 for 7
Kenya won by 3 wickets

at Stafford
East Africa 220 for 7 (K. W. Arnold 54, D. C. Patel 52)
Fiji 132 (B. Desai 4 for 21)
East Africa won by 88 runs

at King's Heath
Bangladesh 67 (L. Thomas 4 for 13)
Bermuda 70 for 3
Bermuda won by 7 wickets

at Old Edwardians
Malaysia 128
Singapore 129 for 4 (F. J. R. Martens 67)
Singapore won by 6 wickets

Bermuda made certain of a place in the semi-finals of the competition when they crushed Bangladesh, their nearest rivals in group two, by 2.45 in the afternoon. Only seventeen-year old Nazem Shiraz reached double figures for Bangladesh whose defeat meant that they had to beat Holland to qualify. Zimbabwe continued their winning way and Canada improved their chances by overwhelming U.S.A.

Tilcon Trophy
30 June

at Harrogate
Yorkshire 181 (B. J. Griffiths 4 for 25)
Northamptonshire 184 for 9 (A. J. Lamb 93, G. B. Stevenson 5 for 31)
Northamptonshire won by 1 wicket

1 July

Gloucestershire 226 (B. C. Broad 72, P. W. Romaines 71, J. D. Inchmore 4 for 50)
Worcestershire 125
Gloucestershire won by 101 runs

2 July
Final
Northamptonshire 101 for 3
Gloucestershire 88 for 3
Northamptonshire won by 13 runs

The final of the Tilcon Trophy was reduced to ten overs by rain, Allan Lamb and Wayne Larkins attacked boldly for Northants, the winners. In the first match of the tournament Tim Lamb hit the last two balls of the innings for four to give Northants a dramatic victory.

30 June, 1 and 2 July

at Bournemouth
Pakistanis 300 for 9 dec (Mansoor Akhtar 87, J. W. Southern 4 for 88) and 101 for 2 dec
Hampshire 85 for 4 dec and 319 for 4 (T. E. Jesty 133, M. C. J. Nicholas 107 not out)
Hampshire won by 6 wickets

With the second day's play lost to the rain, Pakistan and Hampshire conjured some magic on the last day to provide a spectacular result. Hampshire were required to make 317 in 272 minutes and they accomplished the task with nine balls to spare. Jesty hit 133 in 119 minutes and hit 20 fours and 3 sixes. Nicholas provided a more subdued contribution to the innings with his 107 occupying 269 minutes. He hit 13 fours as he and Jesty took Hampshire from 3 for 2 to 178 before Jesty was out having put victory in sight.

I.C.C. Trophy
2 July

at Banbury
Israel 157
U.S.A. 158 for 2 (N. Lashkari 76 not out, K. Khan 65 not out)
U.S.A. won by 8 wickets

at Market Harborough
Gibraltar 55 (V. Pala 4 for 30)
Papua New Guinea 58 for 1
Papua New Guinea won by 9 wickets

at Old Hill
Canada 242 for 8 (I. F. Kirmani 107)
Kenya 197 (G. Musa 53, C. Neblett 4 for 26)
Canada won by 45 runs

at Wroxeter
West Africa 219 for 9 (S. Elliott 75, J. Onyechi 53)
v. **Malaysia**
Match abandoned

at Stratford-on-Avon
Bermuda 240 (L. Thomas 68, E. James 51)
East Africa 175 for 8 (D. Patel 64)
Bermuda won by 65 runs

at Northampton
Netherlands 163 for 8
Bangladesh 167 for 4
Bangladesh won by 6 wickets

Papua New Guinea defeated Gibraltar before lunch and enhanced their chances of reaching the semi-finals where they would be most popular contestants. Bangladesh won their crucial match with Holland with four overs to spare and Bermuda and Canada again showed form although for the Canadians a resurgence to their 1979 standard may have come too late.

NatWest Trophy – Round One

3 July

at Bedford
Bedfordshire 153 for 9
Somerset 154 for 6
Somerset won by 4 wickets
(Man of the Match – R. Dethridge)

at Leicester
Norfolk 164 for 7 (Parvez Mir 55, L. B. Taylor 4 for 34)
Leicestershire 166 for 2 (D. I. Gower 65 not out)
Leicestershire won by 8 wickets
(Man of the Match – D. I. Gower)

at Enfield
Cheshire 104 (P. H. Edmonds 5 for 12)
Middlesex 106 for 2 (W. N. Slack 54 not out)
Middlesex won by 8 wickets
(Man of the Match – P. H. Edmonds)

at Northampton
Ireland 155
Northamptonshire 156 for 3 (P. Willey 72 not out)
Northamptonshire won by 7 wickets
(Man of the Match – P. Willey)

at The Oval
Surrey 279 for 7 (M. A. Lynch 129, G. R. J. Roope 77, S. Davies 5 for 51)
Durham 168 for 6 (S. Greensword 73)
Surrey won by 111 runs
(Man of the Match – M. A. Lynch)

at Hove
Sussex 113 (C. E. B. Rice 6 for 18)
Nottinghamshire 114 for 1
Nottinghamshire won by 9 wickets
(Man of the Match – C. B. E. Rice)

at Edgbaston
Warwickshire 300 for 6 (D. L. Amiss 135, T. A. Lloyd 64, G. W. Humpage 52)
Cambridgeshire 180 (M. S. A. McEvoy 52)
Warwickshire won by 120 runs
(Man of the Match – D. L. Amiss)

The first round of the NatWest Trophy produced no giant-killing performances. At Bedford the home county survived the might of Garner and Botham due mainly to a brave ninth wicket stand of 52 between Dethridge and Williams. Dethridge was run out off the last ball of the innings for 31 and then took the wicket of Vic Marks for 21 runs in the seven overs he bowled. Somerset had no easy time of it. Roebuck, Denning, Richards, Botham and Popplewell were out with only 77 scored, but Rose was at his dourest and Marks scored a brisk 31 to put Somerset in reach of victory.

Edmonds completely bemused Cheshire. His 5 for 12 in 12 overs meant an early finish at Enfield.

Leicestershire and Northamptonshire disposed of weaker opposition in uneventful matches and Warwickshire, with Amiss and Lloyd opening with a stand of 141, went on a run spree against Cambridgeshire for whom ex-Essex opener Mike McEvoy scored 52.

There was an interesting contest at The Oval where Neil Riddell won the toss and asked Surrey to bat. Australian fast medium bowler Simon Davis took the wickets of Pauline, Clinton and Knight with only 16 runs scored. D. M. Smith fell to J. G. D. Smith at 84, but then Roope joined Lynch in a blistering stand of 166. Lynch's 129 was his highest score in a one-day competition and came in 136 minutes. Durham could not match this rate of scoring and were prepared to concede the game when a violent thunderstorm saturated the ground just before 7.30 with eight overs still to be bowled, but both sides agreed to come out again an hour later and complete the sixty overs with some arranged slow bowling from Lynch and Clinton and an agreed lack of aggression from Durham so that honour and the law were satisfied and the Test pitch protected.

The sadness of Sussex continued. From a position of eminence they had sunk to the depths in a week when they were totally outclassed by Nottinghamshire. Without the injured Hadlee to open the attack, Clive Rice decided to use himself as a bowler after a long lay off through back injury. He took three wickets in his first 22 balls and finished with 6 for 18. Green, fifth out, made a brave 41 out of 62, but the Sussex performance was even more dismal than their one at Taunton and the game was over by early afternoon.

3, 4 and 5 July

at Chelmsford

Essex 336 (B. R. Hardie 161, N. Phillip 79) and 175 for 4 dec (K. R. Pont 58 not out, K. S. McEwan 52)
Indians 258 for 7 dec (A. Malhotra 85, G. A. H. M. Parkar 60 not out, D. R. Pringle 5 for 59) and 171 for 5 (R. J. Shastri 74, R. E. East 4 for 49)

Match drawn

at Broughton Ferry

Worcestershire 369 for 8 dec (G. M. Turner 125, D. N. Patel 84, G. E. Goddard 4 for 114) and 189 for 8 dec (Younis Ahmed 53, W. A. Morton 4 for 46)
Scotland 316 for 5 dec (W. E. Donald 92, R. S. Weir 58 not out, R. G. Swan 53) and 128 for 3

Match drawn

3, 5 and 6 July

at Swansea

Pakistanis 356 for 4 dec (Mudassar Nazar 163 not out, Majid Khan 88, Wasim Raja 50 not out)
Glamorgan 155 (Abdul Qadir 5 for 31) and 128 (Abdul Qadir 4 for 20)

Pakistanis won by an innings and 73 runs

at Derby

Yorkshire 291 for 8 dec (J. D. Love 110, R. G. Lumb 74, D. G. Moir 4 for 83) and 200 for 4 (C. W. J. Athey 134, S. N. Hartley 52 not out)
Derbyshire 473 (J. G. Wright 190, I. S. Anderson 82, K. J. Barnett 74, G. B. Stevenson 4 for 114)

Match drawn
Derbyshire 6 pts, Yorkshire 3 pts

at Maidstone

Hampshire 179 and 283 (N. E. J. Pocock 62, R. E. Hayward 59, D. L. Underwood 4 for 34)
Kent 181 (C. J. Tavare 68, M. D. Marshall 6 for 55) and 236 (Asif Iqbal 75, M. D. Marshall 4 for 54)

Hampshire won by 45 runs
Hampshire 21 pts, Kent 5 pts

In their final game against a county the Indians did not fare too well at Chelmsford. Brian Hardie batted with determination and aggression on the Saturday and came to within one run of his career best when he was run out by team-mate Ray East. Although the game was not taken too seriously by Essex, it was important for Derek Pringle who, whatever he had proved to the England selectors, had much to prove to the Essex supporters. He grasped the opportunity by bowling quite splendidly on the Sunday and posing great problems for the Indian batsmen who were perplexed by his quickness and the height from which he delivered the ball. In the second innings Shastri batted with enough confidence to confirm his place as Gavaskar's opening partner for the final Test.

The Pakistanis emphasised their strength by beating Glamorgan in two days. Rich strokes by Mudassar Nazar on the Saturday were supported by a gem of an innings from Majid and some brisk runs by Wasim Raja. Then the leg-spin of Abdul Qadir proved all too much for some leaden footed Glamorgan batting on the Monday and one looked with joy towards the Test series with Pakistan and the promise of the exciting sight of a leg-break bowler operating in international cricket. Remembrance of things past.

The Derby wicket was the ultimate victor in one of the two Schweppes County Championship games played. Yorkshire, in spite of a hundred from Love, were too stolid in their first innings to gain much hope of victory. Derbyshire responded by Wright and Anderson, who both hit career best scores, putting on 242 for the first wicket. Anderson was opening in place of Wood who was injured. Barnett also batted well and Kirsten tried to force an innings victory which looked highly probable when Yorkshire lost Boycott, Lumb and Love for 41. Athey batted with a delicate mixture of caution and attack to reach a career best 134 and reminded the Test selectors that he was fully re-established in confidence. He is still only twenty-four. He and Hartley added 133 and the game was saved.

Malcolm Marshall bowled Hampshire back into the game at Maidstone after they had been dismissed for 179 in their first innings. In their second innings Hampshire batted with resolution right down the order, but owed much to Hayward and, in particular, to Pocock who looked very correct in defence and punctuated his caution with an attacking shot of classical elegance. Kent needed 282 to win in as many minutes and started badly when Benson and Taylor were out for 20. There were some courageous knocks by Tavare, Asif, Cowdrey and Knott, but Woolmer had been struck in the face in the first innings and could not bat. Marshall again exploited the flaws in the wicket although it had improved considerably since the opening day and he was well supported by Emery and some keen fielding. When Emery bowled Jarvis to give Hampshire victory there were but 5.2 overs to spare, but Hampshire had moved into fourth place in the table. Parks' wicket-keeping was again impressive.

4 July

at Swansea

Pakistanis 74 for 4
v. **Glamorgan**
Match abandoned

John Player League

at Derby

Derbyshire 225 for 5 (K. J. Barnett 111, J. G. Wright 61)
Lancashire 122 (S. Oldham 5 for 37)

Derbyshire (4 pts) won on faster scoring rate

at Maidstone

Sussex 254 for 5 (G. D. Mendis 121, I. J. Gould 52)
Kent 181

Sussex (4 pts) won by 73 runs

THE ENGLISH SEASON/287

at Leicester

Warwickshire 213 for 4 (G. W. Humpage 87 not out)
Leicestershire 214 for 4 (D. I. Gower 107)

Leicestershire (4 pts) won by 6 wickets

at Tring

Northamptonshire 164 for 9
Surrey 132

Northamptonshire (4 pts) won by 32 runs

at Leeds

Yorkshire 233 for 8 (C. W. J. Athey 50, P. Bainbridge 4 for 66)
Gloucestershire 95 for 9

Yorkshire (4 pts) won on faster scoring rate

With Illingworth at the helm Yorkshire gained their second victory in the John Player League in successive Sundays. Boycott and Athey gave Yorkshire a fine start and the impetus was maintained by the later batsmen. Rain reduced the Gloucestershire innings to 24 overs and the target to 140, but they were beaten from the time that Broad was run out in the first over.

An opening stand of 100 by Gower and Briers set up Leicestershire's comfortable win over Warwickshire. Gower batted 34 overs to reach his third John Player League century of the season. He hit twelve fours and three sixes and he and Davison added 86 for the second wicket.

Kim Barnett, a young cricketer rich in promise, who hit his first hundred for Derbyshire, 111 v Lancashire, at Derby, John Player League, 4 July.

Rain reduced Lancashire's target at Derby to 187 but they were bowled out in 27.5 overs with Steve Oldham taking the honours. The man of the match for Derbyshire, however, was Kim Barnett who hit his first hundred in any competition and shared an opening stand of 132 with John Wright. It was good to see such a fine and enthusiastic cricketer as Barnett beginning to realise his rich potential.

Northants had little difficulty with Surrey at Tring where the visitors' batting crumpled after Pauline, Knight and Smith had made an assertive start.

With Middlesex idle, Sussex closed the gap at the top of the table when they overwhelmed Kent. Mendis and Gould began with 110 in 19 overs. Mendis hit eight fours and three sixes in his innings which lasted until the thirty-ninth over. It was a superb effort and he gained splendid support from Parker who played a magnificent, if brief, innings when the scoring rate threatened to flag. Geoff Arnold was back in the Sussex attack and bowled well and Kent could never come to terms with the required rate against a consistently accurate array of bowlers.

I.C.C. Trophy

5 July

at Bewdley

Hong Kong 192 for 4 (A. A. Lorimer 72 not out)
Zimbabwe 196 for 3 (A. J. Pycroft 83 not out, J. G. Heron 51)

Zimbabwe won by 7 wickets

at Tamworth

Kenya 210 for 8 (H. S. Mesta 52)
Papua New Guinea 173 (W. Maha 61)

Kenya won by 37 runs

at Redditch

Netherlands 301 for 3 (R. Lifmann 155 not out, R. Schoonheim 117)
Malaysia 178

Netherlands won by 123 runs

at Olton

West Africa 249 (S. Elliott 67, J. Onyechi 53)
Bermuda 252 for 3 (C. Blades 82 not out, G. Brown 78 not out)

Bermuda won by 7 wickets

at Wellesbourne

Israel 246 (R. J. Cottle 90)
Canada 247 for 7 (C. Neblett 79)

Canada won by 3 wickets
Canada won on default

at Solihull

Fiji 219 for 8 (M. Rajalingham 5 for 39)
Singapore 205 for 9

Fiji won by 14 runs

With the top two places in each group already decided the last round of qualifying matches held only academic interest, but they produced some fine cricket and a little controversy.

A contingent of the Israeli party, including the manager Gabriel Kandi, returned home on Saturday, 3 July, following a series of domestic incidents which caused a rift between players and management. The disagreements reached a head during the game against U.S.A. on the Friday and several players packed their bags and left the next day. This was a somewhat ungracious act and left Canada without opponents at Wellesbourne, but some guest players were incorporated to supplement the Israeli team members still left and a very fine game was played albeit that the Canadians had won by default before a ball was bowled.

The outstanding performance was at Redditch where Holland, who had been expected to reach the semi-finals but had not produced their best form, broke records. Lifmann and Schoonheim put on 257 for the first wicket, a record for the competition, and Lifmann's 155 not out was the highest score made in the Trophy games.

Final Group Tables					
Group One					
	P	W	L	NR	Pts
Zimbabwe	7	5	—	2	24
Papua New Guinea	7	4	2	1	18
Canada	7	3	1	3	18
Kenya	7	3	2	2	16
U.S.A.	7	1	2	4	12
Hong Kong	7	2	3	2	12
Gibraltar	7	—	3	4	8
Israel	7	—	5	2	4
Group Two					
	P	W	L	NR	Pts
Bermuda	7	6	—	1	26
Bangladesh	7	4	1	2	20
Netherlands	7	3	1	3	18
Singapore	7	1	2	4	12
Fiji	7	1	3	3	10
West Africa	7	—	2	5	10
East Africa	7	1	3	3	10
Malaysia	7	—	4	3	6

I.C.C. Trophy – Semi-Finals

7 July

at West Bromwich
Bangladesh 124 (K. M. Curran 4 for 28)
Zimbabwe 126 for 2 (J. G. Heron 63 not out)
Zimbabwe won by 8 wickets

at Mitchell & Butler's, Birmingham
Papua New Guinea 153 (I. V. Pala 72)
Bermuda 155 for 4 (C. Blades 69 not out)
Bermuda won by 6 wickets

As expected Zimbabwe and Bermuda reached the I.C.C. Trophy Final, both winning their matches comfortably. Zimbabwe won their match by tea-time with Jack Heron again in bristling form. Kevin Curran won the man of the match with a brisk 44 and four wickets. John Traicos conceded only 11 runs in 10 overs of superbly flighted and controlled off-spin.

Papua New Guinea, one of the most popular sides in the competition, were floundering at 48 for 6 when Vavine Pala went for the bowling and hit 72 to take his side to 153. It was a brave effort by the big all-rounder, but it was not enough to stop Bermuda winning with some ease.

7, 8 and 9 July

at Derby
Northamptonshire 370 for 8 dec (P. Willey 145, R. J. Boyd-Moss 88, C. J. Tunnicliffe 4 for 72) and 179 for 6 dec (D. G. Moir 5 for 53)
Derbyshire 203 (N. Mallender 5 for 30) and 350 for 3 (J. G. Wright 185 not out, P. N. Kirsten 68)
Derbyshire won by 7 wickets
Derbyshire 21 pts, Northamptonshire 8 pts

at Bristol
Sussex 308 for 9 dec (C. M. Wells 100 not out, G. D. Mendis 67)
Gloucestershire 70 (G. S. le Roux 5 for 15) and 150 (I. A. Greig 4 for 66)
Sussex won by an innings and 88 runs
Sussex 23 pts, Gloucestershire 2 pts

at Maidstone
Surrey 326 (D. J. Thomas 64, R. D. V. Knight 57) and 197 for 6 dec (G. S. Clinton 61)
Kent 203 (A. P. E. Knott 53) and 177 for 6 (L. Potter 83 not out)
Match drawn
Surrey 8 pts, Kent 5 pts

at Uxbridge
Leicestershire 399 (J. C. Balderstone 148, B. F. Davison 100, R. W. Tolchard 80 not out) and 75 for 4
Middlesex 168 (N. G. B. Cook 6 for 32) and 316 (P. R. Downton 65, J. E. Emburey 61, W. N. Slack 57, A. M. E. Roberts 4 for 53)
Leicestershire won by 6 wickets
Leicestershire 24 pts, Middlesex 5 pts

at Trent Bridge
Essex 285 (D. E. East 61, N. Phillip 59, K. E. Cooper 5 for 53) and 86 for 0 (B. R. Hardie 50 not out)
Nottinghamshire 122 (J. K. Lever 5 for 63) and 247 (M. A. Fell 108, B. N. French 68, D. L. Acfield 4 for 35, J. K. Lever 4 for 55)
Essex won by 10 wickets
Essex 23 pts, Nottinghamshire 4 pts

at Edgbaston

Warwickshire 303 (D. L. Amiss 84, A. I. Kallicharran 74, J. Simmons 4 for 79) and 238 for 3 (D. L. Amiss 76, T. A. Lloyd 74)
Lancashire 498 for 7 dec (G. Fowler 150, K. A. Hayes 90, D. Lloyd 83, J. Abrahams 51, S. P. Sutcliffe 4 for 154)
Match drawn
Lancashire 5 pts, Warwickshire 4 pts

at Sheffield

Worcestershire 267 (G. M. Turner 112, P. Carrick 6 for 90) and 362 for 9 dec (G. M. Turner 70, J. D. Inchmore 58, D. N. Patel 53)
Yorkshire 424 (G. Boycott 159, P. Carrick 93, D. N. Patel 4 for 142)
Match drawn
Yorkshire 6 pts, Worcestershire 4 pts

at Taunton

Pakistanis 334 for 5 dec (Mansoor Akhtar 153, Mohsin Khan 85) and 218 for 3 dec (Javed Miandad 105 not out)
Somerset 300 for 7 dec (I. V. A. Richards 181) and 54 for 3
Match drawn

Acting Northants' captain George Sharp was left red-faced after his decision not to ask Derbyshire to follow-on when Neil Mallender's return to form burst of 5 for 30 helped dismiss Derbyshire for 203 on the second day. A Peter Willey century, his first Schweppes County Championship century for three years, and another impressive innings by Robin Boyd-Moss had put Northants in a fine position and Derbyshire trailed by 167, but Sharp was anxious not to bat last on what he judged to be a wicket that was breaking up. He decided to bat again, score some brisk runs and give his bowlers time to bowl out Derbyshire on a wicket which he assessed would give them assistance. Derbyshire were set to make 347 in 305 minutes. Wood and Wright added 125 in 34 overs of glorious stroke play. Wright, who had been missed at third slip when 15, batted on with urgent serenity to record his second century of the week and steer Derbyshire to victory with 17 balls to spare, and seven wickets.

Sussex threw off the despair which had gripped them when they had exited from the NatWest Cup and the Benson and Hedges Cup within the space of four days by beating Gloucestershire in two days at Bristol. Arnold returned to the championship side and compensated for Imran who had been badly missed, but it was le Roux and Greig who took main honours in a bowling line-up which was always attacking the batsmen and never moving on to the defensive. The Sussex innings was built on welcome return-to-form innings by Colin Wells and Gehan Mendis. They seized the initiative when the Gloucestershire spinners threatened to take over and Sussex never lost it again. le Roux dismissed Andy Stovold with the first ball of the Gloucestershire first innings and thereafter the batting was very limp.

Sussex's win took them to within one point of Middlesex who suffered their first championship defeat of the season when Leicestershire beat them at Uxbridge. Leicestershire started inauspiciously and were 9 for 2 when Davison

John Barclay. In the early days of July all his intelligence and qualities of leadership were needed to lift Sussex from the pit of gloom into which they descended after their defeats in the Benson and Hedges and NatWest Cups.

joined Balderstone. Brearley had seen his decision to ask Leicestershire to bat justified, but Davison changed his attitude. When Davison was caught and bowled by Williams in the last over before lunch the score was 169 and Davison had scored 100. It was sparkling stuff from a batsman who is among the most exciting, yet underpraised, in the world. Balderstone batted excellently and he and Tolchard added 148 for the fourth wicket. The stand was ended by Slack who took 3 for 17, his first wickets in first-class cricket. A tired Middlesex lost both openers before the close of the first day and the next day Cook spun them out for 160 so that they had to follow on. The last day was a struggle for Leicestershire to overcome some stubborn resistance from Downton and Emburey in particular, but their greatest adversary was the weather. At 3.00 p.m. they started their second innings needing 75 to win. A series of stoppages around the tea interval made haste essential and, it was Davison who saw them home with nine overs to spare.

There were no such thrills at Edgbaston where the bat once more dominated the ball. There were championship bests for Fowler and Kevin Hayes, some more fine batting from Amiss and Kallicharran and an unenviable 4 for 154 for Simon Sutcliffe who bowled fifty overs.

A similar stalemate occurred at Sheffield. Phil Carrick bowled splendidly on the opening day after Glenn Turner had hit his seventy-first century for Worcestershire, a record for the county. On the second day Geoff Boycott reached the one hundred and twenty-ninth century of his career so drawing level with Sir Leonard Hutton. Worcestershire batted solidly throughout the final day to achieve a draw.

Surrey batted consistently at Maidstone and by the end of the second day they had reached a position of dominance, 225 runs ahead with nine wickets in hand. Knight declared after some quick runs on the last morning and set Kent 321 in 260 minutes, but 80 minutes were lost to bad light and rain and Laurie Potter, substitute for Woolmer, batted with great determination to give his side a draw.

The Pakistanis produced some more thrilling strokes at Taunton, but when it seemed that Somerset would flag Viv Richards hit his highest score of the season and put the tourists' attack into perspective.

At Trent Bridge Essex batted first on a pitch of uneven bounce and were soon in trouble, but Turner, Phillip and David East hit them out of trouble and they recovered from 103 for 5 to 285 all out, Lever and David East adding 57 invaluable runs for the ninth wicket. Before the close Hassan was run out and Lever dismissed Robinson, Birch and Rice to leave Notts floundering at 27 for 4 and Todd unwell and unlikely to bat. Notts were quickly dismissed on the second morning and followed on, but Mark Fell, who had batted with great confidence in the first innings, now batted quite magnificently to reach a maiden first-class hundred. He batted for 230 minutes and hit fourteen fours. French joined Fell in a fifth wicket stand of 114 and Hemmings also offered resistance, but Acfield spun out the tail and Essex won with ease early on the last morning and moved into fifth place in the table.

I.C.C. Trophy – Third Place Play-Off

9 July

at Bourneville

Bangladesh 224 (Yousuf Rahman 115, N. Sherazi 52, L. Aukopi 5 for 14)
Papua New Guinea 225 for 7 (W. Maha 60)

Papua New Guinea won by 3 wickets

Yousuf Rahman became the tenth century maker in the tournament and gave Bangladesh a splendid start, but an early afternoon slump was brought about by the medium pace of Laa Aukopi and Bangladesh were all out in the fifth-eighth over. As they had reached 170 without loss in the thirty-seventh over, this was a bitter disappointment, but it still seemed that 225 would be a formidable target for Papua New Guinea. Indeed they were struggling until William Maha and skipper Api Laka came together in a sixth wicket stand of 90 and although Maha was dismissed, Laka made 41 not out and saw his side win a most popular victory. What a pity that no place could be found for these delightful people in the Prudential World Cup of 1983.

THIRD CORNHILL TEST MATCH
England v. India

India were unchanged and England replaced Miller with Allott, which may have seemed a little harsh on Miller after his splendid 98 at Old Trafford, but one would like to have seen his bowling there a little more impressive, a judgement that also applies to Edmonds.

Willis won the toss and Cook and Tavare opened with a stand of 96. It was hard going and neither batsman convinced that he was a Test opener. Both played mainly off the front foot and both had some near misses. They were dismissed in successive overs. Cook was caught at extra cover and Tavare followed, bowled off bat and pad playing across the line.

Lamb was most introspective at the start and there was a placid period. Gower hit some fluent shots and looked set for a big score until he dabbed unwisely at Shastri.

This brought Botham to the wicket with the score at 185 for 3. He immediately hit hard at Shastri and runs started to flow. One powerful blow off Shastri hit Gavaskar who was fielding at silly point and he left the field with a broken bone in the leg and took no further part in the game.

Below: *Randall hit in an unusual place by a return from the field. Kirmani enquires.*
Right: *The beginning of India's problems in the Third Test at The Oval. Gavaskar is helped from the field with a broken bone in his leg after being struck by a fierce hit from Botham when fielding at silly point.*

THIRD CORNHILL TEST MATCH – ENGLAND v. INDIA
8, 9, 10, 12 and 13 July, 1982 at The Oval

ENGLAND

	FIRST INNINGS		SECOND INNINGS	
G. Cook	c Shastri, b Patil	50	c Sharma, b Dev	8
C. J. Tavare	b Dev	39	not out	75
A. J. Lamb	run out	107	b Doshi	45
D. I. Gower	c Kirmani, b Shastri	47	c and b Nayak	45
I. T. Botham	c Viswanath, b Doshi	208		
D. W. Randall	st Kirmani, b Shastri	95		
D. R. Pringle	st Kirmani, b Doshi	9		
P. H. Edmonds	c sub (Parkar), b Doshi	14		
R. W. Taylor*	lbw, b Shastri	3		
P. J. W. Allott	c Sharma, b Doshi	3		
R. G. D. Willis†	not out	1		
Extras	b 3, lb 5, nb 10	18	b 6, lb 8, nb 4	18
		594	(for 3 wkts dec)	191

INDIA

	FIRST INNINGS		SECOND INNINGS	
R. J. Shastri	c Botham, b Willis	66	c Taylor, b Willis	0
D. B. Vengsarkar	c Edmonds, b Botham	6	(3) c Taylor, b Pringle	16
G. R. Viswanath	lbw, b Willis	56	(4) not out	75
Yashpal Sharma	c Gower, b Willis	38	(5) not out	9
S. M. Patil	c sub (N. R. Taylor), b Botham	62		
S. M. H. Kirmani*	b Allott	43		
Kapil Dev	c Allott, b Edmonds	97		
Madan Lal	c Taylor, b Edmonds	5		
S. V. Nayak	b Edmonds	11	(2) c Taylor, b Pringle	6
D. R. Doshi	not out	5		
S. M. Gavaskar†	absent hurt	0		
Extras	b 3, lb 5, nb 13	21	lb 3, nb 2	5
		410	(for 3 wkts)	111

	O	M	R	W	O	M	R	W
Kapil Dev	25	4	109	1	19	3	53	1
Madan Lal	26	8	69	—	11	6	17	—
Nayak	21	5	66	—	5.3	—	16	1
Patil	14	1	48	1				
Doshi	46	6	175	4	19	5	47	1
Shastri	41.3	8	109	3	16	3	40	—

	O	M	R	W	O	M	R	W
Willis	23	4	78	3	4	—	16	1
Botham	19	2	73	2	4	—	12	—
Allott	24	4	69	1	4	1	12	—
Pringle	28	5	80	—	11	5	32	2
Edmonds	35.2	11	89	3	12	5	34	—

FALL OF WICKETS
1–96, 2–96, 3–185, 4–361, 5–512, 6–534, 7–562, 8–569, 9–582
1–12, 2–94, 3–191

FALL OF WICKETS
1–21, 2–134, 3–135, 4–232, 5–248, 6–378, 7–394, 8–396
1–0, 2–18, 3–43

Match drawn

BOTHAM
Above left: *In harmony with Allan Lamb.*
Above right: *He hits Doshi over long-on for six.*
Left: *The reverse sweep which brought his downfall.*

Nayak tried some leg-breaks and though Lamb was slightly troubled, 100 runs came in 20 overs. Lamb was now looking assured, hitting beautifully through the covers. Botham was bludgeoning in all directions until he decided to concentrate on the morrow and England closed at 329 for 3, Lamb 96, Botham 82, and the game already out of India's grasp.

Allan Lamb reached his maiden Test century the next morning and was run out shortly after. It was an accomplished innings, thoughtful and secure, and one now looks to him to assert his personality at international level.

Botham went on his irrepressible way. It was a stirring innings. The man's power is breathtaking, his audacity is nerve-tingling, and yet he harnessed his belligerence to concentration and good sense. He was in part responsible for the running out of Lamb. His reaction was to advance down the wicket to Kapil Dev and hit a perfectly good ball over long-on for six. It was one of four sixes he hit and his innings, which occupied only 225 balls also included nineteen fours. It was marvellous stuff.

His end was inglorious. He chose to play a totally unnecessary reverse sweep and Viswanath, anticipating, ran from slip to catch him. It was annoying, but he dies as he lives – laughing. And he lets us share the joke.

Above: *Madan Lal, caught Taylor, b Edmonds 5.*

The great Kapil Dev rues his error, caught off Edmonds when three short of his hundred, but what delight was here.

Beside Botham anyone would pale, but Randall was in a particularly uncertain mood. He came off for light drizzle when he would have done better to have stayed and was finally stumped five short of his century, an uncharacteristically moody innings.

England were all out for 594 and the only interest remaining was whether or not India could avoid the follow-on.

India had a pair of make-shift openers in Shastri and Vengsarkar and it was surprising that it was the better batsman of the two, Vengsarkar, who was caught early on when the ball looped up to short-leg. Viswanath and Shastri then set about grinding towards the 395 they needed to reach to avoid the follow-on.

In mid-afternoon Willis returned with a fine spell of bowling, generating a fierce pace and troubling the batsmen. Viswanath appeared to be well caught at first slip by Pringle, but, to the surprise of all, the batsman stood his ground. The umpires could not be sure that the low catch had been taken and gave the batsman the benefit of the doubt. There was a time when a fieldsman claiming a catch was sufficient for the batsman to walk. Sadly that time seems to have passed and cricket is the worse for it. It mattered little. Next ball Willis brought one back viciously and the Indian vice-captain was lbw. Justice.

The Third Test, England v India. Above: Randall drives Doshi during his introspective innings of 95. Opposite: *Botham. 208 off 225 deliveries.*

Shastri was brilliantly caught by Botham in a close gully position and Yashpal Sharma, having been missed at forward short-leg, was taken at slip. But the decisive wicket with the second new ball was that of Patil who had been playing with flourish. He hooked a short ball from Botham to long-leg where Neil Taylor, substituting for the injured Randall, ran in to take a memorable catch as he fell forward.

Pringle bowled well without luck and Allott did not bowl well, but this was hardly surprising as his captain, who presumably did not really consider him worth his place in the side, had him fielding fine-leg both ends for long periods.

Kapil Dev and Kirmani batted with great sense on the Saturday and continued in the same vein on Monday. Once more Kapil Dev gave an astonishing display of clean and powerful hitting. Once he hoisted a ball from Ian Botham which pitched outside off-stump over long-on for six, a mighty blow which Botham himself must have envied.

When Kapil Dev drove Edmonds into the hands of Allott at backward point the saving of the follow-on was but twelve runs away. It was glorious stuff. All the more pity then that we had had to wait until one o'clock for a start as Umpire Bird had suggested to the Indians that the light may not be good enough, with which they readily agreed. To have delayed play in the conditions that prevailed was a farce. Forty-two overs were lost in the day and cricket was again the loser.

Cricket lost more on the last day. Cook had been dismissed by Kapil Dev before close on the fourth day and on the last morning we were subjected to a mockery of a great game as Tavare batted 4 hours 10 minutes for 75. Gower batted 70 minutes after lunch for 20 runs. One has the greatest admiration and respect for both of these men, but this was dreadful.

Willis, who, as captain, must take responsibility for this drudgery, declared belatedly just before three o'clock and the farce dragged on.

There was great concern at the end of this series over the financial losses, the drop in revenue, the alarming fall in attendance, and people seemed to be at a loss for an answer. I offer a few suggestions.

(a) We are close to the point of indigestion with Test cricket. We are in danger of killing the goose that lays the golden egg. Indeed, we may have already done so.

(b) This indigestion is not relieved when two countries contest two series within weeks of each other, particularly when the first of the series was played at funeral pace and seemed to have as its sole purpose the game's destruction.

(c) However much sponsorship is put into the game, it is

Indian Touring Team 1982
First Class Matches

BATTING	v. Warwickshire (Edgbaston) 8-10 May 1982		v. Nottinghamshire (Trent Bridge) 12-14 May 1982		v. Yorkshire (Bradford) 15-18 May 1982		v. M.C.C. (Lord's) 19-21 May 1982		v. Kent (Canterbury) 22-24 May 1982		v. Hampshire (Southampton) 29-31 May 1982		v. Northamptonshire (Northampton) 5-7 June 1982		First Test Match (Lord's) 10-15 June 1982		v. Gloucestershire (Bristol) 19-21 June 1982	
S. M. Gavaskar	32	172	23	10	79	—			19	—			29		48	24		
P. A. Roy	9	8	51	—			9	7	3	20			6	17			32	—
D. B. Vengsarkar	72	57*	28	18*			96	—			—	86	19	—	2	157		
G. R. Viswanath	67	—			45	—	32	—			100		21*	106*	1	3	1	—
A. Malhotra	1	79			22	8	5	18	154*	—			15	10	5	0	21	37
S. M. Patil	0	4	34	0			7	3	18	0	23	7					20	34
Kapil Dev	0	6	4	40	—	30			—	—	26	40			41	89		
S. V. Nayak	28	3*			—	14*	0	—	37*	2	33	—	67*		6*	3		6
S. M. H. Kirmani	15	—	32	4			4	4*		5*	65	26					—	—
S. N. Yadav	1*						0											
D. R. Doshi	2	—					—								0	4*		
G. A. M. Parkar			30	13	146	28	0	92					19	32	1	5	6	1
Yashpal Sharma			3	9	48*	26			77*				10	56	4	37	50*	40*
R. J. Shastri			24	—	21	29			4				25*	15*	4	23	51	20
S. Madan Lal			13*	2*	—	28*	19*	11*			32*	4*			6	15	51*	58*
Randhir Singh			0	—			0											
Byes	4	8	4		2		5	2			2	5	8		8	4		
Leg-byes	8	11	6	1	8	2	4	3	3	1	2	8	6	13	1	2	6	
Wides	1		7		1	5		1					3	4	1		2	1
No-balls	3	3			4	1	4		5		1	6	4	11	5	4	11	3
Total	243	351	259	97	376	171	180	143	282	68	277	298	206	197	128	369	245	200
Wickets	10	5	10	6	5	5	10	4	3	3	6	7	5	4	10	10	5	4
Result	D		D		D		D		D		W		D		L		D	

Catches
15 — S. M. H. Kirmani (ct 11/st 4)
9 — D. B. Vengsarkar
8 — G. A. M. Parkar (ct 7/st 1) and G. R. Viswanath
6 — R. J. Shastri and Yashpal Sharma
5 — Kapil Dev and A. Malhotra
3 — S. V. Nayak and S. M. Gavaskar
1 — S. Madan Lal, S. M. Patil, P. A. Roy

BOWLING	Kapil Dev	S. V. Nayak	S. M. Patil	S. N. Yadav	D. R. Doshi	A. Malhotra	S. M. Gavaskar	S. Madan Lal
v. Warwickshire (Edgbaston) 8-10 May 1982	26-4-86-2	28-7-87-2	18-3-27-1	33-10-68-1	34-7-87-0	9-1-37-1	2-0-13-0	
v. Nottinghamshire (Trent Bridge) 12-14 May 1982	16-4-39-5 21.4-8-60-0		10-1-26-2 1-0-2-0					14-4-40-1 18-3-42-1
v. Yorkshire (Bradford) 15-18 May 1982	8-2-26-0 6-1-9-0	8-2-22-0 1-0-4-0		17-4-48-1	26.1-4-85-2			11-1-48-0 6-1-17-0
v. M.C.C. (Lord's) 19-21 May 1982		16-0-80-1 9-1-32-0		24-3-94-0 7-0-35-0				19-2-63-3 12-0-41-1
v. Kent (Canterbury) 22-24 May 1982	19-2-66-1 4-0-9-0	13-3-40-2 7-2-8-0			21.1-8-53-2 32-3-110-2			17-2-73-2 7-1-11-0
v. Hampshire (Southampton) 29-31 May 1982	10-2-34-1 12-1-42-1	13-2-38-0 11-2-45-0	5-1-25-0	30-2-96-0 12-3-55-0	28-8-86-3 14-3-39-1		3-0-10-0	
v. Northamptonshire (Northampton) 5-7 June 1982		22-7-54-5		15-3-37-1	17-3-47-1			
First Test Match (Lord's) 10-15 June 1982	43-8-125-5 10-1-43-3				40-7-120-2 5-3-11-0			28.1-6-99-3 2-1-2-0
v. Gloucestershire (Bristol) 19-21 June 1982		10-1-33-1 6-3-11-0		16-1-49-0	16-4-41-1			12-3-35-2 7-0-28-4
Second Test Match (Old Trafford) 24-28 June 1982	36-5-109-0	12-1-50-0			47.1-17-102-6			35-9-104-3
v. Essex (Chelmsford) 3-6 July 1982		12-1-40-1 11-2-19-1	7-1-14-0 5-2-13-0	24-4-77-3 17-3-45-1				16-1-64-2 5-1-10-0
Third Test Match (The Oval) 8-13 July 1982	25-4-109-1 19-3-53-1	21-5-66-0 5.3-0-16-1	14-1-48-1		46-6-175-4 19-5-47-1			26-8-69-0 11-6-17-0
	255.4-45-810-20 av. 40.50	205.3-39-645-14 av. 46.07	60-9-155-4 av. 38.75	195-33-604-7 av. 86.28	345.3-78-1003-25 av. 40.12	9-1-37-1 av. 37.00	5-0-23-0 —	246.1-49-763-22 av. 34.68

A. P. A. Roy 1-0-14-0   B. D. B. Vengsarkar 0.2-0-2-0

THE ENGLISH SEASON/297

Chris Tavare. If only he could bring the aggression of his Kent play to the Test arena, what a player we would have.

the people who pay to go through the turnstiles who matter most, yet still they are treated with the utmost contempt as we witnessed on the fourth morning at The Oval when, indefensibly, we were made to wait until one o'clock for some cricket. One had hoped that the farce of the Centenary Test at Lord's had taught all some lessons. Obviously, it has not. If players and umpires show a lack of willingness to play, is it surprising that people show a lack of willingness to watch?

(d) Cricket is a game. It is a great and glorious game, but it is still a game. According to the dictionary a game is a contest for amusement and in a world where many are threatened by unemployment and even a nuclear holocaust we need amusement. What we suffered on the last day at The Oval was devoid of all fun, all gaiety and therefore it was unpalatable. The glories of Botham and the Incredible Tests will all too quickly become a dim memory if the spirit is lost and no-one will watch what does not give joy.

(e) There is a resentment against the ban placed upon Graham Gooch and the other players who went to South Africa to play for the Breweries XI. The resentment is born of the belief that we allowed other countries to dictate to us in the composition of our side and there were many who wrote to newspapers and the cricketing magazines and expressed the view that they would not watch an England 'second' eleven while great players languished so that other governments may strike moral attitudes. In most parts of the world people are very tired of politicians and of their pro-

England v. India – Test Match Averages

ENGLAND BATTING

	M	Inns	NOs	Runs	HS	Av	100s	50s
I. T. Botham	3	3		403	208	134.33	2	1
D. W. Randall	3	3		221	126	73.66	1	1
A. J. Lamb	3	5	1	207	107	51.75	1	
C. J. Tavare	3	5	1	178	75*	44.50		2
P. J. W. Allott	2	2	1	44	41*	44.00		
D. I. Gower	3	5	1	152	47	38.00		
P. H. Edmonds	3	3		90	64	30.00		1
G. Cook	3	5		138	66	27.60		2
R. G. D. Willis	3	3	1	35	28	17.50		
D. R. Pringle	3	3		39	23	13.00		
R. W. Taylor	3	4	1	36	31	12.00		

Played in one Test: G. Miller 98.

INDIA BATTING

	M	Inns	NOs	Runs	HS	Av	100s	50s
S. M. Patil	2	2	1	191	129*	191.00	1	1
Kapil Dev	3	4		292	97	73.00		3
G. R. Viswanath	3	5	1	189	75*	47.25		3
D. B. Vengsarkar	3	5		193	157	38.60	1	
S. M. H. Kirmani	3	4	1	110	58	36.66		1
S. M. Gavaskar	3	3		74	48	24.66		
Yashpal Sharma	3	5	1	98	38	24.50		
R. J. Shastri	3	5		93	66	18.60		1
Madan Lal	3	4		52	26	13.00		
S. V. Nayak	2	3	1	19	11	9.50		
D. R. Doshi	3	3	2	9	5*	9.00		

Played in one Test: A. Malhotra 5 & 0; G. A. M. Parkar 6 & 1.

ENGLAND BOWLING

	Overs	Mds	Runs	Wkts	Av	Best	5/inn
R. G. D. Willis	88	11	330	15	22.00	6/101	1
D. R. Pringle	82	22	219	7	31.28	2/16	
I. T. Botham	93.3	16	320	9	35.55	5/46	1
P. H. Edmonds	102.2	35	261	6	43.50	3/89	
P. J. W. Allott	49	9	147	2	73.50	1/51	

Bowled in one innings: G. Cook 1-0-4-0; G. Miller 16-4-51-1.

INDIA BOWLING

	Overs	Mds	Runs	Wkts	Av	Best	5/inn
D. R. Doshi	157.1	38	455	13	35.00	6/102	1
Kapil Dev	133	21	439	10	43.90	5/125	1
Madan Lal	102.1	30	291	6	48.50	3/99	
R. J. Shastri	116.3	29	275	4	68.75	3/109	
S. V. Nayak	38.3	6	132	1	132.00	1/16	

Bowled in one Test: S. M. Patil 14-1-48-1; Yashpal Sharma 3-2-1-0.

ENGLAND CATCHES
9—R. W. Taylor; 5—G. Cook; 2—P. J. W. Allott, D. I. Gower and C. J. Tavare; 1—I. T. Botham, P. H. Edmonds and D. W. Randall and sub (N. R. Taylor).

INDIA CATCHES
7—S. M. H. Kirmani (ct 4/st 3); 5—G. R. Viswanath; 2—S. M. Gavaskar, A. Malhotra, R. J. Shastri and Yashpal Sharma; 1—S. V. Nayak, D. B. Vengsarkar and G. A. M. Parkar (also one as sub).

nouncements on sport. The resentment at the omission of Gooch and company was not lessened by the fact Lamb and other South Africans could play for England without recrimination and return to play in South Africa at the end of the season.

These are personal observations, but they are based on the evidence of conversations and discussions with players and lovers of the game throughout England.

Dilip Doshi, not quite the threat to England that India had hoped.

I.C.C. Trophy Final

A superbly contested final went eventually to the favourites by a comfortable margin and with five overs and two balls to spare, but none could deny that Bermuda had given a splendid account of themselves throughout this wonderful competition whose only blight had been the unkind weather early on.

For the final the weather was glorious and Bermuda batted first, put in by Fletcher. There was a solid start to the innings, but the bowling of Traicos who in an eleven spell before lunch conceded only 16 runs frustrated Bermuda's ambitions of building quickly on the sound foundation.

Brown and Blades did increase the scoring rate in the afternoon with some clean hitting and brisk running. Seventy runs came from the last ten overs of the innings in which Douglas was most prominent.

Zimbabwe had an uncertain start losing Houghton and Heron, who had scored well in the tournament, with only 30 scored. Curran and Pycroft added 48 before Curran fell to Blades and Fletcher went to the same bowler at 110 so that the game was once more in the balance.

Andy Pycroft now took command and he and Hodgson added 67. Pycroft was dropped off a skier in the covers when 31, but thereafter he did not give a chance until he lofted an easy catch to mid-wicket where Lightbourne accepted gratefully, but by then only 45 runs were needed in 16 overs and Zimbabwe cantered home.

We had seen some splendid cricket and some fine cricketers in the competition and one would suggest that the gap between Papua New Guinea, Netherlands, Bermuda and Zimbabwe and first-class international status is not so great as many had imagined.

The storm clouds gather on a beautiful scene. Bermuda v Bangladesh at Kings Heath, Birmingham. Rain plagued the tournament.

I.C.C. TROPHY FINAL: ZIMBABWE v. BERMUDA
10 July 1982 at Leicester

BERMUDA				ZIMBABWE			
G. A. Brown	c Traicos, b Rawson		48	D. L. Houghton*	lbw, b Trott		8
W. A. Reid	b Hogg		13	J. G. Heron	c and b Gibbons		9
S. Lightbourne	b Fletcher		32	K. M. Curran	lbw, b Blades		30
N. A. Gibbons	b Fletcher		1	A. J. Pycroft	c Lightbourne, b Gibbons		82
C. Blades†	c Curran, b Rawson		45	D. A. G. Fletcher†	c Douglas, b Blades		13
E. G. James	run out		8	C. A. T. Hodgson	not out		57
J. Tucker	lbw, b Hogg		18	R. D. Brown	not out		12
A. C. Douglas*	not out		36	P. W. Rawson			
J. L. D. Bailey	c Hough, b Fletcher		4	A. J. Traicos			
A. King	not out		5	E. J. Hough			
W. Trott				H. R. Hogg			
Extras	b 1, lb 15, w 1, nb 4		21	Extras	b 1, lb 8, w 10, nb 2		21
	(for 8 wkts)		231		(for 5 wkts)		232

	O	M	R	W		O	M	R	W
Hogg	10	—	35	2	Trott	11.4	1	27	1
Hough	8	3	28	—	King	3	—	10	—
Rawson	12	1	48	2	James	11	1	41	—
Traicos	12	3	25	—	Gibbons	12	—	64	2
Fletcher	9	1	34	3	Blades	12	2	39	2
Curran	9	1	40	—	Bailey	5	—	30	—

FALL OF WICKETS
1–27, 2–74, 3–78, 4–135, 5–151, 6–161, 7–197, 8–210

FALL OF WICKETS
1–22, 2–30, 3–78, 4–110, 5–177

Zimbabwe won by 5 wickets

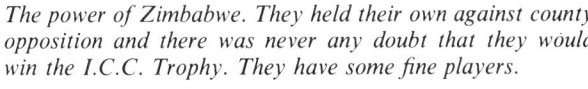
The power of Zimbabwe. They held their own against county opposition and there was never any doubt that they would win the I.C.C. Trophy. They have some fine players.

Top: *The joy of competition. Bermuda jubilant when Bangladesh captain Shafique-ul-Haque is caught at silly mid-on by Gladstone Brown.*

Centre: *Vavine Pala who excited all with his powerful hitting for Papua New Guinea. He lives cricket and trains on beer.*

Above: *Jahangir Badshah of Bangladesh hits out against Zimbabwe in the semi-final, but his side was beaten.*

Top left: *John Traicos, the off-spinner, a former South African Test bowler.*
Top right: *Duncan Fletcher, captain and all-rounder.*

Above: *Andy Pycroft, a prolific scorer and Man of the Match in the final against Bermuda at Leicester.*

Opposite right: *Peter Rawson, a young bowler of great promise.*

Below: *Kevin Curran, another fine all-rounder, and Man of the Match in the semi-final against Bangladesh when he took 4 wickets and scored 44.*

Top right: *Vince Hogg, opening bowler.*
Below right: *Jackie Heron, opening batsman and prolific scorer.*

The moment of triumph. Zimbabwe have won the I.C.C. Trophy and players and managers savour the moment.

G. O. Allen presents the I.C.C. Trophy to Duncan Fletcher, the captain of Zimbabwe. Some of his team-mates record the occasion.

10, 11 and 12 July

at Worcester

Worcestershire 188 (P. A. Neale 68, Abdul Qadir 4 for 30) and 186 (M. J. Weston 93, P. A. Neale 59, Iqbal Qasim 5 for 52, Abdul Qadir 4 for 75)
Pakistanis 467 for 4 dec (Mohsin Khan 165 retired hurt, Zaheer Abbas 147, Mudassar Nazar 75)
Pakistanis won by an innings and 93 runs

10, 12 and 13 July

at Cardiff

Hampshire 270 (C. G. Greenidge 157 not out, M. A. Nash 4 for 63, W. W. Davis 4 for 72) and 70 for 0 dec
Glamorgan 54 for 2 dec and 170 (K. St. J. D. Emery 4 for 19, J. W. Southern 4 for 50)
Hampshire won by 116 runs
Hampshire 19 pts, Glamorgan 4 pts

at Old Trafford

Surrey 374 (A. Needham 134 not out, C. J. Richards 63, R. D. Jackman 60) and 176 for 7 dec (R. D. Jackman 68, J. Simmons 5 for 57)
Lancashire 249 (J. Abrahams 124, A. Needham 5 for 91) and 252 for 6 (C. H. Lloyd 76, J. Abrahams 58)
Lancashire won by 4 wickets
Lancashire 22 pts, Surrey 5 pts

at Coalville

Leicestershire 234 (B. F. Davison 72, J. C. Balderstone 57, G. Miller 8 for 70) and 222 (J. C. Balderstone 75, B. F. Davison 60, G. Miller 4 for 68)
Derbyshire 250 (P. N. Kirsten 84, I. S. Anderson 79, G. Miller 50 not out, J. F. Steele 5 for 60, L. B. Taylor 4 for 58) and 210 for 5 (P. N. Kirsten 102, J. G. Wright 60)
Derbyshire won by 5 wickets
Derbyshire 22 pts, Leicestershire 6 pts

at Northampton

Northamptonshire 252 (R. J. Boyd-Moss 61, R. G. Williams 50, S. Turner 4 for 53) and 307 for 5 (P. Willey 140, W. Larkins 50)
Essex 449 for 6 dec (K. W. R. Fletcher 124, B. R. Hardie 94, K. S. McEwan 61, K. R. Pont 50 not out)
Match drawn
Essex 8 pts, Northamptonshire 4 pts

at Trent Bridge

Middlesex 383 (J. M. Brearley 135, M. W. Gatting 96, M. K. Bore 6 for 134, K. E. Cooper 4 for 121)
Nottinghamshire 190 (J. E. Emburey 4 for 32) and 178 (S. B. Hassan 70)
Middlesex won by an innings and 15 runs
Middlesex 23 pts, Nottinghamshire 2 pts

at Hove

Somerset 358 for 8 dec (P. M. Roebuck 70, V. J. Marks 67) and 192 (I. V. A. Richards 69, D. J. S. Taylor 52, C. E. Waller 4 for 67)
Sussex 295 (I. A. Greig 68, C. M. Wells 65, C. P. Phillipson 64, V. J. Marks 4 for 93) and 234 (I. J. Gould 94, V. J. Marks 4 for 82)
Somerset won by 19 runs
Somerset 24 pts, Sussex 5 pts

at Bradford

Yorkshire 279 (S. N. Hartley 114, D. L. Bairstow 55) and 187 (C. W. J. Athey 73, J. N. Shepherd 5 for 43)
Gloucestershire 266 for 7 dec (P. Bainbridge 103, P. W. Romaines 74) and 201 for 5
Gloucestershire won by 5 wickets
Gloucestershire 22 pts, Yorkshire 6 pts

Left out of the England side for the third Test at The Oval, Geoff Miller joined his Derbyshire colleagues at

Coalville and answered the England selectors in the most positive manner possible by taking a career best 8 for 70 on the opening day as the home county went from 116 for 2 to 234 all out. Derbyshire faded after a second wicket stand of 158 between Kirsten and the rapidly improving Anderson. Miller alone stood firm as the middle order collapsed to John Steele. Leicestershire lost their last eight second innings wickets for 55 runs with Miller again effective, but Derbyshire still had the difficult task of making 207 in 205 minutes. They accomplished this with fourteen balls to spare with Wright and Kirsten making the victory possible with a second wicket stand of 112. Kirsten's innings lasted 170 minutes and he hit thirteen fours in his third century of the season.

Mike Gatting was another to nudge the England selectors. Put in to bat, Middlesex lost Slack and Tomlins for 15, but Brearley and Gatting added 164 with Gatting taking command after lunch to make up for a slow start. He hit Bore onto the pavilion to reach 96 and then was lbw sweeping. It came as a shock, runs looked to be coming to him so easily. Brearley went on serenely and the weakened Notts side lost control of the match. They batted limply, for batting is not their strength, and in spite of a stubborn knock by the inelegant Hassan, they were beaten by an innings.

Sussex lost ground on the leaders. Roebuck played one of his obstinate innings and Richards hit seven fours in an innings of 33. There was a late flourish from Marks and Taylor and Somerset finished the first day in comfort. The second day was much less happy for them. Greig and Phillipson added 102 for the eighth wicket and Sussex (27 for 3 for 93 for 5) got to within 61 of the Somerset total. Garner and Richards were unwell and Somerset finished the day on 52 for 5 with Sussex scenting victory. Richards returned the next day, batted number 8 and scored 69. Taylor the dependable scored 52 and Sussex needed 254 in 220 minutes. In the early stages of their innings Sussex could not maintain the appropriate scoring rate, but the arrival of Gould changed the complexion of the game. He hit three sixes and eleven fours in an innings which lasted 91 minutes before he was run out for 94, his best score for Sussex in the Schweppes County Championship. With him went the hopes of Sussex.

Glamorgan declared 216 behind Hampshire, whom Gordon Greenidge had carried on his shoulders on the Saturday, in order to beat the weather and force a result. Eventually Glamorgan chased a target of 287 in 295 minutes, but they lost with more than an hour to spare. Emery took four of the first five wickets, Southern mopped up the tail and Hampshire maintained their championship challenge.

There were complaints about the general standard of maintenance at Bradford where Yorkshire suffered their first championship defeat of the season. Boycott captained Yorkshire in the absence of Illingworth and was severely criticised when he twice ran out Lumb in the match. Neil Hartley hit a fine hundred and shared a century stand with David Bairstow. Gloucestershire were wilting at 26 for 4, but were saved by Romaines and Bainbridge who added 154. Both were caught behind by Athey, deputising for the injured Bairstow. Romaines hit a career best. In their second innings Yorkshire succumbed to Shepherd and Surridge who exploited the wicket well. Shepherd took five wickets for 9 runs in 23 balls and the Gloucestershire batsmen responded to his achievement by moving placidly to victory in just under three hours.

Northants gave a miserable display on an easy wicket on the first day at Northampton. Stuart Turner was the architect of the Northants' discomfiture as he moved the ball disconcertingly off the seam. Boyd-Moss and Williams gave Northants some respectability, but the Essex batsmen, led by Fletcher, showed the home side what could be achieved on the wicket with a dazzling array of shots on the second day, the last hundred or so runs being scored in semi-darkness. When Northants batted again Carter left at 7, but Larkins and Willey added 129 and a draw became an inevitability as Willey reached his second hundred in seven days before he became one of Pont's three victims.

The exciting strokes of the Pakistanis were again in evidence at Worcester where Zaheer Abbas and Mohsin Khan, who retired with a jarred wrist, added 228 for the third wicket. Earlier Mohsin had shared an opening stand of 164 with Mudassar Nazar. Abdul Qadir's leg-breaks were the undoing of Worcestershire, but the county's second innings began quite remarkably with Weston and Scott putting on 94 of which Weston scored 86. On the last morning Weston took his score to a career best 93 before being caught behind off Iqbal Qasim who was the main destroyer with Qadir. The last eight Worcestershire wickets went down for 64 runs.

The most dramatic happenings were at Old Trafford. Surrey were 152 for 9 when Jackman joined Needham. They attained only one bowling point, but suddenly the last pair mocked the efforts of the earlier batsmen. They closed at 260 for 9 on the Saturday and on the Monday they took the score to 324 before Jackman was bowled by Hughes. Their stand of 172 was only one run off the Surrey tenth wicket record set by Sandham and Ducat in 1921. Needham reached a maiden century in first-class cricket, but his day did not end there for he then proceeded to take a career best 5 for 91 with his well flighted off-breaks. There his glories ended. Abrahams had kept Lancashire in contention with his highest championship score and when Surrey batted again he caught Needham at silly point off Simmons before the close. Knight declared and set Lancashire to make 252 in 164 minutes. With Clive Lloyd in one of his most devastating moods, Lancashire achieved the target with two balls to spare. Abrahams was again in fine form and with twelve needed off the last two overs he hit Lynch for a glorious six before he was run out. Simmons saw the side home. Needham's figures in this innings were 2 for 113 in 15 overs and he and Duncan Pauline were left out of the Surrey side for the NatWest Trophy for staying out beyond the prescribed time during the game with Lancashire.

John Player League

11 July

at Cardiff

Glamorgan 164 for 8
Hampshire 165 for 2 (C. G. Greenidge 92 not out)
Hampshire (4 pts) won by 8 wickets

at Maidstone

Kent 181 for 6 (G. W. Johnson 54 not out)
Somerset 180 for 9

Kent (4 pts) won by 1 run

at Old Trafford

Surrey 172 (C. J. Richards 52, B. W. Reidy 4 for 28)
Lancashire 174 for 3 (C. H. Lloyd 61 not out)

Lancashire (4 pts) won by 7 wickets

at Lord's

Middlesex 214 for 4 (J. M. Brearley 74)
Northamptonshire 198 for 8 (P. Willey 76, W. Larkins 60)

Middlesex (4 pts) won by 16 runs

at Trent Bridge

Leicestershire 114 (N. J. B. Illingworth 4 for 15)
Nottinghamshire 118 for 5

Nottinghamshire (4 pts) won by 5 wickets

at Edgbaston

Warwickshire 181 for 6 (T. A. Lloyd 83)
Gloucestershire 185 for 5 (P. W. Romaines 52)

Gloucestershire (4 pts) won by 5 wickets

at Scarborough

Yorkshire 133 for 9
Essex 134 for 5

Essex (4 pts) won by 5 wickets

Middlesex maintained their form and with half of the John Player League fixtures completed they had won seven and had one abandoned, a formidable record. Northants were their latest victims, but they gave the leaders a fright. Middlesex had batted with customary accomplishment and reached 214 in their 40 overs, but Larkins and Willey countered with an opening stand of 116 in 25 overs. After they were dismissed, however, wickets tumbled and Northants needed 32 off the last over to win. Steele hit two defiant sixes, but it was a forlorn task.

Kent joined Sussex in second place with the narrowest of wins over Somerset. Kent had looked well beaten. They recovered from 81 for 5 when Knott and Johnson added 90 for the sixth wicket, but then lost Ellison injured before he had completed bowling his second over. Roebuck and Denning began with 64 in 15 overs, but the visitors slumped to 94 for 4. Marks and Popplewell added 62 in 13 overs and victory seemed assured, but Jarvis returned to bowl splendidly and snatched victory for Kent.

Hampshire won easily at Cardiff against bottom of the table Glamorgan and Gloucestershire won the contest between the two struggling teams at Edgbaston.

Clive Lloyd hammered Lancashire to victory with more than four overs to spare and Notts won a very low scoring game at Trent Bridge. Illingworth had a League best of 4 for 15.

The Essex bowlers were in miserly mood at Scarborough and restricted Yorkshire to 133 in 40 overs, a total that they could not hope to defend.

NatWest Trophy

14 July

at Chelmsford

Essex 269 for 7 (K. W. R. Fletcher 97)
Kent 139 (S. Turner 4 for 23, N. Phillip 4 for 26)

Essex won by 130 runs
(Man of the Match – K. W. R. Fletcher)

at Southampton

Derbyshire 239 for 5 (P. N. Kirsten 110 not out, J. G. Wright 56)
Hampshire 242 for 4 (C. G. Greenidge 83, J. M. Rice 59)

Hampshire won by 6 wickets
(Man of the Match – P. N. Kirsten)

14 and 15 July

at Taunton

Somerset 271 for 5 (P. W. Denning 73, V. J. Marks 51 not out)
Leicestershire 208 for 9 (D. I. Gower 60, J. Garner 4 for 23)

Somerset won by 63 runs
(Man of the Match – V. J. Marks)

at Cardiff

Glamorgan 169 (R. C. Ontong 54)
Warwickshire 170 for 4 (T. A. Lloyd 52)

Warwickshire won by 6 wickets
(Man of the Match – T. A. Lloyd)

at Trent Bridge

Nottinghamshire 142
Gloucestershire 143 for 1 (A. W. Stovold 76 not out, B. C. Broad 59)

Gloucestershire won by 9 wickets
(Man of the Match – A. W. Stovold)

at Leeds

Worcestershire 286 for 5 (G. M. Turner 105)
Yorkshire 290 for 7 (D. L. Bairstow 92, S. N. Hartley 58, C. M. Old 55 not out)

Yorkshire won by 3 wickets
(Man of the Match – D. L. Bairstow)

15 and 16 July

at Lord's

Middlesex 204 for 9 (J. M. Brearley 66)
Lancashire 202 for 9 (N. G. Cowans 4 for 26)

Middlesex won by 2 runs
(Man of the Match – N. G. Cowans)

David Steele, a sound return to Northants with bat and ball.

Left: *John Rice. His consistent form as Gordon Greenidge's opening partner did much to raise Hampshire to a challenging position in the Schweppes County Championship and the John Player League.*

at The Oval

Northamptonshire 239 for 5 (P. Willey 55, G. Cook 50)
Surrey 242 for 4 (D. M. Smith 103 not out)

Surrey won by 6 wickets
(Man of the Match – D. M. Smith)

There was rain all round the country and only at Southampton and Chelmsford could the games be completed on the first day.

Essex won a surprisingly easy victory over Kent who were without Woolmer and Cowdrey. Essex had a good start from Gooch and Hardie who put up the fifty in twelve overs, but it was Keith Fletcher who dominated the innings with batsmanship of the highest quality. He batted for 146 minutes and was as dismissive of pace as he was of spin. The penultimate over of the innings, bowled by Jarvis, brought Essex twenty runs and Fletcher was out off the first ball of the last over when he was taken on the long-on boundary off the bowling of Underwood. He hit two sixes and six fours. Taylor and Potter began with a stand of 54, but when Turner joined the attack the Kent innings crumbled. Phillip mopped up the tail and the game ended after eight o'clock, the interruptions for rain having been minimal when one considered the deluges only a few miles distant.

Hampshire won with twenty balls to spare and surprised many. Kirsten and Wright, inevitably, had seen Derbyshire to what appeared to be a winning total after being put in to bat. Greenidge and Rice responded with an opening stand of 137, but at that total Wood took the wickets of Greenidge, Nicholas and Jesty in fourteen balls. Rice left at 172, but Hayward and Pocock batted with great good sense, hitting cleanly and running well, and Hampshire moved into the quarter finals.

At Headingley, Glenn Turner hit a sparkling hundred and with support from Neale and Scott and generally sound batting down the order he saw Worcestershire to a formidable 286. Inchmore then began with a fierce spell of bowling which removed Boycott, Lumb, Athey and Love with only 38 scored. Rain brought play to an early close with Yorkshire at 40 for 4 from 16 overs and seemingly well beaten. Bairstow and Hartley had other ideas. Bairstow began cautiously and then launched a blistering and courageous attack. He and Hartley added 95 in 25 overs, Carrick went quickly, but Old joined Bairstow in a decisive stand of 102 in 15 overs. Still Yorkshire needed 51 from the last 38 deliveries. When Bairstow was brilliantly caught by the diving Scott, Yorkshire were 43 runs short of their target. Stevenson hit two sixes off Inchmore who bowled the fifty-seventh over, and the fifty-eighth over brought nine runs. 14 were needed off two overs, but savage blows from Stevenson and Old ended Worcestershire's hopes and when Old hooked the third ball of Warner's last over through mid-wicket Yorkshire had won an astounding victory.

There were no such fireworks at Trent Bridge where the Gloucestershire seam attack reduced Notts to ruins on the first day and Stovold and Broad in an opening stand of 126 strode to victory on the second.

Leicestershire began well at Taunton with Roebuck and Richards dismissed and only 12 scored. Thereafter the game belonged to Somerset. Rose and Denning righted the situation with a stand of 126 and Botham, Marks and Lloyds all contributed good innings. Marks added some cunningly controlled slow bowling to his fifty and snatched the Man of the Match award. Neither he nor any of the other Somerset bowlers ever allowed Leicestershire to reach the required rate of scoring.

Glamorgan surrendered in a dour struggle at Cardiff where Andy Lloyd held Warwickshire together with an innings that lasted nearly three hours.

Kapil Dev could not inspire Northants to victory at The Oval. Northants batted steadily enough on the Thursday after rain had left the ground looking like mid-November on the first day. David Smith saw Surrey home with surprising ease on the Friday. It was his best innings in a limited over competition and Surrey won with seven balls to spare.

It seemed that Lancashire would once more dispose of Middlesex in a knock-out competition when they restricted the home side to 204 on the Thursday, Brearley alone looking comfortable. Lancashire began very badly in reply, losing Fowler and Maynard to Cowans with only 12 scored.

Clive Lloyd went to Selvey at 31, but David Lloyd and David Hughes added 73 before Cowans returned to trap Lloyd lbw. Abrahams, Simmons and Reidy kept Lancashire in contention and Reidy, in particular, was hitting well. Simmons and Allott were both run out and Lancashire started the last over eleven short of victory. Six runs were scampered and victory seemed possible until an accurate throw by Barlow ran out Reidy on the fourth ball of the over. Croft despatched the fifth for two, but swung and missed the last ball to give Middlesex a win by two runs.

14 and 15 July

at Glasgow

Pakistanis 351 for 4 dec (Wasim Raja 174, Javed Miandad 54 not out)
Scotland 111 for 5 (W. A. Donald 53 not out, Imran Khan 5 for 24)

Match abandoned as a draw. No play on second day

Prudential Trophy – First Match: England v. Pakistan

The claims of Gatting could be ignored no longer and he was included in the side for the Prudential Trophy matches. More surprisingly, Eddie Hemmings was included at the expense of Edmonds. Hemmings' selection was well deserved and it was good to see that the selectors were taking note of achievements at county level. Jarvis was also in the party but played in neither match.

The game began and ended in a cascade of glorious shots. Mudassar and Mohsin treated the England bowling with alarming disrespect and their driving through the off-side field was a delight. Anything dropped short was hooked in a grand and disdainful manner and for an hour and a half we enjoyed a feast of elegant shots. The stand ended disastrously when Mohsin pushed Hemmings down the pitch, called for an impossible run and then sent Mudassar back. He was too late and was run out by the bowler. Possibly unsettled by his error, Mohsin was yorked by Botham in the next over. At lunch Pakistan were 128 for 2 in 35 overs.

Miandad and Zaheer threatened more than they achieved. Neither looked completely fit and Zaheer's concentration could not have been helped by the mob invasion when he reached fifty.

All the Pakistan batting looked rich in strokes, but steady bowling and fine fielding restricted them to a score forty or fifty below what they must have hoped for.

Gower opened for England as Cook had been omitted and he displayed some handsome shots until brilliantly caught by the diving Wasim Bari. Tavare carried on steadfastly until bowled by a full toss and this let in Botham to partner Lamb.

Lamb had already reached his half-century before Tavare's dismissal and he had hit Iqbal Qasim for twelve in one over. Sarfraz had injured a hand and Imran apart, there was no bowler who looked likely to trouble the England batsmen. The two hundred came up in the thirty-ninth over and shortly afterwards Lamb reached a magnificent hundred. By the time he was out the match had long been decided.

PRUDENTIAL TROPHY – FIRST MATCH: ENGLAND v. PAKISTAN
17 July 1982 at Trent Bridge

PAKISTAN			
Mudassar Nazar	run out		51
Mohsin Khan	b Botham		47
Zaheer Abbas	lbw, b Pringle		53
Javed Miandad	c Willis, b Pringle		28
Majid Khan	c Willis, b Botham		23
Wasim Raja	c Hemmings, b Botham		14
Imran Khan†	not out		16
Sarfraz Nawaz	not out		2
Wasim Bari*			
Iqbal Qasim			
Sikhander Bakht			
Extras	b 4, lb 4, w 6, nb 2		16
	(for 6 wkts)		250

	O	M	R	W
Willis	11	1	46	—
Botham	11	—	57	3
Pringle	11	1	50	2
Miller	11	1	36	—
Hemmings	11	1	45	—

FALL OF WICKETS
1–102, 2–103, 3–175, 4–208, 5–222, 6–238

ENGLAND		
D. I. Gower	c Wasim Bari, b Sikhander	17
C. J. Tavare	b Imran	48
A. J. Lamb	c Wasim Bari, b Imran	118
M. W. Gatting	not out	37
I. T. Botham	not out	10
D. W. Randall		
G. Miller		
D. R. Pringle		
E. E. Hemmings		
R. W. Taylor*		
R. D. G. Willis†		
Extras	lb 12, w 5, nb 5	22
	(for 3 wkts)	252

	O	M	R	W
Imran Khan	11	2	35	2
Sarfraz Nawaz	11	3	43	—
Mudassar Nazar	5.1	—	26	—
Sikhander Bakht	7	—	34	1
Iqbal Qasim	7	—	49	—
Majid Khan	4	—	25	—
Wasim Raja	2	—	18	—

FALL OF WICKETS
1–25, 2–132, 3–234

England won by 7 wickets

17, 19 and 20 July

at Southend

Essex 262 (K. S. McEwan 116, P. G. Newman 4 for 59) and 261 for 4 dec (B. R. Hardie 77, K. S. McEwan 63)
Derbyshire 130 (J. K. Lever 6 for 48) and 308 (P. N. Kirsten 113, J. H. Hampshire 95, S. Turner 4 for 74, J. K. Lever 4 for 88)

Essex won by 85 runs
Essex 23 pts, Derbyshire 4 pts

at Bristol

Gloucestershire 244 (A. W. Stovold 63, Sadiq Mohammad 53, D. S. Steele 4 for 77, P. Willey 4 for 74) and 193 (Sadiq Mohammad 50, D. S. Steele 5 for 71)
Northamptonshire 401 (G. Cook 101, W. Larkins 92, D. S. Steele 74 not out, Sadiq Mohammad 4 for 42) and 40 for 1)

Northamptonshire won by 9 wickets
Northamptonshire 23 pts, Gloucestershire 4 pts

Allan Lamb, an England success.

at Portsmouth
Hampshire 251 for 9 dec (D. R. Turner 96) and 221 (M. C. J. Nicholas 81, S. T. Clarke 4 for 53, R. D. Jackman 4 for 58)
Surrey 343 for 7 dec (D. J. Thomas 50 not out, D. M. Smith 50) and 131 for 8 (K. St. J. D. Emery 4 for 38, M. D. Marshall 4 for 64)
Surrey won by 2 wickets
Surrey 23 pts, Hampshire 5 pts

at Lord's
Middlesex 363 (K. P. Tomlins 138, N. J. B. Illingworth 5 for 89)
Nottinghamshire 114 (J. E. Emburey 4 for 30) and 138 (P. H. Edmonds 6 for 31)
Middlesex won by an innings and 111 runs
Middlesex 23 pts, Nottinghamshire 2 pts

at Taunton
Somerset 78 (M. A. Nash 5 for 35) and 463 (P. W. Denning 91 not out, J. W. Lloyds 89, P. M. Roebuck 66, P. A. Slocombe 63, V. J. Marks 50, B. J. Lloyd 5 for 155)
Glamorgan 333 for 9 dec (D. A. Francis 127, C. J. C. Rowe 105) and 22 for 0
Match drawn
Glamorgan 6 pts, Somerset 1 pt

at Hove
Leicestershire 208 (N. E. Briers 69, I. A. Greig 4 for 58) and 204 (R. W. Tolchard 57, I. A. Greig 4 for 39)
Sussex 164 (P. W. G. Parker 106, J. F. Steele 5 for 4, J. P. Agnew 4 for 55) and 235 (G. D. Mendis 72, C. M. Wells 52, C. E. Waller 50, N. G. B. Cook 7 for 81)
Leicestershire won by 13 runs
Leicestershire 22 pts, Sussex 5 pts

at Leeds
Yorkshire 365 for 8 dec (G. Boycott 152 not out, P. Carrick 75, C. Lethbridge 4 for 84) and 64 for 1
Warwickshire 189 (D. L. Amiss 73, A. I. Kallicharran 59, S. J. Dennis 5 for 42) and 236 (D. L. Amiss 94, G. W. Humpage 55)
Yorkshire won by 9 wickets
Yorkshire 24 pts, Warwickshire 4 pts

Middlesex's grip on the Schweppes County Championship tightened when they destroyed Nottinghamshire, low in spirit and application, for the second time in a week. The Middlesex batting was not particularly inspiring against a weakened attack, but Tomlins, firmly establishing himself since Barlow's loss of form, and Radley rescued them from 73 for 3 with a stand of 117. Tomlins hit two sixes and thirteen fours in an innings of practicality. Ian Pont and Peter Such bowled commendably on their championship debuts, but Illingworth was by far the most effective of the Notts bowlers. The Notts batting crumpled before Emburey and Edmonds and Middlesex moved to an easy win early on the last day and to a 37 point lead at the top of the table.

Brian Davison. His exciting batting was a major factor in Leicestershire's fine season.

Sussex, their nearest challengers, lost a fascinating game at Hove. Ian Greig bowled well in both innings and Leicestershire were twice dismissed for just over two hundred, but the Sussex batsmen unaccountably failed to press home the advantage their bowlers had given them. In their first innings they reached 158 for 4, thanks to a beautiful knock by Paul Parker, full of graceful aggression, but John Steele took the last five wickets as six fell for six runs. Ultimately, Sussex had to make 249 to win and although Green went quickly, Mendis and Wells put on 100 for the second wicket. Nick Cook dismissed them both and gnawed away at the Sussex batting so that they were limping at 173 for 8. Then Chris Waller hit 50 off 27 deliveries and gave Sussex dreams of glory, but Cook bowled him and took the honours for Leicestershire.

Essex, surviving the trauma of losing Gooch to the first ball of the match, maintained their late challenge for the title by beating fellow contenders Derbyshire at Southend. Ken McEwan and Keith Pont batted well in a fourth wicket stand of 137. McEwan's hundred was a delight, but when he fell to Tunnicliffe Essex collapsed to the Derbyshire seam attack which exploited the conditions well. Before the close, however, Derbyshire had lost Wood, Wright and nightwatchman Moir for 38, and on the Monday John Lever completed the rout. Hardie and McEwan added brisk runs for Essex and Fletcher set Derbyshire the improbable task of scoring 394 to win. Wright, for whom Essex is not a happy county, again failed and Wood and Maher quickly followed so that they were 47 for 3, but Kirsten, who made an accomplished century, and Hampshire added 158. It seemed as if Essex would be denied, but Lever had Kirsten caught behind and Turner took quick wickets in a mid-afternoon spell to bring the points to Essex.

David Steele emulated the success of brother John by taking nine wickets with his left-arm spin bowling at Bristol. Steele also plundered runs in support of Cook and Larkins who put on 175 for the first wicket. Larkins has never batted better than he did for Northants in 1982. When Gloucestershire collapsed a second time to spin Northants had no difficulty in recording their first victory of the season.

It seemed as though Glamorgan would record their first win of the season when, spearheaded by Malcolm Nash, they bowled out Somerset for 78 on the first morning. Francis hit a career best and Rowe his first century for Glamorgan to give their county a first innings lead of 255, but Somerset recovered sanity in the second innings. Roebuck and Slocombe began with a partnership of 137 and thereafter all the batsmen applied themselves to deny Glamorgan their coveted victory, none more so than Peter Denning who finished 91 not out despite being injured.

Warwickshire also remained without success as Boycott completed another century and Simon Dennis bowled with great intelligence, accuracy and hostility. Amiss remained the master craftsman as all about him floundered, Kallicharran apart. Yorkshire's win was their second of the season over Warwickshire. They had beaten no other county.

Hampshire and Surrey, jostling close in the pack behind Middlesex, engaged in a splendid contest at Portsmouth. A fine innings by David Turner, who had had a miserable season and spent much of it in the second team, restored Hampshire's fortunes on the Saturday, but on the Monday they faltered as a consistently even display by the Surrey batsmen gave the visitors a first innings lead of 92. Once more Surrey revealed their depth in batting, Thomas and Needham added an unbeaten 54 for the eighth wicket. A third wicket partnership of 133 between Turner and Nicholas gave some substance to the Hampshire second innings and ensured that Surrey would have a target to chase. Turner was the recipient of an unusual piece of good fortune when umpire Ibadulla bravely reversed a decision after he had first given Turner out lbw. Surrey were set to make 130 in 108 minutes, Clarke and Jackman having brought about a Hampshire collapse and given their side a chance of victory. In the chase for runs wickets fell regularly, but Surrey never gave up their attempt to win. At 119 for 8 Needham joined Thomas who was batting with a runner because of a knee injury. Off the third ball of the last over of the match, bowled by Marshall, Thomas hooked a four to bring his side victory and so avenge their defeat in the equally thrilling contest at The Oval a few weeks earlier.

John Player League
18 July

at Southend

Essex 194 for 9 (N. Phillip 56, K. S. Mackintosh 4 for 37)
Surrey 163 (A. Needham 55)
Essex (4 pts) won by 31 runs

at Bristol

Northamptonshire 180 for 7 (R. G. Williams 82)
Gloucestershire 175 for 9
Northamptonshire (4 pts) won by 5 runs

at Southampton

Lancashire 215 for 5 (D. Lloyd 79)
Hampshire 215 for 9 (M. C. J. Nicholas 76, L. L. McFarlane 4 for 18)
Match tied
Hampshire 2 pts, Lancashire 2 pts

at Lord's

Middlesex 135 (B. Wood 5 for 20)
Derbyshire 137 for 3
Derbyshire (4 pts) won by 7 wickets

at Taunton

Yorkshire 210 for 7 (D. L. Bairstow 64, S. N. Hartley 56)
Somerset 213 for 4 (V. J. Marks 56 not out)
Somerset (4 pts) won by 6 wickets

at Hove

Sussex 183 for 9 (P. W. G. Parker 54, G. J. Parsons 4 for 27)
Leicestershire 169 for 9 (J. C. Balderstone 52, I. A. Greig 5 for 42)
Sussex (4 pts) won by 14 runs

at Worcester

Glamorgan 187 for 8
Worcestershire 186 for 7 (E. J. O. Hemsley 77)
Glamorgan (4 pts) won by 1 run

Middlesex suffered their first John Player League defeat of the season when Barry Wood's movement off the seam and reserve keeper Bernard Maher's five dismissals helped to rout Middlesex for 135 in under 34 overs. The confident Barnett survived the early loss of partner John Wright to combine with the aggressive Kirsten in a second wicket stand of 50 and the reliable John Hampshire in a third wicket stand of 71 so that Derbyshire won with ease to move to within six points of the leaders.

The Derbyshire victory gave great heart to Sussex whose win over Leicestershire took them to within two points of Middlesex with a game in hand. A third wicket stand of 82 between Parker and Wells was the highlight of the

Sussex innings. Briers and Balderstone began with a partnership of 80 for Leicestershire that seemed to put them on the road to victory, but Ian Greig's seam bowling brought about a collapse and they fell well short.

Essex maintained their challenge with their sixth victory in a row. Gooch failed for the second day running and Essex lost their first four batsmen for 44, but Phillip, Pont, Lilley and Turner hit and ran well in spite of some good bowling by Mackintosh. Surrey lost 3 for 22 and never really recovered although Needham, used as an opener, recorded a maiden John Player League fifty.

A splendid innings by Richard Williams, not so long ago regarded as on the verge of the England side, was the outstanding achievement of the day at Bristol where others failed on a green pitch. A seventh wicket stand of 65 in 10 overs between Stephenson and Graveney brought Gloucestershire close, but they could never maintain the required rate of scoring.

A stand of 105 for the fourth wicket between Bairstow and Hartley lifted Yorkshire to 210 at Taunton. Somerset lost their first four batsmen, including acting skipper Viv Richards for a duck, for 107, but Marks and Popplewell scored the remaining runs without mishap and victory came with ten balls to spare.

In their pursuit of tight finishes Hampshire nearly cut it too fine at Southampton. David Lloyd provided the main substance of Lancashire's 215 for 5, but Hampshire were going well at 189 for 3 with Nicholas playing his best Sunday League innings of 76. Then McFarlane, who bowled quite splendidly, bowled Nicholas and Pocock with successive deliveries. Cowley hit briskly for 23 and when the last over began Hampshire needed five to win with three wickets standing. Marshall was run out and Bob Parks caught swinging at the accurate McFarlane. Tremlett was left facing the last ball of the match with three needed for victory. He managed two and the match was tied.

The greatest excitement of the day was at Worcester, however, where the home side needed ten to win off the last over which was bowled by Winston Davis, settling in well as Ezra Moseley's replacement. Humphries hit a four and a two, but was then run out. Inchmore and Warner could only manage a single each so that Glamorgan won their first match against a county in any competition during the season – by one run. They had to thank a containing spell by Nash and Worcestershire were brought close to victory by a third wicket stand of 112 by Neale and Hemsley.

Right: *Eddie Hemmings, an international debut of professional accomplishment.*
Centre: *Sikhander Bakht ponders on the violence of the England batting.*
Far right: *Ian Botham and Mike Gatting savaged the Pakistan bowling in such a manner as to put the game at Old Trafford out of the visitors' grasp. Wasim Bari, keeping wicket, seems to symbolise the anguish of his team by his facial expression.*

Prudential Trophy – Second Match: England v. Pakistan

England played the same side that had won at Trent Bridge, but Pakistan brought in Mansoor Akhtar and Tahir Naqqash for the injured Sarfraz and Javed. Imran won the toss and asked England to bat first on a magnificent wicket. Tavare, Gower and Lamb all batted with a delightful urgency, but it was the batting of Botham and Gatting that was the glory of the day.

Iqbal Qasim had begun by having Allan Lamb caught at the wicket off a ball that turned. Thereafter he was slaughtered. His eight overs cost 76 runs. Four times Botham hit him into the crowd for six, mighty blows.

In eleven overs Botham and Gatting added 84. It was three quarters of an hour of sumptuous stroke play and Gatting placed the Test selectors in the position where his position in the England side became axiomatic. His 76 was made from 82 balls and he was voted Man of the match. The pace of the England innings was not sustained over the final overs, but it mattered little. We had drunk some rich wine.

The England bowling and fielding was better than Pakistan's and for a time it looked as if Pakistan would disintegrate and surrender meekly. They never suggested that they could win, but Wasim Raja and Imran Khan batted bravely and played some fierce shots so that at least they died with honour.

After the pitch invasions at Trent Bridge it was refreshing that the appeals to the crowd at Old Trafford had the desired result and the day was free of incident.

THE ENGLISH SEASON/311

PRUDENTIAL TROPHY – SECOND MATCH: ENGLAND v. PAKISTAN
19 July 1982 at Old Trafford

ENGLAND

D. I. Gower	c Wasim Bari, b Mudassar		33
C. J. Tavare	run out		16
A. J. Lamb	c Wasim Bari, b Qasim		27
M. W. Gatting	run out		76
I. T. Botham	c Raja, b Imran		49
D. W. Randall	run out		6
G. Miller	b Imran		26
D. R. Pringle	not out		34
E. E. Hemmings	c Qasim, b Tahir		1
R. W. Taylor*	not out		1
R. G. D. Willis†			
Extras	lb 16, w 10		26
		(for 8 wkts)	295

	O	M	R	W
Imran Khan	11	1	48	2
Tahir Naqqash	10	—	37	1
Sikhander Bakht	11	—	42	—
Mudassar Nazar	11	—	50	1
Iqbal Qasim	8	—	76	1
Majid Khan	4	1	16	—

FALL OF WICKETS
1–32, 2–54, 3–101, 4–185, 5–217, 6–226, 7–280, 8–284

PAKISTAN

Mudassar Nazar	run out	31
Mohsin Khan	b Pringle	17
Zaheer Abbas	c Randall, b Pringle	13
Mansoor Akhtar	run out	28
Majid Khan	b Miller	5
Wasim Raja	c Botham, b Willis	60
Imran Khan†	c Gower, b Miller	31
Tahir Naqqash	run out	1
Wasim Bari*	b Hemmings	4
Iqbal Qasim	lbw, b Botham	13
Sikhander Bakht	not out	2
Extras	lb 14, w 2, nb 1	17
		222

	O	M	R	W
Willis	8	—	36	1
Botham	8.4	—	40	1
Miller	11	1	56	2
Pringle	11	—	43	2
Hemmings	11	3	30	1

FALL OF WICKETS
1–52, 2–55, 3–82, 4–97, 5–123, 6–183, 7–200, 8–201, 9–213

England won by 73 runs

Far left: Wasim Raja strikes out bravely at Manchester and Pakistan die with honour.
Left: Iqbal Qasim, the sufferer.
Top: Mike Gatting
Above: Imran Khan at Manchester. The captain of Pakistan rests as he considers the hopeless task.

21, 22 and 23 July

at Southend
Essex 250 (G. A. Gooch 60) and 263 for 7 dec (G. A. Gooch 87, D. R. Pringle 51 not out)
Middlesex 229 (W. N. Slack 50) and 47 for 1

Match drawn
Essex 7 pts, Middlesex 6 pts

at Portsmouth
Glamorgan 184 (A. L. Jones 53, K. St. J. D. Emery 6 for 51) and 193 (D. A. Francis 77 not out, T. M. Tremlett 5 for 59, K. St. J. D. Emery 4 for 50)
Hampshire 435 for 2 dec (C. G. Greenidge 183 not out, T. E. Jesty 135 not out, J. M. Rice 57)

Hampshire won by an innings and 78 runs
Hampshire 24 pts, Glamorgan 1 pt

at Old Trafford
Lancashire 397 for 8 dec (J. Simmons 79 not out, G. Fowler 66, D. Lloyd 61, S. J. O'Shaughnessy 56, D. S. Steele 4 for 82) and 215 for 3 dec (D. Lloyd 112 not out, S. J. O'Shaughnessy 50)
Northamptonshire 330 for 5 dec (P. Willey 102, R. J. Boyd-Moss 62 not out, G. Cook 61) and 233 for 6 (G. Cook 66, D. P. Hughes 4 for 50)

Match drawn
Lancashire 6 pts, Northamptonshire 6 pts

at Worksop
Nottinghamshire 329 for 9 dec (E. E. Hemmings 127 not out, A. Sidebottom 5 for 85) and 181 for 2 dec (P. A. Todd 117 not out)
Yorkshire 206 (G. Boycott 91) and 305 for 8 (G. Boycott 82, C. W. J. Athey 76)

Yorkshire won by 2 wickets
Yorkshire 22 pts, Nottinghamshire 6 pts

at The Oval
Surrey 213 (G. Monkhouse 63 not out, H. R. Moseley 5 for 57) and 134 (J. Garner 5 for 28, I. T. Botham 4 for 34)
Somerset 147 (I. V. A. Richards 64, S. T. Clarke 5 for 42) and 204 for 8 (P. M. Roebuck 51)

Somerset won by 2 wickets
Somerset 20 pts, Surrey 6 pts

at Nuneaton

Gloucestershire 240 (A. J. Wright 65, M. W. Stovold 52, C. Lethbridge 4 for 56) and 434 for 5 dec (P. W. Romaines 186, A. W. Stovold 100, P. Bainbridge 75 not out)
Warwickshire 446 (A. I. Kallicharran 173, R. G. D. Willis 63 not out, D. Surridge 4 for 137)

Match drawn
Warwickshire 8 pts, Gloucestershire 4 pts

at Hereford

Kent 321 for 7 dec (M. R. Benson 107, D. G. Aslett 75) and 287 for 6 dec (M. R. Benson 80, A. P. E. Knott 56 not out)
Worcestershire 321 (G. M. Turner 118, D. J. Humphries 60 not out, D. N. Patel 56, G. R. Dilley 6 for 87) and 122 for 2 (G. M. Turner 66)

Match drawn
Worcestershire 6 pts, Kent 5 pts

at Leicester

Leicestershire 354 for 3 dec (D. I. Gower 176 not out, I. P. Butcher 71 not out) and 241 for 9 dec (T. J. Boon 90, R. W. Tolchard 61, Abdul Qadir 6 for 71)
Pakistanis 351 for 3 dec (Mohsin Khan 203 not out, Mansoor Akhtar 65) and 61 for 2

Match drawn

What should have been one of the matches of the season between the leaders of the Schweppes County Championship and one of their most vital challengers ended in a feeble draw and dissension over bad light at Southend. A fine half-century by Gooch, an innings which promised more than it ultimately achieved, was the spark of a brisk Essex first innings. It was a contest between some good batting and some fine bowling and fielding, but it was rather overshadowed by the events concerning Stuart Turner. Twice he fended off lifting balls, one from Cowans and one from Hughes, to be caught in the gully. Both times umpire Oslear called no-ball as he adjudged that they were the second bouncers to be bowled in the over. There were more technicalities on the second day when Middlesex struggled laboriously to match the Essex score. Downton, having pulled a hamstring, batted with a runner. He drove a ball from Phillip and instinctively set off on a run. Both batsmen and runner made their ground, but the ball was returned to David East who broke the wicket and Downton was given out under Law 2, Section 7. It was said that none of the Essex players realised that Downton could be given out, but Brian Hardie had attended a lecture given by Oslear in New Zealand earlier in the year when the umpire had explained the law. Gooch again batted well for Essex and Pringle reached a maiden championship fifty so that Fletcher declared, leaving Middlesex 3¾ hours to make 285. Brearley declined the offer and avidly accepted the chance to leave the field because of the light, a gesture which caused acrimony between himself and the crowd.

Hampshire overtook Essex and moved into third place when they annihilated sad Glamorgan at Portsmouth. On the opening day Kevin Emery returned the best figures of his brief career and Glamorgan, in difficult conditions, were bowled out for 184. Hampshire replied with some scintillating batting, scoring at six runs an over as Greenidge and Rice put on 176 for the first wicket. Jesty joined in the romp on the second day as he dominated the third wicket partnership with Greenidge which produced 251 runs. Greenidge was hampered by a back injury, but he still hit two sixes and twenty-eight fours. Jesty, in his benefit year, hit a six and twenty-two fours. Francis batted bravely, but there was little other resistance offered as Glamorgan surrendered to Emery and Tremlett.

Lancashire and Northamptonshire shared the honours in a high scoring match at Old Trafford and Gloucestershire recovered composure to deny Warwickshire at Nuneaton. Alvin Kallicharran's wonderful season continued and he plundered the Gloucestershire attack to give his side a lead of 206 on the first innings. Andy Stovold and Paul Romaines exposed the limitations of the Warwickshire bowling when Gloucestershire batted again. They shared a second wicket stand of 132 and both reached centuries. Romaines' was his first in first-class cricket and he went on to make 186.

On the eve of the Benson and Hedges Final, Nottinghamshire gained some encouragement at Worksop although Yorkshire were narrow winners so achieving their second victory of the week. The first day had revealed the excitement of a maiden century for Eddie Hemmings, a fine way to celebrate the beginning of an international career. Notts led by 123 on the first innings and scored briskly in their second. Paul Todd, who had the season's fastest century at the beginning of the season since when he had the most miserable of times, showed a heartening return to form with some powerful driving which brought him a hundred in just over three hours. Needing to score 305 to win, Yorkshire were given a good start by Lumb and Boycott, and the pace was maintained throughout the innings in spite of the spasmodic loss of wickets. Victory was achieved with eight balls and two wickets to spare, but Notts were severely handicapped when Hadlee, in his first game after injury, turned an ankle near the close and jeopardised his place for the Final at Lord's the following day.

Somerset, Notts' opponents at Lord's, were on the right end of an exciting finish at The Oval. They trailed on the first innings, but Garner and Botham bowled them back into contention so that they needed 201 to win. They lost 2 for 18 and had Roebuck dropped at the wicket before he had scored. He went on to bat for 3½ hours and make victory possible. At tea, Somerset needed only 60 from their last six wickets, but after tea things went wrong and they stumbled to 153 for 7. It was at this point that Colin Dredge came to the wicket. He attacked right from the start. He and Marks added 37 in half an hour and though Marks was out to Mackintosh, Dredge finished the job.

There was some dreadfully tedious cricket at Hereford where, on a placid pitch, the teams finished level on the first innings, Benson and Turner hitting centuries. Kent batted until tea on the last day and then set Worcestershire the task of scoring 288 in two hours.

There was a flurry of majestic shots at Leicester. Gower announced himself to the Pakistanis with an innings of graceful innocence. Ian Butcher and Tim Boon made their highest scores in first-class cricket. Abdul Qadir again stole the show with his leg-breaks and Mohsin Khan hit a double century of effortless charm.

BENSON and HEDGES CUP
1982

PRIZE STRUCTURE
£42,400 of the £207,000 Benson and Hedges sponsorship of this event will go in prize money for teams or individuals.
The breakdown is as follows:

* The champions will win £10,000 (and hold, for one year only, the Benson and Hedges Cup)
* For the runners-up: £4,500
* For the losing Semi-finalists: £2,200
* For the losing Quarter-finalists: £1,100

ADDITIONAL TEAM AWARDS
The winners of all matches in the zonal stages of the Cup will receive £385.

INDIVIDUAL GOLD AWARDS
There will be a Benson and Hedges Gold Award for the outstanding individual performance at all matches throughout the Cup.
These will be:

* In the zonal matches £60
* In the Quarter-finals £150
* In the Semi-finals £200
* In the Final £300

The playing conditions and Cup records are on the reverse.

HOLDERS: SOMERSET COUNTY CRICKET CLUB

MARYLEBONE CRICKET CLUB

FINAL

15p — NOTTINGHAMSHIRE v. SOMERSET — **15p**

at Lord's Ground, Saturday, July 24th, 1982

Any alterations to teams will be announced over the loud speaker system

NOTTINGHAMSHIRE

#	Player	Dismissal	Runs
1	P. A. Todd	b Garner	2
2	R. T. Robinson	c Richards b Dredge	13
3	D. W. Randall	b Marks	19
4	B. Hassan	c Taylor b Dredge	26
‡5	C. E. B. Rice	b Marks	27
6	J. D. Birch	b Moseley	7
7	R. J. Hadlee	b Garner	11
*8	B. N. French	c Taylor b Botham	8
9	E. E. Hemmings	b Botham	1
10	K. E. Cooper	b Garner	3
11	M. Hendrick	not out	0

B , l-b 5, w 7, n-b 1, ... 13
Total 130

FALL OF THE WICKETS
1...3 2...40 3...40 4...86 5...102 6...106 7...122 8...123 9...130 10...130

Bowling Analysis	O.	M.	R.	W.	Wd.	N-b
Garner	8.1	1	13	3	...	1
Botham	9	3	19	2	3	...
Dredge	11	2	35	2	1	...
Moseley	11	2	26	1	3	...
Marks	11	4	24	2	...	...

SOMERSET

#	Player	Dismissal	Runs
1	P. M. Roebuck	not out	53
2	P. W. Denning	c French b Hendrick	22
3	I. V. A. Richards	not out	51
‡4	B. C. Rose		
5	I. T. Botham		
6	V. J. Marks		
7	N. F. M. Popplewell		
*8	D. J. S. Taylor		
9	J. Garner		
10	C. H. Dredge		
11	H. R. Moseley		

B , l-b 5, w 1, n-b , ... 6
Total 132

FALL OF THE WICKETS
1...27 2... 3... 4... 5... 6... 7... 8... 9... 10...

Bowling Analysis	O.	M.	R.	W.	Wd.	N-b
Hadlee	9	0	37	0	...	...
Hendrick	8	1	26	1	...	...
Cooper	5.1	0	41	0	...	...
Rice	6	2	11	0	1	...
Hemmings	5	0	11	0	...	...

‡ Captain   * Wicket-keeper

Umpires—D. J. Constant & D. G. Evans
Scorers—L. Tomlinson, D. Beckett & E. Solomon

Toss won by—Somerset who elected to field
RESULT—Somerset won by 9 wickets

The Playing conditions for the Benson & Hedges Cup Competition are printed on the back of this score card.

Total runs scored at end of each over:—

Notts.	1	2	3	4	5	6	7	8	9	10	11	12	13	14	15	16	17	18	19	20
	21	22	23	24	25	26	27	28	29	30	31	32	33	34	35	36	37	38	39	40
	41	42	43	44	45	46	47	48	49	50	51	52	53	54	55					

Somerset	1	2	3	4	5	6	7	8	9	10	11	12	13	14	15	16	17	18	19	20
	21	22	23	24	25	26	27	28	29	30	31	32	33	34	35	36	37	38	39	10
	41	42	43	44	45	46	47	48	49	50	51	52	53	54	55					

Benson and Hedges Cup Final – Somerset v. Nottinghamshire

The fears and apprehensions that were nursed about the 1982 Benson and Hedges Cup Final were sadly realised. Somerset, it seemed, were running into form at the right time. The great powers of Garner, Richards and Botham were carefully tuned for the big day. Nottinghamshire, on the other hand, had had a miserable run of form and injury, and even at full strength their batting looked susceptible to the pace and variety of the Somerset attack. Our hope was that Notts might win the toss and give Somerset first use of the wicket so that the pace and guile of Hadlee and Hendrick, if fit, could benefit from the early moisture and probable heavy atmosphere to restrict and trouble the Somerset batsmen to a score within the reach of Notts.

The reverse happened. Brian Rose won the toss and he asked Notts to bat in heavy conditions which the sun failed to penetrate. Todd, a century the day before to relieve the gloom of a depressing season, and Robinson opened the batting against Garner and Botham. It was apparent from the very first over that Notts were not at ease with themselves or the bowling. Somerset grasped the initiative at the start, and they never lost it.

In his second over Garner yorked the unhappy Todd. Randall hit Garner's one loose delivery for four and Robinson looked as if he were composing himself and an innings, but the air was full of Somerset menace.

Dredge and Marks came into the attack. Dredge moved the ball prodigiously. In seventeen overs, however, Notts had got to 40. Robinson swung Dredge away to mid-wicket where Richards took a simple catch with enthusiastic drama. 40 for 2.

In the next over, Marks' first, Randall, the hopes of Nottingham heavily upon his shoulders, unwisely essayed a cut at a ball well up to him which turned a little and left his stumps in disarray. 40 for 3.

This brought Hassan and Rice together. Hassan, the most inelegant of batsmen, but among the most successful for Notts, suggested a confidence lacking elsewhere as he pushed and nudged. Rice, for whom 1982 had not held the same glories as previous seasons, never looks anything else but a player of class, but there was an attendant concern, the feeling at this hour that a cause, desperate and lost, was being fought.

Rice moved down the wicket and hit Marks for six. It was, in truth, the only indignity that the off-spinner suffered in eleven immaculate overs. When Rice tried to repeat the shot he did so with lack of conviction and was bowled. Marks had dismissed Notts' two great hopes and his spell of bowling from which, theoretically, Notts were expected to harvest the majority of their runs, cost but 24. It was the vital contribution in an impressive attack.

In the post lunch period there was total disintegration. Birch hit Moseley on the arm with a fierce drive. In return Moseley knocked his stumps over.

The beginning of a disastrous day for Notts. Paul Todd is bowled by Joel Garner.

Hadlee, less than half fit, smacked a couple of blows, but he never suggested permanence. Hassan, the most effective and confident of the Notts' batsmen, nudged once too often and was caught behind and French fell the same way. The end was swift and 29 balls still unused.

Denning started rather fretfully. He was dropped at slip off Hendrick by Hadlee and at cover by Randall. He was finally caught behind off Hendrick, but there was never any doubt that Somerset would get the runs with great ease.

Richards had not had a good season by his standards, but he left no doubt that he would be at the wicket when the game was over. For Notts it had become a nightmare and they were now reconciled that it was not their day.

It was certainly not Cooper's day. He began with a loosener that was crashed for four and the next ball went the same way. His five overs cost 37 runs and the first ball of his sixth went for four to give Richards his fifty and win the match for Somerset. Richards had already seen Roebuck reach an efficient fifty and all that was left was for Marks to receive the Gold Award and Rose the Cup.

Somerset had triumphed for the second year running and they will rarely have an easier victory. Notts' first final had been a bitter disappointment to them, but nothing could diminish the brave and exciting cricket that had enabled them to reach this stage.

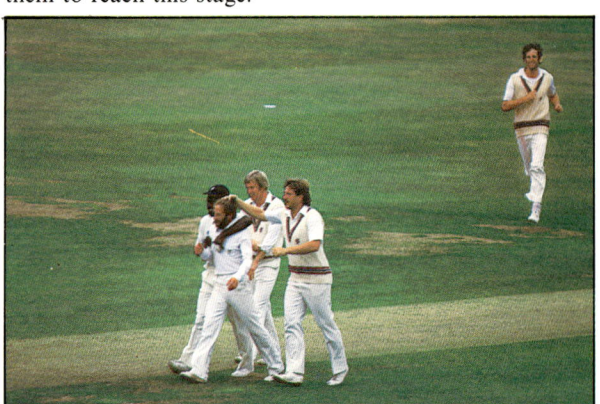

Above: *Despair and elation. Randall is bowled by Vic Marks who receives the congratulations of his team-mates. Lunch, and for Notts only a temporary respite.*

Left: *Richard Hadlee, a bold, defiant gesture from a great player whose lack of complete fitness was a dreadful handicap to Notts.*

Above: *Superman arrives to recharge Somerset batteries after Moseley had received a slight injury.*

Below and right: *Hemmings is bowled by Botham.*

Below: *Roebuck sets about batting Somerset to victory.*

Left: *Roebuck drives Hemmings for four.*
Above: *Viv Richards. The end is near.*

Below: *The sadness of defeat. Clive Rice, The Nottinghamshire captain, receives the loser's award from Hubert Doggart, MCC President.*

Derek Wilson, Managing Director, Gallaher Tobacco Limited, presents Vic Marks with the Gold Award, as player of the match.

The moment of triumph. Brian Rose holds the Benson and Hedges Cup. The Somerset fans swarm over Lord's.

Right: The most exciting bowler to tour England since the days of Sonny Ramadihn. Abdul Qadir, leg-breaks and googlies, in the process of sorcery.

Below: One of England's forgotten men. Bill Athey, a confident and consistent season. A mature and correct batsman. At the age of twenty-five he is a far better player than when he played for England two years ago.

Opposite: Laurie Potter, captain of Young England and, not yet twenty, a dynamic batsman of immense talent.

Right: Ian Gould, rejected by Middlesex, his performances for Sussex, particularly his aggression with the bat, made him a serious contender for the position of reserve wicket-keeper to Bob Taylor in the England party.

24, 25 and 26 July
at Chesterfield
Pakistanis 260 for 9 dec (Zaheer Abbas 51) and 299 for 2 dec (Zaheer Abbas 148 not out, Mudassar Nazar 100 not out)
Derbyshire 257 for 6 dec (G. Miller 72 not out) and 162 (Imran Khan 4 for 27, Sikhander Bakht 4 for 68)
Pakistanis won by 140 runs

24, 26 and 27 July
at Leicester
Leicestershire 289 (R. A. Cobb 63, B. F. Davison 59, D. L. Acfield 4 for 56) and 112 (N. Phillip 5 for 42)
Essex 219 (B. R. Hardie 82, G. A. Gooch 50, N. G. B. Cook 6 for 51, L. B. Taylor 4 for 54) and 157 (G. A. Gooch 85, G. J. Parsons 5 for 25)
Leicestershire won by 25 runs
Leicestershire 23 pts, Essex 5 pts

Pakistan won more friends with their positive approach to the games against the counties. On the eve of the First Test Match they played some excitingly aggressive cricket at Chesterfield and won a convincing victory. They had one of their least successful days with the bat on the Saturday, but in their second innings Mudassar and Zaheer engaged in a thrilling stand of 221 for the third wicket in 105 minutes. Imran declared, leaving Derbyshire 225 minutes in which to make 303 runs. He dismissed both openers and with excellent support from Sikhander he bowled Pakistan to victory.

In the only Schweppes County Championship match, Fletcher won the toss and asked Leicestershire to bat. On a pitch of uneven bounce, the home side laboured against the spin attack of Acfield and Ray East and were dismissed for 289, owing most to the belligerence of Davison. Gooch and Hardie batted with assurance for Essex and 95 came for the first wicket before Hardie fell to Taylor. Essex scored 153 in the pre-lunch session on Monday, and at the interval they were 172 for 3. It was the advent of the slow left-arm of Cook that brought destruction. He had Gooch stumped, having already had Pringle dropped and caught for 0 and McEwan caught. Essex moved into a state of bewildered perplexity and were all out for 219, the last eight wickets falling for the addition of 48 runs. Essex countered in the form of Phillip and Lever who reduced the home side to 104 for 8 by the close and allowed them only 8 more runs on the last morning. This left Essex most of the day in which to make 183. Hardie and Pringle left quickly, but Gooch was

Chris Balderstone, the rock of Leicestershire.

confident and assertive and he and McEwan took the score to 94 before Steele bowled the South African. At tea, with Gooch and Fletcher seemingly steering Essex to victory, the score stood at 132 for 3. Six runs were added after tea when Gooch, hooking at Parsons, was well caught low down on the leg-side by Tolchard behind the stumps. It was the first of Parsons' five wickets in 46 balls which gave him the best return of his career, 5 for 25. Seven wickets fell for 19 runs. Gooch and Phillip had gone at 138. Turner, Fletcher, David East and Lever all went at 152. It was bizarre stuff and after it all Leicestershire found themselves in second place in the table and Essex rued what might have been had they won. Gower suffered a black eye and facial bruising when struck in the face by a hit from Fletcher when fielding close on the off-side.

Ray Illingworth returned to first-class cricket at the age of fifty to captain an ailing Yorkshire. His wisdom, experience and qualities of leadership had a great impact on the side who improved in morale and performance. Here he directs his troops in the John Player League game at Canterbury.

John Player League

25 July

at Swansea

Glamorgan 172 for 6 (A. Jones 52)
Middlesex 133
Glamorgan (4 pts) won by 39 runs

at Bristol

Hampshire 145 for 9
Gloucestershire 146 for 2
Gloucestershire (4 pts) won by 8 wickets

at Canterbury

Kent 162
Yorkshire 164 for 5 (C. W. J. Athey 59)
Yorkshire (4 pts) won by 5 wickets

at Old Trafford

Lancashire 225 for 6 (D. Lloyd 93, C. H. Lloyd 70)
Warwickshire 207 for 5 (T. A. Lloyd 55, Asif Din 55 not out)
Lancashire (4 pts) won by 18 runs

at Northampton

Northamptonshire 213 for 4 (W. Larkins 59, P. Willey 53)
Sussex 215 for 6 (G. S. le Roux 85)
Sussex (4 pts) won by 4 wickets

at Taunton

Somerset 240 for 7 (P. M. Roebuck 83, V. J. Marks 72)
Worcestershire 238 for 7 (M. J. Weston 100)
Somerset (4 pts) won by 2 runs

at The Oval
Surrey 193 for 4 (M. A. Lynch 50)
Nottinghamshire 186 for 7 (C. E. B. Rice 62)
Surrey (4 pts) won by 7 runs

The greatest John Player League surprise of the season saw Glamorgan, who had won their first game only the week before, beat top-of-the-table Middlesex by the considerable margin of 39 runs. Brearley asked Glamorgan to bat and Allan Jones and Alan Lewis Jones responded with an opening stand of 86 that was to prove vital. Rowe and Lloyd boosted the total with some late runs and Lloyd bowled a spell of off-breaks which, with Davis' excellent contribution of 3 for 17 in his 6.4 overs, proved too much for Middlesex.

Their defeat cost Middlesex their place at the top to Sussex who won a remarkable victory at Northampton. Chasing a formidable 214, Sussex lost Mendis, Gould and Parker for 29. Le Roux came in at number five and immediately attacked the bowling. He hit six sixes in a powerful display and when he was out the score was 179 for 6 and Sussex were in sight of victory. Phillipson finished the job, scoring 29 of the last 36 runs, including the winning hit for six over long-on.

Essex and Derbyshire were not engaged and Kent lost to a fine Athey innings and an equally fine contribution of 34 not out from Boycott, batting number five. Lancashire were boosted by a stand of 121 in 22 overs by David Lloyd and Clive Lloyd and always had the beating of Warwickshire so that they drew level on 24 points with Essex, Derbyshire, Kent and Somerset who had a narrow celebratory win over Worcestershire.

Somerset owed much to Peter Roebuck who batted with sense and solidity and to Vic Marks, fresh from his Gold Award at Lord's, who hit sturdily. Both recorded their best scores in the John Player League. They were overshadowed by Martin Weston who, in 34 overs, hit his first century in senior cricket, an impressively aggressive innings which included five sixes and seven fours. He was brilliantly caught and bowled by Botham and Garner's return stemmed the flow of runs. Worcestershire needed 17 off the last over. Alleyne and Warner managed 14, but it was not enough.

A sad Notts side battled bravely against a Surrey side weakened by injury. Clive Rice played an excellent innings for Notts and he and Birch added 103 in 19 overs for the third wicket, but after Rice's dismissal Notts faltered and they lost by 7 runs to complete a dismal week-end.

Gloucestershire, looking unexpectedly sharp and confident in every department of the game, beat Hampshire with considerable ease at Bristol. Hampshire batted poorly against Stephenson and Shepherd while Childs too bowled effectively. An opening stand of 82 by Andy Stovold and Broad made Gloucestershire's task an easy one.

27, 28 and 29 July

at Dublin
Ireland 301 (M. A. Masood 109, J. A. Prior 70) and 213 for 4 dec (J. Short 103, E. McDermott 80)
Wales 214 (W. Harris 64, J. D. Monteith 4 for 52) and 251 (G. Edwards 73, N. Roberts 62, J. D. Monteith 4 for 26)
Ireland won by 49 runs

28, 29 and 30 July

at Southport
Warwickshire 533 for 4 dec (G. W. Humpage 254, A. I. Kallicharran 230 not out) and 111 (L. L. McFarlane 6 for 59)
Lancashire 414 for 6 dec (G. Fowler 126, I. Cockbain 98, J. Abrahams 51 not out) and 226 for 0 (G. Fowler 128 not out, D. Lloyd 88 not out)
Lancashire won by 10 wickets
Lancashire 21 pts, Warwickshire 6 pts

at Northampton
Gloucestershire 357 for 4 dec (A. W. Stovold 212 not out, B. C. Broad 61) and 237 for 3 dec (P. Bainbridge 89, B. Dudleston 78 not out)
Northamptonshire 310 for 9 dec (R. J. Boyd-Moss 53) and 252 for 8 (R. J. Boyd-Moss 114 not out, P. Willey 59, J. H. Childs 4 for 65, F. D. Stephenson 4 for 73)
Match drawn
Gloucestershire 7 pts, Northamptonshire 4 pts

at The Oval
Surrey 450 for 9 dec (M. A. Lynch 118, C. J. Richards 117 not out, G. P. Howarth 74, R. D. V. Knight 54) and 4 for 0
Nottinghamshire 264 (R. J. Hadlee 131, S. T. Clarke 6 for 63) and 187 (C. E. B. Rice 62)
Surrey won by 10 wickets
Surrey 24 pts, Nottinghamshire 5 pts

at Hove
Kent 353 for 8 dec (M. R. Benson 137, C. S. Cowdrey 61, G. S. le Roux 4 for 49)
Sussex 152 (A. M. Green 57, D. L. Underwood 5 for 21, G. R. Dilley 4 for 43) and 434 for 7 dec (C. M. Wells 126, A. M. Green 95, G. D. Mendis 72, G. S. le Roux 70 not out)
Match drawn
Kent 8 pts, Sussex 4 pts

at Worcester
Worcestershire 367 for 8 dec (J. D. Inchmore 68, J. G. Thomas 4 for 52) and 224 for 9 dec (T. S. Curtis 59 not out, R. C. Ontong 4 for 30)
Glamorgan 317 for 5 dec (A. Jones 146 not out) and 125 for 3 (D. A. Francis 58 not out)
Match drawn
Worcestershire 6 pts, Glamorgan 5 pts

Surrey moved into second place in the Schweppes County Championship when they trounced Notts who were experiencing the unhappiest of times. Monte Lynch again demonstrated his maturing craftsmanship with a brisk century, full of good shots, and Surrey batted into the second morning when Jack Richards completed his maiden century in first-class cricket. Notts were soon in disarray to Clarke, but in the afternoon Richard Hadlee played a blistering innings of 131 off 107 balls in 2 hours, 17 minutes. When he came to the wicket Notts were 53 for 5, but even his heroics and some brave batting by Illingworth and Cooper could

Mark Benson. He returned after injury, and hit two centuries in three innings. Amused as he sprawls to make his ground at Canterbury, Benson is an exciting cricketer who, with discipline and constant application, could become one of England's great players.

not save the follow-on and Notts surrendered quietly on the last morning.

At Northampton Andy Stovold hit the first double century of his career. It was an innings of rich stroke-play and helped Gloucestershire to a commanding position. He and Broad opened with a stand of 139 and later Dudleston, returning to the first-class game, made a useful contribution. Northants countered with an even batting display and Gloucestershire, led by Bainbridge and Dudleston, scored briskly and set Northants a target of 285 in 172 minutes. They lost Larkins and Cook for 25, but Willey and Boyd-Moss batted with great panache in adding 87 and Boyd-Moss went on to an impressive first century in the championship. Northants maintained their challenge, but wickets fell to the spin of Childs and the pace of Stephenson and Northants were left 33 short of victory and Gloucester two wickets.

Mark Benson hit his second century in three innings and a career best. Kent had been 48 for 3, but Benson, Johnson and Cowdrey transformed the game and when, on the second day, Underwood and Dilley bowled Sussex out 201 runs short of the Kent total, it seemed that the visitors were heading for an innings victory. Mendis and Green had other ideas and began with a partnership of 160. Wells carried on the recovery with an innings of great confidence and he and le Roux shared a sixth wicket stand of 172 before Sussex declared and the rains came.

Glenn Turner withdrew from the Worcestershire team with appendicitis which meant that we could have seen this magnificent player bat for Worcester for the last time. In his absence the county struggled initially, but they were revived by a wagging tail; they recovered from 134 for 5 to 367 for 8. Glamorgan batted well in reply with Alan Jones, one of the great cricketers of our time, scoring a century full of wisdom and experience. At the second attempt, Worcestershire were a little cautious as was their declaration which asked Glamorgan to make 275 in 135 minutes. When Inchmore took three wickets in five overs the chase was ended.

Compared to the events at Southport, however, these matches were as nothing. Warwickshire batted first and lost Amiss and Dyer with only 6 scored. Lloyd fell to Folley at 53 and this brought Humpage in to join Kallicharran. At 5.50 Humpage was bowled by David Lloyd, but by then the score stood at 523 and Humpage had hit a career best, 254, and Kallicharran had reached his third double century of the season. Their stand of 470 was an English record for the fourth wicket, beating the stand of Abel and Hayward of 448 at The Oval in 1899. The partnership lasted 293 minutes. Humpage hit thirteen sixes in his innings, a total exceeded only by John Reid in New Zealand in 1963. The Lancashire attack, without Allott and Croft, was torn to shreds by some brilliant stroke play. The Lancashire batsmen were undaunted even though they had the unique experience of facing a substitute bowling, David Brown being given special dispensation as Gladstone Small had been called to Edgbaston to stand by for the England side as Pringle was injured. Small returned for the last day. Fowler hit an exciting hundred, Cockbain a career best and the follow-on, to the surprise of most, was easily avoided. Then Les McFarlane took a career best as Warwickshire were inexplicably bowled out for 111. Needing 221 to win, Lancashire achieved the runs without loss, Fowler hitting his second century of the match, and both had been scored with the aid of a runner. Humpage, Kallicharran and the Warwickshire supporters could only look on in utter disbelief. It was one of those matches that will be written about for many years to come, which is no consolation to the long-suffering followers of the Midland county.

FIRST CORNHILL TEST MATCH
England v. Pakistan

Pakistan's only surprise choice was that of Mansoor Akhtar instead of the experienced Majid Khan. England caused more surprise. Cook was omitted and a reluctant Randall moved up to open the innings. Gatting, rightly, was re-called, and Hemmings was given the spinner's place to the exclusion of Edmonds. Hemmings deserved his chance. Most surprisingly, Ian Greig was included. He had had a fairly good season with the ball, but one wondered what the Trevor Jesty's, Robin Jackman's and Stuart Turner's of the world must feel when their seasons of endeavour are ignored year after year and they see young men like Pringle and Greig awarded Test caps on the strength of a season or a month's good form.

Cook and Small were called from their county games to act as stand by for Pringle and Gower, both injured, and, in the event, Pringle did not play, but Cook and Small returned to their counties.

Randall and Tavare opened the England innings in fine weather. Randall batted in a state suggesting frenzy. He hit Imran's first ball for four and then hooked him twice, once perilously. Tahir was erratic and after four overs England had scored 27.

Once Randall lifted his bat and offered no shot at a ball from Imran that moved back at him. He repeated the exercise and was bowled. 29 for 1 in the fifth over, Randall 17.

Tahir was replaced by Sikhander and in the eighth over Lamb played a little leaden-footedly at the away swinger and was well caught by the diving Wasim Bari.

With obvious signs of moisture in the pitch and a feeling of uncertainty about what was to come, Tavare and Gower batted with great caution. Sikhander bowled economically and the introduction of Abdul Qadir added a sense of mystery to the occasion. He worked his fingers and wrist continuously, flicking the ball from hand to hand at the beginning of a run up that suggested an Eastern sorcerer about to cast a spell.

The effect that Qadir had on the day's play cannot be measured in terms of the one wicket that he took, for he troubled all batsmen and wreathed a smoke of psychological uncertainty in the England team.

Gower batted with great good sense and graceful hostility. He survived a ridiculous appeal for a catch at slip and Javed responded to the umpire's 'not out' with unforgivable petulance. The claim for this catch, which so obviously came to the fielder on the half volley, violated an ethical principle of cricket and Javed's reaction violated the manners of the game.

Tavare and Gower had added 127 before Imran returned to find the edge of Gower's bat for Wasim Bari to take a fine diving catch in front of second slip. Botham perished

The Pakistan Touring Team.

Opposite: *The Pakistan support.*

FIRST CORNHILL TEST MATCH – ENGLAND v. PAKISTAN
29, 30 and 31 July, 1 August 1982 at Edgbaston, Birmingham

ENGLAND

	FIRST INNINGS		SECOND INNINGS	
D. W. Randall	b Imran	17	b Imran	105
C. J. Tavare	c Javed, b Qadir	54	c Mohsin, b Imran	17
A. J. Lamb	c Wasim Bari, b Sikhander	6	lbw, b Tahir	5
D. I. Gower	c Wasim Bari, b Imran	74	c Mudassar, b Tahir	13
I. T. Botham	b Imran	2	(6) lbw, b Tahir	0
M. W. Gatting	b Tahir	17	(5) c Bari, b Tahir	5
G. Miller	b Imran	47	b Tahir	5
I. A. Greig	c sub (Haroon), b Imran	14	b Qadir	7
E. E. Hemmings	lbw, b Imran	2	c Mansoor, b Qadir	19
R. W. Taylor*	lbw, b Imran	1	c Qadir, b Raja	54
R. G. D. Willis†	not out	0	not out	28
Extras	b 4, lb 10, w 6, nb 18	38	b 10, lb 11, w 7, nb 5	33
		272		291

	O	M	R	W	O	M	R	W
Imran Khan	25.3	11	52	7	32	5	84	2
Tahir Naqqash	15	4	46	1	18	7	40	5
Sikhander Bakht	18	5	58	1	13	5	34	—
Mudassar Nazar	5	2	8	—				
Abdul Qadir	29	7	70	1	40	10	100	2
Wasim Raja					2.3	2	0	1

PAKISTAN

	FIRST INNINGS		SECOND INNINGS	
Mudassar Nazar	lbw, b Botham	0	lbw, b Botham	0
Mohsin Khan	c Willis, b Botham	26	lbw, b Botham	35
Tahir Naqqash	c Taylor, b Greig	12	(9) c and b Hemmings	39
Mansoor Akhtar	c Miller, b Hemmings	58	(3) c Taylor, b Botham	0
Javed Miandad	c Willis, b Hemmings	30	(4) run out	10
Zaheer Abbas	lbw, b Greig	40	(5) c Taylor, b Willis	4
Wasim Raja	c Tavare, b Willis	26	(6) c Gower, b Willis	16
Imran Khan†	c Taylor, b Willis	22	(7) b Miller	65
Wasim Bari*	not out	16	(8) c Taylor, b Botham	12
Abdul Qadir	lbw, b Greig	7	c Randall, b Miller	9
Sikhander Bakht	c Hemmings, b Greig	1	not out	1
Extras	b 5, lb 2, w 1, nb 5	13	lb 3, nb 5	8
		251		199

	O	M	R	W	O	M	R	W
Botham	24	1	86	2	21	7	70	4
Greig	14.2	3	53	4	4	1	19	—
Willis	15	3	42	2	14	2	49	2
Hemmings	24	5	56	2	10	4	27	1
Miller	2	1	1	—	7.4	1	26	2

FALL OF WICKETS
1–29, 2–37, 3–164, 4–172, 5–179, 6–228, 7–263, 8–265, 9–271
1–62, 2–98, 3–127, 4–137, 5–137, 6–146, 7–170, 8–188, 9–212

FALL OF WICKETS
1–0, 2–29, 3–53, 4–110, 5–164, 6–198, 7–217, 8–227, 9–248
1–0, 2–0, 3–38, 4–54, 5–66, 6–77, 7–98, 8–151, 9–178

England won by 113 runs

almost immediately, beaten by Imran's pace as he prepared to drive, but ended getting tucked up in an ugly fashion.

For Tavare, Qadir had proved incomprehensible and he fell to a bat and pad catch as he played for the leg-break in what transpired to be the top-spinner.

Gatting looked far from the confident and pugnacious man of Middlesex and was bowled off his pads. Miller played with a certainty and classical accomplishment that yet lacks the mark of personality stamped on great batting and he was leading England from the darkness when he swung madly at Imran and was bowled. Hemmings fell lbw the same over.

Taylor was lbw to one that kept low and Greig, having enjoyed some good fortune, was caught off a short pitched delivery, the second of the over. Pakistan had bowled out England in less than a day while 272 runs had been scored. It was marvellous stuff and a tonic to Test cricket.

There was time for one over before the close which was bowled by Botham. He essayed a bouncer second ball on which Mudassar turned his back. He was hit high on the thigh and given lbw. Like all humans, umpires err, and this seemed a poor decision, and, unfortunately, a crucial one. It prompted the Pakistanis to complain later about the inconsistency in the umpiring. It is a difficult job and it is well done, but England touring teams had better reflect a little longer when they complain of umpiring, for it seems that visitors everywhere suffer from a sense of injustice.

The second day was as heady as the first as Pakistan, rich in strokes and talent, threw away a glorious opportunity. Tahir was missed behind off Botham, then caught off Greig, who, mysteriously, had been given the new ball. Mohsin, all dignity and feline aggression, lapsed in concentration after a debate about the changing of the ball and swung childishly at Botham to give Willis a good catch.

Mansoor batted extravagantly, and with a little fortune, until he was caught at square leg sweeping at Hemmings. Hemmings had already accounted for Javed Miandad who, excited by the arrival of a spinner, tried to hit him over the top. Having once succeeded dangerously, he tried again and gave Willis his second catch.

Zaheer threatened to devour England, but he missed a straight ball from Greig. Imran hit lustily and was caught off a skier when he attempted to hook Willis. Wasim Raja was taken at slip and the last two wickets offered little resistance so that England found themselves with an improbable lead of 21 on the first innings which Randall and Tavare increased by 51 before the close. Gloriously, on the second evening, no one was talking of the match in terms of a draw.

On the third day England were bowled out for the second time. There was a middle order of total disaster, brought about by Tahir Naqqash who had easily the best figures of his short Test career. He had Lamb lbw with a break back, Gower then taken at second slip off a fierce edge, Gatting caught behind off an airy shot that saddened his admirers, Botham lbw first ball and Miller bowled as he withdrew his back leg.

Qadir got just reward for some gleeful bowling when he troubled and beat Greig and England were 170 for 7. The eighth to go was Randall at 188, of which he had scored 105. It was a glorious innings, unpredictable like the man, all bounce and belligerence and cheeky innocence.

When Hemmings was out England were 212 for 9 and the match was in Pakistan's grasp, but from this moment on it slipped away from them.

Bob Taylor and Bob Willis batted with a resolution that some of their colleagues must have viewed with a mixture of envy and embarrassment. It was a situation fitted to the temperaments and committed attitude of both men. They defended stoutly, swayed out of the way of some violent bouncers from Imran, and punctuated defence with nudges, deflections, and occasional elegant drives and hearty clouts.

The stand realised 79, a tenth wicket record for England against Pakistan, and Taylor was finally taken at slip after reaching his third fifty in Test cricket. They had raised Pakistan's target to 313 and the initiative was now with England.

There was a delayed start on the Sunday because of bad light and when Mudassar and Mohsin began the Pakistan innings the light was still far from good.

Botham, who had had a bad match with the bat, 2 and 0, took the new ball. His second delivery beat Mudassar and had him lbw without argument. The last ball of the over was a widish outswinger which Mansoor unwisely followed to give Taylor a catch. After one over Pakistan were 0 for 2 and Edgbaston's Sunday crowd was baying for more blood.

Mohsin and Javed steadied the innings, but at 38, Javed fell to a remarkable piece of fielding by Gatting at short-leg. Javed played the ball down and moved forward. Gatting caught the ball in his left hand, transferred it to his right and with a back hand flick threw down the wicket with Javed out of his ground. There have been few more brilliant pieces of fielding in Test cricket.

Mohsin then completely misjudged a ball from Botham and was lbw. Willis showed shrewd leadership in packing the slip and gully area and bowling to Zaheer's strength outside the off-stump. Zaheer took the bait and was caught behind. Wasim Raja once more disappointed and was caught at slip as always seemed likely, just as Wasim Bari always seemed likely to perish as he did, caught behind.

Tahir, who had a fine match, drove splendidly at almost every delivery until he was very well caught and bowled by Hemmings. Imran had remained cool and defensive, but now he drove Hemmings high for two mighty sixes. He reached a gloriously defiant fifty and was last man out, bowled by Miller when he gave himself room to drive on the off. His individual performance had been a great one, but his acceptance of the Man of the match award could in no way disguise his disappointment that Pakistan had thrown away a great opportunity of beating England whom they had matched in every department of the game but concentration.

It had been a thrilling and absorbing contest and if one felt a little sorry for Pakistan, one could feel only excitement for Test cricket and the rest of the series.

Opposite top: Pakistan players leap with delight. Chris Tavare is caught by Javed Miandad at silly mid-off off the bowling of leg-spinner Abdul Qadir. Tavare was in a state of perplexity when facing Qadir. Right: Randall hooks Tahir Naqqash for four. Randall's batting in both innings was always at fever pitch. Far right: Tahir Naqqash, caught Taylor, bowled Greig 12. Ian Greig's first wicket in Test cricket.

Above: *In the previous over, Tahir had had this reprieve off Botham's bowling. The ball flies through the slips at catchable height. Left to right: Taylor, Miller, Tavare, Greig (in balletic pose) and Randall.* Left: *Another wicket for Greig. Abdul Qadir is lbw.* Below: *The opposing captains. Imran Khan, seven wickets in the first innings, hostile fast bowling at its very best, but Man of the Match award is no compensations for defeat. Bob Willis batting. His last wicket stand with Bob Taylor in the second innings turned the match in England's favour.*

Right: *Randall plays no shot at a ball from Imran Khan and is bowled.*

Below: *Tahir Naqqash produced a remarkable spell of bowling in the second innings which gave Pakistan scent of victory.* Left: *First innings victim Mike Gatting registers acute disappointment after edging a ball on to his stumps. The off-bail can be seen lying on the ground as Tahir and Wasim Bari celebrate.* Right: *Geoff Miller is bowled.*

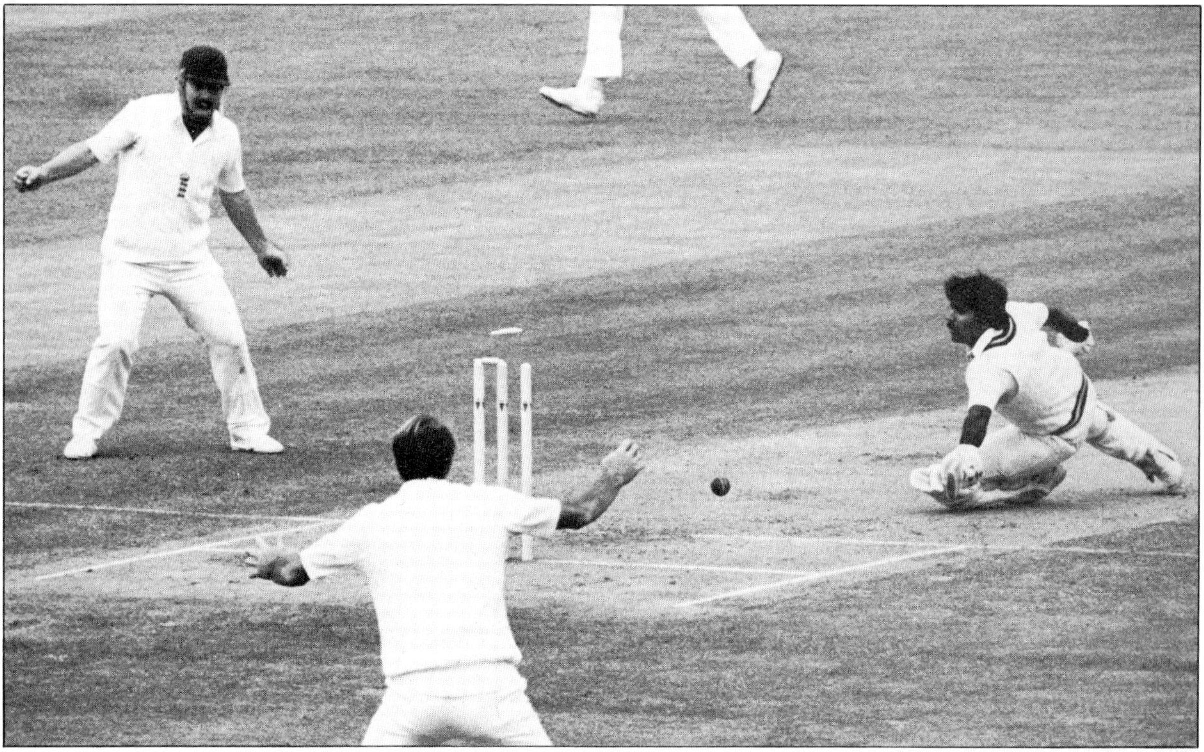

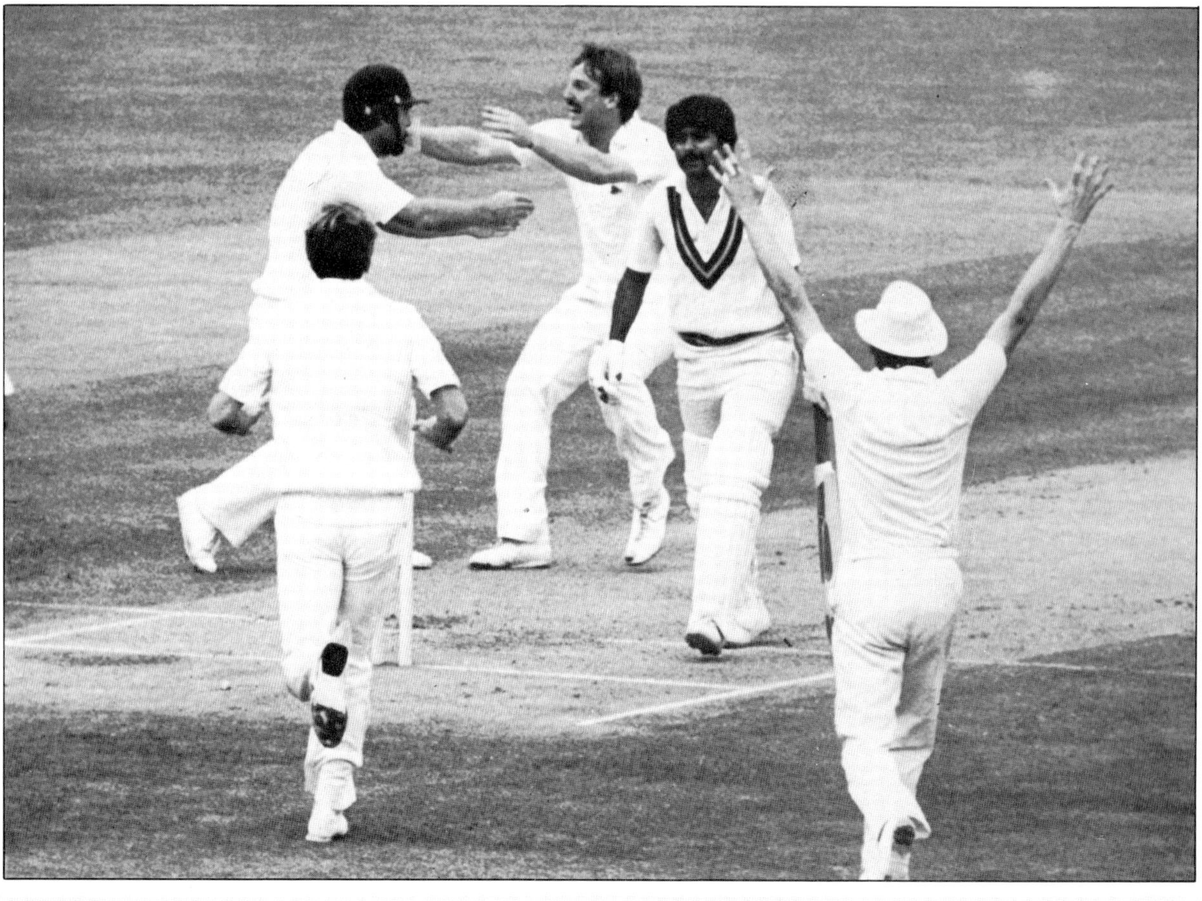

Opposite: *One of the most brilliant pieces of fielding seen in Test cricket. Gatting's back hand flick from short leg runs out Javed Miandad.*

Above: *'Guy the Gorilla Rules – O.K.' Mohsin Khan lbw to Botham and Pakistan face defeat.*

31 July, 2 and 3 August

at Derby
Surrey 401 for 9 dec (G. P. Howarth 121, M. A. Lynch 94, S. Oldham 4 for 88) and 144 for 8 dec (M. A. Lynch 72, D. G. Moir 4 for 43)
Derbyshire 252 for 4 dec (P. N. Kirsten 164 not out) and 240 for 3 (P. N. Kirsten 123 not out, J. H. Hampshire 85)
Match drawn
Derbyshire 5 pts, Surrey 5 pts

at Cardiff
Glamorgan 256 (C. J. C. Rowe 77, N. Phillip 5 for 40) and 138 (K. R. Pont 5 for 17)
Essex 154 for 9 dec and 241 for 3 (K. W. R. Fletcher 83 not out)
Essex won by 7 wickets
Essex 20 pts, Glamorgan 6 pts

at Bournemouth
Hampshire 119 and 157 (T. E. Jesty 50, J. Garner 6 for 57)
Somerset 194 (T. E. Jesty 4 for 31) and 72 (M. D. Marshall 5 for 37, T. E. Jesty 4 for 8)
Hampshire won by 10 runs
Hampshire 20 pts, Somerset 5 pts

at Leicester
Leicestershire 244 for 4 dec (J. C. Balderstone 103 not out)
Gloucestershire 70 (L. B. Taylor 5 for 24) and 129
Leicestershire won by an innings and 45 runs
Leicestershire 22 pts, Gloucestershire 1 pt

at Lord's
Kent 312 for 9 dec (L. Potter 108, G. W. Johnson 86, N. R. Taylor 58) and 191 for 8 dec (L. Potter 55)
Middlesex 250 for 6 dec (J. E. Emburey 73 not out) and 187 for 4 (K. P. Tomlins 62)
Match drawn
Kent 5 pts, Middlesex 3 pts

at Northampton
Northamptonshire 200 for 8 dec and 183 for 6 dec (W. Larkins 110 not out)
Worcestershire 112 (T. M. Lamb 5 for 37) and 112 for 5
Match drawn
Northamptonshire 6 pts, Worcestershire 3 pts

at Trent Bridge
Nottinghamshire 164 (R. J. Hadlee 60, J. D. Birch 56, L. L. McFarlane 4 for 37) and 261 (J. D. Birch 102 not out, S. J. O'Shaughnessy 4 for 66)
Lancashire 165 (J. Simmons 64 not out) and 133 for 3 (D. Lloyd 56)
Match drawn
Nottinghamshire 5 pts, Lancashire 5 pts

at Scarborough
Sussex 230 for 5 dec (C. M. Wells 71 not out) and 197 for 6 dec (P. W. G. Parker 69 not out, P. Carrick 4 for 69)
Yorkshire 150 for 4 dec (G. Boycott 52) and 252 for 4 (G. Boycott 122 not out, J. D. Love 56)
Yorkshire won by 6 wickets
Yorkshire 19 pts, Sussex 3 pts

Rain affected several games and, in spite of a best of the season effort from Tim Lamb and a sparkling hundred by Wayne Larkins, batting better than he has ever done, Northants drew with Worcestershire although they always had the upper hand. There was a similar stalemate at Trent Bridge where John Birch hit a welcome hundred and Jack Simmons showed the wisdom and virtues acquired after fourteen years in the game.

There was a draw of a different nature at Derby where Surrey scored heavily on the first day. Their ambitions of victory were thwarted by two masterful innings by Peter Kirsten who reached his fifth and sixth championship hundreds of the season without being dismissed. As in the first innings, Wood and Wright went cheaply, but Kirsten and Hampshire added 196 to follow their 119 stand of the first innings. In the end, the draw favoured Derbyshire who finished 54 short of victory with 7 wickets standing.

A brilliant innings by Laurie Potter which confirmed the high opinions that had been expressed of him was the highlight of Kent's match at Lord's. Middlesex were handicapped by an injury to Brearley and later to substitute Maru and a draw looked inevitable. Emburey's batting once more impressed and he must now be considered as an all-rounder rather than as just a spin bowler.

Leicestershire moved into second place with a two-day victory over Gloucestershire. Balderstone was the backbone of the Leicestershire innings and, on a dubious wicket, the Gloucestershire batting crumpled twice in a day before Taylor (8 for 33 in the match) and Agnew. To add to Gloucestershire's woe, Phil Bainbridge broke a finger and would miss the NatWest Quarter Final match with Middlesex.

Hampshire also won in two days, a most remarkable victory over Somerset, for whom Viv Richards was twelfth man, not fully fit, at Bournemouth. On the Saturday, Hampshire collapsed from 47 for 0 to 119 all out. Dredge, Davis and Moseley did the initial damage and then Joel Garner took 6 for 9 in 8.1 overs after lunch. Somerset found the uneven bounce equally disconcerting when they batted, Rose having chosen to put Hampshire in, and this time it was Marshall and Emery who took the early wickets with Trevor Jesty destroying the middle order. Garner hit lustily on Monday morning and Somerset had a valuable lead of 75. Hampshire struggled for a second time, but a brave half century in an hour by Jesty, who chose to hit his way out of trouble in difficult conditions, saved them from humiliation. With Somerset needing only 83 to win, the extra half-hour was claimed. They reached 38 for 2 and looked set for a win, but Jesty joined Marshall in the attack and his relentless accuracy combined with the West Indian's pace brought Hampshire an incredible victory. Jesty bowled 10 overs for 8 runs and the wickets of Felton, Marks, Davis and Garner. Bowling unchanged, Marshall had 5 for 37 and Hampshire won by 10 runs.

THE ENGLISH SEASON/335

Jim Love quietly regaining the form for Yorkshire that made him an England prospect.

Boycott led Yorkshire to an exciting win over Sussex. Rain brought about a series of declarations which ended with Yorkshire needing 251 in 3¼ hours. They batted in sunshine and Boycott hit the 131st century of his career. He hit ten fours as he reached his hundred in 168 minutes and then opened his shoulders to hit a six and three more fours as he led Yorkshire gloriously to victory.

On Monday evening Glamorgan stood poised for their first victory of the season. They had batted tediously on the first day and dragged on to the Monday, but Essex had lost Lever with a back injury and Hardie batted at number nine with an injured hand. Fletcher declared 102 behind. A. L. Jones and Hopkins began the second innings with a stand of 67 and though both fell to Turner before the close and Acfield got Ontong, Glamorgan were 99 for 3 and a stricken Essex faced defeat. On the last morning Keith Pont, so often the Cinderella of the Essex side, produced a remarkable spell of swing bowling which brought him a career best 5 for 17 and dismissed Glamorgan for the addition of only 39 runs. Essex needed 241 in 245 minutes, a doubtful task considering their injury problems. Gooch and David East gave them a good start and McEwan played some fine shots, but it was a superb innings by Fletcher who combined with Pont in an unbeaten fourth wicket stand of 85 that brought victory for Essex and a shattering defeat for Glamorgan and their long-suffering followers.

John Player League
1 August

at Derby
Surrey 205 for 7 (G. R. J. Roope 74)
Derbyshire 149 (I. R. Payne 5 for 21)
Surrey (4 pts) won by 56 runs

at Cardiff
Essex 200 for 6 (N. Phillip 84, K. S. McEwan 68)
Glamorgan 184 for 7 (A. Jones 55)
Essex (4 pts) won by 16 runs

at Portsmouth
Somerset 177 for 6 (T. E. Jesty 4 for 45)
Hampshire 180 for 4 (C. G. Greenidge 84)
Hampshire (4 pts) won by 6 wickets

at Leicester
Leicestershire 196 for 4 (N. E. Briers 82)
Gloucestershire 164 for 9 (P. W. Romaines 55, G. J. Parsons 4 for 33)
Leicestershire (4 pts) won by 32 runs

at Lord's
Kent 119
Middlesex 118 for 8
Kent (4 pts) won by 1 run

at Luton
Northamptonshire 272 for 3 (W. Larkins 158, R. G. Williams 79 not out)
Worcestershire 220 (P. A. Neale 102)
Northamptonshire (4 pts) won by 52 runs

at Trent Bridge
Lancashire 192 for 6 (D. Lloyd 80)
Nottinghamshire 186 for 6 (S. B. Hassan 96 not out)
Lancashire (4 pts) won by 6 runs

at Scarborough
Sussex 222 for 7 (P. W. G. Parker 77)
Yorkshire 167 (D. L. Bairstow 54)
Sussex (4 pts) won by 55 runs

Sussex strengthened their position at the top of the John Player League with a comfortable win at Scarborough. An even batting performance, with Paul Parker again pacing the innings intelligently, and some hostile bowling by Arnold and le Roux who reduced Yorkshire to 26 for 3, had Sussex in total command of the game from start to finish.

Middlesex fell six points behind by losing their third match in succession, an incredible defeat at home to Kent. 119 hardly seemed a total that would worry Middlesex, but Kent bowled with commendable accuracy throughout and no Middlesex batsman apart from Cook established himself. Middlesex reached the last over 11 short of victory with

Tim Robinson, the Notts opener. A much improved player.

four wickets in hand. Downton hit eight off the first four balls bowled by Dilley, but he was run out off the fifth. Cook needed to hit three off the last ball, but he was run out going for the second. In many ways Middlesex's final effort was praiseworthy as they had been 7 for 3 and 13 for 4.

Essex maintained their challenge with an easy win at Cardiff, Phillip and McEwan batting excitingly in a stand of 123. Lancashire stayed level with a win over luckless Notts for whom Hassan was again left just short of a hundred.

Hampshire relied again on the brilliant hitting of Greenidge and the accuracy of their seam bowlers, but Somerset had the air of an ailing side, a side with whom all is not well.

Derbyshire slipped out of the title race when they were beaten at home by Surrey. Roope batted well in Surrey's innings and led them to a score of 205. Derbyshire never approached it and Ian Payne's medium pace earned him his best figures in any competition, 5 for 21 in 6.2 overs.

Wayne Larkins played another spectacular innings for Northants as he hit six sixes and twelve fours in a stay of 123 minutes. He was dropped on 8 and he and Richard Williams set up a league record for the third wicket of 215 in 25 overs of glorious hitting. Worcestershire were never in the hunt, but skipper Neale made a maiden John Player League century in under two hours.

Paul Romaines was another to hit a best league score and finish on the losing side. He scored 55 at Leicester, but found little support and the home side, for whom Briers batted with brisk efficiency, won with ease.

NatWest Trophy Quarter-Finals

4 August

at Leeds

Essex 132 (S. Turner 50 not out)
Yorkshire 133 for 1 (M. D. Moxon 78 not out)

Yorkshire won by 9 wickets
(Man of the Match – M. D. Moxon)

at Southampton

Hampshire 119 (D. R. Turner 51, R. D. Jackman 6 for 22)
Surrey 120 for 2 (D. M. Smith 62 not out)

Surrey won by 8 wickets
(Man of the Match – R. D. Jackman)

at Bristol

Middlesex 215 for 8
Gloucestershire 212 for 8 (B. C. Broad 98)

Middlesex won by 3 runs
(Man of the Match – B. C. Broad)

4 and 5 August

at Taunton

Somerset 259 for 9 (I. T. Botham 85, V. J. Marks 55, A. M. Ferreira 4 for 53)
Warwickshire 262 for 5 (A. I. Kallicharran 141 not out, D. L. Amiss 59)

Warwickshire won by 5 wickets
(Man of the Match – A. I. Kallicharran)

The decision to begin the quarter final matches of the NatWest Trophy at 10.00 am proved to be a most unhappy one and in two cases ruined the matches as contests.

At Headingley, Illingworth won the toss and had no hesitation in asking Essex to bat in an atmosphere heavy with forboding. The ball swung violently and the bowlers responded gleefully to the outrageous advantage that they had been given. With Boycott moving the ball menacingly and Sidebottom looking a world-beater, anything could happen, and did. Hardie went at 9, Gooch at 15, and Fletcher and Pont to successive balls at 18. Essex were 51 for 9 when Ray East joined Turner. The conditions had improved considerably and the batting was heroic and dedicated professional application. They added 81, a record last wicket stand for the Gillette–NatWest competitions, and Turner had just reached a memorable fifty when Ray East became the fifth Essex player adjudged lbw. With 60 overs in which to get 133 runs and the weather now favourable to batting, Yorkshire went about their task lightly. Boycott was caught at slip and Athey missed. With 28 runs needed for victory, the heavens opened and the ground was soon covered with pools of water. Unwilling to stay overnight for a lost cause, Essex elected to come out and finish the game in farcical conditions. Pont and Lilley bowled 14 balls and the fielders sloshed after the hits with humour, if little enthusiasm for stopping them, and the game was won. Moxon was named Man of the Match for his accomplished innings, but the cynics, not all of them from Essex, felt that Illingworth should have won the award for winning the toss.

There was a similar situation at Southampton where Knight asked Hampshire to bat and Jackman exploited the heavy, overcast early morning conditions to rout the home side. 17 for 3, 38 for 4, Hampshire had their own heroic Turner, but, as at Leeds, his efforts were not enough, and Surrey won in mid-afternoon with more than 26 overs to spare. The idea of a one-day game is that both sides should bat under similar conditions, on the same wicket, the starting time had made nonsense of this concept.

At Bristol, Brearley decided to bat in conditions a little more favourable than those at Leeds and Southampton, but Middlesex struggled to 63 for 3. The middle order of Gatting, Butcher and Radley batted with great sense and Downton, at number nine, played eminently correctly and intelligently for his invaluable 40 not out. In reply Gloucestershire lost Stovold and Romaines for ducks, but Chris Broad batted gloriously. He found a good partner in the re-emerging Dudleston and they added 90 before the former Leicestershire man fell to Embury. In the forty-third over, with the score on 138, Wright was run out, a disgraceful and unnecessary waste, for Gloucestershire were seizing the initiative. 58 were needed off ten overs. Shepherd could not get going and was caught and bowled by Cowans. Graveney joined Broad and looked purposeful if not immediately middling the ball. At 167, Broad moved out to Slack, missed and was beautifully stumped on the leg-side by Downton, a better player now than when chosen for England. With Broad, who had played one of his greatest innings, went Gloucestershire's hopes. Graveney batted with gallantry and hope, Russell failed bravely and was run out. Nine were needed off the last over, bowled by Slack, but it produced six and Middlesex had won.

Willis won the toss at Taunton and saw his decision to put Somerset in confirmed when Denning, Roebuck, Richards and Rose were back in the pavilion with 91 scored. Then came Botham and Marks. They added 148 in 24 overs with Botham at his most irresistible and Marks unobtrusively effective. Botham had scored only 3 runs in the first 8 overs of his innings, but after lunch he put Warwickshire to the sword, hitting four huge sixes in his stay of 87 deliveries. Rain brought play to a close on the Wednesday with Warwickshire, 74 for 2, needing another 186 to win in 34 overs. Kallicharran had been dropped at mid-wicket when 11 and Somerset rued that lapse the next day. He and Amiss took the score to 183 before Amiss fell to Garner, but nothing could stop Kallicharran who reached his highest score in limited-over cricket. His 141 was achieved off 132 deliveries and included a six, off Garner, and twenty-four fours. It was masterful stuff and although Warwickshire hiccuped a little when Humpage and Oliver fell to successive balls from Dredge, Kallicharran steered them to victory with 6.3 overs to spare.

5 and 6 August

at Slough

Minor Counties 114 for 5 dec and 179 (M. S. A. McEvoy 61, Iqbal Qasim 4 for 36)
Pakistanis 148 for 1 dec (Mansoor Akhtar 83 not out) and 154 for 3 (Mansoor Akhtar 51)
Pakistanis won by 7 wickets

Jalal-ud-Din, added to the Pakistan touring party as a stand-by for the injured Sarfraz, played in this match in which Mansoor batted very well. McEvoy, the former Essex opener, had a fine game with innings of 39 and 61. In dismal weather, only Bailey's first innings declaration made a result possible and the Pakistanis won by seven wickets.

7, 8 and 9 August

at The Oval

Pakistanis 239 for 4 dec (Mohsin Khan 79, Zaheer Abbas 60 not out) and 218 for 4 dec (Haroon Rashid 90, Zaheer Abbas 50 not out)
Surrey 154 for 8 dec and 291 for 9 (R. D. V. Knight 111, Sarfraz Nawaz 6 for 92)
Match drawn

at Edinburgh

Ireland 203 and 167 (J. Clark 4 for 55)
Scotland 315 (R. G. Swan 66, R. S. Weir 65, A. B. M. Ker 58, C. J. Warner 55, S. C. Collett 7 for 82) and 56 for 2
Scotland won by 8 wickets

7, 9 and 10 August

at Swansea

Glamorgan 296 for 5 dec (A. Jones 87, J. A. Hopkins 72 not out) and 178 for 2 dec (A. L. Jones 88, D. A. Francis 68 not out)
Northamptonshire 157 for 2 dec (W. Larkins 82 not out) and 254 for 7 (P. Willey 117, W. Larkins 78)
Match drawn
Glamorgan 3 pts, Northamptonshire 3 pts

at Cheltenham

Nottinghamshire 197 (R. J. Hadlee 64, J. H. Childs 4 for 53, J. N. Shepherd 4 for 86) and 284 for 6 dec (S. B. Hassan 85, C. E. B. Rice 58, J. H. Childs 5 for 112)
Gloucestershire 111 (E. E. Hemmings 5 for 31) and 264 (A. W. Stovold 58, P. M. Such 5 for 112, E. E. Hemmings 4 for 73)
Nottinghamshire won by 106 runs
Nottinghamshire 21 pts, Gloucestershire 4 pts

at Canterbury

Essex 248 (G. A. Gooch 71) and 261 for 4 dec (G. A. Gooch 149)
Kent 209 (D. L. Acfield 4 for 37, D. R. Pringle 4 for 53) and 284 for 8 (C. S. Cowdrey 72 not out, D. G. Aslett 56, M. R. Benson 51)
Match drawn
Kent 6 pts, Essex 6 pts

at Old Trafford

Lancashire 310 for 6 dec (C. H. Lloyd 100, J. Simmons 61 not out) and 30 for 0 dec
Yorkshire 0 for 0 dec and 142 for 3 (G. Boycott 62)
Match drawn
Lancashire 4 pts, Yorkshire 2 pts

at Weston-super-Mare
Somerset 187 (P. M. Roebuck 58, B. C. Rose 53) and 57 (N. G. Cowans 5 for 28, S. P. Hughes 4 for 28)
Middlesex 319 (C. T. Radley 82, W. N. Slack 62, P. R. Downton 59)

Middlesex won by an innings and 75 runs
Middlesex 24 pts, Somerset 5 pts

at Eastbourne
Hampshire 160 (N. E. J. Pocock 50, I. A. Greig 5 for 46) and 240 (M. C. J. Nicholas 73, G. S. le Roux 5 for 60)
Sussex 230 (I. A. Greig 62, J. R. T. Barclay 61, M. D. Marshall 7 for 48) and 122 for 8 (M. D. Marshall 4 for 59)

Match drawn
Sussex 6 pts, Hampshire 4 pts

at Edgbaston
Derbyshire 128 (R. G. D. Willis 6 for 45) and 338 (K. J. Barnett 120, I. S. Anderson 89, G. C. Small 4 for 89)
Warwickshire 284 (D. L. Amiss 60, G. W. Humpage 60, S. Oldham 7 for 78) and 60 for 2

Match drawn
Warwickshire 7 pts, Derbyshire 4 pts

at Worcester
Leicestershire 247 (J. P. Agnew 56, J. D. Inchmore 5 for 59) and 291 for 5 dec (B. F. Davison 139 not out, D. I. Gower 74)
Worcestershire 303 for 7 dec (Younis Ahmed 122, M. J. Weston 68) and 25 for 1

Match drawn
Worcestershire 8 pts, Leicestershire 5 pts

In a glorious game of cricket at The Oval, Surrey and Pakistan defied the weather and contrived a finish as exciting as one could wish. Brisk scoring by Haroon Rashid and Zaheer Abbas enabled Zaheer to declare and set Surrey to make 304 in 226 minutes. They began badly, losing three for 56, but Knight, Roope and Smith batted splendidly, Knight and Roope adding 110 in 79 minutes. Knight reached his hundred in under 2½ hours, but Sarfraz dismissed him and Roope and Surrey needed 47 in 6 overs with four wickets left. They continued to go for the win, but wickets fell to steady bowling and in the end Needham and Mackintosh had to survive for a draw.

In the Schweppes County Championship, Middlesex took a 45-point lead at the top of the table with a remarkable win at Taunton. Somerset laboured on the opening day and Middlesex took a commanding lead before the rain brought play to a close. A solid innings by Radley, who had not had the best of seasons, but was always reliable in a crisis, provided the backbone of the Middlesex innings. The weather had seemed to dictate a draw, but on the last morning Cowans and Hughes bowled the leaders to a spectacular victory, dismissing Somerset for 57 in just over an hour. They bowled fast and straight and made the ball lift frighteningly from just short of a length. Somerset reached 21 before losing a wicket, the two openers, Roebuck and Lloyds, being the only batsmen to reach double figures.

Clive Lloyd hit his sixth century in Roses' matches, a Lancashire record, and Yorkshire forfeited their first innings, but their total lack of enterprise in chasing a target of 341 in 283 minutes made one wonder why.

There were endeavours to beat the weather at Swansea where Northants were set to make 318 in 3 hours. Willey and Larkins, who had batted well in the first innings, led the assault of the Glamorgan bowling after Cook had gone second ball. They added 170 in 116 minutes and Willey reached his fifth century of the season in under 2½ hours. When Willey was caught in the covers at 247, fifth man out, Northants began to look uncertain and after two more wickets had fallen Steele and Tim Lamb batted for a draw.

Nottinghamshire ended their miserable spell with a convincing win at Cheltenham. It was the off-spin of Eddie Hemmings and eighteen-year old Peter Such, a career best 5 for 112 in 30 accurate overs, that clinched victory for Notts.

Essex started brightly at Canterbury with Gooch and McEwan striking the ball to all parts of the field, a cascade of glorious shots, but both fell to Cowdrey, caught at square-leg by Baptiste off poor shots, and Essex collapsed from 168 for 2 to 248 all out. In reply, Kent's batting was dreadful. They ended play an hour early on the Saturday through bad light, an unwise decision if you want people to pay to come and watch you again, and laboured through Monday. The innings folded when Fletcher belatedly turned to spin. After tea Gooch devastated the attack to reach his first first-class hundred of the season. He continued his wonderful display of hitting the following morning when Fletcher declared, leaving Kent 255 minutes to make 301. Taylor again went quickly, and although Benson and Tavare batted confidently, Acfield dismissed them both and gave Essex a grip on the game. Aslett, Johnson and Cowdrey then batted with a freedom not displayed in the first innings and the last twenty overs began with Kent needing 112 and six wickets in hand. Three more wickets went down while only 28 were scored and Kent fell well behind the clock in spite of some brave flourishes from Cowdrey.

Remarkably, the match at Eastbourne ended in a draw. On a wicket which always helped the seam bowlers, Sussex led by 70 on the first innings, Greig and Barclay defying some more magnificent bowling by Marshall. Nicholas batted nobly in the second innings and, helped by Cowley, he negotiated the vagaries of the pitch and the hostility of le Roux to help set Sussex 171 to win in 150 minutes. Mendis was soon lbw to Marshall and it was the West Indian's sustained pace and accuracy that denied Sussex and, indeed, almost brought Hampshire victory.

Bob Willis returned his best championship figures for four years as Derbyshire were routed on the first day at Edgbaston. The great John Wright alone offered any real resistance. Amiss and Humpage helped Warwickshire to a lead of 156 with a fourth wicket stand of 126, but Steve Oldham took the second day's honours with a career best 7 for 78. Warwickshire looked set for their first victory of the season, but Kim Barnett, that most impressively upright young player, hit a maiden century and saved the game. Barnett's fine performance did not receive the acclaim that was due to it as, because of the strike by electricians in Fleet Street, newspapers were not printed and for many it went unnoticed.

There were two heartening performances at Worcester, a

valuable maiden fifty from John Agnew and a brilliant century on his return after injury by Younis Ahmed. Younis reached his century in 222 minutes with a spectacular six off Parsons. He also hit twelve fours. Sadly, Tolchard decided to bat on beyond the point where a result could have been achieved and Worcestershire responded by scoring 25 in 28 overs as the match crawled to a close. The contempt for the public continues, and this in a season where Test receipts were disastrously low.

John Player League
8 August
at Cheltenham
Nottinghamshire 214 for 6 (R. J. Hadlee 100 not out, S. B. Hassan 54)
Gloucestershire 167
Nottinghamshire (4 pts) won by 47 runs

The Saffrons Ground, Eastbourne. A beautiful ground, a doubtful wicket.

at Canterbury
Kent 152 for 9
Essex 154 for 0 (G. A. Gooch 83 not out, B. R. Hardie 67 not out)
Essex (4 pts) won by 10 wickets

at Old Trafford
Lancashire 124 for 0 (G. Fowler 59 not out, D. Lloyd 53 not out) **v. Yorkshire**
Match abandoned
Lancashire 2 pts, Yorkshire 2 pts

at Weston-super-Mare
Middlesex 211 for 9 (W. N. Slack 77, M. W. Gatting 72)
Somerset 197 (J. E. Emburey 4 for 50)
Middlesex (4 pts) won by 14 runs

at Eastbourne
Sussex 192 for 7
Hampshire 179 (A. C. S. Pigott 4 for 33)
Sussex (4 pts) won by 13 runs

at Edgbaston
Warwickshire 137 for 8
Glamorgan 138 for 1 (A. L. Jones 82)
Glamorgan (4 pts) won by 9 wickets

at Stourbridge
Worcestershire 119
Leicestershire 120 for 2 (N. E. Briers 58)
Leicestershire (4 pts) won by 8 wickets

Essex appeared very reluctant to surrender their John Player League title without a struggle. They restricted Kent to a meagre 152 at Canterbury and passed the score without loss and with 11 overs to spare. Hardie set the early pace and he was on 61 and Gooch on 30 at one time. The return of Jarvis prodded Gooch into unrestrained aggression. He hit the first ball of the Kent pace bowler's over for six to reach his fifty and followed it with two more sixes and two fours in the over, and the game was as good as settled.

Sussex, however, maintained their six-point lead at the top. Sussex owed much to Alan Wells who took 17 off the last over of the innings bowled by Emery. It lifted Sussex to 192 and, as the margin of victory was 13, it can be considered crucial. When Hampshire pushed for victory at the end it was the steady bowling of Pigott which thwarted them.

Middlesex held on to second place with a return-to-form win over Somerset. Slack and Gatting added 120 for Middlesex's second wicket and the fine bowling of Emburey in the middle of the Somerset innings clinched the match for the visitors.

The ever-improving batting of Richard Hadlee reached another landmark. He hit his first John Player League century. It came off only 80 balls and included three sixes and ten fours. He followed this with a spell of 2 for 33 and Notts won with ease. Hadlee shared a stand of 96 with Hassan for the second wicket.

Batsmen found runs difficult at Stourbridge, but after Taylor, Parsons, Roberts and Wenlock had shared the Worcestershire wickets when the home side collapsed to 119 all out, Leicestershire had few problems and won with 8.2 overs to spare.

Glamorgan enjoyed more success, this time at Edgbaston where they savaged the home side and won with 13 overs to spare. Nash and Davis bowled so well at the outset that Warwickshire were reduced to 51 for 5 and never recovered. Alan Lewis Jones hit a sparkling 82, his highest score in limited-over cricket, and he and Alan Jones reached the Warwickshire score without being parted. The younger Jones fell to Small with the scores level, which made it possible for Arthur Francis to come to the wicket to see the winning run made.

Rain destroyed the Roses contest when Lancashire looked on their way to a formidable score.

11, 12 and 13 August

at Derby
Lancashire 332 for 5 dec (D. P. Hughes 111, J. Abrahams 90 not out) and 181 for 6 dec (G. Fowler 57, D. G. Moir 4 for 48)
Derbyshire 305 for 7 dec (J. H. Hampshire 101 not out, B. Wood 67, P. N. Kirsten 63)
Match drawn
Lancashire 6 pts, Derbyshire 4 pts

at Chelmsford
Essex 175 (S. Turner 58, K. St. J. D. Emery 6 for 67) and 261 (N. Phillip 73, M. D. Marshall 6 for 103)
Hampshire 351 (T. E. Jesty 106, J. M. Rice 69) and 75 for 2
Match drawn
Hampshire 8 pts, Essex 5 pts

at Cheltenham
Gloucestershire 247 (B. C. Broad 75, N. G. Cowans 5 for 34) and 141 for 7
Middlesex 277 (R. O. Butcher 173, F. D. Stephenson 5 for 69, J. N. Shepherd 4 for 79)
Match drawn
Middlesex 7 pts, Gloucestershire 6 pts

Kevin Jarvis. His form earned a place in the party for the matches with Pakistan, but he played in neither.

at Canterbury
Glamorgan 368 for 7 dec (D. A. Francis 142 not out, E. W. Jones 58) and 235 for 3 dec (A. Jones 136 not out, A. L. Jones 53)
Kent 300 for 8 dec (E. A. Baptiste 69 not out, M. R. Benson 51, W. W. Davis 4 for 83) and 164 for 5 (M. R. Benson 56 not out)
Match drawn
Kent 6 pts, Glamorgan 6 pts

at Leicester
Nottinghamshire 216 (B. N. French 79, A. M. E. Roberts 4 for 53) and 70 (A. M. E. Roberts 5 for 37, L. B. Taylor 4 for 28)
Leicestershire 267 (B. F. Davison 51) and 20 for 0
Leicestershire won by 10 wickets
Leicestershire 23 pts, Nottinghamshire 6 pts

at Weston-super-Mare
Somerset 388 (N. A. Felton 71, P. A. Slocombe 59, N. F. M. Popplewell 55, P. Carrick 4 for 31)
Yorkshire 250 for 4 (G. Boycott 129, R. G. Lumb 81)
Match drawn
Somerset 5 pts, Yorkshire 5 pts

at Eastbourne
Northamptonshire 261 (Kapil Dev 103, W. Larkins 81, A. C. S. Pigott 7 for 74)
Sussex 84 (P. Willey 6 for 17, D. S. Steele 4 for 27) and 119 (D. S. Steele 5 for 32)
Northamptonshire won by an innings and 58 runs
Northamptonshire 23 pts, Sussex 4 pts

at Edgbaston
Warwickshire 447 for 8 dec (A. I. Kallicharran 195, T. A. Lloyd 89) and 143 for 2 dec (T. A. Lloyd 60)
Surrey 318 for 1 dec (A. R. Butcher 187 not out, D. M. Smith 105 not out) and 234 for 9 (R. D. V. Knight 99, S. P. Sutcliffe 4 for 72)
Match drawn
Surrey 5 pts, Warwickshire 4 pts

Indifferent weather hampered several matches and there was no play possible on the last day at Weston-super-Mare. On the second day, Boycott and Lumb put on 178 for the first Yorkshire wicket and Boycott hit 18 boundaries in his 129.

There was no play necessary on the third day at Eastbourne or Leicester. The match at Eastbourne was over one ball after lunch on the Thursday. On an uncertain wicket, which deteriorated rapidly, Larkins and Kapil Dev hit mightily while they could. Kapil Dev hit three sixes and eleven fours as wickets tumbled around him to the bowling of Pigott who had a career best 7 for 74. Waller had already shown that there was turn in the wicket and as soon as the effects of the heavy roller had worn off, Willey and Steele had Sussex at their mercy, 44 for 0 to 84 all out. The following morning Sussex disintegrated again and the pitch was declared unfit for first-class cricket by the umpires.

At Leicester it was the pace of Roberts and Taylor that discomfitted Notts. 37 for 4 in their first innings, Notts were rescued by a career best 79 from wicket-keeper Bruce French. Solid Leicestershire batting throughout the innings brought them a lead of 51. This did not seem a match-winning margin, but Taylor and Roberts, bowling unchanged, dismissed Notts in under 26 overs in 95 minutes.

Leicestershire gained a little on Middlesex in the championship race, the leaders being thwarted by the weather at Cheltenham. Emburey was captain of Middlesex for the first time and saw his side in total disarray when, facing Gloucestershire's 247, they were 30 for 5 at the end of the first day. The sixth wicket fell at 55, still 43 short of saving the follow-on. The damage had been done by Stephenson. Middlesex were steadied by Roland Butcher who first played with the utmost caution and then savaged the home attack to the extent that his last 71 runs came in 47 minutes. The tail-enders assisted him nobly and Simon Hughes helped to add 92 for the last wicket before Butcher was out. He had lifted Middlesex to an improbable lead of 30, but rain restricted play on the last day.

There was rain on the last day at Chelmsford too, and Essex were saved from certain defeat. The home side collapsed to Kevin Emery, who seems to like bowling at Chelmsford, and, inevitably, it was only a brave knock by Turner that gave the score any respectability. Hampshire passed the Essex score with only 3 wickets down and Trevor Jesty consolidated their position with a splendid hundred, driving and pulling disdainfully, and making all wonder why he was not at Lord's with the England side. By the end of the second day, Essex had lost 5 wickets and were still 29 short of avoiding an innings defeat. Phillip batted well the next day, but with nine wickets down, four hours were lost to bad weather, and Hampshire were left needing 86 in 8 overs. They went for the runs in a frenzy, but finished 11 short.

Surrey also finished short at Edgbaston and, ultimately, were thankful to draw. Kallicharran played another magnificent innings on the first day, but centuries from Butcher and Smith in a second wicket stand of 316 in 200 minutes enabled Knight to declare 129 behind. On the last day, Surrey were set 273 in 135 minutes and went bravely at the task. Knight made 99 in 104 minutes before dying bravely, caught at deep mid-wicket. Kallicharran dismissed Needham in the same over and the game swung in favour of Warwickshire. Monkhouse and Mackintosh negotiated the last 20 deliveries to give Surrey a deserved draw.

Alan Jones hit the fiftieth century of his career and reached one thousand runs for the twenty-second season in succession, but Glamorgan still failed to win. Arthur Francis hit a career best and confirmed his recent good form, but some late order thrashing from Baptiste and Ellison took Kent to four batting points and near parity. Lloyd asked Kent to make 304 on the last afternoon and captured 5 wickets for 136, three of them to Ontong, but rain destroyed the chance of a result.

Derby induced a match of uneventful meandering in which David Hughes played another fine innings and Abrahams gave further evidence of how much better a player he had become since being given the confidence of a county cap. Derbyshire relentlessly pursued the Lancashire total, Jackie Hampshire completing his thousand runs with one of his less memorable centuries. On a dismal last day rain was a saviour.

SECOND CORNHILL TEST MATCH
England v. Pakistan

In the Pakistan side, Sarfraz Nawaz replaced Sikhander and Haroon Rashid came in for Wasim Raja. In the England side, Pringle returned for Miller who had chicken-pox and Jackman came in for Willis who was unable to play because of a neck injury sustained in his last wicket stand with Taylor in the First Test. Pleasing as was the selection of Jackman, it was difficult to follow the policy of selectors who, having asked Small and Jarvis to stand by in previous Tests, then turned to Jackman when a place became vacant. Marks was called to join the England party when Miller was deemed unfit, but once more he was omitted from the side.

Imran won the toss and Pakistan displayed the batting talents that we knew they possessed. A brisk opening partnership was followed by a firm partnership between Mansoor and Mohsin which was ended when Mansoor obligingly hit a long-hop to mid-on. Javed was needlessly run out, but Zaheer stayed with Mohsin until the end of the day when Pakistan had reached 295 for 3.

Pakistan had batted with a graceful and engaging freedom on the opening day that put them in a strong positon, but it must be admitted that the England attack looked a very mediocre affair, relying entirely on the durability and endeavour of Botham and Jackman. The contributions from Pringle and Greig were negligible.

Bad light in the morning and heavy rain in the afternoon restricted play on the second day. Zaheer made some glorious flourishes until he played rather lazily at a ball from Jackman which came back at him. Haroon, nervous-

Mohsin Khan in all his glory.

Imran Khan, the inspiration of Pakistan's great victory.

ness patent, was soon lbw to Botham, but Mohsin went on his elegant way and when rain halted play for four hours he was on 199.

On the resumption, frustratingly delayed beyond the point where play seemed possible, Mohsin turned Botham off his legs for a single and ran waving his bat in exultation. He had scored the first double century in a Lord's Test since Martin Donnelly's 206 for New Zealand in 1949. He batted for 491 minutes, faced 383 balls and hit twenty-three fours. Losing concentration, he flicked Jackman to square-leg as soon as he had reached his second century. It was an innings of great charm. Mohsin is a batsman incapable of an ugly gesture. There is majesty in his stature and aristocracy in his strokes. Upright and eager for runs, he was a regal sight.

Wickets fell in a frenzy for quick runs, Imran anxious to compensate for the lost hours. He declared the innings closed overnight and England began Saturday's session needing 229 to avoid the follow-on, on this wicket it seemed a simple task.

Randall began with characteristic frenzy and Tavare with refreshing fluency, but with the score on 16 Tavare played

Ian Botham hits out.

down a lifting ball from Sarfraz and stood immobile and seemingly mesmerised as it spun back slowly onto his stumps. Runs came briskly, which was as well considering the deplorably slow over-rate, thirteen an hour. In this respect, Pakistan were their own worst enemies.

Randall was bowled when he played inside a ball from Sarfraz and after lunch Lamb was caught off a firm bat and pad. Gower, who had not looked a happy captain in the field, looked a positively miserable one with the bat. There is nothing worse than beauty and elegance when it is contorted and as he groped ineffectively against the mysteries of Abdul Qadir and the speed of Imran, one felt a sense of embarrassment, like witnessing Ophelia's madness.

Botham took his cue from Gower and played with the utmost restraint. There was, it seemed, little faith in what batting was to come. One could not help but admire Botham's dedication, but wished that it were possible for him to play his natural game.

Qadir, and all around the bat, appealed vehemently for lbw when Botham, only half-forward, missed an attempted sweep. The appeal was denied by umpire Constant and Qadir reacted in agonised astonishment, which led to a rebuke from the umpire and words from the umpires to Imran. Qadir accepted his rebuke and apologised.

Botham fell to Qadir when he accepted the bait and swung high to Mohsin at fine-leg, rather square, who ran in to take a good catch. With his first belligerent shot, Gower mis-hooked to mid-wicket.

Pringle and Greig lacked the class, experience and ability to deal with Qadir. Hemmings fell to Sarfraz and Taylor was lbw on the back foot to Qadir whose bowling created that same sense of excitement that Ramadhin's had evoked thirty-two years ago.

Jackman joined Gatting, who alone had shown the footwork and positive attitude necessary to cope with the Pakistan bowling, with three runs needed to avoid the follow-on. A debate ensued as to the light and play was ended.

Imran bowled the first over on Sunday morning, the first time we had seen Sunday play in a Test at Lord's. Gatting took a single and Jackman was hit on the toe by the last ball of the over and was out lbw. Pakistan erupted gleefully and England followed-on. It had been a miserable batting display against some good bowling, which might have achieved even more had it been more consistently accurate.

With Tahir absent with an injured back muscle, Mudassar Nazar was used as first change bowler. In his first over he

Above: *Mohsin Khan, helmet discarded, hits through the leg-side field. Gatting takes evasive action.* Below left: *Mohsin has turned Botham to leg and sets off in celebratory style for his two hundredth run.* Below right: *Down, but not out. Robin Jackman reflects on his return to Test cricket.*

Above: *Zaheer Abbas. A majestic scourge.* Below: *Greig hitches his trousers as Jackman and Gower confer. A captain's lot is not a happy one.*

bowled Randall, who played inside the line again, and had Lamb lbw. In his next over Gower followed a gentle away swinger and was caught behind. 9 for 3 and Pakistan had scented a famous victory and the inspiration had come from a most unlikely source.

Tavare did not score until fifteen overs had passed, 67 minutes, but at least he was still at the crease. For Pakistan there was bitter disappointment when rain washed out play for most of the afternoon. Botham and Tavare negotiated what overs remained without mishap.

They continued their partnership the following morning. There was a break for bad light and there were warnings of advancing rain which added a sense of urgency to the play. It took Tavare an hour to add to his overnight score so that he had had two scoreless hours in his innings.

Once more Botham was restrained, but, he still hit the loose ball and showed signs of wishing to hit more. Mudassar returned and Botham drove hard at a short ball which flew to Sarfraz in the gully. Gatting presented Mudassar with his fifth wicket when he drove at a wide delivery and was caught behind, a terrible shot in any circumstances, in these circumstances it seemed like high treason.

Many felt that Imran was wrong not to confront Pringle earlier than he did with Qadir's leg-spin. Once more he fell to the wrist spinner as, in his bemused state, he pushed forward hopefully and was caught at silly mid-off. Mudassar had Greig lbw to give him incredible figures at this stage of 6 for 19.

Tavare reached his fifty after 332 minutes at the wicket. He began to accelerate, not difficult considering what had gone before, but when he had reached 82 he pushed at a ball from the eager and untiring Imran and was caught at second slip by Javed who held the ball at the second attempt.

It is perhaps ungracious to criticise Tavare who had stood firm while others floundered, but had he taken advantage of some of the loose balls that had been bowled to him earlier in his innings, the England score could well have been beyond Pakistan's reach. His dedication and defence were admirable, but in the end cricket matches are decided by the number of runs scored and strokelessness will never win matches, rarely will it save them.

Still bowling with the old ball, Imran had Hemmings caught behind and England's last pair came together with their side 34 runs on and 38 overs remaining.

Taylor was hit on the foot first ball, but he hobbled painfully to join with Jackman in a stand of courage and professional application that almost thwarted Pakistan. Imran finally took the new ball and with it Qadir found the extra bounce to have Jackman taken off bat and pad. When one considers that for most of the innings Imran was without the services of Sarfraz and Tahir, fifty per cent of his attack, the Pakistan achievement was a remarkable one.

Pakistan had 18 overs in which to score 76 runs. Javed and Mohsin, and all Pakistan, knew that this was a moment of glory which must not be missed. In 79 balls, bowled in the gloom as clouds threatened, they reached the goal with panache and ran in excitement from the field, earlier they had graciously declined the umpires' offer to leave for bad light.

It was a memorable, and deserved victory, only their second over England in 35 meetings.

Above: The beginning of England's misfortunes. Tavare watches mesmerised as the ball rolls back on to his stumps and dislodges the off-bail.

Right: Lamb is lucky to escape as his helmet falls and all but knocks down his wicket. Below: Less fortunate. Caught off bat and pad by Haroon Rashid.

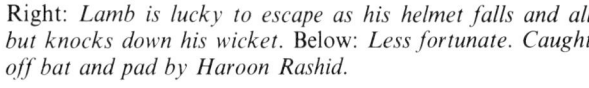

Left: *Positive leadership – Imran Khan.*

Above: *The joy of success. Pakistan appeal.*

Below: *Disbelief. The appeal for lbw against Botham is rejected.*

Below left: *Disbelief. A near miss.*

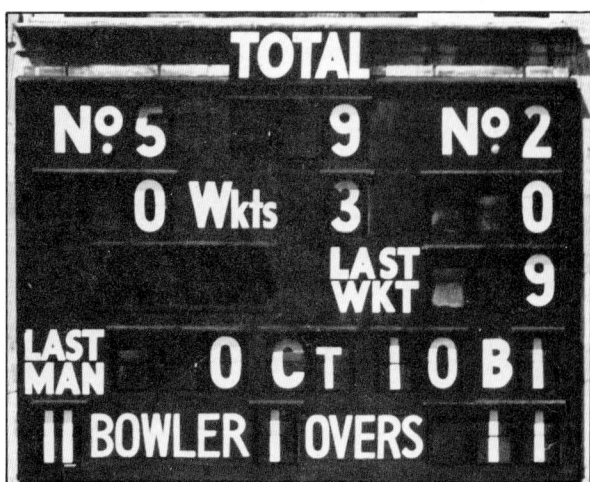

Above: *England's despair. Gower is caught behind to become Mudassar's third victim. The scoreboard tells a melancholy tale. England second innings, 9 for 3.*

Right: *England's improbable destroyer – Mudassar Nazar.*

Below: *Tavare the defiant. Here he hits out in his marathon innings.*

THE ENGLISH SEASON/349

Top left: *The end of Tavare. Javed juggles but catches.*
Right: *The end of Pringle. Leg-spin posed unsolved problems for the young man.*

Above left: *Architects of victory. Abdul Qadir and Imran Khan.*
Right: *Bob Taylor in his valiant effort to save England.*

Right: *The sweet smell of success. Bari leaps. Javed runs.*

SECOND CORNHILL TEST MATCH – ENGLAND v. PAKISTAN
12, 13, 14, 15 and 16 August 1982 at Lord's

PAKISTAN

	FIRST INNINGS		SECOND INNINGS	
Mohsin Khan	c Tavare, b Jackman	200	not out	39
Mudassar Nazar	c Taylor, b Jackman	20		
Mansoor Akhtar	c Lamb, b Botham	57		
Javed Miandad	run out	6	(2) not out	26
Zaheer Abbas	b Jackman	75		
Haroon Rashid	lbw, b Botham	1		
Imran Khan†	c Taylor, b Botham	12		
Tahir Naqqash	c Gatting, b Jackman	2		
Wasim Bari*	not out	24		
Abdul Qadir	not out	18		
Sarfraz Nawaz				
Extras	b 3, lb 8, nb 2	13	b 1, lb 10, w 1	12
	(for 8 wkts)	428	(for no wkt)	77

	O	M	R	W	O	M	R	W
Botham	44	8	148	3	7	—	30	—
Jackman	34	5	110	4	4	—	22	—
Pringle	26	9	62	—				
Greig	13	2	42	—				
Hemmings	20	3	53	—	2.1	—	13	—

FALL OF WICKETS
1–53, 2–197, 3–208, 4–361, 5–364, 6–380, 7–382, 8–401

ENGLAND

	FIRST INNINGS		SECOND INNINGS	
D. W. Randall	b Sarfraz	29	b Mudassar	9
C. J. Tavare	b Sarfraz	8	c Javed, b Imran	82
A. J. Lamb	c Haroon, b Tahir	33	lbw, b Mudassar	0
D. I. Gower†	c Mansoor, b Imran	29	c Bari, b Mudassar	0
I. T. Botham	c Mohsin, b Qadir	31	c Sarfraz, b Mudassar	69
M. W. Gatting	not out	32	c Bari, b Mudassar	7
D. R. Pringle	c Haroon, b Qadir	5	c Javed, b Qadir	14
I. A. Greig	lbw, b Qadir	3	lbw, b Mudassar	2
E. E. Hemmings	b Sarfraz	6	c Bari, b Imran	14
R. W. Taylor*	lbw, b Qadir	5	not out	24
R. D. Jackman	lbw, b Imran	0	c Haroon, b Qadir	17
Extras	b 11, lb 12, w 13, nb 10	46	b 10, lb 19, w 5, nb 4	38
		227		276

	O	M	R	W	O	M	R	W
Imran Khan	23	4	55	2	42	13	84	2
Sarfraz Nawaz	23	4	56	3	14	5	22	—
Tahir Naqqash	12	4	25	1	7	5	6	—
Abdul Qadir	24	9	39	4	37.5	15	94	2
Mudassar Nazar	4	1	6	—	19	7	32	6

FALL OF WICKETS
1–16, 2–69, 3–89, 4–157, 5–173, 6–187, 7–197, 8–217, 9–226
1–9, 2–9, 3–9, 4–121, 5–132, 6–171, 7–180, 8–224, 9–235

Pakistan won by 10 wickets

The moment of history. Mohsin Khan runs from the field in joy and Pakistan have beaten England for only the second time in their cricket history.

14, 16 and 17 August

at Cheltenham
Gloucestershire 322 (A. W. Stovold 83, Sadiq Mohammad 75, J. N. Shepherd 67 not out, J. K. Lever 5 for 78) and 236 for 7 dec (B. C. Broad 66, P. W. Romaines 59)
Essex 303 for 9 dec (K. S. McEwan 91, S. Turner 64 not out, K. R. Pont 50) and 107 for 5

Match drawn
Gloucestershire 7 pts, Essex 6 pts

at Southampton
Hampshire 259 (T. E. Jesty 123, A. J. Webster 5 for 87, A. P. Pridgeon 4 for 75) and 191 for 3 dec (M. C. J. Nicholas 59 not out)
Worcestershire 167 (M. D. Marshall 8 for 71) and 286 for 9 (D. N. Patel 89, Younis Ahmed 59, J. W. Southern 4 for 48)

Worcestershire won by 1 wicket
Worcestershire 21 pts, Hampshire 7 pts

at Leicester
Leicestershire 298 (B. F. Davison 60, J. C. Balderstone 52, G. J. Parsons 51, J. Simmons 4 for 59) and 137 for 9 dec (J. Simmons 5 for 57)
Lancashire 187 for 5 dec (S. J. O'Shaughnessy 55, I. Cockbain 52) and 154 for 5 (C. H. Lloyd 68)

Match drawn
Leicestershire 5 pts, Lancashire 3 pts

at Northampton
Northamptonshire 400 for 5 dec (R. J. Boyd-Moss 137, W. Larkins 105, Kapil Dev 65 not out, R. G. Williams 58) and 228 for 4 dec (Kapil Dev 100 not out, R. J. Boyd-Moss 80 not out)
Derbyshire 275 for 6 dec (J. G. Wright 157) and 117 (N. A. Mallender 7 for 41)

Northamptonshire won by 236 runs
Northamptonshire 22 pts, Derbyshire 4 pts

at Trent Bridge
Somerset 289 (V. J. Marks 64, N. A. Felton 61, J. W. Lloyds 50, K. Saxelby 4 for 51, P. M. Such 4 for 102) and 162 for 2 dec (J. W. Lloyds 86 not out, P. A. Slocombe 50 not out)
Nottinghamshire 200 for 2 dec (S. B. Hassan 89 not out) and 147 (R. T. Robinson 77, V. J. Marks 7 for 51)

Somerset won by 104 runs
Somerset 19 pts, Nottinghamshire 6 pts

at Guildford
Glamorgan 360 for 7 dec (R. C. Ontong 88, J. G. Thomas 84, D. A. Francis 52, C. J. C. Rowe 51 not out) and 316 for 6 dec (J. A. Hopkins 124, R. C. Ontong 110)
Surrey 358 for 5 dec (G. P. Howarth 156 not out, A. R. Butcher 60, D. J. Thomas 58 not out) and 322 for 8 (M. A. Lynch 141 not out, A. R. Butcher 54, S. R. Barwick 4 for 63)

Surrey won by 2 wickets
Surrey 22 pts, Glamorgan 6 pts

at Coventry
Middlesex 360 for 8 dec (C. T. Radley 106, W. N. Slack 72, P. H. Edmonds 62 not out)
Warwickshire 174 (Asif Din 102, W. W. Daniel 5 for 55) and 120

Middlesex won by an innings and 66 runs
Middlesex 23 pts, Warwickshire 3 pts

at Leeds
Yorkshire 304 (C. W. J. Athey 100, G. Boycott 69, G. W. Johnson 5 for 52, D. L. Underwood 4 for 62) and 109 for 1 dec
Kent 164 for 3 dec (M. R. Benson 57 not out) and 142 for 9 (C. S. Cowdrey 51 not out, P. Carrick 4 for 56)

Match drawn
Kent 4 pts, Yorkshire 4 pts

Middlesex took a forty-seven-point lead in the Schweppes County Championship and it now seemed that the title was theirs. On the Saturday they owed much to Slack and the tenacity of Radley. However far away Radley's England days and best form seem to be, he remains one of the most dependable of men when the going is tough. Edmonds came with some late runs in his relaxed manner. He and Radley added 104 for the seventh wicket. One of the features of the Middlesex innings was an eighteen-ball over by Gladstone Small. Small lost his rhythm and was no-balled eleven times. Dropping to half-pace in an effort to regain control, he bowled a wide.

Kallicharran was hurt in the John Player League game at Edgbaston and was unable to bat in either innings of the championship match. Asif Din scored his maiden century and Paul Smith made a creditable 45, and these two players lifted Warwickshire from the depths of 10 for 4 to 152, but could not save the follow-on. Warwickshire subsided limply a second time, slipping from 64 for 1 to 120 all out.

Leicestershire failed to make ground on Middlesex because of interruptions by rain and a lack of courage in forcing a declaration. For Lancashire, Jack Simmons had match figures of 9 for 116 and Steve O'Shaughnessy showed further signs of his maturation as a cricketer.

Rain hampered progress at Trent Bridge, but Somerset snatched a remarkable victory on the last afternoon. Young Felton again showed high promise in the Somerset first innings in which Saxelby bowled well and Peter Such gave another impressive display of off-break bowling for a young man with only half-a-dozen first-class games behind him. Notts declared 89 behind and Somerset scored briskly to set the home side a target of 252 in 168 minutes. The wicket was turning slowly and Robinson, batting with superb judgement, steered Notts to 134 when he was sixth out. It heralded a collapse and four wickets fell in the space of 8 overs for 4 runs. French and Such, scoring his first first-class runs, nearly saved the game for Notts, but Moseley returned to have Such caught behind. The destroyer of Notts was Vic Marks who, rejected by England, returned to his county to record a career best 7 for 51 as he exploited the conditions. Keeping wicket for Somerset was Trevor Gard. It was announced that Derek Taylor would retire at the end of the season – one of the great unsung players of first-class cricket.

massive sixes. 129 were needed off the last 20 overs and in the race, wickets fell. 68 were needed from 10 overs, and 26 were needed off the last three with only two wickets standing, but Lynch hit two sixes, 17 in all, and when Monkhouse clipped the winning runs four balls were left. Lynch's century came in 88 minutes off 78 deliveries.

There were explosions at Northampton too. Centuries by Larkins and Boyd-Moss on the first day swept Northants to a big score, but John Wright's dedication kept Derbyshire in touch. On the last morning Kapil Dev and Boyd-Moss put on 182 for the fifth wicket in 98 minutes of thrilling stroke-play. Derbyshire were set 354 to win in 252 minutes, but Neil Mallender, who had had a poor season, produced a magnificent spell of quick and consistent accurate bowling to dismiss them for 117. Mallender's 7 for 41 was a career best performance.

Gloucestershire recovered from an indifferent start on the Saturday to pass three hundred. Essex laboured in their reply until McEwan and Pont added 103 for the fifth wicket, but it was Turner's hitting that attained respectability. Gloucestershire seemed little interested in pressing for victory and their declaration which asked Essex to make 256 at two runs a minute was far from generous in cloudy conditions. Essex scored 107 in 13 overs of violent hitting, mostly by the spectacular Gooch, but they lost five wickets in the process and the rain came to halt all progress.

Trevor Jesty, who should have been selected for the England side at Lord's in place of some embryo talents, rescued Hampshire from the disgrace of 18 for 5 with his second century in successive matches. Malcolm Marshall

Bobbie Parks. His enthusiastic and stylish wicket-keeping put him among England's best.

Trevor Jesty. His non-inclusion in the England side was incomprehensible.

There was a tense finish at Headingley where Underwood and Johnson had caused great problems to the Yorkshire batsmen after Athey and Boycott had threatened to give them a massive first innings total. Rain caused Kent to declare 140 runs behind and Yorkshire batted for 90 minutes before setting Kent to make 250 in 3¼ hours. Kent struggled on a wet pitch against a varied attack in which Carrick was particularly effective, but Cowdrey batted with great resolution and he and Jarvis defied Yorkshire for seven overs to save the game.

There was a marvellous game of cricket at Guildford. The Glamorgan batting was refreshingly positive on the first day. Alan Jones scored only 11, but in doing so he completed 1000 runs against each of the other sixteen counties. Arthur Francis continued his good form and there were fine innings from Ontong and Thomas, a hard-hit career best. Howarth dominated the Monday with a splendid innings, overcoming early uncertainty to flow into his confident best. He and Thomas had an unbeaten stand of 145 for the sixth wicket. Then came centuries for Ontong and Hopkins, a most welcome one, and Glamorgan declared in mid-afternoon, leaving Surrey 2¾ hours in which to make 319 to win. Surrey attacked from the start with Butcher and Howarth scoring briskly, but the architect of their victory was Monty Lynch who hit a wonderful 141 not out. Batting at number three, Lynch hit eight sixes in his career best innings and led Surrey to a memorable victory. Ten minutes with Clarke produced 35 runs, the pace bowler hitting two then produced the best bowling of his distinguished career, 8 for 71, and Hampshire had snatched an improbable lead of 92 when one considered the depths to which they had sunk on the first day. That lead was built upon and Pocock made a challenging declaration which demanded a response of 284 in 4¼ hours from Worcestershire. Weston and Ormrod opened with a stand of 104 and Younis and Patel added 145 for the third wicket which put Worcestershire in sight of victory. They had needed 110 off the last 20 overs and 40 were needed off the last 10. Southern, whose left-arm spin had been introduced in the last hour, took three wickets and 7 were needed off the last over with three wickets standing. Pridgeon was bowled by the second ball and Patel caught behind off the fourth. Perryman then hit the only ball he received over long-on for six and victory, by one wicket and one ball.

John Player League

15 August

at Cheltenham
Gloucestershire 177 for 8 (A. J. Wright 52)
Essex 172 for 8
Gloucestershire (4 pts) won by 5 runs

at Southampton
Worcestershire 236 for 1 (D. N. Patel 125, J. A. Ormrod 92 not out)
Hampshire 225 (D. N. Patel 4 for 39)
Worcestershire (4 pts) won by 11 runs

at Leicester
Leicestershire 173 for 8 (M. A. Garnham 79 not out)
Lancashire 149 (B. W. Reidy 50, P. B. Clift 4 for 17)
Leicestershire (4 pts) won by 24 runs

at Milton Keynes
Derbyshire 233 for 5 (J. G. Wright 75, C. J. Tunnicliffe 51 not out)
Northamptonshire 238 for 5 (Kapil Dev 75, P. Willey 58)
Northamptonshire (4 pts) won by 5 wickets

at Trent Bridge
Kent 164 (M. R. Benson 77)
Nottinghamshire 168 for 1 (S. B. Hassan 71 not out, C. E. B. Rice 59 not out)
Nottinghamshire (4 pts) won by 9 wickets

at Guildford
Surrey 133 for 9 (R. D. V. Knight 57, A. C. S. Pigott 5 for 28)
Sussex 134 for 6
Sussex (4 pts) won by 4 wickets

at Edgbaston
Middlesex 243 for 9 (K. P. Tomlins 58, W. N. Slack 56, R. O. Butcher 51)
Warwickshire 141 (J. E. Emburey 4 for 25)
Middlesex (4 pts) won by 102 runs

A maiden half-century in the John Player League by Tony Wright helped Gloucestershire to their first win in the Cheltenham Festival. Turner restricted the home side with some accurate bowling, but after his quota was finished Shepherd and Wright boosted the score. Essex seemed set for victory, but wickets fell when batsmen looked set and 12 off the last over proved too much.

Essex's defeat virtually ended their chances of retaining the title. Middlesex crushed Warwickshire at Edgbaston where Kallicharran retired hurt after being struck by a ball from Daniel and the visitors had the advantage of three brisk half-centuries at the beginning of their innings.

Sussex remained six points ahead of Middlesex with a game in hand after gaining a splendid win at Guildford. Rain restricted the match to 33 overs and, chasing Surrey's 133, Sussex were floundering at 87 for 6. A magnificent partnership of 47 in 6½ overs between Parker and Barclay won them the match. They hit hard and ran brilliantly to bring Sussex victory with four balls to spare and showed that whatever else had been lost in a season which promised so much, Sussex were determined to win the John Player League.

Worcestershire devastated the Hampshire bowling. Ormrod and Patel put on 224 for the first wicket, a record for any wicket in the fourteen years of the league. Patel hit his maiden century in the league and Hampshire faced a formidable task. They attacked it bravely and some late hitting by Marshall and Parks nearly brought victory.

Kent slipped further down the table when Notts beat them with three overs to spare, Hassan and Rice shared an unbeaten stand of 123 for the second wicket.

Leicestershire beat Lancashire to draw level with them on 30 points. Clift, returning after his achilles tendon injury which had kept him out of action for most of the season, bowled splendidly. Garnham and Davison, in his benefit match, hit lustily after Leicestershire had started poorly.

Making his John Player League debut at Milton Keynes, Kapil Dev hit the second ball he received for 6. He and Willey added 64 in 8 overs as Northants chased Derbyshire's 233. Barnett and Wright put on 124 for Derbyshire's first wicket and Tunnicliffe hit 51 off 29 balls for a John Player League best score, but Larkins, Willey, Kapil Dev and Boyd-Moss hit Northants to victory with an over to spare.

18, 19 and 20 August

at Leicester
Pakistanis 132 for 7 dec (K. St. J. D. Emery 4 for 46) and 191 for 4 dec (Mudassar Nazar 103 not out)
England 'B' 131 for 3 dec and 72 for 3
Match drawn

This match was ruined by the weather. Cook of Leicestershire, a fine slow left-arm bowler, and Emery, who had a remarkable debut season in first-class cricket, showed to advantage. Mudassar hit his fourth century of the tour on the last morning. The main interest in the match lay in the selection of the England side. Players engaged in the NatWest semi-finals could not be used, but one still wondered at the selectors' policy and planning. After a moderate season was Roebuck really worth an England trial? And Neale? Could they really suggest that Gould had more to offer as wicket-keeper than Parks, David East or two or three others? One was becoming increasingly aware that after five Test matches the selectors and the England side were as uncertain as they had been at the start of the season. On the last day of this match came the news that the ban on the fifteen English players who had represented the South African Breweries in the pseudo-Test series was to stay. As Greig and Lamb were playing for England and Wessels was preparing to open for Australia, one could only conjecture what Gooch, Boycott, Les Taylor and the rest must be thinking. One of the reasons for the retention of the ban was to safeguard the future tours of England by the West Indies, particularly in 1984. Would West Indian cricket survive without a tour to England? Would their players maintain any form if they did not spend nine months of the year playing anywhere but in the West Indies?

NatWest Trophy – Semi-Finals

18 August

at Edgbaston

Yorkshire 216 for 9 (G. Boycott 51)
Warwickshire 219 for 3 (K. D. Smith 113, T. A. Lloyd 66)

Warwickshire won by 7 wickets
(*Man of the Match* – K. D. Smith)

18 and 19 August

at The Oval

Surrey 205 for 9 (A. R. Butcher 53, W. W. Daniel 4 for 24)
Middlesex 80 (S. T. Clarke 4 for 10)

Surrey won by 125 runs
(*Man of the Match* – S. T. Clarke)

A prompt start was possible at Edgbaston where Willis asked Yorkshire to bat when he won the toss, a natural reaction when a match begins at 10.00 am. Warwickshire soon reaped the benefit of winning the toss and of Willis' decision. It was the bounce that Small and Willis achieved that disconcerted the Yorkshiremen. Lumb pushed half-heartedly at Small and Lloyd, who fielded well throughout, took a tumbling catch at slip at the second attempt.

Athey was beaten on the back foot by a Willis delivery that was the first that the bowler had pitched well up. There was a fifteen minute stoppage for drizzle and Love was out, caught at slip, off the first ball bowled on the resumption. Hartley was wastefully run out by Kallicharran's throw and Yorkshire were 52 for 4. Boycott had survived against some fine bowling by Willis, but he had never dominated.

Stevenson made some lusty blows and then tried one too many and was bowled by Lethbridge. The bonus for Warwickshire was Alvin Kallicharran whose gentle off-

Above: *The NatWest semi-final at Edgbaston. Clouds lower, but Warwickshire are triumphant.* Below: *Love is caught at slip by Andy Lloyd.*

Above: *Warwickshire erupt. Athey is lbw to Willis.*
Below left: *The bowler that escaped the expected punishment. Kallicharran bowling his gentle but accurate off-breaks.*
Bairstow watches. Below right: *Boycott reluctantly lbw to Ferreira. The South African was Warwickshire's most successful bowler.*

breaks, aimed mainly at the leg-stump, went mostly unpunished, so confirming the Warwickshire trust in using him as their fifth bowler.

Boycott reached his fifty with a superb shot through the covers off the back foot off Ferreira. The South African exacted immediate revenge by having Boycott lbw although the batsman obviously considered that the ball was going down the leg-side. 99 for 6 and overs evaporating.

Bairstow and Carrick engaged in the most sensible stand of the innings and the post lunch period was most profitable for Yorkshire until Carrick missed an attempted pull at Kallicharran and was lbw. This was in the forty-sixth over, but, under the supervision of Bairstow the last 14 overs produced 65 runs and Yorkshire reached 216, a total far beyond their dreams in the minutes before lunch.

It soon became as nothing, however, as David Smith and Andy Lloyd with complete nonchalance dismissed any bowler that Illingworth confronted them with. Their pacing of the innings was always right and they suffered no alarms. By the time that Lloyd rather lazily flicked Carrick into the hands of mid-on, the score was 139 and Warwickshire were on their way to Lord's.

There was a tremble of apprehension through the Midlands when Kallicharran swept his first ball into the hands

Above: *Malcolm Marshall – the first to a hundred wickets.* Below: *Warwickshire are driven to victory.* Left: *Andy Lloyd and* (right) *David Smith.*

Sylvester Clarke – Man of the Match.

Monte Lynch. An innings of unusual restraint.

of Boycott at deep square-leg. Amiss, the years of accomplishment worn with ease, allayed any fears and Smith continued untroubled.

Smith reached a quite magnificent hundred and then went a little rash. He hit a six and sacrificed his wicket unnecessarily, but he deserved his ruch of blood and his award. Amiss and Humpage scored the remaining eleven and victory came with 27 balls to spare. It had been thoroughly deserved.

Play began 80 minutes late at The Oval and ended after only 14 overs during which Howarth had played at a wide one from Daniel and been caught behind.

Brearley had put Surrey in and must have wondered at the wisdom of his decision next morning as Butcher and Smith scored freely until Butcher was run out. Knight flittered very briefly, but Smith looked good until bowled by Edmonds. Edmonds and Emburey bowled superbly and Gatting contributed some impressive overs of medium pace swing, but Brearley erred in his reluctance to use Daniel early on. The West Indian finished with 4 for 24 and four overs short of his quota.

Cowans was disappointingly wild and fortunate not to be called for more than one wide.

Lynch was surprisingly subdued and it was left to Thomas to provide the fireworks. In spite of his blows, Surrey closed at 205 for 9, a score which would hold few terrors for Middlesex it seemed.

We were mistaken. In the first eleven overs of the Middlesex innings the match was decided in Surrey's favour.

Bowling very fiercely, Clarke sent back Brearley (caught behind), Tomlins (lbw), Slack (caught behind) and Gatting, taken at short leg.

Radley suggested durability, but Monkhouse bowled with a beautiful delivery that moved back off the seam. Emburey was well caught in the gully off a hard hit – Clarke was the catcher. Downton was superbly caught by Richards standing up to Monkhouse and Butcher, the last hope, skied a necessary slog to the square-leg area where Richards ran and caught him.

Middlesex had disintegrated and now only the Schweppes County Championship was within their grasp.

For Surrey, there were hopes that a fourth final in four years might prove lucky.

21, 22 and 23 August

at Old Trafford

Lancashire 120 for 3 dec (D. Lloyd 55)
Pakistanis 93 for 1 (Mansoor Akhtar 53 not out)
Match drawn

21, 23 and 24 August

at Chesterfield

Derbyshire 300 for 5 dec (P. N. Kirsten 105 not out, J. G. Wright 79, G. Miller 52) and 0 for 0
Sussex 202 for 4 dec (P. W. G. Parker 58 not out)
Match drawn
Derbyshire 5 pts, Sussex 4 pts

at Colchester

Essex 502 (K. S. McEwan 128, B. R. Hardie 86, S. Turner 83, G. A. Gooch 72, D. R. Pringle 54, S. P. Sutcliffe 5 for 131)
Warwickshire 249 (P. Smith 68, K. D. Smith 50, N. Phillip 5 for 80) and 113 for 4
Match drawn
Essex 8 pts, Warwickshire 4 pts

at Swansea

Nottinghamshire 318 (R. J. Hadlee 91, S. B. Hassan 73, W. W. Davis 7 for 101) and 202 for 5 (C. E. B. Rice 54)
Glamorgan 249 (A. Jones 103, D. A. Francis 58, E. E. Hemmings 6 for 76)
Match drawn
Glamorgan 6 pts, Nottinghamshire 6 pts

at Folkestone

Kent 324 for 6 dec (M. R. Benson 81, R. A. Woolmer 67, C. S. Cowdrey 54) and 154 for 2 (M. R. Benson 59 not out, G. W. Johnson 59 not out)
Gloucestershire 303 for 7 dec (B. C. Broad 97, Sadiq Mohammad 90)

Match drawn
Kent 7 pts, Gloucestershire 6 pts

at Lord's

Yorkshire 182 (D. L. Bairstow 54 not out, S. N. Hartley 54) and 75 for 1
Middlesex 461 for 5 dec (R. O. Butcher 197, M. W. Gatting 141)

Match drawn
Middlesex 8 pts, Yorkshire 2 pts

at Northampton

Hampshire 268 (C. G. Greenidge 62, N. E. J. Pocock 53, D. S. Steele 6 for 59) and 0 for 1
Northamptonshire 377 for 8 dec (A. J. Lamb 140, P. Willey 51)

Match drawn
Northamptonshire 7 pts, Hampshire 6 pts

at Taunton

Leicestershire 364 for 5 dec (D. I. Gower 111, N. E. Briers 91 not out, R. A. Cobb 63, R. W. Tolchard 50) and 189 for 1 dec (N. E. Briers 93 not out, J. C. Balderstone 88)
Somerset 216 (N. A. Felton 59, G. J. Parsons 4 for 88) and 177 (N. G. B. Cook 7 for 63)

Leicestershire won by 160 runs
Leicestershire 24 pts, Somerset 4 pts

at Worcester

Surrey 536 for 7 dec (A. R. Butcher 162, D. M. Smith 160, R. D. V. Knight 95 not out) and 36 for 0
Worcestershire 305 for 4 dec (D. N. Patel 133, J. A. Ormrod 57)

Match drawn
Surrey 5 pts, Worcestershire 4 pts

Rain so ruined the last day of matches that play was possible to any great extent only at Taunton where Leicestershire snatched victory thanks to a career best by Nick Cook and closed the gap on Middlesex to 31 points.

Leicestershire took full advantage of a good wicket to collect full batting bonus points. There was an elegant, and welcome century from David Gower and good contributions from Cobb, Tolchard and Briers. Briers had the distinction of being not out in the nineties in both innings when his captain declared. Somerset were rather lack-lustre and Balderstone and Briers scored at nearly five and a half an over as Leicestershire sought quick runs in their second innings. The opening partnership was worth 189 in approximately 2½ hours. Somerset needed 338 to win, but as soon as Cook joined the attack their troubles began and Leicestershire's positive approach gave them a deserved victory.

Middlesex were less fortunate. They bowled out a less than impressive Yorkshire on the Saturday, Hartley and, inevitably, Bairstow being the only batsmen to demonstrate the necessary application. On Monday, Butcher and Gatting were in dynamic form and despatched the ball to all parts at Lord's. They came together at 68 for 3 and when they were parted the score was 305. They were together for 60 overs. Butcher, who hit six sixes and eighteen fours, made a career best 197 in under five hours. It was thrilling stuff and with Gatting at his most authoratative and Embury hitting lustily, Middlesex reached 400 in 100 overs. Rain came on the last day as Boycott was digging in.

There was only a few hours play on the last day at Old Trafford after two blank days.

An avalanche of runs at Worcester. Butcher and Smith put on 225 in 70 overs for the second Surrey wicket and then Smith and Knight added 122 for the third. Smith reached a career best 160. Facing the massive score of 536 for 7, Worcestershire were undaunted and Patel's hundred, an innings of quiet charm, suggested a draw which rain confirmed.

Rain also brought a draw at Colchester where Essex were in a most favourable position. Gooch and Hardie began with 130, the hundred up in 62 minutes, Pringle made his top score for the county and Ken McEwan hit 128 in 140 minutes with four sixes and thirteen fours. One wondered at the captaincy of Willis who allowed McEwan to ravage his attack without having to face Small or Willis himself. Turner hit some glorious blows after tea and Essex were out of sight. The wicket began to turn on the second day and Warwickshire had to follow-on. They were struggling a second time when the rain arrived.

Bob Woolmer returned to the Kent side for the first time since he sustained facial injuries against Hampshire. He had, in fact, played in the John Player League game against Essex at Canterbury when he batted number nine, but this was his 'official' return. He did admirably, surviving the early loss of the out-of-form Taylor and batting with confidence. Benson was again in splendid form with fifties in each innings. Gloucestershire responded well through Sadiq and Broad, but Cowdrey broke a little finger and Woolmer had a recurrence of a shoulder injury to handicap Kent while Romaines retired hurt before scoring with a badly bruised thumb.

Kirsten set up a Derbyshire record with his seventh championship century of the season in the rain-doomed match at Chesterfield in which Wright and Miller also displayed their class.

Richard Hadlee continued his excellent batting form which must surely make him the all-rounder of the season. The reliable Hassan, the one batsman of consistency throughout Nottinghamshire's traumas, gave stolid support. Davis had a career best bowling performance for Glamorgan and then came another century for Alan Jones whose non-selection for a Test match in his twenty-five-year career stands like a monument of mockery to generations of selectors.

Allan Lamb, who had a lean season by previous standards, hit a fine century for Northants which, combined with David Steele's productive left-arm spin, put his side well on top against Hampshire. There was no play on the last day due to rain.

John Player League
22 August

at Chesterfield

Derbyshire 151 for 8
Sussex 155 for 7 (C. M. Wells 57)

Sussex (4 pts) won by 3 wickets

at Colchester

Essex 299 for 4 (K. S. McEwan 156 not out, B. R. Hardie 75)
Warwickshire 301 for 6 (G. W. Humpage 74, K. D. Smith 73, T. A. Lloyd 66)

Warwickshire (4 pts) won by 4 wickets

at Swansea

Glamorgan 89 for 4
Nottinghamshire 90 for 1

Nottinghamshire (4 pts) won by 9 wickets

at Folkestone

Kent 271 for 5 (C. J. Tavare 90, N. R. Taylor 74)
Gloucestershire 165 (D. L. Underwood 4 for 15)

Kent (4 pts) won by 106 runs

at Lord's

Middlesex 198 for 6 (J. M. Brearley 73)
Yorkshire 177 for 9 (S. N. Hartley 67)

Middlesex (4 pts) won by 21 runs

at Northampton

Northamptonshire 205 for 8 (W. Larkins 51)
Hampshire 123 (T. M. Lamb 5 for 25)

Northamptonshire (4 pts) won by 82 runs

at Taunton

Leicestershire 180 for 8 (D. I. Gower 58)
Somerset 183 for 4 (B. C. Rose 54)

Somerset (4 pts) won by 6 wickets

at Worcester

Surrey 156 (A. R. Butcher 72)
Worcestershire 65 for 2

Worcestershire (4 pts) won on faster scoring rate

Sussex brought themselves to within one match of winning the John Player League when they won at Chesterfield in a game restricted to 28 overs. Barclay asked Derbyshire to bat and his bowlers, aided by some good catching, whittled away at the Derbyshire batting, only Wood and Anderson defying them for long. At 113 for 2, with Colin Wells in control, Sussex were cruising to victory, but Oldham dismissed Parker and le Roux in the same over and Newman brilliantly caught and bowled Wells. Wood then bowled Greig and had Phillipson caught at 'fly' slip. Barclay played with a determination befitting to the captain of prospective champions and swept Sussex home with three balls to spare.

Middlesex maintained their second place with a strange win over Yorkshire. Yorkshire were 84 for 8 chasing Middlesex's 198, but Hartley and Ramage put on a record ninth wicket stand of 88 to lift the total to 172. It was still too far short of the target and Middlesex won with ease.

Bottom of the table Warwickshire won a sensational victory at Colchester and so ended Essex's hopes of retaining the title. Essex tore the Warwickshire attack to shreds. McEwan and Hardie added 147 in 22 overs. McEwan hit five sixes and seventeen fours in his second century of the week-end. His final 55 runs came off 18 balls and he took 24 off the last over. Ferreira had the unwanted league record of conceding 85 runs off his 8 overs. Essex, it seemed, had won. Warwickshire, morale high from having reached the NatWest Final, had other ideas. David Smith and Lloyd started voraciously. 135 came in 20 overs. Three wickets fell, but Humpage continued the onslaught. Ferreira exacted a small revenge by being there at the close as Paul Smith hit the third ball of the last over for four and victory. Warwickshire had beaten the previous best score by a side batting second in the John Player League by 40 runs.

There was a ten over after tea slog at Swansea and rain ended the day early at Worcester and provided Worcestershire with their first home win of the season.

Tim Lamb, omitted from the championship side, took three Hampshire wickets in his second over. He returned to break the Marshall-Cowley partnership and he finished with 5 for 25. Earlier, Larkins, Allan Lamb and Cook had been the main run providers for the home side.

In a thirty-seven-over match at Taunton, Somerset won off the fourth ball of the last over when Marks turned Clift for four. Somerset had been easing to victory when Rose and Roebuck put on 89 for the first wicket, but Richards and Botham were caught off skiers and the scoring rate declined.

Kent overwhelmed Gloucestershire thanks to an innings of 90 in 79 minutes by Chris Tavare. He hit fourteen fours and a six and he and Benson added 100 for the third wicket off 11 overs. Taylor and Tavare had added 80 in 11 overs for the second wicket and it was good to see Taylor recapturing form and reaching his first fifty in the league.

25, 26 and 27 August

at Colchester

Essex 140 (N. G. B. Cook 6 for 17) and 308 (K. R. Pont 89, G. A. Gooch 88, N. G. B. Cook 6 for 113)
Leicestershire 246 (J. C. Balderstone 114 not out) and 203 for 4 (B. F. Davison 110 not out)

Leicestershire won by 6 wickets
Leicestershire 21 pts, Essex 2 pts

at Cardiff

Glamorgan 279 (A. L. Jones 71, H. Morris 55, I. A. Greig 5 for 103) and 70 for 2 dec
Sussex 49 for 2 dec and 248 for 7 (P. W. G. Parker 68, A. M. Green 59, G. S. le Roux 50, R. C. Ontong 4 for 57)

Match drawn
Sussex 4 pts, Glamorgan 3 pts

at Bournemouth

Gloucestershire 272 (B. Dudleston 111, A. J. Hignell 63, A. W. Stovold 50) and 84 (M. D. Marshall 5 for 33)
Hampshire 294 (T. E. Jesty 121, M. D. Marshall 54) and 64 for 2

Hampshire won by 8 wickets
Hampshire 23 pts, Gloucestershire 7 pts

at Folkestone

Kent 300 for 7 dec (D. G. Aslett 82, A. P. E. Knott 69 not out) and 212 for 8 dec (N. R. Taylor 56, B. J. Griffiths 5 for 71)
Northamptonshire 192 (W. Larkins 68, K. B. S. Jarvis 5 for 94) and 273 for 8 (W. Larkins 71, G. Sharp 58 not out, R. J. Boyd-Moss 54)

Match drawn
Kent 8 pts, Northamptonshire 4 pts

at Blackpool

Worcestershire 145 (P. J. W. Allott 4 for 32) and 148 for 8 (D. J. Humphries 55 not out)
Lancashire 277 (D. P. Hughes 93, S. J. O'Shaughnessy 58, S. P. Perryman 6 for 49)

Match drawn
Lancashire 7 pts, Worcestershire 4 pts

at Lord's

Middlesex 276 (W. N. Slack 79, K. S. Mackintosh 6 for 61) and 157 for 2 dec (W. N. Slack 71 not out, K. P. Tomlins 51)
Surrey 273 for 4 dec (G. P. Howarth 112, A. R. Butcher 82) and 102 (J. E. Emburey 4 for 24)

Middlesex won by 58 runs
Middlesex 18 pts, Surrey 5 pts

A third wicket stand of 146 between Barry Dudleston, who made his first century for Gloucestershire, and Alastair Hignell, who made his highest score of the summer, was ended when Hignell fell to Southern. At that time Gloucestershire were 244 for 4. Then, in an after tea spell, Malcolm Marshall had Dudleston lbw for his hundredth wicket of the season. Stephenson followed next ball and Shepherd became the third victim as Gloucestershire lost their last six wickets for 11 runs. Malcolm Marshall's achievement in becoming the first bowler to take a hundred wickets in the season won him the Swanton Trophy presented by *The Daily Telegraph*. It was a magnificent performance by the twenty-four-year old West Indian, the outstanding bowler of the season.

Hampshire ended the first day badly on 63 for 5. The next day Trevor Jesty, who should have been with the England side at Leeds had the selectors done their job properly, hit his sixth hundred of the season and he and Marshall added 81 for the seventh wicket. Tremlett had first helped Jesty stop the rot with a stand of 92 for the sixth wicket.

When Gloucestershire batted again they were totally destroyed by the bowling of Marshall, Emery, Jesty and Southern and the home side won with ease.

Rain fractured the match at Cardiff. Hugh Morris hit a maiden fifty, Ian Greig, dropped from the England side, took five wickets, Paul Parker scored briskly and elegantly, and Wells reached his thousand runs for the season. Sussex needed 301 in 195 minutes and the target looked possible while Parker was batting, but when he fell to Ontong Sussex settled for a draw and Glamorgan were thwarted once more.

Steve Perryman had his best bowling performance since joining Worcestershire and David Hughes batted well again, this time aided encouragingly by O'Shaughnessy, but Humphries saved the day for Worcestershire with a dogged batting performance, saving his side from defeat which had looked certain at 66 for 7. Warner gave him able assistance.

Kent's young side were denied victory by George Sharp, the Northants wicket-keeper. Needing 321 in 4½ hours, Northants slumped to 208 for 7, mainly due to the accuracy of Ellison, but Sharp played positively and the match was drawn.

The slow left-arm spin of Nick Cook demoralised Essex on the opening day at Colchester and the home side were bundled out in just under 60 overs. Acfield threatened to give Essex parity, but Chris Balderstone played a stout innings of 114, carrying his bat and steering Leicestershire to a lead of 106. Essex batted better at the second attempt with Gooch recapturing form and Keith Pont, so often unjustifiably in the shadows, hit a fine 89 before being last man out. Once more it was Cook who was the main scourge of the Essex batsmen, nagging away on a length and turning the ball just enough to disconcert. Here is a fine prospect who has learned the game by hard work at Leicester. His match figures of 12 for 130 were just reward for fine bowling.

Leicestershire were left 115 minutes in which to score 203. Brian Davison opened with Balderstone and was soon showing magnificent form with his powerful driving. He hit five sixes and five fours and with Roberts, who batted at number four and scored 42, put on 75 in 8 overs of spin. Ray East was unable to show anything like the control that Cook had demonstrated and suffered accordingly. Leicestershire reached their target with sixteen deliveries in hand, a glorious victory which they believed had helped them to come to within easy reach of Middlesex at the top. The news from Lord's came as a shock to them.

Mike Brearley created a surprise when, shortly before the beginning of the match, he asked Fred Titmus, three months short of his fiftieth birthday, if he would play as he believed that the wicket would take spin. Titmus agreed and borrowed kit from his former Middlesex colleagues.

Middlesex batted rather laboriously. Rain restricted play on the second day and Surrey seized the advantage when Howarth and Butcher finished the day still together with the score at 180. They added only eight more runs the following morning and Knight declared three runs behind. Brearley, Slack and Tomlins hit briskly and, to the amazement of all, Brearley declared leaving Surrey 135 minutes in which to make 161.

His assessment of the situation was as precise as ever. Middlesex bowled out Surrey in less than two hours. Emburey (4 for 24), Edmonds (3 for 24) and Titmus (3 for 43) had spun them to defeat as Brearley had anticipated and Middlesex held a 28-point lead over Leicestershire at the top of the Schweppes County Championship table.

THIRD CORNHILL TEST MATCH
England v. Pakistan

England omitted Ian Greig and included Graeme Fowler, the Lancashire left-handed opening batsman, a welcome inclusion after the summer of aridity in opening batsmen. Vic Marks was also included in the side to the exclusion of Hemmings and Jackman retained his place when Pringle reported unfit having cricked his back when stretching after writing a letter. Willis returned to captain the side.

With Sarfraz and Tahir injured, Pakistan created a surprise by including Ehtesham-ud-Din who had taken fourteen wickets in his three Test matches against India in 1980. A somewhat portly veteran seam bowler, Ehtesham-ud-Din had bowled a few overs in the rain-ruined game with Lancashire and had had a very successful season in the Bolton League, but he hardly remained a threat at Test level. Majid Khan was included in the side for the first time in the series and Sikhander Bakht returned.

Imran won the toss and elected to bat. The wicket looked brown and mild in pace. Pakistan had reached 16 without any alarms when a short pitched ball from Botham was diverted into Mohsin's face and from there down the leg side where Taylor leapt to catch the ball. Mohsin was adjudged caught behind the wicket, the ball having brushed his glove before cutting his chin, an injury which needed stitching.

The Pakistanis were not happy with the decision, but they could have no doubts about the fall of the next wicket in the following over when Mansoor lamely fended a lifter from Willis into the hands of short-leg.

Mudassar, revealing something of his true ability, and Javed played with great common sense and mixed watchful defence with flowing drives and vicious pulls off wayward deliveries. Runs came smoothly. Marks bowled some rather innocuous first overs in Test cricket and Gatting swung a few gently.

A hundred runs had been added when Mudassar was out most unluckily. He drove a ball from Botham against his boot from where it spun back on to the stumps.

Jackman had been brought into the attack and proceeded to bowl 35 overs unchanged. His accurate medium pace proved effective both as run stopper and wicket taker. The wicket gave him just a little assistance.

Zaheer hit two fours and then perished to a dreadful shot. Majid Khan, who looked to have so much time to play his shots, became the highest scoring Pakistan batsman in Test cricket, but his stay was all too brief.

The clouds lower and the ball moves menacingly.

England's new opener Graeme Fowler strikes purposefully. Pakistan fielders are close to despondency.

After four hours of restraint Javed was caught in the gully by Fowler who fielded well all day. Wasim Bari played recklessly and was bowled when he aimed an unforgivable swipe. The tail was propped by the wonderfully disciplined Imran. Few men have responded better to the responsibility of leadership than the Pakistan all-rounder. He and Sikhander put on an invaluable fifty and Imran spoiled Jackman's figures by hitting him for 14 in one over.

There was an early disappointment for Fowler, and England, when the Lancashire opener missed a straight ball from Ehtesham-ud-Din and was bowled.

Gatting, in need of runs in Test cricket to dispel the growing opinion that he is not of international quality, and Tavare added 50 before Gatting played back to Imran and was lbw. Next over from Imran saw Tavare turn a lifter into short-leg's hands and two overs later Lamb mis-hooked to square-leg. In nine balls, Imran had taken 3 for 2.

Botham and Gower repaired the damage in a much more purposeful manner than they had done at Lord's. Botham hit about him splendidly. For once Qadir was mastered and Ehtesham-ud-Din was punished before retiring from the field injured.

Right: *Jackman bowls Wasim Bari. No one could fail to applaud the Surrey bowler's sustained accuracy and aggression; not everyone approved of his dramatic gestures.* Below: *Sikhander runs out Randall.*

Gower escapes. Miandad misses a sharp chance off Qadir. Below: Abdul Qadir bowling at Leeds. It was probably his least successful match of the tour.

The fun ended when Botham was caught at long-on by Haroon who was substituting for Mansoor and took three catches in different positions. Randall was run out after a stop-start performance and Marks shouldered arms to a Qadir leg-break which turned out to be a googly and was bowled, a wicket of delight for the bowler and indignity for the batsman.

Taylor batted with determination, but both he and Gower were out before the close. Jackman and Willis resumed for England on the third morning, but Jackman fell to the second ball of the day. England trailed by 19.

The first ball of the Pakistan innings saw Mohsin aim a totally irresponsible drive at Willis – a Sunday League shot. Taylor held a fine catch off the snick down the leg-side, a dismissal which, once more, was not to the Pakistanis' liking. Three runs were scored by Mansoor and Mudassar had the strike for the first time. He tucked back to a short delivery and steered the ball into Botham's hands at third slip. Willis one over. Pakistan 3 for 2.

Javed nursed Mansoor through a difficult period. The less experienced batsman was inclined to rashness and Javed constantly proffered advice in an effort to effect control. Javed himself batted splendidly. Watchful defence was punctuated by some exquisite drives of the very highest quality. Javed has no superior in ability, only in temperament.

He fell to Botham's outswinger launching an unwise drive, he edged and Taylor dived to take a breath-taking catch in front of first slip. For Javed it was another sinful waste, and on the eve of lunch.

Pakistan's lunch was made more inedible when Zaheer

perished almost immediately, lbw to Botham. Zaheer had made a brief and exciting contribution at Lord's, but his Test record over the past few years must suggest that his days as an international player are coming to a close.

There was more success for England after lunch. Mansoor was caught at third slip and Majid was caught at first slip off an attempted cut, and it was possible that we had seen his last Test innings.

Imran must have shuddered at the sinful waste of his batsmen. As at Edgbaston, they had had the match in their grasp and frittered it away. Inevitably, it was Imran himself who showed the necessary application. He lost Bari and Qadir, but Sikhander stayed with him in another profitable stand and played commendably. It was sad that his innings should end controversially. He was given out caught bat and pad by umpire Constant, and indeed the decision seemed a poor one. Imran was out next over after his valiant innings and England needed 219 to win.

The Pakistanis complained bitterly about the umpiring, and about Constant in particular. They had some cause for grievance, but as I wrote in the pages of *Pelham Cricket Year* last year, the only improvements or restoration of values that can be effected in the game are those which find their roots in the hearts of the players. On the fourth morning, shortly before lunch, Javed behaved disgracefully when his ridiculous claim for a slip catch against Tavare was denied. Earlier in the season one had seen a slip fieldsman in a county match claim a catch and persist until umpire Constant gave the decision in his favour when the rest of the field and the batsmen knew that the ball had bounced

Above: *Bob Willis. A decisive opening over in the second innings.* Below: *A surprised and unhappy return to Test cricket. Ehtesham-ud-Din is bowled off his face by Botham for a 'duck'.*

Mansoor caught bat-pad by Gatting.

some two feet in front of the catcher. Pressurising the umpire has become a sullying part of the game. It must be remembered that every time an umpire gives a bad decision, he has done so because a player has appealed in the first place, often when he knows well that the batsman was not out. Panels and neutrals are not the answer to bad decisions, only attitudes.

Tavare and Fowler batted well in an opening stand of 103 and Fowler, in particular, played with an assurance and aggression that marked him as a batsman of character.

Tavare played with confidence until he edged Imran to slip, but he had seemed to have done enough and England

Below: *Mohsin Khan caught Taylor, bowled Botham via his chin.* Right: *David Constant, a man at the centre of a storm, tests the light.*

Above and below: *Sikhander Bakht stands in amazement as he is given out caught bat-pad by Gatting off Marks.*

Imran Khan. An all-rounder and captain of heroic stature.

Javed Miandad hooks Botham for four. A batsman of great charm and vigour, but a temperament of fallibility.

were well set for victory. Gatting had an unhappy start, but he played with resolution. The batsmen rejected the offer to leave the field because of declining light and it improved. Thirteen runs later, Fowler drove rather lazily at Mudassar and was caught behind. He had raised English spirits with his fine display.

In Mudassar's next over Lamb was lbw playing across the line. Gower went in Mudassar's following over when he pushed tentatively at the away swinger and was caught behind. In 16 deliveries Mudassar had taken 3 for 11 and England were 187 for 4.

Pakistan now breathed hope where none had been and Imran bowled at a furious pace. He had the shuffling Gatting lbw and Randall was adjudged out the same way in the same over although he was forward.

In under an hour five wickets had fallen for 21 runs. It

THIRD CORNHILL TEST MATCH – ENGLAND v. PAKISTAN
26, 27, 28, 30 and 31 August 1982 at Headingley, Leeds

PAKISTAN

	FIRST INNINGS		SECOND INNINGS	
Mohsin Khan	c Taylor, b Botham	10	c Taylor, b Willis	0
Mudassar Nazar	b Botham	65	c Botham, b Willis	0
Mansoor Akhtar	c Gatting, b Willis	0	c Randall, b Botham	39
Javed Miandad	c Fowler, b Willis	54	c Taylor, b Botham	52
Zaheer Abbas	c Taylor, b Jackman	8	lbw, b Botham	4
Majid Khan	lbw, b Jackman	21	c Gower, b Botham	10
Imran Khan†	not out	67	c Randall, b Botham	46
Wasim Bari*	b Jackman	23	c Taylor, b Willis	7
Abdul Qadir	c Willis, b Botham	5	b Jackman	17
Sikhander Bakht	c Tavare, b Willis	7	c Gatting, b Marks	7
Ehtesham-ud-Din	b Botham	0	not out	0
Extras	b 1, lb 7, w 4, nb 3	15	lb 6, w 4, nb 7	17
		275		**199**

ENGLAND

	FIRST INNINGS		SECOND INNINGS	
C. J. Tavare	c sub (Haroon), b Imran	22	c Majid, b Imran	33
G. Fowler	b Ehtesham-ud-Din	9	c Bari, b Mudassar	86
M. W. Gatting	lbw, b Imran	25	lbw, b Imran	25
A. J. Lamb	c Mohsin, b Imran	0	lbw, b Mudassar	4
D. I. Gower	c sub (Haroon), b Sikhander	74	c Bari, b Mudassar	7
I. T. Botham	c sub (Haroon), b Sikhander	57	c Majid, b Mudassar	4
D. W. Randall	run out	8	lbw, b Imran	0
V. J. Marks	b Qadir	7	not out	12
R. W. Taylor*	c Javed, b Imran	18	not out	6
R. D. Jackman	c Mohsin, b Imran	11		
R. G. D. Willis†	not out	1		
Extras	b 4, lb 10, w 2, nb 8	24	b 19, lb 16, w 1, nb 6	42
		256	(for 7 wkts)	**219**

	O	M	R	W		O	M	R	W
Willis	26	6	76	3		19	3	55	3
Botham	24.5	9	70	4		30	8	74	5
Jackman	37	14	74	3		28	11	41	1
Marks	5	—	23	—		2	1	8	1
Gatting	8	2	17	—		2	1	4	—

	O	M	R	W		O	M	R	W
Imran Khan	25.2	7	49	5		30.2	8	66	3
Ehtesham-ud-Din	14	4	46	1					
Sikhander Bakht	24	5	47	2		20	4	40	—
Abdul Qadir	22	5	87	1		8	2	16	—
Mudassar Nazar	4	1	3	—		22	7	55	4

FALL OF WICKETS
1–16, 2–19, 3–119, 4–128, 5–160, 6–168, 7–207, 8–224, 9–274
1–0, 2–3, 3–81, 4–85, 5–108, 6–115, 7–128, 8–169, 9–199

FALL OF WICKETS
1–15, 2–67, 3–69, 4–77, 5–146, 6–159, 7–170, 8–209, 9–255
1–103, 2–168, 3–172, 4–187, 5–189, 6–189, 7–199

England won by 3 wickets

England v. Pakistan – Test Match Averages

ENGLAND BATTING

	M	Inns	NOs	Runs	HS	Av	100s	50s
C. J. Tavare	3	6		216	82	36.00		1
D. I. Gower	3	6		197	74	32.83		2
D. W. Randall	3	6		168	105	28.00	1	
I. T. Botham	3	6		163	69	27.15		2
R. W. Taylor	3	6	2	108	54	27.00		1
M. W. Gatting	3	6	1	111	32*	22.20		
E. E. Hemmings	2	4		41	19	10.25		
R. D. Jackman	2	3		28	17	9.33		
A. J. Lamb	3	6		48	33	8.00		
I. A. Greig	2	4		26	14	6.50		

Also batted: R. G. D. Willis 0*, 28* and 1* (two Tests); (one Test) – G. Fowler 9 and 86, V. J. Marks 7 and 12*, G. Miller 47 and 5, D. R. Pringle 5 and 14.

PAKISTAN BATTING

	M	Inns	NOs	Runs	HS	Av	100s	50s
Mohsin Khan	3	6	1	310	200	62.00	1	
Imran Khan	3	5	1	212	67*	53.00		2
Javed Miandad	3	6	1	178	54	35.60		2
Mansoor Akhtar	3	5		154	58	30.80		
Wasim Bari	3	5	2	82	24*	27.33		
Zaheer Abbas	3	5		131	75	26.20		1
Tahir Naqqash	2	3		53	39	17.66		
Mudassar Nazar	3	5		85	65	17.00		
Abdul Qadir	3	5	1	56	18*	14.00		
Sikhander Bakht	2	4	1	16	7	5.33		

Also batted: (one Test) Ehtesham-ud-Din 0 and 0*, Haroon Rashid 1, Majid Khan 21 and 10, Wasim Raja 26 and 16, Sarfraz Nawaz played in one Test but did not bat.

ENGLAND BOWLING

	Overs	Mds	Runs	Wkts	Av	Best	5/inn
R. G. D. Willis	74	14	222	10	22.20	3/55	
I. T. Botham	150.5	33	478	18	26.55	5/74	1
I. A. Greig	31.2	6	114	4	28.50	4/53	
R. D. Jackman	105	30	247	8	30.87	4/110	
E. E. Hemmings	56.1	12	149	3	49.66	2/56	

Bowled in one Test: M. W. Gatting 10-3-21-0; V. J. Marks 7-1-31-1; G. Miller 9.4-2-27-2; D. R. Pringle 26-9-62-0.

PAKISTAN BOWLING

	Overs	Mds	Runs	Wkts	Av	Best	5/inn
Mudassar Nazar	54	18	104	10	10.40	6/32	1
Tahir Naqqash	52	20	117	7	16.71	5/40	1
Imran Khan	178.1	48	390	21	18.57	7/52	2
Abdul Qadir	160.5	48	406	10	40.60	4/39	
Sikhander Bakht	75	19	179	3	59.66	2/47	

Bowled in one Test: Ehtesham-ud-Din 14-4-46-1; Wasim Raja 2.3-2-0-1; Sarfraz Nawaz 37-9-78-3.

ENGLAND CATCHES
12—R. W. Taylor; 3—M. W. Gatting, D. W. Randall, C. J. Tavare and R. G. D. Willis; 2—D. I. Gower and E. E. Hemmings; 1—I. T. Botham, G. Fowler, A. J. Lamb and G. Miller

PAKISTAN CATCHES
8—Wasim Bari; 7—Haroon Rashid (four as sub); 4—Javed Miandad and Mohsin Khan; 2—Majid Khan and Mansoor Akhtar; 1—Mudassar Nazar, Abdul Qadir and Sarfraz Nawaz

was close to being seven; Botham survived a hard caught and bowled chance to Mudassar and Marks was all but bowled by the same bowler. Bad light rescued England who were still 29 runs short of victory with four wickets standing.

There was only forty minutes play necessary on the last morning, but a crowd of some 3,000 watched the contest which remained finely balanced until the very end. Only nine runs had been added to the overnight score when Mudassar had Botham taken at slip, but Taylor batted with an efficiency and confidence that mocked some others in the match and, with Marks having some good fortune, England were steered to victory.

Imran was named Man of the Match and Man of the Series, and none could argue with either award, but they were small compensation for Pakistan who considered that they had been beaten by an inferior team and that they themselves had contributed largely to their own defeat. That was very true. In the first and third Tests they had sacrificed wickets with some dreadful shots, temperamentally they had failed where technically they were superior.

In the final Test they could also reflect on conceding 66 extras, not all of these could be blamed on the wicket-keeper, but, in truth, Wasim Bari did not have a good time behind the stumps. He did not miss chances, but in the basic requirements of keeping wicket, he seemed past his best.

In spite of the acrimony over the umpiring, one can only remember this series with gratitude and the Pakistanis with a sense of joy. Imran was an inspiration and his side bubbled with excitement in their desire to win. They brought to the games with the counties a commitment which has been sadly lacking from touring teams of recent years and they deserve the highest praise for making a tourist v. country game something like the attraction it had been in former years.

They brought to us the wiles of Abdul Qadir, the elegance of Mohsin Khan, the supreme ability and dedication of Imran Khan and much else for which those of us who were privileged to watch them will long be grateful.

Rival captains. A cheerful Willis and a rueful Imran interviewed by Peter West.

28, 30 and 31 August

at Bristol
Gloucestershire 240 (A. J. Hignell 72, Sadiq Mohammad 57, H. R. Moseley 4 for 50) and 328 for 6 (Sadiq Mohammad 66, B. C. Broad 65, A. J. Wright 65)
Somerset 438 for 5 dec (B. C. Rose 173 not out, P. A. Slocombe 78, P. M. Roebuck 63, I. V. A. Richards 58)

Match drawn
Somerset 7 pts, Gloucestershire 3 pts

at Bournemouth
Hampshire 255 (T. E. Jesty 109) and 167 for 8 dec (T. E. Jesty 58, M. C. J. Nicholas 51)
Yorkshire 196 (G. Boycott 72, S. N. Hartley 51, M. D. Marshall 6 for 41) and 217 for 8 (J. W. Southern 5 for 106)

Match drawn
Hampshire 6 pts, Yorkshire 5 pts

at Old Trafford
Kent 159 (P. J. W. Allott 5 for 58) and 218 for 5 dec (D. G. Aslett 60, E. A. Baptiste 51 not out)
Lancashire 105 for 2 dec and 247 for 6 (D. Lloyd 103, D. P. Hughes 63 not out)

Match drawn
Lancashire 4 pts, Kent 1 pt

at Northampton
Leicestershire 263 (B. F. Davison 68, D. S. Steele 5 for 50) and 186 for 7 dec (R. A. Cobb 50 not out)
Northamptonshire 226 (G. Cook 56, J. F. Steele 5 for 45) and 147 for 7

Match drawn
Leicestershire 7 pts, Northamptonshire 4 pts

at Trent Bridge
Nottinghamshire 400 for 5 dec (C. E. B. Rice 144, S. B. Hassan 77, B. N. French 67 not out) and 112 for 4 dec
Derbyshire 251 for 4 dec (B. Wood 124 not out) and 99 for 7

Match drawn
Nottinghamshire 5 pts, Derbyshire 5 pts

at The Oval
Essex 276 (K. R. Pont 75) and 281 for 4 (G. A. Gooch 140, K. W. R. Fletcher 60 not out)
Surrey 304 (A. R. Butcher 90, G. P. Howarth 76, D. L. Acfield 4 for 76)

Match drawn
Surrey 7 pts, Essex 5 pts

at Hove
Middlesex 304 for 9 dec (J. M. Brearley 58, R. G. P. Ellis 50, I. A. Greig 4 for 85) and 198 for 3 dec (J. M. Brearley 100 not out, R. G. P. Ellis 55)
Sussex 251 for 6 dec (J. R. T. Barclay 64, I. A. Greig 55) and 254 for 7 (A. M. Green 99, G. D. Mendis 66)

Sussex won by 3 wickets
Sussex 21 pts, Middlesex 5 pts

at Edgbaston
Worcestershire 368 (Younis Ahmed 110, A. E. Warner 67, T. S. Curtis 51, A. M. Ferreira 5 for 109) and 222 for 4 dec (M. J. Weston 63, P. A. Neale 60 not out)
Warwickshire 250 for 3 dec (A. I. Kallicharran 109 not out, D. L. Amiss 54) and 274 for 9 (T. A. Lloyd 120, D. N. Patel 5 for 76)

Match drawn
Warwickshire 6 pts, Worcestershire 5 pts

The fight at the top of the table saw Leicestershire edge two points closer to Middlesex although Leicestershire were denied victory at Northampton by an hour and a quarter-long stand between Sharp and David Steele. Steele had been a thorn in Leicestershire's side in the first innings with his left-arm spin, but his brother John had proved equally effective with the same manner of bowling for Leicestershire. Tolchard made a generous declaration when he allowed Northants three hours in which to attempt to make 224. His gamble was rewarded when shortly after tea Northants stood at 91 for 6, but then came the stand between Steele and Sharp and Leicestershire had to be content with seven points.

Mike Brearley had a personal triumph in the game at Hove with an unbeaten century in the second innings and Richard Ellis, suggesting he might be a future Middlesex captain, batted impressively. Brearley asked Sussex to make 252 in three hours and fortunes fluctuated. A wonderful opening stand of 168 between Mendis and Green put Sussex on course for victory. Green was quite magnificent and it was thrilling to see a young, uncapped player respond so excitingly to a challenge. Green was caught behind one short of his century, one of Daniel's three victims in as many overs, and, in all Sussex lost seven wickets in eight overs. Undeterred, they still pressed for victory though they needed 54 in less than six overs when le Roux fell to Emburey. They found another young hero in Alan Wells, who had forced his way into the side with his fine fielding and total commitment to the game. He immediately hit Emburey for two sixes and hit an unbeaten 45 as Sussex won with one ball to spare.

There was no such excitement at Bristol where Gloucestershire batted through the final day to gain a draw. Somerset were indebted to some solid batting throughout their innings and a blossoming knock by Rose who batted under four hours and evoked memories of why he was chosen for England not so long ago.

With a Test in progress Trevor Jesty gave the selectors yet another reminder of his name with his seventh century of the season. Once more it was a mixture of technical correctness and eagerness to score that makes him a most attractive player. In contrast, Yorkshire's batting was painful and Malcolm Marshall troubled all batsmen. Southern's slow left-arm nearly bought Hampshire victory, but Bairstow and Sharp were less eager to sell their wickets than some of their team-mates and the match was drawn.

Declarations, a maiden championship fifty by Baptiste and a hundred by David Lloyd could not compensate for the loss of a day's play at Old Trafford.

Barry Wood hit his first hundred of the season to match Nottinghamshire's mammoth first innings total which, thanks to some sparkling batting by Clive Rice, had been reached at four an over. In the end, Derbyshire were brought to the brink of defeat by the offspin of Hemmings and Such, and by their own ineptitude. Barnett and Maher showed the necessary application to save the game.

Warwickshire's dreams of gaining their first championship win of the season leapt and faded at Edgbaston. Younis and Kallicharran, his seventh of the season, both hit hundreds and Warwickshire declared 118 behind. Neale set them to make 341 in 300 minutes and Andy Lloyd, who is gaining in confidence and beginning to look a very good player, hit a splendid hundred to set them on their way. Smith, in an opening stand of 103, Humpage and Din all made good contributions, but wickets fell to Patel and the last pair, Lewington and Sutcliffe, had to survive 16 balls to save the game.

At The Oval, Keith Pont again batted well for Essex and Butcher and Howarth had another fine opening stand of 171 so that Surrey led by 28 on the first innings. Essex batted throughout the last day and Gooch scored one of his less memorable hundreds. The policy and reasoning of the Essex captain, like much else that he does, was not communicated to the public who had to suffer a dreadful final day's cricket.

John Player League
29 August

at Bristol
Somerset 179 for 6 (I. V. A. Richards 88)
Gloucestershire 71 for 2
Gloucestershire (4 pts) won on faster scoring rate

at Southampton
Hampshire 248 for 4 (T. E. Jesty 110 not out, M. C. J. Nicholas 50)
Yorkshire 234 (K. Sharp 62)
Hampshire (4 pts) won by 14 runs

at Old Trafford
Lancashire 148 for 5
Kent 151 for 5
Kent (4 pts) won by 5 wickets

at Leicester
Northamptonshire 166 for 7
Leicestershire 170 for 6 (I. P. Butcher 71, R. W. Tolchard 57 not out)
Leicestershire (4 pts) won by 4 wickets

at Trent Bridge
Derbyshire 145
Nottinghamshire 149 for 4
Nottinghamshire (4 pts) won by 6 wickets

at The Oval
Surrey 174 for 6 (D. B. Pauline 74 not out, M. A. Lynch 56)
Glamorgan 175 for 2 (A. L. Jones 60, C. J. C. Rowe 52 not out)
Glamorgan (4 pts) won by 8 wickets

at Hove
Sussex 228 for 7 (G. D. Mendis 100, I. J. Gould 58, N. G. Cowans 4 for 44)
Middlesex 205 (R. O. Butcher 59)
Sussex (4 pts) won by 23 runs

at Worcester
Worcestershire 242 for 9 (P. A. Neale 57)
Warwickshire 46 for 0
Match abandoned
Worcestershire 2 pts, Warwickshire 2 pts

Trevor Jesty scored his second century on successive days, Ian Butcher and Tolchard added 91 for Leicestershire's fourth wicket against Northants, Jones and Jones began with 96 for Glamorgan at The Oval and rain flittered at Bristol and Worcester.

These events were swamped, however, by the triumph of Sussex over Middlesex, a win which gave them the John Player League title. The event could not have been stage-managed better – the only two contestants for the title meeting on a fine afternoon at Hove.

Sussex batted first and Mendis and Gould gave them just the start that Sussex supporters had dreamed – 134. That Sussex did not turn this start into a score of gigantic proportions was due mainly to some finely controlled slow bowling by Emburey. Gould, though not fully fit, batted well, mostly using his aggression at sensible moments. He was an excellent partner to the more accomplished Mendis who reached a brilliant hundred and then suddenly lost touch, being run out in the thirty-fifth over when the score was 180.

Paul Downton, a surprising and effective number four.

Above: *Sussex* v. *Middlesex at Hove, Sunday, 29 August.*
Below: *Ian Gould prepares to gather. For him victory was particularly meaningful. Two year earlier Middlesex had discarded him.*

Parker ran furiously and hit cleanly and le Roux thumped some lusty shots. In the lemming period Cowans picked up four rather fortuitous wickets.

Middlesex lost Brearley at 22, but Slack, Butcher and Downton, a surprise promotion to number four, all batted well and Middlesex had a chance of victory.

Sussex bowled admirably and fielded brilliantly, apart from the bewildering lapse of a dropped catch by the magnificent Parker. Middlesex slipped behind the required rate and Radley and Cook produced strange and ineffective strokes to try to raise the tempo. Barclay handled his team intelligently and encouragingly. Emburey was run out by yards, Daniel was bowled flailing at Pigott and on the first ball of the last over Hughes was run out. Sussex whooped in joy and fled from the field as the crowd invaded.

It was a thoroughly deserved triumph for a fine all round side who had played with great enthusiasm and skill throughout the year. It was said that, as with all successful sides in all sports, they had attracted an element of support that they would rather have been without and whose interest was mainly in the consumption of beer and the abuse of the visitors.

1, 2 and 3 September

at Derby

Derbyshire 209 (J. G. Wright 107, M. D. Marshall 6 for 60) and 296 for 4 dec (I. S. Anderson 103 not out, J. G. Wright 65, J. H. Hampshire 61)
Hampshire 225 for 9 dec (J. W. Southern 50 not out) and 179 for 5 (D. R. Turner 61 not out)

Match drawn
Derbyshire 6 pts, Hampshire 6 pts

at Chelmsford

Kent 129 (N. R. Taylor 65, J. K. Lever 4 for 57) and 353 for 5 dec (C. J. Tavare 168 not out, A. P. E. Knott 115 not out)
Essex 300 for 6 dec (G. A. Gooch 127, K. R. Pont 58 not out) and 18 for 1

Match drawn
Essex 8 pts, Kent 2 pts

at Leicester

Glamorgan 208 (A. M. E. Roberts 6 for 38) and 145 (A. M. E. Roberts 8 for 56)
Leicestershire 411 for 6 dec (B. F. Davison 119, J. C. Balderstone 118, D. I. Gower 77)

Leicestershire won by an innings and 58 runs
Leicestershire 24 pts, Glamorgan 4 pts

at Taunton

Warwickshire 300 for 6 dec (G. W. Humpage 113, K. D. Smith 67, T. A. Lloyd 55, V. J. Marks 4 for 94) and 216 (C. Lethbridge 87 not out, V. J. Marks 4 for 47)
Somerset 208 for 6 dec and 312 for 5 (I. T. Botham 131 not out, I. V. A. Richards 85, P. A. Slocombe 50)

Somerset won by 4 wickets
Somerset 20 pts, Warwickshire 6 pts

Ian Greig. A valuable all-round contribution in limited-over cricket.

An ambition realised. John Barclay holds aloft the John Player League Trophy.

at The Oval

Surrey 296 (M. A. Lynch 102, D. M. Smith 53, A. C. S. Pigott 5 for 85) and 127 for 4 dec
Sussex 150 for 8 dec (A. M. Green 56, R. D. Jackman 6 for 28) and 71 for 4

Match drawn
Surrey 6 pts, Sussex 5 pts

at Worcester

Nottinghamshire 326 for 6 dec (D. W. Randall 122, R. J. Hadlee 100 not out, J. D. Birch 67) and 230 for 5 dec (J. D. Birch 54 not out, S. B. Hassan 52, P. G. Newport 4 for 76)
Worcestershire 277 (D. J. Humphries 98, Younis Ahmed 50, P. M. Such 4 for 94) and 227 for 7 (Younis Ahmed 114)

Match drawn
Nottinghamshire 8 pts, Worcestershire 5 pts

1 and 2 September

at Scarborough

Pakistanis 177 (Mohsin Khan 52, Haroon Rashid 50, F. D. Stephenson 5 for 64) and 134 (Mohsin Khan 85, N. Gifford 4 for 24)
D. B. Close's XI 357 for 8 dec (M. D. Crowe 104, F. D. Stephenson 63, Abdul Qadir 4 for 106)

D. B. Close's XI won by an innings and 46 runs

Pakistan Touring Team 1982
First Class Matches

BATTING

	v. Middlesex (Lord's) 23–25 June 1982	v. Sussex (Hove) 26–28 June 1982	v. Hampshire (Bournemouth) 30 June–2 July 1982	v. Glamorgan (Swansea) 3–5 July 1982	v. Somerset (Taunton) 7–9 July 1982	v. Worcestershire (Worcester) 10–12 July 1982	v. Leicestershire (Leicester) 21–23 July 1982	v. Derbyshire (Chesterfield) 24–26 July 1982	First Test Match (Edgbaston) 29 July–1 Aug. 1982	v. Surrey (The Oval) 7–9 August 1982	Second Test Match (Lord's) 12–16 August 1982	v. England 'B' (Leicester) 18–20 August 1982
Mudassar Nazar	12* —	211* —	— —	163* —	— —	75 —	— —	22 100*	0 0	43 2*	20 —	9 103*
Mohsin Khan	1 —	151 —	17 0	— —	85 —	165* —	203* —	22 42	26 35	79 —	200 —	39* 24 12
Majid Khan	12* —	0 —	8 45	88 —	16 47	8 —	42 6*	— —	— —	13 36	— —	3 9
Javed Miandad	— —	52* —	— —	— —	29 105*	35* —	— —	— —	30 10	24* 17	6 26*	10* —
Zaheer Abbas	— —	— —	— —	— —	36 41	147 —	— —	51 148*	40 4	60* 50*	75 —	— —
Wasim Raja	— —	— —	40 —	50* —	14* 3	— —	12* 21*	14 —	26 16	5 —	— —	30 38
Imran Khan	— —	— —	— —	— —	— —	— —	— —	46* —	22 65	— —	12 —	— —
Sarfraz Nawaz	— —	— —	7 —	— —	— —	— —	— —	— —	— —	— —	— —	— —
Wasim Bari	— —	— —	45 —	— —	— —	— —	— —	35 —	16* 12	— —	24* —	— —
Iqbal Qasim	— —	— —	3* —	— —	— —	— —	— —	— —	— —	— —	— —	1 —
Sikhander Bakht	— —	— —	— —	— —	— —	— —	— —	4 —	1 1*	— —	— —	— —
Haroon Rashid	— —	— —	32 7*	20 —	— —	— —	8 44*	43 —	— —	1 90	1 —	13 12*
Tahir Naqqash	— —	— —	12 —	— —	— —	— —	— —	— —	12 39	— —	2 —	— —
Abdul Qadir	— —	— —	21* —	— —	— —	— —	— —	0 —	7 9	— —	18* —	— —
Mansoor Akhtar	— —	— —	87 40*	26 —	153 —	2 —	65 5	1 0	58 0	— —	57 —	— —
Saleem Malik	— —	— —	12 —	0 —	— —	— —	25* —	— —	— —	— —	— —	6 0
Salim Yousuf	— —	— —	— —	— —	— —	— —	6* —	— —	— —	— —	15* —	— —
Jalal-ud-Din												
Ehtesham-ud-Din												
Intikhab Alam												
Byes	1	8	3 2	—	7 4	—	4	—	1 5	2 2	3 1	2 4
Leg-byes	—	4	9 3	2	2 3	8	3	1 3	2 3	8 6	8 10	1 2
Wides	—	1	— 1	3	— —	—	—	— 2	— 1	— —	4 1	— 2
No-balls	5	23	4 3	4	2 3	6	1	19 5	5 5	9 6	2 —	18 9
Total	31	450	300 101	356	344 218	467	351	61 260	199 251	199 239	218 428	77 132 191
Wickets	1	2	9 2	4	5 3	4	3	0 9	2 10	10 4	4 8	0 7 4
Result	D	W	L	W	D	W	D	W	L	D	W	D

Catches: 29 – Wasim Bari (ct 22/st 7); 14 – Javed Miandad; 9 – subs.; 8 – Haroon Rashid and Majid Khan; 7 – Salim Yousuf (ct 5/st 2); 5 – Wasim Raja, Mansoor Akhtar and Mohsin Khan

BOWLING

	Imran Khan	Sarfraz Nawaz	Sikhander Bakht	Iqbal Qasim	Mudassar Nazar	Wasim Raja	Tahir Naqqash	Abdul Qadir
v. Middlesex (Lord's) 23–25 June 1982	13–5–15–0 / 7–1–10–4	12–4–41–2	17–4–48–2 / 5–0–14–0	4–1–4–1 / 3–3–0–0	6–1–21–3	1.1–1–0–1 / 2–1–2–0		
v. Sussex (Hove) 26–28 June 1982			12–3–62–1 / 11–2–47–1		3–0–7–0	14–7–26–1 / 8–2–32–0	11–0–49–0 / 18–7–33–1	23.1–6–44–7 / 30.3–7–78–6
v. Hampshire (Bournemouth) 30 June–2 July 1982		7–2–20–2 / 16–2–56–2		18.3–4–57–0		5–0–25–0	8–1–40–0 / 12–3–49–2	6–2–17–2 / 24–4–114–0
v. Glamorgan (Swansea) 3–5 July 1982	14–7–10–2 / 12–3–29–1		17–8–38–2 / 14–4–41–2	9–2–25–0	12–3–41–1 / 10–1–28–2			10.1–2–31–5 / 7–2–20–4
v. Somerset (Taunton) 7–9 July 1982	23.5–2–80–1 / 7–3–6–1	5–0–15–1	20–1–85–3 / 9–6–11–1			3–0–16–0 / 1–0–1–1		27–3–80–2 / 7–2–19–0
v. Worcestershire (Worcester) 10–12 July 1982	9–0–35–0 / 9–2–17–1			12–4–27–2 / 29.4–8–52–5	9–4–21–1		15–4–60–3 / 5–0–38–0	14–5–30–4 / 26–8–75–4
v. Leicestershire (Leicester) 21–23 July 1982			23–7–54–2 / 16–5–35–1	13–0–54–0 / 20–4–68–1		20–4–59–0	23–2–107–1 / 16–7–44–1	6–2–15–0 / 39–14–71–6
v. Derbyshire (Chesterfield) 24–26 July 1982		10–3–16–0	25–5–75–1 / 16–3–68–4		17–5–43–2 / 6–0–22–0	19–5–44–0 / 14–5–25–2		26–9–50–2 / 8–5–7–0
First Test Match (Edgbaston) 29 July–1 August 1982	25.3–11–52–7 / 32–5–84–2		18–5–58–1 / 13–5–34–0		5–2–8–0	2.3–2–0–1	15–4–46–1 / 18–7–40–5	29–7–70–1 / 40–10–100–2
v. Surrey (The Oval) 7–9 August 1982		15–4–33–0 / 20–0–92–6	14–5–34–2 / 15–2–63–0		11–2–26–1 / 11–1–55–1	12–3–34–3 / 7–0–45–0		
Second Test Match (Lord's) 12–16 August 1982	23–4–55–2 / 42–13–84–2	23–4–56–3 / 14–5–22–0			4–1–6–0 / 19–7–32–6		12–4–25–1 / 7–5–6–0	24–9–39–4 / 37.5–14–94–2
v. England 'B' (Leicester) 18–20 August 1982			13–3–27–1 / 6–1–27–0	18–3–47–1 / 5–0–14–2				
v. Lancashire (Old Trafford) 21–23 August 1982	3–2–2–0		10–5–21–0					10–1–24–1
Third Test Match (Leeds) 26–31 August 1982	25.2–7–49–5 / 30.2–8–66–3		24–5–47–2 / 20–4–40–0		4–1–3–0 / 22–7–55–4		22–5–87–1 / 8–2–16–0	
v. D. B. Close's XI (Scarborough) 1–2 Sept. 1982			8–3–30–1	29–7–86–0		9–1–37–0		28–3–106–4
	290.3–76– 621–35 av. 17.74	122–24– 351–16 av. 21.93	326–86– 959–27 av. 35.51	161.1–36– 434–12 av. 36.16	139–35– 368–21 av. 17.52	117.4–31– 346–9 av. 38.44	160–44– 537–15 av. 35.80	452.4–122– 1187–57 av. 20.82

A. P. W. G. Parker absent hurt, A. N. Jones absent hurt (2nd inns.)
B. Saleem Malik 1–0–5–0
C. Zaheer Abbas 0.1–0–0–0
D. Jalal-ud-Din 8–2–16–1 and 4–1–2–0
E. Jalal-ud-Din 21–9–43–1 and 8–1–29–1
F. Ehtesham-ud-Din 14–5–35–0
G. Ehtesham-ud-Din 14–4–46–1

3 September

at Scarborough

Pakistanis 264 for 5 (Mansoor Akhtar 88, Mohsin Khan 76, Javed Miandad 52)
D. B. Close's XI 181

Pakistanis won by 83 runs

The last match of Pakistan's tour saw them beaten in two days by an international eleven in which New Zealander Martin Crowe and West Indian Stephenson were outstanding. A one-day match was hastily arranged for the Friday and Pakistan gained some revenge.

The main interest, of course, was centred on Leicester. A gloomy first day, scarred by rain saw Leicestershire grasp the initiative with Roberts bowling finely. The Leicestershire batsmen then responded quite magnificently. They began their innings 50 minutes before lunch on the second day and lost Cobb almost immediately, but by lunch they were 66 for 1. In the afternoon period 180 were scored from 40 overs. Balderstone threw off his customary caution and batted with relish. Gower found his touch to hit cleanly and effectively and then came the irresistible Davison who led the final assault on the Glamorgan bowling which produced 165 in the last 32 overs before the declaration. Roberts dismissed Alan Lewis Jones before the close and the next day he continued the devastation to return the best match figures, 14 for 94, of his distinguished career. The result was that, with two matches remaining, Leicestershire were only two points behind Middlesex in the race for the Schweppes County Championship.

Elsewhere, Ian Anderson completed a maiden century for Derbyshire in the drawn match with Hampshire, Gooch hit a sparkling hundred for Essex against Kent in a game which the visitors saved through a sixth wicket partnership of 256 between Knott and Tavare and Randall, Hadlee and Younis all prospered at Worcester.

Chris Tavare's 168 not out represented a career best, but once more there was some criticism of the Essex attitude on the final day. They were not finishing the season well.

Monte Lynch hit splendidly for Surrey, but none followed his energetic lead and the game with Sussex was drawn. Surrey's main attention was on the NatWest Final on the Saturday and they had a serious fright when Sylvester Clarke turned an ankle.

Warwickshire, still seeking a victory, were given a good lead by the belligerent Humpage and Rose declared 92 behind on the first innings. Willis set Somerset to score 309 in 4 hours, a task which the home side accomplished with 5 wickets and 80 minutes to spare. This electric scoring rate was brought about by Ian Botham who, coming in at 149 for 4 with 160 still needed in 145 minutes, hit the fastest century of the season and took the Lawrence Trophy. He reached his hundred in 52 minutes off 56 balls. In reaching his hundred he hit eight sixes and eight fours, and, in all, hit ten sixes and twelve fours. After tea, he scored 117 out of 129 in 40 minutes. What more can one say of the man?

On a quieter note, John Wright's century for Derbyshire was his seventh and, like Kirsten, he passed the previous Derbyshire record of six centuries in a season by Townsend in 1933.

National Westminster Bank Trophy Final

There was perhaps some element of surprise that Warwickshire and Surrey should find themselves in the final of the sixty-over knock-out competition. It was Surrey's fourth final in as many years and they were finishing the season with a settled and successful side. Warwickshire, on the other hand, had had few smiles during the season. The brilliant batting of Kallicharran, ably supported by Amiss and Humpage, and now by the emerging opening combination of Lloyd and Smith, had failed to compensate for a weak attack.

Both sides had reached the final by beating more fancied opponents, Surrey having been victorious over the favourites, Middlesex, and Warwickshire having brought off a remarkable win over Somerset in the quarter-final. The contest seemed a simple one – Surrey's attack against the Warwickshire batting, for the Warwickshire bowlers needed a large total to defend.

Knight won the toss on a pleasant morning and, with the early atmosphere still heavy, asked Warwickshire to bat.

Warwickshire's early problems were to put bat to ball and the result was that, in the fourth over, with the score at three, Lloyd shuffled across to Jackman and was lbw. Kallicharran took no immediate risks and it was not until the eighth over that the Midland county reached double figures.

Thomas replaced Clarke who was bowling quickly and with hostility. Jackman was nagging away accurately and when he gave way to Monkhouse Smith relished the change and hit the new bowler straight for two fours. It was a dying gesture. In the next over he played Thomas to leg and as he looked for the single his foot slipped back and dislodged a bail. He left the wicket and looked back in anguish.

Warwickshire were 32 for 2 in the thirteenth over. Kallicharran looked firm, but there was no hint of onslaught or command.

Amiss fretted a little and then played across the line to Thomas and was bowled. Humpage edged and was superbly caught by the diving Richards. Oliver stupidly set off on a run and was sent back, but he had passed the point of no return. Kallicharran, after two promising shots of power and beauty, flashed wildly at Knight and was brilliantly taken at slip by Howarth. Ferreira was adjudged lbw to Clarke, an unlucky decision for the batsman, and Lethbridge was taken at slip, high and one-handed by Howarth. In the twenty-

Jack Richards is airborne, Smith and Howarth leap in hope, but the ball sails past. A rare escape for Warwickshire.

National Westminster Bank Trophy 1982

The County winning the Trophy will receive a prize of £12,000, the losing Finalist £5,500, the losing Semi-finalists £3,250 each and the losing Quarter-finalists £1,600 each.

MARYLEBONE CRICKET CLUB

NatWest Bank Trophy Final

15p SURREY v. WARWICKSHIRE **15p**

at Lord's Ground, †Saturday, September 4th, 1982

SURREY

1	A. R. Butcher	not out	86
2	G. P. Howarth	c Oliver b Lethbridge	31
3	D. M. Smith	not out	28
‡4	R. D. V. Knight		
5	M. A. Lynch		
*6	C. J. Richards		
7	D. J. Thomas		
8	G. A. Monkhouse		
9	S. T. Clarke		
10	R. D. Jackman		
11	K. S. Mackintosh		

B , l-b 4, w , n-b 10, ... 14

Total... 159

FALL OF THE WICKETS
1...80 2... 3... 4... 5... 6... 7... 8... 9... 10...

Bowling Analysis	O.	M.	R.	W.	Wd.	N-b
Willis	7	0	23	0	...	7
Small	8	0	60	0	...	3
Ferreira	6	0	16	0	...	...
Lethbridge	6	1	23	1	...	...
Kallicharran	6.4	1	23	0	...	...

WARWICKSHIRE

1	K. D. Smith	hit wicket b Thomas	12
2	T. A. Lloyd	l b w b Jackman	2
3	A. I. Kallicharran	c Howarth b Knight	19
4	D. L. Amiss	b Thomas	0
*5	G. W. Humpage	c Richards b Thomas	0
6	P. R. Oliver	run out	2
7	M. Asif Din	l b w b Jackman	45
8	A. M. Ferreira	l b w b Clarke	8
9	C. Lethbridge	c Howarth b Knight	4
10	G. C. Small	c Richards b Clarke	33
‡11	R. G. D. Willis	not out	8

B 8, l-b 11, w , n-b 6, ... 25

Total... 158

FALL OF THE WICKETS
1...3 2...32 3...42 4...48 5...51 6...52 7...67 8...74 9...136 10...158

Bowling Analysis	O.	M.	R.	W.	Wd.	N-b
Clarke	11.2	5	17	2	...	1
Jackman	12	2	27	2	...	...
Thomas	11	1	26	3	...	3
Monkhouse	8	0	36	0	...	...
Knight	12	3	14	2	...	...
Mackintosh	3	0	13	0	...	2

Any alterations to teams will be announced over the loud speaker system

RULES—1 The Match will consist of one innings per side and each innings is limited to 60 overs.
2 No one bowler may bowl more than 12 overs in an innings.
3 Hours of play: 10.00 a.m. to 7.00 p.m. In certain circumstances the Umpires may order extra time.

Luncheon Interval 12.30 p.m.—1.10 p.m.   Tea Interval 20 minutes (time according to state of game).

‡ Captain   * Wicket-keeper

Umpires—H. D. Bird & B. J. Meyer   Scorers—J. Hill, S. P. Austin & E. Solomon

†This match is intended to be completed in one day, but three days have been allocated in case of weather interference

Surrey won the toss and elected to field

Surrey won by 9 wickets

Total runs scored at end of each over:

First Innings	1	2	3	4	5	6	7	8	9	10	11	12	13	14	15	16	17	18	19	20
	21	22	23	24	25	26	27	28	29	30	31	32	33	34	35	36	37	38	39	40
	41	42	43	44	45	46	47	48	49	50	51	52	53	54	55	56	57	58	59	60
Second Innings	1	2	3	4	5	6	7	8	9	10	11	12	13	14	15	16	17	18	19	20
	21	22	23	24	25	26	27	28	29	30	31	32	33	34	35	36	37	38	39	40
	41	42	43	44	45	46	47	48	49	50	51	52	53	54	55	56	57	58	59	60

Derbyshire C.C.C. First-Class Matches – Batting, 1982

	v. Worcestershire (Worcester) 5–7 May		v. Somerset (Derby) 12–14 May		v. Lancashire (Old Trafford) 19–21 May		v. Nottinghamshire (Chesterfield) 29 May–1 June		v. Middlesex (Lord's) 2–4 June		v. Gloucestershire (Gloucester) 5–8 June		v. Essex (Chesterfield) 9–11 June		v. Kent (Canterbury) 19–22 June		v. Leicestershire (Derby) 26–29 June		v. Yorkshire (Derby) 3–6 July		v. Northamptonshire (Derby) 7–9 July		v. Leicestershire (Coalville) 10–13 July		v. Essex (Southend) 17–20 July	
B. Wood	24	24	62	—	17	36	19	2†			10	4	0	—	45	—	39*	12			33	28	4	10	20	16
J. G. Wright	10	60	16	59†	24	39	141*	5	9	103†	36	40	34	106	22	—	18*	25	190		38	185*	2	60	13	2
P. N. Kirsten	22	31	11	31†	0	81	0	20	47	80†	143	11	22	4	16	—	—	121†	45	—	10	68	84	102	23	113
J. H. Hampshire	34	17	45	—	54	30	12	0	40	—	52	40	64	81†	37*	—	—	62†	—	—	0	17	6	2	3	95
A. Hill	1	19	22	13	54	13†	0	5	14	18	7*	1	28	24												
G. Miller	21	39	61	—			44	53			38*	—			25*	—			0	—			50*	7		
R. W. Taylor	45	3	10	—	3	0	1	25				4*							7	—						
P. G. Newman	0	18†					5	2†	12	—			18	—					30	—	1	—			11*	17
D. G. Moir	10	11	5	—	3	—	25	—	25	—		4	0	—			7	—	1	—	10	—	1	—	1	0
S. Oldham	12	0*	9*	—	23	—	3	—	22*				0*	—							1*	—	6	—	10	—	3	8*
P. J. Hacker	10*	—	2	—	10*	—	0	—																		
R. J. Finney			39	—																						
I. S. Anderson					8	33*			9	—									82	—	27	—	79	11*	3	11
C. J. Tunnicliffe			0	—							—	40							32	—	38	—	0	17*	37	16
K. J. Barnett							24	—				6	9	0					74	—	22	42*	0	17*	6	19
B. J. Maher							4	—					0	11†							1*	—	11	—	0	1
J. E. Morris																										
S. T. Jefferies																										
A. Watts																										
Byes		6	1			1	1	8	1		5		4				3		2		3	1	1		1	
Leg-byes	6	12	4	2	14	3	4	1	14	1	5	6	9	4	5		3	8	7		3		1		1	6
Wides					1	1	1		1				2						1		2	2				
No-balls	3	7	4	3	5	5	3	2	6	6	5	1	9	11	1		3	1			9	7	1	1	8	4
Total	198	247	291	108	216	242	259	123	228	207	301	157	199	241	151		73	229	473		203	350	250	210	130	308
Wickets	10	8	10	1	10	5	10	6	9	4	9	4	9	3	3		1	2	9†		10	3	10	5	10	10
Result	D		W		D		D		D		D		D		D		W		W		W		W		L	
Points	5		23		6		6		2		6		4		4		20		6		21		22		4	

Fielding figures
31 – R. W. Taylor (ct 27/st 4)
24 – D. G. Moir
21 – B. Wood
19 – I. S. Anderson
16 – G. Miller
14 – J. G. Wright
13 – B. J. Maher and J. H. Hampshire
12 – P. N. Kirsten
11 – K. J. Barnett
 8 – C. J. Tunnicliffe
 6 – S. Oldham
 5 – A. Hill
 4 – P. G. Newman and subs
 3 – P. G. Hacker
 1 – R. J. Finney and A. Watts

English Counties Form Charts

The statistics of all first-class matches are given on pages 378 to 445. The games covered are:

Schweppes County Championship.
Matches against touring and representative sides.

In the batting tables a blank indicates that a batsman did not *play* in a game, a dash (—) that he did not *bat*. A dash (—) is placed in the batting averages if a player had 2 innings or less, and in the bowling figures if no wicket was taken.

fifth over Warwickshire were 74 for 8 and the game was decided.

Quite remarkably, the game had been turned by a steady spell from Knight, who only bowled because Monkhouse failed to settle, and Thomas, whose destruction of three of Warwickshire's leading batsmen rightly earned him the Man of the Match award.

It must also be added that some of the batting was very bad.

Asif Din and Small batted with great good sense and limited aggression. Early on in his innings Asif Din seemed unable to distinguish between a long-hop and a bouncer and treated all as menacing, but his was a courageous innings and ensured that we would see some cricket after lunch.

Small gave good support and was just beginning to swipe well when he edged Clarke to Richards. The ninth wicket stand had lasted 24 overs and produced 62 runs. Willis swotted well and more valuable runs were added before Asif Din was lbw to Jackman. 158 hardly seemed a total that Surrey would fear but it was more than had seemed possible at 11.30.

Right: *A shameful waste. Phil Oliver is run out by yards.*

THE ENGLISH SEASON

	v. Pakistanis (Chesterfield) 24-26 July		v. Surrey (Derby) 31 July-3 August		v. Warwickshire (Edgbaston) 7-10 August		v. Lancashire (Derby) 11-13 August		v. Northamptonshire (Northampton) 14-17 August		v. Sussex (Chesterfield) 21-24 August		v. Nottinghamshire (Trent Bridge) 28-31 August		v. Hampshire (Derby) 1-3 September		v. Yorkshire (Scarborough) 8-10 September		v. Glamorgan (Derby) 11-14 September		Inns	NOs	Runs	HS	Av
	39	13	0	13	2	37	67	—	3	42	16	0*	124*	31	5	18	0	17	19	0	38	4	851	124*	25.02
			8	9	39	11	1	—	157	20	79	0*			107	65	27	9	17	44	39	6	1830	190	55.45
					164*	123*	4	19	63	—	48	5	105*	—	27	29			36	140*	37	7	1941	164*	64.70
	37	40	40	85	1	36	101*	—	—	14*			38	0	6	61	10	7	40	57*	36	6	1264	101*	42.13
																					14	3	219	54	19.90
	72*	40									52	—	1	3	22*	34*	12	12	23	5	22	6	614	72*	38.37
	21	0			2	0					10*	—			0	0	1	1	9	—	19	2	142	45	8.35
	—	7			0	8	13	—	0	6			—	0	5	—	1	1	39*	2	22	4	196	39*	10.88
	—	0			12	—			—	0					9	—	0	12	—	0*	22	1	136	25	6.47
	—	8*			35*	15*			—	0							1*	0			18	10	156	35*	19.50
																					4	2	22	10*	11.00
																					1	—	39	39	39.00
	18	2	11*	—	2	89	24	—	0	5	6	—	45	12	10	103*	29	11	3	38	26	4	671	103*	30.50
					16	9	8	—	13*	6			1*	5	28	—	6	5	10	3	19	2	273	40	16.05
	37	27	21	8*	4	120	2	—	46	12	18	—			9*	—			100*	11	25	5	642	120	32.10
							15*	—	4*	0					2*	—					11	5	49	15*	8.16
	6	12																			2	—	18	12	9.00
	14*	0																			2	1	14	14*	14.00
													0	—							1	—	0	0	0.00
Extras		4	4				9			2		1			6	4			4		4				
	7	4	2	2	4		9		2	6	4		3	2	6	9	2	3	6	7					
			2								2		1	3	8	2	2	1							
	6	5			7	5			1	1	8		6	1				17	8	8					
Totals	257	162	252	240	128	358	305		275	117	300	0	251	99	209	296	137	237	281	268					
	6	10	4	3	10	10	7		6	10	5	0	4	7	10	4	10	10	8	8					
Result	L		D		D		D		L		D		D		D		L		D						
Points	—		5		4		4		4		5		5		6		4		7						

† J. H. Hampshire absent injured

Derbyshire C.C.C. First-Class Matches – Bowling, 1982

	P. G. Newman	P. J. Hacker	S. Oldham	B. Wood	G. Miller	D. G. Moir	P. N. Kirsten	R. J. Finney	I. S. Anderson
v. Worcestershire (Worcester) 5–7 May	19.5–3–73–3 12–2–45–0	23–3–61–5 13–2–53–2	17–4–37–0 5–0–24–0	2–2–0–2 8–2–22–1	5–2–10–0 3–1–15–0	1–0–1–0 2–0–12–2	1–0–3–0		
v. Somerset (Derby) 12–14 May		16–3–57–1 7–2–23–2	19–3–63–6 12.4–2–34–2		17–5–38–2 19–8–32–2	3–0–18–0 25–6–60–3	6–1–18–1	13–5–37–1 1–0–3–0	
v. Lancashire (Old Trafford) 19–21 May		18.1–1–51–5	17–4–57–3	18–6–47–0		6–1–15–0	2–1–5–0		10–1–29–1
v. Notts. (Chesterfield) 29 May–1 June	13–5–50–1 18–0–78–3	14–1–68–1 10–0–31–2	20–6–45–1 24–9–45–2	14–5–45–1	16–5–31–1 4–1–9–0	23–4–62–4 14–4–30–0			
v. Middlesex (Lord's) 2–4 June	11–3–25–0 13–1–72–2	10–4–27–0 19–3–86–3	10–2–18–0 17–0–99–3			9–3–12–0 13–1–45–0			1–0–3–0 4–0–24–0
v. Gloucestershire (Gloucester) 5–8 June			10–2–28–1 7–0–28–1	4–1–22–0	34–14–76–1 19–7–46–2	27–7–94–1 23.2–11–46–4	14–1–51–2 10–3–25–3		
v. Essex (Chesterfield) 9–11 June	30–2–116–2	15–2–74–2	10–1–34–0	18–5–50–0		23–4–93–3	1–1–0–0		
v. Kent (Canterbury) 19–22 June	17–1–62–0 3–0–12–0		23.4–9–52–2 5–0–8–0	12–3–36–0	3–0–10–1	1–0–1–0 1–1–0–0			
v. Leicestershire (Derby) 26–29 June			4–1–9–0			25–8–40–5 15–6–15–2		7–0–15–1 5.4–0–43–2	
v. Yorkshire (Derby) 3–6 July	13.2–4–39–3 12–4–37–1		21–6–54–0 12–5–21–2		14–2–54–0 21–11–45–1	38–14–83–4 30–10–76–0	8–3–9–0		
v. Northamptonshire (Derby) 7–9 July	20–2–79–1 4–1–16–0		13–0–60–0 4–0–11–0	13–2–46–0 1–0–18–0		26–5–72–2 24–8–53–5	6–0–19–1 14–0–43–1		
v. Leicestershire (Coalville) 10–13 July			7–0–25–1 13–1–27–1		44.2–11–70–8 33–7–68–4	35–13–83–1 27–5–65–1	6–1–17–0 7–1–21–0		
v. Essex (Southend) 17–20 July	19.1–3–59–4 15–2–75–2		20–8–50–3 18–2–66–1	16–3–45–2 6–1–19–0		2–1–5–0 11.2–4–42–1			
v. Pakistanis (Chesterfield) 24–26 July	14–1–67–1 16–1–61–0		16–0–41–2	3–0–14–0 3–1–17–0	14.5–3–49–2 16.4–2–57–0	5–1–10–1 17–4–76–0			4–0–19–0
v. Surrey (Derby) 31 July–3 August	16–2–64–2 7–1–43–0	10–1–54–0 7–1–40–2	22–4–88–4 3–0–13–1	22–4–48–0		30–2–85–3 13.4–3–43–4	13–2–44–0		
v. Warwickshire (Edgbaston) 7–10 August	25.2–4–90–3		30–9–78–7 3–0–27–1	5–1–13–0		7–1–13–0 4–3–1–0	4–1–17–0		
v. Lancashire (Derby) 11–13 August	19–4–52–0 9–5–26–0		27–3–64–0 6–0–23–1	18–2–51–0		23–5–65–1 39–21–48–4	7–1–23–1 3–0–22–0		29–19–43–1
v. Northamptonshire (Northampton) 14–17 Aug.	13–2–50–0 5–0–23–1		15–2–59–0 12–2–79–0	23–3–78–1		34–9–106–3 16.3–3–66–1			
v. Sussex (Chesterfield) 21–24 August		12–2–52–0	13–3–36–1	2–2–0–0	13–4–29–0	28–13–42–1			
v. Nottinghamshire (Trent Bridge) 28–31 Aug.	9–1–46–0 8–1–15–1		20.3–3–70–0	15–3–42–0	11–3–42–0 8–2–13–0	23–4–69–2 13–0–59–3			
v. Hampshire (Derby) 1–3 September	16–2–43–1 5–0–31–1			5–2–9–1	15–6–36–1 9–0–38–2	30–8–74–2 13–4–42–1			
v. Yorkshire (Scarborough) 8–10 Sept.	18–3–36–1 13–2–37–0		16–4–31–0 12–3–40–2	4.2–1–12–2 5–0–20–0	8–1–11–1 1–0–6–0	35–16–63–6 5–2–24–0			
v. Glamorgan (Derby) 11–14 September	12.5–1–60–3 14–2–40–2			10–4–28–0 4–1–8–0	25–8–35–1 60–22–118–2	19–3–56–1 52–9–112–5	19–12–31–0		2–2–0–0
	440.3–65– 1622–38 av. 42.68	174.1–25– 677–25 av. 27.08	504.5–98– 1544–48 av. 32.16	231.2–54– 690–10 av. 69.00	413.5–125– 938–31 av. 30.25	811.5–228– 2076–76 av. 27.31	121–28– 348–9 av. 38.66	14–5– 40–1 av. 40.00	62.4–22– 176–5 av. 35.20

a A. Hill 1–0–4–0
b J. H. Hampshire 4–1–26–0
c J. G. Wright 3–0–29–0
d A. Watts 5–1–8–0 and 4–0–23–0

C. J. Tunnicliffe	S. T. Jefferies	K. J. Barnett	Byes	Leg byes	Wides	No balls	Total	Wickets
			2	4		6	194	10
				4	1	9	192	5a
			1	4	1		219	10
			1	2		4	177	10
23–3–68–1			7	3		5	287	10
			2	9	1	7	320	9
				8	2	7	210	7
				2		2	89	0
			1	10	3		340	9
11–2–40–0		5–0–27–0	4	6	1	5	354	5
8–2–29–0		3–0–10–0		3		7	194	10
			1	9	2	7	386	7
24–3–73–5				6	1	10	250	8
				4		4	28	0
21.5–7–53–4			2	1		6	126	10
4–0–18–1		11–2–34–0	4	3	1	2	175	5b
18–8–52–1				2	1	6	291	8c
2–0–4–0		2–0–2–0	2	1		3	200	4
22–5–72–4			1	5		16	370	8
3–0–6–0		6–0–27–0		1	1	3	179	6
6–1–28–0			5	4	1	1	234	10
12.5–0–26–0			5	5		5	222	10
20.4–2–76–1			1	6		20	262	10
8–2–39–0			1	7		12	261	4
	16–2–57–3			1	2	19	260	9
	12–1–52–2	1–0–8–0	1	3		5	299	2
		1–0–3–0	2	6	2	5	401	9
				3	1	1	144	8
20–6–63–0			4	3	20		284	10
2–0–14–1						1	60	2
25–11–65–3			2	2		8	332	5
3–1–7–0		10–6–8–0	1	2		1	181	6
19.2–2–95–1				6		6	400	5
12–1–53–2				1		6	228	4
16–7–27–2				5		11	202	4
25–5–109–2		1–0–8–0	2	7		5	400	5
4–1–12–0				7	1	5	112	4
23–5–49–2				6			225	9d
10–3–25–1		2–0–15–0		2		3	179	5
17–3–45–0			1	10		8	217	10
5.3–2–21–2			1	5		4	158	4
17–10–44–4			1	2		8	234	10
		1.3–0–5–0	2	4	4	8	327	9
383.1–92– 1213–37 av. 32.78	28–3– 109–5 av. 21.80	53.3–8– 147–0 —						

Late defiance. Asif Din.

Gladstone Small takes evasive action during his brave stand with Asif Din.

Essex C.C.C. First-Class Matches – Batting, 1982

	v. Middlesex (Lord's) 5-7 May		v. Sussex (Hove) 12-14 May		v. Cambridge University (Cambridge) 19-21 May		v. Surrey (Chelmsford) 29 May-1 June		v. Somerset (Chelmsford) 5-8 June		v. Derbyshire (Chesterfield) 9-11 June		v. Lancashire (Liverpool) 12-15 June		v. Worcestershire (Ilford) 19-22 June		v. Yorkshire (Ilford) 23-25 June		v. Indians (Chelmsford) 3-5 July		v. Nottinghamshire (Trent Bridge) 7-9 July		v. Northamptonshire (Northampton) 10-13 July		v. Derbyshire (Southend) 17-20 July	
G. A. Gooch	58	—	56	3	35	—	19	71	5	34	7	—	66	—	10	—	28	—	0	0	4	33†	48	—	0	31
A. W. Lilley	20	—	0	39	40	—	13	67	7	5	26	—	39	—	9	—	11*	—								
K. S. McEwan	14	—	28*	31	51	—	14	3	26	13	150*	—	92*	—	20	—			12	52	35	—	61	—	116	63
K. W. R. Fletcher	120	—	64	3			8	122	72	61	16	—	73*	—	45	—			17	—	30	—	124	—	10	35
B. R. Hardie	50	—	1	25	44	—	21	3	76	47	36	—	18	—	55	—	44*	—	161	20	13	50†	94	—	27	77
N. Phillip	37	—	1	56	20	—	27	11†	9	0	23	—			61	—			79	—	59	—	23	—	17	—
S. Turner	28	—	3	22	11	—	74	—	8	21	56	—			24*	—			7	—	31	—	19	—	8	—
D. E. East	10*	—	5	36†	78	—	11	—	8	14†	17	—			10*	—			2	32†	61	—	5*	—	0	—
R. E. East	1	—	7	10	58	—	18	—	3*	44									10	—	0	—			16	—
J. K. Lever			0	0			1	—	0	4											22*	—			2*	—
N. A. Foster			0	7	15	—							36*	—												
K. R. Pont					32	—									2	—			21	58†	7	—	50*	—	38	35*
D. L. Acfield					1*	—	1*	—	4	—									2*	—	3	—			1	—
D. R. Pringle																			0	10						
R. J. Leiper																										

Byes			1	4	1		7	1	7	3	1		1				1		5		4	2	1		1	1
Leg-byes	10		3	6	6		13	8	1	3	9				12		4		16	2	6		15		6	7
Wides	1		1		1		1	1	1		2		1						2		1					
No-balls	6			2	6		1	1	11		7		10		4		2		2	1	9	1	9		20	12
Total	355	0	170	244	399		228	288	238	249	386		300	3	252		90	1	336	175	285	86	449		262	26
Wickets	8	0	10	10	10	5	10	9	10	9	7		3		7		1		10	4	10	0	6		10	4
Result	L		L		W		W		W		D		D		D		D		D		W		D		W	
Points	4		5		—		22		22		8		8		7		3		—		23		8		23	

Fielding figures
74 – D. E. East (ct 66/st 8)
25 – G. A. Gooch
21 – R. E. East
15 – B. R. Hardie
12 – K. W. R. Fletcher
11 – K. R. Pont
 9 – K. S. McEwan
 8 – S. Turner
 7 – D. L. Acfield
 6 – N. Phillip
 5 – J. K. Lever
 4 – A. W. Lilley
 2 – R. J. Leiper
 1 – sub

There was no nonsense about Butcher and Howarth. Against erratic bowling, and the usual quota of Warwickshire no-balls, they reached 20 inside four overs and thirty inside six. Howarth played some superb shots off the back foot and his driving square was exquisite. There seemed no chance of a wicket falling until, in the seventeenth over, Howarth played a dreadful shot to a bad ball and lifted the ball to mid-on where Oliver took the catch falling forward.

Butcher was unperturbed and proceeded to strike the ball to all corners of the ground. He looked a superb player and it was most fitting that he should on-drive Kallicharran for the winning four. Smith, too, had batted well, but, in truth, the bowling was very moderate, and this was a day that Warwickshire would probably rather forget.

Geoff Howarth attempts the preservation of modesty as Harold Bird does running repairs on Anton Ferreira's trousers.

THE ENGLISH SEASON/383

v. Middlesex (Southend) 21–23 July		v. Leicestershire (Leicester) 24–27 July		v. Glamorgan (Cardiff) 31 July–3 August		v. Kent (Canterbury) 7–10 August		v. Hampshire (Chelmsford) 11–13 August		v. Gloucestershire (Cheltenham) 14–17 August		v. Warwickshire (Colchester) 21–24 August		v. Leicestershire (Colchester) 25–27 August		v. Surrey (The Oval) 28–31 August		v. Kent (Chelmsford) 1–3 September		v. Northamptonshire (Chelmsford) 11–14 September			Inns	NOs	Runs	HS	Av
60	87	50	85	2	24	71	149	12	1	5	44	72	—	5	88	34	140	127	0	61	7		38	1	1632	149*	44.10
																							14	1	276	67	21.23
20	7	32	25	36	28	47	4	3	23	91	13	128	—	19	7	49	28	26	—	38	21		37	3	1426	150*	41.94
43	13	2	20	7	83*	19	43	0	19	11	0*	15	—	3	25	26	60*	11	—	10	23		35	4	1233	124	39.77
43	43	82	5	19*	—	25	26	12	34	10	30*	86	—	47	19	9	8	28	2*	12	30		39	5	1432	161	42.11
26	14	22	0	33	—	5	25*	6	73	6	7	24	—	27*	16	21	—	3	—	32	20		32	3	783	79	27.00
21	1*	12	7	1	—	4	—	58	21	64*	11	83	—	9	19	26	—	30*	—				28	4	679	83	28.29
6	23	1	0	5	38	20	—	27	41	6	0	1	—	7	4	6	—		15*	35*	1		32	8	525	78	21.87
7	—	5	4	18	—	22	—	12	0	34	—	20	—	0	13					14*	28		23	2	344	58	16.38
5*	—	0	0	4	—			8	6	5	—	8	—	4	9	11	—	—	—		0		19	3	89	22*	5.56
																							4	1	58	36*	19.33
2	0			5	47*	0	1*	12	5	50	—			9	89	75	31*	58*	—	49	11		24	7	687	89	40.41
		0*	0*	4*	—	2*	—	0*	0*	3*	—	0*	—	0	0*	2*	—				0*		18	14	23	4*	5.75
5	51*	0	1			21	—					54	—					2	—	11	7		10	1	162	54	18.00
																3	0						2	—	3	3	1.50
1	10	5	1		3		3		7	4					4	4	8			11							
1	10	7	9	5	5	3	5	8	16	7	2	7		4	11	5	4	14		10	10						
2				3	2	1	1	2	5	1				1	1	1	1	1	1								
8	4	1		12	11	8	4	15	10	6		4		5	3	1	2			17	10						
250	263	219	157	154	241	248	261	175	261	303	107	502		140	308	276	281	300	18	300	168						
10	7	10	10	9	3	10	4	10	10	9	5	10		10	10	10	4	6	1	7	10						
	D		L		W		D		D		D		D		L		D		D		L						
	7		5		20		6		5		6		8		2		5		8		7						

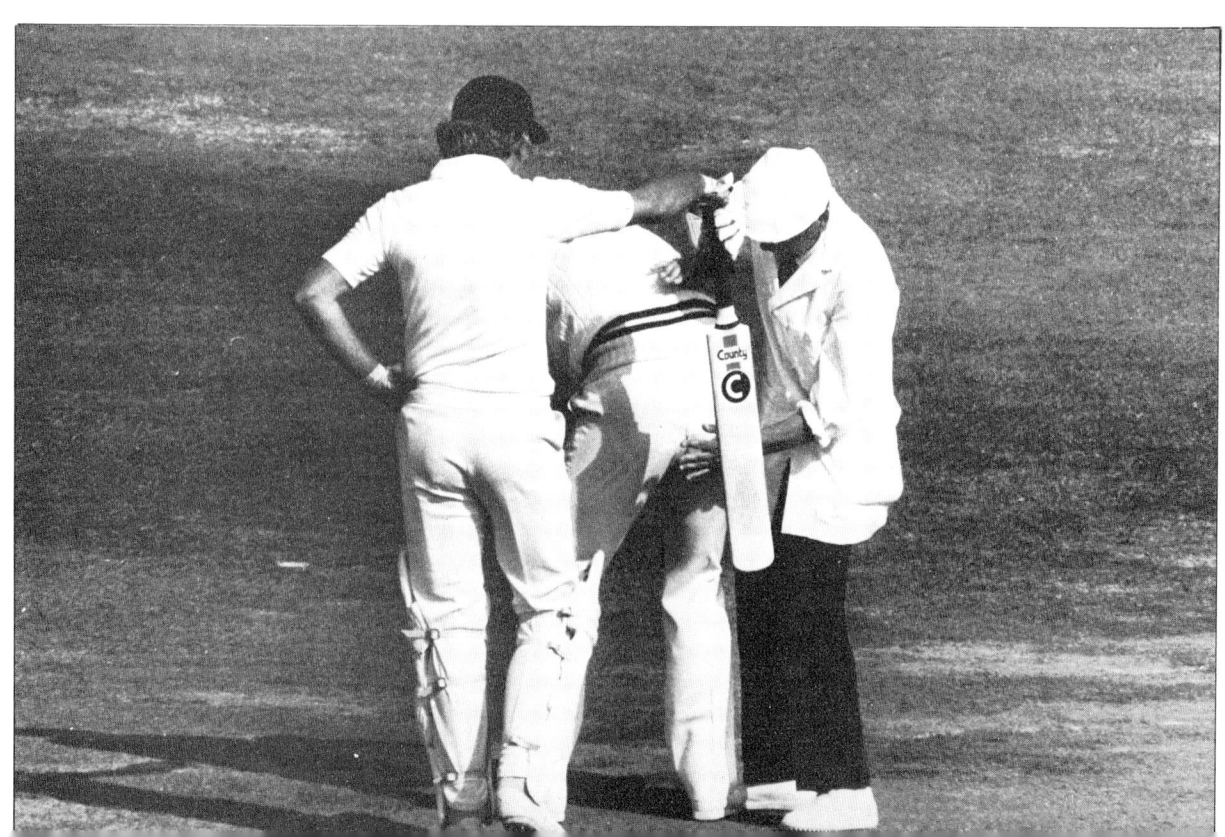

Essex C.C.C. First-Class Matches – Bowling, 1982	N. Phillip	J. K. Lever	N. A. Foster	S. Turner	R. E. East	G. A. Gooch	K. W. R. Fletcher	D. L. Acfield	A. W. Lilley
v. Middlesex (Lord's) 5–7 May	1–0–2–0 14–3–73–2	2–1–6–0 22.2–3–57–1	22–4–83–2	11–2–30–0	31–10–69–3	4–0–17–0			
v. Sussex (Hove) 12–14 May	18–2–81–3	27.4–7–91–5	14–3–69–0	22–2–72–0 6–2–13–0	10–0–39–1	5–0–17–0	0.1–0–4–0		
v. Cambridge University (Cambridge) 19–21 May	12–2–41–5 15.5–4–50–6		16–7–46–3 27–4–93–1	5–2–6–1 15–4–39–3	2–2–0–0 8–2–22–0	5–0–31–0		17–7–16–0	
v. Surrey (Chelmsford) 29 May–1 June	15.1–1–60–6 15–1–80–2	16–4–63–2 17–4–61–5		2–0–4–1 3–2–4–0	2–0–12–0 4.5–0–12–1			2–0–8–1 13–2–22–3	
v. Somerset (Chelmsford) 5–8 June	13–2–31–2 6–0–34–3	19.5–5–28–4 8–2–13–0		2–0–4–0	27–6–80–6		1–0–7–0	30–10–58–1	
v. Derbyshire (Chesterfield) 9–11 June	12–2–26–0 7–0–29–0	30–9–67–3 14–2–45–1	24–9–32–3 8–0–45–1	23–7–37–2 5–2–14–0		7–4–11–0 10–6–55–2		4–3–2–0 17–4–28–0	3–0–10–0
v. Lancashire (Liverpool) 12–15 June	22.4–6–63–3 21–8–43–2		14–2–57–2	22–9–36–1 20–7–50–0	13–5–31–2 16–5–39–0	18–10–21–0	13–0–103–2	13–4–38–2 14–3–31–0	
v. Worcestershire (Ilford) 19–22 June	15–4–29–3 5–2–6–1			4–0–16–0		11–5–14–7 5–0–11–0			
v. Yorkshire (Ilford) 23–25 June	23.4–5–47–3			23–9–37–1	2–2–0–0	29–10–60–4			
v. Indians (Chelmsford) 3–5 July	14–2–41–2 5–1–1–2			7–0–35–0 8–2–16–0	19–5–30–0 15.4–4–9–4	1–0–2–0	4–0–22–0	17–2–46–0 6–1–23–0	
v. Nottinghamshire (Trent Bridge) 7–9 July	10–3–32–1 12–0–47–1	16–2–63–5 13–3–55–4		8.2–3–21–1 4–1–13–0	1–1–0–0 21–7–54–0	1–0–2–0 7–2–31–0		19.5–6–35–4	
v. Northamptonshire (Northampton) 10–13 July	17–2–66–1 9–1–43–0	14–2–36–1 17–3–53–1		27–7–53–4 5–1–15–0	16–9–17–1 9–4–5–0	15–2–36–2 13–4–36–1		11–1–31–1 27–10–45–0	
v. Derbyshire (Southend) 17–20 July	16–2–65–3 16–2–53–0	18.5–4–86 23–7–88–4		1.3–0–7–1 21–1–74–4	21–4–47–2			10–1–36–0	
v. Middlesex (Southend) 21–23 July	15–2–43–1 3–1–13–0	26–9–67–3 8–4–9–1		14–3–27–0	11–2–24–2 5–1–15–0	1–1–0–0	1–0–2–0		
v. Leicestershire (Leicester) 24–27 July	10–1–25–0 18–7–42–5	16–2–40–2 18–3–31–3		16–4–40–1 9–3–25–0	27–9–60–3			24–8–56–4	
v. Glamorgan (Cardiff) 31 July–3 August	30–12–40–5 16–3–24–1	26.5–6–70–1		24.1–10–24–1 18–3–36–2	11–5–23–0	24.2–7–37–3 11.5–4–33–1		12–1–34–0 9–5–14–1	
v. Kent (Canterbury) 7–10 August	20.4–4–55–2 9–0–43–0			22–9–23–0 11–1–32–0	8–3–23–0 13–0–48–1	8–4–6–0	1–0–18–0	16–4–37–4 25–3–84–3	
v. Hampshire (Chelmsford) 11–13 August	19.3–1–66–3 4–0–42–2	25–5–109–1 4–0–27–0		23–3–74–2	6–2–12–1	8–1–17–0		24–6–50–2	
v. Gloucestershire (Cheltenham) 14–17 August	12–1–50–0 10–2–28–0	22–4–78–5 7–2–26–1		13–3–40–2	24–8–65–2 31.5–3–89–3	5–2–14–0		29–5–62–1 25–5–79–3	
v. Warwickshire (Colchester) 21–24 August	16–4–80–4 9–0–39–0	11–1–30–1 14.3–2–49–1			31–10–45–2 2–2–0–1			14.1–3–38–2 6–4–4–1	
v. Leicestershire (Colchester) 25–27 Aug.	14–5–22–1 2–0–11–0	15–1–45–1 12–0–54–2		15–4–22–2	38.1–17–66–2 8–0–80–0			41–18–77–3 8.2–0–50–2	
v. Surrey (The Oval) 28–31 August	14–1–49–3	18.3–5–50–1		20–4–63–0		11–3–30–0		37–7–76–4	
v. Kent (Chelmsford) 1–3 September	7.4–3–13–3 12–0–31–0	25–8–57–4 18–0–59–2		8–3–17–1 15–4–61–0		5–3–4–1 15.5–4–58–1		1–0–5–0 22–3–70–0	
v. Northamptonshire (Chelmsford) 11–14 Sept.	22–5–50–2 5–0–22–0	16–1–80–1 4–0–28–0			22–4–70–2 35–9–105–6			28–4–99–2 33–9–78–1	
	584.1–107– 1842–82 av. 22.46	543.5–112– 1683–72 av. 23.37	125–29– 425–12 av. 35.41	453–117– 1080–30 av. 36.00	490.5–141– 1231–45 av. 27.35	220–72– 541–22 av. 24.59	20.1–0– 156–2 av. 78.00	555.2–129– 1332–45 av. 29.60	3–0– 10–0 —

* J. R. T. Barclay retired hurt ‡ P. A. Todd absent ill b B. R. Hardie 2–0–2–0
† P. I. Pocock absent injured a B. R. Hardie 5–1–18–0

THE ENGLISH SEASON

K. S. McEwan	D. R. Pringle	K. R. Pont	Byes	Leg byes	Wides	No balls	Total	Wickets
							8	0
				18		1	348	8
			1	19	1	5	378	9*
			2	3		1	40	0
				4		2	99	10
			2	3		2	258	10
				6	2	1	132	10
				1	1	8	175	9†
			3	1	4	6	111	10
				6		1	203	10
			4	9	2	9	199	9
				4		11	241	4
				3		9	237	10
6–0–64–1			5	3	1	7	367	5
				2		3	64	10
							17	1
				2	2	4	152	8
	19–5–59–5	9–1–38–0		4		5	258	7
2–0–26–0	5–2–13–0		5	2		3	171	5
				1		3	122	9‡
				9		3	247	9
				5		8	252	10
5–0–30–0		18–3–48–3	2	4	1	7	307	5a
			1	1		8	130	10
				6		4	308	10
	25–5–61–2			5	1	1	229	10
				3	1	2	47	1b
	16–2–55–0		3	9	1		289	10
	8–3–9–2			4		1	112	10
				11	2	15	256	10
		13–3–17–5		6	2	6	138	10
	27–9–53–4		4	4	2	2	209	10
	20.5–4–45–3		5	5	1	3	284	8
			8	4		11	351	10
				6			75	2
			3	6	1	3	322	10
			3	10		1	236	7
	11–3–36–1		2	10	3	5	249	10
	3–0–14–1			3		4	113	4
			1	11	1	1	246	10
				8			203	4
		11–1–23–2	2	7		4	304	10
	14–3–25–1		2	4	1	1	129	10
	15–5–32–2	11–3–32–0		4	2	4	353	5
	22–6–58–1			8	1	10	376	9
			12	1	1	4	251	7
13–0–	185.5–27–	62–11–						
120–1	460–22	158–10						
av. 120.00	av. 20.90	av. 15.80						

Jackman and Willis. Friendly face to face.

Alan Butcher in sumptuous form despatches another ball to the boundary.

Glamorgan C.C.C. First-Class Matches – Batting, 1982

	v. Cambridge University (Cambridge) 21–23 April		v. Warwickshire (Edgbaston) 5–7 May		v. Yorkshire (Leeds) 12–14 May		v. Leicestershire (Cardiff) 19–21 May		v. Gloucestershire (Swansea) 29 May–1 June		v. Somerset (Swansea) 2–4 June		v. Lancashire (Old Trafford) 5–8 June		v. Middlesex (Swansea) 9–11 June		v. Warwickshire (Cardiff) 12–15 June		v. Oxford University (Swansea) 19–22 June		v. Worcestershire (Cardiff) 23–25 June		v. Pakistanis (Swansea) 3–5 July		v. Hampshire (Cardiff) 10–13 July	
A. Jones	103	31	45	14	4	12	5	15	7	94	43	16	2	17	7	17	0	14	98	—	53		17	0	22*	34
A. L. Jones	24	20							4	—	36	12	12	49	8	43	72	0	5				12*	0		3
R. C. Ontong	6	106*	73	3	75	19	25	27	4	152*	4	25	11	4	0	17	7	56					33	41		10
C. J. C. Rowe	23	44	23	0	18	—	2	3	55	21	2	58*	0	1	12	23	20	43*	60*				48	8		27
M. J. Llewellyn	2	61*	25	0																						
G. C. Holmes	68	—	6	29			6	—	46*	5	37	—	4	6					3	—						
E. W. Jones	0	—	22	4	0*	—	3	2																		
B. J. Lloyd	9	—	6*	6	2	—	1	6	9	—	6	0*	0	1	0	1	0	—	4	—			9	18		15*
M. A. Nash	0	—	1	4	31	—	13	37	10	—			0	0			4	0	19	—	10		4	5		9
S. A. B. Daniels	30*	—							73	1	11	—	0*		3*	0	2*	4	14	—	16					
S. R. Barwick	5*	—			0*	—	15	2											10*	3*	24		0	2	—	9
J. A. Hopkins			33	5	80	64	1	0	4	4	75	31	36	23	39	0	10	6	27		24*		4	24	0	2
Javed Miandad			35	96*	50	14*	7	51	29	27	32	27	4	16	66	52	68	27								
D. A. Francis			14	14	30	—	0	23*					16	5	5	1					—		12	0	25	16
T. Davies									66*		0	2	25	8	32	34	8	7	52		4*		6	14*	2*	15
M. N. Davies																			0							
W. W. Davis																							0	6	—	12
J. G. Thomas																										
H. Morris																										
Byes	3		4	11	5		3	3		1	1	4	1						2				4	4		1
Leg-byes	7	2	9	2	5	1	4	2	5	17	6	4	3	3	4	3	20	8	13		4		5	5	2	11
Wides	1	2		1			1		3	2	1						2		1	1						2
No-balls			6	2	15	2	8	8	2	2	5	2	2	4	10	7	1	1	2		1		1	1	3	4
Total	281	266	303	190	322	112	134	184	308	321	226	187	115	131	191	202	250	166	317		86		155	128	54	170
Wickets	9	3	10	10	9	2	10	10	10	4	10	7	10	10	10	10	10	6	10		1		10	10	2	10
Result	D		D		D		L		D		D		L		L		D		D		D		L		L	
Points	—		7		6		3		5		4		4		5		5		—		4		—		4	

Fielding figures
41 – E. W. Jones (ct 37/st 4)
20 – T. Davies (ct 19/st 1)
19 – J. A. Hopkins
14 – B. J. Lloyd
13 – A. L. Jones
12 – R. C. Ontong
10 – M. A. Nash and C. J. C. Rowe
9 – D. A. Francis
7 – Javed Miandad
6 – S. R. Barwick and subs
4 – A. Jones, J. G. Thomas and W. W. Davis
3 – S. A. B. Daniels
2 – G. C. Holmes
1 – M. J. Llewellyn, H. Morris and M. N. Davies

John Player League

5 September

at Derby

Derbyshire v. Gloucestershire

Match abandoned
Derbyshire 2 pts, Gloucestershire 2 pts

at Chelmsford

Essex 159 for 5 (K. S. McEwan 66 not out)
Nottinghamshire 160 for 3 (R. T. Robinson 56)

Nottinghamshire (4 pts) won by 7 wickets

at Abergavenny

Glamorgan 229 for 7 (R. C. Ontong 100)
Northamptonshire 153 for 7

Glamorgan (4 pts) won on faster scoring rate

at The Oval

Surrey 139 for 9
Hampshire 139 for 9 (J. M. Rice 64)

Match tied
Surrey 2 pts, Hampshire 2 pts

THE ENGLISH SEASON/387

at Edgbaston

Warwickshire v. Sussex

Match abandoned
Warwickshire 2 pts, Sussex 2 pts

Rain prevented play in two games and hampered others. Notts, thanks to an impressive spell from Hadlee and an opening stand of 74 by Hassan and Robinson, beat Essex with ease.

At The Oval, Surrey and Hampshire contrived a tie when Lynch caught Tremlett off a skier off the last ball of the match. Earlier Smith, the Surrey left-hander, had been given out 'handled ball'.

Rodney Ontong hit a six and nine fours in his century at Abergavenny.

Asda Trophy

5 September

at Scarborough

Lancashire 212 for 8 (S. J. O'Shaughnessy 80)
Yorkshire 17 for 2

Lancashire won on toss of a coin

6 September

at Scarborough

Nottinghamshire 234 for 6 (S. B. Hassan 58, R. T. Robinson 58)
Derbyshire 236 for 5 (G. Miller 87 not out, K. J. Barnett 54 not out)

Derbyshire won by 5 wickets

Miller and Barnett put on 143 in 23 overs to win the match.

Final

7 September

at Scarborough

Lancashire 163 for 7 (C. H. Lloyd 57)
Derbyshire 164 for 1 (B. Wood 59 not out, J. G. Wright 59)

Derbyshire won by 9 wickets

Glamorgan C.C.C. First-Class Matches – Bowling, 1982

	M. A. Nash	S. A. B. Daniels	S. R. Barwick	B. J. Lloyd	R. C. Ontong	C. J. C. Rowe	Javed Miandad	G. C. Holmes	A. Jones
v. Cambridge University (Cambridge) 21–23 April	18–5–50–2 14–4–38–1	16–1–49–3 5.4–0–19–1	12–3–22–0 10–6–17–0	23.2–9–58–5 28–11–78–1	3–0–27–0 5–1–29–0	5–2–6–0 27–6–64–2			
v. Warwickshire (Edgbaston) 5–7 May	15–4–47–1			16–2–56–3	28–5–85–3	5–2–16–0	26.4–10–52–3		
v. Yorkshire (Leeds) 12–14 May	27–7–95–2 24–2–111–1		15–5–25–0 8–1–16–0	24–3–86–2 2–0–27–0	28–10–73–2 23–4–80–4	10–1–39–1	4–0–21–0	5–2–14–0	
v. Leicestershire (Cardiff) 19–21 May	27–5–72–3		13–1–53–1	21.4–4–55–3	26–9–79–1	7–4–22–0	15–5–30–2		
v. Gloucestershire (Swansea) 29 May–1 June	20–6–39–3 2–1–4–0	14–3–54–1 3–0–26–0		19–2–83–1 21–6–63–2	21–4–72–1 6–3–7–1	1–0–3–0 16–0–60–2	9–1–36–0 3–1–4–0	5–1–17–0	
v. Somerset (Swansea) 2–4 June		18–1–81–1 16.4–5–54–2	21–2–69–1 21–7–44–5	23–4–54–1 25–7–32–0	17–3–47–0 8–1–23–0	11.3–3–36–1	14–7–26–1		
v. Lancashire (Old Trafford) 5–8 June		15–3–58–1 11–2–29–1	24–6–53–1 9–2–22–1	7.2–3–22–2 22.4–3–83–3	24–9–53–4 18–5–52–1		17–5–48–1 3–2–5–0		
v. Middlesex (Swansea) 9–11 June	26.2–4–95–4 3–1–11–0		17–6–42–3 3–1–7–0	16–0–73–1 2.2–1–12–0	20–2–94–1		5–0–42–0 2–0–12–0		1–1–0–0
v. Warwickshire (Cardiff) 12–15 June	23–5–62–2 7–1–29–0	14–1–65–0 9–1–57–2	16–5–56–1 4–1–10–4	36.1–8–92–3 1–0–2–0	20–3–67–1 20–4–61–4	1–1–0–0	3–0–17–0		
v. Oxford University (Swansea) 19–22 June	20–8–40–3 18–5–57–1	7–0–22–0 7–3–9–1	8–4–19–1 10–5–18–1	25.3–6–57–3 26–15–30–1		29–7–67–3 15–7–29–2		8–1–29–0	
v. Worcestershire (Cardiff) 23–25 June	22–9–52–2	19–2–65–3		17.1–2–44–3	25–0–45–2				
v. Pakistanis (Swansea) 3–5 July	12–4–43–0		17–2–69–2	19.4–1–80–0	16–1–81–2				
v. Hampshire (Cardiff) 10–13 July	20–5–63–4 5–1–22–0		12–2–48–1	16–7–39–1	12–2–30–0 4–0–16–0				
v. Somerset (Taunton) 17–20 July	17–3–35–5 18–6–37–0	6–1–37–1		40–4–155–5	5.5–2–10–3 17–6–40–1	24–4–75–0			
v. Hampshire (Portsmouth) 21–23 July	14–3–56–0	11–3–58–0		21–3–79–0	19–3–71–0	8–2–22–0			
v. Worcestershire (Worcester) 28–30 July		13–4–53–1 12–2–30–0		28–5–85–0 9–4–20–0	8–2–32–0 19–8–30–4	4–1–24–0			
v. Essex (Cardiff) 31 July–3 August		9–1–23–1 17–4–47–1		4–1–7–1 14–4–41–0	14–5–28–2 10.2–3–37–0				
v. Northamptonshire (Swansea) 7–10 August			7–0–29–0 16–1–78–2	8–0–27–0 6–0–35–2	12–4–32–1 6–1–34–0	2–0–8–0 6–2–16–0			
v. Kent (Canterbury) 11–13 August	17–7–35–2 12–2–47–1			12–3–35–1 10–1–38–0	16–4–63–0 11–1–42–3				
v. Surrey (Guildford) 14–17 August			7–1–32–0 8.2–0–63–4	21–4–69–1 13–0–81–2	12–2–43–0 14–0–60–1	18–4–95–3 12–0–83–1			
v. Nottinghamshire (Swansea) 21–24 August	20–2–71–0 6–1–16–0			10.5–0–40–2	16–4–43–1 18.4–1–79–3	1–0–3–0			
v. Sussex (Cardiff) 25–27 August			7–3–11–0 11–4–35–2	1–1–0–0 21–4–97–0	16.4–2–57–4 14–0–64–0	6–2–16–0			
v. Leicestershire (Leicester) 1–3 September	11–1–49–1			28–1–121–3	11.5–2–62–1				
v. Gloucestershire (Bristol) 8–10 September			6–2–24–0 15–2–50–1	26.4–8–72–2 7–1–19–0	22–5–76–4 26–8–50–6				
v. Derbyshire (Derby) 11–14 September			23–7–54–1 4–0–15–0	7–1–17–0 8–0–37–1	15.4–3–46–1 21–1–101–3	32–6–83–7 13–1–69–2			
	418.2–102– 1276–38 av. 33.57	223.2–37– 836–20 av. 41.80	324.2–79– 981–32 av. 30.65	688.2–139– 2201–55 av. 40.01	638.1–131– 2059–64 av. 32.17	265.2–57– 898–19 av. 47.26	101.4–31– 293–7 av. 41.85	18–4– 60–0 —	1–1– 0–0 —

8, 9, and 10 September

at Bristol

Gloucestershire 288 (P. Bainbridge 84, W. W. Davis 4 for 69, R. C. Ontong 4 for 76) and 203 (R. C. Ontong 6 for 50)
Glamorgan 177 (E. W. Jones 65, R. J. Doughty 6 for 43) and 319 for 6 (C. J. C. Rowe 70, A. Jones 68, D. A. Francis 63)

Glamorgan won by 5 wickets
Glamorgan 21 pts, Gloucestershire 7 pts

at Old Trafford

Sussex 315 for 6 dec (G. D. Mendis 104, A. M. Green 82) and 223 (J. R. T. Barclay 53, J. Simmons 4 for 60)
Lancashire 301 for 6 dec (G. Fowler 91, S. J. O'Shaughnessy 54 not out, C. H. Lloyd 50) and 152 for 8 (C. H. Lloyd 60)

Match drawn
Sussex 5 pts, Lancashire 4 pts

at Uxbridge

Middlesex 207 (W. N. Slack 68, M. D. Marshall 4 for 67) and 215 (J. M. Brearley 56, M. W. Gatting 50, J. W. Southern 5 for 51)
Hampshire 178 (P. H. Edmonds 6 for 48) and 138 (W. W. Daniel 4 for 31, P. H. Edmonds 4 for 59)

Middlesex won by 106 runs
Middlesex 22 pts, Hampshire 5 pts

at Trent Bridge

Nottinghamshire 400 (J. D. Birch 125, D. W. Randall 65, L. B. Taylor 5 for 101)
Leicestershire 144 (K. E. Cooper 4 for 40) and 151 (P. M. Such 4 for 25, E. E. Hemmings 4 for 70)

Nottinghamshire won by an innings and 105 runs
Nottinghamshire 24 pts, Leicestershire 3 pts

at Taunton

Worcestershire 120 (J. Garner 6 for 42) and 169 (D. J. Humphries 60, I. T. Botham 5 for 50)
Somerset 307 for 9 dec (I. T. Botham 98, I. V. A. Richards 77, S. P. Perryman 5 for 74)

Somerset won by an innings and 18 runs
Somerset 24 pts, Worcestershire 4 pts

at Edgbaston

Warwickshire 381 for 9 dec (G. W. Humpage 146, A. I. Kallicharran 68, N. A. Mallender 5 for 97) and 282 for 8 dec (K. D. Smith 54)
Northamptonshire 333 for 9 dec (A. J. Lamb 97, R. J. Boyd-Moss 63, A. M. Ferreira 4 for 126) and 333 for 5 (P. Willey 96, A. J. Lamb 95 not out, G. Cook 87)

Northamptonshire won by 5 wickets
Northamptonshire 22 pts, Warwickshire 8 pts

Gloucestershire C.C.C. First-Class Matches – Batting, 1982

	v. Oxford University (Oxford) 5-7 May		v. Worcestershire (Bristol) 12-14 May		v. Sussex (Hastings) 19-21 May		v. Glamorgan (Swansea) 29 May-1 June		v. Lancashire (Gloucester) 2-4 June		v. Derbyshire (Gloucester) 5-8 June		v. Worcestershire (Worcester) 9-11 June		v. Surrey (The Oval) 12-15 June		v. Indians (Bristol) 19-21 June		v. Somerset (Bath) 23-25 June		v. Hampshire (Bristol) 26-29 June		v. Sussex (Bristol) 7-9 July		v. Yorkshire (Bradford) 10-13 July	
B. C. Broad	95	—	16	40	4	14	16	25	0	29			36	14	40	23	73	0	23	—			18	44	0	20
P. W. Romaines	32	16*									20	25									—	25	17	9	74	11
Zaheer Abbas	144	—	0	91			39	60	162*	107	30	4			77	0	39	58								
M. W. Stovold	47	—			20	8													3	8						
S. J. Windaybank	8	10*																								
J. N. Shepherd	57*	—	33	16	30	10	1	9*	10	8*	57*	28	—	9*	14	—					—	16*			2	16*
D. A. Graveney	20*	—	8	13	5	49	55*	—	0	—	—	28	—	5*	21	—			12*	—			—	2*	16	20	41*	—
C. R. Trembath																										
A. J. Brassington	—	—	2	5	7*	35	—	—	1	—	—	—	14	—	—	—	—	—	0	—	—	—	1	14	11*	—
J. H. Childs	—	—	0	1	0	8	—	—	0	—	—	—	0	—	—	—	—	—	—	—			0	11*	—	—
D. Surridge	—	—	0*	2*	10	3*	—	—	3	—	—	—	6										5*	9	—	—
A. W. Stovold			27	1	9	54	28	4	12	30	60	0	17	68	12	24	12	0	42	—			29	0	0	5	37
Sadiq Mohammad			36	18	3	12	33	15	43	91	85	33	72	22	10	5	9	15*					8	27
P. Bainbridge			2	14	5	5	101*	1	15	39	34	23*	55*	62	57	44*	61	7*	1	—			—	11	4	8	103	35*
A. J. Hignell			13	23	0	13	31	50*	12	38*	52*	23	44*	11	29	4*			33*	—			—	3	4	6	0	45
R. J. Doughty															2*	—										
E. J. Cunningham																	11*	9	1*	—			5	0	1
D. V. Lawrence																										
F. D. Stephenson																							—	4	0	14
A. J. Wright																										
B. Dudleston																										
R. C. Russell																										
D. Simpkins																										
Byes	2	4	6	4			8		1	3	4		8		6		9		1				1		1	2
Leg-byes	3	3	13	5	3	7	4		5	1	6	3	6	4	3	3	10		1		1		1	13	12	6
Wides	3	3	1			2		3		2	1		1	1	1	2					1		1		3	1
No-balls		1	1	4	2	2	9	5	3	2	5	7	4	1	4	2			2				4	2	1	6	1
Total	411	37	158	237	98	222	325	172	267	350	354	194	320	197	239	163	200	39	104		0	101	70	150	266	20
Wickets	5	0	10	10	10	10	6	5	10	5	5	10	4	6	8	4	6	4	3		0	6	10	10	7	5
Result	W		L		L		D		D		D		D		D		L		D		W		L		W	
Points	—		5		4		8		4		5		4		4		—		3		16		2		22	

Fielding figures
44 – A. J. Brassington (ct 37/st 7)
24 – A. W. Stovold
14 – D. A. Graveney
13 – J. N. Shepherd
9 – P. Bainbridge and A. J. Hignell
8 – Sadiq Mohammad
7 – J. H. Childs
6 – R. C. Russell (ct 4/st 2)
5 – P. W. Romaines and B. Dudleston
4 – B. C. Broad
3 – A. J. Wright and D. Surridge
2 – R. J. Doughty
1 – C. R. Trembath, F. D. Stephenson, Zaheer Abbas and sub

at Scarborough

Derbyshire 137 (A. Sidebottom 6 for 31) and 237 (P. N. Kirsten 140 not out, G. B. Stevenson 5 for 72)
Yorkshire 217 (G. Boycott 57, D. G. Moir 6 for 63) and 158 for 4 (M. D. Moxon 67, C. W. J. Athey 58)

Yorkshire won by 6 wickets
Yorkshire 22 pts, Derbyshire 4 pts

In the penultimate round of Schweppes County Championship matches Glamorgan snatched their first victory of the season when Eifion Jones hit the first ball of the last over of the match, bowled by Doughty, for six. Glamorgan had trailed by 111 runs on the first innings when Richard Doughty returned a career best 6 for 43. Ontong bowled well for Glamorgan when Gloucestershire batted again, but the Welshmen were left with the daunting task of making 315 for victory, the highest score of the match. Alan Jones and Alan Lewis Jones began with a stand of 80. Then Alan Jones and Francis added 56. Rowe joined Francis in an invaluable partnership of 98, Rowe's contribution being 70 which included two sixes and nine fours. Gloucestershire came back into contention when the durable Francis and Ontong went in quick succession to Shepherd. Thomas fell to the same bowler and this left the young Morris and the veteran Eifion Jones to score 38 in nine overs. They ran superbly and hit hard at anything loose before Jones' final blow gave them a memorable victory.

There was equal excitement at Edgbaston where the weakness of the Warwickshire attack was exposed once more. Humpage had hit a thumping century for Warwickshire in the first innings and Willis set Northants to make 331 ir 175 minutes, a formidable task. A partnership of 168 between Willey and Cook for the second wicket laid the foundation for victory, but the winning innings was played by Allan Lamb who came in during the first of the final twenty overs and scored 95 not out, Northants winning with 15 balls to spare. Lamb hit Kallicharran for 30 in one over, three sixes and three fours, and reached 75 in half an hour.

No such excitement at Old Trafford where Lancashire battled for a draw and the young men, O'Shaughnessy and Green, continued to impress. There were good innings from Mendis and Barclay, lately recapturing form, and from Fowler, exuding confidence after his Test success.

Bowlers were mostly on top at Scarborough and Moxon made one wonder why we had not seen more of him.

Botham and Richards were in more furious form at Taunton when, after Garner had bowled out Worcestershire for 120, the England all-rounder hit 98 off 51 balls in an hour, five sixes and twelve fours. Earlier, Richards had hit 77 in 81 minutes and a demoralised Worcestershire were beaten in two days, Botham taking the last 5 wickets in 46 balls while conceding 50 runs.

The main interest, of course, was in the fight for the Championship. Leicestershire suffered a severe blow. They laboured on the first day as Notts, inspired by a John Birch hundred, reached 400 in spite of some good bowling by Cook and Taylor. Sadly, Leicestershire's batsmen failed twice, once to seam and then to the combined off-breaks of Hemmings and the talented Such, reaching such rich reward in his first half-season. Leicestershire were beaten by an innings and their hopes of the title dwindled to an optimistic dream.

There was no slip by Middlesex. On a difficult wicket at Uxbridge, Edmonds bowled them to a first innings lead although they had been dismissed for 207, Slack, Butcher and Monteith, playing his first match of the season and batting at number ten, having worked hard to take them to that total against Marshall's hostility. At their second attempt, Middlesex batted with great resolution, Brearley, in his last home game, and Gatting reaching splendid fifties as the ball began to turn and lift. There was still a chance of a Hampshire victory, but the speed of Daniel wedded to the spin of Edmonds broke the back of the visitors' batting and Middlesex were within four points of the title. Edmonds had match figures of 10 for 107, a telling contribution.

Gloucestershire C.C.C. — First-Class Matches – Bowling, 1982

Match	C. R. Trembath	D. Surridge	J. H. Childs	J. N. Shepherd	D. A. Graveney	B. C. Broad	B. Dudleston	P. Bainbridge	Sadiq Mohammad
v. Oxford University (Oxford) 5–7 May	19.1–4–91–5 / 7–1–30–1	18–7–52–0 / 16.4–7–43–4	26–18–14–2 / 31–12–53–2	25–7–60–3 / 9–6–4–0	31–12–51–2 / 8.2–4–6–2	5–1–17–0			
v. Worcestershire (Bristol) 12–14 May		28–4–78–5 / 15–6–33–1	27–4–40–0	19–3–55–1 / 31.3–8–77–2	25–12–37–7			10–4–23–1 / 7–2–23–0	
v. Sussex (Hastings) 19–21 May		30–6–74–4 / 13.1–5–29–1	9–4–14–0 / 9–2–29–1	33.1–5–75–6 / 12–2–30–0				13–4–44–0 / 3–1–12–1	
v. Glamorgan (Swansea) 29 May–1 June		29–9–79–1 / 26–4–57–2	9–3–19–0 / 13–1–62–0	33–5–116–3 / 14–2–48–0	11–1–46–0	4–0–12–0		28.2–8–59–6 / 22–5–74–2	7–0–25–0
v. Lancashire (Gloucester) 2–4 June		30–10–81–1	15–2–54–0	32–11–82–1	14–1–51–1			28–8–84–2	
v. Derbyshire (Gloucester) 5–8 June		20–8–41–0 / 2–0–22–0	30–7–94–2 / 19.5–6–64–3	11–4–34–1 / 6–1–15–0	32.1–4–99–1 / 15–4–49–4			3–0–14–0	2–1–4–0
v. Worcestershire (Worcester) 9–11 June			21–3–55–0 / 21–7–42–1	18–3–53–0 / 6–1–25–0	31–6–80–1 / 12–4–33–0	5–2–13–0		2–0–11–0	24–3–90–1 / 20–2–76–1
v. Surrey (The Oval) 12–15 June		4–0–27–0 / 5–0–24–0		16–2–67–2 / 24–1–81–4				17.4–2–80–1	
v. Indians (Bristol) 19–21 June		27–10–57–1 / 8–1–36–1	27.1–8–57–1 / 21–5–43–0		16–8–15–1 / 21–7–42–2			20–5–47–1 / 5–0–24–0	
v. Somerset (Bath) 23–25 June		20.1–5–36–3		16–0–59–2	10–4–19–1			9–1–27–0	
v. Hampshire (Bristol) 26–29 June		19–8–26–4		10.5–5–18–2	1–0–4–0				
v. Sussex (Bristol) 7–9 July		15–2–58–1	34–14–68–1		32–12–79–3			14–3–49–1	
v. Yorkshire (Bradford) 10–13 July		27–8–67–3 / 22–11–29–3	26–11–45–0 / 6–3–25–1	19–5–49–2 / 14.3–2–43–5	15–4–33–3 / 7–0–22–0	2–0–10–0		13–2–52–0 / 17–4–62–0	
v. Northamptonshire (Bristol) 17–20 July		27–7–82–3 / 3–0–9–1	27–5–90–0 / 7–3–13–0	28–3–79–0 / 2–0–10–0	44–14–99–3 / 6–4–7–0				18.4–6–42–4
v. Warwickshire (Nuneaton) 21–23 July		37–6–137–4		37–12–87–3	11–0–29–0			19–4–63–2	
v. Northamptonshire (Northampton) 28–30 July			30–14–52–0 / 23–7–65–4	25–7–73–2 / 2–0–16–0	19–3–71–2 / 10–1–65–0		19–8–36–3 / 6–1–20–0		
v. Leicestershire (Leicester) 31 July–3 Aug.		22–5–55–1	23–9–45–1	21.4–6–43–0		5–0–13–1		30–11–72–1	
v. Nottinghamshire (Cheltenham) 7–10 August		22–8–51–2 / 20–8–37–1	24–12–53–4 / 38–11–112–5	22.5–5–86–4 / 25.2–6–66–0				7–0–27–0	6–1–22–0
v. Middlesex (Cheltenham) 11–13 Aug.		25–8–78–0	8–0–25–0	24.3–8–79–4					
v. Essex (Cheltenham) 14–17 August			28–6–88–3 / 2–0–23–0	25.2–9–48–2 / 8–1–44–3	21–5–56–1 / 3–1–5–2	15–5–23–1			
v. Kent (Folkestone) 21–24 August	17–2–62–0 / 6.2–0–36–0		19–1–73–1	25–8–51–1 / 19–3–58–2	17.1–3–46–1				
v. Hampshire (Bournemouth) 25–27 Aug.			22–4–79–3 / 5.3–1–17–0	30–9–64–2 / 7–3–15–0	21–13–29–2 / 6–3–6–1	3–0–16–0	5–1–25–0		
v. Somerset (Bristol) 28–31 August		30–6–109–0	24–5–70–1	30–6–80–0	38–8–116–3			15–0–53–1	
v. Glamorgan (Bristol) 8–10 September			13–4–23–1 / 25–6–75–1	30–10–58–3 / 27–8–78–3	21–7–47–1			19–12–28–0 / 6–1–14–0	24–7–46–1
	49.3–7–219–6 av. 36.50	561–159–1507–47 av. 32.06	663.3–198–1681–38 av. 44.23	739.4–177–2026–63 av. 32.15	498.4–145–1242–44 av. 28.22	39–8–104–2 av. 52.00	37–10–108–3 av. 36.00	301–77–915–19 av. 48.15	101.4–20–305–7 av. 43.57

a P. W. Romaines 5–2–9–0
b Zaheer Abbas 2–0–15–0
c M. W. Stovold 1–0–13–0
d E. J. Cunningham 4–0–13–0
e D. Simpkins 2–0–15–0

R. J. Doughty	F. D. Stephenson	D. V. Lawrence	Byes	Leg byes	Wides	No balls	Total	Wickets
				4		9	230	10
					3	7	217	10a
			5	14	1		222	10
			4	10			184	10
				7		4	218	10
				2		2	104	3
				5	3	2	308	10
			1	17	2	2	321	4
			5	14	1	3	375	5
			5	5		5	301	4
				6		1	157	8
			4	10			369	2b
15–1–62–0				4		3	268	3
19–2–61–1			5	3			150	5
12.4–3–48–3			1	14	4		253	5
10–0–49–0		16–2–50–1	8	6	2	5	245	5
		7–1–24–1	4		1		200	4c
	16–2–45–2			5		9	200	8d
				Innings Forfeited			0	0
	23–6–48–4		1	1		1	99	10
	17.1–3–45–3			9			308	9
				10	6	7	279	10
				4	1	1	187	10
			1	4	1	3	401	10
				1			40	1
	23–4–106–1		6	10	2	6	446	10
	24–6–64–2		3	5	1	5	310	9
	14–1–73–4		2	10	1		252	8
				10		6	244	4
				4	2	1	197	10
			2	15	1	2	284	6
	26–9–69–5			5		6	277	10e
22–4–70–2			4	7	1	6	303	9
3–0–33–0				2			107	5
21–1–80–3			1	7	2	2	324	6
12–1–37–0			1		1	1	134	2
	25.2–5–67–3		5	7		2	294	10
	7–1–25–1			1			64	2
				4	2	4	438	5
20.2–5–43–6			10	6	9		177	10
14.1–2–50–0			2	5	1	1	319	6
149.1–19–	175.2–37–	23–3–						
533–15	542–25	74–2						
av. 35.53	av. 21.68	av. 37.00						

Norman Cowans in action at Uxbridge. A surprise choice for Australia.

Finishing with a flourish. Mike Brearley, the eminence grise of English cricket, in his last home match, Middlesex v. Hampshire at Uxbridge. Bobby Parks keeping wicket.

Hampshire C.C.C. First-Class Matches – Batting, 1982

	v. Leicestershire (Southampton) 5–7 May		v. Oxford University (Oxford) 12–14 May		v. Nottinghamshire (Trent Bridge) 19–21 May		v. Indians (Southampton) 29–31 May		v. Kent (Bournemouth) 2–4 June		v. Surrey (The Oval) 5–8 June		v. Lancashire (Southampton) 9–11 June		v. Somerset (Bath) 19–22 June		v. Sussex (Basingstoke) 23–25 June		v. Gloucestershire (Bristol) 26–29 June		v. Pakistanis (Bournemouth) 30 June–2 July		v. Kent (Maidstone) 3–6 July		v. Glamorgan (Cardiff) 10–13 July	
C. G. Greenidge	26	40†			3*	6	4	156	22	33	8	84	9	62†	35	48†	60	2	—	1	5	0	46	32	157*	38†
J. M. Rice	5	18			9	4	28	16	60	0	23	0	4	50†	29	20	0	5*	—	9			11	9	0	27†
V. P. Terry	5	16†	6																5*			6			9	
T. E. Jesty	31	—			15	5	164*	1	2	52	55	0	2	—	16	—			—	15	45*	133	24	1		
D. R. Turner	22	—	34		0	3									2	—					7	31	9	59	2	—
R. E. Hayward	9	—	29*																							
N. G. Cowley	104	—			0	8	13	—	26	20	0	1	71	—	50	—	—	—	—	7			35	9	31	—
M. D. Marshall	15	—			9	17			14	32	25	24	116*	—	14	—	—	—	—	21			10	22	10	—
R. J. Parks	44	—			0	0	16*	—	6	14†	7*	5	28	—	14	—			—	25			25	12	4	—
J. W. Southern	6*	—					—	—	0	8			16*	—	30*	—			—	9			10	1	12	—
K. St J. D. Emery	0*	—			0*	1			0*	0	1	5†			0	—			—	1*			0*	0†	0	—
C. L. Smith			71	—																						
T. M. Tremlett			18	—	5	0	1	—	0	2	0	3	2	—												
M. C. J. Nicholas			206*	—	21	7	72	54†	5	20	17	14	31	—	37	10*	127*	0*		2	2	107*	1	49	7	—
K. Stevenson																										
S. J. Malone			—	—	2	2†	—	—			2	4														
N. E. J. Pocock							29	—	7	6			5	2	164	—	12	—		0	10*	29†	0	62	20	—
R. A. Smith																					8	1				
M. J. Bailey																										
Byes	17		2		4	1		1	1	1	8		3		6	5	4			1		4	1		1	
Leg-byes	8	3	2		2		3	5	6	14	5	7	6	2	11	2	5	1		1	1	2	5	17	3	4
Wides			2				1			1			2	1	1										3	1
No-balls	9	4				2	5	3	9	18		11	5		3		1			1	6	12	2	10	11	
Total	301	81	370		70	56	336	236	158	221	148	170	458	115	259	85	202	8	0	99	85	319	179	283	270	70
Wickets	9	1	4		9†	10	6	2	10	10	10	10	8	0	10	1	2	1	0	10	4	4	10	10	10	0
Results	D		W		L		L		L		W		W		D		D		L		W		W		W	
Points	8		—		4		—		5		20		24		7		4		0		—		21		19	

Fielding figures
76 – R. J. Parks (ct 70/st 6)
26 – J. M. Rice
23 – C. G. Greenidge
20 – N. E. J. Pocock
15 – T. M. Tremlett
14 – M. C. J. Nicholas
13 – T. E. Jesty
9 – N. G. Cowley
8 – J. W. Southern
6 – D. R. Turner
4 – M. D. Marshall
3 – R. E. Hayward, V. P. Terry and K. St J. D. Emery
2 – C. L. Smith and R. A. Smith
1 – S. J. Malone, K. Stevenson and sub

John Player League

12 September

at Derby
Derbyshire 180 (K. J. Barnett 68, B. Wood 50 not out, W. W. Davis 4 for 24)
Glamorgan 182 for 6 (C. J. C. Rowe 61)

Glamorgan (4 pts) won by 4 wickets

at Chelmsford
Northamptonshire 189 for 9 (A. J. Lamb 104 not out)
Essex 191 for 5 (G. A. Gooch 51)

Essex (4 pts) won by 5 wickets

at Bournemouth
Warwickshire 166 for 6 (Asif Din 56 not out)
Hampshire 170 for 6

Hampshire (4 pts) won by 4 wickets

at Canterbury
Leicestershire 203 for 3 (D. I. Gower 88 not out)
Kent 181

Leicestershire (4 pts) won by 22 runs

THE ENGLISH SEASON

	v. Surrey (Portsmouth) 17-20 July		v. Glamorgan (Portsmouth) 21-23 July		v. Somerset (Bournemouth) 31 July-3 August		v. Sussex (Eastbourne) 7-10 August		v. Essex (Chelmsford) 11-13 August		v. Worcestershire (Southampton) 14-17 August		v. Northamptonshire (Northampton) 21-24 August		v. Gloucestershire (Bournemouth) 25-27 August		v. Yorkshire (Bournemouth) 28-31 August		v. Derbyshire (Derby) 1-3 September		v. Middlesex (Uxbridge) 8-10 September		v. Warwickshire (Southampton) 11-14 September		Inns	NOs	Runs	HS	Av
	6	8	183*	—	24	20	6	38	33	25	3	38	62	0	28	37*	8	12	28	18	10	14	85	31	41	8	1526	183*	46.24
	11	20	57		18	2	0	15	69	17*	1	39	29	0*	0	5	26	16	0	45	15	11			44	4	777	69	19.42
																									6	2	41	16*	10.25
			135*	—	23	50			106	27*	123	30*	46	—	121	9*	109	58	5	38	4	26	35	134	36	8	1645	164*	58.75
	96	46	—	—	15	0	25	14					30	—			42	3	0	61*	30	0	8	13	21	1	459	96	22.95
	16	7																							9	1	169	59	21.12
	22	0			16	26	20	28	7	—	0	—	11	—	1	—			18	21	33	6*			28	1	584	104	21.62
	7	20			0	25	19	42	5	—	44	—	1	—	54	—	0	1	6	0*	29	9	14	28*	31	3	633	116*	22.60
	15	10*			0	5	9	3	1	—	36	—	1	—	17	—	3	8*	12	—	14	13	3	—	30	5	350	44	14.00
							3	3	31*	—	17	—	8*	—	11	—	24	3	50*	—	18*	23	17	—	21	7	300	50*	21.42
	1*	0			0*	0	1	0*	5	—			1	—	2*	—	0*	—	18*	—	0	0*	1*	—	26	15	37	18*	3.36
																									1	—	71	71	71.00
	9*	11			2	3*	17*	10	8	—	6	2			31	—			48	—			1	30	22	3	209	48	11.00
	21	81	4	—	0	2	5	73	39	0	9	59*	6	0*	7	12	26	51	44	9	8	0	67*	—	42	9	1312	206*	39.75
																									5	2	13	4	4.33
	19	0	—	—	15	20	50	8	24	—	1	—	53	—	8	—	2	0	8	3	18	16	25	—	30	2	616	164	22.00
																									2	—	9	8	4.50
																	3	—							1		3	3	3.00
	10	6	19				8				11		5			2			4	2			8		† C. G. Greenidge retired hurt				
	14	10	11		3	2	1	1	4	6	14	18	6		7	1	6	6	6	2	6	2	4	4	‡ M. C. J. Nicholas retired hurt				
	4		4					1			1	2				1								5					
		2	22		3	2	4	4	11		1	3	3		2		6	6		3	4	1	13	2					
	251	221	435		119	157	160	240	351	75	259	191	268	0	294	64	255	167	225	179	178	138	306	261					
	9	10	2		10	10	10	10	10	2	10	3	10	1	10	2	10	8	9	5	10	10	9‡	4					
	L		W		W		D		D		L		D		W		D		D		L		W						
	5		24		20		4		8		7		6		23		6		6		5		24						

at Taunton
Lancashire 143 for 9
Somerset 144 for 3 (I. V. A. Richards 69, I. T. Botham 67 not out)
Somerset (4 pts) won by 7 wickets

at The Oval
Surrey 205 for 3 (A. R. Butcher 70, M. A. Lynch 52 not out)
Yorkshire 198 for 8 (C. W. J. Athey 71, I. R. Payne 4 for 31)
Surrey (4 pts) won by 7 runs

at Hove
Nottinghamshire 185 for 9 (C. E. B. Rice 59, G. S. le Roux 4 for 18)
Sussex 186 for 4 (C. M. Wells 65, P. W. G. Parker 52)
Sussex (4 pts) won by 4 wickets

at Worcester
Middlesex 229 for 6 (P. R. Downton 58 not out, S. P. Perryman 4 for 31)
Worcestershire 212
Middlesex (4 pts) won by 17 runs

With the top two places already decided the last Sunday of the John Player League was mainly a time for reflection in the sun and reluctant leave takings from friends and places.

Sussex rounded off the season in glorious style when they defeated Notts on the last ball of the match and so took their total of points to the record 58.

Middlesex won at Worcester and Botham and Richards hit 115 in 16 overs against Lancashire. The last four overs of their stand produced 65 runs.

Defeats for Warwickshire and Yorkshire confirmed them as seventeenth and sixteenth in the table, and it was a sobering reflection for the Midland county that they also finished bottom of the Schweppes County Championship.

Glamorgan finished with a win and Kim Barnett was awarded his county cap, richly deserved, although his innings could not save Derbyshire.

Pringle was also given his county cap, an honour which Essex had conferred on the bouncing David East the week before. Allan Lamb hit a wonderful hundred for Northants who had lost Willey to the first ball of the match, but Turner and Pont showed common sense at a time when it seemed in short supply and Pont hit the first ball of the last over for six to win Essex the game.

Hampshire C.C.C. First-Class Matches – Bowling, 1982

	M. D. Marshall	K. St. J. D. Emery	T. E. Jesty	J. M. Rice	N. G. Cowley	J. W. Southern	K. Stevenson	S. J. Malone	T. M. Tremlett
v. Leicestershire (Southampton) 5–7 May	20–6–56–2 21.4–6–44–0	25.3–4–84–2 11–6–16–0	27–6–71–6 12–4–31–2	10–0–49–0 7–3–18–0	24–10–48–6	15–8–39–1			
v. Oxford University (Oxford) 12–14 May					9–3–11–0 6–4–7–0	11–4–18–0 18–8–37–2	14–6–35–1 8–4–21–0	23.3–7–55–7 24–10–55–5	19–7–44–2 21–13–10–3
v. Nottinghamshire (Trent Bridge) 19–21 May	23–6–53–3 24–5–52–1	14–5–32–0 15–5–40–3	6.5–1–22–2 5–2–11–0					15–4–53–4 15–3–42–0	22–5–41–1
v. Indians (Southampton) 29–31 May		14–1–62–0 14–1–56–1			26–7–63–1 11–0–54–1	23.4–3–83–3 11–0–64–2		11–1–42–1 19.2–2–74–1	9–4–17–1 5–1–30–2
v. Kent (Bournemouth) 2–4 June	31.2–10–84–5 4–1–9–1	13–3–45–2 3–0–9–0	10–4–12–0		4–0–13–1 14–2–46–1	28–9–77–2 14–4–42–2			8–3–11–0
v. Surrey (The Oval) 5–8 June	20–7–38–3 20.1–6–38–7	19–4–72–3 17–4–41–3	1–0–8–0					8–2–28–1 3–0–10–0	10.1–1–36–3
v. Lancashire (Southampton) 9–11 June	18.1–7–48–5 32–9–108–3	20–5–55–2 26–7–71–3	18–5–56–2 16.3–5–42–2		26–11–54–1	2–0–10–0 17–4–62–0			15–8–22–1
v. Somerset (Bath) 19–22 June	25.1–8–71–3	23–4–80–5	19–7–64–2		1–0–5–0				
v. Sussex (Basingstoke) 23–25 June	16–3–42–4	8–3–29–1	7.5–1–22–1						
v. Gloucestershire (Bristol) 26–29 June	10–2–39–1	12–3–37–2	4–2–10–1		9.4–7–9–2				
v. Pakistanis (Bournemouth) 30 June–1 July		7–1–24–0 4–0–19–0	9–3–20–1	19–5–76–1 6–1–25–0	13.3–3–26–2	26–7–88–4		8–1–50–1 7–2–35–1	
v. Kent (Maidstone) 3–6 July	27.5–9–55–6 21–5–54–4	23–5–49–1 18.4–4–77–2	24–11–57–2 11–1–32–1		22–7–60–2 7–4–13–0	3–2–1–0			
v. Glamorgan (Cardiff) 10–13 July	8–4–8–1 19–6–46–2	7–1–16–1 15–4–19–4	7–0–12–0 12–4–35–0		2–1–2–0	16.1–2–50–4			
v. Surrey (Portsmouth) 17–20 July	23.2–9–66–1 16.3–1–64–4	17–3–60–1 12–0–38–4		18–1–64–1	18–5–59–2				28–8–63–2 4–0–15–0
v. Glamorgan (Portsmouth) 21–23 July	19–2–41–1 24–7–43–1	22–6–51–6 23–10–50–4	6–1–25–0 1–0–4–0	1.3–0–8–1	6–1–19–0				9–3–26–1 32.3–15–59–5
v. Somerset (Bournemouth) 31 July–3 August	19–5–47–3 16–3–37–5	21–5–53–3 5–0–21–1	7–2–31–4 10–4–8–4						11–3–37–0
v. Sussex (Eastbourne) 7–10 August	33–16–48–7 19–5–59–4	15.4–4–43–1 12–3–25–1			15–3–51–1	24–11–37–1 5–1–15–1			22–6–34–0 6–1–11–0
v. Essex (Chelmsford) 11–13 August	14–4–54–3 28–5–103–6	13.1–1–67–6 21–3–48–1				7–2–22–1 8–2–37–0			7–3–7–0 28–12–35–3
v. Worcestershire (Southampton) 14–17 Aug.	22.5–7–71–8 24–8–57–3		10–5–22–1 5–0–18–0		6–0–50–0	8.5–1–48–4		8–1–36–1 9–2–25–0	8–2–23–0 17–1–65–1
v. Northamptonshire (Northampton) 21–24 Aug.	28–4–84–2	21–7–48–3			24–4–96–0	41–10–118–3			
v. Gloucestershire (Bournemouth) 25–27 Aug.	16–1–48–3 13–5–33–5	15–3–75–2 10–2–25–2	17–4–41–1 5–4–4–1		11–0–54–1	11.3–5–18–3 7.4–2–13–2			10–5–19–0
v. Yorkshire (Bournemouth) 28–31 Aug.	32–13–41–6 17–1–44–2	25–8–39–1 6–1–11–1	6–3–8–0			32.5–12–60–1 21–2–106–5			
v. Derbyshire (Derby) 1–3 September	26–9–60–6 10–2–21–0	21–7–50–1 11–2–63–0	14–4–40–1			1–1–0–0 32–3–119–3			20.5–3–50–2 8–1–23–1
v. Middlesex (Uxbridge) 8–10 September	20–3–67–4 17–5–48–3	17–6–51–2 8–0–26–0	7–4–15–0		16–6–26–0 19–2–75–2	11.4–3–34–3 27.2–12–51–5			
v. Warwickshire (Southampton) 11–14 Sept.	26–8–74–5 17–2–53–1	17–5–51–1 15–3–64–3	6–2–11–0 4–0–18–1		20–6–54–1	4.5–0–22–2 11.2–0–43–1			15–7–24–1 19–2–64–3
	822–225– 2108–134 av. 15.73	637–149– 1892–79 av. 23.94	288.1–89– 750–35 av. 21.42	61.3–10– 240–3 av. 80.00	310.1–86– 895–24 av. 37.29	439.5–118– 1314–55 av. 23.89	22–10– 56–1 av. 56.00	150.5–35– 505–22 av. 22.95	354.3–114– 766–32 av. 23.93

* R. A. Woolmer retired hurt, absent hurt
a N. E. J. Pocock 12.5–1–55–0

John Player League Final Table

	P	W	L	T	NR	Pts
Sussex (5)	16	14	1	0	1	58
Middlesex (15)	16	11	4	0	1	46
Leicestershire (14)	16	9	6	0	1	38
Essex (1)	16	9	7	0	0	36
Kent (7)	16	9	7	0	0	36
Hampshire (6)	16	8	6	2	0	36
Nottinghamshire (10)	16	8	6	1	1	36
Northamptonshire (17)	16	8	7	0	1	34
Somerset (2)	16	8	8	0	0	32
Glamorgan (10)	16	6	7	0	3	30
Lancashire (10)	16	6	7	1	2	30
Surrey (7)	16	6	9	1	0	26
Derbyshire (4)	16	6	9	0	1	26
Gloucestershire (16)	16	5	9	0	2	24
Worcestershire (10)	16	5	10	0	1	22
Yorkshire (7)	16	3	10	1	2	18
Warwickshire (3)	16	3	11	0	2	16

(1981 position in brackets)

11, 13 and 14 September

at Derby

Glamorgan 224 (H. Morris 63, C. J. Tunnicliffe 4 for 44) and 327 for 9 dec (A. L. Jones 55, A. Jones 54, D. A. Francis 53, D. G. Moir 5 for 117)
Derbyshire 281 for 8 dec (K. J. Barnett 100 not out, J. G. Thomas 5 for 61) and 268 for 8 (P. N. Kirsten 92, J. H. Hampshire 57 not out)

Match drawn
Derbyshire 7 pts, Glamorgan 5 pts

at Chelmsford

Northamptonshire 376 for 9 dec (A. J. Lamb 106) and 251 for 7 dec (R. E. East 6 for 105)
Essex 300 for 7 dec (G. A. Gooch 61, D. S. Steele 5 for 105) and 168 (D. S. Steele 5 for 44)

Northamptonshire won by 159 runs
Northamptonshire 23 pts, Essex 7 pts

at Southampton

Hampshire 306 (C. G. Greenidge 85, M. C. J. Nicholas 67 retired hurt) and 261 for 4 dec (T. E. Jesty 134)
Warwickshire 191 (M. D. Marshall 5 for 74) and 339 (A. I. Kallicharran 131)

Hampshire won by 37 runs
Hampshire 24 pts, Warwickshire 5 pts

at Canterbury

Kent 250 (N. R. Taylor 82) and 241 (A. P. E. Knott 57, C. J. Tavare 52, G. J. Parsons 4 for 55)
Leicestershire 200 (G. R. Dilley 6 for 71) and 252 (B. F. Davison 100 not out, D. I. Gower 80, D. L. Underwood 5 for 80, G. R. Dilley 4 for 45)

Kent won by 39 runs
Kent 23 pts, Leicestershire 6 pts

Kent C.C.C. First-Class Matches – Batting, 1982

	v. Oxford University (Oxford) 1-4 May		v. Surrey (The Oval) 5-7 May		v. Warwickshire (Dartford) 12-14 May		v. Indians (Canterbury) 22-24 May		v. Somerset (Taunton) 29 May-1 June		v. Hampshire (Bournemouth) 2-4 June		v. Middlesex (Tunbridge Wells) 5-8 June		v. Sussex (Tunbridge Wells) 9-11 June		v. Nottinghamshire (Trent Bridge) 12-15 June		v. Derbyshire (Canterbury) 19-22 June		v. Leicestershire (Leicester) 23-25 June		v. Hampshire (Maidstone) 3-6 July		v. Surrey (Maidstone) 7-9 July	
R. A. Woolmer	126	—	0	62	4	55			31	50	10	32	25	2	203	22†	3	1	12	16†	42	—	3*	—		
N. R. Taylor	127	—	2	82	143*	2	62	18	7	81	16	3	100	1	—	—			40	4†	9*	—	40	13	37	0
C. J. Tavare	125	—	28	10	26	66	39	—	122*	9			1	2					54	—			68	39		
M. R. Benson	120	—	15*	20	0	0	9	41†															1	1	29	2
D. G. Aslett	51*	—									80	11	53	13			19	—	6	0	4*	—				
C. S. Cowdrey	42	—	—	10	42	17	7	19	34	16	49	4	30	14			27	—	11	21	7	—	14	31	5	13
G. W. Johnson	11	—	—	6	0	—	18*	12	1*	—							8	—	35	1	20	—	0	13	0	21
S. Marsh	—	—			10*	—																				
G. R. Dilley			—	13†	3	32	33	—			7	6†			3*	5			11	0	3	—	5	5	1	—
G. D. Spelman																										
K. B. S. Jarvis			—	1							3*	—	0	4			0*	0†	—	—			0	0	1	—
Asif Iqbal			0*	12	55	115†			47	20			13	21	73	—	9	0	65	—			10	75	23	15
A. P. E. Knott				3					5	5	65	—	24	1	30	—	52	13	22	—			18	36	53	38
D. L. Underwood				0					—	—	9	—	8	7	6*	—	4	2	6*	—			2*	11	2*	—
L. Potter							96	118			0	54					43	12†	0	0					5	90†
A. G. E. Ealham							16	31†			7	—														
E. A. Baptiste							14*	—																		
S. N. V. Waterton																										
L. J. Wood							—	—																		
C. Penn									30	—	2	—	7	11†	0	—			4*	—						
S. G. Hinks											1	2†							18	14						
R. M. Ellison																							29	2†		
Byes	2		1	2		4	1	1	4		16		4	1	8		5				1		4			
Leg-byes	6		1	4	10	4		4	13	5	9		3	1	5	1	2	5	6	4			8	6	12	4
Wides	5			3	1	1			1				1				1				1			1	1	1
No-balls	1		1	1	6	1	7	4			6		4	7			1		10	4			11	5	1	
Total	616		48	229	300	297	302	248	302	192	274	106	276	90	424	35	157	57	250	28	55		181	236	203	186
Wickets	6		3	10	7	5	7	4	7	5	10	4	10	10	8	0	10	10	8	0	1		9†	9	10	6
Result	D		L		D		D		D		W		L		W		L		D		D		L		D	
Points	—		4		7		—		7		23		4		24		5		4		0		5		5	

Fielding figures
54 – A. P. E. Knott (ct 46/st 8)
26 – C. S. Cowdrey
20 – G. W. Johnson
13 – C. J. Tavare and R. A. Woolmer
12 – D. G. Aslett
9 – G. R. Dilley
7 – Asif Iqbal, E. A. Baptiste, M. R. Benson and N. R. Taylor
6 – K. B. S. Jarvis, L. Potter and S. Marsh
4 – C. Penn
3 – R. M. Ellison and D. L. Underwood
2 – Subs
1 – S. G. Hinks and S. N. V. Waterton

at Taunton

Lancashire 168 (S. J. O'Shaughnessy 55, I. T. Botham 4 for 44) and 275 (C. H. Lloyd 79, S. J. O'Shaughnessy 62, V. J. Marks 6 for 128)
Somerset 307 (I. V. A. Richards 178, P. A. Slocombe 56, D. P. Hughes 4 for 22, S. J. O'Shaughnessy 4 for 72) and 119 (D. Lloyd 4 for 36)

Lancashire won by 14 runs
Lancashire 21 pts, Somerset 8 pts

at The Oval

Yorkshire 383 for 8 dec (J. D. Love 128, C. W. J. Athey 114 not out) and 209 for 7 dec (M. D. Moxon 54, K. Sharp 52)
Surrey 257 for 1 dec (G. P. Howarth 126 not out, D. M. Smith 100 not out) and 294 for 8 (D. M. Smith 75, A. Sidebottom 4 for 66)

Match drawn
Surrey 4 pts, Yorkshire 3 pts

at Hove

Sussex 257 (J. R. T. Barclay 85, A. P. Wells 70, R. J. Hadlee 5 for 21) and 284 for 6 dec (C. M. Wells 123 not out)

v. Worcestershire (Hereford) 21-23 July		v. Sussex (Hove) 28-30 July		v. Middlesex (Lord's) 31 July-3 August		v. Essex (Canterbury) 7-10 August		v. Glamorgan (Canterbury) 11-13 August		v. Yorkshire (Leeds) 14-17 August		v. Gloucestershire (Folkestone) 21-24 August		v. Northamptonshire (Folkestone) 25-27 August		v. Lancashire (Old Trafford) 28-31 August		v. Essex (Chelmsford) 1-3 September		v. Leicestershire (Canterbury) 11-14 September		Inns	NOs	Runs	HS	Av
												67	—			14	29					22	3	809	203	42.57
2	38	35	—	58	7	12	8	36	1	0	2	8	13	28	56	0	9	65	2	82	41	41	4	1290	143*	34.86
13	10					24	22					42	0					0	168*	34	52	23	2	954	168*	45.42
107	80	137	—			48	51	51	56*	57*	6	81	59*	25	7	48	8	8	13	16	4	30	5	1100	137	44.00
75	11	0	—	12	9	31	56	6	17	37	31			82	18	37	60	19	5	27	24	28	3	794	82	31.76
38	27	61	—	2	24	13	72*	6	12*		51*	54	—					4	10	2	5	35	4	794	72*	25.61
12*	12*	40	—	86	18	10	41	32	4	24*	11	16	59*	6	7	10	25	11*	—	12	0	34	7	582	86	21.55
																						1	1	10	10*	—
1*	—	14*	—	1	23	0	5				0			2*	1	17*	—	3	—	5	0	27	7	199	33	9.95
																						—				
						1	—				0*					5	—	0	—	0	6	15	4	21	6	1.90
				5	—																	17	2	558	115*	37.20
6	56*	32	—	9	42	40	1	15	—		4	44*	—	69*	21	1	22*	9	115*	34	57	32	5	942	115*	34.88
		0*	—	—	—	7*	0*	10*	—		2			—	10*	0	—	1	30	10*	2	22	11	129	30	11.72
39	44	13	—	108	55			0	52	26	4			8	8							21	2	775	118	40.78
																						2	1	47	31*	47.00
		20	—			11	14	69*	10	—	18			42	43	20	51*					12	3	319	69*	35.44
																						—				
				0*	0*																	8	4	54	30	13.50
																						4	1	35	14	11.66
				10	2			35	—					15	25*	0	—	1	—	14	46*	11	3	179	46*	22.37
1	2			1	4	4	5	4	4		4	1	1	3				2				† R. A. Woolmer retired hurt, absent hurt				
13	3			10	4	4	5	17	2	8	3	7		10	4	3	8	4	4	12	3					
1				2	2	2	1	2	1			2	1					1	2	2						
13	4		1	8	1	2	3	17	5	12	4	2	1	10	12	4	6	1	4		1					
321	287	353		312	191	209	284	300	164	164	142	324	134	300	212	159	218	129	353	250	241					
7	6	8		9	8	10	8	8	5	3	9	6	2	7	8	10	5	10	5	10	10					
D		D		D		D		D		D		D		D		D		D		W						
8		8		5		6		6		4		7		8		1		2		23						

Nottinghamshire 274 (R. T. Robinson 109, A. C. S. Pigott 6 for 61) and 269 for 4 (R. T. Robinson 79, D. W. Randall 76, C. E. B. Rice 58 not out, C. E. Waller 4 for 77)

Nottinghamshire won by 6 wickets
Nottinghamshire 22 pts, Sussex 5 pts

at Worcester

Worcestershire 168 (D. J. Humphries 56) and 263 M. J. Weston 64, P. A. Neale 50, M. W. Gatting 4 for 43)
Middlesex 382 (R. O. Butcher 94, P. H. Edmonds 92, M. W. Gatting 61) and 50 for 0

Middlesex won by 10 wickets
Middlesex 24 pts, Worcestershire 5 pts

David Bairstow came down to The Oval and scored 1 and 1 and took one catch as Yorkshire drew with Surrey in a high scoring game which saw Athey and Love add 190 for the Yorkshire fifth wicket and Howarth and Smith add an undefeated 232 at more than five an over for the Surrey second. One reflects on Bairstow because he had come straight from equalling the world record at Scarborough

David Bairstow

Kent C.C.C. First-Class Matches – Bowling, 1982

	K. B. S. Jarvis	G. R. Dilley	R. M. Ellison	R. A. Woolmer	D. G. Aslett	G. W. Johnson	C. S. Cowdrey	D. L. Underwood	C. Penn
v. Oxford University (Oxford) 1–4 May	17–4–58–2 12–6–7–1	15–3–35–0 10–3–21–3	11–6–13–2	14–2–54–1		20–6–49–1 2–2–0–0	7–1–21–0		
v. Surrey (The Oval) 5–7 May	24–5–77–2 8–0–47–0	22.2–1–96–6 9–1–35–0		4–1–14–0			8–4–6–2 1–0–4–0		
v. Warwickshire (Dartford) 12–14 May	16–4–50–1 20–4–80–2	15–6–27–1 17–4–81–1		11–3–28–1		23.5–7–64–0	9–3–31–1 1–0–5–0	36–14–63–5 35–9–104–4	
v. Indians (Canterbury) 22–24 May		17–7–35–0 5–1–5–0				20–7–40–0 2–0–7–0	20–4–60–0 9–2–20–1		
v. Somerset (Taunton) 29 May–1 June	18–3–75–0 11–1–33–0	17–5–59–1 13–1–45–0		7–2–23–0		19–6–48–2	3–0–25–0	23–9–65–4 28–15–47–3	13–0–64–0 4–1–11–2
v. Hampshire (Bournemouth) 2–4 June	16–6–46–3 20–7–53–2				2–0–7–0			23–11–45–3 32.2–6–79–7	5–1–10–1 9–3–21–0
v. Middlesex (Tunbridge Wells) 5–8 June	40–13–113–3	37–4–148–3		7–0–23–0	1–0–3–0		4–1–16–0	24–7–75–1	15–4–38–0
v. Sussex (Tunbridge Wells) 9–11 June	22–7–49–3 21–4–67–2			9–3–22–1	1–0–5–0	11–4–16–1	6–1–19–0 4.3–2–12–2	13.1–4–34–3 31–9–70–2	15–2–63–2 13–3–61–2
v. Nottinghamshire (Trent Bridge) 12–15 June	8–4–18–0 2–0–11–0	10–0–36–0 2–0–8–0			1–0–5–0	14.2–3–36–5	6–0–21–0	25–9–70–5	
v. Derbyshire (Canterbury) 19–22 June	14–6–33–2	11–4–28–1		2–1–2–0			8–1–37–0	2–0–3–0	11.4–1–42–0
v. Leicestershire (Leicester) 23–25 June									
v. Hampshire (Maidstone) 3–6 July	19–7–46–3 27–7–77–2	16.3–3–70–3 25–6–56–3		1–1–0–1		13–5–28–0	20–6–45–3 16–5–61–1	2–0–10–0 15.1–5–34–4	
v. Surrey (Maidstone) 7–9 July	20–3–62–1 10–1–39–1	13–3–64–0	16–1–41–3 14.2–1–52–1			26–11–72–3 15–6–31–1	1–0–1–0	26–10–72–3 23–8–69–3	
v. Worcestershire (Hereford) 21–23 July	18–0–91–1 10–1–54–1	27–5–87–6 5–1–22–1			2–0–13–0	26–6–55–1	3–1–10–0	35–14–75–2 5–0–17–0	
v. Sussex (Hove) 28–30 July	8–1–29–1 18–5–54–0	15–7–43–4 23–7–67–1				29.1–4–119–4 28–7–76–2	18–4–40–0 9–0–49–0	17.3–11–21–5 27–7–63–1	
v. Middlesex (Lord's) 31 July–3 August		15.3–5–37–2 7–1–17–1	12–5–21–0 2–1–4–0			7–1–23–0 8–1–35–1		27–8–57–1 13–1–74–2	6–1–16–0 2–1–1–0
v. Essex (Canterbury) 7–10 August	22–4–73–2 10–1–59–0	7–1–39–1					9–5–19–2 11–0–34–2	20–8–48–1 16–0–60–1	
v. Glamorgan (Canterbury) 11–13 August	25–3–95–2 17–6–32–1		23–6–63–1 6–1–21–0		5–0–18–0 6–1–33–1	18–2–61–1 20–5–46–0	4–1–7–1 9–0–49–1	20–6–34–1 9–3–34–1	
v. Yorkshire (Leeds) 14–17 August	19–6–43–1 4–0–15–0	16–6–34–0 4–0–15–0				12.3–1–52–5 6–0–21–1	4–0–14–0	35–14–62–4 9–2–41–0	
v. Gloucestershire (Folkestone) 21–24 August	16–4–55–0	22–4–72–3		8–3–15–1		11–2–43–1		14–3–41–1	
v. Northamptonshire (Folkestone) 25–27 August	23–4–94–5 15–2–71–1	16–2–52–1 23–4–88–3	13–6–12–3 21.5–8–51–3					7–4–10–1 10–2–28–1	
v. Lancashire (Old Trafford) 28–31 August	7–1–43–1 8–1–28–2	7–2–20–0 13–2–45–1	7–2–14–1 4–1–14–0		3–0–16–0		1–0–2–0	4–4–0–0 17.3–1–96–1	
v. Essex (Chelmsford) 1–3 September	18–1–71–3	16.5–0–88–0 2–2–0–1	9–1–40–0		1–0–4–0 4–1–8–0		12–2–31–0	29–7–51–3	
v. Leicestershire (Canterbury) 11–14 Sept.	20–6–40–1 11–0–38–0	27–7–71–6 12.1–2–45–4	14.4–2–40–3 11–0–60–1			4–0–22–0	2–0–19–0	14–6–19–0 23–6–80–5	
	614–138– 2026–52 av. 38.96	513.2–110– 1691–57 av. 22.66	153.5–35– 433–16 av. 27.06	60–20– 140–6 av. 23.33	84.1–10– 343–7 av. 49.00	330.4–84– 892–26 av. 34.30	166.3–39– 533–14 av. 38.07	690.4–223– 1751–78 av. 22.44	93.4–17– 327–7 av. 46.71

a G. D. Spelman 16–5–44–2 and 7–3–22–1   c S. G. Hinks 1.4–1–5–0
b L. J. Wood 12–1–58–0   d M. R. Benson 4–0–28–0

where he took 11 catches against Derbyshire, including a Yorkshire record 7 in the first innings. Bairstow is a man who deserves to break records for he has never given less than one hundred per cent commitment and enthusiasm. The game is the better for his having played it.

In the end, Surrey needed 346 in 220 minutes, but lost wickets in the rush for runs and Jackman held on for the draw. It was enough to maintain fifth place in the Championship.

Leicestershire's hopes of a miracle faded in defeat at Canterbury where Dilley had his best bowling figures of the season. Runs were never easy in this match and Leicestershire's target of 292 was a heavy one. Gower played a delightful innings of 80 and was third out at 129. It was then that Brian Davison took control with one of his belligerent and heroic innings. He equalled the Leicestershire record of seven centuries in a season, but Kent won with 4.3 overs to spare. It could not detract from the glory of Leicestershire's late challenge for the title, however, for once they had realised that Middlesex could be caught, they had played with a confidence and enthusiasm that was a joy to watch.

Somerset, who had been riding high in the closing weeks of the season, suffered an incredible defeat at the hands of Lancashire. Viv Richards had produced a violent attack on the Lancashire bowling to give Somerset a first innings lead of 139. Richards and Slocombe added 178 for the fourth wicket in 140 minutes. Richards hit two sixes and eighteen fours in his 4 hour 20 minute innings. Clive Lloyd and

Viv Richards

402/BENSON & HEDGES CRICKET YEAR

Lancashire C.C.C.
First-Class Matches – Batting, 1982

	v. Nottinghamshire (Old Trafford) 5-7 May	v. Cambridge University (Cambridge) 12-14 May	v. Derbyshire (Old Trafford) 19-21 May	v. Yorkshire (Leeds) 29-31 May	v. Gloucestershire (Gloucester) 2-4 June	v. Glamorgan (Old Trafford) 5-8 June	v. Hampshire (Southampton) 9-11 June	v. Essex (Liverpool) 12-15 June	v. Middlesex (Lord's) 19-22 June	v. Surrey (The Oval) 23-25 June	v. Worcestershire (Worcester) 26-29 June	v. Warwickshire (Edgbaston) 7-9 July	v. Surrey (Old Trafford) 10-13 July
A. Kennedy	21 0	19 17	3 —	20 43	0 —	9 36	31 15	2 3	33 —	31 —	38 —		
I. Cockbain	11 0		7 —										
D. Lloyd	5 14	54 4	114 —	21 81	108 —	8 30	0 112	29 20			12 —	83 —	6 36
C. H. Lloyd	21 13		73 —	5 15	44 —	0 53†	11 60		93 —	8 —		17 —	34 76
J. Abrahams	40 14	4 14		57 38	33 —	39 1	0 17	53 90	6 —		0 —	51 —	124 58
D. P. Hughes	0 3	106 0		126* 44	66* —	99 17	40 65	6 85†	12 —	7* —	39 —	43 —	20 21
J. Simmons	1 41		3*				50 27	34 —	0 —	6* —	13 —	21* —	2 31†
C. J. Scott	0 15	1 9	1 —			0* —							
P. J. W. Allott	9 8	23 11		30 —		17 —			2 —				
C. E. H. Croft	2* 16		3 —	8* —	—	17 2	18 1	12 —	20 —		2 —	8* —	
L. L. McFarlane	1 0	11 12			—		4* 0		0* —		0* —	—	
F. C. Hayes		0 9						43 —	21* —				
B. W. Reidy		37 11	19 —	19 11	1* —	9 —	15 33†	8 29		5 —	2 —		
I. Folley		17 15	36 —	4 5†	—	18 —			26* —		3 —	14 —	
G. J. Speak		4* 15†	1 —									7 —	
G. Fowler			12 —	32 2	100 —	18 52	2 6	37 122	28 —		28 —	150 —	11 21
M. A. Wallwork													
C. Maynard							20 1	1 2†	16 —	18 —	17 —	7 —	8 1
K. A. Hayes												90 —	4* —
S. J. O'Shaughnessy													11 0*
P. G. Lee													
N. H. Fairbrother													
M. Watkinson													
T. J. Taylor													
R. G. Watson													
Byes	1	8 1	7	5		2 12	7	5	6		5	10	2
Leg-byes	4 5	4	3	15 3	14	4 7	5 8	3 3	11	1	12	8	7 2
Wides		1		6 4	1		2	1	1		2	4	
No-balls	4	20	5	8 9	3	2	14 5	9 7	5		2	6	1 4
Total	120 129	304 128	287	351 255	375	240 212	210 359	237 367	280	78	175	498	249 252
Wickets	10 10	10 10	10	8 6	5	10 6	10 10	10 5	9†	5	10	7	10 6
Result	L	L	D	D	D	W	L	D	D	D	L	D	W
Points	4	—	7	5	7	22	5	3	4	2	0	5	22

Fielding figures
24 – J. Abrahams
23 – C. Maynard (ct 18/st 5)
19 – C. H. Lloyd
18 – D. P. Hughes
14 – J. Simmons
13 – C. J. Scott (ct 12/st 1)
 8 – D. Lloyd
 7 – C. E. H. Croft, A. Kennedy and B. W. Reidy
 5 – G. Fowler
 4 – P. J. W. Allott, I. Cockbain and sub
 3 – L. L. McFarlane, I. Folley, G. J. Speak and M. A. Wallwork
 1 – K. A. Hayes and S. J. O'Shaughnessy

O'Shaughnessy salvaged some pride for Lancashire from what looked like being a total wreck, but Somerset needed only 134 to win. They failed against a varied attack in which David Lloyd took the honours. The wicket was turning, but Somerset's was not a bright performance. This was Derek Taylor's last match and one cannot allow him to go from the game without saying thank you for the warmth of his professional accomplishment which went unrecognised by selectors who prefer to reward fledgling talents which then have the habit of never becoming full grown.

A fledgling talent which, one predicts, will rapidly come to maturity is that of Hugh Morris who batted admirably for his 63 for Glamorgan. Kim Barnett reached his second century of the season and Peter Kirsten left us with a pugnacious 92 in an otherwise undistinguished game.

Allan Lamb hit two centuries in a week-end against Essex, the second was in the John Player League, and David Steele spun Essex to defeat. It was a miserable end to the season for Essex who need to reflect on policies and team composition.

Notts ended on a happier note when they flayed a weakened Sussex attack to reach their target of 268 in 165 minutes with two overs to spare. Robinson followed his first century of the season with an exciting 79 and Randall and

THE ENGLISH SEASON/403

	v. Northamptonshire (Old Trafford) 21–23 July		v. Warwickshire (Southport) 28–30 July		v. Nottinghamshire (Trent Bridge) 31 July–3 August		v. Yorkshire (Old Trafford) 7–10 August		v. Derbyshire (Derby) 11–13 August		v. Leicestershire (Leicester) 14–17 August		v. Pakistanis (Old Trafford) 21–23 August		v. Worcestershire (Blackpool) 25–27 August		v. Kent (Old Trafford) 28–31 August		v. Sussex (Old Trafford) 8–10 August		v. Somerset (Taunton) 11–14 September			Inns	NOs	Runs	HS	Av
													17*	—											12	1	242	43	22.00
			98	—	17	2	0	13*	39	33	52	7			29	—	43	21	11	2	7	4	25	1	492	98	20.50
61	112*	10	88*	17	56	31	—	12	2	—	—	55	—	0	—	29	103	7	11	3	2	35	2	1336	114	40.48
28	—	45	—	3	45*	100	—	34	—	2	68	—	—	35	—	—	31	50	60	32	79	29	2	1135	100	42.03
49	—	51*	—	14	—	41	—	90*	19*	2	17*	—	—	0	—	—	0	27	32	6	26	32	5	1013	124	37.51
14	4	14	—	17	22*	6	—	111	21*	36*	13	1*	—	93	—	—	63*	44	7	5	33	36	9	1303	126*	48.25
79*	5*	—	—	64*	—	61*	—	—	—	15*	11*	—	—	10	—			8*	5*			21	12	487	79*	54.11
		9	—	4	—																	8	1	39	15	5.57
														14	—			5				11	2	135	30	15.00
																						12	3	109	20	12.11
				8	—									3	—							10	3	39	12	5.57
																						4	1	73	43	24.33
																						13	2	199	37	18.09
—	—	—	—	5	—			—	0					10*	—			—	5	5	2*	15	4	165	36	15.00
																						4	2	27	15*	13.50
66	35	126	128*			4	17*	29	57	1	0	27	—					91	11	19	12	31	2	1246	150	42.96
10	—							—	37	—	—	6	—	2	—	1*	5		5*	10	20	19	3	187	37	11.68
9																						3	1	103	90	51.50
56	50	26*	—	0	1	41*	—	5*	8	55	34			58	—	25*	9*	54*	10	55	62	19	7	560	62	46.66
				0	—			—	—					—	—							1		0	0	0.00
																1*	—									
																—	—					—				
																				11	4	2		15	11	7.50

† F. C. Hayes retired hurt

6				2	1	8		2	1	12		2		3				2			5
9	7	13	2	4	3	5		2	2	6	2	4		7		2	2	4	4	3	11
		3			1															1	2
10	2	19	8	10	2	13		8	1	6	2	8		13		5	6			4	1
397	215	414	226	165	133	310	30	332	181	187	154	120		277		105	247	301	152	165	275
8	3	6	0	10	3	6	0	5	6	5	5	3		10		2	6	6	8	10	10
D		W		D		D		D		D		D		D		D		D		W	
6		21		5		4		4		3		—		7		4		4		21	

Rice played sparkling innings. For Sussex, Barclay had shown that 1983 might see him recapture his elusive batting form and the Wells brothers both made exciting and entertaining contributions. Alan Wells has had to be content with winning places in the side for his fine fielding, but, surely, he is a Sussex batsman who will gather a rich harvest in the next few years.

When the England party to tour Australia was announced on the Saturday the name of Trevor Jesty was not among it. Jesty's answer was to pound his eighth century of the season in 82 minutes, two sixes and twenty-two fours. Bob Willis, the England captain, who did not introduce himself into the attack while Jesty was making his main assault, watched thoughtfully and the Hampshire crowd left Willis in no doubt as to their opinion of Jesty's non-selection. Malcolm Marshall broke Lance Gibbs' eleven-year old record of 131 wickets in a season which contained only 22 championship matches. Marshall's sustained hostility over the season when his enthusiasm and endeavour had never flagged had had much to do with Hampshire's success and their well deserved third place. They were a good, happy

Malcolm Marshall

Lancashire C.C.C. First-Class Matches – Bowling, 1982

	C. E. H. Croft	P. J. W. Allott	L. L. McFarlane	J. Simmons	G. J. Speak	I. Folley	D. Lloyd	J. Abrahams	D. P. Hughes
v. Nottinghamshire (Old Trafford) 5–7 May	23–3–96–2	21–3–76–2	15–3–64–4	13.4–3–33–2					
v. Cambridge University (Cambridge) 12–14 May		21–6–62–2	15–3–59–0		6–1–14–0	19–4–40–4	8–1–15–0	13–3–46–0	8.2–2–28–4
		13–6–26–0	5–2–10–0		4–0–18–0	10–5–24–2		6.4–0–27–0	13–2–41–1
v. Derbyshire (Old Trafford) 19–21 May	33–7–88–7				10–1–25–0	20–3–37–3	1–0–4–0		
	20–2–81–0			16–4–42–2	5–0–24–0	10–3–20–0	19–4–49–1		
v. Yorkshire (Leeds) 29–31 May	27–4–103–1	19–5–52–2				12–3–40–0	6–0–20–0	11–3–29–1	1–0–12–0
	15.2–1–51–3	10–1–39–0				6–1–22–0	1–1–0–0		
v. Gloucestershire (Gloucester) 2–4 June	10–0–39–4		12.5–1–62–2			6–0–26–1	16–2–60–1	20–1–52–2	
	11–1–37–1		8–2–31–1			9–0–25–0	13–3–46–0	31–6–77–2	16–3–57–0
v. Glamorgan (Old Trafford) 5–8 June	20–7–42–3	15–5–27–2				15–6–30–2	17–10–23–3	9.3–2–22–2	
	17–5–24–2	16–8–15–0				6–1–7–0			
v. Hampshire (Southampton) 9–11 June	27–3–102–2		23–3–102–1	22–6–53–1			8–1–36–0	7–0–29–0	14–0–63–3
	8.4–0–62–0		5–0–36–0	3–0–14–0					
v. Essex (Liverpool) 12–15 June	23–7–64–1		14–3–62–0	29–8–81–1			7.2–0–28–0	3–0–5–0	
v. Middlesex (Lord's) 19–22 June	26–3–100–4	13–1–67–1		14–2–57–1		5–0–18–0			
v. Surrey (The Oval) 23–25 June	8–4–23–2		5–2–11–0	7–1–36–1		12–3–35–2			
v. Worcestershire (Worcester) 26–29 June	7–1–35–0		16–2–64–4	24–3–71–3		5–0–34–0			
v. Warwickshire (Edgbaston) 7–9 July	16–6–40–0		14–3–56–0	37–10–79–4		17.1–7–23–3	20–5–43–3	21–7–46–0	31–11–65–2
	5–4–5–0		10–2–34–0	24–6–51–1		5–1–6–0	8–2–22–0	14–6–19–2	17.1–7–37–1
v. Surrey (Old Trafford) 10–13 July				33–14–54–2	24–3–78–1	16–4–28–1	3–0–9–0	14–6–19–2	
				25–7–57–5	4–0–17–0	11–2–29–1	15–4–52–1	4–0–13–0	
v. Northamptonshire (Old Trafford) 21–23 July			14–6–55–0	24–0–53–0		7–2–21–1	16–3–42–1	22–2–75–1	23–10–63–2
			9–1–49–0	13–1–46–1		3–0–24–0	3–3–0–0	13–1–40–1	22–7–50–4
v. Warwickshire (Southport) 28–30 July			11–2–90–2	20–2–97–0		15–3–64–1	10.1–1–45–1	15–3–76–0	20–2–79–0
			20–3–59–6	1–1–0–0		11–5–19–1			
v. Notts. (Trent Bridge) 31 July–3 August			14–5–37–4	18.3–9–27–2		11–5–20–3		6–0–18–0	
			1–0–6–1	28.2–10–47–3		17–4–28–0	9–3–9–0	3–0–14–0	16–4–39–0
v. Yorkshire (Old Trafford) 7–10 August		15–6–19–1		14–4–33–1		14–8–11–0	12–6–9–0	7–3–7–0	
v. Derbyshire (Derby) 11–13 August		34–11–74–3		20–3–47–0		6–1–20–0	23.1–5–68–2	6–0–23–1	12–2–36–0
v. Leicestershire (Leicester) 14–17 August	7–3–11–1	22–7–59–0		33.1–13–59–4		8–1–18–1	6–3–19–0	21–5–63–2	
		11–3–33–0		14–1–57–5			1–0–4–0		
v. Pakistanis (Old Trafford) 21–23 Aug.		6–3–9–1	5–0–22–0			1–0–2–0	3–0–10–0	7–2–32–0	
v. Worcestershire (Blackpool) 25–27 August		14.1–4–32–4	4–0–26–2	18–7–31–0		5–2–6–0	13–6–17–1		17–8–23–3
		10–4–16–1	3–0–11–0	25–16–31–3			8–1–24–0	4–3–5–1	
v. Kent (Old Trafford) 28–31 August		25–8–58–5					1–0–4–0	15–6–30–2	
		7–0–22–1					3–0–22–1	11–4–42–0	
v. Sussex (Old Trafford) 8–10 September		21.5–3–72–1		36–11–68–3		20–5–38–0	4–0–14–0	7–0–19–0	14–2–30–1
		7–3–14–0		26–10–60–4		11.5–2–19–1	11–3–23–1	18–3–58–1	12–3–24–3
v. Somerset (Taunton) 11–14 September		14–5–30–1				17–4–50–1	15–0–59–0	19–2–61–0	10–2–22–4
		15–2–29–3				3–0–5–0	15.4–1–36–4	2–0–6–0	11–4–18–1
	304–61–1003–33 av. 30.39	330–94–831–30 av. 27.70	223.5–43–946–27 av. 35.03	538.4–152–1284–49 av. 26.20	53–5–176–1 av. 176.00	311–76–758–27 av. 28.07	297.2–68–801–21 av. 38.14	316.1–61–921–16 av. 57.56	292.3–79–789–31 av. 25.45

a G. Fowler 5–2–11–0; A. Kennedy 7–2–17–1
b A Kennedy 2–0–11–0
c G. Fowler 2–0–2–0; I. Cockbain 2–2–0–0
d T. J. Taylor 3–0–15–0 and 13–1–57–1
e M. Watkinson 5–3–21–0 and 8–1–24–1

B. W. Reidy	P. G. Lee	S. J. O'Shaugnessy	Byes	Leg byes	Wides	No balls	Total	Wickets
			4	6	7		286	10
5-4-7-0				5		5	274	10
15-1-42-0				4		2	159	3
5-1-16-2				14	1	5	216	10
13-5-40-1			1	3	1	5	242	5
14-1-78-2			7	6	2	6	317	6
6-2-19-0				6		1	197	5
7-0-41-0			1	5		3	267	10
8-4-10-1			3	1	2	2	350	5a
17-5-33-3			1	3		2	115	10
18-6-58-0				3		4	131	10
			3	6	1	5	458	8
				2	1		115	0
18-5-48-1			1		1	10	300	3
			5	5		4	267	6b
3-0-19-0			2		1	1	128	5
9-0-46-0			4	4	3	3	264	7
			4	5		7	303	10
			1	5	1	1	238	3
		29-6-89-3		6	1	3	324	10
		5-2-6-0		2			176	7
		2-0-9-0	8	1		3	330	5
			6	8			223	6
		15-2-62-0	1	6	1	2	523	4
		7.1-0-29-3	1	2	1		111	10
	7-1-31-0	6-0-28-1		2		1	164	10
	10-1-34-1	19-3-66-4	3	11	3	1	261	10
				Innings Forfeited				
	10-0-19-1	8-1-32-0		6	1	3	142	3c
		6-1-26-0	2	9			305	7
		15-1-59-1		7		3	298	10
		10.3-1-39-3	2	1		1	137	9
	5-1-17-0			1			93	1
		6-1-19-3	9	4		1	145	10
		10-4-24-0	9	2	1	2	148	8
		14.3-4-24-3		3		4	159	10d
		11-3-37-1		8		6	218	4e
		16-0-60-0	3	6		5	315	6
		3-0-13-0	4	6		2	223	10
		21.1-3-72-4	5	1		7	307	10
		5-2-16-1		7		2	119	10
138-34-	32-3-	209.2-34-						
457-10	101-2	710-27						
av. 45.70	av. 50.50	av. 26.29						

team to watch and they were as proud of Marshall as they were hurt by Jesty's non-selection. On the final day, Warwickshire batted bravely in search of 377 to win and Kallicharran scored his eighth century and became the only batsman to pass 2,000 runs in the season, but Warwickshire finished without a win and bottom of the table.

Shortly after lunch on the first day, Warner lofted Emburey to long-off where Daniel held the catch. This reduced Worcestershire to 168 for 9 and gave Middlesex their fourth bonus point of the match so making them Schweppes County Champions, the fourth time that they had won the title under Brearley's leadership. It was a reward for Brearley's fine, competitive side, rich in talent, strong in selection and tactics. It was some consolation for Gatting, Edmonds and Downton, all of whom had reason to believe that they would be going with the England party to Australia.

Roland Butcher, another forgotten man, Gatting and a nonchalantly aggressive Phil Edmonds thumped Middlesex to a 214-run lead and it was only that batting of the impressive Weston that saw Worcestershire into the last day. Gatting showed his all-round abilities with a good bowling spell.

On the last morning Middlesex won by 10 wickets and Brearley left the scene after making the winning hit.

There was, in a sense, no sadness at Brearley's departure. What more could the man accomplish? In bearing and tactical intelligence he stood above his contemporaries and his greying hair marked him out as the grey eminence of the game. The quickness of the man's mind is a delight whether he is arguing with you about a quote from *The Wild Duck* or reading the wicket at Lord's and forecasting, rightly, to dubious listeners that Surrey would be bowled out for under 150 in their second innings for the wicket would turn. He has had his detractors and there are those

Schweppes County Championship Final Table

	P	W	L	D	Btg	Blg	Pts
Middlesex (4)	22	12	2	8	59	74	325
Leicestershire (8)	22	10	4	8	57	69	286
Hampshire (7)	22	8	6	8	48	74	250
Nottinghamshire (1)	22	7	7	8	44	65	221
Surrey (6)	22	6	6	10	56	62	214
Somerset (3)	22	6	6	10	51	66	213
Essex (5)	22	5	5	12	57	75	212
Sussex (2)	22	6	7	9	43	68	207
Northamptonshire (15)	22	5	3	14	61	54	195
Yorkshire (10)	22	5	1	16	48	51	179
Derbyshire (12)	22	4	3	15	45	64	173
Lancashire (16)	22	4	3	15	48	55	167
Kent (9)	22	3	4	15	55	63	166
Worcestershire (11)	22	3	5	14	43	54	141
Gloucestershire (13)	22	2	9	11	46	55	133
Glamorgan (14)	22	1	8	13	43	60	119
Warwickshire (17)	22	0	8	14	58	53	111

Worcestershire total includes 12 pts from match reduced to one innings.
1981 positions in brackets.

Leicestershire C.C.C. First-Class Matches – Batting, 1982

Player	v. Hampshire (Southampton) 5-7 May		v. Surrey (Leicester) 12-14 May		v. Glamorgan (Cardiff) 19-21 May		v. Northamptonshire (Leicester) 29 May-1 June		v. Yorkshire (Hinckley) 2-4 June		v. Zimbabwe (Leicester) 5-8 June		v. Warwickshire (Leicester) 9-11 June		v. Cambridge University (Cambridge) 19-22 June		v. Kent (Leicester) 23-25 June		v. Derbyshire (Derby) 26-29 June		v. Middlesex (Uxbridge) 7-9 July		v. Derbyshire (Coalville) 10-13 July		v. Sussex (Hove) 17-20 July	
J. C. Balderstone	6	40	94	17	8	—	98	5	67	6			51	7			—		8	9	148	14	57	75	16	20
J. F. Steele	19	22	3	—			5	12*	40	0	63	10*	58	4*					3	12*	1	—	8	0	6	40*
D. I. Gower	5	15	99	61			54	52			32	0			77	—										
B. F. Davison	172	29	31	111	23	—	14	52			6	5	42	12	58*	9			61	45	100	25*	72	60	14	11
N. E. Briers	7	18	13	8	40	—	71	5	106	19					94				1	36	1	—	33	0	69	10
R. W. Tolchard	24	6	0	15*	93*	—	16	17	45	30			5	50*					22	53	80*	2	9	27	4	57
M. A. Garnham	5	38*	24	55	53	—	1	0			6	15	8	10	21	57	0	—	0	—	0	5*				
A. M. E. Roberts	0	18	20	15*	11	—					0	22*			16	3					4	6				
N. G. B. Cook	4	4			10	—	19*	—			—	—			16*	—			7*	2*	5	—	21*	22	29*	0
J. P. Agnew	18	4	4	—							—	—							0	—	14	0	0	17		
L. B. Taylor	0*	2	6*	—	0	—	2*	—		5			9*	—	0*	10			0	—	17	—	2	0*	13	0
G. J. Parsons			22	—	43	—	4	4*	1*	9	9*	—			20	—			9	—	16	—	3	0	1	2
R. A. Cobb					7	—			41	20			64	26	33	33	10	5	6	8	0	20	3	22	32	21
I. P. Butcher					23	—				5*							14	25*								
P. B. Clift							17	18			45	15*											1	1	1	16
T. J. Boon											1	8			4	5*										
G. Forster											22*	—			4	—										
K. Higgs															—	—										
D. A. Wenlock															9	—										
Byes	4	8	4	4	6			5			4	1	1	1	1				2	4		2	5	5	2	
Leg-byes	9	10	9	5	7		7		15	5	11	3	6	9	5	2			1	3	8	1	4	5	15	4
Wides	1					1		1			1		9			1				1	1		1		1	2
No-balls	7		2	1	3		11	3	8	5	18		2	1	2	2			6	2	18		1	5	5	4
Total	281	214	331	292	327		319	174	329	141	284	78	302	196	256	40			126	175	399	75	234	222	208	204
Wickets	10	10	10	5	10		9	7	7	8	7	5	7	7	9	1			10	5	10	4	10	10	10	10
Result	D		W		W		D		D		D		D		D		D		L		W		L		W	
Points	7		24		23		5		7		—		5		—		0		0		24		6		22	

Fielding figures
53 – R. W. Tolchard (ct 45/st 8)
26 – J. F. Steele
19 – N. G. B. Cook
18 – J. C. Balderstone
17 – M. A. Garnham (ct 13/st 4)
16 – B. F. Davison
12 – N. E. Briers
11 – R. A. Cobb
7 – G. J. Parsons
5 – I. P. Butcher
4 – D. I. Gower, A. M. E. Roberts and subs
3 – T. J. Boon
2 – L. B. Taylor and G. Forster
1 – J. P. Agnew, P. B. Clift and D. A. Wenlock

throughout the country who have booed him as he came out to bat, and, indeed, it would be foolish to deny that there are times when he has frustrated and annoyed, but his strength has been that, while always giving total commitment to the game, he has never failed to realise that it is not the most important part of life, but an artistic reflection of life itself and that pain and survival are part of it. I do not think I shall see his like again in my life-time.

The sweet taste of success. Mike Brearley, Mike Gatting and Richard Ellis celebrate the winning of the Schweppes County Championship.

	v. Pakistanis (Leicester) 21-23 July		v. Essex (Leicester) 24-27 July		v. Gloucestershire (Leicester) 31 July-3 August		v. Worcestershire (Worcester) 7-10 August		v. Nottinghamshire (Leicester) 11-13 August		v. Lancashire (Leicester) 14-17 August		v. Somerset (Taunton) 21-24 August		v. Essex (Colchester) 25-27 August		v. Northamptonshire (Northampton) 28-31 August		v. Glamorgan (Leicester) 1-3 September		v. Nottinghamshire (Trent Bridge) 8-10 September		v. Kent (Canterbury) 11-14 September		Inns	NOs	Runs	HS	Av
	4	4	10	3	103*	—	35	4	21	15*	52	14	0	88	114*	12	28	17	118	—	42	48	4	0	41	3	1482	148	39.00
			6	9			33	—	15		44	8			7	24*	18	—			18	0	8	0	31	6	496	63	19.84
	176*	16	37	9			4	74					111	—					77	—	6	6	26	80	21	1	1017	176*	50.85
			59	45	39	—	14	139*	51	—	60	31	14	—	0	110*	68	20	119	—	1	26	19	100*	37	4	1800	172	54.54
			40	5	38	—	33	13	11	—	45	38	91*	93*	36	7	35	6	21*	—	36	12	10	7	38	4	1175	106	34.55
	—	61	6	10	0*	—	2	6*	6	—	13	9	50	—	30	0	13	24*	1	—	11	3	31*	12	38	8	843	93*	28.10
																									17	2	298	57	19.86
	—	22*							25	—					43	42			27	—	0	4	47	13	20	3	338	47	19.88
	—	5	12	0			9	—	33*	—	13	7			0	—	3	—			4*	22	37	0	25	8	284	37	16.70
		0*	2	7			56	—																	12	1	122	56	11.09
			0	4*			24*	—	25	—	6*	6*			0	—	7	0			0	0	0	7	23	8	119	25	7.93
	—	4	41*	0			13	30	24	—	51	8	21*	—	2	—	49	50			10	14*	2	12	32	7	392	51	15.68
	42	13	63	15	27	—	7	11	27	5*	0	9	63	—	0	—	35	6	3	—	0	6	5	14	37	1	760	64	21.11
	71*	1													0	—	12	31							9	3	189	71*	30.33
																	4*	24							6	2	123	45	30.75
	44	90			21	—			13	—	2	3													14	1	210	90	16.15
											2	—													3	1	28	22*	14.00
																									—				
	—	2															4	—							3	—	15	9	5.00

	6	9	3				1	2	5			2			1	3			11			1		
	3	3	9	4		10	5	9	4		7	1	7	3	11	8	7	5	10		1	3	4	6
			1												1								1	2	1
	8	11		1		6	11	3	7		3	1	7	2	1		15	5	24		15	5	5	

	354	241	289	112	244		247	291	267	20	298	137	364	189	246	203	263	186	411		144	151	200	252
	3	9	10	10	4		10	5	10	0	10	9	4	1	10	4	10	7	6		10	10	10	10
	D		W		W		D		W		D		W		W		D		W		L		L	
	—		23		22		5		23		5		24		21		7		24		3		6	

Leicestershire C.C.C. First-Class Matches – Bowling, 1982

	A. M. E. Roberts	L. B. Taylor	J. P. Agnew	N. G. B. Cook	J. F. Steele	N. E. Briers	G. J. Parsons	J. C. Balderstone	P. B. Clift
v. Hampshire (Southampton) 5–7 May	22-7-52-1 8-3-23-0	20-7-63-3 8-0-33-1	17.3-2-73-3 2-0-14-0	17-3-42-1 1-0-4-0	6-0-26-0	3-0-11-1			
v. Surrey (Leicester) 12–14 May	21-2-69-3 14-3-36-1	18-4-48-2	14.1-2-71-2 18-3-72-2		13-4-29-0 23-1-78-1	2-1-5-0	22-2-123-3 15-2-55-1	4-1-10-0	
v. Glamorgan (Cardiff) 19–21 May	18-8-27-5 18.4-6-33-2	17-4-30-2 21-8-31-4		15.2-8-21-2 16-6-39-1			11-1-40-1 18-5-68-3		
v. Northamptonshire (Leicester) 29 May–1 June		19-2-52-1 15-4-46-1		36-11-88-2 32-7-116-3	17-4-50-1	1-0-4-0	16-3-65-0 2-1-4-0	9-1-19-0 19-6-51-4	22-4-69-1
v. Yorkshire (Hinckley) 2–4 June	24-6-70-2 12-2-27-0	22-7-52-5 3-0-13-0		7-1-15-0 18-3-74-4	5-2-3-1 15-1-73-2		15.5-1-74-0 2-1-2-0	2-2-0-0	
v. Zimbabwe (Leicester) 5–8 June			19-2-54-1 8-1-27-0	10-2-47-1 24.5-5-73-3	22-4-49-2		16-3-64-3 12-0-48-1	18-3-51-2 18-3-49-2	
v. Warwickshire (Leicester) 9–11 June	25-4-79-2 25.2-5-61-6			19-6-43-0 8-6-5-0	17-5-37-0		28.3-2-130-2 20-4-71-3	10-0-34-2 5-1-16-0	
v. Cambridge University (Cambridge) 19–22 June		18-5-54-1		7-3-12-1		5-2-11-2	13-2-65-1		
v. Kent (Leicester) 23–25 June	8-7-1-0	3-2-4-0		12-6-16-0			4-1-25-0	4-1-9-1	
v. Derbyshire (Derby) 26–29 June		11-5-21-0 3-0-25-0	2-0-25-0 2.2-0-19-0	8.3-5-7-1 21-2-78-1	3-1-4-0 13-0-46-1		4-0-7-0 6-0-33-0	3-0-19-0	
v. Middlesex (Uxbridge) 7–9 July	16-2-38-0 22.3-7-53-4	18-3-42-3 17-3-60-2		25.4-13-32-6 31-8-87-0	1-1-0-0 22-5-42-2	4-0-24-1	12-1-43-0 10-2-29-1	3-0-6-0	
v. Derbyshire (Coalville) 10–13 July		28-8-58-4 16-1-65-2	10-3-40-0 5-0-14-1	24.2-7-60-1 13-0-55-0	31-8-60-5 18.4-2-54-2		13-5-21-0 5-1-21-0	2-0-8-0	
v. Sussex (Hove) 17–20 July		16-4-44-1 17-4-35-0	17-4-55-4 9-1-24-1	7-1-22-0 19.1-0-81-7	7.3-4-4-5 11-0-66-1		9-2-30-0 4-0-23-0		
v. Pakistanis (Leicester) 21–23 July	13-3-41-0 5-2-13-1		16.3-0-101-0 3.2-0-25-0	18-2-63-2			15-1-87-0 6-2-18-1	4-1-10-0	
v. Essex (Leicester) 24–27 July		23-6-54-4 17-7-42-1	14-3-59-0 12-1-36-0	24.3-8-51-6 14-3-26-1	21.2-13-18-2		9-1-42-0 13-5-25-5		
v. Gloucestershire (Leicester) 31 July–3 Aug.		13.2-4-24-5 12-7-9-3	14-4-16-3 12-1-42-1	18-10-36-2 27-10-56-3	0.3-0-0-1 15-2-28-1	9-1-31-0	11-2-37-2 20-2-87-2		
v. Worcestershire (Worcester) 7–10 August		21-7-41-1	8-0-49-1		10-6-4-1			9-6-3-0	
v. Nottinghamshire (Leicester) 11–13 August	16-4-53-4 13-3-37-5	20-4-58-2 12.4-1-28-4		16-9-25-1	8.5-2-13-2		13-2-48-1		
v. Lancashire (Leicester) 14–17 August		19-8-16-1 6-1-17-1		31.5-12-64-0 22.4-3-69-3	27-10-47-3 10-5-23-1		11-3-21-1 2-0-8-0		
v. Somerset (Taunton) 21–24 August		21-6-36-2 12.1-4-30-1		30.5-9-49-2 35-14-63-7	14-6-24-1 27-10-51-2		23-4-88-4 6-1-18-0		11-5-8-1 3-2-6-0
v. Essex (Colchester) 25–27 August	17-5-38-1 15-3-36-0	19-3-62-2 3-0-13-0		12.5-6-17-6 36-8-113-6	27.2-7-80-3		11-1-13-1 7-0-47-1		
v. Northamptonshire (Northampton) 28–31 Aug.				34.3-13-77-3 24-5-57-3	25-11-45-5 15-5-31-2		14-6-24-0 6-1-27-2	3-3-0-0	16-1-62-1 13-5-30-0
v. Glamorgan (Leicester) 1–3 September	27-9-38-6 22.5-8-56-8	14-5-26-0 17-8-32-0		14.1-5-37-2 12-4-27-0			25-4-77-2 8-4-12-2		9-3-8-0 3-1-11-0
v. Nottinghamshire (Trent Bridge) 8–10 Sept.	24-0-96-1	26-4-101-5		31-10-67-1	17-2-28-1		18-0-87-2	1-0-2-0	
v. Kent (Canterbury) 11–14 September	20-7-41-1 21-8-63-2	24-5-83-3 12-2-17-0		26-11-57-3 26-7-56-2	9.1-5-16-2 18-5-46-2		13-4-39-1 17.3-4-55-4	1-1-0-0	
	428.2-114- 1081-55 av. 19.65	582.1-153- 1465-67 av. 21.86	203.5-27- 816-19 av. 42.94	827.1-252- 2027-87 av. 23.29	470.2-131- 1075-52 av. 20.67	24-4- 86-4 av. 21.50	515.5-89- 1931-50 av. 38.62	78-22- 187-7 av. 26.71	113-27- 294-7 av. 42.00

* P. Bainbridge, retired hurt, absent hurt † J. D. Birch retired hurt
a D. I. Gower 5-2-10-0; R. A. Cobb 4-2-5-0

The Problem of Wickets
Bob Willis

Cricket Year, 1982, had provided more than its share of controversies and surprises. They are reflected upon by England captain *Bob Willis* and associate editor and former England captain *Tony Lewis*:

I believe that wickets are the big problem in the cricket world. Quite simply, if the wickets are not good enough to reflect all cricket's subtleties, the game suffers as a spectacle and for the players. Ideally, a good cricket wicket for a three to five day match should satisfy the following requirements – it should be lively early on with the pace bowler encouraged to slip himself, and it should turn for the spinner as the game goes on. At all times, the wicket should be fast. Thus the stroke players are encouraged and the slow bowler who gets an edge from the batsman will be rewarded. As a fan of slow bowlers myself, I could weep for them sometimes as the nick fails to carry to slip or short leg because the wicket is so slow. That is one of the main reasons why slow bowlers have declined so dramatically in importance in recent years – they are just not being encouraged to develop their skills and experience by groundsmen.

The same applies to fast bowlers in England. The fact that I am still a Test fast bowler in my thirty-fourth year is a matter of great professional pride to me, but it has serious implications for English cricket. Few young fast bowlers are coming through to jostle me out of the Test side because the wickets are so slow in England. You really have to work hard to wring some pace out of these low, unresponsive tracks; you need to be fit, dedicated and philosophical. I am afraid that hard work is not an attitude embraced by many young English fast bowlers these days, something that saddens me – but the fact remains that groundsmen are not encouraging them by turning out lifeless pitches. The game of cricket was not meant to be dominated by batsmen who just nudge and deflect their runs and medium pace trundlers who can wobble the ball around on green wickets. It should be a game of challenge and counter-attack, of variety and subtlety as well as raw aggression. I believe the players would respond continually if the wickets were fast and true, but what are the groundsmen doing about it? I think that they have been let off lightly in recent years and that is mainly due to self-interest…

Counties want to win trophies and there is no doubt their groundsmen are instructed to prepare pitches that suit their bowling strategies. That has gone on for decades, I agree, but in recent years, the trend has been towards dead, slow tracks. In 1981 Nottinghamshire reversed that trend and prepared pitches that yielded positive results. Many in the game accused Nottinghamshire of sharp practice but I was not one of them; you could still play shots at Trent Bridge, and class spinners still picked up a fair share of wickets there. The county championship went to Nottinghamshire that season, but I have no complaints about that. At least the spectators saw genuine entertainment, not those dreadful draws that seem inevitable midway through the second day. On those occasions, the lethargy that envelops the players is all too easily transmitted to the crowd and we lose spectators who vow never to return because the cricket is too dull. On behalf of my fellow professionals, I can only say

Middlesex C.C.C. First-Class Matches – Batting, 1982

Player	v. Cambridge University (Cambridge) 28–30 April		v. Essex (Lord's) 5–7 May		v. Northamptonshire (Lord's) 12–14 May		v. Oxford University (Oxford) 19–21 May		v. Sussex (Lord's) 29 May–1 June		v. Derbyshire (Lord's) 2–4 June		v. Kent (Tunbridge Wells) 5–8 June		v. Glamorgan (Swansea) 9–11 June		v. Yorkshire (Sheffield) 12–15 June		v. Lancashire (Lord's) 19–22 June		v. Pakistanis (Lord's) 23–25 June		v. Surrey (The Oval) 26–29 June		v. Leicestershire (Uxbridge) 7–9 July	
J. M. Brearley	60	—	4*	59	165	21*			7	33	43*	6	33	—			25	18*	0	—			6	40*	5	1
W. N. Slack	114	—	4*	19	44	1	203*	—	85	36	42*	46	51	—	37	11	3	0	15	—	64	9	14	2	10	57
G. D. Barlow	36*	6	—	4	2	37*	28	—	13	9					4	31*					8	0				
M. W. Gatting	3*	164*	—	90	17	—			24	8	—	140	114	—	81	—	38	8*	133*	—	18	4	192	16	21	22
C. T. Radley	—	72	—	25	3	—			32	2	—	9	141*	—	18	—	30	11	1	—	2	2	6	0	6	20
P. H. Edmonds	—	38*	—	19	25*	—			11	0	—	67	2	—					5	—						
J. E. Embury	—	—	—	67*	100*	—	18*	—	13	30	—	40	3	—	0	—	3	—	17	—			54	—	10	61
P. R. Downton	—	—	—	2	—	—			2	9	—	5	7	—	41	—	12	—	0*	—	7	—	1	—	40	65
M. W. W. Selvey	—	—	—	17	—	—											25	—					6	—		
N. F. Williams	—	—	—	27*					0	10*			5*	24	0	—	4	—			6*	—	14*	—	4	18
W. G. Merry	—	—																								
W. W. Daniel									3	—			3*	5*	11*	—	0*	—							8*	0
G. R. Cook							0	—																		
K. P. Tomlins							146	—													3	—	24	—	51	44
N. J. Kemp							37	—	22*	46*			1	1	14	—										
R. J. Maru							—	—							18	—	12	—			13	2*				
R. O. Butcher							29	—					—	4	35	—	122	—	0	—	82	—	7	9*	2	5*	0	13
K. D. James																					1	—				
S. P. Hughes																									0	0*
N. G. Cowans																										
F. J. Titmus																										
R. G. P. Ellis																										
J. D. Monteith																										
Byes	7			4			11		1	4		1					5				2				4	
Leg-byes		9	18		8	4	5		15	10	2	10	11		2	2	4	2	5		9		7	2	2	5
Wides	11	1			2							3	1		2							2	2		2	3
No-balls		2	1		9	4	1		2		2		10		2	1	2		4		6	2			1	
Total	231	292	8	348	379	67	478		230	199	89	340	438		352	45	158	39	267		144	30	330	63	160	313
Wickets	2	2	0	8	5	1	5		10	8	0	9	9		10	0	10	2	6		9	4	9	3	10	10
Result	W		W		W		W		W		D		W		W		D		D		D		D		L	
Points	—		18		24		—		22		4		24		24		5		6		—		5		5	

Fielding figures

61 – P. R. Downton (ct 51/st 10)
24 – M. W. Gatting
22 – R. O. Butcher
20 – W. N. Slack and C. T. Radley
18 – J. M. Brearley
17 – J. E. Embury
13 – W. W. Daniel
8 – N. G. Cowans and K. P. Tomlins
6 – P. H. Edmonds
5 – G. D. Barlow and N. J. Kemp
4 – Subs
3 – C. R. Cook and W. G. Merry
2 – R. J. Maru, M. W. W. Selvey and N. F. Williams

that we would turn in more enjoyable performances if the conditions for play were more satisfactory.

In this scientific age, I cannot understand why something has not been developed that would produce the ideal cricket wicket. Of course, I understand the problems of the groundsmen; the climate in England is very difficult to assess and the clubs do exert undue pressure. Yet the thought nags away at me that not enough has been done on the matter. Too much lip service is paid on wickets by everyone in the game. The shelves at Lord's are cluttered with reports from bygone committees that churned out sonorous warnings on the perils of bad cricket wickets and we modern county captains are no better. Often I sit at captains' meetings where wickets are discussed and think 'here we go again' – because we all go back to our respective clubs and continue to preside over the present situation.

The problem is now world-wide. On my last tours to

THE ENGLISH SEASON/411

	v. Nottinghamshire (Trent Bridge) 10-13 July	v. Nottinghamshire (Lord's) 17-20 July	v. Essex (Southend) 21-23 July		v. Kent (Lord's) 31 July-3 August		v. Somerset (Weston-super-Mare) 7-10 August		v. Gloucestershire (Cheltenham) 11-13 August		v. Warwickshire (Coventry) 14-17 August		v. Yorkshire (Lord's) 21-24 August		v. Surrey (Lord's) 25-27 August		v. Sussex (Hove) 28-31 August		v. Hampshire (Uxbridge) 8-10 September		v. Worcestershire (Worcester) 11-14 September		Inns	NOs	Runs	HS	Av
	135	—	7	—	28	22*	31*	—	7	—					4	—	43	27	58	100*	0	50	31	14*	32	9	1083	165	47.08
	2	—	13	—	50	16	32	15	62	—			7	—	72	—	41	—	79	71*	27	1	68	26	18	32*	40	6	1499	203*	44.08
																											12	3	178	37*	19.77
	96	—			5	—			13	—					141	—					3	50	61	—	25	4	1462	192	69.61
	21	—	45	—			40	40*	82	—	6	—	106	—	7	—	40	—	6	0*					28	3	773	141*	30.92
			41	—	2	—	5	—	28*	—	0	—	62*	—			0	—			5	4	92	—	18	4	406	92	29.00
	18	—	30	—	27	—	73*	7	35	—	35	—	12	—	43*	—	13	—	44	—	15	3	2	—	27	5	773	100*	35.13
	28	—	22	—	46	—	1	7*	59	—	6	—	1	—			24	—	47	—	14	17	20	—	25	2	483	65	21.00
	13	—			36*	—	—	—	—	—			17	—											6	1	114	36*	22.80
																									11	5	112	27*	18.66
																									—				
			21	—			—	—			10	—	2*	—			3	—	16	—	4*	2*	0*	—	15	9	88	21	14.66
											2		36	—											3	—	38	36	12.66
	4	—	138	—	14	3*	33	62	6	—	8	—	6	—			9	51	5	—					17	1	607	146	37.93
																									6	2	121	46*	30.25
																									4	1	45	18	15.00
	29	—	30	—	4	—	20	49	0	—	173	—	11	—	197	—	36	0*	32	33	42	0	94	—	28	3	1058	197	42.32
																									1	—	1	1	1.00
	2*	—	0*	—	0	—			2	—	5*	—											18	—	8	4	27	18	6.75
	10	—	2	—	10	—	—	—	8	—	14	—					0	—	1*	—	0	2	16	—	10	1	63	16	7.00
																	1*	—							1	1	1	1*	—
																			50	55	6	45	1	—	5	—	157	55	31.40
																					36	1			2	—	37	36	18.50
	1		1						6				6				5	5	3	3	1	6	9						
	13		4		5	3	6	4	8		5		10		11		13	1	6	4	7	8	14	3					
	5				1	1							4						1				1						
	6		9		1	2	9	3	3		6		21		11		10	2	8	2	6		5	1					
	383		363		229	47	250	187	319		277		360		461		276	157	304	198	207	215	382	50					
	10		10		10	1	6	4	10		10		8		5		10	2	9	3	10	10	10	0					
	W		W		D		D		W		D		W		D		W		L		W		W						
	23		23		6		5		24		7		23		8		18		5		22		24						

Pakistan and India, the wickets were so slow and lifeless that the game was strangled almost from the first morning of play. In New Zealand, the wickets are mainly green and under-prepared, which gives little encouragement to the spinner and the stroke player. On my first tour to Australia in 1970, the wickets were tremendous: hard, fast, dry, with more and more in it for the slow bowler as the game progressed. Since then, they have deteriorated; Lillee and Thomson prospered on dreadfully prepared ones in 1974/5, and Melbourne gets slower every time I go there. The same applies to the West Indies. With the honourable exception of Barbados, the other Test tracks are slow. With such a magnificent climate, a lot of questions should be asked of West Indian groundsmen, but again nothing is done. The crowds flock to see the Tests, so everything in the garden is rosy – or is it?

I believe that Harry Brind at the Oval has the right idea. He thinks that after a time, wickets just die of old age and the only remedy is to dig the things up and start again. He took this drastic step for the first time at the end of the 1978 season and the result was a succession of good cricket matches at the Oval. Indeed, the Australian captain, Kim Hughes went so far as to say that the pitch for the 1981 Test at the Oval was the best he had ever played on.

It would be interesting to see the results around the counties if the Harry Brind method was adopted. Certainly something must be done – apart from Trent Bridge, Hove, Scarborough and (occasionally) Lord's, there are very few excellent cricket wickets in England. As a result our game is becoming uniform. It is right to blame partly the players for this – we do tend to get a little obsessional and cautious about what is after all our livelihood – but surely we deserve more imagination from our groundsmen? If we were given the proper tools, I feel sure we would do a better job.

Middlesex C.C.C. First-Class Matches – Bowling, 1982	M. W. W. Selvey	W. G. Merry	N. F. Williams	P. H. Edmonds	J. E. Emburey	W. W. Daniel	W. N. Slack	N. J. Kemp	R. J. Maru
v. Cambridge University (Cambridge) 28–30 April	20–6–52–2 11–3–21–1	15–1–76–0 7–1–13–0	13–0–69–2 8–2–20–1	26.3–7–85–2 14–4–42–0	26–8–80–0 11–3–37–0				
v. Essex (Lord's) 5–7 May	22.2–4–63–2		19–0–74–0	19–1–58–1	16–3–41–2	31–3–102–3			
v. Northamptonshire (Lord's) 12–14 May	18–5–56–2 9–5–13–0		14–2–42–1 16.4–4–38–3	13.5–4–22–2 40–14–75–2	18–6–31–3 26–6–50–2	19–5–61–2 21–5–39–3	2–1–2–0		
v. Oxford University (Oxford) 19–21 May		26–7–54–2 13–6–16–0	21–4–58–1 15–2–38–4		18–10–19–2 20–10–22–1			20–6–53–2 9–1–17–0	16.2–9–18–3 21–10–30–4
v. Sussex (Lord's) 29 May–1 June			10–2–35–1 1–0–13–0	20.4–3–40–4 28.5–5–80–8	15–3–38–3 25–5–77–1	12–5–27–1 9–1–20–1		3–0–13–1	
v. Derbyshire (Lord's) 2–4 June			19–4–38–1 5–2–14–0	21.3–6–60–2 24–4–84–0	28–9–50–5 28–3–65–1	20–4–31–1 8–2–16–0		10–2–27–0 3–1–6–0	
v. Kent (Tunbridge Wells) 5–8 June			10–1–64–0 4–0–14–1	42–12–91–4 6.5–3–18–3	28.5–8–68–5 6–2–12–1	14–5–26–1 14–5–37–5		5–0–15–0	
v. Glamorgan (Swansea) 9–11 June			12–3–35–1 15–2–73–0		7–0–36–1 1–0–10–0	15.2–6–36–2 21.5–6–61–9		8–1–21–1 8–2–28–0	3–1–13–0 6–3–3–0
v. Yorkshire (Sheffield) 12–15 June	31–7–66–3 12–1–27–0		8–1–29–0 15–0–60–0		6–2–13–0 17–6–44–1	21.3–3–60–6 12–3–21–2	3–1–13–0		8–3–24–0
v. Lancashire (Lord's) 19–22 June	28–10–58–2	15.2–3–42–1		27–5–71–1	15–4–30–3	23–7–48–2			
v. Pakistanis (Lord's) 23–25 June			6–1–12–0						
v. Surrey (The Oval) 26–29 June	3–0–13–0 7–1–27–0		9–0–40–4 7–2–19–1		6–0–19–0 5–2–10–0	9–1–53–0 16–4–37–6			
v. Leicestershire (Uxbridge) 7–9 July			9–2–34–2		35.3–6–119–1 9.2–3–26–3	16–2–53–2 5–1–15–0	7–1–17–3		
v. Nottinghamshire (Trent Bridge) 10–13 July	22–8–38–1 6–0–24–0				18–6–32–4 23–7–43–2		6–2–22–0 4–2–6–1		
v. Nottinghamshire (Lord's) 17–20 July				11–4–26–2 29.4–16–31–6	20.4–9–30–4 31–16–49–3	10–2–22–1 3–0–6–0	2–0–7–0		
v. Essex (Southend) 21–23 July	16–4–41–1 10–2–30–1			21–8–37–2 27–7–80–3	10–1–30–2 11–0–38–0		2–0–6–0		
v. Kent (Lord's) 31 July–3 August	28.3–13–47–3 3–2–4–0			34–10–74–2 13–3–43–3	22–5–51–2 15–4–52–1	17–5–34–1 5–1–6–1	4–1–9–0 1–0–2–0		
v. Somerset (Weston-super-Mare) 7–10 August				32.2–11–43–3	14–2–33–1		4–2–8–0		
v. Gloucestershire (Cheltenham) 11–13 Aug.				30–10–62–0 17–9–23–2	14–3–50–1 11–1–24–0	10–1–34–1 11–3–30–1	6–1–16–2 4–1–5–0		
v. Warwickshire (Coventry) 14–17 August	8–3–17–2			20–6–30–1 18–6–32–3	12–2–26–0 17–9–21–2	19–5–55–5 11.5–3–29–2	4–0–14–0 4–2–8–2		
v. Yorkshire (Lord's) 21–24 August				20–10–33–2 9.1–4–13–1	13.1–4–28–3 5–0–11–0	11–3–33–2 10–2–27–0	3–0–3–0		
v. Surrey (Lord's) 25–27 August				43–16–67–1 11–3–24–3	43–11–76–1 13.3–2–24–4 2–0–3–0	9–0–24–1			
v. Sussex (Hove) 28–31 August					30–5–57–2 19.5–1–79–3	14.2–3–61–2 10–1–38–3	10–2–29–0 4–0–15–0		
v. Hampshire (Uxbridge) 8–10 September				23.5–7–48–6 22.3–4–59–4	25–5–61–3 5–1–19–1	9–0–23–1 14–6–31–4			
v. Worcestershire (Worcester) 11–14 Sept.				3–2–2–0 6–2–22–0	9–2–18–3 14–3–38–0	11–2–33–0 5–2–13–0	4–0–14–2 7–2–29–0		
	254.5–74–597–20 av. 29.85	76.2–18–201–3 av. 67.00	236.4–34–819–23 av. 35.60	675.4–206–1475–73 av. 20.20	763.5–198–1787–77 av. 23.20	469.5–107–1245–71 av. 17.53	81–18–225–10 av. 22.50	66–13–180–4 av. 45.00	54.2–26–88–7 av. 12.57

a K. P. Tomlins 1–0–5–0 and 1–0–9–0
b J. M. Brearley 1–0–3–0; C. T. Radley 1–0–9–0
* F. C. Hayes retired hurt
c K. D. James 6–1–13–1
d K. P. Tomlins 7–1–31–0
† M. K. Bore retired hurt
e C. T. Radley 3–0–18–0; K. P. Tomlins 3.3–0–28–2
‡ A. I. Kallicharran absent hurt

A Season to Remember
Tony Lewis

'What do they all write about Dad?' my fourteen year old, in-love-with-Ian-Botham-daughter asked. I was sweating through another large bag of mail from *Sunday Telegraph* readers.

'There is more to life than Ian Botham,' I replied.

'Yes,' said daughter number two, 'David Gower.'

'No,' I began to lecture, 'most cricket lovers write to me about South Africa. Sit and listen. Because South Africa has a system of apartheid, which I think means the segregation of its people according to their colour, the white people ruling, and a separate development for the blacks, then all the cricket countries refused to play against them. Even if an England team has one player in it, like Robin Jackman, who has contacts with South Africa, then one of the black sides of the world, say West Indies, India, Sri Lanka or Pakistan may decide not to play against us.'

'That is why Geoff Boycott, Graham Gooch, John Emburey, Derek Underwood and others were banned from playing for England for three years by the England Board of Control... because they went out to South Africa in the Spring and played for a South African Breweries XI. You see they were told that they would end Test cricket. The black countries would refuse to play against a team with those men in it.'

'First question,' said Joanna Lewis. 'But I thought that some of England's players were South African. What about Ian Greig and Allan Lamb?'

'Yes, true. They are South African, but they have British parents and have qualified by residence for England at cricket.'

'But they are still South African.'

'Yes.'

'So, hang on, Dad. The English boys who went to South Africa can't play, because South Africa is out, but the South Africans can.'

I could have added, to complete her confusion, that at the start of the 1982 season, England waited for the word of Mrs Ghandi to hear if she approved of India's short tour of England, and yet at the same time, Indians, Pakistanis, West Indians were all travelling to this country to take their places in county sides; where Sarfraz would play alongside Allan Lamb of Langebaanweg, Cape Province, Imran Khan with Garth le Roux of Sussex and Ian Greig of Queenstown. Zaheer and Sadiq had always been pleased to rub shoulders with the talent of Mike Procter in Gloucestershire.

That is what people are writing about, I told my daughter.

'Doesn't make sense to me,' she opted out.

It made sense to the country's professional cricketers. The Cricketers' Association voted on the fate of the fifteen cricketers who did this short tour of South Africa and by 190 to 35 with 5 abstentions banned them because more cricketers stood to benefit from preserving the present structure of Test cricket than did not.

The Board's ban stuck. A sell out? Bending to blackmail? Heads in the communist noose? All these are descriptions from the letter-writers and the majority would want to see England play South Africa again... to acknowledge the brave efforts made by that country's cricketers to achieve

Northamptonshire C.C.C. First-Class Matches – Batting, 1982

	v. Oxford University (Oxford) 24–27 April		v. Yorkshire (Northampton) 5–7 May		v. Middlesex (Lord's) 12–14 May		v. Surrey (Northampton) 19–21 May		v. Leicestershire (Leicester) 29 May–1 June		v. Nottinghamshire (Northampton) 2–4 June		v. Indians (Northampton) 5–7 June		v. Cambridge University (Cambridge) 9–11 June		v. Somerset (Northampton) 12–15 June		v. Yorkshire (Middlesbrough) 19–22 June		v. Warwickshire (Northampton) 23–25 June		v. Derbyshire (Derby) 7–9 July		v. Essex (Northampton) 10–13 July	
G. Cook	28	22	10	17	12	9			125	3	81	2	3	—			16	52	137	8	112*	—			5	36	26	50
W. Larkins	42	25	118*	59	8	38	15	2	24	28	17	10			16	52	137	8	186	—	4	—	19	6	50	37
R. G. Williams	31	106*	35	0	0	35					52*	42	14	—	141		26	87*			44*	—				
A. J. Lamb	140	—	1	34	55	18	17	63	102	13			25	—					49	—						
P. Willey	100*	14*	5	13*			18	26	14	88*	51	47			64	—	65	70	16	—	3	—	145	27	32	140
T. J. Yardley	20*	2	17	—	39	18	15	0																		
D. S. Steele	—	3	0	29*	52	66	8	36	49*	0			12	9	10	—	65*	—	9*	—			23	16	1	36*
G. Sharp			19	—	4	5*	0	2			—	11	—	28	22	—							9	44*	4	—
Sarfraz Nawaz	—	17	18	—	4	4	25	0	—	14*			—	—	26	—										
N. A. Mallender	—		4	—	3	3	2*	0	—	42			—	1*	0	—							2*	—	16	—
B. J. Griffiths	—		0	—	0	0	0	3							0*	—									10*	—
R. M. Carter					28*	40	24	19*	18*	18	14*	24			79	—	5*	38	28	17	6*	—	35	7	3	1
D. J. Capel									15	0	14	19	4				33	21*	13	60*			17	35*	22	5
D. J. Wild													16	—					21		18*	—				
M. Bamber																	27	31								
T. M. Lamb																	—	11*					5*	—	14	—
R. J. Boyd-Moss																							88	3	61	24*
Kapil Dev																										
R. J. Bailey																										
Byes	2	2				4	1	14	2	1	1	1			1			1					1			2
Leg-byes	1	1	8	6	6	6	7	13	2	8	11	3	3		4	3	4	9	9		1		5	1	5	4
Wides	1							2	1	5						2	8	1		5	1					1
No-balls	1		2	2			1		2	2		1					8	1	2			7	16	3	8	7
Total	366	211	223	160	220	225	133	215	354	233	253	187	204		372	179	302	257	382		65		370	179	252	307
Wickets	4	6	10	4	10	10	10	10	5	8	5	8	10		5	4	5	3	3		2		8	6	10	5
Result	D		D		L		L		D		D		D		W		D		D		D		L		D	
Points	—		5		4		4		7		7						4		5		0		8		4	

Fielding figures
- 54 – G. Sharp (ct 47/st 7)
- 21 – G. Cook
- 19 – D. S. Steele
- 13 – W. Larkins
- 12 – R. M. Carter
- 10 – R. J. Boyd-Moss, P. Willey and N. A. Mallender
- 8 – D. J. Capel and Kapil Dev
- 5 – A. J. Lamb
- 4 – B. J. Griffiths, T. J. Yardley and Sarfraz Nawaz
- 3 – R. G. Williams
- 1 – R. J. Bailey, T. M. Lamb, and sub

multi-racial cricket to say that we are ready to play a game of cricket with you, and that it is not up to us to tell you how to run your own country.

The International Cricket Conference of 1982 refused South Africa a hearing but the spin of events is turning many more unhypocritically towards South African cricketers. Time may soon come for them to stand up and be counted.

Actually, the Indian series of three Tests was a disappointment. There were brilliant individual performances from Ian Botham, Kapil Dev, Sandeep Patil and Bob Willis but the attendances at the Tests were poor. Pakistan attracted more. To watch the Indians, 99,165 spectators paid £411,763; for Pakistan there were 166,189 spectators paying £658,377.

What did we learn? Something, I think, about the marketing of cricket. Remember that England toured India and played six Tests during the previous winter. To follow that series, which was frequently boring, with three more Tests was folly. In older days there would not have been the intense media coverage of an Indian tour. Now, however, television pictures came back nightly, a full press corps beat around the circuit and ball-by-ball commentary was broadcast on Radio Three.

In days when it has become obvious that cricket is a multi-million pound international business you would think

	v. Gloucestershire (Bristol) 17-20 July	v. Lancashire (Old Trafford) 21-23 July	v. Gloucestershire (Northampton) 28-30 July	v. Worcestershire (Northampton) 31 July-3 August	v. Glamorgan (Swansea) 7-10 August	v. Sussex (Eastbourne) 11-13 August	v. Derbyshire (Northampton) 14-17 August	v. Hampshire (Northampton) 21-24 August	v. Kent (Folkestone) 25-27 August	v. Leicestershire (Northampton) 28-31 August	v. Warwickshire (Edgbaston) 8-10 September	v. Essex (Chelmsford) 11-14 September	Inns	NOs	Runs	HS	Av
	101 18*	61 66	47 12	8 5	3 0	6 —	20 1	23 —	21 37	56 22	15 87	5 29	34	2	1067	125	33.34
	92 0	4 44	44 8	13 110*	82* 78	81 —	105 29	0 —	68 71	47 0	7 5	25 44	44	3	1863	186	45.43
	4 —	27 4	14 0	7 0	— 39	23 —	58 4	6 —	34 17	1 32	8 14	21 26	39	4	1087	141	31.05
			30 25		— 2			140 —			97 95*	106 35	19	1	1047	140	58.16
	33 21*	102 34	10 59	49 23	49* 117	23 —	0 7	51 —	28 0	40 10	20 96	43 30	41	6	1783	145	50.94
													7	1	111	39	18.50
	74* —	32* 32*	0 0	47* 19	— 12*	3 —	3* —	44* —	14 15	12 33	31 —	42 16*	36	13	853	74*	37.08
	37 —	— 1*	18 19	2 —		0 —		32 —	3 58*	3 24*	13* —	15 23*	26	7	401	58*	21.10
													8	1	108	26	15.42
			4* —	— —		1 —		8* —	1* 5*	9 —	— —	20* —	17	8	121	42	13.44
	16 —	— —				4* —		— —	6 —	0* —			11	4	39	16	5.57
	7 —												19	6	411	79	31.61
	1 —		46 25	20 0				— —			44 15*	45 6	22	4	460	60*	25.55
			21 1	29 7*									7	2	113	29	22.60
													2		58	31	29.00
	0 —	— —	39* 1*	1* —	5 1*				11 0*	19 —	30* —		13	8	137	39*	27.40
	27 —	62* 3	53 114*	11 14	— 8	1 —	137 80*	7 —	0 54	31 11	63 4	5 24	24	4	885	137	44.25
					— 5	103 —	65* 100*	36 —	4 0	6 13			9	2	332	103	47.42
					10 —				4 3				3	—	17	10	5.66

	1	8 6	3 2		3	4	2	13		1	1 2	12
	4 1	1 8	5 10	7 2	3 10	1	6 1	11	3 3	3 1	3 10	8 1
	1		1 1					6				1 1
	3	3	5	6	11 12	3	6 6	6	6 10	6 1	12 5	10 4
	401 40	330 223	310 252	200 183	157 284	261	400 228	377	192 273	226 147	333 333	376 251
	10 1	56 6	9 8	8 6	2 7	10	5 4	8	10 8	10 7	9 5	9 7
	W	D	D	D	D	W	W	D	D	D	W	W
	23	6	4	6	3	23	22	7	4	4	22	23

the planners could avoid placing two England–Indian series back-to-back. It was the same with the West Indies two years ago. The computer is locked by the rigid pattern of fixtures with Australia, whom England meet every two years, home and away alternatively. It should be unlocked.

No one could expect nine successive Test matches against India, who are not at any sort of peak, to start cricket watchers jangling the money in their pockets and skipping work to grab a day at Lord's, Manchester or the Oval.

Right at the end of the season, I sat at dinner with the former Indian captain, the Nawab of Pataudi who was in London to play a charity game. His 'concern of the year' was not marketing but umpiring. He had seen Keith Fletcher's England complain about Mohammad Ghouse and have him removed from the Test panel. He had seen how India had done the same with David Constant in England and how Pakistan, after their first Test at Birmingham announced to everyone that they would have objected to the two umpires Evans and Palmer standing in any of their remaining Tests. Yes, Pataudi is right, our Test match umpires have become the whipping boys.

Is television the cause of the trouble? Action replays of umpires' decisions are supposed to instruct and clear the air. But what happens if the umpire has made a glaring mistake? It is possible for a batsman to be given out in a Test match, walk back to the dressing room and arrive in time to see an action replay of his dismissal. Not much use when you are back in the hutch, but it can throw all the player's frustration, disappointment and anger in the direction of the umpire. This all comes out as mistrust.

One of the delights of the summer was watching Abdul Qadir, a wrist-spinner, flip through a bewildering repertoire of leg-spin, top-spin, googly. What was not so enthralling was his over-aggressive appealing. He would turn to the umpire, demand the decision in his favour, and mouth abuses when it was not given. If he had got his own way England would never have made twenty-five in any innings.

It brought about a lot of serious and useful discussion about the lbw law. One truth that eventually arrived in everyone's television room at home was that the full toss which hits the front pad down the pitch and which is in line with the stumps need not necessarily be out. The 'dying' full toss, it was argued, could not be presumed to be landing near enough the stumps for it to be assumed it was going straight on.

Yes, there was more understanding, a healthy product, and in the end television had done its job.

However, the effect of all this on umpires was not so clinical. Many were upset, over-aggressive themselves, quick to smart.

Northamptonshire C.C.C.
First-Class Matches – Bowling, 1982

Match	Sarfraz Nawaz	B. J. Griffiths	D. S. Steele	P. Willey	Kapil Dev	N. A. Mallender	R. G. Williams	R. M. Carter	D. J. Capel
v. Oxford University (Oxford) 24–27 April	17–5–62–0 4–1–9–1	18–6–35–2 4–0–12–0	25–7–62–0 7–3–12–1	20–5–63–2 10–4–16–1		13–2–59–0 11–3–28–0	8–1–21–0		
v. Yorkshire (Northampton) 5–7 May	27–5–76–2 17–4–52–2	21–5–59–3 19–7–45–1	5–0–25–0 2–0–19–0	13–1–32–0		22–3–115–2 11–0–56–2			
v. Middlesex (Lord's) 12–14 May	22–3–71–0 7–1–12–1	32–7–105–5 3–0–11–0	16–2–48–0			19–5–70–0 4–0–13–0	8–2–34–0 7.2–2–23–0	10–2–28–0	
v. Surrey (Northampton) 19–21 May	18–4–72–3 14.3–3–33–4	24–5–57–3 14–0–58–3		11–4–40–0		21.1–3–69–3 17–5–40–1		4–1–21–0 9–1–26–2	
v. Leicestershire (Leicester) 29 May–1 June	14–3–38–1 3–0–12–0	21–7–55–2 6–1–17–1	33–8–96–4 24–7–81–1	22–0–69–0 21–10–49–3		13–3–40–1 1–0–4–1			1–0–3–0
v. Nottinghamshire (Northampton) 2–4 June	24–7–54–3 7–3–9–1	18.3–4–53–4 5–1–13–0	11–7–28–2	13–6–12–3 20–12–33–3		16–5–45–0 4–0–38–1	5–5–0–1		3–0–22–0
v. Indians (Northampton) 5–7 June	10–3–21–2	14–3–36–2 8–2–15–1	7–2–26–0 12–2–42–0			11–1–44–0 9–6–10–1	18–5–50–2	6–2–18–0	7–0–37–1
v. Cambridge University (Cambridge) 9–11 June			20.4–9–41–0 10–3–40–2	32–15–45–4 27.2–17–36–3		18–11–31–1 9–3–18–1	21–5–55–0 19–10–25–4		8–3–14–2 4–0–8–0
v. Somerset (Northampton) 12–15 June	12–4–38–0 4–2–10–0	10–1–33–0 3–2–7–0	12.3–4–26–1 12–2–41–0	10–1–44–0		8–2–16–0 4–2–5–0	4–0–19–0	4–1–19–0	4–0–17–0 7–1–23–0
v Yorkshire (Middlesbrough) 19–22 June		11–3–22–2	12–6–20–1	5–2–14–0		8–1–46–0	1–0–2–0		3–0–11–1
v. Warwickshire (Northampton) 23–25 June		6–3–6–1 18–4–40–1	4–0–10–0	23–9–34–1		6–1–28–0 3–0–13–0	7–0–19–0		1.5–1–0–1
v. Derbyshire (Derby) 7–9 July		15–3–33–2 13–1–61–1	22–9–44–1 27–8–79–2	8–2–26–0 29–6–77–0		16–5–30–5 5–0–43–0	6–6–0–1 10–3–27–0		3–0–19–1
v. Essex (Northampton) 10–13 July		28–7–80–3	20–7–53–1	2–1–5–0		25–7–86–0		3–0–16–0	10–0–58–0
v. Gloucestershire (Bristol) 17–20 July		5–1–27–0 8–1–28–1	28–9–77–4 44–17–71–5	36–13–74–4 38.3–12–59–3			7–3–9–2 6–3–13–0	2–0–17–0	
v. Lancashire (Old Trafford) 21–23 July		11.1–0–42–0	28.5–7–82–4 18–2–54–1	30–9–52–2 19–4–34–1		22–6–93–0 6–1–21–0	13–3–47–1 18–4–59–0		
v. Gloucestershire (Northampton) 28–30 July			21–9–39–1 11–3–50–0	18–4–53–0 19–8–33–1		18.3–4–50–1 12–2–46–1	9–1–32–2 5–0–22–0		8–0–51–0
v. Worcs. (Northampton) 31 July–3 August			2–1–4–1 18–9–24–1	15–10–9–3		13–3–52–1 12–2–41–1	4–0–15–0		
v. Glamorgan (Swansea) 7–10 August			17–4–41–1 6–1–14–0	33–10–70–1 9–4–21–0	18–3–59–1 9–1–34–0	18–3–55–0 9–2–22–1	1–0–4–0 10–1–40–0		
v. Sussex (Eastbourne) 11–13 August		2–0–4–0 1–0–16–0	15–4–27–4 20–9–32–5	10.5–4–17–6 20.1–3–41–3	5–0–15–0 1–0–7–0	3–0–6–0			
v. Derbyshire (Northampton) 14–17 Aug.		12–0–53–0 4–2–2–1	31–14–55–1 8–4–13–0	8–1–21–2 7–4–8–0	18–5–33–0 14.2–5–32–1	16–2–55–3 19–8–41–7	15–3–54–0 6–1–14–1		
v. Hampshire (Northampton) 21–24 Aug.		5–1–28–0 0.3–0–0–0	41–19–59–6	33–14–65–1	11.4–3–34–1 1–1–0–1	8–1–30–1	8–1–32–0		
v. Kent (Folkestone) 25–27 August		20–6–61–2 23–5–71–5	14–4–41–2 5–0–19–0	10–3–24–0		20–6–57–0 18–2–59–1	18–4–45–2 20–5–47–2	17–4–49–1	
v. Leicestershire (Northampton) 28–31 Aug.		8–2–15–0	27.5–5–50–5 8.5–3–29–1	32–11–74–1 1–0–2–0	10.4–5–17–2 13–1–57–2	19–4–68–1 9–1–41–2	6.1–1–17–0		
v. Warwickshire (Edgbaston) 8–10 Sept.			22–8–63–1 23–6–57–1	11–2–19–0 8–1–13–0		27–4–97–5 19–9–42–2	10–2–23–3		20–2–87–0 11–2–43–0
v Essex (Chelmsford) 11–14 September			37.2–12–105–4 26–11–44–5	25–6–55–1 17.2–5–32–2		11–1–30–1 7.4–0–31–1	5–1–12–0 19–8–30–2		8–0–39–0
	200.3–48– 569–20 av. 28.48	411.1–92– 1200–46 av. 26.08	755–245– 1846–70 av. 26.37	667.1–223– 1371–51 av. 26.88	139.4–32– 404–9 av. 44.88	561.2–130– 1860–51 av. 36.47	273.3–75– 747–21 av. 35.57	38–7– 145–2 av. 72.50	59.5–5– 263–6 av. 43.83

a W. Larkins 5–2–8–0
b W. Larkins 9–0–38–1
c A. J. Lamb 2–1–1–0; G. Sharp 3–0–19–0
d W. Larkins 2–0–15–0
e W. Larkins 1–0–5–0
f R. J. Boyd-Moss 2–0–26–0

Theories were put forward for neutral umpires or an independent panel. It was dangerous to put back the clock but I did think of the time I toured with one of England's finest umpires, Syd Buller and listened to his gentle arguments. I can see Syd now, squarely at his beer and beef sandwiches in the old colonial foyer of the Galle Face Hotel in Colombo.

Syd was always quiet but firm in his argument for a life of discipline. Talk of a professional Army career, respect for the rank not the person under the pips ... respect for the white coat as much as for the man who wears it ... no fuss ... the nature of authority. Syd Buller's life had order, respect, and trust, all the qualities missing from the England–Pakistan series as far as the Pakistanis and the umpires were concerned.

Of course you have to argue the shifts of social behaviour. Abdul Qadir cursing Constant is much like a school youth balling out a teacher, which is like a skinhead tilting at a policeman. Not will the clock go back. However, it does seem to me that all will be right again in the cricket world as soon as everyone expects to see umpires make mistakes.

There are real, fallible human minds and bodies under those white coats. Unless everyone concedes that, the arguments of the season could get nasty. Pataudi thinks not. 'A phase. We can get out of it. We need to be sure that umpires are the best umpires, and no country goes to the right lengths to make sure of that ... and captaincy must be strong again ... when it is, the fielders close to the wicket will stop pressurising umpires for all those nasty decisions when the ball perhaps flicks bat and pad or maybe doesn't.'

If the season in England had its issues, it had its splendid cricket too. The memory I have taken into the winter is of three mighty all-rounders, Ian Botham, Kapil Dev and Imran Khan.

Kapil Dev was made Man of the Indian series, Imran Man of the Pakistan series. Botham was surely Man of the Season.

Kapil, in Tests scored 41 and 89, 65, 97 ... 292 runs at an average of 73. Imran's scores were 22, 65, 12, 67 not out and 46. Botham took 27 wickets for 798, Imran 21 for 390 and Kapil 10 wickets for 439.

But more than figures they shared the same aggression yet the same self-control. They were brilliant entertainment, yet they were disciplined and responsible. They were aware of each other; they pushed harder to bowl at each other and swung the bat more ferociously when it was their time to hit out. Those confrontations alone made 1982 a season to remember.

Nottinghamshire C.C.C.
First-Class Matches – Batting, 1982

	v. Cambridge University (Cambridge) 24–27 April		v. M.C.C. (Lord's) 1–4 May		v. Lancashire (Old Trafford) 5–7 May		v. Indians (Trent Bridge) 12–14 May		v. Hampshire (Trent Bridge) 19–21 May		v. Derbyshire (Chesterfield) 29 May–1 June		v. Northamptonshire (Northampton) 2–4 June		v. Worcestershire (Trent Bridge) 5–8 June		v. Kent (Trent Bridge) 12–15 June		v. Warwickshire (Trent Bridge) 19–22 June		v. Essex (Trent Bridge) 7–9 July		v. Middlesex (Trent Bridge) 10–13 July		v. Middlesex (Lord's) 17–20 July	
P. A. Todd	52	104*	0	0	4	—			0	0			3	35	0	12					40	68	1	17	11	4
B. N. French	40	—			10	—			38	65*	3	55	4	8	9	—	0	—	—	—						
D. W. Randall	0	29*	52*	32	61	—	29	51			18	67			76	16*			—	—	9	3	48	70	4	0
S. B. Hassan	1	—					7	44	23	28*							66	15*	—	—	9	3	48	70	4	0
J. D. Birch	23	—	15*	—	71	—	6	27			60	6	64	2	46	—	2	—			0	17	11	8	32	0
N. I. Weightman	36	—																								
N. J. B. Illingworth	49	—			11*	—	0	—													2	5*	7	0	12*	9
E. E. Hemmings	0	—			2	—	6	—	3	15*	43	18*	16	2*	0	—	5*	—			8	22				
M. J. Harris	31*	—					41	43*													9	1	12	21	6	7*
K. E. Cooper	38*	—			0	—	19	—			4	—	24	12	2	—	0	—					23*	2*		
M. K. Bore	—	—					0	—	5*	—			7	4*												
R. T. Robinson			11	28*	12	—	14	52	0	35	12	6	5	8	65	28*	41	14*			5	11	37	8	0	40
C. E. B. Rice			46	—	39	—			20	7	87	30	24	30	42	—	39	—			4	0	8	17	12	19
R. J. Hadlee					59	—			37	0	0	3	1	17	19	—	17	—								
M. Hendrick					0	—			29	—	4*	—	1*	—	5	—	0	—			1*	0	14	0*		
C. W. Scott							14	17*																		
K. Saxelby							2*	—	4	—	59*	4*			1*	—	0	—			40	108	4	0	11	34
M. A. Fell									1	36	11	4	37	3			11	—					4	23	4	7
P. Johnson																									16	8
I. L. Pont																									0	0
P. M. Such																										
Byes	7				4				2	8	2		1		7						4	4	2	3		
Leg-byes	2	1	2		6		1	8	7	10	9	8	4	6	14			4			1	9	8	1	2	1
Wides	1				7					2	1	2	1			4		1					1	5	1	
No-balls			5	1			2	9	11	12	7	7	3	7	4	3	2	1			3	3	8	2	1	6
Total	280	134	131	61	286		141	251	180	218	320	210	195	134	290	63	183	35			122	247	190	178	114	138
Wickets	8	0	3	2	10		10	4	10	5	10	7	10	8	10	1	10	0			9†	9‡	10	9‡	10	10
Result	W		D		W		D		W		D		D		W		W		D		L		L		L	
Points	—		—		23		—		21		7		3		23		21		1		4		2		2	

Fielding figures
- 63 – B. N. French (ct 60/st 3)
- 25 – C. E. B. Rice
- 18 – S. B. Hassan
- 16 – R. J. Hadlee
- 14 – E. E. Hemmings and D. W. Randall
- 13 – R. T. Robinson
- 12 – P. A. Todd
- 11 – J. D. Birch
- 10 – K. E. Cooper
- 9 – M. A. Fell
- 7 – P. M. Such
- 6 – M. Hendrick
- 4 – M. K. Bore and N. J. B. Illingworth
- 2 – K. Saxelby, C. W. Scott and subs
- 1 – I. L. Pont

First Class Averages

BATTING

	M	Inns	NOs	Runs	HS	Av	100s	50s
G. M. Turner	9	16	3	1171	311*	90.07	5	3
Zaheer Abbas	16	25	4	1475	162*	70.23	5	7
A. I. Kallicharran	23	37	5	2120	235	66.25	8	5
P. N. Kirsten	21	37	7	1941	164*	64.70	8	6
G. Boycott	21	37	6	1913	159	61.70	6	10
M. W. Gatting	18	34	6	1651	192	58.96	6	5
T. E. Jesty	22	36	8	1645	164*	58.75	8	4
J. G. Wright	21	39	6	1830	190	55.45	7	5
B. F. Davison	22	37	4	1800	172	54.54	7	8
Younis Ahmed	18	29	6	1247	122	54.21	4	7
J. Simmons	18	21	12	487	79*	54.11		4
P. Willey	23	41	6	1783	145	50.94	5	8
D. M. Smith	14	25	4	1065	160	50.71	3	5
Javed Miandad	18	29	8	1051	105*	50.04	1	9
D. P. Hughes	23	36	9	1303	126*	48.25	3	6
C. J. Tavare	20	36	4	1522	168*	47.56	3	7
D. W. Randall	20	33	4	1369	130*	47.20	4	8
J. M. Brearley	20	32	9	1083	165	47.08	3	4
S. J. O'Shaughnessy	11	19	7	560	62	46.66		7
A. J. Lamb	18	30	2	1302	140	46.50	5	
D. I. Gower	20	35	2	1530	176*	46.36	2	12
C. G. Greenidge	21	41	8	1526	183*	46.24	3	4
I. V. A. Richards	20	31	2	1324	181*	45.65	4	5
W. Larkins	24	44	3	1863	186	45.43	5	9
B. C. Rose	21	32	8	1090	173*	45.41	2	5
Imran Khan	16	20	7	588	85	45.23		3

THE ENGLISH SEASON

v. Yorkshire (Worksop) 21–23 July		v. Surrey (The Oval) 28–30 July		v. Lancashire (Trent Bridge) 31 July–3 August		v. Gloucestershire (Cheltenham) 7–10 August		v. Leicestershire (Leicester) 11–13 August		v. Somerset (Trent Bridge) 14–17 August		v. Glamorgan (Swansea) 21–24 August		v. Derbyshire (Trent Bridge) 28–31 August		v. Worcestershire (Worcester) 1–3 September		v. Leicestershire (Trent Bridge) 8–10 September		v. Sussex (Hove) 11–14 September		Inns	NOs	Runs	HS	Av
10	117*	9	27	4	4			4	14	48	14											21	2	461	117*	24.26
19	—	4	6	8	25	8	2	79	5	—	10*	11	2*	67*	6*	8	27*	31	—	30	—	34	6	721	68	25.75
34	0					10	27					18	2			122	45	65	—	16	76	22	3	846	122	44.52
21	21*	1	26	14	29	3	85	26	8	89*	1	73	26	77	17	10	52	14	—	22	37	34	4	970	89*	32.33
0	—	13	5	56	102*	13	43*	13	25*			0	28	30	6	67	54*	125	—	30	11*	35	6	1011	125	34.86
																						1	—	36	36	36.00
13	—	46*	0	1	3																	14	4	158	49	15.80
127*	—					5	32*					1	—	17*	—	2*	—	49	—	18	—	21	8	391	127*	30.07
																						3	2	115	43*	115.00
33*	—	17	0	0*	6	1	—	3	8	—	0	18*	—	—	—	—	—	6	—	0	—	26	5	247	38*	11.76
																		3*	—	0	—	8	5	44	23*	14.66
28	34					43	14	10	0	14	77	59	26	1	37	0	9	12	—	109	79	38	3	984	109	28.11
20	—	31	62	6	33	34	58	0	0	35*	16	28	54	144	33*	5	8	46	—	0	58*	36	3	1095	144	33.18
3	—	131	37	60	12	64	3	20	1	—	16	91	30*	13	0	100*	16	20	—	32	5	28	2	807	131	31.03
																						10	4	54	29	9.00
																						2	1	31	17*	31.00
				1	25	9	—	40	0	—	1	0	—	—	—	—	—	10	—	4*	—	15	5	160	59*	16.00
		0	8	0	0					—	7											18	—	315	108	17.50
				11	4											37*	—					7	1	90	37*	15.00
		0	3*					2	3	—	0											7	1	32	16	5.33
		0	0			0*	—	0*	1*	—	2	0	—									9	3	3	3	0.50
1	1	5	6			3		2				3	2	5	1	2		7	2	4		† P. A. Todd absent ill
13	2	5	6	2	11	4	15	10	1	8		7	9	7	7	4	9	4		2	1	‡ M. K. Bore retired hurt
		1			3	2	1	1					1		1		1		1			§ J. D. Birch retired hurt
7	6	1	1	1	1	1	2	8	3	3	1	7	23	5	5	3	7	11		10	2	The match v. Yorkshire at Harrogate, 26–29 June was abandoned without a ball being bowled.
329	181	264	187	164	261	197	284	216	70	200	147	318	202	400	112	326	230	400		274	269	
9	2	10	10	10	10	10	6	10	9§	2	10	10	5	5	4	6	5	10		10	4	
L		L		D		W		L		L		D		D		D		W		W		
6		5		5		21		6		3		6		5		8		24		22		

	M	Inns	NOs	Runs	HS	Av	100s	50s		M	Inns	NOs	Runs	HS	Av	100s	50s
R. J. Boyd-Moss	23	41	5	1602	137	44.50	5	10	K. W. R. Fletcher	24	36	4	1244	124	38.87	3	6
R. S. Cowan	8	16	4	533	143*	44.41	2	2	A. P. Wells	5	9	3	233	70	38.83		1
I. T. Botham	17	29	1	1241	208	44.32	3	7	D. A. Francis	19	33	5	1076	142*	38.42	2	5
G. A. Gooch	23	38	1	1632	149	44.10	3	11	G. W. Humpage	25	41	4	1407	254	38.02	4	5
W. N. Slack	25	40	6	1499	203*	44.08	2	10	D. L. Amiss	21	38	1	1404	156	37.94	1	9
M. R. Benson	16	30	5	1100	137	44.00	3	7	K. P. Tomlins	13	17	1	607	146	37.93	2	3
C. W. J. Athey	22	38	7	1339	134	43.19	4	8	A. M. Ferreira	8	10	2	303	112*	37.87	1	
Kapil Dev	14	20	2	770	103	42.77	2	5	J. Abrahams	23	32	5	1013	124	37.51	1	7
P. Bainbridge	18	33	8	1069	103	42.76	2	7	Asif Iqbal	11	17	2	558	115*	37.20	1	4
R. A. Woolmer	13	22	3	809	203	42.57	2	4	D. S. Steele	25	36	13	853	74*	37.08		4
R. O. Butcher	21	28	3	1058	197	42.32	3	2	T. A. Lloyd	25	45	5	1432	122	35.80	2	9
J. H. Hampshire	22	36	6	1264	101*	42.13	1	9	Sadiq Mohammad	15	29	1	998	91	35.64		9
B. R. Hardie	24	39	5	1432	161	42.11	1	8	A. Jones	25	47	5	1491	146*	35.50	4	6
G. Fowler	21	35	2	1387	150	42.03	5	5	E. A. Baptiste	9	12	3	319	69*	35.44		2
C. H. Lloyd	21	29	2	1135	100	42.03	1	9	J. E. Emburey	24	27	5	773	100*	35.13	1	4
K. S. McEwan	24	37	3	1426	150*	41.94	3	6	A. P. E. Knott	21	32	5	942	115*	34.88	1	6
S. P. Henderson	10	16	3	531	209*	40.84	1	1	J. D. Birch	22	35	6	1011	125	34.86	2	6
L. Potter	12	21	2	775	118	40.78	2	5	N. E. Briers	23	38	4	1175	106	34.55	1	6
G. Miller	16	26	7	772	98	40.63		6	N. R. Taylor	24	43	4	1340	143*	34.35	3	7
K. R. Pont	16	24	7	687	89	40.41		6	R. G. P. Ellis	13	25	1	823	105*	34.29	1	3
D. Lloyd	23	36	2	1371	114	40.32	5	7	J. G. Varey	7	12	5	239	68	34.14		1
G. P. Howarth	19	32	3	1158	156*	39.93	4	2	B. Dudleston	6	12	1	373	111	33.90	1	1
A. R. Butcher	23	43	5	1514	187*	39.84	4	6	D. R. Pringle	15	26	4	741	127	33.68	1	6
M. C. J. Nicholas	24	42	9	1312	206*	39.75	3	7	J. D. Love	18	29	6	773	123	33.60	2	4
D. W. Varey	19	17	3	548	156*	39.14	1	2	C. E. B. Rice	22	36	3	1095	144	33.18	1	5
J. C. Balderstone	23	41	3	1482	148	39.00	4	8	A. W. Stovold	23	42	1	1350	212*	32.92	2	7

Nottinghamshire C.C.C.
First-Class Matches – Bowling, 1982

	K. E. Cooper	M. K. Bore	N. J. B. Illingworth	E. E. Hemmings	P. M. Such	R. J. Hadlee	M. Hendrick	R. T. Robinson	C. E. B. Rice
v. Cambridge University (Cambridge) 24–27 April	18–6–46–2 18–1–49–3	27–6–65–1 11.2–5–23–2	20–4–63–0 15–3–58–3	30.3–8–71–5 15–8–17–2					
v. M.C.C. (Lord's) 1–4 May	22–8–60–3 9–2–24–0		12–0–51–1 5–1–26–0	15–4–46–3 4–1–12–0		23–7–49–1 7–5–4–1	20–6–50–0 7–2–22–0	4–0–19–0	
v. Lancashire (Old Trafford) 5–7 May	31–13–46–6 17–9–33–3			6–2–20–0		17.1–6–27–3 17.3–5–65–6	16–9–18–1 10–3–26–1		
v. Indians (Trent Bridge) 12–14 May	25–10–57–0 7–1–38–3	35–19–52–4 2.3–1–3–0	12–2–42–0	24–9–44–2 7–0–31–1					
v. Hampshire (Trent Bridge) 19–21 May						18.2–6–25–7 10–4–14–1	16–7–21–2 13.5–6–21–5		
v. Derbyshire (Chesterfield) 29 May–1 June	12–0–45–0 2–1–1–0			35–10–66–3 29–5–48–4		26.5–8–64–5 11–4–18–1	21–8–35–2 10–5–12–1		
v. Northamptonshire (Northampton) 2–4 June	20.1–3–73–1 11–2–30–0	30–10–58–3 12–3–34–0		20–9–55–0 17–3–39–2		13–5–21–1 8–2–21–2	15–7–34–0 7–2–17–0	3–0–22–1	
v. Worcestershire (Trent Bridge) 5–8 June	6–0–12–0 4–1–13–1			9–3–26–0		15–4–59–3 12–1–56–3	12–0–56–3 19–5–49–2		
v. Kent (Trent Bridge) 12–15 June	14–6–21–3 5.1–1–17–3			9–3–14–0 7–1–18–1		23–9–47–3 10–2–13–2	20.3–7–27–3 10–6–4–4		
v. Warwickshire (Trent Bridge) 19–22 June	7–1–20–0		1–0–1–0	9–4–15–1			9–4–12–1		
v. Essex (Trent Bridge) 7–9 July	27–6–53–5 9–1–35–0		12.1–2–59–2 3–0–14–0	20–4–63–1 11–3–34–0			19–3–44–1		18–5–46–1
v. Middlesex (Trent Bridge) 10–13 July	42–10–121–4	49.5–14–134–6	11–2–39–0				19–6–25–0		11–1–39–0
v. Middlesex (Lord's) 17–20 July	37.1–13–77–3		31–6–89–5		23–3–70–0				
v. Yorkshire (Worksop) 21–23 July	19–4–33–2 23–5–57–5		10–3–35–1 4–1–15–0	30–6–83–2 23–6–90–3		16.5–5–33–3 21.5–6–74–1			10–6–10–2 12.5–2–59–1
v. Surrey (The Oval) 28–30 July	32–5–121–3		23–4–68–1		17–5–53–1 1–0–4–0	35–8–79–2			
v. Lancashire (Trent Bridge) 31 July–3 August	17–4–45–3 13–2–38–0		3–1–2–1 2–0–3–0			22–4–26–3 12–4–11–1			17–7–37–1 10–4–15–1
v. Gloucestershire (Cheltenham) 7–10 August	12–4–34–2 10–2–44–0			21.3–8–31–5 32.5–14–73–4	13–5–31–2 30–6–112–5				
v. Leicestershire (Leicester) 11–13 August	33–14–66–2					23–6–79–3 5–2–3–0	18–7–44–3		
v. Somerset (Trent Bridge) 14–17 August	28–4–53–2 2–0–14–0					29–4–102–4 22.4–5–70–1			
v. Glamorgan (Swansea) 21–24 August	32–10–63–2			47.2–19–76–6	10–3–33–0				
v. Derbyshire (Trent Bridge) 28–31 August	14–4–37–0 8–3–14–1			29.5–5–79–2 21–12–17–2	11–0–39–1 14–5–18–3	15–7–32–0 6–1–15–1			
v. Worcestershire (Worcester) 1–3 September	8–4–20–0 8–0–30–2	19–6–37–3 24–8–95–2		27–8–103–3 20–3–62–2	23.3–4–94–4 10–3–29–1	4–1–12–0			
v. Leicestershire (Trent Bridge) 8–10 Sept.	20–6–40–4 16–5–26–1	6–3–5–0 15.3–6–25–4		20–4–43–3 33–15–70–4					
v. Sussex (Hove) 11–14 September	22.3–10–45–1 24–10–68–1	29–17–33–2 18–6–45–1		19–3–62–0 16–6–54–0		16–6–21–5 25–7–59–3			
	685–191–1719–68 av. 25.27	279.1–104–609–28 av. 21.75	164.1–29–565–14 av. 40.35	608–186–1462–61 av. 23.96	232.1–51–737–25 av. 29.48	403.3–124–889–61 av. 14.57	244.2–86–473–26 av. 18.19	7–0–41–1 av. 41.00	78.5–25–206–6 av. 34.33

a N. I. Weightman 1–0–4–0
b D. W. Randall 3.5–1–15–3
* C. G. Greenidge retired hurt
c J. D. Birch 2.3–0–19–1
† A. E. Warner retired hurt, absent hurt
‡ G. M. Turner retired hurt

BATTING cont.

	M	Inns	NOs	Runs	HS	Av	100s	50s
G. S. Clinton	14	23	4	625	172*	32.89	2	
C. M. Wells	23	41	3	1248	126	32.84	3	6
C. J. C. Rowe	25	39	6	1071	105	32.45	1	5
S. B. Hassan	19	34	4	970	89*	32.33		7
K. J. Barnett	18	25	5	642	120	32.10	2	1
M. A. Lynch	23	38	2	1155	141*	32.08	3	4
G. S. le Roux	20	28	5	737	83	32.04		6
D. G. Aslett	16	28	3	794	82	31.76		7
R. M. Carter	11	19	6	411	79	31.61		1
G. Cook	21	43	2	1285	125	31.34	3	7
K. S. Mackintosh	12	10	7	94	31	31.33		
K. A. Hayes	13	22	3	594	152	31.26	1	3
G. R. J. Roope	14	25	7	560	108	31.11	1	1
R. G. Williams	24	39	4	1087	141	31.05	5	9
A. M. Green	14	26	1	776	99	31.04		6
R. J. Hadlee	18	28	2	807	131	31.03	2	4
G. D. Mendis	23	42	2	1840	114	31.00	2	7
R. D. V. Knight	24	40	4	1114	111	30.94	2	7
C. T. Radley	21	28	3	773	141*	30.92	2	2
R. C. Ontong	24	43	4	1205	152*	30.89	3	4
R. D. Jackman	20	22	8	430	68	30.71		3
I. S. Anderson	17	26	4	671	103*	30.50	1	3
I. P. Butcher	6	9	3	182	71*	30.33		1
S. N. Hartley	20	30	9	635	114	30.23	1	4
A. J. Hignell	15	28	6	664	72	30.18		4
K. Sharp	10	18	2	478	115	29.87	1	1
R. Marsden	5	10	1	264	60	29.33		1
N. A. Felton	8	12		346	71	28.83		3
D. L. Bairstow	23	30	9	603	77	28.71		4
S. Turner	23	28	4	679	83	28.29		5
J. R. T. Barclay	22	33	6	761	95	28.18		6
R. C. Broad	22	41		1153	97	28.12		7
R. T. Robinson	21	38	3	984	109	28.11	1	5
R. W. Tolchard	23	38	8	843	93*	28.10		7
P. H. Edmonds	21	22	4	505	92	28.05		4
G. J. Toogood	9	18	4	392	83	28.00		2
P. A. Neale	26	44	8	1006	79*	27.94		5
P. W. Romaines	14	24	2	593	186	27.68	1	2
T. S. Curtis	10	17	4	359	59*	27.61		2
G. Monkhouse	8	10	5	137	63*	27.40		1
T. M. Lamb	13	13	8	137	39*	27.40		
J. A. Ormrod	21	38	2	981	200*	27.25	1	4
J. W. Lloyds	23	39	3	981	132*	27.25	2	3
J. A. Hopkins	23	41	5	978	124	27.16	1	4
N. Phillip	24	32	3	783	79	27.00		4
R. G. D. Willis	18	22	9	351	72	27.00		2
D. N. Patel	25	42	1	1104	133	26.92	1	4
Asif Din	24	34	2	855	102	26.71	1	2
D. J. Humphries	25	37	5	852	98	26.62		7
R. G. Lumb	20	33	1	844	81	26.37		7
P. W. G. Parker	25	43	9	896	106	26.35	1	5
P. A. Slocombe	13	23	1	579	78	26.31		6
P. M. Roebuck	23	40	3	958	90	25.89		10
P. W. Denning	14	22	1	541	91*	25.76		3
B. N. French	23	34	6	721	79	25.75		5
D. A. Graveney	23	30	11	489	55*	25.73		1
C. S. Cowdrey	22	35	4	794	72*	25.61		4
D. J. Capel	14	22	4	460	60*	25.55		1
P. Smith	10	16	1	383	68	25.53		2
E. E. Hemmings	20	25	8	432	125*	25.41	1	
B. Wood	21	38	4	851	124*	25.02	1	2
A. L. Jones	22	38	2	900	88	25.00		6
C. J. Richards	24	38	9	716	117*	24.68	1	4
K. D. Smith	20	34	6	691	67	24.67		5
P. A. Todd	12	21	2	461	117*	24.26	2	1
D. J. Thomas	17	20	3	409	64	24.05		3
I. J. Gould	19	32	3	695	94	23.96		5
N. F. M. Popplewell	16	24	5	451	55	23.73		1
G. B. Stevenson	17	19	4	356	115*	23.73	1	
K. I. Hodgson	8	10	1	213	50	23.66		1
J. N. Shepherd	22	34	9	590	67*	23.60		3
T. Davies	10	16	4	283	66*	23.58		1
P. Carrick	20	21	3	423	93	23.50		2
A. J. Wright	10	19	2	399	65	23.47		2
M. J. Weston	17	31	1	704	93	23.46		6

	K. Saxelby	M. A. Fell	I. L. Pont	Byes	Leg byes	Wides	No balls	Total	Wickets
				7	2		1	259	8a
					7			154	10
					9		4	269	8
				1	1	1		125	4b
				1	4		4	120	10
					5			129	10
	22.2-8-47-4			4	6	7		259	10
	2-0-24-1				1			97	6
	7-1-18-0			4	2			70	9*
	9-4-18-4			1			2	56	10
	6-0-36-0	1-0-4-0		1	4	1	3	259	10
		9-3-33-0		8	1		2	123	6
				1	11			253	5
				1	3		1	187	8c
	10-1-33-3				5	1		166	9†
	10-1-37-2			1	3		1	186	8‡
	17-5-40-1			5	2	1		157	10
								57	10
	9-1-19-1			3	3		1	74	3
				4	6	1	9	285	10
				2			1	86	0
		8-1-20-1	23-2-93-1	1	13	5	6	383	10
				1	4		9	363	10
				4	5		3	206	10
				1	6		3	305	8
			28.4-6-107-2	2	6	2	12	450	9
								4	
	20.2-7-24-2	4-0-15-0		2	4		10	165	10
	10-3-38-1	6-1-21-0		1	3	1	2	133	3
	4-1-11-1				4			111	10
	8-2-21-1			4	10			264	10
	18-4-46-2		3-1-16-0	5	4		7	267	10
			5.1-1-17-0					20	0
	25-5-51-4		19-3-69-0	4	7	3		289	10
	8-2-21-1	17-2-53-0				2	2	162	2
	26-6-61-2			5	3		8	249	10
	19-5-49-1			6	3		6	251	4
	5-0-27-0			4	2	1	1	99	7
				2	7		2	277	10
				9	2			227	7
	15-2-40-3				1		15	144	10
	11-5-20-1			1	3	1	5	151	10
	19-4-72-2			6	7	1	10	257	10
	11-1-46-0			1	6		5	284	5
	291.4-68-	78.5-13-	45-7-						
	799-37	302-3	146-1						
	av. 21.59	av. 100.66	av. 146.00						

Somerset C.C.C. First-Class Matches – Batting, 1982

Player	v. Sussex (Taunton) 5-7 May		v. Derbyshire (Derby) 12-14 May		v. Worcestershire (Worcester) 19-21 May		v. Kent (Taunton) 29 May-1 June		v. Glamorgan (Swansea) 2-4 June		v. Essex (Chelmsford) 5-8 June		v. Northamptonshire (Northampton) 12-15 June		v. Hampshire (Bath) 19-22 June		v. Gloucestershire (Bath) 23-25 June		v. Warwickshire (Edgbaston) 26-29 June		v. Pakistanis (Taunton) 7-9 July		v. Sussex (Hove) 10-13 July		v. Glamorgan (Taunton) 17-20 July	
B. C. Rose	8	43	2	27	33	40*	89	4	97*	63*	2	83*	—		7		45		102*		11	—	12	5		
J. W. Lloyds	11	22	3	8	6	—	41	25	44	25	27	5	132*	102*	16		2	—	22		16	0	10	1	13	89
P. A. Slocombe	10	8	0	41	27	2			0	0											19	17			0	63
P. M. Roebuck	0	1	37	17	50	10	9	73	90	53*			51	38*	7		30	—	0	—	15	1	70	2	0	66
P. W. Denning	2	20	24	13	71	12	21	13	21	2	21	33	—		45		51	—	—				46	3	13	91*
I. T. Botham	66	20	63	26	0	6	20	47			0	46			66		—									
N. F. M. Popplewell	43*	4			11	23*	18*	23	10	5	13	12	—		19		26	—	5	—	0	29*	28	1	25	22
V. J. Marks	51	8	28	6			9	5			1	1	—		12		2	—	14*	—	0	2*	67	24	5	50
D. J. S. Taylor	12	7*	10	13	67	—	6*	0*	14*	4	11	4	—		6		8	—					36*	52	1	3
C. H. Dredge	5	4	35	4			—	4*		0	12*	11	—		17		1*	—	54*		34*		12*	22	4	0
H. R. Moseley	0	—	4*	3*	11*	—				9*			—				0*	—			24*			0	0*	13
R. J. McCool			7	12																						
I. V. A. Richards					5	1	146	—	11	9	3	0	6*	—	25		12	—	135	—	181*	—	33	69	11	36
M. Davis					1	—			—	9															0	6
R. L. Ollis											1	1														
M. Bryant											6	0														
N. Russom													—	—												
J. Garner																	9	—					26	0*		
T. Gard																					0	—				
N. A. Felton																										
G. V. Palmer																										
Byes	1	5	1	1	6			5		1	3		5	4	4				12	4	9	1	2	7		9
Leg-byes	3	7	4	2	9	5	3	1	5	5	1	6	5	5	6		5		9	1	10	3	8	1	3	12
Wides				1	1						4								2		4				2	1
No-balls					4		1	2			8	11	6	1	4	2			17		4		1	1	6	5	1	2
Total	212	150	219	177	298	101	362	200	300	196	111	203	203	152	248		200		305	83	300	54	356	192	78	463
Wickets	10	9	10	10	10	5	7	7	6	8	10	10	1	0	10		8		4	0	7	3	8	10	10	10
Result	D		L		W		D		D		L		D		D		D		D		D		W		D	
Points	6		5		21		7		8		4		4		6		3		7		—		24		1	

Fielding figures
- 45 – D. J. S. Taylor (ct 41/st 4)
- 30 – J. W. Lloyds
- 11 – T. Gard (ct 8/st 3), V. J. Marks and I. V. A. Richards
- 10 – B. C. Rose
- 9 – P. A. Slocombe and C. H. Dredge
- 8 – N. F. M. Popplewell and subs
- 7 – P. M. Roebuck
- 6 – P. W. Denning and H. R. Moseley
- 5 – I. T. Botham
- 4 – N. A. Felton, J. Garner and M. Davis
- 1 – R. J. McCool, M. Bryant, R. L. Ollis and N. Russom

BATTING cont.

	M	Inns	NOs	Runs	HS	Av	100s	50s
G. C. Holmes	7	10	1	210	68	23.33		1
A. Sidebottom	19	18	8	233	44*	23.30		
C. Lethbridge	16	21	5	369	87*	23.06		1
D. R. Turner	15	21	1	459	96	22.95		2
J. P. C. Mills	9	17		389	98	22.88		3
M. D. Marshall	22	31	3	633	116*	22.60	1	1
A. Needham	13	20	6	316	134*	22.57	1	
R. M. Ellison	7	11	3	179	46*	22.37		
R. S. Luddington	10	14	1	290	65	22.30		2
P. J. W. Allott	18	15	5	220	41*	22.00		
A. Kennedy	9	12	1	242	43	22.00		
N. E. J. Pocock	22	30	2	616	164	22.00	1	3
S. A. B. Daniels	11	15	6	197	73	21.88		1
D. E. East	24	32	8	525	78	21.87		2
H. L. Alleyne	8	9	3	130	32	21.66		
N. G. Cowley	23	28	1	584	104	21.62	1	2
G. W. Johnson	22	34	7	582	86	21.55		2
J. W. Southern	19	21	7	300	50*	21.42		1
V. J. Marks	23	33	5	599	71*	21.39		5
A. W. Lilley	10	14	1	276	67	21.23		1
R. E. Hayward	6	9	1	169	59	21.12		1
R. A. Cobb	22	37	1	760	64	21.11		4
G. Sharp	25	26	7	401	58*	21.10		1
P. R. Downton	25	25	2	483	65	21.00		2
I. Cockbain	14	25	1	492	98	20.50		1
S. J. G. Doggart	9	13	1	242	64	20.16		1
A. Hill	7	14	3	219	54	19.00		1
A. M. E. Roberts	14	20	3	338	47	19.88		
M. A. Garnham	11	17	2	298	57	19.86		3
J. F. Steele	20	31	6	496	63	19.84		2

THE ENGLISH SEASON/423

v. Surrey (The Oval) 21-23 July		v. Hampshire (Bournemouth) 31 July-3 August		v. Middlesex (Weston-super-Mare) 7-10 August		v. Yorkshire (Weston-super-Mare) 11-13 August		v. Nottinghamshire (Trent Bridge) 14-17 August		v. Leicestershire (Taunton) 21-24 August		v. Gloucestershire (Bristol) 28-31 August		v. Warwickshire (Taunton) 1-3 September		v. Worcestershire (Taunton) 8-10 September		v. Lancashire (Taunton) 11-14 September				Inns	NOs	Runs	HS	Av
20	6	21	6	53	9	45	—	24	—	4	1	173*		40*	0*	15	—					32	8	1090	173*	45.41
17	0	12	9	16	10	30	—	50	86*	1	33	38	—	22	20	13	—	2	2			39	3	981	132*	27.25
						59	—	4	50*	17	25	78	—	0	50	33	—	56	20			23	1	579	78	26.31
0	51	8	4	58	10	0	—	1	19	29	16	63	—	7	0	22	—	6	0			38	2	914	90	25.38
		25	9	0	5																	22	1	541	91*	25.76
3	0			7	0									41	131*	98	—	5	30			20	1	675	131*	35.52
7	48					55	—	6	—			18*	—									24	5	451	55	23.73
9	44	20	0	0	5			64	—	18	9			21*	—	5	—	13	16			30	3	509	67	18.85
10	0	1	4	2	8	36	—											8	11			26	5	334	67	15.90
5	34*	8	6	1	4	19*	—			18*	1							1	18			26	8	317	54*	17.61
0*	—	9	7*			7	—	0*	—									2*	5*			19	13	113	24*	18.83
																						2		19	12	9.50
64	9			35	0	36	—	29	3	36	0	58	—	26	85	77	—	78	5			31	2	1324	181*	45.65
		4	0	0*	0	5	—	5	—	14	21*											12	1	65	21*	5.90
																						2	—	2	1	1.00
																						2	—	6	6	3.00
																						—				
7	2*	40*	2	1	5*													6	—			11	5	98	40*	16.33
										31	—	3	3					0*	—			5	1	37	31	9.25
		20	19			71	—	61	—	59	32	0	—	43	10	11	—	17	3			12	—	346	71	28.83
										6	27											2	—	33	27	16.50

4	4	10	2	8		7		4		8	5					5										
1	6	4	4	3	1	7		7	2	2	2	4		6	5	20		1	7							
		2						1		3		2		1		1										
		10		3		10			2	1	2	4		1	11	10		7	2							

147	204	194	72	187	57	388		289	182	216	177	438		208	312	307		307	119							
10	8	10	10	10	10	10		10	2	10	10	5		6	5	9		10	10							
	W		L		L		D		W		L		D		W		W		L							
	20		5		5		5		19		4		7		20		24		8							

	M	Inns	NOs	Runs	HS	Av	100s	50s		M	Inns	NOs	Runs	HS	Av	100s	50s
G. D. Barlow	7	12	3	178	37*	19.77			W. W. Daniel	19	15	9	88	21	14.66		
S. Oldham	21	18	10	156	35*	19.50			C. P. Phillipson	16	22	3	274	64	14.42		1
J. M. Rice	23	44	4	777	69	19.42		5	Sarfraz Nawaz	14	9	1	115	26	14.37		
N. Gifford	13	15	7	155	31*	19.37			R. J. Parks	25	30	5	350	44	14.00		
A. E. Warner	11	17	2	287	67	19.13		1	C. M. Old	16	18	3	207	32	13.80		
H. R. Moseley	18	19	13	113	24*	18.83			C. Penn	7	8	4	54	30	13.50		
I. A. Greig	21	28	1	507	109	18.77	1	3	N. A. Mallender	24	17	8	121	42	13.44		
N. F. Williams	12	11	5	112	27*	18.66			R. P. Moulding	10	20	2	242	67	13.44		
J. D. Inchmore	15	19	3	294	68	18.37		2	C. Maynard	17	20	3	227	40	13.35		
B. W. Reidy	9	13	2	199	37	18.09			B. J. Lloyd	25	32	8	318	48	13.25		
C. H. Dredge	20	26	8	317	54*	17.61		1	J. G. Thomas	9	13		172	84	13.23		1
M. A. Fell	10	18		315	108	17.50	1		G. C. Small	25	29	5	309	57*	12.87		1
M. W. Stovold	5	9		154	52	17.11		1	C. F. E. Goldie	9	9		115	31	12.77		
E. J. O. Hemsley	16	24	1	393	49	17.08			C. E. H. Croft	12	12	3	109	20	12.11		
N. G. B. Cook	24	25	8	284	37	16.70			C. E. Waller	23	27	12	181	50	12.06		
R. E. East	21	23	2	344	58	16.38		1	R. W. Taylor	19	29	5	286	54	11.91		1
J. Garner	10	11	5	98	40*	16.33			K. E. Cooper	23	26	5	247	38*	11.76		
S. T. Clarke	22	25		408	52	16.32		1	D. L. Underwood	21	22	11	129	30	11.72		
T. J. Boon	8	14	1	210	90	16.15		1	F. D. Stephenson	8	10	1	105	63	11.66		1
C. J. Tunnicliffe	16	19	2	273	40	16'05			S. R. Barwick	15	18	7	126	24	11.45		
K. Saxelby	14	15	5	160	59*	16.00		1	M. A. Nash	16	20	1	216	37	11.36		
R. K. Illingworth	11	16	4	191	47*	15.91			J. P. Agnew	10	12	1	122	56	11.09		1
D. J. S. Taylor	17	26	5	334	67	15.90		1	T. M. Tremlett	16	22	3	209	48	11.00		
P. R. Oliver	7	9		143	46	15.88			P. G. Newman	19	22	4	196	39*	10.88		
N. J. B. Illingworth	11	14	4	158	49	15.80			M. S. Scott	6	11		118	37	10.72		
G. J. Parsons	24	32	7	392	51	15.68		1	A. J. Pollock	7	8	2	63	19	10.50		
I. Folley	17	15	4	165	36	15.00			A. C. S. Pigott	23	23	7	167	40	10.43		
A. J. Webster	8	10	5	75	25	15.00											
E. W. Jones	15	21	3	268	65	14.88		2	**(Qualification 8 innings, average 10.00)**								
M. K. Bore	8	8	5	44	23*	14.66											

Somerset C.C.C. First-Class Matches – Bowling, 1982

	I. T. Botham	H. R. Moseley	C. H. Dredge	N. F. M. Popplewell	V. J. Marks	J. Garner	P. M. Roebuck	J. W. Lloyds	M. Davis
v. Sussex (Taunton) 5–7 May	14–6–33–2 15–2–47–2	27–10–40–5 6–1–20–1	23–6–80–2 8.2–0–47–0	7–1–22–0	1–0–7–0		1–1–0–0		
v. Derbyshire (Derby) 12–14 May	17–3–55–1 6–1–15–0	15.3–2–40–4 1–0–7–0	19–8–39–2		41–14–103–3 13–1–44–1			5–0–19–0	
v. Worcestershire (Worcester) 19–21 May	16–6–28–2 11.5–3–36–2	13–2–56–1 11–3–27–2						30–7–62–6 28–7–92–3	10–0–35–1
v. Kent (Taunton) 29 May–1 June	14–6–27–0 4–0–42–0	11–2–38–0 2–0–9–0	18–4–52–3 10–0–31–1		25.5–6–98–2 22–3–73–3			29–9–69–2 11–2–32–0	
v. Glamorgan (Swansea) 2–4 June		9.4–2–26–0	17.2–9–23–1 12–0–38–2					30–9–114–6 27–6–107–2	13–2–36–3 5–0–26–0
v. Essex (Chelmsford) 5–8 June	6–3–12–1 16.2–1–54–1		13–3–33–0 5–1–16–0	13–6–23–2 6–0–29–0	24.5–8–59–7 22–6–56–1			6–3–20–0 28–4–88–7	
v. Northamptonshire (Northampton 12–15 June			16–2–53–0 12–4–32–1	17–3–43–2 5–0–28–0	19.4–4–74–0 27–8–76–0				
v. Hampshire (Bath) 19–22 June	23.3–7–48–5 6–1–28–0	16–4–41–1 9–1–33–0	18–6–44–1 9–1–15–1	13–3–45–1	12–2–33–1				
v. Gloucestershire (Bath) 23–25 June		7–2–20–0	5–1–15–0	2–0–9–0	2–2–0–0	8–0–30–0			
v. Warwickshire (Edgbaston) 26–29 June			5–1–21–0	11–2–40–0	51–18–121–7	18–3–47–1		11.5–2–34–2	
v. Pakistanis (Taunton) 7–9 July		8–0–33–0 9–0–31–1	15–3–48–2 6–1–12–0	2–0–15–0 10–1–47–0	36–10–96–1 12.2–3–45–1			16.4–4–59–2 4–0–20–1	7–0–46–0 13–2–41–0
v. Sussex (Hove) 10–13 July		13–5–24–2 11–2–48–2	12–1–46–1 13–3–33–1	3–0–8–1	39.5–13–93–4 24–8–82–4	3–1–3–0		30–5–97–2 8–3–29–0	
v. Glamorgan (Taunton) 17–20 July		22.5–5–75–3 2–0–5–0	28–12–33–3 2–1–7–0		42–13–93–0			12–1–33–0 7–2–15–0	16–2–35–2
v. Surrey (The Oval) 21–23 July	17–7–34–4	18–3–57–5 6–2–9–0	21–5–37–1 5–1–11–0	3–1–3–0	8–1–24–1 14–5–34–0	25.2–6–61–2 20.2–9–28–5	6–1–17–0	4–0–13–0	
v. Hampshire (Bournemouth) 31 July–3 August		8–0–18–1 7–1–22–0	16–4–39–1 18–5–40–3		6–1–15–0 18.2–5–57–5	16.1–7–23–6		5–0–19–1	10–2–33–2
v. Middlesex (Weston-super-Mare) 7–10 August	18–5–52–2		13–5–24–2		27.3–5–99–3	13–3–31–0		21–4–67–2	7–1–25–1
v. Yorkshire (Weston-super-Mare 11–13 August		18–7–41–0	6–2–4–0				6–0–14–0	32–6–84–3	18–4–42–1
v. Nottinghamshire (Trent Bridge) 14–17 Aug.		7–1–26–0 2.3–0–12–2			18–6–53–1 20–6–51–7			15–4–28–0 11–5–44–0	16–1–54–0 9–2–33–0
v. Leicestershire (Taunton) 21–24 August		18–3–79–0 10–2–38–0			37–10–102–2 11.2–3–40–1			23–1–82–2	14–3–56–1
v. Gloucestershire (Bristol) 28–31 August		15.2–2–50–4 2–1–5–0	21–8–49–2 11–0–36–0	2–0–8–0		22–4–53–2 19–6–35–0	12–1–40–1	23–6–57–1 34–4–118–2	
v. Warwickshire (Taunton) 1–3 September	10–2–24–2 14–4–41–1		14–1–59–0 3.2–0–12–2		40–13–94–4 19–9–47–4	12–2–41–0 17–5–25–1	2–1–5–0	10–2–27–0 12–3–50–2	
v. Worcestershire (Taunton) 8–10 September	10.1–2–29–3 7.4–1–50–5		9–0–48–0 21–5–82–1			15–4–42–6 18–9–32–3			
v. Lancashire (Taunton) 11–14 Sept.	14–3–44–4 6.5–2–20–2	7–2–22–1 8–3–33–0	11.5–3–29–2 10–2–26–0		1–1–0–0 44–14–128–6	20–4–62–1 14–8–13–1		12–0–36–1	
	247.4–65–719–39 av. 18.43	320–68–985–35 av. 28.14	446.5–108–1214–35 av. 34.68	94–17–320–6 av. 53.33	661.2–193–1840–65 av. 28.30	259.1–76–583–33 av. 17.66	39–5–109–1 av. 109.00	468.3–98–1463–46 av. 31.80	143–19–481–12 av. 40.08

a R. McCool 9–0–45–0 and 18–2–18–0
b B. C. Rose 1–0–5–0
c D. J. S. Taylor 3–2–1–0; P. A. Slocombe 2–0–8–0
* D. M. Smith retired hurt, absent hurt
d G. V. Palmer 7–3–15–0 and 10–0–42–0
e P. A. Slocombe 1.2–0–2–1
† Younis Ahmed absent hu

BOWLING

	Overs	Mds	Runs	Wkts	Av	Best	5/inn
R. J. Hadlee	403.3	124	889	61	14.57	7/25	4
M. D. Marshall	822	225	2108	134	15.73	8/71	12
K. R. Pont	62	11	158	10	15.80	5/17	1
M. W. Gatting	135	40	343	21	16.33	5/34	1
Imran Khan	484.4	134	1079	64	16.85	7/52	2
W. W. Daniel	469.5	107	1245	71	17.53	9/61	5
J. Garner	259.1	76	583	33	17.66	6/23	3
M. Hendrick	244.2	86	473	26	18.19	5/21	1
G. S. le Roux	467	116	1210	65	18.61	5/15	3
A. M. E. Roberts	428.2	114	1081	55	19.65	8/56	5
F. D. Stephenson	197.3	40	632	32	19.75	5/64	2
S. T. Clarke	659.3	154	1696	85	19.95	6/63	6
J. F. Steele	470.2	131	1075	52	20.67	5/4	3
T. E. Jesty	288.1	89	750	35	21.42	6/71	1
K. Saxelby	291.4	68	799	37	21.59	4/18	
M. K. Bore	279.1	104	609	28	21.75	6/134	
N. G. Cowans	222.3	52	721	33	21.84	5/28	2
L. B. Taylor	582.1	153	1465	67	21.86	5/24	3
P. H. Edmonds	789	242	1786	80	22.10	8/80	3
D. L. Underwood	690.4	223	1751	78	22.44	7/79	5
N. Phillip	584.1	107	1842	82	22.46	6/50	5
W. N. Slack	81	18	225	10	22.50	3/17	
S. J. Malone	150.5	35	505	22	22.95	7/55	2
I. T. Botham	491.4	114	1517	66	22.98	5/46	4
J. E. Emburey	763.5	198	1787	77	23.20	5/50	2
N. G. B. Cook	847.1	257	2093	90	23.25	7/63	6
J. G. Thomas	140	25	514	22	23.36	5/61	1
J. K. Lever	543.5	112	1683	72	23.37	6/48	5
D. R. Pringle	433.1	122	1087	46	23.63	6/33	2
K. St J. D. Emery	659	152	1969	83	23.72	6/51	3
J. W. Southern	439.5	118	1314	55	23.89	5/51	2
T. M. Tremlett	354.3	114	766	32	23.93	5/59	1
R. D. Jackman	677.1	196	1751	73	23.98	6/28	2
J. D. Inchmore	328.2	68	841	35	24.02	7/53	2
G. A. Gooch	220	72	541	22	24.59	7/14	1
A. Sidebottom	495.2	95	1538	62	24.80	6/31	3
E. E. Hemmings	664.1	198	1611	64	25.17	6/76	3
K. E. Cooper	685	191	1719	68	25.27	6/46	2
I. A. Greig	571.1	131	1723	68	25.33	5/46	2
D. P. Hughes	292.3	79	789	31	25.45	4/22	
Sarfraz Nawaz	327.3	72	920	36	25.55	6/92	1
B. J. Griffiths	411.1	92	1200	46	26.08	5/71	2
J. Simmons	538.4	152	1284	49	26.20	5/57	2
S. J. O'Shaughnessy	209.2	34	710	27	26.29	4/66	
D. S. Steele	755	245	1946	70	26.37	6/59	6
C. M. Old	467.2	125	1229	46	26.71	6/76	1
S. P. Hughes	218.5	30	723	27	26.77	4/28	
P. Willey	667.1	223	1371	51	26.88	6/17	1
R. M. Ellison	153.5	35	433	16	27.06	3/12	
P. J. Hacker	174.1	25	677	25	27.08	5/51	2
K. I. Hodgson	198.1	42	625	23	27.17	8/68	1
D. G. Moir	811.5	228	2076	76	27.31	6/63	4
R. E. East	490.5	141	1231	45	27.35	6/80	2
A. C. S. Pigott	483	92	1684	61	27.60	7/74	4
I. Folley	311	76	758	27	28.07	4/40	
H. R. Moseley	320	68	985	35	28.14	5/40	2
D. A. Graveney	498.4	145	1242	44	28.22	7/37	1
R. G. D. Willis	446	89	1444	51	28.31	6/45	2
G. R. Dilley	563.3	124	1833	64	28.64	6/71	2
V. J. Marks	700.4	199	1951	68	28.69	7/51	4
P. M. Such	232.1	51	737	25	29.48	5/112	1
C. E. Waller	605	172	1627	55	29.58	7/67	1
D. L. Acfield	565.2	129	1332	45	29.60	4/35	
M. W. W. Selvey	254.5	74	597	20	29.85	3/47	
K. S. Mackintosh	304.2	59	1023	34	30.08	6/61	1
P. I. Pocock	233	64	632	21	30.09	5/73	1
G. Miller	455.5	135	1058	35	30.22	8/70	1
A. M. Ferreira	243.3	51	789	26	30.34	5/109	1
C. E. H. Croft	304	61	1003	33	30.39	7/88	1
S. J. Dennis	95	16	365	12	30.41	5/42	1
G. C. Small	589.1	106	1925	63	30.55	7/68	1
D. N. Patel	572.2	146	1531	50	30.62	7/42	2
S. R. Barwick	324.2	79	981	32	30.65	5/44	1
W. W. Davis	391.5	70	1296	42	30.85	7/101	1

426/BENSON & HEDGES CRICKET YEAR

Surrey C.C.C. First-Class Matches – Batting, 1982

Player	v. Kent (The Oval) 5-7 May		v. Leicestershire (Leicester) 12-14 May		v. Northamptonshire (Northampton) 19-21 May		v. Essex (Chelmsford) 29 May-1 June		v. Hampshire (The Oval) 5-8 June		v. Oxford University (Oxford) 9-11 June		v. Gloucestershire (The Oval) 12-15 June		v. Sussex (Hove) 19-22 June		v. Lancashire (The Oval) 23-25 June		v. Middlesex (The Oval) 26-29 June		v. Kent (Maidstone) 7-9 July		v. Lancashire (Old Trafford) 10-13 July		v. Hampshire (Portsmouth) 17-20 July	
A. R. Butcher	0	59*	15	151*	19	4	4	8	3	5	10	131	33	79	32	—	0	—	23	1			8	49*	32	9
G. R. J. Roope	7	—	14	4	108	4	11	7	1	9			53*	16*	5	—	20*	—	30*	10	9	41*	21	5
R. D. V. Knight	13	—	17	12	6	65	14	21	0	0	0	104*	19	54	69	—	0	—	0	13	57	8	6	17*	25	14
G. P. Howarth	46	—							19	0	33	—	7	12	0	—	14	—	18	30			29	17	46	8
M. A. Lynch	0	—	6	47	7	0	4	69	67	0			5	30	25	—	0	36			30	15	40	22	0	9	35	25
G. S. Clinton	2	27*	102	5	2	27	1	3	5	4	175*	—	14	39	34	—	0	40			—	26*	33	61	12	—
C. J. Richards	52*	—	61	—			8	4	1	13	61	—	11*	4*	3	—	0	14*			34*	4	13	20	63	6	28	7
R. D. Jackman	2	—	15	—	19	6†	23*	12*	49*	6	52	—			15	—			—	12*	17	—	60	68	—	—
S. T. Clarke	52	—	26	—	10	13	40	31	6	7			—	—	22	—			—	0	16	—	0	6	—	9
P. I. Pocock	6	—	0	7	1	0	1	—																		
P. H. L. Wilson	13	—	0*	—	4*	3																				
D. M. Smith			89	25*	74	19	3	9													36	17			50	9
A. J. Stewart					9	16																				
A. Needham									14	1			6*	19*									134*	1	25*	1*
D. J. Thomas									17	37					5	—					0	64	—	0	—	50*	30*
G. Monkhouse									14	8*			—	—												
K. S. Mackintosh													—	—												
M. Butcher																										
C. Bullen													—	—												
R. G. L. Cheatle															27*	—							1*	—		
D. B. Pauline																					26	22	2	1		
Byes	1			1	1	1			4	2		4	5	1	2		2			9					3	6
Leg-byes	7	3	6	5	5	12	6	1	11	6	3	3	3	14	1			1	1	6	6	6	6	2	13	8
Wides	1		1				2	1						4			1		2	1			1		1	
No-balls	3	1	6	3	7	1	1	8	16	4	5				3			1	6	10	7		1	3	14	
Total	205	90	358	260	272	171	132	175	214	101	345	261	150	253‡	243		128		144	137	326	197	324	176	343	131
Wickets	10	10	10	10	10	10	10	9†	10	10	5	1	5	5	10		5		4	8	10	6	10	7	7	8
Result	W		L		W		L		L		D		W		D		D		D		D		L		W	
Points	19		7		23		4		6		—		20		5		2		3		8		5		22	

Fielding figures
53 – C. J. Richards (ct 50/st 3)
18 – M. A. Lynch
16 – G. P. Howarth
13 – D. M. Smith and G. R. J. Roope
12 – A. R. Butcher
11 – S. T. Clarke
10 – R. D. V. Knight
7 – A. Needham
6 – D. J. Thomas
5 – K. S. Mackintosh
4 – G. S. Clinton, R. D. Jackman and A. J. Stewart
3 – G. Monkhouse and subs
1 – P. I. Pocock, R. G. L. Cheatle and M. Butcher

BOWLING cont.	Overs	Mds	Runs	Wkts	Av	Best	5/inn
J. W. Lloyds	468.3	98	1463	46	31.80	7/88	3
D. Surridge	561	159	1507	47	32.06	5/78	1
J. N. Shepherd	739	177	2026	63	32.15	6/75	2
S. Oldham	504.5	98	1544	48	32.16	7/78	2
R. C. Ontong	638.1	131	2059	64	32.17	6/50	1
P. J. W. Allott	452.4	125	1172	36	32.55	5/58	1
G. B. Stevenson	443.4	88	1474	45	32.75	5/72	1
C. J. Tunnicliffe	383.1	92	1213	37	32.78	5/73	1
G. Monkhouse	131.3	27	395	12	32.91	3/40	
M. A. Nash	418.2	102	1276	38	33.57	5/35	1
C. Lethbridge	304.3	68	977	29	33.68	5/68	1
G. W. Johnson	330.4	84	892	26	34.30	5/36	2
A. J. Pollock	115.5	18	483	14	34.50	5/108	1
C. H. Dredge	446.5	108	1214	35	34.68	3/33	
S. P. Perryman	430.1	111	1216	35	34.74	6/49	3
P. Carrick	568.5	154	1425	41	34.75	6/90	1
N. Gifford	500	157	1080	31	34.83	6/48	1
L. L. McFarlane	223.5	43	946	27	35.03	6/59	1
N. A. Foster	125	29	425	12	35.41	3/32	
R. J. Doughty	149.1	19	533	15	35.53	6/43	1
R. G. Williams	273.3	75	747	21	35.57	4/25	
N. F. Williams	236.4	34	819	23	35.60	4/38	
D. J. Thomas	426.4	109	1284	36	35.66	4/39	
S. Turner	453	117	1080	30	36.00	4/53	
N. A. Mallender	561.2	130	1860	51	36.47	5/41	3
A. P. Pridgeon	463	103	1184	32	37.00	4/39	
A. E. Warner	202.1	34	707	19	37.21	4/73	
N. G. Cowley	310.1	86	895	24	37.29	6/48	1

THE ENGLISH SEASON

v. Somerset (The Oval) 21–23 July	v. Nottinghamshire (The Oval) 28–30 July	v. Derbyshire (Derby) 31 July–3 August	v. Pakistanis (The Oval) 7–9 August	v. Warwickshire (Edgbaston) 11–13 August	v. Glamorgan (Guildford) 14–17 August	v. Worcestershire (Worcester) 21–24 August	v. Middlesex (Lord's) 25–27 August	v. Essex (The Oval) 28–31 August	v. Sussex (The Oval) 1–3 September	v. Yorkshire (The Oval) 11–14 September	Inns	NOs	Runs	HS	Av
0	2	24	4*	9	28	1	17	187*	11	60	54	162	20*	82	1	90	—	8	13	14	47	41	5	1452	187*	40.33
41	7					34*	46															25	7	560	108	31.11
5	43	54	—	49	0	26	111	—	99	10	4	95*	—	16*	7	6	—	6	14	—	35	40	4	1114	111	30.94
34	7	74	—	121	1			0	3	156*	26	25	15*	112	8	76	—	28	24	126*	43	32	3	1158	156*	39.93
9	10	118	—	94	72	0	14	—	15	20	141*	2	—	22	3	38	—	102	23*	—	0	38	2	1155	141*	32.08
		6	0*	4	3																	23	4	625	175*	32.89
7	4	117*	—	47	16*	27	15	—	10	0	21	0	—	0*	5	16	—	0	5*	—	3	36	9	700	117*	25.92
		4	—	1*	0*													1	—	—	40*	19	8	402	68	36.54
11	6	4	—	24	13			—	37	—	17			—	35	0	—	20	—	—	3	25	—	408	52	16.32
																7*	—	10*	—	—	—	8	2	32	10*	5.33
																						4	2	20	13	10.00
2*	—			30	35	105*	18	24	25	160	—	19	17	27	—	53	44	100*	75			25	4	1065	160	50.71
																						2	—	25	16	12.50
0	32	5	—	14	4	5	4*	—	13	—	0	12	—	—	—	11	—	15	—			20	6	316	134*	22.57
				21	2	0	6	—	13	58*	12	44	—	—	—	7	—	28	—	—	8	20	3	409	64	24.05
63*	17	5	—			11*	4	—	4*	—	11*			—	0							10	5	137	63*	27.40
31	1*	17*	—	2*	—			1*	—	—	0*			—	0*	9	—	22	—	—	11*	10	7	94	31	31.33
																						—				
																						2	2	28	27*	—
						9	9															6	—	69	26	11.50

‡ D. M. Smith retired hurt, absent hurt

1	1	2		2			4	1			1	6		7	6	2		8	1		2
8	4	6		6	3	3	11	9	8	13	4	19	1	13	2	7		9	3	7	7
1		2		2	1	1	1	2		2		9		1						1	7
		12		5	1	7	13	14	3	15	6	2		1		4		1		9	13
213	134	450	4	401	144	154	291	318	234	358	322	536	36	273	102	304		296	127	257	294
9‡	9‡	9	0	9	8	8	9	1	9	5	8	7	0	4	10	10		10	4	1	8
L		W		D		D		D		W		D		L		D		D		D	
6		24		5		—		5		22		5		5		7		6		4	

	Overs	Mds	Runs	Wkts	Av	Best	5/inn
H. L. Alleyne	207.3	44	599	16	37.43	4/92	
C. S. Cowdrey	166.3	39	533	14	38.07	3/45	
D. Lloyd	297.2	68	801	21	38.14	4/36	
K. B. S. Jarvis	636	145	1078	54	38.48	5/94	1
G. J. Parsons	515.3	89	1931	50	38.62	5/25	1
B. J. Lloyd	688.2	139	2201	55	40.01	5/58	2
M. Davis	143	19	481	12	40.08	3/36	
N. J. B. Illingworth	164.1	29	565	14	40.35	5/89	1
Kapil Dev	386.2	76	1180	29	40.68	5/39	2
A. I. Kallicharran	154.2	21	578	14	41.28	3/32	
P. G. Newman	458.3	73	1661	40	41.52	4/59	
S. A. B. Daniels	223.2	37	836	20	41.80	3/49	
I. V. A. Richards	265.3	75	671	16	41.93	3/6	
T. M. Lamb	298.5	76	850	20	42.50	5/37	1
J. P. Agnew	203.5	27	816	19	42.94	4/55	
I. S. Curtis	214.4	45	659	15	43.93	5/140	1
J. H. Childs	663.3	198	1681	38	44.23	5/112	1
R. K. Illingworth	260.4	59	811	18	45.05	4/85	
B. W. Reidy	138	34	457	10	45.70	3/33	
C. J. C. Rowe	265.2	57	898	19	47.26	3/67	
J. Cumbes	349.1	71	993	21	47.28	4/47	
A. J. Webster	202.1	36	716	15	47.73	5/87	1
P. Bainbridge	301	77	915	19	48.15	6/59	1
S. P. Sutcliffe	554.3	114	1799	37	48.62	5/151	1
R. D. V. Knight	266.2	61	762	15	50.80	3/34	
A. Needham	359	73	1170	22	53.18	5/91	1
P. Smith	136	21	536	10	53.60	2/47	
T. J. Taylor	165	25	541	10	54.10	5/118	1

	Overs	Mds	Runs	Wkts	Av	Best	5/inn
E. A. Baptiste	186.4	45	671	12	55.91	3/41	
Asif Din	284.1	60	1128	20	56.40	5/100	1
J. Abrahams	316.1	61	921	16	57.56	2/19	
R. W. M. Palmer	219.4	34	849	14	60.64	4/98	
S. J. Ridge	234.1	29	824	13	63.38	4/128	
J. R. T. Barclay	230.2	58	702	11	63.81	3/44	
B. Wood	231.2	54	690	10	69.00	2/0	

(Qualification 10 wickets)

Surrey C.C.C. First-Class Matches – Bowling, 1982

	S. T. Clarke	R. D. Jackman	R. D. V. Knight	P. H. L. Wilson	P. I. Pocock	A. Needham	A. R. Butcher	G. Monkhouse	D. J. Thomas
v. Kent (The Oval) 5–7 May	5–2–7–0 17–2–52–5	7–3–24–2 12–3–55–0	3–1–14–1 7–1–31–1	13.4–2–63–2	3–0–18–1				
v. Leicestershire (Leicester) 12–14 May	29–4–101–4 13–1–70–2	18–5–43–0 6–3–19–1	10–2–45–0 5–0–42–0	22–5–57–2 22–5–46–0	29–9–70–3 18.5–2–105–2				
v. Northamptonshire (Northampton) 19–21 May	19–4–58–5 23.5–5–51–5	19.2–7–39–5 24–10–53–2	3–1–7–0 6–2–17–0	9–5–20–0 7–1–23–0	23–10–42–2				
v. Essex (Chelmsford) 29 May–1 June	21–4–50–3 15–3–49–2	25–14–29–1 16.3–3–57–2	7–2–30–1 14–0–59–0		35.1–12–73–5	6–0–21–0 15–3–49–0	1–0–4–0 16–2–63–1		
v. Hampshire (The Oval) 5–8 June	16–3–44–4 20–7–33–3	14.3–0–52–4 18–3–52–2	6–1–18–0					5–0–23–1	8–3–24–1 17–5–39–4
v. Oxford University (Oxford) 9–11 June		25.5–6–66–4 5–1–9–0	5–3–2–0	18–4–41–1 12–4–33–1		13–7–28–0 17–4–40–1	4–0–21–0 11–4–23–1		
v. Gloucestershire (The Oval) 12–15 June	31–7–76–3 14–3–33–0	33–15–58–3 14–4–25–2	6–2–16–0				3–1–18–0 5–0–31–1	3–1–5–0 7–2–19–1	16.4–3–51–2 8–3–14–0
v. Sussex (Hove) 19–22 June	31–7–70–6 10–4–18–2	35–9–96–1 8–1–43–1	16–3–37–0						22–5–56–2 7–2–24–0
v. Lancashire (The Oval) 23–25 June	11–2–30–1	10–6–9–1							9–0–38–3
v. Middlesex (The Oval) 26–29 June	24.4–7–69–1	27–9–55–4	21–2–52–1						17–2–82–1 7–0–25–1
v. Kent (Maidstone) 7–9 July	23.4–9–44–3 14–2–32–1	13–6–32–2 13–2–45–3	6–0–19–0 5–0–34–1						19–7–33–3 8–2–31–0
v. Lancashire (Old Trafford) 10–13 July	23–8–45–2 10.4–2–42–0	15–5–42–2 4–0–7–0	8–2–23–1			30.3–7–91–5 15–1–113–2			10–1–26–0 10–2–30–1
v. Hampshire (Portsmouth) 17–20 July	21–5–49–1 23.4–6–53–4	28–8–66–2 23–6–58–4	12–4–23–0 19–5–39–2			9–1–27–1 3–0–22–0	2–0–15–0		22–9–28–3
v. Somerset (The Oval) 21–23 July	17–2–42–5 20.2–5–57–2		4.2–1–15–1 17–5–34–3			4–2–5–0		7–0–23–2 8–1–30–0	
v. Nottinghamshire (The Oval) 28–30 July	17.4–3–63–6 17–2–36–3	18–5–52–0 11–1–58–2				11–2–46–1 15.4–6–37–2		7–0–19–0 6–2–11–1	
v. Derbyshire (Derby) 31 July–3 August	15–4–39–0 8–1–22–0	22–2–77–3 16–1–65–2	4–1–19–0			18–2–54–1 9–1–35–0	5–1–33–0		12–3–26–0 8–0–48–0
v. Pakistanis (The Oval) 7–9 August			5–1–8–0 2–0–9–0			9–4–17–0 10.3–2–53–0		24–9–58–0 12–4–40–3	23–6–72–3 15–3–58–1
v. Warwickshire (Edgbaston) 11–13 August	13–6–24–1		18–4–51–1			28–4–82–1 8–1–24–0		14.3–2–62–2 10–2–29–1	32–6–123–3 8–1–34–0
v. Glamorgan (Guildford) 14–17 August	23–5–47–1 16–4–30–2		14–3–30–0			16–2–68–0 38.2–4–102–3	29–5–105–1	17–2–48–0	17–4–80–2 3–0–20–0
v. Worcestershire (Worcester) 21–24 Aug.	14–5–40–0	22–5–66–1				20–0–92–1	3–0–13–0		14–2–47–1
v. Middlesex (Lord's) 25–27 August	17–6–35–0 2–0–13–0		8–2–18–1			25–10–63–2 13–0–44–1	4–0–24–0	11–2–28–1	25–14–43–0 3–0–16–0
v. Essex (The Oval) 28–31 August	20–2–75–3 18–4–41–2		14–6–22–1 4–0–15–0		15–5–43–2 32–8–57–0	2–0–11–0 23–10–46–1	7–2–24–0		17–6–43–2 13–2–48–0
v. Sussex (The Oval) 1–3 September	7–3–17–0	20–7–28–6 8–4–10–1	7–2–12–0		20–2–58–2 14–8–12–1		3–1–5–0		5–2–9–0 11–6–14–1
v. Yorkshire (The Oval) 11–14 September	12–6–26–1 6–2–13–2	32–9–92–2 9–3–22–0	10–5–21–0		23–5–84–1 20–3–70–2		5–0–32–1		28–8–75–2 12–2–27–0
	659.3–154– 1696–85 av. 19.95	572.1–166– 1504–65 av. 23.13	266.2–61– 762–15 av. 50.80	103.4–26– 283–6 av. 47.16	233–64– 632–21 av. 30.09	359–73– 1170–22 av. 53.18	98–16– 411–5 av. 82.20	131.3–27– 395–12 av. 32.91	426.4–109– 1284–36 av. 35.66

a G. S. Clinton 1–0–11–0
b C. J. Richards 1–0–5–0; M. Butcher 1–0–2–0; C. Bullen 9–0–29–0
c G. R. J. Roope 8–5–25–1
d D. B. Pauline 1–0–3–0
e G. R. J. Roope 13–4–30–2 and 6–3–16–0
f G. R. J. Roope 5–2–10–0
g C. J. Ri[chards]

THE ENGLISH SEASON

Review of the Season
David Lemmon

'It was the best of times, it was the worst of times' so might Dickens have said of Cricket Year 1982. On the one hand there was the trauma of the South African connection, the umpiring controversies, Lillee and Javed exchanging gestures and the tedium of India against England, on the other hand there was Botham, Imran, Qadir, Sri Lanka's victory in the one-day international against England and Glenn Turner's triple hundred. If you chose your wine wisely, it was a good year.

In England there was still the joy of county cricket, still watched by thousands and followed by millions.

The ultimate honour went deservedly to Middlesex who, at one time, threatened to win everything. It is good for cricket that they didn't, but this does not detract from their splendour as a team, confident and committed and sensibly selected.

Sussex deserved their success and when they become temperamentally more stable and their batsmen have the patience and belief in their great ability they will win more. Parker had a lean season, but no one will convince me that he is not a very fine player, and it is unlikely that Barclay will again have so poor a time with bat and ball.

Derbyshire had great batsmen in Wright and Kirsten and there was exciting promise from Barnett, Moir and Anderson.

Essex began and ended badly and their team policy is not always easy to discern. Gooch had a morose season, blossoming late, and he cut a sad figure most of the summer. He is a glorious player and a gentle man and his isolation from Test cricket could only make one reflect on the 'sad waste time'. Hardie was both solid and pugnacious, David East was exciting behind the stumps and Phillip had a fine season. Turner touched heroic heights at times and in the

Dallas Moir

430/BENSON & HEDGES CRICKET YEAR

Sussex C.C.C.
First-Class Matches – Batting, 1982

	v. Somerset (Taunton) 5–7 May		v. Essex (Hove) 12–14 May		v. Gloucestershire (Hastings) 19–21 May		v. Middlesex (Lord's) 29 May–1 June		v. Warwickshire (Edgbaston) 5–8 June		v. Kent (Tunbridge Wells) 9–11 June		v. Worcestershire (Hove) 12–15 June		v. Surrey (Hove) 19–22 June		v. Hampshire (Basingstoke) 23–25 June		v. Pakistanis (Hove) 26–28 June		v. Gloucestershire (Bristol) 7–9 July		v. Somerset (Hove) 10–13 July		v. Leicestershire (Hove) 17–20 July	
G. D. Mendis	17	49*	54	8*	5	22	2	4	26	32	29	52	29	—	0	17	5	—	48	114	67	—	16	18	4	72
J. R. T. Barclay	47	—	1*	—	9	17	8	6	77	—	1	23	7	—	87	—					11	—	17	16*	14	6
C. M. Wells	27	13	12	—	88	35	39	16	12	0	41	8	3	—	45	0	20	—	28	59	100*	—	65	27	0	52
P. W. G. Parker	30	39	0	—	33	25*	12	31	6	84*	26	1	74	—	3	10*	0	—			5	—	0	14	106	11
Imran Khan	7	13*	85	—	31	1*	34	40	5	12*	7	39	23	—									68	19	1	4
I. A. Greig	5	—	13	—	8	—	7	9	109	—	5	1	16	—	18	—	18*	—			25	—	64	6		
C. P. Phillipson	0	—	21	—	8*	—	0	26	1	35			10	—	19	—	4*	—	17	3			2	94	0	4
I. J. Gould	12	0	74	26*	14	—	16	22	16	—	6	65	66	—	16	55*	17	—	32	11	24	—	8		0	4
G. S. le Roux	30	—	69	—	7	—	17*	35	53	—	78	42	—	—	83	—	0	—			8	—			0	17
A. C. S. Pigott	3	—	23	—	1	—	13	1*	5	—	1	3	—	—	2*	—	—	—	0	2*	18	—	12	1	1	11
C. E. Waller	4*	—	0*	—	3	—	5	0	8*	—	1*	1*	9*	—	4*	—	—	—	6*	3	12	—	10	2	18	50
D. J. Smith											1	0														
J. R. P. Heath															17	3	19	—	10	12						
A. M. Green																			30	3	29	—	9	21	11	0
A. P. Wells																			17	4						
A. N. Jones																			0	—						
G. G. Arnold																					0*	—	8*	1	0*	2*
R. S. Cowan																										
A. Willows																										
Byes			1	2			3		4	2					4		6		1				12	2		
Leg-byes	8	9	19	3	7	2	6	3	11	4	6	2	17		12		6		7	7	9		3	12	6	6
Wides			1				2				2	1							1				2	1		
No-balls	2	2	5	1	4	2	4		8	4	2	13	21		3		1		12	10			7	3	3	
Total	192	125	378	40	218	104	168	193	343	174	204	251	275		313	85	106		209	228	308		295	234	164	235
Wickets	10	3	9†	3	10	3	10	10	10	3	10	10	8		9	3	6		9‡	8	9		10	10	10	10
Result	D		W		W		L		W		L		W		D		D		L		W		L		L	
Points	5		24		22		5		24		3		23		7		0		—		23		5		5	

Fielding figures
45 – I. J. Gould (ct 40/st 5)
25 – J. R. T. Barclay
24 – C. P. Phillipson (ct 23/st 1)
20 – P. W. G. Parker
18 – I. A. Greig
17 – C. E. Waller
15 – G. S. le Roux
 9 – A. C. S. Pigott
 7 – A. M. Green
 6 – C. M. Wells and D. J. Smith
 5 – G. D. Mendis
 2 – Imran Khan and sub
 1 – R. S. Cowan and A. P. Wells

Ian Anderson

THE ENGLISH SEASON

v. Kent (Hove) 28-30 July		v. Yorkshire (Scarborough) 31 July-3 August		v. Hampshire (Eastbourne) 7-10 August		v. Northamptonshire (Eastbourne) 11-13 August		v. Derbyshire (Chesterfield) 21-24 August		v. Glamorgan (Cardiff) 25-27 August		v. Middlesex (Hove) 28-31 August		v. Surrey (The Oval) 1-3 September		v. Lancashire (Old Trafford) 8-10 September		v. Nottinghamshire (Hove) 11-14 September				Inns	NOs	Runs	HS	Av
4	72	44	7	31	1	21	35	36	—	2	6	15	66	48	1	104	6	0	51			42	2	1240	114	31.00
1	24	8	30*	61	5	14*	1	—	—	—	1*	64	2	3	10*	39	53	95	3			33	6	761	95	28.18
18	126	71*	37	0	27	0	5	9	—	0	31	29	5	6	14	24	33	0	123			41	3	1248	126	32.84
7	6	7	69*	6	25	2	5	58*	—	8*	68	0	2	19*	0	22	0	8	23			39	7	845	106	26.35
				62	0								2	55	1		31					12	3	297	85	33.00
3	11	—	4	7	23*	0	4						8									23	1	477	109	21.68
0	12	10	1	11	5	3	0	38*	—							15	18					22	3	274	64	14.42
1	70*	24*	6	16	18	4	2	24		—	50	46*	7	0	30*	—	0					32	3	695	94	23.96
6*	—	—	—	0*	—	0	20*							0*	—	—	4	40	—			28	5	737	83	32.04
5	—	—	—	0	0*	1	5			—	5*	—	15*			—	9*	5	—			23	7	167	40	10.43
																		0	—			27	12	181	50	12.06
																						3	—	1	1	0.33
																						5	—	61	19	12.20
57	95	26	34	19	6	19	14	21	—	27*	59	6	99	56	0	82	18	15	20			26	1	776	99	31.04
												12*	45*	1	—	15*	39	70	30			9	3	233	70	38.83
29	—	—	—			5	5															4	—	39	29	9.75
																						5	4	11	8*	11.00
																		0	18*			2	1	18	18*	18.00
																		0*	4			2	1	4	4	4.00

	3	3		4		9	8			1	3	6		5	4	3	4	6	1		†J. R. T. Barclay retired hurt
3	3	2	5	5	8	1	5	5		1	3	3	3	7	8	6	6	7	6		‡P. W. G. Parker absent hurt
	1		1							1									1		A. N. Jones absent hurt (second innings)
18	11	8	3	8	4	5	10	11		9	12	15	9	5	4	5	2	10	5		
152	434	203	197	230	122	84	119	202		49	248	251	254	150	71	315	223	257	284		
10	7	5	6	10	8	10	10	4		2	7	6	7	8	4	6	10	10	6		
	D		L		D		L		D		D		W		D		D		L		
	4		3		6		4		4		4		21		5		5		5		

Norbert Phillip

hearts of the Essex followers Pringle is an inadequate replacement for him, but he has time on his side.

Glamorgan struggled for success and their one championship victory came late in the season. Barry Lloyd worked hard to knit the side together and there were distinct signs of improvement. Morris promises much, but the bowling is in need of strengthening.

The same applies to Gloucestershire and Warwickshire. The return of Hogg could help Warwickshire, but what they need most is for Willis to reproduce England form for his county. Surridge faded after a promising start for Gloucestershire, but Stephenson will be a great asset.

Surrey are a very well organised side. They select neither on promise, nor on past glories, but on merit, and they derive maximum return from what, on paper, look to be limited resources. Smith and Howarth had fine seasons and Butcher, with a splendid August, saw lesser players chosen to tour Australia.

Notts had a most miserable mid-season, but they recovered well and the blend of the side looked good at the close. One still had certain doubts about their batting, but Robinson showed he was maturing into a responsible opener and French, whose wicket-keeping improved, scored useful runs.

Somerset had a strange season and their multitude of talents never produced the consistent displays that win

Sussex C.C.C. First-Class Matches – Bowling, 1982	G. S. le Roux	Imran Khan	A. C. S. Pigott	I. A. Greig	J. R. T. Barclay	C. E. Waller	C. M. Wells	I. J. Gould	P. W. G. Parker
v. Somerset (Taunton) 5–7 May	19.1–5–47–5 15.5–2–45–3	21–7–48–1 13–3–42–1	13–3–27–2 8–3–26–3	20–5–86–2 12–4–24–2	1–1–0–0				
v. Essex (Hove) 12–14 May	17–6–39–3 14–1–44–2	20–6–40–4 20.5–2–75–3	10–3–32–1 13–2–53–4	16–4–54–1 12–2–42–1		7–0–18–0			
v. Gloucestershire (Hastings) 19–21 May	8–3–23–2 16.2–2–69–2	15–7–26–4 22–7–44–3	6–0–19–1 17–6–50–3	17.1–7–25–3 16–4–36–1	2–0–5–0	7–4–7–1			
v. Middlesex (Lord's) 29 May–1 June	14–4–22–0 7–1–17–0*	25–13–28–3	19–6–47–5 3–0–9–0	26.4–5–63–4	10–3–39–0 27–9–48–3	14–4–41–1 33–7–78–2			
v. Warwickshire (Edgbaston) 5–8 June	6–2–21–2 9–3–16–3	16.3–4–61–2 9–1–14–2		10–1–38–2	4–1–21–0	25–6–55–3 6.2–3–11–4			
v. Kent (Tunbridge Wells) 9–11 June	14–2–30–0	15–6–24–0	16–2–67–2	29–3–132–3	22–4–72–1	17–2–66–1	4–0–18–1	5.4–2–18–0	5–0–16–0
v. Worcestershire (Hove) 12–15 June	9–4–23–3 10–1–46–3	8.3–2–23–3 8.2–0–33–3		6–0–29–3 12–3–53–2			6–0–15–2		
v. Surrey (Hove) 19–22 June	11–4–25–0		10–1–39–0	18–3–49–2	21–5–57–0	26.3–4–67–7			
v. Hampshire (Basingstoke) 23–25 June	6–3–11–1 4–1–5–1		7–2–30–0 3–2–2–0	10–3–26–0	18.2–6–50–0	23–5–60–1	5–0–15–0		
v. Pakistanis (Hove) 26–28 June			23–4–87–0			34–6–100–0	13.1–3–20–0	3.5–0–5–0	
v. Gloucestershire (Bristol) 7–9 July	11.3–4–15–5 1.5–1–1–1		2–0–10–0 10–2–29–1	10–2–28–2 22–5–66–4	3–1–8–1	4–3–3–1 15–11–20–1			
v. Somerset (Hove) 10–13 July			12–3–34–0 9–3–29–3	17–4–102–3 17–3–36–1	26–9–51–1 9–2–28–0	35–7–94–2 16.5–2–67–4			
v. Leicestershire (Hove) 17–20 July	23–7–50–3 18–6–35–2		14.3–5–44–1 13–3–31–0	24–7–58–4 27–12–39–4	5–0–21–0	17–7–14–1 30.5–13–55–3			
v. Kent (Hove) 28–30 July	22–7–49–4		26–3–105–1		7–1–58–0	16–2–62–0		9–1–19–0	
v. Yorkshire (Scarborough) 31 July–3 August	11–4–23–0 17–2–49–1		14–1–59–2 10–1–33–0		13–0–65–0	15.5–6–35–2 19.4–1–100–3			
v. Hampshire (Eastbourne) 7–10 August	20–6–49–2 28.2–5–60–5		18–5–47–3 19–3–45–3	22.4–7–46–5 27–7–55–0	5–2–15–0	7–1–13–0 27–11–59–2			
v. Northamptonshire (Eastbourne) 11–13 August	11–2–33–0		20.1–4–74–7		11–3–25–0	27–7–96–2	5–2–24–0		
v. Derbyshire (Chesterfield) 21–24 Aug.	25–7–63–2 2–2–0–0		24–5–78–1 1–1–0–0	27.5–11–90–0		22–6–55–2			
v. Glamorgan (Cardiff) 25–27 August	30–7–68–2 4–1–18–1		16–3–66–2 5.4–1–15–1	36–6–103–5 7–1–29–0	4–1–8–0	1–0–4–0	7–3–9–1		
v. Middlesex (Hove) 28–31 August	20–5–64–2 5–1–16–0		10–1–50–1 7–0–41–1	32–8–85–4 7–1–43–0	7–1–17–0	29–20–46–2 11–0–68–1	8–2–24–0 2.3–0–13–1		
v. Surrey (The Oval) 1–3 September	18–2–75–3 4–0–18–0		29–1–85–5 13–1–57–2	22.3–2–71–1 8–0–31–1		13–2–47–1 3–0–17–1			
v. Lancashire (Old Trafford) 8–10 September	15–3–38–2		24–5–68–0 4–1–12–0	9–2–20–1 5–0–19–2	25–6–70–2 10–3–44–3	25–5–72–0 13–2–49–1			
v. Nottinghamshire (Hove) 11–14 September			19.4–4–81–6 14–2–103–0			41–23–71–2 23–2–77–4	7–1–16–0 3–0–22–0		
	467–116–1210–65 av. 18.61	194.1–58–458–29 av. 15.79	483–92–1684–61 av. 27.60	525.5–122–1578–63 av. 25.04	230.2–58–702–11 av. 63.81	605–172–1627–55 av. 29.58	69.4–12–195–5 av. 39.00	9.3–2–23–0 —	5–0–16–0 —

* P. R. Oliver absent hurt
† M. S. Scott absent

a A. P. Wells 12–1–42–0; C. P. Phillipson 14–0–57–1
b A. Willows 13–4–23–0 and 4–0–16–0

c R. S. Cowan 7–0–22–0 and 2–0–12–0

THE ENGLISH SEASON

A. N. Jones	A. M. Green	G. G. Arnold	Byes	Leg byes	Wides	No balls	Total	Wickets
			1	3			212	10
			5	7	1		150	9
			1	3	1		170	10
			4	6		2	244	10
				3		2	98	10
				7	2	2	222	10
			1	15		2	230	10
			4	10	2		199	8
				7		2	205	9*
			1	1			43	9
			8	5	1	1	424	8
				1			35	0
			1	6	2	1	85	9†
				3		3	153	10
			2	1		3	243	10
			4	5		1	202	2
				1			8	1
3–0–11–0	24–2–92–0		8	4	1	23	450	2a
		13–8–9–2	1	1	1	2	70	10
		11–5–12–2		13		1	150	10
	7–1–33–1	8–3–26–0	2	8		6	356	8
	3–1–9–1	7–2–10–1	7	1		5	192	10
		16–4–19–1	2	15	1	5	208	10
		4–1–13–0		4	2	4	204	10
16–3–59–3						1	353	8
8–2–27–0				3	1	2	150	4
			1	3		1	252	4
				1		4	160	10
				1	1	4	240	10
2–0–3–1			2	1		3	261	10
				4	2	8	300	5
							0	0
			4	8	6	3	279	10
				5	3		70	2
			3	6	1	8	304	9
	1–0–8–0		3	4		2	198	3
			8	9		1	296	10
			1	3			127	4
	2–0–24–1		5	4			301	6
	4–0–24–1			4			152	8
		13–2–48–2		2	1	10	274	10b
		6–0–36–0		1		2	269	4c
29–5– 100–4 av. 25.00	60–6– 274–6 av. 45.66	59–23– 89–6 av. 14.82						

B. J. Lloyd

D. M. Smith

434/BENSON & HEDGES CRICKET YEAR

Warwickshire C.C.C. First-Class Matches – Batting, 1982

	v. Cambridge University (Cambridge) 1-4 May		v. Glamorgan (Edgbaston) 5-7 May		v. Indians (Edgbaston) 8-10 May		v. Kent (Dartford) 12-14 May		v. Yorkshire (Edgbaston) 19-21 May		v. Worcestershire (Worcester) 29 May-1 June		v. Oxford University (Oxford) 2-4 June		v. Sussex (Edgbaston) 5-8 June		v. Leicestershire (Leicester) 9-11 June		v. Glamorgan (Cardiff) 12-15 June		v. Nottinghamshire (Trent Bridge) 19-22 June		v. Northamptonshire (Northampton) 23-25 June		v. Somerset (Edgbaston) 26-29 June	
K. D. Smith	10	0*	—		13	—	—		—		31	62*	64	—	2	0	19	0	0	4	0*	—	—	2*	34	—
T. A. Lloyd	95	7*	74	—	87	—	87	9	12	5	0	3	24	63	5	4	3*	32	122	42	12	—	28*	14	20	—
A. I. Kallicharran	—	—	18	—	2	—	10	105*	11	8	235	35			89	12	210	7	38	9	32*	—	2	52*	33	—
G. W. Humpage	22	—	78	—	—		22	64	4	18	15	23	0	121*	22	0	25	11	90*	1	19	—	—	6	8	—
P. R. Oliver	26	—	4	—	2	—	26	46	16	9			—	—												
Asif Din	30*	—	2	—	91	—	27	5	13	5	12	39	15	38*	39	5	16	1	13	55					8	—
P. Smith	34*	—					13	10	15	16			20	—			30	59	35	0						
A. M. Ferreira			4	—	112*	—																				
G. C. Small	—	—	3	—			30*	4	22	5	0	—	57*	—	3	5	—	13	14*	7	—	—			5	—
J. Cumbes	—	—	6	—	—		4*	0*	4	0	4*	—			0*	4*	—	1	—	0*			—	2	0	—
W. Hogg			1	—			—	0*	0*	8																
D. L. Amiss			39	—	—		12	54	39	75	64	21			6	2	49	0	32	38	4	—	10	41	156	—
R. G. D. Willis			27*	—	72	—	4	1	12	2*	7	—			28	9										
C. Maynard					40	—																				
C. Lethbridge											0	2*	0	—			17*	47								
S. P. Sutcliffe											1*	—	17*	—	2	0			0*	—	15	3			8	—
G. Tedstone													9	—												
D. M. Smith													27	—												
S. H. Wootton																										
R. I. H. B. Dyer																			—	0					31*	—
R. K. Maguire																							—	2		
P. J. Hartley																										
D. J. Brown																										
P. J. Lewington																										
Byes	1		4		19		2	8	2		2	1				1	5		12	2	3				11	
Leg-byes	12		9				9	16	3	5	8	9	3	8	7	1	6	4	12	2	3			2	6	
Wides	7							1	1	2			1					1		1						
No-balls	7		11		9		9	4	4	8	1	2	2			2		1	8	5	1		1	4	1	
Total	244	7	280		447		255	327	158	166	380	197	239	230	205	43	381	177	391	169	74		41	123	323	
Wickets	4	0	10		7		8	9	10	10	9	5	8	1	9†	9†	6	10	7	10	3		2	4	10	
Result	D		D		D		D		L		D		W		L		D		D		D		D		D	
Points	—		6		—		6		5		3		—		6		7		8		0		0		5	

Fielding figures
50 – G. W. Humpage (ct 49/st 1)
14 – K. D. Smith
13 – Asif Din
12 – D. L. Amiss and T. A. Lloyd
9 – P. Smith
8 – J. Cumbes and A. I. Kallicharran
7 – C. Lethbridge
6 – G. C. Small
5 – G. Tedstone (ct 4/st 1) and A. M. Ferreira
4 – P. R. Oliver and R. G. D. Willis
2 – C. Maynard, W. Hogg and S. P. Sutcliffe
1 – D. J. Brown, P. J. Hartley and R. I. H. B. Dyer

championships. In a sense they were surprise finalists in the Benson and Hedges competition, but on their day they were very hard to beat.

The troubles of Yorkshire continue in one shape or form. Illingworth's return to the field of play brought discipline, stability and some success, but he is fifty-one and his term of office can only provide a temporary solution. One wonders why Bairstow has not been turned to for leadership, few men give more to the game.

Worcestershire are in a state of rebuilding and familiar faces will be missing next season. Lancashire, too, are rebuilding and there looks to be more optimism at Old Trafford than for some years. Apart from Fowler, O'Shaughnessy impressed among the younger players, but one wonders what will happen when Simmons and Hughes depart. They have given so much and show no sign of a decline. Folley may well supply the thrust that has been missing from the attack.

Northants still bat better than they bowl which also applies to Kent. There are some fine batsmen in the hop county, but there is no sign of a successor to Underwood and Dilley and Jarvis till promise more than they achieve.

Leicestershire did splendidly and might have done even better had Tolchard not been a little too cautious at times. Parsons' figures do not reflect his value, nor his improve-

THE ENGLISH SEASON

v. Lancashire (Edgbaston) 7–9 July		v. Yorkshire (Leeds) 17–20 July		v. Gloucestershire (Nuneaton) 21–23 July		v. Lancashire (Southport) 28–30 July		v. Derbyshire (Edgbaston) 7–10 August		v. Surrey (Edgbaston) 11–13 August		v. Middlesex (Coventry) 14–17 August		v. Essex (Colchester) 21–24 August		v. Worcestershire (Edgbaston) 28–31 August		v. Somerset (Taunton) 1–3 September		v. Northamptonshire (Edgbaston) 8–10 September		v. Hampshire (Southampton) 11–14 September		Inns	NOs	Runs	HS	Av
19	4*	3	2					7	—	21	49*	4	16	50	2	36	42	67	15	25	54	6	28	34	6	691	67	24.67
35	74	3	7	24		23	0	19	12*	89	60	0	25	17	42*	6	120	55	4	0	34	8	27	45	5	1432	122	35.80
74	37	59	8	173	—	230*	0	14	24*	195	14	—	—	26	3	109*	17			68	3	27	131	37	5	2120	235	66.25
7	39*	0	55	17	—	254	21	60	11	15	—	0	1	1	11	23*	34	113	1	146	42	1	6	41	4	1407	254	38.02
		1	13																					9	—	143	46	15.88
26	—			48		—	21	16	—	12	—	102	2	1	32	—	28	24	7	37	34	31	20	34	2	855	102	26.71
										21	—	45	14	68	—			1	2					16	1	383	68	25.53
								25	—					21	16*	—	1			22	41	23	38	10	2	303	112*	37.87
21	—	7	7	22	—	—	0	36	—	11	—	9*	0	8	—	—	1	—	1	2	3*	3	10	29	5	309	57*	12.87
												1	7*											14	7	33	7*	4.71
																								4	2	9	8	4.50
84	76	73	94	33	—	6				60	12	49	10*	6	41			54	8	1	26	42	32	31	0	38	1	1404	156	37.94
				63*	—		24			1	—			2	—					—	48	2*	—	8*	1	16	5	287	72	26.09
																								1	—	40	40	40.00
		3	26	2	—	—	18	4	—					34	—		4	16*	87*	0	7*	43	33	21	5	369	87*	23.06
0	—	0	0	20	—	—	7*			—	—	0	1	1*	—	—	0*	—	0			1	2*	17	7	52	20	5.20
																		9*	7	18*	2			5	2	45	18*	15.00
																								2	—	27	27	13.50
				3	—	—	0																	2	—	3	3	1.50
10	—			17	—	0	0																	5	1	58	31*	14.50
												1	0											3	—	3	2	1.00
4	—	3	8*			—	16																	4	1	31	16	10.33
7*	—																							1	1	7	7*	—
		11*	5					15*	—			0*	—			—	4*							5	3	35	15*	17.50
4	1	4	2	6		1	1	4		6		3	2	2		2		10	12		15		22	†P. R. Oliver absent hurt				
5	5	12	1	10		6	2	3		15	2	2	6	10	3	8	11	4	1	7	5	6	7	‡A. I. Kallicharran absent hurt				
		1		2	2	1	1	20		5	1			3			1						12					
7	1	10	6	6		2			1	8	7	1	5	5	4	12	3		5	12	10	3	2					
303	238	189	236	446		523	111	284	60	447	143	174	120	249	113	250	274	300	216	381	282	191	339					
10	3	10	10	10		4	10	10	2	8	2	9‡	9	10	4	3	9	6	10	9	8	10	10					
D		L		D		L		D		D		L		D		D		L		L		L						
4		4		8		6		7		4		3		4		6		6		8		5						

ment, and Taylor is a terrible loss to the England selectors. Balderstone was a rock and Davison one of the most thrilling sights of the summer.

The rise of Hampshire surprised many, but they are a well balanced, well ordered and committed side. Emery gave Marshall the support that that fine bowler so needed and had the spin department been stronger, success may have been even greater. For me, and for many others, Trevor Jesty was the player of the season and it is cruel that his honest application and abundant talent have gone unrecognised. If there is a disappointment of the season, it must be Peter May and his selectors, who suggested neither policy nor progress and left England supporters, and some players, in a state of bewilderment and dismay.

Trevor Jesty

Warwickshire C.C.C. First-Class Matches – Bowling, 1982

	W. Hogg	G. C. Small	A. M. Ferreira	J. Cumbes	P. Smith	T. A. Lloyd	R. G. D. Willis	Asif Din	C. Lethbridge
v. Cambridge University (Cambridge) 1–4 May	16–5–45–2 10–0–38–1	18–3–51–2 10–0–55–0	25.1–6–60–2 19–0–75–2	16–3–38–1 20–2–66–1	17–2–73–2 7–2–22–0	1–0–2–0			
v. Glamorgan (Edgbaston) 5–7 May	17–1–53–1 4–0–15–1	22–6–64–2 5–2–14–1	29–10–48–4	19.1–3–60–2			24–3–58–1 26–15–38–2	5–2–8–0 30–9–100–5	
v. Indians (Edgbaston) 8–10 May	12–2–30–1 9–2–28–0	12.3–1–47–2 10–2–45–3	21–2–67–3 3–0–19–0	6–0–31–0 27–3–97–2		7–0–29–2 5–0–43–0	14–6–17–2 8–0–33–0	2–0–6–0 12–1–64–0	
v. Kent (Dartford) 12–14 May	20–5–54–2 4–1–21–0	14–2–48–2 11–2–38–0		13.1–2–54–0 21–4–81–2	15–2–47–2 9–2–36–0	5–1–12–0	14–7–38–0 5–3–11–1	10–2–42–1 20–2–88–2	
v. Yorkshire (Edgbaston) 19–21 May	7–0–41–0 6.3–2–14–0	29–7–68–7 7–0–13–1		20–8–34–0	5–0–32–0		23–4–71–2 2–0–3–0	12–4–27–1	
v. Worcs. (Worcester) 29 May–1 June		7–0–54–0 8–3–33–1		9–0–58–0		7–1–22–0	12–0–76–0 5–1–17–0	10–1–29–0	20–1–94–1 11–5–26–2
v. Oxford University (Oxford) 2–4 June		20–6–41–2 18–8–40–3		24–6–60–1 28–7–47–4	10–1–43–0 8–0–36–1	2–1–4–0		11–1–41–0 7–3–18–0	3–1–16–0
v. Sussex (Edgbaston) 5–8 June		21.1–4–68–3 10–0–34–0		25–9–65–3 10–2–27–0			19–6–37–1 8–0–30–1	5–1–19–0 2–1–4–1	
v. Leicestershire (Leicestershire) 9–11 June		19–3–53–1 14–2–41–3		14–2–37–0 3–1–4–0	10–0–34–0 2–1–6–0			2–1–5–0 3–3–0–0	27–4–87–3 20–4–53–1
v. Glamorgan (Cardiff) 12–15 June		18–8–30–2 14–4–29–3		10–0–37–0 17–2–34–0	12–3–35–0			20–7–46–2 6–2–37–0	24.5–5–68–5 17–3–54–2
v. Nottinghamshire (Trent Bridge) 19–22 June									
v. Northamptonshire (Northampton) 23–25 June		5–2–13–1		3–1–8–0					3–1–4–0
v. Somerset (Edgbaston) 26–29 June		24–1–87–2		32.5–9–85–2		1–0–2–0 6–2–37–0		3–2–5–0 7–1–35–0	13–4–47–0
v. Lancashire (Edgbaston) 7–9 July		22–4–69–1						12–0–63–0	
v. Yorkshire (Leeds) 17–20 July		20–4–68–0 8–3–8–0							31.3–9–84–4 9–3–25–1
v. Gloucestershire (Nuneaton) 21–23 July		19–5–43–2 16–2–41–0				11–2–50–0	17–3–64–3 19–5–60–1	7–1–29–1 15–4–52–0	21.1–6–56–4 12–0–45–2
v. Lancashire (Southport) 28–30 July		15–4–38–1 11–2–30–0				1–0–1–0		6–1–35–1 5–0–25–0	14–5–58–0 9–2–27–0
v. Derbyshire (Edgbaston) 7–10 August		10–1–37–1 24–3–89–4	18–7–24–2 21–6–47–3				22–8–45–6 9–4–19–0	17–3–68–0	4–1–7–0 18–4–46–1
v. Surrey (Edgbaston) 11–13 August		10–2–67–1 9–0–32–1			8–1–44–0			1–0–12–0 1–1–0–0	
v. Middlesex (Coventry) 21–24 August		19–0–64–2		31–7–70–3	25–6–67–2				
v. Essex (Colchester) 21–24 August		12–0–70–1	7–0–42–0				12–0–58–1	6–1–29–0	1–0–7–0
v. Worcestershire (Edgbaston) 28–31 August		12–1–57–1 7–0–23–1	29.2–5–109–5 9–3–29–0			10–1–55–1		9–1–37–0 5–0–23–0	12–7–24–0 7–1–13–1 5–1–12–1
v. Somerset (Taunton) 1–3 September		6–0–21–0 7–0–34–1			5–1–12–2 3–0–49–1	13–1–49–0	5–2–13–1 8–0–35–1	5–1–19–0	1–0–14–0
v. Northamptonshire (Edgbaston) 8–10 Sept.		11–2–41–1 10.3–1–52–2	29–4–126–4 8–0–37–0				15–4–70–2 12–1–46–0	4–1–11–1 7–0–63–1	5–0–26–0 7–1–38–0
v. Hampshire (Southampton) 11–14 Sept.		10–5–14–2 14–1–61–0	17–6–62–1 8–2–32–0				13–4–37–1 13–1–46–2	17.1–5–58–3 5–0–38–1	9–0–46–1
	105.3–18–339–8 av. 42.37	589.1–106–1925–63 av. 30.55	243.3–51–789–26 av. 30.34	349.1–71–993–21 av. 47.28	136–21–536–10 av. 53.60	95–24–344–5 av. 68.80	284–64–892–26 av. 34.30	284.1–60–1128–20 av. 56.40	304.3–68–977–29 av. 33.68

a G. W. Humpage 3–0–5–0; D. M. Smith 12–2–45–0
b D. L. Amiss 1–0–8–0
c D. M. Smith 2–0–12–0 and 2–0–2–0
d R. K. Maguire 4–0–32–1
e R. K. Maguire 11–1–33–0
f D. L. Amiss 1–0–6–0
g D. Brown 17–1–66–1; P. J. Hartley 16–6–66–0
h G. W. Humpage 10–3–27–0 and 2.2–0–16–0; P. J. Hartley 18–4–45–2
i R. I. H. B. Dyer 1–0–2–0
j D. Bro...
k D. J. B...
l R. K. M...

Book Reviews

All books which have been received by the editor are reviewed in the following pages. The list of cricket books published during the year is completed by E. K. BROWN, the distinguished book-seller.

CRICKETERS IN THE MAKING,
Trevor Bailey: Queen Anne Press: 118 pp, £7.95
I am no great lover of instructional books, but I like this one. The great merit that it has is that it is simple and a child can learn from it. So many books which aim to teach lose their students in a maze of detail by page three. This books keeps clear until the very end. It is pleasantly illustrated, Patrick Eagar having used as his models boys from the Essex schools side of some four years ago and photographed them to advantage. This guide is heartily recommended for all parents who wish to give their child a helpful manual. Some parents may find it useful themselves.

TOM GRAVENEY'S TOP TEN CRICKET BOOK,
Tom Graveney: edited by Norman Giller: Harrap: 192 pp, £6.95
This is a book of lists, the type of lists one sets down on a piece of scrap paper on a rainy day – ten best left-handers, ten best spinners etc. Much of it is contrived – the spin partners' lists for example – but no doubt it will give pleasure and amusement in the chill of winter.

SLICES OF CRICKET,
Peter Roebuck: George Allen & Unwin: 140 pp, £7.95
This is a collection of essays, character studies and reminiscences by the Somerset batsman. Like most collections it is a mixture and some 'slices' are undeniably better than others, but in many ways this is part of the book's appeal. What is apparent from this volume is that Peter Roebuck has qualities that will make him an outstanding cricket writer (his study of Botham is the best thing that I have read on the great man) if he can eradicate the dressing-room gossip, nicknames and in-crowd intrusions which have become a tiresome part of so many cricket books over the past couple of years.

When he relies on wit and elegant prose that mirrors his batting the achievement is a delight. There is a fine sketch of Gavaskar, a charming piece on Combined Universities' victory over Yorkshire and a lovely assessment of R. J. O. Meyer, and much else.

If I have seemed to emphasise too much the intrusions of trivia, it is because they lessen a book which is so eminently readable and enjoyable as to make one ask for more.

THE SPINNER'S TURN,
Patrick Murphy: J. M. Dent: 208 pp, £7.95
This is Pat Murphy's first book under his own name after some years of 'ghosting'. Not all of these ghosting efforts have been happy ventures and one is pleased to welcome this book where his own voice begins to be heard even if it does stutter from time to time.

The subject is fascinating, but the sense of order, the thesis of the book is somewhat chaotic, and the main line of argument becomes lost because it is divided by character

438/BENSON & HEDGES CRICKET YEAR

Worcestershire C.C.C. First-Class Matches – Batting, 1982

	v. Oxford University (Oxford) 28-30 April		v. Derbyshire (Worcester) 5-7 May		v. Gloucestershire (Bristol) 12-14 May		v. Somerset (Worcester) 19-21 May		v. Warwickshire (Worcester) 29 May-1 June		v. Zimbabwe (Worcester) 2-4 June		v. Nottinghamshire (Trent Bridge) 5-8 June		v. Gloucestershire (Worcester) 9-11 June		v. Sussex (Hove) 12-15 June		v. Essex (Ilford) 19-22 June		v. Glamorgan (Cardiff) 23-25 June		v. Lancashire (Worcester) 26-29 June		v. Yorkshire (Sheffield) 7-9 July	
J. A. Ormrod	66	—	39	47	27	10	21	12	79	43			1	1	200*	93	3	14	9	6*	11	—	23	—	112	70
G. M. Turner	239*	—	4	27	4	0	6	4	311*	32			54	9*									115	—	31	6
P. A. Neale	1	—	5	11*	61	4	29	40	—	17*	1	12	16	9	—	79*	8	40	0	—	14	—	32	—	30	8
Younis Ahmed	70*	—	0	36*	3	84	7	39	—	10	63	75	0	65	114*	—					33		34	—	7	53
D. N. Patel	—	—	48	46	30	47	30	26	88*	22	6	12	5	6	27	4	4	8	0	—	8	—	34	—	1	49
E. J. O. Hemsley			0	0	22	0	10	15			17	24	16	47	—	34*	25	24	0	—	13	—	0	—	25	30
D. J. Humphries			52	11	33	0	69*	30	—	5	0	21	6	32*	—	—	7	0	11	—	28	—	6*	—	1	58
J. D. Inchmore					9	9	0	3			21	—	35*	12	—	—	1	3	9	—	38	—			4	7*
N. Gifford			11	—	11	10*			—	14*			11	0	—	—			4*	8*						
A. P. Pridgeon			4*	—	2	6	17	19	—	12			1	0			1	14*	1	—	21	—				
S. P. Perryman			0	—	0*	0	0	0*	—						0*	0							3*	—	43	10
A. E. Warner			19	—									15*	—							31*	—				
R. K. Illingworth							8	1	—	—	5*	15*					14	51								
M. J. Weston											63	2					3	10	15	3	9	—	6	—	13	24
M. S. Scott											8	4					—	14								
D. B. D'Oliveira											21	3					10	—							8*	22*
H. L. Alleyne											9*	—			—	—	23	20	0	—	0	—				
A. J. Webster																										
P. J. Newport																										
T. S. Curtis																										
R. M. Ellcock																										
Byes	13		2		5	4	2		1	2	2			1	4		1		2		1		4		5	1
Leg-byes	11		4	4	14	10	1	5	19	4	8	10	5	3	10	4	6	3		8	4		9	17		
Wides	1			1	1								1				2				3					
No-balls			6	9			1	2	3	6		1		1		3	1	3	3		2		3		3	7
Total	401		194	192	222	184	199	198	501	167	222	181	166	186	369	268	85	153	64	17	217		264		267	362
Wickets	2		10	5	10	10	10	10	1	6	9	7	9†	8†	2	3	9‡	10	10	1	10		7		10	9
Result	D		D		W		L		D		D		L		D		L		D		D		W		D	
Points	—		5		22		4		5		—		5		5		3		3		2		12		4	

Fielding figures
46 – D. J. Humphries (ct 41/st 5)
20 – D. N. Patel
11 – Younis Ahmed
9 – N. Gifford and G. M. Turner
8 – E. J. O. Hemsley, P. A. Neale and J. A. Ormrod
5 – T. S. Curtis, J. D. Inchmore, R. K. Illingworth and S. P. Perryman
4 – A. P. Pridgeon and M. J. Weston
3 – A. J. Webster
2 – A. E. Warner and D. B. D'Oliveira
1 – H. L. Alleyne, M. S. Scott, P. J. Newport and sub

studies and four somewhat irrelevant Test match reports.

The eighty-eight pages in the middle of the book which deal with the leading spin bowlers since the war are sharp character studies, shrewd assessments of man and ability, and are to be highly commended, but they separate the main contention of the book so that when one reaches page 147 it is almost like beginning again.

This is a pity because there is so much of rich promise in this book, but we have a sense of rushing and one feels that Mr Murphy is a young man in a hurry. If he would give himself a little more time, he has the capacity to produce a memorable book for, in this creditable volume, there is joy, argument and a feeling that the author knows the game.

WARWICKSHIRE CRICKET RECORD BOOK,
compiled by Robert Brooke: Association of Cricket Statisticians: 96 pp, £2.50
All that Robert Brooke does is thorough. He is a relentless pursuer of statistical accuracy and this book, a comprehensive statistical survey of his beloved county, is no exception to his usual high standards. It is neatly presented, beautifully set down so that reference is easy and clear.

One looks forward to the day when each county is represented by a work of comparable standard.

Book Reviews

'TICH' FREEMAN AND THE DECLINE OF THE LEG-BREAK BOWLER,
David Lemmon: George Allen & Unwin: 144 pp, £7.95
This is the first full-length study of the great Kent and England leg-break bowler. Unfortunately, it is not customary for an author to review his own work.

THIS CURIOUS GAME OF CRICKET,
George Mell, with illustrations by Bill Tidy: George Allen & Unwin: 127 pp, £5.95
This is a collection of odd, amusing and bizarre stories from first-class and club cricket. They range from being out 'burnt ball 0' to 'wind stopped play'. They will make good retelling on winter evenings and there is something for everyone.

MIDDLESEX COUNTY CRICKET CLUB REVIEW 1981/82,
edited by Alvan Seth-Smith: 128 pp, £1.50
Three years ago there was no Middlesex handbook and it took the drive and commitment of Alvan Seth-Smith to convince the County that a year-book would be both beneficial and commercially viable. Now in its second year of publication the book has achieved a standard second to none among the county annuals.

It is neat, clear, statistically attractive and eminently readable. There are interesting contributions from Ted Jackson, Russell March, Terence Prittie, whose *Mainly Middlesex* remains one of the most delightful of cricket books, Horace Brearley and novelist Len Grimsey, and there is an article on Harry Lee by David Frith which is reprinted from *Wisden Cricket Monthly*. This is an impressive team and makes good reading, but the man who deserves the highest praise for this splendid achievement is Alvan Seth-Smith.

KEN BARRINGTON; A TRIBUTE,
Brian Scovell: Harrap: 176 pp, £7.95
Harrap are making a donation from the proceeds of this book to The Lord's Taverner's Under 13 competition. It is a nice gesture and it is a worthwhile book. The first part is better than the second. Brian Scovell tells the Barrington story with simplicity and without sentimentality, and it is most readable. The second part of the book comprises appreciations of Barrington by many who played with and against him.

FIGURES ON THE GREEN,
Derek Lodge: George Allen & Unwin: 188 pp, £8.95
Derek Lodge came to prominence with *Wisden Cricket Monthly* although members of The Cricket Society knew much of his fascinating work on statistics before then. His

Worcestershire C.C.C. First-Class Matches – Bowling, 1982

	A. P. Pridgeon	S. P. Perryman	J. D. Inchmore	N. Gifford	D. N. Patel	A. J. Webster	A. E. Warner	R. K. Illingworth	H. L. Alleyne
v. Oxford University (Oxford) 28–30 April	25–6–51–3 14–5–24–0	30–12–62–3 24–13–36–0	13.4–5–22–2 8–3–11–0	18–6–31–1 47–27–55–2	10–1–37–0 37–16–64–1				
v. Derbyshire (Worcester) 5–7 May	26.2–6–66–3 26–11–52–1	24–7–43–2 36.2–9–97–5		4–3–7–0 8–4–13–0			24–3–73–4 26–9–60–2		
v. Gloucestershire (Bristol) 12–14 May	23–6–46–1 22.2–6–56–4	8–2–27–2 12–3–36–1	24–7–53–7 17–2–51–1	3–1–11–0 27–6–62–0	21–12–19–4				
v. Somerset (Worcester) 19–21 May	17–4–33–0 17–3–39–4	29–7–67–2	20.2–5–39–1 10–0–35–1		43–12–82–4 6.2–1–20–0			27–8–61–3	
v. Warwicks (Worcester) 29 May–1 June	15–2–54–1 7–2–15–0	10–2–20–0 4–1–9–0		41–11–100–1 20–1–59–2	40–8–110–2 13–3–60–1			37–9–85–4 19–7–42–2	
v. Zimbabwe (Worcester) 2–4 June			8–0–22–1 7–3–8–0		9–2–32–0 7–0–23–2			10–0–47–0 1–1–0–0	9–1–26–2 5–1–15–0
v. Nottinghamshire (Trent Bridge) 5–8 June	29–8–73–2 9–2–23–1		12–1–61–0 4–1–17–0	33.5–15–48–6 6–1–16–0	15–5–50–2				
v. Gloucestershire (Worcester) 9–11 June	6–0–18–0 7–3–19–0		6–1–9–1 3–0–12–0	35–8–97–2 24–8–73–4	24–6–76–1 15–2–58–1			20–2–74–1 13–5–29–1	
v. Sussex (Hove) 12–15 June	19–3–58–1	15–3–60–3	18–1–70–2					22–6–49–1	
v. Essex 19–22 June	20–6–40–1		26–9–44–1	15–6–34–1				30.3–5–92–4	
v. Glamorgan (Cardiff) 23–25 June	9–1–30–0		7–1–24–0		2–0–7–1			11–7–14–0	
v. Lancashire (Worcester) 26–29 June			5–0–17–0		20–9–46–7	7–1–24–0	6–1–16–0	13.3–2–51–3	
v. Yorkshire (Sheffield) 7–9 July			29–5–82–1	16–6–22–0	51–12–142–4	18–6–39–1	32–4–98–3		
v. Pakistanis (Worcester) 10–12 July		26–4–91–1			19–3–47–1		12–1–64–0	30–3–126–1	
v. Kent (Hereford) 21–23 July			17.3–4–36–2 10–5–11–0		37–10–81–3 41–8–101–3	16–3–55–1 5–1–19–0	13–1–39–1 10–1–40–0	9–2–26–0 40–13–107–2	
v. Glamorgan (Worcester) 28–30 July	18–2–40–1 7–0–35–0		16–3–56–1 7–1–30–3	29–8–57–1 3–1–3–0	28–9–54–2 8–0–29–0			17–3–58–0 6–1–16–0	
v. Northants (Northampton) 31 July–3 August	26–8–47–1 14–2–42–2		22–7–40–3 5–0–6–1	20–8–21–2 24–6–60–0	1–1–0–0				28–4–79–2 21–5–70–3
v. Leicestershire (Worcester) 7–10 August	23–5–63–1 10–5–19–0		24–4–59–5 8.5–0–26–2	25.1–12–28–3 31–5–89–0	3–1–4–0 30–4–88–3				24–5–76–1 3–1–6–0
v. Hampshire (Southampton) 14–17 Aug.	29–5–75–4 16–2–60–0	11–1–45–0 14–5–43–1		22–9–36–1 7–1–26–0		23.1–2–87–5 18–6–39–2			
v. Surrey (Worcester) 21–24 August	25–0–92–1 3.2–0–14–0	23–2–91–1		23–1–82–0	30–4–73–1	29–6–99–2 3–0–21–0			
v. Lancashire (Blackpool) 25–27 August		26–6–49–6			15–3–33–0	29–4–113–2	6.1–4–6–1	15–4–53–1	
v. Warwickshire (Edgbaston) 28–31 August			19–4–78–0 10–1–57–0		4–2–8–0 20–6–76–5	16–4–53–1 16–1–70–1	7–0–42–1 10–0–34–2		
v. Nottinghamshire (Worcester) 1–3 September			20–5–51–0 30–7–81–1		20–6–63–2	16–1–79–0 6–1–18–0	28–5–92–3 9–2–36–0		
v. Somerset (Taunton) 8–10 September			19.5–5–74–5		3–0–48–0		13–3–85–2		21–2–69–2
v. Middlesex (Worcester) 11–14 Sept.		32–8–85–2 7–4–14–0					6–0–22–0	33–6–124–2 3.1–0–15–0	
	463–103– 1184–32 av. 37.00	430.1–111– 1216–35 av. 34.74	328.2–68– 841–35 av. 24.02	482–154– 1030–26 av. 39.61	572.2–146– 1531–50 av. 30.62	202.1–36– 716–15 av. 47.73	202.1–34– 707–19 av. 37.21	260.4–59– 811–18 av. 45.05	207.3–44– 599–16 av. 37.43

a P. A. Neale 2–2–0–0
b Younis Ahmed 5–1–14–0
c J. A. Ormrod 1–0–5–0
d P. A. Neale 4–0–16–0
e R. M. Ellcock 20.1–1–80–3
f T. S. Curtis 2–0–7–0

M. J. Weston	P. J. Newport	E. J. O. Hemsley	Byes	Leg byes	Wides	No balls	Total	Wickets
			1	2	1	4	211	10
			4	7		1	202	3a
				6		3	198	10
			6	12		7	247	8
			6	13	1	1	158	10
			4	5		4	237	10
			6	9		1	298	10
				5		2	101	5
			2	8		1	380	9
			1	9		2	197	5
9–3–10–0			7	9		3	156	3
				2		4	52	2
		5–0–19–0	7	14		4	290	10b
					4	3	63	1
4–0–24–0		1–0–3–0	8	6	1	4	320	4
				4	1	1	197	6
				17		21	275	8
7–1–26–0				12		4	252	7
2–0–6–0				4		1	86	1
			5	12	2	2	175	10
		1.4–0–2–1	7	15	1	16	424	10
18.4–0–61–1	11–0–64–0			8		6	467	4
		13–1–56–0	1	13	1	13	321	7
			2	3		4	287	6
10–3–21–0			15	9	2	5	317	5
			1			6	125	3c
				7		6	200	8
			3	2			183	6
			1	5		11	247	10
9.1–2–33–0			2	9		3	291	5d
				14	1	1	259	10
				18	2	3	191	3
14.2–0–63–2			6	19	9	2	536	7
				1			36	0
			3	7		13	277	10
	13–1–47–1		2	8		12	250	3
	3–0–22–1			1	11	3	274	9
	5–0–29–0		5	4		3	326	6
	15–0–76–4		2	9	1	7	230	5
				20	1	10	307	9
11–2–42–3			9	14	1	5	382	10e
			1	11		2	50	0f
85.1–11–	47–1–	20.4–1–						
286–6	238–6	80–1						
av. 47.66	av. 39.66	av. 80.00						

first book is no disappointment. It is a shrewd, clever and intriguing study of the game through an analysis of its statistics. The book is never dull. It is not simply a statistical catalogue, but an investigation that is thought provoking and convincing. We discover the value or otherwise of the nightwatchman and the weight of the burden of captaincy and much else. It should not be missed.

TEST MATCH SPECIAL,
edited by Peter Baxter: Unwin Paperbacks: 206 pp, £1.75
This popular and companionable book which was reviewed last year is now available in paperback. Handy for pocket and train.

THE FAST MEN,
David Frith: George Allen & Unwin: 178 pp, £7.95
This is another re-issue, only this is a revised and updated edition of David Frith's highly acclaimed book. It is written in a lively style which mirrors the subject matter. It is vigorous and argumentative. Well worth re-reading, obligatory if it has not been read before.

THE INCREDIBLE TESTS 1981,
Ian Botham: Pelham Books: 160 pp, £6.95
The England–Australia series of 1981 caught the public imagination as few series have done and it was right that an account of them should be written. This account is by the man who was at the centre of the action. It is simple, straightforward and has an immediacy that helps rekindle the excitement of the memorable matches.

A HUNDRED YEARS OF THE ASHES,
Doug Ibbotson and *Ralph Dellor*: Rothmans Publications Ltd.: 228 pp, £12.95
This is a simple, telling of the history of the Test matches between England and Australia. It is not a detailed history and much has to be glossed over in the need to compress the wealth of material to a manageable size, but it reads well and informatively. One of its great virtues, however, is its splendid illustrations. There are some historical pictures here and for them alone the book is well worth having.

WISDEN CRICKETERS' ALMANACK 1982,
edited by John Woodcock: Queen Anne Press: 1298 pp, £8.95 (hardback) or £7.95 (paperback)
The 119th edition of the mighty *Wisden* is as good as any that have gone before. In the past two years John Woodcock has tightened and modernised without in any way offending tradition. It remains the invaluable work of reference justly renowned.

PLAYFAIR CRICKET ANNUAL 1982
edited by Gordon Ross: Queen Anne Press: 256 pp, £1.10
Descended from the old *Daily News* and *News Chronicle* cricket annuals, this pocket annual is for me the one indispensable cricket book that is published each year. This year NatWest Bank have added sponsorship to keep down prices and they are to be commended. It contains the usual potted biographies of first-class players in England and all information is easily accessible. The sad thing about this publication is that one of its main contributors, Michael

Yorkshire C.C.C. First-Class Matches – Batting, 1982

	v. Northamptonshire (Northampton) 5-7 May		v. Glamorgan (Leeds) 12-14 May		v. Indians (Bradford) 15-18 May		v. Warwickshire (Edgbaston) 19-21 May		v. Lancashire (Leeds) 29-31 May		v. Leicestershire (Hinckley) 2-4 June		v. Middlesex (Sheffield) 12-15 June		v. Northamptonshire (Middlesbrough) 19-22 June		v. Essex (Ilford) 23-25 June		v. Derbyshire (Derby) 3-6 July		v. Worcestershire (Sheffield) 7-9 July		v. Gloucestershire (Bradford) 10-13 July		v. Warwickshire (Leeds) 17-20 July	
G. Boycott	138	3	134	15			79	21*	13	68	17	56	6	34	9	—	9	—	20	7	159		5	33	152*	24*
K. Sharp	27	20	5	19*	115	20*	0	—	43	0	32	21	47	3												
C. W. J. Athey	18	12	77	100	61*	—	0	5*	90	38*	3	50	47	0	54	—	18	—	0	134	44	—	22	73	13	21*
R. G. Lumb	6	—	10	67	52	15*	1	4	29	72	70	21	3	27	18	—	52	—	74	0	21	—	2	14	4	10
J. D. Love	29	64*	65	4	3*	—			0	4	3	27	0	81*	41	—	2	—	110	0			6	3	13	—
S. N. Hartley	2	2	40*	15*	16	—	7	—					18	60*	1*	—	7	—	2	52*	11	—	114	0	18	—
D. L. Bairstow	77	27*	13	—	4*	—	30	—	70*	7	7	8*	18	—	5*	—	16	—	21	1*	5	—	55	9*	34	—
P. Carrick	5	44	—	—	—	—	0	—	44	—	11	2*	0	6			11	—	3*	—	93	—	2	41	75	—
G. B. Stevenson	34*	—	9	14			115*	—					8*	—			1*	—	37	—	19	—	18	0	6	—
C. M. Old	9*	—	0*	—			27	—			22	4	29	—			2	—	15	—	1	—	10	0	20	—
A. Sidebottom	—	—	—	—			13	—	7*	1*	44*	—	13	—			26*	—			2	—	15*	8		
N. S. Taylor	—	—	—	—																						
S. J. Dennis							—	—																	—	—
J. P. Whiteley							1	—			5*	—														
P. W. Jarvis											—	—							—	—	0*	—	7	0		
R. Illingworth																					30	—				
A. Ramage																										
M. D. Moxon																										
P. A. Booth																										
Byes	4	6	4	2	4		5		7			1	2	6					2		2	7			1	
Leg-byes	10	10	13	9	1		4	2	6	6	7		9	4	1		2		2	1	15		10	4	11	6
Wides			3				7		2		1	2		7			2		1		1		6	1	5	1
No-balls	9	1	7	3	4		3	1	6	1	7		3	8	13		4		6	3	16		7	1	13	2
Total	368	189	380	248	260	35	292	33	317	197	229	192	203	236	142		152		291	200	424		279	187	365	64
Wickets	8	5	7	5	3	0	10	1	6	5	8	6	10	5	4		8		8	4	10		10	10	8	1
Result	D		D		D		W		D		D		D		D		D		D		D		L		W	
Points	8		7		—		23		6		4		6		1		1		3		6		6		24	

Fielding figures
- 56 – D. L. Bairstow (ct 35/st 3)
- 21 – C. W. J. Athey
- 10 – G. Boycott
- 9 – R. G. Lumb and C. M. Old
- 8 – P. Carrick
- 7 – J. D. Love
- 6 – G. B. Stevenson and S. N. Hartley
- 5 – P. W. Jarvis
- 4 – A. Sidebottom and subs
- 3 – J. P. Whiteley and R. Illingworth
- 2 – K. Sharp
- 1 – N. S. Taylor and S. J. Dennis

Fordham, died shortly before publication. He will be missed by all who had the privilege of meeting him.

GREAT ONE-DAY CRICKET MATCHES,
David Lemmon: Pelham Books: 151 pp, £7.95
Again it is not customary to review one's own work desirable as that may be. This is the first attempt to record some of the great matches of limited over cricket.

WISDEN ANTHOLOGY 1940–1963,
edited by Benny Green: Queen Anne Press: 1009 pp, £25
The third anthology in this enthralling series has a special attraction as, for most of us who follow the game and write about it, it covers 'all our yesterdays'. The idea of a *Wisden Anthology* was not a revolutionary one, but Benny Green, like any compiler, was confronted by what to omit and what to include. The success of these volumes is that what he has included is so stimulating, often amusing, sometimes sad. He has achieved not simply a collection of bits of *Wisden*, but a chronological comment on the game over a period of twenty-three years, its development and social changes. It is a remarkable achievement, for it could have so easily gone wrong. We look forward to the last volume.

A SUMMER TO REMEMBER,
Patrick Eagar, with commentary by Alan Ross: Collins: 128 pp, £5.95

v. Nottinghamshire (Worksop) 21–23 July		v. Sussex (Scarborough) 31 July–3 August		v. Lancashire (Old Trafford) 7–10 August		v. Somerset (Weston-super-Mare) 11–13 August		v. Kent (Leeds) 14–17 August		v. Middlesex (Lord's) 21–24 August		v. Hampshire (Bournemouth) 28–31 August		v. Derbyshire (Scarborough) 8–10 September		v. Surrey (The Oval) 11–14 September				Inns	NOs	Runs	HS	Av
91	82	52	122*	—		62		129	—	69	41*	2	40*	72	24	57	4	27	37			37	6	1913	159	61.70
												16	—	4	39			15	52			18	2	478	115	29.87
5	76	19	5	—		2		2	—	100	28*	20	1*	3	7	0	58	114*	19			38	7	1339	134	43.19
1	43	46	—	—		15		81	—	5	34	0	34	0	13							33	1	844	81	26.37
0	39	19*	56	—		38*		14		27	—					0	1*	123	1			29	6	773	123	33.60
9	2	4	35	—		15*		7*		0	—	54	—	51	45*	1	16*	3	28			30	9	635	114	30.23
32	5	4*	19	—		—		—		—		12	—	54*	—	0	44	1	1			29	9	603	77	30.15
34	5	—	10*	—		—		—		—		5	—	2	—	25	5					21	3	423	93	23.50
3	18									29	—	4	—	4	0	3	—	34	—			19	4	356	115*	23.73
0	19*													10	32	5	2					18	3	207	32	13.80
18	6*					—		—		16	—	1	—	4	1*	39	—	12	7*			18	8	233	44*	23.30
										0*	—											1	1	0	0*	—
																		5*	—			1	1	5	5*	—
																						2	1	6	5*	6.00
																						3	1	7	7	3.50
1*	—	—		—		—		—		5	—	15	—	2*	—	33	—	—				6	1	86	33	17.20
								4*	—			0	—									2	1	4	4*	4.00
																36	67	40	54			4	—	197	67	49.25
																0*	—					1	1	0	0*	—

4	1		1			3		1		4		3	5	1	1	2	4					The match v. Nottinghamshire at Harrogate, 26–29 June was abandoned without a ball being bowled.				
5	6	3	3			6		2		12	2	3		15	1	10	5	10	3							
			1					1		1		1		2	1			1								
3	3	2	1			3		8		22	4	6		1		8	4	6	3							

206	305	150	252			142		250		304	109	182	75	196	217	217	158	393	209		
10	8	4	4			3		4		10	1	10	1	10	8	10	4	8	7		
W		W		D		D		D		D		D		D		W		D			
22		19		2		5		4		2		5		22		3					

A glorious pictorial record of the Tests of 1981 by a great photographer who is also a kind and sensitive man. There is apt comment by Alan Ross whose poetic qualities and poetic truth are the right verbal complement for the poetry of these superb pictures.

BOYCOTT: A CRICKETING LEGEND,
John Callaghan: Pelham Books: 220 pp, £7.95
A readable, straightforward account of one of cricket's most debated men by a writer who is obviously one of Boycott's followers and fans.

Allen, David R.	*Sir Aubrey* (Elm Tree)	£12.50
	Samuel Britcher, The Hidden Scorer	£11.50
Arlott, John	*Jack Hobbs: Profile of the Master* (Murray)	£6.95
Berry, Scyld	*Cricket Wallah. With MCC in India and Sri Lanka, 1981–2* (Hodder)	£7.95
Boothroyd, Derrick	*Half a Century of Yorkshire Cricket* (Kennedy Bros., Keighley)	£3.95
Boycott, Geoffrey	*Master Class* (Barker)	£3.95
Brayshaw, Ian	*The Wit of Cricket* (Deutsch)	£4.50
Brearley, Mike	*Pheonix from the Ashes, The 1981 Test Series* (Hodder)	£7.95
Burgess, Mike & Allen, Patrick	*Rothmans Club Cricket Yearbook, 1982* (Rothmans)	£5.50
Cardus, Neville	*The Roses Matches, 1919–1939* (Souvenir)	£9.95
	County Champions (Heinemann)	£7.95
De Selincourt, Hugh	*The Game of the Season.* Intro. by John Arlott. Re-issue	£2.50
Eagar, Patrick	*Test Decade, 1972–1982* (World's Work)	£12.95
Fingleton, Jack	*Batting from Memory* (Collins)	£8.95
Gooch, Graham with Alan Lee	*My Cricket Diary, '81. The West Indies, Australia, India.* (S. Paul)	£6.95
Green, Stephen	*Cricketing Bygones*	95p
Illingworth, Ray & Gregory, Kenneth	*The Ashes. A Centenary* (Collins)	£7.95
Keating, Frank	*Another Bloody Day in Paradise* (Deutsch)	£6.95
March, Russell	*The Cricketers of Vanity Fair* (Webb & Bower)	£9.95
Martin-Jenkins, Chris	*Bedside Cricket* (Dent)	£5.50
Melford, Michael	*Botham Rekindles the Ashes* (Daily Telegraph)	£1.95
Peskett, Roy (ed)	*The Best of Cricket* (Hamlyn)	£5.95
Raven, Simon	*Shadows on the Green* (Blond & Briggs)	£7.95
Rippon, Anton	*Classic Moments of the Ashes* (Moorland Publishing)	£6.95
	The Story of Middlesex C.C.C. (Moorland Publishing)	£6.95

Yorkshire C.C.C. First-Class Matches – Bowling, 1982

	C. M. Old	G. B. Stevenson	A. Sidebottom	S. N. Hartley	P. Carrick	C. W. J. Athey	R. Illingworth	S. J. Dennis	N. S. Taylor
v. Northamptonshire (Northampton) 5–7 May	23–8–56–1 14–5–29–1	26–6–74–3 14–2–50–1	22–5–57–5 14–3–40–1	10–4–17–1 10–5–28–1	4–2–9–0 5–3–5–0				
v. Glamorgan (Leeds) 12–14 May	19–4–40–0 5–1–13–0	25.1–6–68–3 8–3–15–0	31–7–83–4 7–2–21–1	3–0–27–0 10–4–17–0	22–3–68–1 17–3–36–1	4–0–10–0 1–0–7–0			
v. Indians (Bradford) 15–18 May		15–4–44–0 6–4–7–0		2–0–15–0	22–6–62–0 14–3–34–1			16–1–71–1 13–5–32–1	14.4–1–76–2 7–1–31–0
v. Warwickshire (Edgbaston) 19–21 May	29–7–52–3 27–8–76–6	18–5–41–3 9–2–30–1	15.1–4–30–2 21.3–7–34–3		5–1–10–0 2–1–1–0				
v. Lancashire (Leeds) 29–31 May	35–13–91–4 6–2–33–1		24–7–71–2 12–3–43–1		21–8–47–0 21–2–88–2				12–2–45–1 13–1–42–2
v. Leicestershire (Hinckley) 2–4 June	21–7–42–0 13–3–43–2		25–4–72–2 10.1–4–45–3		41–13–106–4 5–0–20–2				
v. Middlesex (Sheffield) 12–15 June	20–5–48–4 6–2–11–1	17–5–46–4 6–0–19–1	16–3–57–1 0.5–0–7–0						
v. Northants (Middlesbrough) 19–22 June	25–5–101–1	21–2–104–0	8.4–0–60–1	8–0–41–1	13–2–27–0				
v. Essex (Ilford) 23–25 June	9.5–0–48–1	6–1–29–0				3–0–6–0			
v. Derbyshire (Derby) 3–6 July	31–7–70–2	24–3–114–4			24–5–64–0	5–0–27–0	22–6–68–0		
v. Worcestershire (Sheffield) 7–9 July	7.3–0–27–1 16–5–54–2	16–4–51–1 21–3–76–1	18–1–58–2 16–3–53–1	2–0–6–0	31–7–90–6 46–19–107–3	4–1–8–0	1–0–1–0		
v. Gloucestershire (Bradford) 10–13 July	25–9–66–1 12–0–35–1	24–5–57–3 10–0–57–1	21–5–56–2 2–0–15–0		11–4–10–0 15–2–60–1				
v. Warwickshire (Leeds) 17–20 July	16–6–32–2 18–3–56–2	18–1–46–2 16.3–3–55–3		5–1–18–0 3–0–11–1	5–0–12–0 8–1–19–0		1–0–1–0 1–0–3–1	15–1–42–5 17–5–67–3	
v. Nottinghamshire (Worksop) 21–23 July	10–2–25–0	18–3–69–1	26–3–85–5 16–3–39–2	15–2–43–0 8–3–23–0	13–5–20–2 22–7–70–0	6–0–24–0	24–11–28–1 14–4–39–0		
v. Sussex (Scarborough) 31 July–3 August			19–1–55–3 4–1–17–0	2–1–4–0	8–4–10–0 22–5–69–4		11–6–20–1 17.4–4–57–1		
v. Lancashire (Old Trafford) 7–10 Aug.			19–4–60–2 26–4–104–2	13–3–37–1 4–1–14–0	10–3–36–0 24.4–13–31–4	4.1–0–16–0	5–1–10–0 28–11–54–0		24.3–7–72–1
v. Somerset (Weston-super-Mare) 11–13 August	22–9–50–3			7–1–23–1					
v. Kent (Leeds) 14–17 August		11–4–23–0 6–1–12–1	9–3–22–0 9–3–11–1		15–2–51–1 24–5–56–4		12–2–39–1 14–5–32–2		7–2–9–1 6–2–18–1
v. Middlesex (Lord's) 21–24 August		26–4–120–1	19.1–0–75–0	9–2–35–0	37–9–80–1		4–0–17–0		
v. Hampshire (Bournemouth) 28–31 Aug.	20–5–47–2 11–3–21–2	11–2–34–1 12–3–35–3	16.1–4–36–3 6–1–15–0		36–11–69–2 25.1–5–58–3		20–9–57–1 13–5–23–0		
v. Derbyshire (Scarborough) 8–10 Sept.	16–4–30–2 10–2–33–1	10–1–42–1 27–9–72–5	15.5–5–31–6 17.5–3–61–3	1–0–1–0			9–0–23–0		
v. Surrey (The Oval) 11–14 Sept.		9–0–32–1 13–2–52–0	10–3–59–0 18–2–66–4	6–0–28–0			11–1–48–0 16–0–67–1	15–1–73–0 19–3–80–2	
	467.2–125– 1229–46 av. 26.71	443.4–88– 1474–45 av. 32.75	495.2–95– 1538–62 av. 24.80	118–27– 388–6 av. 64.66	568.5–154– 1425–41 av. 34.75	27.1–1– 98–0 —	223–65– 587–9 av. 65.22	95–16– 365–12 av. 30.41	84.1–16– 293–8 av. 36.62

a J. D. Love 3–3–0–0
b J. H. Hampshire absent injured
c A. Ramage 17–3–73–1 and 6–0–32–1
d A. Ramage 23–7–69–2
e A. Ramage 21–2–101–0
f A. Ramage 23–2–106–1
g P. A. Booth 1–1–0–0 and 9–2–22–0

	J. P. Whiteley	G. Boycott	P. W. Jarvis	Byes	Leg byes	Wides	No balls	Total	Wickets
					8		2	223	10
					6		2	160	4
				5	5	1	15	322	9
					1		2	112	2a
	19–0–93–1			2	8	1	4	376	5
	13–1–59–2				2	5	1	171	5
		6–1–15–2		2	3	1	4	158	10
		4–0–10–0			5	2	8	166	10
			21–3–68–0		15	6	8	351	8
			8–1–33–0		3	4	9	255	6
	10–0–41–1		10–0–45–0		15		8	329	7
			7–1–23–1		5	5	1	141	8
		2.3–1–1–1			4		2	158	10
					2			39	2
	6–0–30–0				9	1	9	382	3
				1	4		2	90	1
		7–1–19–1	25–4–100–2	2	7	1	1	473	9b
			4–0–24–0	5	9		3	267	10
			13–4–32–2	1	17		7	362	9
		5–1–6–0	19–4–49–1	1	12	3	6	266	7
			9–3–24–2	2	6	1	1	201	5
		2.5–1–12–1		4	12		10	189	10
		3–0–14–0		2	1	2	6	236	10
		9–2–14–2		1	13		7	329	9
		1–0–1–0		1	2		6	181	2
		4–1–5–0	11–4–23–0	3	2		8	203	5c
			5–1–13–0		5	1	3	197	6
				8	5		13	310	6d
								30	0
				7	7	1	10	388	10e
					8		12	164	3
				4	3	2	4	142	9
				6	11		11	461	5f
					6		6	255	10
				2	6	1	6	167	8
		8–3–20–1		4	2		8	137	10g
		5–2–3–0			3	2	17	237	10
					7	1	9	257	1
				2	7	7	13	294	8
	48–1–	57.2–13–	132–25–						
	223–4	120–8	434–8						
	av. 55.75	av. 15.00	av. 54.25						

THE ENGLISH SEASON/445

Sheen, Steven	*The Geoffrey Boycott File* (Hamlyn)	£2.25
Sproat, Iain	*The Cricketers' Who's Who*	
	Hardback	£7.50
	Softback	£4.95
Tinniswood, Peter	*More Tales from a Longroom* (Arrow)	£1.50
Trueman, Fred	*My Most Memorable Cricket Matches* (S. Paul)	£5.95
Tyson, Frank	*The Cricketer Who Laughed* (S. Paul)	£4.95
The Warwickshire Centenary Story		£1.00

The following overseas items have all been on sale in this country in the past year.

Australia

A.B.C. Cricket Book. Pakistan & West Indies in Australia, 1981–2.
Bradman's First Tour. From newspapers collected during the tour (Rigby).
Chappell, Greg. *Unders and Overs. The Controversies of Cricket* (Lansdowne Press).
Chappell, Ian etc. *Chapelli Laughs Again* (Lansdowne Press).
Cricketer (edited Ken Piesse) Monthly magazine, Oct. to April.
Derriman, Phillip. *The Grand Old Ground. A History of Sydney Cricket Ground* (Cassell/Australia).
Piesse, Ken. *Cricket Year.* (Now the only Australian Annual).
Piesse, Ken and Main, Jim. *Calypso Summers.*
Sparke, Garry and McFarline, Peter. *Cricket in Australia. Season 1981–2.*
Tasmanian Cricket Yearbook, 1981–82.
Torrens, Warwick. *Queensland Cricket & Cricketers, 1862–1981.*
Whitington, R. S. *Keith Miller. The Golden Nugget* (Rigby).

Bermuda

The Bermuda Cricket Annual, 1982

India

Indian Cricket Annual, 1981
Bombay Golden Jubilee, 1930–1980

New Zealand

Brittenden, Dick and Cameron, Don. *Test Series '82. Australia in New Zealand* (Reed).
Carman, Arthur. *The 1981 Shell Almanack of New Zealand.*
Payne, Francis. *Rothmans – New Zealand First-Class Cricket, 1980–1.*
D. B. Cricket Annual, 1980.
Souvenir. *Rothmans Australia in New Zealand, 1982.*

Pakistan

Qamar Ahmed (ed.). *The Pakistan Book of Cricket, 1980–1.*

South Africa

Owen-Smith, Michael (ed.). *The 1981 Protea Cricket Annual of South Africa, Vol. 28.*

West Indies

The West Indies Cricket Annual, 1981.

Derbyshire C.C.C.
One Day Matches – 1982

BATTING

	v. Leicestershire (Leicester) 8 May (B.&H.)	v. Leicestershire (Leicester) 9 May (J.P.)	v. Minor Counties (Derby) 15 May (B.&H.)	v. Essex (Derby) 16 May (J.P.)	v. Somerset (Taunton) 23 May (J.P.)	v. Worcestershire (Worcester) 25 May (B.&H.)	v. Yorkshire (Chesterfield) 27 May (B.&H.)	v. Warwickshire (Chesterfield) 30 May (J.P.)	v. Worcestershire (Worcester) 6 June (J.P.)	v. Hampshire (Portsmouth) 13 June (J.P.)	v. Sussex (Derby) 16 June (B.&H.)	v. Kent (Canterbury) 20 June (J.P.)	v. Yorkshire (Derby) 27 June (J.P.)	v. Lancashire (Derby) 4 July (J.P.)	v. Hampshire (Southampton) 14 July (N.W.T.)	v. Middlesex (Lord's) 18 July (J.P.)	v. Surrey (Derby) 1 August (J.P.)
J. G. Wright	60	17	45	7	22	19	19	43	103	—	67	33	13	31	61	56	4	19
A. Hill	21						0		—	6			19					
P. N. Kirsten	77*	22	58	72	4	53	48	28	64*	1	60	37	44	30	110*	36	43
J. H. Hampshire	2	28	—	2	91*	44	66*	79	18	41	3	25	12	11*	18	47*	4
B. Wood	20	22	—	1	27*	106	—	—	—	18*	22	11	31		21	6*	29
G. Miller	8	19	88*	32	81	19	47*	12*	0*	29	33	23		1	0		
K. J. Barnett	8	18	—	26		6		17*		18*	6	19	10	111	15	40	12
R. W. Taylor	20*	5	—	1*	—	6*		—			8	15		—	—	—	—
P. G. Newman	—	9	—		—						1*	0*	19*				2
S. Oldham	—	6	—		—						1*	1	10*				4*
P. J. Hacker	—	6*	—		—												
R. J. Finney		5		—				—							—		7
C. J. Tunnicliffe			0*	3*	—	10*		—			12	4	5				0
B. J. M. Maher															0		
W. P. Fowler											4	29	0	0	9*		
I. S. Anderson															—		20
D. G. Moir																	0
Byes		4	1		1		1		1	3		4	1		1		
Leg-byes	6	5	4	4	9	6		4	6	6	6	4	2	5	6	3	5
Wides	3	4	6	10	2	4	1	3	4	1	1	4			1		2
No-balls	7	2		3		10			7	3		1		2	2	1	1
Total	232	172	202	161	236	284	181	187	203	193	190	186	183	225	239	137	149
Wickets	6	10	2	6	3	6	3	3	2	5	9	10	9	5	5	3	10
Result	L	L	W	W	W	W	W	W	W	L	L	L	L	W	L	W	L
Points	0	0	2	4	4	2	4	4	4	0	0	0	0	4	—	4	0

Fielding figures

- 19 – R. W. Taylor (ct 14/st 5)
- 12 – G. Miller
- 10 – B. J. M. Maher (ct 6/st 4) and B. Wood
- 9 – P. N. Kirsten
- 8 – P. G. Newman and J. G. Wright
- 7 – K. J. Barnett
- 4 – D. G. Moir and J. H. Hampshire
- 3 – C. J. Tunnicliffe and S. Oldham
- 2 – R. J. Finney, I. S. Anderson and W. P. Fowler
- 1 – A. Hill

BOWLING

	P. J. Hacker	S. Oldham	B. Wood	G. Miller	P. G. Newman	C. J. Tunnicliffe	R. J. Finney
(B.&H.) v. Leicestershire (Leicester) 8 May	11-2-49-1	11-1-34-1	11-0-37-1	11-2-46-1	10-2-43-0		
(J.P.) v. Leicestershire (Leicester) 9 May	7-0-38-2	8-0-49-1	7-0-46-0	8-0-35-0	8-0-52-1		
(B.&H.) v. Minor Counties (Derby) 15 May	11-2-43-2	10.3-2-34-3		11-4-17-2		11-1-38-1	11-1-44-2
(J.P.) v. Essex (Derby) 16 May	4-0-22-0	8-1-23-3	8-2-8-4	4-0-13-0	8-0-35-0	8-0-46-1	
(J.P.) v. Somerset (Taunton) 23 May		8-1-35-2	8-2-10-1	4-0-35-1	8-0-45-0	8-0-42-2	2-0-37-0
(B.&H.) v. Worcestershire (Worcester) 25 May	3-0-19-0	10-0-51-2	11-2-49-1	11-0-40-0	11-0-48-4	4-0-32-2	
(B.&H.) v. Yorkshire (Chesterfield) 27 May		11-2-30-0	11-3-25-3	11-2-33-1	11-2-36-2	11-1-42-1	
(J.P.) v. Warwickshire (Chesterfield) 30 May		8-2-23-0	8-0-46-2	8-1-23-2	8-1-40-2	8-0-38-1	
(J.P.) v. Worcestershire (Worcester) 6 June		7-0-27-2	8-0-40-0	8-0-34-2	7-0-39-2	6-0-43-0	
(J.P.) v. Hampshire (Portsmouth) 13 June		8-0-36-2	8-1-27-2	8-0-31-0	8-0-26-1	7.5-0-58-3	
(B.&H.) v. Sussex (Derby) 16 June		10-3-30-2	11-2-34-1	11-2-36-1	10.5-2-40-1	9-1-36-0	
(J.P.) v. Kent (Canterbury) 20 June		8-0-34-2	6-0-42-1	8-1-41-1	8-0-29-1	8-0-33-2	
(J.P.) v. Yorkshire (Derby) 27 June		8-0-38-2	8-0-33-1		8-1-34-0	8-1-23-1	
(J.P.) v. Lancashire (Derby) 4 July	5.5-1-17-2	8-1-37-5		8-1-31-1	6-0-19-0		
(N.W.T.) v. Hampshire (Southampton) 14 July		10-2-47-0	12-3-23-3	12-4-37-0	9-0-36-0	10.4-1-62-1	
(J.P.) v. Middlesex (Lord's) 18 July		6-0-24-2	6.5-0-20-5		3-0-17-0	6-1-21-1	
(J.P.) v. Surrey (Derby) 1 August		8-1-41-1	8-0-35-3		8-0-36-1		4-0-22-2
(J.P.) v. Northants (Milton Keynes) 15 Aug.		6-1-38-1	8-0-40-2	5-0-33-1	8-1-33-0	5-0-37-1	
(J.P.) v. Sussex (Chesterfield) 22 August		6-0-23-3	5-0-27-2	4.3-0-34-0	6-0-25-1	6-0-31-1	
(J.P.) v. Notts (Trent Bridge) 29 August		8-0-26-1	8-0-38-2	8-0-20-0		7.1-0-31-0	
(J.P.) v. Gloucestershire (Derby) 5 September							
(Asda) v. Notts (Scarborough) 6 September		7-0-41-2	10-0-31-2	9-0-51-0	4-0-29-0	10-0-52-2	
(Asda) v. Lancs. (Scarborough) 7 September		8-3-15-1	7-1-22-1	10-3-22-2	10-0-39-0	6-1-11-1	
(J.P.) v. Glamorgan (Derby) 12 September		4-0-30-0	6-0-38-1	8-1-20-1	7.2-0-33-2	3-0-18-0	

A A. Kennedy absent hurt

THE ENGLISH SEASON/447

English Counties Form Charts

The statistics of all limited-over cricket matches follow in pages 446 to 479. The games covered are:

John Player League (J.P.)   Tilcon Trophy (T.T.)
Benson and Hedges Cup (B.&H.)   Asda Trophy (Asda)
National Westminster Bank Trophy (N.W.T.)

Once again averages are not produced as it is felt that they have little relevance in limited-over cricket where batsmen often sacrifice their wickets for quick runs and bowlers are ordered to contain rather than capture wickets.

In the batting tables a blank indicates that a batsman did not *play* in a game, a dash (—) that he did not *bat*.

v. Northamptonshire (Milton Keynes) 15 August (J.P.)	v. Sussex (Chesterfield) 22 August (J.P.)	v. Nottinghamshire (Trent Bridge) 29 August (J.P.)	v. Gloucestershire (Derby) 5 September (J.P.)	v. Nottinghamshire (Scarborough) 6 September (Asda)	v. Lancashire (Scarborough) 7 September (Asda)	v. Glamorgan (Derby) 12 September (J.P.)
75	16	16		40	59	1
1	3	19	3		49*	0
		5	6			
8	41	47	4		50*	50*
24	27	1	87*			10
47	5	2	54*			66
	0*		—	—		0
—	—		—	—		17
—	—	2*	—	—		0
	10					
51*	10	25	21	—		7
—		0				
14*	28	2				5
—		11	—	—		4
5			4			
5	10	6	16	4		5
3	1	4				5
		5	1	2		10
233	151	145	236	164		180
5	8	10	5	1		10
L	L	L	Ab	W	W	L
0	0	0	2	—	—	0

K. J. Barnett	P. N. Kirsten	W. P. Fowler	D. G. Moir
2–0–24–0			
	5–0–29–0		
	2–0–7–0		
	2–0–10–1		
	4–0–27–0	4–0–22–1	
	3–0–21–0		
	4–0–19–0		8–1–29–2
	4–0–13–0		8–3–34–0
			7–0–54–0
			8–0–23–1
			10–3–25–0
			9–1–32–2
	2–1–6–1		8–0–29–0

B	Lb	W	Nb	Total	Wkts
19	1		4	233	5
5	10	1	3	239	4
1	12	7	5	201	10
	8		5	160	9
1	4	2		235	6
	7	2	1	278	9
	6	6		178	10
1	9	3		183	7
	6	3	2	201	7
	12	4		194	9
	6	1	1	194	6
3	10	1		193	7
4	16	5		202	5
1	13	3	1	122	9A
1	6	3	6	242	4
	4	1		135	10
2	15	7		205	7
1	1		1	238	5
4	9	1	1	155	7
	7	1	3	149	4
		Abandoned			
1	2	2		234	6
6	11	4	1	163	7
1	6	1		182	6

Essex C.C.C.
One Day Matches – 1982

BATTING

BATTING	v. Surrey (The Oval) 8 May (B.&H.)	v. Sussex (Hove) 9 May (J.P.)	v. Kent (Chelmsford) 15 May (B.&H.)	v. Derbyshire (Derby) 16 May (J.P.)	v. Hampshire (Chelmsford) 22 May (B.&H.)	v. Hampshire (Chelmsford) 23 May (J.P.)	v. Sussex (Hove) 25 May (B.&H.)	v. Middlesex (Lord's) 30 May (J.P.)	v. Somerset (Chelmsford) 6 June (J.P.)	v. Lancashire (Old Trafford) 13 June (J.P.)	v. Worcestershire (Ilford) 20 June (J.P.)	v. Leicestershire (Harlow) 27 June (J.P.)	v. Yorkshire (Scarborough) 11 July (J.P.)	v. Kent (Chelmsford) 14 July (N.W.T.)	v. Surrey (Southend) 18 July (J.P.)	v. Glamorgan (Cardiff) 1 August (J.P.)	v. Yorkshire (Leeds) 4 August (N.W.T.)
G. A. Gooch	66	1	19	10	2	0	198*	17	21	122	23	10	14	30	0	7	10
B. R. Hardie	16	4	23	32	2	14	17	7	11	53	45	2	8	41	6		0
R. J. Leiper	7																
K. S. McEwan	20	4	55*	28	0	7	0	69	14	76	105*	10	7	19	26	68	8
A. W. Lilley	11	26	2	9	0	3	—	22	7	1*	36	0	21*		22		2
N. Phillip	33*	7	7	2	1	3	—	7	10	0*	20	44	24	29	56	84	1
K. R. Pont	4	16	6	0	15	1*	—	18*	0		4	—	14	21	4		0
S. Turner	13	22	7	1	55*			13	18	—	5	35	14*	0	22	10*	50*
D. E. East	9	2	1	43	30			0	0			0*		2*	16*	7*	5
R. E. East	0*		7		2							0*			0	—	33
J. K. Lever	—	8*	3	15*	4*	—	—	10	1						1*		
K. W. R. Fletcher		7	38	7	5	17*	101*	1	0	—	6	3	36	97	7	7	4
N. A. Foster		8		—		—	—	10									
N. Smith																	
D. R. Pringle										2*		—		7*			8
D. L. Acfield											—						
C. Gladwin																0	
P. J. Prichard																	—
Byes	1				2		1			3		1	1	4		1	
Leg-byes	5	6	9	8	5	3	4	11	6	11	5	4	9	21	13	4	8
Wides	5	4	2		2	4	5	9	2	2	2	1		4	3	2	1
No-balls	1			5	6		1			1				1	1	6	2
Total	191	115	178	160	131	52	327	194	92	269	247	114	134	269	194	200	132
Wickets	8	10	10	9	9	5	2	10	10	3	6	8	5	7	9	6	10
Result	L	L	L	L	W	L	W	L	W	W	W	W	W	W	W	W	L
Points	0	0	0	0	2	0	2	0	4	4	4	4	4	—	4	4	

Fielding figures
21 – D. E. East (ct 18/st 3)
13 – G. A. Gooch
9 – R. E. East and B. R. Hardie
6 – A. W. Lilley, S. Turner and K. W. R. Fletcher
3 – J. K. Lever, N. Smith and N. Phillip
2 – K. R. Pont
1 – N. A. Foster, K. S. McEwan and D. R. Pringle

BOWLING

	J. K. Lever	N. Phillip	S. Turner	G. A. Gooch	K. R. Pont	R. E. East	N. A. Foster
(B.&H.) v. Surrey (The Oval) 8 May	11-1-54-3	11-2-54-1	10-2-41-0	5-0-23-1	7-0-28-1	11-0-53-0	
(J.P.) v. Sussex (Hove) 9 May	8-2-19-2	8-1-33-0	8-1-22-1	2.3-0-16-0			8-1-20-1
(B.&H.) v. Kent (Chelmsford) 15 May	10.5-3-25-0	11-1-32-1	11-3-29-1	10-0-44-1		10-2-24-1	
(J.P.) v. Derbyshire (Derby) 16 May	7.5-0-39-1	7-0-21-3	8-0-38-0	8-2-22-0			8-1-24-1
(B.&H.) v. Hampshire (Chelmsford) 22 May	9.2-4-19-4	10-2-28-2	11-5-12-0	11-1-25-2		11-1-34-1	
(J.P.) v. Hampshire (Chelmsford) 23 May	8-2-26-2	8-1-34-1	8-1-25-2	1-0-7-0			8-0-43-2
(B.&H.) v. Sussex (Hove) 25 May	8-0-39-1	10-0-41-2	9-0-36-3	4.2-0-24-3			11-0-43-1
(J.P.) v. Middlesex (Lord's) 30 May	7-0-59-0	6-0-52-1	8-0-45-0	8-0-31-2			8-0-45-2
(J.P.) v. Somerset (Chelmsford) 6 June	2-0-10-0	8-0-26-1	6-0-19-1	2-0-12-1			
(J.P.) v. Lancashire (Old Trafford) 13 June		6.2-0-13-6	6-0-27-0	8-0-38-1	3-0-20-2	8-0-48-1	
(J.P.) v. Worcestershire (Ilford) 20 June		4-0-14-1	4-1-12-0	8-1-53-0	4-0-26-3	8-0-17-3	
(J.P.) v. Leicestershire (Harlow) 27 June	6-1-9-0	6-1-11-4	6-0-27-1	6-0-17-1		6-1-14-1	
(J.P.) v. Yorkshire (Scarborough) 11 July	8-0-20-1	8-1-29-2	8-0-28-1	8-1-22-2		8-3-21-1	
(N.W.T.) v. Kent (Chelmsford) 14 July	6-1-18-0	7-0-26-4	12-1-23-4			8-1-22-2	
(J.P.) v. Surrey (Southend) 18 July	7.3-1-22-2	7-3-32-3	7-3-30-1	7-0-43-2		8-1-20-1	
(J.P.) v. Glamorgan (Cardiff) 1 August	8-1-34-1	8-0-33-2	8-0-26-1	8-0-30-1		8-0-38-2	
(N.W.T.) v. Yorkshire (Leeds) 4 August		9-3-21-0	11-3-39-0	6-1-15-0	4.2-0-27-1	1-1-0-0	
(J.P.) v. Kent (Canterbury) 8 August	8-0-26-2	7-0-27-3	8-0-24-2	8-1-24-1		4-0-22-1	
(J.P.) v. Gloucestershire (Cheltenham) 15 Aug.	8-0-43-3	8-0-48-1	8-3-13-1	8-0-30-1		7-0-34-0	
(J.P.) v. Warwickshire (Colchester) 22 August	8-0-66-1	5.3-0-36-1	7-0-48-1	4-0-33-1		8-0-54-0	
(J.P.) v. Nottinghamshire (Chelmsford) 5 Sept.	6-0-20-0	8-0-23-1	5.3-0-30-0			8-0-35-0	
(J.P.) v. Northants (Chelmsford) 12 Sept.	8-2-40-1	7-1-16-2	4-0-20-0	7-0-40-2		8-0-25-2	

	v. Kent (Canterbury) 8 August (J.P.)	v. Gloucestershire (Cheltenham) 15 August (J.P.)	v. Warwickshire (Colchester) 22 August (J.P.)	v. Nottinghamshire (Chelmsford) 5 September (J.P.)	v. Northamptonshire (Chelmsford) 12 September (J.P.)
	83*	24	10	18	51
	67*	20	75	19	41
	—	32	156*	66*	8
		8			
	—	16	13	17	9
	—	29	—	1	9*
	—	9	16	18*	16*
	—	2*	—	—	—
	—	1*	—	—	—
	—	20	12*	12	46
	—	—	—	—	—
		8	7		1
	3		6	8	10
	1	1	2		
		2	2		
	154	172	299	159	191
	0	8	4	5	5
	W	L	L	L	W
	4	0	0	0	4

G. A. Gooch

	D. R. Pringle	D. L. Acfield	A. W. Lilley		B	Lb	W	Nb	Total	Wkts
						14	8	1	276	6
						5		1	116	5
					1	12	9	4	180	5
						4	10	3	161	6
						6	5	1	130	10
					1	4	3	1	144	7
					7	14	6	3	213	10
					3	8	2		245	5
	2–0–15–1				1	6	1	1	91	6
		5–0–35–0				3	2	1	187	10
	4–0–11–3					3	1	1	138	10
					4	6	7		85	8
					1	6	4	2	133	9
	8–0–37–0					7	3	3	139	10
						8	4	4	163	10
	6.4–2–9–0		1–0–14–0		2	16	2	3	184	7
	4–0–11–0					2	5	1	133	1
						16	2		152	9
						8	1		177	8
	7–0–50–2				2	10	2		301	6
	8–0–43–1					7	1	1	160	3
	6–0–29–0				2	9	7	1	189	9

Glamorgan C.C.C.
One Day Matches – 1982

BATTING

BATTING	v. Gloucestershire (Bristol) 8 May (B.&H.)	v. Lancashire (Old Trafford) 9 May (J.P.)	v. Kent (Canterbury) 16 May (J.P.)	v. Combined Universities (Cardiff) 22 May (B.&H.)	v. Leicestershire (Cardiff) 23 May (J.P.)	v. Somerset (Swansea) 25 May (B.&H.)	v. Middlesex (Lord's) 28 May (B.&H.)	v. Somerset (Swansea) 30 May (J.P.)	v. Yorkshire (Bradford) 6 June (J.P.)	v. Sussex (Hastings) 20 June (J.P.)	v. Gloucestershire (Ebbw Vale) 27 June (J.P.)	v. Pakistanis (Swansea) 4 July	v. Hampshire (Cardiff) 11 July (J.P.)	v. Warwickshire (Cardiff) 14-15 July (N.W.T.)	v. Worcestershire (Worcester) 18 July (J.P.)	v. Middlesex (Swansea) 25 July (J.P.)	v. Essex (Cardiff) 1 August (J.P.)
A. Jones	67		14	27		3	52					—	37	8	31	52	55
J. A. Hopkins	27	0	7	70	—	2	32	56		6		—	4	13			2
Javed Miandad	34	0	70	49	—	41	59	2					23	54	35	1	37
R. C. Ontong	12	35	84	27		0	1	24		21			23	54	35	1	37
C. J. C. Rowe	4	54	8*	13		54	7	19		11			4	2	3	21*	14
G. C. Holmes	7	10	1	0*	—	1		26		3							
M. J. Llewellyn	2									24		—	5		31	18	
E. W. Jones	5	6	0*										1*	11	1	—	
M. A. Nash	6	2*	—	17*		0	6	17		3			5	0	2		
B. J. Lloyd	1	3	—			28*	0	—		23			17	12	6*	12	0
S. R. Barwick	0*	3	—			3	—	—		12*		—		6			
A. L. Jones		9					8	19		4			48	0	13	30	33
D. A. Francis		6	3											34	30	3	5
T. Davies						10	—	—		10							
A. E. Cordle						10	5*										
S. A. B. Daniels										1*		0			4*	—	
W. W. Davis															2*		
J. G. Thomas																4*	15*
Byes	1	4	1	10		1	4						5	11	2	9	2
Leg-byes	15	12	11	11		9	10	17		7			12	7	20	18	16
Wides	2	4	4	5			9	4		8			3	1	7	3	2
No-balls			2	3			2	1						8	2	1	3
Total	183	148	205	232		162	195	186		132			164	169	187	172	184
Wickets	10	10	6	5		10	8	7		10			8	10	8	6	7
Result	L	L	L	W	Ab	L	L	L	Ab	L	Ab	Ab	L	L	W	W	L
Points	0	0	0	2	2	0	0	0	2	0	2	—	0	—	4	4	0

Fielding figures
14 – E. W. Jones (ct 13/st 1)   5 – D. A. Francis   2 – A. L. Jones and G. C. Holmes
8 – T. Davies (ct 6/st 2)   4 – J. A. Hopkins, R. C. Ontong and   1 – A. Jones, Javed Miandad,
7 – B. J. Lloyd   W. W. Davis   S. A. B. Daniels and M. J. Llewellyn
6 – C. J. C. Rowe   3 – M. A. Nash, S. R. Barwick

BOWLING

BOWLING	M. A. Nash	R. C. Ontong	S. R. Barwick	B. J. Lloyd	G. C. Holmes	C. J. C. Rowe	Javed Miandad
(B.&H.) v. Gloucestershire (Bristol) 8 May	6.2-1-25-2	11-1-36-1	11-1-30-3	11-2-29-1	11-0-38-2	4-0-16-0	
(J.P.) v. Lancashire (Old Trafford) 9 May	8-1-24-0	8-2-17-1	4-0-24-0	5.1-0-33-0	4-0-21-0	3-0-19-0	3-0-10-1
(J.P.) v. Kent (Canterbury) 16 May	8-2-25-2	6-0-22-0	5-0-27-1	8-0-57-0	2-0-23-0	3-0-21-0	3-0-18-0
(B.&H.) v. Combined Univ. (Cardiff) 22 May	5-3-20-1	5-2-11-1	4-1-5-2	9.4-3-26-4			
(J.P.) v. Leicestershire (Cardiff) 23 May	8-0-18-1	6-0-25-0	5-0-25-1				
(B.&H.) v. Somerset (Swansea) 25 May	11-1-31-1	11-0-35-1	11-3-28-3	11-3-25-1			
(B.&H.) v. Middlesex (Lord's) 28 May	11-2-22-0	9-0-56-0	11-1-47-0	11-0-40-1			
(J.P.) v. Somerset (Swansea) 30 May	8-1-42-1	6.3-0-37-1	6-0-33-0	8-0-28-1		3-0-21-0	
(J.P.) v. Yorkshire (Bradford) 6 June							
(J.P.) v. Sussex (Hastings) 20 June	8-0-50-0	8-0-59-1	7-0-37-0	8-0-37-2		1-0-20-0	
(J.P.) v. Gloucestershire (Ebbw Vale) 27 June							
v. Pakistanis (Swansea) 4 July	8-1-18-1		4-0-20-2	7-1-15-0			
(J.P.) v. Hampshire (Cardiff) 11 July	8-1-25-0	8-1-21-0	8-0-40-2	7-1-40-0			
(N.W.T.) v. Warwicks. (Cardiff) 14-15 July	10-5-14-2	11-1-43-0		12-1-40-1		12-1-43-1	
(J.P.) v. Worcestershire (Worcester) 18 July	8-3-17-1	8-0-31-2		8-0-38-1			
(J.P.) v. Middlesex (Swansea) 25 July		5-0-29-0		8-2-18-2			
(J.P.) v. Essex (Cardiff) 1 August		8-0-24-3		8-2-35-0			
(J.P.) v. Warwickshire (Edgbaston) 8 August	8-2-26-3	8-0-30-0		8-0-19-0			
(J.P.) v. Nottinghamshire (Swansea) 22 Aug.	2-0-18-0	1.4-0-15-1	2-0-14-0	1-0-7-0			
(J.P.) v. Surrey (The Oval) 29 August	8-4-8-0	8-0-37-4	6-0-32-1	7-0-46-0			
(J.P.) v. Northants (Abergavenny) 5 Sept.	8-1-21-2	8-0-39-2		4-0-17-0			
(J.P.) v. Derbyshire (Derby) 12 September	8-3-12-0	7.2-0-54-3	8-0-39-1	8-0-31-0			

THE ENGLISH SEASON/451

v. Warwickshire (Edgbaston) 8 August (J.P.)	v. Nottinghamshire (Swansea) 22 August (J.P.)	v. Surrey (The Oval) 29 August (J.P.)	v. Northamptonshire (Abergavenny) 5 September (J.P.)	v. Derbyshire (Derby) 12 September (J.P.)
43*	29	34	2	55
—	5	—	17	6
—	6*	—	100	14
—	17*	52*	16	61
—	—	—	6*	22*
—	—	—	13*	2*
82	25	60	14	8
0*		6*	36	6
—		1	5	
1		8		1
2	6	9	14	6
5		6	5	1
5			1	
138	89	175	229	182
1	4	2	7	6
W	L	W	W	W
4	0	4	4	4

R. C. Ontong

A. E. Cordle	S. A. B. Daniels	W. W. Davis	J. G. Thomas	B	Lb	W	Nb	Total	Wkts
				4	8	1		187	10
					2	2		152	3
					9	4		206	3
				2	2	2		86	10
					5	3		88	3
5-1-18-2				1	3	2		174	8
6-1-12-1					8	1		199	3
11-0-49-1				2	3	1		187	3
9-2-25-1							Abandoned		
	3-0-20-0				6	6	1	251	4
	8-1-35-0						Abandoned		
		4-1-16-0		3	2			74	4
		7.5-1-30-0			2	4	3	165	2
		12-3-21-0		3	3	2	1	170	4
	8-1-45-0	8-1-43-2			6	6		186	7
	8-0-32-3	6.4-0-17-3	8-0-26-1	4	4	2	1	133	10
	8-0-68-0	8-1-36-1	8-2-24-1	1	4	2	6	200	6
		8-2-17-3	8-0-28-2	1	5	8	3	137	8
		2-0-12-0	1-0-13-0	4	6		1	90	1
		8-0-30-1		1	11	6	3	174	6
		8-0-41-1	3-0-24-0	4	2	1	4	153	7
		7-2-24-4			5	5	10	180	10

Gloucestershire C.C.C.
One Day Matches – 1982

BATTING	v. Glamorgan (Bristol) 8 May (B.&H.)	v. Middlesex (Bristol) 9 May (J.P.)	v. Combined Universities (Oxford) 15 May (B.&H.)	v. Lancashire (Old Trafford) 16 May (J.P.)	v. Middlesex (Bristol) 22-24 May (B.&H.)	v. Worcestershire (Bristol) 23 May (J.P.)	v. Somerset (Taunton) 27 May (B.&H.)	v. Sussex (Gloucester) 30 May (J.P.)	v. Surrey (The Oval) 13 June (J.P.)	v. Glamorgan (Ebbw Vale) 27 June (J.P.)	v. Worcestershire (Harrogate) 1 July (T.T.)	v. Northamptonshire (Harrogate) 2 July (T.T.)	v. Yorkshire (Leeds) 4 July (J.P.)	v. Warwickshire (Edgbaston) 11 July (J.P.)	v. Nottinghamshire (Trent Bridge) 14-15 July (N.W.T.)	v. Northamptonshire (Bristol) 18 July (J.P.)	v. Hampshire (Bristol) 25 July (J.P.)
A. W. Stovold	59	1	123	9	65	16	3	85	25		21	6	4		76*	12	49
B. C. Broad	12	43	53	15	16	54	27	59	25		72	26	0	35	59	28	35
Sadiq Mohammad	16	7	23*	11	62	22	9										
Zaheer Abbas	7	23	21					0	63*								
P. Bainbridge	31	19	28*	9	—	13*	80	4*	8				8	35	—	4	—
A. J. Hignell	33	17	—	4	56*	2	34	41	8		17	15	12	23	—	0	—
J. N. Shepherd	9	3	16	5		8*	47	2*	14*		1	13		18*		5	—
D. A. Graveney	2	19		8			49*	—			2		14			41	—
A. J. Brassington	1	11*		11*			5*				6		12			14*	
J. H. Childs	4*	2		—							7		2*	—		7*	
D. Surridge	0	1		—							1*		2*	—		3	
R. J. Doughty			—	18*													
E. J. Cunningham				12					22		4	0*	0				
M. W. Stovold					18*	0	13										
P. W. Romaines											71	23	7	52	2*	19	41*
F. D. Stephenson											1	—	27	2*	—	26	—
A. J. Wright														6			9*
R. C. Russell																	—
B. Dudleston																	
C. R. Trembath																	
Byes	4		3	1	4		1	5	1		2			4		4	1
Leg-byes	8	10	18	7	5	12	21	12	13		8	4	5	6	3	7	8
Wides	1		11				5	1	2		12	1	2	4	3	4	3
No-balls		8	4		1				1		1			2	1		
Total	187	164	300	110	226	128	294	209	182		226	88	95	185	145	175	146
Wickets	10	10	4	8	3	5	7	4	5		10	5	9	5	1	9	2
Result	W	L	W	L	L	W	L	L	L	Ab	W	L	L	W	W	L	W
Points	2	0	2	0	0	4	0	0	0	2	—	—	0	4	—	0	4

Fielding figures
- 14 – A. J. Brassington (ct 12/st 2)
- 10 – A. W. Stovold and D. A. Graveney
- 8 – P. Bainbridge
- 6 – A. J. Hignell
- 5 – J. N. Shepherd
- 3 – A. J. Wright, R. C. Russell, B. Dudleston, B. C. Broad and M. W. Stovold
- 2 – J. H. Childs
- 1 – D. Surridge, F. D. Stephenson, R. J. Doughty, E. J. Cunningham and sub

BOWLING	D. Surridge	J. N. Shepherd	P. Bainbridge	J. H. Childs	D. A. Graveney	R. J. Doughty	Sadiq Mohammad
(B.&H.) v. Glamorgan (Bristol) 8 May	11-2-16-1	11-2-33-2	11-0-40-1	11-3-36-3	10.2-0-40-1		
(J.P.) v. Middlesex (Bristol) 9 May	8-0-30-1	8-0-49-3	8-0-27-1	8-0-36-0	8-1-33-1		
(B.&H.) v. Combined Univ. (Oxford) 15 May	11-2-33-0	11-1-37-3	10-2-27-2		11-2-42-2	11-0-62-1	1-1-0-0
(J.P.) v. Lancashire (Old Trafford) 16 May	8-0-51-0	7-0-36-1	8-0-47-0		7-0-32-2	5-0-23-0	
(B.&H.) v. Middlesex (Bristol) 22-24 May	11-1-31-1	11-3-46-0	7.2-0-38-0	11-1-30-1	9-0-38-2		
(B.&H.) v. Somerset (Taunton) 27 May	11-0-49-3	11-0-70-1	11-1-56-1	11-0-45-1	6-0-40-0		
(J.P.) v. Sussex (Gloucester) 30 May	7.3-0-35-3	7-0-39-1	8-0-49-1	8-1-30-1	8-0-40-1		
(J.P.) v. Surrey (The Oval) 13 June	7-0-51-0	8-1-25-0	4-0-19-0		8-0-31-2	7-0-38-2	
(J.P.) v. Glamorgan (Ebbw Vale) 27 June							
(T.T.) v. Worcestershire (Harrogate) 1 July	5.2-1-10-2	5-0-15-3		11-2-18-0	9-1-35-1		
(T.T.) v. Northants (Harrogate) 2 July	2-0-21-2	1-0-15-0			1-0-23-0	2-0-9-0	
(J.P.) v. Yorkshire (Leeds) 4 July	8-0-26-0		8-0-66-4	8-0-48-0			
(J.P.) v. Warwicks. (Edgbaston) 11 July	8-2-46-1	7-0-27-2	8-0-39-1	5-0-16-0		3-0-22-0	
(N.W.T.) v. Notts (Trent Bridge) 14 July	12-3-17-2	12-3-16-3	12-0-26-1			9-1-32-1	
(J.P.) v. Northamptonshire (Bristol) 18 July	8-2-14-1	8-1-46-1	8-0-40-1	8-0-35-1			
(J.P.) v. Hampshire (Bristol) 25 July	7-1-35-0	7-0-27-3	1-0-5-0	8-0-23-2	8-3-11-1		
(J.P.) v. Leicestershire (Leicester) 1 August	6-0-36-0	7-0-26-1	7-0-32-1		6-0-25-0		
(N.W.T.) v. Middlesex (Bristol) 4 August	12-5-25-1	12-1-47-2		12-4-43-2	12-1-42-1		
(J.P.) v. Notts (Cheltenham) 8 August	8-0-33-0	8-0-59-0		8-0-31-1			
(J.P.) v. Essex (Cheltenham) 15 August		8-0-24-3		8-0-25-0		8-0-40-2	
(J.P.) v. Kent (Folkestone) 22 August		8-1-48-0		6-0-40-0	2-0-16-0	8-0-56-1	
(J.P.) v. Somerset (Bristol) 29 August	8-0-41-0	8-0-50-1	4-0-11-0		7-0-34-3		
(J.P.) v. Derbyshire (Derby) 5 September							

THE ENGLISH SEASON/453

	v. Leicestershire (Leicester) 1 August (J.P.)	v. Middlesex (Bristol) 4 August (N.W.T.)	v. Nottinghamshire (Cheltenham) 8 August (J.P.)	v. Essex (Cheltenham) 15 August (J.P.)	v. Kent (Folkestone) 22 August (J.P.)	v. Somerset (Bristol) 29 August (J.P.)	v. Derbyshire (Derby) 5 September (J.P.)
	0	0	27	14	20	47	
	8	98		28	23	15	
	21					5*	
	3		15	0		—	
	29	9	32	34	22	—	
	10	22*			32*	—	
			2	0*	3		
		4*	2	—	1		
	1*	—	1*			—	
				13	0	—	
					10		
	55	0	23	24	13		
	18	7	0	1			
	0	14	33	52	14	0*	
	7*	10					
			31	16			
			7	2*	6	—	
			2				
	6	11	6	8	16	1	
	5	5		1	2	3	
	1	1	1		3		
	164	212	167	177	165	71	
	9	8	10	8	10	2	
	L	L	L	W	L	W	Ab
	0	—	0	4	0	4	2

Zaheer Abbas

	B. C. Broad	F. D. Stephenson	C. R. Trembath		B	Lb	W	Nb	Total	Wkts
					1	15	2		183	10
					1	6	2		184	7
						11	2	2	216	8
	4–0–19–1					5	2	1	216	4
	5–0–32–0				1	11	2		229	6
	5–0–29–0					13	5		307	6
					1	15	1		210	7
	4–0–27–1				2	10	5	2	210	5
									Abandoned	
		8–0–38–3				6	1	2	123	10
	2–0–9–0	2–0–21–0				2		1	101	3
	8–0–37–1	8–0–47–2				6	2	1	233	8
		8–3–18–3			5	7	1		181	6
		10–3–17–2			3	12	14	5	142	10
		8–1–25–2			1	14	5		180	7
		8–0–36–3				8			145	9
	5–0–26–0	8–0–34–1			10		3	4	196	4
		12–1–45–2				7	4	2	215	9
		8–0–35–2	8–0–51–1			1	2	2	214	6
		8–0–42–1	7–1–30–1		8		1	2	172	8
	8–0–48–2		8–0–55–2			6	1	1	271	5
			5–0–31–2			9	3		179	6
									Abandoned	

Hampshire C.C.C.
One Day Matches – 1982

BATTING

	v. Kent (Canterbury) 8 May (B.&H.)	v. Nottinghamshire (Trent Bridge) 9 May (J.P.)	v. Sussex (Bournemouth) 15 May (B.&H.)	v. Middlesex (Bournemouth) 16 May (J.P.)	v. Essex (Chelmsford) 22 May (B.&H.)	v. Essex (Chelmsford) 23 May (J.P.)	v. Surrey (Southampton) 27 May (B.&H.)	v. Leicestershire (Leicester) 6 June (J.P.)	v. Derbyshire (Portsmouth) 13 June (J.P.)	v. Kent (Basingstoke) 27 June (J.P.)	v. Glamorgan (Cardiff) 11 July (J.P.)	v. Derbyshire (Southampton) 14 July (N.W.T.)	v. Lancashire (Portsmouth) 18 July (J.P.)	v. Gloucestershire (Bristol) 25 July (J.P.)	v. Somerset (Portsmouth) 1 August (J.P.)	v. Surrey (Southampton) 4 August (N.W.T.)	v. Sussex (Eastbourne) 8 August (J.P.)
C. G. Greenidge	56	14	13	32	4	64	1	3	29		92*	83	17	41	84	2	32
J. M. Rice	66	6			11	3	56	13	37	38	21	59	42	7	1	6	27
D. R. Turner	6	18	9	9					12				3	32*	51		2
T. E. Jesty	18	79	18	7	10	17	41	49	19	30*	12	0	23	26	33	12	25
N. G. Cowley	11	8	13	32	7	19	1	11	25	22	—	—	23	6	7*	7	5
V. P. Terry	3	0	9	18	15	10	12	4		—							
R. E. Hayward	5*	30*		18	2	6*	12*					—	44*	2			
M. D. Marshall	21	30*	9*	21	14	2	10	46	0	—	—	—	8	13	—	0	2
T. M. Tremlett	0		25	—	3	—		16	18*		—	—	2*	4		6	12*
R. J. Parks	2		2	2*	7	4*	3*	36*	33				5	4		1	13
K. St. J. D. Emery	0		0	—	1*	—	—	0*	1		—		1*	3*		4*	0
M. C. J. Nicholas			22	32*	44	10	35	12	14	18	31*	0	76	6	6	2	36
S. J. Malone				0				—	1*								
N. E. J. Pocock									1	1*	—	40*	0	24*		15	13
J. W. Southern																	
Byes			4				1	10				1	3		2	5	1
Leg-byes	9	15	2	9	6	4	11	8	12	4	2	6	11	8	12	5	8
Wides		1	1	5	5	3		2	4	1		4	3	2	1	2	1
No-balls	1		2		1	1	2				3	6			2	1	2
Total	198	201	129	185	130	144	194	202	194	116	165	242	215	145	180	119	179
Wickets	10	6	10	7	10	7	7	8	9	4	2	4	9	9	4	10	10
Result	L	W	L	L	L	W	L	W	W	W	W	W	T	L	W	L	L
Points	0	4	0	0	0	4	0	4	4	4	4	—	2	0	4	0	0

Fielding figures:
- 32 – R. J. Parks (ct 30/st 2)
- 12 – C. G. Greenidge
- 8 – T. M. Tremlett
- 6 – T. E. Jesty and M. D. Marshall
- 5 – J. M. Rice and N. E. J. Pocock
- 4 – N. G. Cowley
- 3 – M. C. J. Nicholas
- 1 – D. R. Turner, V. P. Terry, J. W. Southern and K. St. J. D. Emery

BOWLING

	M. D. Marshall	K. St. J. D. Emery	T. E. Jesty	T. M. Tremlett	N. G. Cowley	J. M. Rice	S. J. Malone
(B.&H.) v. Kent (Canterbury) 8 May	11–1–40–1	11–1–30–2	6–0–25–0	11–1–35–2	5–0–27–0	11–2–50–2	
(J.P.) v. Notts (Trent Bridge) 9 May	8–1–16–2	7–0–36–0	8–0–40–3	8–0–33–1	5–0–26–0	4–0–19–1	
(B.&H.) v. Sussex (Bournemouth) 15 May	11–3–35–2	11–3–34–3	8–1–32–0	9–0–43–0	11–2–39–3		5–0–30–0
(J.P.) v. Middlesex (Bournemouth) 16 May	7–1–32–1	7.2–0–24–1	8–1–31–1	8–0–44–2	8–0–36–1		
(B.&H.) v. Essex (Chelmsford) 22 May	11–2–29–2	10–3–24–5	11–4–13–0	11–4–19–1	2–0–5–0	8.3–1–26–1	
(J.P.) v. Essex (Chelmsford) 23 May	7–2–15–2	4–0–17–1	3–0–11–2	1–0–2–0			
(B.&H.) v. Surrey (Southampton) 27 May	11–0–34–1	11–2–53–0	11–1–29–2	11–4–22–2	7–1–21–1	5–0–30–1	
(J.P.) v. Leicestershire (Leicester) 6 June	8–3–24–0	8–2–21–4	5–0–43–0	8–0–40–0	3–0–22–0		8–1–37–1
(J.P.) v. Derbyshire (Portsmouth) 13 June	8–1–27–0	8–1–53–2	8–2–19–0	8–1–33–1			8–1–48–1
(J.P.) v. Kent (Basingstoke) 27 June	8–0–31–5	8–0–45–2					
(J.P.) v. Glamorgan (Cardiff) 11 July	8–2–24–1	8–1–28–2	8–0–38–0	8–0–29–3	8–0–25–1		
(N.W.T.) v. Derby. (Southampton) 14 July	12–1–48–0	12–0–69–1	12–2–28–2	12–4–34–2	12–0–50–0		
(J.P.) v. Lancashire (Portsmouth) 18 July	7–1–43–1	8–0–37–1	8–1–30–2	8–0–58–1	8–0–36–0		
(J.P.) v. Gloucestershire (Bristol) 25 July	6–1–33–0	2–0–6–0	8–0–33–1	8–3–12–0	8–0–39–1	3–0–11–0	
(J.P.) v. Somerset (Portsmouth) 1 August	8–2–27–0	7–1–19–1	8–0–45–4	8–0–32–1	8–1–32–0		
(N.W.T.) v. Surrey (Southampton) 4 August	7–0–29–4	6–0–26–1	5–0–17–0	5.2–1–13–0	10–0–29–1		
(J.P.) v. Sussex (Eastbourne) 8 August	8–0–37–0	8–0–46–1	8–0–44–2	8–2–24–2	8–1–28–1		
(J.P.) v. Worcs. (Southampton) 15 Aug.	8–1–29–0		8–0–37–1	5–0–49–0	7–0–37–0	4–0–25–0	8–1–43–1
(J.P.) v. Northants (Northampton) 22 Aug.	8–1–18–2	8–0–40–0	6–1–48–2	8–1–34–3	8–0–47–0		
(J.P.) v. Yorkshire (Southampton) 29 Aug.	8–1–21–2		8–0–53–2	8–0–32–3	8–0–46–1		8–1–56–2
(J.P.) v. Surrey (The Oval) 5 September	8–3–17–3	8–1–47–0	8–4–12–3	8–1–23–1	7–1–26–1		
(J.P.) v. Warwicks. (Bournemouth) 12 Sept.	8–0–37–1		8–1–23–2	8–0–20–2		8–0–40–0	8–0–36–1

THE ENGLISH SEASON/455

	v. Worcestershire (Southampton) 15 August (J.P.)	v. Northamptonshire (Northampton) 22 August (J.P.)	v. Yorkshire (Southampton) 29 August (J.P.)	v. Surrey (The Oval) 5 September (J.P.)
	34	8	10	14
	25	2	41	64
	12	17	13	21
	38	0	110*	0
	3	34	—	0
	29	32	—	2
	0	2*	—	2
	31	13	—	0*
		0		—
	7		50	2
	2*		—	
	19	0	7*	11
		1		
	1	7	4	6
	21	3	10	12
	3	4	3	5
	225	123	248	139
	10	10	4	9
	L	L	W	T
	0	0	4	2

Mark Nicholas

J. W. Southern

	B	Lb	W	Nb	Total	Wkts
	2	6	2		217	9
		9	7		186	7
	14	16	4	1	248	9
	4	13	2		186	6
	2	5	2	6	131	9
		3	4		52	5
	13		3	2	207	8
	1	15	7	1	211	5
	3	6	1	3	193	5
	1	3	1	3	84	9
	5	12	3		164	8
	1	6	1	2	239	5
		7	3	1	215	5
	1	8	3		146	2
		14	7	1	177	6
	1	2	1	2	120	2
		7		6	192	7
		14	2		236	1
		5	1	1	205	8
2–0–11–0	8	13	5		234	10
		7	7		139	9
		7	3		166	6

Kent C.C.C.
One Day Matches – 1982

BATTING

Batsman	v. Hampshire (Canterbury) 8 May (B.&H.)	v. Surrey (The Oval) 9 May (J.P.)	v. Essex (Chelmsford) 15 May (B.&H.)	v. Glamorgan (Canterbury) 16 May (J.P.)	v. Surrey (Canterbury) 25 May (B.&H.)	v. Sussex (Hove) 27-28 May (B.&H.)	v. Worcestershire (Worcester) 30 May (J.P.)	v. Warwickshire (Edgbaston) 6 June (J.P.)	v. Northamptonshire (Northampton) 13 June (J.P.)	v. Somerset (Canterbury) 16 June (B.&H.)	v. Derbyshire (Canterbury) 20 June (J.P.)	v. Hampshire (Basingstoke) 27 June (J.P.)	v. Sussex (Maidstone) 4 July (J.P.)	v. Somerset (Maidstone) 11 July (J.P.)	v. Essex (Chelmsford) 14 July (N.W.T.)	v. Yorkshire (Canterbury) 25 July (J.P.)	v. Middlesex (Lord's) 1 August (J.P.)
R. A. Woolmer	8		55	22	11		8		1	5		8	33	24			
N. R. Taylor	61	7	14	1		121	33				121	44	14*	13	4	20	13	11
C. J. Tavare	29	5	16	103*	6	3	3	36		3	25		27		12	22	
M. R. Benson	7	97	41*	11	65							2	0	19	24	21	
Asif Iqbal	9	33	1	56*	3		4	29	41*	18	2	3	6	46	15	5	2	6
C. S. Cowdrey	8	48	7	—	66	34	61*	—	40	40	33	4	13	12		8	1
A. P. E. Knott	42*	3	20*		17	2	36		8	7	0	0	4	34	2	31	8
G. W. Johnson	43	1*			1	3			7	3				54*	3		29
G. R. Dilley	0	—	—		3	4	23*	—	33	3	14*	7	2		9	16	24
D. L. Underwood	0						—		6	3*		1	3		1*	1*	0*
K. B. S. Jarvis	0*	—			4*	0	—	—	1*	0		0*	2*	—	0	1*	
L. Potter		23	—	—	30	49	21	45	0	5	27	18		24	45	32	6
C. Penn						2*	0*	—	—		0*		40	—	5	1	8
D. G. Aslett							19		33*	7							6
S. G. Hinks									4								
R. M. Ellison														24	1*		4
E. A. Baptiste																	
Byes	2	2	1		2	1		2	4		3	1		1		1	
Leg-byes	6	13	12	9	3	8	3	5	5	7	10	3	3	10	7	7	10
Wides	2	2	9	4	5		2	2	3	3	1	1	3	4	3	5	3
No-balls		1	4		2	4		1	1	2		3	1	3	3	2	3
Total	217	235	180	206	220	252	219	166	142	207	193	84	181	181	139	162	119
Wickets	9	7	5	3	9	10	6	3	10	10	7	9	10	6	10	10	10
Result	W	W	W	W	W	L	W	W	L	L	W	L	L	W	L	L	W
Points	2	4	4	4	2	0	4	4	0		4	0	0	4	—	0	4

Fielding figures
27 – A. P. E. Knott (ct 26/st 1)
13 – C. S. Cowdrey
10 – G. R. Dilley
9 – L. Potter
7 – C. S. Tavare
6 – M. R. Benson
5 – D. L. Underwood
4 – Asif Iqbal, C. Penn and R. A. Woolmer
2 – G. W. Johnson, K. B. S. Jarvis, N. R. Taylor and subs
1 – E. A. Baptiste and D. G. Aslett

BOWLING

Match	K. B. S. Jarvis	G. R. Dilley	R. A. Woolmer	C. S. Cowdrey	D. L. Underwood	L. Potter	C. Penn
(B.&H.) v. Hampshire (Canterbury) 8 May	10-0-41-3	10.3-1-44-4	11-1-28-1	11-0-50-0	11-4-25-0		
(J.P.) v. Surrey (The Oval) 9 May	7-0-16-1	7-0-32-1		8-1-19-2	8-1-20-1	8-2-27-2	
(B.&H.) v. Essex (Chelmsford) 15 May	9-0-27-2	10-2-20-1	11-1-52-0	11-0-44-1	10.3-3-24-4		
(J.P.) v. Glamorgan (Canterbury) 16 May	8-0-38-2	8-1-34-3	8-0-25-1	4-0-26-0		4-0-30-0	8-0-34-0
(B.&H.) v. Surrey (Canterbury) 25 May	11-1-33-2	11-0-40-1	10.5-2-42-2	9-0-34-1			11-0-34-4
(B.&H.) v. Sussex (Hove) 27-28 May	11-0-58-1	11-0-71-2		9-0-40-1			11-1-48-1
(J.P.) v. Worcestershire (Worcester) 30 May	7.1-0-41-4	6-0-32-1	8-0-30-0	4-0-23-1	8-1-15-1		5-0-45-3
(J.P.) v. Warwicks. (Edgbaston) 6 June	8-0-25-1	8-1-55-1	8-0-29-2		8-4-8-2		8-0-31-1
(J.P.) v. Northants. (Northampton) 13 June	8-0-39-4	8-0-51-1	7-0-31-0	8-0-37-0	8-2-28-0	1-0-7-0	
(B.&H.) v. Somerset (Canterbury) 16 June	11-0-44-3	10.4-2-43-2	11-3-29-1	8-0-27-1	11-2-21-0		
(J.P.) v. Derbyshire (Canterbury) 20 June	7.1-0-45-3	5-0-39-1	8-0-31-2	1-0-1-0	8-0-26-1		8-1-35-2
(J.P.) v. Hampshire (Basingstoke) 27 June	6-1-24-0	8-0-35-1	3-0-17-2		8-1-26-1		5-0-35-1
(J.P.) v. Sussex (Maidstone) 4 July	8-1-41-1	8-0-53-3		8-0-43-1	8-1-26-1		4-0-24-2
(J.P.) v. Somerset (Maidstone) 11 July	8-2-32-3			8-0-33-1	8-1-23-2		8-0-24-2
(N.W.T.) v. Essex (Chelmsford) 14 July	12-1-61-1	12-1-45-2			12-3-40-3		12-1-34-1
(J.P.) v. Yorkshire (Canterbury) 25 July	8-0-41-0	7-0-24-0		8-0-28-1	6-0-21-1		8-0-35-3
(J.P.) v. Middlesex (Lord's) 1 August		8-2-26-2			8-3-14-1	7-0-27-1	8-2-26-0
(J.P.) v. Essex (Canterbury) 8 August	6-1-43-0		8-0-36-0	3-0-17-0	5-0-26-0		
(J.P.) v. Notts. (Trent Bridge) 15 August	6-0-29-0	7-0-34-1			8-2-29-0		
(J.P.) v. Glos. (Folkestone) 22 August	5-0-19-1	5-0-15-0	8-1-27-1	6-0-36-1	6.5-2-15-4		
(J.P.) v. Lancashire (Old Trafford) 29 August	8-0-30-2	8-1-33-1	6-1-22-2		6-1-14-0		
(J.P.) v. Leicestershire (Canterbury) 12 Sept.	8-1-27-1	7-1-22-1			8-0-33-1		

THE ENGLISH SEASON

L. Potter

	v. Essex (Canterbury) 8 August (J.P.)	v. Nottinghamshire (Trent Bridge) 15 August (J.P.)	v. Gloucestershire (Folkestone) 22 August (J.P.)	v. Lancashire (Old Trafford) 29 August (J.P.)	v. Leicestershire (Canterbury) 12 September (J.P.)
	7*		32	12	
	1		74	33	8
	1		90		0
	33	77	44	34	19
	0	5	2*		18
	6	15	—	17*	27
	36	11	21*	11*	
		1	—	—	28
	0	1	—	—	4
	8*	0	—	—	5*
		28			
	34	2		24	43
				9	
		10*		—	21
	8	2	0		2
	16	7	6	9	6
	2	4	1	2	
		1	1		
	152	164	271	151	181
	9	10	5	5	10
	L	L	W	W	L
	0	0	4	4	0

	G. W. Johnson	Asif Iqbal	R. M. Ellison	E. A. Baptiste		B	Lb	W	Nb	Total	Wkts
							9		1	198	10
							5	6	3	128	7
							9	2		178	10
						1	11	4	2	205	6
	2-0-11-0						9	11	3	217	10
	10-0-59-2	3-0-10-0					12	7		305	6
							2	1		189	10
							6	7	3	164	9
							7	3		203	6
	3-0-25-0					4	9	4	2	208	7
							4	4	1	186	10
							4	1		116	4
							8	2		254	5
	4-0-24-0	2.1-0-18-0	1.5-0-4-0			4	12	4	2	180	9
	12-0-59-0					4	21	4	1	269	7
							12	3		164	5
			8-3-14-2				6	2	3	118	8
				6-0-28-0			3	1		154	0
	1-0-1-0		5-0-27-0	6-0-28-0			11	1	8	168	1
				8-0-32-3			16	2	3	165	10
			8-0-39-0			1	6	2	1	148	5
			7-0-40-0	8-0-60-0		1	15	1	4	203	3

Lancashire C.C.C.
One Day Matches – 1982

BATTING	v. Scotland (Old Trafford) 8 May (B.&H.)	v. Glamorgan (Old Trafford) 9 May (J.P.)	v. Gloucestershire (Old Trafford) 16 May (J.P.)	v. Northamptonshire (Northampton) 22 May (B.&H.)	v. Northamptonshire (Bedford) 23 May (J.P.)	v. Warwickshire (Old Trafford) 25 May (J.P.)	v. Nottinghamshire (Trent Bridge) 27 May (B.&H.)	v. Sussex (Old Trafford) 6 June (J.P.)	v. Essex (Old Trafford) 13 June (J.P.)	v. Middlesex (Lord's) 16 June (B.&H.)	v. Middlesex (Lord's) 20 June (J.P.)	v. Worcestershire (Worcester) 27 June (J.P.)	v. Nottinghamshire (Trent Bridge) 30 June (B.&H.)	v. Derbyshire (Derby) 4 July (J.P.)	v. Surrey (Old Trafford) 11 July (J.P.)	v. Middlesex (Lord's) 16 July (N.W.T.)	v. Hampshire (Portsmouth) 18 July (J.P.)
A. Kennedy	72*	0	54	43*	1	79	3	30	6	20	26		6	31	—		
D. Lloyd	76*	25*	12	4	—	9	0	4				46	23	7	40	48	79
J. Abrahams	—	43	5							0	—			—	35	16*
C. H. Lloyd	—	64	72	29*	25*	60	49	10	3	66	52		5	5	61*	11	21
D. P. Hughes	—	16*	—	—		14	4	9*	17	13	18	14*	0	0	17*	42	39
B. W. Reidy	—	—	12*	—	—	19	16	3*	11	6	6		9		—	22	—
J. Simmons									21	33	7	13*	6	0		16	23
P. J. W. Allott						0	10	—		2	12*		2	14		3	
C. E. H. Croft						26*	10		13	9*	1		13	12		2*	
C. J. Scott	—																
L. L. McFarlane				—	—				3					2	—		
M. A. Wallwork			—	—		0*	—										
I. Cockbain		53*				0	14										
G. Fowler			18	27	7	59	30		5	4	30	59	18	31	31	0	26
I. Folley				3*	11*	—		8*	3*	2	—	3*	5*		3*	—	
F. C. Hayes									87	6							
C. Maynard									7	13	17	0	60	28	2	1	—
K. A. Hayes															—		
Byes				1	1			1		5		1	1	1	4	2	
Leg-byes	5	2	5	6	1	14	14	4	3	7	5	11	8	13	13	6	7
Wides	2	2	2	4		1	5	4	2	2	1	2	8	3	3	9	3
No-balls	1		1	1		2			1	3		2		1		2	1
Total	156	152	216	105	56	239	194	93	187	191	178	160	182	122	174A	202	215B
Wickets	0	3	4	2	2	8	9	4	10	9	10	4	10	9†	3	9	5
Result	W	W	W	W	Ab	W	L	L	L	W	L	W	L	L	W	L	T
Points	2	4	4	2	2	2	0	0	0	—	0	4	—	0	4	—	2

Fielding figures 12 – C. Maynard (c 10/st 2) 7 – C. H. Lloyd and M. A. Wallwork   5 – J. Abrahams, G. Fowler and D. P. Hughes   4 – C. J. Scott and C. E. H. Croft   2 – A. Ken
9 – D. Lloyd   3 – P. J. W. Allott and J. Simmons   I. Foll

BOWLING	J. Abrahams	D. Lloyd	B. W. Reidy	J. Simmons	P. J. W. Allott	C. E. H. Croft	L. L. McFarlane
(B.&H.) v. Scotland (Old Trafford) 8 May	2–0–14–1	11–1–21–1	6–0–28–0	11–1–28–0	10–1–27–2	10–4–10–6	4–0–18–0
(J.P.) v. Glamorgan (Old Trafford) 9 May			8–3–23–1	8–1–35–3	7–1–17–1	7.4–0–29–1	8–1–24–3
(J.P.) v. Gloucestershire (Old Trafford) 16 May	1–1–0–0		8–2–24–1	8–2–13–3	7–0–26–1	7–0–19–2	8–1–20–1
(B.&H.) v. Northants (Northampton) 22 May		2–0–3–0	11–3–27–4		8–2–18–2	7.5–2–21–3	
(J.P.) v. Northamptonshire (Bedford) 23 May							
(J.P.) v. Warwickshire (Old Trafford) 25 May		8–0–52–1	11–0–44–0		9–3–22–1	9.5–1–26–3	
(B.&H.) v. Notts (Trent Bridge) 27 May		11–1–45–1	11–0–45–2		11–0–39–1	11–2–35–3	
(J.P.) v. Sussex (Old Trafford) 6 June				2.2–0–19–1	7–0–36–0	5–0–18–0	
(J.P.) v. Essex (Old Trafford) 13 June			8–1–39–0	7–0–52–0		8–0–43–2	7–0–44–0
(B.&H.) v. Middlesex (Lord's) 16 June			11–0–46–1	11–2–17–2	8–1–31–0	8–1–22–1	
(J.P.) v. Middlesex (Lord's) 20 June			8–0–43–0	8–0–33–2	7–0–33–0	8–1–34–3	
(J.P.) v. Worcestershire (Worcester) 27 June			8–0–42–0	8–2–17–5		8–0–29–4	4–0–15–1
(B.&H.) v. Notts (Trent Bridge) 30 June			11–0–53–2	11–4–27–1	10–2–35–0	10.1–2–33–3	
(J.P.) v. Derbyshire (Derby) 4 July				8–0–35–1	8–0–25–0	8–0–60–0	8–0–33–2
(J.P.) v. Surrey (Old Trafford) 11 July	7–1–25–1		8–0–28–4	8–0–34–0			6.5–0–15–2
(N.W.T.) v. Middlesex (Lord's) 15 July	2–0–12–0		12–1–48–2	12–5–20–1	12–5–26–3	12–1–37–0	
(J.P.) v. Hampshire (Portsmouth) 18 July	3–0–23–0	4–0–24–1	6–0–31–0	8–0–45–2			8–0–18–4
(J.P.) v. Warwickshire (Old Trafford) 25 July	8–0–40–1		8–0–46–2	8–1–27–0			8–0–46–1
(J.P.) v. Notts (Trent Bridge) 1 August	3–1–23–1			7–1–25–0			
(J.P.) v. Yorkshire (Old Trafford) 8 August							
(J.P.) v. Leicestershire (Leicester) 15 August			8–0–32–2	8–0–26–0	8–1–32–2		8–0–50–1
(J.P.) v. Kent (Old Trafford) 29 August				7–0–31–2	6.5–2–27–1		
(Asda) v. Yorks. (Scarborough) 5 Sept.					4–0–8–1		
(Asda) v. Derby. (Scarborough) 7 Sept.	7–0–35–1	3–0–13–0		2–0–17–0	4–0–19–0		
(J.P.) v. Somerset (Taunton) 12 Sept.	2–0–29–0	3–0–39–1			5–2–18–2		

A C. H. Lloyd 8–0–26–0   B M. Watkinson 8–1–26–2   C M. Watkinson 3–0–9–1   D N. V. Radford 10–1–28–0   E C. H. Lloyd 3–0–11–0; G. Fowler 1–0–1–0;
H Pilling 0.3–0–12–0

THE ENGLISH SEASON

v. Warwickshire (Old Trafford) 25 July (J.P.)	v. Nottinghamshire (Trent Bridge) 1 August (J.P.)	v. Yorkshire (Old Trafford) 8 August (J.P.)	v. Leicestershire (Leicester) 15 August (J.P.)	v. Kent (Old Trafford) 29 August (J.P.)	v. Yorkshire (Scarborough) 5 September (Asda)	v. Derbyshire (Scarborough) 7 September (Asda)	v. Somerset (Taunton) 12 September (J.P.)
	26						
93	80	53*	10	14	14	6	14
9	26	—	8	47*	38*	0	10
70	33	—	1	19	9	57	11
25	0	—	0		15	14	7
1		—	50				
8*	13*	—	21	38	4	32	
		—	3	7*	—	—	10
			2*				
	4			12	19		18
6		59*	33		18	2	14
			—				0*
—			2	—	1	2*	1
2	2	5	1	1		6	
6	5	5	4	6	9	11	7
5	2		3	2		4	2
1		2	2	1		1	1
225C	182D	124E	149F	148G	212H	163I	143J
6	6	0	10	5	8	7	9
W	W	Ab	L	L	W‡	L	L
4	4	2	0	0	—	—	0

A S. J. O'Shaughnessy played but did not bat
B S. J. O'Shaughnessy played but did not bat
C S. J. O'Shaughnessy played but did not bat
D S. J. O'Shaughnessy and P. G. Lee played but did not bat
E S. J. O'Shaughnessy played but did not bat
F S. J. O'Shaughnessy 9
G S. J. O'Shaughnessy 1, N. Fairbrother and M. Watkinson played but did not bat
H S. J. O'Shaughnessy 80, M. Watkinson 5*
I S. J. O'Shaughnessy 18, N. V. Radford 10*
J S. J. O'Shaughnessy 45*, H. Pilling 3

*, B. W. Reidy, 1 – L. L. McFarlane, S. J. O'Shaughnessy,   † A. Kennedy absent hurt
d subs   N. Fairbrother and M. Watkinson   ‡ Won on toss of coin

I. Folley	A. Kennedy	D. P. Hughes	S. J. O'Shaughnessy	P. G. Lee	B	Lb	W	Nb	Total	Wkts
						8			154	10
					4	12	4		148	10
					1	7			110	8
9–3–26–1						4	1	2	102	10
						Abandoned				
9–1–34–4						5	3		201	10
11–2–33–1					5	8	3	3	216	8
3–0–14–1					4	4	2		97	3
7–1–47–0		3–0–27–0			3	11	2	1	269	3
10–2–18–4					1	3	1		139	10
8–0–37–2					4	12	2		198	7
5–0–20–0						10	5		138	10
11–1–20–0					4	7	3	2	184	6
7–0–53–0	1–0–8–0				4	5		2	225	5
			4–0–25–1	6–1–27–2		14	3	1	172	10
10–1–38–2					12	8	3		204	9
8–0–42–0			2–0–16–0		3	11	2		215	9
8–1–29–1						17	2		207	5
6–0–29–1			6–0–36–3	8–1–32–0		13	2		176	6A
						Abandoned				
			8–1–21–1		11		1		173	8
4–0–17–0			8–0–39–0			9	2		151	5B
									17	2C
4–1–16–0		1–0–8–0	3.3–0–22–0			4		2	164	1D
5–0–17–0			4–0–14–0			1	2		144	3E

Leicestershire C.C.C.
One Day Matches – 1982

BATTING

	v. Derbyshire (Leicester) 8 May (B.&H.)	v. Derbyshire (Leicester) 9 May (J.P.)	v. Worcestershire (Worcester) 15 May (B.&H.)	v. Yorkshire (Leicester) 16 May (J.P.)	v. Yorkshire (Leicester) 22 May (B.&H.)	v. Glamorgan (Cardiff) 23 May (J.P.)	v. Minor Counties (Wellington) 27 May (B.&H.)	v. Surrey (The Oval) 30 May (J.P.)	v. Hampshire (Leicester) 6 June (J.P.)	v. Middlesex (Leicester) 13 June (J.P.)	v. Nottinghamshire (Trent Bridge) 16–17 June (B.&H.)	v. Essex (Harlow) 27 June (J.P.)	v. Norfolk (Leicester) 3 July (N.W.T.)	v. Warwickshire (Leicester) 4 July (J.P.)	v. Nottinghamshire (Trent Bridge) 11 July (J.P.)	v. Somerset (Taunton) 15 July (N.W.T.)	v. Sussex (Hove) 18 July (J.P.)
J. C. Balderstone	89*		100		50	—	5			17	14	18	39		8	16	52
N. E. Briers	11	49	47	10	6	14	6	32	58	61	0	3	20	38	21	13	34
D. I. Gower	7	100	37	45	38	44*	0	115	96		34		65*	107		60	
B. F. Davison	25	53	69*	33	32	22	4	3	30	31	32	6	33*	37	9	4	2
R. W. Tolchard	17	2*	—	5	31*	0*	9	19	3*	4	13	0	—	10*	7	26	12
M. A. Garnham	55	10	4*	2	32*	0	0	5	0	0	1	39	—	1	11	12	8
J. F. Steele	5*			5		—	1*	12	—	25	16	4	—		5	1	14
P. B. Clift	—			4		—		3	0								
G. J. Parsons	—			6*		—	7	7*		5*	18*	3	—		7*	6	0
L. B. Taylor	—			1*		—	5	—		0*	2*	0*	—		2	5*	9*
J. P. Agnew	—					—	1		—			3*					
T. J. Boon		6*		29									0*		26		19
D. A. Wenlock		—		4				5		0		2	—	—	7		7
K. Higgs												0	—	—		6*	1*
A. M. E. Roberts						0				15	8				1	46	
I. P. Butcher																	
N. G. B. Cook																	
Byes	19	5	6	2	1		2	1		3	4		9	2			1
Leg-byes	1	10	8	15	11	5	2	8	15	14	9	6	7	6	4	7	7
Wides		1	6	3	3	3	15	2	7		2	7		4	3	5	1
No-balls	4	3	1	5	6		1		1	2		2	2	2	1	1	2
Total	233	239	278	169	210	88	56	213	211	172	154	95	166	214	114	208	169
Wickets	5	4	3	9	4	3	10	8	5	8	9	8	2	4	10	9	9
Result	W	W	W	W	W	Ab	L	L	W	L	L	L	W	W	L	L	L
Points	2	4	2	4	2	2	0	4	0	—	0		4	0	—	0	

Fielding figures
28 – M. A. Garnham (ct 25/st 3)
11 – R. W. Tolchard
10 – J. F. Steele
9 – D. I. Gower
6 – J. C. Balderstone
5 – J. P. Agnew and G. J. Parsons
4 – L. B. Taylor and D. A. Wenlock
3 – T. J. Boon, B. F. Davison, P. B. Clift and N. E. Briers
2 – A. M. E. Roberts
1 – N. G. B. Cook and I. P. Butcher

BOWLING

	L. B. Taylor	J. P. Agnew	P. B. Clift	G. J. Parsons	J. F. Steele	K. Higgs	D. A. Wenlock
(B.&H.) v. Derbyshire (Leicester) 8 May	11-3-43-2	11-0-59-0	11-1-48-0	11-1-28-1	11-3-38-2		
(J.P.) v. Derbyshire (Leicester) 9 May	7-0-27-1			6.3-0-33-2	7-1-24-4	8-0-35-2	7-0-38-0
(B.&H.) v. Worcestershire (Worcester) 15 May	11-0-35-6			11-1-54-0	11-0-59-0	11-0-56-2	
(J.P.) v. Yorkshire (Leicester) 16 May	8-1-32-1		8-1-35-4	8-1-22-0	8-0-29-1		8-0-37-2
(B.&H.) v. Yorkshire (Leicester) 22 May	11-2-40-1	11-4-26-1	11-0-46-2	11-2-28-3	11-0-58-1		
(J.P.) v. Glamorgan (Cardiff) 23 May							
(B.&H.) v. M. Counties (Wellington) 27 May	11-4-16-0	11-2-35-2		11-1-42-3	5-2-14-1		
(J.P.) v. Surrey (The Oval) 30 May	7-0-31-2		8-0-43-3	8-0-43-1	5-0-14-0	8-0-41-0	4-0-30-1
(J.P.) v. Hampshire (Leicester) 6 June		8-0-36-0	8-0-34-1	8-0-32-3	8-0-33-1	7-0-43-2	1-0-12-1
(J.P.) v. Middlesex (Leicester) 13 June	8-1-24-1			8-0-36-1	8-0-33-2	7.1-0-26-1	
(B.&H.) v. Notts (Trent Bridge) 16–17 June	10.4-0-45-3			11-3-14-1	11-2-28-1	11-2-32-2	
(J.P.) v. Essex (Harlow) 27 June	6-1-26-0	3-0-18-0		6-0-19-4	6-1-8-1	6-1-12-2	
(N.W.T.) v. Norfolk (Leicester) 3 July	12-3-34-4			12-1-40-2	12-3-16-0	12-2-36-0	12-2-27-1
(J.P.) v. Warwickshire (Leicester) 4 July	8-0-16-2			8-0-60-0	8-0-37-2	7-0-55-0	6-0-27-0
(J.P.) v. Notts (Trent Bridge) 11 July	8-2-22-2			8-0-29-0	8-4-7-1		
(N.W.T.) v. Somerset (Taunton) 14 July	12-2-55-2			12-1-52-0	12-1-41-0	12-0-34-0	
(J.P.) v. Sussex (Hove) 18 July	7-1-38-1			7-0-27-4	8-0-26-1	8-0-43-2	8-1-33-1
(J.P.) v. Gloucestershire (Leicester) 1 Aug.		7-0-22-1		8-1-33-4	8-3-24-1		8-0-32-3
(J.P.) v. Worcestershire (Stourbridge) 8 Aug.	8-2-11-2			6.3-0-23-3	8-0-37-0		7-1-29-2
(J.P.) v. Lancashire (Leicester) 15 August	8-0-19-2		8-1-17-4	8-0-36-0	6.3-0-26-2		6-0-41-2
(J.P.) v. Somerset (Taunton) 22 August	8-0-30-2		7.4-0-41-1	8-0-42-0	8-0-37-0		5-0-23-1
(J.P.) v. Northants (Leicester) 29 August			8-1-29-1	8-0-40-0			8-0-33-3
(J.P.) v. Kent (Canterbury) 12 September	8-1-34-1		4-0-42-1	6.2-0-20-3	7-1-34-2		

THE ENGLISH SEASON/461

David Gower

Middlesex C.C.C.
One Day Matches – 1982

BATTING

	v. Gloucestershire (Bristol) 9 May (J.P.)	v. Somerset (Lord's) 15 May (B.&H.)	v. Hampshire (Bournemouth) 16 May (J.P.)	v. Gloucestershire (Bristol) 22–24 May (B.&H.)	v. Nottinghamshire (Lord's) 23 May (J.P.)	v. Combined Universities (Cambridge) 25 May (B.&H.)	v. Glamorgan (Lord's) 28 May (B.&H.)	v. Essex (Lord's) 30 May (J.P.)	v. Leicestershire (Leicester) 13 June (J.P.)	v. Lancashire (Lord's) 16 June (B.&H.)	v. Lancashire (Lord's) 20 June (J.P.)	v. Surrey (Lord's) 27 June (J.P.)	v. Cheshire (Enfield) 3 July (N.W.T.)	v. Northamptonshire (Lord's) 11 July (J.P.)	v. Lancashire (Lord's) 15 July (N.W.T.)	v. Derbyshire (Lord's) 18 July (J.P.)	v. Glamorgan (Swansea) 25 July (J.P.)
J. M. Brearley	10	2	13	70	8	39	10	98	17	0	24	32	12	74	66	16	9
W. N. Slack	0	26	16	5	—	60*	41	52	9	7	63	16	54*	—	13	31	9
M. W. Gatting	0	29*	28	7	0	—	88*	24	21	10	42	36	16*	36	5	0	0
R. O. Butcher	7		24		1		50*	29	5	18	16	9	—	44*	17	0	16
C. T. Radley	107*	2*	60*	18	0	—		7	58*	66	3	29	16	26	23	34	31
G. D. Barlow	7	14	14	33	18*	4*	1		29	0	1		6	11	7		
J. E. Emburey	4	17	2	44*	1	—	—	11*	9	12	18*	6		17*	9	12	15
P. H. Edmonds	33	—		36	0*	—	—	11*		18	6		—				5
P. R. Downton	7*	0*	10*	2*	—	—	—		14*	2*	7*	14*		—	26	7	
W. G. Merry	—															1	13
W. W. Daniel		—	—	—					0		—					7*	
N. F. Williams			—														
M. W. W. Selvey	—		—	—			—	—		1	—	1*		—	10*	1	8*
N. J. Kemp								—									
K. P. Tomlins												0				14	13
S. P. Hughes														—	1*		
N. G. Cowans															0		3
C. R. Cook																	
R. G. P. Ellis																	
Byes	1	3	4	1		1		3		1	4	9			12		4
Leg-byes	6	3	13	11	4	1	8	8	10	3	12	7	2	4	8	4	4
Wides	2		2	2		2	1	2	1	1	2		3	2	6	3	1	2
No-balls		3												4	1		1
Total	184	99	186	229	32	107	199	245	173	139	198	162	106	214	204	135	133
Wickets	7	4	6	6	5	1	3	5	6	10	7	7	2	4	9	10	10
Result	W	W	W	W	Ab	W	W	W	L	W	W	—	W	—	W	L	L
Points	4	2	4	2	2	2	2	4	4	—	4	4	—	4	—	0	0

Fielding figures: 32 – P. R. Downton (ct 24/st 8); 11 – J. M. Brearley; 9 – P. H. Edmonds; 7 – G. D. Barlow, J. E. Emburey and M. W. Gatting; 6 – C. T. Radley and R. O. Butcher; 5 – W. W. Daniel and W. N. Slack; 2 – W. G. Merry, K. P. Tomlins and C. R. Cook; 1 – S. P. Hughes and N. G. Cowans

BOWLING

	W. W. Daniel	W. G. Merry	P. H. Edmonds	J. E. Emburey	M. W. Gatting	W. N. Slack	M. W. W. Selvey
(J.P.) v. Gloucestershire (Bristol) 9 May	8-2-18-0	5.2-1-29-1	8-0-33-3	8-0-25-0	2-0-9-0	8-0-32-2	
(B.&H.) v. Somerset (Lord's) 15 May	7-1-15-0		3-1-4-2	2.3-2-0-2	6-0-15-1	1-0-6-0	11-3-22-2
(J.P.) v. Hampshire (Bournemouth) 16 May	8-0-40-3			8-2-23-1	7-0-27-0	1-0-10-0	8-0-26-2
(B.&H.) v. Glos. (Bristol) 22–24 May	11-1-63-0		11-2-29-2	11-0-37-0			11-3-24-1
(J.P.) v. Nottinghamshire (Lord's) 23 May	7.1-0-39-1		3-0-21-0	1-0-8-0	2-0-16-0		5-0-20-0
(B.&H.) v. Combined Univ. (Cambs.) 25 May	8-1-17-0		11-6-9-3	11-3-20-0	1-0-7-0		5-0-20-3
(B.&H.) v. Glamorgan (Lord's) 28 May	11-4-13-3		11-2-26-0	11-1-40-1			11-2-42-1
(J.P.) v. Essex (Lord's) 30 May	6-0-23-0		8-0-28-1	5-0-32-0	2-0-17-1		8-0-27-4
(J.P.) v. Leicestershire (Leicester) 13 June	8-2-21-1	8-0-44-1		8-0-45-1	8-1-21-2		8-0-27-2
(B.&H.) v. Lancashire (Lord's) 16 June	11-2-32-2		11-2-36-2	11-2-43-1	10-1-33-2	1-0-10-0	11-3-21-1
(J.P.) v. Lancashire (Lord's) 20 June	7.3-0-27-5		8-0-37-1	8-1-50-1	8-0-29-0		6-0-28-2
(J.P.) v. Surrey (Lord's) 27 June	7-0-23-2			8-1-31-1	8-0-30-2		7-0-32-4
(N.W.T.) v. Cheshire (Enfield) 3 July	9-3-15-1	8-1-37-1	12-7-12-5	12-2-26-1	2-1-6-0		6-2-11-1
(J.P.) v. Northamptonshire (Lord's) 11 July		5-0-23-0		7-1-28-2	4-0-22-0	8-0-34-2	8-0-38-1
(N.W.T.) v. Lancashire (Lord's) 16 July				12-1-47-1	4-0-16-0	8-1-27-0	12-4-17-1
(J.P.) v. Derbyshire (Lord's) 18 July	8-2-28-1	4-0-16-0		8-1-15-1		5-0-32-0	8-1-21-0
(J.P.) v. Glamorgan (Swansea) 25 July		7-1-25-1	8-0-29-2	8-0-28-1			7-1-25-0
(J.P.) v. Kent (Lord's) 1 August	8-0-23-3		7-0-23-2	8-0-16-1			8-2-12-1
(N.W.T.) v. Gloucestershire (Bristol) 4 Aug.	9-2-39-2		12-1-34-0	12-2-25-1	3-0-13-0	12-1-51-1	
(J.P.) v. Somerset (Weston-s.-Mare) 8 Aug.	8-2-26-1		8-0-31-0	8-0-50-4	2-0-21-0	6-0-33-1	
(J.P.) v. Warwicks. (Edgbaston) 15 August	4-0-16-0	5-0-33-1	8-1-30-3	7.4-2-25-4			6-0-28-1
(N.W.T.) v. Surrey (The Oval) 18–19 Aug.	8-1-24-4		12-1-34-1	12-3-25-1	12-1-32-1	6-0-22-0	
(J.P.) v. Yorkshire (Lord's) 22 August	8-1-27-1		8-1-21-3	7-0-34-0	3-0-19-1	6-0-21-1	
(J.P.) v. Sussex (Hove) 29 August	8-0-56-0			8-1-20-0		8-0-43-2	
(J.P.) v. Worcs. (Worcester) 12 Sept.			8-2-31-2	8-0-42-3	2-0-17-0	8-0-32-2	

Δ J. M. Brearley 1-0-6-0; R. O. Butcher 0.4-0-4-0. † A. I. Kallicharran retired hurt

THE ENGLISH SEASON/463

	v. Kent (Lord's) 1 August (J.P.)	v. Gloucestershire (Bristol) 4 August (N.W.T.)	v. Somerset (Weston-super-Mare) 8 August (J.P.)	v. Warwickshire (Edgbaston) 15 August (J.P.)	v. Surrey (The Oval) 18-19 Aug. (N.W.T.)	v. Yorkshire (Lord's) 22 August (J.P.)	v. Sussex (Hove) 29 August (J.P.)	v. Worcestershire (Worcester) 12 September (J.P.)
	2	18	13		3	73	8	20
		10	77	56	5	23	31	5
		33	72		6	23		40
	1	27	1	51	21	11	59	42
	2	45	2	0	14	6	18	5
	0							
	29	11	0	26*	8	13	2	29*
	11	7	1	11	13*	—		—
	17	40*	16	13	1	8*	40	58*
				0*				
	—	0*	1*	0	0	—	6	
	—			13				
		9	9	58	0		2	
	0*	2	3*		3	—	14*	—
	45		0		32*	3		
							6	21
			3				2	
	6	7	10	11	2	7	11	5
	2	4	1		2	2	2	4
	3	2	2	4	2		1	
	118	215	211	243	80	198	205	229
	8	9	9	9	10	6	10	6
	L	W	W	W	L	W	L	W
	0	—	4	4	—	4	0	4

Norman Cowans

	N. F. Williams	N. J. Kemp	S. P. Hughes	N. G. Cowans	B	Lb	W	Nb	Total	Wkts
						10		8	164	10
						3	1	1	98	10
	9–1–31–3					9	5		185	7
	8–0–45–0				4	5			226	3
	11–2–64–0					5	3		112	1
					1	9	3	3	105	10
	8.4–3–16–3				4	10	9	2	195	8
	11–0–49–2					11	9		194	10
			8–0–47–3			14			172	8
					5	7	1	3	191	9
						5	2		178	10
					2	5			161	10
					2	7		1	104	10
			10–3–24–2			7	2		198	8
			8–0–44–2		2	6	9	2	202	9
			12–1–50–0	12–3–26–4		3		1	137	3A
				8–1–34–0	9	18	3	1	172	6
				7.1–0–29–3		10	3	3	119	10
				12–3–33–2		11	5	1	212	8
				7.2–1–24–2		7	4	1	197	10
					4	6		1	141	9†
				10–0–43–1	4	11	10		205	9
				8–0–47–2	1	5	2		177	9
			8–0–47–0	8–0–44–4	2	13	1	2	228	7
	6–0–30–1			6.5–0–48–1		6	3	3	212	10

Northamptonshire C.C.C.
One Day Matches – 1982

BATTING	v. Nottinghamshire (Northampton) 8 May (B.&H.)	v. Somerset (Northampton) 9 May (J.P.)	v. Scotland (Glasgow) 15 May (B.&H.)	v. Lancashire (Northampton) 22 May (B.&H.)	v. Lancashire (Bedford) 23 May (J.P.)	v. Warwickshire (Edgbaston) 27-28 May (B.&H.)	v. Nottinghamshire (Trent Bridge) 30 May (J.P.)	v. Kent (Northampton) 13 June (J.P.)	v. Yorkshire (Middlesbrough) 20 June (J.P.)	v. Warwickshire (Edgbaston) 27 June (J.P.)	v. Yorkshire (Harrogate) 30 June (T.T.)	v. Gloucestershire (Harrogate) 2 July (T.T.)	v. Ireland (Northampton) 3 July (N.W.T.)	v. Surrey (Tring) 4 July (J.P.)	v. Middlesex (Lord's) 11 July (J.P.)	v. Surrey (The Oval) 15-16 July (N.W.T.)	v. Gloucestershire (Bristol) 18 July (J.P.)
G. Cook	7	31	11	1	—	1	71		73		44	12	2	38	23	50	2
W. Larkins	13	28	126	7		132	16	27	79	16	1	39	30	23	60	49	6
R. G. Williams	4	23	9*	14	—			66	12	30	3	0*	31*	32	1	7*	82
A. J. Lamb	95	25	81	63		25	45		67*		93	45*	11	9		42	
T. J. Yardley	11	43*	2	5				1									
D. S. Steele	19	22	5*	0		28	3*						—	5	25*		
R. M. Carter	18	7*	—			0	6	4*		4	0		—		3	—	2
G. Sharp	7	1		0		11*	15	—		3	0	—		2	2	—	2
Sarfraz Nawaz	3	—		5		20*	4	11*									
N. A. Mallender	6*			0*			2*			5			—	0	4	—	—
B. J. Griffiths	6			0						1*	0*			11*			
D. J. Wild		—				2		0		0	0	—					
P. Willey			1	0		0	29	5	25	89	6	2	72*	17	76	55	4
D. J. Capel						25	6	79	12*	10	27	—		11	9	—	34*
T. M. Lamb									7	9*			1*	2*		0*	
R. J. Boyd-Moss									1						7	15*	28
Kapil Dev																1	
Byes		1				1	2		2				4		5	1	
Leg-byes	6	13	20	4		12	7	7	8	11	1	2	9	7	7	8	14
Wides		1	4	1			1	3	4	6				4	2	6	5
No-balls		1		2		1				2		1	1		1		
Total	195	196	259	102		258	207	203	282	185	184	101	156	164	198	239	180
Wickets	10	6	5	10		8	8	6	4	10	9	3	3	9	8	5	7
Result	L	W	W	L	Ab	L	L	W	W	L	W	W	W	W	L	L	W
Points	0	4	2	0		0	0	4	4	0	—	—	4	4	0	—	4

Fielding figures: 27 – G. Sharp; 11 – W. Larkins; 10 – G. Cook; 5 – A. J. Lamb, Sarfraz Nawaz and N. A. Mallender; 4 – T. J. Yardley, D. J. Wild; and R. J. Boyd-Moss; 2 – D. S. Steele, D. J. Capel, R. M. Carter, R. G. Williams; and B. J. Griffiths; 1 – P. Willey, T. M. Lamb, Kapil Dev and sub

BOWLING	Sarfraz Nawaz	B. J. Griffiths	N. A. Mallender	R. M. Carter	D. S. Steele	D. J. Wild	P. Willey
(B.&H.) v. Notts (Northampton) 8 May	11-1-42-2	11-2-39-0	11-1-49-0	11-0-49-2	11-1-36-2		
(J.P.) v. Somerset (Northampton) 9 May	8-1-26-3	8-0-29-2			8-0-33-2	8-0-43-1	8-0-44-0
(B.&H.) v. Scotland (Glasgow) 15 May	9-1-21-4	4-0-5-0		5-2-8-1	10.2-1-27-3		11-5-14-2
(B.&H.) v. Lancashire (Northampton) 22 May	7-1-16-0	9-2-23-0	6-2-17-1				11-2-21-1
(J.P.) v. Lancashire (Bedford) 23 May	4-0-11-0	4-1-11-0		3-0-17-0			2.2-0-14-1
(B.&H.) v. Warwicks. (Edgbaston) 27-28 May	10.4-2-36-1	11-0-82-0		1-0-6-0	11-0-31-1	8-1-41-0	11-2-43-1
(J.P.) v. Notts (Trent Bridge) 30 May	8-0-32-2	8-0-21-1	8-1-55-0		5-0-29-1		8-0-45-0
(J.P.) v. Kent (Northampton) 13 June	5.2-2-9-2	5-2-7-1					8-1-31-3
(J.P.) v. Yorkshire (Middlesbrough) 20 June		5-1-8-1	8-0-41-0	5.4-0-53-1			8-0-42-1
(J.P.) v. Warwickshire (Edgbaston) 27 June		8-1-32-0	8-0-53-0				8-0-43-0
(T.T.) v. Yorkshire (Harrogate) 30 June		11-4-25-4				10-0-40-1	11-0-28-1
(T.T.) v. Gloucestershire (Harrogate) 2 July		2-0-7-2		1-0-11-0		2-0-13-0	1-0-11-0
(N.W.T.) v. Ireland (Northampton) 3 July		8-2-22-1	11-4-22-2		12-2-25-2		12-1-24-0
(J.P.) v. Surrey (Tring) 4 July		6-0-9-1	8-0-27-3		5-0-18-2		8-1-24-0
(J.P.) v. Middlesex (Lord's) 11 July		8-0-45-0	8-0-37-2	6-1-29-2			2-0-15-0
(N.W.T.) v. Surrey (The Oval) 15-16 July		11-1-48-1	7-1-25-0				12-3-29-1
(J.P.) v. Gloucestershire (Bristol) 18 July		8-0-49-1	8-0-32-1				8-0-26-1
(J.P.) v. Sussex (Northampton) 25 July			7-1-31-2		2-0-14-0	7-1-43-2	6-1-27-1
(J.P.) v. Worcestershire (Luton) 1 August			8-0-31-3		4-0-29-0	8-0-47-1	8-1-32-3
(J.P.) v. Derby. (Milton Keynes) 15 August		8-0-43-0	5-0-37-1			5-0-22-0	7-0-24-2
(J.P.) v. Hampshire (Northampton) 22 August		5-0-10-2	8-0-44-1				8-1-18-1
(J.P.) v. Leicestershire (Leicester) 29 August			6.4-1-26-1				8-1-31-2
(J.P.) v. Glamorgan (Abergavenny) 5 Sept.			8-0-56-2			8-0-35-0	6-0-35-1
(J.P.) v. Essex (Chelmsford) 12 September			7-0-35-0			7-0-32-1	8-0-35-1

A W. Larkins 2-0-24-0

THE ENGLISH SEASON

	v. Sussex (Northampton) 25 July (J.P.)	v. Worcestershire (Luton) 1 August (J.P.)	v. Derbyshire (Milton Keynes) 15 August (J.P.)	v. Hampshire (Northampton) 22 August (J.P.)	v. Leicestershire (Leicester) 29 August (J.P.)	v. Glamorgan (Abergavenny) 5 September (J.P.)	v. Essex (Chelmsford) 12 September (J.P.)
	13	5*	32	33	24	29	21
	59	158	39	51	5	4	8
	22*	79*	7	5	20	42	19
	45			40		25	104*
	—						
	—	—	2*	32	19*	14*	12
	—		—	—			0*
					0*		0
	53	9	58	17	39	4	0
	1*	—			8		2
	—			15*	12*	9	0
		8	22*	0	0	—	4
			75	5	25	15	
	1	2	1	9	4	2	
	16	5	1	5	3	2	9
	2	6		1	1	1	7
	1		1	1	1	4	1
	213	272	238	205	166	153	189
	4	3	5	8	7	7	9
	L	W	W	W	L	L	L
	0	4	4	4	0	0	0

George Sharp

R. G. Williams	T. J. Yardley	D. J. Capel	T. M. Lamb	Kapil Dev	B	Lb	W	Nb	Total	Wkts
					5	12	1	1	234	7
						5	1	3	184	9
						3	2	2	82	10
3–0–13–0	0.1–0–4–0					6	4	1	105	2
						1	1	1	56	1
						10	5	5	259	4
		3–0–28–1			1	12	4	3	230	5
8–1–38–3			8–0–44–0		4	5	3	1	142	10
		6–1–30–4	7–0–38–1		1	11	2	1	227	10
		8–0–47–3	8–0–38–1			12	2		227	5
5–0–15–0		7–2–27–0	11–3–31–3		3	8	2	2	181	10
		2–0–20–2	2–0–21–1			4	1		88	5
5–0–17–2			8.3–2–25–3		3	16		1	155	10
3–0–16–2			6.4–1–16–2		7	8	6	1	132	10
		8–0–44–0	8–0–33–0			4	6	1	214	4
6–0–26–0			11–0–47–1	11.5–2–41–1	6	14	1	5	242	4
8–0–16–2			8–0–36–3		4	7	4	1	175	9
5–0–23–0		4–0–23–0	8–0–48–1			4	2		215	6
4–0–29–0			7.5–1–38–2		1	12		1	220	10
			7–0–42–0	8–0–52–1	5	5	3		233	5
			8–0–25–5	5.3–0–12–1	7	3	4		123	10
8–0–39–1			8–1–25–0	8–1–38–2	6	4		1	170	6
		8–0–39–2	8–3–20–1			14	5	1	229	7A
8–0–36–0		2–0–9–1	7.1–0–33–2		1	10			191	5

Nottinghamshire C.C.C.
One Day Matches – 1982

BATTING

	v. Northamptonshire (Northampton) 8 May (B.&H.)	v. Hampshire (Trent Bridge) 9 May (J.P.)	v. Warwickshire (Trent Bridge) 15 May (B.&H.)	v. Worcestershire (Trent Bridge) 16 May (J.P.)	v. Middlesex (Lord's) 23 May (J.P.)	v. Scotland (Glasgow) 25 May (B.&H.)	v. Lancashire (Trent Bridge) 27 May (B.&H.)	v. Northamptonshire (Trent Bridge) 30 May (J.P.)	v. Yorkshire (Hull) 13 June (J.P.)	v. Leicestershire (Trent Bridge) 16-17 June (B.&H.)	v. Warwickshire (Trent Bridge) 20 June (J.P.)	v. Somerset (Bath) 27 June (J.P.)	v. Lancashire (Trent Bridge) 30 June (B.&H.)	v. Sussex (Hove) 3 July (N.W.T.)	v. Leicestershire (Trent Bridge) 11 July (J.P.)	v. Gloucestershire (Trent Bridge) 14-15 July (N.W.T.)	v. Somerset (Lord's) 24 July (B.&H.)
P. A. Todd	5		1		1	59	3							34			2
R. T. Robinson	12	24	11	16	45*	0	26	28	25	12	2	0	1	44*	19	16	13
D. W. Randall	45	6	7	0	—	0	21	20		23	14		43	16*		0	19
C. E. B. Rice	44	23	2	7	58*	130*	31	117	82	24	43	32	34	—	21	4	27
J. D. Birch	69	17						24	45	14	47	16	8	—	40*	12	7
R. J. Hadlee	20	20	70	17		32	56	16*	6				55*				11
B. N. French	10	1	14	18	—	0	2	1*	7	0	3	0	6	—	16*	18	8
E. E. Hemmings	9*	23*	10	8		0*	19	—	4	9	17	1	15*			7	1
K. E. Cooper	1*		8*				0*			14	4	0	—			11	3
M. K. Bore	—	—	—		9*					3		0					
M. Hendrick	—	—		12					3*	0*		0					0*
N. J. B. Illingworth		8*									5*				0		
S. B. Hassan		48	99*	12				1		48	19	4	6		2	27	26
M. A. Fell				2	—	4	26	4	28			8			0	6	
K. Saxelby				6			13*	—	9*	3	0	0*					
P. Johnson															4		
I. L. Pont															—	7*	
Byes	5		6			3	5	1	3				4		1	3	
Leg-byes	12	9	7	8	5	8	8	12	15	3	4	10	7	4	5	12	5
Wides	1	7	8	3	3	3	3	4	2	3	2	1	3	7	9	14	7
No-balls	1		1			3	3	3			1		2	9	1	5	1
Total	234	186	244	118	112	242	216	230	232	156	161	72	184	114	118	142	130
Wickets	7	7	7	10	1	6	8	5	8	10	9	10	6	1	5	10	10
Result	W	L	W	L	Ab	W	W	W	T	W	W	L	W	W	W	L	L
Points	2	0	2	0		2	2	2	4	2		4	0		4		

Fielding figures
- 30 – B. N. French (ct 23/st 7)
- 9 – D. W. Randall
- 8 – M. Hendrick and K. E. Cooper
- 7 – M. K. Bore and C. E. B. Rice
- 6 – E. E. Hemmings, J. D. Birch and M. A. Fell
- 5 – R. J. Hadlee
- 4 – R. T. Robinson
- 3 – K. Saxelby
- 2 – I. L. Pont and P. Johnson
- 1 – P. A. Todd and N. J. B. Illingworth

BOWLING

	R. J. Hadlee	M. K. Bore	M. Hendrick	E. E. Hemmings	K. E. Cooper	N. J. B. Illingworth	K. Saxelby
(B.&H.) v. Northants (Northampton) 8 May	10-2-36-1	11-5-11-2	10.3-1-33-6	11-0-55-0	11-3-54-1		
(J.P.) v. Hampshire (Trent Bridge) 9 May	8-3-21-1	8-0-22-1	8-1-36-1	8-0-48-1		8-1-58-2	
(B.&H.) v. Warwickshire (Trent Bridge) 15	8.3-3-22-2	11-3-44-0	9-3-19-3	11-2-39-3	11-0-68-1		
(J.P.) v. Worcestershire (Trent Bridge) 16 May	8-1-27-2	6.1-2-24-1	8-0-27-0	8-0-18-1			6-0-20-0
(J.P.) v. Middlesex (Lord's) 23 May	3-0-14-2		2-0-14-1				
(B.&H.) v. Scotland (Glasgow) 25 May	4-2-4-1	11-2-34-0	5-1-8-0	11-3-24-1			11-2-24-3
(B.&H.) v. Lancashire (Trent Bridge) 27 May	11-2-39-3		11-2-38-1	11-1-28-1	11-2-35-1		11-2-36-2
(J.P.) v. Northants (Trent Bridge) 30 May	8-2-22-2	7-0-38-3	8-0-32-2	8-0-26-0			5-0-44-1
(J.P.) v. Yorkshire (Hull) 13 June	8-2-33-0	8-0-52-1	8-1-38-2	8-2-44-0			8-0-48-2
(B.&H.) v. Leics. (Trent Bridge) 16-17 June		11-1-21-3	11-3-18-2	11-1-32-1	11-3-25-1		11-1-42-1
(J.P.) v. Somerset (Bath) 27 June		3-0-16-0	5-1-30-1	6-0-44-5	8-1-43-0		
(B.&H.) v. Lancashire (Trent Bridge) 30 June	11-2-24-2		10.4-1-37-1	11-2-28-2		11-4-30-1	11-1-51-3
(N.W.T.) v. Sussex (Hove) 3 July			9-2-14-2	12-7-19-0	9-4-10-1		10-0-37-0
(J.P.) v. Leicestershire (Trent Bridge) 11 July		8-2-11-2			8-0-29-2	8-2-15-4	
(N.W.T.) v. Glos. (Trent Bridge) 14-15 July					12-5-17-0	7.4-0-38-0	
(B.&H.) v. Somerset (Lord's) 24 July	9-0-37-0		8-1-26-1	5-0-11-0	5.1-0-41-0	12-6-21-1	
(J.P.) v. Surrey (The Oval) 25 July			8-1-21-0	8-2-30-0	7-1-40-1	8-0-29-1	
(J.P.) v. Lancashire (Trent Bridge) 1 August	8-1-25-0				8-0-34-1	8-0-58-1	8-1-22-1
(J.P.) v. Gloucestershire (Cheltenham) 8 Aug.	8-1-33-2			8-0-33-3	8-0-41-0	7.1-0-28-3	5-0-17-1
(J.P.) v. Kent (Trent Bridge) 15 August					6-0-16-0		8-0-38-3
(J.P.) v. Glamorgan (Swansea) 22 August			2-0-16-1	2-0-16-0			2-0-14-0
(J.P.) v. Derbyshire (Trent Bridge) 29 August	8-0-26-2		8-2-23-2	8-0-26-1	6.1-0-22-3		7-0-33-1
(J.P.) v. Essex (Chelmsford) 5 September	8-1-16-3	8-0-32-2		8-2-29-0	8-0-33-0		7-0-41-0
(Asda) v. Derbyshire (Scarborough) 6 Sept.	10-0-49-1	10-1-37-1		10-1-46-1	10-1-51-0		9-2-32-1
(J.P.) v. Sussex (Hove) 12 September	8-0-33-0	8-1-49-0		8-0-32-0	8-0-25-2		7-0-32-2

THE ENGLISH SEASON

	v. Surrey (The Oval) 25 July (J.P.)	v. Lancashire (Trent Bridge) 1 August (J.P.)	v. Gloucestershire (Cheltenham) 8 August (J.P.)	v. Kent (Trent Bridge) 15 August (J.P.)	v. Glamorgan (Swansea) 22 August (J.P.)	v. Derbyshire (Trent Bridge) 29 August (J.P.)	v. Essex (Chelmsford) 5 September (J.P.)	v. Derbyshire (Scarborough) 6 September (Asda)	v. Sussex (Hove) 12 September (J.P.)
		30	—						
	15		1	18		21	56	58	47
	18		31	—		—		29	2
	62	1	8	59*	46*	34	40*	6	59
	44	13	1		29*	40*	12*	22	5
		13	100*	—	4	5	3	47	22
	7	—	14	—	—	—	5*		4
	9*			—	—	—	—	4*	7
	—	0*	—	—	—	—	—		1
									2*
	—	—	—	—					
	10	96*	54	71*	—	35	40	58	14
	9	2	—		3*				10*
		16	—	—		—	—		
				—					
				4				1	1
	12	13	1	11	6	7	7	2	8
		2	2	1		1	1	2	2
			2	8	1	3	1		1
	186	186	214	168	90	149	160	234	185
	7	6	6	1	1	4	3	6	9
	L	L	W	W	W	W	W	L	L
	0	0	4	4	4	4	4	—	0

Basharat Hassan

M. A. Fell	D. W. Randall	C. E. B. Rice	I. L. Pont	S. B. Hassan	B	Lb	W	Nb	Total	Wkts
						6			195	10
						15	1		201	6
					1	8	3	1	205	10
						4	2		122	4
						4			32	5
11–0–38–2	2–0–4–0				4	7	1	1	149	8
						14	4		194	9
4–0–35–0					2	7	1		207	8
						16	1		232	6
					3	9	2	2	154	9
						8	1	1	185	6
		11.1–3–18–6			1	8	3		182	10
8–0–22–1			8–0–27–0		5	5	2	3	113	10
11–0–36–0			9–2–25–0		2	4	3	1	114	10
		6–2–11–0				3	3	2	145	1
		8–0–62–2				5	1		132	1
		8–0–43–3				5	5	1	193	4
		2–0–6–1			2	5	2	1	192	6
					2	6		1	167	10
8–0–39–2		5–0–28–1	8–0–31–1			7	4	1	164	10
			2–0–16–1	2–0–21–1		6			89	4
						6	4	5	145	10
						8			159	5
					4	16		1	236	5
						11	2	2	186	4

Somerset C.C.C.
One Day Matches – 1982

BATTING

	v. Combined Universities (Taunton) 8 May (B.&H.)	v. Northamptonshire (Northampton) 9 May (J.P.)	v. Middlesex (Lord's) 15 May (B.&H.)	v. Sussex (Hove) 16 May (J.P.)	v. Derbyshire (Taunton) 23 May (J.P.)	v. Glamorgan (Swansea) 25 May (B.&H.)	v. Gloucestershire (Taunton) 27 May (B.&H.)	v. Glamorgan (Swansea) 30 May (J.P.)	v. Essex (Chelmsford) 6 June (J.P.)	v. Warwickshire (Edgbaston) 13 June (J.P.)	v. Kent (Canterbury) 16 June (B.&H.)	v. Surrey (Bath) 20 June (J.P.)	v. Nottinghamshire (Bath) 27 June (J.P.)	v. Sussex (Taunton) 30 June (B.&H.)	v. Bedfordshire (Bedford) 3 July (N.W.T.)	v. Kent (Maidstone) 11 July (J.P.)	v. Leicestershire (Taunton) 14 July (N.W.T.)
B. C. Rose	58	6	18	15	5	15	2	4	3	25	52	49*	9	1*	28*	3	48
P. W. Denning	39	45	20	2	39	8	129	84	4	112*	3	5	71	68*	20	30	73
I. V. A. Richards	36*		6	1	9	29	72	25	18	79	12	0	15	9	6	11	8
P. M. Roebuck	13*	10	0		0	50	44			24	50	30	41	33	21	36	0
J. W. Lloyds	—	31	19	11	7*	28	4	29	4*	3*	7		13*			6	28*
I. T. Botham	—	22	10	0	105	16	15	39*	36		42	15		—		—	45
V. J. Marks		15	14*	8	49*	6		—	6		14	0	14*		31	43	51*
N. F. M. Popplewell		29	3	30	14	2	23*		11	—		—	0	—	15	20	
D. J. S. Taylor		9	1	27	—	4*	—		0*		8*	11	—		15*	0	—
C. H. Dredge		7*	2	13 x	—	10*	—	—		—	—		—	—		1	—
H. R. Moseley		0	0	6*	—	—	—			—						4*	
M. Davis		1*			—	—		—	—							0*	
P. A. Slocombe				14													
N. Russom										—							
J. Garner												1*	59*	12		10	—
T. Gard																	
G. V. Palmer																	
Byes	1			5	1	1		2		3	4	1				4	2
Leg-byes	1	5	3	1	4	3	13	3	6	10	9	7	8	1	3	12	6
Wides	1	1	1	1	2	2	5	1	1	4	4		1		6	4	9
No-balls	1	3	1						1	1	2	2	1		3	2	1
Total	150	184	98	134	235	174	307	187	91	261	208	179	185	112	154	180	271
Wickets	2	9	10	9	6	8	6	3	6	3	7	6	6	2	6	9	5
Result	W	L	L	L	L	W	W	W	L	W	W	W	W	W	W	L	W
Points	2	0	0	0	0	2	2	4	0	4	—	4	4	—	—	0	—

Fielding figures
31 – D. J. S. Taylor (ct 29/st 2)
13 – I. V. A. Richards
10 – N. F. M. Popplewell and I. T. Botham
6 – B. C. Rose, J. Garner and J. W. Lloyds
5 – P. M. Roebuck, P. W. Denning and H. R. Moseley
4 – C. H. Dredge, V. J. Marks and T. Gard (ct 3/st 1)
2 – N. Russom
1 – P. A. Slocombe

BOWLING

	I. T. Botham	H. R. Moseley	C. H. Dredge	V. J. Marks	N. F. M. Popplewell	I. V. A. Richards	P. M. Roebuck
(B.&H.) v. Combined Univ. (Taunton) 8 May	4-0-13-1	9-2-13-3	11-1-43-1	11-2-20-2	4-0-27-0	5-0-9-1	6.2-1-13-2
(J.P.) v. Northants (Northampton) 9 May	8-0-38-0	8-1-24-1	8-0-48-2		4-0-18-2		4-0-19-0
(B.&H.) v. Middlesex (Lord's) 15 May	8-2-22-2	8-3-8-0	4-1-13-0	11-1-31-0		4.4-2-10-1	
(J.P.) v. Sussex (Hove) 16 May	7.3-0-40-2	8-0-29-3	8-2-14-2	8-3-19-2	2-0-25-0	5-0-15-0	
(J.P.) v. Derbyshire (Taunton) 23 May	7.3-0-43-0	8-0-28-1	8-0-61-1	8-0-46-1		7-0-47-0	
(B.&H.) v. Glamorgan (Swansea) 25 May	11-5-24-3	10.3-1-27-2	11-1-27-2	9-1-32-1	2-1-7-0	11-3-35-1	
(B.&H.) v. Gloucestershire (Taunton) 27 May	11-1-62-1	11-2-60-1	11-1-66-1		3-0-13-1	8-1-41-1	
(J.P.) v. Glamorgan (Swansea) 30 May	8-1-30-0	8-0-29-0	8-0-32-4	8-0-30-0			
(J.P.) v. Essex (Chelmsford) 6 June	2-0-11-2		2-0-19-0		2-0-26-2	2-0-9-4	
(J.P.) v. Warwickshire (Edgbaston) 13 June		4-0-49-0		8-0-19-3	6-0-32-1	1-0-7-0	2-0-4-2
(B.&H.) v. Kent (Canterbury) 16 June	11-1-52-4	8-1-37-0	11-0-41-1	11-1-31-2		3-0-12-0	
(J.P.) v. Surrey (Bath) 20 June	7.5-0-47-4	8-0-24-3	2-0-13-0	8-0-34-1		6-0-31-0	
(J.P.) v. Nottinghamshire (Bath) 27 June		8-0-40-5	5-2-15-0				
(B.&H.) v. Sussex (Taunton) 30 June	6-1-20-2	11-5-20-0	4-0-12-1	11-3-25-3			
(N.W.T.) v. Bedfordshire (Bedford) 3 July	11-2-29-0	10-1-38-2	12-3-18-1	6-0-23-0		9-4-15-3	
(J.P.) v. Kent (Maidstone) 11 July		8-2-25-3	8-2-43-1	8-0-24-1		1-0-10-0	
(N.W.T.) v. Leicestershire (Taunton) 15 July	8-2-21-0	12-2-36-0	12-1-34-2	12-1-38-2		4-0-43-1	
(J.P.) v. Yorkshire (Taunton) 18 July		8-0-60-1	8-0-47-3	8-1-19-0		8-0-58-1	
(B.&H.) v. Nottinghamshire (Lord's) 24 July	9-3-19-2	11-2-26-1	11-2-35-2	11-4-24-2			
(J.P.) v. Worcestershire (Taunton) 25 July	8-0-59-2	6-0-49-0	8-0-58-1	8-0-25-2			
(J.P.) v. Hampshire (Portsmouth) 1 August		3-0-24-0	8-0-27-0	8-1-27-2			
(N.W.T.) v. Warwickshire (Taunton) 4-5 Aug.	12-1-59-1	10-0-59-0	7.3-1-48-2	12-1-41-0			
(J.P.) v. Middlesex (Weston-s.-Mare) 8 Aug.	8-1-32-2		8-0-35-1	8-0-54-1			
(J.P.) v. Leicestershire (Taunton) 22 August	8-0-46-1	4-1-21-1		8-0-36-3		1-0-1-1	
(J.P.) v. Gloucestershire (Bristol) 29 August		3-0-16-0	3-0-20-0				
(J.P.) v. Lancashire (Taunton) 12 September	8-0-44-3	8-3-7-3	8-0-36-0	8-0-25-3			

THE ENGLISH SEASON

	v. Yorkshire (Taunton) 18 July (J.P.)	v. Nottinghamshire (Lord's) 24 July (B.&H.)	v. Worcestershire (Taunton) 25 July (J.P.)	v. Hampshire (Portsmouth) 1 August (J.P.)	v. Warwickshire (Taunton) 4-5 August (N.W.T.)	v. Middlesex (Weston-super-Mare) 8 August (J.P.)	v. Leicestershire (Taunton) 22 August (J.P.)	v. Gloucestershire (Bristol) 29 August (J.P.)	v. Lancashire (Taunton) 12 September (J.P.)
	—	23	16	29	7	54		0	
46	22	14	40	4	10				
0	51*	17	13	31	27	13	88	69	
49	53*	83	27	15	2	36	37	4	
5		3	27				0	1	
			5	85	44	18		67*	
56*		72	12	55	27	36*		0*	
49*	—			4	29	16*	20	—	
—		4*	5*	3*	3			—	
—	—	—		0	25*		1*	—	
					11				
					—		18*	—	
—		2*	15*	3	0		3	—	
							—		
				12					
4	5	8	14	14	7	10	9	1	
4	1	9	7	4			3	2	
			1	4	1				
213	132	240	177	259	197	183	179	144	
4	1	7	6	9	10	4	6	3	
W	W	W	L	L	L	W	L	W	
4	—	4	0	—	0	4	0	4	

Brian Rose

M. Davis	J. W. Lloyds	J. Garner	G. V. Palmer		B	Lb	W	Nb	Total	Wkts
					2	6	1		147	10
8-0-33-0					1	13	1	1	196	6
	2-0-6-0				3	3		3	99	4
						5	5	1	153	10
						9	2		236	3
					1	9			162	10
11-1-25-2					1	21	5		294	7
8-0-43-1						17	4	1	186	7
2-0-19-0						6	2		92	10
8-0-32-1	3-0-9-0	8-2-17-3				8			177	10
		10.2-4-22-3				7	3	2	207	10
		8-2-12-2			4	6	4		175	10
		6-3-6-4				10	1		72	10
		9.1-1-24-4			1	3	3	2	110	10
		12-4-24-2			2	2	1	1	153	9
7-1-32-1		8-3-29-0			1	10	4	3	181	6
		12-7-23-4				7	5	1	208	9
		8-2-18-2				5	2	1	210	7
		8.1-1-13-3				5	7	1	130	10
		8-0-25-1			4	12	6		238	7
4-0-19-0	6.2-0-40-1	8-1-26-1			2	12	1	2	180	4
		12-2-45-1			1	7		1	261	5
8-0-50-2		8-0-24-1			3	10	1	2	211	9
		8-0-22-2	8-0-44-0			7	3		180	8
		6.4-1-31-1				1	3		71	2
		8-0-21-0				7	2	1	143	9

Surrey C.C.C.
One Day Matches – 1982

BATTING

BATTING	v. Essex (The Oval) 8 May (B.&H.)	v. Kent (The Oval) 9 May (J.P.)	v. Warwickshire (Edgbaston) 16 May (J.P.)	v. Sussex (The Oval) 22–24 May (B.&H.)	v. Kent (Canterbury) 25 May (B.&H.)	v. Hampshire (Southampton) 27 May (B.&H.)	v. Leicestershire (The Oval) 30 May (J.P.)	v. Gloucestershire (The Oval) 13 June (J.P.)	v. Somerset (Bath) 20 June (J.P.)	v. Middlesex (Lord's) 27 June (J.P.)	v. Durham (The Oval) 3 July (N.W.T.)	v. Northamptonshire (Tring) 4 July (J.P.)	v. Lancashire (Old Trafford) 11 July (J.P.)	v. Northamptonshire (The Oval) 15–16 July (N.W.T.)	v. Essex (Southend) 18 July (J.P.)	v. Nottinghamshire (The Oval) 25 July (J.P.)	v. Derbyshire (Derby) 1 August (J.P.)
A. R. Butcher	39	24	2	80	33	17	29	55	1			2		41	0	44	26
G. S. Clinton	79		63	23	17	15	32				2		18				
R. D. V. Knight	33	3	39	57	31	21	8	49	32	19	2	22	1	36	5	34	31
G. P. Howarth	51*						14	38	2					10			
M. A. Lynch	45	8	31	0	13	14	49	55*	3	42	129	2	21	17	2	50	10
S. T. Clarke	4	8	15	10	11	39	20	8*	0	1	5	10	2	—			
G. R. J. Roope	0	51*	22	11	20	53	5	1	26	8	77	7	35	9*	18	22*	74*
C. J. Richards	2*	1	8	3	8	3	—	—	34	4	20*	3	52	—	24	15	5
R. D. Jackman	—			0	46	12*			4				—				
P. I. Pocock	—			3*	3	—											
P. H. L. Wilson	—	—	0						0	0		0	3*		0	—	
D. M. Smith		3		26	0	13	57			50	27	30		103*			10
D. J. Thomas		1					2*	9	7	23	0*	6	3	—	33		0
G. Monkhouse		15*	14*		12*	2*	—	—	20*	1*		0*	6		5*	—	25
A. Needham			17*						0			0	9		55		
D. B. Pauline											10	30	4	—		17	
K. S. Mackintosh															1	—	—
I. R. Payne															4	—	
Byes			2		13	1	2	4	2	1	7		6				2
Leg-byes	14	5	13	10	9		8	10	6	5	3	8	14	14	8	5	15
Wides	8	6	4	6	11	3	3	5	4		3	6	3	1	4	5	7
No-balls	1	3	1		3	2		2			1	1	5	4	1		
Total	276	128	229	231	217	207	214	210	175	161	279	132	172	242	163	193	205
Wickets	6	7	7	10	10	8	7	5	10	10	7	10	10	4	10	4	7
Result	W	L	L	L	L	W	W	W	L	L	W	L	L	W	L	W	W
Points	2	0	4	0	0	2	4	4	0	0	—	0	0	—	0	4	4

Fielding figures: 32 – C. J. Richards (ct 26/st 6) 8 – M. A. Lynch 4 – I. R. Payne 2 – G. P. Howarth and G. S. Clinton 9 – D. M. Smith, A. R. Butcher and G. R. J. Roope 7 – G. Monkhouse 3 – P. I. Pocock, D. J. Thomas and A. Needham 1 – D. B. Pauline, K. S. Mackintosh and 6 – S. T. Clarke and R. D. V. Knight

BOWLING

BOWLING	S. T. Clarke	R. D. Jackman	P. H. L. Wilson	R. D. V. Knight	P. I. Pocock	G. S. Clinton	D. J. Thomas
(B.&H.) v. Essex (The Oval) 8 May	11-4-38-1	10-0-40-1	11-0-36-1	11-0-28-2	11-2-31-2	1-0-6-0	
(J.P.) v. Kent (The Oval) 9 May	7-1-32-0		3-0-31-0	5-0-33-1	7-0-58-1		8-1-36-3
(J.P.) v. Warwickshire (Edgbaston) 16 May	6.3-0-27-2		6-2-14-2		8-1-20-3		
(B.&H.) v. Sussex (The Oval) 22–24 May	11-2-30-0	11-3-20-2	8.2-0-62-1	11-0-29-2	11-0-70-2		
(B.&H.) v. Kent (Canterbury) 25 May	10.5-2-35-2	11-1-50-3		11-1-56-0	11-0-47-0		
(B.&H.) v. Hampshire (Southampton) 27 May	11-3-25-1	11-2-30-2		11-1-34-0	11-1-27-1		
(J.P.) v. Leicestershire (The Oval) 30 May	8-1-36-2			8-0-46-3			8-0-42-0
(J.P.) v. Gloucestershire (The Oval) 13 June	8-1-16-2		6-0-28-0	8-0-32-1			8-0-48-1
(J.P.) v. Somerset (Bath) 20 June	8-1-21-2		3.2-0-19-0	8-0-32-1			6-0-19-0
(J.P.) v. Middlesex (Lord's) 27 June	8-1-24-2	8-0-39-2	6-0-28-0				7.3-0-25-1
(N.W.T.) v. Durham (The Oval) 3 July	8-2-15-0			12-1-43-0		4-2-2-0	10-2-16-3
(J.P.) v. Northamptonshire (Tring) 4 July	8-0-32-2		8-0-40-2	8-0-26-2			8-2-39-2
(J.P.) v. Lancashire (Old Trafford) 11 July	6-1-33-0		7-0-37-0				6-0-17-0
(N.W.T.) v. Northants (The Oval) 15–16 July	12-2-34-1	12-4-42-1		12-0-41-1	4-0-25-0		12-0-51-1
(J.P.) v. Essex (Southend) 18 July			7-0-41-2	4-0-25-0			8-0-39-1
(J.P.) v. Nottinghamshire (The Oval) 25 July			8-0-38-2	6-0-34-0			
(J.P.) v. Derbyshire (Derby) 1 August				8-0-32-1			4-0-16-0
(N.W.T.) v. Hampshire (Southampton) 4 Aug.	9-2-11-0	10.2-2-22-6		7-1-26-1			7-0-27-1
(J.P.) v. Sussex (Guildford) 15 August	8-1-21-2						5-0-15-0
(N.W.T.) v. Middlesex (The Oval) 18–19 Aug.	7-2-10-4	12-4-20-3					5-2-6-0
(J.P.) v. Worcestershire (Worcester) 22 Aug.				3-0-15-0			3-0-21-0
(J.P.) v. Glamorgan (The Oval) 29 August							7-0-28-1
(N.W.T.) v. Warwickshire (Lord's) 4 Sept.	11.2-5-17-2	12-2-27-2		12-3-14-2			11-1-26-3
(J.P.) v. Hampshire (The Oval) 5 September				8-0-26-2	8-0-17-0		6-2-20-0
(J.P.) v. Yorkshire (The Oval) 12 September				8-0-46-2	8-1-31-1		8-0-32-1

A M. A. Lynch 5-4-1-0 B M. A. Lynch 0.3-0-3-0

THE ENGLISH SEASON/471

	v. Hampshire (Southampton) 4 August (N.W.T.)	v. Sussex (Guildford) 15 August (J.P.)	v. Middlesex (The Oval) 18–19 Aug (N.W.T.)	v. Worcestershire (Worcester) 22 August (J.P.)	v. Glamorgan (The Oval) 29 August (J.P.)	v. Warwickshire (Lord's) 4 Sept (N.W.T.)	v. Hampshire (The Oval) 5 September (J.P.)	v. Yorkshire (The Oval) 12 September (J.P.)
	1	18	53	72		86*	24	70
	23*	57	8	9	7	—	3	—
	28		0		3	31	20	12
	—	15	29*	3	56	—	4	52*
	—	0	4		—			
	—	26		13				
	—	1	10	4	1	—	11	—
	—		6					
						6*		
	62*	0	43	10	4	28*	8	28
	—	0	27	11	1	—	38*	31*
	—	1*	0	4			9	—
				7	7*			
					74*			
		5*	0*	4	—	—	2	
		1		0*	—		0	
	1	1	4	†	1			1
	2	6	11	8	11	4	7	10
	1	1	10	5	6		7	1
	2	1		5	3	10		
	120	133	205	156	174	159	139	205
	2	9	9	10	6	1	9	3
	W	L	W	L	L	W	T	W
		0	—	0	0	—	2	4

R. Knight

G. Monkhouse	A. Needham	G. R. J. Roope	K. S. Mackintosh	I. R. Payne	B	Lb	W	Nb	Total	Wkts
					1	5	5	1	191	8
8–0–27–2					2	13	2	1	235	7
8–0–24–1	8–0–36–2				8	9	2	1	141	10
		1–0–7–0			1	10	5	1	235	7
11–3–20–3					2	3	5	2	220	9
6–0–32–1		5–0–23–1			10	11		2	194	7
8–0–40–0	8–0–37–1				2	8	2		213	8
5–0–23–0	3–0–18–1				1	13	2	1	182	5
8–1–39–3	5–0–39–0				1	7		2	179	6
8–0–27–1					9	7	3		162	7
11–1–38–0			10–3–27–3		1	13	10	2	168	6A
8–3–12–1					4	7	4		164	9
8–2–20–0	8–0–41–3				4	13	6		174	3B
12–0–51–1					5	8	6	1	239	5
8–2–15–2			7–1–37–4	4–0–20–0		13	3	1	194	9
8–1–23–0	3–0–14–0		6–1–27–3	8–0–38–2		12			186	7
8–0–29–2	6–0–27–0		5–0–15–2	6.2–0–21–5	1	5	2	1	149	10
12–2–20–2					5	5	2	1	119	10
8–1–28–2			8–0–37–0	3.2–0–22–1		8	3		134	6
11.5–0–27–3			6–3–11–0			2	2	2	80	10
4–1–18–1			3–1–7–1			2	2		65	2
7–1–21–0	6.3–0–39–1		6–0–32–0	4–0–32–0	8	9	6		175	2
8–0–36–0			3–0–10–0		8	11		6	158	10
6–0–22–3			3–0–14–0	8–1–17–2	6	12	5		139	9
8–0–40–1				8–0–31–4	2	12	1	3	198	8

Sussex C.C.C.
One Day Matches – 1982

BATTING	v. Essex (Hove) 9 May (J.P.)	v. Hampshire (Bournemouth) 15 May (B.&H.)	v. Somerset (Hove) 16 May (J.P.)	v. Surrey (The Oval) 22–24 May (B.&H.)	v. Essex (Hove) 25 May (B.&H.)	v. Kent (Hove) 27–28 May (B.&H.)	v. Gloucestershire (Gloucester) 30 May (J.P.)	v. Lancashire (Old Trafford) 6 June (J.P.)	v. Worcestershire (Horsham) 13 June (J.P.)	v. Derbyshire (Derby) 16 June (B.&H.)	v. Glamorgan (Hastings) 20 June (J.P.)	v. Somerset (Taunton) 30 June (B.&H.)	v. Nottinghamshire (Hove) 3 July (N.W.T.)	v. Kent (Maidstone) 4 July (J.P.)	v. Leicestershire (Hove) 18 July (J.P.)	v. Northamptonshire (Northampton) 25 July (J.P.)	v. Yorkshire (Scarborough) 1 August (J.P.)
G. D. Mendis	8	45	35	6	1	10	18	46	0	46	2	6	0	121	27	11	25
I. J. Gould	36	29	18	56	18	72	16	2	12	14	48	8	4	52	4	17	13
C. M. Wells	9	6	2	30	2	80	31	—	46	3	81*	11	1	14	45	45	30
P. W. G. Parker	8	77	2	0	13	4	20	36*	73	72	1		11	29	54	0	77
Imran Khan	13	0	7	11	4	65*	37	2	11	0							
I. A. Greig	22*	23	0	3	18	39	25	—	2	20*	18*		13	3	15*	2	0
C. P. Phillipson	14*	17*	17	66*	25	5	3	—	36*	2*		0	16	12*	17	44*	31
J. R. T. Barclay| —	0	13*	9	31	—	0*	—	0	—			3	11	—	10*	7*	0
G. S. le Roux	—	13	39	37*	42	11*	43*	1*	7	29	88	46	10	1	6	85	15
A. C. S. Pigott	—	0	8	—	6*	—			8*						2	—	
A. P. Wells	—		1		23	—						5*					
C. E. Waller		3*	—		—	—	—	—	—	—		7	1*		0	—	0*
A. M. Green											0	41					8*
A. N. Jones												2					
G. G. Arnold													0	—	—	—	—
Byes		14		1	7		1	4	1			1	5				6
Leg-byes	5	16	5	10	14	12	15	4	8	6	6	3	5	8	12	4	11
Wides		4	5	5	6	7	1	2	2	1	6	3	2	2	4	2	5
No-balls	1	1	1	1	3					1	1	2	3				1
Total	116	248	153	235	213	305	210	97	206	194	251	110	113	254	183	215	222
Wickets	5	9	10	7	10	6	7	3	8	6	4	10	10	5	9	6	7
Result	W	W	W	W	L	W	W	L	W	W	W	L	L	W	W	W	W
Points	4	2	4	2	0	2	4	4	0	—	4	—	—	4	4	4	4

Fielding figures
28 – I. J. Gould (ct 27/st 1)
15 – J. R. T. Barclay
8 – I. A. Greig and A. C. S. Pigott
7 – C. E. Waller
6 – C. P. Phillipson
5 – G. D. Mendis
4 – A. M. Green, C. M. Wells and G. S. le Roux
3 – A. P. Wells and P. W. G. Parker

BOWLING	Imran Khan	G. S. le Roux	I. A. Greig	A. C. S. Pigott	C. M. Wells	C. P. Phillipson	C. E. Waller
(J.P.) v. Essex (Hove) 9 May	8-1-14-3	8-1-21-2	8-0-25-0	8-1-21-1	5-0-18-3	1.5-0-6-1	
(B.&H.) v. Hampshire (Bournemouth) 15 May	5-2-8-0	4-1-10-1	6-0-20-1	11-2-33-3			8.4-2-25-1
(J.P.) v. Somerset (Hove) 16 May	8-0-30-2	8-2-16-2	8-3-16-1	8-1-41-1			
(B.&H.) v. Surrey (The Oval) 22–24 May	11-2-38-3	11-3-35-1	11-2-48-3	11-2-50-2			
(B.&H.) v. Essex (Hove) 25 May	11-1-62-0	11-0-70-0	11-1-56-0	11-3-66-1			
(B.&H.) v. Kent (Hove) 27–28 May	8-0-23-2	9.5-2-59-4	9-1-44-1	11-0-59-1			
(J.P.) v. Gloucestershire (Gloucester) 30 May		8-0-33-1	8-1-53-3	8-0-40-0			8-0-32-0
(J.P.) v. Lancashire (Old Trafford) 6 June	7-0-29-3	5-0-29-0	6-1-28-0				
(J.P.) v. Worcestershire (Horsham) 13 June	8-1-17-2	7-0-37-1	8-0-36-0	7-0-62-1			5-0-21-1
(B.&H.) v. Derbyshire (Derby) 16 June	11-4-31-1	11-2-57-2	11-1-34-2				11-2-38-2
(J.P.) v. Glamorgan (Hastings) 20 June		3-0-8-1	8-0-29-2	8-1-14-3		3-0-10-0	8-0-31-0
(B.&H.) v. Somerset (Taunton) 30 June		5-0-22-0	4-1-14-0				11-1-29-0
(N.W.T.) v. Nottinghamshire (Hove) 3 July		9-2-32-0	10-2-37-1		2.4-0-15-0		
(J.P.) v. Kent (Maidstone) 4 July		8-0-26-2	8-1-32-0	8-0-42-3			0.2-0-2-1
(J.P.) v. Leicestershire (Hove) 18 July		6-0-27-1	8-0-42-5	8-0-29-1			4-0-20-0
(J.P.) v. Northants (Northampton) 25 July		8-0-39-2	5-0-33-0	6-0-35-1			8-0-17-0
(J.P.) v. Yorkshire (Scarborough) 1 August		6-0-13-3		6.5-0-41-3			7-0-52-0
(J.P.) v. Hampshire (Eastbourne) 8 August		8-0-41-2	8-0-24-2	7.5-0-33-4	2-0-11-1		8-0-22-0
(J.P.) v. Surrey (Guildford) 15 August		6-0-28-2		7-0-28-5	8-1-20-2		4-0-25-0
(J.P.) v. Derbyshire (Chesterfield) 22 August		6-0-33-3	6-0-32-1	5-0-27-1	6-1-20-1		
(J.P.) v. Middlesex (Hove) 29 August		7.1-0-27-3	7-0-44-2	8-0-43-2	6-0-23-0		3-0-16-0
(J.P.) v. Warwickshire (Edgbaston) 5 Sept.							
(J.P.) v. Nottinghamshire (Hove) 12 Sept.		7-0-18-4	8-0-34-0	8-0-44-2	8-0-28-1		3-0-17-1

THE ENGLISH SEASON

	v. Hampshire (Eastbourne) 8 August (J.P.)	v. Surrey (Guildford) 15 August (J.P.)	v. Derbyshire (Chesterfield) 22 August (J.P.)	v. Middlesex (Hove) 29 August (J.P.)	v. Warwickshire (Edgbaston) 5 September (J.P.)	v. Nottinghamshire (Hove) 12 September (J.P.)
	23	10	26	100		7
	29	4	16	58		
	5	19	57	2		65
	21	49*	9	17		52
	0		10	2		
	23*	11	11	8		—
	19	18*	7*	0*		—
	33	10	0	23		24*
	26*	2	4*	—		4*
	—	—	—	—		—
	—	—	—	—		19
			4	2		
	7	8	9	13		11
		3	1	1		2
	6		1	2		2
	192	134	155	228		186
	7	6	7	7		4
	W	W	W	W	Ab	W
	4	4	4	4	2	4

Garth Le Roux

J. R. T. Barclay	P. W. G. Parker	A. M. Green	A. P. Wells	G. G. Arnold	B	Lb	W	Nb	Total	Wkts
						6	4		115	10
9–2–24–3					4	2	1	2	129	10
8–0–24–3					5	1	1		134	9
11–1–42–0					2	10	6		231	10
11–1–62–0					1	4	5	1	327	2
11–1–54–2					1	8		4	252	10
8–0–33–0					5	12	1		209	4
					1	4	2		93	4
4–0–24–1						7	3	1	208	7
11–1–23–1						6	1		190	9
8–1–23–2	1.1–0–2–1					7	8		132	10
11–3–25–0		3–1–4–1	2.1–1–17–1			1			112	2
				8–4–10–0		4	7	9	114	1
6–0–45–2				8–0–27–1		3	3	1	181	10
8–1–25–2				4–0–15–0	1	7	1	2	169	9
7–0–47–1				6–0–22–0	1	16	2	1	213	4
6–0–24–2				8–0–27–2		10			167	10
6–0–36–0					1	8	1	2	179	10
8–0–23–0					1	6	1	1	133	9
5–0–28–1						10	1		151	8
8–0–36–1					2	11	2	1	205	10
							Abandoned			
5–0–32–0					1	8	2	1	185	9

Warwickshire C.C.C.
One Day Matches – 1982

BATTING	v. Nottinghamshire (Trent Bridge) 15 May (B.&H.)	v. Surrey (Edgbaston) 16 May (J.P.)	v. Scotland (Edgbaston) 22 May (B.&H.)	v. Yorkshire (Bradford) 23 May (J.P.)	v. Lancashire (Old Trafford) 25 May (B.&H.)	v. Northamptonshire (Edgbaston) 27–28 May (B.&H.)	v. Derbyshire (Chesterfield) 30 May (J.P.)	v. Kent (Edgbaston) 6 June (J.P.)	v. Somerset (Edgbaston) 13 June (J.P.)	v. Nottinghamshire (Trent Bridge) 20 June (J.P.)	v. Northamptonshire (Edgbaston) 27 June (J.P.)	v. Cambridgeshire (Edgbaston) 3 July (N.W.T.)	v. Leicestershire (Leicester) 4 July (J.P.)	v. Gloucestershire (Edgbaston) 11 July (J.P.)	v. Glamorgan (Cardiff) 14–15 July (N.W.T.)	v. Lancashire (Old Trafford) 25 July (J.P.)	v. Somerset (Taunton) 4–5 August (N.W.T.)
D. L. Amiss	0	1	105*	60	18		10	21	3	23	38	135	25	18	12	11	59
T. A. Lloyd	4	26	29	14	0	40	10	26	2	9	79	64	29	83	52	55	21
A. I. Kallicharran	12	24	29*	8	0	86	21	15	6	2	23	8	45	4	28	12	141*
G. W. Humpage	62	0	—	74*	6	40	27	2	16	12	45*	52	87*	41	39	17	17
P. R. Oliver	4			14		42*		11			18	5*			—		0
Asif Din	61	14	—	13*	20	19*	43	19	31	2	10	13	2	10	2*	55*	6*
A. M. Ferreira	0	38	—	—	45			32									—
G. C. Small	11	4			8	—	7*	14*	0	1	—	8*	—	3*	—	—	—
R. G. D. Willis	37	0				—		1		25*		—		—			—
J. Cumbes	1*				0			3	14*								
W. Hogg	0	2			0												
P. Smith		1					12	7	36								
C. Lethbridge		11*	—	—	13*		20*		57*	14	—			9*			
K. D. Smith			—		83	12	20		13	18		7			28*		8
S. P. Sutcliffe						—											
G. A. Tedstone								2							—		
S. H. Wootton										8	—		7*	0		28*	
K. R. Maguire												—					
R. I. H. B. Dyer															10		
P. J. Hartley															—		
Byes	1	8		1			1						1	5	3		1
Leg-byes	8	9	1	3	5	10	9	6	8	6	12	3	14	7	3	17	7
Wides	3	2		4	3	5	3	7		4	2	5	2	1	2	2	
No-balls	1	1	3	3		5		3	1			1		1		1	1
Total	205	141	167	194	201	259	183	164	177	139	227	300	213	181	170	207	261
Wickets	10	10	1	4	10	4	7	9	10	9	5	6	4	6	4	5	5
Result	L	L	W	W	L	W	L	L	L	L	W	W	L	L	W	L	W
Points	0	0	2	4	0	2	0	0	0	4	—	0	0	—	0	—	—

Fielding figures: 22 – G. W. Humpage (ct 20/st 2) 8 – C. Lethbridge and Asif Din 6 – A. I. Kallicharran 4 – A. M. Ferreira and P. R. Oliver K. D. Smith
9 – T. A. Lloyd 7 – G. C. Small and D. L. Amiss 5 – J. Cumbes 2 – R. G. D. Willis, S. P. Sutcliffe, 1 – P. Smith, W

BOWLING	R. G. D. Willis	G. C. Small	A. M. Ferreira	W. Hogg	J. Cumbes	P. Smith	C. Lethbridge
(B.&H.) v. Notts (Trent Bridge) 15 May	11–4–26–1	11–2–48–1	11–1–44–2	11–0–49–0	11–0–55–2		
(J.P.) v. Surrey (Edgbaston) 16 May	8–0–34–2	8–0–36–1	5–0–43–3	8–0–39–0		4–0–27–0	7–1–32–0
(B.&H.) v. Scotland (Edgbaston) 22 May	10–4–12–2	10–3–34–2	11–1–42–4		11–2–27–1		11–2–37–1
(J.P.) v. Yorkshire (Bradford) 23 May		7–0–41–1	8–0–33–2	7–1–27–2	8–2–36–3		7–0–34–1
(B.&H.) v. Lancs. (Old Trafford) 25 May		11–3–48–2	11–1–44–3	5–1–12–0	11–1–29–0		11–0–55–2
(B.&H.) v. Northants (Edgbaston) 27–28 May		11–2–27–2			11–0–48–2	11–1–65–1	11–1–49–3
(J.P.) v. Derbyshire (Chesterfield) 30 May	8–1–39–0	8–1–30–0			3–0–17–0	5.4–0–21–2	8–0–36–0
(J.P.) v. Kent (Edgbaston) 6 June	7.3–1–30–0	6–2–29–1	4–0–12–0		2–0–23–0	6–1–21–2	
(J.P.) v. Somerset (Edgbaston) 13 June		8–0–49–1			8–0–33–0	8–0–66–0	8–0–43–2
(J.P.) v. Notts (Trent Bridge) 20 June	8–2–10–2	8–1–28–2			7–0–40–1		8–0–42–2
(J.P.) v. Northants (Edgbaston) 27 June		7.5–1–20–3			8–0–41–1		8–0–47–5
(N.W.T.) v. Cambs. (Edgbaston) 3 July	7–1–28–0	9.1–5–12–2			12–3–39–2		
(J.P.) v. Leicestershire (Leicester) 4 July	8–1–22–1	8–0–42–1					
(J.P.) v. Gloucestershire (Edgbaston) 11 July		7.5–1–39–1					7–0–35–1
(N.W.T.) v. Glamorgan (Cardiff) 14–15 July	12–4–21–1	12–2–22–3					12–1–37–1
(J.P.) v. Lancashire (Old Trafford) 25 July	8–0–30–3	8–1–40–2					8–0–32–0
(N.W.T.) v. Somerset (Taunton) 4–5 August	12–1–34–1	12–3–56–3	12–1–53–4				12–1–44–1
(J.P.) v. Glamorgan (Edgbaston) 8 August	7–2–14–0	7–0–39–1				3–0–26–0	6–1–24–0
(J.P.) v. Middlesex (Edgbaston) 15 August		7–0–40–2	7–0–46–0		4–0–32–1	4–0–21–3	
(N.W.T.) v. Yorkshire (Edgbaston) 18 August	12–5–23–1	12–1–39–1	12–2–34–3				12–2–44–1
(J.P.) v. Essex (Colchester) 22 August	8–1–35–2	8–0–43–1	8–0–85–0				6–0–51–1
(J.P.) v. Worcestershire (Worcester) 29 Aug.		8–1–26–3	8–1–39–3			4–0–34–0	6–0–42–1
(N.W.T.) v. Surrey (Lord's) 4 September	7–0–23–0	8–0–60–0	6–0–16–0				6–1–23–1
(J.P.) v. Sussex (Edgbaston) 5 September							
(J.P.) v. Hampshire (Bournemouth) 12 Sept.	8–2–21–1	8–3–18–0	7–0–28–2				8–0–32–2

A R. I. H. B. Dyer 2.3–0–21–0   B S. J. Hartley 4–1–19–0   C T. A. Lloyd 2–0–16–0

THE ENGLISH SEASON/475

Andy Lloyd

	v. Glamorgan (Edgbaston) 8 August (J.P.)	v. Middlesex (Edgbaston) 15 August (J.P.)	v. Yorkshire (Edgbaston) 18 August (N.W.T.)	v. Essex (Colchester) 22 August (J.P.)	v. Worcestershire (Worcester) 29 August (J.P.)	v. Surrey (Lord's) 4 September (N.W.T.)	v. Sussex (Edgbaston) 5 September (J.P.)	v. Hampshire (Bournemouth) 12 September (J.P.)
	17	30	24*		66	0		23
	7	36	66	66	19*	2		20
	2	2*	0	11	—	19		14
	11		5*	74		0		1
	44	—		19		2		
	16	27	—	32	—	45		56*
	1	—		3*	—	8		17
	4*	3*	—	—		33		—
	—		—	—		8*		—
		2						
	8	1		9*				
	4*			—	—	4		11*
	7	5	113	73	23*	12		14
		23						
		0						
	1	4		2		8		
	5	6	6	10	1	11		7
	8		1	2	2			3
	3	1	4		1	6		
	137	141	219	301	46	158		166
	8	9†	3	6	0	10		6
	L	L	W	W	Ab	L	Ab	L
	0	0	—	4	2	—	2	0

G. A. Tedstone   K. R. Maguire and sub   †A. I. Kallicharran retired hurt
gg, S. H. Wootton,

G. W. Humpage	S. P. Sutcliffe	A. I. Kallicharran	Asif Din	K. R. Maguire	B	Lb	W	Nb	Total	Wkts
					6	7	8	1	244	7
						13	4	1	229	7
						10	2	2	166	10
					1	17	4		193	9
6–1–29–1					1	14	5	2	239	8
	11–1–55–0				1	12		1	258	8
		7–0–36–1			1	4	3		187	3
		8–1–34–0	1–0–7–0		2	5	2	1	166	3
4–1–29–0		4–0–23–0			3	10	4	1	261	3
		8–1–22–0	1–0–12–0			4	2	1	161	9
		2–0–15–0		8–0–43–1		11	6	2	185	10
	10–1–40–3	12–2–44–2			3	5		9	180	10
	8–0–52–2	8–0–56–0			9	6	4	2	214	4A
	8–0–29–0	8–1–31–2	4–1–18–1		4	6	4		185	5B
	12–2–27–2	12–1–35–2			11	7	1	8	169	10
	8–0–65–1	8–0–45–0			2	6	5		225	6
		12–1–42–0			12	14		4	259	9
		4–0–22–0			1	2	5	5	138	1
		8–0–47–1		8–0–42–0		11		4	243	9
		12–0–46–1			6	16	3	5	216	9
		8–0–52–0			7	6	2	2	299	4C
		8–0–40–0			4	13	5	3	242	9
6–0–36–1		6.4–1–23–0				4		10	159	1
							Abandoned			
3–0–26–0		5–0–31–1			4	7	2	1	170	6

Worcestershire C.C.C.
One Day Matches – 1982

BATTING

	v. Yorkshire (Leeds) 8 May (B.&H.)	v. Yorkshire (Huddersfield) 9 May (J.P.)	v. Leicestershire (Worcester) 15 May (B.&H.)	v. Nottinghamshire (Trent Bridge) 16 May (J.P.)	v. Minor Counties (Wellington) 22 May (B.&H.)	v. Gloucestershire (Bristol) 23 May (J.P.)	v. Derbyshire (Worcester) 25 May (B.&H.)	v. Kent (Worcester) 30 May (J.P.)	v. Derbyshire (Worcester) 6 June (J.P.)	v. Sussex (Horsham) 13 June (J.P.)	v. Essex (Ilford) 20 June (J.P.)	v. Lancashire (Worcester) 27 June (J.P.)	v. Gloucestershire (Harrogate) 1 July (T.T.)	v. Yorkshire (Leeds) 14–15 July (N.W.T.)	v. Glamorgan (Worcester) 18 July	v. Somerset (Taunton) 25 July (J.P.)	v. Northamptonshire (Luton) 1 August (J.P.)
G. M. Turner	5	47	2	50	79	73	78	18		5	4	17	10	105	8		
J. A. Ormrod	14	8	87	44	45	46	45	6	5	28	12						
D. N. Patel	18	13	90	0	13	3	25	13	5	36	3	6	1	25*	20	0	16
Younis Ahmed	13	4	19	0	17	25	39	8	49	12		29	16				
E. J. O. Hemsley	13	2	28	18*	7	15	2	40	41	32	16		29		77	23	0
M. J. Weston	40		2						8	10	51	2	7	23		109	0
D. J. Humphries	41	30	5	—	4	12*	8	0	15	9	4	4	39	0*	14	19	35
J. D. Inchmore	29	21	4*	—	11	—		4			19*	30	0	6	32*	1*	
N. Gifford	19*	5	0				5	31	1*	—	6		—				
A. P. Pridgeon	9*	2*	13*		5		6	17			0*			—			8
S. P. Perryman	—	—	—		5*	—	10*	19*	—					—	—		2*
P. A. Neale		45*		4*	7	21	26	30	48	46*	1	24	1	42	41	3	102
A. E. Warner					3	—		24*				1	1	—	1*	4*	
H. L. Alleyne									18*							17*	17
D. D'Oliveira											6	0		0		33	23
M. S. Scott												39	4	33	12	8	2
A. J. Webster												1*	2*		—		
T. S. Curtis																	1
D. Banks																	
R. Illingworth																	
Byes		4	1		1									4		4	1
Leg-byes	3	3	18	4	18	5	7	2	6	7	3	10	6	6	6	12	12
Wides	4	3	2	2	9	1	2	1	3	3	1	5	1	13	6	6	
No-balls	2	1	1		2	1	1		2	1	1		2	3			1
Total	210	188	272	122	226	202	278	189	201	208	138	138	125	286	186	238	220
Wickets	8	8	8	4	10	6	9	10	7	7	10	10	10	5	7	7	10
Result	W	W	L	W	W	L	L	L	L	W	L	L	L	L	L	L	L
Points	2	4	0	4	2	0	0	0	0	4	0	—	—	—	0	0	0

Fielding figures:
25 – D. J. Humphries (ct 21/st 4)
12 – E. J. O. Hemsley
6 – D. N. Patel and J. D. Inchmore
5 – G. M. Turner
4 – M. J. Weston
3 – Younis Ahmed, P. A. Neale, A. P. Pridgeon, J. A. Ormrod and M. S. Scott
2 – S. P. Perryman
1 – N. Gifford, A. E. Warner, D. Banks, D. B. D'Oliveira and A. J. Webster

BOWLING

	A. P. Pridgeon	J. D. Inchmore	S. P. Perryman	E. J. O. Hemsley	N. Gifford	D. N. Patel	M. J. Weston
(B.&H.) v. Yorkshire (Leeds) 8 May	8-0-17-1	11-1-45-2	9-2-25-3	6-0-30-3	10-0-51-0	11-1-26-0	
(J.P.) v. Yorkshire (Huddersfield) 9 May	7-2-26-3	5-1-23-1	7-0-41-0	4-0-21-1	8-1-40-1	8-0-31-1	
(B.&H.) v. Leicestershire (Worcester) 15 May	9-1-44-1	7-1-35-0	11-0-47-0	3-0-20-0	11-0-54-1	11-0-42-1	3-0-15-0
(J.P.) v. Notts (Trent Bridge) 16 May	6.5-1-20-3	7-0-18-1	7-1-15-2			8-0-18-1	
(B.&H.) v. M. Counties (Wellington) 22 May	8-2-18-1	11-4-28-2	11-4-28-4			11-3-21-2	
(J.P.) v. Gloucestershire (Bristol) 23 May	8-1-31-2	3.1-0-17-0	4-0-21-1			4-0-27-1	
(B.&H.) v. Derbyshire (Worcester) 25 May	11-1-51-0		11-0-65-0	1-0-5-0	11-0-35-1	11-0-60-2	
(J.P.) v. Kent (Worcester) 30 May	7-0-53-0	8-0-51-3	6-0-30-1	6-0-26-1	8-0-21-1	5-0-33-0	
(J.P.) v. Derbyshire (Worcester) 6 June	7-0-44-1		8-0-50-0	2-0-14-0	5-0-23-1	3-0-31-0	
(J.P.) v. Sussex (Horsham) 13 June	8-0-39-2	4-0-22-1		5-0-26-0	7-1-32-1	1-0-13-0	8-0-36-2
(J.P.) v. Essex (Ilford) 20 June	8-0-62-1	8-0-33-1		4-0-20-1	8-1-52-2	7-0-40-0	5-0-33-0
(J.P.) v. Lancashire (Worcester) 27 June		4-1-9-1				8-0-42-1	8-1-46-1
(T.T.) v. Gloucestershire (Harrogate) 1 July		10.5-2-50-4		11-1-42-1		11-1-40-0	
(N.W.T.) v. Yorkshire (Leeds) 14–15 July		12-2-47-4	12-0-32-0		10-0-68-2	2-0-19-0	12-1-52-0
(J.P.) v. Glamorgan (Worcester) 18 July		8-1-25-1	8-1-26-3			8-0-29-0	
(J.P.) v. Somerset (Taunton) 25 July	8-0-44-0		8-0-43-1			7-0-41-2	
(J.P.) v. Northamptonshire (Luton) 1 August	8-0-43-1		8-0-63-1	4-0-31-0		8-0-48-0	4-0-46-0
(J.P.) v. Leicestershire (Stourbridge) 8 August	6-0-15-1	5-0-18-0				7.4-0-21-0	
(J.P.) v. Hampshire (Southampton) 15 August	7.4-1-25-1		5-0-25-1	7-0-50-1	8-1-27-1	8-0-39-4	
(J.P.) v. Surrey (Worcester) 22 August	5.4-0-25-2		8-1-27-2			6-0-31-1	
(J.P.) v. Warwickshire (Worcester) 29 August							
(J.P.) v. Middlesex (Worcester) 12 September			8-0-31-4	4-0-26-1			4-0-23-0

A R. Illingworth 8-0-45-0

THE ENGLISH SEASON/477

P. A. Neale

	v. Leicestershire (Stourbridge) 8 August (J.P.)	v. Hampshire (Southampton) 15 August (J.P.)	v. Surrey (Worcester) 22 August (J.P.)	v. Warwickshire (Worcester) 29 August (J.P.)	v. Middlesex (Worcester) 12 September (J.P.)
					29
	43	92*	0	9	42
	11	125	26	41	16
		3*	33*	32	2
		—	—	45	45
	0	—	—	7	6
	1	—	—	24	
	26				
	2	—	—		
					1
	1	—	2*	57	29
				2*	0
	0				
	11				
	12				
	3*	—	—	0	9*
		—			
				0	21
	2			4	
	4	14	2	13	6
	3	2	2	5	3
				3	3
	119	236	65	242	212
	10	1	2	9	10
	L	W	W	Ab	L
	0	4	4	2	0

A. E. Warner	H. L. Alleyne	P. A. Neale	Younis Ahmed	A. J. Webster	B	Lb	W	Nb	Total	Wkts
					6	8		1	209	9
					1		1	1	185	7
					6	8	6	1	278	3
						8	3		118	10
8–0–36–2					2	6	5	6	129	10
7.3–4–15–1						12		1	128	5
4–0–19–0					1	6	4	10	284	6
11–1–47–2						3	2		219	6
		6–1–19–0	0.2–0–4–0		1	6	4	7	203	2
				7–0–27–1	1	8	2		206	8
						5	2		247	6
6–1–20–0				8–1–21–0	1	11	8	2	160	4
11–3–27–3				11–0–44–2	2	8	12	1	226	10
11.3–2–45–1					8	13	1	5	290	7
8–0–41–1				8–0–35–1	2	20	7	2	187	8
7–0–49–1	8–0–46–2					8	9		240	7
	8–1–28–1				2	5	6		272	3
	5–0–28–0			8–1–26–1	1	3	5	3	120	2
				4–0–34–0	1	21	3		225	10
	7–0–28–2			8–0–26–2	1	8	5	5	156	10
4.1–0–22–0				4–0–20–0		1	2	1	46	0
8–1–44–0				8–0–51–1		5	4		229	6A

Yorkshire C.C.C.
One Day Matches – 1982

BATTING

	v. Worcestershire (Leeds) 8 May (B.&H.)	v. Worcestershire (Huddersfield) 9 May (J.P.)	v. Leicestershire (Leicester) 16 May (J.P.)	v. Leicestershire (Leicester) 22 May (B.&H.)	v. Warwickshire (Bradford) 23 May (J.P.)	v. Minor Counties (Bradford) 25–26 May (B.&H.)	v. Derbyshire (Chesterfield) 27 May (B.&H.)	v. Glamorgan (Bradford) 6 June (J.P.)	v. Nottinghamshire (Hull) 13 June (J.P.)	v. Northamptonshire (Middlesbrough) 20 June (J.P.)	v. Derbyshire (Derby) 27 June (J.P.)	v. Northamptonshire (Harrogate) 30 June (T.T.)	v. Gloucestershire (Leeds) 4 July (J.P.)	v. Essex (Scarborough) 11 July (J.P.)	v. Worcestershire (Leeds) 14 July (N.W.T.)	v. Somerset (Taunton) 18 July (J.P.)	v. Kent (Canterbury) 25 July (J.P.)
G. Boycott	19			82		2	7		2*	7	54	31	48	1	2	10	34*
K. Sharp	71	4	19	20	40	23	5		40								
G. B. Stevenson	6	0	3	0	6	—	10		1	0	18	1	30	1	28*	28	
C. W. J. Athey	57	1	54	24	19	61*	11		24	45	76	13	50	12	5	1	59
J. D. Love	7	32	9	1	1		60		70	5	3	30	29	28	2	9	3
D. L. Bairstow	9	55	27	13	35	18*	10		18	24	17*	34	11	31	92	64	19
C. M. Old	10	49*	21	15	13	—	3		45	34	6	17	40	1	55*	13	
S. N. Hartley	2	20	6	12	10	2			15*	4	3*	32	16	8	58	56	22
P. Carrick	8*	20	9		20*				—	34	—	2	0	2	5	21*	4*
A. Sidebottom	1		1*	22*	10		10			52*				23*			—
A. Ramage	4*			1*	15		8										
M. D. Moxon		1*	6*														8
S. J. Dennis		—							7	—							
P. W. Jarvis												1	0*		4	—	0*
S. Stuchbury			—		2*		6*		0					9*	—		
R. G. Lumb			8			76	36				4				16		
R. Illingworth												1*					
Byes	6	1	3		1	6				1	4	3		1	8		
Leg-byes	8	1	6	7	17		6		16	11	16	8	6	6	13	5	12
Wides			2		4	3	6		1	2	5	2	2	4	1	2	3
No-balls	1	1	2	2		2			1		2	1	2	5	1		
Total	209	185	168	207	193	193	178		232	227	202	181	233	133	290	210	164
Wickets	9	7	8	9	9	4	10		6	10	5	10	8	9	7	7	5
Result	L	L	L	L	L	W	L	Ab	T	L	W	L	W	L	W	L	W
Points	0	0	0	0	0	2	0	2	2	0	4	—	4	0	—	0	4

Fielding figures
28 – D. L. Bairstow (ct 27/st 1) 8 – K. Sharp 5 – G. Boycott 2 – M. D. Moxon, A. Ramage, 1 – S. N. Hartley, R. G.
9 – C. W. J. Athey 7 – S. N. Hartley 4 – C. M. Old and R. Illingworth P. Carrick and J. D. Love and S. J. Dennis

BOWLING

	C. M. Old	A. Ramage	A. Sidebottom	G. B. Stevenson	S. N. Hartley	G. Boycott	P. W. Jarvis
(B.&H.) v. Worcestershire (Leeds) 8 May	11–0–45–0	11–3–21–1	11–1–45–1	11–1–50–5	9–0–30–1	1–0–10–0	
(J.P.) v. Worcestershire (Huddersfield) 9 May	8–1–23–3			7.3–2–42–1			8–1–34–2
(J.P.) v. Leicestershire (Leicester) 16 May	8–1–24–1		8–0–38–0	8–0–29–1	8–0–37–1		
(B.&H.) v. Leicestershire (Leicester) 22 May	11–2–30–1	10–1–38–2	11–1–38–1	10–0–42–0	11–0–41–0		
(J.P.) v. Warwickshire (Bradford) 23 May	8–1–44–0	5–0–32–0		4.4–0–31–0	4–1–20–1		
(B.&H.) v. M. Counties (Bradford) 25–26 May	11–1–27–1	11–3–34–1	11–3–27–2	11–1–41–2			
(B.&H.) v. Derbyshire (Chesterfield) 27 May	9–0–35–0	5–1–35–1	11–3–30–1	7–1–37–0			
(J.P.) v. Glamorgan (Bradford) 6 June							
(J.P.) v. Nottinghamshire (Hull) 13 June	8–1–29–1		8–1–39–2	8–0–46–2	4–0–28–0		
(J.P.) v. Northants (Middlesbrough) 20 June	8–0–40–1		7–0–45–0	8–0–63–1	2–0–28–0	1–0–10–0	
(J.P.) v. Derbyshire (Derby) 27 June	6–0–16–0			6–0–30–2			8–0–39–3
(T.T.) v. Northants (Harrogate) 30 June	11–1–37–1			11–1–31–5	1–0–8–1		11–1–41–1
(J.P.) v. Gloucestershire (Leeds) 4 July	5–0–16–1			4.5–0–25–2		1–0–1–0	7–1–25–2
(J.P.) v. Essex (Scarborough) 11 July	6.2–1–28–0			6–0–18–0		2–0–12–0	6–0–28–1
(N.W.T.) v. Worcestershire (Leeds) 14 July	6–0–30–0			10–1–30–1		8–1–35–2	12–0–80–0
(J.P.) v. Somerset (Taunton) 18 July	6.2–0–43–0			7–0–42–2			8–0–31–1
(J.P.) v. Kent (Canterbury) 25 July			8–0–22–1				7–0–24–3
(J.P.) v. Sussex (Scarborough) 1 August	8–1–22–0		8–1–36–2	7–0–55–2	1–0–9–0	5–0–19–1	8–0–37–2
(N.W.T.) v. Essex (Leeds) 4 August	10.5–2–22–2		12–2–21–3	10–3–25–3	7–0–16–0	9–2–12–2	
(J.P.) v. Lancashire (Old Trafford) 8 August	8–1–20–0		7–0–40–0	4–1–22–0			
(N.W.T.) v. Warwickshire (Edgbaston) 18 Aug.	11–0–49–0		12–1–47–1	9.3–2–31–0		2–1–12–0	
(J.P.) v. Middlesex (Lord's) 22 August	8–1–19–1	4–0–20–0		5–0–26–1	8–0–46–1		
(J.P.) v. Hampshire (Southampton) 29 Aug.	8–0–40–1	8–0–46–0		7–0–31–2	8–0–65–0		
(Asda) v. Lancashire (Scarborough) 5 Sept.	9–1–24–3		9–0–38–0	7–0–38–2		4–0–20–0	
(J.P.) v. Surrey (The Oval) 12 September			8–0–42–0	8–1–52–1			8–0–45–1

THE ENGLISH SEASON/479

Phil Carrick

† Lost on toss of coin

Benson and Hedges Professional Photographers' Awards

£500 And Golden Trophy For Top Cricket Photograph Taken During 1983 British Season

Cricket provides one of the most satisfying and creative mediums for professional photographers and throughout the year, newspapers and magazines all over the country, publish many outstanding examples.

So that this expertise may be recognised, Benson and Hedges Cricket Year has created the Professional Photographers' Awards.

Published photographs taken at any cricket match in Britain during the 1983 British cricket season, will be reviewed by an eminent panel of experts, all leading figures in the photographic, publishing and cricketing worlds.

The panel will nominate the photograph which in their opinion is the definitive picture of the year, and others worthy of commendation.

The winner will receive £500 and a golden trophy, to be held for one year, and the commended photographers, other monetary prizes.
All these awards will be presented at a Press Luncheon, to be held in London in the Autumn of 1983.